D1499199

SOFTWARE AND MIND

SOFTWARE
AND
MIND

The Mechanistic Myth
and Its Consequences

Andrei Sorin

ANDSOR BOOKS

Designed and typeset by the author with text management software developed by the author and with Adobe FrameMaker 6.0. Printed and bound in the United States of America.

Acknowledgements

Excerpts from the works of Karl Popper: reprinted by permission of the University of Klagenfurt / Karl Popper Library.

Excerpts from *The Origins of Totalitarian Democracy* by J. L. Talmon: published by Secker & Warburg, reprinted by permission of The Random House Group Ltd.

Excerpts from *Nineteen Eighty-Four* by George Orwell: Copyright © 1949 George Orwell, reprinted by permission of Bill Hamilton as the Literary Executor of the Estate of the Late Sonia Brownell Orwell and Secker & Warburg Ltd.; Copyright © 1949 Harcourt, Inc. and renewed 1977 by Sonia Brownell Orwell, reprinted by permission of Houghton Mifflin Harcourt Publishing Company.

Excerpts from *The Collected Essays, Journalism and Letters of George Orwell*: Copyright © 1968 Sonia Brownell Orwell, reprinted by permission of Bill Hamilton as the Literary Executor of the Estate of the Late Sonia Brownell Orwell and Secker & Warburg Ltd.; Copyright © 1968 Sonia Brownell Orwell and renewed 1996 by Mark Hamilton, reprinted by permission of Houghton Mifflin Harcourt Publishing Company.

Excerpts from *Doublespeak* by William Lutz: Copyright © 1989 William Lutz, reprinted by permission of the author in care of the Jean V. Naggar Literary Agency.

Excerpts from *Four Essays on Liberty* by Isaiah Berlin: Copyright © 1969 Isaiah Berlin, reprinted by permission of Curtis Brown Group Ltd., London, on behalf of the Estate of Isaiah Berlin.

Library and Archives Canada Cataloguing in Publication

Sorin, Andrei
    Software and mind : the mechanistic myth and its consequences / Andrei Sorin.

Includes index.
ISBN 978-0-9869389-0-0

    1. Computers and civilization.   2. Computer software – Social aspects.
    3. Computer software – Philosophy.   I. Title.

QA76.9.C66S67 2013   303.48'34   C2012-906666-4

Printed on acid-free paper.

Don't you see that the whole aim of Newspeak is to narrow the range of thought?… Has it ever occurred to you … that by the year 2050, at the very latest, not a single human being will be alive who could understand such a conversation as we are having now?

George Orwell, *Nineteen Eighty-Four*

Disclaimer

This book attacks the mechanistic myth, not persons. Myths, however, manifest themselves through the acts of persons, so it is impossible to discuss the mechanistic myth without also referring to the persons affected by it. Thus, all references to individuals, groups of individuals, corporations, institutions, or other organizations are intended solely as examples of mechanistic beliefs, ideas, claims, or practices. To repeat, they do not constitute an attack on those individuals or organizations, but on the mechanistic myth.

Except where supported with citations, the discussions in this book reflect the author's personal views, and the author does not claim or suggest that anyone else holds these views.

The arguments advanced in this book are founded, ultimately, on the principles of demarcation between science and pseudoscience developed by Karl Popper (as explained in "Popper's Principles of Demarcation" in chapter 3). In particular, the author maintains that theories which attempt to explain non-mechanistic phenomena mechanistically are pseudoscientific. Consequently, terms like "ignorance," "incompetence," "dishonesty," "fraud," "corruption," "charlatanism," and "irresponsibility," in reference to individuals, groups of individuals, corporations, institutions, or other organizations, are used in a precise, technical sense; namely, to indicate beliefs, ideas, claims, or practices that are mechanistic though applied to non-mechanistic phenomena, and hence pseudoscientific according to Popper's principles of demarcation. In other words, these derogatory terms are used solely in order to contrast our world to a hypothetical, ideal world, where the mechanistic myth and the pseudoscientific notions it engenders would not exist. The meaning of these terms, therefore, must not be confused with their informal meaning in general discourse, nor with their formal meaning in various moral, professional, or legal definitions. Moreover, the use of these terms expresses strictly the personal opinion of the author – an opinion based, as already stated, on the principles of demarcation.

This book aims to expose the corruptive effect of the mechanistic myth. This myth, especially as manifested through our software-related pursuits, is the greatest danger we are facing today. Thus, no criticism can be too strong. However, since we are all affected by it, a criticism of the myth may cast a negative light on many individuals and organizations who are practising it unwittingly. To them, the author wishes to apologize in advance.

Contents

Preface

The book's subtitle, *The Mechanistic Myth and Its Consequences*, captures its essence. This phrase is deliberately ambiguous: if read in conjunction with the title, it can be interpreted in two ways. In one interpretation, the mechanistic myth is the universal mechanistic belief of the last three centuries, and the consequences are today's software fallacies. In the second interpretation, the mechanistic myth is specifically today's mechanistic *software* myth, and the consequences are the fallacies *it* engenders. Thus, the first interpretation says that the past delusions have caused the current software delusions; and the second one says that the current software delusions are causing further delusions. Taken together, the two interpretations say that the mechanistic myth, with its current manifestation in the software myth, is fostering a process of continuous intellectual degradation – despite the great advances it made possible. This process started three centuries ago, is increasingly corrupting us, and may well destroy us in the future. The book discusses all stages of this degradation.

The book's epigraph, about Newspeak, will become clear when we discuss the similarity of language and software (see, for example, pp. 411–413).

Throughout the book, the software-related arguments are also supported with ideas from other disciplines – from philosophy, in particular. These discussions are important, because they show that our software-related problems are similar, ultimately, to problems that have been studied for a long time in other domains. And the fact that the software theorists are ignoring this accumulated knowledge demonstrates their incompetence. Often, the connection between the traditional issues and the software issues is immediately apparent; but sometimes its full extent can be appreciated only in the following sections or chapters. If tempted to skip these discussions, remember that our software delusions can be recognized only when investigating the software practices from this broader perspective.

Chapter 7, on software engineering, is not just for programmers. Many parts (the first three sections, and some of the subsections in each theory) discuss the software fallacies in general, and should be read by everyone. But even the more detailed discussions require no previous programming knowledge. The whole chapter, in fact, is not so much about programming as about the delusions that pervade our programming practices. So this chapter can be seen as a special introduction to software and programming; namely, comparing their true nature with the pseudoscientific notions promoted by the software elite. This study can help both programmers and laymen to understand why the incompetence that characterizes this profession is an inevitable consequence of the mechanistic software ideology.

There is some repetitiveness in the book, deliberately introduced in order to make the individual chapters, and even the individual sections, reasonably independent. Thus, while the book is intended to be read from the beginning, you can select almost any portion and still follow the discussion. An additional benefit of the repetitions is that they help to explain the more complex issues, by presenting the same ideas from different perspectives or in different contexts.

The book is divided into chapters, the chapters into sections, and some sections into subsections. These parts have titles, so I will refer to them here as *titled* parts. Since not all sections have subsections, the lowest-level titled part in a given place may be either a section or a subsection. This part is, usually, further divided into *numbered* parts. The table of contents shows the titled parts. The running heads show the current titled parts: on the right page the lowest-level part, on the left page the higher-level one (or the same as the right page if there is no higher level). Since there are more than two hundred numbered parts, it was impractical to include them in the table of contents. Also, contriving a short title for each one would have been more misleading than informative. Instead, the first sentence or two in a numbered part serve also as a hint of its subject, and hence as title.

Figures are numbered within chapters, but footnotes are numbered within the lowest-level titled parts. The reference in a footnote is shown in full only the first time it is mentioned within such a part. If mentioned more than once, in the subsequent footnotes it is usually abbreviated. For these abbreviations, then, the full reference can be found by searching the previous footnotes no further back than the beginning of the current titled part.

The statement "italics added" in a footnote indicates that the emphasis is only in the quotation. Nothing is stated in the footnote when the italics are present in the original text.

In an Internet reference, only the site's main page is shown, even when the quoted text is from a secondary page. When undated, the quotations reflect the content of these pages in 2010 or later.

When referring to certain individuals (software theorists, for instance), the term "expert" is often used mockingly. This term, though, is also used in its normal sense, to denote the possession of true expertise. The context makes it clear which sense is meant.

The term "elite" is used to describe a body of companies, organizations, and individuals (for example, the software elite); and the plural, "elites," is used when referring to several entities, or groups of entities, within such a body. Thus, although both forms refer to the same entities, the singular is employed when it is important to stress the existence of the whole body, and the plural when it is the existence of the individual entities that must be stressed. The plural is also employed, occasionally, in its normal sense – a group of several different bodies. Again, the meaning is clear from the context.

The issues discussed in this book concern all humanity. Thus, terms like "we" and "our society" (used when discussing such topics as programming incompetence, corruption of the elites, and drift toward totalitarianism) do not refer to a particular nation, but to the whole world.

Some discussions in this book may be interpreted as professional advice on programming and software use. While the ideas advanced in these discussions derive from many years of practice and from extensive research, and represent in the author's view the best way to program and use computers, readers must remember that they assume all responsibility if deciding to follow these ideas. In particular, to apply these ideas they may need the kind of knowledge that, in our mechanistic culture, few programmers and software users possess. Therefore, the author and the publisher disclaim any liability for risks or losses, personal, financial, or other, incurred directly or indirectly in connection with, or as a consequence of, applying the ideas discussed in this book.

The pronouns "he," "his," "him," and "himself," when referring to a gender-neutral word, are used in this book in their universal, gender-neutral sense. (Example: "If an individual restricts himself to mechanistic knowledge, his performance cannot advance past the level of a novice.") This usage, then, aims solely to simplify the language. Since their antecedent is gender-neutral ("everyone," "person," "programmer," "scientist," "manager," etc.), the neutral sense of the pronouns is established grammatically, and there is no need for awkward phrases like "he or she." Such phrases are used in this book only when the neutrality or the universality needs to be emphasized.

It is impossible, in a book discussing many new and perhaps difficult concepts, to anticipate all the problems that readers may face when studying these concepts. So the issues that require further discussion will be addressed online, at *www.softwareandmind.com*. In addition, I plan to publish there material that could not be included in the book, as well as new ideas that may emerge in the future. Finally, in order to complement the arguments about traditional programming found in the book, I plan to publish, in source form, some of the software applications I developed over the years. The website, then, must be seen as an extension to the book: any idea, claim, or explanation that must be clarified or enhanced will be discussed there.

Belief and Software

This book is largely a study of delusions – mechanistic delusions. But, whereas in the following chapters we discuss the *logical* aspects of these delusions, in this introductory chapter we concentrate on their *human* aspects.

Belief, as we all know, is stronger than reason. For a person who believes that the number 13 brings misfortune, a hundred logical arguments demonstrating the fallacy of this idea amount to nothing; at the same time, one story of an accident that occurred on the 13th day of a month suffices to validate the idea. Similarly, we will see, it is quite easy to expose the absurdity of the *mechanistic* beliefs. Yet hundreds of millions of people – people who think of themselves as modern and rational – spend a great part of their life engaged in activities that are, essentially, an enactment of these beliefs. Clearly, it would be futile to attempt to understand the mechanistic myth without taking into account its emotional roots.

It is in order to emphasize their primacy, therefore, that I deal with the human aspects of the mechanistic myth before its logical aspects. But this book is concerned, ultimately, with logical thinking. Thus, a second reason for including the study of human nature in the introduction is that it is only a brief discussion of this important topic.

Modern Myths

The historian of religions Mircea Eliade predicts that "the understanding of myth will one day be counted among the most useful discoveries of the twentieth century."[1] Myths used to be considered – along with fairy tales, legends, and fables – merely folklore: picturesque stories transmitted to us from ancient times, perhaps carrying some moral lessons, but generally of little value in the modern world. It is only recently, starting with the work of anthropologists like Bronislaw Malinowski, that we have come to view myths in a new light. These scholars studied the life of primitive societies extant in various parts of the world by living among those people and learning their languages and customs. As these cultures exemplify all early societies, this information, combined with our historical knowledge, has helped us to form a more accurate picture of the capabilities, values, and beliefs of archaic man. Even more importantly, it has helped us to understand the development and nature of our own, present-day culture.

One thing we have discovered from these studies is the critical function that myth fulfils in a human society. Myth, according to Malinowski, "supplies the charter for ritual, belief, moral conduct and social organization."[2] Far from being simply folklore, myths are the foundation upon which the entire social system rests: "Studied alive, myth ... is not symbolic, but a direct expression of its subject matter; it is ... a narrative resurrection of a primeval reality, told in satisfaction of deep religious wants, moral cravings, social submissions, assertions, even practical requirements. Myth fulfills in primitive culture an indispensable function: it expresses, enhances, and codifies belief; it safeguards and enforces morality; it vouches for the efficiency of ritual and contains practical rules for the guidance of man. Myth is thus a vital ingredient of human civilization; it is not an idle tale, but a hard-worked active force."[3]

It is wrong to study a myth by inquiring whether it makes sense. Myths are a sacred tradition, and "the main object of sacred tradition is not to serve as a chronicle of past events; it is to lay down the effective precedent of a glorified

---

[1] Mircea Eliade, *Myths, Dreams, and Mysteries: The Encounter between Contemporary Faiths and Archaic Realities* (New York: Harper and Row, 1975), p. 38.

[2] Bronislaw Malinowski, "Myth as a Dramatic Development of Dogma," in *Malinowski and the Work of Myth*, ed. Ivan Strenski (Princeton, NJ: Princeton University Press, 1992), p. 122.

[3] Bronislaw Malinowski, *Magic, Science and Religion, and Other Essays* (Garden City, NY: Doubleday Anchor, 1954), p. 101.

past for repetitive actions in the present."[4] We must study, therefore, not so much the *text* of a story or legend, as its effects on living society. Myths make absurd claims, but we must ignore their scientific inaccuracy. The "extravagant elements in the myth ... can only be understood by reference to ritual, ethical, and social influences of the story on present day conduct."[5]

A myth, then, must be judged solely by its power to inspire large numbers of people. Blatant impossibilities or inconsistencies do not detract from its power. On the contrary, since it is precisely the fantastic elements in a myth that impress us, they are its most important value. Thus, a story that makes only reasonable and verifiable claims cannot possibly serve as myth.

Eliade notes how quickly our perception of the function of myth has changed, from the belief that it is "only fables," to the appreciation that "a man of the traditional societies sees it as the *only valid revelation of reality*."[6] The function of myth is the exact opposite of what we thought it to be: rather than relying on proven knowledge in their important activities and turning to myths in their diversions, it is actually in their important activities that the primitives rely on myths. Because they are inherited from previous generations, myths are believed to represent unquestionable facts: "The myth is thought to express *absolute truth*, because it narrates a *sacred history*.... Being *real* and *sacred*, the myth becomes exemplary, and consequently *repeatable*, for it serves as a model, and by the same token as a justification, for all human actions."[7] Conversely, something that is not reflected in myths is deemed to be untrue and profane.

The greatest benefit that emerges from the study of myth is not a better understanding of primitive cultures, but a better understanding of our own, modern culture. We must "integrate the myth into the general history of thought, by regarding it as the most important form of collective thinking. And, since 'collective thinking' is never completely abolished in any society, whatever its degree of evolution, one did not fail to observe that the modern world still preserves some mythical behaviour."[8] Thus, "*upon the plane of social living*, there was no break in the continuity between the archaic world and the modern world."[9]

But there seem to be few myths left in the modern world. Moreover, those that still exist do not seem to provide anywhere near the powerful inspiration that myths provided in earlier civilizations. So this important question arises: "If the myth is not just an infantile or aberrant creation of 'primitive' humanity, but is the expression of *a mode of being in the world*, what has become of myths

[4] Malinowski, "Dramatic Development," p. 123.   [5] Ibid.
[6] Eliade, *Myths, Dreams, and Mysteries*, p. 24.   [7] Ibid., p. 23.
[8] Ibid., p. 24.   [9] Ibid.

in the modern world? Or, more precisely, what has taken the *essential* place occupied by myth in traditional societies?"[10] "It seems unlikely that any society could completely dispense with myths, for, of what is essential in mythical behaviour – the exemplary pattern, the repetition, the break with profane duration and integration into primordial time – the first two at least are cosubstantial with every human condition."[11]

The absence of myths in modern society, thus, is an illusion. In reality, because human nature has not changed, modern cultures too are founded on myths. All that has happened is a shift in the type of myths that inspire us: our preoccupations are different from those of our ancestors, so our myths too are different. It is a mistake to study the *old* myths, and to conclude that, since we no longer take *them* seriously, we no longer depend on myths.

To understand the mass delusions that possess our present-day society, we must uncover the myths that shape our collective thinking *today*. Let us briefly review some of these myths.

George Steiner refers to the intellectual, political, and social ideologies of the nineteenth and twentieth centuries as surrogate creeds, anti-theologies, meta-religions, or mythologies.[12] These ideologies emerged as a result of the decline of formal religion since the Renaissance. Thanks to the growth of knowledge, Western man's absolute belief in God, which had guided him for centuries, suddenly came to an end. This created a spiritual vacuum and the longing for a new, equally powerful subject of belief: "Where there is a vacuum, new energies and surrogates arise. Unless I read the evidence wrongly, the political and philosophic history of the West during the last 150 years can be understood as a series of attempts – more or less conscious, more or less systematic, more or less violent – to fill the central emptiness left by the erosion of theology."[13]

Steiner discusses three ideologies: Marxism, Freudian psychoanalysis, and Lévi-Strauss's structuralism. These systems of ideas have several characteristics in common: "totality, by which I simply mean the claim to explain everything; canonic texts delivered by the founding genius; orthodoxy against heresy; crucial metaphors, gestures, and symbols."[14] And it is these characteristics that betray their mythological nature: "The major mythologies constructed in the

---

[10] Ibid.   [11] Ibid., p. 31.

[12] George Steiner, *Nostalgia for the Absolute* (Toronto: CBC Enterprises, 1974), p. 2.

[13] Ibid.

[14] Ibid., p. 4. We will also encounter these three ideologies in chapter 3, where we will see that, unsurprisingly, they are based on pseudoscientific theories.

West since the early nineteenth century are not only attempts to fill the emptiness left by the decay of Christian theology and Christian dogma. They are themselves a kind of *substitute theology*. They are systems of belief and argument which may be savagely anti-religious, which may postulate a world without God and may deny an afterlife, but whose structure, whose aspirations, whose claims on the believer, are profoundly religious in strategy and in effect."[15]

Isaiah Berlin[16] shows that, in their attempt to explain social evolution "scientifically," the modern social theories were compelled to ignore the role played by individuals. Human history, according to these theories, is controlled by some mysterious forces and processes – variously represented as class struggles, cultural clashes, geo-political conditions, technological changes, etc. While described in scientific terms, these mighty forces and processes are perceived as supernatural, mythological entities. They manage to explain social evolution only by remaining unexplained themselves, so in the end, these theories – in reality, pseudosciences – are no different from the religious beliefs of the past: "There has grown up in our modern time a pseudo-sociological mythology which, in the guise of scientific concepts, has developed into a new animism – certainly a more primitive and naive religion than the traditional European faiths which it seeks to replace."[17]

Eliade compares the modern political myths with the classical myths: "Eschatological and millennialist mythology recently reappeared in Europe in two totalitarian political movements. Although radically secularized in appearance, Nazism and Communism are loaded with eschatological elements: they announce the end of this world and the beginning of an age of plenty and bliss."[18]

Both Communism and Nazism were seen by their followers as the modern equivalent of the struggle between good and evil – a common mythological theme. Communism is based on "one of the great eschatological myths of the Middle Eastern and Mediterranean world, namely: the redemptive part to be played by the Just (the 'elect,' the 'anointed,' the 'innocent,' the 'missioners,' in our own days by the proletariat), whose sufferings are invoked to change the ontological structure of the world. In fact, Marx's classless society, and the consequent disappearance of all historical tensions, find their most exact precedent in the myth of the Golden Age which, according to a number of traditions, lies at the beginning and the end of History."[19]

[15] Ibid.
[16] Isaiah Berlin, "Historical Inevitability," in *Four Essays on Liberty* (Oxford: Oxford University Press, 1969).   [17] Ibid., p. 110.
[18] Mircea Eliade, *Myth and Reality* (New York: Harper and Row, 1975), p. 69.
[19] Eliade, *Myths, Dreams, and Mysteries*, pp. 25–26.

As for the other great political myth of the twentieth century, "in its effort to abolish Christian values and rediscover the spiritual sources of the 'race' – that is, of Nordic paganism – Nazism was obliged to try to reanimate the Germanic mythology."[20] Thus, "the 'Aryan' represented at once the 'primordial' Ancestor and the noble 'hero,' ... the exemplary model that must be imitated in order to recover racial 'purity,' physical strength, nobility, the heroic 'ethics' of the glorious and creative 'beginnings.'"[21]

Some of our myths are embodied in literary works, movies, television shows, sports, and popular entertainment. Archaic societies had no need for such distractions, because in their normal life – daily work, hunting, war, family and social activities – they were constantly reenacting sacred myths. Having desacralized our world, and especially our work, we had to invent some useless activities, collective and personal, as substitutes for the reenactment of myths.[22]

For example, a popular myth in current American culture is the myth of the lone saviour: "A community in a harmonious paradise is threatened by evil: normal institutions fail to contend with this threat: a selfless superhero emerges to renounce temptations and carry out the redemptive task: aided by fate, his decisive victory restores the community to its paradisal condition: the superhero then recedes into obscurity."[23] Variations of this myth form the main theme in countless movies and television series, and its popularity can be explained by comparing it with the old religious myths: "The supersaviors in pop culture function as replacements for the Christ figure, whose credibility was eroded by scientific rationalism. But their superhuman abilities reflect a hope for the divine, redemptive powers that science has never eradicated from the popular mind. The presentation of such figures in popular culture has the power to evoke fan loyalties that should be compared with more traditional forms of religious zeal."[24]

Similarly, "the characters of the comic strips present the modern version of mythological or folklore Heroes."[25] For instance, "the myth of Superman satisfies the secret longings of modern man who, though he knows that he is a fallen, limited creature, dreams of one day proving himself an 'exceptional person,' a 'Hero.'"[26]

Cultural fashions – in literature, art, music, philosophy, even science – act in effect as modern mythologies: "One of the fascinating aspects of the 'cultural fashion' is that it does not matter whether the facts in question and their

[20] Ibid., p. 26.   [21] Eliade, *Myth and Reality*, p. 183.

[22] Eliade, *Myths, Dreams, and Mysteries*, p. 37.

[23] Robert Jewett and John S. Lawrence, *The American Monomyth* (Garden City, NY: Anchor/Doubleday, 1977), p. xx.   [24] Ibid.

[25] Eliade, *Myth and Reality*, pp. 184–185.   [26] Ibid., p. 185.

interpretation are true or not. No amount of criticism can destroy a vogue. There is something 'religious' about this imperviousness to criticism.... Their popularity, especially among the intelligentsia, reveals something of Western man's dissatisfactions, drives, and nostalgias."[27]

Paul Kurtz[28] discusses the similarities between classical religions and modern belief systems. He accepts the fact that human beings are susceptible to irrational beliefs, that we are possessed by a "transcendental temptation." But, he says, we must find a way to overcome this weakness, because a society dominated by myths faces great dangers: "The transcendental temptation lurks deep within the human breast. It is ever-present, tempting humans by the lure of transcendental realities, subverting the power of their critical intelligence, enabling them to accept unproven and unfounded myth systems. Can we live without myths? Can we overcome the defect, as it were, in our natures? Is it so rooted in our natures that it cannot be overcome, but will crop up in generation after generation, the forms and functions of the transcendental temptation the same, with only the content different?"[29]

Although the growth of science seems to offer a hope for overcoming it, we must remember that "these are relatively recent developments and of short duration in human history.... The transcendental temptation has held sway for millennia, and to hope to mitigate or obviate its continued power may be to engage in wishful thinking.... What guarantee do we have that science too will not be overwhelmed and superseded by new faiths of unreason commanding human imagination?... One cannot predict the future course of human history with any degree of confidence. Regrettably, often the unthinkable becomes true. Will the unimaginable again overtake us, as we slip into a new dark age of unreason? The only option for us to prevent this is to continue to use the arts of intelligence and skeptical criticism against the blind faiths, old and new.... Is there any hope that a scientific, secular, or humanist culture can develop and prevail, devoid of transcendental myths?... If salvation myths are no longer tenable, what will take their place? The dilemma is always that new faiths and new myths may emerge, equally irrational."[30]

Science, however, has been redefined in our universities to mean a blind pursuit of mechanistic theories – whether sound or not, whether useful or not. Science, thus, has *already* been "overwhelmed and superseded by new faiths of unreason" – by the mechanistic dogma. *The mechanistic belief is the new myth that has emerged to replace the old ones.*

[27] Mircea Eliade, *Occultism, Witchcraft, and Cultural Fashions: Essays in Comparative Religions* (Chicago: University of Chicago Press, 1978), p. 3.

[28] Paul Kurtz, *The Transcendental Temptation: A Critique of Religion and the Paranormal* (Buffalo, NY: Prometheus Books, 1991).   [29] Ibid., pp. 477–478.

[30] Ibid., pp. 481–482.

The Mechanistic Myth

1

In this book we are concerned with one particular myth – the *mechanistic* myth; and we are especially concerned with its latest manifestation – the *software* myth. Mechanism is the belief that everything can be represented as a *hierarchical structure*; that is, as a structure of things within things. This is true, we are told, because every entity is necessarily made up of simpler entities, which are in their turn made up of even simpler ones, and so on, down to some basic building blocks.

Thus, if we want to understand a complex phenomenon, all we have to do – according to the mechanistic doctrine – is discover what simpler phenomena make it up. Then, for each one of those, we must discover what phenomena make *it* up, and so on. Clearly, if we continue this process to lower and lower levels of complexity, we are bound to reach, eventually, phenomena simple enough to understand intuitively. So, by understanding those simple phenomena and the process of simplification that revealed them, we will understand the original, complex phenomenon. Ultimately, working in this fashion, everything that exists in the world can be understood.

Similarly, if we want to build a complicated machine, all we have to do is design it as a combination of subassemblies. Because the subassemblies on their own are simpler than the whole machine, they are easier to design and make. Then, we design the subassemblies themselves as combinations of simpler subassemblies, the latter as combinations of even simpler ones, and so on, down to some small parts that can be made directly.

If we want to study a set of related entities – the people in an organization, the parts stored in a warehouse, the various types of animals – all we have to do is depict them with a hierarchical classification. We divide them first into several categories in such a way that all the entities in a category share a certain attribute. Then, we divide each category into several smaller ones on the basis of a second attribute, and so on, until we reach some categories where the entities share all their important attributes and are therefore very similar. In the case of an animal classification, for example, we may divide them into wild and domestic, the domestic ones into types like horses, chickens, and dogs, and finally each type into various breeds.

If we wonder how linguistic communication works, we start by noting that language is made up of sentences, sentences are made up of clauses, and clauses are made up of words. Words correspond to the facts that exist in the world – nouns for objects, verbs for actions, adjectives for properties, and so on. Thus, since everything in the world can be represented as a hierarchical structure, it seems that what we do when communicating is create hierarchical structures of linguistic elements which correspond to the structures that exist in the world.

Finally, if we want to create large and complex software applications, we must start by breaking them down into modules. We then break down each module into smaller ones, and so on, until we reach some simple software constructs, which we can program directly. This method, clearly, allows us to implement the most complex applications with skills no greater than those required to program the smallest constructs.

It appears, thus, that the mechanists are right: everything in the world can indeed be represented with a hierarchical structure. The explanation for this versatility lies in the two principles that constitute the mechanistic philosophy: reductionism and atomism. Reductionism assures us that everything can be represented as a combination of simpler things; at the same time, atomism assures us that there is an end to this reduction, that we will eventually reach some *elementary* entities, which cannot be further divided into simpler ones. Together, therefore, these principles assure us that every problem can be solved.

The term "mechanism" derives from the fact that in the seventeenth century, when this philosophy was established, the elementary entities were believed to be the simplest *mechanical* entities; namely, bits of matter. All phenomena, in other words – from those encountered in the study of mechanics to those encountered in the study of minds and societies – were believed to be reducible, ultimately, to the phenomena associated with the motion of bits of matter.

Formal reductionism still claims this, although the idea is so absurd that most scientists today avoid discussing it. In any case, rigorous mechanism – that is, a reduction to truly elementary entities – is too difficult to practise, so it is an easier variant that has been adopted in universities as "the method of science." This form of mechanism employs *partial* reductionism, and academics like it because it can make trivial activities resemble scientific research. Thus, to explain a given phenomenon we no longer have to *actually* reduce it to some basic, indivisible entities; we are free to end the reduction at any convenient level, and simply *call* those entities elementary. Theories grounded on this method explain nothing, of course; but they *look* scientific, so the method is very popular.

Mechanism is also described as a method that leads to precise and complete explanations – *mathematical* explanations, in particular. It is easy to see why mathematical models are logically equivalent to the hierarchical structures of mechanism: Mathematical systems are themselves based on hierarchical structures. In a given system, a complex theorem can be expressed as a combination of simpler theorems, which can then be reduced to even simpler ones, and so on, until we reach the premises, axioms, and basic elements upon which the system is founded. Thus, since we can always invent a mathematical system whose entities correspond to entities from the real world, a phenomenon that can be represented with a hierarchical structure can also be represented mathematically.

And indeed, those aspects of the world that have been successfully explained through reductionism and atomism also have exact, mathematical models. They include the subjects studied by sciences like physics, chemistry, and astronomy, and their applications – engineering, manufacturing, construction. Mechanism and mathematics, however, have been far less successful in other areas. Sciences like biology, physiology, and medicine benefit to some extent from mechanistic theories, but their main problems are non-mechanistic. As for those sciences that study human phenomena – psychology, sociology, linguistics, economics, politics, history, anthropology – their problems are almost entirely non-mechanistic. Finally, our software-related activities, despite their dependence on computers and hence on engineering, entail largely non-mechanistic problems.

So the mechanistic principles only *appear* to be universal. In reality, they are useful for some phenomena and useless for others. In three hundred years of mechanistic philosophy, *not one* mechanistic model was successful in the human sciences. Countless mechanistic theories have been advanced, and more are being advanced today than ever before, but when a theory fails no one tries to understand the reason. The response, invariably, is to start working on another mechanistic theory. Reductionism and atomism have been so successful in those fields where they do work that science is now universally identified with mechanism. For most of us, science means simply the attempt to extend the success of mechanism to every other aspect of the world. So an individual is perceived as scientist simply if pursuing a mechanistic theory. No one cares whether the theory works or not, or whether mechanism is valid at all in that particular field. Thus, while known as the method of science, mechanism is now largely the method of charlatanism.

2

The obsession with finding a mechanistic representation for every aspect of the world is especially silly in view of the fact that it is quite easy to see why mechanism *cannot* explain every phenomenon. All that the researchers have to do is study with an open mind any one of their failures. For, when mechanism fails, the reason is always the same: the phenomenon is too complex to be represented with a neat structure of things within things. We will examine these failures in the following chapters, but from what we have discussed so far we can already recognize why mechanism is limited.

In the hierarchical structure that is the mechanistic representation of a phenomenon, what determines the relations between levels is the totality of attributes possessed by the structure's elements. Thus, for the structure to provide an exact and complete explanation, the elements must possess these attributes in such a way that the relations we see in the structure are the *only* relations between them. But this is rarely true.

The entities that make up the world possess *many* attributes, and are therefore interrelated in many different ways. For certain types of phenomena, though, a few of these attributes, and the resulting relations, are much more important than the others; and, sometimes, these attributes also happen to define a hierarchical relationship. Thus, if we agree to *ignore* the other attributes, a hierarchical structure will provide a useful approximation of reality. For these phenomena, then, we note that mechanistic theories work. Putting this in reverse, for certain types of phenomena the other attributes *cannot* be ignored, so the phenomena *cannot* be usefully approximated with a hierarchical structure; for those phenomena, then, we note that mechanistic theories fail.

Recall the earlier examples. Hierarchical classifications of things are possible only if we take into account *some* of their attributes (one attribute, or a small set of attributes, per level) and ignore the others. It is impossible to include *all* their attributes in one classification. Thus, animals can be divided into wild and domestic, into types, and into breeds, as we saw. But this is just *one* way to represent them. The biological classification – dividing animals into classes, orders, families, genera, and species – is based on different attributes, and the resulting hierarchy is different. Tigers and horses belong to different categories (wild and domestic) in one classification, but to the same category (class of mammals) in the other. Clearly, there are many ways to classify animals, all valid and useful; and each classification can take into account only *some* of their attributes. It is impossible to represent *all* their attributes in *one* hierarchical structure. The totality of animals and their attributes is, therefore, a non-mechanistic phenomenon. A mechanistic representation – one structure – is valid only if we agree to study animals from one narrow perspective; it becomes useless as soon as we remember their other attributes.

Similarly, we can represent an appliance as a hierarchy of parts and sub-assemblies only if we restrict ourselves to those attributes that determine their position and function in that appliance. For, the same parts and subassemblies form at the same time *other* hierarchical structures, based on other attributes –

their cost, or supplier, or life expectancy. We purposely design appliances in such a way that the other attributes can be ignored in the manufacturing process. But the attributes *are* important when we study the appliances from *other* perspectives. And the other hierarchies are usually different from the one that represents the physical and functional attributes; for example, parts made by the same supplier may belong in different subassemblies. It is impossible to represent the parts and *all* their attributes in *one* hierarchical structure. Again, a mechanistic representation is valid only if we can restrict ourselves to one view.

Sentences appear to form a neat hierarchy of clauses and words only if we take into account the syntactic structure and ignore the *meaning* of the words. For, the things represented by words possess many attributes, and are therefore related through many structures. Consequently, the words themselves are related through many structures, which are different from the syntactic one. It is impossible to depict, with a syntactic structure alone, everything that a sentence can convey.

Finally, software applications appear to form perfect hierarchies of smaller and smaller entities (modules, blocks of statements, statements) only if we study them from the perspective of *one* attribute. The attributes of a software entity are such things as files, variables, subroutines, and business practices. Software entities possess many attributes, and are therefore related through many structures – one structure for each attribute. The programming theories attempt to simplify programming by forcing us to view each application as a neat hierarchical structure of software entities. Thus, since applications consist in fact of multiple, simultaneous structures, it is not surprising that the theories keep failing.

Mechanism, then, is not the solid scientific concept it is believed to be. Its prestige is due largely to its early successes in the exact sciences, and especially to its successes relative to the scholastic doctrines of the Middle Ages, which it was displacing. Just as the religious philosophy had been accepted for centuries as the absolute truth, the mechanistic philosophy was seen now as an absolute method – a method that can explain everything. Mechanism became, in effect, a new religion. It seems that societies cannot exist without some great ideas to inspire them – ideas that people can accept blindly.

Most of us perform both rational and irrational acts, but the two kinds appear to us equally important. In the easier pursuits, when our knowledge guarantees success, we are completely rational and follow only sound and proven principles. But in difficult pursuits, when our knowledge is insufficient, we behave irrationally. Irrationality, thus, emerges when we have no proven theories to rely on: if we wish to understand a given phenomenon but lack the necessary knowledge (and if, in addition, we believe that all phenomena can be understood as we understand the simple ones), we are bound to invent a fantastic concept and use *it* as explanation. This is how myths are born. People are always in need of myths, because there is always much that is unknown or unpredictable, in any society. Consequently, people always display a blend of rational and irrational thinking, rational and irrational activities.

We like to justify our acts by basing them on accepted concepts, but we are less keen on justifying the concepts themselves. As a result, we perceive the two kinds of activities, rational and irrational, as equally effective. The former become pursuits like science and business, while the latter make up pursuits like magic and superstitions. But the *individual* activities that make up these pursuits are very similar: they are always logical and consistent, always grounded on an accepted concept. The difference is only that the concept is a valid theory in one case and a fantasy in the other.

Thus, as we will see in the course of this book, it is possible for a person, and even an entire society, to engage in activities that are perfectly logical *individually*, while the body of activities as a whole constitutes a delusion. So, to judge whether a certain pursuit is rational or not, it is not enough to study the logic of the *individual* activities which make up that pursuit.

In chapter 3 we will learn that the best way to distinguish between rational and irrational pursuits is by studying, not the successes, but the *falsifications* of an idea. Just as important is how people *react* to these falsifications. Serious researchers react by doubting the idea. Most people, however, react by ignoring the falsifications, or by contriving ways to cover them up. They never admit that the idea has been refuted. This shows that, for them, the idea is not a rational pursuit but a belief.

Astrology, for instance, has been around for thousands of years, and we could always show that it doesn't work. All we have to do is note the predictions made in the course of a year, and then count how many actually materialized. Believers, though, never do this. Similarly, today we can note the mechanistic claims in a field like linguistics, economics, or software, and count how many actually materialize. But, again, believers never do this. Mechanism continues to be trusted, regardless of how successful or unsuccessful it is.

We will see that it *is* possible to distinguish between the two types of thinking, the scientific and the pseudoscientific. And we will see that what the mechanists do is simply ignore the falsifications, just like the traditional pseudoscientists. Thus, our mechanistic theories – while embraced by famous scientists, taught in respected universities, and practised throughout society – form in reality a new kind of pseudoscience.

The conclusion must be that mechanism does not function as scientific doctrine in our society, but as myth. It is precisely the lack of doubts that betrays its mythical status. When a method works, we are not afraid to debate it, modify it, or replace it with a better one. Only concepts that cannot be proved become unquestionable truths. Were mechanism perceived merely as an important research method, we would rely on it in those fields where it is useful, and seek other methods in those fields where it fails. But this is not what we see. Mechanism is considered the *only* valid method of science, in *all* fields. Academics are trained to think mechanistically, and are expected to pursue only mechanistic ideas, regardless of whether these ideas are useful or not. Moreover, non-mechanistic ideas are dismissed as "unscientific," even if shown to be useful. We have redefined science, in effect, to mean simply the pursuit of mechanism. And as a result, our academic institutions have degenerated into a self-serving bureaucracy.

Recall the earlier quotations: modern societies are founded on myths, just like the primitive ones; myths are the most important form of collective thinking; myths are thought to express absolute truth; myths serve as models and as justification for all human action; and so on. Thus, if science and its applications – especially the pursuits we call technology – serve as warrant for our actions and decisions, and if science is grounded on mechanism, then, for us, mechanism serves the purpose of myth. When we judge something as important or unimportant, as useful or useless, as moral or immoral, as valid or invalid, simply by invoking a scientific or technological concept, we judge it in effect by invoking the mechanistic myth.

3

Myths can be good. When people possess only limited knowledge, as in a primitive society, most phenomena they observe are unexplainable. They have nothing to lose then, and much to gain, by attributing these phenomena to some mythical powers. The myths replace their anxiety and fears with a sense of confidence and security. The fact that this confidence is based on false assumptions does not detract from the value of the myths, since the primitives cannot arrive at the correct explanation in any case. If they wish to understand what caused a certain disease, for example, and they know nothing about microorganisms, the assumption that it was caused by sins, or demons, or black magic, is quite effective. As they cannot *cure* the disease, these beliefs provide at least the comfort of knowing its origin. With this comfort they are in a better position to face other problems, so they can accomplish more in those fields in which they *are* knowledgeable.

Thanks to the importance of myths, the individuals who provide myth-related services – magicians, shamans, astrologers – enjoy great respect. Their knowledge, limited as it is to myths, is necessarily specious. Nevertheless, just as the myths themselves fulfil a vital function in society while being in fact unreal, the services provided by these experts are crucial even while being specious. The experts, as a result, become a powerful elite. But this position is well-deserved: if a society benefits from its myths, and if the practice of myths requires a certain expertise, then the individuals who possess this expertise are as essential to society as the myths themselves. Thus, when the myths are good for a society, an elite whose existence depends on these myths is a good elite.

Myths, however, can also be bad. A society may reach a point in its evolution where enough knowledge has been accumulated to attain better explanations than what the myths can provide. Most likely, the new explanations include mythical elements of their own, rather than being completely rational. Even so, being closer to reality, they constitute an improvement. In retrospect, then, the practical benefits of abandoning the old myths are obvious. But the actual transition is difficult. The old myths are usually part of a belief system that had guided society for generations, and it takes more than the promise of an improvement to abandon them. So the same myths that hitherto *served* society are now turning *against* it, by preventing it from enjoying the benefits of the new knowledge. The good myths become bad.

The elite too – those experts whose privileged position depends on the myths – is now turning against society. Because they would be redundant without the old myths, the experts continue to praise their value even as society no longer needs them. Whereas formerly they were *practising* those myths, now they are *enforcing* them. They describe this struggle as an effort to preserve some proven social values, but in reality it is their own privileges that they want to preserve. Thus, when the myths turn from good to bad, the elite too becomes bad.

The best-known transition in Western history is the Renaissance and the Scientific Revolution, which took place between the fifteenth and seventeenth centuries. This is when modern science, expressed through the mechanistic philosophy, replaced the religious myths that had dominated Europe for more than a thousand years. One of the most remarkable aspects of this transition is the ferocity with which the church – guardian of the old myths – fought to prevent it. Previously, the church was perhaps a good elite, insofar as myths like the idea of salvation could provide some comfort in an age when science had little to offer. But now that the real benefits of the growing knowledge exceeded the emotional benefits of myths, the only way the church could maintain its power was by suppressing that knowledge. This was the task of the Inquisition.

Thus, regardless of how one feels about the value of the religious myths in earlier times, we all agree that obstructing the truth, and torturing and burning alive innocent people, is not something that a good elite would do. The myths, and with them the elite, had become bad.

The foregoing analysis should help us to recognize that a similar transition is taking place in our own time. What is being defended now is *mechanism* – the very myth that was being *repressed* in the earlier transition. And the elite struggling to maintain its power is embodied now in our educational institutions – our universities, in particular. The academic bureaucrats are the greatest beneficiaries of the mechanistic myth, as this myth affords them a privileged position in society regardless of whether their activities are useful or not. So it is not surprising to see them defend the mechanistic ideology as fiercely as the church was defending earlier the religious one.

When astrology was important, astrologers retained their position regard-less of whether their predictions were correct or not; when alchemy was important, alchemists continued to be trusted regardless of whether their transmuting methods worked or not; and when religion was important, the church bureaucracy retained its power regardless of whether its promises of salvation materialized or not. Today, *mechanism* is important, so we continue to trust and respect the academic bureaucrats even as the mechanistic theories are failing. As we will see in the following chapters, it is quite easy to prove that these theories are fraudulent; and yet we treat their defenders as scientists, not as charlatans.

As part of its power, the academic elite controls education. And it has used this monopolistic position to turn the process of education into a process of indoctrination: all we are taught is what can be explained mechanistically. Thus, while promoting knowledge, intelligence, and creativity, the academic elite has redefined these qualities to mean, not the utmost that human minds can attain, but merely the skills needed to follow the mechanistic ideology: knowledge of the latest mechanistic theories, the intelligence to appreciate the mechanistic principles, and the creativity to accomplish a task with mechanistic methods alone. Mechanism is not just *practised* – it is *enforced*. Together with the corporations (the other beneficiaries of the mechanistic myth), and protected by irresponsible governments, our universities have brought about a social order that is, in effect, a new form of totalitarianism.

Totalitarian ideologies differ in detail, but their goal is always the same: to create a perfect society. For us, this means a society founded upon solid, mechanistic principles. We have already proved the value of these principles in certain areas – in the exact sciences, for instance, and in manufacturing – so all we have to do now is extend their use to every other aspect of human life.

Here is how we can accomplish this: Since everything can be represented with hierarchical structures, we can improve our performance by breaking down all challenges into simpler and simpler ones. In the end, we will only need to deal with the terminal elements of these structures; that is, with trivial issues. In practice, the structures will be embodied in theories and methods, and the terminal elements will be some simple rules. Thus, just by obeying these rules, anyone will be able to perform tasks that previously demanded much knowledge and experience.

Better still, once we represent our problems with hierarchical structures, we can build devices that embody these structures. Then, to solve a given problem, all we need to know is how to operate a device. The skills required to operate devices are easier than those required to solve problems, so we will all be more productive: first, because devices eliminate the lengthy learning periods we needed in the past, and second, because devices are faster, more accurate, and more dependable than humans.

Finally, with our latest invention, computers, we can implement even those structures that are too large or too complex for the traditional devices. Thanks to the power and versatility of software, practically every human endeavour can be translated into a series of easy acts – the acts required to operate a software device. From simple calculations to difficult decisions, from personal concerns to business issues, we can have a software device for every task. Various types of knowledge are now being incorporated into these devices, and made available to us through easy-to-use menus, lists, buttons, and the like; in other words, through a hierarchical structure of selections, and selections within selections, corresponding to the hierarchical structure that is the knowledge itself. So, just by purchasing a software device, we will be able to perform almost any task without having to develop that knowledge in our own minds.

Our idea of a perfect society, then, is one where all human affairs have been reduced to the simple acts required to follow methods and to operate devices. The methods and devices are developed by various elites – experts who know how to translate the complexity of the world into concepts simple enough for us to understand. The responsibility of the elites is to represent the world with exact, mechanistic theories; and *our* responsibility is to obey these theories. Anything that cannot be represented mechanistically is unscientific, and hence devoid of value. Thus, as our goal is endless progress, we cannot afford to spend any time with non-mechanistic notions, even if we might otherwise enjoy it.

If we doubt the efficacy of this scheme, we only need to recall the progress we have made in our *manufacturing* activities. From the handful of simple consumer products available two hundred years ago, and which few people could afford, we have arrived at today's astounding array of sophisticated products, which almost anyone can afford. And we have accomplished this, not by *increasing*, but by *reducing*, the knowledge and skills of the workers who make these products. The secret for the great progress in manufacturing is found, as everyone knows, in concepts like the assembly line (which permits us to employ unskilled workers and to control their output), division of labour and narrow specialization (which permit us to reduce each individual's education and training, and hence the cost of employment), and, in general, fragmentation of the labour process (which reduces all types of work to simple, routine activities, eliminating the dependence on personal skills or initiative) and scientific management (which creates a rigid environment, where everyone is forced to work in the manner dictated by a superior).

These principles are, clearly, an application of the mechanistic ideology: from a rather haphazard series of activities, the manufacturing process has been turned into an exact system – a system that can be represented with a hierarchical structure. In this structure, the elements are the various components, stages, persons, and activities, and the efficiency of this arrangement is assured by the mechanistic concept itself. So there can be little doubt that, to be as efficient in the other fields as we are in manufacturing, we must follow the same principles. We must modify the entire society to resemble, so to speak, a giant factory: each person, each act, each thought, must be designed to function as an element in a giant structure of things within things. We are currently in the process of implementing this idea in our educational and business activities; and soon we will extend it to all social and personal affairs.

Thus, while this may seem paradoxical, it is a fact that if we want to become more efficient we must be *less* knowledgeable, *less* skilled, *less* experienced. It is our natural tendency to gain knowledge that slows progress. So we must stop trying to develop such old-fashioned qualities as expertise or individuality, and admit that we can accomplish more by being an insignificant part in a great whole. We must allow the elites, who have proved the value of this idea in fields like manufacturing, to design that great hierarchical social structure for us. And we must restrict ourselves to those activities which they prescribe.

This ideology – totalitarianism – is quite old, in fact, and was always appreciated by enlightened leaders. The reason it seems new is that only in the twentieth century it became practical on a large scale. The first attempts,

Communism and Nazism, were rather crude and violent. They were *political* movements, and failed. We learned from these mistakes, however, and we rely now on universities and corporations, instead of political institutions, to implement it. Our totalitarianism is better, and it will succeed.

4

Despite its obvious benefits, totalitarianism is not without critics. The first objection concerns the process of dehumanization that inevitably accompanies it. Thinkers of various outlooks – philosophers, sociologists, science-fiction authors – have been warning us for a hundred years that we are being turned into automatons. The vision of a society where human beings are treated as parts of a giant machine, and restricted to some simple and repetitive acts, is not very appealing – even if this is done in the name of efficiency or progress.

As answer to this objection, we point to the great improvements in standard of living and in life expectancy that all sections of society have enjoyed thanks to totalitarianism. Thus, as in any social project, our decision to pursue this ideology amounts to a compromise: we are trading more and more aspects of our humanity for greater and greater prosperity. This has worked out well so far, and there is no reason to doubt that we can continue this trade in the future. Besides, people don't seem to mind this dehumanization: following rules and methods is easier than developing expertise, and most of us are quite happy to be merely parts of a whole, as this absolves us from responsibility for our acts and choices.

More recently, a second objection has arisen to the totalitarian ideology. This objection concerns the environmental problems associated with infinite progress. Specifically, we are reminded that, even if we agree to become full-fledged automatons in our unending quest for prosperity, we may never get there. Growth is limited by such factors as increasing pollution and diminishing natural resources, so the assumption that an ideology which worked in the past will continue to work in the future is invalid. In other words, our ideology is wrong, not so much because it dehumanizes us, but because at the current rate of growth we will destroy ourselves by ruining the environment *before* we do it by becoming automatons.

Unlike the first one, this objection is gaining in popularity, owing largely to the ease with which we can delude ourselves that we care about the environment. All we need to do is read books and articles, watch television documentaries, and discuss the issue from time to time – while keeping our lifestyles and expectations unchanged. This stratagem permits us to feel concerned and involved, without having to give up anything. In reality, an endless increase in prosperity is possible only through an exponential growth in production and consumption. To prevent the environmental problems, therefore, we would have to reduce our prosperity even more than we would have to in order to prevent our dehumanization. And we already saw what is our attitude on the latter. People who agree to pay for prosperity by living their lives as automatons are not likely to renounce the same prosperity for the benefit of future generations. So, despite its apparent popularity, the second objection will not stop the spread of totalitarianism any more than the first objection did in the past.

It is not these two objections that ought to preoccupy us, however, but a *third* one; namely, the risk that the totalitarianism we are being offered may not be at all what it is said to be. We believe the problem is simply whether the price we pay for progress and prosperity is too high, while the real problem is whether we are getting anything at all for this price. The elites justify the totalitarian ideology by telling us that it is grounded on mechanistic, and hence scientific, principles. But if these principles are becoming less and less useful, the elites are deceiving us – regardless of the price we are willing to pay.

The justification entails a succession of ideologies: mechanism, scientism, utopianism, totalitarianism. The belief in mechanism leads to scientism – the application of mechanistic concepts in the study of minds and societies, where they cannot work. Then, despite the failure of their theories, the mechanists conclude that society can be greatly improved by actually implementing these theories; so, scientism leads to utopianism. Finally, everyone agrees that the only practical way to carry out this project is through totalitarianism: by allowing an elite to control all aspects of society.

Totalitarianism, thus, is justified by pointing to its origin, mechanism. Our infatuation with mechanism is so strong that even when noticing its failures, or its harmful consequences, we still do not question the ideology itself. So we accept and respect the idea of totalitarianism, even when criticizing it, simply because we believe it to be scientific. We have no evidence that totalitarianism works, but we cannot help trusting those who advocate it.

5

The declining usefulness of mechanism has engendered a new phenomenon: charlatanism practised in the name of science or in the name of business. This charlatanism consists in the promise to solve a non-mechanistic problem with mechanistic methods. Since mechanism is universally accepted as "the method of science," we trust implicitly anyone who invokes the mechanistic principles.

Thus, once we decided to measure the value of an idea solely by its mechanistic qualities, it became impossible to distinguish between serious mechanistic ideas and mechanistic *delusions*.

Mechanistic delusions have always been part of our culture. Until recently, however, their harm was overshadowed by the mechanistic *successes*. Today, fewer and fewer problems have simple, mechanistic solutions, so the harm caused by delusions exceeds the benefits derived from successes.

Totalitarianism, in particular, is a mechanistic delusion. We like totalitarianism for the same reason we like all other mechanistic ideas: because it offers what appears to be simple solutions to difficult problems. However, while the pursuit of an ordinary mechanistic delusion means merely a waste of resources, the pursuit of totalitarianism can lead to the collapse of society. For, if the world is too complex to be improved mechanistically, the claimed benefits are a fantasy, while the price we pay for them is real. Our problems are getting bigger, while our minds are getting smaller: if we restrict ourselves to mechanistic thinking, we leave our non-mechanistic capabilities undeveloped; so we cope perhaps with the simple, mechanistic problems, but the complex, non-mechanistic ones remain unsolved, and will eventually destroy us.

In universities, the charlatanism is seen in the activity known as research. The rule is simple: any work that follows the mechanistic principles of reductionism and atomism is deemed scientific, and is therefore legitimate. Whether these principles are valid or not in a given field, or whether the resulting theories work or not, is immaterial. Thus, when faced with a problem in the human sciences, all one has to do is perceive it as a hierarchical structure. The problem can then be broken down into smaller and smaller parts, until reaching problems simple enough to describe with precision. But this method, borrowed from the exact sciences, fails when applied to human phenomena. It fails because human phenomena consist, not of one structure, but of multiple, interacting structures.

So the researchers are admired for the rigour with which they study those small problems, even while the real problem remains unsolved. Clearly, their only defence is that they are following the mechanistic principles. But why should principles that are useful in modeling the material world be accepted without reservation in the study of minds and societies? As soon as we question the value of mechanism in these fields, any research project grounded on mechanism changes from scientific pursuit to mechanistic fantasy. What stands between perceiving these academics as scientists or as charlatans, then, is only our blind acceptance of the mechanistic ideology.

In business, the charlatanism is seen in the activity known as marketing. The elites, we saw, tell us that our future must be based on an endless growth in production and consumption, and that this can only be achieved through mechanistic methods. But if, in fact, there is less and less that *can* be discovered or improved mechanistically, the only way to attain the required growth is by replacing the making of useful things with the making of whatever can be made mechanistically (that is, efficiently and profitably). To put this differently, if the old experts – scientists, inventors, entrepreneurs – cannot keep up with our demand for growth, we must replace them with a new kind of experts: charlatans, who know how to make useless things appear important, and thereby help us to delude ourselves that our system is working just as it did in the past.

Thus, from its modest origin as a complement to trade, the process of selling has become more important than the merchandise itself. The fact that it is possible to cheat people, to persuade them to buy something that is not what it appears to be, is now the driving force of the economy. Deceptive advertising – messages purporting to inform while in reality exploiting human weaknesses and ignorance – is no longer limited to domains like fashion or cosmetics, but covers practically all products and services. Dishonest techniques (testimonials and success stories, background music, pictures of happy faces, and the like) are widely employed in order to influence, distract, and confuse. These techniques are logically equivalent to lying (they are needed precisely because the usefulness of those products and services cannot be proved), but we no longer notice this. Language itself has ceased to be a means of communication, and is used as a kind of weapon: words are carefully chosen, not to convey information, but to deceive and to manipulate.

Finally, and most disturbingly, the idea of "selling" has transcended the domain of commerce and is now found in every activity where there is an opportunity to influence people. From what we say in a résumé to what governments say in their policies, from business meetings to military decisions, from lectures and seminars to television news and documentaries, it is vital that we know how to *persuade* our audience; that is, how to *mislead* – how to use special effects so as to make unimportant things appear important, and important things unimportant.

The fact that we have to lie so much ought to worry us, ought to prompt us to doubt our system. We need more and more lies, obviously, because our *real* achievements do not fulfil our expectations. We have experienced continuous growth ever since the Scientific Revolution, and our world view has evolved accordingly: we have yet to accept the fact that there is a limit to discoveries and improvements. We are still making progress, of course, but at a slower and slower rate. Since the exponential growth that we are accustomed to cannot be sustained indefinitely, we are now supplementing the real growth with an imaginary one, based on fantasies. But instead of interpreting the perpetual increase in charlatanism as evidence that our system is failing, we perceive the charlatanism as a new sort of science, or a new sort of business, and hence its increase as progress.

Much of the current growth, thus, is actually growth in delusions, and in the stupidity necessary in order to accept these delusions. It is as if, having realized that the human capacity for intelligence does not guarantee infinite growth, we are now trying to achieve the same growth by relying instead on the human capacity for stupidity. Like oil and minerals, we treat stupidity as a kind of resource, as something that we can exploit and benefit from. To make the most of this resource, though, human beings must be carefully indoctrinated, in order to neutralize their natural capacity for intelligence. The incessant lies and delusions, then, serve to replace the *reality* that surrounds us with the *fantasies* that – according to the elites – are the world we must strive to create instead.

To summarize, the mechanistic myth has outlived its usefulness. What started as a good myth, helping us to expand our knowledge of the world, has become bad. The same qualities that make mechanism such a useful concept are now turning against us. For, mechanism can only explain *simple* phenomena – those that can be represented with *isolated* hierarchical structures; and in today's world we are facing more and more *complex* phenomena, which can only be represented with *systems* of structures. One reason for the complexity, thus, is that there are fewer and fewer mechanistic phenomena left to be explained. If we want to expand our knowledge today, we must increasingly deal with those phenomena that we chose to ignore in the past – when there were so many simple, mechanistic ones, waiting to be studied. Another reason for the complexity is that, as we keep expanding our knowledge, we are creating ourselves new, non-mechanistic phenomena (the software phenomena are an example).

So the mechanistic myth works against us because it restricts us to mechanistic thinking while our most important problems are non-mechanistic. The past successes of the mechanistic philosophy, together with its irresistible appeal, prevent us from noticing how limited mechanism really is. We are trying to explain everything mechanistically while less and less *is* mechanistic. As a result, we are wasting our resources on absurd ideas, neglecting the real problems. Only *minds* can process complex structures. So, to contend with our current problems, we must develop the highest intelligence and expertise that human minds are capable of. Instead, the mechanistic culture restricts us to novice levels: we are taught to treat every challenge as simple, isolated structures, so we are using only our mechanistic capabilities.

Along with the mechanistic myth, our elites too have turned from good to bad. The elites defend the mechanistic myth because it is through this belief that they hold their privileged position. Thus, as long as we accept mechanism unquestioningly, all they have to do to gain our respect is practise mechanism. If we judged them instead by assessing the validity or usefulness of their ideas, we would realize how little of what they do is important. We would stop respecting them, and they would lose their elitist position.

So we shouldn't be surprised that our elites praise the mechanistic ideology and cover up the failure of the mechanistic ideas. In the past, when most mechanistic ideas were useful, the elites did not have to resort to lies and delusions; they gained our respect through real achievements. Today, the mechanistic ideas are becoming increasingly worthless; so the only way for the elites to maintain their position is through charlatanism, by *fooling* us into accepting mechanistic ideas.

Mechanism, moreover, has become totalitarian: We are asked now, not just to accept the mechanistic delusions promoted by the elites, but to become devoted mechanists ourselves. Like the elites, we must restrict ourselves to mechanistic thinking and adhere to this ideology regardless of whether our activities are successful or not.

Our totalitarianism, thus, is the ultimate mechanistic fantasy. For, if our problems stem from the declining usefulness of mechanism, it is absurd to attempt to solve them through totalitarianism, which only *adds* to our mechanistic practices. So, when listening to the elites, we are moving in the wrong direction: we are *aggravating* the problems. The elites tell us that totalitarianism is necessary in order to become more efficient. But if it is based on mechanism, and if mechanism itself is less and less useful, how can totalitarianism help us?

6

By way of conclusion, let us speculate on the alternatives to mechanism. We saw earlier that all human societies are founded on myths. For us, since the seventeenth century, the most important myth has been the mechanistic philosophy. Usually described as a shift from religion to science, the transition to mechanism was in fact a shift from religion myths to science myths: all we accomplished was to replace one kind of myths with another. Mechanism is not an ultimate concept, but merely an improvement, a better way to represent the world.

The usefulness of mechanism has been exhausted, however, and it can no longer function as myth: rather than helping us to advance our knowledge, it holds us back now, and allows evil elites to exploit us. There is an urgent need to abandon it. But it is highly unlikely that, during the next few decades, we can achieve something that no human society ever could – learn to live without myths. The only practical alternative, therefore, is to replace mechanism with a different myth. We must effect, in our lifetime, the next transition: from this naive, seventeenth-century myth, to a modern one, adequate for our time. If we *must* believe in myths, we should at least choose one that can help us to solve *today's* problems.

We will continue to use mechanism, of course, but only where appropriate. What we want to avoid is the mechanistic *delusions*. In those fields where it works, mechanism remains the best method, the best way to represent the world. So what we must do is demote it: from its position as *myth*, to a more modest position, as *method*. Then, we must turn to the *new* myth for inspiration in solving our complex, non-mechanistic problems.

What is left is to decide what belief should replace mechanism as myth. It is obvious that the new myth must be more than just a more sophisticated variant of the mechanistic method. The greatest challenges we face today do not entail merely a larger number of mechanistic problems, or more involved mechanistic problems, but *non-mechanistic* problems. And there is only one way to solve this type of problems: by using our minds. As we will see in chapter 2, our minds excel at solving precisely the type of problems that mechanism leaves unsolved. In our infatuation with mechanism, we have been neglecting these problems. Moreover, we have been neglecting our own, non-mechanistic capabilities: we have been using only a fraction of the capacity of our minds, only what we need in order to think mechanistically.

The next myth, thus, must be a belief in *the unlimited potential of our minds*. Like all myths, this is a fantasy, since the potential of our minds is not unlimited. But we can *believe* that it is; and the very belief will inspire us. In fact, we are using now so little of this potential that, for all practical purposes, it *is* unlimited. Once accepted as myth, the new belief will motivate us to appreciate and to use our non-mechanistic capabilities. And with these capabilities we will accomplish more than we do now.

This process would be similar to the way mechanism itself functioned in the seventeenth century. As we will see in chapter 1, it was its role as myth, rather than its usefulness as method, that imparted to mechanism its strength. It was the *belief* that its potential is unlimited that inspired the seventeenth-century scientists. Had they perceived mechanism as just a new method of research, they would not have had the confidence to propose those radical theories, and the Scientific Revolution would not have happened. Today there are more mechanistic *delusions* than discoveries, so it is obvious that the potential of mechanism is not unlimited. But this fact did not detract from its value in the seventeenth century. All we have to do, then, is undergo a similar process with the new myth. And this will help us to bring about advances of a different kind: in non-mechanistic knowledge.

If it seems improbable that we can start to believe now in a new myth, we must remember that human societies can adopt any myth. Thus, if we managed to believe for three hundred years that every phenomenon can be represented with a neat structure of things within things (an idea easily shown to be false, as we saw), it shouldn't be so difficult to believe now that the potential of our minds is unlimited.

But regardless of which myth we decide to adopt next, we *must* end our dependence on the mechanistic myth, and on the elites that profit from it. The blind belief in mechanism is destroying our minds, and is preventing us from dealing with our problems. The mechanistic *software* beliefs, in particular, have permitted a powerful *software* elite to arise. In just a few decades, organizations that have in fact little to offer us have attained so much power that they practically control society. As we will see in the course of this book, their power rests almost entirely on mechanistic software delusions, and on the stupidity engendered by these delusions.

Software, thus, has emerged as the most effective means of enforcing the mechanistic dogma. Software should have been our most modern pursuit; instead, degraded by the software elite, it is now merely the most modern way of pursuing a seventeenth-century myth.

The Software Myth

1

The software myth is the idea of software mechanism – the enactment of mechanistic beliefs through software. If traditional mechanism holds that every phenomenon can be represented with a hierarchical structure, software mechanism holds that every phenomenon can be represented with a hierarchical *software* structure. This is true because, once we reduce a phenomenon hierarchically to its simplest entities, these entities can be emulated by means of simple *software* entities. To represent the original phenomenon, all we have to do then is combine these entities hierarchically, and thereby generate a software structure that corresponds to the structure of entities that is the phenomenon itself.

In particular, the phenomena associated with human knowledge can be represented with software. Since any type of knowledge can be reduced hierarchically to simpler and simpler pieces down to some basic bits of knowledge, by incorporating these bits in a software device we can emulate the original knowledge structure. Then, simply by operating the device, anyone will be able to perform the same tasks as a person who took the time to acquire the actual knowledge.

Software devices, thus, are perceived as substitutes for knowledge, skills, and experience. Whereas in the past we needed much learning and practice in order to attain expertise in a given field, all we need to know now, it seems, is how to operate software devices.

One type of knowledge that we have been trying especially hard to represent with software is *programming* knowledge. If software devices are only now gaining acceptance in our businesses and in our homes, their counterparts in the world of programming have existed since the 1960s. Thus, if the use of software devices as substitutes for expertise still sounds plausible for other types of knowledge, we have already had several decades to assess their value in *programming* work. And, as we will see in chapter 7, the claim that there exist substitutes for programming expertise has proved to be a fraud.

The study of software mechanism in the domain of programming can help us to understand, therefore, the delusion of software devices in general. For, it is the same myth that the elites invoke when promoting knowledge substitutes, whether they address programmers or other workers. Programming is the only domain in which we can, today, actually demonstrate the failure of software mechanism and the dishonesty of the software elites. Thus, we must make the most of this experience. If we understand how the software myth has destroyed the programming profession, we will be in a better position to recognize its dangers, and to prevent it perhaps from destroying other fields of knowledge.

2

The reason it is so tempting to think of software development as a mechanistic process is that software applications are indeed hierarchical structures – modules within modules. No matter how large or complex, it seems that an application can always be depicted as a neat structure of software entities, just as a manufactured object can be depicted as a neat structure of parts and subassemblies.

As we do in manufacturing, therefore, we should break down the process of software development into smaller and smaller parts, until we reach software entities that are easy to program. Then, as in manufacturing, we will be able to create applications of any size and complexity by employing inexperienced workers – workers who, individually, can only program small and simple pieces of software.

This idea, known as *software engineering*, is behind every programming theory of the last forty years. But the idea is wrong. We already saw that software applications are in fact *systems* of hierarchical structures, so the structure of modules that appears to represent an application is merely *one* of the structures that make it up. The software entities that constitute the application possess many attributes: they call subroutines, use database fields, reflect business practices, etc. Since each attribute gives rise to a structure, each structure represents a different aspect of the application: one subroutine and its calls, the uses of one database field, the implementation of one business practice, etc. But because they share their elements (the software entities that constitute the application), these structures are not independent. So the only way to develop applications is by dealing with several structures at the same time – something that only minds can do, and only after much practice.

Thus, while software engineering is said to turn programmers from old-fashioned artisans into modern professionals, its true purpose is the exact opposite: to eliminate the need for programming expertise. And this, the elites believe, can be accomplished by discovering scientific (i.e., mechanistic) programming theories, and by restricting programmers to methodologies and development systems based on these theories. The aim is to separate applications into their constituent structures, and further separate these structures into their constituent elements, at which point programmers will only need to deal with small, isolated software entities. For example, the theory of structured programming claims that the only important structure is the one that represents the application's flow of execution, and that this structure can be reduced to some simple, standard constructs; and the theory of object-oriented programming claims that we can treat each aspect of our affairs as a separate structure, which can then be assembled from some smaller, existing structures.

But each theory, while presented as a revolution in programming concepts, is in reality very similar to the others. This is true because they are all based on the same fallacy; namely, on the assumption that software and programming are mechanistic phenomena, and can be studied with the principles of reductionism and atomism. Ultimately, the naive idea of software engineering is a reflection of the ignorance that the academics and the practitioners suffer from. They remain ignorant because they waste their time with worthless theories: they are forever trying to explain the phenomena of software and programming through the mechanistic myth. It is not an exaggeration to say that, for the last forty years, their main preoccupation has been this absurd search for a way to reduce software to mechanics. The preoccupation is also reflected in their vocabulary: programmers call themselves "engineers," and refer to programming as "building" or "constructing" software.

The programming theories, thus, are mechanistic delusions, because they attempt to represent complex phenomena mechanistically. What is worse, instead of being abandoned when found to be useless, they are turned by their defenders into pseudosciences. Here is how: Since neither the academics nor the practitioners are willing to admit that their latest theory has failed, they continue to praise it even as they struggle against its deficiencies. They deny the endless falsifications, and keep modifying the theory in the hope of making it practical. While described as new features, the modifications serve in fact to mask the falsifications: they reinstate the traditional, *non-mechanistic* programming concepts – precisely those concepts that the theory had attempted to eliminate. In the end, the theory's exact, mechanistic principles are forgotten altogether. Its defenders, though, continue to promote it by invoking the benefits of mechanism. Then, after perpetrating this fraud for a number of years, another mechanistic theory is invented and the same process is repeated.

So the software workers are not the serious professionals they appear to be, but impostors. Whether they are academics who invent mechanistic theories, or software companies that create systems based on these theories, or programmers who rely on these systems, very little of what they do is genuine. They appear to be dealing with important issues, but most of these issues are senseless preoccupations engendered by their mechanistic delusions: since our problems rarely have simple, mechanistic answers, there is no limit to the specious activities that one can contrive when attempting to solve them mechanistically.

The mechanistic software ideology, thus, is the perfect medium for incompetents and charlatans, as it permits them to engage in modern, glamorous, and profitable activities while doing almost nothing useful. The software practitioners have become a powerful bureaucracy, exploiting society while appearing to serve it. Less than 10 percent (and often less than 1 percent) of their work has any value. Their main objective is not to help us solve our problems through software, but on the contrary, to create new, software-related problems; in other words, to make all human activities as complicated and inefficient as they have made their own, programming activities.

At the top of this bureaucracy are the software elites – the universities and the software companies. It is these elites that control, ultimately, our software-related affairs. And they do it by promoting mechanistic software concepts: since we believe in mechanism, and since their theories and systems are founded on mechanistic principles, we readily accept their elitist position. But if software mechanism is generally useless, their theories and systems are fraudulent, and their elitist position is unwarranted.

3

Three ingredients are needed to implement totalitarianism: a myth, an elite, and a bureaucracy. And the spread of totalitarianism is caused by an expansion of the bureaucracy: larger and larger portions of the population change from their role as citizens, or workers, to the role of bureaucrats; that is, from individuals who perform useful tasks to individuals whose chief responsibility is to practise the myth.

A characteristic of totalitarianism, thus, is this continuous increase in the number of people whose beliefs and acts are a reflection of the myth. Rather than relying on common sense, or logic, or some personal or professional values, people justify their activities by invoking the myth. Or, they justify them by pointing to certain ideas or theories, or to other activities; but if these in their turn can only be justified by invoking the myth, the original activities are specious.

A totalitarian bureaucracy can be seen as a pyramid that expands downward, at its base. The elite, which forms its apex, uses the myth to establish the system's ideology and to recruit the first bureaucrats – the first layer of the pyramid. Further layers are then added, and the pyramid becomes increasingly broad and deep, as more and more categories of people cease living a normal life and join the bureaucracy. Thus, as the pyramid expands, fewer and fewer people are left who perform useful activities; and the closer an individual is to the top of the pyramid, the greater the number of senseless, myth-related preoccupations that make up his life.

Since the lower layers support the higher ones, the model of a pyramid also explains how social power is distributed under totalitarianism: each layer exploits the layers that lie below it, and the elite, at the top of the pyramid, exploits the entire bureaucracy. Thus, the closer we get to the top, the more power, influence, and privileges we find. In addition, the bureaucracy as a whole exploits the rest of society – those individuals and institutions that have not yet joined it.

The totalitarian ideal is that *all* people in society join the bureaucracy and restrict themselves to myth-related activities. But this, clearly, cannot happen; for, who would support them all? In the initial stages of the expansion, when enough people are still engaged in useful activities, the elite and the bureaucrats can delude themselves that their ideology is working. As more and more people join the bureaucracy, however, the useful activities decline and the system becomes increasingly inefficient. Eventually, the inefficiency reaches a point where society can no longer function adequately, and collapses. It is impossible to attain the totalitarian ideal – a bureaucracy that comprises the entire society.

It should be obvious, then, why the software myth can serve as the foundation of a totalitarian ideology. Since the essence of totalitarianism is endless expansion, the ideology must be based on an idea that appeals to every individual in society. And few ideas can match software in this respect. As we will see in chapter 4, software is comparable only to language in its versatility and potency. Thus, even when employed correctly, without falling prey to mechanistic delusions, software can benefit almost anyone. But when perceived as a *mechanistic* concept, its utopian promise becomes irresistible. The promise, we saw, is that software devices can act as substitutes for knowledge, skills, and experience. So, simply by operating a software device, we will be able to perform immediately tasks that would otherwise require special talents, or many years of study and practice. The promise of the software myth, thus, exceeds even the most extravagant promises made by the old political or religious myths. Consequently, an elite can dominate and exploit society through the software myth even more effectively than the political and religious elites did through the other myths, in the past.

The expansion of the software bureaucracy parallels the spread of computers; and even a brief analysis of this expansion (later in this section) will reveal the process whereby various categories of people are turned into bureaucrats. All it takes is a blind belief in the software myth – something that the elite is fostering through propaganda and indoctrination. Then, judged from the perspective of the myth, activities that are in fact illogical, or inefficient, or wasteful, are perceived as important and beneficial; and the incompetents who engage in these activities are perceived as professionals.

Ignorance, therefore, is what makes the belief in a myth, and hence the expansion of a bureaucracy, possible. An individual who took the time to develop expertise in a certain field cannot also develop irrational beliefs in the same field, as that would contradict his personal experience. Thus, in addition to its versatility and potency, it is its novelty that makes software such a good subject for myth. We allowed an elite to assume control of our software-related affairs without first giving ourselves the time to discover what is the true nature of software. And the elite saw software, not as a complex phenomenon, but as a mechanistic one; in other words, not as a phenomenon that demands the full capacity of the mind, but as one that requires only mechanistic thinking.

Because of this delusion, we have remained ignorant: we depend on software while lacking the skills to create and use software intelligently. Instead of developing software expertise, we wasted the last forty years struggling with the worthless theories and methodologies promoted by the elite. Under these conditions, the emergence of irrational beliefs was inevitable. The software myth, thus, is a consequence of our mechanistic culture and our software ignorance.

4

The first workers to be turned into software bureaucrats were the programmers themselves. From the start, the theorists assumed that programming can be reduced to some simple and repetitive acts, similar to those performed by assembly-line workers in a factory. So, they concluded, programmers do not require lengthy education, training, and practice. If we develop software applications as we build appliances, all that programmers need to know is how to follow certain methods, and how to use certain aids – methods and aids based, like those in manufacturing, on the principles of reductionism and atomism. And to improve their performance later, all we need to do is improve the methods and aids.

Thus, instead of trying to understand the true nature of software and programming, the theorists *assumed* them to be mechanistic phenomena; and the programming profession was founded upon this assumption. Using the mechanistic myth as warrant, programming expertise was redefined as expertise in the use of theories, methodologies, and development aids; in other words, expertise in the use of substitutes for expertise. So what was required of programmers from then on was not programming skills, but merely familiarity with the latest substitutes.

If expertise is the highest level attainable by human minds in a given domain, and incompetence the lowest, programmers were neither expected nor permitted to attain a level much higher than incompetence. And, as society needed more and more software, everyone was convinced that what we needed was more and more of this kind of programmers. The alternative – promoting expertise and professionalism, allowing individuals to develop the highest possible skills – was never considered.

The effects of this ideology can be seen in the large number of software failures: development projects abandoned after spending millions of dollars, critical business needs that remain unfulfilled, applications that are inadequate or unreliable, promises of increased savings or efficiency that do not material-ize. Statistics unchanged since the 1970s show that less than 5 percent of programming projects result in adequate applications. What these statistics do not reveal is that even those applications that are adequate when new cannot be kept up to date (because badly written and badly maintained), so they must be replaced after a few years. The statistics also do not reveal that, with inexperienced programmers, it costs far more than necessary to create even those applications that are successful. And if we remember also the cost of the additional hardware needed to run badly written applications, it is safe to say that, for over forty years, society has been paying in effect one hundred dollars for every dollar's worth of useful software.[1]

The conclusion ought to be that the mechanistic assumption is wrong: programming expertise is not the kind of knowledge that can be replaced with methods or devices, so personal skills and experience remain an important factor. The answer to the software failures is then simply to recognize that, as is the case in other difficult professions, to become a proficient programmer one needs many years of serious education, training, and practice.

In our mechanistic software culture, however, this idea is inadmissible; and someone who suggests it is accused of clinging to old-fashioned values, of resisting science and progress. The only accepted answer to the software failures is that we need, not better programmers, but better theories, methodologies, and development aids. If the previous ones failed, we are told, it is because they did not adhere faithfully enough to the mechanistic ideology; so the next ones must be even more mechanistic. In other words, the only permissible solutions to the problem of programming incompetence are those derived from the mechanistic myth – the same solutions that were tried in the past, and which *cause* in fact the incompetence. No matter how many failures we witness, the mechanistic ideology is never questioned.

The mechanistic software concepts cause incompetence because they are specifically intended as *substitutes* for programming expertise. Thus, it is not surprising that programmers who rely on these substitutes do not advance past the level of novices: they are *expected* to remain at this level.

So the incompetence of programmers, and the astronomic cost of software, are a direct consequence of the mechanistic myth. For the first time, a mechanistic delusion is powerful enough to affect the entire society. Previously, it was only in universities that individuals could pursue a mechanistic fantasy, in the guise of research; and the failure of their projects had little effect on the rest of society. Through software, however, the pursuit of mechanistic fantasies became possible everywhere. Unlike the mechanistic theories in

---

[1] It must be noted that software expenses, and computing expenses generally, are now usually called "investments." Useless concepts can only be promoted through deception: it is easier to make ignorant decision makers *invest*, than it is to make them *spend*, large amounts of money on dubious products and services. Thus, "investment" has joined the deceptive terms "solution" and "technology" in the promotion of software novelties in lectures, articles, advertising, and conversation.

psychology, sociology, or linguistics, the mechanistic *software* theories are not limited to academic research. Being applicable to business computing, they spread throughout society, and degraded the notions of expertise and responsibility in business just as mechanistic research had degraded these notions in universities. Just as the academics perceive their responsibility to be, not the discovery of useful theories but the pursuit of mechanistic ideas, programmers perceive their responsibility to be, not the creation of useful applications but the use of mechanistic software methods.

Millions of individuals are engaged, thus, not in programming but in the pursuit of mechanistic fantasies. Probably no more than 1 percent of the programming activities in society represent useful work; that is, work benefiting society in the way the work of doctors does. We find ourselves today in this incredible situation because programming is a new profession, without established standards of expertise. We allowed the software elite to persuade us that this profession must be based on mechanistic principles, so the standard of expertise became, simply, expertise in mechanistic software concepts. Had we tried first the alternative – giving programmers the time and opportunity to develop the highest knowledge and skills that human beings can attain in this new profession – we would easily recognize the absurdity of the mechanistic concepts, and the incompetence of those who restrict themselves to such concepts. It is only because we take software mechanism as unquestionable truth that we accept the current programming practices as a normal level of expertise. And if we consider this level normal, it is natural to accept also the resulting cost and the failures.

Also, with so many programmers around, new types of supervisors had to be created: more and more employees were turned into software bureaucrats – project managers, systems analysts, database administrators – to oversee the hordes of programmers who, everyone agreed, could not be trusted to develop applications on their own. Again, no one questioned this logic. If the programmers were deemed incompetent and irresponsible, the answer should have been to improve their training. Instead, it was decided to adopt, for software development, the assembly-line methods used in manufacturing; namely, to treat programmers as unskilled workers, and to develop applications by relying on management expertise rather than programming expertise.

So for every few programmers there was now a manager, and for every few managers a higher manager. But the manufacturing methods are inadequate for programming, because software applications are not neat hierarchical structures of subassemblies. Consequently, turning software development into factory-type work did not solve the problem of programming incompetence. It only increased the software bureaucracy, and hence the cost of software, and the failures. (Sociological studies of the programming profession, conducted in the 1970s, show that the main goal of corporate management was not so much to improve programming practices, as to repress the programmers' attitudes and expectations. For example, the theory of structured programming was promoted as the means to turn programming into an exact activity, and programmers into skilled professionals, while its true purpose was the opposite: to *deskill* programmers; specifically, to eliminate the need and opportunity for programmers to make important decisions, and to give management complete control over their work.[2])

Finally, as the benefits expected from mechanistic software concepts are not materializing, new types of bureaucrats must be constantly invented as a solution to the incompetence of programmers. Thus, companies have now employees with absurd titles like architect, systems integrator, data analyst, business intelligence analyst, and report developer. While justified by invoking the growing complexity of business computing, and the growing importance of information technology, the task of these new bureaucrats is in reality to do what programmers should be doing; that is, create and maintain business applications. What masks this fact is that, instead of programming, they try to accomplish the same thing through various end-user tools, or by putting together ready-made pieces of software. But the idea that we can create useful applications in this fashion is based on the same delusions as the idea that programming expertise can be replaced with methods and aids. So it only adds to the complexity of business computing, while the real software problems remain unsolved. This is interpreted, though, as a need for even more of the new bureaucrats, in a process that feeds on itself.

A major role in the spread of the software bureaucracy is played by the organizations that *create* the knowledge substitutes – the software companies. These companies form the elite, of course. But in addition to propagating the mechanistic software ideology, they function as employers; and in this capacity, they are turning millions of additional workers into software bureaucrats.

2 See Philip Kraft, *Programmers and Managers: The Routinization of Computer Programming in the United States* (New York: Springer-Verlag, 1977); see also Joan M. Greenbaum, *In the Name of Efficiency: Management Theory and Shopfloor Practice in Data-Processing Work* (Philadelphia: Temple University Press, 1979). It must be noted, though, that, while ground-breaking and as important today as they were in the 1970s, these studies treat the deskilling of programmers as part of the traditional conflict between management and labour. Their authors were unaware of the fallacies of software mechanism, and that theories like structured programming do not, in fact, work. Thus, the delusion that programmers must be a kind of factory workers – because programming is a kind of manufacturing – constitutes a sociological phenomenon that has yet to be studied.

From just a handful in the 1960s, the software companies have grown in number and in size to become an important part of the economy. And they accomplished this simply by invoking the myth of software mechanism. For, their software and services can be justified only if we accept unquestioningly the mechanistic ideology. Thus, only if we agree that software development is a form of manufacturing will we accept the resulting incompetence, and hence the aids and substitutes supplied by these companies as the answer. Or, putting this in reverse, if we had professional programmers instead of the current practitioners, less than 1 percent of the software supplied by these companies would be needed at all.

What this means is that countless organizations, while operating as legitimate businesses under the banner "technology," are actually engaged in the making and marketing of mechanistic software fantasies. So their employees, no matter how good they may be in these activities – programming, research, management, administration, selling – are not performing work that is truly useful. They belong, therefore, to the software bureaucracy.

The programmers who work for these companies hold a special place in the bureaucracy. They are, in general, better prepared and more experienced than the application programmers. But if their job is to develop the useless systems sold by the software companies, their talents are wasted. These systems may appear impressive to their users, but they cannot replace good applications, nor the expertise needed to create good applications. So, if these systems cannot be a substitute for expertise, the work of those who create them is just as senseless as the work of those who use them. We are witnessing, therefore, this absurd situation: our better programmers are employed to create, not the custom applications that society needs, but some generic applications, or some substitutes for the knowledge required to create custom applications. Instead of helping to eradicate the software bureaucracy, our universities prepare programmers for the software companies, thereby *adding* to the bureaucracy. For, by catering to the needs of software bureaucrats, the system programmers are reduced to bureaucrats themselves.

A different kind of software companies are the enterprises run by the individuals known as industry experts, or gurus. Unlike the regular software companies, the gurus earn their fame personally – as theorists, lecturers, and writers. Their role, however, is similar: to promote the ideology of software mechanism. So they are part of the elite. Also like the software companies, their existence is predicated on widespread programming incompetence and an ever-growing bureaucracy.

Although they seldom have any real programming experience (that is, personally creating and maintaining serious business applications), the gurus confidently write papers and books on programming, publish newsletters, invent theories and methodologies, lecture, teach courses, and provide consulting services. Their popularity – the fact that programmers, analysts, and managers seek their advice – demonstrates, thus, the ignorance that pervades the world of programming. To appreciate the absurdity of this situation, imagine a similar situation in medicine: individuals known to have no medical training, and who never performed any surgery, would write and lecture on operating procedures; and real surgeons, from real hospitals, would read their books, attend their courses, and follow their methods.

While unthinkable in other professions, we accept this situation as a logical part of our *programming* culture. The reason it seems logical is that it can be justified by pointing to the software myth: if what we perceive as programming expertise is familiarity with theories, methodologies, and software devices, it is only natural to respect, and to seek the advice of, those who know the most in this area. So the gurus are popular because they always promote the latest programming fads – which, at any given time, are what ignorant practitioners believe to be the cure for their current difficulties.

Programming was only the first profession to be destroyed by the software myth. Once we agreed to treat programmers as mere bureaucrats, instead of insisting that they become proficient and responsible workers, the spread of the software bureaucracy was inevitable. Every aspect of the degradation that is currently occurring in other professions can be traced to the incompetence of programmers. For, as we increasingly depend on computers and need more and more software applications, if the programmers are unreliable we must find other means to develop these applications. We already saw how new types of managers, and new types of software workers, were invented to deal with the problem of programming incompetence. This did not help, however. So the problem spread beyond the data-processing departments, and is now affecting the activities of software *users*.

Little by little, to help users perform the work that should have been performed by programmers, various software aids have been introduced. They vary from simple programming environments derived from databases or spreadsheets (which promise users the power to implement their own applications) to ready-made applications (which promise users the power to eliminate programming altogether). These aids, however, are grounded on the same mechanistic principles as the development aids offered to programmers, so they suffer from the same fallacies. If the substitutes for expertise cannot help programmers, we can hardly expect them to help amateurs, to create useful applications.

Workers everywhere, thus, are spending more and more of their time doing what only programmers had been doing before: pursuing mechanistic software fantasies. Increasingly, those who depend on computers must modify the way they work so as to fit within the mechanistic software ideology: they must depend on the inferior applications developed by inexperienced programmers, or on the childish applications they are developing themselves, or on the generic, inadequate applications supplied by software companies. The world of business is being degraded to match the world of programming: other workers are becoming as inefficient in their occupations as programmers are in theirs; like the programmers, they are wasting more and more of their time dealing with specious, software-related problems.

But we perceive this as a normal state of affairs, as an inevitable evolution of office work and business management. Because we believe that the only way to benefit from software is through the mechanistic ideology, we are now happy to adopt this ideology in our own work. As software users, we forget that the very reason we are preoccupied with software problems instead of our real problems is the incompetence and inefficiency caused by the mechanistic ideology in programming. So, by adopting the same ideology, we end up replicating the incompetence and inefficiency in other types of work. In other words, we become software bureaucrats ourselves.

Thus, because we do not have a true programming profession, workers with no knowledge of programming, or computers, or engineering, or science are increasingly involved in the design and creation of software applications. And, lacking the necessary skills, they are turning to the knowledge substitutes offered by the software companies – which substitutes address now all people, not just programmers. So, as millions of amateurs are joining the millions of inexperienced practitioners, the field of application development is becoming very similar to the field of consumer goods. A vast network of distribution and retail was set up to serve these software consumers, and a comprehensive system of public relations, marketing, and advertising has emerged to promote the knowledge substitutes: books, periodicals, brochures, catalogues, news-letters, trade shows, conventions, courses, seminars, and online sources.

The similarity to consumer goods is clearly seen in the editorial and advertising styles: childish publication covers; abundance of inane terms like "powerful," "easily," "solution," and "technology"; the use of testimonials to demonstrate the benefits of a product; prices like $99.99; and so on. Thus, while discussing programming, business, efficiency, or productivity, the promotion of the software devices resembles the promotion of cosmetics, fitness gadgets, or money-making schemes. Also similar to consumer advertising are the deceptive claims; in particular, promising ignorant people the ability to perform a difficult task simply by buying something. The software market, thus, is now about the same as the traditional consumer market: charlatans selling useless things to dupes.

Again, to appreciate the absurdity of this situation, all we have to do is compare the field of programming with a field like medicine. There is no equivalent, in medicine, of this transformation of a difficult profession into a consumer market. We don't find any advertisers or retailers offering knowledge substitutes to lay people and inexperienced practitioners who are asked to replace the professionals.

This transformation, then, has forced countless additional workers to join the software bureaucracy. For, if what they help to sell is based on the idea that software devices can replace expertise, and if this idea stems from the belief in software mechanism, all those involved in marketing the knowledge substitutes are engaged in senseless activities.

Finally, let us recall that it is precisely those institutions which ought to encourage rationality – our universities – that beget the software delusions. Because they teach and promote only *mechanistic* software concepts, the universities are, ultimately, responsible for the widespread programming incompetence and the resulting corruption.

In the same category are the many associations and institutes that represent the world of programming. The ACM and the IEEE Computer Society, in particular – the oldest and most important – are not at all the scientific and educational organizations they appear to be. For, while promoting profession-alism in the use of computers, and excellence in programming, their idea of professionalism and excellence is simply adherence to the mechanistic ideology. Thus, because they advocate the same concepts as the universities and the software companies, these organizations serve the interests of the elite, not society.

If this sounds improbable, consider their record: They praise every pro-gramming novelty, without seriously verifying it or confirming its usefulness. At any given time, they proselytize the latest programming "revolution," urging practitioners to join it: being familiar with the current software concepts, they tell us, is essential for advancement. In particular, they endorsed the three pseudoscientific theories we examine in chapter 7, and conferred awards on scientists who upheld them. As we will see, not only are these theories fallacious and worthless, but the scientists used dishonest means to defend them; for example, they claimed that the theories benefit from the rigour and precision of mathematics, while this is easily shown to be untrue. Thus, instead of exposing the software frauds, the ACM and the IEEE Computer Society help to propagate them.

What these organizations are saying, then, is exactly what every software guru and every software company is saying. So, if they promote the same values as the *commercial* enterprises, they are not responsible organizations. Like the universities, their aim is not science and education, but propaganda and indoctrination. They may be sincere when using terms like "professionalism" and "expertise," but if they equate these terms with software mechanism, what they do in reality is turn programmers into bureaucrats, and help the elite to exploit society.

5

The foregoing analysis has shown that our mechanistic software culture is indeed a social phenomenon that is causing the spread of a bureaucracy, and hence the spread of totalitarianism. Every one of the activities we analyzed can be justified only through the software myth – or through another activity, which in its turn can be justified only through the myth or through another activity, and so on. The programmers, the managers, the academics, the gurus, the publishers, the advertisers, the retailers, the employees of software companies, and increasingly every computer user – their software-related activities seem logical only if we blindly accept the myth. As soon as we question the myth, we recognize these activities as what they actually are: the pursuit of mechanistic fantasies.

So the expansion of software-related activities that we are witnessing is not the expansion of some useful preoccupations, but the expansion of delusions. It is not a process of collective progress in a new field of knowledge – what our software-related affairs *should* have been – but a process of degradation: more and more people are shifting their attention from their former, serious concerns, to some senseless pursuits.

In chapter 8 we will study the link between the mechanistic ideology and the notion of individual responsibility; and we will see that a mechanistic culture leads inevitably to a society where people are no longer considered responsible for their acts. The road from mechanism to irresponsibility is short. The belief in mechanism tempts us to neglect the natural capabilities of our minds, and to rely instead on inferior substitutes: rather than acquiring knowledge, we acquire devices that promise to replace the need for knowledge. We accomplish by means of devices less than we could with our own minds, and the devices may even be wrong or harmful, but no one blames us. Our responsibility, everyone agrees, is limited to knowing how to operate the devices.

Today, the incompetence and irresponsibility are obvious in our software-related activities, because these activities are dominated by mechanistic beliefs. But if we continue to embrace software mechanism, we should expect the incompetence and irresponsibility to spread to other fields of knowledge, and to other professions, as our dependence on computers is growing.

A society where all activities are as inefficient as are our software-related activities cannot actually exist. We can afford perhaps to have a few million people engaged in mechanistic fantasies, in the same way that we can afford to have an entertainment industry, and to spend a portion of our time with idle amusements. But we cannot, all of us, devote ourselves to the pursuit of fantasies. Thus, if the spread of software mechanism is causing an ever-growing number of people to cease performing useful work and to pursue fantasies instead, it is safe to predict that, at some point in the future, our society will collapse.

To avert this, we must learn all we can from the past: we must study the harm that has *already* been caused by software mechanism, in the domain of programming. In programming we have been trying for forty years to find substitutes for expertise, so we have enough evidence to *demonstrate* the absurdity of this idea, and the dishonesty of those who advocate it.

Despite its failure in programming, it is the same idea – replacing minds with software – that is now being promoted in other domains. And it is the same myth, software mechanism, that is invoked as justification, and the same elites that are perpetrating the fraud. So, in a few years, we should expect to see in other domains the same corruption we see today in programming, the same incompetence and irresponsibility. One by one, all workers will be reduced, as programmers have been, to software bureaucrats. As it has been in programming, the notion of expertise will be redefined everywhere to mean expertise in the use of substitutes for expertise. As programmers are today, we will all be restricted to the methods and devices supplied by an elite, and prevented from developing our minds.

Thus, if we understand how the mechanistic delusions have caused the incompetence and irresponsibility found today in the domain of programming, we will be able perhaps to prevent the spread of these delusions, and the resulting corruption, in other domains.

Anthropology and Software

If the theories of software engineering are founded on a myth, it is not surprising that they do not work. The software practitioners, though, continue to believe in software mechanism, and this prevents them from gaining knowledge and experience. Thus, because of their ignorance, the world of programming resembles a primitive society. Also, as other professions increasingly depend on computers, and hence on the mechanistic myth, the *users* of software are now prevented from gaining knowledge and experience. So the whole world resembles, increasingly, a primitive society. We can learn a great deal about our software delusions, therefore, by comparing the attitudes of programmers and users with those of the primitives.

Let us turn, then, to the field of social anthropology. In the first subsection, we will study the practice of magic as a complement to proven knowledge. And in the second subsection, we will study the invocation of supernatural powers in general.

Software Magic

1

When analyzing the names of software products,[1] we cannot help noticing the large number of names that evoke magic practices. For example, a popular database management system is called Oracle, a word meaning "prophet" and "prophecy" in antiquity. An application development system is called Delphi, after the location of a temple in ancient Greece where oracles were issued. A network system is called Pathworks; pathworking is a form of group visualization practised by those who believe in the occult. One utility is called Genie Backup Manager; others are called Clipboard Genie and Startup Genie. We also have Install Wizard, Disk Clean Wizard, Search Wizard, Web Wizard, PC Wizard, Registry Wizard, Barcode Wizard, etc. To back up drivers we could use Driver Magician, and to create help files Help Magician. A catalogue of hardware and software products describes certain entries as "magic solutions," and offers discounts on other entries to help us "get more magic for less."[2]

---

[1] As we will see later, the belief that software is a kind of product is one of the fallacies of the software myth. So I use the term "software product" only when I want to stress the absurdity of this concept (as in the present section).

[2] IBM *RS/6000* catalogue (spring 2000), pp. 8, 2.

But to leave no doubt as to the supernatural qualities of their products, many software companies include the word "magic" in the product's name: Network Magic, CADmagic, Barcode Magic, Label Magic, vCard Magic, Brochure Magic, Magic eContact, Image Gallery Magic, Magic Transfer, QS Flash Magic Menu Builder, Screenshot Magic, Magic Styles, Web Design Magic, SCP Button Magic, Magic Internet Kit, Magic Recovery Professional, MagicTracer, Magic Xchange, Macro Magic, AttributeMagic Pro, Color Magic Deluxe, Magic Photo Editor, Magic Speed, Magic Separator, Magic/400, Clipboard Magic, Magic Flash Decompiler, Order Page Magic, MagicWeb, MagicFlare, Magic Window Hider, ZipMagic, Magic TSR Toolkit, Antechinus Draw Magic, Slideshow Magic, Magic Folders, Magic Connection, Magic Mail Monitor, Magic ASCII Studio, Raxso Drive Magic, Magic Writer, File Magic, Magic Blog, Magic Cap, Magic Inventory Management, Magic Calendar Maker, Developer Magic, Magic Link, Magic C++, Spectramagic NX, Magic Net Trace, Exposure Magic, Magic Audio Recorder, MAGic, Word Magic, Voice Magic, Focus Magic, Magic ScreenSaver, Magic Memory Optimizer, Monitor Magic, Pad Magic, PartitionMagic, ClipMagic, SupportMagic, Magic DVD Copier, Backup Magic, SpeechMagic, Video Edit Magic, MagicISO, etc.

Or, software companies adopt the word "magic" for their own name: Computer Magic Inc., InfoMagic Ltd., General Magic Inc., Magic Multimedia Inc., Design Magic Ltd., PC-Magic Software, NeoMagic Corp., Inmagic Inc., Software Magic Inc., Magic Software Enterprises Ltd., Magic Solutions Ltd., PlanMagic Corp., WebMagic Inc., TeleMagic Inc., Imagic Inc., Viewmagic Inc., Geomagic Inc., etc.

In an industry famous for its preoccupation with the latest technological advances, at a time when all we hear is proclamations about progress and the future, one would expect vendors to take special care in *avoiding* terms associated with primitive beliefs, as these associations could hurt their credibility. The opposite is the case, however: the ignorance that pervades the world of software has created an environment where primitive beliefs are again an important factor, so the software vendors *deliberately* employ terms that evoke magic powers.

To those who lack knowledge, the world appears as a mysterious place, full of uncertainties and unexplained events. Superstitions and magic systems are then an effective way of coping with situations that would otherwise cause great anxiety. Irrational beliefs, held by most people in a repressed form even in our modern world, can become dominant and can easily be exploited when ignorance renders rational thinking impossible. And so it is how our society, which is increasingly dominated by software and hence by ignorant software practitioners and users, increasingly resembles the ancient and primitive societies, where priests, magicians, shamans, and prophets were consulted in all important affairs. Far from *avoiding* associations with supernatural forces, software vendors and gurus – today's priests and prophets – know that for ignorant programmers and users it is precisely these associations that matter.

❖

Magic – a pseudoscience – claims that certain objects, spells, or acts have the power to influence persons and events, although this power cannot be explained. Magic theories appear to provide important benefits, but persons who believe in magic must accept these theories without proof. For this reason, magic beliefs tend to manifest themselves as wishful thinking. Magic systems have existed as long as human societies, so they have always reflected our current preoccupations, fears, and desires. Thus, we have had magic systems to help us win battles, attract mates, predict the future, lose weight, and create software applications without programming.

The person who believes in magic refuses to face reality: he clings to his beliefs and disregards all evidence of their falsity. The validity of most magic theories can easily be determined – by carefully monitoring the successes and failures, for example. But the believer never bothers with such details, and is annoyed when someone suggests it. He already *knows* that the theory works. He enthusiastically accepts any success as verification of the theory, while dismissing major failures as insignificant exceptions.

The problem with magic thinking, then, is not so much one of ignorance as one of method. Even when we are ignorant, logical methods of inquiry enable us to test hypotheses, and hence to adopt only those theories that work. We favour theories that promise simple solutions to difficult problems, naturally; but it is precisely these theories that are most likely to be false. The most important advantage we have over primitive societies is not our scientific and technological knowledge, but our logical methods of inquiry. Our capabilities, which had grown only slowly throughout the centuries, have been growing exponentially since we adopted these methods. Those content to invoke specious explanations when reaching the limits of their understanding, instead of seeking to expand their knowledge, are condemned to intellectual stagnation. Their knowledge grows very slowly, or not at all.

Given the success that science had in explaining nature and extending our knowledge, it is not surprising that, until recently, magic practices were considered to be a vestige of our primitive past. All human societies, it was believed, start with magic, and when sufficiently advanced, replace it with science. No society can possibly continue to practise magic once the benefits of scientific thinking are revealed to it. Magic thinking, it was thought, is simply prescientific thinking.

Like the theory of myth, however, the theory of magic has undergone a dramatic shift in the last one hundred years. Far from being a vestige of the past, far from being automatically displaced by science, we understand now that magic beliefs affect a modern society just as much as they do a primitive one. All that has happened is a change in theories. We may no longer believe that weather rituals can bring rain, but we accept many other theories – in economics, linguistics, psychology, sociology, programming – which are, in fact, as scientific as rain magic.

Our reevaluation of the role of magic in society started following the work of anthropologist Bronislaw Malinowski.[3] Malinowski, who studied in great detail the life of primitive peoples, was struck by the continual blending of magic thinking and rational thinking. To a casual observer, the primitives appear to merely add some spurious ceremonies to all their activities. Careful study, however, reveals a surprisingly logical pattern. Magic is not practised at will. For each activity, tradition dictates whether magic is required at all, which magic formula must be used, at what point it should be applied, and which magician is qualified to perform the ritual. The ritual, which may be quite lengthy and elaborate, must be performed with great precision, since any deviation from the formula is believed to weaken its efficacy.

The pattern Malinowski observed is this: when the activity can be performed with confidence, when the primitives expect a certain and easy success, no magic is employed; but when the activity entails a significant degree of uncertainty or danger, magic is deemed necessary. Also, just as one would expect, the greater the uncertainty or danger, the more elaborate the magic employed. This is how Malinowski puts it: "We find magic wherever the elements of chance and accident, and the emotional play between hope and fear have a wide and extensive range. We do not find magic wherever the pursuit is certain, reliable, and well under the control of rational methods and technological processes. Further, we find magic where the element of danger is conspicuous. We do not find it wherever absolute safety eliminates any elements of foreboding."[4]

Primitive people employ magic, then, as an *extension* to their knowledge and capabilities. When they feel that skills and labour alone will allow them to complete a given task, their actions are totally rational. But when they know from experience that despite their skills and labour they may still fail, they resort to magic. This happens in activities like agriculture, hunting, and fishing, which depend on factors that are unpredictable and beyond their

[3] See, especially, his *Coral Gardens and Their Magic* (New York: Dover, 1978), and *Argonauts of the Western Pacific* (New York: Dutton, 1961).

[4] Bronislaw Malinowski, *Magic, Science and Religion, and Other Essays* (Garden City, NY: Doubleday Anchor, 1954), pp. 139–140.

control. They also use magic to complement their rational efforts in matters like health or social relations, which also contain much uncertainty.

2

Programming and software use are saturated with magic practices, but we fail to notice this fact. The reason we fail to notice it is the uncanny similarity between magic practices and rational behaviour: "Magic is akin to science in that it always has a definite aim intimately associated with human instincts, needs, and pursuits. The magic art is directed towards the attainment of practical aims. Like the other arts and crafts, it is also governed by a theory, by a system of principles which dictate the manner in which the act has to be performed in order to be effective."[5]

If we watch the activity of a person while being unfamiliar with the scientific principles underlying that activity, we cannot distinguish between rational and magic practices. Only if our knowledge *exceeds* his, can we recognize which acts contribute to his success and which ones are spurious. Primitive people, when engaged in pursuits like agriculture, feel that technical knowledge and magic rituals are equally important. We, watching them from our position in an advanced society, can recognize that only their technical knowledge contributes to their success, and that their rituals are spurious. At the same time, we ourselves engage in spurious activities in our *software* pursuits, convinced that they are as important as our technical expertise. Thus, only a person with superior programming knowledge can recognize the absurdity of such concepts as structured programming and object-oriented programming.

So it is the similarity of our rational and our irrational acts that we must study if we want to uncover the absurdities in today's software practices. But how can we study this similarity? We are convinced that everything we do is rational – we never perform foolish acts deliberately – so we will always fail to distinguish between the rational and the irrational in our own life. One way, we will see later in this book, is to approach any software concept, product, or theory with due skepticism. As in other disciplines, we can apply logical methods of inquiry to confirm or refute any software claim. Besides, as these methods are universal, they can be used even by those with limited programming knowledge. And when doing this, we discover that most software claims are associated with pseudoscientific theories, propaganda, and charlatanism.

Another way is to study the blending of the rational with the irrational in the lives of primitive people, which, in turn, will help us to recognize the same

[5] Ibid., p. 86.

conduct in our own life. For this purpose, we can find no better examples than the garden and canoe magic systems used in the Trobriand islands of eastern New Guinea, which were so thoroughly documented by Malinowski.

❖

The natives display great agricultural expertise in tending their plantations. They understand, for instance, the properties of the different types of soil, and they know which crops are best suited for each type; they are familiar with the principles of fertilization; and they can identify hundreds of varieties and types of plants. In addition, they are conscientious workers, and they perform skilfully such tasks as preparing the garden, planting the seeds, protecting the growing crops, and harvesting them.

This expertise, however, is always supplemented with magic. The natives can explain, for example, why no crops can thrive in certain areas of their island "in perfectly reasonable, almost scientific language.... At the same time they attribute the supreme fertility of some districts ... to the superiority of one magical system over another."[6] They devise clever ways to protect their crops from pests, and "these practical devices they handle rationally and according to sound empirical rules."[7] At the same time, they build and deploy various structures and objects in their gardens, which, they clearly explain, have no other purpose but magic.

The natives do not use magic because they confuse it with practical work. They realize that invoking magic powers is an entirely different type of act, but they believe it to be just as important: "The two ways, the way of magic and the way of garden work ... are inseparable. They are never confused, nor is one of them ever allowed to supersede the other."[8] The natives know which tasks they must perform through their own skills and work, and they never attempt to use magic as a substitute. Thus, they "will never try to clean the soil by magic, to erect a fence or yam support by a rite.... They also know that no work can be skimped without danger to the crops, nor do they ever assume that by an overdose of magic you can make good any deficiencies in work.... Moreover, they are able to express this knowledge clearly and to formulate it in a number of principles and causal relations."[9]

Malinowski includes two diagrams showing stages in the growth of one of the local crops, drawn from information provided by the natives themselves.[10] It seems that the natives have greater knowledge about their crops than some

---

[6] Bronislaw Malinowski, *Coral Gardens and Their Magic*, vol. 1 (New York: Dover, 1978), p. 75.   [7] Ibid., p. 77.   [8] Ibid., p. 76.   [9] Ibid.
[10] Ibid., pp. 140–141.

modern farmers have about theirs. They can describe in great detail the entire development process, from the time the seed is placed in the ground until the plant matures. There are more than twenty native terms in these diagrams – for various parts of the seed, roots, branches, etc. – showing their keen interest in the botanic aspects of their work.

At the same time, the natives have elaborate systems of magic, which they apply scrupulously throughout the growth process. The magic varies from specialized spells and charms addressing individual parts of the plant, to rituals for their tools and for the whole garden. Most of this magic is performed by professional magicians, who receive fees for their services. There are several magic systems in use, and the natives discuss their relative merits with the same seriousness as programmers discussing their application development systems. Some magic systems are owned by individuals, families, or clans, and in this case others must pay for their use – a practice not unlike our patents and copyrights.

We discover a similar combination of rational and irrational acts in canoe building and the associated fishing and trading activities.[11] The natives build sturdy and attractive craft, their size and design matching their intended use: a simple type for coastal transport, a more elaborate type for fishing, and a relatively large and complex type, carrying more than a dozen men, for long sea voyages. Limited to primitive tools, the building of a dugout canoe is a major construction project for them, demanding coordinated team work and timely contribution from specialists. But they are capable of accurate planning and efficient labour organization. Also, they are familiar with the principles of buoyancy and stability, sailing and navigation. They understand, for example, why the outrigger must have a certain, optimal span, measured as a fraction of the canoe's length: a larger span offers greater stability, but at the same time it weakens the outrigger. And they can explain clearly why one canoe is faster than another, or why, in a storm, they must follow one procedure rather than another. "They have," Malinowski points out, "a whole system of principles of sailing, embodied in a complex and rich terminology, traditionally handed on and obeyed as rationally and consistently as is modern science by modern sailors."[12]

Despite these skills, however, every stage in the building of the canoe is accompanied by a magic ritual, deemed necessary to ensure a fast and safe craft. To pick just one example – which also demonstrates the importance of details in magic – a ritual performed before painting the canoe involves burning under its bottom a mixture of such substances as the wings of a bat,

---

[11] Bronislaw Malinowski, *Argonauts of the Western Pacific* (New York: Dutton, 1961), esp. chs. IV–VI.   [12] Malinowski, *Magic, Science and Religion*, p. 30.

the nest of a small bird, cotton fluff, and grass. "The smoke is supposed to exercise a speed-giving and cleansing influence.... All the substances are associated with flying and lightness. The wood used for kindling the fire is that of the light-timbered mimosa tree. The twigs have to be obtained by throwing at the tree a piece of wood (never a stone), and when the broken-off twig falls, it must be caught by hand, and not allowed to touch the ground."[13] Malinowski describes dozens of additional rites, spells, and ritual performances.

What are we to make of this? How is it possible for people to be so rational, and yet so irrational, at the same time? To answer this, we must start by noting that people appear irrational only when judged from *outside* their system of belief. Judged from *within* that system, their conduct is logical and consistent. All it takes is one unproven concept, one false assumption. An entire system can then be built around it, and even if every theory and method in the system is logically derived, that one assumption will render the system nonsensical.

In the case of magic, the false assumption is that certain objects, spells, and ritual performances have the power to influence people's lives, or the forces of nature, or the course of events. In the case of programming, the false assumption is that software applications are akin to the appliances we build in a factory, so programming is akin to manufacturing; that, like appliances, we can separate an application into independent modules, each module into simpler ones, and so on, down to some small parts; that all we need to know is how to program these small parts, because there exist methods and devices which allow us to build applications from software parts just as we build appliances from physical parts; and that, moreover, we can complete our software manufacturing projects even faster if we start with prefabricated subassemblies – large modules that already contain many parts.

In programming as in magic, many principles and methods have been invented, and organized into logical systems. There isn't much that can be criticized when studying such a system from within itself; that is, when using as criteria of validity only concepts that are part of the system. This is what believers are doing, and why the system appears sound to them.

Thus, an individual who believes in magic will always use magic systems; then, *within a magic system*, his conduct will always be logical. Similarly, theorists and practitioners who assume that programming is similar to man-ufacturing will always pursue *mechanistic* software ideas; then, *within the mechanistic ideology*, their decisions and acts will always be logical.

---

[13] Malinowski, *Argonauts*, p. 140.

But the validity of each part of the system depends ultimately on the validity of that one fundamental assumption, which may well be the only concept linking the system to the real world. If that concept is wrong, the entire system, no matter how logical, becomes worthless. Believers never question that concept. The larger the system they build around it, the smaller and less important the concept appears to be. Eventually, they forget altogether that the concept was never anything but an assumption.

3

We are now in a position to explain the blending of rational and irrational behaviour. Primitive societies are closed societies. Their members follow elaborate traditions – rigid patterns of thought and conduct – in all their activities. The traditions derive from ancient myths, which are the charter and the foundation of their culture.

Among other things, tradition establishes for each activity what is within the power of the individual and what is beyond his power. For the part that is within his power, the individual is expected to act rationally and to display expertise, initiative, and creativity. But what is he expected to do when something is believed to lie beyond his power? Recall Malinowski's critical observation that magic is employed only when the outcome of an activity has a great degree of uncertainty, when the primitives know that their skills alone cannot ensure success. Because their social system does not permit them to acquire skills beyond the boundaries determined by tradition, it must provide them with other means to cope with the more difficult tasks. This is the purpose of magic. Simply by accepting one unproven theory, they gain access to a multitude of new possibilities.

If we divide the world of primitive people into fields they understand and control, and fields that lie beyond their knowledge and capabilities, what magic does is bring the latter into the same category as the former. Magic assures them that the methods they use successfully in those fields they understand can be used equally in fields where their knowledge is inadequate.

The primitives know perfectly well when it is *skills* that they rely on and when it is *magic*. When sailing, for example, if the wind suddenly changes they use a spell to persuade it to return to its original direction. We, with our knowledge and computers, are content to try to *predict* the weather; through magic, however, the primitives believe they can *control* it. But their behaviour is quite logical: they make use of their sailing methods as long as they work, and turn to magic precisely because they realize that adjusting their sails would be ineffective, that it is the wind they must now adjust rather than the sails.

Instructing the wind to change direction appears silly only if we reject the theory that the weather can be controlled. They *accept* this theory; so they apply methods that involve the weather, in the same way they apply methods that involve the sails. Both types of methods appear to them equally rational and effective. *Magic practice is an attempt to use our current capabilities to accomplish tasks that require, in fact, greater capabilities.*

It is important to remember that magic does not ask us to accept a *different* mistaken theory every time. All magic practices are based on *the same* mistaken theory. Besides, this theory is plausible: all it asks us to believe is that we can influence events by means of spells or objects. Magic, thus, makes processes that are impossible appear like a logical extension of processes that are familiar and effective. After all, we do influence the world around us with spoken words, with our bodies, with objects and tools. This is why it is so easy for us to believe in magic, and so difficult to distinguish between our magic activities and our rational ones. We may think that we are performing the same kind of acts, but these acts can have a real and verifiable effect one moment and an illusory effect the next.

And the same is true of *software* magic. In chapter 7 we will see that the mechanistic software theories do not promise any benefits that could not be gained simply through good programming. What the software elites are seeking, therefore, is a substitute for programming knowledge: by incorporating various principles into a methodology, or into a development environment, they hope to get inexperienced programmers to accomplish tasks that require, in fact, great expertise. Following rules and methods, or using built-in features and operations, is easier than acquiring knowledge and skills, and is within the capabilities of inexperienced programmers. Programming systems, thus, are perceived as magic systems: they assure programmers that they can accomplish a difficult task with their current knowledge alone.

Software development has become the most elaborate type of magic ever created by man, but this escapes our notice if we watch only superficially the activities of programmers. For, in their activities, as in those of primitive people, the rational and the irrational blend and overlap continually. We already saw that one can distinguish irrationality only by stepping outside the system of belief that fosters it, so we must also do this for software.

Each software activity appears logical, urgently needed, and perfectly justified – *if* studied in the context of other, similar activities. This is because most software activities are engendered by some previous software activities. We may even be impressed by the incessant changes and innovations, the endless theories, languages, methodologies, and development tools, the thousands of courses, exhibitions, conventions, newspapers, magazines, books, brochures, and newsletters, and the astronomic amounts of money spent by corporations and governments. But if we study these activities, we notice that they only make sense if we accept the unproven theory that software development is akin to manufacturing. This absurd theory has been accepted for so long that it is now routinely invoked as the ideological justification for every software concept, when there is no evidence, much less a scientific foundation, to support it. We saw that with magic, by accepting just one unproven theory, the primitives gain the confidence to handle tasks that lie beyond their capabilities. Similarly, by accepting just one unproven *software* theory, inexperienced programmers can confidently engage in activities that lie beyond *their* capabilities.

Like magic in primitive societies, software magic is quite plausible. After all, we build *physical* structures by assembling standard parts and prefabricated modules, and computer programs appear to have their own kind of parts and modules. We improve our manufacturing methods and tools continually, and programming also appears to involve methods and tools. Moreover, programming methods based on the principles of manufacturing seem to work in simple cases – in the examples found in textbooks, for instance. Thus, extending these methods to the large and complex applications we need in the real world appears to be a logical step, whose validity is guaranteed by the fact that large *manufacturing* projects appear to use the same methods as the small ones; they merely involve more parts and subassemblies.

Also like primitive magic, software magic does not ask us to have faith in a *different* unproven theory for each new concept. All programming methods and systems are based on *the same* theory – the similarity of software development to manufacturing – and this makes its fallaciousness harder to detect. These concepts have become a self-perpetuating belief system: a system that uses its own growth as confirmation of validity. No one seems to remember that the entire system, despite its enormous size and complexity, is based ultimately on a theory that was never proved. (See pp. 511–512.)

❖

Unlike other disciplines, where mechanical analogies may lurk behind a theory but are seldom avowed, the software practitioners are quite outspoken about their attempt to reduce software to mechanics. We *must* make programming like manufacturing, they say. They proudly add mechanical metaphors to their software jargon, and take this as a sign of expertise: we are finally turning software into a professional activity, like engineering. But there is no evidence that programming can be based on manufacturing methods. So, even if programmers actually had the training and experience of engineers (rather than merely *calling* themselves engineers, and using engineering *metaphors*), these skills alone would be of little benefit.

Their claim to expertise through mechanical metaphors is especially amusing, as the belief in software mechanics makes their activities look less and less like expert programming and increasingly like primitive magic. Malinowski called this verbal pattern "the creative metaphor of magic":[14] "It is the essence of magic that, by the affirmation of a condition which is desired but not yet fulfilled, this condition is brought about."[15] The verbal part of a magic formula is typically an elaborate and picturesque series of statements describing the *desired* state of affairs, which, of course, is very different from reality. The person performing the ritual asks, as it were, the forces of nature, or certain objects, to behave in a different manner, or to possess different qualities: "The repetitive statement of certain words is believed to produce the reality stated.... The essence of verbal magic, then, consists in a statement which is untrue, which stands in direct opposition to the context of reality. But the belief in magic inspires man with the conviction that his untrue statement must become true."[16]

So when programmers call themselves "engineers," when they talk about "software engineering" and "building" programs from software "components," they are practising in effect software magic: they are making statements they know to be untrue (or, at least, know to be unproven), hoping that, through their repeated assertion, software phenomena may be persuaded to be like the phenomena we see in manufacturing.

4

Let us return to the blending of the rational and the irrational in software activities. Programmers act quite rationally when working on small and isolated pieces of an application. They know, for example, the importance of expressing correctly the conditions for an iterative statement, and they don't expect their development tools to do it for them. They never question the need to specify certain operations in the proper sequence, or to assign correct values to variables, or to access the right database records. And if the resulting program does not work as expected, it is their own logic that they suspect, not the computer.

---

[14] Malinowski, *Coral Gardens*, vol. 2, pp. 70, 238.   [15] Ibid., p. 70.
[16] Ibid., pp. 238–239.

But this is where their rationality ends. We all know that the difficulties encountered in large and complex applications are not simply the accumulation of a large number of small problems. When a software project fails, or when an application does not provide the solution everyone expected, it is not an individual statement or condition that must be corrected, or the subtotals in a report that are wrong, or a data entry field that is missing – nor even a hundred such problems. Isolated deficiencies may well contribute to the failure of the application, but even when we manage to identify and resolve them, the application remains inadequate. The reason is that applications are systems of interacting structures. And the most serious software deficiencies are those caused by the interactions: we overlooked or misjudged some of the links between structures.

Applications, then, are more than the simple hierarchical structures we wish them to be, more than the neat modules and relations we see in diagrams. All programming theories are based on the idea that we must reduce the application to one structure, and thereby *eliminate* the interactions. This is what we do in manufacturing, the theorists say, so this must also be the answer to our programming difficulties. But it is precisely the interactions that make software such a versatile concept: it is the very fact that we can implement interacting structures through software that lets software adapt so well to our needs. The reason we don't seem to be able to eliminate the interactions, no matter what theory we follow, is that we need these interactions if software is to mirror our affairs accurately.

Only minds can process interacting structures, so the answer to our programming difficulties is programming expertise: the skills attained by working for many years on large and complex applications, and on diverse types of software. In our culture, however, programmers are restricted to simple and isolated tasks. Like the members of a primitive society, they are expected to display knowledge and creativity in those activities deemed to be within their power: programming small parts of an application. Hard work may be required, but the success of these activities is assured. Tradition does not permit them to acquire the higher skills needed to design, program, and maintain whole applications. This is a difficult task, full of uncertainties, for which tradition prescribes the use of magic: methodologies, development tools and environments, database systems, and the like. These aids encourage programmers to think of the application as a system of independent structures and parts, thus reassuring them that their current knowledge suffices. Like primitive magic, software magic creates for programmers the illusion that the difficult and unpredictable tasks are of the same kind as the simple ones: the methodology, the development tools, or the database system will somehow turn those independent structures and parts into a useful application.

It takes an experienced person to recognize how little of what programmers do is rational, and how much effort they waste on spurious activities. Neither the programmers themselves nor a lay person watching them can see this, because irrational programming activities are almost identical to rational ones. Thus, a programmer may spend much time mastering the complexities of a particular development system, and even more time later programming in that system, convinced that this is the only way to enhance his capabilities. If asked to demonstrate the benefits of the system, the only thing he can do is point to its popularity, or describe a particular function that was easy to implement. But he cannot *prove* the need for that system. In reality, the most important factor is his skills. Whatever he managed to accomplish with that system he would have accomplished with any other system, or with no system at all (that is, with a traditional programming language, perhaps supplemented with libraries of subroutines). Like the primitives, though, the programmer remains convinced that his technical knowledge and the magic system are equally important.[17]

Since no one can prove the need for a particular development system, all related activities are specious. But there is nothing to betray their irrationality. Studying reference manuals, attending courses, discussing problems and solutions – all these activities are important, all can be justified. They can be justified, however, only in the context of that development system, only if we do not question the need for it.

As a result, even when they get to know a development system well, programmers are no better off than before. Their programming skills did not improve. They wasted their time acquiring worthless knowledge about yet another methodology, yet another language, yet another theory, instead of improving their skills simply by programming. All they did was learn how to use a new magic system.

It is easy to see that, no matter how many years of practice these programmers have behind them, their real programming experience stays at the level it was after the first year or two. They may be familiar with many magic systems, but they have no skills beyond what the software tradition permits them to acquire. Just like the primitives, they do not confuse programming with magic. They know perfectly well what they can accomplish with their own skills, and

---

[17] The benefits of a system or method can be determined only by way of controlled experiments; that is, experiments designed to isolate and measure a specific variable while eliminating all others, including human factors. Such experiments are practically impossible, and this is one reason why the only meaningful way to determine the value of a system or method is by studying the *failures*, not the successes. (We will discuss this problem in "Popper's Principles of Demarcation" in chapter 3.) Thus, any attempt to defend or promote a concept by pointing to individual successes turns it into a pseudoscience, a fraud.

they turn to magic for the more difficult tasks precisely because they are aware of their limited capabilities.

I have described the rational and irrational activities of programmers, but, increasingly, a similar blend can be seen in the activities of software *users*. They too believe that the only way to improve their performance, or to solve difficult problems, is by relying on software devices. Like the programmers, though, whatever they manage to accomplish is due almost exclusively to their skills, not to those devices. To advance, therefore, they must *avoid* the devices, and practise their profession instead, in order to further improve their skills.

How, then, can we detect irrational activities in our software pursuits? We must beware of those activities that can only be justified if judged from within the software culture. We must not be impressed by how important or urgent these activities seem to be, or how expertly the individual performs them. Instead, we must search for evidence. Any attempt to prove the validity of an irrational act will lead to that unproven theory – the theory that forms the foundation of our software culture. The theory is that there exist systems which help us to break down software-related tasks into smaller and smaller parts, so all we need to know is how to use these systems and how to solve simple problems. This is what we do in manufacturing, and software is no different.

Software propaganda has succeeded in shifting our definition of programming expertise from its traditional, commonsensical meaning – the skills needed to solve a difficult problem, or to complete an important task – to its modern meaning: familiarity with the latest theories and methodologies, avoiding programming and using instead ready-made pieces of software, etc. We are expected to measure the expertise of software practitioners, not by assessing their real contribution, but by how many development tools they have tried, how many courses they have attended, how many computer magazines they are reading, and how acquainted they are with the latest "solutions" and "technologies" – the latest ideas, products, announcements, and rumours.

Companies need programmers, but one wouldn't think so just by reading job offer advertisements. For, the required qualifications we see in these advertisements are not what one would think is expected of programmers; namely, proven expertise in solving a company's business problems with software. Depending on the current fad, the requirements are for experience with object-oriented systems, or 4GL systems, or client-server systems, or relational database systems, or CASE tools, or a particular language or development aid or environment; that is, knowledge of one magic system or another. Companies are looking for magicians, not programmers.

Software Power

1

The term *mana*, which comes from Melanesian, was introduced in anthropology at the end of the nineteenth century by R. H. Codrington. This term, usually translated as *power*, denotes a supernatural force, a mythical essence, "an atmosphere of potency that permeates everything."[1] Since then, it has been found that archaic peoples throughout the world believe in its existence. Although we now refer to this concept as mana, it has equivalent terms in many languages: for some peoples of India it is *sakti* or *barkat*, for the African Pygmies *megbe*, for the Iroquois *orenda*, for the Hurons *oki*, for the Dakota *wakan*, for the Sioux *wakanda*, for the Algonquins *manito*.[2] It is believed that this force exists everywhere in the universe, and that any person can use it to accomplish tasks he would otherwise find impossible. The force is said to derive from a number of sources, such as ghosts, spirits, and gods.

Mana can reveal itself in almost anything: a tree, a stone, an animal, and even in such things as a gesture, a sign, a colour, and a season of the year.[3] A typical use of mana may be as follows:[4] An individual would go alone to some isolated spot, where, after fasting, prayer, and exposure to the elements, a spirit might come and point to him a plant. That plant would then become a source of good luck, and the individual would employ this power to ensure success in his endeavours. He might carry with him at all times something symbolizing the plant, and perhaps also offer it to others.

Mana is different from magic. Mana is a universal force available to anyone at any time, and to be used in any way the individual desires; magic, on the other hand, requires formal practice: its power is in the spell and ritual, and magic formulas have an exact significance. Mana exists in nature and can manifest itself in objects, acts, or ideas; magic power resides in man, and magic formulas can only be transmitted from one person to another.[5] Thus, while primitive man may use both magic and mana, most anthropologists agree that, despite their similarity – the belief in supernatural powers that can enhance a person's limited capabilities – they form two different concepts. Sometimes,

---

[1] Ernst Cassirer, *Language and Myth* (New York: Dover, 1953), p. 63.

[2] Mircea Eliade, *Myths, Dreams, and Mysteries: The Encounter between Contemporary Faiths and Archaic Realities* (New York: Harper and Row, 1975), ch. VI passim.

[3] Ibid., p. 132.

[4] Guy E. Swanson, *The Birth of the Gods: The Origin of Primitive Beliefs* (Ann Arbor: University of Michigan Press, 1964), p. 7.

[5] Bronislaw Malinowski, *Magic, Science and Religion, and Other Essays* (Garden City, NY: Doubleday Anchor, 1954), p. 77.

mana is taken as the general concept, and magic as one particular application of it. As we will see in this subsection, software practitioners and users, too, consider mana a more general concept than their formal magic systems.

❖

The words "power," "powerful," "empower," etc., are so common in computer-related discourse that it is almost impossible to describe a new product without the use of them. We have come to expect them, and we doubt the efficacy of the product if these words are missing. After all, we already have thousands of software and hardware products, so the only justification for a new one is that it is more "powerful." An analysis of these words, however, reveals that the power of a product is usually perceived, not as certain qualities, but in the sense of mana – as *supernatural* power.

From the many meanings the dictionary offers for the word "power," it is obvious that the one current in computer matters is *the capability to effect something.* We can immediately divide this function into two kinds. First, "power" can simply stand for a list of qualities. For example, if one computer is faster than another, or if one text editor has better editing features than another, we may say that they are more powerful. When used in this sense, "power" is an abbreviation: an abstract term we can employ without fear of confusion, since we all know what it stands for. If asked, we could readily describe the superior features we subsumed under "power."

Even a casual examination of books, articles, advertising, or conversations makes it clear, however, that "power" is hardly ever used in this precise sense. In its more common sense, "power" is still used as an abstract term, but *without being defined.* Abstract terms are so common in everyday discourse that we seldom stop to think whether we know what they stand for. So, when encountering an undefined abstract term, we tend to assume that it stands for the list of things we *expected,* or *wished,* to see at that point. When encountering "power" without an explanation, then, we assume that it means what it would mean if used legitimately, although now it is just a slogan.

Here are some typical uses of "power" and its derivatives in computer-related discourse: "Powerful software solutions for midsize companies."[6] "Discover the power of Primus Internet services."[7] "Empowering the Internet generation."[8] "Empowered with these capabilities, your company can charge ahead intelligently and efficiently ...."[9] "Power tools for power applications."[10] "Powering comprehensive unified communications solutions."[11] "Wireless

---

[6] http://whitepapers.techrepublic.com.com/.   [7] Primus Canada, adv. pamphlet.
[8] Cisco Systems, adv.   [9] http://www.jda.com/.
[10] Microsoft Visual Basic 2.0, adv. pamphlet.   [11] http://www.myt3.com/.

inventory systems give you the power to have accurate information in real time ...."[12] "Open source empowers the user more than proprietary software can."[13] "Empowering Software Development Environments by Automatic Software Measurement."[14] "Business innovation powered by technology."[15]

When it does not describe precise and verifiable capabilities, "power" is intended to convey something mysterious, supernatural – mana. For the primitives, the belief in mana, like the belief in magic, is a substitute for personal knowledge: "Mana is a substance or essence which gives one the ability to perform tasks or achieve ends otherwise impossible."[16] Similarly, modern individuals believe that a given product or concept has the power to enhance their capabilities, but they don't feel they have to understand how this power acts.

Now, products of all kinds promise us power – weight-loss gadgets, money-making schemes, self-help instructions, and so forth. But in no other field is the promise of power as widespread as in software-related matters. We can see this not only in the frequent use of "power," "powerful," "empower," etc., but also in the long list of software products whose *name* includes "power" (this use of "power," needless to say, is always in an undefined sense): PowerEncoder, Power Keeper, PowerCrypt, PowerPoint, PowerGraphs Toolkit, NXPowerLite, PowerShadow, PowerOLAP, Power Booleans, IT PowerPAC, Power Edit, PDF Power Brand, PowerShop ERP, PowerGREP, RoutePower 32, Animation Power, PowerCinema, PowerPassword, PowerPulse, Bill Power, PowerBackup, HTML PowerSpell, PowerExchange, PowerPressed, Power Office, PowerKey Pro, PowerConvert, HedgePower, PowerBuilder, PowerDesk Pro, PowerDraw, Power Translators, PowerDirector, PowerProducer, Power Solids, Power Print, EMail Developer's Power Suite, PowerUpdate, PowerERP, Power Accounting, OptionPower, Power LogOn, Powerpak, PowerPack, PowerGEM, PowerTerm, PowerChain, PowerBSORT, PowerTCP Emulation, PowerSuite, PowerRecon, ELX Power Desktop, PowerTicker, PowerAnalyzer, Power Broker, Jobpower, PowerBASIC, Powershell, PowerWebBuilder, PowerWEB, PowerPlan, ES Power PDF Creator, PowerToys, PowerMerge, PowerCOBOL, PowerCenter, DQpowersuite, PowerPath, PowerVideoMaker, SQL Power Architect, Power Sound Editor, PowerBoot, PowerISO, etc.

We can account for the abundance of "power" names in software products only if we remember the ignorance that software practitioners and users suffer from, the limited skills that our software culture permits them to acquire. Faced with the difficult problem of developing, using, and maintaining serious

---

[12] http://findmysoftware.com/.   [13] http://www.netc.org/.

[14] Book title, 11th IEEE International Software Metrics Symposium.

[15] Front cover banner, *Information Week* (1999–2007).

[16] Swanson, *Birth of the Gods*, p. 6.

applications, modern people, like the primitives, end up seeking aid from the only source they believe to be available – supernatural forces.

Few people, of course, would admit that they are using a software product because its name includes "power." But the software vendors know better. The ability of a product's name to influence a buying decision, and the associations created in a person's mind between the product and the idea conveyed by its name, are well understood in advertising. The software vendors are simply exploiting the belief in the supernatural, which has been retained, in a repressed form, even by modern man. This belief surfaces in moments of insecurity, or anxiety, or fear, when, like our ancestors, we feel impotent against some great perils. Since ignorance is a major source of insecurity, the large number of products with "power" names merely reflects the large number of difficult situations that ignorant programmers and users are facing.

Similarly, the phrase "power tools" is often used by software vendors to name sets of software devices: LG Power Tools, Engineering Power Tools, SQL Power Tools, HTML PowerTools, Windows Powertools, PowerTools PRO for AOL, TBox Power Tools, jv16 Power Tools, Rizone's Power Tools, Creative Element Power Tools, Nemx Power Tools, Power Tools for ArcGIS, Rix2k Extreme Power Tools, CodeSite Power Tools, etc. And the phrase is also popular in book titles: Java Power Tools, Unix Power Tools, Linux Power Tools, Mac OS X Power Tools, Scripting VMware Power Tools, Windows Developer Power Tools, DOS Power Tools, LEGO Software Power Tools, AutoCad Power Tools, Windows XP Power Tools, Wordperfect 6 Power Tools, Foxpro 2.0 Power Tools, Visual Basic .NET Power Tools, Netcat Power Tools, Novell Netware Power Tools, etc.

The vendors, clearly, want us to associate a software utility, or the information found in a book, with the efficacy of electricity; that is, with the kind of energy used by real power tools like drills and saws. But, without an actual explanation, the meaning of this "power" remains vague, just like the "power" in a name. So, in the end, we perceive it the same way – as mana.

2

Much has been learned about the way the primitives interpret mana, from linguistic and ethnological analyses of the archaic languages. The conclusion has been that "mana" is not simply a word, like "power." We must use a multitude of concepts to convey in a modern language its full meaning: "sacred, strange, important, marvellous, extraordinary";[17] also "remarkable,

---

[17] Paul Radin, quoted in Eliade, *Myths, Dreams, and Mysteries*, p. 129.

very strong, very great, very old, strong in magic, wise in magic, supernatural, divine – or in a substantive sense … power, magic, sorcery, fortune, success, godhead, delight."[18]

Cassirer notes that "the idea of mana and the various conceptions related to it are not bound to a particular realm of *objects* (animate or inanimate, physical or spiritual), but that they should rather be said to indicate a certain 'character', which may be attributed to the most diverse objects and events, if only these evoke mythic 'wonder' and stand forth from the ordinary background of familiar, mundane existence…. It is not a matter of 'what', but of 'how'; not the object of attention, but the sort of attention directed to it, is the crucial factor here. Mana and its several equivalents do not denote a single, definite predicate; but in all of them we find a peculiar and consistent *form of predication*. This predication may indeed be designated as the primeval mythico-religious predication, since it expresses the spiritual 'crisis' whereby the holy is divided from the profane."[19]

The idea of the *sacred*, especially in its sense as the opposite of the profane, expresses even better, therefore, how the primitives perceive mana. This is significant, if we want to understand the belief in *software* power. Like mana, software power is a potency that can manifest itself in diverse concepts and entities, so it does not describe their *type* but their *character*. By asserting that a thing has power, the believer says, in effect, that he perceives it as belonging in the domain of the sacred rather than the ordinary.

So the belief in software power, like the primitive beliefs, is a belief in the existence of miraculous capabilities – capabilities which cannot and need not be explained. In the following passage, Eliade describes the concept of mana, but this can just as easily describe the concept of *software* power: "Among the 'primitives' as among the moderns, the sacred is manifested in a multitude of forms and variants, but … all these hierophanies are charged with *power*. The sacred is strong, powerful, because it is *real*; it is efficacious and durable. The opposition between sacred and profane is often expressed as an opposition between the *real* and the *unreal* or pseudo-real. Power means *reality* and, at the same time, *lastingness* and *efficiency*."[20]

Software power, then, is the modern counterpart of mana. We can confirm this by noting the many similarities between the two beliefs. First, and most

---

[18] Nathan Söderblom, quoted in Cassirer, *Language and Myth*, p. 66.

[19] Cassirer, *Language and Myth*, pp. 65–66.

[20] Eliade, *Myths, Dreams, and Mysteries*, p. 130. (The term *hierophany* was coined by Eliade to denote any manifestation of the sacred.)

significantly, everyone realizes that supernatural power acts like a tool, or like an appliance: we can benefit from it directly, without having to gain new knowledge. Thus, the primitives understand that "mana is an object, not a body of skills and abilities which are obtained through learning. Access to it is acquired, in the sense that a house or a wife or a spear is acquired, that is as a gift, as a purchase, or through the performance of appropriate acts."[21] Similarly, the believers in *software* power do not expect to acquire any skills by using software devices. They understand that this power is a *substitute* for knowledge and experience. Vendors, in fact, make this point the main attraction of software devices: simply by purchasing one, you gain access to a power that will allow you to accomplish your tasks immediately.

Second, supernatural power is perceived by everyone as a truly general potency. For the primitives, mana "is not so much the idea of ... particular embodiments, as the notion of a 'power' in general, able to appear now in this form, now in that, to enter into one object and then into another."[22] Similarly, the great variety of means by which we can acquire *software* power shows that believers do not associate it with *specific* things – a company, a product, a function – but with a universal potency that can materialize in any software-related concept. It can appear in development environments as well as in applications, in database systems as well as in utilities, in user interface as well as in computations.

And, although we are discussing *software* power, we must note that this universal potency can materialize in anything else associated with computers. Thus, it can appear in whole computers (Power Mac, PowerBook, PowerEdge, AcerPower, Power Spec, Prime Power), and also in the *parts* of a computer, and in related devices: in a monitor ("empower your business with advanced display technology,"[23] "... these stylish, powerful and efficient monitors improve the atmosphere of any desktop"[24]), a graphics card ("Radeon 7500 is a powerful and versatile graphic solution,"[25] "GeForce GTX 480 powers interactive raytracing"[26]), a hard drive ("fast performance and huge capacity to power today's storage-hungry applications"[27]), a motherboard ("empowered by integrated graphics and Intel Hyper-Threading Technology ...,"[28] "it delivers awesome power ..."[29]), a scanner ("empower your information management with digital technology"[30]), a network device (PowerConnect switch), a mouse

[21] Swanson, *Birth of the Gods*, p. 6.   [22] Cassirer, *Language and Myth*, p. 63.
[23] NEC Corp., adv.   [24] http://www.samsung.com/.
[25] http://ati.amd.com/.   [26] http://www.nvidia.com/.
[27] Seagate ST3160316AS Barracuda 7200.12, http://www.tigerdirect.ca/.
[28] Asus P4V8X-MX motherboard, http://ca.asus.com/.
[29] Gigabyte GA-X58A-UD3R motherboard, http://www.acousticpc.com/.
[30] Ricoh Aficio scanners, *The Ricoh Report* (Nov. 2000).

(Power Wheelmouse, PowerScroll), a storage system (PowerVault), a CD device (PowerCD, PowerDisc), a processor (PowerPC), a camera (PowerShot), or a microphone (PowerMic). And it can appear even in such concepts as a newsletter (IBM PowerTalk, APC PowerNews), a business relationship (Samsung Power Partner program), a panel discussion (Power Panels[31]), a trade show ("over 700 high-powered exhibits"[32]), or a course ("a powerful 3-day course"[33]).

Lastly, the term "power," like "mana," is employed in a variety of grammatical roles. Analyzing the ways in which the Sioux use "wakanda," McGee notes that "the term was applied to all sorts of entities and ideas, and was used (with or without inflectional variations) indiscriminately as substantive and adjective, and with slight modification as verb and adverb."[34] Similarly, through its derivatives, "power" is used indiscriminately as noun, adjective, verb, and adverb. Let us see some examples.

As noun: "Discover the power of MetaFrame and WinFrame software."[35] "Relational database power made easy."[36] "The power to build a better business Internet."[37] "This empowerment is most visible in backend solutions like servers and networks."[38] "Experience the power of software instrumentation."[39] "SaaS Business Empowerment programs are designed to help Progress' SaaS partners focus on the early-stage fundamentals …."[40] "Accrisoft Freedom web empowerment software provides all the tools you need …."[41] "… AutoPlay Media Studio gives you the power to quickly create just about any software application you can dream up."[42] "IT empowerment with ITSM education from Hewlett-Packard."[43] "Enjoy visual power."[44]

As adjective: "Powerful network storage software with built-in intelligence and automation …."[45] "Discover hundreds of new uses for this empowering tool."[46] "Visual Two-Way-Tools for power programming."[47] "Powerful software for solving LP, NLP, MLP and CGE models."[48] "Control your duplicate files with this powerful utility."[49] "This powerful feature allows affiliates to

---

[31] Comdex Canada Exhibition (1995), adv. pamphlet.
[32] Database and Client/Server World Exposition (1994), adv.
[33] Global Knowledge, adv. pamphlet.
[34] William McGee, quoted in Cassirer, *Language and Myth*, p. 68.
[35] Citrix Systems, Inc., adv. pamphlet.
[36] Borland Paradox for Windows, adv. pamphlet.
[37] Oracle Corp. iDevelop 2000 event, adv. pamphlet.
[38] http://www.netc.org/.
[39] http://www.ocsystems.com/.
[40] http://web.progress.com/.
[41] http://accrisoft.org/.
[42] http://www.indigorose.com/.
[43] Hewlett-Packard Company, adv.
[44] Microsoft Visual Basic 2.0, adv. pamphlet.
[45] http://www.compellent.com/.
[46] http://www.indigorose.com/.
[47] Borland Delphi, adv. pamphlet.
[48] http://web.uvic.ca/.
[49] http://www.kewlit.com/.

create advertising channels."[50] "Simple, useful and powerful software tools."[51] "Powerful database design made simple."[52] "A powerful software tool to tweak, optimize, maintain and tune up your Windows XP ...."[53] "Develop powerful Internet applications."[54] "Create powerful, dynamic Windows programs."[55] "A powerful, easy-to-use process improvement tool."[56]

As verb: "Oracle software powers the Internet."[57] "We can power you, too."[58] "Empowered by innovation."[59] "MV Software has been powering business solutions for over two decades."[60] "Empower employees to collaborate and innovate."[61] "Windows Principles: ... empowering choice, opportunity, and interoperability."[62] "XML: powering next-generation business applications."[63] "Learning powered by technology."[64] "Utoolbox.com ... is powered by a dedicated team of professionals."[65] "Empowering software engineers in human-centered design."[66] "Empowering software debugging through architectural support for program rollback."[67] "Powering the lean, consumer-driven supply chain for manufacturers worldwide."[68] "We can empower your organization through adoption of IT Service Management ...."[69] "Data Query empowers the end user to create reports ...."[70] "Empowering software maintainers with semantic web technologies."[71] "Powering on demand applications."[72] "Powering the digital age."[73]

As adverb: "Accurate Shutdown is a powerfully automatic software that turns off your computer at the user-specified time."[74] "RSConnect Suite corporate management software: ... powerfully simple, powerfully quick."[75] "QSR software ... provides a sophisticated workspace that enables you to work through your information efficiently and powerfully."[76] "XP Picture Manager can correct your photos powerfully and quickly."[77] "The building blocks of

[50] http://www.qualityunit.com/.   [51] http://www.utoolbox.com/.
[52] SDP Technologies S-Designor, adv. pamphlet.
[53] http://www.freedownloadscenter.com/.
[54] Microsoft Visual Studio 6.0, adv. pamphlet.
[55] Borland Turbo Pascal for Windows 1.5, adv. pamphlet.
[56] IEEE Computer Society Press, *LearnerFirst Process Management*, adv. pamphlet.
[57] Oracle Corp., adv.   [58] Dell Computers, adv.
[59] http://www.nec.com/.   [60] http://www.mvsoftware.com/.
[61] Cisco Systems, adv.   [62] http://www.microsoft.com/.
[63] http://www.dbmag.intelligententerprise.com/.
[64] Brochure subtitle, U.S. Dept. of Education, *Transforming American Education* (2010).
[65] http://www.utoolbox.com/.   [66] http://portal.acm.org/.
[67] http://iacoma.cs.uiuc.edu/.   [68] http://www.jda.com/.
[69] Global Knowledge, *IT and Management Training* catalogue (Dec. 2006), p. 12.
[70] Oracle Discoverer/2000, adv. pamphlet.   [71] http://www.rene-witte.net/.
[72] https://www-304.ibm.com/.   [73] http://www.swiftdisc.com/.
[74] http://www.accuratesolution.net/.   [75] http://www.necpos.com/.
[76] http://www.qsrinternational.com/.   [77] http://www.softtester.com/.

virtual instrumentation include powerfully productive software ....".[78] "HP StorageWorks Command View EVA software provides you with a powerfully simple storage management experience ....".[79] "The intelligent technology in our electrical calculation software powerfully calculates and performs your electrical calculations and designs ....".[80] "Powerfully advanced mailing software."[81]

In addition, the phrase "powered by" is commonly used in promotional slogans to mention a given product, in place of a phrase like "made by," "works with," or "employs." Some examples of this practice: "powered by Google," "powered by IBM," "powered by Sun," "powered by AOL Mail," "powered by Microsoft Access," "powered by XMB," "powered by Cognos," "powered by FIS," "powered by Mozilla," "powered by HitsLink," "powered by PayPal," "powered by WebsiteBaker," "powered by Trac," "powered by ATI," "powered by Merril Lynch," "powered by Geeklog," "powered by vBulletin," "powered by eBay Turbo Lister," "powered by GetSimple," "powered by TAXWIZ," "powered by nexImage," "powered by MindTouch," "powered by Joomla," "powered by ShopFactory," "powered by Network Solutions," "powered by Sothink."

3

As programmers and as users, we wish to benefit from the power of software, but without taking the time to develop software expertise. Consequently, we have come to regard this power as the kind of power that we can *acquire*. And it is through the devices supplied by software companies that we hope to acquire it. So, when describing their devices as powerful, the software companies are simply exploiting this belief.

Like all beliefs we carry from our primitive past, the belief that certain devices possess a mysterious power can only be dispelled through learning. As in other domains, once we possess the necessary skills in software-related matters, we can easily recognize which devices are helpful and which ones are fraudulent. In a rational society, this education would be the responsibility of the software elites – the universities, in particular. In our society, however, the opposite is taking place: since the elites can profit far more by exploiting society than by educating it, ignorance and primitive beliefs serve their interests. Thus, only if we remain ignorant will we believe that their devices, which are based on mechanistic concepts, can solve our complex problems. So the elites are doing all they can to *prevent* us from developing software knowledge.

---

[78] http://www.scientific-computing.com/.   [79] https://ads.jiwire.com/.
[80] http://solutionselectricalsoftware.com/.   [81] http://www.satorisoftware.co.uk/.

Software devices can replace expertise only in solving *mechanistic* problems; that is, problems which can be broken down into simpler and simpler ones, and hence modeled with isolated hierarchical structures. Most problems we want to solve with software, however, are non-mechanistic. They can only be represented as systems of interacting structures, so they require a human mind, and expertise. The problems associated with programming, particularly, are of this kind. In the end, less than 1 percent of the software devices we are offered are genuine, beneficial tools; the rest are fraudulent. What distinguishes the latter is their claim to solve complex, non-mechanistic problems; in other words, to act as substitutes for minds. They address naive programmers and users, promising them the power to accomplish tasks that require, in fact, much knowledge and experience.

So the software elites are not responsible organizations, but charlatans. They present their devices as the software counterpart of the traditional tools and instruments, but at the same time they invoke the notions of magic and supernatural power. They tell us that we need these devices in the same way that engineers and doctors need theirs. But the tools and instruments we use in engineering and in medicine are promoted on the basis of real qualities, and provide real benefits. Their vendors do not exploit our ignorance and irrationality when persuading us to use them. Clearly, then, if *software* devices must be promoted in this fashion, it is because they are generally useless, because the possession of an imaginary power is their only quality. To put it differently, if software devices were promoted by demonstrating their *real* benefits, we would use only the few that are truly useful.

The harm caused by this charlatanism extends, however, beyond the waste of time and resources. For, when restricted to the mechanistic knowledge required to operate devices, we forgo all opportunities to develop complex, non-mechanistic knowledge. Without this knowledge we cannot solve our complex problems. But if we believe that it is only through devices that we can solve them, we continue to depend on devices, and hence to restrict ourselves to mechanistic knowledge, in a process that feeds on itself. The only way to escape from this vicious circle is by expanding our knowledge, so as to exceed the mechanistic capabilities of devices. And we cannot do this as long as we agree to depend on them. Thus, by enticing us with software devices, the elites ensure our perpetual ignorance. They prevent us from gaining knowledge and also from solving our problems.

The propaganda depicts the software elites as enligthened leaders who are creating a new world for us – a world with higher and higher levels of efficiency. But now we see that the reality is very different: they are fostering ignorance and irrational beliefs, so they are creating a *less* efficient world. When presenting their devices as magic systems or as sources of supernatural power, they are encouraging us to behave like the primitives. This degradation started with the software practitioners, in their programming activities. Now, as our dependence on computers is spreading, it is increasingly affecting everyone, in every activity.

Bear in mind, though, that it is not software or programming that causes this degradation, but *mechanistic* software and programming, the kind promoted by the software elites. Mechanistic software-related activities restrict us to mechanistic thinking, thereby preventing us from using our natural, non-mechanistic capabilities. Left alone, without software elites and the mechanistic dogma, human beings would learn to develop and use software as effectively as their minds permit them. Complex software phenomena, and complex software knowledge, would then join the many other complex structures that make up human existence. Our software-related activities would then *enhance* our minds, as do other complex phenomena (the use of language, for instance).

CHAPTER 1

Mechanism
and Mechanistic Delusions

The Mechanistic Philosophy

Three doctrines have dominated Western science and culture since the seventeenth century: reductionism, atomism, and mechanism. Reductionism claims that every phenomenon can be represented, through various transformations (or reductions), as a combination of *simpler* phenomena. Atomism claims that there is an end to reductionism, that every phenomenon can be reduced, ultimately, to some *elementary* entities – some building blocks (or atoms) that cannot be divided into simpler parts. Mechanism adds to reductionism and atomism the claim that every phenomenon can be reduced to *mechanical* phenomena – and hence, ultimately, to the phenomena associated with the motion of bits of matter.

Mechanism was the fundamental doctrine of the Scientific Revolution. It was called the new philosophy, to distinguish it from the scholastic philosophy, which had dominated Europe throughout the Middle Ages. Scholasticism had been worthless as a scientific doctrine, because it prevented its followers from expanding their knowledge of the world. Mechanism, on the other hand, is ideally suited for research in the natural sciences, as it encourages a logical breakdown of complex problems into simpler ones.

With the mechanistic philosophy, scientists working in fields like astronomy, physics, and chemistry quickly found explanations for phenomena that had baffled their predecessors for centuries. These spectacular successes have continued ever since, and have served to establish mechanism as the undisputed method of science: "By the middle of the nineteenth century mechanics was widely acknowledged as the most perfect physical science, embodying the ideal toward which all other branches of inquiry ought to aspire. Indeed, it was the common assumption of outstanding thinkers, physicists as well as philosophers, that mechanics is the basic and ultimate science, in terms of whose fundamental notions the phenomena studied by all other natural science could and should be explained."[1]

The failure of mechanism to explain phenomena in other fields, notably in the human sciences, has been as spectacular as its success in the natural sciences; but this has done nothing to reduce its dominating position in our culture. Despite occasional claims to the contrary, mechanistic theories are still considered, just as they were in the seventeenth century, the only valid scientific theories: science *is* mechanism.

We are interested in mechanism because we want to understand the nature of our mechanistic *delusions*; in particular, the nature of our mechanistic *software* delusions. We suffer from a mechanistic delusion when we attempt to apply the mechanistic principles in a field where they cannot work. And, because of our blind faith in mechanism, much of present-day science is in reality a pursuit of mechanistic fantasies. Software, in particular, gives rise to *non-mechanistic* phenomena; and yet, our software theories are based entirely on mechanistic concepts.

One reason for our mechanistic delusions is that we fail to recognize the mechanistic nature of our theories. Mechanism today is rarely expressed through reductions to mechanical phenomena and particles of matter, or through analogies to machinery, as was the case earlier. So, if we continue to associate mechanism exclusively with these concepts, we are liable to overlook our current fallacies.

Mechanism today manifests itself mostly in the belief that everything can be represented as a hierarchical structure of entities; that is, as a neat structure of things within things. In this chapter, we will see that the hierarchical concept is logically equivalent to the traditional mechanistic concepts. Once we understand this, it will be easier to recognize the mechanistic nature of our theories. The hierarchical model will also help us to understand why so many phenomena *cannot* be represented with mechanistic theories.

[1] Ernest Nagel, *The Structure of Science: Problems in the Logic of Scientific Explanation*, 2nd ed. (Indianapolis: Hackett, 1979), p. 154.

❖

The mechanistic myth has its roots in our desire to understand the world completely, and in our belief that this is possible. For, so long as we don't expect to understand each and every phenomenon, we can simply attribute to some transcendental powers those events that we cannot explain, and then carry on with our affairs.

As soon as we demand complete explanations, we are faced with the task of deciding what answers are good enough to count as explanations. The accepted answers in antiquity and in the Middle Ages were rather circular: the weight of an object is due to a quality that causes heaviness; an object bends or breaks according to a quality that causes elasticity; and so on. "Explanations" like these lead nowhere, obviously, and it is not surprising that Western science advanced so slowly during these periods. Since it is easy to find such circular answers, few scientists felt the need to seek the underlying causes, or to verify hypotheses through experiments.

The tendency in early times, thus, was to try to explain a phenomenon by seeing it as the source of other phenomena, rather than by analyzing its origins. Those who recognized the futility of this approach concluded that, to explain the phenomenon, they had to study its causes, not its effects; and then they saw it as consisting of other, simpler phenomena, which are easier to explain. This, in time, led to the mechanistic idea: "When we ask 'why?' concerning an event, we may mean either of two things. We may mean: 'What purpose did this event serve?' or we may mean: 'What earlier circumstances caused this event?' The answer to the former question is a teleological explanation, or an explanation by final causes; the answer to the latter question is a mechanistic explanation. I do not see how it could have been known in advance which of these two questions science ought to ask, or whether it ought to ask both. But experience has shown that the mechanistic question leads to scientific knowledge, while the teleological question does not."[2]

Once we agree that the only way to understand a phenomenon is by studying its causes, we must decide where to stop. We may well succeed in explaining a particular phenomenon in terms of other, simpler phenomena, and then explaining *those* in terms of even simpler ones, and so on. Which phenomena, though, are the ultimate explanations? That is, at which phenomena can we stop, being certain that we understand them?

The answer, of course, is *never*. But it is the fundamental assumption of the mechanistic doctrine that we all understand, intuitively, simple *mechanical*

---

[2] Bertrand Russell, *A History of Western Philosophy* (New York: Simon and Schuster, 1972), p. 67.

operations. So, if we manage to reduce a given phenomenon to mechanical phenomena, we can declare it to be "understood."

For many phenomena – light, heat, chemical reactions, human feelings – no obvious reduction to mechanical phenomena exists. Nevertheless, mechanism assumes that these phenomena, too, are the result of simpler ones, displayed by some minute particles; and that it is the mechanical properties of those particles that cause, ultimately, the observable phenomena.

We are comfortable with mechanical phenomena because we deal with objects in our everyday activities. We tend, therefore, to perceive everything in the universe as similar to these objects, except for being perhaps much larger, or much smaller, or much faster. We feel that we really understand something only if we can apprehend it with our senses, if we can see or touch it. And, although we admit that certain things cannot be seen or touched as we can common objects, we visualize them nevertheless as similar in nature. Anything else simply doesn't count as understanding.

Thus, the physicists of the seventeenth century attempted to understand complex natural phenomena by assuming that they are ultimately caused by things which, although minute and invisible, resemble familiar devices and processes: "They were always looking for hidden mechanisms, and in so doing supposed, without being concerned about this assumption, that these would be essentially of the same kind as the simple instruments which men had used from time immemorial to relieve their work."[3] Even in the late nineteenth century, the great scientist Lord Kelvin candidly admitted that he understood something only if he could make a mechanical model of it.

In conclusion, mechanism is not an exact, unquestionable concept, but only a *convention*. It is a method that defines "understanding" as the acceptance of some facts with which we are naturally comfortable, and gives us hope that we can explain everything else in terms of these facts.

A belief in mechanism entails a belief in *determinism*: mechanistic theories claim that the future state of a system can be predicted from its current state with any degree of accuracy we want. The greatest success of mechanism, Newton's theory of gravitation, exemplifies this belief: if we know the state of the bodies in the solar system at a particular instant, we can indeed determine their position at any other instant, in the past or in the future. From early successes like this, scientists and philosophers gained the confidence that all

---

[3] E. J. Dijksterhuis, *The Mechanization of the World Picture* (New York: Oxford University Press, 1969), p. 497.

phenomena yet to be explained – not just in physics or astronomy, but also in such fields as psychology, linguistics, and politics – would prove to be, in the end, equally mechanistic.

The most famous expression of this belief is the statement made at the beginning of the nineteenth century by the great mathematician Laplace. The whole universe, he claimed, is a deterministic system consisting of particles of matter acting upon one another according to the law of gravitation; thus, a being who possessed sufficient intelligence to note the state of these particles at a given instant and to solve the relevant equations, could accurately predict every future occurrence in the universe – every entity and every event, every fact and every bit of knowledge. This enthusiasm was shared by most scientists: "When nineteenth-century physicists subscribed to determinism as an article of scientific faith, most of them took for their ideal of a deterministic theory one that defines the state of a physical system in the manner of particle mechanics."[4] Strict determinism, however, has been shown since then to be both philosophically and scientifically naive.

Let us pause for a moment and recall the purpose of this discussion. We must study the history of mechanism if we are to understand our mechanistic delusions; and we must understand these delusions in order to recognize our *software* delusions. For, as we will see later, all programming principles, theories, and methodologies invented in the last forty years, despite their great number and variety, can be described with one phrase: *attempts to reduce software to mechanics*.

And it is only because of our long mechanistic tradition that the software charlatans can deceive us with the notion that software problems are a new kind of mechanical problems. Without this bias, it would be obvious to anyone that software phenomena are not the type of phenomena that can be reduced, mechanistically, to simpler ones.

New programming ideas are being introduced every year, all promising a dramatic improvement in programming practices. But once we understand their mechanistic roots, we can easily recognize their similarity. Thus, when analyzed, these ideas reveal a common assumption: software applications consist of neat structures of modules and operations, just as appliances consist of neat structures of subassemblies and parts; so, instead of acquiring programming expertise, we can create applications simply by imitating the methods used to build appliances in a factory. Applications are said to be made of

[4] Nagel, *Structure of Science*, p. 282.

"components," which must be assembled using the methods of "software engineering." Programmers are called "engineers," and are encouraged to use terminology borrowed from the field of manufacturing. They no longer write, but "build" or "construct" applications. They work in "software factories" and design "data warehouses."

This mechanistic software ideology is taught in universities, is promoted in books and periodicals, and is supported by businesses and governments with vast amounts of money. But when we search for a logical basis to the belief that the methods of manufacturing can be applied to programming, we find none. All we find is the classic idea that any process can be reduced to simpler ones, and that this reduction can be repeated again and again, down to some processes that are simple enough to implement directly – an idea that was never shown to be true for software.

In reality, then, our software-related pursuits – the so-called information technology revolution, the activities we identify with progress and the future – are steeped in a naive, seventeenth-century mechanistic mentality.

Reductionism and Atomism

1

The earliest documented mechanistic theory, the *atomistic* philosophy, was developed in Greece during the fifth century BC by a school of philosophers we have come to call atomists. This philosophy was founded by Leucippus and Democritus, but was based on the work of earlier Greek philosophers, Empedocles, Parmenides, and Anaxagoras. These thinkers sought to understand the nature of matter and space, and asked questions such as these: What are things ultimately made of? Is space continuous, and thus infinitely divisible into smaller and smaller parts? Or is it discrete, and thus a line of a certain length is composed of a finite number of segments, and segments within segments? They noticed that substances can change into other substances – through heating or mixing, for example; also, animals that eat grass seem to convert the grass into flesh and bones. This means that each substance may have bits of other substances in it, ready to be released through certain processes. Or, more likely, all substances consist of some common elementary entities, and it is the way these entities are combined that determines the observable qualities of each substance.

The atomists concluded that everything is made up of small particles, or atoms, which are infinitely hard and hence indivisible and indestructible. The atoms are surrounded by empty space and are constantly in motion, colliding and mingling with one another. They come in many shapes and sizes, and the combination of these properties and their motion produces the large-scale phenomena that we observe. The atomists imagined the behaviour of these particles by comparing their interaction to the movement and collision of small objects in a container, or insects in the air, or pebbles in a stream, or grains in a sieve. Thus, while accepting the existence of things that are too small to detect with our senses, the atomists had to visualize them, nonetheless, as similar in nature to the objects encountered in everyday life.

Ancient atomism was a truly mechanistic theory, in that it attempted to explain all phenomena, not just the composition of matter, through reduction to mechanical properties. Sensations and feelings, for example – sight, smell, pain, pleasure – also had to be explained as the result of the collision and interaction of atoms. There is nothing in the universe but atoms and the void, claimed the atomists. Everything is based, ultimately, on matter and motion.

The atomistic philosophy was later embraced by Epicurus, and Epicureanism remained popular in the Roman Empire until the fourth century AD. Then, atomism was forgotten. Centuries later it was remembered, though, owing largely to the book *On the Nature of the Universe*, written in 55 BC by the philosopher and poet Lucretius. Atomism could not be verified, of course, so it was nothing more than speculation. Nevertheless, it greatly influenced the world view of those who accepted it.

After the decline of the ancient civilizations, not much happened in Western science until the Renaissance. Then, during the Scientific Revolution, the ancient atomistic theories were revived and became known as *corpuscular* theories of matter. Their claims had not changed: all phenomena must be explained through the science of mechanics, and hence through reduction to some small and indivisible particles, or corpuscles. Despite the passage of two millennia, scientists could not imagine a world that consisted ultimately of anything but objects and processes which, while invisible, are similar to those we observe in everyday life: "The view became current that all the operations of nature, all the fabric of the created universe, could be reduced to the behaviour of minute particles of matter, and all the variety that presented itself to human experience could be resolved into the question of the size, the configuration, the motion, the position and the juxtaposition of these particles."[1]

It was Pierre Gassendi who introduced ancient atomism in Europe, and the corpuscular notion was quickly embraced by most scientists, including

---

[1] Herbert Butterfield, *The Origins of Modern Science: 1300–1800*, 2nd ed. (London: Bell and Hyman, 1957), p. 120.

Galileo, Descartes, Boyle, Huygens, Newton, and Leibniz. Innumerable theories were brought forward in an attempt to explain natural phenomena
through the motion of particles: solidity and fluidity, rigidity and elasticity,
heat and cold, evaporation, condensation, sound, light, colour, taste, etc. These
theories explained nothing, of course. They were rather silly conjectures
expressing the imagination of the scientists: what they thought particles ought
to be like in order to cause those phenomena. There are heat-producing atoms,
for instance, and cold-producing atoms, and it is their relative influence that
we detect as heat and cold. Solidity of bodies is produced by specially shaped
particles that interlock. Melting occurs when heat atoms penetrate the tight
spaces between particles. Gravitational attraction is explained as particles
emitted from one body and affecting the second body. Vision is explained as
the pressure of particles that fill the space between the source of light and
the eye.[2]

Thanks to the vagueness of these conjectures, several theories could easily
be formulated by different scientists to explain the same phenomenon. Often,
more than one theory was conceived by the same scientist. Thus, although
seriously proposed as explanations, the corpuscular theories were mere speculations: "Everything remains in the vaguely qualitative sphere, so that there
is no question of an experimental verification of the truth of the theories
in question. On the ground of a curious kind of corpuscular imagination,
explanatory hypotheses are formulated which may be considered more or less
plausible, but which cannot be verified in any way."[3]

It is hard to admit today that the greatest scientific minds of that epoch – the
epoch we have come to call the century of genius – could engage in such absurd
speculations. And it is even harder to admit that the same minds, while
engaged in these corpuscular fantasies, produced the brilliant work from
which modern science was born. This chapter in the history of science has
been told many times, but seldom accurately. Being heirs to the scientific
tradition inaugurated by these men, we naturally tend to remember their
genius and to forget their mistakes. But we are also heirs to their mechanistic
delusions, and if we want to understand our current scientific fallacies we must
start by examining theirs. In the following pages, therefore, I want to show the
interdependence of scientific thinking and mechanistic delusions, which can
help to explain why even today we are liable to confuse one with the other.

[2] E. J. Dijksterhuis, *The Mechanization of the World Picture* (New York: Oxford University Press, 1969), pp. 416, 427–429.   [3] Ibid., p. 430.

2

Let us recall the origin of the mechanistic doctrine. The early scientists believed that mechanics is the only exact discipline, that the motion of objects is the only phenomenon with a complete explanation, so we must explain all other phenomena by reducing them to mechanics. This belief gave rise to two types of mechanical reductionism, which are still very much with us today. The first one, which may be called *formal* reductionism, is the belief that all phenomena can be reduced ultimately to the simplest mechanical phenomena (the motion of particles of matter), which can then be explained mathematically. The second one, an *informal* reductionism, is the belief that natural phenomena can be explained merely by showing that they are analogous to mechanical devices (since, in principle, these devices can be reduced to simpler and simpler parts, and ultimately to the particles of formal reductionism); clockworks, the most complicated machines in earlier times, were a common model.

The two types of reductionism exist side by side. Scientists prefer *formal* reductions, but, as these theories seldom work, they need some informal analogies as backup. Thus, in the seventeenth century, formal reductionism was represented by the corpuscular theories; but these theories were only speculations, so to support their claims the scientists also described the world informally as a giant machine, with God acting as the master engineer who created it, set it in motion, and is perhaps still supervising its operation.

Today, formal reductionism is represented by theories that attempt to reduce phenomena to simpler ones, in the hope that the latter will be reduced to even simpler ones, and so on, ending eventually with phenomena that can be depicted with mathematical models. But we also use *informal* models and analogies to describe these theories. Linguist Noam Chomsky, for example, maintains that it is possible to explain with mathematical precision how a sentence is derived from words, simply by studying its linguistic characteristics. He maintains, therefore, that there is no need to take into account such imprecise factors as the knowledge present in the mind, or the context in which the sentence is used. But his theory does not work, so Chomsky is obliged to add an informal model to support it: he postulates an innate language faculty that we possess as part of our genetic structure, so an exact theory of language is no less plausible than an exact theory of the heart or the kidneys; and he defends the idea of an innate language faculty by pointing to the many other innate qualities – our propensity to develop arms rather than wings, for instance.

To take another example, the software theories attempt to reduce program-ming phenomena – which include in fact many unpredictable business, social, and personal aspects – to precise methods and to formal models, on the assumption that software applications can be treated as neat hierarchical structures of software entities. But these theories do not work, so their proponents support them with informal analogies: they add that these theories must be valid because software development resembles manufacturing and construction activities, and in these activities the concept of hierarchical subassemblies works well.

At first sight, the informal analogy invoked by a reductionist to support his theory may look like additional evidence of its validity. The need for an informal analogy, however, is evidence of its *failure*. If the formal theory worked, the scientist would need no additional, informal evidence to back it up. As it is, the formal theory provides the dignified image that makes the claim appear "scientific," while the informal analogy is the distraction that masks the failure of the theory and reassures us that there must be something in it after all, so it is worth pursuing. Some of these theories generate "research programs" that continue for years and decades, without anyone realizing that they are in fact worthless, pseudoscientific notions.

Returning to the seventeenth-century scientists, we notice the following, peculiar fact. Even as they claimed strict allegiance to the mechanistic doc-trine, even while proposing endless corpuscular theories and clockwork models of the world, their important work – the theories we remember them by – had nothing to do with their mechanical speculations. On the contrary, they were based on deductive reasoning, empirical verification, and solid mathematical principles. They modernized algebra, invented calculus and analytic geometry, and founded the theory of probability; they made discover-ies in optics, hydrostatics, pneumatics, physiology, chemistry, and astronomy; all this and more they accomplished within a century. This was the century in which all scientists claimed that mechanics is the only pure science, so everything else must be explained in terms of mechanics; and yet, none of their important theories during this period had to be confirmed through reduction to mechanics.

The greatest irony is that Newton's theory of gravitation, the culmination of seventeenth-century science, was the least mechanistic theory of all. It introduced a mysterious force called gravitational attraction, which horrified everyone, because it was contrary to the accepted mechanistic doctrine. Mechanism asserts that motion can be transmitted from one body to another only by intuitively understandable means; that is, through direct contact and by pushing, like colliding billiard balls. Gravitational force, on the contrary, acts at a distance and by pulling. Newton's contemporaries accused him of relapsing into the medieval belief in occult qualities, of betraying science by abandoning the mechanistic conception of nature. Newton, a mechanist himself, defended gravitational force on the ground that it could be confirmed empirically, and that it was not a primary quality but the result of some hidden mechanical phenomena yet to be discovered. He could not explain it, but he was convinced that one day a mechanistic explanation would be found for it too. He even suggested such a theory himself (a corpuscular theory involving the ether – the substance believed to fill the void between the celestial bodies).

There is an obvious contradiction here. On the one hand, these great scientists sincerely believed that all phenomena must be explained through formal reductions to mechanical operations, or at least through informal analogies. On the other hand, they did not hesitate to advance theories that stand on their own, based on observation, logic, and mathematics. But this contradiction is resolved once we understand that the corpuscular theories, and the informal analogies, served in reality only as *metaphors*.

The reductionistic and atomistic concepts inherent in these metaphors gave scientists the confidence to search for new and better explanations. Believing in reductionism and atomism is, in effect, believing that every problem has a solution, that every phenomenon can be explained. These concepts assure us that all things can be divided into smaller things, reaching eventually parts small enough to be considered elementary. At that point, we will know all that can be known: "Physical atomism is more than logical analysis. It is the assumption that there is a quantitative limit to division, that small ultimate units exist.... Atomism has rightly been described as a policy for research.... But atomism is not merely a policy or a method which has proven brilliantly effective at certain levels of material analysis; it is also a positive assumption regarding ultimate structure. *This assumption has a powerful psychological appeal, for it suggests a limited task with high rewards.* If there really exist ultimate units, we have only to discover their laws and all their possible combinations, and we shall be all-knowing and all-powerful, like gods. So it seems."[4]

Had the seventeenth-century scientists suspected how complex the world really is, they might not have dared look for explanations. Had they known that three centuries later we would still lack a complete understanding of the universe, of matter, of nature, of life, of intelligence, they would have felt

[4] Lancelot L. Whyte, *Essay on Atomism: From Democritus to 1960* (Middletown, CT: Wesleyan University Press, 1961), pp. 14–15 (italics added).

unqualified to propose those sweeping theories. But the belief in mechanism inspired them with confidence: assured that the world is well-ordered and fairly simple, they concluded that all natural phenomena can be explained with a few principles – the same principles that govern the behaviour of common objects and devices.

This belief is evident in their corpuscular fantasies. For instance, they postulate the existence of smooth particles and oddly shaped particles to describe phenomena like fluidity and solidity, simply because these phenomena resemble the effects produced by piles of smooth objects and oddly shaped objects;[5] and they describe magnetism as a vortex of particles shaped like screws, matching appropriately threaded particles present in iron (and magnetic polarity as the existence of particles shaped like right-handed and left-handed screws).[6] Westfall describes this "imaginary construction of invisible mechanisms to account for phenomena" as "the occupational vice of mechanical philosophers."[7]

Nor did this naivety end when the scientists discovered the *real* theories – which they did, not through their corpuscular fantasies, but through careful observation and experimentation. Although the real theories did not depend on corpuscular ideas, they went back and modified the corpuscular theories to agree with the facts revealed by the real theories.

The mechanistic belief was like the belief in a religious myth: it motivated the scientists to great feats of intellect, and they could not abandon it even when recognizing its fallaciousness. They could continue to accept the corpuscular theories and the machine analogies precisely because they were so vague, and because they had no bearing on the real theories anyway.

It is, again, Newton's persistent belief in a mechanistic explanation for gravitational attraction even after proving his great theory – which, being based on the concept of force, *contradicted* that belief – that is paradigmatic of the mechanistic obsession. Then, still failing to find a mechanistic explanation but unwilling to abandon mechanism, his followers in the eighteenth century quietly modified the meaning of mechanism to *include* the new concept of force. Eventually, "Newton's concept of force, which had been rejected as essentially unmechanistic [earlier], came to be regarded as precisely the most characteristic feature of a mechanistic conception of nature."[8]

It was their naivety as much as their acumen that led the early scientists to recognize mechanism – the combination of reductionism and atomism – as

[5] Dijksterhuis, *Mechanization*, p. 428.
[6] Richard S. Westfall, *The Construction of Modern Science: Mechanisms and Mechanics* (New York: Cambridge University Press, 1977), pp. 36–37.   [7] Ibid., p. 41.
[8] Dijksterhuis, *Mechanization*, p. 497.

an effective method of discovery. It was their belief that all the mysteries of the world are ultimately accessible to the human mind, that they are merely a collection of puzzles waiting to be solved. With this belief comes the confidence that the phenomena we observe on a large scale, and which we do not understand, must be caused by some phenomena that exist on a smaller scale. So it is those phenomena that we must study. Then, even if we are wrong and those phenomena are not the elementary causes we thought they were, we only need to treat *them* as the large scale phenomena, and repeat the process. Eventually, we are bound to reach the lowest level: the elementary entities and processes that cause everything else.

Consciously or not, therefore, anyone who believes in determinism and in the existence of complete explanations will become a believer in reductionism and atomism. Indeed, if we define *understanding* as a process similar to knowing how a complicated machine works, there is no other way to understand than by perceiving all phenomena as systems of things within things, waiting for us – just like the subassemblies of a machine – to take them apart and study, one level at a time.

But this method, while useful in disciplines like physics and chemistry, is only partially effective in disciplines like biology and physiology, and is totally useless in those disciplines that deal with mental capabilities or human relations. This is true because reductionism and atomism are valid only for *independent* phenomena; that is, when the lower-level phenomena can be isolated and studied separately. When the lower-level phenomena share some of their elements, they interact, and isolating them alters the nature of the high-level phenomenon by severing the interactions.

The early scientists were unaware of this limitation, and were convinced that *all* phenomena would eventually be explained mechanistically. It is this naivety that must be stressed – not to denigrate their work, but to recognize the same mistake in our own beliefs. It would be historically inaccurate to see the adoption of the mechanistic philosophy as the result of a careful consideration of research methods. It was the result of a naive view of the world: the belief that the world is simpler than it really is.

When scientists today attempt to describe with neat models the human mind, or human communication and relations, or economic phenomena, or the process of software development, they are guilty of the same naivety – the childish belief in a simple and well-ordered world. Although scientists have been attempting for three centuries to reduce everything to mechanics, this has succeeded only for phenomena that can indeed be isolated, and hence approximated with mechanistic theories. All other attempts have resulted in mechanistic delusions.

We are continuing in this tradition, but with one important difference.

Whereas the earlier delusions rarely went beyond academic discourse, the current mechanistic theories immediately become fashionable and influential. No matter how worthless, they are accepted with enthusiasm by experts and laymen, by universities, corporations, and governments – while the non-mechanistic theories, even when successful, are dismissed as "unscientific." We have redefined science to mean simply the pursuit of mechanism, and we no longer care whether a theory works or not, or whether an idea is useful or not, as long as it is mechanistic. As a result, we are wasting more and more of our resources on mechanistic delusions. Moreover, because the pursuit of a mechanistic delusion is just like the pursuit of a pseudoscientific theory, our society is increasingly dominated by crackpots and charlatans. Finally, with the mechanistic *software* theories and their repercussions – the destruction of knowledge and minds, the promotion of totalitarianism – our mechanistic delusions have reached the point where they are threatening civilization itself.

To summarize, the function of mechanism is mainly as myth. In both their informal theories (the analogies of phenomena with machines) and their formal theories (the reduction to particles), the early scientists never insisted on a perfect mechanistic representation, and were ready to overlook deficiencies and contradictions. All that mattered was to discover a theory that worked.

What made mechanism such a powerful myth were the twin concepts of reductionism and atomism. These concepts gave the scientists both the confidence to advance revolutionary theories and the methods to verify them: "The dream of final atomic knowledge seized many Western scientific minds, consciously or unconsciously guiding them to unexpected discoveries which in a sense justified the dream."[9] "In our not fully successful attempts at reduction, especially of chemistry to physics, we have learned an incredible amount.... Thus from the point of view of method, our reduction programmes have led to great successes, even though it may be said that the attempted reductions have, as such, usually failed."[10]

Final atomic knowledge was never attained, but the *belief* that such knowledge is possible has helped us reach levels of knowledge that otherwise we might not even have envisaged. If we doubt the value of mechanism, we need only compare the spectacular advances in natural science during the century of the Scientific Revolution with the stagnation during the preceding

[9] Whyte, *Essay on Atomism*, p. 15.
[10] Karl R. Popper, *The Open Universe: An Argument for Indeterminism* (London: Routledge, 1988), p. 146.

one thousand years. Mechanism acted merely as a motivating force, as a psychological aid. But the fact that it is mainly a myth does not lessen its value in those fields where reductionism and atomism lead to useful theories. The danger is to conclude that mechanism is a universal method of science, and to apply it with the same confidence in fields where it is worthless. Its powerful psychological appeal works then *against* science, by preventing us from trying other, possibly better, research methods.

3

Let us examine today's formal reductionism. To explain how phenomena like chemical reactions or human intelligence can be reduced to the motion of bits of matter, scientists postulate several stages of reduction. These stages parallel the academic disciplines known as physics, chemistry, biology, psychology, and sociology. Thus, today's formal reductionism is a more sophisticated variant of the corpuscular theories of the seventeenth century, which attempted rather crudely to reduce all phenomena *directly* to particles of matter.

This is what today's reductionism claims: Starting with physical phenomena, we must either reduce them directly to mechanical phenomena, or explain them as the external manifestation of the motion of particles. For chemical phenomena, we note that all substances consist of particles like molecules and atoms, so we should be able to explain all chemical phenomena in terms of particles – that is, as physical phenomena; and the physical phenomena can then be reduced to mechanics, as usual. Biological systems (plants, animals, human beings) consist of organic matter whose chemical composition is understood, so biology can be reduced to chemistry; chemistry can then be reduced to physics, and physics to mechanics. The human brain is just another organ, so human behaviour and mental acts, ultimately governed by brain and body, are reducible to biology, and then to chemistry, physics, and mechanics. Finally, a human society is nothing but a collection of human beings, so all social phenomena can be explained in terms of the behaviour of individuals; they can be reduced, therefore, to biology, chemistry, physics, and mechanics.

The neatness of these reductions makes formal reductionism look like a proven principle, but the resulting theories are as naive as the corpuscular fantasies of the seventeenth century. The earlier scientists were trying to explain all phenomena directly as the motion of particles, and this is why their theories look so silly today. But modern, multistage reductionism only *seems* more logical. The actual claim is the same; namely, that all phenomena can be reduced to mechanics. It is merely divided into several smaller claims, which individually are less ambitious and hence more plausible.

Like the earlier ones, the modern theories are ultimately grounded on the belief that everything can be explained in terms of simpler phenomena, with which we are already familiar. The only successful reduction to date has been that of physics to mechanics. Chemistry has been largely, but not completely, reduced to physics, and only isolated parts of biology have been reduced to chemistry; many biological processes, and particularly the phenomenon of life, remain immune to reduction. As for the reduction of psychology to biology, or sociology to psychology, they remain fantasies.

By limiting their work to separate steps of the grand reduction project, today's mechanists can delude themselves that their theories are less absurd than the earlier ones. A scientist would attract ridicule today if he advanced a theory that reduces social phenomena or human intelligence to the motion of atoms. But some scientists *are* attempting to reduce intelligence to simpler phenomena – to basic mental acts, for instance; and others *are* attempting to reduce social phenomena to individual minds, or mental acts to neurological functions, or neurological functions to chemistry. Because each reduction is seen as a small step, today's theories appear sensible – unlike the earlier ones, which attempted a direct reduction to mechanics. All these scientists are convinced that they are working on important projects, on theories that are likely to succeed. So, *as a group*, they still believe in the ultimate reduction of intelligence and social phenomena to the motion of bits of matter. If there appears to be a difference from seventeenth-century mechanism, it is only an illusion created by the current academic specialization. The earlier scientists were generalists, so they believed all disciplines to be reducible to mechanics; today's scientists are specialists, so they are only concerned with reducing their own discipline, to some other discipline.

Thus, in addition to the naivety of the early mechanists, today's scientists suffer from self-deception. On the one hand, they are restricting their theories to individual disciplines; on the other hand, each reduction project can succeed only if those below it have already succeeded. So, in the end, there is no difference between claiming that biology, psychology, and sociology can be reduced to mechanics, and claiming separately that biology can be reduced to chemistry, psychology to biology, and sociology to psychology. If mechanism is valid, all these reductions must succeed; so we should be able to explain every phenomenon in terms of particles of matter, just as the early scientists said.

Not only do today's scientists believe that fragmentary mechanism can be a substitute for true mechanism, but even within their own disciplines they avoid a full reduction. Thus, they usually attempt to explain a complex biological phenomenon by reducing it, not to chemical phenomena, but merely to simpler biological ones. Similarly, they attempt to explain mental phenomena by reducing them, not to biology, but to simpler mental phenomena; and they attempt to explain social phenomena by reducing them, not to the psychology of individuals, but to simpler social phenomena.

In conclusion, to be consistent, one cannot believe in partial reductionism without believing at the same time in the possibility of a total reduction. So today's mechanists are contradicting themselves when working on separate phenomena while rejecting the earlier mechanistic ideas.

This self-deception is especially blatant in the study of the mind. Minds give rise to phenomena that, if one believes in mechanism, can only be explained if all the simpler phenomena (down to physiological processes, and even physical processes) are fully understood. So, strictly speaking, no one should even try to discover mechanistic theories of mind before we understand how particles of matter give rise to basic mental phenomena. Scientists, however, believe that it is possible to explain mental phenomena by starting, not with physical, nor even with biological, phenomena, but with some rather high-level concepts: simple mental acts, bits of behaviour, small linguistic entities, and the like. The scientists hope to explain how the mind works, but without the burden of explaining its dependence on lower-level phenomena – on the brain, on neurons and molecules. These theories keep failing, but the scientists continue to believe that the mind can be explained through partial reductionism. (We will study some of these theories, and their pseudoscientific nature, in the following chapters.)

The self-deception, thus, is believing in reductionism and atomism without adhering strictly to these principles. The scientists want the power promised by mechanism, but without the rigours demanded by serious mechanistic theories. Clearly, since they are pursuing reduction projects in *all* disciplines, today's scientists believe that mechanism involves a continuous series of reductions – from the most complex phenomena down to particles of matter. At the same time, they expect to discover useful mechanistic theories for each phenomenon separately. Logically, a scientist ought to wait until the phenomena of lower complexity than his are successfully reduced to even simpler phenomena. Instead, each scientist believes that he can explain his particular phenomenon even if the lower-level ones are unexplained, so his project can lead to a useful theory regardless of the state of the other projects.

4

Few of us realize how much of our academic research, and how many of the ideas that guide our society, are but mechanistic delusions. The reason we accept absurd theories time and again, and thus repeat the mistakes of the past, is that we don't know how to identify a mechanistic theory.

Psychologists, linguists, sociologists, and software theorists may no longer attempt to reduce their problems to particles of matter or to clockwork models, and they may even criticize the mechanistic doctrine. When we study their theories, though, we find nothing but mechanistic beliefs. One mechanistic theory after another are being invented, and hailed as scientific breakthroughs. We clearly see that they do not work, but we remain convinced that they are valid. And we do not recognize their similarity to the *past* theories, which also did not work, and which no one is taking seriously any longer. It is our failure to recognize their common mechanistic grounding that tempts us to accept each one as novel and important.

Our task now is to find that common concept – the concept shared by all mechanistic theories. We have already determined that the corpuscular theories of the seventeenth century, the atomistic theories of antiquity or of modern physics, and the analogies to machines and manufacturing, are *metaphors*. Reductionism and atomism provided the actual method, while the metaphors provided only psychological support. The metaphors may change, but the underlying methods do not. So, if we want to find that common concept, we must search for the simplest model that provides the functions of reductionism and atomism. It is not hard to see what that model is: the hierarchical structure (see figure 1-1). Clearly, this structure embodies both functions: if we move from the top element toward the terminal elements – that is, from the highest level of complexity to the lowest – the elements at each level are reduced to the simpler elements of the lower level; and the terminal elements are the structure's atoms – its basic building blocks, or alphabet.

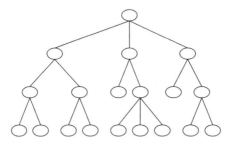

Figure 1-1

We can use the hierarchical structure to model anything that can be depicted as a system of things within things. Thus, to represent the atomistic and corpuscular theories, the terminal elements of the hierarchy are the particles, and the top element is the object or phenomenon described by the theory. When the mechanistic metaphor is a machine, the terminal elements are the simplest operations, the top element is the whole machine, and the intermediate elements are the various subprocesses.[11]

So the hierarchical structure can represent any mechanistic theory and any mechanistic phenomenon. This is true because the elements and relations can stand for anything – physical entities, processes, bits of knowledge, pieces of software, and so forth. The hierarchical concept is what matters, what provides the mechanistic qualities: describing the elements at one level of complexity as combinations of elements from the lower level provides the reductionistic quality, and basing the entire structure on a relatively small set of terminal elements provides the atomistic quality.

Thus, the hierarchical concept can be equated with mechanism because it is the simplest concept that provides the two fundamental properties of the mechanistic method, reductionism and atomism. Let us call *immediate* metaphors the traditional mechanistic metaphors of particles and machines; the hierarchical concept is then the *hidden* metaphor. The hierarchical metaphor is inherent in every mechanistic metaphor; that is, we can always reduce an immediate metaphor to a hierarchical model. The immediate metaphors are expendable, but the hidden, hierarchical metaphor is always present. So, if we want to determine whether a theory is mechanistic, all we have to do is verify whether it can be represented with a hierarchical model. We must not be distracted by the immediate metaphors that accompany the theory; if based ultimately on the hierarchical concept, it is mechanistic.

In the case of software theories, the most popular immediate metaphors are from engineering, but we must not take them too seriously. It is the hidden metaphor that we must look for. And indeed, whether or not employing engineering metaphors, the software theorists resort in the end to hierarchical structures. In fact, they misunderstand and misrepresent the engineering practices altogether. They claim that software development must resemble engineering projects, but even for an informal metaphor their notion of engineering is highly distorted. If we remember the hidden hierarchical metaphor, however, we can easily understand the source of their engineering delusions. What the software theorists like in engineering – what they wish to emulate in software development – is the high degree of success, the precision, and the predictability. They superficially study the engineering practices, and, lacking engineering knowledge, all they see is the use of hierarchical structures: the design of complicated objects as modules within modules. They conclude that this is all there is to engineering, failing to realize that the hierarchical concept was their own metaphor, their own delusion.

---

[11] We will study hierarchical structures, which I also call simple structures, in the next section. They are introduced here in order to complete the present argument.

We like the hierarchical concept because it is reassuring: its reductionism and atomism create the illusion that it can explain any phenomenon and solve any problem. Guided by this belief, we see hierarchical structures everywhere we look. These hierarchies, as well as their ability to create large structures from simple elements, are real enough; but it is a mistake to conclude that this is the most complex concept possible. What creates richness and complexity in the world is not a large number of levels or elements, nor a large number of hierarchies, but the *interaction* of hierarchies.

There are indeed hierarchies in engineering projects, as there are in software projects. But on their own, without the expertise and creativity contributed by human minds, they would remain simple, mechanistic concepts. The software theorists see the hierarchies of engineering, but they underrate the knowledge added by individuals, and which cannot be reduced to hierarchical structures. Thus, they fail to see the *non-mechanistic* aspects of the engineering practices. In programming, the non-mechanistic aspects are even more important, and there is very little that can be accomplished with independent hierarchical structures.

5

To understand the influence of mechanism on science we must also consider the role of mathematics. Science became practically synonymous with mathematics in the seventeenth century, at precisely the time when it became mechanistic. This is hardly a coincidence.

Mathematical systems are hierarchical structures: in a given system, we start with a few basic concepts and create more complex ones by combining, one level at a time, concepts from the previous level; or, conversely, we analyze a complex concept by breaking it down into simpler ones, one level at a time, until we reach the basic concepts. Thus, mathematics and mechanism employ the same hidden metaphor. The concepts of a mathematical system are the entities that make it up, and the functions and theorems that use these entities.

The first mathematical system designed as a hierarchical structure was Euclid's geometry. Euclid, who worked in Alexandria from around 300 BC, collected all the geometrical knowledge accumulated by his predecessors and organized it as one book, the *Elements*. As is well known, he started with a small number of elementary assertions – assertions that appear to state self-evident truths, and can therefore act as premises. Then, by logically combining them, he showed how to demonstrate the truth of more and more complex assertions. The premises, the theorems built from them, those built from the former ones, and so on, form a perfect hierarchical structure, and the progression from one level to the next is based on logical deduction. This guarantees the validity of the theorems at the higher levels, which are too complex to prove directly. And, even though Euclid dealt mainly with geometry, this principle became the foundation of all of mathematics. The simplicity of the idea, coupled with the seemingly unlimited complexity of the entities, functions, and theorems that can be created, explains perhaps our infatuation with hierarchical structures.

Even in ancient times mathematics was appreciated for its ability to solve practical problems. But it was only at the time of the Scientific Revolution, when mechanism became a universal research method, that its ability to represent natural phenomena was recognized. Since mathematics and mechanism are both based on the hierarchical metaphor, it was at this time that science, mathematics, and mechanism became practically indistinguishable. Kepler and Galileo were convinced that "the structure of the external world was essentially mathematical in character and a natural harmony existed between the universe and the mathematical thought of the human mind."[12] They likened the universe to an open book, but a book written in the language of mathematics: we can read it, so we can discover all the secrets of nature, but only through mathematics.

Descartes went further and *identified* science and knowledge with mathematics. He was impressed by "the long chains of simple and easy reasonings by means of which geometers are accustomed to reach the conclusions of their most difficult demonstrations,"[13] and decided to adopt the hierarchical method for all fields of knowledge. Moreover, he says, he "had little difficulty in determining the objects with which it was necessary to commence, for [he] was already persuaded that it must be with the simplest and easiest to know."[14] He believed, in other words, that all we have to do is represent everything as entities within entities, and ensure that the starting elements of these structures are simple enough to understand directly. Then, if we rigorously follow the hierarchical links, if we "always preserve in our thoughts the order necessary for the deduction of one truth from another,"[15] we will be able to create all the knowledge that human minds can attain.

It matters little to us whether the popularity of mechanism was enhanced by the successful use of mathematics, or whether, conversely, scientists adopted mathematics as tool because it was based on the same metaphor as mechanism. What is significant is the transition to the modern world view that took place at this time and involved both mechanism and mathematics: "The

---

[12] Dijksterhuis, *Mechanization*, p. 404.
[13] René Descartes, *A Discourse on Method* (London: Dent, 1912), p. 16.   [14] Ibid.
[15] Ibid.

mechanization of the world-picture during the transition from ancient to classical science meant the introduction of a description of nature with the aid of the mathematical concepts of classical mechanics; it marks the beginning of the mathematization of science, which continues at an ever-increasing pace in the twentieth century."[16] All scientists in the seventeenth century shared in the new belief that "nature has to be described in mathematical language and that it can only be understood by man to the extent that he can describe its workings in that language."[17]

Since mathematics is based on the hierarchical concept, the mathematical belief expressed in the last sentence – a belief that continues to guide us even today – can be summarized as follows: to understand a phenomenon means to be able to represent it with a hierarchical structure. But this, as we saw earlier, is also the idea of mechanism. The mathematical belief, therefore, is identical to the mechanistic belief. Mathematical models are mechanistic models.

If mathematics is identical to mechanism, it too can represent accurately only *deterministic* phenomena; it too is useless, therefore, for phenomena involving minds and societies, which are indeterministic. All mechanistic delusions in the human sciences, we will see later, stem from the belief that complex human phenomena can be represented with exact, mathematical models.

Similarly, despite many exact aspects, software-related phenomena involve minds and societies; so they are, in the end, indeterministic. The idea of defining and developing software applications with the formal tools of mathematics is, therefore, absurd. Accordingly, all programming theories based on this idea – the relational database model, structured programming, and the like – are mechanistic delusions.

The theorists look at software and see that, just like Euclid's geometry, applications are ultimately made up of some basic elements (the individual operations), which are simple enough to verify directly. Why can't we, then, simply combine these elements hierarchically into more and more complex ones (blocks of operations, modules, and so on), each one guaranteed to work perfectly (because built from previously proven elements), until we reach the complete application? Why can't we, in other words, apply Descartes's method, said to work for all human knowledge, to the knowledge embodied in a software application? Programs are nothing but parts within parts, so we should be able to build applications of any size and complexity with geometrical precision, simply by designing them as strict hierarchical structures.

---

[16] Dijksterhuis, *Mechanization*, p. 501.   [17] Ibid.

This is what, in one form or another, is promised by all theories and methodologies. But, as we will see, this promise cannot be fulfilled. The hierarchical concept is useful in geometry because the hierarchical structures represented by geometrical theorems are a *direct mapping* of the world of lines, angles, and objects that geometry is concerned with; so a geometrical structure provides a one-to-one correspondence to the real structure. The phenomena we wish to represent with software, on the other hand, are systems of interacting structures. We may perhaps succeed in mapping *each aspect* of a given phenomenon into a software structure, but we cannot develop the application by implementing these structures separately. Since the actual structures interact, the corresponding software structures must interact too, if the application is to represent the phenomenon accurately. To treat this phenomenon as we do geometrical problems, we must first separate it into its constituent structures. But if we ignore the interactions, then even if we successfully program the individual structures, the application will not reflect reality. (We will discuss the concept of interacting structures later in this chapter, and software structures in chapter 4.)

6

Having equated the hierarchical structure with mechanism, we can define it as the model that represents all mechanistic phenomena, and all mechanistic theories. Our next task is to study this model. Then, we will extend it so as to represent *non-mechanistic* phenomena; this will be a system of *interacting* hierarchies.

I call the mechanistic model a *simple structure*, and the non-mechanistic one a *complex structure*. We will make good use of these models later, when we study various phenomena and the theories that attempt to explain them, and especially when we study *software* phenomena. These models will help us to determine whether a given phenomenon can be represented with a simple structure (in which case it can be explained mechanistically), or whether it can only be represented with a complex structure (in which case no mechanistic theory can explain it).

These models will also help us to understand why it is so easy to fall prey to mechanistic delusions. Because a complex structure appears to be just a collection of simple structures, it is tempting to try to explain the complex phenomenon by studying several simple phenomena in isolation. We will see that, in the final analysis, what all mechanistic theories do is attempt to represent a certain phenomenon with simple structures. This idea works when the phenomenon is reducible to simpler phenomena, but fails when it is not.

Mechanistic theories provide complete and precise explanations. Those who believe in mechanism claim that *all* phenomena can be explained, so their particular phenomenon *must* have a mechanistic theory. If the current theory does not work, they say, it will be improved, or a better one will be discovered in the future. With our models, we can see that this optimism is unwarranted when the phenomenon can only be represented with a complex structure, because no theory can provide a complete and precise explanation for complex phenomena.

I want to emphasize again that it is not mechanism in itself that is the target of this criticism, but the mechanistic *dogma*. Mechanism is an important concept, and we must always start by determining whether a given phenomenon can be usefully represented with a mechanistic model. When successful, such models are invaluable. Our concern here is with mechanistic *delusions*, which stem from the belief that *every* phenomenon can be represented with a mechanistic model.

History abounds with mechanistic delusions, especially following the Scientific Revolution. In our own time, however, they have reached epidemic proportions. One reason may be that we have pushed our knowledge beyond the capability of deterministic models. As we will see presently, even the *successful* mechanistic theories are only *approximations* of reality, because nothing in the world can be purely mechanistic. So, as we expand the range of phenomena that we wish to explain, only complex structures, which are indeterministic, can act as models. But we have yet to reach the level of scientific maturity where we can admit that some phenomena lie beyond the explanatory power of mechanistic principles. So we continue to invent mechanistic theories, whose determinism is comforting, even as we note that they fail to explain these phenomena.

Philosopher Karl Popper reminds us that our sciences are founded on conventions: the simplicity, determinism, and universality we seek to attain with our scientific theories are criteria we have invented ourselves, because this is the only way that we, human beings, can practise science. But theories are only *models* of the world, so no matter how successful some of them are, it doesn't mean that the world itself is simple, deterministic, and regular. We prefer simple theories, but "the world, as we know it, is highly complex; and although it may possess structural aspects which are simple in some sense or other, the simplicity of some of our theories – which is of our own making – does not entail the intrinsic simplicity of the world."[18]

Similarly, we prefer deterministic theories, because they are relatively easy to test; but "it seems no more justifiable to infer from their success that the

---

[18] Popper, *Open Universe*, p. 43.

world has an intrinsically deterministic character than to infer that the world is intrinsically simple.... The method of science depends upon our attempts to describe the world with simple theories: theories that are complex may become untestable, even if they happen to be true.... We have much reason to believe that the world is unique: a unique and highly complex – perhaps even infinitely complex – combination of occurrences of interacting processes. Yet we try to describe this unique world with the help of *universal* theories. Do these theories describe universal features of the world, regularities? Or is universality, like simplicity, a characteristic merely of our theories – perhaps of our theoretical language – but not of the world?"[19]

The conclusion we must draw is this: We defined science long ago as a body of narrow, mechanistic principles. But if we are ambitious enough to attempt to understand those aspects of the world that lie beyond the explanatory power of mechanistic principles – aspects like our mental capabilities, our social affairs, or our software pursuits – then we must also be wise enough to supplement these principles with new ones, adequate for complex phenomena. For, if we continue to believe that complex phenomena can be explained mechanistically, we will be exploited forever by the cranks and charlatans who, under cover of science, promise to solve our complex problems with mechanistic methods.

Simple Structures

1

The model I call *simple structure* is the hierarchical structure introduced in the previous section (see figure 1-1, p. 85). Thus, I also call this model a simple hierarchical structure.

A hierarchical structure is a system of things within things. Hierarchies are usually represented as inverted trees, with the branches spreading downward; but they can also be drawn with the branches spreading upward or sideways. Hierarchical structures have *levels*: two or more *elements* at one level are combined to form an element at the next higher level. These combinations signify the *relations* between elements: the value of an element at a particular level is a function of the values of the elements at the lower level and the particular *operation* that combines them. At the highest level there is only one element, whereas at the lowest level there are usually many elements. Different branches may have a different number of levels, so the *terminal*

---

[19] Ibid., pp. 44–45.

elements (the elements at the lowest level) may actually be at different levels relative to one another.

When studying the hierarchy by moving from low to high levels, it is more appropriate to call the terminal elements *starting* elements. And, since it is common to view hierarchical structures both ways, the two terms, "terminal" and "starting," are used interchangeably for these elements.

The *definition* of a hierarchical structure must include its starting elements, its operations, and the various rules for using them; that is, everything we need in order to derive all valid alternatives for that hierarchy – all possible ways to combine elements, and all the values that the top element can display.

The designation of levels as low and high, although matching the inverted tree representation, has a different reason. Even if we reverse the tree and show the terminal elements at the top, these are still the lowest levels; and the element at the bottom is still called the *top* element. The reason for designating the terminal elements as the lowest level is the way hierarchical structures are used: the terminal elements are the simplest entities of the structure, and the elements at any given level are more complex than those at the next lower level (because one element is the result of an operation between several lower-level elements). The hierarchical levels indicate, therefore, *levels of complexity*.[1]

The hierarchical structure is an extremely versatile model. The elements in the structure can stand for almost anything – physical objects, persons, processes, events, situations, categories, ideas, linguistic entities, pieces of software – and the connections between them can represent any kind of operations. The structure is completely general, therefore, and can model any system involving neatly related "things within things." There is no limit to the number of levels, elements, or operations, so the structure can be extended indefinitely. Let us briefly examine some common uses of the hierarchical model.

Most classification systems are hierarchical. If we imagine a structure starting with the element *life* at the top, a simple classification is as follows: the top element branches into the elements *animals* and *plants*, one level down; the element *animals* branches into *domestic* and *wild*; *domestic* includes the elements *dogs*, *horses*, *chickens*, and so on; *dogs* includes various *breeds*, and each breed finally branches into the terminal elements – the individual animals we call dogs. In a classification, the operations are the criteria whereby the elements at one level are combined to form the next higher level. The only

---

[1] Do not confuse this complexity with the complexity of complex structures. Although the same word is used, the two types of complexity are so different (as will become evident later) that it is always obvious from the context which one is meant. In simple structures, the complexity is caused by the shift from low to high levels within one structure; in complex structures, it is caused by the interaction of several simple structures.

elements that are real things are the terminal elements; the elements at higher levels are abstract concepts that reflect the way we choose to group these things.

We find another example of hierarchies in human organizations like corporations, governments, and armies. The elements in these structures can be the units (departments, divisions, sections) or the people who make up or head these units (managers, commanders, workers); the terminal elements are the smallest units or the actual individuals; and the operations indicate how the elements at one level are grouped to form the elements of the next higher level.

Natural systems like organisms can be seen as hierarchical structures. The human body consists of subsystems (nervous, digestive, respiratory, etc.), which in their turn consist of various organs (heart, kidneys, etc.); organs are made up of specialized parts, and these parts are made up of cells, the terminal elements. Similarly, artificial systems like cars and appliances are designed as hierarchical structures. A car consists of a number of subassemblies, which are composed of simpler subassemblies, and so on, down to the thousands of individual components that are the terminal elements.

We will encounter many other hierarchies later. The examples we have examined, however, already allow us to discuss the most important characteristics of the hierarchical structure. We note, first, that hierarchies are easy to understand when their elements are physical objects. Since physical structures are common and obvious, we have no difficulty visualizing their elements, levels, and operations. But, while simple structures make indeed excellent models for physical structures, this is their least interesting application. We are going to use simple structures to model such phenomena as knowledge, language, and software. Unlike physical objects, the elements and levels in these structures may not be obvious, and the relations may not resemble assembly operations, so the hierarchy may be more difficult to visualize.

We note, next, that the hierarchical model is useful for both analysis and synthesis. When used for analysis, we move from high to low levels: given a complex problem, for instance, we divide it into simpler problems, which become the elements at the next lower level; and we repeat this process of division until we reach problems that are simple enough to solve directly. When used for synthesis, we move from low to high levels: we start with simple concepts, for instance, and combine them into more and more complex ones. A hierarchical tree diagram can be viewed, therefore, as a process that moves in both directions. The elements at the lowest level remain the simplest in the structure; but they can be either terminal elements (when we move from high to low levels) or starting elements (when we move from low to high levels). We can study a physical system, for example, either starting from the completed structure and moving toward the individual parts (in an analysis, or disassembly operation), or starting from the parts and moving toward the higher levels (in a synthesis, or assembly operation).

Some confusion often arises between the *definition* of a hierarchy and the tree diagram used to *represent* it. In the tree diagram, many elements at the lowest level combine into fewer and fewer elements, until we reach just one element at the top. The concept of a hierarchy, however, appears to imply the opposite: we start with just a few values for the elements at the lowest level (a limited "alphabet"), and by combining these elements, more and more values are possible for the elements at the higher levels. But there is no contradiction here. A tree diagram depicts *one instance* of the hierarchy, not its definition; it shows one particular set of values for the starting elements, and the combinations leading to the corresponding value of the top element. To *define* the hierarchy we usually employ other methods – rules, descriptions, formulas, etc. It is impractical to depict the definition itself with tree diagrams, but we can visualize it like this: we would start by drawing all possible trees (perhaps an infinite number of them); then, if we looked at *all* these trees, we would see *the same few* starting values repeated in all the trees at the lowest level, a greater variety of values at the intermediate levels, and the greatest variety of values for the top element (as many values perhaps as there are trees).

2

Let us discuss next the concept of abstraction. To abstract means to leave something out, to extract one aspect out of a whole. And hierarchical structures, clearly, function as systems of abstraction. When we combine the elements of one level through a particular operation to form the next higher level, what we do is abstract, from all the attributes possessed by these elements, those attributes that are important in the relation between the two levels. Thus, while hierarchical operations can take many forms, it is ultimately the attributes of elements, and the abstraction of attributes, that determine how one level gives rise to the next.

This is easy to understand in a classification. When we recognize a great number of dogs as members of a particular breed, what we do is extract, from all the attributes that distinguish each dog, those attributes that are relevant in identifying the breed. So, we may consider the dog's colour and the shape of its ears, but ignore its internal organs and its age. Similarly, when we move to the next level (dogs), we abstract the attributes that distinguish dogs, regardless of their breed, from other kinds of domestic animals; and on the following level (domestic animals), we abstract the attributes that distinguish domestic from wild animals.

Let us look at another hierarchy, a physical structure this time. The transmission of a car consists of subassemblies within subassemblies, on several levels, down to the smallest parts. Here we abstract from the attributes of an individual part, those attributes relevant to the operation of the subassembly to which it belongs, and ignore the others. So for a gear we may note attributes like dimensions and number of teeth, but ignore its date of manufacture. The resulting subassembly has its own set of attributes, but, when combining it with other subassemblies, we abstract only those attributes relevant to the operation of the subassembly at the *next* level. Finally, when the transmission is installed in a car, we ignore its internal details altogether and abstract only attributes like size, weight, and function.

We saw earlier that the levels in a hierarchy indicate levels of complexity: the higher the level, the higher the complexity of the elements, because the value of those elements is affected by more and more elements from lower levels. Now we see that levels have a second and related significance: as we move to higher levels, we increase the degree of abstraction. For this reason, the hierarchical levels are also called *levels of abstraction*. Through abstraction, we lose at each level some of the details that were important at the lower level. What we gain is the ability to deal with just one element. This is beneficial when we can ignore the lower levels, when only the attributes at a particular level are important. Thus, we can discuss the concept of animals without having to think of individual creatures; and we can make use of the car's transmission while knowing nothing about its internal operation. We couldn't even think of animals in general if we had to recall every single one; and it would be difficult to design or build a car if we had to deal with the smallest parts, without subassemblies.

The concept of abstraction leads us to one of the two fallacies born from the popularity of the hierarchical model. We will discuss this fallacy in detail later, but a brief introduction is in order.

We saw that moving to higher levels increases the complexity of the elements, as each element is the result of many operations and elements from lower levels. This may tempt us to associate higher levels with "power": just by moving to higher levels we seem to be getting something for nothing. If the top element of the structure is our goal – as in a manufacturing project, or when creating a structure of knowledge in the mind – then, we may think, it is foolish to start from a low level. For, the higher our starting level, the more complex the starting elements, and the faster we will reach the top. This belief leads in practice to the principle that we should always attempt to start with the largest subassemblies available – whether the subassemblies are physical objects or pieces of knowledge. In programming, the subassemblies are pieces of software, and this principle has engendered an endless series of theories that promise (often using these very words) higher levels of abstraction, as if this were such an obvious benefit that no discussion is needed.

But, while levels impart to hierarchical structures their "power," it is not always beneficial to start from higher levels. A high-level element does indeed replace a whole combination of elements and operations, but it can only replace *one* combination. Thus, as we move to higher levels and higher complexity, we suffer an *impoverishment* in the values possible for our starting elements. As a result, all levels above them, including the top one, will be impoverished. We do indeed shorten our route to the top element, but we lose many alternatives in its value. In an extreme case, when our starting level is the top element itself, there can be only one alternative.

To start from higher levels, then, we must accept the consequences of abstraction. For example, when we start with the concepts of *white*, *blue*, *red*, and so on, there are many ways to perceive an object; but if we replace them with one concept, *colour*, we must accept any colour, and we may even lose the idea of colour differences altogether. And if we go even further and replace *colour*, *shape*, *size*, and so on, with one higher-level concept, *quality*, we will no longer be able to differentiate objects at all. What we will have done, in effect, is replace an infinity of objects of different sizes, shapes, and colours, with only one object. Such an object is an abstract concept, useless as a starting element in any project, except perhaps for creating even more abstract concepts.

The higher the level we start from, the less detailed are our starting elements. This principle can be useful, as we saw: we design cars in such a way that the worker who installs the transmission doesn't need to understand how it works. But we should be wary of applying this principle whenever we see a structure of things within things. Computers and software, for instance, are important tools, and specific applications can be of great benefit. If, however, instead of studying each application we are content with the high-level, abstract concept "technology," we will accept any software novelty, useful or useless.

The consequences of abstraction can be even more serious, of course. Millions of citizens who enthusiastically vote for "freedom," "democracy," "rights," "socialism," or "equality," but without understanding clearly the meaning of these abstract concepts, vote in effect for words; so they can easily bring to power a dictator who uses these words but whose intentions are the opposite of what the words stand for. It happened more than once, as we well know. Similarly, millions of software practitioners who enthusiastically embrace ideas like "software engineering," "object-oriented programming," or "relational databases," and equate them with software progress, embrace in effect words, and bring to power evil organizations whose intentions are the opposite of progress: the prevention of programming skills and software freedom, and, ultimately, the destruction of all human knowledge and freedom.

Complex Structures

1

Given the versatility of the simple hierarchical structure, one may wonder: how can there be anything else? It is precisely this versatility that has led to our mechanistic delusions, to the belief that nothing lies beyond the modeling power of the simple structure. Everything around us, it seems, fits into one hierarchy or another, so there is no need for another model.

But all these hierarchies are not, in fact, simple structures. Let us consider an ordinary object. We immediately notice that it has a shape. And, since all objects have shapes, through this attribute it is related to other objects. The simplest way to represent this relation is as a three-level hierarchy: the top element, which represents all objects, branches into two elements – the category of objects with this particular shape, and the category of objects with any other shape; and these two elements branch into the terminal elements – the individual objects. (See figure 1-2. More elaborate hierarchies can be created, with categories within categories, if we consider also the details of the objects' shape; but here we only need the simplest one.)

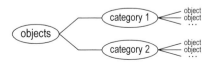

Figure 1-2

The object also has other attributes – colour, size, texture, weight, etc.; and each one relates it to other objects, since all objects have these attributes. These relations too can be represented as three-level hierarchies, and each hierarchy would likely be different (two objects can have, for instance, the same shape but different colours).

The object has, in fact, many attributes, and hence many relations with other objects. No matter how we study this object, we can find a hierarchy where it belongs quite naturally: through its colour, it is part of a hierarchy that relates objects according to their colour; through its location, it is part of a hierarchy that relates objects according to their location; and so on. We can find relations based on its uses, or its manufacturer, or the ratio between its weight and its length, or the age of the person who owns it. Clearly, we can continue the list of attributes indefinitely. Nor are these relations and hierarchies a figment of our imagination; they are as real as the objects and attributes themselves. And, while the starting elements in the example were physical objects, we can follow the same logic starting with any other entities. Thus, we can think of any number of attributes relating persons, events, situations, or concepts.[1]

Recall the idea behind simple structures: at each level, a certain operation combines several elements to form an element for the next higher level. The critical condition is that these operations be precisely defined, so that, given the value of the lower-level elements, we can determine the value of the resulting higher-level element. This condition ensures the determinism of simple structures, but restricts the kinds of relations possible between a particular structure and the external entities – those entities that do not concern it. Specifically, whatever relations exist between its elements and the rest of the world must not alter the nature of its own, internal relations.

Ideally, then, a simple structure is completely isolated from the rest of the world. But we just saw that this is impossible, that there are no entities which are isolated from all other entities. Since each entity has attributes – and has, in fact, a large number of *significant* attributes – it is necessarily related to all the other entities that have the same attributes. Each attribute causes the entity to be an element in a different hierarchy, so the entity is an element in several hierarchies at the same time. As a result, no structure can be isolated from all the other structures.

If a structure shares some of its elements with other structures, the value of its top element depends also on other factors, besides the lower-level elements and their operations: it depends on the elements and operations of the other structures. Thus, when sharing elements, structures interact. And consequently, the behaviour of each structure will be different from its behaviour when isolated. Its definition – in particular, the operations specifying how elements are combined from one level to the next – is no longer sufficient. To describe its behaviour, we must also take into account the structures it interacts with. But the behaviour of each one of those structures is itself affected by the interactions, so it too deviates from the structure's definition. Clearly, then, if we place no restrictions on the interactions, the only

---

[1] A note on terminology: In this book, "entity" and "element" are used to refer to the same things, but from different perspectives. Objects, categories, processes, pieces of software, etc., are *entities*, and at the same time they are *elements* of structures. So, while the two terms refer to the same types of things and are often interchangeable, "entity" is generally used for the thing in itself, and "element" to stress its role in a structure.

way to study the behaviour of one structure is by studying the system of structures as a whole.

Let us call *complex structure*, thus, a system of two or more interacting simple structures.

2

The most important difference between simple and complex structures, and probably the one most difficult to understand, is this: a simple structure can represent the relations created by *only one* attribute; we need a complex structure if we want to represent the relations created by *multiple* attributes. Let us examine this problem.

Recall, first, the three-level structure that represents the relations created by each attribute (figure 1-2). In this structure, one element stands for the category of entities for which the attribute has a particular value, and the other for the category with any other value. We are going to use this type of structure to show how entities are related through their attributes, but bear in mind that this is only a simplified representation.

Attributes can have a whole range of values, and even categories of ranges, so a complete structure would require many levels and many elements on each level. If the attribute is colour, for example, we can have light, medium, and dark on the first level, various colours within these categories on the next level, a division into shades on additional levels, and finally the terminal elements – the groups of entities that have a precise hue. And if the attribute is the time when events occur, we can have years on one level, the twelve months on the next level, then days of the month, hours of the day, etc., down perhaps to fractions of a second. Note that, no matter how many levels and how many elements per level we create, these structures remain correct hierarchies as long as the elements are depicted strictly as categories within categories.

It is for this reason that we can ignore here the additional levels, and limit ourselves to the simplified hierarchy, as if the attribute had only two significant values. The actual structure is much larger, but the additional details are unimportant; all we want is to confirm that elements which share more than one attribute cannot be represented with a simple structure. To put this differently, if it is impossible to combine several attributes in a *simplified* hierarchy, there is no point in demonstrating this problem with the larger, actual hierarchies.

❖

Here is why one structure cannot represent more than one attribute, when attributes may be shared by all entities. If we want to represent several attributes with one structure, we must use one of them for the top element and the rest for the lower elements, within one another, as if each attribute were a finer detail of the previous ones. This problem is illustrated in figure 1-3. If we start with the totality of entities, then *E100*, *E110*, etc., are the categories of entities formed when separating them, repeatedly, based on their attributes (*A1*, *A2*, and *A3*). Each attribute has only two values, and the *E* digits designate the combinations of values that define the various categories. But this is an incorrect hierarchy, because the attributes are repeated: each one must be included for each branch created by the previous attributes. In reality, entities that possess several attributes possess them all in the same way, not as one within another. Thus, the diagram is incorrect because it shows some attributes as subordinate to others while the attributes are, in fact, independent of one another.

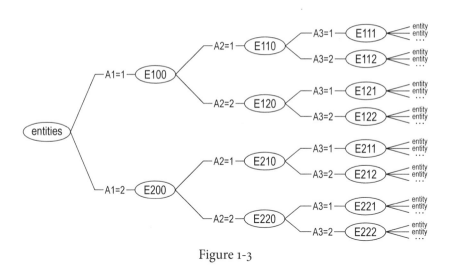

Figure 1-3

In addition to the repetition of attributes, we note the absurdity of this representation in that we can depict the attributes in any order while the terminal elements remain the same: *A3* within *A2* within *A1* (as in figure 1-3), or *A2* within *A1* within *A3* (as in figure 1-4), etc. This freedom means that the structure is illogical. Real entities cannot possess the same attributes in several ways.

A simple structure, therefore, does not represent real entities and attributes correctly: this is neither the way entities actually exist, nor the way we perceive them. We can develop a replica of the complex phenomenon *in our mind*, but we cannot represent the phenomenon with a precise diagram. All we can do is depict the three attributes as *separate* structures, while knowing that the terminal elements are in fact the same in all three structures (see figure 1-5). We will discuss this problem in greater detail in chapter 4.

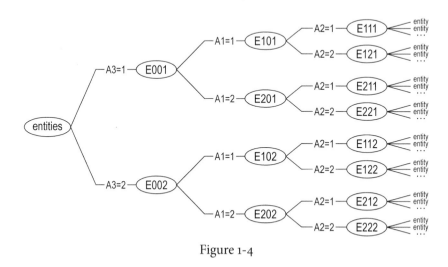

Figure 1-4

When each attribute is shared by only *some* of the entities, it may be possible to include several attributes in one structure, as one within another. In figure 1-6, for instance, while *A1* is shared by all the entities, *A2* and *A3* are shared by fewer entities, and *A4, A5, A6*, and *A7* by fewer still. None of the entities that possess *A5*, for example, possess *A6*. The final structure *is* a correct hierarchy, since attributes are no longer repeated. Moreover, there is only one

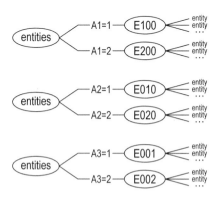

Figure 1-5

way to depict them: we cannot modify their order here as we could in the structure of figure 1-3, where all entities possess all three attributes. *A6*, for example, *must* be within *A3*, since only *some* entities possess *A3* and *A6*, and the others possess *A3* and *A7*. Also, it is impossible to redraw the structure so as to place *A3* within *A6*, rather than *A6* within *A3*.

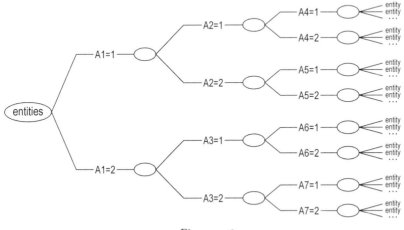

Figure 1-6

One can argue, however, that in fact we can *never* represent a combination of attributes in one hierarchy, as in figure 1-6. This is true because, even when an element does *not* possess an attribute, it still belongs, logically, to the structure established by that attribute: instead of being part of a branch with a particular value, the element is part of a branch called "does not possess the attribute" (as in figure 4-8, p. 361). In other words, because not possessing an attribute may be as significant as possessing it, we can combine several attributes in one hierarchy only when we can indeed ignore the cases where an attribute is not possessed by an element. (Thus, we cannot ignore these cases in *software* structures; for, attributes affect the performance of an application just as significantly when *possessed* by a software element as they do when *not possessed*. For example, an application will malfunction either because a database field is used when it shouldn't be, or because it is not used when it should be. We will discuss software structures in chapter 4.)

Very few phenomena, in the end, consist of entities that possess a perfect combination of attributes – a combination that permits all attributes to be represented together in one hierarchy, as in figure 1-6. The classification of animals provides a good illustration of this problem. An attribute describing their teeth, to pick just one example, is shared by animals that belong to different branches of the formal classification (the neat hierarchy of classes, orders, families, genera, and species). In other words, if we classified animals through a hierarchical structure based on their teeth, the hierarchy would be different from the formal one. Thus, since they possess many attributes of this type, animals are related through many hierarchies at the same time; and the only way to represent these relations in one diagram is by repeating attributes, as in figure 1-3. The formal classification avoids this repetition and remains a correct hierarchy simply because the scientists who designed it restricted themselves to attributes that *can* be represented within one another, as in figure 1-6. It is an artificial classification – correct, but capable of depicting only *some* of the relations between animals. It is impossible to represent *all* their relations with one hierarchical structure.

If you still don't see why the repetition of attributes in a structure indicates that the structure is complex, look at it this way: If entities belonging to different categories (say, *E100* and *E200* in figure 1-3) possess the same attribute (*A2*, in this case), and some of them (those belonging to *E110* and *E210*) even possess the same *value* of that attribute, it means that these entities are logically related; and, through this relation, they form a hierarchical structure that is different from the structure we see in the diagram. This second structure reflects the way the entities possess the attribute *A2*; but it is not manifest – because it is dispersed throughout the structure shown in the diagram – so to detect it, we must identify and combine *in our mind* the categories concerned. (*A3*, thus, gives rise to a third structure, and in its case we must identify and combine in our mind other categories.) Redrawing the diagram as *A1* within *A2* would not solve the problem, of course: the structure representing *A2* would then be manifest, but the one representing *A1* would not.

3

Hierarchical structures are models of reality, and if we can have two kinds of structures, simple and complex, it is because there exist two kinds of phenomena: those that can be represented as simple structures, and those that can only be represented as complex structures. We have equated simple structures with mechanism, so we can call the complex structures *non-mechanistic*. It is the central tenet of my argument that complex structures cannot be reduced to simple ones, and therefore certain aspects of reality cannot be represented with mechanistic models.

The immediate consequence of this claim is that the methods we have developed for studying mechanistic phenomena are inadequate for complex ones. These are the *deterministic* methods – those that attempt to represent a phenomenon with precision. They include, specifically, mathematics and software. The fact that many phenomena cannot be represented mathematically is well known. What is more interesting for us is that the same phenomena – namely, indeterministic phenomena – cannot be represented with software either. Thus, complex phenomena cannot be exactly simulated or explained with software (although they can be *approximated* with software). Note, however, that software can *generate* complex phenomena: a running application is a system of interacting structures, and its behaviour cannot be represented with a mechanistic model.

At first sight, it may not be obvious why complex structures cannot be reduced to simple ones. If complex structures are nothing but systems of interacting simple ones, why can't we study the simple ones individually with mechanistic methods, and then combine the results so as to predict the behaviour of the system as a whole? The reason is the mutual influence of interacting structures: one structure affects the others at the same time *it* is affected by *them*, so they cannot be studied separately. While a solution may be found in trivial cases, no solution is possible for real-world phenomena. In general, the structures can share any number of elements, at any number of levels; they can overlap and intersect in any conceivable fashion.

This becomes evident if we recall the long list of attributes that an entity can possess, each attribute causing it to be an element in a different structure. Since the same entity can be an element at different levels in different structures (when we have several levels of detail for each attribute), an interaction can arise through a feedback loop, as follows: element *e* in structure *A* is also an element in structure *B*, so it affects the elements at higher levels in *B*; but if one of these elements is shared with structure *A* and is at a lower level in *A* than *e* is, then *e* will be affected by *B*, thus closing the loop. With this feedback, the value of the top elements in *A* and *B* may well be unpredictable. Also, a loop can link more than two structures (*A* to *B* to *C* to *A*), and several loops can exist at the same time. In practice, such interaction is not only possible, but probably very common.

The conclusion we must draw from the foregoing analysis is that there can exist no simple structures in the world, but only complex ones. This is true because any element of a simple structure, if one existed, would also be part of other structures, through its other attributes, thus making the simple structure immediately part of a complex one.

But we saw that many phenomena *can* be represented as simple structures, so how can we explain the contradiction? The answer is that those structures which appear to be isolated simple structures are *approximations* of the phenomena. Although their elements take part in the operations of several structures, the operations of one structure are much more important than the others. Or, to put it differently, the attributes that determine their relations in one structure are much more important than the attributes that make them part of other structures. If this is true for all the elements in the structure, the structure behaves in practice approximately like an ideal, isolated simple structure. It is entirely up to us to decide what level of approximation is acceptable, and that depends on how we plan to use the structure.

Classifications of things, for instance, are possible only if we take into account *some* of their attributes, and ignore the others. The formal biological classification of animals is a perfect hierarchy of classes, orders, families, etc., as noted earlier, only because we agreed to consider just *a few* of their attributes. If we wanted to include *all* their attributes, no simple hierarchical structure would be possible. The totality of animals, with the relations generated by all their attributes, is a complex phenomenon, and can be represented only with a complex structure. But in our studies of animals we needed a strict hierarchy, so we settled for an *approximation* of the phenomenon.

The most famous example of mechanistic approximation is Newtonian mechanics – the theory that, for two centuries, served as a model for all phenomena involving matter and force. Then, the growth in knowledge pointed to some anomalies in its predictions, and it was replaced with a more accurate mechanistic model: Einstein's theory of relativity. But we continue to use the Newtonian model where its approximations are useful, because it is simpler. There are difficulties with the relativistic model too, and scientists, including Einstein, have been searching for a better theory. Einstein predicted that one day his theory would be replaced by an even more accurate one, and would then be seen as merely a better approximation of reality than Newton's. Despite repeated failures, however, he continued to believe in complete determinism: he was convinced that the next theory would also be mechanistic. Many scientists today doubt that a mechanistic model can provide a complete explanation for all phenomena, from the smallest particles to the whole universe.

4

Once we recognize that mechanistic theories can provide only degrees of approximation and not a complete explanation, we begin to understand why it is so easy to fall prey to mechanistic delusions. The problem is not that mechanistic theories provide only approximations. This is not a weakness, but their strength; for, if we insisted on a perfect representation of reality, we would never find a working theory and the world would appear incomprehensible. Approximate theories about the world are the only explanations we can hope to find in a world where no phenomenon can be totally isolated, where none is truly mechanistic. And we can often expect improvements in these models as our knowledge, methods, and instruments progress.

The problem, rather, is to determine whether the approximations are practical, whether they can model the world accurately enough to be useful. It is childishly easy to find a mechanistic theory for a particular phenomenon if we don't care how poorly it approximates reality. As we saw earlier, there are patterns and regularities, and hence hierarchies and mechanistic models, everywhere we look. What this means is that we can always find some formulas or diagrams that match reality fairly well in certain situations.

And this is how a mechanistic delusion is born. Formulas and diagrams always look neat. So, even though the model works only in a few situations, we are tempted to conclude that, being neat, it must be important. After all, it is acceptable for a model to provide only an approximation. One day, we think, it will be accurate enough to be useful.

The anomalies displayed by a mechanistic model when approximating a complex phenomenon spring from the fact that it is a simple structure struggling to represent a complex one. Since it can represent *only one* of the structures that make up the phenomenon, we must ignore the interactions between this structure and the others. We must ignore, in other words, those attributes that relate its elements to the other structures. The more important the ignored attributes, the stronger the interactions with the other structures, and the poorer the approximation when these interactions are ignored.

It is this simple explanation that the mechanists fail to grasp. They notice the abnormal relations that exist between the elements of one level and the next – the deviations from the structure's definition. But their assumption of isolation prevents them from recognizing these anomalies as interactions with other structures. Since they only see one structure, they conclude that the anomalies are caused by some deficiencies in the structure's definition; so they try to correct these deficiencies. They may work with a tree diagram or with a mathematical representation of the model. They may modify or add elements, operations, branches, or levels, and they may even diverge from a hierarchical appearance. But they never give up the requirement for complete determinism. They fail to see that, no matter what changes they make, if the behaviour of the resulting structure can be described completely and precisely, it is still a deterministic model, still a simple structure. Even if it no longer looks like a tree diagram, we know that there exists a hierarchical structure (although perhaps a very complicated one) that precisely describes its behaviour.

Some of this work may improve the model, but the need for enhancements never ends: the model never reaches a state where it can provide a practical approximation of the complex phenomenon. All the time, however, the mechanists are convinced that they are making progress, that what they are doing counts as research. They believe that, if the process of improving a mechanistic model often leads to a working theory in the exact sciences, it must also be effective in *their* discipline. But this process succeeds in the exact sciences because *there* we can often isolate a simple structure from the complex whole and use it as an approximation. In disciplines that deal with human minds or human societies, the links between the interacting structures are too strong to be ignored. There seldom exists one dominating structure, and any research project that assumes so becomes a mechanistic delusion: a futile attempt to approximate a complex structure with simple ones.

❖

Note the informal nature of this discussion. Terms like "interaction" and "feedback" are quite vague, but I cannot improve on this. I will make no attempt, for instance, to draw several simple structures and somehow connect their elements to depict a complex structure; or to find some equations that explain how the behaviour of a simple structure is modified by its interaction with the others; or to develop some software that simulates these interactions. Many researchers fall into this trap, failing to see that, no matter how they approach this problem, their work always amounts to the same thing: an attempt to reduce a complex structure to simple ones. This is an impossible task, because what it seeks, in effect, is to represent an indeterministic phenomenon with a deterministic model.

Thus, the structures I described earlier (where entities are related through each one of their attributes) are merely a way to demonstrate the interactions caused by shared attributes. It is impossible to analyze the actual interactions, or the results. If we could perform such an analysis, if we could describe the interactions with precision, if we could explain and predict them with diagrams or equations or software, then we would have no complex structures to begin with. For, if the behaviour of a particular complex structure could be exactly described, there would perforce exist a certain simple structure that displayed exactly the same behaviour. This is true because simple structures are logically equivalent to deterministic theories and methods: any phenomenon that can be described precisely and completely can be represented with a simple hierarchical structure.

I don't need better arguments, because what I claim, ultimately, is only this: all phenomena are complex structures, and are irreducible to simple ones (i.e., deterministic models); while some can be approximated with simple structures, for others no useful approximation exists. If I hold this thesis, I need to prove nothing. What I have done is shift the burden of proof onto those who claim otherwise – onto the reductionists – which is the only logical way to address this problem. I hold that the normal state of affairs in this world is complexity, so it is up to those who insist that the world is simple, or those who promise to reduce complexity to simplicity, to prove their claims. A problem is deemed to have no solution until one is found: we wouldn't take someone seriously if he maintained that all problems have solutions, so there is no need to *actually* solve a given problem. Yet this is exactly the position taken by those who confidently set about to reduce a complex phenomenon to simpler ones, without trying first to solve what is in fact the primary problem: whether mechanistic methods can work at all for that phenomenon.

We must not forget that mechanism is only a doctrine, not unlike the religious doctrines of the past, and true scientific thought does not accept methods on the strength of their popularity or past reputation. We must not let the early successes of mechanism tempt us to see it as the only valid method of science. It must earn our respect like any other method, by solving *today's* problems.

5

Let us examine a few complex phenomena and interpret them as complex structures. The simplest complex structure is probably the phenomenon arising when three bodies attract one another according to the law of gravitation, in what is known as a *three-body* system. The attraction of the bodies in a *two-body* system, like the earth and the moon, and consequently their motion, can be described mathematically with fairly simple equations. If we add just one more body, however, as in the system comprising the sun, the earth, and the moon, we can no longer have an exact mathematical representation. The phenomenon of combined attractions in a three-body system is so complex that it is impossible to express the motion of the bodies analytically for a general case.[2] Intuitively, we can see the difficulty of describing the interaction between A and B if at the same time B interacts with C, and C interacts back with A. When more than three bodies are involved (*n-body* systems), the phenomenon is, of course, even more complex.

---

[2] It is possible for special cases, as when one of the masses is small enough (relative to the other two) to be negligible; otherwise, the motion can be calculated with various methods of successive approximation.

What we witness here is more than just an increase in complexity from two to three bodies, which would merely necessitate more complicated equations. The two kinds of systems appear to create entirely different phenomena. But the bodies in a three-body system are not different from those in a two-body system; and it is the same gravitational force that governs their motion. We must conclude, therefore, that the two phenomena are very similar in reality, and only appear different to *us*, when we try to represent them with our mathematical, and hence mechanistic, models.

The two-body system is a simple structure. We can view it as a trivial hierarchy of two levels: the two bodies, *A* and *B*, are the terminal elements, gravitational attraction is the operation performed on them, and the system as a whole is the resulting higher-level element. The three-body system is a complex structure. One way to view it is as a system of three simple structures (three two-body systems: *A* and *B*, *A* and *C*, *B* and *C*), which share elements and therefore interact with one another. It is not surprising that we can find a mathematical representation for two-body systems but not for three-body systems, since we already know that only phenomena which are simple structures can be reduced to mathematical models. Any attempt to find an exact model for a three-body system amounts to an attempt to reduce a complex structure to simple ones, which is impossible.

Another complex phenomenon is the recognition of a human face. Even though we can easily *recognize* familiar faces, we cannot as easily *describe* them. That is, we cannot depict in words a familiar face with sufficient precision so that someone unfamiliar with it could recognize it as easily as *we* do. And this is not due to a deficiency in our languages; for, if we were permitted to create new words or even to invent a new language to describe faces (using perhaps a special notation, as we do in mathematics), we wouldn't know what words or symbols we needed. This is what we do, in essence, when programming a computer to recognize complex patterns, and the performance of this type of software is always inferior to our own capabilities. We can recognize a face because the mind can process complex structures. Describing the same face with a system of symbols reduces the recognition process to simple structures, and this can only *approximate* the actual phenomenon.

When we recognize a face, our mind processes it as a whole, not by reducing it to simpler patterns first. We don't know how the mind does it, but we can try to understand this process by representing it as a complex structure. It is obvious that we do not remember faces by storing picture-like images of them, but by storing certain information about them. For example, we can recognize a face – even a barely familiar one – from any angle, not just as we previously saw it. There can be little doubt, therefore, that we recognize faces thanks to their attributes: the size, shape, and proportion of the various parts of the face; the relations between sizes, shapes, and proportions; the combinations of relations and proportions; and possibly even the combinations of these combinations.

If I wanted to describe to you the face of a person I know well, so that you could recognize that person in a crowd, I would have to be aware of all these attributes, relations, and combinations. But these facts do not exist in my mind in a form that I can use consciously. I never had them separated and classified in my mind, not even when I first learned to recognize that face; for, I didn't learn to recognize it by matching it with a list of attributes. So the best I could do is watch or visualize that face, and convey to you its attributes – most of which I would probably notice for the first time. Then, if we are both skilled in this task, you may even manage to recognize that person using my instructions.

At that point, you are acting the way a computer would; namely, matching faces with a list of attributes. But as you get to know that person, you will begin to recognize his face instantly, intuitively, as I do. You will not simply run that "program" – that list of instructions – in your mind faster and faster. You will have acquired some knowledge which lets you recognize that face *without* matching it with a list of attributes; but you will have no idea what that knowledge is. If asked to describe the face, you would have to draw up a list of attributes, as I had done earlier.

We can think of a number of individual processes that make up the complex process of face recognition: we may perceive the basic arrangement of the principal parts (eyes, nose, mouth, chin, hair) as a generic template that we interpret as a human face, the actual faces being then particular deviations from this template; we may perceive the sizes of these parts as big or small, their shapes as round or long, their proportions as average or not, and so on. Each one of these processes could be represented with a simple structure, because the elements and relations that make it up can be precisely described. But these structures share their elements – the various parts of a face – so the whole process of face recognition must be a complex structure. When we describe a face with words, we create in effect an approximation of the complex structure by means of several simple structures; and, depending on the face and the description, this may provide a useful substitute for the process of recognition.

❖

Our linguistic capability provides another example of complex phenomena. We will study the important subject of language and its relation to software later, but we can already see why our capacity for language is not a mechanistic phenomenon.

When we think of language, we immediately think, in the case of written text, of a hierarchical structure of letters, words, sentences, and paragraphs; and in the case of speech, we think of a hierarchical structure of phonemes, words, sentences, and ideas. We can also view each sentence, though, as a hierarchical structure of grammatical units – words, phrases, clauses. Moreover, in addition to being an element in the structures just mentioned, each word has a meaning: it names a thing like an object, an action, or a concept. This makes it an element in yet another structure, one including related objects, actions, or concepts. But we saw that entities have in fact *many* attributes, and are therefore related in many different ways. So, through the entities they represent – through their meanings – words are elements in *many* additional structures. Language is possible because the mind can process all these structures simultaneously.

The phenomenon of language, thus, is the interaction of many structures. It can have no precise representation, no mechanistic model, and this ought to be obvious to anyone who thinks about it. This has not stopped scientists and philosophers throughout history, though, from attempting to find a mechanistic model. Nor has this stopped them from searching for an artificial language – a language they hope would have the same potency as the natural ones while being simpler, and hence reducible to a mechanistic model. (We will study these delusions in chapter 4.)

The reason it is tempting to seek a mechanistic model for language is the ease with which we can discover and isolate linguistic structures. All we have to do is extract one of these structures from the whole phenomenon of language. Then, if we base a theory on this structure, the theory is guaranteed to work for *some* sentences. In general, it is easy to find a simple structure that represents *approximately* a complex one, and hence a mechanistic theory that *approximates* a complex phenomenon. These approximations typically yield theories that work in some situations but not in others, and this explains their occasional success. Thus, if the approximation is useful, we may be doing valuable research. In the case of language, however, the interactions are too strong. Consequently, no mechanistic theory can usefully approximate the whole phenomenon of language.

Abstraction and Reification

1

Two great fallacies arise from mechanistic thinking. Let us discuss first the fallacy I mentioned earlier, when we studied simple hierarchical structures: the belief that starting from higher levels of abstraction confers certain benefits. We saw that, as we raise the level of our starting elements, we reduce the number of values possible for the elements at the higher levels. Ultimately, we reduce the number of values that the top element, our final goal, can take.

Starting from higher levels of abstraction, thus, causes an *impoverishment* – a reduction in alternatives. The versatility of the hierarchical structure derives, not from a large number of possible values for the starting elements, but from the large number of combinations of values generated at the higher levels. For a hierarchy to be practical, the number of values we start with must be small. To attain a large number of values at the top level, we increase, instead, the number of levels and the types of operations that relate them.

When starting from a higher level, we could still have, in principle, as many values as we had at that level previously. We could, in other words, define as a set of starting values the *combinations* of values occurring at that level when our starting level was the lower one. In practice, though, this set would be so large that we would use only a fraction of it. Thus, when we lose the lower levels of a hierarchy we are bound to lose also many combinations of values.

Starting with only twenty-six letters in the English alphabet, for instance, we can create thousands of words one level up, and an infinite number of sentences on the next level. If we were to start with *words*, each word having its own symbol (that is, an elementary symbol, independent of the symbols of the other words, just as the symbols for letters are now independent of one another), our language would be impoverished. We would have to limit our vocabulary to a practical size (say, a few hundred symbols), and communication would be very limited. And if we were to skip one more level and start with *sentences* (assigning a symbol to each sentence and restricting ourselves to, say, a few hundred sentences), communication would break down completely.

Note that this fallacy can be committed even with simple structures, since it involves only one hierarchy; so it can be committed even when a mechanistic model is otherwise adequate. I will use the term *abstraction* to describe this fallacy, but bear in mind that "abstraction" also refers to the normal transition from one level to the next. Abstraction, therefore, means both the process of generalization that is part of any hierarchical structure, and the mistaken view that we can skip the lower levels of the structure. (Although the sense in which the term is used will be obvious from the context, I will sometimes use the whole phrase, "fallacy of abstraction," for the second sense.)

It is especially easy to commit this fallacy when the elements of the hierarchy are abstract concepts. We may think of the "average" man or woman, for example, or the "typical" salesman or accountant, and this may be a useful concept. But we can never *meet* an average or typical person; there is no such being. So when we treat an actual person, or think of ourselves, according to this idea, we are committing the fallacy of abstraction. In a hierarchy, if the average person is an element at a certain level of abstraction, it subsumes millions of real individuals who are elements at a lower level. The elements at the lower level are real things, whereas those at the higher level are abstract concepts. This situation is found in many hierarchies. (Classifications, for instance, have actual things at the lowest level, and categories of things – i.e., abstract concepts – at the higher levels.)

But the fallacy of abstraction is not limited to a transition from concrete things to abstract concepts. It can be committed even when both levels have concrete things (as with the words and sentences we saw previously), or when both levels have abstract concepts. The fallacy occurs whenever we start illegitimately from a higher level of abstraction. When we accept the elements at the higher level as *starting* elements, what we do is perceive them mistakenly as similar in nature to those at the lower level, as providing the same versatility. So the consequence of abstraction is a reduction in alternatives: *the structure is impoverished through the destruction of levels.*

It is easy to see how this fallacy can be exploited, if an elite gains control of the levels of abstraction in an important structure. Our alternatives may be restricted even as we think that we are gaining something. The elite can tempt us to start from higher levels by promising us expedience: why start from low-level elements when high-level elements are available? Since each high-level element includes a combination of many low-level ones, the elite tells us, we will reach the top element, our goal, much faster.

Now, when the high-level elements are provided *in addition* to the low-level ones, as an *option*, we may well find them more effective in certain situations, and we are committing no fallacy in using them. But they are usually provided as a *substitute* for the low-level elements, not as an option. Once we lose the lower levels, we lose countless alternatives for the top element – alternatives that may be important. If we forgo those alternatives, our life will be impoverished. And if we do want them, we will depend on the elite, which alone can access the low levels. Having lost the capability to create those alternatives on our own, we are at the mercy of the elite every time we need a new alternative.

Abstraction can be subtle. A common way of losing alternatives without

realizing it is by confusing freedom of choice with a large number of alternatives. But a large number of possible values for the top element may be only an
illusion of freedom: we may have a large number of values, even an infinite
number, and still be severely restricted.

This problem is related to the unusual properties of large numbers. To
understand this, imagine a system represented by a structure where the
elements are numeric values, and the top element – the result of various
operations, performed on several levels – can be any integer. The top element,
thus, can have any one of an infinite number of values. Now imagine that,
through the elimination of one level, we restrict it to integers divisible by 10; we
are left with only one tenth of the original values, but we still have an infinite
number of them. And if we eliminate further levels and thereby restrict the top
element to integers divisible by 100, and then to integers divisible by 1,000, and
so on, we are left each time with only one tenth of the values previously
possible. There will be fewer and fewer values, but we will continue to have,
nevertheless, an *infinite* number of values.

So, even though the alternatives for the top element are being reduced to the
point where the system may become useless, if we judge it by the sheer *number*
of alternatives we may feel that we haven't lost much; after all, there are still an
infinite number of them. This paradox is obvious in a trivial structure like the
one just described, especially if we are already familiar with all the alternatives.
But it may be hard to detect in a structure where the values possible for the top
element consist of *novel* alternatives – alternatives which we never encountered
before, and which we cannot even imagine in advance. In this case, we may not
even realize that we are missing alternatives.

The more ignorant we are, the easier it is for an elite to gain control of the
levels of abstraction in structures on which we depend, and to exploit us by
eliminating alternatives. Thus, widespread programming incompetence has
permitted the software elites to establish a sort of business best described as
software charlatanism. The chief goal in this business is to destroy levels: under
the pretext of efficiency, the elites are constantly raising the level of abstraction
in development systems. When starting from higher levels, they tell us, we
reach the top level – the complete application – much sooner. Certain features
may no longer be possible, it is true, but we still have an *infinite* number of
alternatives. So we can implement about the same applications as before.

We commit the fallacy of abstraction, however, if we interpret the infinity
of alternatives as evidence that we have lost only a few. This will become
clearer when we discuss the second mechanistic fallacy, reification, because the

two fallacies are usually committed together. Applications comprise *many* structures, not one; so when starting from higher levels we lose also the low-level *links* between structures, and with that further alternatives.

We are aware of lost alternatives only if we once had them. If we had to abandon words, for example, and restrict ourselves to ready-made sentences and ideas, we would immediately recognize the dramatic impoverishment in language-related processes. But programming is a new human endeavour, and the software charlatans gained control of our software-related affairs, and restricted them, before we could discover all possible alternatives – all the ways that human minds can find to create and use software. Software controlled by an elite is the only software we have ever had, so we cannot know what we have lost.

To enable us to create useful applications, the elites often restore some of the low levels. But they do it through some complicated means, which they control. So, instead of being free to create any application, we now depend on the elites for their high-level systems, and also for the low-level elements that had previously been available to us directly. (We will study this charlatanism in "The Delusion of High Levels" in chapter 6.)

2

If the fallacy of abstraction can be committed with simple structures alone, the second mechanistic fallacy is committed with complex structures; specifically, when we extract the simple structures from the whole that is a complex structure.

We already know that a mechanistic theory employs a simple structure to approximate a complex phenomenon. The approximation is achieved by isolating one structure – one aspect of the phenomenon. This is a legitimate procedure when the isolated structure approximates the complex one well enough to be useful; in other words, when its interactions with the other structures are much weaker than its internal relations. If, however, we attempt to extract a structure when the interactions are too strong to be ignored, we are committing a fallacy: the resulting simple structure is not a useful approximation of the actual phenomenon; if employed as model, it will not represent correctly the behaviour of the complex structure. I call this fallacy *reification*, borrowing a term that is already used to describe similar fallacies.

In philosophy, reification is often used to describe the fallacy of perceiving an abstract or hypothetical concept as a real thing. We do this, for example, when we treat transcendental entities as similar in nature to the concrete things of everyday life. Outside philosophy, however, the idea of reification has gained a broader meaning and is used in any situation where this type of fallacy is committed. In psychiatry, for example, reification describes a common thought pattern displayed by schizophrenic patients. Many schizophrenics are incapable of comprehending a particular topic while viewing it as part of a context. They extract it from the complex reality and treat it as a separate entity, or they attach it to a wrong context. Most topics, however, have different interpretations in different contexts, so schizophrenic conversation and behaviour is often incoherent. To take another example, in certain social theories, reification (along with notions like alienation and false consciousness) is used to describe our tendency to perceive human lives and societies as made up of separable parts. We isolate a person's knowledge or skills, for example, from the whole that is his existence, and thereby distort our social relations. It seems logical then to rate and to purchase a person's skills or time as if they were objects the person owned.

What is common to these examples is a mechanistic form of thinking: an illegitimate attempt to reduce a complex phenomenon to a simple one by taking something that is part of a whole, something that cannot possibly exist in isolation, and treating it as a separate thing. Since that aspect can exist as a separate thing only in our imagination, what this type of thinking does is objectify an abstract concept. It is quite appropriate, therefore, to use the term "reification" for the fallacy we are considering here – separating a complex structure into simple ones. If the simple structure we attempt to isolate has strong links to the others, it can exist as a separate structure only in our imagination. While the complex structure represents reality, the individual simple structures that constitute it are imaginary: they cannot exist as separate things. Or, more accurately, when viewed as independent structures they represent a *different* reality – an approximation of the complex structure. The fallacy is in the belief that the approximation is close enough to be useful.

A round and red object is always both round and red. It cannot have only shape or only colour, so it cannot occur separately in a structure of shapes or in a structure of colours; it *must* exist in both structures at the same time. In our imagination, we may be able to extract the object's roundness or redness. We may be able, that is, to construct an isolated hierarchical structure of shapes with no colours, or a structure of colours with no shapes – structures that would function as classifications of objects (see figure 1-2, p. 98). But these structures cannot exist in reality. If shapes and colours are defined as attributes of objects, the only structures of shapes and colours that can exist in reality are those that interact and make up a complex structure, because they always share their elements (the objects).

We can represent shapes or colours with hierarchical diagrams of categories, describe them in words, or define them with codes. What these devices do is convert our imaginary structures into real ones, and they may be useful when we can study each structure on its own; for instance, when only the shape or only the colour of objects is important. But if *both* are important, then the two structures interact, and the diagrams and codes are a form of reification: we convert into real things, concepts that can exist only in our imagination. At this point, it may seem quite natural to treat objects on the basis of diagrams or codes, as if these devices embodied the same knowledge as the complex structure that represents the actual objects.

We can view, for example, all the objects in the world as a simple hierarchy with two branches leading to two categories, round objects and other objects. Our round and red object will then be one of the terminal elements branching out of the round-objects category. We can also classify all the objects in the world into red objects and other objects, and our object will be one of the terminal elements in this hierarchy too: an element branching out of the red-objects category. But clearly, the terminal elements in these two hierarchies represent the very same objects. Since an object cannot be in two places at the same time, these hierarchies do not represent reality, although they are correct from the perspective of the *individual* attributes. The only way to take into account *both* attributes, roundness and redness, at the same time – which is the way they actually exist – is by treating the whole phenomenon of objects and their attributes as a complex structure. In our mind we can readily do so (because the mind can process complex structures), and this is why we can *perceive* objects as being round and red at the same time. But we cannot represent this phenomenon accurately with mechanistic models (because it is impossible to combine several attributes in one hierarchical structure when the attributes are possessed by all the elements, see pp. 100–104).

To put this differently, if objects and their attributes could be represented with mechanistic models we would be able to represent the world with software, and our computers would perceive reality just as *we* do. But, in fact, we cannot program a computer to perceive even that single round and red object as it really is, as humans perceive it. If we represent the two attributes as two code systems, for example, the computer will "see" first one code and then the other; but it cannot see both codes at the same time. The attributes, however, do exist together in reality, so we must conclude that the computer does not represent the phenomenon exactly as it is.

Thanks to its ability to process data quickly, the computer may provide an *approximation* of a complex structure – if we manage to reduce the phenomenon to its most important structures and interactions. For example, we could use *one* system of codes instead of two, and represent *combinations* of shapes and colours; the computer will then "see" the roundness and redness simultaneously. But this method, while adequate in the trivial case of one object and two attributes, breaks down in practical applications, when we must represent *many* entities and *all* their attributes. And the reason is not only that there is no computer fast enough to simulate so many interactions, but that we don't even know how to identify for the computer all the structures involved, and all their interactions. (It is for this reason that the research program known as artificial intelligence, which tries to make computers perceive the world as humans do, could not advance beyond trivial situations. We will return to this issue in chapter 2.)

Three kinds of structures exist in the process of reification: the complex structure, which alone reflects reality, and which is the only true representation of the complex phenomenon; the simple structures that exist only in our imagination, when we view the complex structure as several interacting structures; and the real, reified simple structures that we create from the imaginary ones. The fallacy consists in thinking that the real structures we created ourselves represent the same phenomenon as the imaginary ones.

It is easy to demonstrate the fallacy: when we reconnect the real structures the way we think the imaginary ones were connected, we will not re-create the same phenomenon as the one represented by the original, complex structure. In practice, if our intent was to reduce the complex structure to simple ones, what we see is that our model, theory, or method does not work as we expected: it does not explain the complex phenomenon adequately; it cannot account for all the alternatives that constitute the phenomenon. *For a phenomenon that is a complex structure, the only exact representation is the phenomenon itself.*

Recall the complex structures we studied earlier. We may well think of a three-body system as made up of three two-body systems, but these two-body systems can exist only in our imagination. We may be able to separate, for example, any two of the bodies from the third one (or perhaps the two did exist once as a separate system); but this isolated two-body system behaves differently from the two bodies that are part of the three-body system. We have two kinds of two-body systems: the real ones, and those we visualize as making up the three-body system; and the latter *must* be imaginary. If we separated bodies A and B as one system, how could we separate at the same time A and C as a second system? A cannot be in two places at the same time. The phenomena peculiar to complex structures are caused precisely by the fact that its elements belong to several structures at the same time.

Similarly, when recognizing a face we may well *imagine* several separate processes, but these processes cannot be separated. There may exist, for example, a process involving the size of the nose. But it doesn't follow that we can view this process as a separable structure. To separate it from the other processes that make up this phenomenon, we would have to separate the nose from the face; and this would alter the other processes that involve the nose. So the simple structures that exist as separate things *in reality* (sizes, proportions, combinations – big eyes, long face, etc.) are not the same kinds of things as the equivalent simple structures that are part of the face recognition phenomenon, and which can exist only in our imagination.

We also note the fallacy of reification in the study of language. Linguists start by extracting language from its complex human context; then, they go even further and extract various aspects of language – syntax or semantics, for instance. Language, however, could not possibly exist separately from the human beings who use it; and human societies would not be what they are, were the form of language different. The two evolved together and are inseparable. We may view the linguistic and human structures – syntax, word meaning, social relations, individual behaviour, cultural traditions – as separable phenomena, if we want. But, clearly, they can exist as isolated phenomena only in our imagination: separating any one of them would separate many elements that also belong to the others, so they cannot actually exist as independent structures. The *real* phenomena studied under these labels are different, therefore, from the *imaginary* phenomena we perceive as parts of the phenomenon of language. The real phenomena constitute a reification, and this is why studying them cannot help us to understand the phenomenon of language.

3

We saw previously that abstraction – treating the higher-level elements of a structure as starting elements – impoverishes the structure by reducing the number of alternatives for the top element. Now we see that the effect of reification, too, can be described as an impoverishment. Similarly to abstraction, the impoverishment manifests itself as a reduction in the number of alternatives for the top element; but this reduction derives from a loss of interactions rather than a loss of levels.

The impoverishment caused by reification is probably even more severe than the one caused by abstraction, because even more alternatives are lost now. It is more difficult to recognize this loss, though, because we cannot describe the interactions between structures (which is where the loss occurs in reification) as precisely as we can the relations between the elements and levels of each structure (which is where the loss occurs in abstraction).

We are tempted to separate structures when we want to understand a

complex phenomenon. Separating structures, however, severs the links between them – links that create in fact the complexity. The complexity is due
to the unspecifiable alternatives: those values or states which are caused
by interactions, and which cannot be predicted from the properties of the
individual structures. Reification eliminates the unspecifiable alternatives, and
hence the indeterminism, but it is precisely this indeterminism that imparts to
complex phenomena their richness and potency. It is silly to try to understand
a complex phenomenon by eliminating the interactions, since this destroys
its complexity: what is left is only the simpler, deterministic phenomena
represented by the individual structures.

   It is obvious, then, why reification is such a tempting fallacy. The only way
to understand a complex phenomenon is by studying it as a whole, by relying
on the mind's ability to process complex structures. (Understanding is then
taken as an informal concept, not in the mechanistic sense of breaking down
the phenomenon into simpler ones.) Thus, if there is a way to understand a
complex phenomenon, it entails a great deal of knowledge and experience,
intuition and creativity. Reification simplifies the task by separating it into
isolated structures, which can be handled by researchers who lack these
qualities. With isolated structures, they can apply mechanistic methods; in
particular, separating the structures into even simpler ones. But mechanistic
methods are futile in the case of complex phenomena. The isolated (real)
structures studied by the mechanists are not the same as the (imaginary)
structures that make up the phenomenon. So, even if they make good progress
in their study of the isolated structures, the mechanists contribute nothing to
the understanding of the phenomenon.

   Isolated phenomena, thus, are academic inventions, reifications of complex
phenomena, and their study seldom has a practical value. In the domain of
programming, the fallacy of reification has given rise to the theories of
software engineering, to concepts like structured programming and object-
oriented programming. These theories have generated an enormous amount
of academic research (not to mention the effort wasted by those who try to
use them), while contributing nothing to the real issue – the advance of
programming knowledge. Expert programming entails a capacity for complex
software structures, because those phenomena we want to represent with
software are complex; and the only way to develop this capacity is through
lengthy practice. Reification creates isolated software phenomena – simple
structures that reflect isolated aspects of reality. These structures are then
within the capabilities of inexperienced programmers, but the problems
associated with the original, complex phenomena remain unsolved.

I want to stress again how easy it is to confuse the structures we interpret as the components of a complex phenomenon, and which are only imaginary, with some independent, real structures. Even *describing* complex structures as "interacting simple structures," as I do here, is a form of reification (because it suggests that the simple structures were once, or could also exist as, independent structures). We use such phrases because we have no other way to discuss this subject, but we must not forget that those simple structures exist only as a combination, only as the complex phenomenon. They cannot exist on their own. The *real* structures that we think are their identical counterpart are indeed independent, but they represent different phenomena: if we combine them, we will not reconstruct the complex phenomenon. *Thinking* of interacting simple structures may help us to understand the complex structure, but we must go no further.

It is with language, again, that the differences between the imaginary and the real structures are easiest to observe. We may think of language as one of the many phenomena that, together, make up a human society; but this is where we should stop. The very idea of "language" as a distinct subject of study is an absurdity. The (real) phenomenon studied by the academic discipline known as linguistics is not the same as the (imaginary) phenomenon of language that exists only as part of a human society. Were it the same, we would be able to implement our linguistic theories with software and then converse with our computers just as we do with people.

It is generally accepted that the difficulty of programming computers to understand language is not due to the intricacy of the language structures, but to the fact that every word, every expression, every idea, has rich meanings – meanings which depend on such knowledge structures as the current context, related ideas, and previous experiences. It is impossible to store this type of knowledge in a computer, because the only way to acquire it is by "being in the world": by being born human, by having a body, by growing up in a human society. This knowledge cannot be reduced to a number of independent structures – facts, methods, processes – with language structures among them. It is a complex structure, the result of many interacting phenomena, and hence possible only in a human mind.

4

The two mechanistic fallacies, abstraction and reification, are usually committed together. It is easy to see why: we are tempted to abstract because we want to start from higher levels; but to abstract we need simple structures, so we first reify the complex structure. Reification impoverishes the complex structure by eliminating the interactions between its component structures; and abstraction impoverishes each structure by reducing the number of levels. Each fallacy contributes its own kind of impoverishment, but the result is the same: a reduction in the number of alternatives for the values of the high-level elements.

Note that when we commit both fallacies we seldom keep the reified structures separate. We still need a complex structure, usually; so we combine the impoverished structures and allow them to interact again. But the number of interactions and alternatives possible now, with the low levels missing, is only a fraction of those present in the original phenomenon.

Note also that, while reification can be committed even without abstraction, abstraction always entails reification. Thus, we may reify a complex structure but retain the low levels of the individual structures; and the only alternatives lost would then be those resulting from the interactions. But we cannot start from higher levels in the complex structure without also causing some reification. The interactions between structures are due to the shared elements, especially at the lower levels, so when we lose these elements we lose levels *and* interactions. The higher the level we start from, the greater the effect of abstraction, but also of reification, because fewer elements are left that can be shared.

So, when we commit both fallacies it doesn't matter whether we view this process as abstraction, or as reification followed by abstraction, or as committing the two fallacies at the same time. All three interpretations are equivalent to committing abstraction on the individual structures while still part of the complex structure (because this abstraction would also reify them). Destroying the lower levels of the complex structure directly is, therefore, the same as committing reification first, then abstraction on the individual structures, and then allowing the impoverished structures to interact again. The result in both cases is a complex structure where the interactions and alternatives previously generated by the low-level elements are missing.

It should now be obvious why the model of simple and complex structures can help us in the two subjects that concern us in this book: the failure of mechanistic theories to explain complex phenomena, and the methods employed by charlatans to deceive us.

Regarding the first subject, both fallacies consist in the belief that we can simplify the complex structure that represents a complex phenomenon and still represent the same phenomenon. The simplification, though, causes an impoverishment: the resulting structure can represent only a fraction of the alternatives that constitute the complex phenomenon. So what we are depicting now is no longer the original phenomenon. If explanation means accounting for all the alternatives displayed by the phenomenon, the mechanistic theories fail because they can only account for a small portion of these alternatives.

Regarding the methods used to deceive us, the same model can explain how they work. What the charlatans do, in essence, is tempt us to commit the two fallacies; they tempt us, in other words, to hold in our minds an impoverished picture of reality, of the facts and events that constitute our existence. Just like the scientists who construct invalid mechanistic theories about the world, we end up developing invalid mechanistic notions about our personal, social, or business affairs. It is not difficult then for the charlatans to exploit us.

This process is well understood for language. Practically everything in a human society is related to language: culture, traditions, social relations, knowledge, communication. Reasoning, in particular, would be impossible without language: no theory ever offered a satisfactory explanation of reasoning without also involving language, or vice versa. So it is not surprising that those who want to deceive us – leaders, gurus, visionaries, advertisers – always attempt to control language. And they achieve this by impoverishing it: instead of a rich vocabulary and precise ideas, they use slogans, jargon, and standard phrases, which subsume many meanings and hence obliterate the differences between them. They also invent new terms, or use old terms in a new sense, but without properly defining them; so these terms too subsume, in effect, many meanings. The charlatans, thus, employ forms of communication that start with high-level elements: their messages appear to convey information, while expressing in fact only vague, misleading notions. This practice makes it hard for us to connect these messages to our prior knowledge, and without the benefit of prior knowledge we are more easily deceived. Recalling the mechanistic fallacies, the deception is achieved by raising the level of abstraction, but also through reification; for, when losing the low-level elements, we also lose the low-level links between the language structures and other knowledge structures.

If the complex structure is our existence, and the simple structures that make it up are the various aspects of life and of language, then a reduction in the ideas conveyed by language will impoverish not just communication but also other aspects of our life. By destroying alternatives in language, the charlatans can also destroy alternatives in our knowledge, in our beliefs, and in our expectations.

An extreme form of language manipulation was described by George Orwell in his account of a hypothetical society where English was replaced with Newspeak – an artificial language specially devised to control minds. By restricting the vocabulary to carefully selected words, Newspeak limits mental processes to high levels of abstraction and prevents people from linking knowledge structures. This makes it impossible to develop any thoughts that contradict the official ideology. (We will study linguistic manipulation, and Newspeak, in chapter 5.)

Since software is acquiring in our society the same role as language, if we reify and abstract software we should expect to see similar effects. Software, in fact, exemplifies even better how the combination of the two mechanistic fallacies can be used to exploit us, because this has already happened – in the world of programming, at least. (Reification and abstraction in language and in software are discussed in chapters 4, 5, and 6.)

Software is one structure among the many structures that make up society: our affairs are increasingly dependent on computers, and hence on software; and our business and social relations increasingly reflect our dependence on software practitioners. For institutions as much as for individuals, knowledge and thinking are increasingly linked with software, in the same way they are linked with language. But, like language, software lends itself to abstraction and reification: we are just as easily tempted to start from higher levels of abstraction, and to treat the various aspects of software as separable processes.

Thus, it is common to think of a software application as an entity that interacts with the world only through its specifications, or parameters, or input and output; in other words, through means that can be defined precisely and completely. Once we commit this fallacy, we are likely to think of programming – the act of creating that application – as a project that can be separated from the other aspects of our affairs. Moreover, it is easy to commit further reifications *within* the act of programming: we extract certain software processes (user interface, reporting, database operations, etc.) and treat them as independent structures, linked to the rest of the application through precise specifications. But these processes share their elements (the software entities that constitute the application), so they form structures that interact with one another. Finally, these structures interact with the structures created by the business, social, and personal issues reflected in the application. All structures are different aspects of the same phenomenon – the complex phenomenon of software development and use – and we sever the links between them when addressing them separately.

In addition to *reifying* the application, we are tempted to raise the level of abstraction of the starting elements within the isolated structures. And this further reduces the number of alternatives that can be implemented. The interactions between the software processes that make up an application, and between these processes and our affairs, must take place at low levels of abstraction (as low as the individual operations), because this is the only way to represent with software the *details* of our affairs. The experts, nevertheless, manage to convince us that starting from higher levels affords us efficiency, or standards, or "power." The higher levels come in the form of programming aids – methodologies, development tools and environments, database systems.

Another way to start from higher levels of abstraction is to use ready-made applications. Since these applications cannot include all possible alternatives, they function in effect as high-level expedients. When relying on ready-made software, therefore, we lose low-level elements *and* low-level links – the links between software structures, and between software structures and the structures that make up our affairs. So we commit both fallacies, abstraction and reification, and the result is the same as when relying on programming aids: impoverished applications. As we saw earlier, committing both fallacies can be interpreted either as abstraction on the complex structure directly, or as reification followed by abstraction on the separated structures (see p. 123). With software, we see now, using ready-made applications is equivalent to the first interpretation, while using programming aids is equivalent to the second one.

As a consequence of these fallacies, more than 90 percent (and perhaps as much as 99 percent) of the cost of business computing is due to adopting new applications and programming aids over and over; in other words, to solving software-related problems instead of business problems. The reason for this incredible inefficiency is the incompetence of programmers. The complex phenomena of software can only be understood as a whole, and this requires great expertise. Programmers need to isolate software processes and to start from higher levels because they cannot deal with the complex software structures directly. But higher starting levels allow fewer alternatives. The resulting structures are impoverished, and so are the structures they interact with – those structures that make up the business environment. This impoverishment manifests itself in the inadequacy of applications: some of the alternatives – that is, some of the business needs – cannot be met. And this perpetual inadequacy compels businesses to seek new applications and new programming aids all the time.

Now that we have developed our mechanistic and non-mechanistic models, we can study complex phenomena and the failure of mechanistic explanations by representing them with these models. For each phenomenon, we must do two things: first, determine that it is in fact the result of several interacting phenomena, so it can only be represented with a system of interacting structures; then, show that the proposed explanations are mechanistic, that they attempt to represent the phenomenon with isolated simple structures. We will use these models frequently in the following chapters.

The only way to study a complex phenomenon mechanistically is by extracting one of its structures. This is the fallacy of reification, which is always present; we may or may not also find the second fallacy, abstraction. Scientists underestimate the links which that particular structure has to the other structures, and conclude that on its own it can provide a practical approximation of the complex phenomenon. Once they isolate a simple structure, any number of mechanistic theories present themselves to explain that one reified phenomenon; but the original, complex phenomenon remains unexplained. Sometimes, the scientists extract *several* structures, hoping to explain the complex phenomenon by somehow combining their separate, mechanistic explanations.

We recognize a theory as mechanistic when it is deterministic, when it promises a complete and exact explanation, when it is based on reductionistic and atomistic concepts. It may use simple hierarchical structures directly, but it may also use a machine model, or a mathematical method, or diagrams, or software. Regardless of the concept or model employed, we already know that if it is deterministic it is also mechanistic, so there exists a simple hierarchical structure that could represent it. That structure may be large and unwieldy, but we don't have to create it, or even to visualize it. We can continue to study the theory in its given form (mathematics, diagrams, software, etc.), and keep in mind that it is logically equivalent to a simple hierarchical structure.

Scientism

1

Most attempts to explain complex phenomena mechanistically are found in the human sciences: in psychology, sociology, linguistics, economics, anthropology, history, politics, etc. And we must add programming and software use to this category, because, apart from their precise and deterministic aspects, these activities are performed in a social context; they are, therefore, subject to the same processes that make all human activities complex, and hence non-mechanistic, phenomena.

It is not hard to understand why these fields have engendered so many mechanistic theories. They deal with our most important concerns, and at the same time they are the most complex phenomena we know. So we are anxious to discover models that can explain and predict, just like the models we use in physics or astronomy; and we forget that we are now dealing with indeterministic phenomena, which cannot be represented with exact models.

Human phenomena always involve interacting structures, starting with those that occur in one mind and ending with those that involve many minds in a society. Each one of us has many characteristics, roles, and preoccupations: we are workers, parents, friends, neighbours, citizens, spouses, investors, consumers, drivers, clients, patients; we have fears, wishes, beliefs, hopes, memories, plans; we use and own objects; we have bodies. The list of things that make us what we are is practically endless. But the important thing is that we are all of these things at the same time, all the time.

Each one of these attributes places us in a different structure; for example, a structure of people, events, activities, locations, or beliefs. We are the elements of many structures at the same time, so a human existence is a complex structure. We cannot even *identify* all these structures, much less separate them from one another. Even as we are engaged in one activity, or think of one subject, we are influenced by everything else that makes us what we are. At any instant, we are the repository of countless experiences, traditions, emotions, propensities, and pieces of knowledge. Our minds provide the interactions that make our individual lives complex structures, and each one of us provides the interactions that make society a complex structure. We are, each one of us, both the result and the cause of the many interacting structures that make up society.

It ought to be obvious, then, that it is impossible to study *any* aspect of individual or social life in isolation. Yet this is precisely what we do in the academic disciplines called psychology, sociology, linguistics, and so on. The disciplines are separated as if our behaviour, our social relations, or our use of language were separate phenomena. Various theories assume that I am either a man, or a programmer, or a speaker, or a consumer, or a hundred other things. But I am *all* these things *at the same time*. How could I be only one thing at a time? I am not running several unrelated programs simultaneously, like a multitasking computer. It is my mind and body, which are always there, that cause the endless interactions between these roles.

If we seek a theory that explains only one particular aspect of human life, we must extract that aspect from the complex whole. We must treat it as a simple structure, and assume that its interactions with the other structures are weak enough to be ignored. But this is rarely true, so the approximations created by these theories are very poor. We already saw that language can be explained only through non-mechanistic theories – theories that take into account *all* the knowledge present in a mind. And the same is true of our other capabilities and acts, as individuals and as society.

2

Scientism is a derogatory term used to describe mechanistic delusions: the application of mechanistic concepts in fields where they cannot work, and especially in the human sciences. Scientism is the opposite of science; it is a dogmatic approach to research, embraced by those who are incapable of discovering useful theories. Mediocre scientists prefer to stress *methods* rather than *results* as the criterion by which the value of research is measured. Only exceptional people can make a real contribution, but almost anyone can follow methods. Through their dominating influence in academia and in society, these bureaucrats have shifted the definition of science to match their incompetence: the practice of science in many disciplines today means an interminable "research program" – activities that must obey the mechanistic principles, but need not produce any useful results.

Here are three views: "Scientism is the profoundly unscientific attempt to transfer uncritically the methodology of the physical sciences to the study of human action."[1] Scientism describes "an attitude which is decidedly unscientific in the true sense of the word, since it involves a mechanical and uncritical application of habits of thought to fields different from those in which they have been formed. The scientistic as distinguished from the scientific view is not an unprejudiced but a very prejudiced approach which, before it has considered its subject, claims to know what is the most appropriate way of investigating it."[2] "The progress of modern science has been due to its rigorous confinement to the measurable aspects of elements of experience which are contained in a causal system. But science does not encompass nor does it profess to encompass all human experience. Science seeks to approximate the truth about the world only within the limitations of specific and rigorously defined contexts. No true scientist will claim more; no educated layman should expect more. Yet the vulgarization of science – scientism – has led many people, including not a few scientists who have lost sight of the philosophical foundations of their craft, to assert that science holds the key to *all* problems of human experience."[3]

These views, expressed many years ago, show that we have been aware for a

[1] Murray N. Rothbard, "The Mantle of Science," in *Scientism and Values*, eds. Helmut Schoeck and James W. Wiggins (Princeton, NJ: D. Van Nostrand, 1960), p. 159.

[2] F. A. Hayek, *The Counter-Revolution of Science: Studies on the Abuse of Reason*, 2nd ed. (Indianapolis: Liberty Fund, 1979), p. 24.

[3] Robert Strausz-Hupé, "Social Science Versus the Obsession of 'Scientism,'" in *Scientism and Values*, eds. Schoeck and Wiggins, p. 223.

long time of the limitations of mechanism. This has not stopped it from spreading, however. Although many thinkers have shown why mechanism cannot work in the human sciences, the mechanistic temptation is too great to resist. This is true because there are no easy alternatives, if we seek an exact theory.

For complex phenomena, the approximations provided by mechanistic theories are not close enough to be practical. It is highly improbable that we can discover a theory which explains and predicts with great accuracy individual or group behaviour. And if we ever do, it would be a *non-mechanistic* theory, because it would have to explain many of our capabilities and actions at the same time. Its model would be a complex structure, and hence impossible to represent with diagrams, mathematics, or software. Such a theory might evolve in the mind of one person (because minds can process complex structures), but that person would be unable to describe it to others with precision, as we explain mechanistic theories. This superior knowledge would manifest itself in the form of correct decisions and predictions, and would be interpreted as the result of intuition or personal experience.

In our mechanistic culture, however, such a theory would be rejected as "unscientific." Researchers, therefore, do not even try to discover non-mechanistic explanations. They are trained to think only in mechanistic terms, to see the world as nothing but isolated hierarchical structures, so they can discover nothing better than mechanistic theories even when non-mechanistic explanations exist. We are caught in the mechanistic trap: we only permit ourselves to discover theories that cannot work.

If mechanism leads to scientism, scientism leads to utopianism – the belief that society can be greatly improved by implementing some rational or scientific plan. Thus, modern utopian ideas tend to parallel contemporary scientific knowledge. Their enthusiasm reflects the latest successes in the natural sciences, and the belief that similar successes are possible in the human sciences. Not surprisingly, utopian theories have been multiplying at an ever increasing rate since the Scientific Revolution. Utopian ideas never work, of course, and few were attempted on a large scale. Nevertheless, they have been an important factor in the evolution of social thinking.

The most striking characteristic of utopianism is that it always leads to totalitarianism; that is, a society where individual freedom is sacrificed in the name of an ideal, where an elite controls the political, social, and even personal life of every citizen. Central control is deemed necessary in order to maximize efficiency in industry, commerce, education, and all other public domains.

This efficiency, it is believed, will ultimately benefit all people by permitting the elite to create a perfect society.

The history of scientific utopianism in Western culture starts with Plato's ideal society in the *Republic*. Karl Popper,[4] in his study of totalitarian philosophy, traces its roots to Plato's theory of forms or ideas. According to this theory, all objects, attributes, and processes in the real world derive from a set of pure and abstract ideas. The ideas depict the original, perfect forms, while the real things derived from them are deviations from these forms. The idea of a circle, for example, is a perfect circle. There can be only one perfect circle, and that is an abstract concept; the actual circles found in the world are only approximations.

Plato disliked the political turmoils and the drift toward democracy that were taking place in his time, favouring instead a stable and unchanging society – a society founded upon sound political principles. According to his theory of ideas, there must exist an idea of the perfect social system, and the reason why societies in the real world are so changeable and corrupt must be that they are deviations from that system. It should be possible, therefore, to deduce rationally what the perfect society ought to be like. This he does, and the result is the depiction of a totalitarian state.

Like all utopias, Plato's ideal society can only be realized if we disregard the interests of the individual. Society is to be ruled by an elite – a body of highly trained experts who, Plato feels, are alone qualified to make political decisions. Thus, using what seems to be irrefutable logic but is in fact scientism, Plato promoted totalitarianism as the best form of government. This escaped the notice of most interpreters until quite recently, when the similarities between Plato's imaginary state and the totalitarian ideas of our own time became evident.

While in Plato's utopia the rulers had to be highly trained in the sciences and in mathematics, Francis Bacon took this idea to its extreme: in his utopia, *The New Atlantis*, the rulers *are* scientists. There is no politics, as the chief preoccupation of the rulers is scientific research and technological development. All the inhabitants of his imaginary island are supremely happy, thus illustrating Bacon's belief that science and technology will solve all personal and social problems.

Bacon is known as the founder of modern science, but not because of any discoveries of his own. This honour is due to the fact that he was the first to specify and promote the new methods of empirical research – observation, experimentation, inductive logic – while also being an influential philosopher

---

[4] Karl R. Popper, *The Open Society and Its Enemies*, vol. 1, *The Spell of Plato*, 5th ed. (Princeton, NJ: Princeton University Press, 1966).

and public figure. So, although most contemporary scientists were already using these methods in their work, it was Bacon's reputation that made them respectable. It is interesting, however, that for someone who stressed the importance of logical methods of inquiry, Bacon found it unnecessary to apply such methods to his vision of the ideal society. He takes it for granted that scientific and technological advances can be used to improve human lives and human societies just as we use them to improve things in the material world. He assumes – without trying to verify this assumption – that if each need and desire can be addressed separately by specialists, this is bound to create happy individuals and hence an ideal society. He gives no thought to the complex interactions that take place in a society, and how these interactions might affect the implementation of his vision.

In the modern era, the first attempt to implement a utopian idea took place in France during the revolution of 1789. This attempt resulted immediately in a totalitarian society, followed after a few years of failures by an even more oppressive regime – the Napoleonic dictatorship. A variety of mechanistic social theories were developed in Europe during the next one hundred years, eventually giving rise to the two greatest utopian concepts, and hence totalitarian systems, of our time: Communism and Nazism.

Albert Salomon and F. A. Hayek,[5] among others, have studied the growth of social scientism in the nineteenth century, and its totalitarian tendencies. They trace its origins to Henri de Saint-Simon and Auguste Comte, the French thinkers credited with founding sociology. These thinkers were quite outspoken about their vision. The only way to have a perfect society, they said, is by designing it scientifically, from scratch. Then, an elite should control it, scientifically. Individual freedom is an unscientific concept, and its abolition must be the first step in any project whose goal is social progress. Thus, while seeking a system that benefits all citizens, these thinkers ended up advocating totalitarianism as the answer. This is the type of absurdity that scientistic beliefs lead to: "The early sociologists made one fatal mistake: they placed their faith in the methods of natural science. In their fervent hopes for an intellectual revolution, they believed that knowledge about human beings was of the same sort and could attain the same precision as that of physics or biology.... But the application of scientific progress to rational transformation of society in the name of a humanitarian ideal ended in a clearly articulated vision of a totalitarian society."[6] We will return to this subject in "Totalitarian Democracy" in chapter 8.

[5] Albert Salomon, *The Tyranny of Progress: Reflections on the Origins of Sociology* (New York: Noonday Press, 1955); Hayek, *Counter-Revolution of Science.*
[6] Salomon, *Tyranny of Progress*, pp. 103–104.

❖

We are interested in utopian thought because, if we understand how utopian social concepts are born from mechanistic social theories, we will be in a better position to understand how our mechanistic *software* theories are engendering today a new sort of utopia: the Age of Information. By exposing the similarities – the ignorance of the elites, the pseudoscientific nature of their theories, the use of propaganda instead of reasoned argument, the need for deception to cover up failures – we may be able to recognize the totalitarian tendencies of our software culture, and to avoid perhaps the mistakes of the past.

Scientistic social theories, we recall, offer solutions by separating the complex phenomenon that is a human society into isolated aspects; in other words, by separating a complex structure into its constituent simple ones. Human beings are seen as members of political systems, or production systems, or educational systems, or communities, or families, or organizations. But human beings are elements in these structures, and in many others, *at the same time*. They are, in fact, the shared elements that cause these structures to interact. In our imagination, it is not difficult to find precise, mechanistic methods to improve any *one* aspect of society. It usually seems possible to improve that aspect simply by modifying or replacing the structure that represents it. When we try to implement these changes, however, we find that it is impossible to isolate that aspect from the others. What we may see in practice is that people are reluctant to adopt the changes because these changes affect negatively other aspects of their life, or that the other aspects affect the one modified so that the promised benefits do not materialize.

For example, we may have nothing in principle against a centrally planned economy. But in order to implement such an idea, the elite must decide which social institutions are important and which ones are not, must determine what goods are to be available and their prices, must control everyone's education and training, must restrict individual choices in selecting a career, and so on. Even if it were sincere when claiming that it wanted to control only one thing, the elite would end up controlling *all* aspects of life. The utopian system would become totalitarian.

Similarly, our software elites may be sincere when claiming that all they want is to improve the way we create and use software. But if everything we do depends directly or indirectly on computers, the only way to control software is by controlling *all* aspects of our existence. Thus, a society can become totalitarian through a utopian software ideology as easily as it can through a utopian economic, political, or religious ideology.

Their ideology notwithstanding, all totalitarian systems are alike. The elites are so confident in their plans that they cannot understand our doubts. How important are individual rights compared to the vision of a perfect society? They attribute our resistance to ignorance, to our failure to appreciate the ultimate benefits of totalitarianism. They alone are knowledgeable enough in these matters, so it is their duty to persuade us to accept the new system, for our own good. And if this necessitates deception, propaganda, indoctrination, or even force, then they must carry out these unpleasant tasks, because achieving that dream is more important than the rights of the individual. In any case, these are only temporary measures, which will become unnecessary once we are all enlightened enough to accept the new system on our own accord.

3

The influence of the natural sciences on the social sciences took place in two stages.[7] In the period encompassing most of the seventeenth century, social thinkers, impressed by the successes of the new mechanical and mathematical concepts, looked for ways to apply the same concepts in their own fields. After Newton's publication of the *Principia*, however, their expectations grew accordingly: they became convinced that a *universal* theory can be found, similar to Newton's theory of universal gravitation, which would explain all social and individual behaviour.

No useful theories based on mechanical models were ever discovered in the human sciences, but a brief survey of these attempts may help us later to recognize our *software* delusions. We immediately notice the use of mechanical terms to describe mental and social phenomena: "mass," "attraction," "motion," etc. Similarly, the software experts describe *programming* concepts with mechanical terms: applications are "assembled" from software "components," are "built" by software "engineers," and so forth. We recognize in both cases the same circular, fallacious logic: The experts *assume* that a given phenomenon can be reduced to mechanics, so they adopt mechanical notions *before* discovering a useful mechanistic theory. As a result, models and terms that have a precise meaning in mechanics are only metaphors in the other fields, where they are employed illegitimately. But now, these very metaphors are taken as evidence that the theory is valid.

Thus, John Locke and the other empiricist philosophers applied the model of contemporary mechanics to the working of the mind: "The mind was treated as if it were a box containing mental equivalents of the Newtonian

[7] I. Bernard Cohen, *Interactions: Some Contacts between the Natural Sciences and the Social Sciences* (Cambridge, MA: MIT Press, 1994), pp. 101–102.

particles."[8] Everything we know, the empiricists claimed, originates with the simple sensations perceived by our bodies; these sensations result in simple ideas, or atoms of thought; and the complex ideas that constitute knowledge and reasoning are combinations of these simple ideas, in the same way that physical objects are combinations of some elementary particles.[9] David Hartley, who introduced the concept of associations of ideas, explained them as purely mechanical processes: each type of sensation is transmitted as a different type of vibration through the nerves and causes a corresponding vibration in the cerebral material, which then becomes predisposed to vibrate in that way. This results in a simple idea, and when different vibrations occur simultaneously, these ideas become associated. Ultimately, "Hartley's associationalist psychology led to a mechanical theory of creativity.... The creative function of the mind consisted of breaking down complex ideas into their component parts and rearranging them into new ideas. That is, the imagination functioned in a purely mechanical way – simply rearranging parts into new wholes."[10]

George Berkeley tried to explain social relations by viewing them as mutual attraction between people; and David Hume claimed that the phenomenon of associations of ideas can be explained as a form of attraction. Both indicated Newtonian mechanics as the source of their inspiration, comparing their concepts of attraction to the gravitational attraction between physical masses.[11]

Charles Fourier, one of the founders of socialism, created a utopian social theory based on Newtonian mechanics. (A few communities in France and in America actually attempted to implement this theory.) He "claimed to have discovered an equivalent of the gravitational law, one that applied to human nature and social behavior."[12] He had a "calculus of attraction" and a "calculus of harmony," and claimed that his "laws of social motion" were superior to Newton's laws of physical motion.[13]

Many economists were impressed by the science of mechanics. Leon Walras, for example, published an article titled "Economics and Mechanics," in which he "argued that identical differential equations appear in his analysis of economics and in two examples from mathematical physics: the equilibrium of a lever and the motion of planets according to gravitational celestial mechanics."[14] Vilfredo Pareto claimed that "pure economics is a sort of mechanics or akin to mechanics."[15] Pareto, as well as Fisher, drew up detailed tables showing many concepts from mechanics and their counterparts in

[8] Isaiah Berlin, *The Age of Enlightenment: The 18th Century Philosophers* (New York: Mentor, 1956), p. 18.   [9] Ibid.

[10] David F. Channell, *The Vital Machine: A Study of Technology and Organic Life* (New York: Oxford University Press, 1991), p. 44.   [11] Cohen, *Interactions*, p. 19.

[12] Ibid., p. 20.   [13] Ibid.   [14] Ibid., p. 41.

[15] Vilfredo Pareto, quoted ibid.

economics.[16] J. E. Cairnes claimed that the principles of economics are identical in character to the physical principles of the laws of gravitation and motion.[17] In the end, "with a sense of security coming from the use of equations homologous to those in physics, the new economics assumed the metaphor of rational mechanics."[18]

Harvey's discovery of the principles of blood circulation, occurring as it did when the mechanical philosophy was beginning to dominate science, contributed greatly to the view that the body works just like a machine. Few doubted that, like blood circulation, all physiological functions would ultimately prove to be nothing but mechanical operations: "The 'new philosophy' no longer accepted organic development as self-explanatory. Rather, it insisted on analysing all natural processes into fixed patterns of mechanical action and interaction. The bodies of animals, quite as much as inanimate objects, were to be regarded as configurations of material parts, moving and interacting like the pieces of a machine."[19] "At first the machine served only as an analogue for biological processes.... But as mechanical philosophy became successful as a method of explanation, people no longer saw the machine as simply an analogue for life – life became literally mechanical."[20]

Although Harvey himself recognized that most biological phenomena cannot be reduced to mechanics, his work was vulgarized by Descartes and the other mechanists. What emerged as a result was the school of mechanical biology called iatromechanics.[21] Some scientists applied Newtonian mechanics directly, and attempted to explain physiological functions and diseases as the effect of forces they believed to act between organic particles.[22] Most theories, however, were directed toward finding parallels between organisms and machines, on the assumption that live systems work on the same mechanical, hydraulic, or pneumatic principles as the machines of that period.

It was easy enough to find parallels to mechanical operations when superficially studying, say, the movement of limbs. But the iatromechanists attempted to explain *all* physiological functions as mechanical operations: digestion, metabolism, respiration, reproduction, sensation – no function lay beyond the power of their imagination, and they invented machine-like operations to explain them all. Although they believed that they saw evidence to confirm their theories, these theories were only speculations: "For the most part, iatromechanics was simply irrelevant to biology.... Beside the subtlety of

---

[16] Ibid., pp. 44–47.   [17] Ibid., p. 42.   [18] Ibid.

[19] Stephen Toulmin and June Goodfield, *The Architecture of Matter* (Chicago: University of Chicago Press, 1982), p. 168.   [20] Channell, *Vital Machine*, p. 30.

[21] Richard S. Westfall, *The Construction of Modern Science: Mechanisms and Mechanics* (New York: Cambridge University Press, 1977), p. 94; Channell, *Vital Machine*, p. 36.

[22] Channell, *Vital Machine*, p. 39.

biological processes, the 17th century mechanical philosophy was crudity itself.... In fact iatromechanics made no significant discovery whatever."[23]

The movement culminated with the work of Julien Offray de la Mettrie, *Man a Machine*, published in 1748. This philosophical treatise went beyond Descartes's mechanistic doctrine by asserting that not just the human body but also the phenomena of mind and life are mechanical in character. Everything concerning human beings, therefore, can be explained by applying the principles of motion to organic matter.

The political theory of Thomas Hobbes was very advanced for his time, and influenced several generations of thinkers. Hobbes, however, was also interested in the natural sciences, and his political theory reflects this: "He was fully convinced that a science of politics or of human society must be similar to a natural science, based on two primary concepts: movement and matter or substance, in accordance with what was known as the 'mechanical philosophy.'"[24] In *Leviathan*, Hobbes likened the state to a great animal, combining the mechanical theory of Galileo and the physiological theory of Harvey into a political theory. The state had been likened to a live body by earlier political thinkers, but Hobbes modified this concept into that of "a great animal machine, acting like an animal but composed of mechanical parts."[25] He "used the new discoveries in physiology to transform the organismic concept of the body politic by giving it a mechanical basis in conformity with Descartes's reductionistic philosophy. The political and social world of Hobbes is a hybrid kind of organic structure operating mechanically and conceived under the sign of Galileo, Descartes, and Harvey. His system of society was a collection of human beings acting as 'mechanical systems of matter in motion.'"[26]

Hobbes had great admiration for the deductive methods of science, as illustrated by the theorems of geometry, and believed that a perfect society could be attained if we found a way to apply these methods to social relations: "Were the nature of human actions as distinctly known, as the nature of quantity in geometrical figures," all irrational and dishonest motives would disappear, and mankind would enjoy "an immortal peace."[27] The method of science "was said by Hobbes to lead to predictive rules for a human science and so to produce a guide for obtaining predictable results in the domains of ethics or morals and of political action. In short, Hobbes envisioned a social science that would have some of the same qualities of exactness and of predictability as the physical sciences."[28]

---

[23] Westfall, *Modern Science*, p. 104. [24] Cohen, *Interactions*, p. 120.
[25] Ibid.   [26] Ibid., p. 123.   [27] Thomas Hobbes, quoted ibid., p. 121.
[28] Ibid.

In France, too, in the decades preceding the Revolution, political thinkers held that human phenomena are similar to the phenomena studied by the exact sciences. So, they concluded, it should be possible to design a perfect society simply by emulating the methods employed in those sciences. The Revolution was, in effect, an attempt to implement such a society. Thus, Morelly claimed that a science of morality can be developed, "as simple and as self-evident in its axioms and consequences"[29] as a mathematical system. He assumed that there existed in nature an ideal, objective pattern of human affairs, which he perceived as "a social mechanism, a 'marvellous automatic machine.'"[30] Similarly, Mably "strove for scientific certainty in social and human affairs. He believed that politics could develop from the most conjectural into a most exact science, once the recesses of the human heart and passions had been explored, and a scientific system of ethics defined."[31] And Condorcet was convinced that the events of the Revolution proved that a general method of investigation had been found, equally applicable to the exact sciences and the human sciences: "Once this instrument had been applied to morals and politics, a degree of certainty was given to those sciences little inferior to that which obtained in the natural sciences."[32]

The most flagrant manifestation of scientism is to be found, however, not in previous centuries but in our own time. The mechanistic fallacies that dominated the human sciences in the mid-twentieth century were denounced, in an exhaustive and scathing study, by the eminent sociologist Pitirim Sorokin.[33] Still, even though considered a classic, this study did not put an end to mechanistic theories.

In its simplest form, this scientism manifests itself in the use of jargon, neologisms, pompous terms, and platitudes. This practice, mockingly called by Sorokin "speech disorders," includes the "blind transference of terms and formulas from the natural sciences into sociology and the related disciplines. The net result of the transference is a distortion of the precise meaning the terms have in the natural sciences and a contamination of the social sciences by terms that now become either meaningless or vague. Being incomprehensible, such terms impress the uninitiated as exact and 'scientific.'"[34] With innumerable examples, Sorokin shows that any definitions and explanations based on such terms are meaningless, because the terms themselves are not

---

[29] J. L. Talmon, *The Origins of Totalitarian Democracy* (New York: Praeger, 1960), p. 17.
[30] Ibid.   [31] Ibid., p. 18.   [32] Ibid.
[33] Pitirim A. Sorokin, *Fads and Foibles in Modern Sociology and Related Sciences* (Chicago: Henry Regnery, 1956).   [34] Ibid., p. 22.

properly defined. To take just one case of "speech disorders" cited by him: "'Every psychological activity may be ordered to a *two-dimensional plane (surface)* where organism and goal represent certain spatial regions within *the surface...*' 'Psychological activity of all sorts will be ordered to a *path*, and may be said to represent *locomotion* in the psychological field.' This psychological field is a 'topological medium,' with 'fluidity,' 'cohesiveness,' 'permeability,' 'hodological space,' etc."[35]

Another imitation of the exact sciences is the concept of operationalism. Operationalist methods (which consist of precise definitions, experiments, and measurements), while important in disciplines like physics and chemistry, are worthless in the human sciences: "As usual, without the necessary study of the real nature of operationalism, of its role in the progress of the natural sciences, of its limitations and doubtful elements, and forgetting the important role of pure intuition, deduction, and nonoperational induction in the progress of science and wisdom, our sociologists, psychologists, and anthropologists were converted into ardent operationalists and began *en masse* to apply operational method on their study of social, cultural, and mental phenomena. A sort of operational orgy rapidly spread throughout these disciplines."[36]

G. K. Zipf, for example, using operational preciseness, arrives at this fantastic definition of an organism: "A movable mathematical point in time-space, in reference to which matter-energy moves in such a way that a physical situation exists in which work is expended in order to preserve a physical system from a final gravitational and electromagnetic equilibrium with the rest of universe."[37] S. C. Dodd, in his so-called system of operationally defined concepts for sociology, attempts to explain social change with terms borrowed from physics, but he does not actually define any operational procedures. "Instead," Sorokin notes, "he simply takes the terms with their symbols (like T for time) from the physical sciences and concludes that by such a transference he has satisfactorily solved the problem of operationally defined concepts for sociology."[38] So the resulting theory, despite the presence of equations similar to those we find in physics, is nonsensical: "However impressive this simplified transcription of physical concepts and their symbols looks, in application to 'societal' time, duration, change, acceleration, and force, these definitions are empty and useless. For *they do not give any real unit* for the measurement of social change or of its acceleration, velocity or force."[39]

T. Parsons and R. F. Bales claim that social action can be explained with such notions as the principle of "inertia," the principle of "action and reaction," and

---

[35] Ibid., p. 25, citing J. F. Brown and K. Lewin.   [36] Ibid., p. 32.
[37] G. K. Zipf, quoted ibid., p. 30.   [38] Ibid., p. 41.   [39] Ibid.

the principle of "virtual displacements." But, while valid in mechanics, in a social theory these principles are merely "distorted transcriptions" and "logical and empirical nonsense."[40]

Some of the authors of mechanistic social theories are not sociologists at all. For instance, P. W. Bridgman is a physicist, and J. Q. Stewart is an astrophysicist. Their avowed goal is to find "uniformities in social behaviour which can be expressed in mathematical forms more or less corresponding to the known patterns in physical science."[41] So they attempt to express such psychosocial concepts as people, activities, interactions, and desires in physicalist terms like social mass, social temperature, and social distance. Stewart "views the social universe as six-dimensional or made up of six 'social quantities' or 'fundamental categories': 'distance, time, mass, temperature, electric charge, and number of molecules,' whatever social interpretation is to be given to each of these 'dimensions' or 'social quantities.' We are told further that 'this list [of six dimensions] makes social physics in its dimensional structure isomorphic with physical science,' that is, 'there is a complete and trustworthy analogy between two or more situations' which entitles one 'to transfer equations from physics to politics.'"[42]

Some scientists propose theories that are based directly on the concepts of reductionism and atomism. They maintain that there exist social *atoms* – elementary social particles that are the smallest units of psychosocial phenomena. The social atoms are small groups of individuals (families, for instance), whose relations are simple and irreducible and can therefore be described with precision. (In a social atom, these scientists say, the relations between individuals are nothing but forces of attraction and repulsion, just like the forces operating within the atoms studied by physics.) We should be able, then, to discover an exact theory for the entire society simply by representing larger and larger groups as neat structures of social atoms. But Sorokin shows that these theories are mistaken: members of a society interact in complex ways, and no group can be isolated from the others and described with precision.[43]

The modern mechanistic theories, says Sorokin, are not only worthless but also unoriginal. These scientists seem to be unaware of the mechanistic delusions of the past, and are merely repeating the work previously "performed by a legion of social and psychological scribes hoping to establish a new 'social physics,' 'social mechanics,' 'social geometry,' or 'social energetics.' ... Contrary to their claims to being revolutionary, contemporary 'social physicists,' econometrists, psychometrists, sociometrists, and ethicometrists are

---

[40] Ibid., pp. 246–247.   [41] J. Q. Stewart, quoted ibid., p. 188.

[42] Ibid., p. 189, citing J. Q. Stewart (brackets in the original).   [43] Ibid., ch. 10.

merely continuing centuries-old operations."[44] After analyzing hundreds of claims, Sorokin concludes that "the recent period has not produced anything remarkable in the field of general systems of sociology and psychology."[45]

❖

This brief survey of mechanistic thinking will suffice for now. It is important to recognize, though, that similar idiocies are being pursued even today, by scientists working in famous universities. And we should perhaps ponder over the prospects of a society that not only tolerates this intellectual corruption, but holds the scientists and their institutions in high esteem. If you feel this judgment is unfair, you will see in "Popper's Principles of Demarcation" (in chapter 3) that it is possible to determine whether a given activity constitutes true scientific research, or whether it is pseudoscientific. Accordingly, mechanistic theories like these can be shown to be worthless pursuits.

We will continue our study of scientism in the next three chapters, where we will examine the mechanistic delusions that concern us the most. By learning to recognize the common mechanistic foundation of these theories, we will be in a better position to understand our *software* delusions, which also spring from mechanistic thinking. The study of scientism, thus, can help us to see our software ideology in the broader context that is our mechanistic culture: given this tradition, the emergence of software mechanism was inevitable.

[44] Ibid., p. 110.   [45] Ibid., p. 310.

CHAPTER 2

The Mind

The most pernicious consequence of a mechanistic culture is the disparagement of human capabilities. Because the human environment consists of complex phenomena, the brain has evolved to help us cope with complex structures. We possess naturally, therefore, non-mechanistic capabilities. And we exercise these capabilities every time we do something through personal experience, skills, creativity, and intuition; in other words, simply by knowing how to do it, rather than by following rules and methods.

As we will see in the present chapter, practically all mental acts involved in normal, intelligent behaviour require *non-mechanistic* knowledge. In our mechanistic culture, however, all knowledge that cannot be reduced to simple hierarchical structures is deemed "unscientific," and hence unimportant. We admit that intuition and other personal forms of knowledge are useful in certain fields – in the arts, for instance – but otherwise we prefer knowledge that can be precisely described. Consequently, we are neglecting our superior, non-mechanistic capabilities, and restricting ourselves to the mechanistic ones; that is, to those capabilities we share with our machines. But our most important problems are non-mechanistic. So these problems remain unsolved, and we even cease noticing them. Pleased with our success in solving simple, mechanistic problems, we increasingly ignore the important, complex ones.

Mind Mechanism

We have a special interest in the mechanistic theories of mind, for they are more than just another example of mechanistic delusions. Scientists search for mechanistic explanations of the mind because these explanations would enable them to create models of human intelligence. But in the age of the computer it is more than intellectual curiosity, or the scientist tradition, that motivates this work. Mechanistic models can be implemented with software, so the search for mechanistic theories of mind is ultimately an attempt to replace minds with software; that is, to find substitutes for human intelligence.

It is relatively easy to study the effects of mind substitutes when software *exceeds* human capabilities – in complicated calculations, for example. But what are the social consequences of mind substitutes when software is *inferior*? We will examine this issue later, in "Replacing Minds with Software." For now, it suffices to remember the connection between the two subjects we are discussing here: the *non-mechanistic* capabilities of human beings and the *mechanistic* theories of mind. Restricted as they are to simple structures, the mechanistic models, and hence the substitutes based on them, can never attain the capabilities of human minds.

The mechanistic philosophy, we recall, is the combination of reductionism and atomism, the belief that every phenomenon can be described as a system of things within things. Our infatuation with mechanism started in the seventeenth century, when philosophers and scientists equated nature with mathematics. All natural phenomena, as well as the phenomena related to human life, were seen as simple structures and hence amenable to mathematical treatment. In particular, the working of the mind – the way we acquire knowledge, develop skills, or solve problems – was represented as simple structures.

We attribute this idea to Descartes, because he was the first to describe it in detail. Any problem, he claimed, any inquiry, can be broken down hierarchically into smaller and smaller parts, until we reach parts that are simple enough to understand directly. Thus, all human knowledge can be represented with hierarchical structures. And consequently, everything that is within the capabilities of the mind can be expressed in a form similar to the deductive system of mathematics: "The long chains of simple and easy reasonings by means of which geometers are accustomed to reach the conclusions of their most difficult demonstrations, had led me to imagine that all things, to the knowledge of which man is competent, are mutually connected in the same way, and that there is nothing so far removed from us as to be beyond our reach, or so hidden that we cannot discover it."[1]

While Descartes's view was becoming the accepted model of mind, there remained a few dissenters, who claimed that much of our problem-solving ability is intuitive rather than mathematical. The best known of these dissenters is Pascal, a contemporary of Descartes, and himself a distinguished mathematician and scientist. Pascal held that we are capable of two types of thinking, the mathematical and the intuitive, and that we need both: "We know the truth not only through our reason but also through our heart.... Principles are felt, propositions proved, and both with certainty though by different means."[2] Those "accustomed to the clearcut, obvious principles of mathematics and to draw no conclusions until they have clearly seen and handled their principles ... become lost in matters requiring intuition, whose principles cannot be handled in this way."[3]

Descartes, too, recognized the need for intuitive thinking, but he believed it to be necessary only in understanding the *terminal* elements of a knowledge structure; that is, those concepts whose truth we accept as self-evident, because there are no antecedent concepts to deduce it from. All other knowledge, he believed, can be represented exactly and completely by reducing it hierarchically to the terminal elements.

Following Descartes, philosophers of all persuasions – rationalists and empiricists, idealists and realists – proposed theories of mind which assumed that the phenomena of knowledge and learning can be explained mechanistically. Some mental capabilities, however, always remained unexplained; so, in reality, none of these theories worked. In the twentieth century, despite the continuing popularity of the mechanistic view of mind, some philosophers came to accept the fact that a great part of our knowledge cannot be formally defined or described. The best known of these philosophers are Ludwig Wittgenstein, Martin Heidegger, and Maurice Merleau-Ponty. Far from being only peripheral, these philosophers say, the informal knowledge that we develop in the mind is essential for intelligent behaviour.

In the last five decades, we have learned a great deal about our mental capabilities from the work done in the field of computer science known as artificial intelligence. Ironically, though, what we have learned is the exact opposite of what research in artificial intelligence set out originally to prove. The aim was to create software that simulates human intelligence, and the

---

[1] René Descartes, *A Discourse on Method* (London: Dent, 1912), p. 16.
[2] Blaise Pascal, *Pensées* (London: Penguin Books, 1966), p. 58.   [3] Ibid., p. 211.

computer was seen as the device through which we could actually implement – and hence, finally vindicate – our mechanistic theories of mind. What we discovered instead is that these theories, which had been accepted by countless generations of thinkers, fail blatantly when implemented with actual models.

The attempt to emulate human intelligence with software can succeed only for those mental capabilities that are simple enough to be approximated with isolated hierarchical structures; in other words, for mental acts that can be separated from the complex phenomena of the real world. Unsurprisingly, it was this type of acts that researchers chose in their initial projects. They interpreted the immediate successes as evidence that their mechanistic theories were correct, and concluded that machine intelligence of any level can be attained simply by extrapolating those methods; that is, by building larger and larger hierarchical structures. This led to the now famous proclamations made by some of the most respected scientists in the 1960s – namely, that within a few years computers would be intelligent enough to do everything that human minds can do. Some examples: "Extrapolating the recent rapid gains that have been made, we can forecast with some confidence that a decade hence we shall have a reasonably comprehensive theoretical understanding of the processes of human problem solving."[4] "Technologically ... machines will be capable, within twenty years, of doing any work that a man can do."[5] "Within a generation, I am convinced, few compartments of intellect will remain outside the machine's realm – the problems of creating 'artificial intelligence' will be substantially solved."[6]

It is not the naivety of artificial intelligence that concerns us here, though, but its mechanistic roots. All theories that attempt to explain mental acts rely, ultimately, on the concept of hierarchical structures. Whether the simplest elements – the knowledge atoms – are believed to be bits of information, or sensations, or innate functions, to account for actual knowledge and behaviour these elements must be combined hierarchically into more and more complex ones. There is no other way to explain higher levels of knowledge within a deterministic philosophy. So, whether we attempt to explain intelligent acts by breaking them down into successively simpler parts, or whether, conversely, we start with some elementary capabilities and combine them into successively larger parts, it is always the mechanistic concepts of reductionism and atomism that we invoke; specifically, we try to explain intelligence as some atomic entities combined hierarchically through completely specifiable relations.

[4] Herbert A. Simon, *The Shape of Automation: For Men and Management* (New York: Harper and Row, 1965), pp. 89–90.   [5] Ibid., p. 96.

[6] Marvin L. Minsky, *Computation: Finite and Infinite Machines*, (Englewood Cliffs, NJ: Prentice Hall, 1967), p. 2.

The rationalist theories of Descartes and Leibniz, the empiricist theories of Locke and Hobbes, the modern theories of behaviourism and linguistics, are all founded ultimately upon the idea of simple hierarchical structures. Before we had computers, philosophers and scientists could only create hierarchies that were small enough to study manually. Noting how powerful the hierarchical concept was, they imagined that there is no limit to the complexity we can reach with it; all we need, they thought, is a way to create hierarchies with a sufficiently large number of elements, levels, and relations. They had no means to verify this assumption, so they could remain confident that the complexity of human knowledge is simply the result of a very large hierarchical structure created somehow in the mind. The only reason they could not prove this, they believed, was that they had no tools to create models of such large hierarchies.

After centuries of speculations, software finally afforded us the opportunity to create large hierarchical structures, and thereby implement the mechanistic theories of mind. But instead of vindicating these theories, as it was hoped, the software models refuted them. Thus, the failure of the software models of mind became an unintentional refutation of *all* mechanistic theories of mind: "Thanks to AI [artificial intelligence] research, Plato's and Kant's speculation that the mind works according to rules has finally found its empirical test in the attempt to use logic machines to produce humanlike understanding. And, after two thousand years of refinement, the traditional view of mind has shown itself to be inadequate."[7]

The more sophisticated our software becomes, the more obvious are the limitations of the mechanistic models, and the greater ought to be our respect for the unique capabilities of our minds. The failure of artificial intelligence has taught us nothing, however. Few people realize that the failure of mechanistic software concepts in the much broader and more important domain of business application development is due to the same delusion: the belief that human minds can be represented with mechanistic models, and hence human knowledge and skills – in this case, programming expertise – can be replaced with formal methods and with software devices.

---

[7] Hubert L. Dreyfus and Stuart E. Dreyfus, *Mind over Machine: The Power of Human Intuition and Expertise in the Era of the Computer* (New York: Free Press, 1988), p. 98. See also Hubert Dreyfus's classic study of the fallacies of artificial intelligence: *What Computers Still Can't Do: A Critique of Artificial Reason* (Cambridge, MA: MIT Press, 1992). Through philosophical arguments, Dreyfus shows why the very idea that a machine can display human-like understanding is mistaken.

Innumerable theories, methodologies, development tools, and programming languages have been invented as substitutes for programming expertise, and all have failed to provide real benefits. The reason is that mechanistic substitutes can replace only the *simple* aspects of programming. Still, the failures are described as temporary setbacks, to be resolved by the "next generation" of methods and devices. So we continue to see the same delusions, the same claims, and the same failures year after year.

We are witnessing an incredible spectacle: Our software experts, those individuals to whom we have entrusted our future, are claiming in effect that their vision of the future is a world where human beings – that is, *we* – no longer matter. Their projects can be summed up quite simply as attempts to prove that software devices are better than human minds. These projects repeatedly fail, but instead of recognizing their failure as evidence of the superiority of our minds and taking pride in our capabilities, we continue to be fooled. Instead of admitting that our software experts are in fact impostors and charlatans, we accept their excuses, keep admiring them, and pay them to try again to prove that their devices are better than our minds.

Models of Mind

1

Let us take a closer look at the non-mechanistic capabilities of the human mind. Recall the process of face recognition: while we can easily *recognize* a familiar face, we cannot *describe* that face precisely enough to enable someone unfamiliar with it to recognize it as easily as *we* do (see pp. 110–111). Thus, when we know a face, we possess a type of knowledge that cannot be expressed as methods or rules. We can readily *use* this knowledge, but we cannot explain how we do it. What this means is that the only way to acquire this knowledge is by allowing it to *develop* in our mind; we cannot acquire it by learning some facts. The mind has the capacity to create, as it were, an internal replica of a phenomenon, and it does this simply by being exposed to that phenomenon.

We acquire a similar type of knowledge when we learn to recognize a voice on the telephone. We can recognize, in fact, the voices of dozens of people by hearing just a word or two; yet we cannot describe *how* we do it. As in the case of face recognition, a person already familiar with a certain voice cannot describe that voice to us so that we would recognize it if we heard it; the only way to acquire this knowledge is through our own experience. Nor can we transmit this knowledge to others once *we* have acquired it.

Note how different this knowledge is from the knowledge of isolated facts like birth dates or telephone numbers, which we can precisely convey to others in words or symbols. And it is not the *simplicity* of these facts that allows us to describe them with precision, for we can also describe with precision the make-up of a complicated machine with thousands of parts and connections. What makes these phenomena precisely describable is that they are reducible to simple structures. The process of recognizing faces or voices, on the other hand, is a *complex* structure – a system of interacting structures.

For a phenomenon that is a complex structure, the only exact representation is the phenomenon itself. We saw that some complex phenomena can be *approximated* with simple structures, by representing them with mechanistic models (rules, mathematics, software, etc.). And, even though our mind has the capacity for complex structures, our knowledge – the replicas created by the mind – is still only an approximation of the actual phenomena. But, being complex structures themselves, the approximations created by the mind are closer to the actual phenomena than are the mechanistic approximations. The mind, therefore, can usefully approximate many phenomena that cannot be usefully approximated with mechanistic models.

We note two facts characteristic of non-mechanistic knowledge. First, this knowledge cannot be transferred directly, fully developed, into the mind; the only way it can arise is by developing inside the mind from the isolated bits of knowledge that reach the mind. Second, the only way this knowledge can develop in the mind is through repeated exposure to the phenomena associated with it; that is, through personal experience.

Using the concept of simple and complex structures, we can say that this knowledge does not inhere in the bits of knowledge detected by our senses. The bits of knowledge form simple structures, and the knowledge consists of the complex structures created by the *interaction* of these simple structures. It is the mind's capacity to discover the interactions that permits us to deal intelligently with the complex phenomena surrounding us.

2

Philosopher Gilbert Ryle used the terms *knowing that* and *knowing how* to distinguish between the two kinds of knowledge we are discussing here.[1] *Knowing that* refers to the knowledge of isolated facts and rules – knowledge we can describe precisely and completely. *Knowing how* refers to the knowledge acquired through personal experience, by being exposed to certain situations

---

[1] Gilbert Ryle, *The Concept of Mind* (Chicago: University of Chicago Press, 1984), p. 28.

and by performing certain acts. This latter knowledge enables us to behave intelligently, but we cannot describe it in terms of facts and rules. *Knowing how*, thus, cannot be reduced to *knowing that*.

When acquiring a skill, we start by learning facts and following rules; but when we attain expertise, our skilled performance is due, not to memorizing many facts and rules, but to our experience. Intelligent behaviour requires both *knowing that* and *knowing how*. The mechanistic doctrine, though, claims that our mind is only capable of *knowing that*. Our apparent *knowing how*, according to this doctrine, is merely the result of combining in the mind various bits of *knowing that*. Mechanism must deny the existence of *knowing how* because it maintains that every phenomenon can be explained precisely and completely.

Ryle attributes modern mind mechanism to the traditional theory of mind, which he calls "with deliberate abusiveness ... 'the dogma of the Ghost in the Machine.'"[2] This dogma, inaugurated by Descartes, endows us with two separate entities, bodies and minds. The body is a physical thing that functions just like a machine, so we can analyze its operation with the same methods we employ in the study of mechanical devices. The mind, however, is a rather mysterious thing: it does not exist in space, so we cannot see it, nor describe its operation mechanically; all we can do is observe the external results of its workings, as manifested through the body. The body and the mind must interact continually, but we cannot see the means of interaction either. A human being, therefore, is somewhat like a machine operated by a ghost.

At first, this concept placed the mind safely beyond the reach of mechanistic theories; but the relief was short-lived. The mechanists acknowledge the intelligent capabilities of human beings, and they recognize that the body itself is incapable of intelligence. This is why they postulate a ghostly device and attribute to *it* the mysterious acts known as intelligence. However, while admitting that this invisible device is different from the material body, the mechanists insist that its operation need not be different from the mechanical operation of the body. The ghost and its tools may be invisible, but it is still possible to study them with the familiar principles of reductionism and atomism.

So, in the end, the mind too became the subject of mechanistic theories. The mechanistic theories of mind claim that knowledge, skills, and intelligence can be explained through a reduction to simpler parts, leading ultimately to some elementary bits of knowledge, skills, and intelligence. What the ghostly mechanism of the mind does when we engage in an act of thinking or intelligent behaviour is to combine those invisible bits using some mysterious

[2] Ibid., p. 15.

instructions, and then pass the invisible result of this process to our body, where we notice it as speech or movement of limbs.

But, if this is true, it means that whenever we perform an intelligent act we do two things: first we perform some internal calculations, deliberations, or planning (swiftly and unconsciously), and *then* we perform the actual act. Ryle shows that this view is absurd, that when we behave intelligently or skilfully we perform only one thing: that intelligent or skilful act.[3] If we believe that intelligent or skilful behaviour is the result of other mental acts, we have to explain *those* acts as the result of yet other acts, and so on. But there are no final, atomic, indivisible mental acts: "The regress is infinite, and this reduces to absurdity the theory that for an operation to be intelligent it must be steered by a prior intellectual operation.... 'Intelligent' cannot be defined in terms of 'intellectual,' or 'knowing *how*' in terms of 'knowing *that*'; 'thinking what I am doing' does not connote 'both thinking what to do and doing it.' When I do something intelligently, i.e. thinking what I am doing, I am doing one thing and not two."[4]

3

Ryle's ghost is only one of a whole army of invisible workers that had to be drafted by scientists and philosophers to serve in their mechanistic models of mind. It is impossible, in fact, to invent a theory that "explains" the working of the mind without having to postulate the existence of some invisible agents who perform some invisible work on behalf of the owner of the mind. Mechanistic mind models, therefore, are compelled to commit what is known as the *homunculus* fallacy:[5] the belief that, to explain a mental process, all we have to do is describe it as an internal rather than an external phenomenon.

For example, to explain vision – how we perceive as real objects the images formed on the retina – the mechanists might postulate a mind model that has a visual module for scanning and interpreting these images. But this model is specious. All it does is shift the definition of vision from a capability of the person to a capability of the mind: instead of saying that the mind lets the person see, the model says that the visual module lets the mind see. The phenomenon of vision remains as unexplained as before. The scanning and interpreting operations attributed to the visual module are not an explanation of vision; they are, in fact, the phenomenon that the model was supposed to explain. This mistake is called a homunculus fallacy because the explanation

---

[3] Ibid., pp. 30–32.   [4] Ibid., pp. 31–32.
[5] *Homunculus* means "little man" in Latin; this phrase is explained in the next paragraph.

amounts to a claim that there is a little man in the mind who performs the operations needed to produce the phenomenon in question. What exactly are those operations, and how the little man knows to perform them, is left unanswered. (Thus, because of their circularity, the homunculus theories of mind resemble the inane scholastic explanations of the Middle Ages: fluidity is that quality of a substance which causes it to flow, elasticity is that quality of an object which causes it to bend rather than break, etc.)

Mechanism, we saw in chapter 1, has been exceptionally successful in explaining natural phenomena. So what the mind mechanists are attempting now – and what most research in artificial intelligence and cognitive science amounts to – is to combine the homunculus concept with the mechanistic concept. Since mechanism works in other fields, they say, it *must* work also for minds. They admit that the homunculus concept on its own is erroneous, but they believe that its circularity can be resolved if we combine it with the principles of reductionism and atomism; specifically, if instead of one little man performing one task we assume a hierarchical structure where many little men perform tasks of different complexity at different levels of abstraction.

Philosopher Daniel Dennett, for example, expresses a common view when saying that this idea has helped us, if not to understand how the mind works, at least to confirm some of our mechanistic theories of mind.[6] He attacks the homunculus theories, but is enthusiastic about their potential when fortified with mechanistic principles. He evidently fails to see that this combination merely replaces one delusion with another. He believes that if the tasks performed by the little men become progressively simpler as we move to lower levels, this model constitutes real progress.[7] But the model constitutes progress only *if* the mind is a mechanistic phenomenon; if it is not, the only progress made is to replace the homunculus fallacy with the mechanistic fallacies.

Let us examine these delusions more closely. Since most mechanistic models of mind are now grounded on some combination of homunculus and mechanistic fallacies, by exposing these fallacies we can show the futility of *all* mechanistic theories of intelligence.

To explain or understand a phenomenon within the mechanistic doctrine means to represent it, through a series of reductions, as the result of some elementary processes that are simple enough to understand directly: bits of matter, simple facts, basic mathematical operations, small pieces of software,

---

[6] Daniel C. Dennett, *Brainstorms: Philosophical Essays on Mind and Psychology* (Cambridge, MA: MIT Press, 1981), pp. 119–123.   [7] Ibid., p. 123.

and the like. Thus, we can hope to explain a phenomenon in this sense only if we accept *unquestioningly* that it can be represented as a simple hierarchical structure.

So, to explain the mind we must *assume* that it can be treated as a simple structure; that an intelligent act is the high-level manifestation of some simpler operations, which occur at a lower level; and that those operations are the result of even simpler ones, and so on, down to some operations that are simple enough to be accepted implicitly. Theories differ in the level of reduction claimed to be necessary; some are bold enough to continue the reduction down to the mind's "hardware" (the brain), but most theories in psychology, cognitive science, and artificial intelligence stop at some low level of the mind's "software" (the immaterial mental processes). No matter what level each theory considers low enough to count as explanation, though, to effect the reduction they must all treat the mind as a simple hierarchical structure: the lowest-level elements perform certain operations, the results become the elements that take part in the operations of the next higher level, and so on.

This structure, and all its elements and operations, are imaginary, of course. The mechanists agree that this is only a model, a way to account for the intelligent behaviour we observe from outside. But they insist that the model can be as successful in explaining the working of the mind as similar models are in explaining *physical* phenomena.

Philosophers like Ryle criticize the mechanistic theories of mind by showing that their reductionistic principles are untenable: attempting to explain mental acts hierarchically leads to an infinite regress, so the idea is fallacious. The mind mechanists, though, are not impressed by these objections, and argue in the traditional mechanistic manner: by bringing as evidence the very thing which they are supposed to prove.

Characteristic of all mechanistic thinking is that it starts by *assuming* that there exists a mechanistic model of the phenomenon in question: all phenomena can be explained, and "explanation" means a mechanistic model. The mechanists do not see the need to confirm first that a mechanistic model can exist at all; their task, they believe, is only to *discover* that model. As a result, they see nothing wrong in invoking the principles of reductionism and atomism as a justification of their confidence, when in reality it is precisely these principles that are in doubt. And so, all mechanistic theories end up begging the question. This is a consequence of identifying science, research, and explanation with mechanism, and forgetting that mechanism is only a convention, that it can explain some phenomena but not others.

❖

Let us see how this question-begging logic is used to justify the mechanistic models of mind. The little men and their operations, the mechanists remind us, exist only in our imagination. Their only function is to help us explain the complex mental phenomena by replacing them with combinations of simpler phenomena. The hierarchical levels do not strictly exist: as soon as we explain the first level through the operations performed at the second, lower level, we can dispose of the first level altogether; that level is in fact nothing but the result of the operations of the lower level. Then we dispose of the second level in the same way, once we explain it through the operations of the third level. And we continue this process to lower and lower levels. The only real operations, and hence the only little men that we need to retain, are those at the lowest level, in the terminal elements of the hierarchy. But, because this level is very low, its operations are so simple that we can dispose of those little men too: we can explain the operations, for example, as the result of some trivial physiological functions. This logic – a perfect example of reductionism and atomism – appears impeccable: it seems that we can have our imaginary hierarchical levels and little men after all, and at the same time ground our theory on solid bits of organic matter whose existence no one can doubt.

In this argument, the hierarchical structure of operations in the mind is perceived to be similar to other structures of things within things. In a classification of animals, for example, we invent levels like dogs, species, and genera, but ultimately the only physical entities that really exist are the terminal elements – the animals themselves. The levels of classification exist only in our imagination; no physical entity *dogs* exists in addition to the dogs themselves. Similarly, in a structure like a city we have districts, streets, and buildings, the buildings have walls, and the walls are made up of bricks; but the only physical entities that really exist are the bricks. We can view the entire city as nothing but bricks combined in a hierarchical structure. The buildings and the city do not exist *in addition* to the bricks.

But the structure that best resembles the mind, say the mechanists, is the hierarchical structure of modules and subassemblies that make up a complicated machine – a computer, for instance. We build machines as parts within parts, and we describe their function as operations within operations. In the end, though, the only entities that actually exist are the basic components, the lowest level of the hierarchy. The subassemblies and the machine do not exist *in addition* to these components.

The mechanistic theories assume that the mind can be viewed just like these hierarchical structures. The only physical entities that actually exist are the smallest elements of the brain – perhaps the neurons. The higher levels, up to the mental acts we note as intelligence, are only combinations of states (or values) displayed by these elements. We have no idea how this structure works, the mechanists admit, but there is no reason to doubt that it exists, that its levels and operations can be discovered. The only reason we haven't succeeded so far is that it is such a complicated structure. We notice, for example, that some intelligent acts – a process of decision making or problem solving, for instance – can be represented as a hierarchical structure of simpler and simpler acts. True, this structure describes only hypothetical mental acts, and we don't know how to continue it down to the level of physical entities; and true, it explains only the simpler decision-making or problem-solving situations. But this is just the beginning; we are evidently making progress, and one day we will understand all levels and operations, and explain all intelligent behaviour.

The mechanists *start* with the assumption that the mind works like a machine, and then necessarily conclude that it can be explained as we explain the working of machines. They propose models based on reductionistic and atomistic principles, so they are committing the fallacy of assuming what in fact needs to be proved. For, the mind may or may not work like a machine; and if it does not, if it is a phenomenon like so many other natural phenomena that cannot be explained mechanistically, then their theories are bound to fail. The search for a mechanistic model of mind is, thus, a mechanistic delusion.

4

The futility of mechanistic mind models becomes obvious if we remember that they could work only if our mental processes were indeed simple structures. But the brain has evolved to help us cope with our natural environment, which consists of interacting phenomena. It has developed, as a result, the capacity for interacting structures, and this permits us to acquire knowledge that demands complex structures. We already know that complex structures cannot be reduced to simple ones, so a mechanistic model of mind can only *approximate* our mental capabilities. Like all mechanistic approximations, this can be done through reification: by extracting *one* of the simple structures that make up the complex knowledge structure. This method may yield useful approximations for our simple skills, when one knowledge structure is dominant and its interactions with the others can be ignored. But it is useless for our advanced capabilities, when the interactions between structures are important.

Thus, the logic we examined previously (whereby some hypothetical levels are assumed in order to explain the high-level processes in terms of low-level ones, and at the same time dismissed in order to account for the fact that only the low-level processes actually exist) works well for animal classifications, or cities, or machines. It works for these systems because we *purposely* design them as independent hierarchical structures. Specifically, we take into account *some* of the attributes possessed by their elements, and ignore the others; and we do this because we find the resulting approximation useful. In knowledge structures, though, *all* attributes are important, so this logic cannot explain the working of the mind. Mental acts cannot be usefully approximated with a neat structure of operations within operations, as an animal classification can with a structure of dogs within breeds, species, and genera; or as a city can with bricks within walls, buildings, streets, and districts; or as a machine can with components within modules and subassemblies.

Mechanistic mind models must reconcile the evident existence of trivial, low-level physiological processes, with the equally evident existence of complex intelligent acts. And they must accomplish this within the ideal of strict determinism; that is, with precise methods, diagrams, software, and the like. Given these requirements, the mind mechanists are compelled to commit the fallacy of reification, and all mind models end up alike: a hierarchical structure where some simple processes are the starting elements, and the complex intelligent acts are the top element. Some of these models may be very involved, but we must not let their sophistication deceive us. We already know that all deterministic theories – all models based on reductionism and atomism – are logically equivalent to simple hierarchical structures.

If the first fallacy (reification) is to represent the mind with a simple structure, the second fallacy (abstraction) is to use as starting elements relatively high-level entities: the mechanists stop their reductions of little men long before reaching the *basic* mental phenomena. No one knows what is the lowest level in mental phenomena, but even if we agree to take physiological entities like neurons as starting elements, the mechanists do not get anywhere near this level. Their starting elements are such entities as bits of knowledge, small behavioural acts, and simple logical operations; in other words, entities that are not at all basic mental phenomena. They defend their models by invoking the principles of reductionism and atomism, but at the same time they violate these principles and start from relatively high levels.

It is not surprising, therefore, that these models do not work. Mechanistic mind models fail to explain intelligence because their starting elements are not atomic and independent, as starting elements must be. In addition to the one structure that the mechanists recognize, these elements belong to many *other* structures, all formed from the elements that make up the *lower* levels – those levels that the mechanists ignore. The different values of the top element represent the various intelligent acts that the models must explain. And the models fail because they can account for only *some* of these values – those we would see if the starting elements were indeed atomic and independent. They cannot account for the many alternatives resulting from interactions occurring at the lower levels.

If all we want is to approximate some simple, specific mental capabilities – capabilities that can be isolated from the others – the search for mechanistic models may result in practical applications. But it is futile to search for mechanistic models capable of general intelligence, or for mechanistic theories that explain the working of the mind. This search is equivalent, in either case, to searching for a way to represent with simple structures the complex knowledge structures present in a mind – structures which can be acquired only by being a person, by having a body, by living in a society, and by engaging in the infinite variety of activities that make up a normal life. We cannot discover a model of mind because no such model can exist. The great capabilities of the mind arise largely from the knowledge structures that each one of us develops through personal experiences; that is, through exposure to a complex environment. A model of mind (as might be implemented with software, for example) cannot be exposed to such experiences, and therefore cannot attain the knowledge structures that make intelligence possible. Nor can we copy this kind of knowledge fully developed from a real mind into a model, any more than we can copy it from one mind into another.

When the mind mechanists seek to understand how the mind works, what exactly are they searching for? What do they expect to discover? Only a little reflection reveals that there is nothing to find; in a sense, we *already know* how the mind works. All we have to do is recognize that, when we perform an intelligent or skilful act, this act is not divisible into simpler acts. As Ryle points out again and again: "Overt intelligent performances are not clues to the workings of minds; they are those workings."[8]

We only run into trouble and keep searching for theories if we view the mind as a sort of machine instead of a natural phenomenon, and hence intelligence as a structure of operations within operations. It is this belief that tempts us to search for a model in the form of a simple structure. Consider other natural phenomena: The heavenly bodies simply move – they don't solve equations first. It is we who invented mathematical models to represent their motion. This phenomenon is in reality the complex result of many interacting processes, but we find the mathematical approximation useful. Biological phenomena too are the result of interacting processes, and they too manage to

[8] Ryle, *Concept of Mind*, p. 58.

occur without mathematics. It is we, again, who search for exact theories to explain them; but now we are less successful, because these phenomena are more complex than the physical ones, and cannot be usefully approximated with simple structures. The human mind is the most complex biological phenomenon. Mental acts are the result of countless interacting processes, and no useful approximation with simple structures is possible.

Tacit Knowledge

1

The best way to observe the development of non-mechanistic knowledge is by studying the process of skill acquisition. Natural skills like face recognition and language processing we practise continuously from the time we are born, and for this reason they may be difficult to assess. Special skills, however, we acquire all the time: using a tool, driving a car, playing a game, programming a computer – we all learn to perform a great variety of tasks. So the process of skill acquisition – that is, approaching a new type of challenge as novices and then improving our performance through personal experience – is a phenomenon we can readily observe in ourselves and in others. Moreover, we can examine this phenomenon for a wide range of skills, from those we master in a few hours to those we improve continually over the years.

Hubert Dreyfus and Stuart Dreyfus, in their comparison of human skills to computer capabilities, distinguish five stages in the process of skill acquisition: novice, advanced beginner, competent, proficient, and expert.[1] The most noticeable change as one progresses from novice to expert is the shift from rule-following, machine-like behaviour to an intuitive and holistic response. The novice responds to a given situation as if it were made up of simpler parts, and as if it could be decomposed into these parts, because his limited experience only permits him to recognize isolated parts. He is incapable, therefore, of responding intelligently to situations that are not a neat structure of simpler situations. The expert, who was exposed to thousands of situations in the past, has developed knowledge that permits him to cope with new situations directly. His mind, it seems, extracted from the previous situations a kind of knowledge that he can apply in new situations, although he cannot express this knowledge in the form of rules or methods.

As novices acquiring a new skill, we learn to identify specific facts relevant

---

[1] Hubert L. Dreyfus and Stuart E. Dreyfus, *Mind over Machine: The Power of Human Intuition and Expertise in the Era of the Computer* (New York: Free Press, 1988), ch. 1.

to that skill; and we also learn various rules or methods for the appropriate actions. The facts we identify are *context-free* elements, and we learn them as isolated bits of knowledge; namely, knowledge that can be used directly, without reference to the overall context.[2] Thus, as novices, all we can do is break down each situation into recognizable context-free elements, and act according to the rules we learned. At this stage we behave just as a computer does when executing the instructions defined in a program. For example, a novice driver applies standard rules of speed and distance without further consideration of particular traffic conditions; a novice physician attempts to diagnose a disease by matching mechanically the symptoms he observes with the rules he learned; a novice programmer writes small and isolated bits of software by following standard methods, and with no need to consider the broader context of the whole application.

We progress from the novice stage after contending with a large number of real-world situations. This experience increases the number and complexity of rules and context-free elements we know, but it does more than that. Through repeated exposure to similar situations, we learn to identify situations that only *resemble* those that can be identified through rules. For example, we can recognize an object or a face even from an angle from which we never saw it before; as drivers, we can cope with traffic situations that are only similar to previously encountered ones; as programmers, we can use a certain software concept even for a problem that we face for the first time.

This new capability greatly extends the range of situations that we can cope with, by allowing us to recognize *context-dependent*, or *situational* elements – elements that vary from one situation to another.[3] No rules can help us to identify situations that contain such elements; so we learn to recognize them directly, holistically. But we cannot tell *how* we do it. We cannot tell in what ways the new situation is different from previous ones. We do not recognize it by following rules, nor by breaking it down into simpler, familiar elements. We simply recognize it.

Another quality we acquire on the way to expertise is *personal involvement* in our acts. As novices we act in a *detached* manner: because all we do is follow rules provided by others, we do not feel committed, nor responsible for the outcome of our acts. As experienced performers we are deeply involved, because our acts are determined by our own experiences.[4] The new knowledge both affects and is affected by our other knowledge. Having performed those acts many times and under many different conditions, they become associated in our mind with many experiences. Eventually, we no longer think of the new knowledge as a distinct skill; it becomes part of ourselves: "An expert's skill has

[2] Ibid., p. 21.   [3] Ibid., p. 23.   [4] Ibid., p. 26.

become so much a part of him that he need be no more aware of it than he is of his own body."[5]

Along with personal involvement, it is the ability to act *intuitively* that increasingly distinguishes our performance as we gain expertise. Intuition, in this sense, does not mean wild guessing or supernatural inspiration. It is a practical, valuable know-how: the ability to respond intelligently, without following rules or methods, in complex situations. And we can develop this ability only by being exposed to many similar situations. We need to develop intuitive knowledge because most situations in a complex environment are not identical to some predefined, or previously encountered, situations; nor are they made up of simpler situations. The only way to act intelligently in complex situations, therefore, is by responding intuitively to whole patterns, including patterns we face for the first time. We must recognize these patterns without decomposing them into some constituent elements.[6]

An important point, thus, is that expert performance in any field entails intuitive knowledge. To put it differently, when following rules and methods we do *not* display the highest performance that human beings are capable of.

The process of skill acquisition can be summarized by saying that it is "the progression *from* the analytic behavior of a detached subject, consciously decomposing his environment into recognizable elements, and following abstract rules, *to* involved skilled behavior based on holistic pairing of new situations with associated responses produced by successful experiences in similar situations."[7]

A novice pilot uses the controls to guide the airplane; an expert pilot simply experiences flying: the controls, and even the airplane, become an extension to his body. A novice air traffic controller watching the blips on a radar screen interprets them analytically; an expert controller sees, in effect, the airplanes themselves. A novice chess player moves the pieces according to learned rules and strategies; a master player identifies with the game positions: he no longer sees himself as player, but as participant in a world of opportunities, threats, strengths, and weaknesses.[8]

Interestingly, when we attain expertise in a professional skill we behave just as we do when exercising *natural* skills – skills like walking, talking, or recognizing objects. We are all experts in natural skills: when we walk, we don't consciously control our legs following laws of balance; when we talk, we don't put together words following rules of grammar; we simply *perform* these activities. We have the opportunity to observe beginner levels in natural skills when studying the performance of people who suffer from mental disorders. Individuals suffering from agnosia, for example, have difficulty

---

[5] Ibid., p. 30.   [6] Ibid., pp. 28–29.   [7] Ibid., p. 35.   [8] Ibid., pp. 30–31.

recognizing familiar objects, and it is significant that their behaviour resembles the behaviour displayed by all of us when acquiring a new skill: they have to mentally break down each object into parts and features before recognizing it. These individuals fail to function adequately in everyday activities because they are restricted to analytical and logical behaviour. Without the capacity for intuitive and holistic thinking, they are forever novices in ordinary human skills.[9] Other interesting disorders are those of autistic and schizophrenic individuals (we will examine these cases in the next section).

Consider also the skill of visual perception. We learn to perceive the world around us while growing up, just as we learn to talk. But we cannot explain, for example, how we recognize objects – their shape, size, and distance – from the two-dimensional images they form on the retina; we do it effortlessly, intuitively. The only occasion we have to observe novice performance in this skill is when studying individuals who were born blind and begin to see late in life. These individuals must *learn* to distinguish objects visually, and they do it by analyzing them and memorizing their features. They behave just as we all do when acquiring a new skill.

The most important lesson from the study of skill acquisition is that a computer program cannot emulate the involved and intuitive performance of human beings. Since it is this kind of performance that we display when attaining expertise, we must conclude that computers, which are detached and analytic, cannot reach expert skill levels. Thus, in activities where a skill level lower than expertise is insufficient, human minds cannot be replaced with software. Programming, for instance, is such an activity; and this is why development systems – which are, in effect, attempts to replace programming expertise with software – fail to provide any measurable benefits.

2

A similar view was expressed by scientist and philosopher Michael Polanyi,[10] who called the kind of knowledge that can exist only in a mind – the knowledge that we can possess but cannot describe – *tacit* knowledge. (Tacit knowledge, then, is what I called complex, or non-mechanistic, knowledge.) Polanyi created a philosophy of knowledge that recognizes the participation of the subject in the process of knowing, as opposed to the traditional view that knowledge is always objective and impersonal. All knowledge, Polanyi says,

---

[9] Ibid., p. 64.
[10] Michael Polanyi, *Personal Knowledge: Towards a Post-Critical Philosophy*, corr. ed. (Chicago: University of Chicago Press, 1962).

has tacit aspects. Most importantly, tacit knowledge plays a part in our most rational pursuits, even in science. No science learning or practice, and no scientific discovery, would be possible if we were to rely exclusively on *specifiable* facts and methods.

Tacit knowledge manifests itself in that *"we can know more than we can tell."*[11] We have the capacity to develop and use complex knowledge structures, but we cannot explain how we do it: "We know a person's face and can recognize him among a thousand, indeed among a million. Yet we usually cannot tell how we recognize a face we know. There are many other instances of the recognition of a characteristic appearance – some commonplace, others more technical – which have the same structure as the identification of a person. University students are taught in practical classes to identify cases of diseases and specimens of rocks, plants and animals. This is the training of perception that underlies the descriptive sciences. The knowledge which such training transmits cannot be put into words, nor even conveyed by pictures; it must rely on the pupil's capacity to recognize the characteristic features of a physiognomy and their configuration in the physiognomy…. What the pupil must discover by an effort of his own is something we could not tell him. And he knows it then in his turn but cannot tell it…. [This] exemplifies not only that the subsidiary elements of perception may be unspecifiable, but shows also that such tacit knowledge can be *discovered*, without our being able to identify what it is that we have come to know. This holds equally for the learning of skills: we learn to ride a bicycle without being able to tell in the end how we do it."[12]

Scientism, we saw in chapter 1, is the attempt to apply in the human sciences the methods of the exact sciences. Modern scientists believe that phenomena related to living things can be precisely explained, just like mechanical phenomena, through reductionism and atomism. Accordingly, they reject the need for tacit knowledge in disciplines like psychology, physiology, and biology. But many of the phenomena related to living things are unspecifiable: we cannot find a mathematical theory that explains the whole of a plant or animal. These phenomena consist of interacting processes, which must be observed simultaneously; so the only way to study them is through direct observation of the phenomena themselves.

Our study of living things, therefore, must depend on our capacity for tacit learning and knowing, and ultimately on personal experience. Exact

---

[11] Michael Polanyi, *The Tacit Dimension* (Gloucester, MA: Peter Smith, 1983), p. 4.

[12] Michael Polanyi, "The Logic of Tacit Inference," in *Knowing and Being: Essays by Michael Polanyi*, ed. Marjorie Grene (Chicago: University of Chicago Press, 1969), p. 142 – paper originally published in *Philosophy* 41 (1966): 1–18.

theories cannot replace the tacit knowledge developed in the mind of each individual scientist: "Morphology, physiology, animal psychology – they all deal with comprehensive entities. None of these entities can be mathematically defined, and the only way to know them is by comprehending the coherence of their parts.... Our knowledge of biotic phenomena contains a vast range of unspecifiable elements, and biology remains, in consequence, a descriptive science heavily relying on trained perception. It is immeasurably rich in things we know and cannot tell.... An attempt to de-personalize our knowledge of living beings would result, if strictly pursued, in an alienation that would render all observations on living things meaningless. Taken to its theoretical limits, it would dissolve the very conception of life and make it impossible to identify living beings."[13]

What is true of biology is also true of those disciplines concerned with human behaviour and human societies. The complex human phenomena studied by these disciplines are the result of interacting processes that take place in the minds of individual subjects, and between different minds; and these interactions, we saw, cannot be precisely specified. Consequently, a scientist may get to understand some of these phenomena after observing them for a long time, while being unable to describe his knowledge to others. It is the tacit aspects of his knowledge that he cannot describe – those aspects that reflect the interactions.

The theories that attempt to reduce mental processes to exact models – in behaviourism and cognitive science, for example – claim in effect that it is possible to explain precisely and completely all human knowledge. They are bound to fail, though, because they ignore the tacit, unspecifiable aspects of knowledge.

The scientists who advance these theories believe that, if they can *recognize* certain processes which occur in other minds, they should be able to represent these processes with exact models. But *they* can recognize mental processes containing tacit aspects because *they themselves* have a mind, which in its turn is capable of developing tacit knowledge; so they can create similar processes in their own minds.[14] When attempting to express their knowledge about the other minds in the form of mathematical or software models, they must leave behind the tacit aspects, which can only exist in their minds – and of which, moreover, they are not even aware. The models, then, will represent only the *mechanistic* aspects of their knowledge, and will provide a poor approximation of it: "The claim of cybernetics to generate thought

---

[13] Ibid., pp. 150–152.

[14] It is, in fact, for this reason that we can communicate at all with one another and get to share knowledge, values, and traditions – complex phenomena rich in tacit aspects – while the actual communication is limited to simple structures like symbols and sounds.

and feelings rests ... on the assumption that mental processes consist in explicitly identifiable performances which, as such, would be reproducible by a computer. This assumption fails, because mental processes are recognized to a major extent tacitly, by dwelling in many particulars of behaviour that we cannot tell."[15]

Most significantly, tacit knowledge is essential even in the exact sciences. There are "unformalizable mental skills which we meet even in that citadel of exact science, that show-piece of strict objectivity, the classical theory of mechanics."[16] We can understand a mathematical theory only if we understand also the concepts underlying the theory, when and how to apply it, and so on. Being largely informal, this kind of knowledge cannot be represented with precise rules or methods. We cannot teach or learn it as we teach or learn the theory itself. We cannot reduce it to simpler elements, as we can the theory itself, leading ultimately to some basic atoms of knowledge. And yet, we must possess this kind of knowledge if we are to practise science at all. Scientists, evidently, acquire it and use it, although they cannot describe with precision what they acquire or how they do it. They do it simply by growing up in a particular society, by being part of a scientific community, by learning and practising within a certain cultural environment. On the whole, "the ideal of a strictly explicit knowledge is indeed self-contradictory; deprived of their tacit coefficients, all spoken words, all formulae, all maps and graphs, are strictly meaningless. An exact mathematical theory means nothing unless we recognize an inexact non-mathematical knowledge on which it bears and a person whose judgment upholds this bearing."[17]

Even though mathematics forms a perfect hierarchical structure, its fundamental principles – the terminal elements – are not atoms of absolute truth, but informal axioms and conventions. Concepts like *number* and *infinity*, for instance, can only be understood intuitively. The attempts to revolutionize mathematics by reducing it to logic, which gave rise to a large number of complicated theories in the first decades of the twentieth century, generally failed. Such attempts necessarily result in contradictions and circular arguments. For example, to avoid depending on our intuitive notion of what the number *one* means, the symbol "1" would be defined with a lengthy chain of expressions employing a formal symbolic language, but which depend in the end on an informal interpretation of words like "one." This is well understood today, but few scientists saw the futility of these projects at the time.

---

[15] Polanyi, "Tacit Inference," p. 152.

[16] Michael Polanyi, "The Unaccountable Element in Science," in *Knowing and Being*, ed. Grene, p. 106 – paper originally published in *Philosophy* 37 (1962): 1–14.

[17] Michael Polanyi, "Sense-Giving and Sense-Reading," in *Knowing and Being*, ed. Grene, p. 195 – paper originally published in *Philosophy* 42 (1967): 301–325.

In conclusion, "a mathematical theory can be constructed only by relying on *prior* tacit knowing and can function as a theory only *within* an act of tacit knowing, which consists in our attending *from* it to the previously established experience on which it bears."[18] And if mathematics depends on personal, informal knowledge, so must all science. Ultimately, all types of knowledge contain unspecifiable aspects: "*All knowledge falls into one of these two classes: it is either tacit or rooted in tacit knowledge.*"[19]

3

Let us see how the two kinds of skills we have been examining can be explained if we interpret the phenomenon of mind as the processing of simple and complex structures. Skills described as *knowing that*, and requiring only isolated, context-free bits of knowledge, arise from processing *simple* structures in the mind; so they reflect *mechanistic* capabilities. Skills described as *knowing how*, and requiring intuitive, tacit knowledge, arise from processing *complex* structures; so they reflect *non-mechanistic* capabilities. (See pp. 148–149, 157–158). The phenomena we are exposed to may be simple or complex. But the mind has the capacity to create replicas of both kinds of phenomena, so we can develop both kinds of knowledge.

The mind treats all phenomena the same way. Its function is to discover the structures that best depict the phenomena it is exposed to; in particular, the relations between the elements of these structures. For simple phenomena, it needs to discover only the relations *within* structures; but for complex phenomena, it discovers also those *between* structures. The mind, of course, doesn't "know" that some structures are simple and others complex; it discovers all relations the same way. But when the relations are between elements belonging to different structures, the result is non-mechanistic knowledge.

The relations cannot be acquired directly through the senses, but must be developed by the mind; and the mind can only develop them through repeated exposure to a particular phenomenon. The mind always starts by discovering the relations within the individual structures (because stronger or more common, perhaps); but after further exposure it also discovers the relations between elements of different structures.

This is indeed what we observe in the process of learning, when we acquire new knowledge and skills. At first, as novices, we develop the ability to deal with *isolated aspects* of the new knowledge – the simple structures. After gaining further experience, we can deal with larger parts – the complex

---

[18] Polanyi, *Tacit Dimension*, p. 21.   [19] Polanyi, "Sense-Giving," p. 195.

structures. To cope with situations where the interactions between structures are weak, we need to deal only with individual structures, so mechanistic knowledge suffices. But when the interactions are important, we need non-mechanistic knowledge.

I have stated that the mind can process both simple and complex structures, but in reality no knowledge structure can exist in the mind on its own, isolated from the others. Recall our conclusion in chapter 1: no phenomenon is totally isolated, so all phenomena surrounding us are complex structures. Since the brain has evolved to help us cope with our environment, the knowledge we develop in the mind must mirror the actual phenomena; so our knowledge too comprises only complex structures.

Even a basic concept like *one plus one is two*, which can be easily represented as a simple structure, cannot exist in the mind on its own – the way it might exist in a computer, for instance. It is precisely the fact that this concept can be related to others that allows the mind to combine it with existing knowledge structures. Thus, the only way to acquire and use this new concept is by relating it to concepts like *one, number,* and *addition,* by relating *these* concepts to the objects we add and to the effects of addition, and by relating then *these* concepts to others yet.

But, just as some phenomena in the world are only weakly related to others and can be usefully approximated with simple structures, so the knowledge structures in the mind form mutual links that are stronger or weaker, depending on the phenomena they mirror, and can sometimes be usefully approximated with simple structures. This is perhaps what leads the mind mechanists to believe that *all* knowledge can be represented with simple structures.

It is the interactions between structures that transform a group of isolated simple structures into a complex structure. This may be hard to understand, because it is precisely the interactions that cannot be completely described, as can the structures themselves. It is these interactions that define the complex phenomena, and hence also the knowledge structures which mirror these phenomena. It is not too much to say that in complex knowledge structures the interactions *are* the knowledge.

Consider, for example, the word "beauty," the abstract concept of beauty, and the way we recognize beauty. As children growing up in a particular culture we learn all these things, but we don't know how this happens. Clearly, these notions taken separately are meaningless. Can we learn how to recognize beautiful things without knowing that beauty can exist? Can we learn that beauty exists without knowing that we can refer to concepts like beauty with words? Can we learn the meaning of the word "beauty" without knowing already how to recognize beautiful things? The circle is endless. The way we learn about beauty as children is by learning all these notions at the same time. We usually have no difficulty learning about beauty, but if we had to write instructions for aliens, explaining how to recognize beautiful things, we wouldn't know how to do it. Nor can we program a computer to appreciate beauty as *we* do, although we can store the word "beauty" in its memory, and we can implement with software any facts or rules related to beauty. The reason for these difficulties is that most of our knowledge of beauty is contained, not in facts or rules, not in the isolated knowledge structures related to beauty, but in the *interactions* between these structures – and also in the interactions with *other* knowledge structures, for the concept of beauty is related to other concepts.

Human knowledge inheres mostly in the interactions between concepts, rather than in isolated facts and rules; and, unlike facts and rules, these interactions can seldom be specified completely and precisely. Complex knowledge, thus, can exist only in the phenomena themselves and in the mind. The only way to learn about beauty is by being exposed to the structures related to beauty and letting the mind discover the interactions. And we would reach the same conclusion if we analyzed any other concept. It is only when we forget how much of our knowledge is based on interacting structures that we try to imitate intelligence with deterministic models – which, no matter how sophisticated, can only represent simple structures.

The best way to appreciate the importance of these interactions is by studying the process of learning – the acquisition of knowledge. It is on such occasions that we notice how often the knowledge that develops in the mind is, in fact, several kinds of knowledge that are acquired together. The best-known case is that of language. All studies of linguistic skills conclude that language is inseparable from thinking and knowledge. As children, we learn to speak at the same time we learn everything else, and it is generally agreed that intelligence and verbal ability grow together. We must have the capacity to learn the word for beauty and how to recognize beauty at the same time, otherwise we could learn neither.

As already noted, acquiring natural skills early in life is similar to acquiring professional and general skills as adults, but this latter process we can more readily observe and study. Thus, a process similar to the acquisition of linguistic knowledge together with other knowledge takes place whenever we have to communicate in order to develop a complex skill. Polanyi takes the interpretation of chest X-rays as example.[20] A medical student learns to diagnose pulmonary diseases from X-ray pictures by observing diverse cases while listening to an expert radiologist comment on the various features in technical language. Since both the pictures and the verbal descriptions are unintelligible to a novice, they must be learned together.

At first, the student is completely puzzled, for all he can see is light and dark patches; he cannot even distinguish the lungs, let alone the disease. He listens to the expert's explanations, but he can see in the pictures nothing of what the expert is describing. After several weeks, however, after studying in this fashion many different cases, the X-ray pictures slowly turn into a rich panorama of significant details: physiological variations and signs of disease. And then the student also begins to understand the expert's explanations. Although he still sees only a fraction of what an expert can see, both the pictures and the comments are beginning to make sense: "Thus, at the very moment when he has learned the language of pulmonary radiology, the student will also have learned to understand pulmonary radiograms. The two can only happen together. Both halves of the problem set to us by an unintelligible text, referring to an unintelligible subject, jointly guide our efforts to solve them, and they are solved eventually together by *discovering* a conception which comprises a *joint understanding* of both the words and the things."[21]

The process whereby an expert interprets X-ray pictures cannot be separated into two distinct structures – the technical description of X-ray pictures, and the identification of lung physiology and disease. Nor is the description a structure *within* the identification, or the identification a structure *within* the description. The process of interpretation and diagnosis is the *interaction* of these structures (and probably other structures too), and this complex knowledge structure can only exist in a mind. The experienced radiologist cannot convey his expertise to the student directly, because he can only communicate with the student through the simple structures of images and descriptions. The knowledge, therefore, must develop in the mind of each student through personal experience; it consists in the complex structure that is the *combination* of those structures.

I want to conclude this discussion with another example of tacit knowledge: the unusual skill of chick sexing – determining the sex of newly born chicks.

---

[20] Polanyi, *Personal Knowledge*, p. 101.   [21] Ibid. (italics added).

The reason it is important to sort chicks as early as possible is that egg producers need only pullets, so it is uneconomical to grow both pullets and cockerels. The differences at birth are very subtle, though, so the sorting accuracy of an unskilled person is not much better than 50 percent – the equivalent of guessing. Some recognition rules *have* been developed, based on anatomical details; but because each detail individually is unreliable, the best accuracy that a worker can achieve by following these rules is about 70 percent. Speed in this work is as important as accuracy, and sorters who merely follow rules cannot improve their speed either.

The Japanese, however, discovered in the 1920s that experienced sorters could achieve much better results by relying entirely on intuition. After sorting more than a million chicks, these workers had learned to distinguish chicks almost instantly and very accurately. But they were doing it through a combination of visual and tactile clues of which they themselves were unaware; that is, they could not explain what it was that they had learned to recognize. Their expertise, therefore, could not benefit other workers. So the way a novice could acquire this skill remained unchanged: sorting a large number of chicks and developing the same intuition. With intuitive sorting, an expert can attain rates exceeding one thousand chicks per hour, with an accuracy of 98 percent.

Following its success in Japan, the method of intuitive sorting was adopted all over the world. It is still being practised, but it is becoming less and less important, as chick hatchers now prefer breeds in which the chicks can be distinguished by their feathers (so they can be easily sorted even by unskilled workers).

Much studied by psychologists, this skill is an excellent example of tacit knowledge. Although the recognition process remains a mystery, it is probably similar in nature to other skills that involve intuitive pattern recognition – recognizing faces, for instance (see pp. 110–111). Since an expert sorter needs only about three seconds (which includes the handling operations), he is presumably distinguishing the chick immediately, the way we recognize a familiar face. So this *must* be an intuitive act; the sorter is not merely applying some recognition rules quickly.

Also, the learning process itself must be intuitive. There isn't much that an experienced worker can teach an apprentice, apart from confirming whether he was right or wrong about a particular chick. And this, indeed, is how workers are trained. Each apprentice, therefore, must discover on his own, unconsciously, the various patterns; and he does it simply by examining a large number of chicks. So the learning process, too, is similar to face recognition: we learn to recognize faces simply by seeing them many times.

Let us say that there are hundreds of basic variations in chick anatomy, and perhaps even some variations within the basic ones. Even so, a worker who examines millions of chicks will come across each variation many times, and will eventually develop in his mind a set of familiar patterns. He will learn to distinguish these variations, just as we all learn to recognize hundreds of faces after seeing them repeatedly. And he cannot tell what it is that he learned to recognize, any more than we can tell how we recognize those faces. Perhaps the set of familiar patterns in his mind includes only the basic variations, and he recognizes the other patterns as variations of the basic ones – the way we recognize a familiar face from different angles.

The process of face recognition, we saw, is a complex structure: it entails several interacting recognition processes (simple structures). Similarly, we can think of several structures that make up the chick anatomy, so the process of distinguishing a chick must include several structures; for example, recognizing relations between the sizes, shapes, or proportions of some chick parts, or relations between these relations, and so on. These structures interact, because they exist at the same time and share their elements – the chick parts. This makes the whole recognition process a complex structure.

To follow recognition rules, a worker needs only mechanistic knowledge. This permits him to recognize *separately* the individual structures, and his performance is restricted to those patterns obvious enough to identify in this manner; that is, those for which the links between structures can be ignored. When attaining expertise, the worker's knowledge includes the *interactions* between structures. His performance improves because this complex knowledge permits him to recognize additional patterns – those for which the links between structures are important.

4

The study of unusual skills like chick sexing demonstrates that seemingly mysterious capabilities can be accounted for through the concept of tacit knowledge. These skills are striking because they are unusual – we would find similar capabilities if we studied *normal* activities. Normal skills are more difficult to observe, though, because we practise them all the time and take them for granted. We acquire them naturally and effortlessly while growing up, and this is why we are liable to forget that they are in fact important and impressive skills.

It is when artificial intelligence researchers fail to simulate with software what are for us simple, everyday tasks, that we are reminded how important is our *unspecifiable* knowledge. Thus, an unusual skill that can be acquired under controlled conditions stands out and provides a striking example of tacit knowledge, but we must bear in mind that it merely brings to attention what are in reality *normal* human capabilities.

The fact that we can acquire unusual skills also casts doubt on the theories that postulate *specialized* higher mental functions. Although we cannot doubt that all mental acts are based ultimately on the physiological characteristics of the brain, and that there exist specialized functions at the *lower* cognitive levels, we have no reason to assume that we need a great variety of mental processes to produce intelligent behaviour. Since we can acquire so many skills (skills as diverse as distinguishing chicks, interpreting X-rays, and programming computers), it is unlikely that we use specialized mental functions for any one of them, and more likely that we possess some *generic* mental capabilities, which take part in *all* mental acts. If we use generic capabilities to acquire one skill, then why not others? If we use them for chick recognition, why not also for face recognition, which seems so similar? And why not also for linguistic skills, and for all other intelligent acts?

No one would seriously suggest that we possess an innate chick sexing faculty, because then we would have to conclude that we possess a separate faculty for every other skill that we can acquire. Yet this is precisely what many theories of mind suggest. Chomskyan linguistics, for example, confidently assumes that we possess an innate *language* faculty. But if we can perform remarkable mental feats in diverse areas without specialized mental functions, why do we need specialized functions for language? Our linguistic capabilities are so closely linked to other mental capabilities that it is for language, particularly, that we do *not* need to postulate specialized functions. We certainly have a faculty for language; but this is the same faculty that takes part in visual perception, in understanding music, in driving cars, in programming computers, and in every other intelligent act. (See pp. 270–273.)

The mind mechanists cannot deny the role played by tacit knowledge in intelligent behaviour, but they refuse to accept it as an irreducible mental process. All their attempts to reduce tacit knowledge to simpler knowledge, however, have failed. Our non-mechanistic model of mind is less ambitious: if there is so much evidence both for the existence of tacit knowledge and for the existence of mental capabilities common to all forms of intelligence, we are content with a model that incorporates these two facts. The mechanistic models fail because they attempt to explain mental acts by treating them as isolated processes: simple hierarchical structures of operations, relations, and bits of knowledge. Our model represents the working of the mind as one complex structure – countless interacting structures. In practice, we can often approximate it with *separate* complex structures; we can treat one skill, for example, as several interacting knowledge structures, but without relating it to all the structures that make up the mind. And sometimes we can even approximate mental acts with isolated *simple* structures; in this reduced version, the model works as a mechanistic one.

Tacit knowledge is the knowledge that can develop only in a mind, and is therefore unspecifiable; it is knowledge that manifests itself in that "we can know more than we can tell." In our model, this knowledge is embodied in the *interactions* between structures. We can acquire and express knowledge only if it is specifiable, only as simple structures (in the form of symbols or sounds, for instance). Our communication with the world is limited, therefore, to mechanistic processes. The interactions that develop in the mind are a reflection of the interactions that exist in the complex phenomena we are exposed to. When we learn something, the mind creates an approximate replica of the phenomenon by discovering the interactions; later, when we perform an intelligent act, the mind uses the interactions found in that replica. The interactions can exist only in the phenomenon itself and in the mind; they cannot be transmitted directly between the mind and the environment through our senses or bodies.

So what we notice as intuition is the external manifestation of tacit knowledge, an expression of the interactions. It is impossible to explain intuition by taking into consideration only the simple structures we detect in our environment. This is why we cannot explain, for example, how we recognize faces, or distinguish chicks, or communicate with language. But if we describe intuitive knowledge as a complex structure, the interactions provide the critical pieces needed to account for the intelligent acts. The model, however, cannot explain the interactions themselves: complex structures cannot be reduced to a precise and complete description of their constituent simple structures, plus a precise and complete description of their interactions.

This is an informal model. But we don't need a more precise one, because, unlike the mechanistic models, ours is not intended to *explain* intelligence. Its purpose, on the contrary, is to show that it is *impossible* to explain mental acts with exact theories, as we explain the working of machines. Its purpose, in other words, is to show that the principles of reductionism and atomism alone cannot account for intelligence. What this model claims, in effect, is that there can be no deterministic model of mind – no model that can be implemented with tools like mathematics or software. It claims that the concept of complex structures is the only way to account for the phenomenon of mind, and complex structures can exist only as natural phenomena; we can describe them, but we cannot implement them with mechanistic means.

Creativity

1

Unusual mental capabilities like technical talent, poetic ingenuity, and appreciating art or humour do not appear to have much in common. They are closely
related, however, insofar as they can all be described with a model of mind that
takes into account the interaction of knowledge structures. Moreover, when
studying these unusual capabilities we recognize that they are caused, in fact,
by the same mental processes that give rise to *normal* performance. What
we will learn from their study, therefore, is this: if we cannot explain or
emulate *extreme* capabilities, we cannot hope to explain or emulate *normal*
intelligence either. When observed from the lower levels of mental processes,
the performance of a genius is not very different from that of an average
person. The mind always works the same way, and the difference between the
extremes of mental capabilities is smaller than it appears.

The mind mechanists keep inventing models that emulate trivial mental
acts, in the belief that these models will be improved later to handle complex
tasks. Our study, however, will challenge this principle. A mechanistic model
may succeed in emulating an isolated mental act, but without emulating the
capabilities of the mind. (A calculator, for instance, can add numbers correctly
without understanding the meaning of addition as *we* do.) Thus, there is no
reason why a model that emulates simple mental acts, but working differently
from a human mind, should reach even an average level of intelligence later,
when improved.

❖

In our discussion of intelligence and creativity we encounter frequently the
term *context*. We find, for example, that intelligent behaviour must take the
context into account, or that the correct interpretation of an item depends
on the context. While the notion of context – in the sense of situation, or
conditions, or circumstances – is well understood, I want to take a moment to
show how it fits within the model of complex structures. Then, we will be able
to refer to contexts in the study of intelligence and creativity without having to
interpret them as structures each time.

Recall the discussion of complex structures in chapter 1 (pp. 98–100).
The entities that function as elements in structures have a large number of
attributes; and each attribute relates them in a particular way to other entities,
thereby forming one simple structure. A physical object, for example, has a
shape, a colour, a weight, a date of creation, an owner, and so forth; it belongs,

therefore, to several structures of objects at the same time – a different structure for each attribute. And these structures interact, because they share their elements – those objects.

A context can be seen as a set of attributes, not unlike the regular attributes of an entity, but which exist *in addition* to the regular ones. The context includes attributes related to time and space (day or night, summer or winter, indoor or outdoor, a specific room or building), to a social setting (a specific town, a public place, the company of friends), to a personal situation (being in a good mood, or sick, or frightened), and so on. Thus, the context attributes are generally *more variable* than the regular ones. It is obvious that, as is the case with the regular attributes, the number of attributes that determine a context can be very large. It is also obvious that an entity *must* have some attributes that determine a context, in addition to its regular attributes, which remain the same from one context to the next. Just as its regular attributes place the entity in various structures and relate it to other entities that have those attributes, the context attributes place it in other structures yet.

This model explains why the context plays such an important part in the interpretation of a given situation. We already know that any entity is an element of a complex structure. But now we see that this structure includes, in addition to the structures formed by its regular attributes, which are constant, the structures formed by the *context* attributes, which are changeable. This makes the entity a somewhat different entity in different contexts, just as a change in its regular attributes (its shape or colour, for instance) would make it a different entity. To interpret correctly an object, or an event, or a process, its current context is as important as are its physical attributes, or its uses, or its effects. Because of the changing nature of the context attributes, we need greater knowledge to cope with the complex structure when it includes a context, than we do when the context is unimportant, or when something always occurs in the same context. The reason, obviously, is that we have to deal with more structures.

Recall also the observation we made earlier on the acquisition of skills. As novices, we start by recognizing only the *context-free* aspects of a new domain – the structures reflecting attributes that remain the same in all contexts. As we gain expertise, however, we learn to recognize also the *context-dependent* aspects of that domain – those structures that include the context attributes. (See p. 158.) The process of skill acquisition entails, therefore, an increase in our ability to recognize complex structures *and* their variations in different contexts; in other words, the ability to cope with structures that are more and more complex.

2

When we think of creativity, we usually think of outstanding accomplishments in science, art, music, poetry, or literature. Creativity in these fields, however, is only one aspect of a wide range of intelligent performance – a range that includes normal, everyday activities. We may not realize it, but we have to be creative just to behave normally. When the mechanistic models of mind fail to display what is called common-sense knowledge and understanding, it is human creativity that they cannot reproduce.

Much has been written on creativity, and a frequent observation is that a creative act produces something totally new, yet relatively simple. What is striking is the novelty, not the complexity, of the result. It is as if the mind searched through a large number of combinations of pieces of knowledge and retrieved a combination that did not exist before. The combination is not random, but especially interesting, or useful, or attractive.

Here is how Jerome Bruner expresses this view: "An act that produces *effective surprise* – this I shall take as the hallmark of a creative enterprise.... Surprise is not easily defined. It is the unexpected that strikes one with wonder or astonishment."[1] Whether the creation consists in a scientific discovery, a work of art, a poem, or a solution to a mundane problem, when we try to explain the new concept we find that it can always be described as a combination of *existing* concepts. On analysis, there are no new facts in the new concept. If we want to describe it as new knowledge, the knowledge is in the combination, not in the individual facts: "I would propose that all of the forms of effective surprise grow out of combinatorial activity – a placing of things in new perspectives."[2] In literature, a great story may be nothing more than novel combinations of human qualities and situations. A poem may be largely new metaphors, words and meanings combined in original and imaginative ways. A technological discovery may be simply a novel combination of processes and applications.

Henri Poincaré,[3] who studied the process of discovery in mathematics, observes that the discovery of new laws is like searching through many combinations of known facts and principles until the right combination is found. The search and selection are performed by the unconscious mind, although they must be preceded and followed by conscious work. But the mind

---

[1] Jerome S. Bruner, *On Knowing: Essays for the Left Hand*, rev. ed. (Cambridge, MA: Harvard University Press, 1979), p. 18.   [2] Ibid., p. 20.
[3] Henri Poincaré, *Science and Method* (New York: Dover, 1952).

does not work like a machine: "It is not merely a question of applying certain rules, of manufacturing as many combinations as possible according to certain fixed laws. The combinations so obtained would be extremely numerous, useless, and encumbering. The real work of the discoverer consists in choosing between these combinations with a view to eliminating those that are useless, or rather not giving himself the trouble of making them at all. The rules which must guide this choice are extremely subtle and delicate, and it is practically impossible to state them in precise language; they must be felt rather than formulated."[4]

All we can tell is that the combinations generated in the mind "are those which, directly or indirectly, most deeply affect our sensibility."[5] Thus, they reflect the knowledge already present in the mind: a mathematician is sensible to combinations that may result in a new mathematical law, while a poet is sensible to combinations that may result in a new metaphor. Discovery is an act of selection – the selection of facts "which reveal unsuspected relations between other facts, long since known, but wrongly believed to be unrelated to each other.... Among the combinations we choose, the most fruitful are often those which are formed of elements borrowed from widely separated domains."[6]

We can summarize these remarks by saying that discovery is the creation of links between knowledge structures that existed previously in the mind but were unrelated. The mind does not *generate* combinations of concepts, of course, and does not *select* combinations, although this may be a useful way of picturing the process of discovery. The combinations are the interactions between structures, which always exist. As we saw earlier, all knowledge structures in the mind are connected as part of one complex structure, but most links are very weak. So the mind can be viewed as a combination of many *separate* complex structures, formed where the links are stronger. The selection that is the act of discovery occurs when the links *between* some structures strengthen; and this typically follows a period of intensive mental activity involving those structures. At that point, a new complex structure is formed.

Bruner notes a similar process in artistic creativity. Works of art like paintings and sculptures achieve their effect by connecting two disparate mental structures: themes or contexts that normally evoke entirely different, even contradictory, feelings. A great work of art manages to accomplish this with economy, using a "compact image or symbol that, by its genius, travels great distances to connect ostensible disparities."[7] One theme, for instance, may be rooted in pragmatic, common-sense knowledge, while the other may

[4] Ibid., p. 57.   [5] Ibid., p. 58.   [6] Ibid., p. 51.
[7] Bruner, *On Knowing*, p. 65.

be a fantasy; the work of art creates then in our mind a new experience, which is the fusion of the two existing ones: "An image is created connecting things that were previously separate in experience, an image that bridges rationality and impulse."[8]

But it is not enough that the *artist* link those structures; we, the beholders, must participate, through individual effort. The artist can communicate with us only through separate images (i.e., simple structures). We must *discover* the links between these images, and the act of discovery constitutes the artistic experience. The difference between great and mediocre art is that great art makes it easy for us to discover the links: "Where art achieves its genius is in providing an image or a symbol whereby the fusion can be comprehended and bound."[9] Comprehending art is a creative act: we must *relive*, as best we can, the original creative act of the artist. And the only way to do this is through a process similar to the process of learning we examined in the previous section: we expose ourselves to the phenomenon and let our mind discover the links between structures, thus creating a new knowledge structure, similar to the one that existed in the artist's mind.

We cannot discuss creativity without mentioning the process of metaphoric thinking. Metaphors are phrases employed in a figurative rather than a literal sense. Metaphors, thus, attempt to connect two knowledge structures on the basis of a relation that is normally very weak, even illogical. Some examples: "time flies" (can time pass faster than normal?), "warm colour" (can colours have a temperature?), "flood of tears" (can a few drops cause an inundation?).

Clearly, then, metaphoric thinking – at work both when inventing and when comprehending metaphors – depends on our capacity to connect knowledge structures that have little in common. But, as we have already seen, this is the mental capability we display when acting creatively. Comprehending metaphors, as much as inventing them, is an act of creativity, of discovery. The metaphor does not work by *connecting* the structures in our mind, but by inviting us to *discover* the connection. Poetry, for instance, is largely metaphoric language, and what makes it enjoyable is the opportunity it affords us to discover new connections. Were these connections *explained*, rather than expressed through metaphors, reading poems would constitute an entirely different experience.

Bruner suggests that the metaphoric mode of thinking is a creative act common to art and science, so scientific discovery and artistic creation have a lot in common.[10] Now we see, though, that it is more accurate to say that scientific discovery, artistic creation, and metaphoric expression are all rooted in a fundamental mental process: combining knowledge structures.

[8] Ibid., p. 62.   [9] Ibid., p. 72.   [10] Ibid., pp. 65–66.

❖

Arthur Koestler[11] is another thinker who found that all forms of creativity derive from the connection of previously independent mental structures. He coined the term *bisociation* for this process, distinguishing it from what takes place within *individual* structures, where only previously established facts, rules, and relations are involved: "The term 'bisociation' is meant to point to the independent, autonomous character of the matrices which are brought into contact in the creative act, whereas associative thought operates among members of a single pre-existing matrix."[12] Koestler uses various terms to convey the idea of mental structures: frames of reference, associative contexts, types of logic, codes of behaviour, universes of discourse, and matrices of thought.[13] He shows how such diverse acts as scientific discovery, aesthetic experience, poetic expression, and understanding humour can be explained as different external manifestations of the same basic mental process. There is a similarity, for instance, "between the scientist seeing an analogy where nobody saw one before, and the poet's discovery of an original metaphor or simile.... In the scientist's [discovery] process two previously unconnected frames of reference are made to intersect, but the same description may be applied to the poet's ... discovery of a felicitous poetic comparison."[14]

Koestler includes humour in the range of creative acts, since understanding comical situations – jokes, satire, irony, wit, puns – is in effect an act of discovery.[15] Like the other types of creativity, humour is due to new connections formed between existing mental structures. In scientific discovery, we saw, two previously independent structures are combined and become one. The same thing happens in art and poetry, but here the relation between the two structures remains tenuous: they represent opposing themes, like reality and fantasy, so we can only *imagine* the new combined structure. In the case of humour, the two structures are totally incompatible; they represent different contexts, so they cannot be logically combined at all.

The pattern underlying all types of humour is this: We are exposed first to one structure, which creates a certain context and certain expectations; then, we are exposed to the second structure, which creates an entirely different context. Our mind attempts to combine the two, but this is impossible. Whereas mentally we can quickly shift from one context to the other, emotionally we cannot, and the tension created by this conflict is released through the reflex action of laughter or smiling. The structures are perfectly logical on their own, but they represent incompatible contexts. Individually, they evoke

---

[11] Arthur Koestler, *The Act of Creation* (New York: Macmillan, 1964).

[12] Ibid., p. 656.   [13] Ibid., p. 38.   [14] Ibid., p. 320.   [15] Ibid., chs. I–IV.

simple, logical, well-known situations; it is their unrelatedness that causes the tension.

Almost any pair of unrelated contexts can be used to produce humour. The simplest kind of humour is created by using words or phrases with double meaning (for example, one literal and the other figurative, or one in common usage and the other in specialized usage). Comic situations can be created with coincidences, cases of mistaken identity, or confusion of time and occasion – all causing the collision of incompatible contexts. The opposition between man and machine, the human and the automaton, has a long tradition in humour (for example, Charlie Chaplin's classic scenes in *Modern Times*). Mind and matter form another successful opposition (for example, the absent-minded genius bumping into a lamppost – the great mind defeated by a simple object).

In jokes, the opposition between two contexts may be more subtle, but it is still the source of their humour. Here is an example: In a store, the check-out line is long and slow, and a man at the end of the line loses his patience. "I am going to complain to the manager," he tells his neighbour, and leaves. A moment later he returns and takes his place back in line. "What happened?" inquires his neighbour. "The line of people waiting to complain to the manager," he explains, "is even longer." Why do we find this amusing? We are asked to combine two incompatible contexts: one is the situation of a long waiting line and the expectation of a resolution – familiar and logical; the other is the situation of a person choosing the shorter of two waiting lines – also familiar and logical, but the two contexts clash.

Here is another example: A man in a restaurant tells the waiter, "Please bring me a coffee without cream"; and the waiter replies, "Sorry, sir, we have no cream. May I bring you instead a coffee without milk?" One context here is the familiar situation of a person preferring black coffee, and the other is the equally familiar situation of a waiter suggesting a substitute for an item. The two situations are logical individually, but their combination is senseless.

3

We have identified the combination of knowledge structures as the mental process that leads to creativity. And, while easy to observe in the work of exceptional minds – in science, art, or poetry – the same process occurs in lesser mental acts: in the acts performed by any one of us when appreciating art or humour, when using words in a figurative sense, and, in the end, when engaged in any intelligent activity. Another way to confirm the importance of interacting knowledge structures is by noting what happens when there is a deficiency in processing these structures, in individuals suffering from mental disorders. We saw that researchers who study creativity reach a mind model based on interacting structures; it should not surprise us, therefore, that researchers who study mental disorders also reach such a model.

The term *schizophrenia* (literally, split mind), introduced in 1908 by Eugen Bleuler, expresses his observation that patients behave as if their thought processes were separated and could not be combined properly. Bleuler suggested that the mental processes of schizophrenics are fundamentally similar to those of normal persons; these processes differ only under certain conditions, and then the difference is nothing more than a failure to respond appropriately to a particular situation. The problem is not that the schizophrenic is incapable of certain thought patterns, but that he is unable to match his thoughts to the current context. If the mind works by combining structures, then schizophrenia can be described as a disorder that prevents the mind from connecting structures as a normal mind does: it fails to connect a particular structure to others, or connects it to the wrong ones. This results in behaviour that appears strange when judged by accepted standards. In extreme cases, the schizophrenic cannot function adequately in society.

The failure of schizophrenics to connect mental structures is described by psychiatrists with such terms as "disconnectedness," "thought blocking," "concreteness," and "overinclusive thinking."[16] The term "reification" is sometimes used – the term we adopted for the fallacy of ignoring the interactions in a complex structure. The following examples show that seemingly unrelated disorders can be traced to the same deficiency if we use a mind model based on interacting structures.[17]

The world of the schizophrenic is fragmented. Patients report that they are flooded with thoughts and sensations, and cannot put the pieces together into a coherent pattern. They notice the colour or the shape of an object, rather than simply *seeing* the object. They notice in turn the eyes or nose or hair of a person, rather than the face as a whole. They notice isolated words when reading a book or in a conversation, and fail to grasp the meaning of the whole sentence. They are distracted by small details – details that normal individuals integrate tacitly into whole patterns; they are disturbed by irrelevant background sounds, for instance, or they become acutely aware of mild sensations or parts of their own body. Many schizophrenics find it impossible to watch television, because they cannot connect the image and sound into a coherent whole – they have to concentrate on one or the other; also, they are confused by images or sounds that are too complex or change too fast, since they can only

---

[16] E. Fuller Torrey, *Surviving Schizophrenia: A Family Manual* (New York: Harper and Row, 1985), p. 17; Theodore Lidz, *The Origin and Treatment of Schizophrenic Disorders* (Madison, CT: International Universities Press, 1990), p. 54.

[17] The examples are from Torrey, *Surviving Schizophrenia*, pp. 8–22 passim.

assimilate them a bit at a time. They fail to put together all the sensory data in a typical social situation: they notice each movement and word separately, so the people's behaviour appears strange to them. An action as simple as getting a drink of water can become a problem, as the schizophrenic must concentrate on each step and detail – hold cup, turn tap, fill cup, drink water. Delusions and hallucinations, the best-known symptoms of schizophrenia, can be explained as the failure to integrate mental structures and sensations correctly; they are "a direct outgrowth of overacuteness of the senses and the brain's inability to synthesize and respond appropriately to stimuli."[18]

At each moment, our mind processes many external stimuli and internal thought patterns, but normally it has no difficulty combining these structures into the most appropriate complex structure. It is this capacity to connect new bits of knowledge, and also to connect them to previous knowledge, that is impaired in schizophrenic minds. The disturbance may affect vision, or hearing, or touch, or thoughts, or emotions, or actions, but the underlying deficiency is the same: the schizophrenic mind can only process one structure at a time. Within each structure, it can be as good as a normal mind. But we cannot function adequately in everyday situations without the capacity to connect structures, because most situations consist of interacting structures.

Even more interesting is the tendency of schizophrenics to connect mental structures *incorrectly* (rather than not at all), a disorder described as loose associations, or derailment of associations.[19] This disorder is interesting because, in addition to affecting their thought patterns, it is seen in their language; it serves thus to support the thesis that the phenomenon of language involves all knowledge structures present in the mind.

The language of schizophrenics often includes jumbled words, as they fail to match words and thoughts. While being highly significant to the patient, sentences may be incomprehensible to others. Schizophrenics also tend to interpret all language literally, so they have difficulty with sentences where words are used figuratively. They cannot appreciate the meaning of proverbs, for example, as they attempt to interpret them literally.[20] Metaphoric language, we saw, relies on the mind's capacity to connect knowledge structures that are only weakly related; and this capacity is limited in schizophrenics. Alternatively, their own language may appear metaphoric, when they create meaningless connections.

Autism is another disorder that can be described as a failure of the mind to combine structures correctly. Autistic individuals "cannot easily understand

---

[18] Ibid., p. 23.   [19] Ibid., p. 17; Lidz, *Schizophrenic Disorders*, p. 53.
[20] J. S. Kasanin, ed., *Language and Thought in Schizophrenia* (New York: W. W. Norton, 1964), pp. 72–88; Torrey, *Surviving Schizophrenia*, p. 19.

language that is flippant or witty, and … instead they are excessively literal.… Sometimes their comments are perceived as inappropriate by others, as rude or as funny, or else over-polite."[21] This is because they have difficulty matching their response to the current context.

Whereas the normal mind can form coherent wholes by correctly combining mental structures, this capacity is diminished in autistic individuals. Their behaviour, as a result, is characterized by detachment.[22] In isolated situations they may perform as well as, or even better than, normal individuals; but when the correct response depends on recognizing the broader context, their behaviour appears strange: "In everyday life we cannot afford too many errors of literal interpretations; we seek interpretations that are coherent within a wider context that takes in social and cultural experiences."[23]

4

What conclusions can we draw from this analysis? In the previous section, in our discussion of learning and skill acquisition, we noted that we can explain all forms of intelligent behaviour through the phenomenon of tacit knowledge, and that this phenomenon can be represented as a system of interacting structures. Thus, the mind's capacity for complex structures is all we need in order to account for our capability to acquire diverse skills. Now a different study of mental performance takes us to the same mind model: we explained diverse forms of creativity as the capacity to process complex structures; and we saw that even a slight deficiency in this capacity is immediately noticeable as mental disorder, and prevents a person from behaving normally. We must conclude, therefore, that we benefit from this capacity not only when exceptionally creative, but also in ordinary activities. The knowledge that allows us to cope with everyday situations, as much as the knowledge responsible for great feats of creativity, is grounded on the mind's capacity for complex structures.

Only a model based on interacting structures can account for what we know about the mind. By adopting this model, we affirm that no *mechanistic* models of mind are possible. In our model, mental acts are complex structures, and complex structures cannot be reduced to simple ones. This model claims, therefore, that mental acts cannot be reduced to simpler operations.

The mind mechanists claim the opposite: the mind works like a machine, they say, and can be emulated with models based on algorithms, rules, and

---

[21] Uta Frith, *Autism: Explaining the Enigma* (Oxford: Blackwell, 1989), p. 134.
[22] Ibid., p. 100.   [23] Ibid., p. 178.

databases of facts; it is true that today's models display only limited intelligence, but there is no reason why they cannot be improved. By putting together what we have just learned about the mind, however, we can demonstrate the absurdity of this idea.

If we think of the mind as a sort of machine, we will inevitably conclude that the capabilities we observe from outside are a reflection of the complexity of the internal processes: as in a machine, the more sophisticated the mind processes, the more intelligent the resulting acts will be. This is why the mind mechanists attempt to improve the performance of their models by refining the algorithms, increasing the number of stored facts and rules, and so on. This, after all, is how we improve our machines, or our software systems. If today the models can only emulate minds of very low intelligence, the mechanists say, we will find ways to improve them, just as we improve everything else we build. The models will progress, one step at a time, through the entire range of capabilities – from low to normal to superior intelligence.

This is their expectation, but when we analyze the mind's performance we realize that this expectation is unwarranted. For, the mind's performance cannot be rated using a scale of capabilities. We do not recognize any processes in the mind that change as the mind's capabilities increase. On the contrary, we find the same processes in a deficient mind as we do in a normal or superior mind. The capabilities displayed by these minds overlap. The only quality that differentiates them is an ability to create the right connections between knowledge structures; and what determines the right connections depends largely on phenomena external to the mind, and which, moreover, cannot be defined with precision.

Thus, it is impossible to improve the performance of a mind model by enhancing its capabilities, because the chief determinant of performance is not its capabilities but its interaction with the environment to which it is exposed. We note that a superior mind is more likely to connect the right knowledge structures, but we cannot define this capacity in terms of some internal mental processes. What we find, in other words, is that the mind's tremendous information processing capability, impressive as it is, does not explain intelligence. What gives rise to intelligent performance is the fact that the mind belongs to a human being who has a body, grows up in a society, and is exposed to the countless phenomena that make up a normal life. It is its interaction with the environment that lets the mind accumulate the complex knowledge structures which determine its future performance, and there is no other way to create these structures.

The mistake of the mind mechanists, therefore, is not just to underestimate the capacity of the mind, but to see intelligence as the result of computational processes. So they conclude that they can enhance the performance of their models by improving the algorithms or the hardware. No matter how much the models are improved, however, they can never attain human intelligence, simply because they cannot emulate the *existence* of human beings; that is, their interaction with a complex environment.

We saw that creativity is the result of connecting knowledge structures which were previously unrelated. If we think of the mind as a sort of machine, it is tempting to conclude that we can become more creative simply by increasing the number of connections between structures. And that, similarly, to enhance the creativity of a mind model, all we have to do is increase the number of connections between *its* structures. But we can easily show that this is not the case.

We have to be creative, for example, to recognize a pen. Pens come in an endless variety of sizes, shapes, colours, and mechanisms, as pen manufacturers never stop conceiving new designs. Despite this challenge, though, we usually have no difficulty recognizing (visually) as pen an object we have never seen before. We do this by considering some of its attributes and ignoring others, and by taking into account many clues, including the context in which we encounter it. Using this information and our previous experiences, we determine that the object fits best in the category of pens.

Imagine now a software model of mind that has difficulty recognizing pens. How could we enhance its capabilities? We know that *we* recognize a new pen by generating new links between knowledge structures. With an unusual pen, the links between the structures formed in our mind when we first see it, and the pen-related structures that already exist in our mind, are very weak; and our creativity consists in discovering these links. But we cannot enhance the model's creativity simply by instructing it to connect as many structures as possible.

Consider how our mind works. If our creativity were limited to the strongest links, we would recognize as pens only those objects that are practically identical to previously encountered pens; we would always be right, but we would fail to recognize most *new* pens. And if we did not limit our creativity, and connected even structures with very weak links, then we would indeed recognize all new pens; but at the same time we would mistake for pens most elongated objects we encounter. In both cases we would act abnormally, and would fail to function properly in everyday situations. When we act normally, it seems that our creativity is neither too low, nor too high, but just right. What is "right," though? What range of pen-recognition creativity represents normal, intelligent behaviour? Although we can identify this behaviour in people and notice any deviation from it, we cannot define it with precision. And if we cannot define it, how could we emulate it in a mind model?

Normal behaviour combines the rational and the irrational, the logical and the illogical. We must be sufficiently illogical (and thus sufficiently creative) to be prepared at any time to recognize as pens objects that are inconsistent with our established conception of pens, and at the same time sufficiently logical (and thus sufficiently uncreative) to avoid seeing pens where there are none. The term "arational" describes, perhaps, this type of behaviour.[24]

It is not only with pens, of course, that we need this unspecifiable blend of rationality and irrationality in order to act normally. Every object has its own narrow range of creativity that we identify as normal behaviour, and so has every feeling, sound, idea, phrase, or situation. We are never exposed to a thing in isolation from all other things, so we associate with certain contexts everything we know: we connect every knowledge structure to other structures. We cannot specify what is normal behaviour, or what is the right degree of creativity, because these qualities do not have measurable values. They are not processes that can be measured or improved as we measure or improve the performance of machines. Depending on the context, new connections between mental structures may appear either as an act of creativity or as mental disorder: the same act may be intelligent one moment and absurd the next.

The only way to assess whether a certain act is correct, or intelligent, or normal, is by noting the context in which it occurred; for the chief criterion that determines whether an act is right or wrong is how appropriate it is in the current context. So, if we wanted to bring the behaviour of a mind model closer to that of humans, we would have to improve its ability to recognize the current context, just as *we* are (intuitively) aware at all times of the context we are in. But then, all we would have done is shift the problem from having to specify what is a correct response, to having to specify how to distinguish one context from another. We recognize contexts tacitly, by combining many pieces of knowledge. Contexts, just like mental acts, are complex structures, and hence irreducible to precise rules and definitions. We cannot improve the mind model by defining contexts, therefore, any more than we could by defining what is an intelligent response.

To recognize a pen, we are helped by noticing that it lies on a flat surface, rather than hanging in a tree; we are also helped by knowing that the surface is a desk, and to recognize the desk we are helped by perceiving it as a piece of furniture in a room, which we do because we know what it means to be in a

---

[24] Hubert L. Dreyfus and Stuart E. Dreyfus, *Mind over Machine: The Power of Human Intuition and Expertise in the Era of the Computer* (New York: Free Press, 1988), p. 36.

room, and so forth. Clearly, if we want to define a context we run into an infinite regress, as we attempt to define each piece of knowledge in terms of other pieces of knowledge, and then define *those* in terms of others yet. Nor are these recognition processes neat structures of things within things. The structures share elements – objects in the immediate environment, for instance – and hence interact. Like the context itself, the process whereby we recognize the current context is a complex structure.

At any moment, we are influenced by such facts as where we are, what happened moments before, specific objects or people, the sensations received by our senses, cultural background, expectations about the future, and all the related thoughts. Only by tacitly combining these facts can we arrive at the correct interpretation of the current context; and the slightest deficiency in this process leads to abnormal behaviour. The strange responses of schizophrenic or autistic persons can be attributed to their failure to assess correctly the current context; that is, their failure to combine all the clues into one complex structure.

It is notable that the failure of artificial intelligence programs to attain significant performance levels has been attributed to the impossibility of conveying to them all the details they need in order to identify the current context. Contexts are called *frames* in artificial intelligence, and this problem is known as the frame problem. Just like schizophrenic and autistic persons, artificial intelligence programs tend to interpret a given situation too literally, too logically. And we cannot improve their performance by improving the software, because the knowledge structures they lack can only be created by a human mind through exposure to a human environment.

The following passage describes the importance of context in explaining the abnormal behaviour of autistic individuals, but it could just as easily explain the failure of the software models of mind: "Context is at once the most essential ingredient in full intentional communication, and the one feature that distinguishes it from bare message transmission. The hallmark of the latter is the piecemeal handling of information. In principle, there is nothing wrong with this. On the contrary, this mode of information processing guarantees stability: the same code always means the same thing, as in a computer. In everyday human communication this guarantee does not apply. Here, there is an *obligation* to use context. This means often having to say 'it depends.' The meaning of any utterance in word or gesture can only be properly understood by *not* treating it piecemeal, but placing it in context."[25]

No matter how elaborate the software models are, they remain mechanistic; so they can only deal with the complex structures of a context by separating

[25] Frith, *Autism*, p. 180.

them into simple structures. Thus, even if they managed somehow to account for most structures, they would still lack the essential information contained in the *interactions* between structures. This is why the performance of mechanistic models of mind cannot advance beyond that of individuals who suffer from mental disorders.

We note the same problem in understanding humour. We saw that humour is the result of trying to connect two mental structures which cannot be logically combined. But if we wanted to design a model of mind that understands humour, we would find it an impossible task: we wouldn't know how to instruct it to recognize pairs of structures that cause humour.

Consider how our mind recognizes a funny situation: we must be rational enough to understand the logic of each structure on its own, and at the same time irrational enough to attempt to combine them; then, we must be rational enough again to recognize the absurdity of this attempt. Only thus can we appreciate the humour inherent in the situation. If our mind fails to grasp the logical parts of the situation, then we cannot understand it at all and we are accused of being stupid. And if we understand the situation so well that we instantly see its absurdity and do not even try to combine the two incompatible structures, then we can see nothing funny and we are accused of lacking a sense of humour. We have to be both logical and illogical, and there is only a narrow range that is "right," that is deemed normal behaviour. But we cannot define this range with precision; and if we cannot define it, how could we design a software model of mind that understands humour?

Recall the joke about the waiter suggesting milk instead of cream. A software mind model processing that story would not recognize it as a joke. The model would notice the absurdity of the dialogue, and would immediately optimize the text – by replacing the dialogue with one statement, simply requesting black coffee. Computers have no sense of humour. They are completely logical, because we design them that way. But imagine that we wanted to improve the model so that, in addition to being logical, it would understand our jokes. How could we do it?

We all know, of course, that there are no definitions or specifications for understanding humour. The range of behaviour that is "right" is not a value that can be measured or improved. If humour springs from the conflict between two knowledge structures, a model of mind must recognize this conflict. But it can only recognize the conflict if it understands the two structures as *we* do; that is, if these structures are connected to *other* knowledge structures. To appreciate that joke, for instance, the model would have to be familiar with our coffee drinking habits, with our restaurant customs, with the functions of cream and milk, with the concept of choice, and so on.

But possessing many knowledge structures is not enough. In the case of humour, too, the model must be able to recognize contexts – combinations of structures – and we already saw that this is an unspecifiable process. We notice how delicate this process is when a remark meant to be funny becomes absurd or insulting as the context changes (on a different occasion or with different listeners), or when people with a different cultural background fail to understand a certain type of humour. In both cases, the problem is that some of the knowledge structures in the minds of those exposed to that humour are different from the structures needed to complete the humorous situation. But it is impossible to specify with precision which structures are wrong and how to correct them.

It is, again, by studying mentally impaired individuals that we notice how difficult it is to specify what is normal behaviour. Mental disorders and humour both manifest themselves as shifts between unrelated mental structures, and only the context can tell us which one we are witnessing: "Such shifts from one realm into another are very frequent with schizophrenics, and therefore the patients' statements sometimes strike one as witticisms."[26]

Whether we observe creativity, or humour, or any other act of discovery, the mental process is the same – generating new connections between knowledge structures – and to judge the result we must know the context: "When two independent matrices of perception or reasoning interact with each other the result … is either a *collision* ending in laughter, or their *fusion* in a new intellectual synthesis, or their *confrontation* in an aesthetic experience. The bisociative patterns found in any domain of creative activity are tri-valent: that is to say, the same pair of matrices can produce comic, tragic, or intellectually challenging effects."[27]

Now, one may argue that it is not important that models of mind be so advanced that they display creativity, or appreciate art or humour. But this, of course, is not the issue. If the same mental processes that take part in creative acts, aesthetic experiences, and humour also take part in normal behaviour, then if we cannot emulate these unusual mental acts we cannot hope to emulate normal human intelligence either. In other words, functioning normally in everyday situations already requires the *full* capacity of the mind. Emulating highly creative acts, therefore, is *not* more difficult than emulating normal behaviour – not if "more difficult" means faster computers, or more advanced algorithms, or more facts and rules.

---

[26] Kasanin, *Schizophrenia*, p. 121.   [27] Koestler, *Act of Creation*, p. 45.

5

Mind mechanism, then, is the belief that human skills and intelligence can be replaced with software devices. In the next section we will examine the social consequences of this fallacy, but let us first analyze its origin; namely, the assumption that it is possible to emulate the mental capabilities of human beings by separating intelligence into independent knowledge structures.

Normal behaviour depends on generating the right connections between knowledge structures; and what is "right" on each occasion depends on the existing structures and connections, which themselves were generated on earlier occasions through the "right" connections, and so on. What we recognize as knowledge and intelligence is embodied in the structures and connections developed by the mind when we were exposed to certain phenomena. Although we must not underrate the data processing capabilities of the brain, it is ultimately our experiences that determine our knowledge. So, even if we join the mind mechanists and hope to have one day a device with the same capabilities as the brain, the only way to emulate human knowledge would be to expose the device to a human environment.

But how could a computer be designed to live the life of a human being? No one expects to have mind models of this kind, of course. Thus, because they deny the need to emulate *all* of a person's existence, the mind mechanists reject, in effect, the concept of learning. Specifically, they reject the fact that the intelligence required to cope with a certain environment can only be acquired through exposure to that environment. If the device must have knowledge that does not come from interacting with its environment, the only alternative is to program somehow this knowledge directly into the device – through algorithms, rules, and databases of facts. This explains the attempts to reduce human intelligence and skills to a mechanistic representation, as only mechanistic concepts can be translated into software concepts. And this explains also the attempts to emulate only one act at a time: implementing only one knowledge structure, the mechanists believe, is easier than trying to incorporate in a model *all* the knowledge of a human being. But these ideas are fallacious.

To behave intelligently, we must recognize at any moment the context we find ourselves in. This context is a complex structure, and we recognize it because we are already familiar with the interacting structures that make it up. If we try to isolate some of these structures, we end up losing the interactions; besides, we discover that they too are made up of interacting structures, which are made up of others yet, and so on. The only way to recognize a context, therefore, is intuitively: we must recognize it as a whole, by processing all its structures simultaneously. We *can* recognize contexts, but we cannot explain how we do it. Because so many knowledge structures are involved in this process, we must conclude that we use a great part of our knowledge every time we recognize a context.

Returning to the previous examples, there are no specific mental processes for recognizing pens, or for understanding coffee jokes; consequently, there is no specific pen recognition skill, or coffee jokes skill, that one can acquire. The knowledge we need in order to behave intelligently in these situations is about the same as the knowledge we need in a thousand other situations. We can find no knowledge structure that, when isolated from our other knowledge, embodies the intelligence required to perform a particular act. The idea that models of mind can be programmed to perform specific intelligent acts is, therefore, nonsensical. This can succeed for *context-free* acts, which can indeed be isolated from the others and approximated with simple structures (data processing tasks, for instance), but not for the general acts we perform in everyday situations. To put it differently, the only way to program a mind model to emulate *one* of our intelligent acts is by programming it to emulate *most* of our acts. The mind mechanists admit that the latter task is too ambitious, so they address the simpler one. They don't see that the simpler one is only an illusion.

It is because no knowledge structure in the mind can be isolated from the others that normal behaviour is so hard to define. If we stay within one structure, we are *too logical* – and our behaviour is considered abnormal. We *must* connect knowledge structures, but then we find that, from the infinity of possible links, very few are right: only those that reflect the current context. If we allow more links, we become *too illogical* – and our behaviour is again considered abnormal. Normal behaviour, thus, is far from being banal behaviour. When we behave normally we display great expertise – expertise in recognizing contexts.

The same mental processes are involved in everything we do: when behaving normally as much as when displaying expertise, creativity, or humour. No one knowledge structure can be isolated from the others, because no mental act can be represented mechanistically. This is why it is no easier to program a mind model to display intelligence in one specific act than to program it to display the general intelligence of a person, and no easier to program it to display normal, common-sense behaviour than to program it to display expertise, or creativity, or humour.

Replacing Minds with Software

1

The greatest challenge facing us today is to recognize how the mechanistic delusions are shaping the future of our society. And it is the mechanistic *mind* delusions that are the most dangerous, because how we think of our mental capabilities affects our decisions in all fields where knowledge and skills play a part. Thus, "what we do now will determine what sort of society and what sort of human beings we are to become. We can make such a decision wisely only if we have some understanding of what sort of human beings we already are. If we think of ourselves only as repositories of factual knowledge and of information processing procedures, then we understand ourselves as someday to be surpassed by bigger and faster machines running bigger and more sophisticated programs. Those who embrace that limited conception of intelligence welcome the change with enthusiasm."[1]

The danger we face when perceiving human minds as a kind of machine is getting to depend on charlatans who promise us devices that are better than our minds. For, once we replace knowledge and skills with devices and stop using our non-mechanistic capabilities, we will indeed become inferior to devices. We will then *have* to depend on devices, and our minds will be further degraded, in a process that feeds on itself.

I have devoted so much space to mind mechanism because it is more than just another mechanistic delusion. The belief that we can build models of mind leads in practice to the belief that there exist substitutes for knowledge and skills. The delusion that it is possible to embed human intelligence in a device has now gone beyond the speculations of artificial intelligence: it has escaped the academic confines, and is increasingly influencing our business and social decisions. Our belief in mind mechanism has given rise to a phenomenon that may be called *the culture of knowledge substitutes.*

Thus, instead of developing certain knowledge, we expect a software device to function as a substitute for that knowledge. And it is this fantastic idea that has allowed the software companies to rise to their glamorous and dominating position. These companies cannot provide knowledge substitutes, of course – no one can. But the bytes they sell us in those colourful boxes produce illusions that act very much like the religious or political illusions of the past, tempting us with promises of salvation, of easy solutions to difficult problems.

---

[1] Hubert L. Dreyfus and Stuart E. Dreyfus, *Mind over Machine: The Power of Human Intuition and Expertise in the Era of the Computer* (New York: Free Press, 1988), p. 206.

❖

Mind mechanism is the most widespread of our mechanistic delusions, and is a factor in many other delusions, including our language and software theories. Mind mechanism is typical of what I have called *the new pseudosciences* – the subject of the next chapter.

Scientists who engage in these worthless pursuits can create entire academic disciplines out of nothing more substantial than a mechanistic fantasy. They start by making an extravagant claim and presenting it in the form of a theory: an explanation for a complex phenomenon, or a solution to a complex problem. This generates a great deal of excitement, even though everyone can see that the theory is only a speculation, a wish. Its foundation on mechanistic principles – which principles are accepted unquestioningly – is what makes the theory credible, imparts to it a "scientific" image, and persuades everyone that it will soon be useful.

The theory appears to work in a few cases (as mechanistic approximations always do), and this gives the scientists additional confidence. Since they are now convinced that it is an important contribution, a "research program" is initiated: a long series of modifications, which make the theory increasingly complicated and thereby mask its shaky foundation. These modifications often result in mechanistic solutions to isolated problems – problems discovered when trying to apply the theory, and perceived now to be part of the research. Encouraged by these successes, the scientists are convinced that they are making progress, that these solutions will be combined one day into an answer to the *original* problem. Non-mechanistic phenomena, however, cannot have mechanistic explanations. So the theory never works, and is eventually abandoned. But we learn nothing from these delusions: new mechanistic theories, equally fallacious, always emerge to replace those that failed.

2

Our chief concern in this book is a specific pseudoscience: the belief that knowledge and skills can be replaced with software. In particular, we are concerned with the belief that *programming* knowledge and skills can be replaced with software – the belief that there exist substitutes for programming expertise.

We hear about innovations like application development environments, object-oriented languages, relational databases, or computer-aided software engineering, and we see the many software devices that embody these ideas. Every year, there are hundreds of new versions of these devices, thousands of books, periodicals, and courses promoting them, millions of practitioners struggling to assimilate the endless novelties, and billions of dollars being spent by society to support it all. And even a casual study would reveal that it is these innovations and the resulting complexity, rather than the software applications themselves, that constitute the chief preoccupation in the world of programming.

Accordingly, a person unacquainted with programming must think that programming substitutes are indispensable for creating applications. This impression would be reinforced by the fact that, for the last forty years, the notion of programming substitutes has been upheld by professors and gurus, taught in famous universities, endorsed by professional associations, approved by renowned experts, and embraced by corporations large and small in their effort to improve programming practices.

Faced with this reality, the lay person must conclude that the need for programming substitutes, and for their perpetual changes and ever increasing complexity, is based on solid theories, or on irrefutable evidence. That person would be surprised, therefore, when he found out that no such theories or evidence exist. He would be surprised to hear that these innovations are totally unnecessary for developing or maintaining software applications; that their sole purpose is *to eliminate the need for programming expertise*; and that the enormous social and economic structure we have created around them is merely a system of belief – a system founded on the *assumption* that we can invent substitutes for programming expertise.

In chapter 7 we will see that the programming substitutes are mechanistic delusions: despite their variety, they are all based ultimately on the principles of reductionism and atomism – on the belief that programming tasks can be neatly broken down into simpler and simpler tasks. But we can already see the part played in software delusions by the delusions of *mind* mechanism. For, the very notion of programming substitutes must assume that the mental processes involved in programming can be precisely specified, represented with rules and methods, and then implemented with software. And this assumption is identical to the assumption of mind mechanism; namely, that human knowledge and skills can be emulated with mechanistic models. Thus, the programming substitutes are in effect models of mind, substitutes for human intelligence.

The mechanists notice the various processes that make up a software application – the business practices embodied in it, the subroutines, the database, the flow of execution, the data entry or display operations – and conclude that each process can be extracted from the whole act of programming and dealt with separately. Once this idea is accepted, any number of methodologies, theories, or development tools can be invented for each isolated process, all claiming great improvements in programming productivity. Typically, these expedients attempt to simplify programming by providing higher-level starting elements.

In these concepts, we recognize the two fallacies of mechanistic thinking: reification (the belief that we can separate the simple structures that make up a complex phenomenon) and abstraction (the belief that we can start from higher levels without losing any alternatives at the top level). By reifying complex programming phenomena into simple structures, the software mechanists hope to replace the difficult task of programming a whole application with the easier task of programming separately each one of its processes. This reification also opens the way to abstraction: less work and lower programming skills are required to complete the application if we start from higher levels within each process; in other words, if our starting elements are modules or operations that already incorporate many others. With this method, it is believed, applications of any size and complexity can be created even by inexperienced programmers.

Although useful in domains like manufacturing and construction, this method is inadequate for software-related phenomena; it is inadequate because these phenomena consist, not of processes *within* processes, but of *interacting* processes. In an application, the various software processes interact with one another, and also with the personal, social, and business processes affected by that application. A software process is not a structure *within* other software processes, or *within* a business process; nor is a business process a structure *within* a software process. Thus, software-related phenomena can only be represented with *complex* structures. Thanks to its non-mechanistic capabilities, the human mind can successfully deal with these phenomena. But the only way to create in our mind the complex knowledge structures that reflect the complex software phenomena is through personal experience: by being exposed to these phenomena for many years. We *can* acquire programming expertise; but, like other difficult skills, this takes a long time.

3

When the mechanists claim that programming methods and devices can reduce or eliminate the need for programming – and can therefore act as substitutes for the programming skills of humans – how are we to understand the claim? Since models of mind can emulate only those mental functions that can be represented mechanistically, the claim is in effect that programming is such an easy challenge that it requires only mechanistic knowledge. But is this true?

Programming methods and devices are based on the assumption that the various activities in software development can be represented with *simple* structures; namely, independent mental acts and independent pieces of software related to one another only through the precise definition of a hierarchy. We saw, however, that practically everything we do requires our mind's capacity for *complex* structures. Is programming, then, an exception? Is it simpler than recognizing faces or voices, or driving a car, or interpreting X-rays, or distinguishing chicks? Is it simpler than coping with everyday situations, or understanding jokes or metaphors? Can we program without being able to recognize contexts? Since it is absurd to think that programming is simpler than everything else we do, the burden of proof rests on those who claim it is: those who claim that there can exist mechanistic substitutes for programming knowledge.

The software mechanists, of course, do not claim that programming is easy. On the contrary, they say, we need the substitutes precisely because programming is difficult and there is no other way to simplify it. But note the contradiction: their attempt to simplify programming through mechanistic theories is equivalent to claiming that programming *is* a simple activity – so simple that it can be reduced to exact, fully specifiable structures of things within things. This contradiction stems from the same fallacy that mechanists have being committing for centuries (we will study this fallacy in chapter 4): They see the richness of a complex phenomenon (minds, language, software, etc.), and the simplicity of the hierarchical concept, and they wish to have both: they wish to use simple hierarchical structures to represent the complex phenomenon. They fail to understand that it is precisely the fact that the phenomenon is complex, and hence irreducible to simpler ones, that gives it its richness and potency.

This explains why programming theories, methodologies, tools, and aids, no matter how sophisticated, have so little effect on programming productivity. Programming is one of the most difficult tasks that we have ever had to perform; and it is so difficult precisely because there is no way to reduce it to a mechanistic representation, and we must depend therefore on personal experience. It is similar, in this respect, to our linguistic or visual performance. Like these other acts, programming can only be performed by human minds, because it depends on our capacity for complex knowledge. It involves discovering the right connections between many knowledge structures: the various concepts that make up the application, technical details, business matters, and even personal and social concerns. And, like all intelligent acts, it requires the full capacity of a mind.

So, in the end, the issue is this: Are programming skills a mechanistic phenomenon? Or are they a complex phenomenon, like our linguistic capability and the many other skills that cannot be reduced to simpler mental acts? Our software pursuits are based on the assumption that our software-related problems are mechanistic, so programming can be restricted to mechanistic acts. But, as we have seen here, all the evidence indicates that this assumption is mistaken: software involves complex phenomena, so programming requires complex knowledge. Thus, we must accept the conclusion that our current software pursuits are largely mechanistic delusions.

Unlike other mechanistic delusions, however, which did not survive for long in the real world, outside academia, the software delusions keep growing and are now spreading throughout society. Thus, the ideology of software mechanism has become the greatest mass delusion in history: a myth more powerful and widespread than all the religious and political systems of belief we had in the past.

But how did this happen? How was it possible for the software elites, in just a few years, to reach the point where they practically control society through this myth? By persuading us to shift our preoccupations from *real* problems to *software-related* ones. The shift occurred first for programmers; then, the incompetence it caused in application development forced the *users* of software to undergo a similar transformation. (We will study this evolution in chapter 6.) Whether the victims are programmers or other workers, it is the same belief – software mechanism – that leads to the change in preoccupations.

Typically, the software mechanists start by promising us solutions to *real* business, social, or personal concerns. Because of our mechanistic tradition, we fail to see that only *mechanistic* problems can have software solutions, so we believe all their claims. For the simple, mechanistic problems, their solutions work well, and these successes enhance their credibility. These successes, however, do not guarantee that software will also solve our complex, non-mechanistic problems – those requiring human expertise. But, even though software fails in those tasks, just by depending on software we create a whole category of problems we did not have before: software-related problems. Since we do not doubt the mechanistic ideology, we continue to believe that the original, real problems can be solved with software. So we seek solutions to the new, software-related problems, hoping that by solving *them* we will solve the original ones. Since most software-related problems are mechanistic, we can usually solve them with mechanistic means – which entail even more software. But these software solutions are only solutions to the *software-related* problems, which we created ourselves, not to the *original* problems.

Every time we adopt a piece of software, we get to depend on *it*, instead of depending on some other expedient or on our own skills. And even if that software does not solve our real problems, we continue to depend on it and must deal with the problems it generates. So the software elites control our life simply by persuading us to accept software solutions. We need more and more software solutions because we have more and more software-related problems. Our real problems may remain unsolved, but as long as we believe that they can be solved with software we continue to adopt new types of software, and thus create new types of software-related problems, for which we need new software solutions, and so on.

The more difficult it is to solve our real problems with software, the more software solutions we will try, and the more software-related problems we will have. Attempting to find a substitute for a complex phenomenon – a difficult human skill like programming, for instance – is guaranteed to generate a never-ending series of software problems and solutions, of software innovations and devices, precisely because it is an impossible quest. Eventually, a great part of our life is taken by software preoccupations that have little to do with our real problems. But in our infatuation with mechanism we fail to notice this. On the contrary, we *like* our new, software-related problems. We like them because they seem to have easy solutions: we always seem to be *solving* problems. Besides, the software propaganda makes us feel modern and successful simply by *having* this type of problems.

It is this shift in preoccupations – from the real problems to the spurious, software-related ones – that has allowed the software elites to gain so much power. As with any tool, there is nothing wrong in depending on software devices when they are indeed the best answer. It is not from *solving* problems that the elites derive their power, however, but from the exact opposite: *preventing* us from solving problems. For, if the problems are so complex that only a human mind can solve them, then by depending on software devices we forgo the opportunity to develop the skills that *could* solve them. The devices will provide only limited answers, or no answers at all; but we will continue to depend on them, and on the elites behind them, because we will no longer have our own expertise as measure.

Since the only thing the elites can offer us is software devices, they must ensure our dependence on these devices regardless of their degree of usefulness. And the simplest way to achieve this is by degrading the concept of expertise: from the difficult skills needed to solve important problems, to the easy skills needed to operate software devices. This – the prevention of true expertise – is the final goal of the software elites. For, only in a world where we can no longer use the full capacity of our minds do the software devices outperform us. The reason it appears to us that the software elites are indispensable is that we are becoming increasingly dependent on them for software solutions to the software-related problems we created when we adopted some other software solutions. To *these* problems they can indeed provide answers; and this keeps increasing their prestige and influence, even as they are preventing us from developing our minds and from solving our *real* problems.

4

The programming profession is the only field in which the destruction of knowledge and skills caused by software mechanism is now complete. The incompetence of programmers, therefore, provides the best illustration of the delusion of knowledge substitutes; and the programming theories are the best medium for studying this delusion. (This is the subject of chapter 7.)

It is not hard to see why the programming profession was so easy to destroy: unlike other skills, programming lacks a tradition that could act as standard of expertise. We have centuries of tradition in writing, for example. We already know what good prose is, so if the mechanists claimed that certain language devices can replace the talent and expertise of humans, we would simply compare the results, and recognize the absurdity of their claims. In programming, however, we had no time to attain a similar wisdom before this activity was taken over by incompetents and charlatans.

We have had many opportunities to observe the work of talented programmers. But, while in other professions it was always the performance of the *best* workers, in programming it was the performance of the *mediocre* ones, that was taken as the highest level we should expect. From the start, the official doctrine was to avoid relying on exceptional individuals (because they are hard to find) and to degrade programming to an activity that can be performed even by the least experienced practitioners. The software theorists, we were promised, will show us how to replace programming expertise with methods, tools, and aids. Thus, while in other professions education and training took years, and expertise was attained only after decades, programmers were trained in weeks or months, and were not expected to ever attain expertise.

I have stated that the software elites can control our life by inducing us to shift our preoccupations from real problems to spurious, software-related ones. In the case of programming, the real problem was how to create and maintain software applications efficiently and reliably. This is a difficult task, demanding much knowledge and experience; but there are enough men and women who can acquire the necessary skills, if given proper education and training, and the opportunity to practise. Programming is no different in this respect from other difficult professions – medicine, for instance. As in other professions, we may use methods, tools, or aids, but it is our own expertise that is the critical factor. No methods, tools, or aids can replace this expertise, because it can exist only in a mind. The expertise is embodied in the complex knowledge structures formed in the mind through lengthy exposure to the complex phenomena of programming.

Thus, if the problem is programming expertise, the answer is a great deal of programming practice – which should not surprise us. But it is a fundamental assumption in our software culture that programming is different from other professions; that creating software applications is akin to the routine work performed by assembly workers when putting together appliances from prefabricated parts; and that the software elites have invented methods and systems which allow us to create applications in this fashion. So, rather than practising for many years to attain programming expertise, it is believed that programmers can accomplish the same tasks merely by using these methods and systems.

And so it is how programming expertise was redefined to mean expertise in the use of substitutes for expertise. The preoccupation of programmers shifted from developing their skills and creating useful applications, to learning how to use programming substitutes. The problem shifted from improving their knowledge of programming to improving their knowledge of ways to *avoid* programming.

It was evident from the start, though, that the substitutes do not work: applications took too long to develop, or were never completed, or were inadequate. Still, no one wanted to give up the idea of programming substitutes, so the conclusion was that we needed better substitutes, not better programmers. And when the new substitutes also failed to replace expertise, the conclusion was, once again, that we needed different substitutes. Thus, changes in programming theories, methodologies, environments, languages, and tools became the chief preoccupation of all software practitioners.

This is still true today. After forty years of failures, the doctrine of programming substitutes continues to define this profession. The substitutes, in fact, are now even more complicated and are changing even more frequently, so programmers are wasting even more time with them. Every software deficiency is blamed on the current programming environment, tools, or methods, and is used to justify the next round of changes. Programming incompetence is never suspected. As in the past, the level of a novice is considered the highest level of knowledge that we can expect from a programmer. No matter how many years of experience they have, programmers are rarely required to perform a task they could not have performed after the first year or two of practice.

A programmer's expertise is measured, not by his ability to develop and maintain software applications, not by his skills in solving important problems, but by how many methodologies, programming languages, or development environments he is acquainted with, or how many computer periodicals he reads, or how many courses he attended. He must be aware of the latest releases and versions of software products, of announcements and rumours. These are the kind of qualifications that companies are looking for when hiring a programmer; that is, how well he conforms to the mechanistic software ideology. Often, just a few months of experience with a particular system is the only qualification needed.

By degrading the programming profession, by lowering the definition of programming expertise to mean expertise in the use of programming substitutes, the original problem – how to create and maintain applications efficiently and reliably – has been replaced with a multitude of *software* problems. The work of programmers has been degraded to the point where they are only expected to know a number of facts, rather than possess a body of knowledge and skills recognizable as a profession. We have all but forgotten that programming practice ought to mean simply the solution of business or social problems through software. Only the smallest part of a programmer's activities is directly related to this objective.

To understand why this inefficiency is seldom evident, we must remember how common it is for programmers to perform activities that, while perceived as important and urgent, are in reality spurious: dealing with the problems generated by programming substitutes. And, even though what I have said applies mainly to *application* programmers, we must not forget that the work of *system* programmers consists almost entirely in creating the substitutes needed by the application programmers. Thus, no matter how successful or impressive is the creation of the programming tools, development environments, or database systems themselves, this is a spurious activity.

And so are the other activities engendered by the programming substitutes. Were the application programmers experienced professionals, there would be no need for the programming substitutes, or the organizations that sell them, or the schools that teach how to use them, or the conventions that promote them, or the publications that explain, advertise, and review them. It is only because we have forgotten the real purpose that computers and software ought to have in society that we are not outraged by the stupidity of these preoccupations.

❖

As our dependence on computers is growing, the cost of programming incompetence is becoming a social issue that affects us all, because the businesses and governments that depend on incompetent programmers simply pass the cost to the rest of society. The cost to society caused by the destruction of programming skills exceeds probably one trillion dollars a year, globally – money that ultimately ends up in the pockets of the software elites and the software bureaucrats. We need only recall the so-called Y2K date problem (the need to modify the existing applications to handle correctly dates beyond 1999, which cost society hundreds of billions of dollars), to recognize the immense power that software practitioners derive from providing solutions to problems they create themselves. Nor is this problem as unique as it appears. It stands out because it was due to the same deficiency in millions of programs, but it is otherwise similar to all the other software-related problems.

The present consequences of programming incompetence, however, while important, are small compared to what the future holds. Programming is only the first type of knowledge to be destroyed by the software elites. Others will follow, as our dependence on software is spreading beyond the dependence on inadequate business applications. We can already recognize similar delusions, for example, in the kind of software known as office productivity systems, which attempts in effect to replace a variety of skills – skills that take many years to acquire – with acts that anyone can learn to perform in a few days. Similarly to what happened in programming, the preoccupation of managers and office workers is shifting: from improving their skills to learning how to use substitutes for these skills, and from providing professional services to searching for solutions to the endless problems generated by the substitutes. The expertise of office workers is increasingly measured, not by their ability to perform important tasks, but by how well they are acquainted with software devices. Valuable knowledge that can only develop in a mind is being destroyed and replaced with inferior substitutes.

Each time we replace human expertise with substitutes that are in fact only illusions, we lose our capacity to solve the *real* problems, because we forgo the opportunity to develop, through practice, the complex knowledge needed to solve those problems. What is worse, we add to our software-related problems, and thus increase our dependence on software charlatans.

This makes our study of software mechanism in the domain of programming even more important: not only does it help us understand why knowledge substitutes cannot work, and why we must encourage expertise and responsibility among programmers; not only can it help us derive greater benefits from our computers and at the same time save society trillions of dollars, which can then be directed toward better causes than the support of a software bureaucracy; but it can help us anticipate the consequences of replacing human expertise with mechanistic substitutes in *other* fields of knowledge. If we understand how the mechanistic fallacies have contributed to our software delusions in the domain of programming, we can perhaps learn to recognize and avoid the formation of software delusions from mechanistic fallacies in other domains.

CHAPTER 3

Pseudoscience

The mechanistic view of mind we studied in the previous chapter is only one of the many mechanistic delusions being pursued in universities today under the cloak of science. In the present chapter, I propose to study some of the other delusions, and to show that they all share a set of obvious characteristics.

This study has a dual purpose. First, we will expose the intellectual corruption of the academics – a corruption inevitable when mechanism changes from a mere hypothesis into a principle of faith. Second, we will establish methods for determining whether a given theory, or discipline, or research program, represents a legitimate scientific activity or is nothing more than a system of belief. In addition, this study will help us later, when we examine the greatest mechanistic delusions of all time – our software theories. For, software mechanism has grown out of the mechanistic culture that pervades the academic world.

Even more harmful than the promotion of pseudoscientific theories are the political consequences of this mechanistic culture. If we believe that complex phenomena of mind and society can be modeled with exact theories, we are bound to believe also the utopian promises of totalitarianism. Thus, even though *failing* as scientific theories, the mechanistic notions promoted in universities are helping various elites – the software elite, in particular – to implement totalitarian ideologies.

The Problem of Pseudoscience

1

A pseudoscience is a system of belief that masquerades as scientific theory. The list of pseudosciences, ancient and modern, is practically endless: astrology is founded on the belief that the heavenly bodies influence human affairs on earth; phrenology claims that we can determine various personality traits from the shape of a person's skull; graphology claims that we can determine traits from a person's handwriting; dowsing maintains that it is possible to discover underground water just by walking over an area; alchemy holds that it is possible to transmute base metals into gold. Other pseudosciences are based on the belief in psychic phenomena, visits from aliens, faith healing, prophecy, magical objects, and so on.

Astrology has been with us for five thousand years, but most pseudosciences lose their popularity over time and are replaced by new ones. The continuing appeal of pseudoscience rests on its promise of simple solutions to difficult problems, as opposed to the relatively modest claims made by science. Widespread education has not eradicated what seems to be a basic human need – our craving for supernatural powers – and it has been noted that pseudosciences, superstitions, and the belief in the paranormal are actually on the rise throughout the modern world.[1]

A distinguishing characteristic of pseudoscience is the acceptance of a hypothesis as unquestionable truth, and the refusal to review it later in the light of falsifying evidence. Whereas serious researchers insist on careful and objective tests of validity for their theories, pseudoscientific theories depend on the enthusiasm of the practitioners and the credulity of their followers. When subjected to controlled experiments, the success rate of these theories is usually revealed to be no better than chance. Pseudoscientific theories do not work, but believers interpret the chance successes as evidence of their truth, and belittle the significance of the failures. It is important to note that the practitioners' sincerity is often above suspicion; it is precisely their *belief* that prevents them from recognizing the falsity of their theories. But because there are no serious validity tests, pseudosciences also attract many charlatans – practitioners who knowingly deceive the public.

Despite their variety, the traditional pseudosciences have been addressing the same concerns since ancient times: our fears and desires, our longing for omnipotence and immortality. But today the mechanistic delusions are

---

[1] See, for example, Paul Kurtz, *The Transcendental Temptation: A Critique of Religion and the Paranormal* (Buffalo, NY: Prometheus Books, 1991).

fostering a new kind of pseudosciences: various academic pursuits that are part of modern disciplines and spheres of knowledge. And they are also fostering a new kind of pseudoscientists: researchers, professors, and theorists working in universities and other institutions. While these academic pursuits resemble scientific research, they belong to the pseudoscientific tradition insofar as they too are founded on a hypothesis that is taken as unquestionable truth. The hypothesis is that all phenomena can be explained with the mechanistic principles of reductionism and atomism. Although this belief is different from the beliefs upon which the traditional pseudosciences are founded, the ensuing pursuits acquire a similar character: they become systems of belief that masquerade as scientific theories. Thus, I call these pursuits *the new pseudosciences*. The new pseudosciences belong to the class of theories we examined in chapter 1 under scientism.

Like the traditional ones, the new pseudosciences do not work. Also like the traditional ones, blatant falsifications leave their supporters unperturbed. Instead of recognizing falsifications as a refutation of their theory, pseudoscientists think their task is to *defend* it; so they resort to various stratagems to make the theory appear successful despite the falsifications. Their work, thus, while resembling scientific research, is in reality a series of attempts to save from refutation an invalid theory.

We saw in chapter 1 how mechanistic delusions lead to futile pursuits (see pp. 106–108). If the phenomenon in question can only be represented with a complex structure – if, in other words, it cannot be usefully approximated by separating it into simpler, independent phenomena – the only way to explain it is by studying it as a whole. This is a difficult, often impossible, task. The researchers believe that a simple structure – in the form of a mechanistic theory, or model – can represent the phenomenon accurately enough to act as explanation. So they extract one of the simpler phenomena from the complex whole, hoping that a mechanistic model based on it alone will provide a good approximation of the whole phenomenon. They are committing the fallacy of reification, but they see this act as a legitimate method, sanctioned by science.

Science sanctions this method only for *mechanistic* phenomena. The researchers cannot know in advance whether their subject is indeed mechanistic, so the possibility of explaining the complex phenomenon by isolating the simpler phenomena that make it up is only an assumption. To validate this assumption, they must arrive at a successful explanation of the original phenomenon; specifically, they must discover a mechanistic approximation that is close enough to be useful. But even when they find explanations for the isolated phenomena, the researchers fail to explain the original, complex phenomenon. We know, of course, why: the complex phenomenon includes the *interactions* between structures, and these interactions were lost when they separated the structures. They mistakenly assumed that the interactions are weak enough to be ignored, so the model based on reified structures does not represent the actual phenomenon accurately enough.

In their work, these researchers may be following the strictest methods. In their study of the isolated structures, their theories and procedures may be faultless. Thus, their activities may be indistinguishable from those of real scientists. The more complex the problem, the more opportunities there are to separate it into simpler problems, then to separate these into even simpler ones, and so on.

It is obvious, then, why the mechanists perceive these activities as important work. At any point in time, what they are doing resembles true research – the kind of work that in the exact sciences brings about great discoveries. Consequently, solving one of the isolated problems is seen as progress, as a contribution to the solution of the original problem. Besides, the theory does work in certain cases. It is in the nature of poor approximations to work in some cases and not in others, but the mechanists interpret the odd successes as evidence that their ideas are valid.

At this stage, they have forgotten that the entire project is based on the *assumption* that the original phenomenon can be explained mechanistically. The assumption is wrong, so all these activities – no matter how rational and scientific they may appear when judged *individually*, and no matter how successfully they may solve *isolated* problems – constitute a delusion. Not surprisingly, no theory that explains the original phenomenon is ever found. Modern mechanistic pseudosciences last several years, or several decades, and then they are quietly abandoned.

What is especially striking in pseudosciences, thus, is to see people engaged in activities that are entirely logical *individually*, even while the body of activities as a whole constitutes a delusion. All it takes is one wrong assumption; and if this assumption is never questioned, the research is nonsensical no matter how rational are the individual activities.

By its very nature, therefore, the mechanistic assumption engenders pseudosciences: If we assume that a non-mechanistic phenomenon can be explained by breaking it down into mechanistic ones, we will end up studying the latter. So, like real scientists, we will be engaged at all times in the exact work associated with mechanistic phenomena. We will be pursuing a delusion, but this will not be evident from the *individual* activities. The only way to recognize the delusion is by questioning the mechanistic assumption itself.

❖

If it is so easy to fall prey to mechanistic delusions, how can we differentiate between those scientists engaged in important research and those who pursue hopeless, pseudoscientific ideas? Clearly, if we agree that science means simply the pursuit of mechanistic theories, regardless of whether they work or not, it is no longer possible to distinguish true scientists from crackpots and charlatans.

Note that it is not the *failure* of these theories that must concern us. Ambitious or revolutionary ideas often prove to be mistaken, so the risk that a theory may eventually fail should not prevent us from pursuing it. What we must question, rather, is whether the pursuit of a theory should be considered science simply because the theory is mechanistic. Science ought to mean the pursuit of *sound* theories: mechanistic ones for mechanistic phenomena, and non-mechanistic ones for complex phenomena.

Is there a way to avoid this enormous waste of resources – and, worse, its consequences? For, if we take the *software* theories as an indication of where this degradation can lead, the consequences are the destruction of knowledge, a return to the irrationality of the Dark Ages, and a totalitarian society. Once we recognize that software phenomena are non-mechanistic, any research program based on mechanistic software notions looks absurd, no different from the research program of the alchemists or the astrologers. It is only through the mechanistic hypothesis – namely, the assumption that any phenomenon can have a mechanistic model – that the software theories can be said to belong in the domain of science, rather than pseudoscience.

Thus, we have reached perhaps a critical point in history, where there is an urgent need to revise our conception of science. If the software delusions are an indication, the survival of our civilization may well depend on our decision whether or not to retain mechanism as an article of scientific faith.

2

Since mechanistic delusions undermine logical thinking in the same way that other delusions did in the past, the problem we are facing is a problem that has preoccupied philosophers for centuries: In our quest for new knowledge, how can we avoid irrational thinking, fallacious arguments, and unsound judgment? If what we discover is really new, how can we know whether it is true? For, the only way to be absolutely sure that something is true is by proving it on the basis of *previous* knowledge – knowledge whose truth is established. But then, a successful proof will also indicate that it depends entirely on facts we knew before, leading to the conclusion that it is not really new. It seems, therefore, that we can gain new knowledge only if we do not also expect to be certain of its truth. This inference is very disturbing, as it suggests that the advance of knowledge depends entirely on something rather doubtful: the human capacity for faultless reasoning.

Many methods have been suggested for improving our thinking habits – methods ranging from rules of common sense to procedures of formal logic. In the seventeenth century, for instance, Francis Bacon, who stressed the importance of experimentation and logical thinking in scientific research, described four categories of reasoning errors (which he called "idols of the mind"). And in the nineteenth century, John Stuart Mill popularized a set of methods that can be used in any experimental inquiry to check the validity of hypotheses and to avoid drawing mistaken conclusions.

To the traditional principles we must add a new one if we want to guard against *mechanistic* delusions: Before attempting to explain a phenomenon by separating it into several independent phenomena, we must first prove that the interactions between these phenomena can be ignored. In other words, we must determine that the original phenomenon can indeed be modeled with simple structures. Since only mechanistic phenomena lend themselves to this treatment, if we commence our project by isolating structures we merely beg the question: we start by assuming the very fact that needs to be determined – the mechanistic nature of the phenomenon. Thus, if the project is to be considered science and not speculation, we must start by proving that the links *between* structures are weak relative to the links *within* structures; specifically, we must prove that they are weak enough to be ignored. And if such a proof is impossible, the phenomenon must be deemed non-mechanistic. Any search for a mechanistic theory is then known in advance to be futile, so it cannot be considered a serious scientific activity.

In particular, most phenomena involving human minds and societies consist of interacting structures, and weak links between these structures are the exception. Scientists isolate these structures precisely because they want to avoid the complexity generated by their interactions. They fail to see, though, that once they eliminate the interactions they are no longer studying the original phenomena. So we must not be surprised when, years later, they are still searching for a useful model. But we must remember that, by applying a simple logical principle, they could have avoided this futile work.

No system has been found that can guarantee sound reasoning while also permitting creativity, innovation, and discovery. The problem of reconciling these conflicting ideals remains a difficult one. Descartes believed that the "geometrical method" is the answer: if we treat all knowledge as simple hierarchical structures, we will discover, without ever falling into error, everything the human mind can comprehend. Only in a world limited to mechanistic phenomena, however, could such a naive method work. And it is precisely his legacy – the belief that non-mechanistic phenomena, too, can be explained with the geometrical method – that engenders the new pseudosciences.

This problem has evolved into what is known today as the problem of *demarcation*: how to differentiate between scientific and pseudoscientific theories. The best-known and most successful principles of demarcation are those developed by Karl Popper. These principles can be used to assess, not only formal theories in the traditional disciplines, but any concepts, statements, and claims. In the domain of software, particularly, we can use them to assess notions like structured programming, the relational database model, and software engineering in general. These notions are in effect empirical theories, insofar as they make certain claims concerning the benefits of various methods or aids. The principles of demarcation will help us to determine whether these theories express important software concepts, or whether they are pseudosciences.

Popper's
Principles of Demarcation

1

Sir Karl Popper, generally recognized as the greatest philosopher of science of the twentieth century, created a philosophy of knowledge and progress that can be applied consistently in all human affairs. It is useful for scientific theories as well as social and political ideas, for difficult decisions as well as common, everyday puzzles.[1]

Popper held that it is impossible, in the empirical sciences, to *prove* a theory; so we can never be sure that our knowledge is correct or complete. The only way to advance, therefore, is through a process of trial and error, by learning from our mistakes: we must treat all ideas and theories as *tentative*

---

[1] See, in particular, these books by Karl Popper: *Conjectures and Refutations: The Growth of Scientific Knowledge*, 5th ed. (London: Routledge, 1989); *The Logic of Scientific Discovery* (London: Routledge, 1992); *Realism and the Aim of Science* (London: Routledge, 1985).

solutions, as mere conjectures, and we must never cease to doubt them. It is our responsibility, in fact, to attempt to refute our own theories – by subjecting them to severe tests. And we must always try to find better ones. In this way, our theories will keep improving, and we will get nearer and nearer to the truth. But, because the world is so complex, this process can never end. Indeed, even if one day we do arrive at the truth, we will have no way of knowing that we did.

Theories turn into worthless pursuits when their supporters choose to ignore the falsifying evidence. Unlike true scientists – who seek the truth and know that their theories, even when apparently successful, may be mistaken – pseudoscientists believe their task is simply to defend their theories against criticism.

Popper considered demarcation to be "the central problem of the theory of knowledge."[2] It must be noted that he sought to distinguish the empirical sciences not only from pseudosciences, but also from metaphysics and purely logical theories. He recognized the value of these other types of knowledge; but, he said, they are different from the empirical sciences. For example, some theories considered scientific today originated in antiquity as pseudosciences, so even as pseudosciences they must have been useful; and purely logical systems like mathematics, while not part of the real world but our invention, can provide invaluable models (by *approximating* the real world). Any theory, thus, can be useful. But the theories of empirical science occupy a special position, because they alone permit us to develop knowledge that matches reality. So, if we want to improve our knowledge of the world, we must have a way of determining whether a given theory belongs to one category or the other.

It may seem odd to place the rigorous theories of pure mathematics in the same category as pseudosciences. These theories *are* alike, though, when viewed from the perspective of empirical science; that is, when judged by their ability to represent the world. The mechanistic *software* theories provide a nice illustration of this affinity. The structured programming theory, for instance, and the relational database theory, are founded upon mathematical principles. But these principles reflect only minor and isolated aspects of the phenomenon of software development, not whole programming projects. In their pure form, therefore, these theories are useless for creating serious applications, because they do not approximate closely enough the actual software phenomena. They became practical (as we will see in chapter 7) only after renouncing their exact, mathematical principles and replacing them with some vague, informal ones. And this degradation is one of the distinguishing characteristics of

[2] Karl R. Popper, *The Logic of Scientific Discovery* (London: Routledge, 1992), p. 34.

pseudoscience: the experts continue to promote their theory on the basis of its exactness, even while annulling, one by one, its exact principles.

Mechanistic software theories, thus, can exist only as purely logical systems and as pseudosciences; and in either form they cannot be part of empirical science. Empiricism stipulates that theories be accepted or rejected through actual tests, through observation and experiment. As logical systems, the mechanistic software theories were tested in the real world, and failed; and in their modified form, as pseudosciences, these theories offer no exact principles to begin with, so they cannot be tested.

2

Popper's interest in a criterion of demarcation started in his youth, when he "became suspicious of various psychological and political theories which claimed the status of empirical sciences, especially Freud's 'psychoanalysis,' Adler's 'individual psychology,' and Marx's 'materialist interpretation of history.'"[3] Popper was struck by the *ease* with which one could find confirming evidence for these theories, despite their dubiousness. A Marxist could find evidence of the class struggle in every event and every news item, and also in the *absence* of certain events or news items. A Freudian or Adlerian psychoanalyst could find confirming evidence of Freud's or Adler's psychological theories, respectively, in every act performed by every person; and had a person acted differently, that behaviour too could have been explained by the same theory. Any event seemed to fit quite naturally within these theories. In fact, one could not even *imagine* an event that would have contradicted them.

While these dubious theories were so easily *verified*, Popper was impressed by how easy it was to *falsify* a true scientific theory. Einstein, for example, boldly predicted several events from his theory of relativity, and declared that if they did not occur as stated he would simply consider the theory refuted.

Popper realized that it was precisely the *ease* with which a theory can be confirmed that *reduces* its scientific value, and this led him to his criterion of demarcation: "But were these theories testable?... What conceivable event would falsify them in the eyes of their adherents? Was not every conceivable event a 'verification'? It was precisely this fact – that they always fitted, that they were always 'verified' – which impressed their adherents. It began to dawn on me that this apparent strength was in fact a weakness, and that all these 'verifications' were too cheap to count as arguments.... The *method of looking for verifications* seemed to me unsound – indeed, it seemed to me to be the

---

[3] Karl R. Popper, *Realism and the Aim of Science* (London: Routledge, 1985), p. 162.

typical method of a pseudoscience. I realized the need for distinguishing this method as clearly as possible from that other method – the method of testing a theory as severely as we can – that is, the method of criticism, the *method of looking for falsifying instances*."[4]

Several years later, Popper recognized that the problem of demarcation is closely related to the classical problem of induction, and that the two had to be considered together.[5] The problem of induction is this: When we develop a theory in the empirical sciences, we draw general conclusions from a limited number of observations and experiments; we reason from singular facts to general statements; we believe that we can explain an infinite number of situations that have yet to occur, from the study of a finite number of situations that we observed in the past. This concept – induction – is indispensable in science, for we could have no theories without it. Logically, however, induction is invalid, because there is no justification for deriving general laws from the observation of unique events. The only way to practise science, therefore, is by trusting the principle of induction even as we know that it is invalid.

But there can be no doubt that induction *does* work: our knowledge *has* been increasing, and this shows that we *can* draw valid conclusions from past events, and we *can* have useful theories. We accept induction, therefore, simply because it works; and it works because there are regularities in the world: some future events *will* be similar to past ones, so it is possible to discover theories and to make predictions, especially if we are content with approximations.

Unfortunately, this expectation of regularities also tempts us to see patterns where there are none, leading us to fallacious thinking and irrational behaviour. Pseudosciences and superstitions are theories that predict future events from current knowledge, just like the theories of empirical science. For example, if we concluded once that a certain event was caused by a psychic force, we will attribute to this force other events in the future; and if we noticed once a black cat while a tragic event took place, we will avoid black cats in the future. With pseudosciences and superstitions, thus, we also use induction; we also draw general conclusions from the observation of a few events; so we also reason from particular facts to general statements. The only difference from science seems to be that our observations are less careful, so our conclusions are less accurate and our predictions less successful.

The belief in induction is closely related to the belief in causality. We must accept both principles in order to develop theories, and both stem from the way our mind works: we expect to find regularities in our environment. When

---

[4] Ibid., pp. 162–163.

[5] For Popper's views on induction, see ibid., ch. I, and his *Objective Knowledge: An Evolutionary Approach*, rev. ed. (Oxford: Oxford University Press, 1979), ch. 1.

an event occurs simultaneously with another, or shortly thereafter, we tend to conclude that they must be related, that one caused the other or perhaps a third one caused both. This belief is reinforced by the belief in induction, when we observe a repetition of that pattern.

As with induction, though, no matter how often we notice the pattern, we have no logical grounds to conclude that there is a causal relation between the two events. We feel that such a relation is likely, of course, just as we feel that an event which occurred frequently in the past is likely to recur in the future. But these are strictly subjective notions, which spring from our habits of mind, from our natural tendency to expect regularities. According to the theory of probability, if we observed only a finite number of events and there are an infinite number of future events, the probability of predicting anything about those future events from the past ones is the first number divided by the sum of the two, which is practically zero.

Causality and induction, then, are hardly the solid and objective foundation we would like to have for our empirical sciences. It is true that science, unlike pseudoscience and superstitions, demands more observations before concluding that one event causes another; and it is true that scientific theories are more than just our expectation to see in the future a repetition of past events. Nevertheless, it is disturbing that our scientific knowledge has the same foundation as our superstitions: our habits of mind, our inclination to expect regularities, perhaps a propensity resulting from the evolution of the brain.

If you think these problems ought to concern only philosophers, remember the sad story of the chicken that believed in causality and induction. The chicken noticed, day after day, that the farmer sheltered it, fed it, and watched its health. After observing this pattern for many days, the chicken felt justified to conclude that the farmer's acts were motivated by love, and that it would enjoy the same comfort in the future. Soon after, though, the farmer killed the chicken and ate it – which had been his intent, of course, from the start.

What philosophers are trying to determine is whether, from the information available to it, the chicken could have known the truth.[6] Or, rather, they are trying to determine whether *we*, from our current knowledge, can arrive at the truth. For, at any given time, we are in a position not very different from that of the chicken: we must make decisions about *future* events by using the doubtful theories we developed from the observation of relatively few *past* events. And when, recognizing the limitations of our personal knowledge, we

---

[6] It is Bertrand Russell who first noted the chicken's quandary.

listen to scientists and experts, to corporations and universities, to governments and media, all we do is trust the doubtful theories that *others* developed from those few past events.

For example, when we accept the programming methods concocted by software theorists because they seem to work with some simple textbook examples, or when we judge the value of a software system from a few "success stories" or "case studies," we are using in effect a few past events to make decisions about the future. But how can we be sure that we are not making the same mistake as the chicken?

So, if the problem of demarcation is how to distinguish our scientific from our pseudoscientific theories, the problem of induction is that *all* theories are logically unjustifiable, so there is no real difference between the scientific and the pseudoscientific ones in any case.

The problem of induction and its disturbing implications were first studied by David Hume, who resigned himself to complete skepticism. His conclusions had a profound influence on the development of Western thought, as they cast doubt on the possibility of rationality and objective knowledge: "The growth of unreason throughout the nineteenth century and what has passed of the twentieth is a natural sequel to Hume's destruction of empiricism.... It is therefore important to discover whether there is any answer to Hume within the framework of a philosophy that is wholly or mainly empirical. If not, there is no intellectual difference between sanity and insanity.... This is a desperate point of view, and it must be hoped that there is some way of escaping from it."[7]

Popper found a solution to Hume's problem of induction, and to the skepticism engendered by it, through his solution to the problem of demarcation: "If, as I have suggested, the problem of induction is only an instance or facet of the problem of demarcation, then the solution to the problem of demarcation must provide us with a solution to the problem of induction."[8] He agrees that induction and past confirmations are insufficient to prove a theory; but he does not agree with the conclusion drawn by the earlier philosophers – namely, that this limitation will forever prevent us from distinguishing between our rational theories and our delusions.

What Popper proposes is to combine the methods of induction, which are indispensable for discovering new theories but cannot prove them, with the

---

[7] Bertrand Russell, *A History of Western Philosophy* (New York: Simon and Schuster, 1972), p. 673.

[8] Karl R. Popper, *Conjectures and Refutations: The Growth of Scientific Knowledge*, 5th ed. (London: Routledge, 1989), p. 54.

methods of *deduction*, which cannot create new knowledge but *can* prove statements. Deduction allows us to prove the validity of a statement by showing that it can be derived logically from other statements, which are known to be valid. Mathematical and logic systems, for example, are based on deduction: a conclusion is derived by combining premises; a new theorem is demonstrated by combining previous, simpler theorems. With strict deduction, there can be no knowledge in a new statement that is not already contained in the original ones (this is what guarantees the validity of the new statement). But, even though they do not create new knowledge, the methods of deductive logic are still important, because the new statements may express the same knowledge more clearly, more economically, and more usefully.[9]

Popper was impressed by the *asymmetry* between trying to *prove* a theory and trying to *refute* it. A theory is a universal statement that makes a claim about a large, perhaps infinite, number of events. Consequently, any number of confirmations are insufficient to prove its validity. At the same time, just one event that *contradicts* the theory is sufficient to *refute* it. Imagine, for instance, that we wanted to verify the universal statement "all swans are white" (one of Popper's favourite examples). No matter how many white swans we observe, these confirmations would not verify the statement, for we could never be sure that we saw all the swans in the world; but observing just one black swan would suffice to *refute* the statement.

This is how Popper explains his idea: "My proposal is based upon an *asymmetry* between verifiability and falsifiability; an asymmetry which results from the logical form of universal statements. For these are never derivable from singular statements, but can be contradicted by singular statements. Consequently it is possible by means of purely deductive inferences (with the help of the *modus tollens* of classical logic) to argue from the truth of singular statements to the falsity of universal statements."[10]

Modus tollens states that, if we know that whenever p is true q is also true, then if q is found to be false we must conclude that p is false. So what Popper says is this: if p stands for any one of the assertions that make up a theory, and q stands for any one of the conclusions derived from this theory, then just one instance of q being false will refute the theory.[11] In other words, while no number of "q is true" claims that are true suffices to *prove* the theory, just one "q is false" claim that is true suffices to *refute* it.

---

[9] The induction discussed here must not be confused with the method known as *mathematical induction*, which employs in fact deduction.

[10] Popper, *Scientific Discovery*, p. 41.   [11] Ibid., p. 76.

❖

The first thing we learn from Popper's discovery is how absurd is the popular belief that we must *verify* our theories, that we must search for *confirming* evidence. For, no matter how many confirmations we find, these efforts can prove nothing. Rather than attempting to show that a theory is valid, we must attempt to show that it is *invalid*; and the theory will be accepted as long as we *fail* in these attempts. It will be accepted, not because we proved its truth (which is impossible), but because we failed to prove its falsity.

Thus, if we sincerely attempt to refute our theories, if we agree to accept only those that pass the most severe tests we can design, our knowledge at any point in time is guaranteed to be as close to the truth as we can get. This, says Popper, is all we can hope to achieve: "Assume that we have deliberately made it our task to live in this unknown world of ours; to adjust ourselves to it as well as we can; to take advantage of the opportunities we can find in it; and to explain it, *if* possible (we need not assume that it is), and as far as possible, with the help of laws and explanatory theories. *If we have made this our task, then there is no more rational procedure than the method of trial and error – of conjecture and refutation:* of boldly proposing theories; of trying our best to show that these are erroneous; and of accepting them tentatively if our critical efforts are unsuccessful."[12]

With this method we combine, in effect, the benefits of induction and deduction. In our search for new theories, we can now use induction as often as we want. We need no longer worry about our habits of mind – about our inclination to expect regularities. Ideas revealed to us in our dreams are as good as those discovered through formal research methods. We can use our imagination and creativity freely, and we can propose theories that are as bold and original as we like. We can do all this because we need no longer fear that our thought patterns may be wrong, or that our conclusions may be mistaken. The discovery of a theory is now only the first stage. The theory is accepted provisionally, and it is in the next stage that the most important work is done: attempting to refute the theory by subjecting it to severe tests.

If we allowed the *uncertainty of induction* in order to *discover* the theory, we rely on the *certainty of deduction* in order to *refute* it. We benefit from deductive logic in two ways. First, as noted earlier, in the knowledge that the failure to pass even one test will prove that the theory is invalid. Second, we must use deductive methods – formal logic, mathematics, established theories, controlled experiments – in the tests themselves. It is pointless to devote any effort and to insist on deductive methods for tests that *verify* the theory; for, no

[12] Popper, *Conjectures and Refutations*, p. 51.

matter how scrupulous these tests are, each confirmation of the theory does not increase significantly the likelihood of its validity (since there will always remain an infinite number of unverified instances). Instead, we must devote this deductive effort to tests that try to *falsify* the theory. Logically, we can learn little or nothing from any number of instances that confirm it, but we can learn a great deal from just one instance that falsifies it.

Popper's solution, thus, has rescued the principle of empiricism – the requirement that theories be accepted or rejected on the basis of observations and experiments – from the destructive consequences of induction. All we must do is replace the principle of *accepting* a theory on the basis of *confirming* evidence, with the principle of *rejecting* the theory on the basis of *refuting* evidence. Empiricism "can be fully preserved, since the fate of a theory, its acceptance or rejection, is decided by observation and experiment – by the result of tests. So long as a theory stands up to the severest tests we can design, it is accepted; if it does not, it is rejected. But it is never inferred, in any sense, from the empirical evidence. There is neither a psychological nor a logical induction. *Only the falsity of the theory can be inferred from empirical evidence, and this inference is a purely deductive one.*"[13]

What Popper's solution amounts to, in essence, is a trade. We agree to give up the dream of knowing with certainty whether a theory is true or false; in return, we save the ideals of empiricism, the possibility to distinguish rationality from irrationality, and the hope for intellectual progress.

3

If the correct way to judge theories is by subjecting them to tests that try to falsify them, it follows that we cannot even consider theories that do not lend themselves to tests and falsification. This quality, then, is the criterion of demarcation that Popper was seeking: "Not the *verifiability* but the *falsifiability* of a system is to be taken as a criterion of demarcation.... I shall require that its logical form shall be such that it can be singled out, by means of empirical tests, in a negative sense; *it must be possible for an empirical scientific system to be refuted by experience.*"[14]

Most people think that to test a theory means to show that it works, so they choose for their tests situations that confirm the theory. But such tests are worthless: "It is easy to obtain confirmations, or verifications, for nearly every theory – if we look for confirmations."[15] The criterion of demarcation

---

[13] Ibid., p. 54.   [14] Popper, *Scientific Discovery*, pp. 40–41.
[15] Popper, *Conjectures and Refutations*, p. 36.

prescribes the opposite; namely, for a theory to be included in the domain of empirical science, there must exist tests that, if successful, would *falsify* it. Thus, scientific theories are falsifiable; theories that are unfalsifiable are pseudoscientific.

It is important to understand the difference between the two qualities, *falsifiable* and *falsified*. The criterion of demarcation is not concerned with the theory's validity, or with its usefulness; it only determines whether the theory should be considered part of empirical science. If our tests – our attempts to find falsifications – are successful, the theory is rejected; if unsuccessful, it is accepted. But it must be falsifiable to begin with, in order for us to be able to *apply* the tests; and this quality is what makes it scientific.

A scientific theory is always falsifiable, but it may or may not be eventually falsified by tests (and even if falsified, and then abandoned, it does not lose its scientific status). Pseudoscientific theories, on the other hand, are unfalsifiable, so they can never be falsified by tests. They are, therefore, untestable. The fact that they are never falsified makes them appear successful, but in reality they are worthless; for, they do not earn their success by *passing* tests, as do the scientific theories, but by *avoiding* tests. We will examine shortly how theories can be made unfalsifiable, but we can already see the simplest way to accomplish this: by keeping their predictions vague and ambiguous, so that any event appears to confirm them. (This is typically how pseudosciences like astrology manage to appear successful.)

The principle of falsifiability can also be expressed as follows. A scientific theory makes a statement about a universe of events, dividing them into two categories: those events it permits and those it forbids. The more specific the statement (i.e., the less it permits and the more it forbids), the more valuable the theory: "Every 'good' scientific theory is a prohibition: it forbids certain things to happen. The more a theory forbids, the better it is."[16] A falsification of the theory takes place when one of the forbidden events is observed to occur. So, a good scientific theory is also a theory that is relatively easy to falsify: because it forbids many more events than it permits, it actually helps us to specify tests that, if successful, would refute it.[17]

A good theory, therefore, makes a bold statement and takes great risks:

---

[16] Ibid.

[17] Thus, for an object moving at a certain speed in a given time period, a theory stating *The distance is the product of speed and time* is better than one stating *The greater the speed, the greater the distance*. The number of events permitted by the theory (i.e., the *correct* combinations of values) is much smaller in the first case than in the second; and the number of events forbidden by it (i.e., the *incorrect* combinations of values) is much larger. This difference is what makes the first theory easier to test, and hence, if invalid, to falsify. So this difference is what makes it more valuable.

"Testability is falsifiability; but there are degrees of testability: some theories are more testable, more exposed to refutation, than others; they take, as it were, greater risks."[18] (We hope, of course, that these tests will fail and the theory will be accepted. But the failure or success of tests, and the consequent acceptance or rejection of the theory, is a separate issue. The criterion of demarcation merely prescribes that such tests be possible.) Whereas a good scientific theory forbids a great deal, a pseudoscientific theory forbids little or nothing: any conceivable event belongs to the category of permitted events. Thus, it takes no risks. Nothing can falsify it. It is worthless precisely because it appears to work all the time: "A theory which is not refutable by any conceivable event is non-scientific. Irrefutability is not a virtue of a theory (as people often think) but a vice."[19]

Recall the problem of the growth of knowledge (the fact that we can never be certain of the validity of our current knowledge) and the conclusion that the only way to progress is by trial and error. Since we cannot *prove* our theories, we must accept them with caution; we must doubt them, try to show that they are wrong, and continue to search for better ones. Seen from this perspective, a theory that cannot be falsified is a dead end: because we cannot show that it is wrong even if it is, we can never reject it; we must accept it on faith, so it is not a scientific idea but a dogma.

Published in 1934, Popper's principles of demarcation were misunderstood and misinterpreted from the beginning. Nevertheless, these principles are well known today, and are often used to expose pseudosciences. Most philosophers and scientists respect them. At the same time, we notice that few of us actually use these principles to decide whether to accept or reject a theory; that is, few of us seriously attempt to falsify our theories by subjecting them to severe tests. The mistaken belief that we must prove a theory by searching for confirmations continues to guide our decisions; and, incredibly, it affects even academic research.

It is easy to see the reason for this delusion. We tend to fall in love with our theories. We cannot bear to see them criticized. And it is even more difficult to accept the idea that it is *our* responsibility, if we are serious workers, to attack our theories. It takes a great deal of intellectual integrity, which most of us lack, to consciously design tests through which we may refute our own ideas. So, although we appreciate the falsification principle, we find it hard to adhere to it. In the end, we succumb to the temptation of *confirming* evidence.

[18] Popper, *Conjectures and Refutations*, p. 36.   [19] Ibid.

Another reason why we cannot trust verifications is that our observations are subjective and open to interpretation: "Observations are always collected, ordered, deciphered, weighed, in the light of our theories. Partly for this reason, our observations tend to support our theories. This support is of little or no value unless we consciously adopt a critical attitude and look out for refutations of our theories rather than for 'verifications.'"[20] In other words, we must design our tests in such a way that their success would constitute a *falsification* of the theory, not a confirmation. The observations collected in a particular test are significant only if that test sought to *falsify* the theory; they are meaningless when the test sought to *confirm* it. Thus, "every genuine *test* of a theory is an attempt to falsify it, or to refute it."[21]

Moreover, we must specify the nature of the tests, and which results should be interpreted as confirmation and which ones as falsification, at the time we propose the theory – and then *stay* with these criteria. This reduces the temptation to avoid tests found later to falsify the theory, or to modify the theory to fit the results of tests: "*Criteria of refutation* have to be laid down beforehand; it must be agreed which observable situations, if actually observed, mean that the theory is refuted."[22]

Popper stresses an important aspect of the testing procedure: the requirement for "*the severest tests we have been able to design*" and for "*our sincere efforts to overthrow*" the theory.[23] Only if we resort to such severe tests and sincere efforts does their failure count as an indication of the theory's validity. Popper calls these results *corroborating evidence*: each failed test provides additional support for the theory (although, of course, not a proof). The qualities "severe" and "sincere" in these requirements are not subjective assessments of the researcher's attitude; they are exact, technical concepts.[24] Specifically, they mean that only *comprehensive* attempts to falsify the theory count as tests; that is, only tests which, given all current knowledge, are the most likely to falsify the theory.

[20] Popper, *Aim of Science*, p. 164.

[21] Popper, *Conjectures and Refutations*, p. 36. Popper appears to be using the terms "falsify" and "refute" interchangeably. Although the difference is often subtle, in this book I use "falsify" for the individual tests, and "refute" for the theory as a whole. Since one falsification suffices to refute it, a theory that is "falsifiable" is also "refutable," and if "falsified" it is also "refuted"; but the two terms still refer to different aspects of this argument.   [22] Ibid., p. 38 n. 3.

[23] Both quotations are from Popper, *Scientific Discovery*, p. 418.

[24] Karl R. Popper, "Replies to My Critics," in *The Philosophy of Karl Popper*, vol. 2, ed. Paul A. Schilpp (La Salle, IL: Open Court, 1974), p. 1079.

4

Before continuing this study, let us pause for a moment to reflect on the significance of what we have learned. For, we can already recognize how far Popper's principles are from the *actual* way we accept new ideas and theories. We have been aware of these principles for many years, and it is an indication of the irrationality and corruption of our present-day society that we continue to base our decisions on confirmations rather than on falsifications.

It should be obvious that we must apply these principles, not only to scientific theories, but also to everyday personal and business decisions; for example, to the adoption of a new product. Products are in effect theories, not unlike the theories of empirical science, insofar as they make certain claims – claims that can be verified or falsified through experiments. So, if we want to make the best decisions possible from the knowledge available to us, we must follow the same methods when considering a new product as we do when considering a scientific theory. Since many of these products greatly affect our life, there is no reason to treat them less seriously than we do our scientific theories.

The methods employed in promotional work like advertising and public relations offer a striking example of fallacious decision-making principles. Promotions are based entirely on *confirming* evidence – typically in the form of testimonials, or case studies, or success stories. These promotional devices describe a few applications of a product, asking us to interpret them as evidence of its usefulness. Most people believe that the issue here is one of veracity: if the claims are honest, the product must indeed be as useful as it appears. But the honesty and accuracy of the claims are irrelevant, since, from Popper's principles, the very idea of assessing the usefulness of a product by means of confirming evidence is unsound. (Still, it is worth noting that, technically, the use of isolated testimonials or success stories *is* dishonest, even if the claims themselves are true. It is dishonest because it does not include the *whole* truth – i.e., all pertinent cases; and this omission is, logically and legally, equivalent to lying. The similarity of this argument to Popper's principles is hardly coincidental: since these principles are based on logic, a claim that ignores them does not reflect reality, so it is necessarily untrue.)

We see this type of promotion everywhere: in books and periodicals, on radio and television, for ordinary consumer products as well as major corporate and government issues. From pain remedies to management theories, from fitness gadgets to software systems, this type of promotion is so prevalent because it is effective; and it is effective because it exploits our natural tendency to draw general conclusions from the observation of a small number of events – the same tendency that leads us, as we saw, to develop superstitions as readily as we develop sound theories.

But from Popper's principles we know that confirming instances prove nothing, that it is the *falsifying* instances that we must examine. What this means in practice is that the successes may be due to some unusual conditions. So we could learn a lot more by studying the *failures*. We might find, for example, that the failures exceed by far the successes, or that our situation resembles more closely those situations where the product failed than those where it succeeded.

Instead of being deceived by these promotional tricks, then, we could use them to our advantage. For, now we know that the promoters select a few confirming instances precisely because this is the only evidence they have, because the product is *not* as useful as they claim. We know that if they were honest, they would seek and discuss the *falsifying* instances – of which there are always thousands.

The link between promotions and theories is easy to recognize when we examine the *way* the promoters present their products and the *way* we assess them. The promoters propose, in effect, a theory – the theory that a given product has certain qualities and provides certain benefits; and we, on our part, develop in our mind a similar theory about its qualities and benefits. Like all theories, this theory makes certain claims and predictions regarding future situations and events; for example, the prediction that certain operations would be performed faster, or better. Logically, therefore, both the promoters and we must accept or reject this theory, not by searching for confirmations, but by subjecting it to severe tests: by sincerely attempting to falsify it. We would then accept it – we would adopt, that is, the product – only as long as we cannot falsify it, only if it survives the harshest possible criticism.

Not only do we not observe this principle, but we ignore the many falsifications (situations where the product does not work as expected) that present themselves even without deliberate testing. By ignoring these falsifications, or by belittling their significance, we render in effect the theory unfalsifiable: we accept its claims and predictions in an act of faith. Our decision-making process when adopting a product on the basis of confirming instances is, thus, an irrational act, just like accepting superstitions.

Even more disturbing is that we find this fallacy – relying on confirmations – in the most respected sources. What is the most common method of deception in advertising is also found in professional, business, and even academic publications. Articles that purport to inform or educate us, for example, are little more than stories about specific situations. Decades after Popper has shown us why we must base our decisions on falsifications, our entire culture continues to be founded on the absurd search for confirmations. It seems that we have given up the quest for knowledge and reason, and have resigned ourselves instead to our natural tendency to irrationality.

The most blatant demonstration of this irrationality can probably be found in the world of software and programming, which, because of widespread ignorance, resembles the world of primitive man. (We studied the similarity of software-related beliefs to primitive beliefs in "Anthropology and Software" in the introductory chapter.) Respected trade and business publications routinely extol the merits of software concepts on the strength of isolated success stories. Thus, while Popper's principles state that *one* falsification suffices (logically, at least) to refute a concept, thousands of falsifications lie all around us (instances where a software concept was *not* useful) without even being mentioned in those publications. What ought to be the most important evidence in assessing a given concept – the failures – is deliberately ignored.

If the method of selecting ideas and theories through criticism – by attempting to falsify them rather than confirm them – appears to us too severe, it may help to remember that we only feel this way about our *current* theories. We find this method perfectly logical when judging *old* theories, which have already been discredited. It is when recalling those theories that we appreciate the wisdom of Popper's principles, because with old theories we have no difficulty recognizing how absurd is the method of searching for confirmations.

Consider, for example, geocentrism – the theory that the earth is the centre of the solar system and the universe. When we believed that the planets, the sun, and the stars revolve round the earth, we had no difficulty *confirming* this theory. After all, everything in the sky appears to move, and the ground under us appears stationary. For centuries the idea that the earth is rotating and flying through space was ridiculed. So how did we eventually reject the wrong theory and accept the heliocentric one? We did that by noting the *falsifications* of geocentrism, not its confirmations; that is, not by dismissing, but by *studying*, the discrepancies between the phenomena predicted by the theory and those actually observed. Looking back, we can easily see now that the *only* way we could progress past our geocentric delusion was by ignoring the confirmations and accepting the falsifications. Had we continued to test the theory by searching for confirmations, we would be discovering confirming instances to this day, and we would still believe that the planets and the sun are moving round the earth. And the same is true of *all* knowledge: we can only make progress by taking the falsifications of our theories seriously – indeed, by *searching* for falsifications.

It is also interesting to note that serious programmers, even if they have never heard of Karl Popper, scrupulously apply the falsification principle when testing their software. A new piece of software is similar to a theory in empirical science, in that it makes certain claims about some events – claims that can be tested through experiments and observation. Specifically, we predict that, given certain data, certain effects will occur when using the software. Thus, similarly to a theory, we assess a new piece of software by subjecting it to tests: we *accept* it as long as our tests *fail* – fail, that is, to contradict the predictions; and we *reject* it if the tests *succeed* – succeed, that is, in refuting its claims. (The rejection is only temporary, of course: we modify the software to correct the errors – creating, as it were, a new theory – and then we repeat the tests.)

It is easy to see that this testing procedure amounts to an implementation of Popper's falsification principle: we don't test the software by searching for confirmations, but by trying to falsify it. Even when an application has many errors, there are countless situations where it runs correctly; in other words, situations that *confirm* the claims made by the software. But, while it is gratifying to see our new software run correctly, we understand that it is silly to restrict testing to these situations. We all agree that the only effective way to verify software is by specifically searching for those situations where deficiencies may be found; in other words, those situations most likely to *falsify* the claims made by the software. Imagine testing software by searching for confirmations; that is, restricting ourselves to situations where it runs correctly, and avoiding situations where it may fail. We would never find errors, so the application would appear perfect, when in reality it would be unverified, and hence worthless.

The reasons for accepting or rejecting theories, or concepts, or products are very similar logically to the reasons for accepting or rejecting new software. Thus, to recognize the absurdity of accepting concepts and products on the strength of confirmations – testimonials, case studies, success stories – all we need to do is imagine what it would be like to accept a new piece of software by testing only those situations where we already know that it is correct.

5

To summarize, two principles make up Popper's criterion of demarcation between scientific and pseudoscientific theories: first, the theory must be *falsifiable* (an unfalsifiable theory cannot even be considered, because we have no way to test it); second, we accept a theory because it passes tests that attempt to *falsify* it, not because we find confirming evidence. If we remember these principles, it is not difficult to recognize pseudoscientific theories and irrational ideas, because what their defenders do is cover up the fact that they are being falsified; and the only way to accomplish this is by disregarding the two principles.

We all wish our theories to be proved right; that is, to remain unfalsified when exposed to the reality of tests and criticism. But unlike good theories, which remain unfalsified because they are useful and make correct predictions, the unscientific ones remain unfalsified thanks to the dishonest stratagems employed by their defenders: they are made unfalsifiable from the start, or become unfalsifiable later.

The simplest way to avoid falsifications is to make the theory unfalsifiable from the start. This is typically done by formulating the claims and predictions in such a manner that they cover most eventualities, so the theory cannot be effectively tested. Thus, the claims are so vague that almost any subsequent event appears to confirm them. The fact that the theory cannot be tested – and therefore is never falsified – makes it look successful, but we already saw the fallacy of accepting a theory when all we have is confirmations. A theory is successful when it *passes* tests, not when it *avoids* tests.

Popper uses Freud's and Adler's psychoanalytic theories as examples of theories that were unfalsifiable from the start.[25] It is important to emphasize again that the issue here is not whether these theories are valid, but whether, in the absence of any means to test them, they are scientific; in other words, whether we can rely on their interpretations. There probably is a great deal in them that is important. Few question, for instance, the concept of an unconscious mind, or that childhood experiences affect us later in life. And, on the whole, no one denies that these theories have contributed greatly to our understanding of human behaviour. However, "those 'clinical observations' which analysts naively believe confirm their theory cannot do this any more than the daily confirmations which astrologers find in their practice. And as for Freud's epic of the Ego, the Super-ego, and the Id, no substantially stronger claim to scientific status can be made for it than for Homer's collected stories from Olympus. These theories describe some facts, but in the manner of myths. They contain most interesting psychological suggestions, but not in a testable form."[26]

The most common stratagem, however, is not to make a theory unfalsifiable from the start, but to make it unfalsifiable later. Most pseudoscientific theories start by being falsifiable, and thus indistinguishable from the scientific ones. They are, therefore, testable. But when in danger of being falsified by certain events, their defenders find a way to save them. One can save an invalid theory

---

[25] Popper, *Conjectures and Refutations*, p. 37.   [26] Ibid., pp. 37–38.

by avoiding tests, or by testing it without sincerely attempting to refute it, or by studying only situations that confirm it, or by ignoring the falsifications (claiming that the tests were wrong, or belittling their significance).

Although crude, these stratagems are quite effective. I will not dwell on them, though, for it is the more sophisticated stratagems that we want to examine: those employed, not by propagandists, advertisers, or irrational people, but by the academics and the experts who create the new pseudo-sciences. The trick they use is to suppress the falsifications as they occur, *one at a time*. And they suppress them by *modifying* the theory; specifically, they *expand* the theory so as to make the falsifying situations look like a natural part of it.

Thus, while the theory remains testable and falsifiable *in principle*, it is rendered unfalsifiable *in fact*, by incorporating into it every falsifying situation. What the pseudoscientists are doing is *turning falsifications of the theory into new features of the theory*. This stratagem may be difficult to detect, because the theory appears, at any given moment, very similar to the serious, scientific theories. It only differs from them when threatened by a falsifying situation. At that point, rather than being abandoned, it expands so as to swallow that situation – thus eliminating the threat. This task accomplished, it appears again to be a serious theory – until threatened by another falsifying situation, when the same trick is repeated.

Popper called the tricks used to avoid falsifications "immunizing tactics or stratagems,"[27] since their purpose is to immunize the theory against falsifications. Popper anticipated some of these tactics, but recognized that new ones can be easily invented.[28] He singled out the stratagems that modify a theory in order to make it correspond to the reality that would have otherwise refuted it – the trick I have just described. We will examine these stratagems in detail later, when discussing specific pseudosciences.

To combat these stratagems, Popper added a third principle to his criterion of demarcation: a theory, once formulated, cannot be modified. If we want to modify our theory (to save it from being falsified by evidence), we must consider the original theory refuted and treat the modified one as a *new* theory: "We decide that if our system is threatened we will never save it by any kind of *conventionalist stratagem*.... We should agree that, whenever we find that a system has been rescued by a conventionalist stratagem, we shall test it afresh, and reject it, as circumstances may require."[29]

---

[27] Popper, "Replies to My Critics," p. 983. (Popper attributes this phrase to Hans Albert.)

[28] Popper, *Scientific Discovery*, pp. 81–82.

[29] Ibid., p. 82. "Conventionalist stratagem" is the term Popper used earlier, before adopting "immunizing stratagem." It derives from the conventionalist philosophical doctrine, which holds that a theory may be used even if falsified by observations (ibid.).

Recall the interpretation of theories as statements that permit certain events and forbid others. Recall also that a good theory makes very specific claims, and hence permits relatively few, and forbids most, events. Falsifying events are those events that are forbidden by the theory but do occur. Since a pseudoscientific theory forbids little or nothing, almost any event is compatible with its predictions; and consequently, it has little empirical value. Viewed from this perspective, stratagems that modify a theory in order to suppress the falsifying events reduce the number of events the theory forbids. They succeed in rescuing the theory from refutation, but at the price of reducing its value. A theory may start by making bold claims, but if it is repeatedly expanded so as to transfer previously forbidden events (which are now found to falsify the claims) into the category of permitted events, its empirical value is no longer what it was originally. It becomes increasingly unfalsifiable (that is, permits more and more events), and eventually worthless – no different from those theories which are unfalsifiable (that is, permit most events) from the start.

Popper uses Marxism as an example of theories that start by being falsifiable but are later modified by their defenders to match reality. Some of Marx's original ideas were serious studies of social history, and as such they made predictions that were testable. It is, in fact, because they were testable that they were falsified by subsequent historical events. The events, therefore, *refuted* the theory. "Yet instead of accepting the refutations the followers of Marx reinterpreted both the theory and the evidence in order to make them agree. In this way they rescued the theory from refutation; but they did so at the price of adopting a device which made it irrefutable … and by this stratagem they destroyed its much advertised claim to scientific status."[30]

It is always unscientific to trust a theory unconditionally; and it is this dogmatic belief that prompts its defenders to try to rescue the theory, even at the risk of turning it into a pseudoscience. We can understand now even better the requirement to doubt and criticize our own theory, to subject it to tests that sincerely attempt to refute it. Clearly, the immunizing stratagems – which aim to suppress falsifications – violate this requirement, and hence exclude the theory from the domain of science. Scientists know that they must *doubt* and *attack* their theory; pseudoscientists think their task is to *defend* their theory.

Because they do not question the validity of their theory, the pseudoscientists are bound to interpret a falsification as an insignificant exception. They

---

[30] Popper, *Conjectures and Refutations*, p. 37.

feel justified then to modify the theory to make it cope with that situation. They do not deny that the theory is deficient; what they deny is that it has been refuted. They don't see the modification of the theory as a dishonest move, but as an improvement. They believe that only a few such exceptions exist, and that their effort to make the theory match reality constitutes serious research work.

This delusion is enhanced by the fact that the falsifications are discovered *one at a time*; so each falsification looks like a small problem, and also like the only one left. But in the case of pseudoscientific theories there is no end to falsifications. The reason these theories keep being falsified is that their claims are fantastic, and thus unattainable. Pseudosciences typically attempt to explain a complex phenomenon through some relatively simple concepts. Since the simple concepts do not work, the falsifying events are not exceptions but an infinity of *normal* occurrences. By the time the theory is modified to cope with them all, there is nothing left of the simplicity and exactness it started with.

The only way the pseudoscientists can deal with these "exceptions" is by incorporating them into the theory. And they accomplish this by contriving various extensions, which they describe as enhancements, or new features. The extensions, thus, are only needed in order to bring the falsifying events into the realm of events that the theory can be said to explain. So their true effect is not to *improve* the theory, but to *degrade* it – by reducing its rigour and precision. In the end, the patchwork collection of features ceases to be a theory. Its defenders, though, still fascinated by the beauty of their original fantasies, continue to believe in it and to expand it.

All mechanistic *software* theories, we will see in this book, start by being testable and falsifiable but are later modified in order to suppress the falsifications. Consider, for example, the theory behind the relational database model (we will study it in detail in chapter 7). This theory started by claiming that, if we separate the database from the rest of the application, and if we agree to "normalize" our files, we will be able to represent the database structures with a formal system. This will ensure that the result of database operations reflects accurately the stored data. Moreover, we will access the data from a higher level of abstraction: every database requirement will be expressed simply as a mathematical combination of relational operations. Ultimately, the relational model will turn database programming into an exact, error-free activity.

Now, an experienced programmer would immediately recognize the absurdity of this concept, without even using it in a real application: since the database structures interact with the other structures that make up the application, and since most of these interactions occur at the low level of records and fields, it is impossible to separate the database operations from the other types of operations, or to raise their level of abstraction. So the relational model was essentially an academic concept, unconcerned with reality. For example, in order to restrict programming to high-level operations on normalized files, it had to assume that processors and disk drives have infinite speed.

Still, despite its absurdity, the relational model was a falsifiable theory. And if one does not expect practicality from software concepts, it was even an interesting theory. It became testable when software companies decided to implement it in actual database systems – systems intended to serve real business requirements. At that point, needless to say, it was refuted. But instead of studying the reasons and admitting that the relational model has no practical value, its advocates started a long series of "enhancements": they suppressed the falsifications by expanding the model so as to include the falsifying situations. This made the theory unfalsifiable, and the relational database model became a pseudoscience.

Strict data normalization, for instance, was found to be impractical, so the concept of "denormalization" was introduced; now a file could be either normalized or not – a reversal of a fundamental relational principle, and a return to the pragmatic criteria of the traditional design methods. Then, separating the low-level database entities from the other entities of the application was found to be impractical, so various alternatives were introduced in the guise of new relational features. The purpose of these "features" was to move more and more parts of the application into the database system, and thereby reduce the need to link the database structures to the application's other structures.

In the end, as the invention of a new relational feature to suppress each new falsification proved too cumbersome, SQL, a simple database language originally intended just for queries, was expanded into a *programming* language. Although quite primitive in its new role, SQL allows us to deal with most falsifications through the traditional expedient of programming. In other words, SQL restored in a complicated and roundabout manner the low-level links between database entities, and between database entities and the other types of entities – links which the traditional programming languages had been providing all along. So SQL, while described as a relational database language, is not used to *implement* the relational principles, but to *override* them. For example, the relational model restricts us to manipulating whole files or logical portions of files, and SQL permits us to bypass this restriction: now we can specify operations for individual fields and records, and we can control these operations by means of conditional and iterative constructs, just as we do when using the traditional file operations.

Thus, there is nothing left of the idea of high levels in today's relational database systems. As it turned out, the restriction to relational operations is much too awkward and inefficient. Nor is there anything left of the promise to separate the database structures from the application's other structures. In fact, most modifications made to the relational model were prompted by the need to restore the low-level interactions between these two types of structures. So the relational model could be rescued only by expanding it to include the very features it had originally excluded, and from the exclusion of which it had derived its simplicity and formality.

If this fact escapes the notice of software practitioners, it is because the features were given new names. Thus, the relational theory also exemplifies another practice frequently found among pseudoscientists: the use of new and pompous terminology for the features introduced to suppress falsifications. This trick serves to mask the fact that these are not new features at all, but reversals of claims: reinstating well-known and indispensable concepts, which the theory had attempted to eliminate in its quest for simplicity.

Recall Popper's principle that a theory which was modified to escape refutation must be treated as a different theory: its claims must be assessed afresh, and it must be subjected to the same severe tests as a new theory. Imagine now that the relational concepts were introduced for the first time today, as they are found in the latest relational systems. In other words, we would be exposed from the start to the complexity and inefficiency of these systems, and we would have to assess their *current* benefits and drawbacks. It is safe to say that no one would see the point in adopting these systems. It would be obvious to everyone that the so-called relational model is merely a more complicated variant of the *traditional* database model. The relational theory established its reputation through its *original* claims – precisely those claims that had to be abandoned later in order to save it.

The relational theory, thus, exemplifies yet another deceptive practice employed by pseudoscientists: advertising the original benefits even after the theory was modified, its principles were forsaken, and those benefits were lost. The chief claim of these theories is that they enable us to solve complex problems with relatively simple methods. It is this combination of power and simplicity, this promise to give us something for nothing, that makes them so enticing. (The relational theory, for example, did not promise any capabilities that the traditional, low-level file operations did not already provide. What it claimed was that the restriction to high-level operations made the database concept so simple that inexperienced programmers too would enjoy those capabilities.) And when this promise proves later to be a fantasy, when the theory is expanded to incorporate the falsifying situations and thereby loses its simplicity, its advocates continue to defend it by invoking the benefits of the *original* theory. But all we have to do is remember the principle that a modified theory must be treated as a different one, to recognize the dishonesty of this stratagem.

6

Popper's criterion of demarcation is one of the most important contributions to the theory of knowledge and to the philosophy of science. It provides an excellent solution to the problem of distinguishing between science and pseudoscience – between true research and the pursuit of delusions. It is a sad reflection on our civilization, therefore, that in the period of time since these principles were discovered, our delusions have been multiplying and flourishing at an even higher rate than before. We can observe this not only in the traditional pseudosciences (which attract the ignorant and the gullible), or in the useless products and concepts (which are, as we saw, similar logically to pseudosciences), but also in the new pseudosciences, including the software pseudosciences, which are practised in universities and corporations. We must take a moment to investigate this phenomenon.

When there exists a simple method for recognizing worthless pursuits, one would expect scientists to adopt it and to rely on it in their work. And when this method can detect delusional thinking, not only in scientific research but in all our affairs, one would expect scientists, philosophers, and teachers to explain it to the rest of us. The intellectuals have failed in this task, however, and have left the education of society to advertisers, propagandists, and charlatans. But, what is worse, they have ignored the method even in their own work. As we will see later in this chapter, academic research means today, more often than not, simply the pursuit of a mechanistic idea. And when the idea turns out to be a fantasy, research becomes the pursuit of a pseudoscience: looking for confirmations and for ways to cover up the falsifications. What masks this degradation is the formal tone in which these worthless activities are reported.

Popper's demarcation principles are well known, of course. But instead of being used to assess theories, concepts, and products, they have become a topic of debate in the philosophy of science.[31] The debates involve issues such as these: When facing a falsification, how can we decide what is closer to the

---

[31] For examples of these debates, see Paul A. Schilpp, ed., *The Philosophy of Karl Popper*, 2 vols. (La Salle, IL: Open Court, 1974).

truth, the claim that the theory was falsified or the claims made by the theory? Or, when two theories remain irrefutable, or when both are refuted but in different degrees, how can we determine which theory is the better one? Popper recognized these problems, and he addressed them on many occasions. But it is important to understand that these philosophical subtleties are irrelevant when we employ his principles only as a criterion of demarcation, which was his original intent. We don't have to concern ourselves with any fine points when all we want is a way to recognize as early as possible a worthless idea. Thus, no philosophical subtleties can vindicate the frauds we are studying in this book. (Could the settlement of such issues correct the fallacies of behaviourism, or universal grammar, or structured programming, or the relational database model? The principles of demarcation expose the uselessness of these theories no matter how we choose to interpret the finer points.)

To understand why the academics prefer to ignore the true significance of Popper's principles, let us imagine what would happen if they applied these principles to their theories. Clearly, if they did that, most research work in disciplines like psychology, sociology, linguistics, economics, and programming would have to be classified as pseudoscientific. Thus, their failure to observe the demarcation principles doesn't stem from a concern with the finer philosophical points, but from professional dishonesty. They cannot *afford* to recognize the importance of these principles; for, if they did, they would have to admit that most of their work is not scientific research but a pursuit of mechanistic fantasies.

The mechanists are in an awkward position: they cannot *reject* Popper's principles, because their validity is obvious; but they cannot accept them either. So they resolve this conflict by debating their philosophical meaning instead of studying their practical applications. In addition, they deliberately *misinterpret* the principles. Some scientists and philosophers, for example, misinterpret them as a method of discovering new theories, and conclude that they are inadequate for that purpose; others misinterpret them as a study of the social and psychological aspects of scientific discovery, and end up treating them as an alternative to Kuhn's famous theory of scientific revolutions.[32] Popper's ideas were misinterpreted, in fact, even when judged by their fundamental philosophical aspects; for example, they were mistakenly viewed as merely an attempt to base the criteria of meaningfulness on falsifiability instead of verifiability.[33]

[32] Thomas S. Kuhn, *The Structure of Scientific Revolutions*, 2nd ed. (Chicago: University of Chicago Press, 1970).

[33] See, for example, Popper, "Replies to My Critics," pp. 967–974.

So Popper had to spend much of his career explaining again and again his demarcation principles, correcting the misinterpretations, and repeating over and over what he had said clearly in his original writings. He called the mistaken views "the Popper legend": "There were books in which I had protested against the various parts of the legend, and older books and papers to which I referred in these protests, and which needed only to be read to disprove the legend. Nevertheless, the legend grew, and it continues to grow."[34] And regarding his solution to the problem of induction, he remarks: "Few philosophers have taken the trouble to study – or even to criticize – my views on this problem, or have taken notice of the fact that I have done some work on it. Many books have been published quite recently on the subject which do not refer to any of my work, although most of them show signs of having been influenced by some very indirect echoes of my ideas; and those works which take notice of my ideas usually ascribe views to me which I have never held, or criticize me on the basis of straightforward misunderstandings or misreadings, or with invalid arguments."[35]

The most common error, and the most important, is to interpret his criterion of demarcation as a requirement to *actually* falsify a theory through experiments, when in fact it is the requirement for a theory to be falsifiable *in principle*: we must be able to specify some conditions that, *if* they occurred, would falsify the theory. (Of course, if we can design *actual* tests, so much the better.) Popper agrees that it may be impossible to actually falsify a theory, but he stresses that this is not required by his demarcation criterion: "An entire literature rests on the failure to observe this distinction…. And the difficulties, in many cases the impossibility, of a conclusive practical falsification are put forward as a difficulty or even impossibility of the proposed criterion of demarcation…. This would all be of little importance but for the fact that it has led some people to abandon rationalism in the theory of science, and to tumble into irrationalism. For if science does not advance rationally and critically, how can we hope that rational decisions will be made anywhere else? A flippant attack on a misunderstood logical-technical term [falsifiability] has thus led some people to far-reaching and disastrous philosophical and even political conclusions."[36]

---

[34] Popper, "Replies to My Critics," p. 963.

[35] Karl R. Popper, *Objective Knowledge: An Evolutionary Approach*, rev. ed. (Oxford: Oxford University Press, 1979), p. 1.   [36] Popper, *Aim of Science*, pp. xxii–xxiii.

The New Pseudosciences

The Mechanistic Roots

In the following subsections, we are going to examine some of the greatest mechanistic delusions of our time. I ignore here the fads that emerge continually in the human sciences – fads like those we encountered in "Scientism" in chapter 1. Although any one of these delusions can be shown to display the characteristics of a pseudoscience, examining them would be an interminable task. I will single out, instead, three major theories – or, rather, systems of theories – which are among the most influential intellectual movements of our time: the psychological theory of behaviourism, the social theory of structuralism, and the linguistic theory of universal grammar. The first two are now defunct, but the third one is still drawing a large number of believers.

Unlike the lesser fads, which last only a few years and attract relatively few scientists, the three theories I have selected for study dominated their respective fields for many decades. Also, their founders and supporters are world-famous scientists: men like Noam Chomsky, B. F. Skinner, Jean Piaget, and Claude Lévi-Strauss are among the best-known intellectuals of the twentieth century. As these three delusions became major research programs, they are good examples of the new pseudosciences. The discussion, however, is not meant to be a complete study of their fallacies. What I want is only to bring out their common characteristics (which they also share with the *software* pseudosciences, as we will see in chapter 7): their mechanistic foundation, and their dishonest methods. Here is a summary of the common characteristics.

Scientists who uphold these theories regard mechanism as undisputed truth. That is, the possibility of arriving at a useful solution or explanation through reductionism and atomism is not taken as hypothesis, but as established fact. It is this dogmatic attitude that prevents them from accepting the evidence later, when their theories fail. They notice a structure – a certain regularity, or uniformity, or pattern – in the phenomenon they are investigating, and immediately conclude that this structure can form the basis of a mechanistic theory.

The structure they noticed is, of course, one of the structures that make up the complex phenomenon. Their mistake is to assume that its interactions with the other structures can be ignored. They believe that a *simple* structure (their mechanistic theory, which reflects the one structure they noticed in the phenomenon) can provide a useful approximation of the *complex* structure (the whole phenomenon). When they base their theory on one structure, when they assume that it alone can represent the phenomenon, these scientists commit the fallacy of reification: they extract that structure from the complex whole, and thereby sever its interactions (which are, in fact, the most important part of the phenomenon). And even when they do recognize that one structure alone cannot represent the phenomenon, they still expect to find a mechanistic theory, by somehow combining several structures.

The mechanistic nature of the theory can manifest itself in one or more of these features: the use of atomistic and reductionistic concepts; the use of hierarchical concepts or diagrams, of neat systems of things within things; the use of other precise diagrams, or rules, or methods, or mathematical representations. As we know, all these models are logically equivalent to a simple hierarchical structure. Mechanistic theories, in the end, always claim the same thing; namely, that a precise and relatively simple diagram, or formula, or procedure can describe and explain a complex phenomenon. They claim, in other words, that it is possible to find a deterministic representation for an indeterministic phenomenon.

Up to this point, the scientists are only guilty of wishful thinking. They are convinced that a mechanistic approximation can explain their phenomenon, so they naively emulate the methods employed in fields like physics or astronomy, where mechanistic approximations are indeed useful. But when their theory proves to be inadequate, instead of abandoning it, they forsake their responsibility as scientists and turn it into a pseudoscience: they search for confirmations; they ignore or suppress the falsifications; and, to deal with those falsifications that cannot be denied, they incorporate them into the theory.

Specifically, the scientists repeatedly expand the theory by adding various features, principles, and conditions to make the falsifying situations appear to be part of it. They coin pretentious terms for these modifications, to make them look like novel and important concepts, when in reality their function is to reinstate old, informal concepts – precisely those concepts that the original theory had tried to exclude. Often, they describe the modifications with terms like "transformation" or "normalization," borrowed from mathematics; but, whereas in mathematics these are exact operations, in pseudoscience they are makeshift, artificial conversions, invented in order to bring the falsifying instances into the range of events that the theory can be said to account for.

It is the mechanistic dogma, in the final analysis, that fosters these pseudosciences. Even when an idea starts as an honest attempt to explain a phenomenon, even if it starts as a falsifiable and testable concept, the belief in mechanism is bound to make it unfalsifiable. If a theory is grounded on mechanism and mechanism is accepted unquestioningly, a falsifying instance is necessarily interpreted as an anomaly, a rare exception. Its supporters, therefore, see nothing wrong in ignoring the falsification, or in modifying the theory to cope with it. They verify their theory and confirm that it does indeed obey the mechanistic principles. So the theory, they conclude, cannot possibly be wrong. If its predictions are contradicted by a certain event, something must be wrong with that event; or perhaps the theory needs an adjustment.

Now, if these falsifications were limited to a few cases, they would indeed be exceptions, and the mechanistic theory would provide a useful approximation. But in mechanistic delusions the falsifications never cease, and the theory must be modified again and again to match reality. It then becomes an unfalsifiable, and hence worthless, concept. Its supporters, though, do not consider this activity to be dishonest, or unprofessional, or illogical. On the contrary: because the mechanistic ideology has redefined science to mean the pursuit of mechanistic concepts, even when these concepts are useless, an activity that tries to save a mechanistic theory from refutation is seen as the very model of scientific work.

Behaviourism

1

The first of the modern mechanistic pseudosciences was the psychological theory known as *behaviourism*. There aren't many behaviourists left today, but for more than half a century, and as late as the 1960s, behaviourism was the dominant school in academic psychology, especially in American universities. In addition, behaviourism had a profound influence on sociology and the other human sciences.

Described as *behavioural science* – the science of human behaviour – behaviourism was seen by its advocates as an effort to turn psychology into an exact science, like physics. Psychological theories, the behaviourists claimed, will not be as successful as the theories of the exact sciences as long as they deal with the subjective and unscientific concept known as the mind. The exact sciences deal with real entities – entities that can be observed and measured. So, if psychology is to become an exact science, we must stop searching for theories of the mind, and confine ourselves to the study of human *behaviour*; namely, those human acts that can be observed, measured, and subjected to experiments.

Behaviourism, thus, rejected the traditional subjects of psychology – consciousness, knowledge, intelligence, memory, volition, emotions, beliefs, desires, fears, etc. These phenomena, the behaviourists say, are nothing but the combination of some elementary units of behaviour; and, once we identify those units, we will be in a position to describe with precision all human acts. As in physics, therefore, we must trust the principles of reductionism and atomism, and search for the smallest bits of behaviour, the simplest human acts that can be observed: reflexes, blinking of eyelids, the movement of a finger or limb, and the like. These elementary acts are the behavioural atoms: the building blocks from which all human acts are made up, including those complex acts we attribute to intelligence. Behaviourism asserts, in other words, that there are no hidden, private, internal processes – processes requiring the invention of a concept like the mind. All human acts can be explained as a combination of simple mechanical processes, which can be observed and assessed objectively by an experimenter.

Human beings learn to display a particular combination of behavioural atoms by interacting with their environment. The basic unit of interaction is the *stimulus-response* mechanism, or S-R: an event in the environment provides the stimulus, and the organism produces the response. The responses are the behavioural atoms just mentioned; and the stimuli are the simplest events that can be perceived by the organism with its senses (the presence of a certain object, or light, or sound). When the organism is exposed to various stimuli and tries various responses, it gradually discovers certain associations between the stimuli and the responses. The associations it discovers are those that produce pleasant experiences or prevent unpleasant ones. The phenomenon whereby the organism establishes these associations is called *reinforcement*, and is taken to be a propensity of all organisms. The process whereby an organism acquires a certain set of S-R units is called *conditioning*.

The connections between stimuli and responses – the S-R units – are thus the basic elements from which all interaction between the organism and its environment is made up. The interaction is assumed to be strictly sensori-motor: the stimuli affect the senses, and the responses are muscular or glandular reactions. Ultimately, all human acts can be explained through a reduction to combinations of S-R units. There is nothing else.

The era of behaviourism started in 1913, when John B. Watson, generally viewed as its founder, published his "behaviourist manifesto": the proclamation that psychology must be practised as an objective science, and that its goal must be, not just to observe, but to predict and control human behaviour. In other words, the task of psychologists is to study and manipulate human minds, just as other scientists study and manipulate physical entities.

Historically, behaviourism was a continuation of the mechanistic theories of mind originated two centuries earlier by John Locke, David Hume, and David Hartley. These theories, which later became known as associationism, maintained that all knowledge can be explained as combinations of various knowledge atoms connected through stronger or weaker associations.

The early behaviourists gained additional confidence from the work of physiologist Ivan Pavlov, who investigated the process of conditioned reflexes in dogs: after learning to associate the presence of food with a certain stimulus (a specific sound or image), the dog would salivate even when this stimulus alone, without any food, was presented. This seemed to prove the stimulus-response theory – for *reflex* responses, at least. The behaviourists also liked the theory of Edward Thorndike, who experimented with cats and explained their learning behaviour as nothing more than trial and error and conditioning – a process that requires no intelligence.

Although even this limited evidence was later shown to be tenuous, the behaviourists saw nothing wrong in extrapolating it to explain, not only *all* animal behaviour, but also *human* behaviour, and even human *intelligence*. Thus, experiments with animals – especially rats – and a preoccupation with their simplest acts became the distinguishing features of behaviourism. For several decades, scientists were trying to understand human intelligence by studying the behaviour of rats through trivial experiments in which the animals were rewarded with food for performing some simple acts. An endless variety of such experiments were designed, all for the purpose of studying and measuring with precision the process of animal conditioning. One ingenious device, for instance, invented by Skinner and known as the Skinner box, consists of a small cage equipped with a mechanism that releases a food pellet into a tray when the animal inside presses a lever. It also includes means for automatically controlling this reward and for counting and recording the animal's attempts. Through such experiments, scientists can determine the rate of learning and extinction of various patterns of behaviour under different conditions.

The behaviourists justified their experiments with animals by claiming that human behaviour, while more complex than the behaviour of rats, is not *qualitatively* different; it is only a more complicated combination of the same atoms of behaviour. The purpose of their experiments is to restrict the animal's environment so as to isolate and study these atoms. Obviously, we cannot subject *people* to experiments in a laboratory. But, whether we study animals or humans, at the lowest levels we are observing the same phenomena. Just as the same bricks are used to build both small and large buildings, the atoms that make up animal behaviour can also be used to explain *human* behaviour.

2

Behaviourism did not work, of course. It failed to explain even the behaviour of rats, let alone that of humans. It was successful only in those experiments that created a highly impoverished, artificial environment – an environment in which the animals were almost forced to display the kind of responses the experimenters expected of them. When observed in their natural environment, the animals' behaviour remained quite unpredictable, and the behaviourist theories were useless.

Like all mechanistic delusions, behaviourism extracted from the complex structure that constitutes the phenomenon in question (animal or human intelligence, in this case) a simple structure (the patterns of visible behaviour, in this case), assuming that one structure could explain the whole phenomenon. Now, there is no doubt that animals and humans are affected by their environment, that they sense stimuli and exhibit responses, and that there exists a process of associations and reinforcement which occurs somehow in conjunction with their experiences. But these patterns and regularities cannot be extracted and studied in isolation. They are only *some* of the structures that make up the existence of animals and humans, and when studying them on their own we ignore their interactions with the other structures. This is why the behaviourist model can only account for the simplest kind of behaviour – the kind for which the interactions with the other structures are indeed weak enough to be ignored.

Even for a mechanistic theory, behaviourism was very naive. In particular, it tried to explain everything with *chains* of S-R units, rather than structures of elements within elements. It claimed, in effect, that a trivial two-level hierarchy (S-R units as terminal elements and behaviour as the top element) can account for all knowledge and intelligence. Unlike most mechanistic theories, it did not try to build large, multilevel hierarchical models, so it did not even exploit fully the concepts of reductionism and atomism.

We must not be surprised that such a naive theory did not work. But let us see how, instead of admitting that it was refuted by evidence, its supporters turned it into a pseudoscience. First, they adopted the simple tactic of looking for confirmations and ignoring the falsifications. They designed their experiments not as severe tests, not as attempts to *falsify* the theory, but as means to *verify* it; specifically, as means to produce the results they wanted to see. Since they wanted to confirm that behaviour can be reduced to simple elements, their experiments consisted in creating restricted environments, in which the rats could perform *only* simple acts (pressing a bar, for instance). When the environment was more complex (finding their way in a maze, for instance), the rats frequently displayed unexpected and more intelligent behaviour, which could not be readily explained. Since Thorndike wanted to prove that the only way cats can learn is by trial and error, he designed his experiments so that the only way to solve the problem was by trial and error. In other experiments, when confronted with different challenges, cats were shown to act more intelligently.[1]

The tactic, thus, consisted in simplifying and restricting the experimental environment until the animals' behaviour was reduced to a small number of trivial, isolated acts, at which point the scientists could indeed confirm their hypothesis of behavioural atoms. In this artificial environment, models based on S-R chains did indeed provide a useful approximation of behaviour, but only because, out of the whole range of normal behaviour, the animals were restricted to isolated S-R structures. It was this limited behaviour that the model explained. When used to explain their normal, natural behaviour, which includes many interacting structures, the model failed.

Another tactic used by behaviourists to confirm their conditioning theories was, obviously, the choice of animals. Rats and pigeons were the preferred subjects in their experiments precisely because it was found that these creatures, being particularly docile and rather stupid, were most likely to display the kind of behaviour these theories postulated.

While the behaviourists were busy confirming over and over their theories with contrived experiments, their critics had no difficulty finding falsifications. The most common problem was the failure to reproduce in the real world the results observed in artificial laboratory conditions. If exposed to conditioning experiments while in their natural environment, animals ranging from pigs to whales were found to behave unpredictably, contradicting the laboratory theories.[2] These falsifications were ignored by behaviourists. Also ignored were the "experiments on experimenters," which showed that the laboratory measurements of rat performance that were so confidently accepted by everyone were in fact biased, and merely reflected the expectations of the individual experimenters.[3]

So for half a century, while the world believed that these scientists were studying human psychology, what they were studying was not even animal psychology, but some technicalities related to experiments designed to confirm

[1] Arthur Koestler, *The Act of Creation* (New York: Macmillan, 1964), pp. 568–571.

[2] Kellar Breland and Marian Breland, "The Misbehavior of Organisms," cited in Lawrence LeShan, *The Dilemma of Psychology: A Psychologist Looks at His Troubled Profession* (New York: Dutton, 1990), pp. 76–78.

[3] R. Rosenthal and K. L. Fode, "The Effect of Experimenter Bias on the Performance of the Albino Rat," cited in Koestler, *Act of Creation*, p. 568.

their fantasies: "In spite of the impressive mathematical apparatus, and the painstaking measurements of 'rates of response,' 'habit-strength,' 'fractional anticipatory goal-responses,' and the rest, rarely in the history of science has a more ambitious theory been built on shakier foundations."[4]

3

Let us examine next how behaviourists used the other pseudoscientific tactic to make their theory unfalsifiable: repeatedly modifying the theory by incorporating into it the falsifying situations. The original theory postulated that all behaviour can be reduced to chains of S-R units, and that both the stimuli and the responses are small, atomic units, which can be observed and measured experimentally. Apart from trivial experiments, however, behaviour could not be reduced to S-R chains, and responses could not be reduced to elementary movements. Thus, because the evidence did not agree with the theory, behaviourists made the theory agree with the evidence – by expanding it to account for those situations that it could not explain. Also true to the pseudoscientific tradition, they invented impressive terms to describe the extensions. This served to mask the fact that the extensions were not new features but reversals of the original claims. What the extensions accomplished, essentially, was to reinstate the complex and inexplicable capabilities traditionally attributed to a mind – capabilities which had been specifically excluded earlier, because they could not be measured or reduced to atomic units.

For example, to account for the unaccountable responses, Edward Tolman held that there are two kinds of behaviour: higher levels, or *molar*, and lower levels, or *molecular*; and only the molecular levels can be explained with S-R units. Behaviour at the molar level is an *emergent* phenomenon and cannot be reduced to, or explained in terms of, molecular units. Edwin Guthrie invented a similar concept: the movements of the organism are low levels of behaviour, while the complex acts are high levels; and acts cannot be explained in terms of movements alone. These extensions introduced some mysterious processes between the stimulus and the response, which explained previously unexplainable responses only by remaining unexplained themselves, and were therefore a radical departure from the original goal of strict reductionism.

Tolman also introduced the concept of *intervening variables*. These variables – described as subjective and unexplainable phenomena that somehow occur between the stimulus and the response – served to revive the traditional,

---

[4] Koestler, *Act of Creation*, p. 568.

informal concept of *mental* acts. The informal concept of *drives* was also revived, and was profitably employed to explain certain types of behaviour. And to combat the limitations of the atomic behavioural units, Tolman introduced "sign-Gestalt expectations," which used the *holistic* concepts of Gestalt psychology – a reversal of the *atomistic* principles of behaviourism.

So, little by little, the traditional psychological concepts were reinstated, and were incorporated into behaviourism in the guise of new features. The behaviourists continued to use S-R chains to explain trivial responses, and reverted to the traditional, informal concepts whenever they had to describe complex forms of behaviour.

By the time of B. F. Skinner, the last and best known of the great behaviourists, the countless "enhancements" made the theory sufficiently different from its original version to earn it the title *neobehaviourism*. Skinner added his own enhancements, of which the most important was a complete obliteration of the original meaning of stimuli and responses. And, although in his experiments he never progressed beyond chains of simple S-R units with rats and pigeons, he confidently extrapolated these results into the most fantastic theories of human knowledge and human society.

Thus, in his Skinner boxes he managed to shape the behaviour of pigeons so as to make them perform some relatively complex and unusual acts; for example, walk to a certain wall of the box and peck at a coloured disk there. He achieved that by reinforcing, in several stages, various movements which the bird had performed randomly in the direction of the disk, thus creating a chain of conditioned S-R units that looked like one purposeful act. From successes such as this, Skinner boldly concluded that everything human beings learn is also in the form of simple S-R chains, and human acts that appear purposeful or intelligent are only illusions, just as the pigeon's act was an illusion.

He could not confirm this hypothesis, nor describe how various intelligent or creative acts can be reduced to chains of S-R units. What he did instead was modify the meaning of "stimulus" and "response" to match whatever acts had to be explained. For his rats and pigeons, these terms retained their original meaning of elementary sensations and movements. But for human behaviour, the terms expanded to include, respectively, such complex acts as reading a letter and then reacting emotionally to its contents, or being threatened with a weapon and then surrendering one's wallet, or noticing merchandise displayed in an alluring fashion and then purchasing something. Thus, the concept of stimulus and response became so vague that it could account for any human act, thereby rendering the whole theory unfalsifiable. Moreover, the requirement to reduce complex acts to combinations of behavioural atoms – to the movement of a finger or an eyelid, for example – was forsaken. By now behaviourism had completely abandoned its original goal of being an exact science of behaviour. Judged by their own standards, the behaviourists were now mere charlatans.

Using the new, high-level concept, Skinner even managed to describe linguistic performance (which behaviourists called "verbal behaviour") as nothing but stimuli and responses. Again, he makes no attempt to reduce language-based communication to elementary S-R units (which might be the movement of the tongue or lips, or the vibration of the eardrum). Instead, stimulus and response refer now directly to such complex behaviour as creating and understanding sentences, formulating a challenging question, or returning an intelligent answer. Skinner's naive views of language attracted a scathing criticism from linguist Noam Chomsky, in a review that became somewhat of a classic.[5]

Some say that the demise of behaviourism was hastened by Chomsky's criticism and the rising popularity of his own theories of mind; others say that it was the rise of cognitive science and the theories that depict the mind as a computing device. Either way, the shift exemplifies a spectacle common in the academic world: one pseudoscience is replaced with another; one popular theory is displaced by another, which seems very different, when in reality both are rooted in the mechanistic culture and suffer therefore from the same fallacy – the belief that non-mechanistic phenomena can be represented with mechanistic models.

Structuralism

1

The movement known as *structuralism* was popular in one form or another for much of the twentieth century, especially in Europe. It flourished in the 1960s and 1970s, and had adherents even in the 1980s. Few remember it today. Structural linguistics, however, which acquired a life of its own through the work of Noam Chomsky, continues to dominate the study of language; I treat it, therefore, as a separate pseudoscience (see the next subsection, "Universal Grammar").

The structuralists noticed that, despite their immense variety, human activities, languages, societies, customs, and institutions display many regularities. The reason for this uniformity, the structuralists say, is that all human acts are governed ultimately by the working of the brain. Thus, since human brains

---

[5] Noam Chomsky, "A Review of B. F. Skinner's *Verbal Behavior,*" *Language* 35, no. 1 (1959): 26–58.

are the same everywhere, from the most primitive societies to the most advanced, we should not be surprised to find the same patterns in the various aspects of their cultures.

Up to this point, the structuralist idea is quite sensible. When expressed informally, it is neither ambitious nor original. This modest idea, however, is only the *basis* of the structuralist philosophy. The important claim is that the biological characteristics of the brain can be described mathematically. These characteristics constitute, as it were, an alphabet of human propensities; and, once we discover this alphabet, we will be able to depict with precision every human accomplishment as a function of the human propensities.

The structuralists claim, in other words, that it is possible to represent mathematically all human capabilities; and, since the various types of human activities are in the end combinations of these capabilities, they too can be represented mathematically. Human activities, therefore, are no different from the phenomena studied by physics or chemistry. Thus, anthropologist Claude Lévi-Strauss, the most famous structuralist, claimed that the customs of all societies that ever existed are nothing but "certain combinations from a repertoire of ideas which it should be possible to reconstitute [and depict as] a sort of periodical chart of chemical elements, analogous to that devised by Mendeleev. In this, all customs, whether real or merely possible, would be grouped by families and all that would remain for us to do would be to recognize those which societies had, in point of fact, adopted."[1]

We recognize structuralism as one of those mechanistic theories that attempt to reduce to mathematics the complex phenomena studied by the human sciences. Structuralism is especially ambitious, though, in that it does not limit itself to one discipline, but claims that *all* human activities can be reduced to *the same* mental operations. Disciplines like anthropology, linguistics, psychology, sociology, political science, and philosophy can be turned into exact sciences, no different from physics or chemistry, simply by discovering the elementary human propensities. One day, the structuralists say, we will be able to explain everything in the human universe – every sentence we utter, every custom and tradition, every piece of literature and folklore, every work of art, every musical composition, every type of social organization, and even our clothes fashions and our cooking and eating habits – with equations as precise as the equations of physics.[2]

---

[1] Claude Lévi-Strauss, *Tristes Tropiques*, p. 60, quoted in Howard Gardner, *The Quest for Mind: Piaget, Lévi-Strauss, and the Structuralist Movement* (New York: Knopf, 1973), p. 118.

[2] It must be stressed that these were actual claims, made as late as the 1970s and 1980s. Respected scientists were actually working on theories that attempted to represent mathematically these aspects of human life.

❖

Historically, structuralism has its roots in some of the linguistic theories proposed in the 1930s. Roman Jacobson, among others, showed that all languages share a set of common features. This, however, becomes evident only when studying the smallest elements of language: the sounds that make up phonemes. These sounds (the atoms of verbal communication) are based on a small set of elementary features. Moreover, it is possible to describe these features in terms of *binary opposites*: a phoneme is voiced or unvoiced, nasal or oral, etc. This discovery gave linguists hope that the phenomenon of language can be represented with a mechanistic model: since any sentence, in any language, can be expressed as a combination of phonemes, we should be able to reduce sentences to exact structures of sounds, and hence explain the phenomenon of language mathematically.

No one has achieved this, of course, and we know why. Language is a complex phenomenon, a system of interacting structures. The mechanists isolate these structures and study them separately, hoping to find one that can explain, alone, the complex phenomenon. The structure created by sounds plays indeed a part in language, but it interacts with the others: the meaning of words, the context in which we use a sentence, syntax rules, voice stress, and various knowledge structures present in the mind. It is impossible to explain the whole phenomenon of language with *one* structure, no matter how accurate that structure is. Thus, a theory that tries to represent language as sound structures alone is very naive – as naive as one, like Chomsky's, based on syntactic structures alone. If we view the richness of language as the large set of alternatives for the top element of a complex structure, then an isolated structure cannot explain language because it cannot account for all the alternatives: when we separate the structures we lose their interactions, and with them many of the alternatives.

But without waiting for a confirmation of the phoneme theory with actual languages, the structuralists extrapolated it to cover, not only language, but all human capabilities. Thus, Lévi-Strauss maintained that all aspects of culture, all human activities, can be seen as forms of communication, and hence as languages; and if all *languages* seem to be based on a small set of common elements, we should also expect to find an analogous set of common elements in all *cultures*. He then proceeded to analyze hundreds of myths and customs collected from primitive societies, searching for their common elements. This analysis, according to Lévi-Strauss, is a process of *decoding*. The various myths or customs may look very different from one another, and may appear disordered, complicated, or illogical, but this is because we only see their *surface structures*; it is their *deep structures* that we must study, and it is at these low levels that we will discover the common elements. As in the phoneme theory, the atomic concepts of human knowledge form pairs of binary opposites: left/right, good/bad, male/female, day/night, up/down, cold/warm, and so forth. Myths and customs, and all other aspects of a culture, can be reduced to combinations of such binary concepts.

We can start with any myth or custom, therefore, and through a process of *transformations* we will arrive at a structure similar to that of another myth or custom, belonging perhaps to a different society. The transformations convert a surface structure – the story told by a myth, the costume worn by a woman, the painting or carving of an object, the rules observed in a certain social setting, the food eaten on a certain occasion – into the common, atomic concepts; that is, into one of the two parts of various pairs of opposites. At this low level, all myths, customs, traditions, and institutions reveal similar structures; and the chief component of these structures is a play between opposing themes. Since the atomic concepts, according to the structuralist theory, are a reflection of the basic capabilities of the mind, it seems that an important function of the brain is to classify experiences into opposite categories.

While anthropologists like Lévi-Strauss were analyzing myths and customs, other structuralists were using similar techniques to analyze works of art, of literature, or of historiography. Their goal was the same: to find the set of basic elements (the building blocks, or alphabet) from which a whole body of works is constructed. They tried to show, for instance, that the meaning of a novel, or poem, or painting is only a surface structure; that it can be reduced, through a process of transformations, to a deep structure; and that, at this level, we find the same atomic concepts as in another novel, or poem, or painting.

Psychologist Jean Piaget believed that all human intelligence can be reduced to a small set of binary operations that are very similar to the basic operations of mathematical logic. As we grow up, our mind acquires new operations and learns to combine them into more and more complex logical structures. This theory, he claimed, is all we need in order to explain how humans perform intelligent acts of increasing complexity.

To reduce intelligent behaviour to binary operations, Piaget suggested various transformations, analogous to those defined in modern algebra: "The algebra of logic can help us to specify psychological structures, and to put into calculus form those operations and structures central to our actual thought processes."[3] He tried to prove his theory by subjecting children of various ages to intelligence tests of increasing levels of difficulty. The purpose of these

---

[3] Jean Piaget, *Logic and Psychology*, p. xvii, quoted in Margaret A. Boden, *Piaget* (London: Fontana, 1979), p. 80.

experiments was to explain the intellectual development of the child in terms of basic logical operations. If, for example, a four-year-old child correctly solves a problem which a three-year-old child cannot solve, Piaget explains this progress by identifying some logical operators or transformations that are required to arrive at the solution, and concludes that they are only acquired by the mind at four.

The structuralists are fascinated by a rather trivial quality of binary operations: they can be combined to generate complex patterns while starting with operands that have only two values (*yes* and *no, 0* and *1*, etc.). For example, certain problems and solutions can be represented with a hierarchical structure, if we employ this structure as a decision tree; that is, as decisions within decisions, where each decision involves two alternatives. We know that only *mechanistic* knowledge can be represented with simple hierarchical structures; but the structuralists believe that *all* knowledge can be reduced to such decision trees, and hence to the binary elements and operations known as Boolean logic (the same elements and operations used in digital circuits).

The inanity of the structuralist theories is evident in these silly analogies of minds to computers (which are far more naive than the ideas of artificial intelligence – themselves futile mechanistic pursuits, as we saw in chapter 2). Computers do indeed perform complex tasks by reducing them to simple binary operations, but the use of the word "binary" is the only thing that computer logic has in common with structuralism. Unlike the vague transformations of structuralism, computer operations can be explained completely and precisely, down to the last bit.

Thus, using terms and concepts borrowed from logic, Piaget describes the "Boolean operations" and "truth tables" that allegedly can be employed to explain human intelligence.[4] An important set of logical operations, for instance, which appears only in adult intelligent behaviour, is the "quaternary group" of operations called INRC (which stands for Identity, Negation, Reciprocity, and Correlativity, or inversion): "What we have here is a group of four transformations of which the operations of a two-valued propositional logic supply as many instances as one can form quaternaries from the elements of its set of subsets.... The group INRC has for its elements, not the 4 cases of a truth table for 2 variables, but the 16 combinations of its set of subsets (or, for 3 variables, the 256 combinations, and so on). Because of its greater complexity, the INRC group does not make its appearance psychologically until early adolescence, whereas ... simpler models of groups of 4 elements are accessible to 7 and 8 year olds."[5]

[4] See chapter 4, p. 332 for a brief discussion of Boolean operations and truth tables.
[5] Jean Piaget, *Structuralism* (New York: Harper and Row, 1971), pp. 31–32 n. 9.

What Piaget is saying here is that, as our mental capabilities develop, we can handle problems that involve more facts and more combinations of facts, because we can process larger decision trees. This is undoubtedly true, but it doesn't follow that we can represent mental processes with mathematical logic. The reason, again, is that mental processes are complex structures: when our mind develops, we gain the capacity to handle, not just increasingly large decision trees, but *interacting* decision trees. The simple structures suggested by Piaget constitute, in effect, a mechanistic mind model; and, like all mechanistic approximations, in simple situations this model may well be adequate.

Lévi-Strauss, too, takes the binary operations of computers as evidence of the validity of structuralism. For example, after struggling to find some connection between the wind and a flatfish in a certain myth, he concludes that they both function as "binary operators," because both have *yes/no* qualities (the flatfish can be seen from one angle but not from another, and the wind can either blow or not). So, "we could only understand this property of the myth at a time when cybernetics and computers have come to exist in the scientific world and have provided us with an understanding of binary operations which had already been put to use in a very different way with concrete objects or beings by mythical thought."[6] It is hardly necessary to point out the absurdity of this comparison of myth-logic to computer logic.

Edmund Leach is another structuralist fascinated by the binary operations of computers: "In some respects and in some circumstances, the products of expressive action (e.g. ritual sequences, mythological texts, poems, musical scores, art forms) show marked pattern similarity to the output of a digital computer, and when we attempt to decode such message-bearing systems we usually find that binary discriminations of the *yes/no* type are very prominent."[7] But the only "decoding" that Leach manages to perform through his analogy to computers is some speculative interpretation of a few isolated cultural elements, no better than the interpretation reached through any other type of analysis.

2

As pseudoscientific theories go, structuralism is not very sophisticated: it belongs to the category of pseudosciences that are unfalsifiable from the start. These theories, we saw earlier, manage to escape refutation by making claims

[6] Claude Lévi-Strauss, *Myth and Meaning* (New York: Schocken Books, 1979), p. 23.
[7] Edmund Leach, *Culture and Communication: The Logic by which Symbols are Connected* (New York: Cambridge University Press, 1976), p. 57.

so vague that any event appears to confirm them. In the case of structuralism, it is the concepts of transformations and binary opposites that are vague and make the theory unfalsifiable.

In mathematics, transformations are well-defined operations, but the structuralists employ this term freely, whenever they want to show that one aspect of culture is related to another. In particular, they don't restrict themselves to a *fixed* set of transformations; rather, for every pair of stories, customs, or works of art which they wish to relate, they feel free to invent, if necessary, a new type of transformation. Clearly, we can always find some common elements in different aspects of culture. So, if what we seek is *any* relation, with just a little imagination we can relate any stories, customs, works of art, and so forth. The transformations are meaningless, therefore, precisely because they are guaranteed to work: there are no aspects of culture that *cannot* be related through one transformation or another. This guarantee makes the concept unfalsifiable, and hence worthless.

This weakness was pointed out by many critics. Philip Pettit, for example, after analyzing structuralism in general and Lévi-Strauss's work in particular, concludes: "The objection to Lévi-Strauss's method … is that the sort of hypothesis that he puts up in the analysis of [myths] is just not falsifiable."[8] "The method is hardly more than a licence for the free exercise of imagination in establishing associations between myths."[9] Lévi-Strauss divides a myth into a number of elements, selecting those elements that best fit his purpose. Then, he relates them to the elements of another myth in any way he chooses: he may call them "equivalent," or "inverted," or "symmetrical," or anything else. In the end, "if the only constraints put on transformation are that it be achieved by a set of rules then anything can be transformed into anything: you make up the rules as you go along. Thus with a modicum of ingenuity, any two myths could be presented as transformations or versions of one another."[10]

Similarly, the concept of binary opposites is not restricted to a set of well-defined attributes, like left/right, male/female, or light/dark, but is extended to fit any situation. As a result, any number of contrasts can be found between the elements of a myth, or between the elements of two different myths. A particular animal, for instance, can be contrasted with a human; or, if a land animal, with a fish or bird; or, if it hunts by day, with one that hunts by night; or, if it has coloured stripes, with one that has no stripes; and so on. These pairs of attributes are indeed binary opposites, and they represent valid relations; but this doesn't mean that myths can be analyzed mathematically. The elements of myths have *many* such attributes, so myths are connected through many

---

[8] Philip Pettit, *The Concept of Structuralism: A Critical Analysis* (Berkeley: University of California Press, 1975), p. 88.   [9] Ibid., p. 96.   [10] Ibid., p. 90.

structures at the same time, one for each attribute. The totality of myths constitutes a complex structure.

The structuralists use terms like "isomorphism," "dimensions," "axes," and "matrices" to describe how the individual structures overlap and interact. But, while having a precise meaning in mathematics, these terms are only vague analogies in structuralism. Thus, Lévi-Strauss claims that "the algebra of the brain can be represented as a rectangular matrix of at least two (but perhaps several) dimensions which can be 'read' up and down or side to side like the words of a crossword puzzle."[11] The use of terms like "matrix," however, is the only thing that the "algebra of the brain" has in common with real algebra.

Using this sort of mathematics, Leach attempts to show that three stories from the Bible "have the same general structure and ... reflect the same narrative impulse."[12] He presents the various elements of these stories in a complex diagram full of blocks and arrows that suggest binary opposites in three or four dimensions.[13] Most of these opposites are contrived, as usual, but even if we accept them the diagram has no mathematical meaning. It is hard to see the point in this kind of analysis, since those conclusions that make sense – the recurring theme of good and evil, for instance – can be reached without structuralism's mathematical pretenses.

Lastly, Piaget's reduction of intelligence to mathematical logic has been shown by more than one critic to be inconsistent and ambiguous, and hence meaningless.[14] Thanks to the vagueness of his mathematics, however, the theory appears to be confirmed by almost any experiment. Thus, "it is often possible to amend Piaget's claims so as to take account of new, apparently conflicting, evidence. But this possibility may sometimes seem too strong for comfort, suggesting that his theory is so vague as to be virtually unfalsifiable."[15]

One reason why the structuralists fail to note the failure of their theories is that they always look for *confirmations*. We saw earlier that the correct way to assess a theory is by looking for *falsifications*; that is, by subjecting it to tests that attempt to *refute* it. Confirmations are worthless because, no matter how many we find, they cannot prove that the theory is valid.

The structuralists, thus, are convinced that all myths, customs, literature, etc., can be reduced to common structures through transformations, so they approach a new case, not by trying to show that it *cannot* be so reduced, but by *expecting* to find a common structure. As a result, when no meaningful interpretation is forthcoming, they keep analyzing it until they find *some*

---

[11] Edmund Leach, *Claude Lévi-Strauss* (Chicago: University of Chicago Press, 1974), p. 55.

[12] Howard Gardner, *The Quest for Mind: Piaget, Lévi-Strauss, and the Structuralist Movement* (New York: Knopf, 1973), p. 152.   [13] Ibid., p. 153.

[14] Margaret A. Boden, *Piaget* (London: Fontana, 1979), pp. 82–83.   [15] Ibid., p. 153.

similarity or contrast to another case. The harder it is to find a meaningful transformation, the closer that situation is to being a *falsification* of the theory. But the structuralists interpret even the most contrived analysis as confirmation: the structure is especially subtle, they say, and it takes a more complex transformation to decode it. Others, though, did not fail to notice the dishonesty of this procedure: "Not a few critics complain that Lévi-Strauss is *overly* clever; that he makes distinctions and syntheses where data are lacking or ambiguous; that he ignores information incompatible with his theories and overemphasizes the limited amount of information in their favour."[16]

In general, both Lévi-Strauss and Piaget have been criticized for employing imprecise terms, descriptions, and methodologies, for presenting as facts what are in reality subjective assessments, and for their inclination to interpret the results of experiments as confirmations of their theories when other explanations are also possible.[17]

The structuralist movement is a particularly morbid manifestation of our mechanistic culture, and a vivid demonstration of the resulting corruption. It is not surprising that serious workers were outraged by structuralism's inane theories and its unwarranted claims to scientific status. Stanislav Andreski, for example, in his harsh criticism of Lévi-Strauss's ideas, calls his meaningless symbols and transformations "crazy formulae" and "pseudo-mathematical decorations,"[18] and the graphic depictions of sexual matters from the life of primitive peoples, with their transformation into pseudo-mathematical representation, "surrealist pornography."[19]

Andreski is especially annoyed by the immense popularity that such worthless theories have among intellectuals: "No doubt the chief reason why Lévi-Strauss's inconsequential musings about applications of mathematics to the study of culture have found such a wide acclaim is that they affect many people as hallucinogenic incantations.... One of the great attractions of this kind of poetry masquerading as science is that it would be very difficult to invent a topic more remote from everything that matters in social life, and better fitted for a non-committal conversation among pseudo-intellectual international bureaucrats of most divergent outlooks and loyalties."[20]

---

[16] Gardner, *Quest for Mind*, p. 158.   [17] Ibid., pp. 219–221.
[18] Stanislav Andreski, *Social Sciences as Sorcery* (London: André Deutsch, 1972), p. 133.
[19] Ibid., p. 135.   [20] Ibid., pp. 135–136.

Universal Grammar

1

The linguistic theory of Noam Chomsky, based on the concept known as *universal grammar*, is seldom mentioned without being called revolutionary; even its critics agree that it has revolutionized the study of language. More than that, its influence has spread into related fields, notably psychology and the philosophy of mind.

Although it has its origins in earlier theories of structural linguistics, Chomsky's theory, first developed in the 1950s, is much more rigorous – and much more ambitious. Chomsky is searching for a theory, or model, that would account for each and every grammatical sentence in a particular language; in other words, a formal system of rules that can generate (just like a native speaker familiar with that particular language) all correct sentences, while avoiding the incorrect ones. This kind of formal grammar, which emulates a native speaker's knowledge, he called *generative grammar*. Due to the nature of its rules, it is also known as *transformational grammar*.

The study of grammar is, for Chomsky, the most important part of linguistics, and he believes that the traditional and structuralist theories failed to provide an adequate explanation of language because they were not formal enough. His project calls for a *mathematical* analysis of grammar, which would eventually allow any sentence to be formally described as a precise structure of linguistic elements: "Mathematical study of formal properties of grammars is, very likely, an area of linguistics of great potential."[1]

After half a century, however, Chomsky's theory still doesn't work. It has gone through innumerable versions; it has spawned countless sub-theories; it has grown into a fantastic array of rules and principles; but it still has not achieved its goal – a mechanistic model of the phenomenon of language. It can account for many aspects of language, of course, but this means very little: we know how easy it is to find mechanistic *approximations* of non-mechanistic phenomena. And the ultimate goal of Chomskyan linguistics remains as ambitious as ever: not an approximation, but a complete, formal description of all natural languages.

The fact that a theory which doesn't work can be so popular and influential in academic circles; its foundation on nothing more substantial than the observation of a few patterns and regularities; the practice of avoiding refutation by constantly expanding it to incorporate the falsifying instances; the

---

[1] Noam Chomsky, *Aspects of the Theory of Syntax* (Cambridge, MA: MIT Press, 1965), p. 62.

preoccupation with isolated mechanistic problems, the individual solution of which is interpreted as progress toward the explanation of the original, complex phenomenon – these characteristics make universal grammar an excellent example of the new pseudosciences.

A commonly expressed view is that, even if it will ultimately turn out to be mistaken, this theory will have made an invaluable contribution to linguistics by showing that it can be studied with the same methods as the exact sciences: "We must at least envisage the possibility that Chomsky's theory of generative grammar will be dismissed one day, by the consensus of linguists, as irrelevant to the description of natural languages.... I personally believe, and very many linguists will share this belief, that even if the attempt he has made to formalize the concepts employed in the analysis of languages should fail, the attempt itself will have immeasurably increased our understanding of these concepts and that in this respect the 'Chomskyan revolution' cannot but be successful."[2]

The fallacy of this view, of course, is that if the theory turns out to be mistaken it is precisely because mechanistic theories cannot explain the phenomenon of language. In this case, then, it will have made no contribution whatever to linguistics, nor to the understanding of the mind. Even more serious, we will see in the next section, is the fact that mechanistic delusions of this kind are causing great harm to society, by promoting a diminished view of our capabilities and responsibilities as individuals.

2

Chomsky maintains that our linguistic capacity has little to do with learning or culture. It is a biological trait, an *innate* human faculty: "The structure of particular languages may very well be largely determined by factors over which the individual has no conscious control and concerning which society may have little choice or freedom."[3]

Thus, Chomsky says, our language faculty is akin to an organ, and we must study it in the same way we study the function of organs. Every sentence we utter or comprehend is a reflection of this language organ, and it is possible to describe with mathematical precision the working of this organ by analyzing the structure of sentences. The task of linguistics, therefore, is to discover a model that can represent all the sentences that humans utter and comprehend when they use natural languages. This model will then help us to understand

---

[2] John Lyons, *Chomsky*, 3rd ed. (London: Fontana, 1991), p. 153.
[3] Chomsky, *Theory of Syntax*, p. 59.

how our mind processes language. And, since we probably have similar mental organs for performing other intelligent acts, the language model will also increase our general knowledge of the mind.

Chomsky is basing his hypothesis of an innate language faculty on a number of observations. For example, while the thousands of spoken languages and dialects appear very different from one another, on closer analysis they reveal common characteristics. Thus, sentences in all languages seem to have a neat hierarchical structure: they can be divided into distinct grammatical units (noun phrases, verb phrases, prepositional phrases, etc.), which can be further divided into parts (component phrases), then into words (nouns, verbs, adjectives, etc.), and finally into morphemes and phonemes (the smallest speech elements). Also, sentences in all languages can be modified to yield related forms: past or future tense, negative or passive meaning, etc. Languages may differ in the way the elements are combined into hierarchical structures, or in the way the modified forms are derived, but it seems that a small number of categories can account for all possible variations.

Another observation is how quickly and effortlessly children learn the particular language spoken in their community: without consciously studying the language, they acquire by the age of four or five a significant subset of the adult language, and by the age of twelve or fourteen practically the whole adult language. Thus, despite its complexity, children are capable of acquiring a language simply by being exposed to it – without having to learn its rules of grammar, and without even knowing that such rules exist. This fact contrasts, for example, with the lengthy and arduous learning process we must undergo to acquire a second language as adults. It also contrasts with the *general* mental development displayed by children: at an age when they are already proficient language users, their logical and mathematical abilities, for example, are still poor and can only be improved through painstaking learning.

We also note that all normal adults in a certain community manage to acquire the same language, despite otherwise great variations in level of education or in intellectual capabilities. It is also well known that a child will acquire whatever language he is exposed to: an English child growing up in a Japanese-speaking community will acquire Japanese just like a Japanese child.

But perhaps the most striking phenomenon is the *creativity* inherent in the knowledge of a language: individuals who acquired a language without even being aware of its rules of grammar can, nevertheless, produce an infinite number of original sentences that are grammatically correct. Also, they can instantly recognize whether a sentence they hear is grammatical or not (without being able to explain why), and they can understand the meaning of complicated sentences they have never heard before. Moreover, they accomplish this although the sentences they hear spoken in their community while growing up, and through which they presumably learned the language, are usually an impoverished and incorrect sample of that language.

All these facts, says Chomsky, can be explained only if we assume that human beings possess, as part of their genetic structure, a *language faculty*. There is no obvious reason for different languages to share so many important characteristics, or, for that matter, to have those particular characteristics in the first place. But this is readily explained if we assume that they are all governed by the same factors: certain limitations of the human mind. An innate language capacity also explains why all humans acquire a language so quickly and easily: we become proficient language users without having to consciously learn the language because, in a sense, we already know the language. We don't learn to grow arms, or to breath, or to digest food. Our organs develop and perform specific functions without any participation from us, so why should language be different? Since verbal communication confers such obvious evolutionary advantages, the human body has evolved a specific language capacity, just as it has evolved so many other functions and organs.

The language faculty is unique to human beings; it is a species-specific aptitude, like dam building for beavers or navigation for migratory birds. We are born with the capacity to acquire language, but at the same time, because this aptitude is part of our genetic structure, we are severely restricted in the type of languages that we can acquire naturally. The similarities we observe in the various languages are a reflection of these restrictions.

Also, the fact that it is so much easier for a child to acquire at an early age the complex system of rules that make up a natural language – while having such a hard time acquiring a system like mathematics, which is simpler – points to the special position occupied by language in our mental capabilities. Our brain is wired, so to speak, for natural languages, but not for other knowledge systems. Actually, acquiring a language is not a learning process at all, but more akin to the growth of an organ. Although there are variations among individuals, just as there are variations in height or lung capacity, the basic language faculty is the same for all human beings. And since any human being can acquire any language, we must conclude that it is not the features specific to a particular language, but the characteristics common to all languages, that form the innate language faculty.

Chomsky calls this set of common characteristics *universal grammar*: "Let us define 'universal grammar' (UG) as the system of principles, conditions, and rules that are elements or properties of all human languages not merely by accident but by [biological] necessity.... Thus UG can be taken as expressing 'the essence of human language.' UG will be invariant among humans."[4]

---

[4] Noam Chomsky, *Reflections on Language* (New York: Pantheon Books, 1975), p. 29.

Children acquire so easily whatever language they happen to be exposed to because they don't actually have to *learn* the language: since they already possess the knowledge of universal grammar, all they have to do is find out, as it were, how universal grammar is implemented in that particular language.

Chomsky believes that one day we will discover the physiological roots of these innate mental functions in the brain. In the meantime, we should be able to discover the principles of universal grammar – discover, that is, a theory, or model, that exactly represents it – simply by studying the languages themselves.[5] In fact, it doesn't even matter which language we study: whether we start with English or Chinese or Latin, we should reach the same model, because universal grammar includes only what is common to all languages. The comparative study of languages can perhaps help us to discover their common characteristics, but otherwise we may as well search for the model of universal grammar by studying the language we know best. Thus, Chomskyan linguistic concepts are derived largely from English sentences.

3

Chomsky's notions of a language faculty are, of course, pure speculations. His entire theory is grounded on the innateness hypothesis, but few people notice that the hypothesis itself is necessary only in order to account for a mechanistic theory of language. Typical of mechanistic question-begging, Chomsky started with the *assumption* that there exists a mechanistic theory of language, was then compelled to contrive an innateness hypothesis to explain linguistic phenomena mechanistically, and finally used this hypothesis as warrant for his research program. (Grounding a theory on biological and evolutionary hypotheses, instead of presenting it as a body of speculations, makes it more respectable.) The idea whose truth needs to be proved – the existence of a mechanistic explanation of language – is used as the starting point, as an assumption. This circularity is blurred by the enormous number of technical and complex aspects, and by their formal and rigorous treatment, which make the theory look like a serious scientific pursuit when in reality it is just another mechanistic delusion.

It is because people don't appreciate how fantastic its claims are that this theory is taken seriously at all. It would be instructive, therefore, to analyze its fallacies in some detail. And there is a second reason why we must devote more time to this pseudoscience than we did to behaviourism and structuralism: since the mechanistic language delusions have contributed to our mechanistic

[5] Ibid., p. 36.

software delusions, this analysis will help us later to understand the fallacies of *software* mechanism. Language and software fulfil a similar function – allowing us to mirror the world in our mind and to communicate with it; so it is not surprising that they engender the same type of delusions. (We will study this similarity in chapter 4.)

Linguistics is concerned with the study of the various aspects of language, especially phonology, morphology, syntax, and semantics. Some theories stop at the level of phonemes, morphemes, or words, but Chomsky's generative grammar, like other modern linguistic theories, is concerned with the structure of entire sentences. Significantly, linguists do not attempt to study elements of language that are more complex than sentences; they do not try to interpret, for example, the meaning of an argument encompassing several sentences. This, they say, is the task of philosophy, not linguistics.

But in normal discourse the meaning of sentences depends usually on the context in which they are used. Thus, if linguistics restricts itself to the study of isolated sentences, it must admit that there are certain aspects of language which necessarily lie beyond its range of explanations. And indeed, most linguistic theories are content to study only *some* aspects of language. Chomsky, though, claims that it is possible to discover a formal model that provides a complete and exact explanation of *all* possible sentences; specifically, a model that generates all the grammatical sentences in a given language and avoids the ungrammatical ones. In other words, he claims that we can account for all possible uses of a language from its grammar alone, without being concerned with the contexts in which the language might be used. But does this claim make sense?

In normal speech we rarely use words in isolation, so we rarely express a simple, rigid meaning of a word. When used in sentences, words can have more meanings than one could deduce by studying the words in isolation; it is the interactions between words – the complex structures generated in the mind when we interpret sentences – that provide the additional information. Similarly, we seldom use isolated sentences; a sentence is normally part of a context, and its meaning is affected by the meaning of the other sentences, by the interaction between its words and those of the other sentences, and also by any number of factors involving the persons who utter and interpret the sentences.

Thus, while there is much that can be learned about language by studying individual words and sentences, we cannot expect to detect all the information that a sentence can convey by studying it in isolation, any more than we can detect all possible meanings of a word by studying it in isolation. Yet this is precisely what Chomsky is attempting to do. He criticizes those linguistic theories that are content with an incomplete and informal analysis of sentences, and claims that it is possible to find an exact, mathematical model that accounts for all the information conveyed by a sentence. But how can a model based on isolated sentences accomplish this?

Chomsky studies isolated sentences because he knows that it is impossible to find a mechanistic theory for the whole phenomenon of language – which would be tantamount to searching for a mechanistic theory of all human knowledge. To recognize the futility of searching for a mechanistic representation of knowledge, we only need to recall the many attempts made by philosophers to find an exact correspondence between language and knowledge (we will examine some of these attempts in chapter 4). By studying isolated sentences, Chomsky reifies in effect small portions of language, and hence small portions of knowledge, from the complex phenomenon of human intelligence. By severing the interaction of these sentences with other knowledge structures, he gets closer to a mechanistic representation of language. But what he is studying now is no longer the whole phenomenon of language.

And Chomsky goes even further: not only does he extract individual sentences from their context, but he separates the syntax of the reified sentences from their semantics. Thus, he makes the bold claim that the syntax and the meaning of a sentence are independent structures and can be analyzed separately. As evidence, he notes the following two sentences: "colorless green ideas sleep furiously" and "furiously sleep ideas green colorless."[6] As speakers of English we recognize both sentences as meaningless, but for different reasons: the first sentence, although meaningless in many ways, is perfectly grammatical, while the second one is not; we can easily recognize certain syntactic elements in the first sentence, while in the second one we recognize none and end up treating each word as a separate phrase. It is as if we had a feeling of familiarity with the first sentence, but not with the second one, even though we hear both for the first time; we can memorize, for example, and recall the first sentence more easily than the second one.[7] This and other facts give Chomsky the confidence to postulate the independence of syntax from meaning. It is chiefly the syntactic structure of a sentence that determines how we interpret it: we feel more comfortable with the first sentence, although both are meaningless, because, being grammatical, our language organ can more readily cope with it.

Chomsky, thus, decided to ignore the meaning of sentences – their semantic aspect – altogether: universal grammar is independent of meaning, and we should be able to discover a precise and complete model of the language

---

[6] Noam Chomsky, *Syntactic Structures* (The Hague: Mouton, 1957), p. 15.
[7] Ibid., p. 16.

faculty without getting involved with the semantic interpretation of sentences. He agrees that we use both syntax and semantics to create and interpret sentences; but he argues that we can develop separately theories of syntax and of semantics.[8] In any case, syntax is the more important component, and it is the syntactic structure of sentences that is the essential element in a scientific study of language: "Despite the undeniable interest and importance of semantic and statistical studies of language, they appear to have no direct relevance to the problem of determining or characterizing the set of grammatical utterances."[9] "Grammar is best formulated as a self-contained study independent of semantics. In particular, the notion of grammaticalness cannot be identified with meaningfulness."[10]

The independence of syntax from meaning is, of course, just another hypothesis Chomsky had to adopt in order to find a mechanistic model of language. Thus, he observes that all attempts made by previous linguists to include aspects of semantics led to vague and unsatisfactory theories.[11] But, apart from a few examples and arguments, he made no serious attempt in his original theory to show why the two can be separated. He made it clear, in fact, that the main reason he prefers to view syntax as an independent subject is that this approach offers the only hope for a rigorous study of language: "The motivation for this self-imposed formality requirement for grammars is quite simple – there seems to be no other basis that will yield a rigorous, effective, and 'revealing' theory of linguistic structure."[12]

So, like the man who is looking for his keys under a streetlamp, not because that is where he lost them but because that is where there is light, Chomsky candidly admits that he is searching for a mechanistic theory simply because mechanistic theories are exact and "revealing." This they are, of course; but a revealing theory of *language* can be discovered only if there is something to reveal – only if language is indeed a mechanistic phenomenon.

Whether it is the reification of individual sentences from a discourse or the reification of syntax or semantics from a sentence, the goal is to break down a complex knowledge structure into several simple ones – which can then be represented with mechanistic models. The phenomenon of language is the result of many interacting structures (see p. 112). It is easy to identify some of the structures that make up a sentence, but just because we can identify them it doesn't follow that we can explain language by studying them separately.

---

[8] Ibid., ch. 9.   [9] Ibid., p. 17.   [10] Ibid., p. 106.
[11] Ibid., pp. 93–94.   [12] Ibid., p. 103.

Thus, structures like the syntax of a sentence, or the meaning of its words, or the context in which it is used, occur together; and they interact, because they share their elements. Moreover, their elements are not just the words, but also pieces of knowledge that, while not part of language, affect our interpretation of the sentence.

To convey the flavour of these issues, I will mention just one of the problems studied by Chomskyans – the problem of ambiguity. The sentence "John lost his book" can mean either that John lost his own book or that he lost another man's book. A generative grammar based on syntactic rules, like the one developed by Chomsky, can indeed resolve this ambiguity (by treating the sentence as one phonemic string generated from two different syntactic structures, one for each meaning). This may tempt us to conclude that we can account for multiple interpretations of a sentence with a model based on syntax alone, without depending on word meaning or the context in which the sentence is used. But the sentence "John lost his way," although syntactically identical to the previous one, can have only one meaning: losing his own way. And we can only account for this discrepancy with a model that uses *both* syntax and word meaning in the interpretation of sentences.[13]

The difficulties encountered by Chomsky and his followers, with the original theory as well as its innumerable variations, are due to the fact that the impoverished model of language he reached through repeated reifications cannot explain all possible sentences. His theory does indeed provide a mechanistic model of language, but only by failing to explain the *whole* phenomenon of language. The model ignores the interactions between structures, and it is these interactions that give language its richness. As is the case with all mechanistic delusions, Chomsky wishes to have both the richness of a complex phenomenon and the simplicity of a mechanistic model – an impossible goal. When he separated the complex phenomenon of language into simpler ones – when he severed the interactions – he renounced, in effect, the original project.

Chomsky's mechanistic theory of language is a fantasy, and we must not be surprised that it doesn't work. We should examine, though, how Chomsky and his followers react to its falsifications. The original concepts were expressed in the form of a falsifiable theory, and Chomsky himself recognizes the importance of falsifiability as a criterion of demarcation.[14] But, while *introduced* as a testable and falsifiable theory, universal grammar became unfalsifiable soon thereafter, when its defenders started to modify it in order to suppress the falsifications. The theory was turned into a pseudoscience, thus, by the

---

[13] For this example, as well as other, similar problems, see Chomsky, *Reflections on Language*, ch. 3.   [14] Ibid., p. 37.

decision to *expand* it, rather than abandon it, each time an aspect of language was found that could not be accounted for through the existing principles.

4

Let us briefly review the original concepts. Chomsky's first model of a generative grammar consisted of three components: the phrase-structure component, the transformational component, and the morphophonemic component. The phrase-structure component provides the rules for generating *phrase markers*; these are the *underlying strings*, or *deep structures*, of linguistic elements. The transformational component provides a set of *transformational* rules, which convert the underlying strings into *surface structures* – the final, grammatical sentences. The morphophonemic component provides the interpretation rules for converting the surface structures into the phonemic strings that make up speech.

The rules of the phrase-structure component show us how to generate an underlying string as a hierarchical structure of lexical elements. Thus, a sentence is built from certain elements, those elements from smaller ones, and so on, down to the lexical atoms – the words and morphemes that make up the underlying strings. There are only about a dozen phrase-structure rules. Thus, the top element of the hierarchy is a sentence, *S*, and is derived by concatenating a noun phrase, *NP*, and a verb phrase, *VP*; *VP* is derived by concatenating a *Verb* and an *NP*; *Verb* is composed of an optional auxiliary, *Aux*, and an actual verb; *Aux* is a morpheme like *will* or *may*, or a form of the verbs *have* or *be*; and so on. By combining and repeatedly applying these phrase-structure rules, it is possible to generate an infinite number of underlying strings. And any string generated in this fashion will eventually result in a grammatical sentence.

An underlying string may have to be further modified, by applying one of the transformational rules. The transformations manipulate words and morphemes in various ways; for instance, they modify their relative position in the string. Transformations are required in order to generate sentence constructions like negation, passive voice, and past tense, which cannot be generated directly by the hierarchical phrase-structure rules. In other words, a transformational rule must be defined for each surface structure that cannot be derived directly from a deep structure.[15]

It must be emphasized that all these rules were specified in a formal and precise manner – precise enough, for example, to be implemented as

---

[15] Chomsky, *Syntactic Structures*, pp. 111–114.

a computer program. Chomsky recognized that the rules he described in his original model were imperfect, that they did not adequately define all grammatical English sentences; but he was convinced that a perfect model was attainable. In particular, he described only a small number of transformations. It was chiefly through transformations that the model was expected to improve in the future, as this concept seemed versatile enough to generate any sentence. We only need to analyze all possible sentence constructions, he believed, and determine the transformations that generate them, and we will end up with a formal definition of the whole English language.

5

The origin of the Chomskyan delusion is not without interest, and is worth therefore a short digression. The study of formal grammars and languages, along with the study of automata (abstract machines that are mathematically related to formal languages, in that they can generate or process statements expressed in these languages), formed a new and exciting field in the 1950s. The theories discovered in those days had immediate applications in the emerging discipline of computer science, in both hardware and software design. The theories of programming languages, in particular, and of compilers (the software tools that translate them into the lower-level languages of the hardware), were a direct application of the theories of formal languages.

Scientists saw great potential in the fact that a relatively simple system of specifications was all they needed in order to define a grammar or a machine, which could then generate an infinite number of different strings of elements. The principle behind this power is recursion: performing an operation with certain elements, then with the resulting elements, and so on. By nesting elements within elements hierarchically, scientists could build mathematical models of grammars or automata that displayed very complex behaviour while their definition remained completely specifiable and relatively simple.

It was natural perhaps to think that nothing lay beyond the capabilities of such mechanistic models. Reassured by the mathematical foundation of these concepts (established in the preceding two decades by pioneers like Alan Turing), and fascinated by the first computers (which were already demonstrating the practicality of these ideas), many scientists concluded that they had finally found the answer to the great mysteries of knowledge and mind: the capabilities of the models they had already built resembled the simpler capabilities of the mind; computers afforded the means to build models of any complexity; therefore, to attain a model with the full capabilities of the mind, they only needed to apply the same principles on higher and higher levels. Mind mechanism – the belief that reductionism and atomism can explain the concept of mind – had entered the computer age.

Viewed from this perspective, Chomsky's fantasy is the linguistic counterpart of the other mechanistic mind fantasies of that period – fantasies which became known as artificial intelligence. The naive optimism of that period has been preserved for posterity through the ludicrous statements made by a number of scientists; namely, that computer models of the whole phenomenon of human intelligence would be attained within a few years (see p. 145).

It is significant that, although not directly involved, Chomsky always approved of the principles and goals of artificial intelligence. And it is quite irrelevant that Chomsky himself only worked on *models* of grammar: since his project calls for a complete and precise definition of natural languages, this definition could always be used to develop a computer program. Thus, his project too is, in effect, a search for a mechanistic model of mind, an attempt to replace human intelligence with software (the delusion we discussed in chapter 2).

Now, Chomsky had done some of the original work on formal languages, so he was familiar with the properties and capabilities of a series of grammars that had already been investigated – grammars called *regular* (or *finite-state*), *context-free*, *context-sensitive*, and *phrase-structure*.[16] Each one of these grammars is more powerful than the preceding one, in that it can generate a greater variety of statements. Context-free grammars, for instance, are more versatile than regular grammars, and are powerful enough to serve as the foundation of programming languages. The neat hierarchical structures of elements generated by context-free grammars are well-suited for the construction of software statements, modules, and applications, as they can grow to any size while remaining unambiguous and basically simple (and hence easily processed by compilers).

Chomsky showed that these grammars are too weak to generate all the sentences people use in a natural language like English, and he assumed that all we need for this task is a grammar that is even more powerful than the phrase-structure type. He also assumed that a formal grammar powerful enough to describe a natural language would be an extension of the existing grammars, just as each one of *those* grammars was an extension of the preceding one. His original model clearly reflects this belief: the phrase-structure component is the implementation of a grammar that was already understood, while the new, transformational component provides the extension (it modifies the resulting

---

[16] For a discussion of these grammars (including Chomsky's early contributions), see, for example, John E. Hopcroft and Jeffrey D. Ullman, *Formal Languages and Their Relation to Automata* (Reading, MA: Addison-Wesley, 1969).

strings so as to generate new types of sentences). The transformational rules were expected, in other words, to cope with all the differences between natural languages like English and simple, formal systems such as programming languages. The few transformations that Chomsky proposed were precisely specified, using a mathematical representation, just like the other rules that define formal grammars. He evidently hoped that, with additional work, it would be possible to discover a complete set of transformations, and the English language would be shown to be merely a more complex system than the others – something akin to a sophisticated programming language.[17]

This background also accounts for his view that grammar is independent of the *meaning* of words and sentences. A programming language, after all, can be defined without a knowledge of the actual applications that will eventually be created in that language. Similarly, a natural language must be studied "as an instrument or a tool, attempting to describe its structure with no explicit reference to the way in which this instrument is put to use."[18]

For Chomsky, then, there is a difference in degree, but not in kind, between human minds and the human environment that gives rise to natural languages, and the machines controlled by means of programming languages. This diminished view of humanity is an inevitable consequence of the mechanistic dogma.

6

Let us return to the main issue: the pseudoscientific nature of Chomsky's theory, the practice of modifying and extending it in order to escape refutation. The principal feature of the original theory was the claim that a natural language can be fully specified without taking into account the meaning of words and sentences or the context in which they are used. This idea, and hence the possibility of a formal definition of an entire language with a

---

[17] A computer program is a system of interacting structures, so what is completely specifiable is only the individual structures. The program's run-time performance depends on the interactions between these structures, and is therefore a non-mechanistic phenomenon. It is silly, therefore, to strive to reduce natural languages to a formal system resembling our programming languages, seeing that even computer programs, whose language *already is* a formal system, cannot have mechanistic models. What the mechanists fail to understand is that the software entities which make up a program, as much as the linguistic entities which make up a sentence, belong to several structures at the same time; and mechanistic models cannot represent the resulting interactions. We will study this problem in chapter 4. The mechanistic *software* theories are failing, therefore, for the same reason the mechanistic *language* theories are failing.

[18] Chomsky, *Syntactic Structures*, p. 103.

relatively simple system of rules and principles, is what made the theory famous. The subsequent development of the theory, however, consisted mainly in the discovery of types of sentences that *cannot* be explained without resort to meaning, followed by the modification of the theory to make it explain these sentences too. And this was usually accomplished by reinstating some *traditional* grammatical concepts, which do take meaning into account. The response to each falsification, in other words, was to turn it into a new feature of the theory. The following discussion is only a brief survey of this evolution, as it is impossible to mention here all the theories and sub-theories that have formed, at one time or another, the school of Chomskyan linguistics.

Just a few years after proposing his original theory, Chomsky introduced a series of major modifications.[19] (The new model became known as the *standard* theory.) There were changes in the phrase-structure component (now called the base component) and in the transformational component, but the most startling change was the introduction of a *semantic* component: deep structures were now processed both syntactically and semantically, so the resulting surface structures had both a syntactic structure and a meaning.

The new theory was more complicated than the original one, and more obscure. Neither theory worked – that is, neither went beyond a few examples and suggestions for future research – so both were mere speculations. But even as speculation, the new theory was a step backward: not only was its claim that semantics plays a role in the interpretation of sentences a blatant reversal of the original principles, but it left more questions unanswered. What was left for future research was not just some rules or transformations, as was the case earlier, but major problems in all sections of the model. We were now further away from a formal model of language, but this situation, instead of being recognized as a refutation of universal grammar, was interpreted as progress. What impressed people was, again, Chomsky's authoritative tone and the formal treatment of the problems; in other words, the fact that issues involving phrases, verbs, or pronouns were studied like issues in the exact sciences. The fact that few solutions were actually offered, and that most problems were merely stated, without even an attempt to solve them, made no difference.

Chomskyans allowed semantics into their grammatical model because they believed that a set of rules can be found to define with precision the relations between word meaning and syntax. No such rules exist, of course, but the search for them has been a major issue ever since. Chomskyans still do not admit that the interpretation of a sentence is related to the entire knowledge structure present in the mind, so in the new theory (and in all subsequent ones) they isolate various aspects of syntax, and search for ways to relate

---

[19] Chomsky, *Theory of Syntax.*

them formally to the meaning of words. To pick just one example, Chomsky proposed at one time a system of *concept categories* (animate or not, abstract or not, etc.) to determine whether the use of certain types of words is valid in specific situations.

The application of semantic rules to deep structures was eventually abandoned, and was replaced by a new model (known as the *extended standard theory*), in which the semantic functions are performed mainly on surface structures. But to retain the links to the syntactic structures, a complicated *trace* sub-theory was developed to allow the transfer of such information as the position of words in the sentence, from the deep structures to the surface structures. In the meantime, other linguists proposed a theory of *generative semantics*, which tried to build the meaning of sentences from the meaning of smaller elements.

None of these theories worked, so the next step was to replace the entire transformational philosophy, which was based chiefly on systems of rules, with a new model, based on *principles and parameters*. Chomsky argues now that languages can be described as sets of principles, where each principle can be implemented only as one of the alternatives permitted by universal grammar. All languages are basically the same, the only difference being in the implementation of these principles; and language acquisition consists in the unconscious discovery of the correct alternatives for a particular language. It is as if our language organ had a number of switches, all set at birth in a neutral position and ready to accept any value (from among the values permitted by universal grammar). What we do when acquiring the first language is set these switches to one value or another.

This is how Chomsky describes the new concept: "The principles are language-independent and also construction-independent; in fact, it appears that traditional grammatical constructions (interrogative, passive, nominal phrase, etc.) are taxonomic artefacts, rather like 'terrestrial mammal' or 'household pet.' These categories, with their special and often intricate properties, result from the interaction of fixed general principles, with parameters set one or another way. Language acquisition is the process of determining the values of parameters. There are no 'rules of grammar' in the traditional sense: rather, language-invariant principles and values for parameters of variation, all indifferent to traditional grammatical constructions."[20]

This text is typical of Chomsky's writing style: he is describing some linguistic fantasies, but by presenting these fantasies in an authoritative tone he makes them look like a scientific revolution.

---

[20] Noam Chomsky, "Chomsky, Noam" self-profile, in *A Companion to the Philosophy of Mind*, ed. Samuel Guttenplan (Oxford: Blackwell, 1995), p. 161.

The new theory, Chomsky declares, is "a conception of language that [departs] radically from the 2500-year tradition of study of language."[21] Unfortunately, while elements "of the picture seem reasonably clear" (to Chomsky, at least), "a great deal is unknown, and clarification of principles regularly opens the doors to the discovery of new empirical phenomena, posing new challenges. Though much less is understood, something similar must also be true of the lexicon, with the links it provides to the space of humanly accessible concepts and signals."[22]

Thus, Chomsky admits, what is "much less understood" than the part of which "a great deal is unknown" is (as always) the interaction between language structures and the other structures that make up human knowledge; in other words, the actual, complex phenomenon of language, as opposed to the reified, mechanistic phenomena studied by linguists.

Note again his authoritative tone, even as he is describing what are, in fact, mere speculations. For example, while admitting that we know practically nothing about a certain phenomenon, he confidently asserts that certain aspects are "reasonably clear," and that "something similar must also be true" of others. This is the same confidence that brought us the previous theories, all now forgotten. So now we have a new revolutionary theory that is mere speculations and doesn't work, to replace Chomsky's other theories that revolutionized linguistics though they were mere speculations and didn't work.[23]

Note also, in that passage, the statement about "new empirical phenomena" being regularly discovered and "posing new challenges." This assertion illustrates how pseudoscientific thinking distorts the idea of research – from an effort to discover the truth, to an effort to save a theory from refutation: "new empirical phenomena" is a euphemistic term for the falsifications of the theory, while the "challenges" constitute the search for ways to turn these falsifications into new features; that is, ways to expand the theory so as to account for them and thus escape refutation.

It is instructive to take a look at some of the principles that make up the new model:[24] *X-bar* theory deals with phrase structure and lexical categories and

---

[21] Ibid., pp. 160–161.   [22] Ibid., p. 161.

[23] Like the previous theories, the new one did not last long. In the following years many of its principles were abandoned, and by the late 1990s another linguistic revolution – another batch of speculations – was being promoted: the so-called minimalist program.

[24] See, for example, Noam Chomsky, *Knowledge of Language: Its Nature, Origin, and Use* (Westport, CT: Praeger, 1986).

their mutual relationships. *Theta* theory deals with the thematic roles (agent, patient, goal) played by elements in a sentence. *Case* theory deals with the assignment of case (nominative, accusative, genitive) to noun phrases. *Control* theory deals with the subject of infinitival clauses (the relation between the missing subject and the other elements in the sentence). *Binding* theory deals with the problem of expressions that refer or not to the same entities as other expressions in the sentence (as in constructions involving pronouns or anaphors). *Bounding* theory deals with the movement of grammatical units from one place in the sentence to another (as when deriving passive or interrogative constructions).

What is immediately striking about these principles, or sub-theories, is that each one deals with a single, isolated aspect of grammar. There are many other, similar principles in the new model, and additional ones are known but little has been done to study them. New principles, Chomskyans say, will undoubtedly be discovered in the future. And to cover any grammatical cases that may remain unexplained no matter how many principles and sub-theories will be discovered, the concepts of *core* and *periphery* have been introduced.[25] Every language, it appears, has two types of grammatical constructions: the core is that part of language explained by universal grammar, while the periphery includes those aspects of language that somehow evolve outside the scope of universal grammar.

The theory, thus, has become blatantly unfalsifiable, as any conceivable sentence and any aspect of grammar is now guaranteed to be accountable: either it is explained by the known principles, or it will be explained by principles yet to be discovered, or it doesn't need to be explained at all, because it belongs to the periphery. Little by little, Chomskyan linguistics has turned into a full-fledged pseudoscience.

If we compare the new principles to the original theory, what we notice is the evolution from a simple and elegant model that made bold and sweeping claims, to a collection of distinct and rather complicated theories that deal with isolated and minute aspects of grammar. It is also interesting that these aspects are not unlike those studied by *traditional* grammars. So, if we ignore the new terminology, many of these concepts are in fact a reinstatement of older grammatical concepts, which had been excluded by the original theory when it claimed that a relatively simple system of rules can explain a whole language. And we must recall that it was its simplicity and elegance that made the original model so attractive in the first place. Thus, Chomskyan linguistics continues to benefit today from its original prestige, even though its current features and claims are, in many respects, the exact opposite of the original ones.

[25] Ibid., p. 147.

Chomskyans stress now the benefits of the "modular" approach to the study of language: each sub-theory forms an independent module, which can be studied separately, while the modules also interact and work together as one system – the language faculty. Chomskyans draw block diagrams to depict these mental language modules and their interactions; and they connect the blocks with arrows, and use terms like "input" and "output" to describe the alleged data flow in the mind. The entire language faculty is treated then as one module among the many modules of the mind (the other faculties), which are believed to be relatively independent while interacting and working together to produce intelligence. It is hardly necessary to point out the mechanistic nature of this model: Chomsky's study of language and mind looks now just like an engineering project whose difficulty was originally underestimated.

This evolution is typical of mechanistic delusions: Chomsky started with a fantastic claim – the claim that a fairly simple model can provide an exact and complete explanation for the phenomenon of language. To make such a claim, he had to *assume* that the phenomenon is mechanistic in nature; namely, that it can be explained by explaining separately the simpler phenomena which appear to make it up. This led to the reification of language from the whole phenomenon of human knowledge, the reification of syntax from the phenomenon of language, and, finally, the reification of individual aspects of syntax. The reductionistic procedure looks perfectly logical – if we forget that the mechanistic nature of the phenomenon is only a hypothesis. With this hypothesis, we can always break down a phenomenon into simpler and simpler ones. Eventually, we are certain to reach phenomena that are simple enough to explain with mechanistic models – with rules, diagrams, mathematics, etc.

It is clear, then, why Chomskyans believe that they are making progress. They keep finding explanations for isolated grammatical phenomena, and they believe that these explanations will one day be combined into an explanation of the original phenomenon. But language is a complex phenomenon. So even if one day they manage to identify all its constituent structures, their model will still not work, because mechanistic models cannot represent the *interactions* between structures.

It is interesting that the new theory specifically depicts language as the result of many *interacting* principles of grammar, all sharing the same linguistic elements. The theory describes, therefore, a complex structure; and these principles are, quite correctly, some of the simple structures that make up the phenomenon of language. Chomskyans, however, still fail to see that it is impossible to explain a complex structure by explaining separately its constituent structures. And they still fail to see that the phenomenon of language involves, not only grammatical structures, but many other knowledge structures present in the mind.

7

Chomsky compares our current linguistic knowledge with our knowledge of physics before Galileo. He modestly admits, with each new model, that these are only beginnings, that there is much work left to be done. He believes that, just as Newton synthesized the knowledge of his time and discovered the laws of universal gravitation, a similar breakthrough will take place one day in linguistics, when someone will discover a unified theory of language.[26]

Chomsky's belief in language mechanism is unshakable: he does not doubt for a moment that the phenomenon of language can be explained, just like gravitation, through reductionism and atomism. Viewed in this light, the practice of modifying the theory to account for contradicting empirical evidence may look like a legitimate research method – a way to improve the theory. Recalling Popper's principles, however, the scientist must sincerely attempt to *refute* his theory. If he modifies it to avoid the falsifications, he does the opposite: he attempts to *save* the theory. The scientist must specify, when proposing his theory, what events or situations, if observed, would refute it. And if subsequent tests reveal such events or situations, the correct response is to declare that theory refuted, propose a *new* theory, and specify what events or situations would refute *it*.

If we keep this principle in mind, it becomes clear that Chomsky is not trying to refute his theory, but to save it. We must not be confused by his endless models; these models are not really new theories that replace previously refuted ones, but different versions of the *same* theory. Chomsky's theory is not just a formal model of grammar, but the system comprising a model of grammar *and* the idea of an innate universal grammar. One cannot exist without the other. The search for a mechanistic model of grammar is motivated by the innateness hypothesis – the hypothesis that humans possess a language faculty which is akin to an organ. *This hypothesis* is, in the end, Chomsky's thesis, what has made the whole theory unfalsifiable and hence pseudoscientific. The innateness hypothesis never changed, and it is in order to save *it* from refutation that all those models of grammar – all the theories, sub-theories, and principles – had to be invented, modified, and extended.

But why is the innateness hypothesis so important? Why does Chomsky defend it at all costs? Because, he frequently asserts, it is the only logical alternative. An innate language faculty is the only way to account for the ease

[26] See, for example, Noam Chomsky, *Language and Politics* (Montréal: Black Rose Books, 1988), p. 418.

and speed with which children learn a language, especially when we consider the impoverished sample they are exposed to; it is the only way to account for their ability to create correct sentences which have little resemblance to those they heard before; and so on. Since we can think of no other explanation, says Chomsky, we must accept the hypothesis of an innate language capacity.

But is it true that there are no alternative explanations? Only if we assume that language is a mechanistic phenomenon do we have to resort to an innateness hypothesis. If we admit that there are complex phenomena in this world – phenomena which cannot be explained through reductionism and atomism – then an alternative hypothesis is that the linguistic capability of humans is a complex phenomenon.

The circularity characteristic of mechanistic thinking is, again, obvious. Because he wishes to explain language with a mechanistic theory, Chomsky must conceive a second mechanistic theory: the innateness hypothesis (which is, in effect, the notion that there exists in the mind a thing whose operation can be described with precision). Then, he uses this hypothesis as warrant for his linguistic theory. Chomsky must assume both language mechanism and mind mechanism at the same time. One mechanistic assumption is adduced to justify another. The mechanistic philosophy is invoked to defend the mechanistic philosophy.

Since the entire Chomskyan project is grounded on the innateness hypothesis, we should perhaps investigate the soundness of this hypothesis. In our discussion of skill acquisition, we concluded that it makes no sense to postulate the existence of specialized high-level mental functions (see "Tacit Knowledge" in chapter 2). We saw that the same model of mind can account for any skills: general skills acquired simply by belonging to a human society (using language, interpreting visual sensations, recognizing social contexts), and specific skills selectively acquired by each individual (playing chess, interpreting X-rays, programming computers). We develop the necessary knowledge by being exposed to the phenomena – that is, the complex structures – which embody that knowledge. Our mind discovers the simple structures (the regularities) in the information captured by the senses, and creates an approximate replica of the complex structures by discovering also the interactions.

Complex structures can exist only in the phenomena themselves and in the mind; they cannot be transferred directly into a mind, because our senses communicate with our environment only through simple structures (through systems of symbols or sounds, for instance). The complex structures formed in the mind manifest themselves as non-mechanistic knowledge: we can *use* this knowledge, but we cannot precisely describe what we know. In other words, we cannot reduce this knowledge to simple structures. Non-mechanistic knowledge is the type of knowledge we possess when we reach expertise in a particular skill.

The human brain may well have some specialized low-level innate functions, like those found in simpler animals. And such functions may even take part in our verbal acts. But it is both absurd and unnecessary to postulate innateness in order to explain *high-level* mental capabilities; that is, to assume specialized faculties to account for *particular* skills, as Chomsky does.

It is absurd, first, from an evolutionary perspective: low-level functions, or instincts, play a dominant part in the behaviour of simple organisms, and the brain has evolved precisely in order to confer the advantages of learning. It makes no sense to assume that language – the most human-specific faculty, perhaps our most complex capability – is handled mostly by innate functions, while the *learning* functions of the brain, which have evolved specifically as an improvement over innate functions, play only a secondary part.

Another reason why the innateness hypothesis is absurd is that it leads to the conclusion that we possess a specialized faculty for each skill we can acquire. We might perhaps accept the innateness hypothesis for those skills acquired early in life by all humans – using language, recognizing faces, etc. But we saw that there is no fundamental difference between these natural skills and the skills related to a particular culture or occupation, which can be acquired at any age. All skills can be accounted for through a mind model based on complex knowledge structures.

Recall the skills we studied in "Tacit Knowledge." No one would suggest that we possess a specialized faculty for playing chess, or for interpreting X-rays, or for distinguishing chicks. Humans can acquire thousands of different skills, so we must conclude that the *same* mental capabilities are used in all of them. And if we can acquire so many skills using some generic mental capabilities, why do we have to assume that some other skills – like the use of language, which also can be accounted for by the same model of mind – are innate? The innateness hypothesis is unnecessary if we accept the existence of complex mental structures. Chomsky postulates specialized mental faculties, not because of any evidence that such faculties exist, but because this is what he needs for his mechanistic mind model.

And what about those linguistic phenomena Chomsky says can only be explained by an innate language capability? The fact that languages have so many common features, and the fact that children learn a language so quickly and easily, can be explained, just as Chomsky says, by an innate characteristic: our brain has developed the capability to process hierarchical knowledge structures. So this characteristic may well be reflected in our languages too: in each one of the various structures, including the grammatical structures, that make up the phenomenon of language. What Chomsky chooses to interpret as a specialized *language* capability – the mind's capacity for hierarchical structures – is a *general* capability. It is a capability that can be observed in *all* mental acts.

For example, when we see a face we perceive its elements and attributes as structures, not as isolated parts; we don't notice one eye, then the chin, then the nose, then the other eye; we don't study the elements randomly, or left to right, but unconsciously perceive them as several facial structures that exist at the same time. An expert chess player doesn't perceive a position by examining the pieces on the board in a certain sequence, but by unconsciously recognizing many overlapping and interacting logical structures. Similarly, we don't make sense of a sentence by combining words randomly, or left to right, but by detecting structures of grammar and of meaning. We perceive *everything* as structures, but this is masked by the fact that these structures share their elements, so we perceive them simultaneously. As we saw in "Tacit Knowledge," only when *inexperienced* in a certain domain do we notice the individual structures separately.

As for the creative aspect of language – our capability to utter and comprehend an infinite number of sentences that only resemble, and only in unspecifiable ways, those we heard before – it too is not peculiar to linguistic skills, but common to all skills. The distinguishing aspect of expertise, we saw, is the capability to recognize new situations intuitively. As novices, we can only cope with a new situation mechanically; that is, by following rules and by decomposing it into familiar elements. After a great deal of practice, however, when we reach expertise, we can cope with new situations directly, holistically. Expertise, therefore, permits us to cope also with *complex* situations, which cannot be precisely described as a combination of familiar elements.

Thus, we can recognize a familiar face from any angle, or from any distance, or in any light, or in a photograph; that is, when the image formed on the retina only *resembles* the previous images. And we cannot describe with precision how we recognized the new image, nor in what ways it resembles the previous ones. An experienced radiologist correctly interprets X-ray pictures that are necessarily only *similar* to others he saw previously. Expert chess players recognize positions that are only *similar* to previously encountered ones. To drive a car we must be able to handle random traffic situations, which at best *resemble* previously encountered ones. Moreover, we need this capability not only with specific skills, but to perform any intelligent act. We need it, in fact, just to behave normally in everyday situations; in this case we need it in order to recognize *contexts* that only resemble previous ones.

So, if this capability is used in all mental acts, why not also in the acquisition of language? Language is a complex structure, and the child discovers its constituent structures, including the grammatical structures and their interactions, simply by being exposed to it – as is the case with other skills. Also like other skills, the child manages to cope with novel situations; that is, he can create and understand sentences that only *resemble* previous ones. The complex knowledge the child acquires in the case of language includes the grammar; so, as is the case with any non-mechanistic knowledge, he can benefit from his knowledge of grammar without being able to describe what he knows.

In conclusion, the innateness hypothesis – the foundation of Chomskyan linguistics – is not as solid as Chomsky believes. And without this foundation, his theory is left as just another mechanistic mind delusion: just another system of belief, and no more of a science than behaviourism or structuralism. Despite the preciseness observed by most Chomskyans in their work, their models can lead nowhere if the project itself is unsound. No matter how many rules or principles they study, or how successful they are in reducing each one to a formal representation, these reified structures cannot improve our understanding of the phenomenon of language, nor of the human mind. There is no innate language faculty, and universal grammar is a mechanistic fantasy.[27]

Consequences

Academic Corruption

In the previous section we studied some of the more influential mechanistic delusions of our time – modern pseudosciences pursued in universities and accepted by large numbers of scientists. By discussing these pseudosciences here I am making a statement; namely, that I view our *software* delusions as a social phenomenon belonging to the same tradition. (The *language* delusions, as a matter of fact, have contributed *directly* to the software delusions. We will study this link in chapter 4.)

The theories of software engineering – the relational database model, structured programming, object-oriented programming, and the like – are in

---

[27] More than a few thinkers have criticized Chomskyan linguistics, of course, sometimes with arguments very similar to those presented in the foregoing discussion. No criticism, however, and no falsifications, can affect the popularity of a mechanistic idea among the academic bureaucrats.

the domain of programming what behaviourism, structuralism, or universal grammar are in the human sciences: mechanistic delusions, naive attempts to represent complex phenomena with exact models. They are the work of academic bureaucrats: individuals who cannot make a real contribution to their discipline or to society, and who hide their incompetence by imitating the methods of the exact sciences. Through this imitation they appear to be engaged in serious research, while pursuing in fact a pseudoscience.

One consequence of the mechanistic dogma, thus, is the intellectual corruption it fosters. These theories do not work, and they cannot possibly work; but because mechanism is taken as unquestionable truth, each falsification is seen as a challenge – the challenge to find ways to *deny* that it is a falsification. The theory becomes then unfalsifiable: it changes from a naive hypothesis to a full-scale system of belief, a pseudoscience.

This mechanistic culture is what allows now the *software* elites to deceive society, with *their* mechanistic concepts. For it is in universities and other research institutions that the software fantasies emerge: among individuals whose programming experience is limited to textbook examples, to trivial problems and neat solutions. To them, the possibility of finding exact models for complex, real-world software phenomena is as certain as is the possibility of finding exact models for complex psychological, social, or linguistic phenomena to their colleagues in the human sciences. The software fantasies do not seem so extraordinary once we recognize their grounding in the mechanistic ideology, and their similarity to the other academic fantasies; nor is extraordinary the dishonesty of their promoters and the evolution of the theories into pseudosciences.

It is impossible to assess the price we pay for these mechanistic obsessions and their ramifications. We cannot even imagine the progress we might have made in the human sciences, had the effort wasted on futile mechanistic theories been invested in other directions, more likely to increase our understanding of human minds and human relations; specifically, in theories that attempt to explain whole human phenomena, rather than break them down into simple and independent processes as if they were engineering projects.

Another consequence of our mechanistic obsessions is the prevention of expertise and responsibility. Workers in all fields are expected to follow blindly the principles of reductionism and atomism, rather than to search creatively for solutions and explanations. Instead of seeking to increase and broaden their knowledge, these two principles – which are taken as "the method of science" – allow them to equate expertise with narrow specialization: knowing as little as possible is perceived as a virtue, as a sign of professionalism. And if a narrow domain still requires too much knowledge, workers invoke these principles again and again, until they finally reach those low levels in the structure of knowledge where even the most ignorant people can be experts – levels where they only need to deal with trivial and isolated problems.

This trend has affected all occupations that involve knowledge and skills, but is especially noticeable in research work. Science has been redefined: an individual is considered a great scientist simply for discovering a mechanistic theory, regardless of whether the theory works or not. Thus, a mechanistic culture rewards mediocrity and discourages creativity. To be successful in academia, an individual must think like a bureaucrat and must accept blindly the mechanistic doctrine. Moreover, creative individuals who could make an important contribution are ignored, or see their work branded as "unscientific," simply because they reject the mechanistic principles and try to deal holistically with complex phenomena.

And this trend is just as widespread in our software-related activities – in universities, in business, and now even in our personal affairs. An individual is considered knowledgeable simply for accepting the latest mechanistic software concepts, regardless of whether these concepts are valid or not. To be successful in a software-related career, an individual must have the temperament of a bureaucrat, must restrict himself to mechanistic practices, and must display an unwavering allegiance to whichever authority is supporting the doctrine of software mechanism.

Psychologist Abraham Maslow[1] suggests that mechanistic beliefs are a sign of immaturity and insecurity. Instead of seeking to understand the complex reality, the mechanists prefer the comfort of artificial, narrow domains, where it is easy to find theories: "Science, then, can be a defense. It can be primarily a safety philosophy, a security system, a complicated way of avoiding anxiety and upsetting problems. In the extreme instance it can be a way of avoiding life, a kind of self-cloistering. It can become – in the hands of some people, at least – a social institution with primarily defensive, conserving functions, ordering and stabilizing rather than discovering and renewing.... The greatest danger of such an extreme institutional position is that the enterprise may finally become functionally autonomous, like a kind of bureaucracy, forgetting its original purposes and goals and becoming a kind of Chinese Wall against innovation, creativeness, revolution, even against new truth itself if it is too upsetting."[2]

In many academic disciplines, and in our software pursuits, our culture increasingly resembles the culture of primitive societies, or of the West during the Dark Ages, or of totalitarian states. What characterizes these cultures is their dogmatic value system, grounded on belief instead of logic. In our culture the dogma is mechanism. This is a scientific rather than religious or

[1] Abraham H. Maslow, *The Psychology of Science: A Reconnaissance* (South Bend, IN: Gateway, 1966).   [2] Ibid., p. 33.

political dogma, but its consequences are the same: intellectual stagnation; an ignorant population susceptible to irrational ideas, and hence to deception and propaganda; and, in the end, a society dominated by corrupt elites that exploit these weaknesses.

❖

In the following subsections, I want to discuss the social and political consequences of mechanistic thinking. Specifically, I want to show that the mechanistic theories promoted in our universities, even though invalid, are shaping the future of our society – by fostering totalitarianism.

The reason we must study the consequences of mechanism is that the belief in *software* mechanism has created the conditions for mechanistic theories to be actually implemented in society. The concepts promoted by mechanistic theories in sociology, psychology, and linguistics have undoubtedly influenced our world view, but they were never implemented on a large scale. These theories may pervade the academic world, but they have no direct application in business, or in politics, or in our social or personal affairs.[3] The mechanistic *software* theories, on the other hand, promise immediate benefits to everyone. They are appealing because they address the use and programming of computers, and we now depend on computers in practically every activity.

For example, corporate managers who have never heard of structuralism, and who would probably dismiss its fantastic claims, accept software ideas described as "solutions," without realizing that these ideas are based on the same mechanistic delusions as the structuralist theories. And liberal politicians who have never heard of behaviourism, and who would never endorse its totalitarian policies, accept the utopian promises of the "information revolution," without realizing that these promises are based on the same vision as the behaviourist theories.

So we accept mechanistic *software* theories, which are just as worthless as the traditional ones, not because we understand their principles better, but because their claims address immediate concerns. And we do not recognize their common totalitarian aspects any better than we do their common mechanistic principles. Thus, to recognize the totalitarian tendencies of the *software* theories, we must start by examining the totalitarian tendencies of the *traditional* mechanistic theories. (These two types of theories are the subject of the next two subsections.)

---

[3] We must remember, though, that totalitarian systems like Nazism and Communism *were* founded on mechanistic social and economic theories. And, as we will see in chapter 8, the democratic systems too are moving in this direction.

The Traditional Theories

1

What do all mechanistic delusions have in common? If we represent as structures the phenomena they try to explain, then what they all claim is that it is possible to account for all the values of the top element from the values of the starting elements. For behaviourism, the starting elements are bits of behaviour, and the top element comprises all possible behaviour patterns and intelligent acts. For structuralism, the starting elements are bits of knowledge or logic, and the top element comprises all human knowledge, accomplishments, social customs, and institutions. For universal grammar, the starting elements are words and elementary sounds, and the top element comprises all valid sentences and some of the knowledge embodied in sentences. So these theories claim that we can explain precisely and completely, starting with some simple elements, all possible manifestations of the human phenomenon in question – mental acts, social behaviour, linguistic competence, etc.

The significance of the claims is evident, therefore, when the phenomena are seen as structures. We immediately notice that the theories describe *simple* structures. They may use diagrams or equations rather than a structure; but we know that if they attempt to provide a precise explanation, they are deterministic models, so they could also be represented with a simple structure. And we also know why these theories do not work: because the phenomena they try to model can be usefully represented only with *complex* structures.

The fact that they do not work, thus, is not surprising. It is important to note, however, the *claim*, or the *expectation*, that they work. The scientists who defend these theories *wish* them to work. Specifically, they *wish* the phenomena to be simple structures, and the top element to be precisely describable in terms of the low-level elements. But if the phenomena are in reality complex structures, if they are the result of interactions between the simple structures the scientists recognize and some *other* structures, then what these scientists do in effect is deny the importance of those other structures; that is, they deny their bearing on the value of the high-level elements. And what are those other structures? They are the phenomena created by human minds: the knowledge, the experience, the creativity, the intuition of individual human beings.

When behaviourists say that intelligent behaviour can be computed from elementary units of behaviour, or when structuralists say that knowledge and social customs can be computed from elementary bits of logic, or when linguists say that sentences can be computed from words, what they claim in effect is that there is nothing between the low levels and the high levels that is unpredictable. They claim, thus, that we can describe the high levels in terms of the low ones just as we describe the operation of a machine in terms of its subassemblies and elementary parts.

But in the case of human beings and human societies, the high levels *are* unpredictable; and this unpredictability is what we understand as creativity, free will, and indeterminism. The indeterminism is caused by the complexity of interacting structures: the knowledge structures formed in individual minds, and the structures formed by many minds in a society. The structures studied by behaviourists, structuralists, and linguists are indeed among the structures that make up minds and societies. Taken alone, though, these structures cannot explain entire human phenomena; and this is why their theories do not work. In the end, the failure of the mechanistic theories constitutes corroborating evidence (to use Popper's principle) for *non-mechanistic* social and psychological theories: for theories that endow human beings with free will and unbounded creativity.

Mechanistic theories fail because they do not recognize the unique knowledge structures that can develop in a mind. Thus, the failure of these theories ought to enhance our respect for the potential of human beings, for the creativity of each individual. Instead, the scientists insist that these are not failures but merely setbacks, that they *will* eventually find mechanistic theories of mind and society.

Our mechanistic culture has given rise to this incredible spectacle: in a democratic society, in the name of science, renowned professors working in prestigious universities believe it is their duty to prove that human beings have no value. For, by denying the bearing that the knowledge structures present in our minds have on the structures studied by their theories, these scientists deny the unique contribution that each individual can make. By claiming that human phenomena can be explained with mechanistic theories, they claim in effect that these phenomena can be explained without taking into account the knowledge structures developed by individual minds.

❖

And this is not all. Although these theories do *not* work, the mechanists use them to draw sweeping conclusions about man and society – the kind of conclusions that one would draw if the theories *did* work. Specifically, they maintain that human freedom and creativity are only illusions, prescientific notions, not unlike the ancient beliefs that the earth is the centre of the universe, or that Man was created in God's image. Hence, just as science has shown that the earth is merely another planet, and that Man is merely a higher animal, we must trust science again and resign ourselves to the fact that we cannot be truly creative: everything we do is dictated by our genetic structure, or by our environment, or by other factors over which we have no control. Human beings are in reality nothing but machines – complicated ones perhaps, but machines nevertheless.

Thus, Skinner could only confirm his behaviourist theory in contrived laboratory experiments with rats and pigeons, but concluded that there is an urgent need to apply this science of behaviour to the shaping of human minds and societies. All human acts are the result of external influences, he says, and it is a mistake to believe that we are free and responsible agents. So, rather than allowing ourselves to be controlled by whoever has the power to influence us – parents, teachers, friends, advertisers – it is best to allow a hardheaded government and expert behaviourists do that. These elites would use objective principles and rigorous methods to shape the personality of each individual starting from birth, and thereby create a society of perfect citizens: "What we need is a technology of behavior.... But a behavioral technology comparable in power and precision to physical and biological technology is lacking."[1] This is where the science of behaviourism can help: the conditioning techniques that seem to work for the rats and pigeons trapped in a Skinner box in a laboratory must now be used for the people that make up modern society.

What prevents us from creating this progressive system is our democratic prejudices; that is, our naive belief in human freedom and dignity – notions that the science of behaviourism, according to Skinner, has shown to be illusory anyway: "The conception of the individual which emerges from a scientific analysis is distasteful to most of those who have been strongly affected by democratic philosophies."[2] Skinner was so confident in the potential of behaviourism to solve our social problems that he wrote a science-fiction novel to depict the kind of society we could create through behavioural technology.[3]

It is significant that Skinner's ideas were very popular and became somewhat of a cult in America, especially among intellectuals. It is also significant that most of those who *rejected* Skinner's utopia did so because they found his behavioural technology objectionable on humanistic, not scientific, grounds: how outrageous that a professor from Harvard University is promoting totalitarianism. Few realized that the first objection to behaviourism must be that it is a pseudoscience, that it does not work, that it is founded on fallacious concepts of mind and society. And what ought to be outrageous is that our universities foster the corrupt environment where pseudoscientists like Skinner can peddle their theories.

[1] B. F. Skinner, *Beyond Freedom and Dignity* (New York: Knopf, 1972), p. 5.
[2] B. F. Skinner, *Science and Human Behaviour* (New York: Free Press, 1965), p. 449.
[3] B. F. Skinner, *Walden Two* (New York: Macmillan, 1948).

The structuralist theories work no better than the behaviourist ones, but their defenders do not hesitate to conclude that human freedom and creativity, in the sense in which we generally understand them, are mere illusions. When we acquire skills and knowledge, when we invent something or solve a problem, when we develop social customs and institutions, all we do in reality is select various acts from a predetermined range of alternatives – the range for which our brains are biologically wired.

Thus, Lévi-Strauss held that the set of possible social customs is analogous to the periodic table of chemical elements: all a society does when adopting a certain custom is select, perhaps randomly, one of the slots available in this table. And Piaget held that the mental development of children is analogous to an increase in the number of levels in a hierarchical structure of binary operations – the structure which is built into the human brain, and which, ultimately, determines our mental capabilities. As individuals or as societies, human beings can be no more creative or free than programmed computers. What we like to think of as creativity and free will is only an illusion caused by the large number of available alternatives.

The case of Chomsky and his universal grammar is especially interesting, because Chomsky himself draws attention to the harmful influence that theories of mind can have on social and political ideologies. He stresses that the innateness hypothesis behind his linguistic theory postulates a view of human nature in the *rationalist* tradition. Rationalist philosophers, starting with Descartes, held that we possess certain mental capabilities simply by being born human; and, although we acquire much knowledge later, our innate capabilities restrict and structure forever what we can know. The rival philosophical school of *empiricism*, on the other hand, holds that human minds are empty at birth, that everything we know comes from interacting with our environment, and that there are no innate restrictions on the kind of knowledge we can acquire.

Chomsky points out that the rationalist view is conducive to ideologies that defend freedom, equality, and respect for the individual, whereas the empiricist view is conducive to ideologies that support authoritarianism, inequality, and exploitation. Specifically, if human beings are empty organisms at birth, as the empiricists say, this means that by their very nature they have no rights; so there is nothing wrong in moulding them to fit a certain policy. Thus, theories like behaviourism, ideologies like Nazism and Communism, and even democratic systems where various elites are permitted to control society, demonstrate the danger of the empiricist view: the leaders can invoke the idea of human nature to justify the control of knowledge. Rationalists, on the contrary, respect the fundamental rights of the individual – the right to live free, to develop any personality, to pursue any lifestyle – simply by recognizing that human beings possess from birth some important and immutable faculties.[4]

Accordingly, says Chomsky, while rationalism appears to postulate a more limited view of human capabilities, it is in fact the one philosophy that defends individual freedom and creativity. He admits that the hypothesis of an innate language faculty restricts the types of languages that humans can acquire, and the types of sentences – and hence also the types of ideas – that they can create; and he admits that, if everything we can know is governed by innate faculties, similar restrictions apply to all other kinds of knowledge. But, he reassures us, we needn't worry that these restrictions limit our creativity or freedom, because we still have a very large number – indeed, an infinite number – of alternatives *within* the boundaries of innate capabilities. We can create an infinite number of sentences, for instance, despite the severe restrictions imposed by universal grammar.

Chomsky's thesis, however, is fallacious and dangerous. We can agree with him that the concept of empiricism has been distorted and abused by certain ideologies. And, even without accepting his hypothesis of innate faculties, we can agree that our mental capabilities are structured and restricted by certain biological characteristics. But these facts do not warrant his conclusions.

Chomsky's mistake is to assume that, if our mental capabilities lie within a certain range, we should be able to discover a deterministic model that accounts for all possible human acts (because these acts necessarily derive from that range of capabilities). His mechanistic theory of mind compels him to *degrade* the definition of creativity: from the capacity to perform *unpredictable* acts, to the capacity to *select* an act from a predetermined range of alternatives. The traditional view is that creativity gives rise to an infinity of alternatives, and, in particular, to alternatives that were not known in advance. Chomsky, though, believes that we can *account* for these alternatives – simply by inventing a deterministic model that generates an infinity of sentences, ideas, and types of knowledge. But the infinity displayed by a deterministic model is only a fraction of the *real* infinity of alternatives that human minds can develop. (This, obviously, is why his theory doesn't work.)

Chomsky speaks eloquently of human freedom and creativity, but at the same time he attempts to determine with precision all the manifestations of creativity. He seems oblivious to the self-contradiction. For, if there were ways

[4] See, for example, Chomsky's *Language and Politics* (Montréal: Black Rose Books, 1988), pp. 594–595, and *Reflections on Language* (New York: Pantheon Books, 1975), pp. 127–133.

to account for all possible human acts, it would be absurd to call the quality involved in performing these acts "creativity." No surprises would be possible – no exceptions, no novelty, no originality. Anything an individual would do could be shown to be derivable independently of that individual. To put this differently, if Chomsky's theory worked, we could implement it with software; a computer would then perform exactly the same acts as human beings (would generate, for example, the same sentences and ideas), but could the computer be said to be free or creative in the human sense? Determinism is the opposite of freedom, but Chomsky wants to have both: Chomsky the humanist is concerned with freedom, while Chomsky the scientist is searching for a theory that would make a mockery of freedom by showing that a programmed machine can be identical intellectually to a free human being.

Just like the mechanistic theories of mind in the field of artificial intelligence, Chomsky's theories are, in effect, an attempt to replace human minds with software. And, with microprocessors becoming more and more powerful, some of these theories can already be implemented with just one semiconductor chip. They may not state it, and they may not even realize it, but what all these researchers are claiming, essentially, is that we will soon be able to replace human beings with inexpensive devices. The important point, again, is that although these theories do *not* work, the researchers, and the lay people who trust them, are convinced that soon they *will* work, and are therefore developing a world view that reflects these theories. Nor should we forget that our society is already dominated by political and business elites who hold the same conviction, and who are planning our future accordingly. It is not difficult to imagine the kind of future these elites are preparing for us, if they believe that human beings are not very different from expendable semiconductor chips.

In conclusion, Chomsky's preference for a rationalist theory of mind, rather than an empiricist one, is irrelevant when rationalism is supplemented with a *mechanistic* theory of mind. It makes little difference which philosophy one starts with, if one ends by claiming that deterministic models of mind are possible.

Chomsky's case, then, is a good example of the corruptive effect of the mechanistic dogma. Through writings and lectures, he has become known throughout the world as a humanist. His efforts as a scientist working in the mechanistic tradition, however, are harming the humanistic cause more than his efforts as a humanist can help it.

Geoffrey Sampson[5] notes that Chomsky's impoverished definitions of freedom and creativity provide the common philosophical foundation for both

[5] Geoffrey Sampson, *Liberty and Language* (Oxford: Oxford University Press, 1979).

his linguistic and his political theories. As language users, Chomsky says, we are restricted genetically to certain types of grammatical constructions; hence, the creativity we display in speech is in reality only the capacity to select utterances from a certain range of alternatives. Similarly, as citizens, we are restricted genetically to certain types of achievements; hence, there is nothing wrong in defining freedom as merely the right to pursue any ideas within a prescribed range of alternatives: "Chomsky has misappropriated the term 'creative' as he misappropriated the term 'free.' In each case he uses the term in a sense that conflicts with its standard usage; but, by contrasting 'freedom,' or 'creativity,' in his impoverished sense with something that is even further removed from the notion usually associated with the respective word, he invites us to overlook the fact that what we usually mean by the word is something different from both his alternatives."[6]

Chomsky contrasts his theories to those of authoritarian ideologies, which deny freedom and creativity altogether, and which hold that human nature must be moulded to fit a general plan. When presented from this perspective, his own views appear enlightened and liberal. His theories are dangerous precisely because he appears to be defending freedom while defending, in fact, not the traditional concept of freedom, but an impoverished version of it: "The adverse consequences of scientism stem from its assumption that all human phenomena can be analysed by the scientific method; creativity is an exception, since acts which are truly creative cannot, by definition, be predicted. To the question 'Who, in the contemporary intellectual world, most stresses the importance of human creativity?', the answer must undoubtedly be Noam Chomsky.... Yet, when we ask what Chomsky means when he calls men creative, he turns out to refer to our ability to behave in conformity to certain fixed, rigorous rules."[7]

2

By way of summary, I want to show how the mistaken conclusions drawn by these scientists can be traced to the mechanistic fallacies. The scientists are evidently fascinated by the fact that simple structures, when used as mechanistic models, can generate a large number of different values for the top element. They can generate, in fact, an *infinite* number of values. Depending on the theory, these values represent the different alternatives displayed by individuals or societies in their knowledge, their behaviour, their traditions, their sentences, etc. So, the scientists conclude, mechanistic models can

[6] Ibid., p. 106.   [7] Ibid., pp. 107–108.

account for *all* possible alternatives: all knowledge and behaviour of an individual, all customs and language uses of a society, and so forth.

But a large number of values – even an infinite number – does not necessarily mean that the model can account for *all* possible alternatives. We can demonstrate this with a simple example. It is easy to create a device (a piece of software, for instance) that generates numeric values according to certain rules: values limited to a given range, or values that are prime numbers, or integers. Consider now the set of all numeric values. Although the subset of integers is an infinite number, in practice there are infinitely more fractions than integers (there are, in fact, an infinite number of fractions between any two integers). Consequently, while accounting for an infinity of values, a device that generates integers accounts for an infinitely small subset of all possible numeric values. There are many similar examples, so it is important to bear in mind that an infinite number of alternatives may not mean *all* the alternatives.

What these scientists are seeking is a fully specifiable model that can account, nevertheless, for all the alternatives displayed by human minds. They hope to find, in other words, a deterministic model that can account for indeterministic phenomena – for the creativity and unpredictability of human acts. They are misled by the infinity of alternatives that their mechanistic systems can generate, and conclude that they have discovered such a model. They misinterpret this infinity of alternatives as equivalent to creativity and unpredictability – equivalent, that is, to all possible alternatives. As we just saw, it is easy for a mechanistic system to generate an infinity of values in a given domain while failing to account for all values possible in that domain. Thus, the infinity that the scientists notice in their models is *not* the infinity that gives rise to indeterminism, to creativity and unpredictability. Mechanistic theories fail because, even though explaining an infinity of acts, this infinity is a small subset of all possible human acts. (We will study this fallacy in greater detail in chapter 8; see pp. 828–831.)

The scientists start with a reasonable hypothesis: the idea that human beings are restricted in the types of knowledge they can acquire, and in their behaviour patterns, by some innate capabilities. Now, no one can doubt that the basic human faculties *are* bounded by some low-level physiological processes occurring in the brain. The high-level phenomena of mind and society must then reflect these limitations, just as our physical characteristics and abilities reflect our genetic code.

But, to be consistent, the scientists ought to build their theories starting from those low-level physiological processes (from neurons, for instance). Instead, the starting elements in their structures are relatively high-level entities: for linguists they are phonemes and words; for behaviourists they are simple movements, reflexes, and the like; for structuralists they are the binary opposites found in thought, or in stories and traditions. These are not the simplest entities from which human phenomena are made up, but merely the smallest entities that we notice or understand. The scientists believe that they can start their projects from any level of abstraction they like, so they choose high levels, which are more convenient. They base their theories on mechanistic processes assumed to occur at low physiological levels; but then they ignore the low levels, and the many intermediate levels, and build their models starting from some arbitrary, relatively high-level, entities.

Their mistake, thus, is to use as building blocks in their models, elements that are not independent. Elements like words, or limb movements, or pieces of mental logic, are related – both mutually and to other *types* of elements; so they give rise to complex, not simple, structures. They are related because they serve as elements in other structures too, besides the particular structure that each scientist is concerned with. All these structures are formed at the same time from the low-level physiological elements, so they reflect the countless interactions that take place at levels *lower* than the level where the scientists decided to start their projects.

When ignoring the interactions – when assuming that those starting elements are independent – the scientists separate the one structure that forms their particular project from the complex structure that is the human phenomenon. The top element in the complex structure represents all the alternatives that human beings can display; and the theory fails because it can account for only *some* of these alternatives – the ones that would occur if those starting elements were indeed independent. The theory may well account for an infinity of alternatives, but this is still a small fraction of the alternatives that constitute the actual phenomenon. When attempting to represent a complex phenomenon with a simple structure, and when starting from higher levels, the scientists are committing both fallacies, reification and abstraction. The dramatic reduction in alternatives is then the impoverishment that these fallacies inevitably cause.

We can understand now why these scientists are convinced that freedom and creativity are illusory, that what we perceive as free will is merely the freedom to select any act from a predetermined range of alternatives. They base this notion on the existence of low-level physiological elements, and on the assumption that, *in principle*, we can account for all the alternatives generated by these elements. At the same time, they admit that they *cannot* develop their models starting from these elements. So they continue to claim that freedom and creativity mean just a selection of alternatives, even while starting their models from much higher levels – as if the infinity of alternatives they *can* account for were the same as the infinity generated by the low-level elements. They are seeking mechanistic explanations, but they are *not* following the

mechanistic doctrine: a model cannot explain mechanistically a given phenomenon unless the starting elements are atomic and independent, and *their*
starting elements are neither. (Even the low-level physiological elements,
which they *fail* to reach, are only *assumed* to be atomic and independent.)

The scientists believe that it will soon be possible to explain all the alternatives and thereby account for the full range of possible human acts. But
this optimism would be warranted only if their theories were completely
mechanistic. They admit that they cannot find a true mechanistic explanation
– a continuous series of reductions from the human phenomena to some
atomic and independent entities – but they refuse to take this failure as
evidence that human phenomena are indeterministic, and hence unexplainable
with mechanistic theories.

Thus, no matter how we feel about mechanism and about mechanistic
explanations of human phenomena, the conclusions drawn by these scientists
are unjustified simply because their theories are fallacious even *within* the
mechanistic doctrine. The indeterminism, the creativity and unpredictability
of human minds, are precisely this impossibility of finding a set of atomic and
independent entities for the starting elements.

The Software Theories

1

The evil concepts of mind and society engendered by the traditional mechanistic theories are being implemented already, without anyone noticing,
through the mechanistic *software* theories. While our democratic system
has safeguards to protect society from the political consequences of the
traditional mechanistic delusions, no safeguards exist to protect us from the
ideas promoted by the software elites. And few of us recognize the similarity
between the social systems envisaged by the traditional mechanists, and which
we reject as totalitarian, and those promoted by software experts and by the
software companies, and which we perceive as scientific and progressive.

Recall the distinguishing characteristic of the mechanistic delusions we
studied in this chapter: the claim that, in a complex structure, it is possible to
derive with precision the value of the top element from the values of the
starting elements. The complex structure represents a complex human or
social phenomenon, so what the mechanists are claiming is that a simple
structure – a deterministic model – can account for all possible manifestations
of the complex phenomenon. They are claiming, in other words, that the other
structures that are part of the phenomenon are unimportant. But the other

structures are the knowledge structures present in human minds, or the social structures formed by the interaction of many minds. So, by making this claim, the mechanists are depreciating the role played by each mind in the complex phenomenon. The reason these theories are failing is that the assumption is wrong: the contribution made by individual minds is in reality an important part of the phenomenon.

In the case of software theories, the complex structures comprise the various activities performed by people when developing and using software applications. And what the software theories claim is that it is possible to account for the top element of these structures from a knowledge of their starting elements. Accordingly, we should be able to replace the knowledge involved in those activities with formal methods and, ultimately, with software devices based on these methods.

In programming activities, the starting elements are details like the definitions and statements used in an application, the fields in data files or display screens, and the software-related acts in the human environment where the application is used. The top element consists of the combinations of operations performed by these applications, and the business, social, and personal needs they serve. The knowledge and experience of programmers and users provide the structures that, together with the structures formed by the elements just mentioned, give rise to the complex phenomena observed when a social or business environment depends on software.

The software theories, though, claim that these are not complex, but mechanistic, phenomena: the top element can be described, precisely and completely, as a function of the starting elements. Whether they invoke mathematical principles or the similarity of programming to manufacturing, the appeal of these theories is understandable. Let us design our applications as hierarchical structures, we are told, as neat structures of independent modules. We should then be able to develop applications of any size and complexity simply by combining these software parts, one level at a time: starting with some atomic entities whose validity is established, we will create larger and larger software subassemblies – each one guaranteed to be correct because built from proven parts – until we reach the top element, the complete application.

All theories, and all methodologies and development environments, are grounded on this principle. But the principle is invalid, because even the smallest software elements share attributes, and are therefore interrelated. Thus, like the mechanistic theories of mind and society, the software theories praise reductionism and atomism, and at the same time they violate these principles by using starting elements that are not atomic and independent. Also like the traditional theories, the software theories are failing because these elements give rise to multiple, interacting structures. Applications, and software-related activities generally, are not the simple hierarchical structures the mechanists assume them to be. (We will study the various types of software structures in chapter 4.)

2

Psychologists, sociologists, and linguists think that mechanistic theories can account for all the alternatives displayed by individuals and societies: all possible manifestations of knowledge, behaviour, customs, language, and so forth. Their theories account for only *some* of the alternatives, but despite these failures, the scientists conclude that what human minds do is simply select various acts from a predetermined range of alternatives: what we perceive as free will or creativity is an illusion caused by the large number of alternatives that minds can select from. Let us see how the mechanistic *software* theories lead to the same conclusion.

Like the mind mechanists, the software mechanists are searching for a deterministic model that can account for indeterministic phenomena – software-related phenomena, in this case. Specifically, they hope to find a mechanistic model that can account for all the alternatives displayed by human minds when engaged in software development and use. And they think that if a model can account for an infinite number of alternatives, this means that it can account for *all* the alternatives.

But we saw how easy it is for a mechanistic model to display an infinity of values while accounting, in fact, for only a small subset of the possible values. The alternatives in software-related phenomena are all the applications that can be implemented with software, and all the business, social, and personal aspects of programming and software use. These alternatives constitute an infinite number, of course. And, as is the case with the other theories, the infinity of alternatives that make up the real software phenomena is infinitely greater than the infinity of alternatives that a mechanistic model can account for. The difference is seen in the perpetual need for new programming theories – a need arising, obviously, from the failure of the previous ones.

While the mind mechanists attempt to represent with exact models *mental* phenomena, the software experts attempt to represent with exact models *software-related* phenomena. This must be possible, they argue, because the totality of software-related human acts can be described with precision as a function of some low-level elements. We should be able to build software devices, therefore, which incorporate these elements. These devices will then allow us to generate any software-related structure – that is, any alternative of the phenomena of programming and software use – without ever again having to start from the low levels.

True to the mechanistic doctrine, the software experts attempt to explain complex software phenomena by repeatedly reducing them to simpler ones. And in so doing they commit both fallacies, reification and abstraction: they take into account only one structure, failing to see that software entities are related in several ways at the same time; and they stop the reduction long before reaching the lowest levels.

The experts notice that in processes like manufacturing we benefit from the mechanistic principles while starting our structures, nevertheless, from high-level elements (prefabricated subassemblies), and they conclude that software-related processes, too, can start from high levels. They also notice that physical entities can function as starting elements only if independent, and they conclude that software entities, too, can be independent: just as, in a physical structure, the internal properties of one subassembly are unrelated to those of the others (so that we can build them independently of one another), the internal operation of each software module can be unrelated to those of the others.

Both conclusions, however, are unwarranted. While it is true that we can build software structures starting from independent, high-level elements, if we limited ourselves to such structures we could represent with software only *a fraction* of our business, social, and personal affairs.

The experts treat software development as a manufacturing process because they don't appreciate how much richer are human phenomena than physical ones. The number of alternatives lost when we start from high levels and when we separate structures in *physical* phenomena is relatively small, and we gain important benefits in return; when we ignore the low levels and the links between structures in *human* phenomena, we lose an infinity of important alternatives.

Simple structures and high-level starting elements – that is, the use of standard parts and subassemblies – are acceptable in activities like manufacturing because there are only a few kinds of tools, appliances, vehicles, etc., that are useful, or convenient, or economical. The same is not true, however, in mental and social phenomena. There is an infinity of sentences, ideas, customs, cultures, forms of knowledge, and types of behaviour that are correct, or practical, or suitable. Unlike physical processes, therefore, our models of human phenomena cannot be restricted to simple structures, and cannot start from high levels. For, the loss of alternatives is then so severe that the benefits of simple structures and high starting levels become irrelevant: the number of human acts the model can explain, relative to those it cannot explain, is too small for it to be useful.

Software-related phenomena, in particular, despite their dependence on physical structures like computers, are largely *human* phenomena, because they entail various intellectual and social processes. Consequently, simple software structures and high-level starting elements can account for only *some* of the alternatives, just as the mechanistic models of mind and society can explain only *some* aspects of human phenomena.

3

The immediate benefit of software mechanism is thought to lie in explaining the phenomenon of programming itself. If we view as hierarchical structures not just the applications but also the activities and the mental acts involved in developing applications, we should be able to account for all the values displayed by the top element; that is, all the combinations of applications, requirements, software concepts, etc. We will then search for some *high-level* entities that can be used as starting elements in these structures. And, once we discover these entities, we will no longer have to develop applications starting from low levels.

Everyone agrees that it is possible to develop all conceivable software applications if starting with *low-level* elements. The promise of software mechanism, thus, is not to enable us to perform tasks that we could not perform otherwise, but to perform them more easily: less work and lower skills are needed to reach the top element – the application, the business system – when starting with higher-level elements. So what software mechanism promises us in effect is devices that would permit us, not only to attain everything that can be attained through software, but to attain it sooner, and with less knowledge. This is true, we are told, because the infinity of applications possible when starting from the higher levels is about the same as the infinity we could create by starting from the low levels.

It is not surprising that the scientists make such fantastic claims; after all, these ideas are nothing but the software counterpart of the theories of mind that mechanists have been proposing for centuries. What *is* surprising is that we all accept the claims now, and that we continue to accept them even as we see them refuted in practice.

A little thought will reveal the true nature of these claims. We are told that software devices will permit us to create *any* software applications, or to address *any* software-related matters, *without* the need to develop all the knowledge that human minds *can* develop. So, by stating this, the experts admit in effect that we *can* attain greater knowledge; we simply *do not need* that extra knowledge. But if we *are* capable of greater knowledge in software-related matters, we necessarily could, through that knowledge, perform certain tasks, or develop certain ideas, or create certain applications, or make certain discoveries, that we cannot *without* it. To say that those additional alternatives are unimportant, that they represent an insignificant part of the potential achievements of human minds, and that they can be forsaken, is to make an astonishing statement about the future of humankind. For, we can only judge how important or unimportant those alternatives are by *having* them first; we cannot know in advance how human knowledge will evolve, or what our future needs and capabilities will be.

By making such statements, the software elites are claiming in effect the right to decide what knowledge and mental capabilities we, and future generations, are permitted to acquire. They see themselves as an enlightened vanguard: they are the select few who can appreciate the future of software, so it is their duty to guide us.

It is in the interest of the elites to maintain a general state of ignorance in all software-related matters, and the mechanistic software ideology is an essential part of this plan: we perceive the theories, methodologies, and devices as expressions of software science, even as they are preventing us from using our minds. By controlling the way we create and use software, the elites are restricting those aspects of our life that depend on software to a certain range of alternatives. But few of us realize just how narrow this range is, how many alternatives are lost when we are limited to mechanistic software thinking.

We would have no difficulty recognizing a similar limitation in areas in which we are already knowledgeable – other professions, or naturally acquired skills. Programming, however, was taken over by incompetents and charlatans before a body of responsible professionals could emerge; and as a result, we believe that what these impostors are doing is the utmost that a society can attain in the domain of programming. Since the programming we see is the only kind we have ever had, we cannot know how limited and inefficient our software-related affairs are. We cannot even imagine a society where programmers are as competent in their work as other professionals are now in theirs; that is, a society where programmers are permitted to attain the highest skill levels attainable by human minds.

The mechanistic software ideology, thus, fosters incompetence among programmers – but also among software *users*, because their performance is impaired by the inadequate applications. These conditions, then, impoverish our life by limiting our expectations in all software-related matters to only a fraction of the possible alternatives: those that can be accounted for through mechanistic concepts. Although our minds are capable of non-mechanistic knowledge, and we could therefore have infinitely more alternatives in our software-related affairs, as long as we limit ourselves to mechanistic thinking we cannot know what these alternatives are. We trust the software devices provided by the elites, while the real purpose of these devices is to induce a state of ignorance and dependence. We like the many alternatives that we gain so easily through devices, and we are convinced that they constitute *all* the alternatives. We are unaware of the *missing* alternatives, because the only way to attain them is by starting our software-related structures from lower levels; that is, by *avoiding* the devices, and developing instead programming expertise.

Again, we can easily understand this for other types of knowledge, in areas in which we have had the time to become proficient. We all use *language*, for example, starting with low-level elements – with words. We also know that, when expressing wishes or ideas, we do more than just build linguistic structures; what we do is combine our linguistic knowledge with other types of knowledge. Hence, if we have difficulty expressing ourselves, we know that language devices would not solve the problem.

Imagine now a society where an elite suggested that we use language by starting with higher-level elements – with ready-made sentences and ideas. Thus, instead of *creating* sentences and ideas, we would have to express ourselves by combining the ready-made ones produced by certain devices; and instead of increasing our knowledge and our linguistic capability, we would learn only how to operate these devices. Even without recalling the mechanistic fallacies, or the difference between simple and complex structures, we sense intuitively that this could not work, that we would lose something. We sense that, even if we could still create an infinity of ideas, it would be impossible to create the same variety of ideas as we do now, starting with words. And we realize that, by restricting the use of language, the elite would impoverish all knowledge and all aspects of our life.

We accept in the domain of software, thus, mechanistic concepts and theories that we would immediately dismiss in the case of language. We accept them because we fail to see that they serve the same purpose: to restrict our knowledge, our values, and our expectations. (We will return to this subject in chapters 5 and 6.)

4

The mechanistic theories of mind, we saw, claim that we can account for all the alternatives in human knowledge, behaviour, language, customs, and so forth; and they conclude that no creativity is involved in mental acts, that what we perceive as creativity is merely the selection and combination of bits of knowledge leading to a particular alternative. In the mechanistic *software* theories, the counterpart of this belief is the belief that we can account for all possible alternatives in software-related phenomena. If we can account for all the alternatives, the conclusion must be that we can account for all possible applications, and also for the processes that take place in the mind when creating applications. So what we perceive as creativity and originality in the work of an experienced programmer is only an illusion: what the programmer really does in his mind at every stage of software development is akin to selecting and combining bits of programming knowledge in order to generate one of the applications.

More accurately, what the software theorists say is that programmers *could* create applications in this manner, so it is wrong to depend on such inexact resources as personal knowledge. Professional programming entails nothing but rules, standards, principles, and methods. Only old-fashioned practitioners rely on unscientific notions like skill, experience, or intuition. In other words, the theorists say, programming phenomena are deterministic: practically all the work involved in developing a particular application, or in modifying it later, can be specified precisely and completely from a knowledge of the requirements – just as the steps needed to build a car or an appliance can be specified in advance from a knowledge of their physical characteristics.

So, if we can account for all software applications that human minds can create – if there is nothing indeterministic, or unpredictable, in what programmers do – we should be able to replace programming knowledge with devices. The devices known as development environments, for example, materialize this idea by providing high-level starting elements. They simplify programming by minimizing the number of levels between the starting elements and the final application. Programming expertise, clearly, is becoming redundant, since even novices can now create applications. It is also interesting to note the trend in these devices to reduce the programmer's involvement to a series of selections, and selections within selections. The process of programming – the definition of files and variables, the specification of operations and conditions – has given way to a process of *selections*: instead of a blank screen where we can enter our definitions and specifications freely, we find colourful screens replete with menus, lists, icons, buttons, and the like. This structure of selections within selections attempts to emulate, obviously, the hierarchical structure believed to constitute the mental part of programming: the selection and combination of bits of knowledge leading to one of the alternatives, to a particular application.

The devices, thus, are an embodiment of the software theories. And, since the software theories are the counterpart of the traditional mechanistic theories of mind, we are witnessing the actual implementation of the idea that human creativity is an illusion, that the mind works simply by selecting and combining bits of knowledge within a predetermined range of alternatives. The substitutes for human intelligence – the models of mind that the mechanists were proposing all along in psychology, sociology, and linguistics – have finally found their practical expression in the world of programming. While the traditional mechanists were content with speculations and theories, the software mechanists are actually replacing human intelligence with devices.

We have already discussed the consequences of mind mechanism: by claiming that all human acts can be explained – by claiming, therefore, that human beings are incapable of truly creative, or unpredictable, acts – the traditional mechanistic theories can lead to a society where freedom, expertise, and creativity are redefined to mean the selection of acts from the range of alternatives sanctioned by an elite. In the world of programming, clearly, the shift has *already* occurred: the software theories assume that programmers are capable of nothing more creative than using programming substitutes, and this has given rise to the belief that it is these substitutes that are important, not the individual minds. This, in turn, has led to the belief that we must depend on the companies which provide the substitutes, and that the only way to improve our programming practices is by constantly adopting new versions of the substitutes.

Both the traditional theories and the software theories, thus, lead to the belief that human intelligence can be replaced with deterministic models. But, whereas traditional mechanism has had so far no serious consequences outside academia, *software* mechanism is causing great harm – by distorting our conception of knowledge and skills. Like the traditional ones, the theories behind the programming substitutes have been repeatedly refuted. Yet, while the theories themselves are failing, our belief in substitutes has become a self-fulfilling idea: Because we assume that programmers cannot advance beyond their current level, we encourage them to depend on substitutes. Consequently, no matter how many years of experience they have, their programming skills remain at the same low level – the level needed to use substitutes. Given this state of affairs, the adoption of the next substitute always appears to be the only way to improve their performance. So they waste their time assimilating yet another theory, or methodology, or language, instead of simply programming and improving their skills. And so the fallacy feeds on itself.

Human beings, as a matter of fact, *can* attain higher skill levels. It is only because programmers are forced to stay at novice levels that their capabilities do not exceed those of the substitutes. Recall the process of skill acquisition we studied in "Tacit Knowledge" in chapter 2: the skills and knowledge of a novice programmer constitute *simple* structures, just like the structures on which the mechanistic software theories are based; only when attaining expertise can the programmer's mind process the *complex* structures that make up software phenomena. Expert programmers outperform the substitutes because their minds can cope with whole software phenomena, while the substitutes can only cope with isolated aspects of them.

So it is the dependence on programming substitutes that is preventing the emergence of a true programming profession. Application programming has been so degraded that it now entails nothing more difficult than the performance of acts which almost anyone can master in a year or two. We are underrating the potential of our minds, and we have forgotten that there exist levels of knowledge and skills higher than those reached after a year or two of practice. In effect, we are degrading our conception of human intelligence to the level attainable by the mechanistic substitutes for intelligence.

5

We saw how the mechanistic ideology has affected the programming profession. The most serious consequence of software mechanism, however, is not the destruction of *programming* knowledge, but the destruction of the *other* kinds of knowledge – knowledge that took centuries to develop. The belief that intelligence can be replaced with devices is already spreading into other domains, especially in our business-related pursuits.

In one activity after another, we see the claim that it is possible to account for all the alternatives in that activity, discover the starting elements that give rise to these alternatives, and then incorporate the elements in a software device. In all activities, we are told, what the mind really does is combine some elementary bits of knowledge into knowledge structures, one level at a time, just as we build cars and appliances. By providing directly some high-level starting elements – prefabricated knowledge subassemblies, as it were – the devices eliminate the need for each one of us to develop in our minds the low-level elements and the combinations leading to the high levels. The lengthy and arduous period of learning and practice is a thing of the past: all we need to know now is how to operate software devices. In one occupation after another, we are told that it is unnecessary, even wrong, to rely on personal experience. Anyone can perform the same tasks as the most experienced worker simply by selecting and combining the ready-made, high-level elements available through these devices.

The devices known as office productivity systems, for example, which address office workers, are the counterpart of the development systems used by programmers. Instead of claiming that we can account for all the alternatives in programming activities, the software companies claim now that we can account for all the alternatives in *business-related* activities. Instead of software concepts that programmers can use as substitutes for programming expertise, the office systems promise software concepts that replace the skills of office workers.

And here too we see the trend to provide these concepts in the form of selections, and selections within selections, rather than permitting the user to combine freely some low-level elements. Here too, therefore, the system attempts to emulate what are believed to be the mental acts of an experienced person: selecting and combining hierarchically, one level at a time, the bits of knowledge leading to one of the alternatives.

As in the case of programming systems, the fact that an office system can generate an infinity of alternatives in business-related matters is mistaken as evidence that these devices can generate *all* possible alternatives. But this infinity is only a fraction of the infinity that an experienced worker can implement by starting from low levels, through the complex knowledge structures developed in his mind. Software devices cannot replace business-related knowledge any more than they can programming knowledge.

The fallacy, again, lies in providing starting elements that are not atomic and independent. We are lured by these devices only because we forget that the knowledge required to perform a difficult task constitutes, not an isolated structure, but a system of interacting structures: it includes many knowledge structures besides the neat hierarchical structure of selections that can be embodied in a software device. The different values of the top element – values representing the various acts performed by an experienced mind – are determined largely by the *interactions* between structures. The most important interactions occur at levels lower than the starting elements provided by devices, because it is low-level elements like variables and individual operations that are shared by the software structures, business structures, and knowledge structures which together make up the phenomena of office work. These interactions are lost when replacing minds with devices, and this is why a device can display only *some* of the alternatives displayed by a mind – those alternatives that can be represented with isolated simple structures.

To conclude, I want to stress again the link between the mechanistic theories of mind and the delusion of software devices. If we believe that it is possible to account for all the alternatives displayed by human beings in their mental acts, we will necessarily conclude that it is possible to describe human intelligence as a function of some starting mental elements; that the creativity of human minds is an illusion; and that everything the mind does can be explained as we explain the working of a machine. It should be possible to represent a person's mind, therefore, with a simple structure where the elements and levels correspond to the knowledge developed by the mind, and the values of the top element correspond to the various acts performed by that person.

What is left is to implement this structure by means of a software device. Then, any person operating the device will be able to perform the same acts as the person whose mind the device is emulating. All that human beings do, in reality, is operate devices. So, why depend on a device like the mind, which is inefficient and unreliable and, moreover, can only develop knowledge structures through painstaking learning and practice, when we can purchase modern software devices that already contain these structures?

In the domain of programming, we have already replaced minds with devices. Now, as our reliance on computers is growing, the software elites are degrading all activities where human knowledge and skills play a part, in the same way they have degraded the activity of programming. They are modifying our conception of knowledge and skills to mean simply a dependence on software devices. They are instilling in us the belief that our intelligence, our work, our initiative, our experience, can be reduced to the process of selecting and combining operations within the range of alternatives provided by these devices. They are shifting our definition of expertise, creativity, and responsibility from their traditional meaning – to do a good job, to solve an important problem, to make a real contribution – to merely knowing how to use the latest software devices.

CHAPTER 4

Language and Software

Software is written in programming languages – formal systems of communication that bear a superficial resemblance to our natural languages. Just as natural languages like English, Spanish, or Chinese allow us to communicate with the world, and thereby acquire knowledge and create in our minds an image of reality, so programming languages allow us to communicate with our computers. And, since we depend on computers in practically everything we do, programming languages allow us, ultimately, to communicate with the world, and to create in our minds perhaps a new and different image of reality.

Our programming languages are joining our traditional languages as means of communication, as ways to express ideas, as social devices that shape our life and culture. It is not surprising, therefore, that we have transferred to the domain of programming and programming languages, perhaps unconsciously, many notions from the domain of human communication and natural languages. In particular, we have transferred some of our mechanistic delusions about the phenomenon of language.

The issues involving programming languages concern not programmers alone, but all members of society. Persons who never program computers but make decisions involving software, or use software applications, or use products and services supplied by organizations that depend on software,

are all indirectly affected by our conception of programming activities and programming languages. This is true because, if this conception is reflected in the qualities of the software that we all indirectly depend on, it will necessarily be reflected also in our own capabilities and accomplishments.

Our interaction with computers, then, in any capacity and at any software level, depends on software written by various people using programming languages – software that depends in its turn on other software, and so on. If programmers communicate directly through programming languages, others communicate through software applications created with these languages. Thus, given the complete dependence of society on software and on programming, our conception of programming languages is of more than academic interest. If we are to depend on software as much as we depend on our natural languages, it is important that we understand how software functions as a means of communication.

The Common Fallacies

1

Let us review first our language and software fallacies. Most people, if asked what is the purpose of programming languages, would agree that it is similar to the purpose of natural languages. All languages, it seems, are systems of symbols, definitions, and rules, employed to convey instructions or information. Speaking, along with programming, entails the translation of knowledge from one representation – mental forms, social situations, natural phenomena – into another: words and sentences in the case of speech, operations and statements in the case of programming.

So the resulting sentences or statements, we believe, reflect the original knowledge in a different form and medium. Sentences describing wishes, or feelings, or states of affairs, or scientific facts, or logical arguments, are perceived by most of us to be verbal representations of those things – representations created by selecting appropriate words and arranging them according to certain rules of grammar. And the act of communication takes place, presumably, when the person hearing or reading these sentences translates them, somehow, into a mental representation that resembles the original one. Similarly, programs designed to address specific business requirements in inventory management, production scheduling, or text processing are thought to be software representations of those requirements.

With programming languages as with natural ones, then, we perceive the structures created with language to be *pictures* of the world, replicas of reality.

We believe that the role of language is to generate structures which provide a *one-to-one correspondence* to the knowledge or events we want to represent: each entity in the real world – each object, process, or event – must have its corresponding counterpart in the structures created with language; then, and only then, will utterances correctly express facts or ideas, and programs correctly represent our requirements.

Another term commonly used to describe this relationship is *mirroring*. An even better term is *mapping*: just as a map provides a one-to-one correspondence to those aspects of a territory that we want to represent graphically, our utterances and our programs correspond to, or map, those aspects of the world that we want to express through language. Lastly, the term *isomorphism* is sometimes used to describe these one-to-one relationships: the structures we create with language are isomorphic to the phenomena that occur in the world.

A second quality we believe to be shared by programming languages and natural languages is their hierarchical character. It seems that sentences can always be represented as hierarchical structures of linguistic entities – clauses, phrases, words; in addition, words can be classified hierarchically on the basis of their meaning. Similarly, it seems that any piece of software can be broken down hierarchically into smaller and smaller software entities. Our mechanistic view of the world tempts us to perceive all phenomena, including language and software, as systems of things within things.

Thus, if we believe that all phenomena can be represented with hierarchical structures, and believe also that languages generate hierarchical structures, it is not surprising that we see languages as mapping systems. We do not doubt for a moment that all aspects of reality can be represented precisely and completely in one language or another. If we assume that the simplest elements of language (words, for instance) correspond to the simplest elements of reality (individual objects or actions, for instance), all we need to do is combine these elements into more and more complex ones, on higher and higher levels. Each level in the structure created by language will then correspond to a more complex aspect of reality. Similarly, if the simplest *software* elements correspond to the simplest parts of our affairs, by combining these elements hierarchically we will generate software applications that represent more and more complex aspects of our affairs.

These, then, are our language and software fallacies. Our naive view of language – the belief that language can provide a one-to-one correspondence to reality, which stems from the belief that both language and reality can be represented with neat hierarchical structures – forms one of the oldest mechanistic delusions in Western history. It has misled philosophers and scientists for centuries, and it is now distorting our perception of software and programming.

The fundamental mistake in this view is, of course, reification. The structures we create with language do indeed represent the world, but not on their own. Languages are human inventions, so they cannot exist independently of their human users. As a result, language structures always interact with the other knowledge structures present in human minds, and with the structures formed by human societies. Thus, it is not through language alone but through the totality of these structures that we can hope to understand the world; that is, to attain a close correspondence to reality. The fallacy is the same, whether we expect a one-to-one correspondence between our world and the sentences of a language, or between our affairs and the statements of a software application.

In the domain of logic, the language fallacy has given rise to the belief in the existence of an ideal language. The ideal language is an artificial language, or a modified natural language, which, being logically perfect, would permit us to represent with mathematical precision everything that can exist in the world. The search for the ideal language culminated in the twentieth century with the work of philosophers like Bertrand Russell and Rudolf Carnap. These philosophers held that knowledge can always be represented by means of a language, and that science and philosophy are in fact little more than attempts to represent the world through various types of languages.

These philosophers also believed that the world has a certain logical structure – a structure that can be discovered. But we will not discover it as long as we try to mirror it in our natural languages, because these languages are imperfect, ambiguous and illogical. It is this defect, more than anything else, that prevents us from understanding the world and finding answers to our inquiries. Thus, Russell remarked that "almost all thinking that purports to be philosophical or logical consists in attributing to the world the properties of language."[1] We set out trying to mirror the world in language, and we end up, instead, perceiving the world as similar to our illogical languages.

So, the argument continues, if we represented reality in a logically perfect language, we would find the correct answers simply by expressing our inquiries in that language. This is what we do when we represent the world in the perfect language of mathematics – in astronomy, for instance. It is because we have found a way to represent the world with a perfect language that we are so

---

[1] Bertrand Russell, quoted in Irving M. Copi, "Artificial Languages," in *Language, Thought, and Culture*, ed. Paul Henle (Ann Arbor: University of Michigan Press, 1965), p. 107.

successful in the exact sciences and in engineering; so we should try to find an equally logical language for the other kinds of knowledge.

But the argument is wrong, because most aspects of the world are too complex to represent with logical languages like mathematics. Our natural languages appear ambiguous and illogical precisely because we use them to represent this complexity. No language can represent with precision the complex aspects of the world.

In the domain of programming, the language fallacy has given rise to our software delusions, to the notion of software engineering, to theories like structured programming, to methodologies, development tools, and programming environments – all stemming from the belief that the problem of programming is the problem of creating exact hierarchical structures of software entities. We believe that the answer to our programming problems lies in inventing programming concepts that are logically perfect, and in the use of application development systems based on these concepts.

Thus, because programming systems can generate hierarchical structures, we ended up attributing to the world the properties of these systems: we ended up believing that those aspects of the world that we wish to represent with software are neat hierarchical structures. But the world is *not* a neat structure, so the neat software structures are seldom adequate. We continue to believe, though, that the problem is the inexactness of the software structures, so the answer must be to improve our programming systems.

The language fallacy, then, has given rise to our preoccupation with programming languages, methodologies, tools, and environments, to the belief that these inventions are the most important aspect of software development, and that the adoption of more and more elaborate versions is the only way to improve our software representation of the world.

This preoccupation, this search for the perfect programming system, is the software counterpart of the age-old search for the perfect language. Instead of overcoming our mechanistic language delusions, we have augmented them with mechanistic *software* delusions.

2

We are interested in the modern theories of a perfect language – the theories that have emerged since the seventeenth century – for it is from these language delusions that our software delusions were ultimately born. Umberto Eco,[2]

---

[2] Umberto Eco, *The Search for the Perfect Language* (Oxford: Blackwell, 1997). The title of the next section reflects this book's title.

however, notes that the idea of a language that mirrors the world perfectly was preoccupying philosophers long before the Scientific Revolution. An attempt to explain how language corresponds to reality can be found even in Plato's dialogues. On the whole, "the story of the search for the perfect language is the story of a dream and of a series of failures.... [It is] the tale of the obstinate pursuit of an impossible dream."[3]

If the search for a logically perfect language has been based since Descartes on mechanistic notions, earlier theories were based on mystical or religious notions. One theory, for instance, was inspired by the biblical story of Babel: In the Garden of Eden there was only one language – the language God used to speak to Adam. This was a perfect language, but it was lost at Babel, when Man started to build a mighty tower in an attempt to reach the heavens. This arrogant project incurred the wrath of God, who decided to stop it by confounding the language used by the workers. Construction was disrupted, the tower was never finished, and we have suffered ever since the confusion of a multitude of illogical languages. Thus, the belief in a perfect language can be seen as an attempt to restore the ideal state of the Beginning: a language that mirrors reality perfectly would enable Man to again understand his world, attain omniscience and happiness, and perhaps communicate with God.

An early example of this belief, Eco notes, is the linguistic project of Dante Alighieri, started in 1303. Dante, who is best known as poet and philosopher, attempted to create a poetic language that would serve the needs of an ideal society – a language suited for expressing truth and wisdom, and capable of accurately reflecting reality. "Opposing this language to all other languages of the confusion, Dante proclaimed it as the one which had restored that primordial affinity between words and objects which had been the hallmark of the language of Adam."[4]

Interpreters have concluded that Dante, influenced by even earlier scholars, believed that the divine gift received by Adam was not so much a language as the *capacity* to understand and create languages – a view similar to Chomsky's idea of an innate language faculty (see "Universal Grammar" in chapter 3): "What God gave Adam ... was neither just the faculty of language nor yet a natural language; what he gave was, in fact, a set of principles for a universal grammar."[5] And what Dante believed to be the most important characteristic of these principles was the capability to provide a one-to-one correspondence to the actual world. This capability is what he saw as the distinguishing quality of a perfect language – that quality which our natural languages have lost, and which he strove to restore through his poetic language: "It seems most likely that Dante believed that, at Babel, there had disappeared the perfect *forma*

---

[3] Ibid., p. 19.   [4] Ibid., p. 35.   [5] Ibid., p. 44.

locutionis [i.e., linguistic model] whose principles permitted the creation of languages capable of reflecting the true essence of things; languages, in other words, in which the *modi essendi* of things [i.e., their essence] were identical with the *modi significandi* [i.e., their representation]."[6]

George Steiner points out that every civilization had its version of Babel in its mythology.[7] Thus, the belief in a language that mirrors reality stems perhaps from a common human need to understand the world. And the one-to-one correspondence provided by such a language derives from its divine nature: "The vulgate of Eden contained, though perhaps in a muted key, a divine syntax – powers of statement and designation analogous to God's own diction, in which the mere naming of a thing was the necessary and sufficient cause of its leap into reality.... Being of direct divine etymology, moreover, [it] had a congruence with reality such as no tongue has had after Babel.... Words and objects dovetailed perfectly. As the modern epistemologist might put it, there was a complete, point-to-point mapping of language onto the true substance and shape of things."[8]

Throughout history we have been searching for an ideal language, motivated by the belief that language can provide an exact correspondence to reality – the same belief we recognize in modern linguistics. We should not be surprised, therefore, that this mechanistic view of language has prompted twentieth-century thinkers like Russell, Carnap, and Chomsky to propose linguistic theories that are so similar to the mystical notions held by medieval scholars. Nor should we be surprised that our *software* theories, which arose out of the same mechanistic culture and are grounded on the same beliefs, make the same mistake: they regard the relationship between *programming* languages and reality just as the linguistic theories regard the relationship between *natural* languages and reality.

Ancient or modern, founded on mysticism or science, all attempts to find an ideal language, or a logically perfect language, have been sheer fantasies. It is important, however, to recognize their common fallacy. Philosophers recognize the potency of language, its power to describe and explain the world, to express knowledge and ideas; and they also recognize the power and simplicity of hierarchical structures, their ability to represent apparently complex phenomena with neat systems. These philosophers believe, then, that

[6] Ibid., p. 45.

[7] George Steiner, *After Babel: Aspects of Language and Translation*, 2nd ed. (Oxford: Oxford University Press, 1992), p. 59.   [8] Ibid., pp. 60–61.

it is possible to combine the potency of language with the neatness of a hierarchical structure. The terminal elements of the hierarchy (the words, typically) would correspond directly to the basic objects, processes, and events that make up the world; and the rules that define the relations between elements in language would correspond to the natural laws that govern the relations between the real things. Since such a system would provide an exact correspondence between words and reality, it would constitute a perfect language.

What these philosophers fail to see is that the potency of language derives, not from a capability to mirror the world through one-to-one correspondence, but from its capability to generate interacting structures. The structures formed by language elements interact with one another, and also with the knowledge structures present in human minds, and with the structures formed by human societies. It is the complex structures generated by these interactions that are the source of richness and potency in language.

It is futile, therefore, to try to explain the world by inventing a language that is better, or more logical, than our natural languages. For, if we cannot explain a complex phenomenon, the problem is not the imperfection of our languages but the complexity of the world, and also the lack of certain knowledge structures in our minds. If we are at all capable of understanding a certain phenomenon, we will understand it through any language, for the language structures themselves play only a small part in this process. It is their interaction with the other knowledge structures present in our minds that gives rise to the intelligence we need to understand a complex phenomenon.

And so it is with our *software* structures. If our applications fail to answer our needs (fail, that is, to provide an exact correspondence to the world), the problem is not the imperfection of our programming languages or development tools, but the complexity of the world, and the lack of adequate knowledge structures (that is, programming skills) in our minds. Consequently, it is futile to seek a solution by improving the programming languages or the development tools. As is the case with natural languages, the richness and potency of software derives, not from a capability to mirror the world perfectly (something no programming language or tool can do), but from its capability to generate interacting structures; namely, structures that interact with one another, with the knowledge structures present in our minds, and with the structures formed by our social and business affairs. It is the complex structures emerging from these interactions that we observe as software benefits.

Therefore, when the benefits are not forthcoming, improving the *language* structures will not solve the problem; it is the *knowledge* structures that we must improve. For, the programming languages themselves play only a small part in this process, and, in any case, they are already adequate. It is not a new language or a new development system that we need, but greater programming knowledge.

The Search for the Perfect Language

1

Let us start with the philosophies of the seventeenth century. The three great rationalists, Descartes, Spinoza, and Leibniz, believed that everything can be represented in the form of a deductive system; namely, as a hierarchical structure similar to the system of mathematics. Their philosophies varied in detail, but were all based on the vague notion of *substances* (the hypothetical things that make up the world).

Substances are taken to be independent of one another. In particular, the material world is made of one kind of substance, and mental processes are made of a different kind. There are objects that occupy physical space, attributes that can be perceived, and events that can be observed to occur in time; then, there are their mental counterparts – the notions we hold in the mind when we are aware of these objects, attributes, and events. The real things are said to have an *extension*, while thoughts and feelings do not. There were difficulties in explaining how the material world interacts with the mental one (as when a thought causes the movement of a limb), but these difficulties could usually be resolved by postulating divine intervention in one form or another.

In their effort to explain the world mathematically – that is, with simple structures – the rationalists had to assume that it is made up of several independent aspects, each one consisting of a different substance. They could not explain the *real* world – the complex structure – mathematically, so they extracted various aspects, thinking that by explaining each one separately they would eventually explain the world. And two aspects they always had to separate were the material and the mental.

Thus, Descartes's system "presents two parallel but independent worlds, that of mind and that of matter, each of which can be studied without reference to the other."[1] Spinoza held that the world is only one substance, one system,

---

[1] Bertrand Russell, *A History of Western Philosophy* (New York: Simon and Schuster, 1972), p. 567.

but had to separate the physical from the mental anyway. He interpreted them as two attributes, each one providing "complete and adequate knowledge of the essence of a single substance. Thought and extension each represents reality as it essentially is, and each attribute gives a *complete* account of that reality."[2] Leibniz preferred a system called *monadology*, according to which the world is a hierarchical structure of *monads*: atomic entities that form independent substances while also being related through the mystical quality known as "pre-established harmony." Leibniz was trying to explain how physical and mental structures, which are different substances and do not interact, can nevertheless influence each other: some of the properties of monads give rise to physical structures, and others to mental structures, but the pre-established harmony keeps the two kinds of structures synchronized at all times.

The dichotomy of mind and matter has remained a major problem of philosophy. This problem can be described as the problem of accounting for mental phenomena by means of mechanistic theories: explaining how it is possible for such phenomena as knowledge, consciousness, intelligence, and emotions, which have no material existence, to arise in a world made up of material entities. It ought to be obvious that mental phenomena are complex structures, and thus irreducible to deterministic models; but such an explanation is inadmissible in a mechanistic culture like ours. So, for over three hundred years, one philosophy after another has been advanced in an attempt to bridge the gap between the mental and the material worlds; that is, to reduce mental phenomena to physical processes. Today's theories of artificial intelligence, for example, are merely the modern equivalent of the mechanistic fantasies of the seventeenth century: just another attempt to account for consciousness and intelligence by means of deterministic models.

Returning to the rationalist philosophers, we can understand why they liked the two-world conception of reality – the separation of reality into a material world and a mental world. By accepting this notion, they abandoned in effect the goal of understanding the real world, and replaced it with the lesser challenge of understanding the material and the mental worlds independently. Now they were able to apply the mechanistic principles, reductionism and atomism, to two separate worlds, which individually are simpler than the real one.

In the material world, this has resulted in the spectacular advances in science and technology of the last three centuries. In the mental world, the benefits of the mechanistic methods have been much more modest. The reason is that mechanistic theories and models, as embodied in mathematical systems and other simple hierarchical structures, can provide only *approximations* of

[2] Roger Scruton, *Spinoza* (Oxford: Oxford University Press, 1986), pp. 56–57.

reality. In the material world, many phenomena are sufficiently independent – sufficiently isolated from other phenomena – for these approximations to be useful. But the phenomena created by human minds cannot be studied in isolation, because they are closely linked. Moreover, they are linked to the phenomena of the material world. A mental world separated from the material world can exist only in our imagination. In practice we cannot observe a person's actual thoughts or feelings, but only the phenomena that arise when those thoughts and feelings interact with the material world.

The conclusion must be that processes occurring in a mind cannot be studied as we do those involving physical objects. Searching for a theory that explains mechanistically mental phenomena is an absurd pursuit, so we must not be surprised that so little progress has been made in disciplines like psychology and sociology. If there exists a way to explain mental phenomena, it must involve the study of the complex structures of the real world – structures created by the interaction of the phenomena of one mind with those of other minds, and with those occurring in the material world. This may well be an impossible challenge.

When the rationalist philosophers addressed themselves to the problem of language, they naturally tried to solve it as they had tried to solve the problem of mind: by separating language from the complex reality. Just as they had separated the real world into mental and material worlds, they treated language as yet another world – a third kind of substance, capable of independent existence. They believed that if such matters as grammar and word meaning were fairly well understood on their own, there was no reason why they could not discover a complete theory of language, a model that explained with precision every aspect of it. And, needless to say, "they held that a truly systematic conception and formation of language could be obtained only through the application of the method and standards of mathematics."[3] Language, they believed, is a mechanistic phenomenon, a system of things within things, and must be investigated in the same way as the phenomena of the material world.

Language, however, is a *complex* structure, the result of many interacting structures; and it involves not only linguistic structures like syntax and semantics, but also various knowledge structures present in the mind, and the structures that make up the context in which it is used. Since they could not

[3] Ernst Cassirer, *The Philosophy of Symbolic Forms*, vol. 1, *Language* (New Haven: Yale University Press, 1955), p. 127.

explain the whole phenomenon of language, the rationalists attempted to create exact linguistic models by reducing language to one of its component structures; typically, a structure based on grammar, or one based on word meaning. But this reification can yield only a crude approximation of the whole phenomenon.

The rationalist philosophies of the seventeenth century ended up depicting reality, thus, as three independent structures: the material, the mental, and the linguistic. These three structures were seen as three parallel worlds, each one reflecting reality, and each one being a reflection of the others.

But the notion of three parallel and independent worlds did not originate with the rationalists. It went back, in fact, at least to the thirteenth century, when a group of scholars called Modistae "asserted a relation of *specular* correspondence between language, thought and the nature of things. For them, it was a given that the *modi intelligendi* [i.e., mental forms] and, consequently, the *modi significandi* [i.e., symbolic forms] reflected the *modi essendi* [i.e., actual forms] of things themselves."[4] They believed, in other words, that the linguistic symbols we use to express knowledge correspond to both the knowledge held in the mind and the actual things depicted by that knowledge.

It is this fallacy – the idea that language structures can map mental structures and material structures perfectly, coupled with the idea that all three are neat hierarchical structures and hence amenable to mechanistic treatment – that we can recognize in all the theories we are examining here, down to the theories of our own time. The fallacy can manifest itself in one of two ways: the philosophers believe that *natural* languages form simple structures, and therefore any language, if carefully employed, can reflect perfectly the mental world or the material world (also taken to form simple structures); or they believe that an *artificial* language based on a simple structure can be invented – a language which would reflect perfectly the mental or the material world. Let us start by examining how these two beliefs influenced the philosophies of the seventeenth century; then, we will study their influence in the twentieth century, and how they gave rise to the current *software* delusions.

2

The most naive manifestation of the language fallacy was the belief that it is possible to use ordinary language to build systems of logical concepts, simply by arranging these concepts into neat hierarchical structures that emulate the deductive method of mathematics.

---

[4] Umberto Eco, *The Search for the Perfect Language* (Oxford: Blackwell, 1997), p. 44.

In a mathematical system we start with a small number of axioms, and derive simple theorems by showing that their validity can be logically deduced, or demonstrated, from these axioms. Then, we derive more complex theorems by deducing them from the simple ones; and we continue this process with more and more complex theorems, on higher and higher levels. Ultimately, by creating a hierarchical structure of theorems, we can confidently determine the validity of very difficult ones.

The rationalist philosophers believed, as we saw, that language can provide an exact, one-to-one correspondence to the material and the mental worlds, and that all three can be represented with simple hierarchical structures. So, they concluded, if they expressed their arguments in ordinary language very carefully, the resulting sentences would function just like the axioms and theorems of mathematics: they would start with simple assertions about the world – assertions whose truth no one doubts, and which could therefore act as axioms; then, they would formulate more and more ambitious statements by moving up, one level at a time, and expressing each statement as a logical combination of statements from the previous level.

This method, they believed, is identical to the deductive method employed in mathematics, so it should allow us to determine the truth of the most difficult statements. But language mirrors reality, so these demonstrations will function at the same time as demonstrations of certain states of affairs that exist in the world. Simply by manipulating sentences, then, we will be able to determine the validity of any concept, including concepts that cannot be verified directly.

Thus, with this method Descartes needed only a few pages of text to "establish the existence of God, and the distinction between the mind and body of man."[5] The logic system through which he "establishes" these facts includes: ten definitions (for example, definition I is "By the term *thought* ... I comprehend all that is in us, so that we are immediately conscious of it...."[6]); seven postulates, which preface and explain ten axioms (for example, axiom I is "Nothing exists of which it cannot be inquired what is the cause of its existing...."[7]); and four theorems, or propositions, with their demonstrations.

Similarly, in the *Ethics*, Spinoza presented his entire philosophy in this fashion. The book consists of definitions, postulates, axioms, propositions, demonstrations, and corollaries, arranged in five hierarchical structures, just like mathematical systems. Spinoza addresses such topics as the existence of God, knowledge and emotions, the relation between matter and mind, the power of reason over passion, and human freedom. And Samuel Clarke,

---

[5] René Descartes, *A Discourse on Method* (London: Dent, 1912), p. 229.   [6] Ibid.
[7] Ibid., p. 232.

another philosopher of that period, presented in the form of a mathematical system his ideas on religion and morals.

We are not concerned here with the content or merit of these theories, but only with their mathematical pretences. These philosophers were convinced that, by mimicking in ordinary language the deductive methods of mathematics, they were actually proving their "theorems." This delusion is easy to understand if we remember their belief that the knowledge embodied in a set of sentences can form a self-contained system, an independent structure. They fail to see that the reason we can comprehend these sentences at all – the reason they can communicate their ideas to us through language – is the common knowledge structures that both they and we *already hold* in our minds. Thus, it is the *combination* of this previous knowledge and the knowledge found in the new sentences that forms, in reality, their philosophical systems.

The sentences themselves may or may not form a perfect hierarchical structure, but in either case the new knowledge is the result of several interacting structures. What we derive from reading the axioms, propositions, and demonstrations is not just a new and independent structure of neatly related concepts, but the complex structure formed by the interaction of these concepts and many *other* concepts, which already exist in our minds. For, if this were not the case, if all the concepts required to understand a philosophical system were contained in the structure of sentences alone, we could implement them as a *software* system – by storing the definitions, axioms, and propositions in the elements of a hierarchical data structure. Then, simply by interpreting the high levels of this structure, the computer would understand the idea of good and evil, or the meaning of reason and passion, or the value of freedom, just as *we* do – a preposterous notion.

The delusion becomes obvious, thus, when we represent these verbal theorems as simple and complex structures. Entities can function as the starting elements of a simple structure only if atomic and independent, otherwise they give rise to a *complex* structure. The rationalist philosophers invoke the mechanistic principles of reductionism and atomism, but do not, in fact, follow them rigorously: they employ as starting elements – as definitions, postulates, and axioms – entities that are neither atomic nor independent. To use as definition, postulate, or axiom a sentence like the ones previously quoted, we must know the meaning of its words, understand the facts asserted, and place these facts in the current context. So we must appreciate its significance, and we do this by analyzing and interpreting it on the basis of *previous* knowledge – the same knowledge that helps us to appreciate the significance of the *other* definitions, postulates, and axioms. Thus, since the starting elements are interrelated, what these philosophers are building is not an isolated hierarchical structure but a system of interacting structures.

These philosophers also fail to see that if they could use the neat, deductive methods of mathematics with these topics, they wouldn't need all those sentences in the first place. They could substitute symbols like x and y for the starting elements, and then restrict themselves to manipulating these symbols with equations, as we do in mathematics. It is precisely because they need to express concepts that *cannot* be represented mathematically – specifically, because they want us to link the new structures with some *other* knowledge structures – that the philosophers use *verbal* theorems and demonstrations. They need the words because it is only through the multiple meanings of words that we can link these structures. But then, how can they continue to believe that those verbal hierarchies function as isolated structures, as mathematical systems? Since their method is unsound, their conclusions are unwarranted, and this casts doubt on their entire philosophy.

This is what George Boole showed nearly two centuries later.[8] We know Boole as the mathematician who established modern symbolic logic, and in particular, what is known today as Boolean logic – the system that provides the mathematical foundation for (among other things) digital electronics, and hence computers. In Boolean logic, entities are reduced to the values 0 and 1, or *False* and *True*, and are manipulated with logical operators like AND, OR, and NOT; large and intricate hierarchical structures can be built starting with these simple elements and operations.

Like the rationalist philosophers, Boole held that a logic system is not limited to mathematical problems, but can also be used with general propositions. Unlike them, however, he recognized that it is adequate only in situations that can be reduced to a symbolic form. Thus, he criticized Spinoza and Clarke, showing that the ideas they attempted to prove with deductive methods do not lend themselves to this treatment. As a result, their philosophical systems – which continue to be seen even today as impeccable – are not as sound as they appear: "In what are regarded as the most rigorous examples of reasoning applied to metaphysical questions, it will occasionally be found that different trains of thought are blended together; that particular but essential parts of the demonstration are given parenthetically, or out of the main course of the argument; that the meaning of a premiss may be in some degree ambiguous; and, not unfrequently, that arguments, viewed by the strict laws of formal reasoning, are incorrect or inconclusive."[9]

Boole checked some of Spinoza's and Clarke's demonstrations by substituting symbols for their verbal propositions, and then reproducing their verbal arguments by means of logical formulas. Thus, he notes that some of the

[8] George Boole, *The Laws of Thought* (New York: Dover, 1958), ch. XIII.
[9] Ibid., p. 186.

original definitions and axioms turn out to be vague or ambiguous when we try to represent them with precise symbols. And, even when they can be accurately reduced to logical formulas, he notes that some of the conclusions cannot, in fact, be logically derived from the premises.

3

So far we have examined the belief that natural languages can be used like mathematical systems. The most common manifestation of the language fallacy, however, is the belief that our natural languages are hopelessly inadequate for expressing rational thought; that only a formal system of symbols and rules can accurately reflect reality; that we must start from scratch, therefore, and *invent* a perfect language.

Descartes, who held that the totality of human knowledge can be represented, as it were, with one giant structure of things within things, envisaged the possibility of a universal language that would express this knowledge: all we have to do is create a hierarchical linguistic structure that matches, element for element, the whole structure of knowledge. He believed that "just as there is a very definite order among the ideas of mathematics, e.g., among numbers, so the whole of human consciousness, with all the contents that can ever enter into it, constitutes a strictly ordered totality. And similarly, just as the whole system of arithmetic can be constructed out of relatively few numerical signs, it must be possible to designate the sum and structure of all intellectual contents by a limited number of linguistic signs, provided only that they are combined in accordance with definite, universal rules."[10] Unfortunately, Descartes admitted, the only way to design such a language is by first determining all the elements in the hierarchy of knowledge – a task that would require "the analysis of all the contents of consciousness into their ultimate elements, into simple, constitutive 'ideas.'"[11]

Descartes never attempted this project, but his immediate successors did: "In rapid sequence they produced the most diverse systems of artificial universal language, which, though very different in execution, were in agreement in their fundamental idea and the principle of their structure. They all started from the notion that [the totality of knowledge is ultimately based on] a limited number of concepts, that each of these concepts stands to the others in a very definite factual relation of coordination, superordination or subordination, and that a truly perfect language must strive to express this natural hierarchy of concepts adequately in a system of signs."[12]

---

[10] Cassirer, *Symbolic Forms*, p. 128.   [11] Ibid.   [12] Ibid.

Two language systems designed as a hierarchical classification of concepts were those of George Dalgarno and John Wilkins.[13] These men attempted to classify all known objects, attributes, qualities, relations, actions, etc., into one giant hierarchical structure. Each one of these entities was believed to occupy a precise place in the structure of knowledge, and to form therefore one of the terminal elements in the structure of words that mirrors the structure of knowledge. But familiar words can be misleading, so Dalgarno and Wilkins invented elaborate systems of symbols to represent these elements, as well as rules of grammar to combine them into sentences. It was widely believed that an artificial language of this kind, designed in the form of a logic system, would enable scientists and philosophers to express ideas more effectively than it is possible with our natural languages. And few doubted that such languages can, indeed, be invented.

Among the seventeenth-century language fantasies, it is Leibniz's work that has probably received the most attention. Although Leibniz did not actually attempt to create a language system, he was preoccupied with the relation between language and knowledge throughout his career. Leibniz's work was guided by two beliefs. First, anything that is complex – mental as much as material – is necessarily made up of simpler things; and these things, if still complex, are made up of even simpler things, and so on, ending eventually with some elements that are no longer divisible into simpler ones. These elements function, therefore, as an "alphabet": they are the building blocks from which everything is made up.

This, of course, is a belief in reductionism and atomism. Applying these principles to mental entities, Leibniz held that there must exist an "alphabet of human thought": a set of simple, elementary concepts that constitute the building blocks of all knowledge, of all science and philosophy, of all truths known or yet to be discovered. It is the use of imprecise natural languages to express ideas that leads us into error and slows down intellectual progress. With an alphabet of thought we could formulate inquiries logically, solve problems rationally, and quickly expand our knowledge. All we would have to do is combine the basic elements of thought into more and more complex concepts, one level at a time, following precise rules. We could then deal safely with concepts of any complexity, because their validity would be guaranteed by the method's formality.

Leibniz's second belief, thus, was that a logical language is not limited to helping us express what we already know, but can also help us attain *new* knowledge. The language of mathematics, for example, allows us to represent very large numbers, or very complex relations, by starting with a small set of

---

[13] See, for example, Eco, *Perfect Language*, chs. 11–12.

symbols and rules. By combining and manipulating these symbols logically on paper, we have made great discoveries about the real world; that is, about the actual, physical entities represented by the symbols. These discoveries, clearly, could not have been made by observing or manipulating the physical entities themselves.

Similarly, Leibniz believed, a language based on an alphabet of thought would enable us to make progress in any domain involving rational thinking. He called the symbols used to represent concepts *characters*, and the language *universal characteristic*. This language, he believed, would function as a sort of calculus: "It is obvious that if we could find characters or signs suited for expressing all our thoughts as clearly and exactly as arithmetic expresses numbers or geometrical analysis expresses lines, we could do in all matters *insofar as they are subject to reasoning* all that we can do in arithmetic and geometry. For all investigations which depend on reasoning would be carried out by the transposition of these characters and by a species of calculus."[14] Thus, Leibniz was convinced that it is possible to invent a language "in which the order and relations of signs would so mirror the order and relations of ideas that all valid reasoning could be reduced to an infallible, mechanical procedure involving only the formal substitution of characters."[15]

The fallacy of these language systems lies in the belief that human knowledge can be represented with *one* hierarchical structure. We recognize this as the fallacy of reification. When a hierarchical classification of concepts is used as the basis of a universal language, what is wrong is not the classification, which in itself may be accurate and useful. The reason the system fails is that there are *additional ways* to classify the same concepts, on the basis of other attributes, or characteristics, or criteria (see pp. 100–104).

Only elements that are atomic and independent can function as starting elements in a simple hierarchical structure; and it is impossible to find such elements in the phenomenon of knowledge. The concept of a flower, for example, is an element in many hierarchical structures: a structure that depicts the botanical aspects of flowers, a structure that depicts the business of flowers, a structure that depicts social customs involving flowers, and so forth. These structures are not distinct subsets of a hierarchical structure of knowledge, but different structures that share some of their elements. The concept of a flower,

[14] Gottfried Leibniz, quoted in Donald Rutherford, "Philosophy and Language in Leibniz," in *The Cambridge Companion to Leibniz*, ed. Nicholas Jolley (New York: Cambridge University Press, 1995), p. 234.   [15] Ibid., p. 231.

therefore, is not a starting element in the structure of knowledge. And breaking it down into even simpler concepts would not help; for, were the lower-level elements independent of other structures, the concept of a flower itself would be independent.

When Leibniz attempts to discover the alphabet of human thought by repeatedly breaking down complex concepts into simpler ones, what he fails to see is that, at each level, he is taking into account *only one* of the attributes that characterize the concepts of that level. There are always other ways that a concept can be expressed as a combination of simpler ones. We can stop, in fact, at any level we like and call its elements the alphabet of thought; but these elements always have other attributes besides those we took into account, so they are part of other structures too. These elements, therefore, are not independent, so they cannot function as the starting elements of a simple hierarchical structure.

Thus, there are *many* hierarchical structures, not one. And these structures interact, because they exist at the same time and share their elements. When we acquire knowledge, our mind develops structures matching *all* these classifications, and their interactions. This is why we can *acquire* and *use* knowledge, while being unable to represent the same knowledge with rules or diagrams. The knowledge is embodied largely in the *interactions* between structures, and it is these interactions that can exist in a mind but not in a mechanistic model.

It is not difficult, then, to find some building blocks of human thought. But, while the elements at any level could be called the alphabet of thought, they would not serve this function as Leibniz hoped (in the way the building blocks of mathematics are the foundation of mathematical systems). We could indeed create the entire human knowledge from these elements, but only by taking into account *all* their attributes: we would combine the elements through many structures simultaneously, and thereby build a *complex* structure.

For example, if we decide that certain *words* should function as the alphabet of thought, it is not enough to see them as the elements of *one* structure. Since the things depicted by words have more than one attribute, they belong to a different structure through each attribute. Thus, when words are used to express ideas, their meanings give rise to many structures: just as the things themselves link, through their attributes, the structures that *constitute* reality, the words depicting these things link in our mind the knowledge structures that *mirror* reality. Knowledge, therefore, like reality itself, is a complex structure, and cannot be represented with one hierarchy, as Leibniz hoped. (We will return to this problem in the next section.)

But perhaps Leibniz *did* recognize the limitations of simple structures. In the passage previously quoted, for instance, he emphasizes that his system would be useful "in all matters *insofar as they are subject to reasoning.*" His error, therefore, is perhaps not so much in believing that *all* knowledge can be represented with simple structures, as in failing to see how little *can* in fact be so represented; that is, how little is "subject to reasoning," if we define reasoning in the narrow sense of mathematical reasoning. For, if we did that, we would have to declare almost all knowledge as *not* being subject to reasoning. His system could indeed work, but only if we restricted our mental acts to whatever can be accomplished with neat mathematical methods; in other words, if we restricted human thought to the capabilities of machines.

4

We cannot leave this early period without recalling the satire of Jonathan Swift. Through imaginative writing, Swift ridiculed the society of his time, and especially the ignorance, hypocrisy, and corruption of the elites. From politics to religion, from education to morals, from arts to science, he fearlessly questioned all accepted values. In his best-known work, *Gulliver's Travels*, the hero finds himself in some strange lands, giving Swift the opportunity to expose the preoccupations of the contemporary British society by projecting them in modified and exaggerated forms onto the fictional societies of those lands.

Now, one of the things that Swift detested was the excesses of the mechanistic philosophy, which by the end of the seventeenth century had become for most scientists practically a new religion: the belief that mechanistic theories can explain any phenomenon; the obsession with finding a neat model that would describe the whole world; and, of course, the search for an artificial language that would mirror reality perfectly.

In his voyage to Laputa, Gulliver has the occasion to visit the Grand Academy of Lagado, where hundreds of "projectors" are engaged in fantastic research projects: ideas that promise extraordinary benefits to society, although so far none of them work. Here Swift is ridiculing the Royal Society and other institutions, which, in their infatuation with mechanism, were studying quite seriously all sorts of utopian schemes. And some of these schemes involved the improvement of language. (In 1668, for example, the Royal Society appointed a commission of distinguished scientists to study the possible applications of the language invented by John Wilkins, mentioned on p. 314.[16])

Swift recognized the absurdity of the mechanistic language theories; specifically, the belief that the totality of knowledge can be represented with exact,

[16] Eco, *Perfect Language*, p. 229.

mathematical systems. To satirize these theories, he describes the language machine invented by one of the professors at the Academy: a mechanical contraption that generates random combinations of words. Simply by collecting those combinations that form meaningful sentences, the professor tells Gulliver, one can generate effortlessly any text in a given domain: "Every one knows how laborious the usual method is of attaining to arts and sciences; whereas by his contrivance, the most ignorant person at a reasonable charge, and with a little bodily labour, may write books in philosophy, poetry, politics, law, mathematics and theology, without the least assistance from genius or study."[17] (We will discuss the delusion of language machines in greater detail in chapter 6; see pp. 458–461.)

Then, to ridicule the idea that the elements of language mirror the world through one-to-one correspondence, Swift describes another research project: abolishing language altogether and communicating instead directly through physical objects (which would obviate both the need to produce sounds and the need to translate words from one language into another): "Since words are only names for *things*, it would be more convenient for all men to carry about them such *things* as were necessary to express the particular business they are to discourse on."[18]

Our challenge today is to recognize that our preoccupation with programming languages and systems stems from delusions that are the software counterpart of the language delusions of previous ages. When a programming theory claims that our affairs constitute a neat hierarchical structure of concepts, and therefore applications should be built as neat hierarchical structures of modules, we are witnessing the same fallacy as in Leibniz's idea of human knowledge and the mathematical language that would represent it.

Structured programming methodologies, object-oriented systems, fourth-generation languages, not to mention pursuits like Chomskyan linguistics and artificial intelligence – these are the projects that Gulliver would have found the professors of the Grand Academy engaged in, had Swift lived in our time. And the language machine that permits ignorant people to write books on any subject has its counterpart today in the application development environments, programming tools, database systems, and other software devices that promise ignorant programmers and users the power to generate applications "without writing a single line of code." (We will study these delusions in chapters 6 and 7.)

---

[17] Jonathan Swift, *Gulliver's Travels and Other Writings* (New York: Bantam Books, 1981), p. 181.   [18] Ibid., p. 183.

5

Let us pass over the dozens of other language proposals and go straight to the last years of the nineteenth century, when the modern theories of language and meaning were born. The first thing we notice is that there is little difference between these theories and the earlier ones, as the passage of two centuries did not alter the two fundamental beliefs: that there exists a one-to-one correspondence between language and reality, and that both can be represented as simple hierarchical structures.

A major concern of twentieth-century philosophy has been the formal analysis of language structures – not in the linguistic sense, but as regards their *meaning*; specifically, the study of the relationship between statements and reality. One of the aspects of this study has been the attempt to derive and interpret the meaning of ordinary sentences using the methods of formal logic; that is, to determine from the grammatical and logical structure of a sentence whether it describes something that actually exists in the world. This is how Irving Copi puts it: "The linguistic program for metaphysical inquiry may be described as follows. Every fact has a certain ontological form or structure. For a given sentence to assert a particular fact, the sentence must have a grammatical structure which has something in common with the ontological structure of the fact. Hence, on the reasonable expectation that sentences are easier to investigate than the facts they assert, the examination of sentences will reveal metaphysical truths about the world."[19]

But, philosophers say, while the world has presumably a neat and logical structure, our natural languages do not, so we will never be able to understand the world through ordinary language. We must design, therefore, a special language: "The relevance of constructing an artificial symbolic language which shall be 'ideal' or 'logically perfect' to the program for investigating metaphysics by way of grammar is clear. If we have a 'logically perfect' language, then its structure will have something in common with the structure of the world, and by examining the one we shall come to understand the other."[20] Copi points out, however, that "even if an 'ideal' or 'logically perfect' language could be devised, the proposed program for investigating the logical or ontological structure of reality by investigating the syntactical structure of an 'ideal' language is impossible of fulfillment."[21] The reason is simple: if a

---

[19] Irving M. Copi, "Artificial Languages," in *Language, Thought, and Culture*, ed. Paul Henle (Ann Arbor: University of Michigan Press, 1965), p. 108.   [20] Ibid., p. 109.
[21] Ibid., p. 110.

language is to mirror reality perfectly, we must understand reality before we design that language, thus contradicting the original goal of designing the language in order to understand reality.

These linguistic theories demonstrate once again the circularity that characterizes mechanistic thinking. The philosophers attempt to describe the world with languages based on simple structures because they *assume* that the world has a neat hierarchical structure. They start by assuming the truth of what, in fact, needs to be proved. For, the structure of the world is what they do not know, what those languages were meant to uncover. In other words, they use their mechanistic fantasy about the world to justify their mechanistic fantasy about language. Actually, the world is not a simple structure but the interaction of many structures, so it is not surprising that these languages do not work. It is *because* they are logically perfect that they cannot mirror the world. Thus, the mechanistic language dream – a complete analysis of language and knowledge through mathematical logic – was never attained.

The first philosopher to investigate this possibility was Gottlob Frege, who rejected the view that a precise language like the symbolic language of mathematics can represent only the formal aspects of knowledge. He held that *all* human thought can be reduced to a precise language – a language that can "be taken care of by a machine or replaced by a purely mechanical activity."[22] Frege, however, "recognized from the very beginning that for most sentences of natural languages 'the connection of words corresponds only partially to the structure of the concepts.' But instead of drawing Kant's defeatist conclusion, Frege attempted to identify what others would call a 'perfect language,' a fragment of German that expressed perspicuously the content of what we say."[23]

The language fragment Frege was seeking had to fulfil two conditions: "(a) Every German sentence has a translation into this fragment, and (b) the grammatical form of every sentence in this fragment mirrors isomorphically the constituents of the content it expresses, as well as their arrangement in that content.... In effect, the idea was to produce a language in which, even though inference was based on meaning, one need no longer think about meanings ... since one could now restrict oneself to the signs 'present to the senses' and their symbolic correlations."[24] What Frege was seeking, thus, was a symbolic system that would fulfil for all the knowledge we can express in a natural language like German, the same function that the symbolic language of mathematics fulfils for that portion of knowledge we can express mathematically.

---

[22] Gottlob Frege, quoted in J. Alberto Coffa, *The Semantic Tradition from Kant to Carnap* (New York: Cambridge University Press, 1993), p. 65.

[23] Coffa, *Semantic Tradition*, p. 64.   [24] Ibid., p. 66.

And, once this perfect language is discovered, the interpretation of the meaning of sentences will be automatic. By translating all discourse into this language, we will be able to determine whether a given statement is meaningful or not "by a purely mechanical activity": all we will have to do is manipulate symbols, just as we do in mathematics.

❖

In the first two decades of the twentieth century, it was Bertrand Russell and Ludwig Wittgenstein who made the greatest contribution to the philosophy of language. And, since the two men collaborated during this period, their theories have much in common. Wittgenstein's most important work, however, was done later. For this reason, and because Wittgenstein's philosophy is especially important to us, I will discuss it separately in the next section.

Russell based his philosophy of language on a theory he called *logical atomism* – the analysis of language using the principles of atomism and mathematical logic. He developed and modified this philosophy over a period of more than forty years, yet his goal remained the same: to find a formal, mathematical language that can express with preciseness all knowable facts, and hence all mental processes. His goal, in other words, was to represent human knowledge and thought with a neat structure of concepts within concepts. And although the theory never worked, Russell continued to believe in the possibility of such a language to the end of his life: "There is, I think, a discoverable relation between the structure of sentences and the structure of the occurrences to which the sentences refer. I do not think the structure of non-verbal facts is wholly unknowable, and I believe that, with sufficient caution, the properties of language may help us to understand the structure of the world."[25]

Thus, Russell's linguistic project is an excellent example of the futile struggle to reduce complex phenomena to simple structures. It is also an example of the corruptive effect of our mechanistic culture – the effect I described in chapter 3 in connection with Chomsky's work (see p. 282): Russell was a professional logician and philosopher, but his mechanistic beliefs compelled him to pursue absurd linguistic theories, not unlike those of crank intellectuals. He was also a humanist, but at the same time he was convinced that the phenomena of knowledge and intelligence can be explained with deterministic theories. He failed to see that what he was trying to prove was, in effect, that human minds are no different from machines. While as humanist he was

[25] Bertrand Russell, *An Inquiry into Meaning and Truth*, rev. ed. (London: Routledge, 1995), p. 341.

concerned with freedom, justice, and peace, as scientist he promoted theories that, although invalid, undermine our respect for human beings.

❖

Russell stresses the mechanistic nature of his philosophy of language. The principles of reductionism and atomism figure prominently in his theory, and it is obvious that the formal language he is seeking would form a simple hierarchical structure: "My own logic is atomic, and it is this aspect upon which I should wish to lay stress."[26] Thus, Russell maintains that there are two kinds of entities, "simples" and "complexes."[27] Simples are the atoms of thought, what we find at the limit of analysis, and are represented in language with symbols (or names). Complexes are those entities that can still be divided into simpler ones; they are not represented with symbols, since they are merely combinations and relations of simples: "I confess it seems obvious to me (as it did to Leibniz) that what is complex must be composed of simples, though the number of constituents may be infinite."[28]

We have yet to discover this symbolic language, Russell admits, but we can assume that it will have several levels of abstraction, and that the levels will reflect the actual facts: the complexity of the elements at each level will match the complexity of the facts described by these elements: "I shall therefore ... assume that there is an objective complexity in the world, and that it is mirrored by the complexity of propositions."[29] Basic language elements will represent simple facts directly, and combinations of elements will represent complex facts: "In a logically perfect language the words in a proposition would correspond one by one with the components of the corresponding fact, with the exception of such words as 'or', 'not', 'if', 'then', which have a different function. In a logically perfect language, there will be one word and no more for every simple object, and everything that is not simple will be expressed by a combination of words."[30]

The simplest facts are those that are not deduced from other facts; that is, facts of which we are aware through direct knowledge or perception. (Russell's term for this awareness is *acquaintance*.) An example of a simple fact is "the possession of a quality by some particular thing."[31] More complex facts occur when two or more facts are combined with relations; for example, "A gives B to C."[32] Russell calls all these facts *atomic facts*, and the language elements that express them *atomic sentences*. He then defines certain operations –

[26] Bertrand Russell, *The Philosophy of Logical Atomism* (Peru, IL: Open Court, 1985), p. 157.   [27] Ibid., p. 173.   [28] Ibid.   [29] Ibid., p. 58.
[30] Ibid.   [31] Ibid., p. 59.   [32] Ibid.

substitution, combination, generalization – by means of which increasingly complex propositions can be built.[33] For example, the operation of combination connects atomic sentences with words like *or*, *and*, *not*, and *if-then*, and yields *molecular sentences*; thus, "the truth or falsehood of a molecular sentence depends only upon that of its 'atoms.'"[34]

Russell calls "the assemblage of sentences obtained from atomic judgments of perception by the three operations of substitution, combination, and generalization, the *atomistic* hierarchy of sentences."[35] The principle of atomicity "asserts that all propositions are either atomic, or molecular, or generalizations of molecular propositions; or at least, that [if this is not true of ordinary languages] a language of which this is true, and into which any statement is translatable, can be constructed."[36]

Russell's mistake, like Leibniz's, is the mistake we note in all mechanistic delusions; that is, whenever scientists attempt to represent complex phenomena with simple structures (see pp. 315–317). They praise reductionism and atomism, but the starting elements in their structures are *not* atomic and independent, as starting elements must be. Russell calls his theory atomic, but his "atomic facts" are not atomic at all: they are relatively high-level elements. His logical atomism could perhaps work, but only if the reduction ended with some truly atomic and independent entities. Russell cannot perform such a reduction, so he starts his structure from certain "facts." But even those facts that he assumes to be perceived directly (like the possession of a quality by an object) are not really "simple": we appreciate their significance by relying on previous experiences and on the current context; that is, on the same knowledge we use to understand *other* facts. These facts are, therefore, interrelated. They derive from elements and interactions occurring at *lower* levels, so they form multiple, interacting structures. They are not the starting elements of a simple structure, as Russell assumes.

6

Let us turn next to the philosophical school called *logical positivism* (also known as logical empiricism), which flourished between the 1920s and the 1950s. Its best-known members were Moritz Schlick, Friedrich Waismann, Rudolf Carnap, Otto Neurath, and A. J. Ayer. Logical positivism was concerned with *verifiability*; namely, ways to determine from the logical structure of a sentence whether the facts it describes can actually occur.

---

[33] Russell, *Meaning and Truth*, pp. 194–197.   [34] Ibid., p. 195.   [35] Ibid., p. 197.
[36] Ibid., p. 266.

The logical positivists held that a sentence is meaningful only if what it says can be logically broken down into a combination of some basic statements – statements simple enough to verify through direct observation. A sentence is true if the basic statements are found to be true, and false otherwise; but in either case it is meaningful. And sentences that cannot be reduced to such basic statements must be considered, not just false, but meaningless. This view of meaningfulness (which is similar to that found in other mechanistic theories of knowledge) is useless as criterion of demarcation, however.

The logical positivists were attempting to establish a revolutionary ideology: a scientific philosophy, grounded entirely on verifiable propositions. As part of this project, they were trying to reduce all knowledge to a system of propositions related through the precise rules of symbolic logic. And they believed that a strict criterion of demarcation is essential, in order to ensure that the system includes all the scientific propositions and none of the metaphysical or meaningless ones. Their criterion, however, was so strict that it ended up labeling as meaningless practically all sentences, including the theories of empirical science. The reason is that only trivial statements and theories can be reduced to facts that are verifiable through direct observation. Almost all knowledge is based, ultimately, on various *hypotheses* about the world; that is, on assertions which cannot be verified.

Consequently, much of the subsequent work of the logical positivists consisted in searching for a way to resolve this difficulty, and to formulate a practical criterion of demarcation. But, as Popper showed, it is impossible to determine with absolute certainty the truth or falsehood of empirical propositions. Popper criticized the logical positivist project, and held that a criterion of demarcation must be based on falsifiability, not verifiability (see "Popper's Principles of Demarcation" in chapter 3).

Logical positivism was committed to the mechanistic principles of reductionism and atomism. Its chief contribution to the mechanistic culture was the *linguistic* interpretation of science: the attempt to reduce all scientific knowledge to a logical analysis of sentences. Thus, the mechanistic principles were to be applied, not directly to scientific knowledge, but to the *sentences* in which this knowledge is expressed (on the familiar assumption that linguistic structures mirror through one-to-one correspondence the reality they describe).

The logical positivists believed that there is no need to take into account such imprecise information as the context in which a sentence is used. They held that the *logical structure* of a sentence, if properly analyzed, contains all the information we need to determine whether what it expresses is meaningful or not. And if this is not entirely true of natural languages, they argued, we can undoubtedly invent a precise language into which and from which we can translate our sentences. Then, by expressing knowledge in *this* language, we will automatically restrict ourselves to meaningful propositions.

Many attempts were made over the years, especially by Carnap and Neurath, to design that precise language upon which all knowledge could be based. Some theories, for example, involved "protocol sentences": isolated statements that describe such simple and verifiable facts as the position of an object, a particular attribute, a movement, or the time of day. Since reality is ultimately made up of such simple facts, it was argued, the sentences describing these facts can act as the basic elements of discourse. We should be able, then, to express any proposition as a combination of these sentences. Other theories claimed that the language of *physics* must be considered the basic language of knowledge. The basic elements would then be sentences that describe simple processes in space and time. Since everything in the world is ultimately based on elementary physical processes, we should be able to reduce all propositions to linguistic structures built from sentences that describe basic physical processes.

None of these theories worked, but this did not stop the logical positivists from promoting an ambitious project – called *the unity of science* – which, they claimed, would be one of the benefits of a precise language. The unity of science is the culmination of the scientistic dream: a reduction of all knowledge, of all the theories from all sciences, to a common, universal representation. Carnap believed that this is the only way for science to advance, and that only the language of physics can provide a universal representation. We may well develop other universal languages, he says, but such languages would always be reducible to the language of physics: "Every systematic language of this kind can be translated into the physical language.... Because the physical language is thus the basic language of Science *the whole of Science becomes Physics*."[37]

Needless to say, the phenomena studied by sciences like biology, psychology, and sociology must also be reduced to the language of physics. The reason we have not been as successful in these disciplines as we have in physics is that their languages are specialized, and hence limited, unlike the language of physics, which is universal. Their reduction to the language of physics is, therefore, the only way to make progress in these disciplines.[38]

Recall the discussion of formal reductionism in chapter 1 (pp. 82–84): mechanists claim that everything in the world – from material entities to biological phenomena, mental acts, and social life – can ultimately be reduced to physics; and physics can be reduced to mechanics, to the motion of bits of

---

[37] Rudolf Carnap, *The Unity of Science* (Bristol: Thoemmes, 1995), p. 97.
[38] Ibid., p. 100.

matter. Viewed in this light, logical positivism, along with the concept of the unity of science, is just another manifestation of the reductionistic project – but in a linguistic dress. Since these philosophers believe that language structures can mirror the world through one-to-one correspondence, they inevitably invent theories that postulate, instead of the traditional reduction of biology, psychology, and sociology to the motion of bits of matter, the reduction of the *sentences* employed in these disciplines to *sentences* describing bits of matter.

7

The language delusions of the first half of the twentieth century are reflected in the software delusions of the second half. Our software delusions stem from the same fallacy: the belief that a language – a formal system of rules and symbols – can generate hierarchical structures that mirror reality perfectly. This was the belief of Russell and Carnap, but, while the language delusions are limited to theories, we are actually *implementing* their software counterpart.

The software counterpart of the search for the perfect language is the search for the perfect programming language, or the perfect development system, or the perfect database model, or the perfect application. We recognize it in the endless succession of programming theories, methodologies, environments, languages, and tools, and the perpetual changes, versions, and "generations."

The belief in a perfect language, like the mechanistic doctrine of which it is part, has undoubtedly influenced our conception of language and knowledge, of mind and society. But this is where the harm ended. Its software counterpart – the belief in a perfect programming system – is just as fallacious, yet the mechanists are now asking us to alter our lives, and to lower our expectations, in order to conform to software theories based on this fallacy. Despite the continued belief in a logically perfect language, we never downgraded our conception of human capabilities to what can be represented with simple structures – the only structures possible in such a language. But this is precisely what we do with software when we agree to depend on mechanistic concepts (theories, methodologies, programming aids, ready-made applications), whose express purpose is to restrict us to simple knowledge structures.

It bears repeating: The potency of language and software derives from their ability to mirror reality. They do not mirror reality, however, through structures that provide a one-to-one correspondence to the world. The world consists of complex structures, whereas the entities that make up language and software give rise to simple structures. What mirrors reality is the *interactions* between the structures of language or software, and between these and other knowledge structures.

The greatest thinkers of the twentieth century fell victim to the language fallacy and could not see that their ideas were practically identical to the language fantasies of earlier times. So we should not be surprised that so many people today fall victim to the software and programming fallacies. Russell and Carnap built elaborate logic systems, which may even be faultless, but which cannot represent reality – because the premises of one-to-one correspondence between language and reality, and of a simple hierarchical structure that can represent all knowledge, are both invalid. Similarly, mechanistic software theories may be faultless as logic systems, but are useless in practice, because they start from the same invalid premises. They cannot represent reality any better than can the language theories.

Russell, even after forty years of futile search for a language that would represent logically all knowledge, still did not admit that human minds hold types of knowledge which cannot be reduced to simple structures of symbols.[39] But, as we saw in chapter 2, practically all types of knowledge consist, in fact, of *complex* structures. No one has managed to represent the act of recognizing contexts, for example, as a precise structure of elementary mental acts; yet recognizing contexts is something we all do, continually and effortlessly. Thus, the knowledge involved in this act cannot be mapped perfectly in a language like the one proposed by Russell. It cannot be mapped in *any* language, because it consists of *interacting* structures, and a neat system of symbols can only map *individual* structures.

Similarly, the concepts of software engineering – the relational database model, object-oriented systems, structured programming, and the like – claim that the reality we want to represent with software can be mapped perfectly into hierarchical structures of symbols. But these concepts cannot work, because reality consists of *interacting* structures. For software as for language, it is the interactions that are lost when we attempt to map reality with precise systems of symbols. And when these interactions are important, the resulting systems can provide only a poor approximation of reality.

The language and software theories, thus, are part of the same project: the attempt to reduce to neat hierarchical structures the complex phenomena that make up the world. For software as for language, it is the same world that we try to map with simple structures of symbols, so there is no reason to expect the software theories to succeed where the language theories have failed.

[39] Russell, *Meaning and Truth*, pp. 327–330.

Wittgenstein and Software

1

Ludwig Wittgenstein is regarded by many as the most influential philosopher of the twentieth century. Although he made contributions in many areas, notably in the philosophy of mathematics and the philosophy of psychology, his chief concern was language; namely, how ordinary sentences describe the world and express ideas.

Wittgenstein is famous for having created two different systems of thought, one in his youth and the other later in life, both of which greatly influenced the views of contemporary philosophers. His later ideas represent in large part a criticism and rejection of the earlier ones, and it is this change that makes Wittgenstein's philosophy so important today. For the change is, quite simply, a repudiation of the mechanistic doctrine.

His early theory – a model of language that provides an exact, one-to-one correspondence to reality – is generally considered the most rigorous system of this kind ever invented. Then, in his later philosophy, he shows not only that his earlier ideas were wrong, but also that no such system can exist. Thus, while in his early work he is attempting to find an exact linguistic representation of the world, in his later work he is trying to prove the *impossibility* of such a representation. Wittgenstein's later views, we will see presently, match the concept of complex structures and my claim that complex structures cannot be reduced to simple ones. What he is saying, in essence, is that he was wrong when he believed that complex phenomena can be represented with simple structures; that they can only be represented as systems of interacting structures; and that these systems cannot be described exactly, as can the simple structures.

Thus, unlike those philosophers who continue to believe in mechanism despite their failure to discover a useful theory, Wittgenstein created what everyone accepted as a great theory, and then saw it as his task to doubt it, and ultimately to abandon it.[1] Russell and the logical positivists, in particular, liked only his earlier theory; they rejected his later views, and persisted in the futile search for an exact linguistic representation of the world.

Wittgenstein's repudiation of mechanism has been known and studied since the 1930s, and his popularity has been increasing ever since. His ideas are

---

[1] Recall what we learned in "Popper's Principles of Demarcation" in chapter 3: serious thinkers *doubt* their theory and attempt to *refute* it, so they search for *falsifications*; pseudoscientists believe they must *defend* their theory, so they search for *confirmations*. Thus, Wittgenstein's shift demonstrates the value of Popper's principles.

quoted and discussed in many contexts, and have engendered an enormous body of secondary literature by interpreters and commentators. At the same time, we note that *mechanistic* theories of mind, of intelligence, of knowledge, of language, continue to flourish. Most scientists, thus, continue to represent complex human phenomena with simple structures; so they claim, in effect, that it is Wittgenstein's *early* concepts that are valid and his *later* concepts that are wrong. These scientists do not explicitly reject his non-mechanistic ideas; they simply ignore the issues he addresses in his later work, and which, if properly interpreted, clearly show the futility of searching for a mechanistic theory of mind.

In chapter 3 we saw that Popper's principles of demarcation are greatly respected, while their practical applications are largely disregarded (see pp. 230–232). The academics manage to accept and to disregard these principles at the same time by *misinterpreting* them: they ignore their value as a criterion of demarcation, and treat them instead as just another topic in the philosophy of science.

Similarly, the academics cannot reject Wittgenstein's later theory, but they cannot accept it either, because accepting it would be tantamount to admitting that their own work is merely a pursuit of mechanistic fantasies. So they resolve the dilemma by *misinterpreting* Wittgenstein's ideas: by perceiving them as a topic fit for philosophical debate, instead of recognizing their practical applications. Norman Malcolm observes that even philosophers fail to appreciate the significance of Wittgenstein's non-mechanistic ideas: "The dominant currents in today's academic philosophy have been scarcely touched [by Wittgenstein's later work, which] has been read but its message not digested. As has been aptly said, it has been assimilated without being understood."[2]

And what about our *programming* theories and practices? If they too grow out of the belief that the function of language is to map reality through one-to-one correspondence, then Wittgenstein's shift from his early to his later theory may well be the most important topic in the philosophy of software. But this shift – arguably the most celebrated event in twentieth-century philosophy, and a challenge to all mechanistic concepts of mind – is completely ignored in the world of programming. Even a casual study of our programming theories reveals that they all reflect Wittgenstein's *early* theory, which claimed that there is an exact correspondence between language and the world. They ignore the evidence he brought later to show the impossibility of such a correspondence.

[2] Norman Malcolm, *Nothing is Hidden: Wittgenstein's Criticism of his Early Thought* (Oxford: Blackwell, 1986), p. ix.

2

Wittgenstein presented his early theory in the small book *Tractatus Logico-Philosophicus*, published in 1921. Like Russell's theory of language, his theory is known as *logical atomism*; but, while the two theories are generally similar, they differ in many details. Wittgenstein started with Russell's ideas, but Russell often acknowledged that his own theory was influenced by Wittgenstein's work.

Superficially, Wittgenstein's theory makes the same assertions as the theories we have already discussed; namely, that there is a one-to-one correspondence between language and reality, and that both have a hierarchical structure. What sets his theory apart is the fact that his is the only *complete* system – simple, clear, and almost free of fallacies. Wittgenstein accomplished this feat by keeping his arguments abstract, and by excluding from his system certain types of knowledge: he insisted that it is not the task of logical analysis to search for explanations in such matters as feelings, morals, or beliefs. From all the universal language systems, Wittgenstein's is the only one that can be said to actually work. But this was achieved simply by restricting it to a small portion of reality. As he himself realized later, practically all phenomena, and the sentences representing them, must be excluded from his neat system if we want it to work.

The hierarchy that makes up Wittgenstein's system has four levels, and hence four kinds of elements: the top level is the world, which is made up of facts; facts are made up of atomic facts, and atomic facts are made up of objects. This hierarchy is perfectly mirrored in the hierarchy of language, which also has four levels and four kinds of elements: language, at the top level, is made up of propositions; propositions are made up of elementary (or atomic) propositions, and elementary propositions are made up of names. Each level and each element in one hierarchy stands in a one-to-one correspondence to the matching level and element in the other hierarchy. Thus, the totality of the world is represented by the totality of language, each fact is represented by a proposition, each atomic fact by an elementary proposition, and each object by a name. This system is illustrated in figure 4-1.[3]

Wittgenstein is careful not to define or interpret the meaning of these elements – what the objects, names, facts, and propositions actually are in the world and in language – thus leaving the system as an entirely abstract idea. He

[3] The diagram is adapted from K. T. Fann, *Wittgenstein's Conception of Philosophy* (Oxford: Blackwell, 1969), p. 20.

maintains that such definitions and interpretations are outside the scope of
language, that it is impossible to convey them with precision, and that we must
try to understand the system as best we can from his description. We need only
recall the failure of the other language systems, which did attempt to define
with precision the elements of their hierarchies, to appreciate Wittgenstein's
reluctance to discuss them. We are free to interpret "names" as words and
"propositions" as sentences; but we must bear in mind that, if we insist on such
interpretations, the system will cease to be an abstract idea and will no longer
work. Objects, names, facts, and propositions must remain, therefore, technical
terms, and their use in this system must not be confused with their traditional
meaning.

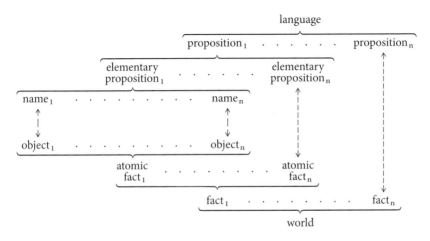

Figure 4-1

What Wittgenstein does explain is the *relations* between the various levels
and elements. Objects are the most basic constituents of the world, and the
names that correspond to them in language are the most basic constituents of
language. In practice we may be unable to determine whether a particular
entity is indeed an object or is a higher-level element, but this is unimportant.
The theory simply assumes that objects exist, that the world consists ultimately
of entities which are not divisible into simpler ones. And it is to these entities
that the names correspond. For each object in the world there exists a name,
and only one name, in language.

An atomic fact is a certain configuration of objects, and an elementary
proposition is a matching configuration of names. Wittgenstein calls the
relation between an atomic fact and its corresponding elementary proposition
"picturing." By this he means what we called mirroring, or mapping: a one-to-

one correspondence akin to the correspondence between a map and the territory, or between a musical score and the sounds. Elementary propositions describe all possible states of affairs in the world, those that actually exist as well as those that we can only imagine. Thus, an elementary proposition can be either true or false: it is true if the atomic fact it represents exists in reality, and false if the atomic fact does not exist. An important issue, stressed by Wittgenstein, is the *independence* of elementary propositions: the truth or falsity of one elementary proposition does not depend on the truth or falsity of others. Corresponding to this, the existence or non-existence of one atomic fact is independent of other atomic facts.

At the next level, Wittgenstein's propositions are *truth functions* of elementary propositions. Truth functions – a familiar concept in logic and digital electronics – perform logical operations such as AND, OR, and NOT on one, two, or more logical operands. The operands, as well as the result of the operation, can have one of two values (called *truth values*): *False* and *True*, or a low and high state, or *0* and *1*. The operation of truth functions can be illustrated by means of *truth tables* – tables that show the result of the operation for any combination of truth values of the operands. The columns in the table denote the operands and the result, and additional columns are often included for the result of intermediate operations. The rows in the table show all possible combinations of operand values; thus, since each operand can be either *False* or *True*, there will be two rows for one operand, four for two operands, eight for three operands, and so on. The truth table in figure 4-2, for example, shows a truth function with three operands.[4]

a	b	c	a OR b	(a OR b) AND c
F	F	F	F	F
F	F	T	F	F
F	T	F	T	F
F	T	T	T	T
T	F	F	T	F
T	F	T	T	T
T	T	F	T	F
T	T	T	T	T

Figure 4-2

[4] The result of AND is *True* when both operands are *True*, and *False* otherwise; the result of OR is *True* when either operand is *True*, and *False* otherwise; NOT takes only one operand, and negates its value: *True* to *False*, *False* to *True*. Wittgenstein was not the first to employ truth tables, but it was his pragmatic use of them, and the popularity of his book, that established this concept in modern logic.

In Wittgenstein's system, the operands are the elementary propositions, so the truth or falsity of a proposition is completely determined by the truth or falsity of its constituent elementary propositions. In other words, depending on the truth function that defines a particular proposition, certain combinations of truth values for its elementary propositions will yield a true proposition, while the other combinations will yield a false one. (The truth table that defines a given proposition may involve a large number of operands, and therefore a huge number of rows. Remember, though, that the system is only an abstract concept.)

But propositions in language correspond to facts in the world. We already saw that the atomic facts that make up facts are in a one-to-one correspondence to the elementary propositions that make up propositions, so the truth or falsity of elementary propositions mirror the existence or non-existence of the atomic facts. Consequently, the truth function that determines the truth or falsity of a proposition also determines the existence or non-existence of the corresponding fact: whether a fact exists or not in the world depends entirely on the truth function and on the existence or non-existence of the atomic facts that make it up.

The world is as it is, and the function of language is to describe it. All possible facts, and all possible propositions, no matter how complex, can be expressed as truth functions of atomic facts and elementary propositions, respectively. This system, therefore, represents both the world and the language that mirrors it. It represents even facts that do *not* exist in the world: these are the combinations of atomic facts for which the truth functions yield *False*. Facts that do not exist are mirrored in language by combinations of elementary propositions for which the same truth functions yield *False*: false assertions ("snow is black," "the sun moves round the earth"), fictional stories, and the like.

All these propositions, says Wittgenstein, true or false, are *meaningful* propositions. They must be distinguished from those propositions that cannot be expressed as truth functions (because their truth or falsity does not depend exclusively on the truth or falsity of some elementary propositions). For example, no truth function can describe the situation where the same combination of truth values for the elementary propositions yields, unpredictably, sometimes *True* and sometimes *False*. And they must also be distinguished from those propositions that simply say nothing; for example, a proposition that is always *True*, regardless of the truth values of its elementary propositions (a tautology), or one that is always *False* (a contradiction). Such propositions, says Wittgenstein, are *meaningless*, because they do not mirror facts that either exist or do not exist in the world.

Meaningless propositions, it turns out, form a large part of our discourse:

philosophy, religion, ethics, metaphysics, and much of everyday language consist chiefly of such meaningless propositions. Even logic and mathematics consist of meaningless propositions, because they do not represent facts, but are self-contained deductive systems: they are purposely designed so that, if one follows their rules, one always expresses the truth. Thus, purely deductive systems assert nothing about the world. Only the propositions of empirical science can be said to be meaningful, to mirror facts. Wittgenstein does not deny the value of the other propositions; he merely says that they do not reflect facts from the real world. To say that they are meaningless overstates the case, but this uncompromising position – this arrogance – was an important aspect of his early philosophy.

❖

Although only an abstract concept (unlike the language systems we examined earlier), Wittgenstein's theory was received with enthusiasm. Everyone was fascinated by its simplicity and by its apparent power to explain the world, and it was generally seen as a real improvement over the others.

But Wittgenstein's system is no improvement. Like the others, it is an attempt to determine by strictly mechanical means, through a logical analysis of linguistic elements and without taking into account the context in which they are used, whether or not the facts they represent exist in the world. It seems to be an improvement because it restricts the universe of meaningful propositions to a small fraction of those used in ordinary discourse. Thus, his neat system appears to work because Wittgenstein permits into it only those aspects of the world that *are* neat, while branding everything else as meaningless.

In the end, very little is left that is *not* considered meaningless. In fact, even the propositions of empirical science must be excluded, because they can rarely be reduced to the system's terminal elements – to names pointing to simple, irreducible objects. (In other words, the system is incompatible with the fundamental tenet of empirical science – the requirement that propositions be accepted only if they can be verified through direct observation.) Thus, similarly to the ideas of logical positivism (see p. 324), Wittgenstein's view of meaningfulness is in effect a criterion of demarcation based on verifiability. Popper, who held that a criterion of demarcation must be based on falsifiability (see "Popper's Principles of Demarcation" in chapter 3), pointed out this weakness shortly after the *Tractatus* was published.[5]

---

[5] Karl R. Popper, *Conjectures and Refutations: The Growth of Scientific Knowledge*, 5th ed. (London: Routledge, 1989), pp. 39–40.

❖

It should be obvious why Wittgenstein's early theory can help us to understand the origin of our software delusions. If we accept his system as the best expression of the mechanistic language delusion – the belief that language mirrors the world through one-to-one correspondence, and that both can be represented with hierarchical structures – we recognize our software delusions as an embodiment of Wittgenstein's theory.

The programming theories claim that the world can be mirrored perfectly in software if we design our applications as hierarchical structures of software elements: operations, blocks of operations, larger blocks, modules. To use Wittgensteinian terminology, these elements are software propositions that correspond to specific facts in the world, each proposition consisting of a combination of lower-level propositions. In a perfect application, the software propositions at each level are independent of one another; and the truth or falsity of each one (that is, whether or not it mirrors *actual* facts) is completely determined by its lower-level, constituent propositions. Each software element is, in effect, a truth function of its constituent elements. (Most software applications, however, need more than the two levels that Wittgenstein allows for propositions in his system.)

These theories fail because they try to represent with neat structures, facts that are not independent and are not made up of elementary facts in the precise way expected by the software propositions. Just as Wittgenstein's theory accepts only a small fraction of the totality of propositions, and brands the rest as meaningless, the programming theories accept only a small fraction of the totality of *software* propositions: those corresponding to facts that *can* be represented with neat structures of lower-level facts. Most situations in the real world, however, are not neatly structured. Most situations can only be mirrored with software propositions that are, in the Wittgensteinian sense, meaningless: propositions that *cannot* be expressed as exact functions of independent lower-level propositions.

Unfortunately, we cannot write off these situations as Wittgenstein does in his system. For, if we did, there would be practically no situations left for which software applications are possible. Thus, what is wrong with the programming theories is not that they let us create *bad* applications, but on the contrary, that they restrict us to *logically perfect* applications: to simple hierarchical structures of software propositions. And, just as is the case with the meaningful propositions in Wittgenstein's system, we can represent with logically perfect applications only a small fraction of the facts that make up the world.

3

Let us examine next how Wittgenstein changed his views, and what his new philosophy of language means to us. After writing the *Tractatus*, Wittgenstein felt that he had no further contribution to make to philosophy, and for nearly ten years he pursued other interests. Although his theory was becoming increasingly popular and influential, he himself was becoming increasingly dissatisfied with it. By the time he returned to philosophy he had new ideas, and he continued to develop them for the rest of his life. He wrote only one book expounding his later philosophy: the posthumously published *Philosophical Investigations*. Several other books, though, consisting largely of transcripts of his notes and lectures, have been published since then. As in the *Tractatus*, his ideas are interconnected and cover many fields, but we are interested here only in his central concern: how language represents knowledge, thought, and reality.

Wittgenstein admits now that, if we want to understand how language mirrors reality, we cannot restrict ourselves to neat linguistic structures and formal logic. We cannot assume that only those propositions which can be expressed with truth functions are meaningful. All normal uses of language have a meaning, simply because they fulfil certain social functions. So, instead of *ignoring* those propositions that cannot be reduced to neat structures of linguistic entities, we should conclude that they cannot be so reduced because the reality they mirror cannot be reduced to neat structures of facts: "The more narrowly we examine actual language, the sharper becomes the conflict between it and our requirement [i.e., our wish]. (For the crystalline purity of logic was, of course, not a *result of investigation*: it was a requirement [i.e., a wish].)"[6]

Wittgenstein notes that complex entities are complex in more than one way; that is, there are several ways to break down a complex entity into simpler parts. It is impossible, therefore, to define a precise, unique relationship between the parts and the complex whole.[7] If the complex entities are facts, or propositions that mirror these facts, there is always more than one way to represent these facts and propositions as a function of simpler facts and propositions. So if we want to depict these entities with a hierarchical structure, we will find *several* hierarchies through which a particular complex entity is related to simpler ones.

---

[6] Ludwig Wittgenstein, *Philosophical Investigations*, 3rd ed. (Englewood Cliffs, NJ: Prentice Hall, 1973), §107.   [7] Ibid., §47.

A chessboard, for example, is a complex entity: we can view it as a config-uration of sixty-four squares, but we can also view it as eight rows of squares, or as eight columns, or as various arrangements of pairs of squares, or as combinations of squares and colours.[8] Clearly, there are many ways to describe a chessboard as a structure of simpler elements, and all these structures exist at the same time.

A more difficult example is the notion of a game.[9] Each of the various activities we call games has a number of distinguishing characteristics, but there is no one characteristic that is common to all of them. There are ball games, board games, card games, and so on; some are competitive, but others are mere amusements; some call for several players, while others are solitary; some require skill, and others luck. This means that there is no set of principles that would permit us to determine, simply by following some identification rules, whether a given activity is or is not a game. But, in fact, even without such principles, we have no difficulty identifying certain activities as games. So it seems that games have a number of similarities, for otherwise we would be unable to distinguish them as a specific type of activity. And yet, despite these similarities, we cannot represent them through a neat classification of activities.

Just like the word "game," says Wittgenstein, the meaning of most words and sentences is imprecise; it depends largely on the context in which we use them. The meaning of linguistic entities is imprecise because the reality they mirror is an imprecise structure of facts. No methods or rules can be found to relate all the meanings of words and sentences, in all conceivable contexts; so we must think of them simply as *families* of meanings. Thus, Wittgenstein coined the phrase "family resemblance" to describe the complex relationship between facts, or between the linguistic entities that correspond to facts: "And the result of this examination is: we see a complicated network of similarities overlapping and criss-crossing.... I can think of no better expression to characterize these similarities than 'family resemblances'; for the various resemblances between members of a family: build, features, colour of eyes, gait, temperament, etc. etc. overlap and criss-cross in the same way."[10]

No methods or rules can describe *all* the resemblances between the mem-bers of a family. Their family relationship can be accurately represented, of course, with the hierarchical structure known as the family tree. But this relationship reflects only *one* of their attributes. If we classified in a hierarchical structure the relationship that reflects another attribute (height, or eye colour, or a particular facial feature), that hierarchy will not necessarily match the family tree. Each attribute gives rise to a different classification. Thus, the

---

[8] Ibid.   [9] Ibid., §66.   [10] Ibid., §§66–67.

resemblance of family members is the result of several hierarchies that exist at the same time – hierarchies that overlap and intersect.

Similarly, if we classified the activities we call games on the basis of one particular attribute (number of players, level of skill, use of a ball, etc.), we would end up with a different hierarchy for each attribute. It is impossible to create a hierarchy with *game* as the top element, the individual games as terminal elements, and their categories as intermediate elements – not if we want to capture in this hierarchy *all* their attributes. Instead, there are *many* such hierarchies, a different one perhaps for each attribute. All have the same top element and the same terminal elements, but different intermediate elements. And all exist at the same time.

This, incidentally, is true of all classifications. We classify plants and animals, for example, into a hierarchy of classes, orders, families, genera, and species on the basis of *some* of their attributes, while ignoring the others. It is impossible to capture *all* their attributes in one hierarchy. The current hierarchy is useful to biologists, but we could easily create different ones, on the basis of other attributes. Since the plants and animals are the same, all these hierarchies exist at the same time.

We must take a moment here to clarify this point. When I say that one hierarchy cannot capture all the attributes of entities like games, what I mean is that a *correct* hierarchy cannot do so. For, one can always draw a tree diagram in the following manner: assuming for simplicity only three attributes and only two or three values for each attribute, we divide games into, say, ball games, board games, and card games; then, we divide *each one* of these elements into games of skill and games of luck, thus creating six elements at the next lower level; finally, we divide *each one* of these six elements into competitive and amusing, for a total of twelve categories. This structure is shown in figure 4-3.

Clearly, if we limit games to these three attributes, any game will be a terminal element in this structure, since it must fit within one of the twelve categories: ball games that require skill and are competitive, ball games that require skill and are amusing, etc. The intermediate elements are the categories that make up the various levels; and the attributes are represented by the branches that connect one category to the lower-level ones.[11]

---

[11] Note that it is irrelevant for the present argument whether we treat the use of a ball, a board, and cards as three values of one attribute (on the assumption that no game requires more than one of them), or as three separate attributes (each one having two values, *yes* and *no*); only the intermediate levels and elements of the classification would differ. This is true in general, and I will not repeat it in the following discussion. We can always reduce a classification to attributes that have only two values (*use* or not, *possess* or not, *affect* or not, etc.), simply by adding levels and categories. Thus, since logically there is no difference between multivalued and two-valued attributes, I will use both types in examples.

This structure, however, although a tree diagram, is not a true hierarchy. It captures all three attributes, but it does so by *repeating* some of them; *competitive*, for instance, must appear in six places in the diagram. While such a classification may have its uses, it does not reflect reality: it does not represent correctly the actual categories and attributes. We don't hold in the mind, for example, six different notions of competitiveness – one for ball games that require skill, another for ball games that require luck, and so forth. We always know in the same way whether a game is competitive or amusing; we don't have to analyze its other attributes first. To put this in general terms, we don't perceive the attributes of games as *one within another*.

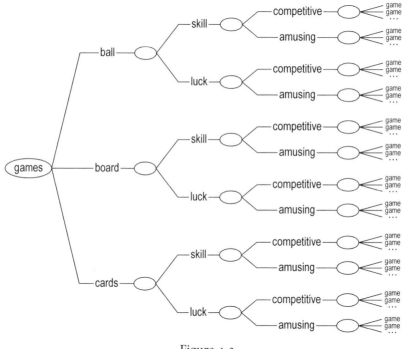

Figure 4-3

There is another way to look at this problem. The order in which we showed the three attributes was arbitrary. We can create another tree diagram by dividing games first into competitive and amusing, then each one of these two elements into games of skill and games of luck, and then the resulting four elements into ball games, board games, and card games, as in figure 4-4; and we end up with the same twelve elements as before. If *this* structure reflected reality, rather than the first one, we would indeed have only one way to perceive competitive and amusing games; but now we would be using four different methods to decide whether a game is a card game: one for competitive games that require skill, another for competitive games that require luck, and so forth. Again, this is silly: we always know in the same way whether a game is a card game. And, even if we were willing to admit that this is how we distinguish games, why should we prefer one way of arranging the attributes rather than the other? Since this situation is absurd, we must conclude that this is *not* how we perceive games, so this type of structure does not reflect correctly our knowledge of games and their attributes. A correct hierarchy must include each attribute only once, and no such hierarchy exists.

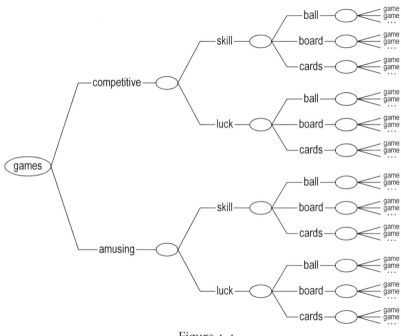

Figure 4-4

Thus, it seems that we can distinguish games *in our mind* on the basis of several attributes simultaneously, but we cannot represent this phenomenon with a simple hierarchical structure. The only way to represent it is as *several* structures, one for each attribute, while remembering that our mind does not, in fact, perceive these structures separately (see figure 4-5). The top element (the concept of games) and the terminal elements (the individual games) are the same in all three structures, and they are also the same as in the previous structures.

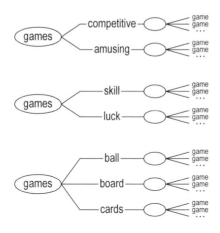

Figure 4-5

Intuitively, we can easily see why it is impossible to depict all the attributes in one hierarchy. If the attributes are independent – if the possession of a certain attribute by a game is independent of its possession of other attributes – then any attempt to depict all the attributes in one hierarchy is bound to distort reality, because it must show some attributes as subordinate to others.

I used the concept of hierarchical classifications in the foregoing analysis because it is especially suitable for studying Wittgenstein's problem of family resemblance. This concept was introduced in chapter 1, along with the concept of complex structures (see pp. 100–104). But I want to stress that this analysis is new – it is *not* how Wittgenstein, or the many philosophers who interpreted his work, studied the problem. They did little more than *describe* it. The problem, again, is to understand how our mind discovers that several entities are related through their attributes even though no one attribute has the same value for all entities, and to understand also why it is impossible to represent this apparently simple phenomenon mechanistically. The concept of hierarchical classifications can be seen, therefore, as a model for studying Wittgenstein's problem. And, while still informal, this model provides a more accurate depiction than the discussions found in philosophy texts. (We will make good use of this concept later, for both language and software structures.)

So, Wittgenstein concludes, we must give up the idea of reducing facts, and the linguistic entities that mirror these facts, to perfect hierarchical structures: "We see that what we call 'sentence' and 'language' has not the formal unity that I imagined, but is the family of structures more or less related to one another."[12] Wittgenstein coined the phrase "language games" to describe the relationships that turn linguistic entities – sentences, expressions, even individual words – into families of entities. Language games replace in his new theory what was in his earlier system the neat hierarchy of propositions, and serve to mirror in language the "games" that exist in the world: the complex structures of facts that replace in the new theory the neat hierarchy of facts of the earlier system.

All activities performed by people in a society are, in the final analysis, akin to games: they form structures that are indefinite and overlapping, rather than formal and independent. The linguistic structures are an inseparable part of these activities, so they too are indefinite and overlapping. Thus, we cannot state with precision what is a meaningful proposition, simply because we cannot find any characteristics that are common to all meaningful propositions. The concept of language can only be defined informally, as a collection of interrelated linguistic structures: "Instead of producing something common to all that we call language, I am saying that these phenomena have no one thing in common which makes us use the same word for all – but that they are *related* to one another in many different ways. And it is because of this relationship, or these relationships, that we call them all 'language.'"[13]

Like the propositions of the earlier system, the totality of possible language games forms the structure we recognize as language. Also like the propositions, language games do it by creating complex elements from simpler ones, and thus higher levels of abstraction from lower ones. But this is no longer a simple hierarchical structure. The relations that generate the elements at one level from those at the lower level cannot be defined with precision, as could the truth functions of the earlier system. Because the elements are related through several structures simultaneously, the only way to describe this relationship is informally, as "family resemblance."

Wittgenstein's "family resemblance" is, obviously, the type of phenomenon that requires the model of a complex structure. Recall our discussion of complex structures in chapter 1 (pp. 98–104). We saw that any entity has a number of attributes, each one relating it to other entities which have that attribute. Any entity, therefore, is an element in a different structure for each one of its attributes. But all these structures exist at the same time; so they interact, because they share these elements.

The family tree is a perfect hierarchy, but this structure alone does not determine all the resemblances. We could classify the members of a family according to other attributes, and each classification would be a different structure. These structures exist at the same time and share their terminal

---

[12] Wittgenstein, *Philosophical Investigations*, §108.   [13] Ibid., §65.

elements (the people themselves), so they interact. The phenomenon of family resemblance is a complex structure, and cannot be described precisely and completely as a function of the people.

We note the same situation in the relations between games – the phenomenon that inspired the phrase "language games." A game is related to other games through all its attributes, and each attribute gives rise to a different structure. The games are the terminal elements shared by these structures, and this phenomenon – the existence of activities perceived as games – is a complex structure. It is impossible to describe the concept of games, precisely and completely, as a function of the individual games.

The incorrect hierarchies in figures 4-3 and 4-4 reflect, then, the futility of attempting to reduce a complex structure to simple ones. Also, since simple structures are logically equivalent to deterministic systems, the impossibility of depicting several attributes in one structure demonstrates the indeterministic nature of these phenomena.

What Wittgenstein's new theory does, essentially, is mirror in language a greater portion of reality than did his earlier theory. Propositions mirror facts, and Wittgenstein acknowledges now that there exist facts which cannot be expressed with precision as a function of simpler facts. The only way to mirror them in language is by *permitting* those propositions which the earlier theory branded as meaningless; that is, those propositions which *cannot* be expressed as a logical function of simpler linguistic elements. Such propositions are not meaningless, Wittgenstein says now. Language is a social device, and its function is to assist us in our everyday activities. A proposition must be deemed meaningful, therefore, simply if it helps us to perform an act, or if it describes an aspect of human life. The imprecise language we use in everyday discourse is a reflection of the imprecise nature of our life, so we must accept it as meaningful. The meaning of a word or sentence must be determined by its use, not through formal logic.

The price we pay for mirroring in language a greater portion of reality is having to give up the preciseness of the earlier theory: we must be content with the imprecise concept of language games. To use our own terminology, the complexity of the world cannot be represented accurately enough with mechanistic models, so we need non-mechanistic ones, which must remain informal.

It is significant that Wittgenstein did not attempt to improve his earlier theory by *expanding* it: he did not attempt to make the theory match more facts by adding rules, or levels, or types of elements. When he realized that a mechanistic theory cannot work, he did not hesitate to abandon the mechanistic dogma. This attitude stands in sharp contrast to the attitude of the other thinkers who start with mechanistic theories. Scientists who search for mechanistic theories of language, mind, and society, or software experts who invent mechanistic programming theories, continue to defend mechanism even when they see their theories falsified. They resort then to the pseudoscientific practice of *expanding* their theories: they add more and more features to make the theories cope with those conditions that would otherwise falsify them (see pp. 225–226).

Wittgenstein recognized the dishonesty and futility of these attempts, and this is why his work is so important today. He started with the same mechanistic delusions and created a great mechanistic theory; but unlike the other thinkers, he realized that the methods of the exact sciences cannot explain language and the mind, and settled for a less ambitious, and less formal, theory – a non-mechanistic one. If "explanation" means exact methods and theories, he frequently asserts, then the phenomenon of language cannot be *explained*, but only *described*: "We must do away with all *explanation*, and description alone must take its place."[14]

S. S. Hilmy,[15] after studying Wittgenstein's unpublished manuscripts and notes, concludes that his later philosophy is essentially a rejection of the prevailing notion that the "scientific way of thinking" – namely, reductionism and atomism – is as important in the study of human minds as it is in physics. Wittgenstein's philosophy, thus, is a struggle against the scientistic current of his time – a current in which he himself had been caught earlier, and which, despite his legacy, the passage of more than half a century, and the failure of countless mechanistic theories of mind, is just as strong today.

4

What can we learn from Wittgenstein's later philosophy that can help us in our software pursuits? We already saw that mechanistic programming theories are in the domain of software what Wittgenstein's *early* theory is in the domain of language. The early theory claims that language mirrors reality, that both can be represented with perfect hierarchical structures, and that there is a one-to-one correspondence between propositions and facts – between the levels and elements that make up language and those that make up the world. Similarly,

---

[14] Ibid., §109.
[15] S. Stephen Hilmy, *The Later Wittgenstein: The Emergence of a New Philosophical Method* (Oxford: Blackwell, 1987), esp. ch. 6.

the programming theories claim that software applications mirror reality through neat hierarchical structures of software entities (operations, blocks of operations, modules), which correspond on a one-to-one basis to the facts that make up our affairs.

When the programming theories insist that applications be designed as neat structures of entities within entities, they do so because of our belief that the world can be represented with neat structures of things within things – the same belief that engenders mechanistic *language* theories. Since it is the same world that we want to mirror in language and in software, it is not surprising that we end up with similar language and software theories.

In his later theory, Wittgenstein shows us that the world cannot be represented with formal hierarchical structures; that facts are related to other facts in many different ways at the same time; and that these complex relationships can only be expressed informally – as families, or systems, of facts. Then he shows us that, since language mirrors the world, we find similar relationships in language. This is why everyday discourse consists of informal language games and families of linguistic entities, rather than formal structures of propositions.

But if it is the same world that we try to mirror in our software applications, why do we expect simple *software* structures to succeed where simple *linguistic* structures fail? Our programming theories can be no more formal, no more exact, than our language theories. Following Wittgenstein, we could call our software applications – the structures of operations and modules – software games; and we must accept the fact that these applications cannot be the neat hierarchical structures we wish them to be.

The fundamental principle of software mechanism is that the entities which make up an application constitute *only one* logical structure. We are told that applications must be designed as perfect hierarchical structures, so we draw block diagrams and flowcharts that depict operations within operations, modules within modules. Having done this, we are convinced that the software modules themselves are as independent from one another as the blocks which represent them on paper. We are convinced, in other words, that the modules are related to one another only through the lines connecting the blocks in the diagram. We conclude, then, that the main difficulty in programming an application is the process of analysis: the discovery of the particular hierarchical structure which corresponds to the structure of facts that make up the requirements. For, once we establish this one-to-one correspondence between software and reality – once we discover the software entity that corresponds to each entity in our affairs, from the most general to the simplest – it is relatively easy to translate the resulting structure into a programming language.

This principle, stated in one form or another, forms the foundation of all programming theories. But the principle is invalid, because it is impossible to reduce reality to a hierarchical structures of facts, and perforce impossible to reduce software applications to a hierarchical structures of software entities. The principle is invalid because facts form, not one, but many hierarchical structures. Software entities, therefore, if they are to reflect the facts, must also be related through many structures at the same time.

We saw that real entities (objects, processes, events, concepts – facts, in Wittgensteinian terminology) have a large number of attributes, and are elements in a different structure through each attribute. The corresponding software entities, too, have a large number of attributes (using files and variables, calling subroutines, being affected by business rules, etc.), and are elements in a different structure through each attribute. Thus, the block diagram we believe to depict the application's logic is merely *one* of these structures. No matter how strictly we design the application as independent entities (as a neat structure of operations within operations, modules within modules), these entities will also be related through other structures, besides the structure we see in the diagram. All these structures exist at the same time and share their elements – those software entities thought to be independent. An application, therefore, is a complex structure, just like the reality it mirrors, and no diagram can capture *all* the relations between the software entities.

That structure we perceive to be the application's logic – let us call it the *main* structure – is perhaps the most obvious, and may well represent some of the most important operations or relations. But just because the other structures are less evident, and we choose to ignore them, it doesn't mean that they do not affect the application's performance.

Note how similar this phenomenon is to the phenomenon of language. Nothing stops us from inventing theories based on *one* of the structures that make up sentences: their syntactic structure, like Chomsky, or their logical structure, like Russell and Carnap. But this will not provide an explanation of language. These theories fail because language consists of many structures, not one, and it is their totality that determines the meaning of sentences. Moreover, it is not only linguistic structures that play a part in this phenomenon. The structures formed by the other knowledge present in the mind, and those formed by the context in which the sentences are used, are also important. And the same is true of software: the performance of an application is determined, not only by the syntactic structure formed by its elements, or by the logical structure that is the sequence of their execution, but by *all* the structures through which they are related.

Wittgenstein discusses many situations where reality cannot be reduced to one simple structure, but his two famous examples – games and families, which we examined previously – already demonstrate the similarity of language and software. Thus, there is no one hierarchical structure with the concept of games as the top element and the individual games as the terminal elements – not if we want to classify games according to *all* their attributes. Instead, we find *many* structures with these top and terminal elements. Nothing stops us from considering one of them, perhaps the one dividing games into competitive and amusing, as the only important structure; but this will not explain completely the concept of games.

Similarly, there is no one hierarchical structure with a particular software application as the top element and some elementary operations as the terminal elements – not if we want to describe the application completely. There are *many* such structures, each one reflecting a different aspect of the application. Nothing stops us from interpreting the application's block diagram or flowchart as its definition, or logic; but if we do, we should not be surprised if it does not explain its performance completely. (The structures that make up software applications are the subject of the next section.)

Software Structures

1

To understand how the software entities that make up an application can form several hierarchical structures at the same time, think of them as similar to *linguistic* entities, since both are reflections of entities that exist in the world. A software entity can be a module, a block of statements, and even one statement. And, insofar as they reflect real processes or events, the software entities possess, just like the real entities, not one but *several* attributes; so they must belong to a different structure through each one of these attributes. The attributes of a software entity are such things as the files, variables, and subroutines it uses. Anything that can affect more than one software entity is an attribute, because it relates these entities logically, thereby creating a structure.

I want to discuss now some common principles we employ in our applications, and which I will call simply *software principles*. What I want to show is that it is these principles that endow software entities with attributes, and serve, therefore, to relate them.[1]

A software principle, then, is a method, a technique, or a procedure used in the art of programming. An example is the sharing of data by several elements of the application; this principle is implemented by means of database fields

---

[1] As is the case throughout this book, the terms "entity" and "element" refer to the same things, and are usually interchangeable. See p. 99, note 1.

and memory variables. Another example is the sharing of operations; this principle is typically implemented by means of subroutines. A principle frequently misunderstood is the sequence in which the application's elements are executed by the computer; this principle is implemented through features found, implicitly or explicitly, in each element. The user interface, and the retrieval of data through reports and queries, are also examples of principles. Lastly, the methods we use to represent our affairs in software constitute, in effect, principles. The principles we will study in this section are: practices, databases, and subroutines. (We will further study software principles later in the book, particularly in chapter 7, when discussing various software theories.)

I will refer to the individual instances of software principles as *software processes*: each case of shared data or shared operations, each business practice, each report or query or user interface, is a process. And each process endows the application's elements with a unique attribute, thereby creating a unique structure – a unique way to relate these elements. Ultimately, these structures reflect the various *aspects* of the application: each aspect corresponds to a process, and each process gives rise to an attribute, and hence a structure. An application may comprise thousands of such structures.

2

Let us start with those processes that reflect the various *practices* implemented in the application – the countless rules, methods, and precepts that are embodied in the application's logic. Practices can be divided into two broad categories: those related to the activities we want to translate into software, and those related to the methods we employ in this translation. Let us call the first category *business practices*, and the second one *software practices*. Business practices include such processes as the way we invoice a customer, the way we deal with surplus inventory, and the way we calculate vacation pay. And software practices include such processes as reporting, inquiry, file maintenance, and data entry.

Practices necessarily affect software elements from different parts of the application. They create, therefore, various relations between these elements – relations that do not parallel the relations created by the main structure. If, for example, we depict with a hierarchical diagram one of the practices implemented in the application, the diagram will not be a distinct section of the main diagram, although the practice *is* part of the application's logic. The implementation of practices, thus, creates *additional* structures in the application – structures that share their elements with the main structure.

As an example of practices, consider the case of back orders. One way a distributor can handle back orders is as follows: when the quantity ordered by a customer exceeds the quantity on hand, the order is placed on hold, the customer is informed, special messages and forms are generated, and so on; the order is revived later, when the necessary quantity becomes available. Another way to handle back orders, however, is by allowing the quantity on hand to go negative: the order is processed normally, thus reducing the quantity on hand below zero; steps are taken to ensure the product in question is ordered from the supplier before the order's due date; when the product is received, the quantity on hand is restored to zero or to a positive value.

It is obvious that the implementation of a back-order process will not only affect *many* elements of the application, but will affect them in different ways depending on the back-order method chosen. And it is just as obvious that the relations between these elements, as seen from the perspective of the back-order process alone, may not be the same as the relations created by the application's main structure. The main structure will probably reflect such aspects of reality as the functions selected by users from a menu, the responsibilities of the different departments, or the daily operating procedures. Thus, while the software elements that make up the application must reflect the main structure, some of these elements must also reflect the particular back-order process chosen: variables and fields may or may not have negative values, back-order data is or is not printed, purchase orders are or are not issued daily, and so on.

This sharing of elements, moreover, will not be restricted to the high levels of the structure, but will affect elements at all levels, from entire modules down to individual operations. The back-order process, in other words, cannot be implemented as an independent piece of software connected to the rest of the application simply through some input and output links. If we represent the application with a block diagram that depicts the main structure, we will not find the back-order process as one particular block in the diagram; rather, it is part of many blocks, and it connects therefore these blocks through a structure that is different from the one depicted by the diagram.

To understand why a process is in fact a structure, think of the application from the perspective of this process alone, while ignoring all its other functions. Seen from this perspective, the application can be depicted as a hierarchical structure that divides the application's elements into two categories, those affected and those unaffected by the process. The former may then be classified into further categories, on lower and lower levels, according to the way the process affects them, while the latter may be classified into categories reflecting the reasons why they are unaffected. Finally, the lowest-level elements will be the individual statements that make up the application. But these elements are also the elements used by the main structure, so the application can be said to consist of either structure, or of both structures at the same time.

The back-order process is only an example, of course, only one of the hundreds of practices that make up a serious application. Each one of these processes, and each one of the other *types* of processes (databases, subroutines, user interface, and so on), forms a different structure; but all exist at the same time, and all use the same software elements. An application *is*, in effect, these processes; it consists of countless structures, all interacting, and the main structure is merely one of them. The idea that an application can be depicted as a perfect hierarchical structure of independent elements is, therefore, nonsensical. Note that this situation is inevitable: a serious application *must* include many processes, and a process *must* affect different parts of the application. The very purpose of processes is to *relate* – in specific ways, on the basis of certain rules or requirements – various parts of our affairs, and hence various parts of the software application that mirrors these affairs.

An application, thus, is a system of interacting structures, not the simple structure we see in diagrams. The other structures are hidden, although we could describe them too with neat diagrams if we wanted. We would need a different diagram, though, for each structure, and the main difficulty – the task of dealing with many structures together – would remain. Because the structures share the application's elements, we must take into account many structures, and also many interactions, at the same time. And it is only our minds – our knowledge and experience – that can do this, because only minds can process complex structures.

It is interesting to compare this system of structures with the system of structures created by *language*. Think of a story describing a number of people, their life and physical environment, their knowledge and activities, their desires and fears. We may consider the main structure of the story to be the structure of linguistic entities, so the story can be viewed as a hierarchy of paragraphs, sentences, and words. In addition, we can view each sentence as a hierarchy of grammatical entities. And if we take into account the *meaning* of the words, we can discern many other structures. Their meaning reveals such entities as persons, objects, and events, all of which have a number of attributes. These entities are related in the story, so for each attribute there exists a structure that relates in a particular way the *linguistic* entities, in order to reflect the relations between the *real* entities.

The fact that we can understand the story proves that the author successfully conveyed to us the relations between persons, objects, and events, permitting us to discover those structures; for, without those structures, all we would see is the *linguistic* relations. But the structures share their elements – they use the same words, phrases, and sentences; so the story is a system of interacting structures, although only the linguistic ones are manifest. We can discover from the story such structures as the feelings that people have toward one another, or their family relationships, or the disposition of objects in a room, or the sequence of events; and these structures do not parallel the linguistic structure.

Each structure in the story is, simply, one particular way of viewing it, one of its aspects. If we view the story from one narrow perspective, if we interpret, relate, and analyze its elements to reflect one aspect while ignoring all others, we end up with one of these structures. But, clearly, all structures exist at the same time. In the case of language, then, we have no difficulty understanding why the same elements are used in several structures simultaneously. No one (apart from misguided linguists) would claim that the only thing that defines a story is its structure of linguistic entities, or its structure of grammatical entities. So why do we expect a *software* system to be completely defined by its main structure? In software applications, as in stories, the elements are always connected through diverse relations – relations that are not part of the main structure and cannot be predicted from it. This is not an accident, nor a sign of bad programming or writing, but the very nature of these systems. It is precisely this quality that makes those symbols, when processed by a human mind, a meaningful story or software application, rather than a collection of independent structures.

3

Let us examine next the software principle known as *database*, which also gives rise to complex relations between software entities.[2] Databases are the means through which software applications use data, especially the large amounts of data stored in external devices like disks. Data records are read, written, modified, and deleted in many places in the application. And an application may use hundreds of files, and millions of records, connected through intricate relations and accessed through thousands of operations.

The purpose of databases is to relate the various data entities in ways that mirror the relations connecting the *real* entities – those entities that make

---

[2] The term "database" refers to any set of logically related files, not just those managed formally through a database system. And consequently, the term "database operations" includes not just the high-level operations of a database system, but also the traditional file operations. These terms are discussed in greater detail in chapter 7 (see pp. 686–687).

up our affairs. Database theories encourage us to describe with elaborate definitions and diagrams the data structures; that is, the relations formed by files, records, and fields. And this is a fairly easy task, because most of these relations can indeed be designed (individually, at least) as simple hierarchical structures. But the theories ignore the relations created at the same time by the database *operations*. These operations access the database from different elements of the application, and therefore relate these elements logically.[3]

As is the case with the other types of processes, the effect of database operations can be represented with hierarchical structures. To discover one of these structures, all we need to do is view the application from the perspective of one particular field, record, or file; that is, classify the application's elements according to the operations performed with that field, record, or file, while ignoring their other functions. In most applications we can find a large number of such structures, all using the same elements, and thus interacting with one another and with the structures representing the other processes.

It is impossible for database operations *not* to create structures that relate diverse elements. The very essence of the database principle is to connect and relate various parts of the application by means of data that is stored in files and indexes. We seldom access a set of related files in only one place in the application: we modify fields in one place and read them elsewhere; we add records in one place and delete them elsewhere; we interpret the same records on the basis of one index in one place and of another index elsewhere.

For example, if the program stores a certain value in a database field in one place and makes decisions based on that value in other places, all these places will necessarily be linked logically. They form a structure that, very likely, does not parallel the main structure, nor one of the structures formed by the other processes. For, could this particular relation be expressed through another structure, we wouldn't need that database field to begin with. We need a number of structures precisely because we need to relate the various parts of the application in several ways at the same time. The data stored in the database, together with the operations that access it, provides the means to implement some of these relations. And, just as is the case with the other processes, the structures formed by database operations are seldom manifest;

---

[3] Although *individually* the file relationships are simple hierarchical structures, a file is usually related to *several* other files, through the same fields or through different fields; and these relationships can seldom be depicted as one *within* another. The totality of file relationships in the database, therefore, is not one structure but a system of interacting structures. This fact is obvious (for instance, if we tried to depict with one hierarchy all the file relationships in a complex application, we would find it an impossible task), so I will not dwell on it. I will only discuss here the structures generated by the database operations, which are less obvious.

we only see them if we separate in our imagination each structure – each set of related elements – from the other structures that make up the application.

Note also that databases merely create on a large scale the kind of relations that memory variables – any piece of storage, in fact – create on a smaller scale. Each variable we use in the application gives rise to a structure – the structure formed by the set of elements that modify or read that variable. And these structures interact, because most elements use more than one variable. Moreover, each element is part of other processes too (part of a business practice, for instance), so the structures created by memory variables also interact with the other *types* of structures.

Thus, let us call *shared data* the broader software principle; namely, all processes based on the fact that the same piece of storage – a database field as well as a memory variable – can be accessed from different elements in the application.

4

Let us study, lastly, the software principle known as *subroutine*. A subroutine is a piece of software that is used (or "called") in several places in the application. Subroutines are software modules, but their ability to perform the same operations in different contexts endows them with additional qualities. (The software entities known as subprograms, functions, procedures, and objects are all, in effect, subroutines.)

We already saw how the practices implemented in the application, as well as the operations performed with databases and memory variables, create multiple, simultaneous structures. But it is with subroutines that the delusion of the main structure is most evident, because subroutines serve both as elements of the main structure and as means of relating *other* elements. The software theorists acknowledge one function, but not the other, so they fail to appreciate the complex role that subroutines play in the application.

The programming theories praise the concept of modularity and the notion of structured, top-down design. Since a module can call other modules, and those can call others yet, and so on, it is possible to create very large hierarchical structures of modules. Thus, the theories say, applications of any size and complexity can be developed by breaking them down into smaller and smaller modules, until reaching modules simple enough to program directly. The application's main structure will then be a hierarchical block diagram where the blocks are the modules, and the branches are the relations between the calling and the called modules. This diagram will represent accurately the application's performance.

We already know why the theories are wrong: the modules are related, not only through the main structure, but also through the structures formed by practices and shared data. And when some of the modules are subroutines, there are even more structures. If a module is used in several places, those places will be linked logically – because they will perform, by way of the shared module, the same operations. It is quite silly to start by deliberately designing two software elements in such a way that they can share a subroutine, and to end by claiming that they are independent; and yet this is exactly what the theories ask us to do. The very fact that a set of operations is useful for both elements demonstrates the existence of a strong logical link between these elements.

So, while *separating* the application into independent elements, subroutines *connect* into logical units *other* parts of the application. Each subroutine, together with its calls, forms a hierarchical structure – a structure that involves some of the application's elements but is different from the main structure, or from the structures formed by the other subroutines, or by the other types of processes. We can picture this structure by viewing the application from the perspective of that subroutine alone, while ignoring its other functions. The structure would represent, for example, the elements that call the subroutine, classifying them according to the ways in which the subroutine affects them.

Only if every module in the application is used *once*, can we say that the sole relations between modules are those depicted by the main structure. When this is true (and if the modules are not related through any other processes), the software theories may well work. But this trivial case can occur only in textbook examples. In real applications most modules are used more than once. As we divide the application into smaller and smaller parts, we are increasingly likely to encounter situations where the same operations are required in different places – situations, that is, where modules become subroutines. This, of course, is why subroutines are so common, why they are such an important programming expedient. The theories are right to encourage modularity; their mistake is to ignore the structures created by the subroutines.

Subroutines are a special case of a broader software principle – a principle that includes all the means of performing a given operation in different places in the application. Consider, for instance, the operation of incrementing a counter, or the operation of comparing two variables, or the operation of adding a value to a total. (It doesn't have to be the *same* counter, or variables, or total; what is shared is the *idea*, or *method*, of incrementing counters, of comparing variables, of updating totals.) We don't think of these operations as subroutines, but they play, by means of individual statements, the same role that subroutines play by means of modules: they perform the same operation in different contexts. Thus, we can implement these operations as subroutines if we want, but this is rarely beneficial. (Some do become subroutines, in fact, when translated by the compiler into a lower-level language.) Whether physically repeated, though, or implemented as subroutines and called where needed, we have no difficulty understanding that what we have is one operation performed in several places. So, *in our mind*, we are already connecting the application's elements into various logical structures, a different structure for each operation.

We must also include in this broader principle those subroutines that are implemented *outside* the application; for example, those found in subroutine libraries. Let us call them *external* subroutines, to distinguish them from those belonging to the application. The external subroutines are themselves modules, of course, so they may be quite large, and may invoke other modules in their turn. But all we see in the application is their name, so from the perspective of the application they are like the simple operations we discussed previously. Also like those operations, an external subroutine will relate the calling elements logically if called more than once, giving rise to a structure. (Their similarity to simple operations becomes even clearer when we recall that functions available only through external subroutines in one language may well be available through built-in operations in another, specialized language.)

Let us call *shared operations*, therefore, the broader software principle; namely, all processes based on the fact that the same set of operations can be performed by different elements in the application.

Since each process gives rise to a structure, the application is not just the elements themselves, but also the structures formed by these elements, and the interactions between these structures. If the structures represent various aspects of the application, if their purpose is to implement certain relations that exist between the application's elements in addition to the relations established by the main structure, then the interactions simply reflect the simultaneous occurrence of these relations. To put this differently, the complex structure that is the application cannot be approximated with one structure – not even the main structure – because the links between the individual structures are too strong to be ignored. Since each structure is an important aspect of the application, if we ignore the links caused by just one structure the application is bound to be inadequate in at least one class of situations.

The fallacy that all software theories suffer from is the notion that software modules are independent elements: it is assumed that their internal operations are strictly local, and that they are related to other modules only through their input and output. Their internal operations are indeed hidden from the other modules, but only if judged from a certain perspective (from the perspective of the flow of execution, for instance). Even a module that is invoked only once is rarely independent – because it is usually related to other modules, not just through its input and output, but also through the various processes of which it is part (business practices, for instance).

But the belief in module independence is especially naive for modules that are shared, because, in addition to the relations caused by various processes, their very sharing gives rise to a set of relations. The structure created by calling a subroutine in different places is a reflection of a requirement, of a logical link between these places – a link that must exist if the application is to do what we want it to do. This link is the very reason we use a piece of software that can be invoked in several places. We *need* to relate these places logically; for, if we didn't, we would be using only modules that are invoked once. (And it is merely a matter of interpretation whether the subroutine itself is independent and the elements that call it are not, because related logically through it, or the subroutine too is part of the structure and hence related logically to these elements.) Ultimately, we need the principle of shared modules for the same reason we need the other software principles: to relate the application's elements in many different ways at the same time.

Note that it is not by being one *physical* entity that a subroutine relates the elements that call it. What matters is the *logical* link, so even if we made copies of the subroutine – each call referring then to a different physical entity – the logical link, and hence the structure, would remain. (This is what happens, in essence, when we repeat individual operations – those small pieces of software we decide not to turn into subroutines.)

5

Recall Wittgenstein's example of games. We concluded that games cannot be correctly represented with one hierarchical structure, because it is impossible to capture in one classification all the attributes that games can possess. Instead, we need several structures, one for each attribute, and it is only this *system* of structures that completely represents the concept of games. In other words, there are many structures with the concept of games as the top element and the individual games as the terminal elements; and all these structures exist at the same time. We saw that the only way to account for all the attributes in one structure is by *repeating* some of the attributes at the intermediate levels. But this is no longer a correct hierarchy; moreover, it does not reflect the way we actually perceive games and their attributes. In a correct hierarchy each attribute appears only once.

It is relatively easy to see this problem in hierarchies that depict classifications and categories, but we encounter it in any complex phenomenon. Recall
the case of stories. We concluded that a story is a system of interacting
structures, where each structure is one particular way of relating the linguistic
elements that constitute the story. Each structure, then, depicts one aspect of
the story, one attribute. So, if the story is the top element and some small
linguistic parts (say, sentences) are the terminal elements, the only correct
structures are those that depict its attributes separately. These structures are
imaginary, however. Since the top element and the terminal elements are the
same in all of them, they cannot exist as separate structures in reality. Thus, to
understand the story we must combine them in the mind, and the result is a
complex phenomenon: we cannot depict the combination with a simple
hierarchical structure. This problem is similar to the problem of depicting in
one structure the attributes of games.

For example, referring to one person or another, and referring to one event
or another, are attributes of the linguistic elements that make up the story.
Consider a trivial story involving only two persons, *P1* and *P2*, and two events,
E1 and *E2*. Figure 4-6 shows the four structures that represent these attributes;
and, for simplicity, each attribute has only two values, *Y* and *N*: a given element
either is or is not affected by it. Each structure, then, divides the story's
sentences into two categories (with no intermediate levels of detail): those that
refer to, and those that do not refer to, *P1*; those that refer to, and those that do
not refer to, *E1*; and so on. While each combination of two categories includes
all the sentences in the story, and is therefore the same for all attributes, the
sentences in the individual categories may be different.

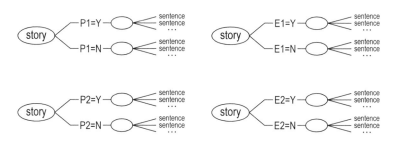

Figure 4-6

Since each sentence possesses all four attributes, these structures interact;
so the story is the system comprising all of them. When we read the story, we
easily picture such situations as a person involved in two different events,
a person involved in neither event, or two persons involved in the same

event. Thus, we can hold in the mind the structures of persons and events simultaneously (because minds can process complex structures), but we cannot represent this phenomenon with one structure.

To combine the four attributes in one structure, we must depict them as *one within another*. For example, we can start with *P1*, include in each of its two branches the two branches of *P2*, and then similarly include *E1* and *E2*. But this is an incorrect hierarchy. Attributes of entities are independent concepts: when an entity possesses several attributes, it possesses them in the same way, not as one within another. The need to repeat attributes, and the fact that we can combine them in any order we like, indicate that this structure does not reflect reality. The only way to depict more than one attribute in one structure is by showing all but the first as *subordinate* to others, while in reality they are independent.

This structure is shown in figure 4-7 (to reduce its size, half of the lower-level elements were omitted). There are sixteen categories of sentences: starting from the top, those that refer to both persons and both events, those that refer to both persons and only to *E1*, those that refer to both persons and only to *E2*, and so on, down to those that refer to neither person and neither event. The diagram clearly demonstrates the need to depict the attributes as one within another – the cause of their repetition. It also demonstrates the multitude of possible combinations: instead of ordering the levels of categories as *P1-P2-E1-E2*, we could order them as *P2-P1-E2-E1*, or as *E1-P1-E2-P2*, etc. While the top element and the terminal elements would be the same, the

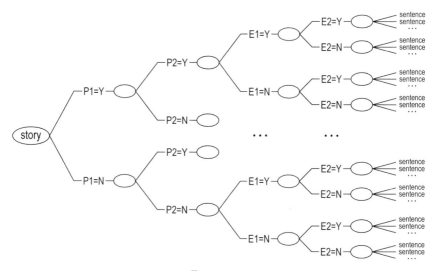

Figure 4-7

intermediate levels would differ. So, when attempting to combine attributes, we end up with several structures depicting the same story. And the absurdity of this situation indicates that these structures do not reflect the actual relationships. In reality, when reading the story, there is only one way to understand the relationships between persons and events.

To appreciate this problem, it may also help to contrast the complex phenomena of games and stories with those situations that *can* be adequately represented with simple structures. A physical structure like the transmission of a car can be described completely and accurately with a hierarchical structure where the individual components are the terminal elements, and the various subassemblies form the levels of abstraction. If, however, we consider such attributes as the colour of the components, or their weight, or the date they were made, or the age of the workers who handle them, we will find that each attribute relates them in a different way. We can view the same transmission, therefore, as a system of many different structures, one structure for each attribute: the top element and the terminal elements are the same in all structures, but the intermediate elements and levels differ. (Levels can be used, for example, to represent increasingly fine details: in the structure depicting the manufacturing date, they may be the year, month, and day; in the structure depicting the colour, they may be light and dark, and various shades; and so on.)

What distinguishes this system of structures from the system that makes up a story is the fact that the structure which concerns us the most – the one depicting the interconnection of components and subassemblies – is very weakly linked to the structures formed by the other attributes. In other words, the other attributes have little or no bearing on our main structure. So, even though the assembly of a transmission gives rise to a complex phenomenon, just like a story or the concept of games, in practice we can ignore the interactions between the main structure and the others. As a result, the hierarchical diagram of components and subassemblies provides an excellent approximation of the whole phenomenon.

Note that if we become interested in other details too – if, for instance, we require a study of that assembly plant, the business of transmission manufacturing, the workers and their life – the phenomenon will change. In the new phenomenon, attributes like a part's manufacturing date or a worker's age are as important as the attributes that affect the operation of the transmission. And consequently, the structures they generate and their interactions can no longer be ignored. Thus, the neat tree diagram depicting the components and subassemblies will no longer provide an adequate approximation of the whole phenomenon.

6

Contrary to the accepted programming theories, software applications are more akin to games and stories than to physical structures like car transmissions. Thus, software applications cannot be correctly represented with only one hierarchical structure. The software entities that make up an application – entities as small as individual operations and as large as entire modules – are affected by various processes; in particular, they call subroutines, use memory variables and database fields, and are part of practices. Since a process usually affects several entities, it serves also to relate them. It endows the entities, therefore, with an attribute, and the attribute creates a hierarchical structure in the application. So there are as many structures as there are processes. We see these structures when we study the application from the perspective of one subroutine, or one memory variable, or one database field, or one practice.

Thus, there is no hierarchy where the entity *application* is the top element, and the individual statements or operations are the terminal elements – not if we want to depict *all* the attributes possessed by these elements. Instead, there are *many* such structures, all using these elements. And it is only this system of simultaneous, interacting structures that completely represents the application.

As in the case of games and stories, the only way to represent all the attributes with one structure is by *repeating* some of them throughout the intermediate levels; and this will not be a correct hierarchy. For instance, if the calling of a particular subroutine is one attribute, then in order to include it in the same structure as another attribute we must repeat it at the intermediate levels. The structure will *look* like a hierarchy, but we know that this was achieved by showing several times what is in fact one attribute. It is impossible to indicate which elements call the subroutine and which ones do not, without this repetition (impossible, that is, if the structure is to include also the other processes implemented in the application – the other subroutines, the business practices, and so forth). The only way to show the subroutine only once is with its own, separate structure. But the terminal elements in this structure are software elements used also by the other processes, so this structure cannot exist on its own, separately from the others; they form the application together.

We encounter the same problem, of course, for any other process. For any one attribute, the only way to prevent its repetition is by creating its own structure. Only by showing the application's elements from the perspective of one attribute and ignoring their other functions can we have a diagram where the attribute appears only once. If we want to represent the entire application with one structure, then all attributes but one must be repeated, and shown as *subordinate* to others, in order to account for the combinations of attributes. But the attributes are not related in this manner in the actual application, so this structure does not represent it correctly. When a software element possesses several attributes, they are all possessed in the same way, not as one within another.

This problem is illustrated in figure 4-8. As with the structures of games and stories we studied previously, in order to emphasize the problem I am showing a trivial, purely hypothetical situation. The only purpose of this example is to demonstrate that even simple applications give rise to complex structures.

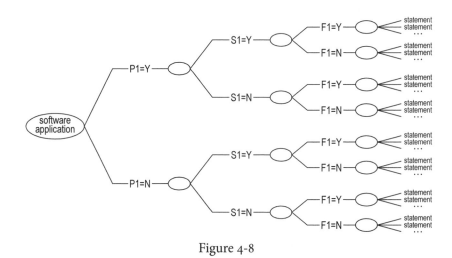

Figure 4-8

There are only three processes, and hence three attributes: *P1* is a particular practice implemented in the application, *S1* is the calling of a particular subroutine, and *F1* is the use of a particular database field. Moreover, each attribute has only two values, *Y* and *N*: a given software element either is or is not affected by a process. In other words, in this simple application there is only one way to be part of that practice (which is unrealistic, of course, even for a simple application), one way to call that subroutine (there are no parameters or returned values, for instance), and one way to use that field (its value can only be read, for instance). The terminal elements of this structure are some small software parts, say, statements. So there are eight categories of statements: those that are part of the practice, call the subroutine, and use the field; those that are part of the practice, call the subroutine, and do not use the field; those that are part of the practice, do not call the subroutine, and use the field; and so on.

The diagram clearly shows why two of the attributes, *S1* and *F1*, must be repeated: if we start with *P1*, the structure can be said to represent the application from the perspective of *P1*; then, the only way to include the other attributes is by depicting each one *within* the categories created by the previous attributes. And it is just as clear that we could draw the diagram by showing the attributes in a different order: we could start with *F1*, for example, and follow with *P1* and *S1*; *F1* would no longer be repeated, but *P1* and *S1* would. The fact that some attributes must be repeated, and that the same application can be represented with different structures, indicates that these structures do not reflect reality.

Figure 4-9 shows the structures that represent the three attributes separately. Like the separate structures of games in figure 4-5 (p. 341), or those of stories in figure 4-6 (p. 357), these *are* correct hierarchies. But, like the others, these structures are imaginary: since the top element and the terminal elements are the same in all three, they cannot actually exist separately. Each statement possesses the three attributes, so the structures interact. It is their combination, a complex structure, that constitutes the application. And we are able to create applications for the same reason we are able to understand stories or the concept of games: because our mind can process complex structures.

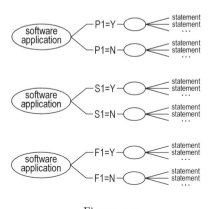

Figure 4-9

Note that there are no intermediate levels in these structures; that is, no intermediate categories of statements. This is due to the assumption that the attributes have only two values, *Y* and *N*. In a real application, most attributes generate a structure with several levels of detail: categories within categories, reflecting the many ways in which a process can affect a statement, or the many reasons it does not affect a statement. But even with the additional levels, these structures remain correct hierarchies if they continue to represent individual attributes. It is only the attempt to combine all the attributes in one structure that is wrong.

It is obvious that any application can be represented with a classification-style diagram like the one in figure 4-8. And, while a real application may have thousands of attributes and elements, the problem would be the same: since all attributes but one must be repeated, the diagram would not reflect reality. Only a system of structures like those in figure 4-9 represents the application correctly. Thus, by showing that one structure is inadequate, classification-style diagrams remind us that applications consist of interacting structures; so they help us to understand the nature of software. We don't have to actually draw the diagrams, of course; we only need to know that such diagrams exist.

In contrast, diagrams like flowcharts represent only *one* aspect of the application; for example, the flow of execution, or the logic of a particular business practice. By emphasizing one structure and obscuring the others, these diagrams lead to the delusion that applications can be reduced to one structure, the *main* structure; the other structures, we think, can be ignored, or eliminated, or handled separately. With classification-style diagrams it is more difficult to make this mistake, because in these diagrams all structures look alike: since we can draw the diagram with the attributes in any order, it is obvious that *all* structures are important.

The delusion of the main structure is demonstrated by the naive theory known as structured programming. This theory holds that programs can be designed as a strict hierarchical structure of software elements, and gives us methods whereby, supposedly, any piece of software can be transformed into such a structure. But the theory looks only at the *flow-control* structures, ignoring the *other* structures formed by the same elements. Moreover, the recommended transformations do not *eliminate* the unwanted flow-control structures, but merely replace them with structures based on shared data or shared operations. The purpose of the new structures, therefore, is to relate the program's elements in various ways; in other words, to restore, by different means, the links originally provided by the flow-control structures.

What the transformations do, then, is replace the original complex structure, which has *many* flow-control structures plus *many* structures of other types, with a different complex structure, which has *one* flow-control structure plus *even more* structures of other types. If we study only the flow-control type, the program does indeed look now like a neat hierarchy of software entities. If, however, we also take into account the other types, we find that it consists of many interacting structures, just as before.

Because in the program's flowchart the flow-control structures are obvious while the others are not, the advocates of structured programming believe that the program was reduced to one structure. The fallacy, thus, lies in the belief that transformations which reduce the *flow-control* structures to one structure reduce the program itself to one structure. (Actually, the fallacy of structured programming is even greater: as we will see in chapter 7, the flow-control structure itself remains a system of interacting structures; besides, the transformations are rarely practical.)

7

We wish to represent our software applications with neat tree diagrams, and we wish to have software entities that are independent of one another. We appreciate the benefits of these two principles, but we fail to recognize their impossibility in practice. These principles are related, since both are necessary in order to implement simple hierarchical structures. We apply them successfully in our manufacturing and construction activities, where we create large hierarchical structures of independent *physical* entities; and we try to create software applications by applying these principles to *software* entities.

Software, however, like language, is different. The *physical* structures we design and build are our invention, so we deliberately restrict ourselves to simple hierarchical structures in order to ensure their success. With software and language, on the other hand, we want to mirror facts, processes, and events that *already exist* in the world, and which can only be represented with *complex* structures. If we restricted ourselves to simple hierarchical structures, we would be able to represent in software and in language only the simplest phenomena, or we would have to tolerate poor approximations of the complex phenomena. Simple structures are inadequate if we want to represent the world as it actually is, if we want to mirror reality.

Software entities, we saw, are independent only when viewed as elements of *one* structure; for instance, the application's main structure, or a particular process. And this independence is illusory, because they are, at the same time, elements in *other* structures. We can treat them as independent entities, and as elements of a simple structure, only if we ignore the roles they play in the other structures, and the interactions that these multiple roles give rise to. The only way to attain independence of software entities is by ensuring that each entity is used in only one structure; but then our applications would no longer mirror reality.

I want to emphasize again that the complex structures we generate with our software applications are inevitable. The interactions that occur between software elements are not necessarily a sign of bad programming; we must expect them even in well-designed applications. The software mechanists tell us that we need their theories and programming aids in order to reduce these interactions, but now we understand why these theories and aids cannot help us: if we accept them and restrict our applications to isolated structures of software entities, the applications will not reflect correctly our affairs.

The complex relations that arise in our applications are, thus, an important *quality* of software. Their existence demonstrates that, like language, software *can* have interacting structures, and *can* mirror the world accurately. Instead of trying to *avoid* these relations, then, we must increase our programming expertise so that we can successfully deal with them. We *must* create software structures that share their elements, because this is the only way to mirror, in software, phenomena which themselves consist of structures that share their elements.

In conclusion, the versatility of software is due to the ability to relate the elements of an application in various ways by using the same files, variables, operations, and subroutines in different elements. We need this ability in order to implement processes, and we need processes in order to represent the world. It is the programmer's task to create, for each process, the structure that relates the application's elements in the manner required by that process. And he must do this with many processes at the same time, because this is how the actual facts are related in the world. The very purpose of practices, and of shared data and operations, is to mirror in software those aspects of our affairs that *already* form different structures with the same elements in the real world. So we must not be upset, but pleased, when we end up with interacting structures in software.

If software involves complex structures, software development requires human minds. How, then, can the programming theories and aids help us? Being mechanistic systems, they can only represent *isolated* software structures. So, just to consider them, we must commit the fallacy of reification: we must separate the countless processes that make up an application. The main structure, the practices embodied in the application, the database, are held to represent independent logical structures – structures that can be studied and programmed separately. The reason we are asked to reify these structures is that, within each structure, the theories and aids can offer us the means to start from higher levels of abstraction. Thus, we are also tempted to commit the fallacy of abstraction. Less programming and lower programming skills are needed when starting from higher levels; and this, ultimately, is seen as the chief benefit of programming tools, database systems, and development environments. But when committing the two fallacies, we lose most of the interactions; so our applications will not represent the world accurately.

❖

To recognize the absurdity of programming theories and aids, all we need to do is imagine a similar situation for language. The equivalent of the software industry, and the theories and devices that act as substitutes for programming expertise, would be a *language* industry. Instead of learning how to use language to acquire and to express knowledge, we would learn how to use various systems provided by language companies as substitutes for linguistic competence. And instead of simply communicating through language, we would spend most of our time and resources assimilating an endless series of linguistic innovations – new languages, theories, methodologies, and devices. The equivalent of software development tools and aids would be linguistic tools and aids that promise higher levels of abstraction. These devices would extract individual structures from the complex phenomenon of language – the syntax of a sentence, the logic of an argument, the aspects of a story – addressing each one in isolation. Within each structure, the devices may even do what they promise; but this would not help us to use language, because language structures interact, and we need the ability to deal with all of them simultaneously.

The only thing that language companies could offer us, then, is a way to start from higher levels of abstraction within each structure. We would have to use a set of ready-made sentences and ideas, for example, instead of creating our own, starting with words. This would perhaps expedite the generation of individual structures, but at the cost of reducing the number of alternatives for the concepts we represent with language. The interactions between language structures occur not only at the level of sentences and ideas, but also at the low level of words: it is the meaning of individual words that usually determines the attributes of linguistic elements – attributes which ultimately cause the interactions. If we could no longer express ourselves starting with words, many interactions would become impossible – not only between language structures, but also between the language structures and other knowledge structures.

What this means in practice is that many ideas, or stories, or kinds of knowledge, or forms of discourse, would also become impossible. The consequence of linguistic reification and abstraction, thus, is not just an impoverishment in language structures and in the kind of concepts that can be represented with language. Because these concepts are linked with all human knowledge, our entire existence would be impoverished. Other knowledge structures we hold in our minds – our thoughts, feelings, beliefs, and expectations, which interact with the linguistic structures – would be restricted to a small number of alternatives.

And so it is with programming. When we start from higher levels of abstraction, and when we separate the various aspects of an application, we end up with impoverished software; that is, software which represents only a fraction of the possible alternatives. We *can* mirror our affairs in software, but only if we start from low levels. We cannot if we rely on mechanistic programming theories and on ready-made pieces of software.

What is worse, as software is acquiring a social role similar to that of language, an impoverishment in the alternatives that we represent with software will affect us just as it would for language: other knowledge structures we hold in our minds – structures that appear unrelated to software but interact, in fact, with the software structures – will be impoverished at the same time. This threat is what we will examine in the next two chapters.

CHAPTER 5

Language as Weapon

In this chapter and the next, we will study the consequences of mechanistic delusions in the domains of language and software. We will see, specifically, how language and software are being used to control the minds of large numbers of people: how they have been turned into weapons, into means of domination and exploitation.

Mechanistic Communication

Language and software, we saw, are similar, insofar as both are systems of representation and communication. But they do not function, as the mechanistic theories claim, by directly mirroring reality with structures of symbols; that is, language structures and software structures do not simply *map* the real world. The reality we seek to represent consists of complex structures, while the strings of symbols employed in language and in software can form only simple structures. These simple structures, though, interact with one another and with other knowledge structures. And it is the complex structures resulting from these interactions that mirror reality.

In language structures – in the manifest structures that make up discourse – grammatical conventions and word meanings give rise to additional structures, all sharing the same words. We recognize them as the various *aspects* of a message, story, or argument (see pp. 350–351). But because they use the same linguistic entities, these structures interact. Only a mind can grasp the complex meanings of the manifest language structures, because only minds can process all the structures simultaneously.

In software structures – in the manifest structures that make up software applications – it is the software *processes* that give rise to additional structures (see pp. 347–348). And, as in the case of language, these structures use the same software entities. They interact, therefore, and only a mind can grasp the complex meanings of the manifest software structures. With software or with language, we *can* mirror the world; but we do it through the complex structures developed in our mind, not by merely mapping the world in software structures or language structures.

To understand how charlatans use language and software to exploit us, we must remember how the process of communication works, for it is by disrupting this process that they deceive us. Language and software work by permitting us to link structures in the mind, and these links must start at low levels of abstraction. This is true because, if our goal is to develop knowledge structures that mirror the world accurately, we must be able to re-create in our mental structures *all* the interactions that occur between the *actual* structures. So, to deceive us, the charlatans prevent us from creating complex knowledge structures. And they accomplish this by forcing us to commit the fallacies of reification and abstraction: they restrict us to high levels of abstraction and isolated structures, instead of encouraging us to start with low-level elements and to discover the interactions between structures.

In language, the charlatans keep inventing new terms when the existing ones are, in fact, perfectly adequate. The use of new terms, especially when not defined or explained, prevents us from linking the new notions to our previous knowledge structures. Sometimes the terms are purposely misleading, in order to tempt us to link these notions to the wrong knowledge structures. Thus, because the terms are not properly defined, they convey vague and abstract notions. These notions become the starting elements of our new knowledge structure. But because they form an isolated structure and are at a high level of abstraction, they restrict our final knowledge, and hence our conception of reality, to a small number of alternatives.

So it is not the invention of new terms that deceives us, but the lack of definition. Were the new terms carefully defined and explained, their high level would be harmless: the details of the explanation would function then as low-level elements, linking the new structures to our existing knowledge. But the prevention of these links is precisely what the charlatans intended, the reason they invented new terms in the first place.

In software, the charlatans force us to depend on theories and aids that address isolated aspects of programming and limit us to high levels of abstraction. As a result, we cannot create the proper links between the various software structures that make up an application, and between these structures and the structures that make up our social or business affairs; so our applications remain inadequate. Moreover, by restricting us to isolated software structures and high-level elements, the software charlatans prevent us from developing the knowledge whereby we *could* create useful applications; so we continue to depend on their theories and aids, while we could accomplish more with our own minds.

Both language and software deception, thus, work by restricting us to mechanistic thinking. When we are forced to commit the two mechanistic fallacies, we are forced in effect to use language and software as if they were simple structures, thereby losing their most important quality – the capability to mirror the world through *complex* structures. Our performance is reduced then to the level of machines. Machines can *only* handle simple structures; *we* have the capacity for complex structures, but if we do not make use of this capacity we are no better than machines.

We are going to study this deception now, first in language and then, in the next chapter, in software. Our main interest is software, but it will be helpful to examine first how *language* is used to deceive and exploit us. We have already established the similarity of language and software, and the similarity of our language and software delusions; thus, apart from the obvious value of recognizing language deception, this study will also help us later to recognize *software* deception.

Language manipulation was never complete, not even in totalitarian societies, because no institution can have that much power. With software, however, the elites have reached almost complete control. We are permitting them to deceive and exploit us through software because we do not understand the role of software in society as well as we do that of language. Had an elite attempted to exploit us by manipulating language as the software elites are now exploiting us by manipulating software, we would have easily recognized their totalitarian intentions. Thus, if we see how powerful is mind control through language, even when the manipulation forms only a small part of our whole use of language, we will better appreciate the consequences of mind control through *software*, where the manipulation is almost total.

The Practice of Deceit

1

Acquiring knowledge by way of language is very different from developing the same knowledge directly, from the actual phenomenon. When we develop knowledge through our own experience, we are exposed to all the structures that make up the phenomenon. In our mind, we develop links between these structures, and between them and prior knowledge structures, and this is how we form the new knowledge structure that reflects the phenomenon. With linguistic communication, on the other hand, the message acts as a *substitute* for the actual phenomenon and for our exposure to it. All we can do now to attain the new knowledge is combine the structures we detect *in the message* with our prior knowledge structures. It is impossible for this knowledge to be as accurate as the knowledge developed through direct experience, so the most we can expect is knowledge that is *close* to reality.

Now, if the author of the message *wants* us to attain knowledge that is close to reality, he will formulate the message in a manner that helps us to arrive at the truth. In other words, an honest message is a message that helps us to attain knowledge which is as close as possible to the knowledge we would attain through exposure to the phenomenon itself. A dishonest author does the opposite: he formulates the message in a manner that forces us to attain knowledge that is very different from reality. And if we believe that our new knowledge reflects the truth, we will conduct ourselves in ways that may be against our interest. This is how linguistic deception is used to exploit us.

The challenge faced by those who want to control us through language is how to limit and distort knowledge without actually telling lies. They must make us feel that we are being informed when in reality we are being deceived. And they accomplish this (as we saw in the previous section) by restricting us to mechanistic thinking.

A message constitutes *only one* of the structures that make up knowledge. It is merely a string of sounds or symbols conforming to certain conventions – a simple structure. Only by combining the meaning of its words with our prior knowledge, using these conventions, can we detect the other structures. When communicating through language, therefore, the receiver of the message is at a great disadvantage, because he must start with just one structure.

The reification caused by a deceptive linguistic message serves to isolate the new knowledge structure from those already in the mind. It prevents us from forming the links that would create the proper knowledge, and provides the deceivers with an independent structure – a structure whose elements they can control. They can now force us, within this structure, to accept as starting elements terms that constitute in fact high levels of abstraction. This abstraction, we already know, limits the number of alternatives we can have for the top element of the structure. What this means in practice is that the knowledge we acquire through their message is restricted to a very narrow range, often only one alternative.

Typically, the deceivers use abstract concepts that already evoke in our mind the simple ideas of good or bad, important or unimportant, useful or useless, and so forth; that is, they use concepts that are "good" when they want us to think positively about something, and concepts that are "bad" when they want us to think negatively. These abstract concepts become the lowest-level elements of the new knowledge structure. No real knowledge is possible when starting with abstract concepts, so we end up simply associating the message with "good" or with "bad," just as the deceivers wanted.

2

Slogans and prejudicial labels are examples of terms wrongly employed as starting elements in a knowledge structure. They are high-level linguistic entities that invite us to think of whole classes of situations, objects, or persons as either good or bad, instead of starting from lower levels, where we could learn about each individual case.

For example, a popular contemporary slogan is "technology" – a highly abstract term that subsumes a great number of diverse concepts, processes, and products. And, needless to say, we all perceive technology as "good." This combination makes "technology" the ideal term for all the charlatans who want to influence us. What they do, in essence, is modify their claims by substituting "technology" for the particular ideas, products, or services they offer us. But to make an informed decision we must start from low levels of abstraction: we must understand individual items and properties. Only by combining these details with other knowledge structures can we discover all possible alternatives; that is, all possible values for the top element of the larger knowledge structure, which may be a purchase decision, the way we view our responsibilities, and the like. So the charlatans plant in our minds an isolated element – the abstract linguistic entity "technology," which we already interpret as good – and tempt us to treat it as a *starting* element. They are impoverishing our knowledge by restricting it to trivial structures. (We will study the slogan "technology" more closely in the next section.)

Other words that have become slogans are "solution," "powerful," "easily," and "quickly." We use terms like these as low-level linguistic elements, although they are high-level entities. Each one subsumes many diverse concepts, but it is no longer possible to assess the individual concepts objectively. The slogan reduces them all to one concept, "good."

But with so much language abuse going on, our existing abstract terms were insufficient. The charlatans, thus, had to coin new terms – terms that can be quickly assimilated by the public and associated with "good" or with "bad." And because it is not easy to add new words to a widespread language, other methods have been developed.

One method is to create acronyms.[1] We perceive acronyms as mere abbreviations, as a way to shorten discourse that involves frequent and lengthy phrases. The proliferation of acronyms in contemporary public discourse, however, is due largely to their usefulness as abstract terms. For, once an acronym is accepted and becomes part of our linguistic communication, it functions just like a word. We quickly forget (if we ever knew) the phrase that the acronym stands for, and the meaning of this phrase, and assimilate instead the associations created for the acronym by its author.

So, by way of acronyms, any charlatan can add terms to our common language – terms whose interpretation he controls, and which will support concepts that serve his interests. If an individual or an institution attempted to add some new *words* to the English vocabulary, we would likely ignore them; but we readily accept *acronyms*, without realizing that they fulfil, in fact, the same function. Since an acronym is a new term, it has no links to our prior knowledge, so we must accept whatever interpretation we are given. Simply by including the acronym in a particular context, for instance, its author can make it appear "good," thereby forcing us to perceive it, and any other concepts associated with it, positively.

Thus, speaking of political acronyms like NATO, SEATO, UN, and AEC, Herbert Marcuse points out that they conveniently "help to repress undesired questions"[2] one might ask if analyzing the original words, as the ideas represented by the acronyms may be quite different from the meaning of those words: "The abbreviations denote that and only that which is institutionalized in such a way that the transcending connotation is cut off. The meaning is fixed, doctored, loaded. Once it has become an official vocable, constantly repeated in general usage, 'sanctioned' by the intellectuals, it has lost all cognitive value and serves merely for recognition of an unquestionable fact."[3]

Similarly, William Lutz notes that acronyms like ICBM, SLBM, IRBM, INF, RDF, and SDI are used to alter our perception of such important matters as nuclear war: "Nuclear doublespeak is filled with acronyms which are cool,

---

[1] Strictly speaking, "acronym" refers to abbreviations pronounced as words, as opposed to those pronounced as distinct letters; but in this book I use the term for both types.

[2] Herbert Marcuse, *One-Dimensional Man: Studies in the Ideology of Advanced Industrial Society*, 2nd ed. (Boston: Beacon, 1991), p. 94.   [3] Ibid.

precise, rational, and authoritative. Those who use these acronyms appear to possess such qualities themselves, and they appear knowledgeable and objective when discussing nuclear weapons and war. Acronyms also allow those discussing nuclear war to distance themselves from the horrible reality of such a war."[4]

The world of computers and software is notorious for its infatuation with acronyms, as the elites incessantly try to instill new concepts in our minds – concepts that we are to perceive as "good" without actually understanding them (IT, OO, CASE, GUI, RAD, SOA, RISC, etc.). We use these terms as if they described specific things, when they are in fact linguistic entities of a high level of abstraction. They subsume countless lower-level elements – particular ideas, methods, situations, and implementations – but we seldom think of those elements when we see the acronyms. Instead, we perceive the acronyms themselves as starting elements, and thus impoverish many other knowledge structures: if we consider the acronyms "good," all thoughts involving them become simple and predictable. (We will return to the subject of acronyms in the next two sections.)

3

We saw how the charlatans employ acronyms as a way of introducing new, abstract terms. The most common method of coining an abstract term, however, and the most subtle, is not by inventing a new term but by using an *existing* term in a *new* sense. In its established sense, the term has a precise and well-known meaning; in its new sense, on the other hand, its meaning is at a higher level of abstraction. So, while looking familiar, the term is in fact a different linguistic entity.

This combination of familiarity and novelty is what confuses us. Because the charlatans do not define or explain its new sense, the term functions in effect as a high-level element: without a proper definition, it subsumes many possible meanings, often a whole range of meanings, from good to bad. At the same time, its familiar sense links the term to prior knowledge, thereby associating it with a precise meaning, good or bad. The deception is achieved, thus, by forcing us to interpret an abstract term – and consequently the facts it stands for – as good or as bad, while the reality is very different. It goes without saying that the creation of a new sense for an old term is not prompted by a lack of adequate words. The charlatans do it solely in order to force us to start from a higher level of abstraction without being aware of it.

4 William Lutz, *Doublespeak* (New York: HarperPerennial, 1990), p. 268.

To see how this works in practice, let us analyze a few cases selected at random from the hundreds of language abuses we encounter every day, and which have become a distinguishing characteristic of public discourse. It is not so much individuals that abuse language, as our social and political establishments, and our corporations. And we should take this opportunity to ponder over the future of a society whose institutions believe they have the right to use language (and now also, increasingly, software) to deceive and exploit the public.

Logging companies, concerned with their image as destroyers of forests, frequently use the term "harvesting" to describe the cutting of trees. Now, we know what harvesting *crops* means. But harvesting *trees* is a new term, which, moreover, is undefined. It is an abstract entity, because it can be interpreted in a number of ways: new trees will grow next year, like cereals, or a new forest will develop in a hundred years, or no forest will ever grow again. Without a definition, the term is too vague, too abstract, to function as a starting element in this knowledge structure; it conveys no real information. At the same time, by choosing the word "harvesting" for the new term, the companies want us to adopt the *first* interpretation; that is, to link their term to the wrong structure. Their intention, therefore, is to instill in our minds a high-level element with a meaning that is very different from reality. A valid knowledge structure must start from *low-level* elements, from the *details* that make up this issue. Only by starting from low levels can we retain all the alternatives for the top element – which reflects many social and environmental concerns – so that we can select the alternative closest to reality. This is precisely what the logging companies are preventing us from doing when forcing us to start from a high level of abstraction.

A mail-order catalogue offers us an "exacting reproduction" of the G.I. wristwatch issued by the U.S. Army in WWII.[5] We all know what an *exact* reproduction is, but not what an "exacting" one is (and when it comes to reproductions, we don't care how exacting, but only how exact, they are). Lacking a definition, the new term represents a high level of abstraction: it subsumes such interpretations as exact, or similar, or similar externally but not internally. The choice of "exacting" for the new term, however, tempts us to adopt the first interpretation. Again, the advertiser is creating a high-level element, and is forcing us to treat it as a *starting* element (whose meaning, moreover, is different from reality). The knowledge structure we develop with this element – our perception of the reproduction as exact or inexact – will be impoverished: its top element will be limited to one alternative.

[5] Hammacher Schlemmer catalogue (holiday 1998), p. 90.

❖

Since most product descriptions consist of statements that appear to make bold promises while saying in fact practically nothing, catalogues and the shelves of retail stores provide an inexhaustible supply of examples of deceptive language. As in any form of advertising, the purpose of this deception is to present a product that does little or nothing, or nothing out of the ordinary, so as to make us believe that it will perform a difficult or even an impossible task. It is not my intention to engage in an analysis of deceptive advertising, but only to show that the most common method of deception is the use of high levels of abstraction. And language makes it easy: Advertisers need only invent a new sense for a given term, while leaving that sense undefined. Since all words look alike, regardless of their level of abstraction, this move can easily trick us into mistaking a high-level term for a low-level one.

If the engine of your car leaks oil, you may like the promise made by a product called Engine Stop Leak – a fluid that, when poured into the oil pan, "stops internal and external oil loss." We read the following description: "Formulated to: improve high temperature oil viscosity, gently condition rubber seals and gaskets."[6] The name of the product, which is prominently displayed, constitutes an authoritative and unambiguous claim; and the description appears to support the claim by explaining how the product works. But the name of a product is just a phrase; it is not a commitment, so the manufacturer can use any words, no matter how deceptive. It is worth noting, therefore, before anything else, this deliberate discrepancy between the precise language of the *name*, which creates no liability, and the evasive language of the *description*, which is the only place where we could find an accountable claim. For, not only doesn't the description make a real claim, but it functions in fact as *disclaimer*.

The sentence that makes up the description consists of several levels of disclaiming, and because of the nature of English sentences, we must study it backward, starting from the end. There are two statements here, as the product appears to act both on oil and on seals and gaskets. Starting with the seals and gaskets, it "conditions" them, but we are not told what conditioning a seal or a gasket means in this context. Thus, because it is undefined, this term can mean almost anything. To stop a leak, the product must make the material *expand*; but if this is your interpretation of "conditioning," remember that this is only wishful thinking: it could also mean the opposite, making the material shrink, which would worsen the leak. (If "expand" is what they meant, why didn't they simply say this?) In any case, whatever "conditioning" is, it is

_____

[6] Wynn's Canada Ltd.; both quotations are package text.

canceled by the qualifier "gently," which is too vague to mean anything; for example, the conditioning may be so gentle that it has no visible effect, one way or the other. As for the first statement, the product will "improve" the oil viscosity. To stop a leak, what we need is an *increase* in viscosity; but, again, it is wishful thinking that tempts us to interpret "improve" as "increase." As it stands, "improving viscosity" is a new and undefined term, so it can mean any action, including *reducing* the viscosity. (If "increase" is what they meant, why didn't they simply say this?) In any case, whatever it means happens only at a "high" temperature, and we are not told what "high" means; "high" can therefore be any value, including a temperature never reached by your engine.

Lastly, just in case the two levels of disclaiming in each statement are insufficient, the description prefixes the whole sentence with one additional disclaimer, "formulated." This term means that the product is made from specific substances: it was not concocted randomly, nor picked from a tree. So it seems to be just a bombastic note. However, it also means that the *only* thing the manufacturer claims is that the product was *formulated* (or designed, or intended) to act as the statements say – not that it *will* act that way. The formula may be wrong, this term suggests, so the product may well have no effect, and may even have the opposite effect.

This product may be useful or useless, but we cannot determine which from its description. All the description does, in fact, is exploit our wishes and fantasies: it tells us what we want to hear, while canceling its own statements. Nor are these promises more deceptive than those made by the thousands of other products, services, and ideas that we are offered every day. (Few products are *totally* useless, of course; in most cases the promises are simply much greater than, or very different from, what the product actually does. Still, even if not a complete lie, a deceptive description accomplishes the same thing; for, were that description replaced with a clear explanation of what the product will and will not do, few of us would buy that product, or buy it at that price.)

We must never forget the power of language: it takes an expert but a few minutes to construct one of these deceptive sentences, which can then exploit millions of people – people who foolishly believe that they can trust our social institutions, governments, manufacturers, retailers, or media.

If you doubt the power of language, consider this: without the benefit of language, the only way to make us buy and use such products would be by threatening us with a weapon. Thus, the use of deceptive language is a kind of weapon: a form of violence, a means of coercion. The reason we do not see it this way is that it has become such an important part of our culture. Lutz agrees: "Power in modern society resides in language. Those who know how to use language can wield great power. Doublespeak is an effective use of the language of power, the language of control, the language of manipulation."[7]

Let us analyze one more description, if you are still looking for products that can help you maintain your car. This time we have a spray can containing a transparent solution, and described as follows: "Specially formulated to give excellent results in resisting the growth of rust caused by stone chipping or scratching ...."[8] Here too, it is best to study the sentence starting from the end. What is the use of this spray? Are we expected to discover the paint nicks caused by stones and scratches as soon as they occur and spray them regularly from then on to prevent rust? Maybe so, but the manufacturer doesn't really say anything about preventing rust. What is "growth of rust"? Rust is the result of a chemical process; it doesn't grow, like plants. Rust growth, therefore, refers to a new and undefined process. Perhaps it really means what you hope it does – iron oxidation. But you needn't be too concerned with its real meaning, because, in any case, the spray doesn't *prevent* it. It can only "resist" it, and we are not told what "resisting" means; so this action is undefined, and hence too vague to be usefully assessed. Fortunately, you needn't be concerned with this either, because the spray doesn't really claim to resist, but only to "give excellent results" in resisting; and excellence can be interpreted to mean any level, from 1 to 100 percent of the desired outcome, depending on the task. (For example, resisting the process called rust growth may be so difficult that 1 percent is indeed an excellent result.)

Lastly, we note that this substance is "specially formulated." This, as always, means that it was *only* formulated, or designed, to do what those statements say. The formula or design may be anywhere from good to bad, the sentence suggests, so the substance may in fact do nothing, and may even make matters worse. If you counted, there are four levels of disclaiming. Each disclaimer raises the message to a higher level of abstraction, and we are deceived because the sentence appears to describe facts, not abstract concepts.

Thanks to its subtlety, the term "formulated" is quite popular as disclaimer. Here are additional examples of formulated products: "Specially formulated to take the guesswork out of plastic repair."[9] "Formulated to relax or excite, aromatic essential oils are refreshing ...."[10] "Formulated to help reduce the appearance of hyperpigmented age spots."[11] "Formulated to be better."[12] "Specially formulated to provide maximum protection for our high carbon tool

---

[7] William Lutz, *The New Doublespeak* (New York: HarperPerennial, 1997), p. 16.

[8] Krown Rust Control System, package text.

[9] Plastic repair system, http://www.kent-automotive.com/.

[10] http://www.skinenergizer.com/.

[11] Bremenn Research Labs Lumedia, http://www.skinstep.com/.

[12] Baytec rotational cast systems, http://www.bayermaterialscience.com/.

steel blades."[13] "Formulated to provide a synergistic 'all purpose' formula."[14] "Specially formulated to influence skin health and beauty."[15]

Instead of being "formulated," a product can be "engineered," because this term, too, can act as disclaimer: while appearing to be merely a pomposity, its real task is to suggest that the product was *only* engineered – or designed, or intended – to do what the following statements say. The engineering itself, the sentence implies, may be good or bad. Some examples: "Engineered to help restore power, performance and efficiency …."[16] "Heavy-duty 2" steel pipe frame engineered for easy assembly."[17] "Engineered to work together."[18] "Engineered to perform better."[19] "Dedicated to providing a complete solution engineered to meet your needs."[20] "A generator engineered to perform in Canadian climate."[21] "Engineered to meet the demanding needs of capability-class High Performance Computing (HPC) applications …."[22] "Precision engineered to help increase workflow efficiency …."[23]

If you still can't see why "formulated" and "engineered" are in reality disclaimers, imagine the same statements *without* these terms. If we omit them (and if we ignore the additional disclaimers), the preceding statements become simple and unambiguous: "improves oil viscosity," "takes the guesswork out," "is better," "relaxes," "reduces the appearance," "gives excellent results," "restores power," "easy assembly," "meets your needs." Thus, it is precisely in order to *avoid* accountable claims like these that advertisers prefix them with "formulated" or "engineered."

Terms like "resists," which we encountered in the previous analysis, belong to a family of words that deceivers love to use because of their effectiveness as disclaimers:[24] "helps," "aids," "acts," "works," "fights," "controls," etc. The disclaimer replaces, or is attached to, a familiar term, which on its own describes an exact process: prevent, relieve, protect, etc. Although it appears to be similar to the familiar term, or merely a stylistic embellishment, the function of the disclaimer is in fact to *modify* the meaning of the familiar term

---

[13] Steele Armor blade coating, http://tradknives.com/.
[14] Blockbuster AllClear, http://www.goodhealthnaturally.com/.
[15] AKN Skin Care, http://www.naturesway.com/.
[16] Slick 50 Plus engine treatment for older engines, package text.
[17] ShelterLogic auto shelter, Canadian Tire brochure.
[18] Oracle Database 10g and Application Server 10g, adv. pamphlet.
[19] http://www.oracal.com/.   [20] http://www.tamlinsoftware.com/.
[21] http://hondacanada.ca/.   [22] Cray XT5 computer, http://www.cray.com/.
[23] Sharp MXM623–MXM753 workgroup document systems, http://www.oiinc.ca/.
[24] Cf. Lutz, *Doublespeak*, pp. 85–93.

– modify it even to the point of *annulling* it. Some examples: "prevents cavities" becomes "helps prevent cavities"; "eliminates dandruff" becomes "fights dandruff"; "reduces your appetite" becomes "controls your appetite"; "relieves the symptoms of colds" becomes "acts to relieve the symptoms of colds." While the first statement in each pair makes a real claim, the second one only *appears* to do so.

Note that, strictly speaking, terms like "improve," "increase," and "reduce" are themselves disclaimers, because we are not told what is the *degree* of improvement, increase, or reduction. Thus, while the claim itself is real, the actual change could be insignificant. So the qualifying word provides, in effect, a *second* level of disclaiming. In phrases like "works to improve," "helps to increase," and "acts to reduce," the words "works," "helps," and "acts" annul a claim that may already be meaningless.

The most common disclaimer is "help," as in the following examples: "Firewall Plus ... helps block hackers."[25] "Fit two A4 size pages on screen to help double working efficiency."[26] "... using Dell PowerConnect switches to help maximize data flow across your network."[27] "Plant sterols help lower cholesterol."[28] "Helps provide exceptional grip ... helps increase water evacuation ... helps provide flatter footprint ...."[29] "Filter helps remove 99% ...."[30] "Minwax Wood Finish penetrates the wood pores to help seal and protect the wood."[31] "Specially coated to help prevent loss of data and minimize errors."[32] "There is a product that can help protect you.... With these notifications, you can help stop unauthorized charges on your credit card .... They are your powerful allies to help fight fraud."[33] "... helps protect you against credit fraud.... help protect you against identity theft ...."[34] "Our superior insight helps deliver outstanding results."[35] "See how technology partners like you are using the Microsoft Partner Program to help achieve greater success."[36]

It is easy to see why these uses of "help" are dishonest. In some, the qualified term ("lower," "increase," "protect," "fight," "exceptional grip," "flatter footprint," "outstanding results," "greater success") is already vague, and hence meaningless – because the improvement could be insignificant, as explained previously. In the others, the term is precise and forceful, but this merely renders the use of "help" even more absurd. Take "help maximize," for instance:

[25] McAfee Personal Firewall Plus, Staples buying guide, Sep.–Dec. 2004.
[26] Asus VW-224U widescreen monitor, http://www.tigerdirect.ca/.
[27] Dell Computers, adv.   [28] Becel pro.activ, adv. pamphlet.
[29] Traction T/A tires, http://www.bfgoodrichtires.ca/.
[30] Filtrete room air purifier, Canadian Tire brochure.
[31] Minwax Product Guide.   [32] Floppy disks, Office Place catalogue (1998).
[33] CIBC, adv. pamphlet.   [34] RBC, adv. pamphlet.
[35] http://www.scotiacapital.com/.   [36] Microsoft Canada, adv. pamphlet.

something is either maximized or not – this process cannot be qualified. Similarly, something is either minimized or not, is blocked or not, is doubled or not, is removed 99% or not, is sealed or not, is prevented or not, is stopped or not. It is illogical to qualify these processes, so the purpose of "help" is strictly to mislead.

We encounter "help" so frequently that it has become difficult to distinguish its *legitimate* uses; that is, limiting a claim that remains, nevertheless, important (as in, "Wearing your safety belt during a crash helps reduce your chance of hitting things inside the vehicle or being ejected from it."[37]). It is hardly necessary to point out the risks a society takes when it allows serious discourse to become indistinguishable from deceptive messages.

The way these disclaimers work is as follows: The disclaimer, or the phrase created by the combination of the familiar term and the disclaimer, describes a *new* concept, but this concept is never defined or explained. Because of its vagueness, the new concept is an entirely different entity from the familiar and exact processes. It constitutes a higher level of abstraction, since it subsumes *several* processes; so it can mean achieving anywhere from 100 to 0 percent of what is achieved by an exact process.

Thus, "controls your appetite" doesn't mean "reduces your appetite"; it is a new concept, which, being undefined, can mean anything – from reducing your appetite, to doing nothing, to increasing it; it is at a higher level than any one process, because it subsumes several. Similarly, "fights odours" doesn't mean "reduces odours"; it is a new and undefined concept, which subsumes such diverse concepts as fighting and defeating odours, and fighting but losing the battle against odours. And "helps you achieve your financial goals" doesn't mean "contributes significantly toward your financial goals"; it subsumes the full range of meanings, from contributing a great deal, to contributing nothing. So these disclaimers deceive us just like those we studied earlier: by tempting us to apply the knowledge and associations we hold for a familiar term to a new linguistic entity, which is at a higher level of abstraction.

But these examples are liberal, because, as we saw previously, the disclaimers are seldom applied directly to the claim. They are used on two or more levels, each term disclaiming in turn the phrase created by the previous ones: "fights odours," "helps fight odours," "formulated to help fight odours"; "controls your weight," "helps control your weight," "acts to help control your weight"; "improves performance," "helps improve performance," "engineered to help

---

[37] General Motors, *1997 Cadillac Owner's Manual.*

improve performance." Each level of disclaiming takes us to a higher level of abstraction, although in practice just one disclaimer creates a level high enough to render the original claim meaningless.

4

William Lutz, who has been exposing language abuse for many years, coined the term *doublespeak* for language that is intended to deceive while pretending to inform: "Doublespeak is language that pretends to communicate but really doesn't. It is language that makes the bad seem good, the negative appear positive, the unpleasant appear attractive or at least tolerable. Doublespeak is language that avoids or shifts responsibility, language that is at variance with its real or purported meaning. It is language that conceals or prevents thought; rather than extending thought, doublespeak limits it."[38] Lutz has collected an endless list of abuses from the language of politicians and government officials, the military, product labels, business communication, schools and universities, advertising and public relations, economics and investment, and medical services. He agrees that most language abuse involves new terms whose meaning is left undefined.

Above all, says Lutz, the responsible use of language is an obligation we all share, because linguistic communication is such an important aspect of society. So we must all fight to prevent language abuse. If we allow language to be turned from a means of communication into a means of domination, we are contributing, in effect, to the destruction of our values: "Language is not irrelevant to the foundations of an ordered society; it is essential. The irresponsible use of language leads to the destruction of the social, moral, and political structure that is our society, our culture, our nation. The irresponsible use of language corrupts the core of an ordered, just, moral society. Those who misuse language to mislead and deceive contribute to the destruction of the belief in the role of language in the life of the nation, and to the destruction of the nation.... We must fight to reassert the primacy of the responsible use of language by everyone, from individual citizen to political leader. We must fight to make the responsible use of language the norm, the requirement, for the conduct of public affairs."[39]

Here are some examples of the types of language abuses discussed by Lutz. When companies dismiss workers, they avoid terms like "laying off" and resort instead to doublespeak to mask the unpleasant reality.[40] Layoffs are described

---

[38] Lutz, *Doublespeak*, p. 1.   [39] Lutz, *New Doublespeak*, p. xi.
[40] The following examples are from Lutz's *Doublespeak* and *New Doublespeak*, passim.

as "workforce adjustments," "negative employee retention," "downsizing our personnel," correcting "imbalances of forces or skills," "reducing duplication," "involuntary severance," "skill-mix adjustment," "employee repositioning," or "vocational relocation." A company can "release surplus labor," initiate "a career alternative enhancement program," or engage in "a refocusing of the company's skills set." And the employees are not laid off, but become "redundant," "unassigned," "disemployed," "involuntarily leisured," "non-renewed," "surplussed," "displaced," are placed on "non-duty, non-pay status," are "involuntarily separated from the payroll," or are "selected" to participate in a "career transition program."

Politicians at all levels of government are careful to avoid the unpopular terms "tax" and "tax increase"; so they resort to doublespeak to increase taxes without appearing to do so.[41] A tax increase can be "user fees," "wage-based premium," "revenue enhancement," "receipts strengthening," "recapture of benefits," "replacement of revenues," or a way to "update the revenue mechanism." Additional doublespeak in the body of documents described as "tax reforms" or "tax simplifications" make these documents incomprehensible to the uninitiated, and serve in fact to conceal such ongoing policies as shifting the tax burden from corporations and wealthy individuals to the common citizen.

The doublespeak of the military, frequently used in their specifications and reports, is among the most sophisticated:[42] a nail is an "interfibrous friction fastener"; a hex nut is a "hexiform rotatable surface compression unit"; a hammer is a "multi-directional impact generator" or a "manually-powered fastener-driving impact device"; a pencil is a "portable, hand-held communications inscriber." Intentionally or not, the pedantic and overly detailed language used by the military ends up making everything appear more complicated than it really is, which helps to justify failures and exorbitant costs. For example, if you read that some equipment "suffered dramatically degraded useful operational life owing to the fact that a $2,000 hexiform rotatable surface compression unit underwent catastrophic stress-related shaft detachment," as one report stated, you will not react as you would if you read the simple truth; namely, that the equipment failed because a nut worth a few cents broke.

Deceptive language is useful not only to make an unimportant thing appear important or a simple thing appear complicated; it can be just as effective in creating the opposite effect. Deceivers try to make something important or complicated appear trivial when they want to belittle their responsibility or

---

[41] The following examples are from Lutz, *Doublespeak*, ch. VII.
[42] The following examples are from Lutz, *Doublespeak*, ch. VI.

liability for failures, or to underrate the costs or hazards associated with a project.[43] Thus, the death of patients in hospitals is called "negative patient care outcome," or "terminal living," or a "terminal episode"; and a medical error causing death is a "therapeutic misadventure" or a "diagnostic misadventure of a high magnitude." Similarly, the risks of nuclear power plants are discounted by officials through doublespeak like the following: An accident is an "event," an "unusual event," an "unscheduled event," an "incident," an "abnormal evolution," a "normal aberration," or a "plant transient"; and if an "abnormal occurrence" occurs too frequently, it becomes a "normally expected abnormal occurrence." Earthquakes, potentially disastrous for nuclear power plants, are merely "seismic events." A fire is an "incendiary event" or a "rapid oxidation." An explosion is an "energetic disassembly," an "energy release," or a "rapid release of energy." A meltdown is a "core disruptive accident."

In all these examples we recognize the same form of linguistic deception: raising the level of abstraction by using an existing term in a new sense and leaving the new sense undefined. The lack of definition endows the term with a number of interpretations, thereby turning it into a high-level element; and our familiarity with its old sense tempts us to interpret the term in the same way as before, although it is now an entirely different linguistic entity. Thus, we end up with a trivial structure, where an abstract element acts as starting element and also holds a certain meaning – the meaning the deceivers want us to accept. This structure has little value as a knowledge structure, because we cannot derive all the alternatives for its top element. Having started from a level that is too high, we are restricted in effect to one alternative – an alternative, moreover, that is very different from reality.

5

Although raising the level of abstraction is harmful, we must keep in mind that it is not the higher levels that must be blamed. Combining elements into increasingly high levels of abstraction is the most important feature of hierarchical structures, the source of their power and versatility. And knowledge structures, too, benefit from this feature: no real knowledge would be possible if all we did were to combine simple elements on one level.

The harm is done, thus, not by the high levels themselves, but when we commit the fallacy of abstraction: when we think that a high level is low enough to act as *starting* level. There is nothing wrong with high-level elements if we reached them on our own, starting from low levels; that is, if we formed

---

[43] The following examples are from Lutz, *Doublespeak*, passim.

them by combining elements, one level at a time. When doing so, we create in the mind a knowledge structure whose top element can have all possible values: the values derived from low-level elements, and from low-level interactions with other knowledge structures. When *starting* from a high level, however, we can no longer do this; what is left then is an impoverished knowledge structure – one where the top element can have only a small number of values, and perhaps none correct.

The deceivers construct their message in such a way that it appears to provide low-level elements while providing, in fact, only high-level ones. Thus, the reason we cannot create an adequate knowledge structure is that there is no real knowledge in their message: the message contains vague terms – terms that can have several meanings.

This analysis also shows us how to *fight* this type of deception: by re-creating the full structure. First, we must recognize that the terms are high-level elements. Then, instead of using them and their mistaken interpretation as starting elements, we must seek the *actual* low levels. One way to do this is by investigating all possible interpretations, which may require the study of additional sources of knowledge. What we would be doing, essentially, is simulating the process whereby we develop that knowledge through personal experience, rather than acquiring it from linguistic messages. When developing knowledge through personal experience we start with low-level elements, so we end up with *complete* knowledge structures – structures that include *all* the alternatives. Only linguistic messages can lure us with impoverished knowledge, because only with language can the deceivers invent high-level elements that look like low-level ones. Clearly, if we managed to create in our mind the same knowledge structure that we would have created had we been directly exposed to the events leading to that knowledge, no deception would be possible. Being already familiar with all the alternatives, we would easily recognize the falseness of the alternative that we are asked to accept.

The Slogan "Technology"

1

I mentioned in the previous section the use of slogans to deceive and to prevent thought. Slogans are expressions representing high levels of abstraction but used in a way that tempts us to perceive them as *low-level* linguistic entities. To illustrate the power of slogans to shape knowledge, and hence the power that an elite can attain through language, let us analyze what may well be the greatest slogan of all time – the term "technology."

Everyone agrees that technology has acquired in our culture the kind of prestige and aura formerly held only by such notions as God. It will be interesting, therefore, to see how much of its authority is due in fact to something as simple as linguistic manipulation. We will find that, as in all forms of sloganeering, the purpose of the term "technology" is to raise the level of abstraction of a phrase; specifically, to alter its meaning so that the *high-level* elements of a knowledge structure become *starting* elements. Ultimately, its purpose is to prevent us from judging critically a particular matter by forcing us to think instead of a much broader subject.

❖

"Technology" is an abstract term denoting the body of concepts, means, and methods employed in the pursuit of some practical goals. In its most general sense, it refers to the totality of knowledge and techniques used by a society to satisfy its material needs. In a more restricted sense, it refers to the application of a body of knowledge and methods in a specific domain: information technology, automotive technology, communications technology, mining technology, space technology, metal-processing technology, prosthesis technology, etc. In its narrowest sense, "technology" can refer to a particular set of concepts and procedures *within* a field: digital technology within the field of communications, cold-forging technology within the field of metal processing, etc.

Like all abstract terms, then, "technology" plays an important linguistic role by subsuming a number of ideas. If the meaning of these ideas is understood, the ability of the word to represent high levels of abstraction helps us to think about or discuss complex matters.

The abundance of the term "technology" in contemporary discourse reflects, undoubtedly, the growing number of occasions when we encounter the application of one technology or another. Much of this abundance, however, springs from a phenomenon that is best described as an *inflation* in the use of this term: "technology" is used to describe narrower and narrower areas. Instead of defining a significant range of activities, or an important body of concepts and methods, the term is increasingly applied to specific situations.

Thus, "we have the technology" to do something may simply mean having a certain device; "we are using an older technology" may mean using an older device; "we are upgrading the technology" may mean buying a new device; "a technology company" may mean an electronics company; "developing new technologies" may mean writing some new software; "using a different technology" may mean using different software; "a technology career" may mean an involvement with software; "a technology investment" may mean purchasing a computer; "its technologies" may mean a company's products, or services, or capabilities; and so on.

Here are some actual examples of this style: "Adobe InDesign includes technology for exporting files directly to Adobe Portable Document Format."[1] "Can be used as the ideal technology for backup or storage."[2] "The intelligent technology in our electrical calculation software …."[3] "Canada's banks [and other organizations] expect to have their technology fully prepared."[4] "Five bottom-line technologies."[5] "Older engines can benefit from using Slick 50 Plus, fortified by unique technology …."[6] "Many [mid-sized firms] apply technology to virtually every part of their business."[7] "Our books are a simple way to learn from the experts about the latest technologies from Intel."[8] "Governments can get into [trouble] when they rush to embrace technology they don't really understand…. [One province] so far has spent $185-million developing new technologies under the flag of the Health Canada Infoway…. The objective is to create a national network of electronic medical records and other, related technology…. Without the in-house expertise to develop new technology, the provinces have relied upon contractors …. 'My biggest concern has always been technology investments.' … 'This is highly sophisticated technology.'"[9]

Just as common is the use of "technology" to describe individual notions or products. The following expressions, taken from the thousands encountered in brochures, periodicals, catalogues, and websites, demonstrate this practice: desktop technology, RISC technology, relational technology, C++ technology, CASE technology, Windows technology, point and click technology, plug and play technology, call center technology, client/server technology, data warehouse technology, object technology, document management technology, cloud technology, ebook technology, text-to-speech technology, web-to-host technology, dual monitor technology, 90 nanometer technology, optical image stabilization technology, perpendicular recording technology, retina display technology, 2.4 GHz technology, V.90 technology, IntelliSense technology, Complete-Compare technology, ColorSmart technology, Q-Fan2 technology, CrossFire technology, WhisperDrive technology, iTips technology, Senseye

[1] Adobe Systems, *Adobe InDesign 2.0 User Guide*, p. 375.

[2] http://www.ahinc.com/.   [3] http://solutionselectricalsoftware.com/.

[4] Government of Canada, year 2000 preparedness, adv.

[5] Article title, *Momentum: The Microsoft Magazine for Midsize Business* (Oct. 2005).

[6] Slick 50 Plus engine treatment for older engines, package text.

[7] "Firms See Link Between Innovation and Technology," *Computing Canada* (Oct. 6, 2006), p. 20.   [8] http://noggin.intel.com/.

[9] "Technology in health care: big trouble when mishandled," http://www.globeandmail.com/ (Oct. 9, 2009).

imaging technology, AMD64 technology, Data Lifeguard technology, cPVA technology, Flash Scan technology, ClearType technology.

Anyone, thus, can take a device, or a method, or a feature, and confidently call it a technology. A sentence will always appear more authoritative if it includes the word "technology," and as everyone is trying to take advantage of its mystique, we encounter this word now in almost any context. So we see "technology" in expressions where it is obviously spurious – expressions where we were content previously with such terms as "system," "feature," "method," "technique," "procedure," or "process"; or, we see it in expressions where neither "technology" nor any other term is necessary, as the thing being described can stand alone, on the strength of its own meaning.

2

To confirm this inflation, let us analyze the phrase "MMX technology," coined by Intel Corporation in 1997 for a new feature of its Pentium processor. Intel is best known as the maker of the processors used in IBM-compatible personal computers. And, continually since 1979, Intel has been introducing new versions of these processors, each time adding new features. The feature called MMX (multimedia extension) includes special data types and instructions, and its purpose is to improve the performance of applications that require intensive computations with graphics or sound data. These computations often involve the repeated execution of one simple operation with several simple operands. The new instructions take advantage of this fact and speed up the computations by executing several operations in parallel; for example, they add at the same time four related values to four others.

Now, Intel had introduced many enhancements before MMX; and, if compared with those enhancements, the novelty, complexity, or scope of MMX, or its impact on the application's performance, can be described as average. So why did Intel decide to call MMX a technology, while the previous enhancements – many of which were broader and more significant – were simply called features, or improvements? The most likely answer is that Intel succumbed to the "technology" inflation.

This can be demonstrated by comparing MMX with another enhancement: the numeric processing feature, which greatly speeds up mathematical operations. This feature had been available since the earliest processors as a separate device, called NPX (numeric processor extension). And, starting with the i486 processor in 1989, the feature became the FPU (floating-point unit), an internal and faster element. But, even though the FPU and the NPX were much more complex than MMX, and much more important, Intel never referred to them as "FPU technology" or "NPX technology." More than that, MMX uses the FPU registers, and the MMX instructions can even be seen as nothing but an enhancement of the FPU.

We are witnessing, thus, an absurd situation: while the FPU (with its great impact on *many* types of applications, including multimedia, and with a broader scope and complexity) is merely a *feature*, MMX (intended *mainly* for multimedia applications, and logically just part of the FPU) is a *technology*. The term "technology" – a high level of abstraction, which must describe a whole domain – is applied here to an entity that is, however we look at it, at a *lower* level than a level that is *too low* to be called a technology.

This absurdity reflects the effect of the "technology" inflation over a period of ten years. As a result, some of Intel's technical manuals started to look quite silly: while dozens of important and impressive features of the Pentium processor were mentioned simply by their names or acronyms, MMX was regularly followed by "technology." (Example: "The MMX technology intrinsics are based on a new _m64 data type to represent the specific contents of an MMX technology register."[10] Twice in one sentence, "MMX" is used adjectivally to modify the noun "technology," and then the whole phrase, "MMX technology," is used adjectivally to modify another noun. To comprehend this sentence, we must read it by omitting the word "technology.") But Intel did not call MMX a technology just to use this expression in its manuals. Now it could coin the famous slogan "with MMX technology," which was displayed everywhere the latest Pentium processors were mentioned. And this slogan was taken over by every computer maker that used these processors, and by every dealer that sold the computers, and was repeated ad nauseam in advertising and sales literature.

The phrase "MMX technology" also exemplifies what is the most common method of presenting something – a particular concept, or process, or feature – as a technology: instead of simply allowing an appropriate term to describe that thing, the sloganeers construct an expression out of that term and the word "technology." Since we perceive "technology" as a whole domain, this usage makes a specific thing appear bigger and more important than it actually is. Thus, the expression "with MMX technology" means exactly the same thing as does "with MMX," but it tempts us to perceive MMX as a broader, and hence more important, notion.

The inflation is also demonstrated by the fact that, while in the *many years* preceding MMX it is hard to find a *single* use of "technology" with these

---

[10] Intel Corporation, *IA-32 Intel Architecture Software Developer's Manual*, vol. 2, *Instruction Set Reference* (2001), p. 3-9. (The "intrinsics" are C language extensions that provide access to the MMX features.)

processors and the related innovations, Intel has resorted to this practice *many times* in the *few years* since. Some examples:[11] Hyper-Threading technology, vPro technology, Viiv technology, Centrino mobile technology, Memory Pipeline technology, Extended Memory 64 technology, Flex Memory technology, Matrix Storage technology, Virtualization technology, Quiet System technology, Active Management technology, I/O Acceleration technology, Performance Acceleration technology, Clear Video technology, GMA 900 graphics technology, Zone Rendering technology, LaGrande technology, SpeedStep technology, Trusted Execution technology, QuickData technology.

3

Let us see now how the deception is achieved. Grammatically, the term describing the concept, or process, or feature is demoted to the role of qualifier: it becomes an adjectival element modifying the noun "technology." Since what is being described is fully defined by the original term, "technology" is always superfluous. But this word has become such a familiar and striking slogan that it is invariably *it* that claims our attention. Thus, from an unnecessary element, this usage turns "technology" into the most important part of the expression.

Logically, the altered phrase deceives us by forcing our thoughts to a higher level of abstraction. Instead of allowing us to create a rich knowledge structure in the mind, starting with low-level elements, the expression shifts the emphasis to a high-level element – "technology." Instead of thinking of the term describing the particular concept, process, or feature, and all the facts associated with it, we are tempted to use the abstract term "technology" (which suggests a whole domain) as the *starting* element of the new knowledge structure. Being forced to create in the mind an impoverished structure, we are prevented from gaining any real knowledge. The expression appears to describe something important, when in fact it is just a slogan.

It is senseless to use "technology" when referring to a *specific* thing, and yet this usage is now widespread. The term "technology," when qualified by the name of a thing, defines a body of principles or techniques that is reflected *entirely* in that thing; so it defines a technology that is, essentially, that thing alone. But then, if one thing can be a technology, why not everything else? If one specific concept, process, or feature is a technology, why not *every* concept, process, and feature? We reach the absurd conclusion that there are as many technologies as there are concepts, processes, features, methods, techniques, procedures, systems, and so forth. Clearly, if we agree to call *specific* things

[11] Terms used on http://www.intel.com/ (Dec. 2006).

"technology," the term cannot also retain its *abstract* sense; that is, a body of concepts, means, and methods that defines a whole domain, and hence subsumes *many* things. We are deceived precisely because we continue to perceive "technology" as a global term, referring to a large body of things, even as we see it applied to only one thing.

Let us analyze some of these expressions. "Java technology"[12] refers presumably to everything that is related to the Java programming language – definitions, principles, methods, and so forth. But simply "Java" or "Java language" would suggest exactly the same thing. There does not exist a body of principles or techniques that are part of the technology of Java, but are not also part of what is encompassed by the programming language Java. The very existence of this language implies the definitions, principles, methods, etc., related to it; in other words, what I have just listed as its technology. The language Java and a technology called Java must be one and the same thing.

But "technology" is used for even narrower areas. For example, "Oracle relational technology"[13] refers to the particular implementation of relational database principles found in the system called Oracle. The technology of the Oracle relational database system subsumes, presumably, all the principles, methods, software, etc., related to this system. But the phrase "Oracle relational system" describes the same thing, since it implies the principles, methods, software, etc., related to this system. There cannot exist two different domains – the Oracle relational system, and the Oracle relational technology; one is the same as the other.

A printer is said to incorporate "straight paper path technology"[14] – a feature of the paper-feeding mechanism. This technology subsumes, presumably, all the issues related to a straight paper path. But the fact that the printer has a straight paper path already implies all the issues related to a straight paper path. So, when saying that the printer incorporates straight paper path technology, we cannot mean more than what we mean when simply saying that it has a straight paper path. The domain known as straight paper path technology is the same as the domain of the issues related to a straight paper path.

The same argument could be repeated for the other expressions. Thus, desktop technology is the same as desktop computers, 2.4 GHz technology is the same as 2.4 GHz telephones, WhisperDrive technology is the same as the WhisperDrive feature, data warehouse technology is the same as data warehouse software, 90 nanometer technology is the same as the 90 nanometer process, and so on.

[12] For example, Sun Microsystems training course, adv. pamphlet.
[13] For example, "Oracle object technology is a layer of abstraction built on Oracle relational technology," *Oracle Database Application Developer's Guide*, http://www.download.oracle.com/.   [14] Brother HL-660 laser printer, package text.

❖

An indication of the trend to use "technology" to denote almost anything is the frequent use of the plural, "technologies." Logically, it is senseless to use the plural: since "technology" already means an indefinite number of principles, methods, etc., employed in a particular pursuit, the plural can add nothing. And indeed, in the past the plural was used only in the rare situations where several domains of technology had to be mentioned together (as in, "use of capital cost allowance ... to allow companies to write down equipment used in information, energy, and environmental technologies"[15]). But now that "technology" is used for small and specific things, we encounter its plural very frequently, as a pompous substitute for "systems," "methods," "techniques," "processes," "concepts," or "features."

Some examples: "The MSDN Library is an essential resource for developers using Microsoft tools, products, and technologies."[16] "On this page you can browse technologies currently available on Adobe Labs.... You can find technologies that may interest you by reviewing related technologies."[17] "Small to medium-sized suppliers [will not require] an expensive investment in traditional EDI technologies."[18] "Discover solutions that leverage the newest cyber-security techniques and technologies."[19] "HR suite of tips, tactics and technologies to attract, retain and train skilled workers."[20] "A new generation of methods and technologies has arrived."[21] "Now includes Service Pack 2 with advanced security technologies."[22] "Businesses can take advantage of Internet technologies without sacrificing performance or security."[23] "A guide to the technologies frequently used in Web-enabled teaching and learning activities."[24] "An overview of some different computer cooling technologies."[25] "See the latest technologies."[26]

As part of the inflation, we note also the large number of companies whose *name* includes "technology," or "technologies." There are probably thousands of such companies, with names varying from the simple XYZ Technology Ltd. to wordy ones like Exquisys Software Technology Ltd., Photo Violation Technologies Corp., and Critical Outcome Technologies Inc. In reality, "technology"

---

[15] "The $10-billion plan to help manufacturing compete globally," http://www.globeand mail.com/ (Feb. 6, 2007).   [16] http://msdn.microsoft.com/.
[17] http://labs.adobe.com/.   [18] https://delphi.portal.covisint.com/.
[19] Infosecurity Canada conference and exhibition (2003), adv. pamphlet.
[20] CATA conference (1999), adv. pamphlet.
[21] Database and Client/Server World conference (1997), adv. pamphlet.
[22] Microsoft Windows XP upgrade CD, package text.
[23] "Surviving the Unexpected," *Computing Canada* (Nov. 3, 2006), p. 10.
[24] http://www.umuc.edu/.   [25] http://www.windowsnetworking.com/.
[26] Solution City exhibition (2006), adv. pamphlet.

hardly ever serves to identify the type of business. Its purpose is to mislead us, by forcing us to associate a specific product or service with a universal and glamorous concept.

And it is not just in advertising and propaganda that we find this style; more and more *individuals* are now using it, in order to enhance their own discourse. Since calling things "technology" imparts a tone of authority to any statement, people everywhere have learned to take advantage of this inflation. Thus, when mentioning a particular product or concept, if we refer to it as a technology we can more effectively impress our listeners. In addition, we can delude ourselves that what we are saying is more important than it actually is.

Also, while this slogan is found mostly in the area vaguely known as high technology, we increasingly see it everywhere. Some examples: People watching instant replay in a tennis event on television "had access to replay technology."[27] To reduce referee mistakes, soccer officials are discussing "the possibility of using goal-line technology."[28] A type of motor oil uses "SuperSyn technology."[29] A ball pen refill "contains advanced ink technology."[30] A scrub sponge uses "unique antimicrobial Stayfresh technology."[31] An air conditioner uses "dripless technology."[32] A fitness device "has air power technology to help you work out."[33] Some winter tires use "Microbit technology, which incorporates thousands of crushed walnut shells into the tread compound."[34] An adjustable wrench uses "gripping technology far superior to standard wrenches."[35] Some windshield wiper blades use "flex shell technology," while others use "special water repellent technology."[36] Some vacuum cleaners use "WindTunnel technology," while others use "Root Cyclone technology."[37] An office paper punch uses "One-Touch technology."[38] A cooking device uses "Vapor technology."[39] A kettle uses "quiet boil technology."[40] A clothes dryer uses "a new vacuum technology."[41]

[27] "Instant replay makes U.S. Open debut," http://www.globeandmail.com/ (July 18, 2006).
[28] "Blatter rules out video replay, but FIFA will discuss new goal technology," http://www.globeandmail.com/ (June 29, 2010).
[29] Mobil synthetic motor oil, package text.
[30] Parker ball pen refill, package text.
[31] 3M Scotch-Brite all-purpose scrub sponge, package text.
[32] Noma air conditioner, Canadian Tire brochure.
[33] AirClimber fitness device, https://www.airclimbertrial.com/.
[34] http://www.toyotires.ca/.
[35] HK1 adjustable wrench, Canadian Tire brochure.
[36] Reflex, Hybrid and WetTec wiper blades, Canadian Tire brochure.
[37] http://hoover.com/, http://www.dyson.com/.
[38] Staples high-capacity 3-hole punch, package text.
[39] http://www.360cookware.com/.
[40] KE9200S kettle, http://www.sunbeam.com.au/.
[41] DryMate clothes dryer, http://www.yankodesign.com/.

❖

To summarize, when applied to a particular thing, "technology" adds nothing to the meaning of the words describing that thing. A specific term – "process," "method," "system," "feature," etc. – would function equally well; or simply the *name* of that thing would suffice to describe it. Thus, when applied to a particular thing, "technology" is strictly a slogan. Its purpose is to deceive us, to make us perceive an ordinary thing as an important notion – important enough to name a whole domain of technology after it.

Calling things "technology" forces our thoughts to a higher level of abstraction: instead of examining the *details* of a given issue, we are restricted to a broad and vague concept – technology. Also, without the lower levels we cannot link that issue to our previous knowledge, so it remains isolated: it does not enhance our minds the way it would if we faced it through personal experience. Finally, because technology in general is a good thing, we are compelled to perceive anything called "technology" positively. In other words, deprived of the normal means of evaluating a new idea, we end up simply accepting it.

Thus, like all slogans, "technology" impoverishes knowledge by restricting us to mechanistic thinking. When we agree to treat a high-level concept like technology as the *starting* element of a knowledge structure, we are committing the fallacy of abstraction; and when we fail to link this knowledge structure with others, we are committing the fallacy of reification. The new knowledge is impoverished because we are left with only a small fraction of the possible combinations of elements. Our minds have the capacity for complex knowledge structures: we *can* start from low levels, and we *can* link structures. So the purpose of slogans is to neutralize this quality, in order to prevent us from developing in our minds all possible alternatives.

Another fact worth noting is how the guardians of the English language are reacting to the spread of "technology" sloganeering. Some dictionaries, in their entry for the word "technology," have recently added a definition for its incorrect use (i.e., in specific instances), while listing also its traditional definition (i.e., a global term). Now, it is true that dictionaries must reflect the current use of a language, even if incorrect; so, if the use of "technology" to describe specific things is now prevalent, it must indeed be included. But dictionaries are also educational. This is why certain entries have a qualifier like *archaic*, *slang*, or *substandard*. Similarly, then, the use of "technology" to denote specific things ought to be described as *propagandistic*. By leaving the new definition unqualified, the dictionaries legitimize, in effect, the misuse of this word. "Technology" cannot function as both a global and a specific term, so it is absurd to list both definitions without an explanation.

4

In "technology" sloganeering, the phrase we encounter most frequently is "information technology," or "IT." This phrase and its acronym are so widespread, in fact, that they have acquired a reputation of their own. They deserve, therefore, a special analysis.

Information technology is the large domain encompassing computers, software, and related systems; so the phrase itself represents a valid application of the term "technology." What is wrong, rather, is the *way* in which the phrase is used. It ought to be used only when discussing the *whole* domain, which is what "information technology" stands for. Instead, we encounter it in reference to narrow and specific aspects of this domain – individual computers, programs, people, tasks, etc. The absurdity of this practice is masked by the fact that it is the acronym, "IT," rather than the whole phrase, "information technology," that is most often used: IT management, IT department, IT consultant, IT professional, IT staff, IT infrastructure, IT budget, IT job, IT training, IT career, IT problem, IT equipment, IT project, IT spending, IT investment, IT planning, IT initiative, etc.

The key term in this domain is, obviously, "information." So it is this term alone that ought to be used as qualifier: information worker, information project, information equipment, and so forth. The phrase "information technology" is then merely a particular use of the term, needed when we must describe the whole domain. What the propaganda has achieved, thus, is to substitute this global sense for the original qualifier. And as a result, the whole domain of information technology is invoked every time we discuss a computer, a piece of software, a person, a project, or any other detail from this domain. This forces our thoughts to a higher level of abstraction: we may be discussing small and concrete entities, but we are thinking in fact of a large and abstract concept – the whole domain of information technology. So we end up perceiving ordinary things as more important than they actually are.

We accept expressions like "IT manager," "IT department," and "IT budget," for instance, only because we saw them repeated a thousand times in the past. To recognize their absurdity, all we have to do is expand the acronym. Thus, while "IT manager" sounds important, "information technology manager" sounds silly: how can a person manage the universal, abstract concept of information technology? Similarly, "IT department" sounds important, but what is an "information technology department"? How can something be a department of an abstract concept? "IT budget," too, sounds important; but what is an "information technology budget"? How can a company have a budget for the abstract concept of information technology? The proper description, again, is "information manager," "information department," and "information budget." It is absurd to use the whole domain as qualifier.

The same is true of any other expression: Does an IT project encompass the whole domain of information technology? Does an IT course teach the abstract concept of information technology? Is an IT career a career in a philosophical, abstract subject?

Thus, while appearing to be just an abbreviation, "IT" serves to control minds. As acronyms always do, it raises the level of abstraction of an expression, thereby preventing us from interpreting it correctly. Even the whole phrase, "information technology," forces our thoughts to a level that is too high – because it invokes the whole domain when discussing, in fact, specific things; but the acronym takes us to an even higher level. Although "information technology" is used incorrectly, we still see the words – so we can reflect on their meaning and recognize the mistake, as we did a moment ago; with "IT," on the other hand, this is no longer possible.

By eliminating the words, and hence the lower levels, acronyms numb the mind. They stand for certain ideas, but they prevent us from linking these ideas to our previous knowledge. Ideas are high levels of abstraction, and we discover their meaning when we understand the meaning of the words at the lower levels. By eliminating the words, acronyms obstruct this process. They turn whole ideas into simple, starting elements. These elements, moreover, come with a ready-made, predefined meaning, which we must accept.

The meaning we accept for IT is "strategic business advantage," "critical success factor in a changing economy," "powerful tool in today's competitive environment," etc. But we did not discover this meaning on our own, by combining bits of previous knowledge. We acquired it ready-made, through messages encountered in publications, lectures, and advertising. Instead of treating it as the top element of a particular knowledge structure, we use the acronym "IT" as a *starting* element in *new* knowledge structures. In reality, the domain of information technology is not a phenomenon *within* the other phenomena that make up our existence; it *interacts* with them. Now, however, we perceive it as a building block of those phenomena. So, if the notion of IT is distorted, we will perceive everything associated with it – IT budget, IT department, IT consultant, IT project, IT investment – as more important than it actually is.

❖

We saw that "information technology" and "IT" are used mostly for propaganda. Logically, they should be used only on the rare occasions when the whole domain of information technology is discussed; instead, we find them in reference to small and specific things. But we can also demonstrate the propagandistic nature of this practice in a different way: by comparing the phrase and the acronym with their counterparts in other technologies.

Automotive technology is the domain of activities related to the design and manufacture of vehicles. But we rarely see the phrase "automotive technology," simply because we rarely need to refer to the whole domain. And we hardly ever see the acronym, "AT"; after all, if the phrase itself is rarely used, there is no need to abbreviate it. The key term in this domain is "automotive." And indeed, this word alone is used as qualifier when referring to specific aspects of the domain: "automotive company," "automotive worker," "automotive industry," "automotive research," "automotive career," and so on. We don't see expressions like "automotive technology company" or "automotive technology worker"; nor do we see "AT company" or "AT worker." To duplicate the usage current in information technology, we would have to refer to our cars as "AT equipment," to car mechanics as "AT specialists," and to a car purchase as "AT investment."

Let us take a specific example. The label of an AC/DC adapter designed to charge the battery of laptop or notebook computers includes this note: "For use with Information Technology Equipment."[42] The closest equivalent in the automotive field would be a car battery charger carrying the note, "For use with Automotive Technology Equipment." If we ever came across such a charger in a store, we would find the note (and the capitals) ludicrous. In fact, we would probably fail to understand the note, and we would have to ask the salesperson whether the charger worked with a car battery. The note for the computer adapter is, in reality, just as ludicrous; yet we find it perfectly logical. This shows how successful has the "information technology" propaganda been.

Let us examine another area. Space technology is the domain of activities related to the exploration of outer space. The key term now is "space," and this word alone is used as qualifier: "space program," "space research," "space vehicle," and so on. And, although we do encounter the phrase "space technology" more often than we should (as a result of the general "technology" inflation), it is still used mostly to describe the whole domain. It is hard to find expressions like "space technology budget" or "space technology manager." As for "ST," if used at all, it is as a legitimate abbreviation when discussing the whole domain – not in phrases like "ST program" or "ST research." We don't refer to satellites as "ST equipment," nor to astronauts as "ST professionals."

Lastly, medical technology is the domain of activities involving the application of science and engineering in health-related matters. As we would expect,

[42] Delta Electronics adapter ADP-30JH B.

"medical technology" is used only for the whole domain, and we hardly ever see the acronym, "MT." The word "medical" alone is used as qualifier: "medical research," "medical equipment," "medical personnel," and so on. We don't refer to a particular X-ray machine as "MT equipment," nor to technicians as "MT workers," nor to a medical laboratory as an "MT company."

The same arguments could be repeated for any other field: environmental technology, mining technology, farming technology, maritime technology, etc. Only in information technology, then, is language manipulation so widespread. And the explanation is simple: In the other fields we get more or less what we expect, relative to what we invest in them. In our computer-related activities, on the other hand, the inefficiency is so high that the elites must constantly *fool* us into accepting their ideas. This is especially true of software ideas. If we were to judge the importance of their activities objectively, we would find that less than 10 percent of what the software bureaucrats are doing has any value. In fact, the only evidence we have for the effectiveness of software theories, methodologies, tools, and applications is found in "success stories" and "case studies." (As we learned in "Popper's Principles of Demarcation" in chapter 3, the very fact that we are asked to rely on this type of evidence proves that the ideas are pseudoscientific.) Thus, since the software novelties rarely work as claimed, the use of deception is an important factor in their promotion. And the manipulation of language is part of this deception: by encouraging us to misuse the abstract terms "information technology" and "IT," the elites prevent us from noticing the details; without details we cannot tell the difference between useful and useless, or between good and bad, so our computer-related activities appear more important and more successful than they actually are.

Orwell's Newspeak

1

George Orwell was no scholar, but his last work, *Nineteen Eighty-Four*, with its analysis of mind control through language, remains to this day one of the most important studies of totalitarianism. Because it is written largely in the form of a novel, it is often misinterpreted as a dystopian tale, or as a prophetic fantasy. Only when we ignore the irrelevant details can we appreciate its depth and accuracy, and its value as a model of totalitarian systems.

As journalist and essayist, Orwell displayed greater insight into social and political matters, and into the function of language in society, than most philosophers and linguists. And when we study his earlier writings, we recognize that *Nineteen Eighty-Four* is a synthesis of ideas which had preoccupied him for many years.[1] Totalitarian oppression, he pointed out, is found not only in political movements like Nazism or Communism, but in any social system where dogmas replace rational thinking. Thus, he believed that even the democratic countries are drifting toward one form of totalitarianism or another.

We will explore the significance of Orwell's model later, when we study software totalitarianism (in chapter 8). Here we are concerned mainly with his analysis of language manipulation, which complements our discussion in the previous sections. The way language is used to control minds in his hypothetical society can be recognized as an exaggerated, satirical form of the deception and exploitation found in our own society. So we should perhaps stop to consider whether our relatively mild language manipulation, along with our business-driven culture of mind control, is in fact not a *final* level of degradation, but only a stage in our continuous progression toward totalitarianism that Orwell feared.

In Orwell's Oceania, in 1984, Newspeak was the official language. It was in the process of replacing English, but this was a slow change, since it is difficult to make people forget a language they already know. Although derived from English, Newspeak was a thoroughly modified and simplified language. Its main purpose was to enforce conformity to Ingsoc, the current totalitarian ideology. It was expected that Newspeak would finally supersede English by about 2050.

"The purpose of Newspeak," Orwell explains, "was not only to provide a medium of expression for the world-view and mental habits proper to the devotees of Ingsoc, but to make all other modes of thought impossible. It was intended that when Newspeak had been adopted once and for all and Oldspeak [English] forgotten, a heretical thought – that is, a thought diverging from the principles of Ingsoc – should be literally unthinkable, at least so far as thought is dependent on words. Its vocabulary was so constructed as to give exact and often very subtle expression to every meaning that a Party member could properly wish to express, while excluding all other meanings and also the possibility of arriving at them by indirect methods. This was done partly by the

---

[1] See, for example, these three essays: "Literature and Totalitarianism," in *The Collected Essays, Journalism and Letters of George Orwell*, vol. 2, eds. Sonia Orwell and Ian Angus (London: Penguin Books, 1970); "The Prevention of Literature," in *Collected Essays*, vol. 4; "Politics and the English Language," in *Collected Essays*, vol. 4. We will examine these writings in "Orwell's Model of Totalitarianism" in chapter 8.

invention of new words, but chiefly by eliminating undesirable words and by stripping such words as remained of unorthodox meanings, and so far as possible of all secondary meanings whatever."[2]

The last sentence in the foregoing quotation summarizes the methods whereby, in Orwell's view, language can be employed to control minds: inventing new words, and eliminating words or word meanings. These methods, unsurprisingly, parallel the methods of language manipulation practised by our own charlatans. As we saw earlier, the aim of language manipulation is to impoverish thought through abstraction and reification: people are prevented from discovering the details associated with a certain message, and from connecting this message to previous knowledge structures. Since the designers of Newspeak had greater power, it is even easier to recognize the efficacy of these methods in Newspeak. In particular, they were not only *adding* new words and meanings, but also *eliminating* words and meanings.

2

Let us see first how Newspeak forced people to reify knowledge structures. The chief means was the elimination of words: "Quite apart from the suppression of definitely heretical words, reduction of vocabulary was regarded as an end in itself.... Newspeak was designed not to extend but to *diminish* the range of thought, and this purpose was indirectly assisted by cutting the choice of words down to a minimum."[3] Eliminating words restricts thought by preventing people from developing and expressing certain ideas altogether, or by altering their intended meaning, as people are forced to express those ideas through the remaining words: "Newspeak, indeed, differed from almost all other languages in that its vocabulary grew smaller instead of larger every year. Each reduction was a gain, since the smaller the area of choice, the smaller the temptation to take thought."[4] In the end, thought becomes both unnecessary and impossible, having been replaced with the simpler act of selecting from a small vocabulary the words and phrases appropriate for the occasion. Putting together sentences and ideas is then reduced to a mechanical and predictable process, determined largely by the language itself.

More subtle than the elimination of words is the elimination of meanings; that is, the restriction of words to one rigid meaning. For example, "the word *free* still existed in Newspeak, but it could only be used in such statements as 'This dog is free from lice' or 'This field is free from weeds.' It could not be used

---

[2] George Orwell, *Nineteen Eighty-Four* (London: Penguin Books, 1983), pp. 257–258.
[3] Ibid., p. 258.   [4] Ibid., p. 265.

in its old sense of 'politically free' or 'intellectually free,' since political and intellectual freedom no longer existed even as concepts, and were therefore of necessity nameless."[5]

Recall our discussion in "Mechanistic Communication." A linguistic structure – a story, for instance – consists of many interacting knowledge structures. We recognize these structures as the various *aspects* of the story. The words that make up the story provide the links between these structures. And it is by combining these structures in the mind, and by combining them also with other knowledge structures present in the mind, that we create the new, complex structure needed to understand the story.

Words can function as links between structures because they hold for us many meanings – meanings we assimilated in the past by encountering the words in diverse contexts. Thus, words can have many meanings because the things they represent can have many attributes. Each attribute gives rise to a different structure by relating the things which possess that attribute, and hence the words representing these things, in a particular way. Just like the things themselves, then, the words belong to several structures at the same time (one structure for each attribute), thereby causing these structures to interact.

The important point is that it is largely through these diverse meanings that complex knowledge structures are possible, because only when words act as links between structures can we combine simple structures into complex ones. So, by restricting each word to one meaning, the designers of Newspeak try to prevent the formation of complex knowledge structures. As Syme, the Newspeak expert, explains to Smith: "Don't you see that the whole aim of Newspeak is to narrow the range of thought?... Every concept that can ever be needed will be expressed by exactly *one* word, with its meaning rigidly defined and all its subsidiary meanings rubbed out and forgotten."[6]

To deceive us, the present-day charlatans must *tempt* us, by means of cleverly constructed sentences, to reify their linguistic messages; that is, to treat them as independent structures. With Newspeak, by eliminating words and meanings, the language itself performs this task: the linguistic structures give rise to simple, isolated knowledge structures, which the mind cannot easily connect with other structures. This is the kind of knowledge that machines can also hold, so human intelligence is restricted to the level of machines.

---

[5] Ibid., p. 258.   [6] Ibid., p. 49.

3

Let us see now how Newspeak raised the level of abstraction. Recall what is the fallacy of abstraction: impoverishing language structures by treating high-level linguistic entities as *starting* elements. But abstraction, as we know, also causes reification: when losing the low-level language elements we also lose the low-level links between language structures, and between language structures and other knowledge structures. In the end, not just language but all knowledge is impoverished.

In Newspeak, as in the present-day languages, a number of methods were employed to raise the level of abstraction. One method was to invent new words, meant to express only abstract concepts: "The special function of certain Newspeak words ... was not so much to express meanings as to destroy them. These words, necessarily few in number, had had their meanings extended until they contained within themselves whole batteries of words which, as they were sufficiently covered by a single comprehensive term, could now be scrapped and forgotten."[7] Since the new words subsumed many different terms, they covered a wide range of meanings; they functioned, therefore, as high levels of abstraction. They rendered the low-level terms meaningless by erasing the differences between them: "A few blanket words covered them, and, in covering them, abolished them."[8] No real knowledge is possible when the starting elements of the knowledge structures are abstract concepts.

In Newspeak this method was used mostly for words related to political matters: "words, that is to say, which not only had in every case a political implication, but were intended to impose a desirable mental attitude upon the person using them."[9] The new terms were always compound words, abbreviations formed from the syllables of two or three words: "Thinkpol" for Thought Police, "Minitrue" for Ministry of Truth, "goodthink" for politically correct views, etc.

In the present-day languages we don't limit this practice to political terms, but extend it to any domain where language can be used to control minds. Our languages are not as advanced as Newspeak, though, so we must create new terms by combining two or three *entire* words. In the domain of software, for instance, we have replaced countless notions and particulars with a few blanket terms – "information technology," "software engineering," "object-oriented," "client/server," etc. On the other hand, we also create new terms by reducing

---

[7] Ibid., p. 262.   [8] Ibid.   [9] Ibid., p. 260.

phrases to *acronyms* (that is, complete abbreviations); so in this respect, at least, our languages are more advanced than Newspeak. But, despite these differences, our new terms fulfil the same function as the political terms in Newspeak: they abolish the specific meanings, and "impose a desirable mental attitude upon the person using them."

We have already discussed the use of acronyms as a way to raise the level of abstraction, thereby obscuring the meaning of the original words and impoverishing the new knowledge structures (see pp. 373–374, 395–396). But it is worth quoting in full Orwell's perceptive analysis, probably the first serious study of this phenomenon: "Even in the early decades of the twentieth century, telescoped words and phrases had been one of the characteristic features of political language; and it had been noticed that the tendency to use abbreviations of this kind was most marked in totalitarian countries and totalitarian organizations. Examples were such words as *Nazi, Gestapo, Comintern, Inprecorr, Agitprop.* In the beginning the practice had been adopted as it were instinctively, but in Newspeak it was used with a conscious purpose. It was perceived that in thus abbreviating a name one narrowed and subtly altered its meaning, by cutting out most of the associations that would otherwise cling to it. The words *Communist International*, for instance, call up a composite picture of universal human brotherhood, red flags, barricades, Karl Marx, and the Paris Commune. The word *Comintern*, on the other hand, suggests merely a tightly knit organization and a well-defined body of doctrine. It refers to something almost as easily recognized, and as limited in purpose, as a chair or a table. *Comintern* is a word that can be uttered almost without taking thought, whereas *Communist International* is a phrase over which one is obliged to linger at least momentarily. In the same way, the associations called up by a word like *Minitrue* are fewer and more controllable than those called up by *Ministry of Truth*. This accounted not only for the habit of abbreviating whenever possible, but also for the almost exaggerated care that was taken to make every word easily pronounceable."[10]

Euphony, thus, was a major consideration in Newspeak. Ease of pronunciation and recognition made discourse possible mechanically, without thinking, as the new word alone – rather than the original words, with their complex meanings and associations – formed now the lowest level of abstraction: "What was required, above all for political purposes, were short clipped words of unmistakable meaning which could be uttered rapidly and which roused the minimum of echoes in the speaker's mind.... The intention was to make speech, and especially speech on any subject not ideologically neutral, as nearly as possible independent of consciousness."[11]

[10] Ibid., p. 264.   [11] Ibid., pp. 264–265.

Again, Orwell discusses political terms, but this principle can be used to make speech independent of consciousness in any domain. In the domain of software, for instance, short and easily pronounceable acronyms (IT, MIS, GUI, CASE, OOP, JAD, RAD, COM, OLE, OCX, CORBA, RIA, AJAX, SOA, ESB, EAS, EII, LAN, WAN, SAN, ODBC, TCM, BI, BPM, BPR, ERP, OLAP, OLTP, OSS, OMT, DOC, XML, SML, CMS, CRM, MRP, etc.[12]) serve this purpose well. By quickly reading or pronouncing the acronyms, instead of consciously articulating the original words, we avoid the associations those words might arouse in the mind. So the acronyms act as new words. They represent high levels of abstraction, but they become *starting* elements in the knowledge structures developed by their users.

Another way to raise the level of abstraction in Newspeak was by simplifying the grammar. In most cases, one word functioned as both noun and verb, while adjectives, adverbs, and inflections (plural, negative, comparison of adjectives) were derived from the same word by means of standard affixes. This reduction was enhanced by the general elimination of words, previously mentioned. And, as is always the case with abstraction, the elimination of word alternatives also reduced the links between knowledge structures. Newspeak tried, in effect, to turn words into a system of codes, and thereby reduce linguistic communication to machine-like performance: "All ambiguities and shades of meaning had been purged out of them. So far as it could be achieved, a Newspeak word of this class was simply a staccato sound expressing *one* clearly understood concept."[13]

For example, "good" was the only word retained from the hundreds of words related to goodness and badness. Words like "splendid" and "odious" were eliminated. The word for "bad" was "ungood," "better" and "best" became "gooder" and "goodest," and "well" became "goodwise." Only two higher levels of goodness were possible, "plusgood" and "doubleplusgood," which meant, approximately, "very good" and "extremely good." Other families of related words were similarly formed, starting with one basic word and abolishing the variants, the irregularities, and the old inflections.

When we use diverse words to express an idea – nouns, verbs, negative forms, levels of emphasis – we do more than specify different codes. Words like "excellent," "bad," "superb," "inferior," "wonderful," "lousy," and the many others, are more than mere marks on a scale of goodness and badness. Each

---

[12] The deciphering of these acronyms will be left (as they say in textbooks) as an exercise for the reader.   [13] Orwell, *Nineteen Eighty-Four*, p. 258.

one of these words has its own meanings, its own associations, and if we replace them with a system of codes we destroy the links between the idea of goodness and badness and our other knowledge. To put it differently, even if the new language still permits a hundred levels of goodness and badness, by defining them as mere marks on a scale we restrict our thinking to what a machine can do: the mechanical selection of an appropriate value. Without the variety of meanings provided by words, we lose the interactions between the different aspects of knowledge.

But in fact these codes comprise only a *few* values, not a hundred, so one value stands for many alternatives. The codes, therefore, are of a higher level of abstraction than the original words. The regularity and the standard affixes amplify this reduction: although several words can be constructed from a basic word, they are not really different words. "Good" and "ungood," for example, do not express different concepts in the way "good" and "bad" do. The designers of Newspeak saw this clearly: "In the end the whole notion of goodness and badness will be covered by only six words – in reality, only one word."[14] The idea of goodness and badness as we know it will cease to exist if the only way to express it is with one word and some prefixes and suffixes. Thus, the structure of goodness and badness – itself reified, isolated from other knowledge structures through the destruction of the alternative words – is further impoverished by raising the level of abstraction.

4

Recall the logically perfect languages we examined in chapter 4. Leibniz, Frege, Russell, and Carnap would have been quite comfortable in Orwell's totalitarian society – in their capacity as scientists, at least – because in this society their mechanistic theories would indeed work. Newspeak, after all, is in many ways the perfect language they were all seeking. For instance, a logically perfect language permits only a direct, one-to-one correspondence between words and things: "In a logically perfect language, there will be one word and no more for every simple object …."[15] And in Newspeak, "every concept that can ever be needed will be expressed by exactly *one* word, with its meaning rigidly defined."[16]

The purpose of a perfect language, we saw, is to express with mathematical precision all possible knowledge – all the facts that can occur in the world, and

[14] Ibid., p. 49.
[15] Bertrand Russell, *The Philosophy of Logical Atomism* (Peru, IL: Open Court, 1985), p. 157.   [16] Orwell, *Nineteen Eighty-Four*, p. 49.

all the thoughts that can occur in a mind. Since these scientists believed that such a language can exist, the conclusion must be that their conception of knowledge and mind is similar to the diminished one found in totalitarian societies. This degradation is the inevitable result of the mechanistic dogma. What all mechanists do, in the final analysis, is attempt to prove that human beings are merely complicated machines; and this idea, Orwell says, is the root of totalitarianism.

Thus, Orwell's main contribution has been to make us aware of the link between language and totalitarianism; specifically, the ease with which language can be used to control knowledge and minds, and hence the lives of millions of people. Long before writing *Nineteen Eighty-Four*, Orwell was protesting against the language abuses he observed around him: advertisers, lecturers, pamphleteers, politicians – anyone who wanted to influence large numbers of people started by manipulating language. While common in the totalitarian countries of that period, Orwell was disturbed to see this practice spreading also in the democratic ones. Language manipulation is so convenient, he concluded, that no one who benefits from it can resist the temptation of perpetrating it: "The connexion between totalitarian habits of thought and the corruption of language is an important subject which has not been sufficiently studied."[17]

Living in a democratic society, therefore, does not protect us from an elite that attempts to control our life through language. And the fact that a real society cannot actually reach the level of manipulation depicted in *Nineteen Eighty-Four* does not lessen the danger. This is a model, not a prophesy. Orwell chose to describe an unrealistic, extreme form of mind control in order to demonstrate the *potential* of language manipulation. His message is clear: by restricting language to its mechanistic aspects, an elite can restrict mental processes to the level of machines.

Thus, Orwell's second contribution has been to make us aware of the link between language and mechanism. As we saw, the language manipulation he describes reflects the two mechanistic fallacies, reification and abstraction. Although he doesn't use the term "mechanism," it is obvious – both from *Nineteen Eighty-Four* and from his earlier writings – that he understood the difference between mechanistic and non-mechanistic thinking. In particular, he recognized the indeterminism and creativity inherent in language, and the impossibility of building a device with the linguistic capabilities of human beings; in other words, precisely what the mechanists fail to understand (recall the linguistic theories we examined in chapters 3 and 4).

For example, in one of his essays, Orwell comments on the "mechanizing

---

[17] George Orwell, "Editorial to *Polemic*," in *Collected Essays*, vol. 4, p. 188.

process"[18] that was replacing the work of individuals in literature, movies, radio, publicity, and journalism: "It would probably not be beyond human ingenuity to write books by machinery."[19] But this is true, he explains, only because language has already been so degraded that what is being written for the masses is comparable to what can be produced by a machine. This type of writing is done by hacks and bureaucrats who work like automatons, following instructions received from their superiors. And he concludes: "It is probably in some such way that the literature of a totalitarian society would be produced .... Imagination – even consciousness so far as possible – would be eliminated from the process of writing."[20] Mechanism and totalitarianism expand together.

Orwell's ultimate message, then, is about the link between mechanism and totalitarianism. What the elite wants is to control people, and the simplest way to achieve this is by controlling their minds: by forcing people to think like automatons. The mechanistic philosophy, Orwell warns us, leads to totalitarianism. His model uses language because this is what he understood best, and because this is indeed an effective way to control minds. But, in fact, any widespread human phenomenon can be restricted by an elite to its mechanistic aspects, and used to implement totalitarianism. Thus, in our time, *software* has emerged as such a phenomenon. (We will study this subject in chapters 6 and 8.)

[18] George Orwell, "The Prevention of Literature," in *Collected Essays*, vol. 4, p. 92.
[19] Ibid.
[20] Ibid., p. 93. Clearly, the imaginary, extreme language abuses invented by Orwell for the totalitarian society of *Nineteen Eighty-Four* (mind control through language, book writing by machines, etc.) were inspired by the *real* abuses he observed in the *democratic* societies of his time.

CHAPTER 6

Software as Weapon

Our discussion in the previous chapter – the use of language to deceive and exploit – had a dual purpose. First, we benefited by discovering the methods employed by charlatans to turn language from a means of communication into a tool of manipulation. From the present-day deceivers to Orwell's totalitarian society, we saw that the aim of linguistic manipulation is to distort knowledge. And this is accomplished by forcing us to commit the mechanistic fallacies of reification and abstraction. Specifically, the charlatans force us to create isolated and impoverished knowledge structures in our minds. They prevent us from using those natural capabilities of the mind that allow us to process complex structures, and our mental processes are reduced to the level of machines.

But the main reason for the study of linguistic manipulation was to demonstrate the immense power inherent in language – the power to control minds. Then, if we understand the similarity of language and software, and of linguistic manipulation and software manipulation, we can better appreciate how the same power can be attained through software.

We already know that language and software fulfil a similar function: mirroring the world and communicating with it. And we also know that they work in a similar manner: by creating systems of interacting structures from linguistic and software entities, respectively. Having established that reification and abstraction are the methods whereby language is used to control minds, what we must do now is study our *software* delusions, and how the software elites are using these delusions to exploit us.

What we will find is that the very methods we recognize as means of deception and manipulation in language – forcing us to separate knowledge structures and to start from higher levels of abstraction – form in software an open doctrine. Whereas the language charlatans try to *hide* the fact that they are employing these methods, the software charlatans are quite candid about it: separating software structures and starting from higher levels, they keep telling us, is the most effective way to develop software.

But software is becoming as important as language, so the conclusion must be that our elites are attaining through software the same power over human minds that the elite in Orwell's hypothetical society attains through language. Thus, while no elite in a real society can ever attain the power to control *language* to the degree that this is done in Orwell's society, our software elites already have that power in controlling *software*. And, if not stopped, they will eventually control our minds as effectively as the elite controls minds in Orwell's society.

A New Form of Domination

The Risks of Software Dependence

I have stated that the elites can control knowledge by means of software just as they can by means of language, but I must clarify this point. I am not referring here to the *direct* use of software to control, acquire, or restrict knowledge. This discussion is *not* concerned with such well-known software dangers as allowing an authority to decide what information is to be stored in databases, or allowing the centralized collection of information about individuals. Nor is it concerned with the use of deceptive language in software propaganda, as in calling everything "technology," or "solution." Important as these dangers are, they are insignificant compared to the dangers we face when an elite controls *the way we create and use software.*

The other dangers we understand, and if we understand them we can perhaps deal with them. But we have yet to understand what it means for a society to depend on software as much as it depends on language; and consequently, we do not realize that it is just as important to prevent an elite from controlling software as it is to prevent one from controlling language. This ignorance can be seen in the irresponsible attitudes of our political leaders, of our corporations and educational institutions, and ultimately of every one of us: we are watching passively as the software elites are increasing their power and control year after year; and we continue to trust and respect them, even as they are creating a world where the only thing left for us to do is to operate their devices.

Thus, while the other forms of software abuse would lead to familiar forms of exploitation, what concerns us here is *a new form of domination*. We are facing a new phenomenon, a new way to control knowledge and thought, which could not exist before we had computers. The dependence of a society on software is a new phenomenon because software and programming are new phenomena. We have been inventing tools for millennia, but the computer is unique in that it is programmable to a far greater extent than any other tool we have had. Software, therefore, is what gives the computer its potency; and the act of programming is what controls this potency. No other human activity – save the use of language – is as far-reaching as programming, because no other activity involves something as potent as software.

This is the first time since humans developed languages that we have invented something comparable in scope or versatility. Software resembles language more than anything else: both systems permit us to mirror the world in our minds and to communicate with it. At the same time, software is sufficiently different from language to mask the similarity (we can easily invent new programming languages, for example, but not natural ones). As a result, we fail to appreciate the real impact that software has on society, and the need for programming expertise and programming freedom. And we have fallen victim to the fallacies of the software myth: the belief that software is a kind of product, and that software applications must be built as we build appliances; the belief that we need elaborate tools for these manufacturing projects, and hence a software industry to supply these tools; the belief that development methodologies and environments can be a substitute for programming expertise; the belief that it is better to program and maintain complex business systems by employing large teams of inexperienced programmers, analysts, and managers, instead of one professional; and the belief that the highest programming skills that human minds can attain, and that society needs, are those possessed by the current practitioners.

It is not surprising that we are unprepared for the consequences of programming, since we did not take sufficient time to learn what programming really is.

Originally, we set out merely trying to develop a particular kind of machine – a fast, programmable calculator. Instead, we stumbled upon a system that gives us a whole new way to use our minds, to communicate, to represent the world. But we continue to regard programming as we did originally, as an extension to the engineering effort required to build the hardware; that is, as an activity akin to manufacturing, and which must be performed in the same fashion. We still fail to see that the skills needed to program computers are more akin to those needed to use language. Programming projects cannot be neatly broken down, like manufacturing activities, into simpler and simpler tasks. Programming skills, therefore, entail a capacity for complex structures. They can be acquired only through lengthy exposure to the phenomena arising from developing and maintaining large and complex applications.

There can be little doubt that within a few decades humans will interact with the world around them by means of software as much as they do now by means of language. Software lends itself to this task just like language, and there is no reason why we should not depend on our newly discovered programming capabilities, just as we depend on our linguistic capabilities. We must ensure, however, the right conditions: first, programmers must have the same competence with software as normal humans have now with language; and second, the activities involving programming and software must be, like those involving language, free from controls or restrictions. A society that allows an elite to control its software and programming faces the same danger as a society that allows its *language* to be controlled: through language or through software, the elite will eventually control all knowledge and thought, and will reduce human minds to the level of machines.

The form of domination that we are studying here can emerge, therefore, when a society depends on software but lacks the necessary programming competence. As Orwell points out, an elite could achieve complete control through language only by forcing us to replace our language with an impover-ished one, like Newspeak, which demands no intelligence. In our present-day society, exploitation by way of language is necessarily limited, because we are all competent language users. Few programmers, however, attain a level of software competence comparable to our linguistic competence. Accordingly, the world of programming is already an Orwellian world: it resembles a society that lacks linguistic competence.

Our dependence on programming aids, and on the organizations behind them, stems from the incompetence of programmers. Programmers need these devices because they are not permitted to attain the level of programming competence of which human minds are naturally capable. But programming aids are only poor substitutes for programming expertise, because, unlike minds, they can only deal separately with the various aspects of programming.

As a result, applications based on these substitutes cannot represent the world accurately, just as statements in Newspeak cannot.

And, just as people restricted to Newspeak cannot realize how limited their knowledge is, *we* cannot realize how limited our *programming* knowledge is, because this is the only kind of programming we have. Just as the people in Orwell's society are forced to depend on the linguistic tools provided by their elite, and their knowledge is shaped and restricted by these tools, our programmers are forced to depend on the devices provided by the software companies, and their knowledge is similarly shaped and restricted. Only mechanistic software concepts, only beliefs that reinforce the software myth, can enter their minds. Programming expertise for them means expertise in the use of substitutes for programming expertise.

By preventing programming competence, then, an elite can use software to control and exploit society, just as language could be used if we lacked *linguistic* competence. The programming aids, and the resulting applications, form a complex world that parallels the real world but has little to do with it. Their chief purpose is to support a large software bureaucracy, and to prevent the emergence of a body of competent and responsible programmers. And if the software bureaucrats no longer deal with the real world, we have to reshape our own views to match theirs. To the extent that our society depends on software, and hence on this software bureaucracy, we *all* live in an Orwellian world: we are all forced to perceive our work, our values, our expectations, our responsibilities, in ways that serve the interests of the software elites.

It is unlikely that Orwell's extreme form of mind control through language can ever happen in the real world, but this is unimportant. Orwell's world is a model, not a prophesy. We must appreciate its value as model, therefore, rather than feel self-complacent because it cannot happen. And when we study it, we recognize that its importance is growing as our dependence on software is growing, because this dependence increases the possibility of an elite controlling our minds through software as the elite in the model does through language.

In our current software culture, the degree of control that an elite can attain through software is not limited by an existing condition, as control through language is limited by our linguistic competence; it rests solely on how much we depend on software. The reason the software elites do not have complete control over our minds today is not our software competence, but the fact that we do not yet depend completely on software. And if our dependence on software is growing, by the time we depend on software as much as we depend now on language it will be too late to do anything. At that point, to use Orwell's model, we will live in a world where Newspeak finally replaces English. Our chief means of thinking, of communicating, of representing the world, will be a simple system requiring only mechanistic knowledge – not because software structures cannot involve complex knowledge, but because there will be no one to create or use the kind of software that requires the full capacity of the mind.

Dependence on software, coupled with software ignorance and programming incompetence – this is what the software elites are trying to achieve. They are persuading us to give up our dependence on knowledge and skills (means through which we *know* how to become competent) and to replace it with a dependence on software (means which they control, and through which they can *prevent* us from becoming competent).

The Prevention of Expertise

1

We probably fail to recognize software domination because the idea of mind control through software is so incredible. Before we had software, only political organizations could carry out such a totalitarian project. And we have yet to accept the fact that an elite can control society through software as effectively as a political elite could through traditional means of domination.

To understand this danger, we must make the most of what we know today. We cannot afford merely to wait and see, because the resulting conditions would likely be irreversible. We must study, for example, the similarity between the role of software in society and that of language. Since we all agree that language can be used to control and restrict thought, we must ensure complete software freedom even if we still cannot see clearly how the software elites can turn software into a means of domination. We should simply assume that they will use software as they would language, had they the opportunity to control language as they do software.

Even more importantly, we must study those aspects of society that are *already* controlled by the software elites: those aspects that form the world of programming itself. Studying the world of programming affords us a glimpse of the future, of the time when the entire society will be controlled by these elites. It was easy to degrade the notion of programming expertise because, this being a new field, there were no established values, as there are in the traditional professions. As a result, the highest level of expertise we believe to be needed in programming is one that in other professions would be considered the level of novices.

We have been involved with software for more than half a century, so by now we could have had a sufficient number of expert programmers; namely, men and women whose skills represent *the utmost that human minds can attain in the domain of programming.* This is how we define expertise in other professions, and this is what we should expect of programmers. Instead, what we find is a software *bureaucracy*: a social system whose chief doctrine is the *prevention* of programming expertise.

We have programmers who are incapable of performing anything but small and isolated programming tasks, and who are not even expected to do more. We have managers who read "success stories" in childish computer publications, and search for ready-made applications and other programming substitutes instead of allowing their own programmers to gain the necessary skills. We have professors and gurus who teach the principles of "software engineering" – which claim that programming is like manufacturing, so what we need is unskilled labourers who know only how to assemble "prefabricated software components." We have software companies that supply practitioners with an endless series of "software tools" – elaborate development and business systems that promise to eliminate the need for programming. And, addressing the incompetence engendered by this corrupt culture, there are thousands of books, magazines, newspapers, brochures, advertisements, catalogues, trade shows, newsletters, courses, seminars, and online sources, all offering "solutions."

Few people realize that this whole bureaucracy could be replaced with a relatively small number of real, expert programmers. This is true because only a fraction of the work performed by the current practitioners is actually useful; that is, directly related to the creation and maintenance of applications. Most of their work consists in solving the problems generated by their dependence on aids and substitutes.

We have no equivalent bureaucracy in other professions. We have surgeons, pilots, engineers, musicians, military commanders, writers, repairmen, and so forth. And we understand that, to reach expertise in a difficult profession, an individual needs many years of education, training, and practice, a sense of personal responsibility, and perhaps special talents as well. We don't attempt to replace a surgeon with a dozen ignorant individuals, and defend the decision by claiming that the work of a surgeon can be broken down into simpler tasks, as in manufacturing.

We don't do this in other professions because we took the time to determine what is the *highest* level that human beings can attain in those fields. We made *that* level our definition of expertise, and we measure everyone's performance against that level. We understand that the more difficult the profession, the longer it takes to attain expertise, and the fewer the individuals who can succeed; and we give these individuals the time and the opportunity to develop their capabilities. We never tried to contend with this problem by reducing our expectations, as we do in programming. We never concluded that, given the urgent need for surgeons, the answer is to debase the definition of expertise to match the level of the available, of the inexperienced, individuals.

We treat programming differently from other professions because this serves the interests of the software elites. In just a few years, an unprecedented propaganda system has made the software myth the greatest system of belief in history, and we now take for granted in the domain of programming, notions that we would dismiss as absurd in other domains. The software practitioners have become a powerful, self-serving bureaucracy, but we continue to regard them as saviours. The reason we fail to see that they are *exploiting* society, not serving it, is that we have no other form of programming as measure. Programming controlled by a bureaucracy is the only programming we know, the only kind we have ever had.

An important element of the software myth is the belief that the typical work currently performed by programmers represents the highest level of competence we should expect in this profession. And if they have difficulty with their applications, it is not greater programming knowledge that they need, but more programming aids and substitutes. Thus, individuals with just a year or two of training and experience – which consist largely in the use of aids and substitutes – have reached the highest knowledge expected of them. The only knowledge they will acquire from then on is how to use the *future* aids and substitutes. This doctrine fits well within the ideology promoted by the software elites, as it ensures continued incompetence among programmers. It also ensures the complete dependence of programmers, and of those using their applications, on the software companies supplying the aids and substitutes. Lastly, this doctrine serves to weaken the programmers' sense of responsibility: what they perceive as their main concern is the problems generated by the aids and substitutes, rather than the real social or business problems that software is supposed to solve.

As a result, no matter how many years of practice programmers have behind them, their real programming experience remains as it was after the first year or two. This is true because the aids and substitutes limit their work to simple and isolated bits of programming, whereas successful application development demands the capacity to deal with many software processes simultaneously. This incompetence also explains why most applications are inadequate, and why most programming work consists in replacing existing applications, which programmers cannot keep up to date.

If we can benefit from studying the similarity of software and language, and from studying the world of programming and the delusions of the software myth, then we can benefit even more from studying these topics together; specifically, from studying the link between the mechanistic ideology and the incompetence of programmers.

We should regard the world of programming as the result of an unintended social experiment: an attempt to replace human expertise with software. The experiment has failed, but we can learn a great deal from this failure. We must create, to begin with, the social and business environment where a body of expert programmers can evolve. The software elites are doing everything in their power to prevent this, of course, since widespread programming incompetence is a critical factor in their plan of domination. A true programming profession will not only stop the flow of trillions of dollars from society to the software elites and bureaucrats, but will lead to better software and, ultimately, greater benefits from computers.

Moreover, by abolishing the software bureaucracy we will prevent the software elites from corrupting other aspects of society. For they are using the power gained from controlling the world of software, to degrade other professions and occupations just as they have degraded programming. If allowed to continue, they will soon force us all to depend on knowledge substitutes instead of our minds. Like programmers, we will all be reduced to the level of novices. As programmers do now, we will all live in a world where expertise is neither possible nor necessary, where the only thing left to do is to operate the devices supplied by the software elites.

2

To understand the concept of software domination, we must start by recalling what we learned in chapter 2 about the mind. We can acquire the most diverse kinds of knowledge and skills: using language, recognizing faces, playing games, programming computers – the kind of knowledge we all share simply by living in a society, as well as specialized knowledge related to individual lifestyles and occupations. But all knowledge and skills, ultimately, involve our mind's capacity for complex structures. When exposed to a new phenomenon, and hence to the new knowledge embodied in that phenomenon, we start by noting the *simple* structures that make it up, the patterns and regularities. What we note, in other words, is those aspects that can be represented with facts, rules, and methods. Being limited to simple structures, our performance at this point resembles that of a software device. We progress from novice to expert by being exposed to that phenomenon repeatedly. This permits our mind to discover, not only more structures, but also the *interactions* between structures; and this in turn permits it to create a replica of the *complex* structures that make up the phenomenon. Thus, when we reach expertise our performance exceeds that of software devices, which are forever restricted to simple structures.

We communicate with the world around us through our senses, which receive information in the form of simple structures (patterns of symbols and sounds, for instance). Complex structures, therefore, can exist only in the phenomenon itself and in the mind; we cannot acquire them through our senses directly from the phenomenon, or from another mind. Consequently, the only way to attain expertise in a given domain is by giving our mind the opportunity to create the complex structures which reflect the phenomena of that domain. And this the mind can do only through repeated exposure to those phenomena; in other words, through personal experience.

Human acts require the capacity for complex structures because most phenomena we face consist of interacting structures. They consist of entities (objects, persons, processes, events) that have many attributes, and belong therefore to many structures at the same time – one structure for each attribute. To put this differently, we can always view ourselves and our environment from different perspectives, while the entities that constitute our existence are the same. So the entities form many structures; but the structures interact, because they share these entities. We rarely find a structure – a particular aspect of our life – whose links to the other structures are so weak that it can be extracted from the complex whole without distorting it or the others.

This recapitulation was necessary in order to remind ourselves of the conclusion reached in chapter 2, and its significance. We note that most mental processes, most knowledge and skills, involve *complex* structures. And we note also that software devices are based on *simple* structures. As substitutes for human intelligence, therefore, software devices are useful only for the rare tasks that can be represented with simple structures; specifically, those tasks that can be separated from others.

On the one hand, then, practically everything we do involves the full capacity of the mind, and cannot be broken down into simpler mental processes. On the other hand, we agree to depend more and more, in almost every domain, on software devices – which attempt to eliminate the need for expertise by reducing knowledge to simple structures. How can we explain this contradiction?

Our software delusions stem from our mechanistic delusions. Our most popular theories of mind claim that human intelligence can be represented with mechanistic models – models based on precise diagrams, rules, methods, and formulas. And, even though these theories keep failing, we also believe now that it is possible to represent intelligence with mechanistic *software* models. Thus, the promoters of mind mechanism can claim, for the first time, to have *actual* devices – software devices – that emulate human intelligence. Anyone with a computer can now perform any task, including tasks requiring knowledge that he lacks. All he needs to do is purchase a software device which contains that knowledge.

We have always used tools to simplify tasks, or to improve our performance; so the idea that a device can enhance certain types of knowledge and skills, or help us perform some tasks faster or better, is not new. If we view software as a device of this kind, the claims are easily justified: the computer, with the programs that run on it, is the most versatile tool we have ever invented; and it can enhance our capabilities in many tasks.

The software claims, though, do not stop at the kind of claims traditionally advanced for devices. The claims are extended to encompass *intelligent* acts; that is, acts involving non-mechanistic knowledge, and hence complex knowledge structures. But devices can represent only *simple* structures. So, to replace those acts with software, we must first separate the complex knowledge structure into several simple ones.

Software domination, thus, starts when we are tempted to commit the fallacy of reification. We believe the claim that knowledge and skills can be replaced with software devices because we already believe that intelligent acts can be broken down into simpler intelligent acts. This belief tempts us to reify the phenomenon of intelligence, and commit therefore, with software, the fallacy already committed by the mechanistic theories of mind: the separated knowledge structures are no longer what they were when part of the complex knowledge; they lose the interactions, so even when we manage to represent them faithfully with software, the knowledge embodied in them is not the same as the original, complex knowledge.

But reification is only the first step. Now that we have independent structures, we are tempted to start from higher levels of abstraction within each structure as we replace it with software. We can be more productive, the experts tell us, if we avoid the low levels of software and start with higher-level elements – with elements that already contain the lower levels. Thus, we also commit the second fallacy, abstraction: we believe that we can accomplish the same tasks as when starting with low-level elements. Starting from higher levels impoverishes the structure by reducing the number of alternatives for the value of the top element; that is, the top element of a software structure that is already a reified, and hence inaccurate, representation of the real knowledge. What this means in practice is that an inexperienced person will accomplish by means of software devices only a fraction of what an experienced person will with his mind alone.

The two fallacies can be seen clearly in the domain of programming. We are told that the most effective way to develop applications is by starting from high levels of abstraction. Specifically, we should avoid programming as much as possible, and use instead software entities that already include many elements: ready-made applications (or, at least, ready-made modules and components), and the built-in operations provided by development tools and environments. To benefit from these high levels, however, we must view our applications, mistakenly, as separable software processes. Each business or software practice, each case of shared data or operations, is a process; and each process represents one aspect of the application, one structure (see pp. 360–363). These structures exist at the same time and use the same software entities, so it is their totality that constitutes the application. If we separate them, we may indeed manage to program each structure starting from higher-level elements; but the resulting application will reflect only poorly the original requirements. We *can* create applications that mirror reality, but only if we have the expertise to start from low levels and to deal with all the processes together.

3

We are now in a position to understand the concept of software domination. The software elites are exploiting our mechanistic delusions; specifically, our belief that software can be a substitute for non-mechanistic knowledge. We see software successfully replacing human minds in *some* tasks, and we trust the elites when they promise us similar success in other tasks. We believe that there is only a quantitative, not a qualitative, difference between the knowledge involved in mechanistic and non-mechanistic tasks, and we allow the elites to exploit this belief.

So the mechanistic delusions act like a trap. If we believe that a given task can be replaced with software, we do not hesitate to depend on that software and on the organization behind it. We enthusiastically devote our time to that software, instead of using it to gain knowledge. But if the task is non-mechanistic, the time we devote to software will be wasted. By luring us with the promise of immediate answers to our complex problems, the elites prevent us from developing our minds. So, not only does software fail to solve those problems, but it also prevents us from gaining the knowledge whereby we *could* solve them. In the end, we have nothing – neither a software expedient, nor the knowledge needed to perform the task on our own. We are caught, thus, in the software variant of the traditional mechanistic trap: we believe in the existence of mechanistic solutions for non-mechanistic problems, so we restrict ourselves to precisely those methods that cannot work.

We get to depend on software because the promise is so enticing. The promise is, essentially, that software can solve important problems in a particular field by acting as a substitute for the knowledge needed in that field. So, instead of taking the time to acquire that knowledge, we can solve the problems right away, simply by buying and operating a piece of software. And the reason we believe this promise is that we see similar promises being fulfilled in tasks like calculations and data processing, where software does indeed allow novices to display the same performance as experts. For tasks involving interacting knowledge structures, however, the promise cannot be met. Software can be a substitute only for knowledge that can be neatly broken down into smaller, simpler, and independent pieces of knowledge – pieces which in their turn can be broken down into even smaller ones, and so on – because this is the only way to represent knowledge with software.

When we depend on software in situations involving complex knowledge structures, what we notice is that it does not work as we expected. But, while software fails to provide an answer, we never question the mechanistic assumptions. We recognize its inadequacy, but we continue to depend on it. And this dependence creates a new *kind* of problems: software-related problems. We don't mind these new problems, though, and we gladly tackle them, because we think that by solving *them* we will get the software to solve our original problems. Most software problems involve isolated knowledge structures, and have therefore fairly simple, mechanistic solutions. Since these solutions often entail additional software, they generate in their turn software problems, which have their own solutions, and so on.

The more software problems and solutions we have, the more pleased we are with our new preoccupations: all the time we seem to be *solving* problems. So we spend more and more time with these software problems, when in fact they are spurious problems generated by spurious preoccupations, in a process that feeds on itself. We interpret our solutions to software problems as progress toward a solution to our real problems, failing to see that, no matter how successful we are in solving software problems, if the original problems involve complex knowledge we will never solve *them* with software. In the end, content with our software preoccupations, we may forget the real problems altogether.

Bear in mind that it is not software dependence in itself that is dangerous, but the combination of this dependence with software ignorance. There is nothing wrong in depending on software when we possess software expertise. It is only when we separate software structures from other knowledge structures, and when we restrict ourselves to high-level elements, that our dependence on software can be exploited; in other words, when our software knowledge is at a mechanistic level.

Recall the language analogy. We attain linguistic competence by starting with *low-level* linguistic elements – morphemes and words, with all their uses and meanings – and by creating language structures that interact with the other knowledge structures present in the mind. This is how we form the complex mental structures recognized as intelligence. No linguistic competence or intelligence would be possible if we had to create our language structures starting with ready-made sentences and ideas, or if we treated them as independent structures. Similarly, software expertise can be attained only by starting with *low-level* software elements, and by treating the software structures that we create with our programs, not as independent structures, but as part of the complex structures that make up our affairs. And this is precisely what the software elites are *preventing* us from doing.

We are exploited through software because of the belief that it is possible to benefit from software without having to develop software expertise. We understand why we could not benefit from *language* without having linguistic competence, but we fail to see this for software. When we trust the elites and get to create and use software in the manner dictated by them, we end up with a combination of several weaknesses: programming incompetence; failure to solve our problems with software, because of the inadequacy of our applications; a growing preoccupation with spurious, software-related problems; and a perpetual dependence on the elites for solutions to both the real and the spurious problems – a dependence that is futile in any case, because only we, with our minds, can hope to accomplish those tasks that require complex knowledge. It is not difficult for the elites, then, to exploit us.

The Lure of Software Expedients

1

Software domination is based on a simple stratagem: consuming people's time. Forcing us to waste our time is the simplest way to keep us ignorant, since, if we spend this time with worthless activities, we cannot use it to improve our minds. The software elites strive to keep us ignorant because only if ignorant can normal people be turned into bureaucrats, into automatons.

Our time, in the end, is all we have, our only asset. Whether we count the hours available in a day or the years that constitute a life, our time is limited. What we do with our time, hour by hour, determines what we make of our lives. We can squander this time on unimportant pursuits, or use it to expand as much as we can our knowledge and skills. In the one case we will accomplish whatever can be done with limited knowledge, and we will probably live a dull life; in the other case we will make the most of our minds, and we have a good chance to live a rich life and to make a contribution to society.

It is not too much to say that, as individuals living in a free society, we are, each one of us, responsible for a human life – our own – and we have an *obligation* to make the most of it. Like freedom itself, realizing our human potential is a *right* we all have; but, just like freedom, this right is also a *duty*, in that we are all responsible for its preservation by defending it against those who want to destroy it. Specifically, we must strive to expand our minds *despite* the attempts made by an elite to keep us ignorant. Only thus, only when each individual *and* each mind counts, can the idea of freedom survive.

Conversely, preventing an individual from realizing his or her potential, from making the most of his or her mind, amounts in effect to an attempt to destroy a life; so it must be considered a crime nearly as odious as murder. Seen from this perspective, our software elites could be described as criminal organizations, since forcing us to squander our time is one of the principles of their ideology.

The software elites consume our time by creating an environment where our activities are far below our natural mental capabilities. When we depend on their concepts and devices, we end up spending most of our time acquiring isolated bits of knowledge, or solving isolated problems. Being simple and mechanistic, these activities do not allow us to create complex knowledge structures in our minds – the kind of knowledge that constitutes skills and experience. We can recognize this in that our capabilities do not progress on a scale from novice to expert, as they do in the traditional fields of knowledge. (Thus, no matter how many of these problems we solve, the next one will demand about as much time and effort.) In any case, mechanistic concepts cannot help us to solve our *complex* problems; so we are wasting our time both when acquiring the mechanistic knowledge and when using it.

Without exception, the software devices are presented as simple, easy to use, requiring little knowledge, and demanding an investment of just a few minutes, or perhaps a few hours. It is a sign of our collective naivety that, in a world which is becoming more complex by the day, we believe in the existence of some devices that can provide immediate answers to our problems, and that this power is ours to enjoy just for the trouble of learning how to operate them. This childish belief can be understood only by recognizing it as the software variant of our eternal craving for salvation: the performance of some simple acts, we think, will invoke the assistance of fabulous powers. This is the same belief that permitted so many other elites to exploit us in the past.

Many of these devices are indeed simple, just as their promoters claim. But they are simple precisely because they are generally useless, because they *cannot* solve our complex problems. As we saw, they are based on the delusion that complex structures – our problems, or the knowledge required to solve them – can be broken down into simple structures, and hence replaced with mechanistic expedients like software. The mechanistic knowledge required to use the software, together with the mechanistic capabilities of the software itself, is believed to provide a practical substitute for the complex knowledge required to solve the problems. But no combination of simple structures can replace a complex knowledge structure, because this kind of knowledge can develop only in a mind, and only after much learning and practice.

When we trust the software elites, we are exploited more severely and in more ways than we think. For, the waste of time and the prevention of knowledge reinforce each other, impoverishing our lives and degrading our minds to the point where we can no longer understand what is happening to us. This is an important point, and we must dwell on it.

We saw that the promise of immediate solutions to our problems tempts us to depend on mechanistic software expedients – ready-made pieces of software, or software tools and aids. These devices are based, ultimately, on reified structures and high levels of abstraction, so they demand only mechanistic thinking. Complex knowledge becomes both unnecessary and impossible, as all we need to do is select and combine various operations within the range of alternatives provided by a device.

We agree to depend on mechanistic expedients because we believe this is the most effective way to accomplish a given task, when in fact most tasks require *non-mechanistic* knowledge. But it is important to note that there is a second process at work here: if we spend our time engaged in activities requiring only mechanistic thinking, we lose the *opportunity* to develop complex, non-mechanistic knowledge. We have the *capacity* for non-mechanistic knowledge, but we will not take the time to *develop* it as long as we believe that the simpler, mechanistic knowledge suffices. So our knowledge remains at mechanistic levels, and we continue to depend on the mechanistic expedients, even though they are inferior to our own capabilities.

What distinguishes human minds from devices is the capacity to develop complex knowledge. But, as we saw in chapter 2, the only way to attain complex knowledge is through personal experience: by engaging in activities that require that knowledge, by being exposed repeatedly to the complex phenomena that embody it. Thus, in some domains we need many years of learning and practice to attain the knowledge levels recognized as expertise. Mechanistic knowledge, on the other hand, can be acquired fairly quickly. (See pp. 157–159.)

The promise of mechanistic solutions to complex problems is, then, a trap. When inexperienced, and hence limited to mechanistic knowledge, the mechanistic expedients do indeed exceed our skills. It is only later, when we develop non-mechanistic knowledge, that we will outperform them. But we will never reach that level if we get to depend on mechanistic expedients from the start, because this very dependence deprives us of the opportunity to develop non-mechanistic knowledge.

This degradation – restricting us to mechanistic thinking, to a fraction of our mental capabilities – is the goal of the software elites when tempting us with mechanistic expedients. The prevention of non-mechanistic knowledge is a critical element in their plan of domination, because they must ensure that we remain inferior to their devices, and hence dependent on them.

We can choose only one of the two alternatives: either pursue activities demanding mechanistic knowledge (because they are easy and immediately accessible), or take the time to develop non-mechanistic knowledge. Mechanistic knowledge (following rules and methods, operating a software device) we can quickly acquire at any time, while non-mechanistic knowledge (the experience to perform complex tasks, the creativity to solve important problems) requires many years of learning and practice.

The software elites encourage us to choose the first alternative. This choice brings immediate rewards and is hard to resist, but it restricts us forever to mechanistic thinking. To prefer the second alternative, we must appreciate the potential of our minds. This choice amounts, in effect, to an investment in ourselves: we decide to forgo some easy and immediate benefits, and, instead, take the time to develop our minds. But we can make this choice only if we already have an appreciation of non-mechanistic knowledge, only if we realize how much more we can accomplish later, when we attain this type of knowledge. And we can develop this appreciation only if, when young or when novices in a particular field, we note around us both mechanistic and non-mechanistic knowledge, and learn to respect those who possess the latter – because their skills exceed ours by far.

The software elites, however, are creating a culture that fosters mechanistic thinking – a culture where non-mechanistic capabilities offer no benefits, as we are all expected to stay at about the same skill level. More and more, in one occupation after another, the only thing we have to know is how to use a software system. The notions of expertise, creativity, professionalism, and responsibility are being degraded to mean simply the skill of following methods and operating devices. As we depend increasingly on mechanistic knowledge alone, non-mechanistic knowledge is becoming redundant: we have fewer and fewer opportunities to either develop it or use it.

By creating a culture where all we need is mechanistic knowledge, the elites make it impossible for us to discover the superiority of *non-mechanistic* knowledge. We are trapped in a vicious circle: we start by being inexperienced and hence limited to mechanistic knowledge; at this point our performance is inferior to their devices, so the elites easily persuade us that the only way to improve is by using devices; as we get to depend on devices, the only knowledge we acquire is the mechanistic knowledge required to operate them; so our skills remain below the level of devices, and we believe that we must continue to depend on them. The only way to escape from this trap is by developing non-mechanistic knowledge, and thus becoming superior to the devices. But this takes time, and time is precisely what we do not have if we squander it on a preoccupation with devices. As long as we trust the elites, therefore, we are condemned to using only the *mechanistic* capabilities of our minds; we are condemned, in other words, to staying at novice levels forever.

Let me put this differently. To control our life, the software elites must induce a state of permanent ignorance and dependence. And they achieve this by persuading us to trust their mechanistic expedients – concepts, theories, methods, devices – while these expedients can rarely solve our real problems. Consuming our time by keeping us preoccupied with their expedients is a critical factor in the process of domination, because the elites must prevent us from using this time to develop our minds. And promoting worthless expedients is an integral part of this process: they wouldn't give us useful ones even if they could. Only expedients that do *not* work can be employed to consume our time; only by *not* solving our problems can they add to our spurious, software-related preoccupations. No domination would be possible if we were asked to depend on the elites only in those few situations where their expedients are indeed superior to our minds (that is, where a complex phenomenon can be usefully approximated with simple structures).

Promoting mechanistic expedients, thus, ensures our continued dependence in two ways at once: by restricting our knowledge and skills to levels even lower than those attained by the expedients, and by consuming our time with the endless preoccupations generated by the expedients.

2

It may be useful to recall our software preoccupations, although we are already spending so much time with them that they are well known. Installing new software, seeking technical support, downloading updates, studying lists of "frequently asked questions," checking the latest notes on a website, reading computer magazines, discovering "undocumented features," running virus protection utilities, printing online manuals, trying to get different pieces of software to work together – these are some of the activities we must perform when involved with software. But these are only the incidentals. We must also include the time required to learn to use the software (the features and options we have to assimilate, how to specify and combine them, keeping up with changes from one version to the next), and the time we take to actually use it, once we get to depend on it.

These activities require almost exclusively mechanistic knowledge: they consist of isolated and fairly simple tasks, which cannot help us to develop an important body of knowledge or skills. We note this in that almost everyone, regardless of age or experience, has to deal with the same kind of problems; and almost everyone manages to solve them. We also note it in that, no matter how many of these problems we faced in the past, we will still face similar ones in the future. In other words, the proportion of time we must devote to software-related problems does not decrease significantly with experience.

Anyone who encountered software-related problems is familiar with the feeling of satisfaction experienced when finally uncovering the answer. The answer is usually a simple fact; for instance, learning that we must select one option rather than another in a particular situation. But instead of being outraged that we had to spend time with an activity so simple that we could have performed it as children, we perceive it as an essential aspect of our work, so we believe that we have learned something important. Although we don't think of this activity as a form of amusement, we experience the satisfaction of solving a puzzle. And even if it is true that we must now spend a great part of our time solving puzzles instead of addressing real problems, it is significant that these are *trivial* puzzles, demanding only a fraction of our mental capabilities. Clearly, there is no limit to the number of software-related puzzles that we can find, and hence the time we must take to deal with them, if we agree to depend on concepts and products that cannot solve our real problems to begin with.

Any activity, method, or tool entails some incidental preoccupations, so we cannot expect to benefit from software without investing some time; and we may even have to spend part of this time dealing with trivial issues. Thus, what I am trying to show here is *not* that our collective preoccupation with software is too great relative to the benefits we derive from it. Such deficiency we could attribute to the novelty of software and to our inexperience. We could then conclude that this condition is transient, and that we will eventually become as able in our software pursuits as human beings can be – just as we have become in other domains.

What I am trying to show, rather, is that this interpretation is wrong, that our incompetence is getting worse not better, that our software preoccupations do not reflect a natural process of intellectual evolution. On the contrary: the incompetence is deliberately fostered by the software elites as part of a monstrous plan of domination founded on our mechanistic delusions, and made possible by our growing dependence on computers – a plan whose goal is to degrade the mind of every human being on earth.

Our continued ignorance in software-related matters – programming, in particular – is essential in this plan of domination, because software knowledge, like linguistic knowledge, is related to all other types of knowledge. *Software* ignorance and dependence, thus, are only the means to bring about *total* ignorance and dependence. It is in order to induce this collective ignorance and dependence that the software elites are exploiting our mechanistic delusions, and the consequent software delusions. For, as long as we believe that knowledge and skills can be replaced with mechanistic concepts, we will inevitably conclude that we must depend on organizations that produce devices based on these concepts – just as we depend on organizations that produce appliances, detergents, or electricity.

In reality, to succeed in software-related activities – programming, in particular – we need *skills*. And, like other skills, these new skills depend on our own capabilities and experience. Also like other skills, they demand the full capacity of the mind, and, to attain expertise, many years of learning and practice.

The software elites are promoting the notion of knowledge substitutes precisely because these substitutes are worthless. It is precisely because they cannot replace skills, and hence fail to solve our problems, that we constantly need new ones and spend so much time with them. By consuming our time with the petty preoccupations generated by these substitutes, the elites are preventing us from developing skills, thus ensuring our continued incompetence and dependence.

Were we permitted, as society, to develop software skills as we develop skills in other domains – were we permitted, in other words, to attain the highest level that human minds can attain in software-related matters – the issues of incompetence and waste of time would not even arise. We would then be, quite simply, as good in these new skills as we can possibly be; and we would take as much time with our software preoccupations as is justifiable. This is how we progressed in other domains, and there is no reason to view software and programming differently. It is unlikely that we have already reached the highest level, or that we are advancing in that direction, since we are using now mostly *mechanistic* knowledge; in other domains, it is our *non-mechanistic* capabilities that we use when we attain expertise. The software elites can persuade us to prefer their mechanistic substitutes to our own minds only because, as society, we have no idea how good we can actually be in software-related matters: we never had the opportunity to find out.

All skills – whether easy or difficult, acquired early in life or later – entail the same mental processes. Interpreting visual sensations, recognizing social contexts, diagnosing diseases, playing musical instruments, flying airplanes, repairing appliances, teaching children, managing warehouses – we can acquire almost any skill, but the only way to acquire it is by performing the activities involved in that skill, and by allowing our mind to discover the complex knowledge structures which constitute that skill. For no other skills can we find an elite that prevents us from using the full capacity of our mind, or forces us to use methods and devices instead of expanding our knowledge, or redefines expertise to mean expertise in the use of substitutes for expertise. From all the skills we can acquire, only those associated with software and programming seem to have engendered such notions, and the reason is simple: these skills are *more complex* than the others, and hence misunderstood. They are so complex, in fact, that they permit us to use our mind and view the world in entirely new ways. They are comparable in scope only to our linguistic skills.

For other skills we had centuries to determine what are the highest levels of competence attainable by humans. We discovered that the longer we practise the better we become, and this is especially true of the complex skills. It is rare to find a field of knowledge where a certain performance level can be said to be the highest level attainable; sooner or later, someone will appear and show us that an even higher level is possible. So, while in other fields we all agree on the meaning of personal experience and know how difficult it is to attain expertise, in our software pursuits we believe the charlatans who claim that experience and expertise are no longer needed, that they can be replaced with methods and devices.

We are witnessing, thus, an absurd situation: Our software pursuits may well demand the most complex type of knowledge we ever created. At the same time, we believe this type of knowledge to be simpler than all the others, so simple that it demands only a fraction of our mental capabilities. All we need to know, we are told, is how to use the methods and devices designed to *replace* this knowledge.

So it is the complexity itself that allows charlatans to deceive us. We became infatuated with software too quickly, without taking the time to appreciate the true meaning and the implications of software knowledge. We still do not understand what can happen when a society depends on software while software is controlled by an authority. This is why we continue to accept the absurd notions promoted by the software elites; in particular, the notion that software is a kind of product, and that we need a software industry. It is precisely because software knowledge is so difficult that we are tempted by theories which tell us that we can enjoy the benefits of software without taking the time to develop software knowledge.

3

We wouldn't believe charlatans who told us that we could enjoy the benefits of language without learning to speak properly – by using, instead, various expedients designed to act as substitutes for linguistic knowledge; but we believe the charlatans who claim the same thing for software. The similarity of language and software, we saw in chapter 4, can help us to understand our software delusions. Let us take a moment, therefore, to imagine what would happen if we allowed an elite to control language as the software elites are controlling software.

Imagine that we lived in a society where a language elite would persuade us that, instead of learning to use language, we must learn to operate various devices that somehow fulfil our communication needs. The elite would also persuade us that, instead of starting with words, we must use ready-made sentences and ideas supplied by language companies. It should be obvious that under these conditions we would enjoy only a fraction of the benefits of language, even as our preoccupations with language-related problems would multiply.

Our language preoccupations are insignificant now, but this is because we are all competent language users. We all take the time (when growing up) to develop linguistic knowledge, and we do this, not by *avoiding* the use of language, but by *using* language. We don't try to communicate by combining ready-made sentences and ideas, but by creating our own, starting with words. Thus, we don't expect to benefit from language by replacing linguistic knowledge with substitutes. We recognize that the potency of language lies, not in the structures of words and sentences themselves, but in their ability to interact with the knowledge structures we hold in the mind, thereby giving rise to even richer knowledge structures.

It is not difficult to invent devices that generate linguistic structures for us, but this would be of little value. It is complex structures that we need, if we want knowledge that mirrors the world accurately. And the only way to create the complex structures is by allowing our mind to process and link all knowledge structures, including the linguistic ones, starting from low-level elements. If we tried to bypass this process and use instead ready-made linguistic structures, we would lose the low-level interactions, and hence limit ourselves to a fraction of the alternatives possible. To put it differently, we would limit ourselves to a fraction of the knowledge that we *are* capable of attaining. Instead of helping us to communicate, language would become a source of problems – the spurious problems generated by our dependence on simple structures.

The linguistic problems in this imaginary society would be caused, just like the software problems in our own society, by the limitations of mechanistic knowledge. If we limited ourselves to high-level starting elements, we would be using only our mechanistic capabilities, and our non-mechanistic ones would remain undeveloped. If we believed that this is the only way to have language, we would not be surprised when we failed to express our thoughts or feelings, or failed to understand a message, or failed in any other task that depends on language – just as we are unsurprised now when noting that our software applications are inadequate. We would simply look for answers within the range of solutions available to us.

We would assume, for example, that we needed a different device: perhaps an improved version that runs faster, or makes longer sentences, or includes more adjectives. We wouldn't know how much more we can accomplish with our *non-mechanistic* capabilities, so we would keep trying the endless devices and ready-made linguistic structures provided by the language elite. The time we currently take to develop our linguistic skills, simply by *using* language, we would waste with the problems generated by the language devices. Year after year, instead of improving our knowledge of language, and through language our knowledge of the world, we would be improving only the trivial skills required to operate language devices. We would worship the language elite – just as we now worship our software elites – convinced that the devices are essential linguistic tools, when in fact their purpose would be to *prevent* us from using language effectively.

This imaginary society resembles, of course, the one described by George Orwell (see "Orwell's Newspeak" in chapter 5). It is a society where language is restricted to its mechanistic aspects in order to restrict thinking to the level of machines. It is not the impoverishment of *language* that is the ultimate goal of the elite, but the impoverishment of all knowledge. Since language structures take part in most structures formed in the mind, by controlling language and by impoverishing mental structures the elite can then program and control human beings as readily as we program and control machines.

And if we recall the similarity of software and language, and their common role in society – to help us communicate, and to help us mirror reality in our minds – it is not difficult to see that an elite can create through software the same kind of society it could create through language. If the only software structures we develop are the impoverished ones permitted by our software elites, then our knowledge, beliefs, and expectations will be restricted to a small set of alternatives. Thus, by degrading software to its mechanistic aspects, the elites can degrade minds and restrict thinking to the level of machines, just as they could by degrading language. The equivalent of Newspeak in our society is software created with development systems and methodologies, or software that comes ready-made. If, as society, we limit ourselves to this impoverished software, by the time we depend on software as much as we depend now on language our minds will be as degraded as the minds of the people in Orwell's society.

This has *already* happened in the domain of programming. Our values in programming are so low that neither the software practitioners nor those who depend on their work can tell the difference between expertise and ignorance, between professional performance and irresponsible decisions, and even between the success and failure of an application. What we expect of software practitioners is not to complete an important task, or to solve a real problem, or to make a measurable contribution to their organization, but merely to know how to use the latest development tools, or how to deal with small pieces of an application, or how to put together some ready-made software parts. In short, they are only expected to perform some simple and isolated acts – acts which can be learned by almost anyone in a few months, and which can rarely fail. There is hardly any need for complex knowledge in their work, so we consider them expert practitioners simply because they are engaged in these acts. Our collective conception of expertise in the domain of programming has been so degraded that we are ready to believe that the work performed by incompetents represents the highest level of knowledge attainable by human minds.

And, as the same degradation of knowledge and values is spreading into other occupations, we can already envisage a society where all types of work have been reduced to the performance of some simple acts; that is, a society where the idea of expertise has lost its meaning, as the only thing left for people to do is to follow rules and methods, and to operate software devices.

If it is difficult for us to imagine a society where *language* was degraded to its mechanistic aspects, this is because we already know that we *can* become competent language users, and that we do *not* have to depend on language companies for our linguistic needs. With language we already know that we *can* start from low levels of abstraction, and that we *must* link the language structures to the other types of knowledge if language is to perform its functions. The software elites are preventing us from attaining in software the level of competence we have attained in language, but we fail to see this. There is no reason why we could not become as good in programming as we are with language, no reason why we could not create complex software structures as effectively as we are creating complex language structures.

If our society is to depend on software as much as it depends on language, ideally we all ought to be competent programmers, just as we are all competent language users. Realistically, though, we must admit that we do not all have the necessary talents; nor can we all devote our time to developing programming expertise and to creating software applications. But the solution is no different from what we do in other fields: only *some* members of society become professional practitioners, and the rest depend on them.

It is significant that those who reach expertise in a particular skill are as comfortable in that skill as we all are in naturally acquired skills – in the use of language, for instance. Thus, they perform much of their work intuitively, rather than by following rules and methods. And this, in fact, is the only way to perform tasks requiring complex knowledge (see "Tacit Knowledge" in chapter 2).

It is also significant that very few *programmers* reach this level of expertise in *their* profession. They believe that mechanistic knowledge is the only knowledge needed, so they deprive themselves of the opportunity to practise: instead of simply creating and maintaining applications, they waste their time assimilating endless concepts, languages, and methodologies. As a result, they keep acquiring some useless knowledge over and over, while their actual programming experience remains where it was after the first year or two. They accumulate various bits of knowledge in the form of simple, isolated structures, instead of developing the complex knowledge structures that constitute expertise. Were programmers permitted to attain the highest level their minds are capable of – as we do in other professions, and as we do with language – we would easily recognize the absurdity of the mechanistic software theories.

4

Our preoccupation with *ease of use* deserves a brief analysis. Software – applications, development systems, utilities – is always promoted with the claim that it is easy to use. I want to show, however, that the belief in easy-to-use software is a mechanistic delusion. The notion "easy to use" is, strictly speaking, meaningless.

Like any tool or device, a piece of software cannot be any easier to use than whatever effort is required to accomplish a given task. The only sensible claim, therefore, is that it is *well-designed*. A lathe, for example, even if well-designed, is necessarily more difficult to use than a chisel. And so it is with software: all we can expect of a particular business application, or a particular development tool, is that it be well-designed. Once this requirement is fulfilled, the notion "easy to use" becomes irrelevant: that software will be as easy or as difficult to use as software can be in a particular situation.

Now, we see the claim "easy to use" for *all* types of software – for business and for home, for programmers and for end users. We never see software described, for example, with the warning that we need much knowledge, or many months of study and practice, in order to enjoy its features. Thus, as we are becoming dependent on software in practically everything we do, if all this software is also easy to use, we reach the absurd conclusion that human beings will never again have to face a challenging situation.

The delusion of easy-to-use software becomes clearer if we recall the other quality commonly claimed for software – *power*. Just as all software devices are said to be easy to use, they are also said to be powerful. The two qualities are often claimed together, in fact, as in the famous phrase "powerful yet easy to use." By combining the two qualities, the following interpretation presents itself: we believe that software devices embody a certain power, and we perceive ease of use as the ease of invoking this power.

The only power that can inhere in a software device is its built-in operations; that is, higher levels of abstraction for our starting elements. And it is the higher levels that also make the device easy to use. The power and ease of use are illusory, however: high starting levels make the device convenient when our needs match the built-in operations, but awkward or useless otherwise.

We saw this with the language analogy: we have *less* power when starting with ready-made sentences; we must start with *words* if what we want is the capability to express any conceivable idea. Similarly, if true software power is the capability to implement any software system, the only way to have this power is by starting with *low-level* entities. Like claiming ease of use, therefore, claiming power for a software device is nonsensical: what is usually described as power is the exact opposite of software power. Moreover, since ease of use can be attained only by providing higher starting levels, and hence by *reducing* the power of the device, claiming both power and ease of use at the same time is especially silly.

Putting all this together, it is obvious that the software elites want us to think of software as an assortment of devices that have the power to solve our problems, while all *we* have to do is *use* them. The only thing left for us to do from now on is operate software devices; and this we can learn in a matter of hours. This notion is absurd, as we just saw, and yet we enthusiastically accept it. The elites are plainly telling us that we will no longer have the opportunity to use the full capacity of our minds, that our sole responsibility will be to perform tasks so simple that anyone can learn to perform them in a short time. But instead of being outraged, we welcome this demotion; and, to rationalize it, we interpret our diminished responsibility as a new kind of expertise.

❖

The elites also claim that software devices will enhance our creativity, by taking over the dull, routine activities. With higher starting levels, the elites tell us, we can reach the top element of a given structure much sooner. Why waste our time and talents with the details of the low levels, when the functions built into these devices already include all the combinations of low-level elements that we are likely to need? When starting from low levels we squander our superior mental capabilities on trivial and repetitive tasks; let the computer perform this tedious work for us, so that we have more time for those tasks demanding creativity. Just as successful managers and generals deal only with the important decisions and leave the details to their subordinates, we should restrict ourselves to high-level software entities and leave the details to the computer.

It is easy to show the absurdity of these claims. We are told to give up the details, and to use instead ready-made entities, so that we have more time for the important work, more time to be creative. But our work *is* the development of high-level entities from low-level ones. In one occupation after another, the software elites are redefining the concept of work to mean the act of combining the high-level entities provided by their devices. To be creative, however, we must be able to arrive at *any one* of the possible alternatives; and this we can do only by starting with *low-level* entities. Moreover, we are offered software devices in *all* fields of knowledge, so we cannot even hope that the time we perhaps save in one type of work will permit us to be more creative in another.

Returning to the language analogy, if a writer used ready-made sentences instead of creating new ones, starting with words, we would study his work and recognize that he is not being *more* but *less* creative. Clearly, fewer ideas can be expressed by selecting and combining ready-made sentences than by creating our own, starting with words. And this is true for all types of knowledge: the higher the level we start with, the greater the effect of reification and abstraction, and the fewer the alternatives for the top element. So it is absurd to claim that we can be more creative by avoiding the low levels, seeing that it is precisely the low levels that make creativity possible.

Managers and generals who make good decisions only *appear* to start from high levels. In reality, their decisions involve knowledge structures that interact at low levels, at the level of details. But this is largely intuitive knowledge, so all we can observe is the top element of the complex structure; that is, the final decision. (See "Tacit Knowledge" in chapter 2.) They developed their knowledge over many years, by dealing with all structures and all levels, low and high. This is the essence of personal experience. Were their knowledge limited to the high levels, to those selections and combinations that can be observed, then anyone could quickly become a successful manager or general – simply by learning to select and combine some high-level entities.

This delusion is also the basis of the software devices known as expert systems – one of the sillier ideas in artificial intelligence. Expert systems claim that it is possible to capture, in a specially structured database, the knowledge possessed by a human expert in a given domain. The database consists of answers that the expert provides to certain questions – questions formulated so as to simulate various decision-making situations. Then, for a real problem, simply by interrogating the system, anyone should be able to make the same decisions that the expert would make. The fact that such devices are being considered at all demonstrates the degradation in the notions of expertise and responsibility that we have already suffered. As we saw in "Tacit Knowledge," expertise is the level where a person does *not* have to rely on rules, methods, and databases of facts (see pp. 159–160). Thus, the device can capture only the *mechanistic* aspects of the expert's knowledge; and consequently, a person using it will not emulate an expert but a novice.

Another claim we see is that software devices enhance our creativity by giving us new forms of expression. And this claim, too, is empty. Software does indeed allow us to express ourselves and to view the world in new ways, as does language. But, as in the case of language, we can only enjoy this quality if we develop our structures starting with *low-level* entities. For, only then can we discover all possible interactions between the software structures, between software structures and the other structures that exist in the world, and between software structures and the knowledge structures present in our minds. If we get to depend on software devices, and hence on *high-level* software entities, we will not only fail to develop all possible alternatives in the new, software-related matters, but we will lose alternatives in the knowledge and skills that we had in the past. In the end, we will have *fewer* alternatives than before, *fewer* ways to express ourselves. Thus, far from *enhancing* our creativity, software devices are in fact degrading our minds, by forcing us to spend more and more time with activities requiring largely mechanistic knowledge.

❖

Power and ease of use, thus, are specious qualities. The elites tell us that software devices can have these qualities because they want to replace our traditional conception of expertise with a dependence on these devices. They want us to believe that all the knowledge that matters inheres now in software devices, so all *we* have to know is how to operate them. The implicit promise is that, thanks to these devices, we don't need to know anything that we don't already know – or, at least, anything that we cannot learn in a short time.

So the elites are downgrading our conception of expertise by reducing to a minimum the range from novice to expert. If all we have to know is how to operate software devices, the difference between novice and expert is just the time taken to acquire this knowledge. Where we thought that one needs many years of study and practice to attain expertise in a difficult field, we are told that this type of knowledge is obsolete. The propaganda makes it seem modern, sophisticated, and glamorous to perform a task by operating a software device, and unprofessional or old-fashioned to perform it by using our minds. Consequently, we are according more importance to our methods and tools than we do to the results of our work. Increasingly, we are judging a person's knowledge and skills by his acquaintance with software devices, instead of his actual capabilities and accomplishments. Increasingly, it doesn't even matter what the results are, as the main criterion for assessing a professional activity is whether the person is using the latest software devices.

5

Recall the pseudosciences we studied in chapter 3. I stated there that our software delusions belong to the same tradition, that they are a consequence of the same mechanistic culture. With our software theories we are committing the same fallacies as the scientists who pursue mechanistic theories in psychology, sociology, or linguistics. When we waste our time with the spurious problems generated by our mechanistic software concepts, we are like the scientists who waste their time studying the mechanistic phenomena created by reifying human phenomena. Just as those scientists cannot explain the complex phenomena of mind and society by explaining separately the simple, mechanistic phenomena, *we* cannot solve our complex social or business problems by solving the simple, software-related problems.

These mechanistic delusions I have called *the new pseudosciences*, and we saw that they are similar to the traditional pseudosciences – astrology, alchemy, and the rest. They are similar in that they too are systems of belief masquerading as scientific theories, and they too are based on a hypothesis that is taken as unquestionable truth. In the case of the new pseudosciences, the hypothesis is that mechanism can provide useful explanations for complex phenomena – for phenomena involving human minds and societies, in particular. The mechanists are, in effect, today's astrologers and alchemists: respected thinkers who attract many followers, even though their theories do not work.

Before we had software, it was only in the academic world that one could spend years and decades pursuing a mechanistic fantasy. One could hardly afford to fall prey to mechanistic delusions in business, for instance. But through software, the ignorance and corruption engendered by mechanistic thinking is increasingly affecting the entire society: corporations, governments, individuals. Through software, we are all asked now to accept fantastic mechanistic theories – theories that promise to solve our problems with practically no effort on our part. Through software, the entire society is returning to the irrationality of the Dark Ages: we are increasingly guided by dogmas instead of logic, by beliefs instead of reason.

When we believe that a software device can replace knowledge, skills, and experience, we are committing the same mistake as the scientists who believe that mechanistic theories can explain human intelligence and social phenomena. So if all of us now, not just the academics, are wasting our time with pseudoscientific theories, we must ask ourselves: Can we afford this corruption? Can our civilization survive if *all* of us engage in futile mechanistic pursuits? When mechanistic theories fail in the academic world, the harm is limited to a waste of resources, and perhaps a lost opportunity to improve our knowledge through better theories. But what price will we pay if we create a society where *all* theories fail?

As we are modifying our values and expectations to fit the mechanistic ideology, we are adopting, in effect, mechanistic theories – theories on our capabilities as human beings, or on our responsibilities as professionals. And since these software-based theories suffer from the same fallacies as the traditional mechanistic theories, they too must fail. But what does it mean for *these* theories to fail? Since what they claim is that we can accomplish more by depending on software devices than by developing our minds, a failure of *these* theories means that we are making a wrong decision about ourselves: we mistakenly assume that our minds can be no better than some mechanistic expedients. Thus, when we decide to leave our non-mechanistic capabilities undeveloped and to depend instead on mechanistic expedients, we are causing, quite literally, a reversal in our intellectual evolution: we are choosing to degrade our conception of intelligence to a mechanistic level, and to create a world where there is no need or opportunity to exceed this level.

Let us interpret the new pseudosciences in another way. The equivalent of a world where we depend on software while being restricted to mechanistic software theories is an imaginary world where the *traditional* mechanistic theories – those explaining minds and societies – actually work. Since these theories fail to explain our *real* intelligence and behaviour, in the imaginary world we would have to alter minds and societies to fit the theories. To comply with the linguistic theory of universal grammar, for example, we would restrict our sentences, and the associated thoughts, to what can be depicted with exact diagrams and formulas; similarly, to comply with behaviourism or cognitive science, we would restrict our behaviour and mental acts to patterns that can be precisely explained and predicted; and to comply with the theories of structuralism or the social sciences, we would restrict our institutions, customs, and cultures to activities that can be described mathematically.

These theories reflect the diminished view that mechanists have of human beings – the view that our acts can be explained with precision, because our capabilities are like those of complicated machines. The scientists who invent and promote mechanistic theories wish them to work, of course. But the theories can work only if we are indeed like machines, so we must conclude that these scientists *want* us to be like machines. And if we, the subjects of these theories, also wanted them to work – if we agreed, as it were, to satisfy the wish of their authors – we would have to restrict our capabilities to what these theories can explain and predict. In other words, we would have to mutate into automatons.

What has saved us from this fate so far is not wisdom – for, if we had that wisdom we would have abandoned the mechanistic ideology already – but the fact that none of these scientists had the power to make us conform to their theories. Through software, however, it has finally become possible for the mechanists to realize their dream: a world where human beings can be designed and controlled as successfully as we design and control machines. The world that we can only *imagine* through the traditional mechanistic theories, we are actually creating through our mechanistic *software* theories. Whereas we can still think, learn, speak, and behave while ignoring the mechanistic theories of mind and society, we are forced to create and use software according to mechanistic theories. But if we are to depend on software in all aspects of our life – including those aspects studied by the theories of mind and society – then by following mechanistic software theories we *are*, in effect, mutating into the automatons that the mechanists wish us to be.

Remember, though, that it is not software dependence in itself that is harmful. On the contrary, if we were permitted to use it freely, as we use language, software would *enhance* our mental capabilities, as does language. The danger lies in the dependence on software while software knowledge is restricted to its mechanistic aspects – a policy intended to prevent us from using the full capacity of our minds.

❖

The decision we are making now is more than a choice; it is a commitment. As individuals and as society, we are making a commitment; namely, to invest in software expedients rather than our minds.

As individuals, we reaffirm this commitment when we consent to depend on software devices that are inferior to our own minds; when we spend time solving a specious, software-related problem, instead of expanding our knowledge to deal with the real problem; and when we degrade our conception of professionalism and responsibility, from the utmost that human beings can do, to merely knowing how to use software devices. As society, we reaffirm this commitment when our corporations and governments, instead of encouraging their workers to develop expertise, spend vast amounts of money on projects that increase their dependence on the software elites.

As individuals, if we are wrong, our knowledge in ten years, for instance, will not be much greater than what it is at present. We will waste that time acquiring worthless bits of knowledge; specifically, knowledge of ways to avoid the need for real knowledge. If we make this choice, of course, we will be unable to recognize our own ignorance in ten years; so for the following ten years we will make the same choice, and so on, and we will remain for the rest of our lives at the present level. As society, if we are wrong, within a few decades we will be where we were centuries ago: in a new dark age, ruled by elites that know how to exploit our ignorance and irrationality.

The decision we are making now is a commitment because we cannot choose both alternatives. If software mechanism is our decision, we will need only mechanistic capabilities; so we will leave our superior, non-mechanistic capabilities undeveloped. If we are wrong, we cannot reverse this decision later: if we choose the mechanistic alternative, in any domain, we will not practise; and practising is the only way to develop non-mechanistic knowledge. If we lose our appreciation of non-mechanistic knowledge, we will forget, in one occupation after another, that we *are* capable of more than just following methods and operating software devices.

This is precisely what has happened in the domain of programming. The superior alternative – personal knowledge and skills – is always available, in principle: any programmer, any manager, any company, could choose to ignore the official software ideology and treat programming as we do the other professions. Yet, despite the evidence that programming aids and substitutes are inferior to human expertise, we continue to trust the software elites and their mechanistic theories. In the domain of programming, we have already lost our appreciation of non-mechanistic knowledge.

Software Charlatanism

Software exploitation, we saw, plays on our mechanistic delusions; namely, on the belief that problems requiring complex knowledge can be broken down into simpler problems, which can then be solved mechanistically. When the software charlatans tempt us with the promise of easy answers to difficult problems – answers in the form of software devices – what they do is tempt us to commit the mechanistic fallacies, reification and abstraction. For, only if we commit these fallacies will we believe that software devices can be a substitute for the complex, non-mechanistic knowledge required to solve those problems.

In the present section, we will examine how the mechanistic delusions manifest themselves in various software-related activities; that is, how the two mechanistic fallacies lead to *software* delusions, and how these delusions are being exploited by the software elites. The world of programming, in particular, consists almost entirely of delusions, and we will study them in detail in chapter 7. Here, the programming delusions are mentioned briefly, just to show how they are contributing to delusions in other software-related activities.

The Delusion of High Levels

1

Recall our discussion in "Software Structures" in chapter 4. Software applications are complex structures, because they can be viewed from different perspectives. Each aspect of an application is one of its processes, one of the simple structures that make up the complex structure. Thus, each subroutine together with its uses, each database field or memory variable together with the associated operations, each business rule or programming method, can be seen as a simple structure. But these structures are not independent. Although in our imagination we can separate them, in reality they share their elements (the software entities that make up the application), so they interact.

Take, for example, subroutines.[1] The use of subroutines is usually shown as part of the application's flow-control logic – those neat diagrams said to define precisely and completely the flow of execution. Subroutines, though, give rise to *additional* relations between software elements – relations that are not seen

---

[1] As in chapter 4, I subsume under "subroutine" any software entity that is used in several parts of the application – modules, functions, procedures, objects, etc. (see p. 353).

in a diagram that represents their calls. Each subroutine, along with its uses and effects, forms a hierarchical structure. One way to depict this structure is as follows: the application (the top element) branches into two categories, those software elements that are affected by the subroutine and those that are unaffected; then, the first category branches into more detailed ones, on one or more levels, reflecting the various ways the subroutine affects them, while the second category branches into more detailed ones reflecting the various reasons the subroutine does *not* affect them; finally, the categories branch into the low-level elements – the blocks of statements and the individual statements that make up the application.

It is not difficult to see that, if we do this for different subroutines, the resulting structures will be different. The terminal elements, however, will be the same; for, in all structures, the terminal elements are the application's statements. Thus, since these structures share their elements, they are bound to interact. So there is no one structure that can represent *all* the subroutines. The only way to represent the subroutines and their calls accurately is as a system of interacting structures. The neat diagram that claims to represent the flow of execution does indeed reduce the application to a simple hierarchical structure, but it does this by distorting reality; specifically, by showing only *some* of the relations that subroutines create between software elements (the calls themselves).

Each subroutine, thus, constitutes *one* aspect of the application, one way of viewing it. But there are other ways yet of viewing the application, besides the use of subroutines. We can view it, for example, from the perspective of each set of related data entry operations, or each shared variable or database field, or each business practice implemented in the application. Like subroutines, each one of these processes constitutes one aspect of the application, and can be represented with a hierarchical structure that describes its effects on the software entities that make up the application. And, along with the structures generated by subroutines, these structures share their terminal elements (the software entities we find at the low levels).

A software application, then, is all these structures, and the difficulties we face in programming are due largely to having to deal with many of them at the same time. Clearly, if a software element is shared by several structures, we must take into account all of them if we are to program the element correctly. Most software deficiencies are due to overlooking the links between structures – links caused by this sharing of elements: the programmer takes into account the effect of an operation on some of the structures, but fails to recognize its effect on others. We must accept the fact that software applications are non-mechanistic phenomena: the interactions between their constituent structures are too complex to represent with mechanistic means like rules, diagrams, or mathematics. To put it differently, the approximations possible with mechanistic models are rarely accurate enough for software applications.

If we forget that applications are complex phenomena, we may think of programming as simply identifying all the structures and interactions, dealing with them separately, and then combining the results. But this would amount to reducing a complex structure to simple ones, and we already know that this is impossible. Even *thinking* of these structures separately is an illusion, since they can only exist as *interacting* structures. We may refer to them informally as separate structures (this is the only way to discuss the issue), but we must bear in mind that they exist only in our imagination; what exists in reality is the complex structure, the whole phenomenon. Thus, if we create the application by dealing with those structures separately, we will likely end up with a *different* phenomenon – a different application. What we will notice in practice is that the application does not work as we expected, and the reason is that some of the interactions are wrong, or missing.

Programming, therefore, requires the capacity for complex structures. So it requires a human mind, because only minds can develop the complex knowledge structures that can mirror the complex phenomena of programming. As programmers, we are expected to combine in our mind the various aspects of an application. We are expected, thus, to develop knowledge that cannot be precisely specified (with rules or diagrams, for instance). And we *can* develop this type of knowledge, because minds can process complex structures.

Nor is this an unreasonable demand. What we are expected to do in programming is no different from what we have to do most of the time simply to live a normal life. Recall the analysis of stories (pp. 350–351). We are all expected to combine in our mind the various aspects of a story that we hear or read. This, in fact, is the only way to understand it, because it is impossible to specify precisely and completely all the knowledge embodied in a story. We understand a story by *discovering* this knowledge. Authors can convey to us, through the expedient of words and sentences, almost any ideas, situations, arguments, or feelings. Complex knowledge that exists in one person's mind can be reproduced with great accuracy in other minds by means of language. We derive *some* of this knowledge from the individual structures – from sentences, and from each aspect of the story. Most of the knowledge, however, inheres not in individual structures but in their *interactions*. We discover these interactions by processing the structures. We develop the complex knowledge that is the story by unconsciously combining its structures in our mind, and combining them also with the knowledge structures already present in the mind. Linguistic communication is possible because we have the capacity to combine knowledge structures, and because we already possess some knowledge that is the same as the author's.

If we tried to express by means of independent structures all the knowledge we derived from a story, we would find it an impossible task, because a complex structure cannot be reduced to simple ones. What we would lose is the interactions. Even if we managed somehow to identify all the elements and all the aspects of the story, we could not identify all their interactions. To put this differently, if we could reduce the story to a set of precise specifications, we could program a computer to understand that story exactly as *we* do – a preposterous notion; or, the fact that a machine cannot understand stories as *we* do proves that stories, and linguistic communication generally, involve complex structures.

And so do software applications. The software theories, then, are wrong when claiming that applications can be programmed with the methods used in building physical structures. In manufacturing and construction we can restrict ourselves to mechanistic methods because we purposely restrict our physical structures to neat hierarchies of parts and subassemblies. But software applications are more akin to stories than to physical structures. This is true because we employ software, as we do language, to represent the world, and our concerns and affairs, which consist of complex phenomena. The potency of software, like that of language, lies in its ability to generate complex structures. If we restricted ourselves to mechanistic methods, as we do in manufacturing and construction, we would use only a fraction of this potency; and we would be unable to create linguistic or software structures that represent the world, or our concerns and affairs, accurately.

We can detect in the individual structures *some* of the knowledge that constitutes the application. But much of this knowledge inheres in the *interactions* between structures. We cannot specify it precisely and completely, therefore, any more than we can specify precisely and completely all the knowledge that inheres in a story. If we reduce this knowledge to precise specifications – as we are obliged to do when strictly following mechanistic programming methods – we must necessarily leave some of it out, and the application will not work as we expected.

It is impossible to create adequate software applications with mechanistic methods for the same reason it is impossible to create or understand *stories* with mechanistic methods. But we know that we can, by relying on the non-mechanistic capabilities of our mind, create and understand complex linguistic structures. We also can, therefore, by relying on the same non-mechanistic capabilities, create complex *software* structures; namely, applications that mirror the complexity of the world. This is the meaning of programming expertise.

We are so easily deceived by the mechanistic software theories because we like their promise. The promise, essentially, is that methods and devices simple enough to be used by almost anyone can be a substitute for programming expertise. And we believe this promise because we fail to see that to accept it means to commit the two mechanistic fallacies, reification and abstraction.

The software theories appear to make programming easier because they treat applications, or the activities involved in creating applications, as separable into independent parts: database operations, display operations, reporting operations, and so on. There are indeed many aspects to an application, as we saw, but these are rarely independent structures. The software theories invite us to reify programming and applications because, once we have independent structures, they can tempt us to start from higher levels of abstraction within each structure. By the time we commit both fallacies, what is left of programming is indeed easy. But it is easy because the concept of programming, and the resulting software, were impoverished: many of the functions we could implement before are no longer possible.

All software theories, in the final analysis, make the same claim: the task of programming can be simplified by starting the development process from higher-level software elements; and we can accomplish this by allowing various expedients – methodologies, software tools, built-in operations – to act as substitutes for the knowledge, experience, and work necessary for creating the lower levels. But this would be possible only if applications consisted of independent structures.

Let us briefly examine how this claim manifests itself in some of the theories and devices promoted by the software elites. The theory known as structured programming encourages us to view the application as a neat hierarchical structure of software elements, which can then be developed independently, one level at a time; but we can do this only if we take into account just one aspect of the application – namely, the sequence of execution of its elements – and ignore the links that the other aspects cause between the same elements. The relational database theory claims that databases can be designed as independent structures, interacting only at high levels with the structures formed by the other aspects of the application; but this is true only in very simple situations. Many development environments provide built-in operations for the user interface, claiming in effect that these operations can be separated from the other aspects, or that the interactions between them occur only at high levels; but in most applications the user interface interacts with the other processes at the low level of statements and variables. Systems like spreadsheets and report writers claim that users can create simple applications without programming – by combining instead some high-level, built-in operations; but even simple applications involve aspects that interact at low levels, and require therefore programming in one form or another. The concept of ready-made components or objects is based on the assumption that business systems of any complexity can be "built" from high-level software elements, just as cars and appliances are built from prefabricated subassemblies; but the assumption is wrong, because, unlike physical components, software components must also interact at the lower levels that are their internal operations.

2

To demonstrate the fallacy of high starting levels, let us analyze a specific situation. A common requirement, found in most business applications, is to access individual fields in database files. The application's user may need to see the phone number or the outstanding balance of a customer, or the quantity in stock of a certain part; or he may need to modify the address of a customer, or the description of a part. Very often, these operations involve more than one file; for example, a customer is displayed together with its outstanding invoices, or a part together with its sales history. Typically, the user specifies some values to identify the records: customer number, invoice number, range of dates, etc. The program displays certain fields from those records, and the user is perhaps permitted to modify some of them. These can be isolated fields (thus giving the user the opportunity to see or modify any files and fields in the database), but most often they are groups of fields logically associated with specific functions: inventory control, financial information, shipping activity, etc. If we also include such options as adding new records and deleting existing ones, we may refer to this category of operations as *file maintenance* operations.

Now, file maintenance operations constitute fairly simple programming tasks. Moreover, much of this programming is very similar in all applications. So it is tempting to conclude that we can replace the programming of file maintenance operations with a number of high-level software elements – some built-in procedures, for example. We should then be able to generate any file maintenance operation by combining these high-level elements, rather than starting with the individual statements and operations of a traditional programming language. I want to show, though, that despite the simplicity and repetitiveness of file maintenance programming, it is impossible to start from higher-level elements.

The illusion of high levels arises when we perceive software as a combination of separable structures, or aspects. There are at least two aspects to the file maintenance operations: database operations and user interface operations. So, to keep the discussion simple, let us assume that these two aspects are the only important ones. If we think of each aspect separately, it is quite easy to imagine the higher levels within each structure, and to conclude that we can start from higher levels. We may decide, for example, that most database operations can be generated by starting with some built-in procedures that let us access specific records and fields; and most interface operations, with some built-in procedures that display individual fields and accept new values. Thus, by specifying a few parameters (file and field names, index keys, display coordinates, etc.), we should be able to generate, simply by invoking these procedures, most combinations of database operations, and most combinations of interface operations.

We commit the fallacy of abstraction, however, if we believe that the alternatives possible when starting from higher levels are about the same as those we had before. The temptation of high levels is so great that we are liable to perceive an application as simpler than it actually is, just so that we can rationalize the reduced flexibility. It takes much experience to anticipate the consequences of the restriction to high levels. For, it is only later, when the application proves to be inadequate, when important requirements cannot be met and even simple details are difficult to implement, that the impoverishment caused by abstraction becomes evident.

But abstraction became possible only through reification – only after separating the two structures, database and user interface. And reification causes its own kind of impoverishment. We can indeed view file maintenance operations from the perspective of either the database or the interface operations, but only in our imagination. In reality, the file maintenance operations consist of *both* the database and the interface operations. Separately, these operations can indeed be represented as simple structures, because we can identify most of their elements and relations. But when part of an application, these operations interact, giving rise to a complex structure. It is this complex structure that constitutes the real file maintenance operations, not the two imaginary, reified simple structures.

Reification impoverishes the complex structure by destroying the interactions between its constituent structures. When we lose the interactions, we also lose many alternatives for the top element of the complex structure. Each alternative at this level represents a particular file maintenance operation, which may be required by some application. Certain interactions are still possible, of course – those that can be generated by combining the high-level, built-in procedures. The alternatives resulting from these interactions are the file maintenance operations that can be implemented even after reification and abstraction. Most interactions, however, take place at low levels, so they can only be implemented with such means as statements, variables, and conditions; that is, with programming languages. And these interactions are no longer possible once we lose the lower levels. The two fallacies, thus, contribute together to the impoverishment of the complex structure that is the application. They are usually committed together, and it is seldom possible, or necessary, to analyze them separately.

To appreciate why it is impossible to eliminate the low levels, all we have to do is think of the details that a programmer faces when implementing a typical file maintenance operation. Thus, the user may want to see only some of the fields at first, and then various other fields depending on the values present in the previous ones; or he may need to scan records, forward or backward, rather than ask for specific ones; in one application the user may want to see detailed information, in another only a summary; in one situation some of the fields may always be modified, in another the fields may be modified only under certain conditions; in some applications, modifying a field must produce a change in other fields, and perhaps in other files too; and so on.

Clearly, the number of possible requirements, even for relatively simple operations like file maintenance, is practically infinite. But the important point is that this variety, and the details that make up these requirements, entail the low levels of *both* the database and the interface operations. To implement a particular requirement, therefore, we need not only low-level software elements in both kinds of operations, but elements that can be *shared* by these operations; in other words, exactly what abstraction and reification would *prevent* us from creating. For example, to display a field depending on the value of another field, we must formulate conditional statements involving particular fields and display operations; and to display details from one file along with the summary of another, we must create a small piece of software that reads records, accesses fields, performs calculations and comparisons, and displays values.

Each requirement reflects a particular file maintenance operation; each one is, therefore, an alternative value for the top element of the complex structure formed by the interaction of the database and display operations. If we agree that a programmer must be able to implement *any* file maintenance operation, and hence to generate *any* alternative, it is obvious that he must be able to create and combine all the low-level elements forming the database operations, and all the low-level elements forming the display operations (and probably other low-level elements and operations too). The use of low levels helps us avoid both fallacies: it lets us generate all the alternatives within each structure, *and* the alternatives resulting from the interaction of the two structures.

If you still have doubts about the importance of the low levels, look at it this way: if just *one* low-level element is not available, at least one file maintenance operation will be impossible to implement; and if this alternative happens to be required, the application will be inadequate. Each alternative of the top element is the result of a unique combination of elements at the lower levels.

So, the only way to ensure that *any* alternative can be implemented is to retain the low-level elements.

Since each alternative is unique, no matter how many alternatives we have already implemented, or are available through built-in procedures, the next application may still have to be programmed starting with low-level elements. Only naive and inexperienced practitioners believe that they can have the versatility of the low levels while being involved only with high levels. In reality, the simplicity promised for high-level operations is achieved precisely by reducing the number of alternatives. It takes the experience of many applications to recognize in a given situation whether we can or cannot give up the low levels.

Note that we never question the need for low-level elements in the case of language. We may well *think* of the various aspects of a story separately; but we all agree that, if we want to retain the freedom to express any idea, we must start with the low-level elements of each aspect – and, moreover, with elements that can be *shared* by these aspects. Only words fulfil both requirements. No one would seriously claim that there exist methods or devices which enable us to start with ready-made sentences and still express any idea.

3

File maintenance was only an example, of course. A major application comprises *thousands* of aspects, most of them more involved than a database or display operation. Besides, we seldom encounter situations where only two aspects interact, as in our simplified file maintenance example. Even there, to discuss realistic situations we had to consider, in addition to the database and display operations, various business practices. These practices are themselves aspects of the application, so they add to the number of structures that must interact. We saw this, for instance, when I mentioned the small piece of software that accesses records and fields, performs calculations and comparisons, and displays values: a small element comprising just a few statements must be shared, nevertheless, by several processes – database, display, and one or more business practices – because this is the only way to implement an operation that involves these processes.

It is hardly necessary, therefore, to demonstrate the need for low levels in real applications, in situations involving thousands of aspects, after showing the need for them even in situations with two aspects. Rather, what I want to show is how the mechanistic fallacies, and the software delusions they engender, lead to software charlatanism. All forms of software exploitation are based, ultimately, on the delusion of high levels that we have just examined.

❖

The deception starts when we are offered some software that promises to enhance our capabilities; namely, software that will allow us to accomplish tasks requiring knowledge that we, in fact, lack. We are promised, in other words, that simply by operating a software device we will be in the same position as those whose skills and experience exceed ours. The promise, it must be emphasized, is not that we will quickly acquire the missing knowledge. On the contrary, the promise is specifically that we don't need to learn anything new: the power to perform those tasks resides in the device itself, so all we need to know is how to operate it.

As programmers, we are offered various tools, development environments, and database systems. We are told that these devices will enable us to create, quickly and easily, applications which otherwise would take us a long time to program, or which are too difficult for us to program at all. The promise, therefore, is that these devices will function as substitutes for programming expertise: through them, we will achieve the same results as programmers who have been developing and maintaining applications successfully for many years.

As users, we are offered various productivity systems, or office systems. We are told that these devices will solve our business problems directly, eliminating the need for programming. Or, we are offered ready-made applications or pieces of applications, and we are told that they will enable us to manage our business just as we would with custom applications created specially for us.

For programmers as for users, the promises are supported with the explanation that the software devices offer higher levels of abstraction: they simplify development by allowing us to start from higher-level elements, bypassing the difficult and time-consuming task of creating the lower levels. The higher-level elements appear in a variety of forms, but, essentially, they are built-in operations or ready-made pieces of software.

No matter what form the higher levels take, the underlying assumption is the same: the work involved in creating a software application is similar to a manufacturing project, so the application can be seen as a neat structure of things within things – parts, modules, subassemblies. Thus, as in manufacturing, the larger the building blocks, the faster we will complete the project. We should avoid programming, therefore, and start instead with the largest modules and subassemblies available: software entities that already contain the lower-level parts. The use of large building blocks benefits us in two ways: by speeding up the software manufacturing process, and by demanding lower skills. Less time, less knowledge, and less experience are needed to assemble a software structure from modules, than to design and build it from basic components. In the extreme case of ready-made applications, the manufacturing process is eliminated altogether: the starting level is then the top element itself, the complete application.

If software exploitation begins with the lure of high levels, the next stage is, needless to say, the disappointment. As programmers, we still cannot create complex and reliable applications; as users, we still cannot manage our affairs as we hoped. The software devices do provide the promised higher levels, and we can perhaps accomplish some tasks that we could not have accomplished without them. What we find, rather, is that the higher levels are rarely beneficial. If we want to start from higher levels, we must give up the flexibility afforded by the low levels. If we want the benefits of built-in operations and ready-made modules, of less work and easier challenges, we must be content with a fraction of the alternatives otherwise possible. Unfortunately, only rarely is this practical: only rarely can we restrict our affairs to the few alternatives provided by the software devices. The greater the promised benefits, the higher must be the starting levels, and the more severe the reduction in alternatives. The deception, thus, consists in promoting the benefits of higher starting levels while masking their concomitant drawbacks.

We adopt these devices and become dependent on them because we are seduced by slogans like "powerful" and "easy to use." We fail to see that these two qualities are contradictory: easy-to-use devices can be powerful only if we redefine power to mean, not the ability to implement *any* operations, but the ability to implement *some* operations easily. Clearly, if ease of use is claimed, all the power must inhere in the devices themselves, in their built-in capabilities. This means that they may perform well those operations that are built in, but they cannot perform other operations at all; and no device can have all conceivable operations built in.

The only way to implement *any* operations that may be required is by starting with low-level elements. So the software charlatans must provide the low levels if we are to use their devices at all. Their challenge, therefore, is how to reinstate the low levels, and how to make us start from these low levels, while we continue to believe that we are working at high levels. And they do it by implementing the low-level features *within* the high-level environment, as *extensions* to the high-level operations.

The low levels were always available to us – in the form of traditional programming languages, for example. So, if low levels are what we need, there is nothing the elites can give us that we did not have all along. The theories and methodologies, the programming tools and fourth-generation languages, the database and reporting systems, serve in reality the same purpose: they provide some of the low-level elements we need, and the means to link software structures, while pretending to be high-level environments.

The third stage in the process of exploitation, then, is the reinstatement of the low levels. To make their devices useful, the elites must restore the very concept that the devices were meant to supersede. Any device that does *not* provide this functionality is eventually abandoned and forgotten, even by the naive people who believed the original claims, simply because it is useless. (The full-fledged CASE environments, which actually tried to materialize the fantasy of creating entire applications "without writing a single line of code," are an example.)

We will waste no time, thus, examining the devices that do *not* restore the low levels. Let us treat them simply as fraudulent products, no different from the other forms of deception employed by charlatans to exploit gullible people – weight-loss contraptions, back-pain remedies, money-making schemes, and the like. As explained earlier, it is not the traditional means of exploitation, but the new form of domination, that concerns us: the use of software to consume our time and prevent us from gaining knowledge and experience. Eliminating the low levels and then restoring them in a different and more complicated form is an important factor in this domination, as it permits the elites to destroy software freedom and to establish the dependence on their devices. And we are fooled by these charlatans because the devices are based on software theories invented in universities, and described as "scientific."

Recall the principles of demarcation between science and pseudoscience, which we studied in chapter 3. Mechanistic software theories claim that we can create applications by starting with high-level elements. So, when this idea proves to be worthless and the charlatans "enhance" their devices by restoring the low-level capabilities, what they do in reality is turn the falsifications of those theories into new features. And this, we saw, is the stratagem through which fallacious theories are rescued from refutation. Thus, mechanistic software theories are intrinsically pseudoscientific.

Here are examples of software devices that were enhanced by restoring the low levels: The so-called fourth-generation languages started by promising us a higher level than the traditional, third-generation languages; but the only way to make them practical was by restoring, one by one, the features found in the traditional languages (loops, conditions, individual variables, etc.). The relational database systems started by claiming that the database can be treated as separate structures, interacting only at high levels with the other structures of the application; but they became practical only after adding countless new features, and whole programming languages, in order to restore the low-level links between these structures (for instance, the capability to access individual records directly, through file scanning loops). Systems like report writers and spreadsheets started by claiming that their high-level features are adequate for our requirements; but they ended up incorporating many traditional features, and even programming languages, in order to provide the low-level operations needed in real-world situations.

To summarize, high-level environments that restore the low levels exploit us in two ways. First, we get to depend on some new and complicated programming methods, arising from the idea of using low-level elements as an extension to high-level ones. The traditional method – creating high-level elements from low-level ones – is simple and natural; it follows a concept we all understand intuitively, and confers complete programming freedom. The new methods, on the other hand, are contrived – absurd and unnecessary; their purpose is to maintain the illusion of high levels, and to induce dependence on proprietary development systems. Second, these systems provide only *a few* of the low-level features available through the traditional methods, only the minimum necessary to fool us. So they remain, essentially, high-level environments, lacking the versatility of a general-purpose language. Each low-level feature is presented as a powerful enhancement, and this obscures the fact that these features are merely a more complicated version of features we always had – in the traditional programming languages.

4

The charlatans promise us power, but all they can give us is higher levels of abstraction. So, once they persuade us to adopt their devices, they must restore the essential low levels, while continuing to promote the devices as high-level environments. It is not too much to say, then, that the only real difference between these devices is how they mask the deception; namely, how they prevent us from noticing that we are working, in fact, at *low* levels.

It is precisely because their chief purpose is to deceive us – to persuade us that they possess some important qualities – that the devices end up so complicated and inefficient. The so-called non-procedural languages, for instance, are promoted with the claim that we only need to tell the computer now *what* to do, not *how* to do it. This sounds like a novel programming concept, as if we could almost talk to the computer and tell it what we need done. In reality, these languages merely incorporate a number of high-level elements in the form of built-in operations. And this concept is available in any programming language in the form of libraries of subroutines: ready-made functions providing levels of abstraction that are as high as we want.

But, whether we use subroutines or non-procedural languages, some of our starting elements must still be at low levels, because it is impossible to implement all conceivable requirements by relying entirely on ready-made, high-level elements. The non-procedural languages look impressive when all we need is one of their built-in operations (these are the examples we see in textbooks and in advertisements, of course), but are more awkward than a traditional language in any other situation. This is true because, in order to make them appear as novel concepts, their authors must make them different from the traditional programming languages; and this also makes them more complicated.

It is common in these languages, for example, when what we need is not just one of the built-in operations, to find long and tangled statements. A procedure that in a traditional language involves conditions, loops, and the use of variables, may turn up in a non-procedural language, in an extreme case, as *one* statement. But, while being perhaps shorter than the procedure, the statement is not, in fact, a higher-level entity: since its clauses must be specified with precision and in detail, they do not constitute a higher level of abstraction.

Thus, in SQL (the most popular database language), we often see statements containing more than a dozen lines, when a number of related database operations must be specified together. These long statements can become extremely complicated, as the programmer is forced to cram into one expression a whole series of related operations. Instead of the familiar structure of loops and conditions found in traditional languages, and which an experienced programmer understands intuitively, we now have an artificial and unwieldy set of specifications. But because the definitions, loops, and conditions are no longer manifest, this complicated piece of software is unlike a traditional language, so we can delude ourselves that what we are doing is no longer programming: "we are only telling the computer what to do, not how to do it."

What we are telling the computer is, however, the same as before. First, the level of abstraction is about the same as in a traditional language (this, after all, is why we needed SQL, why we could not simply use the high-level relational operations). Second, the resulting statements are still the reflection of many structures, which interact and must be kept in the mind simultaneously. In other words, all the difficulties we had before are still there; and because we wanted to *avoid* programming, we must now cope with these difficulties through programming means that are more complicated and less efficient than the traditional ones. (We will examine the SQL fraud in "The Relational Database Model" in chapter 7; see pp. 808–815.)

Let us look at another concept that promises higher levels and, instead, makes programming more complicated. This concept is based on the belief that specifying an operation by selecting it from a list of options, rather than by typing a command or a statement, represents a higher level of abstraction.

Most development environments have features based on this delusion. Like the non-procedural languages, creating applications by selecting things from lists is seen as a novel, high-level concept: all we do now, it seems, is tell the computer what we need, and it automatically generates pieces of software for us, even the entire application.

In reality, whether we select options or write statements, our starting elements must be a combination of high-level operations and low-level ones. Thus, even when we communicate with the system by selecting built-in operations, we must create the application's structures – its unique processes, or aspects – and the links between structures. For, if this were not the case, if our contribution were limited to making selections, the only applications we could create would be random and useless combinations of built-in operations.

With a traditional language, we tell the computer what to do by formulating statements, definitions, and expressions. With the new concept, we are shown lists of options, and options within options, and we tell the computer what to do by selecting entries from these lists. This creates the illusion that we are not programming, that all we must know is how to *select* things. What we must know, though, is the same as before; only the way we apply this knowledge is different.

In principle, one can specify anything by selecting options, but only with trivial requirements is this method more expedient than typing statements. The devices are promoted, however, for *all* applications. Clearly, no one would adopt them if told that they are meant only for novices, or only for solving simple and isolated problems. Thus, the devices must maintain the illusion that, no matter how complex the requirements, all we ever do is make selections; and this is why they end up making programming *more* difficult. But if we believe that one can accomplish more with these devices than without them, we will agree to perform any acts, no matter how illogical, just so that we can use them.

We encounter this delusion, for instance, in the development environments called *visual*, and in those called *by example*. Thus, the concept *query by example* claims to give users the means to perform certain database operations without programming. The concept sounds as if, instead of formulating queries, all we had to do now is show the system some examples of what we need. In reality, since there is no way for a database system to know what we need without being given precise information, we must provide the same specifications as before; and, because we wanted to avoid the traditional method of formulating queries, we end up with a more complicated one.

Thus, to tell the system which records to read, instead of expressing through a traditional language a condition like "products with price less than 100 and quantity in stock greater than 10," we must perform a number of selections: we select from a list of files "product," then from a list of fields "price," then from a list of relational operators "less," then the value 100, then three more selections for "quantity," "greater," and 10, and finally, from a list of logical operators, "and." Even such trivial acts as the entry of a numeric value like 100 can be reduced to a process of selections: we have all seen systems where a number is displayed for us, and we are expected to increment or decrement it with the mouse until it reaches the desired value. This method takes longer than simply typing the value, but it is an important part in the delusion of high levels: we are now only *selecting* a value, not *specifying* it.

It ought to be obvious that in order to select the right field, operation, or value we must know what these notions are, must appreciate the consequences of each selection and of our particular combination of selections, must understand the significance of operations like "less" or "and" when applied to database fields and records, and so on. Also, the query is meaningless as an isolated function; it is part of an application, so we must be aware at the same time of the application's other aspects, and of the other uses of those files, records, and fields. In other words, to select the right things we must deal with details and with interacting structures, so the new method does not represent a higher level of abstraction: we must have almost the same programming skills as when specifying those things with statements.

The knowledge that is no longer required – remembering what operations are available, for instance, or the correct format of a statement – is the *easy* part of programming, the *mechanistic* knowledge. These devices impress ignorant practitioners, who lack even this basic knowledge (and are unaware of the required *complex* knowledge lying beyond it), and who, therefore, believe that a substitute for *it* is all they will ever need in order to create applications. Experienced programmers refuse to use these devices, not because they cling to the old methods, as the propaganda tells us, but because they recognize how insignificant their benefits are.

The devices, thus, introduce elaborate procedures as a substitute for the *simple* knowledge involved in programming, but they cannot replace the difficult, *complex* knowledge, which can only develop through personal experience. The immensity of the environment, and the endless novelties that must be assimilated in order to use it, mask the fact that it is still our own skills, not the device, that solve the difficult programming problems. In the end, all the device does is sit between us and our applications, forcing us to express our requirements in more complicated ways than we would through traditional programming. Moreover, despite its low-level features, the device still prevents us from implementing all conceivable alternatives.

5

The most flagrant manifestation of software mechanism, thus, is the obsession with ways to avoid programming. Serious programming is indeed a difficult pursuit, but so are other professions. And it is only in programming that the main preoccupation of practitioners has become the *avoidance* of the knowledge, skills, and activities that define their profession. The ignorance pervading the world of programming is so great that the obsession with ways to avoid programming forms its very ideology. The irrationality of this obsession can be observed in this strange phenomenon: as programmers and managers are taught that programming must be avoided at all costs, they end up accepting with enthusiasm any theory or system that claims to eliminate the need for programming, even when this makes application development *more* difficult.

It is important to remember the origin of this stupidity: our mechanistic culture, and the software delusions it has engendered. For, only if we perceive software applications as mechanistic phenomena will we attempt to break down applications into independent structures and to start from higher-level elements; and only then will we accept the software devices that promise to help us in these attempts. The devices, we saw, provide higher starting levels for isolated software structures. The development environments through which they do it, no matter how novel or sophisticated, serve only to deceive us, to prevent us from noticing that all we are getting is some built-in operations. So the higher levels are nothing but a proprietary implementation of a simple and well-known programming concept – subroutines.

Were they not blinded by their mechanistic delusions, software practitioners would easily recognize that the programming aids are only replacing their simple, mechanistic activities, and that successful application development entails *non-mechanistic* knowledge. One can attain non-mechanistic knowledge only through personal experience. Thus, as long as they are guided by mechanistic beliefs and seek progress through programming substitutes, the software practitioners deprive themselves of the opportunity to gain this experience. They are trapped, therefore, in a vicious circle: the only knowledge they believe to be required is the mechanistic knowledge they are trying to replace with devices; consequently, they interpret each disappointment, not as evidence of the need for additional, non-mechanistic knowledge, but as a shortcoming of the particular device they are using; so, instead of gaining the additional knowledge through programming, they merely look for another device, and repeat the whole process in a slightly different way.

It is worth repeating these facts, because they are perhaps not as obvious as they appear here. How else can we explain the failure of society to notice the incompetence of our programmers? Endless justifications are being suggested to explain why we must disregard, in the case of programmers, notions that we accept implicitly in any other profession; particularly, the need for personal experience in the tasks defining the profession. For programmers, we have redefined the idea of experience to mean experience in using substitutes for experience.

And so it is how the delusion of software mechanism has given rise to that famous phrase, "without writing a single line of code." When referring to a programming substitute, this phrase is a promise; namely, that the device will permit us to create applications, or pieces of applications, without any programming. This promise is seen as the most desirable quality of a software device, and software companies will do almost anything in order to realize it – even invent, as we saw previously, devices that make application development more difficult. What matters is only the claim that we no longer have to "write code" (write, that is, statements or instructions).

It is not surprising, of course, to see this phrase employed for devices addressing software *users* – office workers, managers, amateur developers, and the like. Since no device can allow someone without programming knowledge to perform tasks requiring programming, the claim is a fraud. But we can understand the *wish* of naive people to have such a device, and consequently their exploitation by charlatans. What is surprising is to see the same phrase employed for devices addressing *programmers* – those individuals whom one would expect to possess programming expertise (and hence to have no use for such devices), to be proud of their programming capabilities, and even to enjoy programming.

The fact that the software charlatans employ the same means of deception in both cases ought to draw attention to the absurdity of our software culture: individuals whom we all consider professional programmers have in reality about the same knowledge, ambitions, and expectations as average computer users; like mere users, their chief preoccupation is to improve, not their *programming* skills, but their skills in *avoiding* programming.

And it is not just the software companies that foster these delusions. Researchers in universities participate by inventing mechanistic software theories, the business media by promoting worthless software concepts, corporations by employing programmers who rely on aids and substitutes, governments by permitting the software bureaucracy to exploit society, and in the end, each one of us by accepting this corruption. For, simply by doing nothing, by continuing to worship the software elites and to depend on the software bureaucrats, we are in effect supporting them. The cost of the mechanistic software delusions (probably exceeding one trillion dollars a year globally) is passed in the end to society, to all of us. So, just by doing nothing, we are in effect paying them, each one of us, thousands of dollars every year, and helping them in this way to increase their domination.

6

In chapter 4 we discussed Jonathan Swift's criticism of the mechanistic ideology that was sweeping the scientific world at the end of the seventeenth century; in particular, his attack on the mechanistic language theories (see pp. 317–318). The idea that there is a one-to-one correspondence between language and knowledge, and the idea that languages can be studied, designed, and improved as we do machines, were seen in Swift's time as a foregone conclusion, and were defended by pointing to the successes of mechanism in the natural sciences. Thus, even though the mechanistic theories of language were mere speculations, most scientists were taking them seriously. To ridicule these beliefs, Swift has his hero, Gulliver, describe to us the language machine invented by a professor at the Grand Academy of Lagado.[2]

The machine is a mechanical device that contains all the words of the English language, and their inflections. By manipulating a number of cranks, the operator can instruct the machine to generate random combinations of words. And by selecting those combinations that constitute valid phrases and sentences, the professor explains, any person intelligent enough to operate the machine – intelligent enough, that is, to turn the cranks – can produce any text in a particular field of knowledge. Thus, a person with no knowledge of philosophy, or history, or law, or mathematics, can now write entire books on these subjects simply by operating the machine.

The professor emphasizes that his invention is not meant to help a person acquire new knowledge, but on the contrary, to enable "the most ignorant person" to write in any field "without the least assistance from genius or study."[3] The machine, thus, will allow an ignorant person to generate any text without having to know anything he does not already know. And this is possible because the person will generate the text (as we say today in programming) "without writing a single line."

Now, one could certainly build such a machine, even with the mechanical means available in the seventeenth century. Swift is not mocking the technical aspects of the project, but the belief that the difficulty of developing ideas is the mechanical difficulty of combining words. If we hold this belief, we will

---

[2] Jonathan Swift, *Gulliver's Travels and Other Writings* (New York: Bantam Books, 1981), pp. 180–183.   [3] Ibid., p. 181.

inevitably conclude that a machine that helps us to manipulate words will permit us to perform the same tasks as individuals who possess knowledge, talent, and experience.

It is obvious that the quality of the discourse generated by a language machine depends entirely on the knowledge of the operator. The machine can indeed produce any text and any ideas, but only by randomly generating all possible combinations of words. So, in the end, it is still the human operator that must decide which combinations constitute intelligent sentences and ideas. Although it appears that the machine is doing all the work and the person is merely operating it, in reality the machine is replacing only the *mechanical* aspects of language and creativity.

Thus, a person using the machine will not accomplish anything that he could not accomplish on his own, simply by writing. Now, however, since he is only *selecting* things, it can be said that he is generating ideas "without writing a single line." Whatever the level of intelligence of a person, it is in fact more difficult to generate a piece of text by operating this machine than by directly writing the text. But if we believe that it is the *mechanical* acts involved in writing that make writing difficult, or if we have to employ as writers individuals known to be incapable of writing, we might just decide that language machines make sense.

Returning to our software delusions, we indeed believe that the difficulty of programming lies in its *mechanical* aspects, in combining pieces of software; and, what is worse, we indeed have to employ as programmers individuals known to be incapable of programming. So we have decided that *programming* machines make sense.

The similarity between Swift's hypothetical language aid and our real *programming* aids is striking. We note, in both cases, devices that address ignorant people; assure them that they don't need to know anything they don't already know; promise them the power to perform tasks that require, in fact, much knowledge; and reduce their involvement to a series of selections.

The similarity is not accidental, of course. We already know that our software delusions and our language delusions stem from the same belief; namely, the belief that the elements of software structures and language structures correspond on a one-to-one basis to the elements that make up reality. So we must not be surprised that devices based on *software* delusions end up just like the device invented by a satirist to mock the *language* delusions.

Swift was trying to demonstrate the absurdity of the mechanistic language theories by exposing their connection to the belief that a mechanical device can replace human knowledge. But today, through the mechanistic *software* theories, we are actually attempting to realize this fantasy: we are building *software* devices to replace human knowledge – programming knowledge, in particular. Concepts that were only academic speculations in Swift's time, easily ridiculed, have become a reality in our time in the world of software. The kind of device that three centuries ago was only a fantasy – a satirical exaggeration of a delusion – is actually being built today by software companies, and is being used by millions of people.

❖

There is no better way to illustrate the essence of software charlatanism than by imagining how the professor from Lagado would design his language machine today. He would make it a software device, of course, rather than a mechanical one. And, as a matter of fact, it is quite easy to design a software system that allows anyone – including persons who are normally unable to express themselves – to produce books in any domain "without writing a single line." To imagine this device, all we have to do is combine the concepts implemented in Swift's language machine with those implemented in our software systems.

The promise, thus, would be the familiar claim that the only thing we need to know is how to operate the device, and that this knowledge can be acquired in a short time. To operate the mechanical language machine, all they did was turn cranks; to operate a modern language machine, all we would do is "point and click" with a mouse. We are assured, in both cases, that the power of the device is ours to enjoy "at a reasonable charge, and with a little bodily labour,"[4] and only by making selections: we would never have to write a single sentence. The phrase we would use today is "powerful yet easy to use."

Let us examine some of the possibilities. Instead of typing words, we can have the system display them for us in the form of selections within selections. If, for example, we need the sentence "the dog runs," we first select the grammatical function by clicking on *noun*; this displays a list of noun categories, and we select *animal*; within this category we select *domestic*, and finally *dog*; what is left is to click on *singular* and *definite article*. Then, for "runs" we select the grammatical function *verb*, which displays a list of verb categories; we select *action*, within this category we select *motion*, and finally *run*; we then click on *present tense*, *third person*, and *singular*, and the complete sentence is displayed for us.

The popular expedient of *icons* could be profitably employed to help even illiterate persons to use this system: if tiny pictures were used to depict words, categories, and grammatical functions (a picture of a dog for "dog," an animal together with a man for "domestic," a running figure for "run," one and two

---

[4] Ibid.

objects for "singular" and "plural," etc.), even those of us who never learned to read and write could benefit from the power of language machines.

It is obvious that, with such a system, anyone could generate text on any subject without writing a single line. And future versions could introduce even more powerful features – built-in sentences, for instance. Instead of words, we would be able to select entire sentences, and even entire paragraphs, from lists of alternatives representing classes and categories of topics. With only a little practice, anyone would then be able to generate page after page of exquisite text just by pointing and clicking.

The more elaborate this imaginary language system becomes, the easier it is to recognize its similarity to our software systems – our programming aids, in particular. But, while few people would be deceived by a language machine, the whole world is being deceived by the software charlatans and their application development machines. Not even illiterates could be persuaded to try a device that promises to replace writing skills. But the most important individuals in society – decision makers working in universities, corporations, and governments – keep trying one software theory after another, and one programming substitute after another, convinced that a device can replace *programming* skills.

❖

Recall also our discussion in "The Software Theories" in chapter 3. Scientists believe that a device based on selections can replace human knowledge because they see intelligence and creativity, not as the indeterministic phenomena they are, but as the process of selecting a particular mental act from a predetermined range of alternatives. So they conclude that it is possible to *account* for human knowledge. Specifically, they claim that high-level forms of intelligence can be described with mathematical precision as a function of some low-level mental elements: all grammatically correct sentences that a person can utter can be predicted from the individual words, all behaviour patterns can be explained as a combination of some simple bits of behaviour, and all social customs can be described in terms of some basic human propensities.

This idea leads to the belief that we can incorporate in a device – in a software system, for instance – the low-level elements, and the methods used to derive from them the high-level ones. The device would then be a substitute for intelligence: by selecting and combining the high-level elements generated by the device, anyone would be able to perform the same tasks as a person who generates *in his mind* high-level elements starting with low-level ones. The device would replace, in effect, the experience of a person who took the time to develop whole knowledge structures, starting from low levels.

The fallacy, we saw, lies in the belief that the alternatives created when starting with high-level elements are about the same as those possible when starting from low levels. In reality, we would be limited to a small fraction of the possible alternatives. The impoverishment is caused by abstraction, but also by reification, because when we lose the low levels we also lose the links between the particular knowledge structure that is our immediate concern, and all the other structures present in the mind. This impoverishment explains why mechanistic theories of mind can represent only *some* aspects of human intelligence, and why ignorant persons equipped with software devices can accomplish only *some* of the tasks that experienced persons can with their minds alone.

7

Whether addressing programmers or software users, an *honest* development system simply provides low-level elements and the means to combine them so as to create the higher levels. The low levels come (for programmers, at least) in the form of general-purpose programming languages; and, when practical, higher levels are available through existing subroutines. Systems that provide *only* high levels, and claim that it is possible to create any application in this manner, are dishonest: they invariably end up reinstating the low levels in a different, and more complicated, form. These systems are for programming what language machines are for writing: not useful tools, but means of deception and exploitation. Their purpose, we saw, is to induce ignorance and dependence, by consuming our time and preventing us from improving our skills.

Honest systems allow us to create the higher levels on our own, and to select any subroutines we like. With honest systems, therefore, we can choose any combination of low-level elements and built-in operations. Dishonest systems provide an environment with high starting levels, and add the low levels as a special feature. The software charlatans have reversed, in effect, the principles of programming: instead of a simple system based on low levels, where we can create the high levels independently, they give us a complicated environment based on high levels, where the low levels are provided as "enhancements." What we had all along in any programming language – the low levels – is presented now as a new and powerful feature of their high-level environment. Instead of programming being the standard development method, and the high levels a natural outcome, they make the high levels the standard method, and turn programming into a complicated extension.

Clearly, if we use a general-purpose development system, if we want to create original applications, and if these applications require a particular level of detail and functionality, our lowest-level elements must be the same mixture of variables, conditions, loops, and statements no matter what development method we use.

The software charlatans prefer environments based on high levels because this is how they can induce dependence. A system based on low levels and subroutines leaves us free to develop and maintain our applications in any way we like. The dishonest systems lure us with the promise of high starting levels, but must include the low levels anyway. They lose, therefore, the only benefit they could offer us. But, because we trusted them and based our applications on their high levels, we will now depend forever on them and on the software companies behind them. While no dependence is possible when using traditional development methods, it is quite easy to control our work, our time, our knowledge, and our expectations through systems based on high levels. For, instead of simply developing applications and expanding our programming skills, we are now forced to spend most of our time with the problems generated by the systems themselves, with complicated concepts, with special languages, and with their endless changes.

The only time a high-level system is justified is when its functions cannot be effectively implemented as subroutines. This is the case, typically, in systems meant for highly specialized applications. Thus, operations involving indexed data files can be added as subroutines to any language. They are more convenient when implemented in the form of statements (as in COBOL), but it would be silly to adopt a new language, or a whole development environment, just for this reason. On the other hand, the features found in an advanced file editing system cannot be simply added to a language as subroutines, because, by its very nature, the editing system must have its own environment (windows, commands, special use of the keyboard, etc.). And what an honest system does, in this case, is make it as easy as possible to transfer the files to and from other systems.

It is worth repeating here that "subroutine" refers to a broad range of high-level software elements, including functions, procedures, subprograms, and the like, which may be explicit or implicit. This term refers, thus, to any elements that can be implemented as a *natural extension* of a general-purpose programming language. The subroutines that perform file operations, for example, are implemented by way of functions in a language like C, but we see them as ordinary statements in a language like COBOL. The important point is that the foundation of the application be a general-purpose language, not the high-level entities of a development environment. The level of this language may vary, depending on the application; thus, parts of the application, if restricted to narrow, specific domains, can often be developed in a higher-level language.

And I refer to individual statements, conditions, iterations, etc., as "low-level" software elements only because they are lower than subroutines, or built-in operations, or the high-level functions provided by development environments. But these "low-level" elements are what we find, in fact, in general-purpose languages (like COBOL and C) called "high-level" (to distinguish them from assembly languages, which use true low-level elements).

This confusion in terminology is due to the software mechanists, who have distorted the meaning of low and high levels by claiming that it is possible to raise forever the level of the starting elements. Thus, the term "fourth generation" (4GL) was coined for the languages provided by development environments, and "third generation" for the traditional high-level languages, in order to make environments look like an inevitable evolution. Assembly languages were declared at the same time to be "second generation," and machine languages, which use even lower-level elements, "first generation."

The level of these languages, however, has little to do with an advance in programming concepts. Thus, the first three "generations" are still in use today, and will continue to be, because the lower levels are the only way to implement certain types of operations. It is true that, historically, we started with low-level languages and only later invented the high-level ones; but this doesn't prove that there can exist general-purpose languages of even higher levels. And it is true that, in most programming tasks, we were able to replace low-level languages with high-level ones without reducing the functionality of the resulting applications; but it doesn't follow that we can repeat this success, that we can develop the same applications starting from even higher levels.

Everyone agrees that it is more efficient to start from higher levels, and that we should use the highest-level entities that are practical in a given situation. But, as we saw earlier, for typical business applications this level cannot be higher than what has been called third generation. Consequently, the fourth generation is not, relative to the third, what the third is relative to the second. (Thus, the most advanced features that can be added naturally to a second-generation language will not turn it into a third-generation one; but most features found in fourth-generation languages can be added naturally to any third-generation one.) While we may agree that the first three generations represent a certain progression in programming concepts, the fourth one is a fraud. Not coincidentally, it was only when the fourth one was introduced that the term "generation" was coined; formerly we simply had "low-level" and "high-level" languages.

It is precisely because no further "generations" are possible beyond the third one (in the case of general-purpose languages and general business applications) that the software mechanists were compelled to reverse the principles of programming; that is, to provide low levels within a high-level environment, instead of the other way around. To put it differently, the only way to make a 4GL system practical is by reinstating the traditional, third-generation concepts; but, to maintain the illusion of higher starting levels, the software companies must provide these concepts from within the 4GL environment.

A fourth-generation language, in the final analysis, is merely a third-generation language (assignments, iterations, conditions, etc.) plus some higher-level features (for display, reporting, etc.), bundled together in a complicated development environment. A programmer can enjoy the same blend of low and high levels by starting with traditional languages (COBOL, C, etc.) and adding subroutines and similar features, created by himself or by others.[5]

8

As an example of development environments, let us examine the communications systems. If what we need in our business applications is high-level operations in the domain of communications (say, transferring data under various protocols between computers, or converting files from one format to another), nothing could be simpler than providing these operations in the form of subroutines. We could then develop the applications in any programming language we like, and invoke these operations simply by specifying a number of parameters.

Needless to say, this is *not* how the popular communications systems make their operations available. What programmers are offered is a whole environment, where the operations are invoked interactively. Then, because the interactive method is impractical when the operations must be part of an application, these systems also provide a "powerful feature": a programming language. (To further distract us, euphemisms like "scripts," "macros," or "command files" are employed to describe the resulting programs.) In short, we are taken back to the lower levels of traditional programming. But we

---

[5] In forty years of programming – from simple utilities and applications to large data management systems and business systems – I have never encountered a situation where I could benefit from a commercial development environment. Even when the project calls for a higher-level programming method, I find it more expedient to implement my own, simple, customized environment (by means of "third-generation" and "second-generation" languages) than to depend on those monstrous systems sold by software companies.

already had programming languages; all we wanted was a few high-level communications operations. Instead, we must get involved with, assimilate, and then become dependent on, yet another system, another language, another software company, and the related documentation, newsletters, seminars, websites, version changes, bug reports, and so on.

Most of these activities are spurious, in that they are caused, not by the communications operations we needed, but by the environment we were forced to adopt in order to have these operations. And, what is worse, the languages that come with these environments are more primitive and less efficient than the general-purpose languages we already had. Only ignorant programmers, of course, can be deceived by this fraud; true professionals recognize that these systems are unnecessary, that their sole purpose is to prevent programming freedom. The popularity of development environments, and the ease with which practitioners can be persuaded to depend on them, demonstrates therefore the incompetence that pervades the world of programming. It is in the interest of the software companies to maintain this incompetence. Thus, by providing environments instead of honest development systems, they ensure that programmers waste their time with spurious activities instead of expanding their knowledge and experience.

As explained previously, programmers are deceived by the development environments because they trust the mechanistic software theories, which claim that it is possible to create applications by starting with high-level software entities. While this may work in narrow, specialized fields, or when the details are unimportant, it is rarely true for general business applications. Systems based on high levels are dishonest, therefore, because they make claims that cannot possibly be met.

Communications systems are only one kind of environment, of course. If we are to depend on development environments for our high-level operations, we will also need systems for display, for user interface, for database operations, for graphics, for reporting, for system management, etc. – each one with its own language, documentation, newsletters, seminars, bugs, changes, and so on.[6]

Development environments must include programming languages because their high-level operations, no matter how impressive they may be on their own, are only useful when combined with *other* operations. An application is not simply a series of high-level operations. The operations provided by one

---

[6] Thus, software reseller Programmer's Paradise boasts on its catalogue cover, "20,000+ software development tools" (for example, the issue Nov–Dec 2008). Perhaps 1 percent of them are genuine programming tools. The rest are environments and the endless aids needed to deal with the problems created by environments. Individuals who need such tools are not true programmers, but a kind of users: just as there are users of accounting systems and inventory management systems, *they* are users of development systems.

system are related to those provided by another, and also to the operations developed specifically for that application. The relations between these operations occur mainly at low levels, so they must be implemented through conditions, loops, statements, and variables; in other words, through the same low-level elements as those found in the traditional programming languages. Like the language machine we examined previously, the environments promise us high levels, but provide in reality the same mixture of levels we had all along. To develop a given application we need the same knowledge as before, but applying that knowledge is now much more difficult.

The complications created by this charlatanism are so great that a new kind of system had to be invented, whose only purpose is to help programmers and users connect the operations of the other systems or transfer data from one system to another; its only purpose, thus, is to solve the problems created by the idea of software environments. These new systems come, of course, with their own environments, languages, procedures, documentation, newsletters, seminars, bugs, changes, and so on. Another kind of system engendered by software charlatanism is the one meant to standardize the operations provided by other systems – to sit above them, as it were, and make their diverse operations available in a common format. Every software company tries to establish *its* system as the standard one, but this struggle merely results in even more facts, languages, procedures, documentation, reviews, etc., that programmers must assimilate.

These complications, to repeat, are a result of the reversal of programming principles: instead of starting with low-level elements and creating the higher levels freely, programmers are forced to develop applications starting with high-level elements. The low levels are then provided only *through* the development environments, and *through* the high levels, thus establishing the dependence.

A system based on low levels and subroutines *also* offers the benefits of high-level elements, and without inducing any dependence. After all, we already have many programming languages – languages better than those we must learn with each development environment; and through these languages, we can create software levels that are as low or as high as we want. Software companies do not promote environments because our general-purpose languages are inadequate, but because traditional concepts like subroutines would not allow them to control our work and our applications as do these environments. Were the high-level operations provided simply as subroutines, our general-purpose languages would provide everything we need to relate them and to create the higher levels. So instead of large software companies, and instead of our incessant preoccupation with their systems, we would simply have independent programmers giving us subroutines, and independent programmers creating and maintaining applications. When we realize how much power the software companies attain through the concept of development environments, it is easy to understand why they like the mechanistic software theories: these theories provide the ideological justification for reversing the traditional programming principles, and hence for their environments.

❖

The ultimate consequence of programming incompetence, then, is the domination of society by the software elite. Programmers are expected to be mere bureaucrats, operators of software devices; so they are not accountable for their applications as other professionals are for their work. If the responsibility of programmers is limited to the use of development systems, it is, in effect, the software companies behind these systems that control the resulting applications.

Consider this language analogy: We can be praised or blamed for what we say because we are free to create any sentences and express any ideas. But if we lived in a society where sentences and ideas could only be produced with some language machines supplied by an elite, the conception of responsibility and knowledge would be different. If everyone believed that language machines are the only way to express ideas and to communicate, we would be judged, not by what we say, but by how skilled we are at operating the machines. Moreover, if the only thing we knew were how to operate these machines, there would be very little intelligent discourse in society. But that would be considered a normal state of affairs. In the end, the only knowledge possible would be the ready-made sentences and ideas built into these machines by the elite.

It is obvious that an elite could dominate society if it could prevent us from developing linguistic competence, and if it could consume our time with worthless linguistic theories and devices. We have no difficulty understanding this for language, but we are allowing it to happen through software. Software and language, though, fulfil similar functions. Thus, incompetence and charlatanism in software will have, in the end, the same consequences as they would in language. If we allow ignorance and exploitation in our software pursuits, by the time we depend on software as much as we depend today on language our society will be completely dominated by the software elite.

Through careful indoctrination, the knowledge of corporate managers is shaped to serve the interests of the software companies. They are encouraged, not to help their organizations use computers effectively, but on the contrary, to make the use of computers as complicated and expensive as possible, and to accept the dependence on software companies. This is accomplished by promoting the mechanistic software ideology. An important factor in this ideology is the reliance on software devices – programming aids, development environments, ready-made pieces of software – in preference to the expertise and work of individuals. But software devices can only replace the *simple* aspects of programming. The complex problems remain unsolved, forcing everyone to search for newer devices, in a never-ending process. So the mechanistic ideology guarantees programming incompetence, and hence a perpetual preoccupation with software devices.

To summarize, the only thing that software companies can give us is higher levels of abstraction for our software elements; and this is precisely what *cannot* help us. The higher levels come in the form of built-in operations that address isolated software structures (that is, individual aspects of an application). They cannot help us because these structures must interact at low levels, and when we start with high-level elements we can no longer implement the links between structures. Starting from high levels impoverishes the complex structure that is the application (by reducing the number of alternatives for the value of the top element). This impoverishment is caused both by abstraction (reducing the alternatives within each structure) and by reification (severing the links between structures). As a result, we can implement only a fraction of the possible combinations of elements, and our applications are not as useful as software can be.

Systems based on high starting levels can be beneficial for creating *simple* applications, especially if these applications are in narrow domains (statistics, for example, or text editing, or graphics), and if they are only weakly linked to other applications. They are useless for creating *general* applications, though, because in this case we cannot give up the lower levels. The mechanistic software theories, and the development environments based on them, assume that the various types of operations that make up an application (database, display, user interface, etc.) can be implemented as independent processes. But this is a fallacy, because most operations in an application must interact, and the interactions must take place at low levels. This is why any attempt to implement general applications through high-level systems leads in the end to the reinstatement of the low levels, in a more complicated way.

The conclusion must be that we don't need software companies. Practically all software supplied by these companies – development environments, system and database management tools, ready-made applications – is based on the notion of high levels. It is true that only large companies can create and support these complicated systems, but if high levels cannot help us, then these systems, while impressive, are worthless. At the same time, the kinds of systems that *can* help us – customized applications, libraries of subroutines, simple tools based on low levels – are precisely what can be created by individual programmers.

This fact is no more a coincidence than the equivalent fact that language machines supplied by large companies could not replace the linguistic performance of individual persons. For software as for language, even the most sophisticated knowledge substitutes can replace just the simple, mechanistic aspects of knowledge. Only with our minds, through personal experience, and by starting from low levels of abstraction, can we hope to attain the complex knowledge needed to solve our problems.

The Delusion of Methodologies

1

So far we have discussed the development of applications mainly from the perspective of programmers. Let us see now how the mechanistic delusions affect the expectations of the *users* of applications – those individuals whose needs are to be embodied in the new software.

When developing a new application, managers familiar with the relevant business practices cooperate with analysts and programmers. The resulting software, thus, will reflect not only programming skills, but also the knowledge and experience of users. And the mechanistic theories and methodologies expect these individuals to express their knowledge and their requirements precisely, completely, and unambiguously; that is, to reduce knowledge and requirements to a form that can be used by analysts and programmers to develop the application. We will examine this absurdity in a moment, but first let us briefly discuss the alternative.

Instead of developing custom software, users can procure ready-made (or what is known as packaged, or canned) applications. With this alternative, the application is available immediately, thus bypassing the lengthy and difficult stages of design and programming. From what we have already discussed, though, it should be obvious that packaged applications are part of the same delusion as all ready-made, or built-in, pieces of software: the delusion of high levels, the belief that one can accomplish the same tasks by starting from high-level software elements as when starting from low-level ones. This delusion finds its ultimate expression in the idea of ready-made applications: the starting level is then the top element itself, the complete application, and the impoverishment is total. From the infinity of alternatives possible for the top element when *programming* the application, we are now left with only one alternative: the particular combination of operations built into the package by its designers. Most packages include options, of course, for some of their built-in operations. But combinations of options still provide only a fraction of the combinations of operations that may be required by an organization. So, in the end, packages remain a poor substitute for custom applications.

Organizations are tempted by the promise of packaged applications because they underestimate the limitations they will face later, when they get to depend on this kind of software. And even when the users realize that the package permits them to implement only *some* operations, and addresses only *some* of their needs, they still fail to appreciate the real consequences of inflexible software. What they tend to forget is that their needs and practices evolve continually, so their software applications must evolve too. It is difficult enough to judge whether a certain application can answer our *current* needs (the only way to be absolutely sure is by running it live, by *depending* on it); but it is impossible to assess its usefulness for the next ten years, simply because we cannot know *what* our needs will be. No one can predict the changes that an organization will face in the future. How, then, can anyone expect a piece of software that is based on a particular combination of built-in processes and operations to cope with such changes?

Note that it is not the *quality* of the application that is at issue here: no matter how good and useful it is today, and even if the company supporting it will bring it up to date regularly in the future, it will always be a *generic* piece of software, designed to answer only that subset of needs common to many organizations; it cannot possibly adapt to the specific needs of every one of them.

It is quite incredible, thus, to see so many organizations depend on packaged software; and they do, not just for minor applications, but also for their important business needs. Most packages fail, of course, so we must not be surprised at the frequency with which these organizations try new ones. The failure of a package rarely manifests itself as major deficiencies, or as software defects. What we see typically is a failure to answer the needs of its users, something that may only become evident months or years after its adoption. Since this type of failure is so common, the reason why organizations continue to depend on packages is, clearly, not their usefulness, but the incompetence of the software practitioners: if programmers lack the skills necessary to create and maintain applications, ready-made software, however unsatisfactory, becomes an acceptable expedient.

More subtle and more harmful than the inadequacy of an application is the tendency of users to lower their expectations in order to match its limitations. In other words, instead of rejecting an inadequate application, they modify the way they conduct their affairs so as to be able to use it. To help them rationalize this decision, the software elites stress the importance of adopting the latest "technologies" – relational databases, object-oriented environments, graphic user interface, client-server systems, and so forth. Ignorant users are impressed and intimidated by these concepts, so they end up interpreting the application's shortcomings as modern and sophisticated features which they don't yet appreciate. Thus, instead of objectively assessing the application's usefulness, they merely judge it by how closely it adheres to the software innovations promoted by the elites, even if these innovations are worthless. So, in the end, the application appears indeed to satisfy their requirements; but this is because they agreed to replace their true requirements with spurious ones.

2

Having established that packages are rarely a practical alternative for serious applications, let us return to the subject of software *development*. Developing their own applications is what many organizations must do, even if lacking the necessary skills, because this is the only way to have adequate software.

An application, we recall, consists of many structures, all sharing the same software entities (see "Software Structures" in chapter 4). These structures are the various *aspects* of the application – the processes implemented in it. Each structure, thus, is one way of viewing the application; and it is this system of interacting structures that constitutes the actual application. Although in our imagination we can treat each aspect as a separate structure, the only way to create the application is by dealing with several structures at the same time. This is true because most entities in a piece of software – most statements and modules – are affected by several aspects of the application, not just one. When writing a statement, for example, it is seldom sufficient to think of only *one* logical structure; we may well perceive a particular structure as the most important, but the same statement is usually an element in other structures too. It is this capability of software entities to be part of several structures simultaneously, and hence link them, that allows software applications to mirror our affairs. This capability is important because our affairs consist of processes and events that already form interacting structures.

If this is what software applications actually are, let us review what the software theories assume them to be. Applications, the theories tell us, must be developed following a *methodology*. Although many methodologies have been proposed, all are ultimately founded on the same fallacy; namely, the belief that it is possible to reduce a software application to a *definition*. The definition of an application is a set of specifications (formal descriptions, flowcharts, block diagrams, and the like) believed to represent, *precisely and completely*, the actual software. Methodologies, thus, are a manifestation of the mechanistic belief – the belief that a complex structure (the software application, in this case) can be reduced to simple ones.

To define an application, users and analysts spend many hours discussing the requirements – the business practices that are to be embodied in the application. This activity is known as analysis and design, and the methodologies prescribe various steps, which, if rigorously followed, are said to result in a complete definition; namely, a definition that represents the application as precisely as drawings and specifications represent a house or a car. It is believed, thus, that a set of mechanistic expedients can capture all the knowledge inhering in a complex phenomenon: the structures that make up the application, their interactions, and their effects when the application is running.

The reason we start with a definition, of course, is that we prefer to work with specifications rather than the statements of a programming language. Deficiencies, for example, are easier to correct by modifying the definition than by rewriting software. Thus, we are told, if we follow the methodology, we should be able to create the entire application in the form of a definition, and then simply translate the definition into a programming language. To put this differently, the methodologies claim that it is possible to represent an application with expedients other than the software itself – expedients that are simpler than software, and accessible to users and programmers alike. Although simpler than the actual application, these expedients represent it completely and precisely. The definition *is*, in effect, the application.

The fallacy of this claim ought to be obvious: if it were possible to express by means of diagrams, flowcharts, etc., all the details of the application, we wouldn't need programming languages. For, a compiler could then translate the definition itself into the machine language, and we wouldn't need to write the programs. In reality, definitions are simpler than programs precisely because they do *not* include all the details that the programs ultimately will.

So definitions are *imprecise* and *incomplete* representations of the application. They are useful only because people can interpret them, because people can add some of their own knowledge when converting them into software. One reason why definitions are simpler than programs, thus, is that they need not be perfect. An error in the program can render the application useless, but in the definition it is harmless, and may even go unnoticed. The impossibility of translating automatically definitions into software proves that definitions are incomplete, faulty, and ambiguous, and require human minds to interpret and correct them.

But an even more important reason why definitions are simpler than programs is that they represent *separately* the software structures that make up the application. The difficulty in programming, we saw, is dealing with several structures simultaneously. Our programming languages permit us to create software entities that can be shared by diverse structures, and this is why it is possible to develop useful applications. In a definition, on the other hand, we usually specify each structure separately: the business practices, the database relations and operations, the display and report layouts – we strive to represent each one of these processes clearly, so we separate them. Even if we *wanted* to relate them in the definition it would be difficult, because the diagrams, flowcharts, and descriptions we use in definitions are not as versatile as programming languages. Definitions are simpler than programs, thus, because most specifications do not share their elements, as software structures do. What this means is that a definition *cannot* represent the application precisely and completely. So the methodologies are wrong when claiming that definitions are important.

The fallacy of definitions is easy to understand if we recall the concept of simple and complex structures. A definition is, in effect, the reification of a complex structure (the application) into its constituent simple structures. It is, thus, an attempt to reduce a complex phenomenon to a mechanistic representation. This can be done, as we know, only when the separated structures can usefully approximate the actual phenomenon. In the case of software phenomena, this can be done for trivial requirements. For typical business applications, however, mechanistic approximations are rarely accurate enough to be useful. In the end, we like software definitions for the same reason we like all other mechanistic concepts: because of their promise to reduce complex problems to simple ones. Definitions are indeed simpler than the applications they represent, but they are simpler because they are only approximations.

Thus, since applications cannot be represented accurately by any means other than the programs themselves, the conclusion must be that definitions are generally irrelevant to application development. They may have their uses, but their importance is overrated. No definition can be complete and accurate, and an application created strictly from a definition is useless. Application development cannot be reduced to a formal activity, as the software theorists say. Since no one can specify or even envisage all the details, and since most details will change anyway (both before and after the application is completed), it is futile to seek a perfect set of specifications. Some brief and informal discussions with the users are all that an experienced programmer needs in order to develop and maintain an application.

❖

The failure of the mechanistic concepts in the early days were so blatant that the software gurus had to modify their methodologies again and again. The invention of new methodologies, thus, became a regular spectacle in the world of programming, and there were eventually nearly as many methodologies as there were gurus. (Most methodologies are known by the name of their creators, a practice borrowed apparently from the world of fashion design.)

Some methodologies tried to eliminate the rigidity of the traditional development phases, and introduced notions like prototyping and stepwise refinements; others attempted to modify the traditional roles played by users, analysts, and programmers. But, in the end, no matter how different they may appear to the casual observer, all methodologies are alike. And they are alike because they all suffer from the same fallacy: the belief that indeterministic phenomena – the applications, and their development and use – can be treated as mechanistic processes. The idea of methodologies, thus, is just another manifestation of the belief that programming expertise can be replaced with some easy skills – the skills needed to follow rules and methods.

The similarity between the various methodologies is betrayed by the trivial innovations their creators introduce in an effort to differentiate themselves. For example, they use pretentious terms to describe what are in fact ordinary features, in order to make these features look like major advances. But most ludicrous is their preoccupation with the graphic symbols employed in diagrams, as if the depiction of processes, operations, and conditions with one symbol rather than another could significantly alter the outcome of a development project. For example, the traditional rectangular boxes are replaced with ovals, or with a shape resembling a cloud, or a bubble, or one known as a bubtangle (a rectangle with rounded corners). And we must remember that these idiocies are discussed with great seriousness in books and periodicals, and are taught in expensive courses attended by managers and analysts from the world's most prestigious corporations.

Programming methodologies, thus, are like the development environments we discussed previously: they provide elaborate systems to replace the *easy* aspects of programming, those parts demanding mechanistic knowledge; but they cannot replace what are the most important and the most difficult aspects, those parts demanding complex knowledge. Since the same knowledge is required of people to create a serious application whether or not they use a methodology, the methodologies, like the development environments, are in the end a fraud. They are another form of software exploitation, another way for the software elites to prevent expertise and to induce dependence on systems and devices which they control.

When a methodology appears successful, its contribution was in fact insignificant. For, why should some techniques that work for one organization fail to work for others? It is the people, obviously, that made the difference. When people have the necessary knowledge, they will develop applications with or without a methodology; and when they lack this knowledge, no methodology can help them. Development environments, we saw, promise programmers and users higher levels of abstraction, and then trick them into working at low levels, as before. Similarly, methodologies promise them simpler, high-level concepts, and then demand the same skills as before. In both cases, this charlatanism complicates the development process, so inexperienced practitioners are even less likely to succeed. Besides, they waste their time now assimilating worthless concepts, instead of using it to improve their skills by creating and maintaining applications.

3

The delusion of methodologies and definitions is reflected in the distorted attitude that everyone has toward the subject of *maintenance*. Software maintenance is the ongoing programming work needed to keep an application up to date. And all studies agree that, for most business applications, this work over the years exceeds by far the work that went into the initial development. We should expect the theorists, therefore, to propose more solutions to the problems arising in maintenance than to those arising during development. What we find, though, is the exact opposite: all theories and methodologies deal with the creation of new applications, and barely mention the subject of maintenance. Moreover, we find the same distorted attitude among corporate managers: maintenance is treated as incidental work, is avoided whenever possible, and is relegated to the least experienced programmers.

In reality, the obsession with new applications is a reaction to the problem of programming incompetence: because programmers cannot keep the existing applications up to date, new ones must be developed. But without proper maintenance the new ones quickly fall behind, so the users find themselves in the same situation as before. At any given time, then, companies are either installing new applications, or struggling with the current ones and looking forward to replacing them. The software elites encourage this attitude, of course, as it enhances their domination. They present the latest fads – fourth-generation or object-oriented systems, CASE tools or relational databases, graphic interface or distributed computing – as revolutionary advances, and as solutions to the current problems. Their applications are inadequate, the companies are told, because based on old-fashioned software concepts. They must replace them with new ones, based on these advances.

So the preoccupation with new applications helps everyone to rationalize the failure of maintenance. It takes great skills to modify a live application quickly and reliably: much programming experience, and a good understanding of the existing functions. In contrast, creating a new application from a definition, as the methodologies recommend, is relatively easy. It is easy because the neat definition is only a simplified version of the actual application. As we saw, definitions can only *approximate* the true, complex needs. But the belief that the next application can be precisely defined inspires everyone with confidence, so a new development project always looks like a wise decision.

To put this differently, practitioners prefer a new application to maintenance because new projects make self-deception possible. A methodology permits them to create, instead of the *required* application, an imaginary, simpler one: the application matching a neat definition and their limited skills. And when *that* application proves to be inadequate, the practitioners still do not suspect their practices. They blame the changing requirements, or the imperfection of the original specifications. They refuse to see these facts as a reality they must cope with, as the very essence of business software. So, instead of accepting the facts, they continue to claim that their practices are sound, and that precise definitions are possible. In other words, if reality does not match the mechanistic software principles, something is wrong with reality.

In new development projects, then, self-deception helps practitioners to deny their failures and to cling to the easy, mechanistic concepts. And they dislike maintenance because, in this type of work, self-deception cannot help them. Each maintenance project is relatively small and well-defined, so it is harder to replace it with an imaginary, simpler one. Ultimately, in maintenance work it is harder to find excuses for failures.

We note a marked discrepancy between the *perception* and the *reality* of applications. On the one hand, everyone strives to create a perfect application – by following a strict methodology, and by using the latest development systems. It is far more expensive to modify the software itself later, we are told, so we must eliminate the imperfections in the design stage. This is why definitions are important. On the other hand, all studies show that less than 5 percent of new applications are adequate. The others must be modified if they are to be used at all, and many are so different from the actual requirements that they must be abandoned. Moreover, even those that are adequate must immediately start a process of ongoing modifications, simply because business requirements change constantly.

Thus, whether it is the original differences (due largely to the fact that no definition can reflect the actual requirements) or the future ones (due to the normal, unpredictable changes in requirements), it is obvious that modifying business applications is an essential programming activity. Yet, for over forty years, all theories and methodologies have been attempting to create "perfect" applications; that is, applications matching some fixed specifications, and requiring as few changes as possible. In reality, all software changes are alike – whether due to faulty specifications, or varying user preferences, or the need for additional features, or the adoption of new business rules, or some external factors. So, if we must be able to deal with endless changes in any case, the idea of a perfect application is meaningless, and there is no point in trying to design one initially.

It is wrong, in fact, even to think of maintenance as modifying the application. The role of business software is to satisfy, at any given time, the current needs. An application, therefore, must be seen as that particular software system which accomplishes this. Business needs change constantly, so the application must change too. Thus, rather than first developing an application and then maintaining it, it is better to think of this work as a continuous, never-ending development.

We find further evidence of the distorted attitude toward maintenance in the notion of application *life cycles*. All experts agree that applications cannot last more than a few years. So, even while encouraging us to create a new one, they warn us to prepare for its demise. Borrowed from biology, the idea of life cycles holds that software resembles live things, so the existence of an application can be divided into stages: birth (definition of requirements), growth (development and testing), maturity (normal operation), and death (obsolescence). Each application represents a cycle, and is followed by another one, and then another one, forever.

But this is an absurd idea, contrived specifically in order to justify the need for new applications. Software, by its very nature, is modifiable. In principle, then, an application never needs to be replaced; it only needs to be kept up to date. Everyone acknowledges the need for changes, and acknowledges also the inability of programmers to implement them. So the idea of life cycles was introduced as a compromise: every few years, a new application is created in order to implement *together* all the changes that should have been implemented *one at a time* in the past. The theorists and the practitioners can now defend the lack of proper maintenance, and hence the need for a new application, by invoking the idea of software life cycles. This logic, however, is circular; for, the idea of life cycles was itself an invention, a response to the incompetence that prevents proper, *ongoing* maintenance.

Instead of trying to eradicate the incompetence, everyone looks for ways to rationalize it.

Business software can fulfil its promise only if it is as changeable as the business issues themselves: inflexible business software can be as bad as inflexible business practices. Thus, replacing the whole application from time to time is a poor substitute for the ability to satisfy new needs as soon as they arise. So the ultimate price we pay for distorting the subject of maintenance is having to depend on perpetually inadequate applications. This is true because, even though an inadequate application is eventually replaced, it reaches that condition gradually, one unsatisfied requirement at a time. This means that it was *always* inadequate, even in its period of normal use. The difference between that period and the time when it is actually replaced is only in the *degree* of inadequacy; namely, how far it is from the users' actual needs, how many unsatisfied requirements have accumulated to date.[1]

4

The delusion of methodologies and definitions is also demonstrated by the failure of CASE (Computer-Aided Software Engineering, see pp. 535–536). The elimination of programming from the process of application development was seen by most theorists as the undisputed next step in development tools, as the ultimate benefit of software engineering. Ambitious CASE systems were promoted for a number of years with the claim that managers and analysts could now create directly, without programming, applications of any complexity – simply by manipulating block diagrams, flowcharts, and the like, on a computer display. The system would guide them in creating the definition, and would then translate the definition automatically into software.

The belief that an application can be generated automatically is a logical consequence of the belief that a definition can represent all the knowledge embodied in an application. (Could definitions do that, automatic programming would indeed be possible.) The CASE fantasy, thus, was born from the

---

[1] The longest I maintained one of my applications is thirty years (until the manufacturing company using it ceased production). This was a complex, integrated business system, which combined all the computing needs of that company. At any given time there was a list of requirements, some of them urgent; but I always implemented them, so no one ever saw the need for new applications. The system kept growing, and was eventually a hundred times larger than it had been in the first year, due to countless new functions; but no one perceived these developments as new applications. Most work, though, was in modifying existing parts (replacing or adding features and details). Again, a properly maintained application never needs to be replaced, because it always has what the users need.

concepts of methodologies and definitions that we have just discussed –
concepts which *continue* to dominate the programming theories, despite the
failure of CASE. No one seems to realize that, if CASE evolved from these
concepts, its failure proves the fallaciousness of these concepts too. Let us
analyze this connection.

Even when following a methodology, people do more than implement rules
and standards. The software created by programmers contains more than
what the analysts specified in their definition, and the definition created
by analysts contains more than what the users specified in their requirements.
Each individual involved in the development of the application has the
opportunity to add some personal knowledge to the project, but this is
largely an unconscious act. Simply to *understand* a set of requirements or
specifications, the person must *interpret* them; that is, he must combine the
knowledge found in the document with some previous knowledge, present in
his own mind. For, if this were not the case, if the only thing that analysts and
programmers did were follow rules and methods, then a person who knows
nothing about software or about a particular company, but who can follow
rules and methods, could also develop applications.

The knowledge missing from the formal requirements and specifications,
and hence contributed by individuals, varies from general facts on computers
and software to details specific to their organization, and from common
business practices to the knowledge shared by people living in a particular
society. It is precisely because most people already possess this kind of knowledge that we take it for granted and do not include it in instructions and
documents. Recall also that the most important part contributed by human
minds constitutes *non-mechanistic* knowledge: not isolated knowledge structures, but the complex structure that is their totality. The capacity for non-
mechanistic knowledge must be provided by human minds because it cannot
exist in simple structures like instructions or diagrams.

Thus, all the people involved in the development of an application may be
convinced that they are following the rules prescribed by the methodology,
while depending on personal knowledge and experience to fill in the missing
pieces, or to resolve the ambiguities and inconsistencies found in specifications. If the application is successful, they will praise the methodology,
convinced that it was the principles of software engineering that led to their
success. Most likely, they will not realize that it was in fact their own minds that
provided the most important part (the non-mechanistic knowledge), and that
the principles, theories, and methods addressed only the simple part (the
mechanistic aspects of the project).

Clearly, if the methodology provides only mechanistic principles while our
activities are mostly non-mechanistic, the only way to use a methodology is by

taking its practical parts and ignoring or overriding the rest. People may be convinced that they are *following* the methodology, when they are using it *selectively*. So it is not too much to say that, to develop an application success-fully, people must work *against* the methodology: if they rigorously followed the mechanistic principles, they would never complete the application. Thus, when a software project is successful, this is not *due* to the methodology but *despite* it.

And it is during programming that people make the greatest contribution. For it is in programming, more than in any other activity, that people have the need and the opportunity to override the rules imposed by a mechanistic methodology. So it is the programmers – more than the managers with their specifications, or the analysts with their definitions – that must use the non-mechanistic capabilities of their minds. We can perhaps delude ourselves in the early stages of development that specifications and definitions represent the application completely and precisely. But if we want to have a useful application, we must permit human minds to deal at some point with the missing pieces, with the ambiguities, and with the inconsistencies. It is during programming, therefore – when the application is created and tested, when it must mirror reality if it is to be used at all – that the delusions of formal methodologies and precise definitions, of neat diagrams and flowcharts, must come to an end.

It should be obvious, then, why CASE failed. The CASE systems were based on methodologies: they literally incorporated some of the popular methodologies, thus allowing managers and analysts who wished to follow a particular methodology to do so through a software system rather than on their own. The system could now *force* people to follow the methodology, eliminating the temptation to omit or modify some of the steps – what was believed to be the chief cause of development failures. Since the methodology was now part of the development environment, the experts claimed, anyone could enjoy its benefits; and since the resulting specifications and definitions were stored in the computer, the system could use them to generate the application automatically, eliminating the programming phase altogether.

CASE failed because it eliminated the opportunities that people had to *override* the methodologies and definitions. By automating the development process, CASE made it impossible for people to contribute any knowledge that conflicted with the mechanistic software theories. They could only use now trivial, mechanistic knowledge, which is insufficient for developing serious applications. What CASE eliminated – what the software mechanists thought was the cause of development failures – was in fact the very reason why methodologies and definitions appeared occasionally to work: the contribution made by people when, out of frustration, and perhaps unconsciously, they were using their non-mechanistic capabilities to override the methods, rules, and specifications. Thus, the failure of CASE proves that people normally contribute to the development process a kind of knowledge – non-mechanistic knowledge – that cannot be replaced with formal methodologies and theories.

There is another way to look at this. A CASE environment is logically equivalent to a traditional development environment where the users, the analysts, and the programmers follow a methodology *rigorously*; where analysis and design, specifications and definitions, theories of programming and testing, are all implemented exactly as dictated by the principles of software engineering; where everyone refrains from *interpreting* the specifications or the definitions; where no one uses personal knowledge to add details to the formal documents, or to resolve ambiguities and inconsistencies. A CASE environment is equivalent to all this because, when the methodologies and programming theories are part of the development system, people are *forced* to follow them rigorously.

Logically, then, the only difference between a CASE environment and a traditional environment is the non-mechanistic knowledge contributed by people – the knowledge that *cannot* be incorporated in a CASE system. So, if CASE failed, we must conclude that this knowledge plays a critical part in a development project. With traditional development methods, when people possess this knowledge the project is successful, and when they do not the project fails. In a CASE environment, people had no opportunity to use this knowledge, whether they possessed it or not; so the result was the same as when people used traditional development methods *and* lacked this knowledge. The promoters of CASE did not recognize the need for this knowledge. They believed that mechanistic knowledge suffices for developing applications; and, since mechanistic knowledge can be embodied in software devices, they believed that the contribution made by people can be reduced to the knowledge required to operate these devices.

The main purpose of this argument, you will recall, is not to show the absurdity of CASE, but to show how the failure of CASE demonstrates the fallaciousness of all methodologies and definitions – which, in turn, demonstrates the fallaciousness of all mechanistic software theories. For, it is software mechanism – the belief that applications consist of independent structures, which can be fully and precisely specified – that is the fundamental delusion. This delusion leads to the delusion that programming expertise can be replaced with rules and methods, which then leads to the notion of methodologies and definitions, and eventually to CASE. The CASE systems merely implemented formally what the theories had been claiming all along, what practitioners had been trying before to do manually. So the only logical explanation for the failure of CASE is that these theories are invalid.

The Spread of Software Mechanism

1

The study of software mechanism reveals some disturbing trends. We note a marked shift in our preoccupations: from solving real problems, to dealing with the problems created by the tools we invent to solve these problems. We have to address more and more issues, and these issues are becoming more and more complicated, while moving further and further away from our real concerns. Each issue begets new kinds of problems, which did not exist before but which are now urgent, because they must be solved before we can return to the original problem.

Simple programming problems – which require only a human mind and experience – gave rise to theories of programming, which evolved into complicated methodologies and programming tools, and finally became the monstrous development environments we see today. What started simply as programming became a preoccupation with programming theories and languages, with tools and environments. We also note a tendency to spread this inefficiency into broader domains: from the world of programming itself to the organizations that use software, and then to the rest of society. Issues that ought to concern only programmers end up affecting the users of their applications, who must now deal with some new, software-related problems in addition to their own problems; and these new problems affect then those people with whom the software users are involved. In the end, the entire society is spending more and more of its resources solving spurious, software-related problems, instead of addressing real concerns.

These three trends – making activities more complicated than necessary, shifting the preoccupation from real to spurious issues, and spreading the inefficiency into broader domains – are related, of course. They are different aspects of the same phenomenon, different manifestations of the delusion of software mechanism. Let us briefly examine this phenomenon.

Since the mechanistic software theories are invalid, the software practitioners who follow them keep failing. Their belief in software mechanism acts then as defence, as a way to deny reality. The reality, we saw, is that their failures are due to incompetence – an incompetence fostered by the very theories they follow. For, in addition to leaving unsolved the programming problems they promise to solve, the mechanistic theories prevent practitioners from gaining the expertise that *could* solve them.

There is no limit to the number of trivial issues that we can contrive if we believe that any problem can be solved by breaking it down into simpler ones. By replacing the original, complex problem with a multitude of isolated and relatively simple issues, ignorant practitioners can delude themselves that they are working toward the solution of the complex problem. They have redefined, in effect, the challenge of programming: from developing software to solve real problems, and at the same time improving their skills, to searching for ways to reduce these problems to simple ones that match their capabilities.

The mechanistic doctrine, thus, helps the software practitioners to rationalize their failures. Instead of the difficult task of creating and maintaining applications, they can now perform activities so simple that they cannot possibly fail. The problems that the applications were supposed to address may remain unsolved, but the new problems always have solutions, so the practitioners are pleased with their accomplishments. The belief in software mechanism, thus, permits them to shift the definition of their profession, from solving real problems to solving their own, simpler problems.

What is left is to persuade those who trust them – their employers, and the rest of society – that what they are doing is the utmost that can be accomplished in the domain of programming. But this is easy in a society dominated by mechanistic beliefs. The concepts of software engineering are deemed "scientific" – because based on mechanistic principles – and are therefore readily accepted by everyone. Given our mechanistic culture, it is the *truth* that is hard to accept. We have enough evidence that the most important part of programming is knowledge, talent, skills, and personal experience; in other words, the traditional form of expertise. And yet, it is the fallacious theories and the programming substitutes based on them that are promoted in computer publications, taught by professors and gurus, and endorsed by institutes and associations.

Permitting the software practitioners to fool us with their mechanistic theories is no different from permitting researchers to fool us with mechanistic theories in the human sciences. We saw in previous chapters how the mechanistic doctrine has corrupted academic research in fields like sociology, psychology, and linguistics, turning in effect these disciplines into pseudo-sciences. Invalid mechanistic theories are being pursued for years and decades, and are then abandoned only to be replaced with other mechanistic theories. The "research" performed by these scientists is merely a preoccupation with the spurious, mechanistic problems they themselves keep creating when breaking down the complex phenomena of mind and society into simpler phenomena. They never explain the actual phenomena; but, despite their delusions and their failures, we continue to trust them, and the universities, and the mechanistic philosophy. It is not surprising, therefore, that we have come to trust in the same way the software practitioners, even as we see them preoccupied largely with the spurious, mechanistic problems they themselves keep creating, and despite their failures.

So those who depend on software learned to deny the reality of software failures just like the practitioners themselves. Software users can see the failure of their applications as clearly as the software practitioners can see the failure of their theories. But, just as the belief in software mechanism helps the practitioners to rationalize their programming failures, this belief helps now those who depend on software to rationalize the failure of their applications.

The software practitioners, we saw, rationalize their failures by expanding the original problem into a vast and complicated array of trivial activities. The real problem – creating and maintaining software applications to address business or social issues – is a well-defined one. It is a difficult problem, however, requiring much expertise, so the software practitioners hide their incompetence by replacing it with a great number of isolated, simple problems. They can then concentrate on *these* problems, and delude themselves that they are making progress toward the solution of the original one. This technique has been so successful in the domain of programming that the *users* of software have now adopted it, in order to rationalize their own failures. Instead of addressing real issues, they are modifying their activities and lowering their expectations to match the inferior applications they depend on.

The software propaganda has succeeded in convincing us to accept a state of affairs that no one would tolerate in other domains. Failures that would be preposterous in manufacturing, or construction, or utilities are considered normal for software applications. The users of applications notice that programmers are using complicated methodologies and development tools, and are calling themselves "software engineers," and conclude that they are like other professionals. Instead of being outraged by the inefficiency and incompetence they note in software development, the users of applications allowed the creators of those applications to persuade them that software-related problems must form an important part of *their own* preoccupations. Thus, assured that the programming they see is the only kind of programming possible, software users started to expand their own problems into a vast array of trivial, software-related activities. Solving software-related problems, they are now convinced, is the only way to make progress toward the solution of their real problems.

2

When studying the spread of software mechanism, and the resulting incompetence and corruption, it is useful to distinguish three stages. The first stage, now complete, involves the world of programming itself: the programming profession has been almost totally destroyed by the mechanistic dogma, and the inefficiency in those activities directly related to programming exceeds 90 percent (and is sometimes as high as 99 percent). To put this differently, if we had true professionals instead of the present programmers, society would pay less than one tenth of the current cost to derive the same benefits from software as it does now. (In fact, with true professionals we would derive *greater* benefits at one tenth the cost, because the present programmers are far from delivering the best possible applications.)

Programming expertise has been redefined, as I have already remarked, from knowledge of programming to knowledge of ways to *avoid* programming. Solving a problem simply through programming is considered old-fashioned, while attempting to solve it by means of development environments, ready-made pieces of software, and other high-level concepts is seen as modern and professional, no matter how inefficient and expensive is the result. Programming expertise, in other words, means expertise in the use of substitutes for expertise. The responsibility of programmers is limited to operating software devices, or following methodologies, or being aware of the latest theories. They are not accountable for their work: what matters is not whether their applications are useful or not, but whether their activities conform to the current software ideology.

When an application fails, no one is blamed. People cannot be blamed when their responsibility is limited to operating devices, or to following rules and methods. The conclusion is typically that they did not use the latest "solutions" or the latest "technologies." So the project is simply abandoned, and another one is started – perhaps with a different development environment and different hardware – while all the people involved continue to be trusted and respected. (We will return to this subject in "Software Irresponsibility" in chapter 8.)

A nice demonstration of the first stage is provided by the evolution of Microsoft Corporation – the most aggressive of the software elites. Microsoft started with simple and useful programming tools, but the more successful it became, the larger and more complicated became its systems. Eventually, every tool grew into a huge environment, where the actual programming issues are hidden in a maze of unnecessary features, options, rules, and standards –

all a result of raising the level of abstraction in software development. The effort involved in using Microsoft development environments (and any other environment that depends on the Microsoft operating systems) is due largely to the environments themselves, not our real programming needs. Microsoft has attained, thus, the goal of the first stage: to destroy the possibility of intelligent and responsible programming by forcing programmers to waste their time with spurious problems; to prevent programmers from improving their skills by making their work dependent, not on personal knowledge, but on development environments; and, ultimately, to reduce all programmers, regardless of experience or potential, to mere operators of software devices.

❖

The second stage, now well under way, involves the world of business: corporations, governments, financial institutions, and the like – those organizations that have been heavy users of computers for many years, as well as those that started more recently. Workers in these organizations are undergoing now, in their own fields, the same indoctrination as the one that led to the destruction of the programming profession. And as a result, the same incompetence, inefficiency, and irresponsibility that characterize the world of programming are increasingly affecting all business. Although we are observing now office workers rather than programmers, and the *use* of software rather than its development, the similarity of this stage to the earlier one is striking.

The second stage started when the users of software realized that programmers did not, in fact, provide an acceptable level of service: new applications took too long to create, or were never finished, or were inadequate; simple modifications that should have been implemented in a day or two took months, or were never done, or did not work. Frustrated by this state of affairs, and convinced that this was the only kind of programming possible, the users fell into the same trap as the programmers themselves: they accepted the solutions proposed by the software elites – the same solutions that had led to programming incompetence, and hence to their current problems, in the first place. As before, the solutions consisted, not in improving anyone's skills, but in means to avoid the need for programming. Incredibly, the elites turned now to the users themselves, offering them software devices that would eliminate their dependence on programmers: ready-made applications and, when these proved to be inadequate, user-oriented software development tools.

Asking users to depend on generic applications, or to develop their own, was tantamount to acknowledging the incompetence of programmers, and hence the failure of the mechanistic programming theories. No one recognized this obvious fact, however. So the same elites that were preventing programming expertise were seen now by their victims – by the users of software – as saviours. The incompetence of programmers, we saw, is due to the mechanistic theories, which force them to depend on aids and substitutes instead of improving their programming skills. They are restricted to mechanistic knowledge, which is the same as staying forever at the level of novices. By invoking the same theories, the elites could now deceive and exploit the *users* of software, and prevent expertise also in other occupations.

The first end-user aids were simple software tools for database query, reporting, spreadsheets, and the like. These tools, needless to say, could not fulfil the promises made for them: they could not be a substitute for serious applications. So the users found themselves dependent on these aids, and on the software companies behind them, even as their needs remained unsatisfied. But, again, no one questioned the software concepts leading to these aids, nor the honesty of the elites. It was the aids that were suspected, so the same process of expansion that had occurred earlier for the programming aids started for the end-user aids. The simple tools grew into large office systems, complete with programming languages, heavy instruction manuals, and proficiency courses. Each new version made them more complicated, until they finally became the monstrous software environments we see today.

These systems, clearly, are the counterpart of the development environments employed by programmers. Also like the development environments, they are fraudulent, in that they do not eliminate the need for programming expertise: to create serious applications, their users need almost the same knowledge as they would if relying on programming languages. They are called *productivity* systems, but this is a spurious term, as its true meaning is the opposite of its literal one. The purpose of these systems is to *reduce* productivity, by consuming everyone's time with software-related activities. And they accomplish this by replacing the dependence on personal knowledge with a dependence on software devices. Like programmers before them, workers in various fields are now prevented from practising their profession and from improving their skills. Increasingly, the only thing they learn is how to operate software devices: how to select and combine functions from a range of alternatives.

Just as the programming environments can replace only the *easy* parts of software development, the office systems can replace only the *easy* parts of software use – the parts requiring *mechanistic* knowledge. No matter how elaborate they are, these systems cannot replace the parts demanding *non-mechanistic* knowledge, and hence human minds. The real problems, thus, remain unsolved, but everyone believes that the only answer is to acquire even more software devices. Like programmers, office workers now remain at novice levels, because, instead of practising, they waste their time with the problems generated by their software tools. Just like programming expertise, the expertise of office workers has been redefined to mean the skill of using substitutes for expertise.

In one occupation after another, the responsibility of people is being lowered, from the traditional one – solving a real problem, making a valuable contribution – to merely knowing how to deal with software-related issues. In some occupations, the simple skills needed to operate a particular software device – skills that can be acquired by almost anyone in a few days – are already considered more important than a lifetime of experience.

A demonstration of the second stage is provided, again, by the evolution of Microsoft Corporation. Having destroyed the concept of expert and responsible programming, Microsoft turned to the world of business. The purpose of its office systems is to raise the level of abstraction in office work; to enforce the perception that any task can be reduced to a combination of some built-in functions, thus making everyone dependent on software devices; to waste workers' time with the problems generated by this dependence, thereby preventing them from gaining knowledge and experience; and, ultimately, to reduce all workers, regardless of position or skills, to mere operators of software devices.

The third stage involves the spread of software mechanism into the rest of society – into our homes and personal affairs, in particular. This stage has just begun, and it is hard to predict how software mechanism will affect our life; that is, to predict what will be the equivalent, in our personal affairs, of the incompetence, the inefficiency, and the corruption that we see now in programming and in business. Judging by the previous stages, however, we can expect an ever-growing dependence on software environments and on the companies behind them; specifically, a dependence on systems that promise to solve our important problems while addressing in reality only the simple ones. In the guise of information, or education, or entertainment, more and more types of software devices will be invented, desktop and mobile, and we will spend more and more of our time with the trivial preoccupations engendered by their use.

Thus, we will have fewer and fewer opportunities to use or to develop non-mechanistic knowledge. Our definition of expertise, creativity, and responsibility will be degraded, in everything we do, to mean simply the skill of selecting and combining the functions provided by software devices. The goal of the elites now is to make all human activities as insignificant and inefficient as they have made programming and office work; to make us all as ignorant as they have made programmers and office workers, by forcing us to depend on their systems instead of improving our minds; and, ultimately, to reduce all human beings on earth to mere operators of software devices.

❖

The three stages overlap, of course, and this analysis may not be entirely accurate. The distinction is still useful, however, because it helps us to observe the progression of software mechanism: its expansion, outward, from the narrow domain of programming into all aspects of human existence. By studying the first stage, which is now complete, we can perhaps foresee the evolution of the other two stages. (This study is the subject of the next chapter, "Software Engineering.")

We should try to imagine a society where all people are as inefficient and irresponsible in their pursuits as the software practitioners are in theirs today. And, by studying the past and current rate of expansion, we should try to estimate how long it will take the software elites to bring about this condition. The frightening conclusion would be that, within a few decades, the second and third stages will also be complete. So we should ask ourselves whether a modern society can function at all when everyone's knowledge is at the low levels we see today in programming. Programmers can be as incompetent as they are only because the rest of us are willing to pay the cost of their inefficiency; that is, willing to support a software bureaucracy. But if we, too, were to be like that, who would support us all?

It is significant that the software elites are not content with merely *exploiting* society – something they have already accomplished, in the first stage. Their objective is not just to extract, through the software bureaucracy, vast amounts of money from society. In their plan of domination, the second and third stages are as important as the first, and they will not stop until every person is turned into an active member of the software movement.

Like all totalitarian ideologies, the software revolution is a mass movement. It is not founded on authoritarianism, but on mind control: people are not threatened, but indoctrinated; they must become devoted followers, and participate, on their own accord. Physical force is needed only against those who, despite the indoctrination, still fail to appreciate the benefits of the new social order.

Viewed in this light, the three stages of the software movement parallel the evolution of political totalitarian movements like Nazism and Communism. The revolution starts with a core of believers – who eventually become the elite, or the Party – and spreads outward, bringing increasingly broad segments of the population into its ranks. The revolution cannot end until every person and every event in society conforms to its ideology. But because the ideology is based on pseudoscientific, fallacious notions, it cannot actually work. The initial phase, when only a small portion of society is involved, usually appears successful, and this gives the believers confidence in their utopian visions. (The software movement is currently in this stage.) The initial phase appears successful, not because the ideology is valid, but because the few who embrace it deceive and exploit the rest of society. As the movement spreads, however, more and more people are turned into bureaucrats who merely serve the ideology, and fewer and fewer are left who do real work and can be exploited. Society becomes increasingly corrupt and inefficient, and eventually destroys itself. (See also the related discussion in the introductory chapter, pp. 30–31.)

CHAPTER 7

Software Engineering

Introduction

My task in this chapter is to show that the body of theories and activities known as software engineering forms in reality a system of belief, a pseudo-science. This discussion is in many ways a synthesis of everything we learned in the previous chapters: the model of simple and complex structures, the two mechanistic fallacies, the nature of software and programming, the structures that make up software applications, the mechanistic conception of mind and software, the similarity of software and language, the principles of demarcation between science and pseudoscience, the incompetence of the software practitioners, and the corruption of the software elite. There are brief summaries here, but bear in mind that a good understanding of these topics is a prerequisite for appreciating the present argument, and its significance.

In chapter 6 we examined the three stages in the spread of mechanistic software concepts: the domain of programming, the world of business, and our personal affairs (see pp. 486–491). And we saw that, while the first stage is now complete, the others are still unfolding. Judged from this perspective, the present chapter can also be seen as a study of the *first* stage. Since this stage involves events that took place in the past, its study can be exact and objective. We can perhaps still delude ourselves about the benefits of software mechanism in our offices or in our homes, but we cannot in the domain of programming; for, we can *demonstrate* the absurdity of the mechanistic theories, and the resulting incompetence and corruption.

To perform a similar study for the other two stages, we would have to wait a few decades, until they too were complete. But then, it would be too late: if we want to prevent the spread of software mechanism in other domains, we must act now, by applying the lessons of the first stage.

The similarities of the three stages are not accidental. It is, after all, the same elite that is controlling them, and the same software concepts that are being promoted. Common to all stages is the promise to replace human minds with software: with the methods and systems supplied by an authority. And this plan is futile, because mechanistic concepts can replace only the *simple* aspects of human intelligence. The plan, thus, has little to do with enhancing our capabilities. It is in reality a new form of domination, made possible by our mechanistic delusions and our increasing dependence on computers.

As we read the present chapter, then, we must do more than just recognize how the mechanistic ideology has destroyed the programming profession. We must try to project this phenomenon onto other fields and occupations, and to imagine what will happen when all of us are reduced, as programmers have been, to mere bureaucrats.

The programming theories have not eliminated the need for programming expertise. All they have accomplished is to *prevent* programmers from developing this expertise, thereby making software development more complicated, more expensive, and dependent on the software elite instead of individual minds. Similarly, the software concepts promoted now for our offices and for our homes serve only to prevent us from developing knowledge and skills, and to increase our dependence on the software elite. What we note is an attempt to reduce all human activities to the simple acts required to operate software devices. But this is an impossible quest. So, like the programmers, we will end up with nothing – neither the promised expedients, nor the expertise to perform those activities on our own.

At that point, society will collapse. A society dominated by a software elite and a software bureaucracy can exist only because the rest of us are willing to support them. It is impossible, however, for *all* of us to be as incompetent and inefficient in our pursuits as the programmers are now in theirs. For, who would support the entire society?

The Fallacy of
Software Engineering

1

The term *software engineering* was first used in the late 1960s. It expresses the view that, in order to be as successful in our programming activities as we are in our engineering activities, we must emulate the methods of the engineering disciplines. This view was a response to what became known as the software crisis: the realization that the available programming skills could not keep up with the growing demand for software, that application development took too long, and that most applications were never completed, or were inadequate, or were impossible to keep up to date.

Clearly, the experts said, a new programming philosophy is needed. They likened the programmers of that era to the old craftsmen, or artisans, whose knowledge and skills were not grounded on scientific principles but were the result of personal experience. Thus, concluded the experts, just as the traditional fields have advanced since modern engineering principles replaced the personal skills of craftsmen, the new field of software will advance if we replace personal programming skills with the software equivalent of the engineering principles.

So for the last forty years, the imminent transition from software art to software engineering has been the excuse for every new theory, methodology, development environment, and database system. Here are just a few out of the thousands of statements proclaiming this transition: "Software is applying for full membership in the engineering community. Software has grown in application breath and technical complexity to the point where it requires more than handcrafted practices."[1] "Software development has often been viewed as a highly individualistic art.... The evolution of software engineering in the 1970s and 1980s came from the realization that software development is better viewed as an engineering task ...."[2] "Software engineering is not alone among the engineering disciplines, but it is the youngster. We can learn a great deal by studying the history of other engineering disciplines."[3] "Software development currently is a craft.... Software manufacturing involves transferring the twin

---

[1] Walter J. Utz Jr., *Software Technology Transitions: Making the Transition to Software Engineering* (Englewood Cliffs, NJ: Prentice Hall, 1992), p. xvii.

[2] Ed Seidewitz and Mike Stark, *Reliable Object-Oriented Software: Applying Analysis and Design* (New York: SIGS Books, 1995), p. 4.

[3] Gerald M. Weinberg, *Quality Software Management*, vol. 1, *Systems Thinking* (New York: Dorset House, 1992), p. 295.

disciplines of standard parts and automated manufacture from industrial manufacturing to software development."[4] "We must move to an era when developers design software in the way that electronic engineers design machines."[5] "Software engineering is modeled on the time-proven techniques, methods, and controls associated with hardware development."[6] "Calling programmers 'software engineers' emphasizes the parallel between developing computer programs and developing mechanical or electronic systems. Many practices that have long been associated with engineering ... have increasingly been adopted by data processing professionals."[7] "We as practitioners must change. We must change from highly skilled artisans to being software manufacturing engineers."[8] "We now have tools and techniques that enable us to do true software engineering.... With these tools we can build software factories.... We have, working today, the basis for grand-scale engineering of software."[9]

The first thing we note in the idea of software engineering is its circularity. Before formulating programming theories based on engineering principles, we ought to determine whether software can indeed be developed with the methods we use to build cars and appliances. There are many human activities, after all, for which these methods are known to be inadequate. In chapter 2 we saw that, from displaying ordinary behaviour to practising a difficult profession, our acts are largely *intuitive*: we use unspecifiable knowledge and skills, rather than exact methods. This is true because most phenomena we face are complex; and for complex phenomena, our natural, non-mechanistic mental capabilities *exceed* the exact principles of science and engineering. Thus, whether this new human activity – programming – belongs to one category or the other is what needs to be determined. When the software theorists *start* their argument by claiming that programming must be practised

[4] Stephen G. Schur, *The Database Factory: Active Database for Enterprise Computing* (New York: John Wiley and Sons, 1994), p. 9.

[5] James Martin, *Principles of Object-Oriented Analysis and Design* (Englewood Cliffs, NJ: PTR Prentice Hall, 1993), p. 40.

[6] Roger S. Pressman, *Software Engineering: A Practitioner's Approach* (New York: McGraw-Hill, 1982), p. 15.

[7] L. Wayne Horn and Gary M. Gleason, *Advanced Structured COBOL: Batch and Interactive* (Boston: Boyd and Fraser, 1985), pp. 2–3.

[8] Sally Shlaer, "A Vision," in *Wisdom of the Gurus: A Vision for Object Technology*, ed. Charles F. Bowman (New York: SIGS Books, 1996), p. 222.

[9] James Martin, *An Information Systems Manifesto* (Englewood Cliffs, NJ: Prentice Hall, 1984), p. 37.

as an engineering activity, they start by assuming the very fact which they are supposed to prove.

While evident in each one of the foregoing quotations, the circularity is even better illustrated by the following passage: "This book is written with the firm belief that software development is a science, not an art, and should be managed as any other engineering project. For our purposes we will define 'software engineering' as the practical application of engineering principles and methods ...."[10] The author, thus, starts by admitting that the idea of software engineering is based on a *belief*. Then, he adds that software development should be managed as "any other" engineering project; so he treats as *established fact* the belief that it is a form of engineering. Finally, he *defines* software engineering as a form of engineering, as if the preceding statements had demonstrated this relationship.

Here is another example of this question-begging logic: "In this section we delineate software engineering and the software engineer.... The first step in the delineation is to establish a definition of software engineering – based upon the *premise* that software engineering is engineering – that will serve as a framework upon which we can describe the software engineer."[11] The authors, thus, candidly admit that they are *assuming* that fact which they are supposed to determine; namely, that software development is a form of engineering. Then, after citing a number of prior definitions that claim the same thing (also without proof), and after pointing out that there are actually some important differences between programming and the work of the engineer, the authors conclude: "Software engineering, in spite of the abstract nature and complexity of the product, is *obviously* a major branch of engineering."[12] The word "obviously" is conspicuously out of place, seeing that there is nothing in the two pages between the first and second quotation to prove that software development is a form of engineering.

This fallacy – defining a concept in terms of the concept itself – is known as *circular definition*. Logically, the theorists ought to start by investigating the nature of programming, and to adopt the term "software engineering" only after determining that this activity is indeed a form of engineering. They start, however, with the wish that programming be like engineering, and their definition ends up reflecting this wish rather than reality. Invariably, the theorists *start* by calling the activity "software engineering," and *then* set out searching for an explanation of this activity! With such question-begging reasoning, their conclusion that software development is a form of engineering

[10] Ray Turner, *Software Engineering Methodology* (Reston, VA: Reston, 1984), p. 2.
[11] Randall W. Jensen and Charles C. Tonies, "Introduction," in *Software Engineering*, eds. Randall W. Jensen and Charles C. Tonies (Englewood Cliffs, NJ: Prentice Hall, 1979), p. 9 (italics added).   [12] Ibid., p. 11 (italics added).

is not surprising. Nor is it surprising that the same experts who promote the idea of software engineering also promote absurd theories like structured programming or object-oriented programming: we can hardly expect individuals who fall victim to an elementary logical fallacy to invent sensible theories.

The second thing we note in the idea of software engineering is a distortion of facts. When the theorists liken the current programmers to the old craftsmen, they misrepresent both the spirit and the tradition of craftsmanship. The craftsmen were highly skilled individuals. They developed their knowledge over many years – years of arduous training as apprentices, followed by years of practice as journeymen, and further experience as masters. The craftsmen were true experts, in that they knew everything that could be known in their time in a particular field. Another way to describe their expertise is by saying that they were expected to attain the highest level of proficiency that human minds can attain in a given domain.

When likening programmers to craftsmen, the software theorists imply that the knowledge and experience that programmers have in their domain is similar to the knowledge and experience that craftsmen had in theirs; they imply that programmers know everything that can be known in the domain of software, that they have attained the utmost that human minds can attain in the art of programming. But is this true?

Let us recall what kind of "craftsman" was the programmer of the 1960s and 1970s – the period when this comparison was first enunciated. The typical worker employed by a company to develop software applications had no knowledge whatever of computers, or electronics, or engineering, and only high-school knowledge of such software-related subjects as science, logic, and mathematics. Nor was he required to have any knowledge of accounting, or manufacturing, or any other field related to business computing. Most of these individuals drifted into programming, as a matter of fact, precisely because they had no skills, so they could find no other job. Moreover, to become programmers, all they had to do was attend an introductory course, measured in *weeks*. (In contrast, the training of engineers, nurses, librarians, social workers, etc., took years. So, compared with other occupations, programmers knew nothing. Programming was treated, thus, not as a profession, but as *unskilled labour*. This attitude never changed, as we will see throughout the present chapter. Despite the engineering rhetoric, programmers are perceived as the counterpart, not of engineers, but of assembly-line workers.)

Not only did programmers lack any real knowledge, but they were prevented from gaining any real experience. Their work was restricted to trivial programming tasks – to small and isolated pieces of an application – and no one expected them to ever create and maintain whole business systems. After a year or two of this type of work, they were considered too skilled to program, so they were promoted to the position of systems analyst, or project manager, or some other function that involved little or no programming. Because it was deemed that their performance was the highest level attainable by an average person, many such positions were invented in an attempt to turn the challenge of software development from a reliance on programming skills to a reliance on management skills; that is, an attempt to create and maintain software applications through a large organization of incompetents, instead of a small number of professionals.[13]

From the beginning, then, the programming career was seen, not as a lifelong plan – a progression from apprentice to master, from novice to expert – but as a brief acquaintance with programming on the way to some other career. Programmers were neither expected nor permitted to expand their knowledge, or to perform increasingly demanding tasks. Since it was assumed that dealing with small and isolated programming problems represents the highest skill needed, and since almost anyone could acquire this skill in a few months, being a programmer much longer was taken as a sign of failure: that person, it was concluded, could not advance past the lowly position of programmer. The programming career ended, in effect, before it even started. Programming became one of those dubious occupations for which the measure of success is how soon the practitioner ceases to practise it. Thus, for a programmer, the measure was how soon he was promoted to a position that did *not* involve programming.

The notion of craftsmanship entailed, of course, more than just knowledge and experience. It was the craftsman's devotion to his vocation, his professional pride, and a profound sense of responsibility, that were just as important for his success. By perceiving programming as a brief phase on their way to some other occupation, it was impossible for programmers to develop the same qualities. Thus, even more than the lack of adequate knowledge and experience, it is the lack of these qualities that became the chief characteristic of our programming culture.

---

[13] While the whole world was mesmerized by the software propaganda, which was portraying programmers as talented professionals, the few sociologists who conducted their own research on this subject had no difficulty discovering the reality: the systematic deskilling of programmers and the bureaucratization of this profession. The following two works stand out (see also the related discussion and note 2 in "The Software Myth" in the introductory chapter, pp. 34–35): Philip Kraft, *Programmers and Managers: The Routinization of Computer Programming in the United States* (New York: Springer-Verlag, 1977); Joan M. Greenbaum, *In the Name of Efficiency: Management Theory and Shopfloor Practice in Data-Processing Work* (Philadelphia: Temple University Press, 1979).

So the occupation of programming became a haven for mediocre individuals, and for individuals with a bureaucratic mind. Someone who previously could do nothing useful could now hold a glamorous and well-paid position after just a few weeks of training – a position, moreover, demanding only the mechanical production of a few lines of software per day. Actually, it soon became irrelevant whether these lines worked at all, since the inadequacy of applications was accepted as a normal state of affairs. All that was required of programmers, in reality, was to conform to the prescripts laid down by the software elite. It is not too much to say that most business applications have been created by individuals who are not programmers at all – individuals who are not even apprentices, because they are not *preparing* to become programmers, but, on the contrary, are looking forward to the day when they will no longer have to program.

In conclusion, if we were to define the typical programmer, we could describe him or her as the exact opposite of a craftsman. Since the notion of craftsmanship is well understood, the software theorists must have been aware of this contradiction when they formulated their idea of software engineering. Everyone could see that programmers had no real knowledge or experience – and, besides, were not *expected* to improve – while the craftsmen attained the utmost knowledge and experience that an individual could attain. So why did the theorists liken programmers to craftsmen? Why did they base the idea of software engineering on a transition from craftsmanship to engineering, when it was obvious that programmers were not at all like the old craftsmen?

The answer is that the theorists held the principles of software mechanism as unquestionable truth. They noticed that the programming practices were both non-mechanistic and unsatisfactory, and concluded that the only way to improve them was by making them mechanistic. This question-begging logic prevented them from noticing that they were making contradictory observations; namely, that programmers were incompetent, and that they were like the old craftsmen. Both observations seemed to suggest the idea of software engineering as solution, when in fact the theorists had accepted that idea implicitly to begin with. The alternative solution – a culture where programmers can become *true* software craftsmen – was never considered.

Barry Boehm,[14] in a paper considered a landmark in the history of software engineering, manages to avoid the comparison of programmers to craftsmen only by following an even more absurd line of logic. He notes the mediocrity of programmers, and concludes that the purpose of software engineering must

---

[14] Barry W. Boehm, "Software Engineering," in *Milestones in Software Evolution*, eds. Paul W. Oman and Ted G. Lewis (Los Alamitos, CA: IEEE Computer Society Press, ©1990 IEEE) – paper originally published in *IEEE Transactions on Computers* C-25, no. 12 (1976): 1226–1241.

be, not to create a body of skilled and responsible professionals, but on the contrary, to develop techniques whereby even incompetent workers can create useful software: "For example, a recent survey of 14 installations in one large organization produced the following profile of its 'average coder': 2 years college-level education, 2 years software experience, familiarity with 2 programming languages and 2 applications, and generally introverted, sloppy, inflexible, 'in over his head,' and undermanaged. Given the continuing increase in demand for software personnel, one should not assume that this typical profile will improve much. This has strong implications for effective software engineering technology which, like effective software, must be well-matched to the people who must use it."[15]

Boehm, evidently, doesn't think that we ought to determine first whether programming is, in fact, the kind of skill that can be replaced with hordes of incompetents trained to follow some simple methods. Note also his idea of what "effective" software generally must do: not help people to develop their minds, but keep them at their current, mediocre level. This remark betrays the paternalism characteristic of the software elite: human beings are seen strictly as operators of software devices – devices which they, the experts, are going to design. Thus, the "easy-to-use" software environments upon which our work increasingly depends today, both as programmers and as users, are, clearly, the realization of this totalitarian vision.

2

The absurdities we have just examined are the type of fallacies one should indeed expect to find in a mechanistic culture like ours. But we cannot simply dismiss them. For, if we are to understand how the pseudoscience of software engineering grew out of the mechanistic ideology, we must start by studying this distortion of the notions of programming and craftsmanship.

The theorists who promoted the idea of software engineering had, in fact, very little programming experience. They were mostly academics, so their knowledge was limited to textbook cases: small and isolated programming problems, which can be depicted with neat diagrams and implemented by way of rules and methods. Their knowledge was limited, in other words, to software phenomena simple enough to represent with exact, mechanistic models. A few of these theorists were mathematicians, so their preference for formal and complete explanations is understandable.

And indeed, some valuable contributions were made by theorists in the

---

[15] Ibid., p. 67 n. 3.

1950s and 1960s, when the field of software was new, and useful mechanistic concepts were relatively easy to come by: various algorithms (methods to sort tables and files, for instance) and the principles of programming languages and compilers are examples of these contributions.

The importance of the mechanistic concepts is undeniable; they form, in fact, the foundation of the discipline of programming. Mechanistic models, however, can represent only simple, isolated phenomena. And consequently, mechanistic software concepts form only a small part of programming knowledge. The most important part is the *complex* knowledge, the capacity to deal with many software phenomena simultaneously; and complex knowledge can only develop in a mind, through personal experience. We need complex programming knowledge because the phenomena we want to represent in software – our personal, social, and business affairs – are themselves complex. Restricted to mechanistic concepts, we can correctly represent in software only phenomena that can be isolated from the others.

So it was not so much the search for mechanistic theories that was wrong, as the belief that *all* programming problems are mechanistic. The theorists had no doubt that there would be future advances in programming concepts, and that these advances would be of the same nature as those of the past. They believed that the field of software would eventually be like mathematics: nothing but neat and exact definitions, methods, and theories.

This conviction is clearly expressed by Richard Linger et al.,[16] who refer to it as a "rediscovery" of the value of mathematics in software development. They note that the early interest in mathematical ideas faded as software applications increased in complexity, that the pragmatic aspects of programming seem more important than its mathematical roots. But they believe this decline in formal programming methods to be just a temporary neglect, due to our failure to appreciate their value: "Thus, although it may seem surprising, the rediscovery of software as a form of mathematics in a deep and literal sense is just beginning to penetrate university research and teaching, as well as industry and government practices…. *Of course, software is a special form of mathematics* …."[17]

The authors continue their argument by citing approvingly the following statement made by E. W. Dijkstra (the best-known advocate of "structured programming"): "As soon as programming emerges as a battle against unmastered complexity, it is quite natural that one turns to that mental discipline whose main purpose has been for centuries to apply effective structuring to

---

[16] Richard C. Linger, Harlan D. Mills, and Bernard I. Witt, *Structured Programming: Theory and Practice* (Reading, MA: Addison-Wesley, 1979), pp. vii–viii.

[17] Ibid., p. viii (italics added).

otherwise unmastered complexity. That mental discipline is more or less familiar to all of us, it is called Mathematics. If we take the existence of the impressive body of Mathematics as the experimental evidence for the opinion that for the human mind the mathematical method is indeed the most effective way to come to grips with complexity, we have no choice any longer: *we should reshape our field of programming in such a way that, the mathematician's methods become equally applicable to our programming problems, for there are no other means.*"[18]

The delusion of software mechanism is clearly seen in these claims. What these theorists see as complexity is not at all the *real* complexity of software – the complexity found in the phenomena I call complex structures, or systems of interacting structures. They consider "complex," systems that are in fact *simple* structures, although perhaps very large structures. They praise the ability of mathematics to master this "complexity"; and indeed, mechanistic methods can handle simple structures, no matter how large. But it is not this kind of complexity that is the real problem of programming. The theorists fail to see that it is quite easy to deal with this kind of complexity, and it is easy precisely because we have the formal, exact tools of mathematics to master it. The reason why practitioners neglect the mathematics and continue to rely on informal methods is that, unlike the professors with their neat textbook examples, *they* must deal with the *real* complexity of the world if they are to represent the world accurately in software. And to master *that* complexity, the formal methods of mathematics are insufficient.

Note the last, emphasized sentence, in each of the two quotations above. These confident assertions clearly illustrate the morbidity of the mechanistic obsession. The theorists say that software is, "of course," a form of mathematics, but they don't feel there is a need to prove this claim. Then, they assert just as confidently that "we should reshape" programming to agree with this claim, treating now an unproven notion as established fact. In other words, since the mechanistic theories do not seem to reflect the reality of programming, we must modify reality to conform to the theories: we must restrict our software pursuits to what *can* be explained mechanistically. Instead of trying to understand the *true* nature of software and programming, as real scientists would, these theorists believe their task is simply to enforce the mechanistic doctrine. The idea that software and programming can be represented mathematically is *their* delusion; but they see it as their professional duty to make us all program and use computers in this limited, mechanistic fashion.

Thus, although it was evident from the beginning that the mechanistic concepts are useful only in isolated situations – only when we can extract a

[18] E. W. Dijkstra, "On a Methodology of Design," quoted ibid. (italics added).

particular software structure, or aspect, from the complex whole – the theorists insisted that the difficulty of programming large and complex applications can be reduced to the easier challenge of programming small pieces of software. They believed that applications can be "built" as we build cars and appliances; that is, as a combination of modules, each module made up of smaller ones, and so on, down to some small bits of software that are easy to program. If each module is kept independent of the others, if they are related strictly as a hierarchical structure, the methods that work with small bits of software – rules, diagrams, mathematics – must hold for modules of any size. The entire application can then be built, one level at a time, with skills no greater than those required to program the smallest parts. All that programmers need to know, therefore, is how to handle isolated bits of software.

So the idea of software engineering is based, neither on personal experience, nor on a sensible hypothesis, but merely on the mechanistic dogma: on the belief that any phenomenon can be modeled through reductionism and atomism.

By the mid-1960s, most software concepts that are mechanistic and also practical had been discovered. But the theorists could not accept the fact that the easy and dramatic advances were a thing of the past, that we could not expect further improvements in programming productivity simply by adopting a new method or principle. They were convinced that similar advances would take place in the future, that there exist many other mechanistic concepts, all waiting to be discovered. To pick just one example, they noticed the increase in programming productivity achieved when moving from low-level to high-level languages, and concluded that other languages would soon be invented with even higher levels of abstraction, so the same increase in productivity would be repeated again and again. (The notion of "generations" of languages, still with us today, reflects this fantasy; see pp. 464–465.)

To make matters worse, just when major improvements in programming concepts ceased, advances in computer hardware made *larger* applications possible. Moreover, continually decreasing hardware costs permitted more companies to use computers, so we needed *more* applications. This situation was called the software crisis. The theorists watched with envy the advances in hardware, which continued year after year while programming productivity stagnated, and interpreted this discrepancy as further evidence that programming must be practised like engineering: if engineering concepts are successful in improving the computers themselves, they *must* be useful for software too.

The so-called software crisis, thus, was in reality the crisis of software mechanism: what happened when the mechanistic principles reached the limit of their usefulness. The crisis was brought about by the software theorists, when they declared that programming is a mechanistic activity. This led to the belief that anyone can practise programming, simply by following certain methods. So the theorists founded the culture of programming incompetence, which eventually caused the crisis. They recognized the crisis, but not its roots – the fallacy of software mechanism. They aggravated the crisis, thus, by claiming that its solution was to treat programming as a form of engineering, which made programming even more mechanistic. Software mechanism became a dogma, and all that practitioners were permitted to know from then on was mechanistic principles.

Deprived of the opportunity to develop complex knowledge, our skills remain at a mechanistic level – the level of novices. Craftsmanship – the highest level of knowledge and skills – is attained by using the mind's capacity for complex structures, while mechanistic thinking entails only simple structures. So what the theorists are promoting through their ideas is not an intellectual advance, but a reversal: from complex to mechanistic thinking, from expertise to mediocrity, from a culture that creates skilled masters to one that keeps programmers as permanent novices.

The software crisis was never resolved, of course, but we no longer notice it. We no longer see as a crisis the inefficiency of programmers, or the astronomic amounts of money spent on software, or the $100-million failures. We are no longer surprised that applications are inadequate, or that they cannot be kept up to date and must be perpetually replaced; we are regularly replacing now, in fact, not just our applications but our entire computing environments. We don't question the need for society to support a large software bureaucracy. And we don't see that it is the incompetence of programmers, and the inadequacy of their applications, that increasingly force other members of society to waste their time with spurious, software-related activities. What was once a crisis in a small section of society has become a normal way of life for the entire society.

The software crisis can also be described as the struggle to create useful applications in a programming culture that permits only mechanistic thinking; specifically, the struggle to represent with simple software structures the complex phenomena that make up our affairs. It is not too much to say that whatever useful software we have had was developed, not *by means* of, but *in spite* of, the principles of software engineering; it was developed *through craftsmanship*, and while fighting the restrictions imposed by our corrupt programming culture. Had we followed the teachings of the software theorists, we would have no useful applications today.

3

The software theorists, we saw, distorted both the notion of craftsmanship and the notion of programming to fit their mechanistic fantasies. They decided *arbitrarily* that programming is like engineering, because they had already decided that future advances in programming principles were possible, and that these advances would be, like those of the past, mechanistic. They likened incompetent programmers to craftsmen because they saw the evolution of practitioners from craftsmen to engineers as a necessary part of these advances. The analogy – an absurdity – became then the central part of the idea of software engineering. Mesmerized by the prospect of building software applications as successfully as engineers build physical structures, no one noticed the falsity of the comparison. Everyone accepted it as a logical conclusion reached from the idea of software engineering, even as software engineering itself was only a wish, a fantasy.

The theorists claimed that programming, if practised as craftsmanship, cannot improve beyond the level attained by an average programmer. But they made this statement without knowing what *real* software craftsmanship is. They saw programmers as craftsmen while programmers lacked the very qualities that distinguished the old craftsmen. Programming, as a matter of fact, is one of those vocations that can benefit greatly from the spirit of craftsmanship – from personal skills and experience – because it requires complex knowledge. If we are to liken programmers to the old craftsmen, we should draw the correct conclusion; namely, that programmers too must have the highest possible education, training, and experience. (And it is probably even more difficult to attain the highest level of expertise in the field of programming than it was in the old fields.)

Had we allowed programmers to develop their skills over many years, to perform varied and increasingly demanding tasks, and to work in ways that enhance their minds, rather than waste their time with worthless concepts – in other words, had we created a programming culture in the spirit of craftsmanship – we would have had today a true programming profession. We would then realize that what programmers must accomplish has little to do with engineering; that mechanistic knowledge (including subjects like mathematics and engineering), crucial though it is, is the *easy* part of programming expertise; that it is the *unspecifiable* kind of knowledge (what we recognize as personal skills and experience) that is the most difficult and the most important part.

The software theorists note the higher levels of knowledge attained by certain individuals, but they cannot explain this performance mechanistically; so they brand it as "art" and reject it as unreliable. We could always find exceptional programmers; but instead of interpreting their superior performance as evidence that it *is* possible to attain higher levels of programming skills, instead of admitting that the traditional process of skill acquisition is the best preparation for programmers, the mechanists concluded the opposite: that we must *avoid* these individuals, because they rely on personal knowledge rather than exact theories.

Distorting the notions of craftsmanship and programming, however, was not enough. In order to make software mechanism plausible, and to appropriate the term "engineering" for their own activities, the software theorists had to distort the notion of engineering itself. Thus, they praise the principles of engineering, and claim that they are turning programming into a similar activity, while their ideas are, in fact, childish imitations of the engineering principles.

It is easy for the software theorists to delude themselves, since they know even less about engineering than they know about programming. They praise the power and precision of mathematics; and, indeed, the real engineering disciplines are grounded upon exact and difficult mathematical concepts. *Their* theories, on the other hand – when not plain stupid – are little more than informal pieces of advice. Far from having a solid mathematical foundation, the software theories resemble the arguments found in self-help books or in cookbooks more than they do engineering principles. The few theories that are indeed mathematical have no practical value, so they are ignored, or are made useful by being downgraded to informal methods. The most common form of deception, we will see, is to promote a formal theory by means of contrived, oversimplified case studies, while employing in actual applications only the downgraded, informal variant. Thus, whereas real engineering is a practical pursuit, *software* engineering works only with trivial, artificial examples.

The software theorists also misrepresent engineering when they point to the neat hierarchical structures – components, modules, prefabricated subassemblies – as that ideal form of design and construction that programming is to emulate. Because they know so little about engineering, all they see in it is what they wish programming to become, what they believe to be the answer to all programming problems, as if the concept of hierarchical structures were all there is to engineering. They ignore the creativity, the skills, the contribution of exceptional minds; that is, the *non-mechanistic* aspects of engineering, which are just as important as the formal principles and methods.

Clearly, without the non-mechanistic aspects there would be no inventions or innovations, and engineering would only produce neat structures of old things.

The software theorists refuse to acknowledge the informal aspects of engineering because, if they did, they would have to admit that much of programming too is informal, non-mechanistic, and dependent on personal skills and experience. In programming, moreover, our non-mechanistic capabilities are even more important, because, unlike our engineering problems, nearly all the problems we are addressing through software – our social, personal, and business affairs – form systems of interacting structures.

In conclusion, the idea of software engineering makes sense only if we agree to degrade our conceptions of knowledge and skills, of craftsmanship and engineering, of software and programming, to a level where they can all be replaced with the mechanistic principles of reductionism and atomism.

The early software theorists were trained scientists, as we saw, and made a real contribution – at least where mechanistic principles are useful. But it would be wrong to think that *all* software theorists are true scientists. By upholding the mechanistic software ideology, the early theorists established a software culture where incompetents, crackpots, and charlatans could look like experts.

Thus, someone too ignorant to work in the exact sciences, or in the real engineering disciplines, could now pursue a prestigious career in a software-related field. Just as the mechanistic software culture had made it possible for the most ignorant people to become programmers, the same culture allowed now anyone with good communication skills to become a theorist, a lecturer, a writer, or a consultant. Individuals with practically no knowledge of programming, or computers, or science, or engineering became rich and famous simply by talking and writing about software, as they could hypnotize programmers and managers with the new jargon. Also, because defining things as a hierarchical structure was believed to be the answer to all programming problems, anyone who could draw a hierarchical diagram was inventing a new theory or methodology based on this idea. Thousands of books, newsletters, periodicals, shows, and conferences were created to promote these idiocies.

Finally, as the entire society is becoming dependent on software, and hence on ignorant theorists and practitioners, we are all increasingly preoccupied with worthless mechanistic ideas. Thus, the ultimate consequence of the mechanistic software ideology is not just programming incompetence, but a mass stupidity that the world has not seen since the superstitions of the Dark Ages. (If you think this is an exaggeration, wait until we study the GOTO superstition – the most famous tenet of programming science.)

Software Engineering
as Pseudoscience

1

Let us start with the *definition* of software engineering. Here are three definitions frequently cited in the software literature: "Software engineering is that form of engineering that applies the principles of computer science and mathematics to achieving cost-effective solutions to software problems."[1] "The practical application of scientific knowledge in the design and construction of computer programs and the associated documentation required to develop, operate, and maintain them."[2] "The establishment and use of sound engineering principles (methods) in order to obtain economically software that is reliable and works on real machines."[3]

At first sight, these statements look like a serious depiction of a profession, or discipline. Their formal tone, however, is specious. They may well describe a sphere of activities, but there is nothing in these definitions to indicate the *usefulness*, or the *success*, of these activities. In other words, even if they describe accurately what software practitioners are doing (or ought to be doing), we cannot tell from the definitions themselves whether these activities are essential to programming, or whether they are spurious. As we will see in a moment, an individual can appear perfectly rational in the pursuit of an idea, and can even display great expertise, while the idea itself is a delusion.

These definitions are correct insofar as they describe the programming principles recommended by the software theorists. But we have no evidence that it is possible to develop actual software applications by adhering to these principles. We saw in the previous section that the very term "software engineering" constitutes a circular definition, since it was adopted without determining first whether programming is indeed a form of engineering; it was adopted because the software theorists *wished* programming to be like engineering (see pp. 495–497). And the same circularity is evident in the

---

[1] Anthony Ralston and Edwin D. Reilly, eds., *Encyclopedia of Computer Science*, 3rd ed. (New York: Van Nostrand Reinhold, 1993), p. 1218.

[2] Barry W. Boehm, "Software Engineering," in *Milestones in Software Evolution*, eds. Paul W. Oman and Ted G. Lewis (Los Alamitos, CA: IEEE Computer Society Press, ©1990 IEEE), p. 54 – paper originally published in *IEEE Transactions on Computers* C-25, no. 12 (1976): 1226–1241.

[3] F. L. Bauer, quoted in Randall W. Jensen and Charles C. Tonies, "Introduction," in *Software Engineering*, eds. Randall W. Jensen and Charles C. Tonies (Englewood Cliffs, NJ: Prentice Hall, 1979), p. 9.

definitions just cited: software engineering is "that form of engineering," is "the practical application of scientific knowledge," is "sound engineering principles." In all three cases, the definition merely expresses the unproven idea that software engineering is a form of engineering.

The definition of software engineering, thus, is not the definition of a profession or discipline, but the definition of a wish, of a fantasy. The fallacy committed by the advocates of software engineering is to think that, if it is possible to *define* a set of principles and methods so as to formally express a wish, then we should also be able to practise them and *fulfil* that wish.[4]

Recall what a pseudoscience is: a system of belief masquerading as scientific theory. Accordingly, the various principles, methods, and activities known as software engineering, no matter how rational they may appear when observed individually, form in reality a pseudoscience.

If it is so difficult to distinguish between sensible and fallacious definitions, or between useful and spurious activities, in the domain of programming, it will perhaps help to examine first some older and simpler delusions.

Consider superstitions – the idea that the number 13 brings misfortune, for instance. Once we accept this idea, the behaviour of a person who avoids the number 13 appears entirely rational and logical. Thus, to determine whether a particular decision would involve the value 13, that person must perform correctly some calculations or assessments; so he must do exactly what a mathematician or engineer would do in that situation. When a person insists on redesigning a device that happens to have thirteen parts, or kilograms, or inches, his acts are indistinguishable from those of a person who redesigns that device in order to improve its performance; in both cases, the changes entail the application of strict engineering methods, and the acts constitute the pursuit of a well-defined goal. When the designers of a high-rise building decide to omit the thirteenth floor, they must adjust carefully their plans to take into account the discrepancy between levels and floor numbers above the twelfth floor. And lawyers drawing documents for the units on the high floors must differentiate between their level, which provides the legal designation, and the actual floor number. These builders and lawyers, then, perform the same acts as when solving vital engineering or legal problems.

---

[4] In "Software Magic" (in the introductory chapter), we studied the similarity between mechanistic software concepts and primitive magic systems; and we saw that magic systems, too, entail the formal expression of wishes and the meticulous practice of the rituals believed to fulfil those wishes.

Note that the activities performed by believers, and by anyone else affected by this superstition, are always purposeful, logical, and consistent. Watching each one of these activities *separately*, a casual observer has no reason to suspect that the ultimate objective is simply to avoid the number 13. In fact, even when we *are* aware of this objective, we may have no way of recognizing the *uselessness* of these activities. Thus, we could formally define these activities as "the practical application of scientific and engineering knowledge to the prevention of misfortune." But, obviously, just because we can define them it doesn't mean that they are effective.

Consider also a system of belief like astrology. Astrologers must follow, of course, the position of the heavenly bodies, and in this activity they behave just like astronomers. The interpretation of these positions involves various principles and methods, some of which have been in use for millennia; so in this activity, too, astrologers must display professional knowledge and skills. A person who cancels a trip because an astrological calculation deems travel hazardous is clearly concerned with safety, and acts no differently from a person who cancels a trip because of bad weather. Astrologers employ certain principles and methods – tables that relate traits to birth dates, for example – to assess the personality of people and to explain their behaviour; but psychologists also use various principles and methods to assess personality and to explain behaviour.

So, as in the case of superstitions, just by watching each activity *separately*, an observer cannot suspect that astrology as a whole is a delusion. Within this system of belief – once we accept the idea that human beings are affected by the position of the heavenly bodies – all acts performed by practitioners and believers appear purposeful, logical, and consistent. A formal definition like "the practical application of astronomic and mathematical principles to the prediction of future events" describes accurately these activities. But being definable doesn't make these activities sensible. As in the case of superstitions, their definition is the definition of a wish.

And so it is for software engineering. Recall the definitions cited earlier: "that form of engineering that applies the principles of computer science and mathematics to achieving cost-effective solutions to software problems," etc. We wish programming to be a form of engineering; but, just because we can express this wish in a formal definition, it doesn't follow that the methods and activities described by this definition form a practical pursuit like traditional engineering. We note that millions of practitioners follow the mechanistic theories of software engineering, and each one of these activities appears purposeful, intelligent, and urgent. But no matter how logical these activities are when observed *separately*, the body of activities as a whole can still constitute a delusion. As we will see in the present chapter, the pseudoscientific nature of the mechanistic software theories is easily exposed when we assess them with the principles of demarcation between science and pseudoscience (see "Popper's Principles of Demarcation" in chapter 3).

2

Pseudosciences are founded on hypotheses that are treated as unquestionable truth. (In the theories we have just examined, the hypothesis is that certain numbers, or the heavenly bodies, influence human affairs.) Scientific theories also start with a hypothesis, but their authors never stop *doubting* the hypothesis. Whereas pseudoscientists think their task is to *defend* their theory, serious workers know that theories must be *tested*; and the only effective way to test a theory is by attacking it: by searching, not for confirmations, but for falsifications. In empirical science it is impossible to *prove* a theory, so confirmations are worthless: no matter how many confirmations we find, we can never be sure that we have encountered all possible, or even all relevant, situations. At the same time, just one situation that falsifies the theory is sufficient, logically, to refute it. The correct approach, therefore, is to accept a theory not because it can be defended, but because it cannot be refuted; that is, not because we can confirm it, but because we cannot falsify it.

It is easy to defend a fallacious theory: all we have to do is restrict our studies to cases that confirm its claims, and ignore those cases that falsify it. Thus, while a scientific theory is required to *pass* tests, pseudosciences appear to work because they *avoid* tests. If we add to this the practice of continually *expanding* the theory (by inventing new principles to cope with the falsifications, one at a time), it should be obvious that almost any theory can be made to look good.

A popular pseudoscientific theory becomes a self-perpetuating belief system, and can reach a point where its validity is taken for granted no matter how fallacious it is. This is because its very growth is seen by believers, in a circular thought process, as proof of its validity. Whenever noticing a failure – a claim that does not materialize, for instance – they calmly dismiss it as a minor anomaly. They are convinced that an explanation will soon be found, or that the failure is merely an exception, so they can deal with it by modifying slightly the theory. They regard the system's size, its many adherents, the large number of methods and formulas, the length of time it has been accepted, as a great logical mass that cannot be shaken by one failure. They forget that the system's great mass was reached precisely because they always took its validity for granted, so they always dismissed its failures – *one at a time*, just as they are now dismissing the new one.

A theory can be seen as a body of provisional conjectures that must be verified empirically. Any failure, therefore, must be treated as a falsification of the theory and taken very seriously. If believers commit (out of enthusiasm, for example) the mistake of regarding any success as confirmation of the theory while dismissing the failures as unimportant, the system is *guaranteed* to grow, no matter how erroneous those conjectures are. The system's growth and popularity are then interpreted as evidence of its validity, and each new failure is dismissed on the strength of this imagined validity, when in fact it is these very failures that ought to be used to *judge* its validity. This circularity makes the theory unfalsifiable: apparently perfect, while in reality worthless.

❖

Pseudosciences, thus, may suffer from only one mistaken hypothesis, only one false assumption. Apart from this mistake, the believers may be completely logical, so their activities may be indistinguishable from true scientific work. But if that one assumption is wrong, the system as a whole is nonsensical.

It is this phenomenon – the performance of activities that are perfectly logical individually even while the body of activities as a whole constitutes a delusion – that makes pseudosciences so hard to detect, so strikingly like the real sciences. And this is why the principles of demarcation between science and pseudoscience are so important. Often, they are the only way to expose an invalid theory.

Any hypothesis can form the basis of a delusion, and hence a pseudoscience. So we should not be surprised that the popular *mechanistic* hypothesis has been such a rich source of delusions and pseudosciences. Because of their similarity to the traditional pseudosciences, I have called the delusions engendered by the mechanistic hypothesis *the new pseudosciences* (see pp. 203–204). Unlike the traditional ones, though, the new pseudosciences are pursued by respected scientists, working in prestigious universities.

Let us recall how a mechanistic delusion turns into a pseudoscience (see pp. 204–205, 233–235). The scientists start by committing the fallacy of reification: they assume that a model based on one isolated structure can provide a useful approximation of the complex phenomenon, so they extract that structure from the system of structures that make up the actual phenomenon. In complex phenomena, however, the links between structures are too strong to be ignored, so their model does not represent the phenomenon closely enough to be useful. What we note is that the theory fails to explain certain events or situations. For example, if the phenomenon the scientists are studying involves minds and societies, the model fails to explain certain behaviour patterns, or certain intelligent acts, or certain aspects of culture.

Their faith in mechanism, though, prevents the scientists from recognizing these failures as a refutation of the theory. Because they take the possibility of a mechanistic explanation not as hypothesis but as fact, they think that only *a few* falsifying instances will be found, and that their task is to *defend* the theory: they search for confirming instances and avoid the falsifying ones; and, when a falsification cannot be dismissed, they *expand* the theory to make it explain that instance too. What they are doing, thus, to save the theory, is *turning falsifications of the theory into new features of the theory*. Poor mechanistic approximations, however, give rise to an *infinity* of falsifying instances; so they must expand the theory again and again. This activity is both dishonest and futile, but they perceive it as research.

A theory can be said to work when it successfully explains and predicts; if it must be expanded continually because it fails to explain and predict some events, then, clearly, it does *not* work. Defending a mechanistic theory looks like scientific research only if we regard the quest for mechanistic explanations as an indisputable method of science. Thus, the mechanists end up doing in the name of science exactly what pseudoscientists do when defending *their* theories. When expanding the theory, when making it agree with an increasingly broad range of situations, what they do in effect is annul, one by one, its original claims; they make it less and less precise, and eventually render it worthless (see pp. 225–226).

Since it is the essence of mechanism to break down complex problems into simpler ones, the mechanistic hypothesis, perhaps more than any other hypothesis, can make the pursuit of a delusion look like serious research. These scientists try to solve a complex problem by dividing it into simpler ones, and then dividing these into simpler ones yet, and so on, in order to reach isolated problems; finally, they represent the isolated problems with simple structures. And in both types of activities – dividing problems into simpler ones, and working with isolated simple structures – their work is indistinguishable from research in fields like physics, where mechanism *is* useful. But if the original phenomenon is non-mechanistic, if it is the result of interacting phenomena, a model based on isolated structures cannot provide a practical approximation. So those activities, despite their resemblance to research work, are in fact fraudulent.

Being worthless as theories, all mechanistic delusions must eventually come to an end. The scientists, however, learn nothing from these failures. They remain convinced that the principles of reductionism and atomism can explain all phenomena, so their next theory is, invariably, another mechanistic delusion. They may be making only one mistake: assuming that any phenomenon can be separated into simpler ones. But if they accept this notion unquestioningly, they are bound to turn their theories into pseudosciences.

3

The purpose of this discussion is to show how easy it is for large numbers of people, even an entire society, to engage in activities that appear intelligent and logical, while pursuing in fact a delusion; in particular, to show that the mechanistic software pursuits constitute this type of delusion. Our software delusions have evolved from the same mechanistic culture that fosters delusions in fields like psychology, sociology, and linguistics. But, while these other delusions are limited to academic research, the software delusions are affecting the entire society.

Recall how a mechanistic software theory turns into a pseudoscience. Software applications are systems of interacting structures. The structures that make up an application are the various *aspects* of the application. Thus, each software or business practice, each file with the associated operations, each subroutine with its calls, each memory variable with its uses, forms a simple structure. And these structures interact, because they share their elements – the various software entities that make up the application (see pp. 347–348).

The mechanistic software theories, though, claim that an application can be programmed by treating these aspects as *independent* structures, and by dealing with each structure separately. For example, the theory of structured programming is founded on the idea that the *flow-control* operations form an independent structure; and the database theories are founded on the idea that the *database* operations form an independent structure.

Just like the other mechanistic theories, the software theories keep being falsified. A theory is falsified whenever we see programmers having to override it, whenever they cannot adhere strictly to its principles. And, just like the other mechanists, the software mechanists deny that these falsifications constitute a refutation of the theory: being based on mechanistic principles, they say, the theory *must* be correct.

So instead of *doubting* the theory, instead of severely testing it, the software mechanists end up *defending* it. First, they search for confirmations and avoid the falsifications: they discuss with enthusiasm the few cases that make the theory look good, while carefully avoiding the many cases where the theory failed. Second, they never cease "enhancing" the theory: they keep expanding it by contriving new principles to make it cope with the falsifying situations as they occur, one at a time.

Ultimately, as we will see in the following sections, all software theories suffer from the two mechanistic fallacies, reification and abstraction: they claim that we can treat the various aspects of an application as independent structures, so we can develop the application by dealing with these structures separately; and they claim that we can develop the same applications by starting from high levels of abstraction as we can by starting from low levels. The modifications needed later to make a theory practical are then simply a reversal of these claims; specifically, restoring the capability to link structures and to deal with low-level entities. In the end, the informal, traditional programming concepts are reinstated – although in a more complicated way, under new names, as part of the new theory. So, while relying in fact on these informal concepts, everyone believes that it is the theory that helps them to develop applications.

❖

Our programming culture has been distinguished by delusions for over forty years. These delusions are expressed in thousands of books and papers, and there is no question of studying them all here. What I want to show rather is that, despite their variety and their changes over the years, all software delusions have the same source: the mechanistic ideology. I will limit myself, therefore, to a discussion of the most famous theories. The theories are changing, and new ones will probably appear in the future, but this study will help us to recognize the mechanistic nature of any theory.

In addition to discussing the mechanistic theories and their fallacies, this study can be seen as a general introduction to the principles and problems that make up the challenge of software development. So it is also an attempt to explain in lay terms what is the *true* nature of software and programming. Thus, if we understand why the mechanistic ideas are worthless, we can better appreciate why personal skills and experience are, in the end, the most important determinant in software development.

Structured Programming

Structured programming occupies a special place in the history of software mechanism. Introduced in the 1970s, it was the first of the great software theories, and the first one to be described as a *revolution* in programming principles. It was also the first attempt to solve the so-called software crisis, and it is significant that the solution was seen, even then, not in encouraging programmers to improve their skills, but in finding a way to eliminate the *need* for skills.

Thus, this was the first time that programming expertise was redefined to mean expertise in the use of substitutes for expertise – methods, aids, or devices supplied by a software elite. This interpretation of expertise was so well received that it became the chief characteristic of all the theories that followed.

Another common characteristic, already evident in structured programming, is the enthusiasm accompanying each new theory – an enthusiasm that betrays the naivety of both the academics and the practitioners. Well-known concepts – the hierarchical structure, the principles of reductionism and atomism – are rediscovered again and again, and hailed as great advances, as the beginning of a *science* of programming. No one seems to notice that, not only are these concepts the same as in the previous software delusions, but they are the same as in every mechanistic delusion of the last three centuries.

Structured programming was the chief preoccupation of practitioners and academics in the 1970s and 1980s. And, despite the occasional denial, it continues to dominate our programming practices. The reason this is not apparent is our preoccupation with more recent theories, more recent revolutions. But, even though one theory or another is in vogue at a given time, the principles of structured programming continue to be obeyed as faithfully as they were in the 1970s. The GOTO superstition, for example, is as widespread today as it was then.

Finally, it is important to study structured programming because it was this theory that established the software bureaucracy, and the culture of programming incompetence and irresponsibility. The period before its introduction was the last opportunity our society had to found a true programming profession. For, once the bureaucrats assumed control of corporate programming, what ensued was inevitable. It was the same academics and gurus who invented the following theories, and the same programmers and managers who accepted them, again and again. The perpetual cycle of promises and disappointments – the cycle repeated to this day with each new methodology, programming aid, or development environment – started with structured programming. Since the same individuals who are naive enough to accept one theory are called upon, when the theory fails, to assess the merits of the next one, it is not surprising that the programming profession has become a closed, stagnating culture. Once we accepted the idea that it is not programming expertise that matters but familiarity with the latest substitutes for expertise, it was inevitable that precisely those individuals *incapable* of expertise become the model of the software professional.

The Theory

1

To appreciate the promise of structured programming, we must take a moment to review the programming difficulties that prompted it. Recall, first, what is the essence of software. The operations that make up a program are organized in logical constructs – mostly conditions and iterations – which reflect the relations between the processes and events we want to represent in software. A typical software module, therefore, is not just a series of consecutive operations, but a combination of blocks of operations that are executed or bypassed, or are executed repeatedly, depending on various run-time conditions. Within each block, we can have, in addition to the consecutive operations, further conditions and iterations. In other words, these constructs can be nested: a module can have several levels of conditions within conditions or iterations, and iterations within conditions or iterations. Blocks can be as small as one operation, or statement, but usually include several. And if we also remember that certain operations serve to invoke other modules at run time, then, clearly, applications of any size can be created in this manner.[1]

The conditional construct consists of a condition (which involves, usually, values that change while the application is running) and two blocks; with this construct, the programmer specifies that the first block be executed when the condition is evaluated as *True*, and the second block when evaluated as *False*. (In practice, one of the two blocks may be empty.) The iterative construct consists of a condition (which involves usually values that change from one iteration to the next) and the block that is to be executed repeatedly; with this construct, the programmer specifies that the repetition continue only as long as the condition is evaluated as *True*. (Iterative software constructs are known as *loops*.) Conditions and iterations are *flow-control* operations, so called because they control the program's flow of execution; that is, the sequence in which the other kinds of operations (calculations, assigning values to variables, displaying data, accessing files, etc.) are executed by the computer.

Modifying the flow of execution entails "jumping" across blocks of operations: jumping forward, in order to prevent the execution of an unwanted

---

[1] Some definitions: *Block* denotes here any group of consecutive, related operations (not just the formal units by this name in block-structured languages). *Operation* denotes the simplest functional unit, which depends on the programming language (one operation in a high-level language is usually equivalent to several, simpler operations in a low-level language). *Statement* denotes the smallest executable unit in high-level languages. Since structured programming and the other theories discussed here are concerned mainly with high-level languages, "statement" and "operation" refer to the same software entities.

block, or jumping backward, in order to return to the beginning of a block that must be repeated. These jumps are necessary because the sequence of operations that make up a program constitutes, essentially, a one-dimensional medium. Physically (in the program's listing, or when the program resides in the computer's memory), all possible operations must be included, and they can appear in only one sequence. At run time, though, the operations must be executed selectively, and in one sequence or another, depending on how the various conditions are evaluated. In other words, the *dynamic* sequence may be very different from the *static* one. The only way to execute the operations differently from their static sequence is by instructing the computer at various points to jump to a certain operation, forward or backward, instead of continuing with the next one. For example, although the two blocks in a conditional construct appear consecutively (both in the listing and in memory), only one must be executed; thus, the first one must be bypassed when the second one is to be executed, and the second one must be bypassed when the first one is to be executed.

It is the programmer's task to design the intricate network of jumps that, when the application is running, will cause the various operations to be executed, skipped, or repeated, as required. To help programmers (and the designers of compilers) create efficient machine code, computers have a rich set of *low-level* flow-control features: conditional and unconditional jump instructions, loop instructions, repeat instructions, index registers, and so forth. These features are directly available in low-level, assembly languages, and their great diversity reflects the important role that flow-control operations play in programming. In high-level languages, the low-level flow-control features are usually available only as part of complex, built-in operations. For example, a statement that compares two character strings in the high-level language will use, when translated by the compiler into machine code, index registers and loop instructions.

The jump operation itself is provided in high-level languages by the GOTO statement (often spelled as one word, GOTO); for example, GOTO L2 tells the computer to jump to the statement following the label L2, instead of continuing with the next statement. While it is impossible to attain in high-level languages the same versatility and efficiency as in assembly languages, the GOTO statement, in conjunction with conditional statements and other features, allows us to create all the flow-control constructs we need in those applications normally developed in high-level languages.

Programmers, it was discovered from the very beginning, cannot easily visualize the flow of execution; and, needless to say, without a complete understanding of the flow of execution it is all but impossible to design an application correctly. What we note is software defects, or "bugs": certain operations are not executed when they should be, or are executed when they shouldn't be.

Serious applications invariably give rise to intricate combinations of flow-control constructs, simply because those affairs we want to represent in software consist of complex combinations of processes and events. It is the *interaction* of flow-control constructs – the need to keep track of combinations of constructs – that poses the greatest challenge, rather than merely the *large number* of constructs. Even beginners can deal successfully with *separate* constructs; but nested, interacting constructs challenge the skills of even the most experienced programmers. The problem, of course, is strictly a human one: the limited capacity of our mind to deal with combinations of relations, nestings, and alternatives. The computer, for its part, will execute an involved program as effortlessly as it does a simple one. Like other skills, though, it is possible to improve our ability to deal with structures of flow-control constructs. But this can only be accomplished through practice: by programming and maintaining increasingly complex applications over many years.

The flow-control constructs, then, are one of the major sources of programming errors. The very quality that makes software so useful – what allows us to represent in our applications the diversity and complexity of our affairs – is necessarily also a source of programming difficulties. For, we must *anticipate* all possible combinations, and describe them accurately and unambiguously. Experienced programmers, who have implemented many applications in the past, know how to create flow-control constructs that are consistent, economical, streamlined, and easy to understand. Inexperienced programmers, on the other hand, create messy, unnecessarily complicated constructs, and end up with software that is inefficient and hard to understand.

Business applications must be modified continuously to keep up with the changing needs of their users. This work is known as maintenance, and it is at this stage, rather than in the initial development, that the worst consequences of bad programming emerge. For, even if otherwise successful, badly written applications are almost impossible to keep up to date. This is true because applications are usually maintained by different programmers over the years, and, if badly written, it is extremely difficult for a programmer to understand software developed and modified by others. (It was discovered, in fact, that programmers have difficulty understanding even *their own* software later, if badly written.)

Without a good understanding of the application, it is impossible to modify it reliably. And, as in the initial development, the flow-control constructs were found to be especially troublesome: the more nestings, jumps, and alternatives there are, the harder it is for a programmer to visualize, from its listing, the variety of run-time situations that the application was meant to handle. The deficiencies caused by incorrect modifications are similar to those caused by incorrect programming in the initial development. For a live application, however, the repercussions are far more serious. So, to avoid jeopardizing their applications, businesses everywhere started to limit maintenance to the most urgent requirements, and the practice of developing new applications as a substitute for keeping the existing ones up to date became widespread. The ultimate consequences of bad programming, thus, are the perpetual inadequacy of applications and the cost of replacing them over and over.

❖

These, then, were the difficulties that motivated the search for better programming practices. As we saw earlier, these difficulties were due to the incompetence of the application programmers. But the software theorists were convinced that the solution lay, not in encouraging programmers to improve their skills, but in discovering methods whereby programmers could create better applications while remaining incompetent. And, once this notion was accepted, it was not hard to invent such a method. It was obvious that inexperienced programmers were creating bad flow-control constructs, and just as obvious that this was one of the reasons for programming inefficiency, software defects, and maintenance problems. So it was decided to prevent programmers from creating their own flow-control constructs. Bad programmers can create good applications, the theorists declared, simply by restricting themselves to the existing flow-control constructs. This restriction is the essence of structured programming.

Most high-level languages of that time already included statements for the basic flow-control constructs, so all that was needed to implement the principles of structured programming was a change in programming style. Specifically, programmers were asked to use one particular statement for conditions, and one for iterations. What these statements do is eliminate the need for explicit jumps in the flow of execution, so the resulting constructs – which became known as the *standard* constructs – are a little simpler than those created by a programmer with GO TO statements. The jumps are still there, but they are now implicit: for the conditional construct that selects one of two blocks and bypasses the other, we only specify the condition and the two blocks, and the compiler generates automatically the bypassing jumps; and for a loop, the compiler generates automatically the jump back to the beginning of the repeated block.

Since we *must* use jumps when we create our own flow-control constructs, what this means is that, if we restrict ourselves to the standard constructs, we will never again need explicit jumps. Or, expressing this in reverse, simply by avoiding the GOTO statement we avoid the temptation to create our own flow-control constructs, and hence inferior applications. GOTO, it was proclaimed, is what causes bad programming, so it must be avoided.

Now, good programmers use the standard constructs when suitable, but do not hesitate to modify them, or to create their own, when specialized constructs are more effective. These constructs *improve* the program, therefore, not complicate it. Everyone could see that it is possible to use GOTO intelligently, that only when used by incompetents does it lead to bad programming. The assumption that programmers cannot improve remained unchanged, however. So the idea of eliminating the need for expertise continued to be seen as an important principle, as the only solution to the software crisis.

The main appeal of structured programming, thus, is that it appears to eliminate those programming situations that demand skills and experience. This, it was hoped, would reduce application development to a routine activity, to the kind of work that can be performed by almost anyone.

Substitutes for expertise are always delusions, and structured programming was no exception. First, it addressed only *one* aspect of application development – the design of flow-control constructs. Bad programmers, though, do *everything* badly, so even if structured programming could improve this one aspect of their work, other difficulties would remain. Second, structured programming does not really eliminate the need for expertise even in this one area. It was very naive to believe that, if it is possible *in principle* to program using only the standard constructs, it is also possible to develop *real* applications in this fashion. This idea may look good with the small, artificial examples presented in textbooks, but is impractical for serious business applications.

So, since programmers still have to supplement the standard constructs with specialized ones, they need the same knowledge and experience as before. And if they do, instead, restrict themselves to the standard constructs, as the theory demands, they end up complicating *other* aspects of the application. The aspects of an application are the various structures that make it up, and the difficulty of programming is due to the need to deal with many of these structures at the same time. Structured programming succeeds perhaps in simplifying the flow-control structure, but only by making the other structures more involved. And, in any case, programmers still need the capacity to deal with interacting structures. We will study these fallacies in detail later.

2

So far we have examined the *informal* arguments – the praise of standard flow-control constructs and the advice to avoid GOTO. These arguments must be distinguished from the *formal* theory of structured programming, which emerged around 1970. The reason we are discussing both types of arguments is that the formal theory never managed to displace the informal one. In other words, even though it was promoted by its advocates as an exact, mathematical theory, structured programming was in reality just an assortment of methods – some sensible and others silly – for improving programming practices. We will separate its formal arguments from the informal ones in order to study it, but we must not forget that the two always appeared together.

The informal tone of the early period is clearly seen in E. W. Dijkstra's notorious paper, "Go To Statement Considered Harmful."[2] Generally acknowledged as the official inauguration of the structured programming era, this paper is regarded by many as the most famous piece of writing in the history of programming. Yet this is just a brief essay. It is so brief and informal, in fact, that it was published in the form of a letter to the editor, rather than a regular article.

Dijkstra claims to have "discovered why the use of the GOTO statement has such disastrous effects,"[3] but his explanation is nothing more than a reminder of how useful it is to be able to keep track of the program's dynamic behaviour. When carelessly used, he observes, GOTO makes it hard to relate the flow of execution to the nested conditions, iterations, and subroutine calls that make up the program's listing: "The unbridled use of the GOTO statement has an immediate consequence that it becomes terribly hard to find a meaningful set of coordinates in which to describe the process progress."[4]

This is true, of course, but Dijkstra doesn't consider at all the alternative: a disciplined, intelligent programming style, through which we could *benefit* from the power of GOTO. Instead of studying the use of GOTO under this alternative, he simply asserts that "the quality of programmers is a decreasing

[2] E. W. Dijkstra, "Go To Statement Considered Harmful," in *Milestones in Software Evolution*, eds. Paul W. Oman and Ted G. Lewis (Los Alamitos, CA: IEEE Computer Society Press, ©1990 IEEE) – paper originally published in *Communications of the ACM* 11, no. 3 (1968): 147–148. An equally informal paper from this period is Harlan D. Mills, "The Case Against GO TO Statements in PL/I," in Harlan D. Mills, *Software Productivity* (New York: Dorset House, 1988) – paper originally published in 1969.

[3] Dijkstra, "Go To Statement," p. 9.

[4] Ibid. The term "unbridled" is used by Dijkstra to describe the *free* use of jumps (as opposed to using jumps only as part of some standard constructs).

function of the density of GOTO statements in the programs they produce,"[5] and concludes that "the GOTO statement should be abolished from all 'higher level' programming languages."[6] His reasoning seems to be as follows: since using GOTO carelessly is harmful, and since good programmers apparently use GOTO less frequently than do bad programmers, then simply by prohibiting everyone from using GOTO we will attain the same results as we would if we turned the bad programmers into good ones.

The logical answer to the careless use of GOTO by bad programmers is not to abolish GOTO, but to encourage those programmers to improve their skills. Yet this possibility is not even mentioned. In the end, in the absence of any real demonstration as to why GOTO is harmful, we must be satisfied with the statement that "it is too much an invitation to make a mess of one's program."[7] What is noteworthy in this paper, therefore, is not just the informal tone, but also the senseless arguments against GOTO.

These were the claims in the late 1960s. Then, the tone changed, and the claims became more ambitious. The software theorists discovered a little paper,[8] written several years earlier and concerned with the logical transformation of flow diagrams, and chose to interpret it as the mathematical proof of their ideas. (We will examine this "proof" later.) Adapted for programming, the ideas presented in this paper became known as the *structure theorem*.

Convinced now that structured programming had a solid mathematical foundation, the theorists started to promote it as the beginning of a new science – the science of programming. Structured programming was no longer seen merely as a body of suggestions for improving programming practices; it was the only correct way to program. And practitioners who did not obey its principles were branded as old-fashioned artisans. After all, rejecting structured programming was now tantamount to rejecting science.

It is *this* theory – the *formal* theory of structured programming – that is important, for it is *this* theory that was promoted as a programming revolution, was refuted in practice, and was then rescued by being turned into a pseudoscience. We could perhaps ignore the informal claims, but it is only by studying the formal theory that we can appreciate why the idea of structured programming was a fraud. For, it was its alleged mathematical foundation that made it respectable. It was thanks to its mathematical promises that it was so widely accepted – precisely those promises that had to be abandoned in order to make it practical.

Thus, a striking characteristic of structured programming is that, even after

[5] Ibid.   [6] Ibid.   [7] Ibid.
[8] Corrado Böhm and Giuseppe Jacopini, "Flow Diagrams, Turing Machines and Languages with Only Two Formation Rules," in *Milestones*, eds. Oman and Lewis – paper originally published in *Communications of the ACM* 9, no. 5 (1966): 366–371.

becoming an exact, mechanistic theory, it continued to be defended with *informal* arguments. Its mathematical aspects imparted to it a scientific image, but could not, in fact, support it. So, while advertised as a scientific theory, structured programming was usually presented in the form of a programming methodology, and its benefits could be demonstrated only for simple, carefully selected examples. Moreover, its principles – the GOTO prohibition, in particular – became the subject of endless debates and changes, even among the academics who had invented them.[9]

When a mechanistic theory works, all we need in order to promote it is a mathematical proof. All we need, in other words, is a formal argument; we don't have to resort to persuasion, debates, justifications, case studies, or testimonials. It is only when a theory fails, and its defenders refuse to accept its failure, that we see both formal and informal arguments used side by side (recall our discussion in chapter 1, pp. 76–77).

It is impossible to discuss structured programming without stressing this distinction between the formal and the informal concepts. For, by pointing to the *informal* concepts, its advocates can claim to this day that structured programming was successful. And, in a sense, this is true. It is in the nature of informal concepts to be vague and subject to interpretation. Thus, since some of the informal principles are sensible and others silly, one can always praise the former and describe them as "structured programming." The useful principles, as a matter of fact, were known and appreciated by experienced programmers even before being discovered by the academics; and they continue to be appreciated, despite the failure of structured programming. But we must not confuse the small subset of useful principles with the real, mathematical theory of structured programming – the theory that was promoted by the scientists as a revolution.

It is because of their mathematical claims that we accepted structured programming, and the other software theories. Deprived of their formal foundation, these theories are merely collections of programming tips. So the effort to cover up their failure amounts to a fraud: we are being persuaded to depend on the software elites when in reality, since the formal theories are worthless, the elites have nothing to offer us.

---

[9] Here are two sources for the *formal* theory: Harlan D. Mills, "Mathematical Foundations for Structured Programming," in Harlan D. Mills, *Software Productivity* (New York: Dorset House, 1988) – paper originally published in 1972; Suad Alagić and Michael A. Arbib, *The Design of Well-Structured and Correct Programs* (New York: Springer-Verlag, 1978). And here are two sources for the *informal* theory: Harlan D. Mills, "How to Write Correct Programs and Know It," in Mills, *Software Productivity* – paper originally published in 1975; Edward Yourdon, *Techniques of Program Structure and Design* (Englewood Cliffs, NJ: Prentice Hall, 1975).

3

The formal theory of structured programming prescribes that software applications, when viewed from the perspective of their flow of execution, be treated
as simple hierarchical structures. Applications are to be implemented using
only three flow-control constructs: sequential operations, conditions, and
iterations. And it is not just the basic elements that must be restricted to these
constructs, but the elements at all levels of abstraction. This is accomplished by
nesting constructs: the complete constructs of one level serve as elements in the
constructs of the next higher level, and so on. Thus, although the elements keep
growing as we move to higher levels, the constructs remain unchanged.

The sequential construct is shown in figure 7-1 (the arrowheads in flow
diagrams indicate the flow of execution). It consists of one operation, *S1*. At the
lowest level, the operation is a single statement: assigning a value to a variable,
performing a calculation, reading a record from a file, and so on.

Figure 7-1

The conditional construct, IF, is shown in figure 7-2. This construct consists
of a condition, *C1*, and two operations, *S1* and *S2*: if the condition is evaluated
as *True*, *S1* is executed; if evaluated as *False*, *S2* is executed. In most high-level
languages, the IF statement implements this construct: IF *C1 is True,* THEN
perform S1, ELSE *perform S2.* Either *S1* or *S2* may be empty (these variants are
also shown in figure 7-2). In a program, when *S2* is empty the entire ELSE part
is usually omitted.

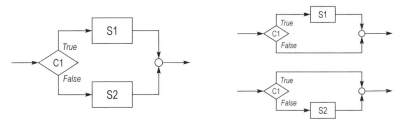

Figure 7-2

The iterative construct, WHILE, is shown in figure 7-3. This construct consists of a condition, *C1*, and one operation, *S1*: if the condition is evaluated as *True*, *S1* is executed and the process is repeated; if evaluated as *False*, the iterations end. In many high-level languages, the WHILE statement implements this construct: WHILE *C1 is True, perform S1*.

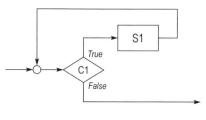

Figure 7-3

To build larger pieces of software, any number of constructs can be connected consecutively: sequential, conditional, and iterative constructs can be combined in any order by connecting the exit of one construct to the entry of the next one. This method of combining constructs is trivial, however. It is only through nesting that we can create the countless combinations of operations, conditions, and iterations required in a serious application.

All three constructs share an important feature: they have one entry and one exit. When viewed from outside, therefore, and disregarding their internal details, the three constructs are identical. It is this feature that makes nesting possible. To nest constructs, we start with one of the three constructs and replace the operation, *S1* or *S2* (or both), with a conditional or iterative construct, or with two consecutive sequential constructs; we then similarly replace *S1* or *S2* in the new constructs, and so on. Thus, the original construct forms the top level of the structure, and each replacement creates an additional, lower level.

This nesting method is known as *top-down design*, and is an important principle in structured programming. To design a new application, we start by depicting the entire project as one sequential construct; going down to the next level of detail, we may note that the application consists in the repetition of a certain operation, so we replace the original operation with an iterative construct; at the next level, we may note that what is repeated is one of two different operations, so we replace the operation in the iterative construct with a conditional construct; then we may note that the operations in this construct are themselves conditions or iterations, so we replace them with further constructs; and so on. (At each step, if the operation cannot be replaced directly with a construct, we replace it first with two simpler, consecutive operations;

then, if necessary, we repeat this for those two operations, and so on.) We continue this process until we reach some low-level constructs, where the operations are so simple that we can replace them directly with the statements of a programming language. If we follow this method, the theorists say, we are bound to end up with a perfect application.

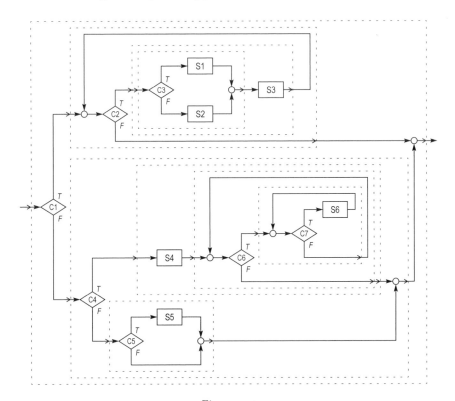

Figure 7-4

The flow diagram in figure 7-4 illustrates this concept. This diagram includes four conditional, three iterative, and two sequential constructs, nested in various ways. Although the format of these constructs is identical to the simple format shown in the previous diagrams, this is obscured by the fact that some of the operations are themselves constructs, rather than simple boxes like *S1*. The dashed boxes depict these constructs, and serve at the same time to indicate pictorially the levels of nesting. (The innermost boxes represent the lowest level, and it is only in these boxes that the constructs' format is immediately recognizable.) Note also the additional arrowheads, drawn to indicate the entry and exit of each dashed box. The arrowheads emphasize that, regardless of their nesting level, the constructs continue to have only one entry and one exit.

Each dashed box encloses a complete construct – a construct that acts as a single operation in the higher-level construct to which it belongs. When viewed as part of the higher-level construct, then, a dashed box acts just like the box depicting a sequential construct. In other words, the internal details of a given construct, including the lower levels of nesting that make it up, are irrelevant when we study only the constructs at higher levels. (So we could ignore, as it were, the diagram shown inside the dashed box, and replace the entire box with one sequential construct.) An important benefit of this nesting concept is that any construct can be replaced with a functionally equivalent construct, both during development and during maintenance, without affecting the rest of the application. A programmer, thus, can develop or modify a particular construct while knowing nothing about the constructs at higher and lower levels. All he needs to know is the entry and exit characteristics of the constructs at the next lower level.

This is all that practitioners need to learn about the theory of structured programming. Programs developed strictly as nested constructs, and their flow diagrams, are *structured* programs and diagrams. And, the theorists assure us, it has been proved through mathematical logic that any software application can be built in this fashion.

Structured programs can be as large as we want, and can have any number of levels of nesting. It is recommended, nevertheless, for practical reasons, to divide large programs into modules of no more than about a hundred lines, and to have no more than about five levels of nesting in a module. In complicated programs, we can always reduce the number of nesting levels by creating a separate module for the constructs below a given level, and then replacing that whole portion with a statement that invokes the module. Logically, there is no difference between the two alternatives, and smaller modules are easier to understand and to maintain. (From the perspective of the flow of execution, descending the nesting levels formed by the local constructs is the same as invoking a module and then descending the levels of constructs in that module.) Invoking a module is a single operation, so it can be part of any construct; constructs in the invoked module can then invoke other modules in their turn, and so on. Large applications, thus, are generally built by adding levels of modules rather levels of constructs. A module may be invoked from several constructs, of course, if the same operations are required in several places; the module then also functions as subroutine.

Regarding the GOTO issue, it is obvious now why GOTO statements are unnecessary: quite simply, structured programs require no explicit jumps (since all the necessary jumps are implicit, within the standard constructs). The purpose of structured programming is to create structures of nested constructs, so the absence of GOTO is merely a consequence. This is an important point, and in sharp contrast to the original, *informal* claim – the claim that GOTO must be avoided because it tempts us to create messy programs. Now we have the *proof* that GOTO is unnecessary in high-level languages (in fact, in any language that provides the three standard constructs). We have the proof, therefore, that any application can be created without using GOTO statements. GOTO is not bad in itself, but because it indicates that the program is unstructured. Structured programs do not need GOTOs.

To conclude, structured programming is concerned with the flow of execution, and claims that the solution to our programming difficulties lies in designing applications as structures of nested modules, and the modules as structures of nested flow-control constructs. We recognize this as the mechanistic claim that any phenomenon can be represented as a structure of things within things. Structured programming, thus, claims that the flow of execution can be extracted from the rest of the application; that it can be reduced to a simple hierarchical structure, the *flow-control* structure; and that, for all practical purposes, this one structure *is* the application. The logic of nesting and standard constructs is continuous, from the simplest statements to the largest modules. It is this neatness that makes the notion of structured programming so enticing. All we need to know, it seems, is how to create structures of things within things. We are promised, in effect, that by applying a simple method over and over, level after level, we will be able to create perfect applications of any size and complexity.

The Promise

No discussion of the structured programming theory is complete without a review of its promotion and its reception. For, the enthusiasm it generated is as interesting as are its technical aspects.

Harlan Mills, one of the best-known software theorists, compares programming to playing a simple game like tic-tac-toe. The two are similar in that we can account, at each step, for all possible alternatives, and hence discover exact theories. The only difference is that programming gives rise to a greater number of alternatives. Thus, just as a good game theory allows us to play perfect tic-tac-toe, a good programming theory will allow us to write perfect programs: "Computer programming is a combinatorial activity, like tic-tac-toe.... It does not require perfect resolution in measurement and control; it only requires correct choices out of finite sets of possibilities at every step. The difference between tic-tac-toe and computer programming is complexity. The purpose of structured programming is to control complexity through theory and discipline. And with complexity under better control it now appears that people can write substantial computer programs correctly.... Children, in learning to play tic-tac-toe, soon develop a little theory.... In programming, theory and discipline are critical as well at an adult's level of intellectual activity. Structured programming is such a theory, providing a systematic way of coping with complexity in program design and development. It makes possible a discipline for program design and construction on a level of precision not previously possible."[1]

Structured programming is a fantasy, of course – a mechanistic delusion. As we know, it is impossible to reduce software applications, which are complex phenomena, to simple hierarchical structures; so it is impossible to represent them with exact, mathematical models. Everyone could see that even ordinary requirements cannot be reduced to a neat structure of standard constructs, but it was believed that all we have to do for those requirements is apply certain *transformations*. No one tried to understand the significance of these transformations, or why we need them at all. And when in many situations the transformations turned out to be totally impractical, still no one suspected the theory. These situations were blatant falsifications of the theory; but instead of studying them, the experts chose to interpret the difficulty of creating structured applications as the difficulty of adjusting to the new, disciplined style of programming. No one wondered why, if it has been proved mathematically that any application can be written in a structured fashion, and if everyone is trying to implement this idea, we cannot find a single application that follows strictly the principles of structured programming.

Thus, even though it never worked with serious applications, structured programming was both promoted and received – for twenty years – with the enthusiasm it would have deserved had it been entirely successful.

---

[1] Harlan D. Mills, "Mathematical Foundations for Structured Programming," in Harlan D. Mills, *Software Productivity* (New York: Dorset House, 1988), pp. 117–118 – paper originally published in 1972. As I have already pointed out (see p. 502), what the software theorists call complexity (i.e., the large number of alternatives) is not the *real* complexity of software (i.e., what makes software applications complex structures, systems of interacting structures). It is impossible to develop applications simply by accounting for the various alternatives, as Mills proposes, because we cannot *identify* all the alternatives.

To appreciate the reaction to the idea of structured programming, we must ignore all we know about complex structures, and imagine ourselves as part of the mechanistic world of programming. Let us think of software applications, thus, as mechanistic phenomena; that is, as phenomena which *can* be represented with simple hierarchical structures. The idea of structured programming is then indeed the answer to our programming difficulties, in the same way that designing physical systems as hierarchical structures of subassemblies is the answer to our manufacturing and construction difficulties.

One promise, we saw, is to reduce programming, from an activity demanding expertise, to the performance of relatively easy and predictable acts: "It is possible for professional programmers, with sufficient care and concentration, to consistently write correct programs by applying the mathematical principles of structured programming."[2] The theorists, thus, are *degrading* the notion of professionalism and expertise to mean *the skills needed to apply a prescribed method.* (I will return to this point in a moment.)

So, to program an application we need to know now only one thing: how to reduce a given problem, expressed as a single operation, to two or three simpler problems; specifically, to two consecutive operations, or a conditional construct (two operations and a condition), or an iterative construct (one operation and a condition). What we do at each level, then, is replace a particular software element with two or three simpler ones. Developing an application consists in repeating this reduction over and over, thereby creating simpler and simpler elements, on lower and lower levels of abstraction. And the skill of programming consists in knowing how to perform the reduction while being certain that, at each level, the new elements are logically equivalent to the original one. But this skill is much easier to acquire than the traditional programming skill, because it is the same types of constructs and reductions that we employ at all levels; besides, each reduction is a small logical step.

Eventually, we reach elements that are simple enough to translate directly into the statements of a programming language. So we must also know how to perform the translation; but this skill is even easier than the reductions – so easy, in fact, that it can be acquired by almost anyone in a few weeks. (This work is often called coding, to distinguish it from programming.)

The key to creating correct applications, then, is the restriction to the standard constructs and the assurance that, at each level, the new elements are logically equivalent to the original one. These conditions are related, since, if we restrict ourselves to these constructs, we can actually prove the equivalence mathematically. Ultimately, structured programming is a matter of discipline:

[2] Richard C. Linger, Harlan D. Mills, and Bernard I. Witt, *Structured Programming: Theory and Practice* (Reading, MA: Addison-Wesley, 1979), p. 3.

we must follow this method *rigorously*, even in situations where a different method is simpler or more efficient. Only if we observe this principle can we be certain that, when the application is finally translated into a programming language, it will be logically equivalent to the original specifications.

This is an important point, as it was discovered that experienced programmers have difficulty adjusting to the discipline of structured programming. Thus, they tend to ignore the aforementioned principle, and enhance their applications with constructs of their own design. They see the restriction to the standard constructs as a handicap, as a dogmatic principle that prevents them from applying their hard-earned talents.

What these programmers fail to see, the theorists explain, is that it is precisely this restriction that allows us to represent software elements mathematically, and hence prove their equivalence from one level to the next. It is precisely because we have so little freedom in our reductions that we can be certain of their correctness. (In fact, the standard constructs are so simple that the correctness of the reductions can usually be confirmed through careful inspection; only in critical situations do we need to resort to a formal, mathematical proof.)

So what appears as a drawback to those accustomed to the old-fashioned, personal style of programming is actually the *strength* of structured programming. Even experienced programmers could benefit from the new programming discipline, if only they learned to resist their creative impulse. But, more importantly, *inexperienced* programmers will now be able to create good applications, simply by applying the principles of top-down design and standard constructs: "Now the new reality is that ordinary programmers, with ordinary care, can learn to write programs which are error free from their inception.... The basis for this new precision in programming is neither human infallibility, nor being more careful, nor trying harder. The basis is understanding programs as mathematical objects that are subject to logic and reason, and rules for orderly combination."[3]

I stated previously that the software theorists are degrading the notions of expertise and professionalism, from their traditional meaning – the utmost that human beings can accomplish – to the trivial knowledge needed to follow methods. This attitude is betrayed by the claim that structured programming will benefit *all* programmers, regardless of skill level. Note the first sentence in the passage just quoted, and compare it with the following sentence: "Now the new reality is that professional programmers, with professional care, can learn to consistently write programs that are error-free from their inception."[4]

---

[3] Ibid., p. 2.
[4] Harlan D. Mills, "How to Write Correct Programs and Know It," in Mills, *Software Productivity*, p. 194 – paper originally published in 1975.

The two sentences (evidently written by the same author during the same period) are practically identical, but the former says "ordinary" and the latter "professional." For this theorist, then, the ideas of professional programmer, ordinary programmer, and perhaps even novice programmer, are interchangeable. And indeed, there is no difference between an expert and a novice if we reduce programming to the act of following some simple methods.

This attitude is an inevitable consequence of the mechanistic dogma. On the one hand, the software mechanists praise qualities like expertise and professionalism; on the other hand, they promote mechanistic principles and methods. Their mechanistic beliefs prevent them from recognizing that the two views contradict each other. If the benefits of structured programming derive from reducing programming to methods requiring little experience – methods that can be followed by "ordinary" programmers – it is precisely because these methods require only mechanistic knowledge. Expertise, on the contrary, is understood as the highest level that human minds can attain. It entails *complex* knowledge, the kind of knowledge we reach after many years of learning and practice. Following the methods of structured programming, therefore, cannot possibly mean expertise and professionalism in their traditional sense. It is in order to apply these terms to mechanistic knowledge – in order to resolve the contradiction – that the theorists are degrading their meaning.

If the first promise of structured programming is to eliminate the need for programming expertise, the second one is to simplify the development of large applications by breaking them down into small parts. Each reduction from a given element to simpler ones is in effect a separate task, since it can be performed independently of the other reductions. Then, for a particular reduction, we can treat the lower-level reductions as either the same task or as separate, smaller tasks. In this fashion, we can break down the original task – that is, the application – into tasks that are as small as we want. Although the smallest task can be as small as one construct, we rarely need to go that far. For most applications, the smallest tasks are the individual modules; and it is recommended that modules be no larger than one printed page, so that we can conveniently study them.

When each module is a separate task, different programmers can work on different modules of the same application without having to communicate with one another. This has several benefits: if a large application must be finished faster, we can simply employ more programmers; we can replace a programmer at any time without affecting the rest of the project; and later, during maintenance, a new programmer only needs to understand the logic of individual modules.

With the old style of programming, the complexity of applications, and hence the difficulty of developing and maintaining them, seems to grow exponentially with their size. The time and cost required to develop a new application, or to modify an existing one, can be unpredictable; adding programmers to a project rarely helps; large projects often become unmanageable and must be abandoned. With structured programming, on the other hand, the complexity and the difficulty do not grow with the application's size. No matter how large, an application is no more difficult to develop than is its largest module. The only difference we should see between large and small applications is that large ones take longer, or involve more programmers; but the time and cost are now predictable. What structured programming does, in the final analysis, is replace the challenge of developing a large system of *interrelated* entities, with the easier challenge of developing many small, *separate* entities.

The greatest promise of structured programming, however, and the most fantastic, is the promise of error-free applications; specifically, the claim that structured programming obviates almost entirely the need to test software, since applications will usually run perfectly the first time: "By practicing principles of structured programming and its mathematics you should be able to write correct programs and convince yourself and others that they are correct. Your programs should ordinarily compile and execute properly the first time you try them, and from then on."[5]

Top-down programming, we saw, entails the repeated reduction of elements to simpler ones that are logically equivalent. So, if we perform each reduction correctly, then no matter how many reductions are required, we can be certain that the resulting application will be logically equivalent to the original specifications. (The application may still be faulty, of course, if the *specifications* are faulty; structured programming guarantees only that the application will behave exactly as defined in the specifications.)

Fantastic though it is, this claim is logical – *if* we assume that applications are simple hierarchical structures. Here is how the claim is defended: Since the equivalence of elements in the flow-control structure can be proved mathematically at each level in the top-down process, and since the statements in the resulting application correspond on a one-to-one basis to the lowest-

[5] Ibid.

level elements, the application *must* be correct. In other words, what we create in the end by means of a programming language is in effect the same structure that we created earlier by means of a diagram, and which we could prove to be correct.

We should still test our applications, because we are not infallible; but testing will be a simple, routine task. The only type of errors we should expect to find are those caused by programming slips. And, thanks to the discipline we will observe during development, these errors are bound to be minor bugs, as opposed to the major deficiencies we discover now in our applications (faulty logic, problems necessitating redesign or reprogramming, mysterious bugs for which no one can find the source, defects that give rise to other defects when corrected, and so on). Thus, not only will the errors be few, but they will be trivial: easy to find and easy to correct. This is how Mills puts it: "As technical foundations are developed for programming, its character will undergo radical changes.... We contend here that such a radical change is possible now, that in structured programming the techniques and tools are at hand to permit an entirely new level of precision in programming."[6]

The inevitable conclusion is that, if we adhere to the principles of structured programming, we will write program after program without a single error. This conclusion prompts Mills to make one of those ludicrous predictions that mechanists are notorious for; namely, that programming can become such a precise activity that we will commit just a handful of errors in a lifetime: "The professional programmer of tomorrow will remember, more or less vividly, every error in his career."[7]

It is important to note that these were serious claims, confidently made by the world's greatest software theorists. And, since the theorists never recognized the fallacy of structured programming, since to this day they fail to understand why its mathematical aspects are irrelevant, they are still claiming in effect that it permits us to create directly error-free applications. By implication, then, they are claiming that all software deficiencies and failures of the last thirty years, and all the testing we have done, could have been avoided: they were due to our reluctance to observe the principles of structured programming.

The final promise of structured programming is to eliminate programming altogether; that is, to *automate* the creation of software applications. This was not one of the original ideas, but emerged a few years later with the notion of

---

[6] Mills, "Mathematical Foundations," p. 117.   [7] Mills, "Correct Programs," p. 194.

CASE – software devices that replace the work of programmers. (This promise is perfectly captured in the title of a book written by two well-known experts: *Structured Techniques: The Basis for CASE.*[8])

As with the other claims, if we accept the idea that applications are simple hierarchical structures, the claim of automatic software generation is perfectly logical. Structured programming breaks down the development process into small and simple tasks, most of which can be performed mechanically; and if they can be performed mechanically, they can be replaced with software devices. For example, the translation of the final, low-level constructs into the statements of a programming language can easily be automated. Most reductions, too, are individually simple enough to be automated. The software entities in CASE systems will likely be different from the traditional ones, but the basic principle – depicting an application as a hierarchical structure of constructs within constructs – will be the same.

Application development, thus, will soon require no programmers. An analyst or manager will specify the requirements by interacting with a sophisticated development system, and the computer will do the rest: "There is a major revolution happening in software and system design.... The revolution is the replacement of manual design and coding with automated design and coding."[9] So, while everyone was waiting for the promised benefits of the structured programming revolution, the software theorists were already hailing the *next* revolution – which suffered from the same fallacies.

This, then, is how structured programming was promoted by the software elites. And it is not hard to see how, in a mechanistic culture like ours, such a theory can become fashionable. The enthusiasm of the academics was shared by most managers, who, knowing little about programming, saw in this idea a solution to the lack of competent programmers; and it was also shared by most programmers, who could now, simply by avoiding GOTO, call themselves software engineers. Only the few programmers who were already developing and maintaining applications successfully could recognize the absurdity of structured programming; but their expertise was ridiculed and interpreted as old-fashioned craftsmanship.

The media too joined in the general hysteria, and helped to propagate the structured programming fallacies by repeating uncritically the claims and

---

[8] James Martin and Carma McClure, *Structured Techniques: The Basis for CASE*, rev. ed. (Englewood Cliffs, NJ: Prentice Hall, 1988). CASE stands for Computer-Aided Software Engineering.   [9] Ibid., p. 757.

promises. *Datamation*, for instance, a respected data-processing journal of that period, devoted its December 1973 issue to structured programming, proclaiming it a revolution. The introductory article starts with these words: "Structured programming is a major intellectual invention, one that will come to be ranked with the subroutine concept or even the stored program concept."[10]

The Contradictions

1

Now that we have seen the enthusiasm generated by the idea of structured programming, let us study the contradictions – contradictions which, although well known at the time, did nothing to temper the enthusiasm.

Structured programs, we saw, are pieces of software whose flow of execution can be represented as a structure of standard flow-control constructs. Because these constructs have only one entry and exit, a structured piece of software is a structure of hierarchically nested constructs. The structure can be a part of a module, an entire module, and even the entire application. The flow diagram in figure 7-4 (p. 527) was an example of a structured piece of software.

Our affairs, however, can rarely be represented as neat structures of nested entities, because they consist of *interacting* processes and events. So, if our software applications are to mirror our affairs accurately, they must form systems of *interacting* structures. What this means is that, when designing an application, we will encounter situations that *cannot* be represented with structured flow diagrams.

The theory of structured programming acknowledges this problem, but tells us that the answer is to change the way we view our affairs. The discipline that is the hallmark of structured programming must start with the way we formulate our requirements, and if we cannot depict these requirements with structured diagrams, the reason may be that we are not disciplined in the way we run our affairs. The design of a software application, then, is also a good opportunity to improve the logic of our activities. Much of this improvement will be achieved, in fact, simply by following the top-down method, since this method encourages us to view our activities as levels of abstraction, and hence as nested entities.

---

[10] Daniel D. McCracken, "Revolution in Programming: An Overview," *Datamation* 19, no. 12 (1973): 50–52.

So far, there is not much to criticize. The benefits of depicting the flow of execution with a simple hierarchical structure are so great that it is indeed a good idea, whenever possible, to design our applications in this manner. But the advocates of structured programming do not stop here. They insist that *every situation* be reduced to a structured diagram, no matter how difficult the changes or how unnatural the results. In other words, even if the use of standard constructs is *more complicated* than the way we normally perform a certain activity, we must resist the temptation to implement the simpler logic of that activity.

And this is not all. The theorists also recognize that, no matter how strictly we follow the top-down design method, some situations will remain that cannot be represented as structured diagrams. (It is possible to prove, in fact, that whole classes of diagrams, including some very common and very simple cases, cannot be reduced to the three standard constructs.) Still, the theorists say, even these situations must be turned into structured software, by applying certain *transformations*. The transformations complicate the application, it is agreed, but complicated software is preferable to unstructured software.

The ultimate purpose of these transformations is to create new relations between software elements as a replacement for the relations formed by explicit jumps, which are prohibited under structured programming. (We will study this idea in greater detail later.) And there are two ways to create the new relations: by sharing operations and by sharing data. I will illustrate the two types of transformations with two examples.

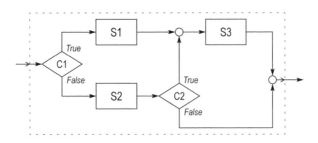

Figure 7-5

Figure 7-5 shows the flow diagram of a requirement that, although very simple, cannot be reduced to standard flow-control constructs. This is a variation of the standard conditional construct: the condition *C1* and the operations *S1* and *S2* form the standard part, but there is an additional operation, *S3*. This operation is always executed after *S1*, but is executed after *S2* only if *C2* is evaluated as *True*. The requirement, in other words, is that an operation which is part of one branch of a conditional construct be also executed, sometimes, as part of the other branch. And if we study the diagram, we can easily verify that it is unstructured: it is not a structure of nested standard constructs. Standard constructs have only one entry and exit, and here we cannot draw a dashed box with one entry and exit (as we did in figure 7-4) around any part of the diagram larger than a sequential construct.

Note that this is not only a *simple* requirement, but also a very common one. The theory of structured programming is contradicted, therefore, not by an unusual or complicated situation, but by a trivial requirement. There are probably thousands of situations in our affairs where such requirements must become part of an application.

The problem, thus, is not *implementing* the requirement, but implementing it under the restrictions of structured programming. The requirement is readily understood by anyone, and is easily implemented in any programming language by specifying directly the particular combination of operations, conditions, and jumps depicted in the diagram; in other words, by creating our own, non-standard flow-control construct. To implement this requirement, then, we must employ *explicit* jumps – GOTO statements. We need the explicit jumps in order to create our own construct, and we need our own construct because the requirement cannot be expressed as a nested structure of standard constructs.

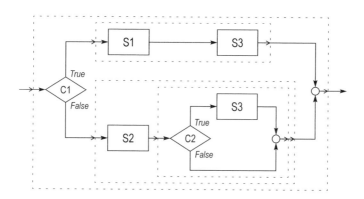

Figure 7-6

But explicit jumps are forbidden under structured programming. So, instead of creating our own construct, we must modify the flow diagram as shown in figure 7-6. If you compare this diagram with the original one, you can see that the transformation consists in duplicating the operation S3. As a result, instead of being related through an explicit jump, some elements are related now

through a shared operation. The two diagrams are functionally equivalent, but
the new one is properly structured (note the dashed boxes depicting the
standard constructs and the nesting levels). In practice, when *S3* is just one or
two statements it is usually duplicated in its entirety; when larger, it is turned
into a subroutine (i.e., a separate module) and what is duplicated is only the
call to the subroutine.

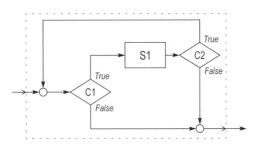

Figure 7-7

Figure 7-7 is the flow diagram of another requirement that cannot be
reduced to standard constructs. This is a variation of the standard iterative
construct: the condition *C1* and the operation *S1* form the standard part, but
the loop is also controlled by a second condition, *C2*. The requirement is to
terminate the loop when either *C1* or *C2* is evaluated as *False*; in other words,
to test for termination both before and after each iteration. But the diagram
that represents this requirement is unstructured: it is not a structure of nested
standard constructs. As was the case with the diagram in figure 7-5, we can find
no portion (larger than the sequential construct) around which we could draw
a dashed box with only one entry and exit.

This is another one of those requirements that are common, simple, and
easily implemented by creating our own flow-control construct. One way is
to start with the standard iterative construct and modify it by adding the
condition *C2* and a GOTO statement (to jump out of the loop); another way is
to design the whole loop with explicit jumps.

To implement the requirement under structured programming, however,
we must modify the diagram as shown in figure 7-8. This modification
illustrates the second type of transformation: creating new relations between
elements by sharing data, rather than sharing operations. Although functionally equivalent to the original one, the new diagram is a structure of nested
standard constructs. Instead of controlling directly the loop, *C2* controls
now the value of *x* (a small piece of storage, even one bit), which serves as
switch, or indicator: *x* is cleared before entering the loop, and is set when *C2*

yields *False*. The loop's main condition is now a combination of the original condition and the current value of *x*: the iterations are continued only as long as both conditions, *C1* and *x=0*, are evaluated as *True*.[1]

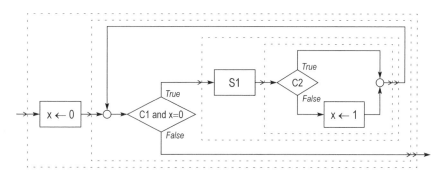

Figure 7-8

It must be noted that only the transformation based on shared data is, in fact, necessary. Structured programming permits any transformations, but the one based on shared operations is not strictly needed; it is merely the simpler alternative in the case of diagrams like that shown in figure 7-5. In principle, we can resort to memory variables to reduce any diagram to a structured format.

These examples demonstrate some basic situations, but we can think of any number of other, similar requirements (to say nothing of more complicated ones) that are easier to implement directly, with non-standard flow-control constructs, than through transformations: a loop nested in a conditional construct and the need to jump from inside the loop to outside the conditional construct; two or more levels of nested conditions and an operation common to more than two elements in this construct; two or more levels of nested iterations and the need to terminate the outermost loop from inside the innermost one; and so on.

Note that the issue is not whether constructs based on transformations are or are not better than constructs based on explicit jumps. Duplicating pieces of software, or using variables as switches, may well be the best alternative in one situation, while creating specialized flow-control constructs may be preferable in another. Ultimately, it is the programmer's task to implement the most effective flow-control structure for a given requirement. The real issue, thus, is

---

[1] The symbol ← inside the blocks denotes the assignment operation. When using variables as switches, only two values (such as 0 and 1) are needed.

the validity of the claim that a restriction to standard constructs simplifies development, guarantees error-free applications, and so forth. This claim, we will see, is a delusion.

2

Let us review the concept of software structures and attributes (see "Software Structures" in chapter 4). Software applications are complex structures, systems of interacting structures. The elements of these structures are the various entities that make up the application: statements, blocks of statements, larger blocks, modules. The attributes of software entities are those characteristics that can be possessed by more than one entity: accessing a particular file, using a particular memory variable, calling a particular subroutine, being affected by a particular business rule, and so forth. Attributes, therefore, relate the application's elements logically: each attribute creates a different set of relations between the application's elements, thereby giving rise to a different structure. There is a structure for each attribute present in the application – a structure reflecting the manner in which the elements are affected by that attribute. We can also describe these structures as the various *aspects* of the application.

Although an application may have thousands of attributes, any one element has only a few, so each structure involves only *some* of the application's elements. We saw, though, that it is useful to treat *all* the application's elements as elements of *every* structure; specifically, to consider for each element *all* the attributes, those that affect it as well as those that do not, because *not* possessing an attribute can be as significant as possessing it. This is clearly revealed when depicting each attribute with a separate, classification-style diagram: first, we divide the application's elements into those affected and those unaffected by the attribute; then, we divide the former according to the ways they are affected, and the latter according to the reasons they are unaffected.

But even when restricting our structures to those elements that actually possess the attribute, we find that, because they possess *several* attributes, most elements belong in several structures at the same time. And this sharing of elements causes the structures to interact. Thus, a software element can be part of business practices, use memory variables, access files, and call subroutines. Software elements must have several attributes because their function is to represent real entities. Since our affairs comprise entities that are shared by various processes and events, the multiplicity of attributes, and the consequent interaction of structures, is not surprising: it is precisely this interaction that allows software to mirror our affairs. So it is quite silly to attempt to reduce applications to independent structures, as do structured programming and the other mechanistic theories, and at the same time to hope that these applications will represent our affairs accurately.

Although there is no limit to the *number* of attributes in an application, there are only a few *types* of attributes (or what I called *software principles*). Thus, we may need a large number of attributes to implement all the rules and methods reflected in the application, but all these attributes can be combined under the type *business practices*. Similarly, the use of subroutines in general, as well as the repetition of individual operations, can be combined under the type *shared operations*. And accessing files, as well as using memory variables, can be combined under the type *shared data*.

An important type are the *flow-control* attributes – those attributes that establish the sequence in which the computer executes the application's elements. An element's flow-control attributes determine when that element is to be executed, relative to the other elements. Each flow-control attribute, thus, groups several elements logically, and relates the group as a whole to the rest of the application. The totality of flow-control attributes determines the performance of the application under all possible run-time conditions.

The flow-control attributes are necessary because computers, being sequential machines, normally execute operations in the sequence in which they appear in memory. But, while the operations that make up the application are stored in memory in one particular order (the static sequence), they must be executed in a different order (the dynamic sequence), and also in a different order on different occasions. In a loop, for instance, the repeated block appears only once, but the computer must be instructed to return to its beginning over and over; similarly, in a conditional construct we specify two blocks, and the computer must be instructed to execute one and bypass the other. Any element in the application, in fact, may have to instruct the computer to jump to another operation, forward or backward, instead of executing the one immediately following it. Thus, since it is the elements themselves that control the flow of execution, the flow-control features are attributes of these elements.

The flow-control attributes can also be described as the various means through which programming languages allow us to implement the *jumps* required in the flow of execution; that is, the *exceptions* to the sequential execution. The most versatile operation is the explicit jump – the GOTO statement, in most languages. Each GOTO gives rise to a flow-control attribute, which relates logically several elements: the one from which, and the one to which, the jump occurs, plus any others affected by the jump (those bypassed, for instance).

Most jumps in high-level languages, however, are implicit. The construct known as *block* (a series of consecutive operations, all executed or all bypassed) defines in effect a jump. Other implicit jumps include exception handling (jumping automatically to a predefined location when a certain run-time error occurs), the conditional construct (jumping over a statement or block), and the iterative construct (jumping back to the beginning of the loop). Additional types of jumps are often provided by language-specific statements and constructs. All jumps, though, whether explicit or implicit, serve in the end the same purpose: they create unique flow-control attributes. With each jump, two or more elements are related logically – as viewed from the perspective of the flow of execution – and this relationship is what we note as a particular flow-control attribute.

As is the case with the other types of attributes, an element can have more than one flow-control attribute. For example, the execution of a certain element may need to be followed by the execution of different elements on different occasions, depending on run-time conditions. Also like the other types of attributes, each flow-control attribute gives rise to a structure – a *flow-control* structure in this case. Although a flow-control structure usually affects a small number of elements, here too it is useful to treat *all* the application's elements as elements of each structure. For, it may be just as important for the application's execution that an element is *not* affected by that particular flow-control attribute, as it is that the element *is* affected. Take, for instance, the case of design faults: the sequence of execution is just as wrong if two elements are *not* connected by a jump when they should be, as it is if two elements *are* connected by a jump when they shouldn't be.

3

Having established the nature of software applications, and of software structures and attributes, we are in a position to understand the delusions of structured programming. I will start with a brief discussion; then, in the following subsections, we will study these delusions in detail.

To begin with, the theorists are only concerned with the *flow-control* structures of the application. These structures are believed to provide a complete representation of the running application, so their correctness is believed to guarantee the correctness of the application. The theorists fail to see that, no matter how important are the flow-control structures, the other structures too influence the application's performance. Once they commit this fallacy, the next step follows logically: they insist that the application be designed in such a way that all flow-control structures are combined into one; and this we can accomplish by restricting each element to *one* flow-control attribute.

Clearly, if each element is related to the rest of the application – from the perspective of the flow of execution – in only one way, the entire application can be designed as one hierarchical structure. This, ultimately, a mechanistic representation of the entire application, is the goal of structured programming. For, once we reduce applications to a mechanistic model, we can design and validate them with the tools of mathematics.

We recognize in this idea the mechanistic fallacy of reification: the theorists assume that one simple structure can provide an accurate representation of the complex phenomenon that is a software application. They extract first *one type* of structures – the *flow-control* structures; then, they go even further and attempt to reduce all structures of this type to *one* structure.

The structure we are left with – the structure believed to represent the application – is the nesting scheme. The neat nesting of constructs and modules we see in the flow diagram constitutes a simple hierarchical structure. Remember that both the nesting and the hierarchy are expected to represent the *execution* of the application's elements, not their static arrangement. The sequence of execution defined through the nesting scheme is as follows: the computer will execute the elements found at a given level of nesting in the order in which they appear; but if one of these elements has others nested within it, they will be executed before continuing at the current level; this rule is applied then to each of the nested elements, and so on. If the nesting scheme is seen as a hierarchical structure, it should be obvious that, by repeating this process recursively, every element in the structure is bound to be executed, executed only once, and executed at a particular time relative to the others.

So the nesting concept is simply a convention: a way to define a precise, unambiguous sequence of execution. By means of a nesting scheme, the programmer specifies the sequence in which he wants the computer to execute the application's elements at run time. The nesting convention is, in effect, an implicit flow-control attribute – an attribute possessed by every element in the application. And when this attribute is the *only* flow-control attribute, the nesting scheme is the only flow-control structure.

Recall the condition that each element have only one entry and exit. This, clearly, is the same as demanding that each element be connected to the rest of the application in only one way, or that each element possess only one flow-control attribute. The hierarchical structure is the answer, since in a hierarchical nesting scheme each element is necessarily connected to the others in only one. Thus, the principle of nesting, and the restriction to one entry and exit, one flow-control attribute, and one hierarchical structure are all related.

It is easy to see that the software nesting scheme is the counterpart of the *physical* hierarchical structure: the mechanistic concept of things within things that is so useful in manufacturing and construction, and which the software theorists are trying to emulate. The aim of structured programming is to make the flow of execution a perfect structure, a structure of *software* things within things. Just as the nesting scheme of a physical structure determines the *position* of each part and subassembly relative to the others, so the nesting scheme of a software application determines when each element is *executed* relative to the others. While one structure describes space relationships, the other describes time relationships; but both are strict hierarchies.

We can also express this analogy as follows. Physical systems can be studied with the tools of mathematics because their dynamic structure usually mirrors the static one. The sequence of operations of a machine, for instance, closely corresponds to the hierarchical diagram of parts and subassemblies that defines the machine. In software systems, on the other hand, the dynamic structure is very different from the static one: the flow of execution of an application does not correspond closely enough to the flow diagram (the static nesting of constructs and modules).

By forcing the flow of execution to follow the nesting scheme, the advocates of structured programming hope to make the dynamic structure of the application mirror the static one, just as it does in physical systems. It is the discrepancy between the dynamic structure and the static one that makes programming more difficult and less successful than engineering. We know that hierarchical systems can be represented mathematically. Thus, if we ensure that the flow diagram is a hierarchical nesting scheme, the flow of execution will mirror a hierarchical system, and the mathematical model that represents the diagram will represent at the same time the *running* application.

This idea – the dream of structured programming from the beginning – is clearly stated in Dijkstra's notorious paper: "Our powers to visualize processes evolving in time are relatively poorly developed. For that reason we should do ... our utmost to shorten the conceptual gap between the static program and the dynamic process, to make the correspondence between the program (spread out in text space) and the process (spread out in time) as trivial as possible."[2]

And here is the same idea expressed by other academics *twenty years* later: "Programs are essentially dynamic beings that exhibit a flow of control, while the program listing is a static piece of text. To ease understanding, the problem is to bring the two into harmony – to have the static text closely reflect the

---

[2] E. W. Dijkstra, "Go To Statement Considered Harmful," in *Milestones in Software Evolution*, eds. Paul W. Oman and Ted G. Lewis (Los Alamitos, CA: IEEE Computer Society Press, ©1990 IEEE), p. 9 – paper originally published in *Communications of the ACM* 11, no. 3 (1968): 147–148.

dynamic execution."[3] "The goal of structured programming is to write a program such that its dynamic structure is the same as its static structure. In other words, the program should be written in a manner such that during execution its control flow is linearized and follows the linear organization of the program text."[4]

This wish betrays the naivety of the software theorists: they actually believed that the enormously complex structure that is the flow of execution of an application can mirror the simple diagram that is its static representation. And the persistence of this belief demonstrates the corruptive effect of the mechanistic dogma. There were thousands of opportunities, during those twenty years, for the theorists to observe the complexity of software. Their mechanistic obsession, however, prevented them from recognizing these situations as falsifications of the idea of structured programming.

Now, a running application could, in principle, be a strict nesting scheme – a system of elements whose sequence of execution reflects their position in a hierarchical structure. This is what structured programming appears to promote, but it should be obvious that no serious application can be created in this manner. For, in such an application there would be no way to modify the flow of execution: every element would consist of nothing but one operation or several consecutive operations, would always have to be executed, always executed once, and always in the sequence established by the nesting scheme. The application, in other words, would always do the same thing. This is what we should expect, of course, if we want the execution of a software application – that is, its representation in time – to resemble the nesting scheme of a physical structure. After all, a physical structure like an appliance is always the same thing: its parts and subassemblies always exist, and are always arranged in the same way.

The theorists recognize that software is more versatile than mechanical devices, and that we need more than a nesting scheme if we want to create serious applications. So, while praising the benefits of a single flow-control structure, they give us the means to relate the application's elements in additional ways: the conditional and iterative constructs. The purpose of these constructs is to *override* the nesting scheme: they endow the application's

---

[3] Doug Bell, Ian Morrey, and John Pugh, *Software Engineering: A Programming Approach* (Hemel Hempstead, UK: Prentice Hall, 1987), p. 17.

[4] Pankaj Jalote, *An Integrated Approach to Software Engineering* (New York: Springer-Verlag, 1991), p. 236.

elements with additional flow-control attributes, thereby creating flow-control structures that are additional to the nesting scheme. Consequently, the application is no longer a strict nesting scheme of sequential constructs. It is a nesting scheme plus other structures – a *system* of flow-control structures. The two constructs, thus, serve to restore the multiplicity of structures and the complexity that had been eliminated when the theorists tried to reduce the application to one structure.

Because the application is still a nesting scheme of constructs with only one entry and exit, the theorists believe that the nesting scheme alone continues to represent the running application. The additional flow-control structures are not reflected in the nesting scheme, so it is easy to ignore them. But, even though they are not as obvious as the nesting scheme, these structures contribute to the complexity of the application – as do the structures created by shared data or operations, and by business or software practices, also ignored by the theorists because they are not obvious.

Finally, the hierarchical nesting scheme with its sequential constructs, and the enhancement provided by the two additional constructs, appear to form a basic set of software operations – basic in that they are the only operations needed, in principle, to implement any application. As a result, the theorists confuse these three types of constructs with the set of operations that forms the *definition* of a hierarchical structure (the operations that combine the elements of one level to create the next one). This leads to the belief that, by restricting ourselves to these constructs, we will realize the original dream: a flow of execution that mirrors the static nesting scheme, and is therefore a simple structure. This also explains why we are asked to convert those flow-control structures that cannot be implemented with these constructs, into other *types* of structures. But if the true purpose of the conditional and iterative constructs is to create additional flow-control structures, this conversion is futile, because the flow of execution is no longer a simple structure in any case.

There are so many fallacies in the theory of structured programming that we must separate it into several stages if we are to study it properly, and to learn from its delusions. These are not chronological stages, though, since they all occurred at about the same time. They are best described as stages in a process of degradation. We can identify four stages, and I will refer to them simply as the first, second, third, and fourth delusions. Bear in mind, however, that these delusions are interrelated, so the distinction may not always be clear-cut.

The first delusion is the belief that one structure alone – a flow-control structure – can accurately represent the performance of the application.

The second delusion is the belief that the standard constructs constitute a basic set of operations, whereas their true role is to restore the multiplicity of flow-control structures lost in the first delusion.

The third delusion is the belief that, if it is possible *in principle* to restrict applications to the standard flow-control constructs, we can develop *actual* applications in this manner. We are to modify our requirements by applying certain transformations, and this effort is believed to be worthwhile because the restriction to standard constructs should reduce the application to one structure. What the transformations do, though, is convert the relations due to flow-control attributes into relations due to other types of attributes, thereby adding to the other types of structures.

The fourth delusion is the notion of inconvenience: if we find the transformations inconvenient, or impractical, we don't have to *actually* implement them; the application will have a single flow-control structure merely because the transformations can be implemented *in principle*. The transformations *are* important, but only when convenient. This belief led to the reinstatement of many non-standard flow-control constructs, while the theorists continued to claim that the flow of execution was being reduced to a simple structure.

Common to all four delusions, thus, is the continuing belief in a mathematical representation of software applications, error-free programming, and the rest, when in fact these qualities had been lost from the start. Even before the detailed analysis, therefore, we can make this observation: When the software experts were promoting structured programming in the 1970s, when they were presenting it as a new science and a revolution in programming, all four delusions had already occurred. Thus, there never existed a useful, serious, scientific theory of structured programming – not even for a day. The movement known as structured programming, propagandized by the software elites and embraced by the software bureaucrats, was a fraud from the very beginning.

The analysis of these delusions also reveals the pseudoscientific nature of structured programming. The theory is falsified again and again, and the experts respond by *expanding* it. They restore, under different names and in complicated ways, the *traditional* programming concepts; so they restore precisely those concepts which they had previously rejected, and which must indeed be rejected, because they *contradict* the principles of structured programming.

The four delusions are, in the end, various stages in the struggle to rescue the theory from refutation by making it cope with those situations that falsify it. Structured programming could be promoted as a practical idea only after most of the original principles had been abandoned, and the complexity of applications again accepted; in other words, at the precise moment when it had lost the very qualities it was being promoted for. What was left – and what was called structured programming – was not a scientific theory, nor even a methodology, but merely an informal, and largely worthless, collection of programming tips.

The First Delusion

The first delusion is the delusion of the main structure: the belief that one structure alone can represent the application, since the other structures are unimportant, or can be studied separately. In the case of structured programming, the main structure is the nesting scheme: the hierarchical structure of constructs and modules. The static nesting scheme is believed to define completely and precisely the flow of execution, and hence the application's dynamic performance (see pp. 544–546).

If the goal of structured programming is to represent applications mathematically, the theorists are right when attempting to reduce them to a simple structure. As we know, mechanistic systems, as well as mathematical models, are logically equivalent to simple structures. Thus, it is true that only an application that was reduced to a simple structure can have a mathematical model. The fallacy, rather, is in the belief that applications *can* be reduced to a simple structure.

Like all mechanists, the software theorists do not take this possibility as hypothesis but as fact. Naturally, then, they perceive the *flow-control* structure (the sequence in which the computer executes the application's elements) as the structure that determines the application's performance. So, they conclude, we must make *this* structure a strict hierarchy of software entities. And this we can do by making the nesting scheme (which is simply the implementation of the flow-control structure by means of a programming language) a strict hierarchy.

But the flow-control structure is not an independent structure. Its elements are the software entities that make up the application, so they also function as elements in other structures: in the various processes implemented in the application. Every business practice that affects more than one element, every subroutine used by more than one element, every memory variable or database field accessed in more than one element, connects these elements logically, creating relations that are different from the relations defined by the flow of execution. This, obviously, is their purpose. It is precisely because one structure is insufficient that we must relate the application's elements in additional ways. Just like the flow-control structure, *each one* of these structures could be designed, if we wanted, as a perfect hierarchy. But, while the individual structures can be represented mathematically, the application as a whole cannot. Because they share their elements, the structures interact, and this makes the application a non-mechanistic phenomenon (see p. 542).

No matter how important is the flow-control structure, the other structures too affect the application's performance. Thus, even with a correct flow-control structure, the application will malfunction if a subroutine or variable is misused, or if a business practice is wrongly implemented; in other words, if one of the other structures does not match the requirements.

So, if the other structures affect the application's performance as strongly as does the flow-control structure, if we must ensure that every structure is perfect, how can the theorists claim that a mathematical representation of the flow of execution will guarantee the application's correctness? They are undoubtedly aware that the other structures create additional relations between the same elements, but their mechanistic obsession prevents them from appreciating the significance of these simultaneous relationships.

The theory of structured programming, thus, is refuted by the existence of the other structures. Even if we managed to represent mathematically the flow-control structure of an entire application, this achievement would be worthless, because the application's elements are related at the same time in additional ways. Like all attempts to reduce a complex phenomenon to a simple structure, a mathematical model of the flow-control structure would provide a poor approximation of the running application. What we would note in practice is that the model could not account for all the alternatives that the application is displaying. (Here we are discussing only the complexity created by the other *types* of structures. As we will see under the second delusion, the flow-control structure itself consists of interacting structures.)

All we can say in defence of software mechanism is that each aspect of the application – the flow of execution as well as the various processes – is indeed more easily designed and programmed if we view it as a hierarchical structure. But this well-known quality of the hierarchical concept can hardly form the basis of a formal theory of programming. Only rarely are strict hierarchies the most effective implementation of a requirement, and this is why programming languages permit us to override, when necessary, the neat hierarchical relations. Besides, only rarely is a mathematical representation of even one of these structures, and even a portion of a structure, practical, or useful. And a mathematical representation of the entire application is a fantasy.

Note how similar this delusion is to the linguistic delusions we studied in previous chapters – the attempts to reduce linguistic communication to a mechanistic model. In language, it is usually the syntax or the logic of a sentence that is believed to be the main structure. And the mechanistic theories of language are failing for the same reason the mechanistic *software* theories are failing: the existence of other structures.

It would have been too much, perhaps, to expect the software theorists to recognize the similarity of software and language, and to learn from the failure of the linguistic theories. But even without this wisdom, it should have been obvious that software entities are related in many ways at the same time; that the flow-control structure is not independent; and that, as a result, applications cannot be represented mathematically. Thus, the theory of structured programming was refuted at this point, and should have been abandoned. Instead, its advocates decided to "improve" it – which they did by reinstating the old concepts, as this is the only way to cope with the complexity of applications. And so they turned structured programming into a pseudoscience.

The Second Delusion

1

The second delusion emerged when the theorists attempted to restore some of the complexity lost through the first delusion. An application implemented as a strict nesting scheme would be trivial, its performance no more complex than what could be represented with a hierarchical structure of sequential constructs. We could perhaps describe mathematically its flow of execution, but it would have no practical value. There are two reasons for this: first, without jumps in the flow of execution – jumps controlled by run-time conditions – the application would always do the same thing; second, without a way to link the flow-control structure to the structures that depict files, subroutines, business practices, and so forth, these processes would remain isolated and would have no bearing on the application's performance.

Real-world applications are complex phenomena, systems of interacting structures. So, to make structured programming practical, the theorists had to abandon the idea of a single structure. In the second delusion, they make the *flow-control* structure (supposed to be just the nesting scheme) a complex structure again, by permitting *multiple* flow-control structures. In the third delusion, we will see later, they make the whole application a complex structure again, by restoring the interactions between the flow-control structures and some of the other *types* of structures. And in the fourth delusion they abandon the last restrictions and permit any flow-control structures that are useful. The pseudoscientific nature of this project is revealed, as I already pointed out, by the reinstatement of concepts that were previously excluded (because they contradict the principles of structured programming), and by the delusion that the theory can continue to function as originally claimed, despite these reversals.

The second delusion involves the standard conditional and iterative constructs. Under structured programming, you recall, these two constructs, along with the sequential construct, are the only flow-control constructs permitted. Because it is possible – in principle, at least – to implement any application using only these constructs and the nesting scheme, the three constructs are seen as a basic set of software operations.

The theorists look at the application's flow diagram, note that the flow-control constructs create levels of nesting, and conclude that their purpose is to combine software elements into higher-level elements – just as the operations that define a simple hierarchical structure create the elements of each level from those of the lower one. But this conclusion is mistaken: the theorists confuse the hierarchical nesting scheme and the three constructs, with the concept of a hierarchy and its operations.

Now, in the flow diagram the constructs do appear to combine elements on higher and higher levels; but in the running application their role is far more complex. The theorists believe that the restriction to a nesting scheme and standard constructs ensures that the flow-control structure is a *simple* structure, when the real purpose of these constructs is the exact opposite: to make the flow-control structure a *complex* structure.

This is easy to understand if we remember why we need these constructs in the first place. The conditional and iterative constructs provide (implicit) jumps in the flow of execution; and the function of jumps is to override the nesting scheme, by relating software elements in ways *additional* to the way they are related through the nesting scheme. We need the two constructs, thus, when certain requirements cannot be implemented with only one flow-control structure. As we saw earlier, the ability of an element to alter the flow of execution, implicitly or explicitly, is in effect a flow-control attribute (see pp. 543–544). Jumps override the nesting scheme by creating additional flow-control attributes, and hence additional flow-control structures. (We will examine these structures shortly.)

So the whole idea of standard flow-control constructs springs from a misunderstanding: the theorists mistakenly interpret the sequential, conditional, and iterative constructs as the *operations* of a hierarchical structure. To understand this mistake, let us start by recalling what *is* a hierarchical structure.

In a hierarchical structure, we combine a number of relatively simple elements (the *starting* elements) into more and more complex ones, until we reach the top element. The set of starting elements can be described as the basic building blocks of the hierarchy. At each level, the new elements are created by performing certain *operations* with the elements of the lower level. Thus, the elements become more and more complex as we move to higher levels, while the operations themselves may remain quite simple. The *definition* of a hierarchy includes the starting elements, the operations, and some rules describing their permissible uses.

The fallacy committed by the advocates of structured programming is in perceiving the three standard constructs as *operations* in the hierarchical structure that is the nesting scheme. The function of these constructs, in other words, is thought to be simply to combine software elements (the statements of a programming language) into larger and larger elements, one nesting level at a time. In reality, *only the sequential construct* combines elements into higher-level ones; the function of the conditional and iterative constructs is not to combine elements, but to generate multiple flow-control structures.

To appreciate why the conditional and iterative constructs are different, let us look at other kinds of structures and operations. In a physical structure, the starting elements are the basic components, and the operations are the means whereby the components are combined to form the levels of subassemblies. When the physical structure is a device like a machine, its performance too can be represented with a structure; and the operations in this structure are the ways in which the *working* of a subassembly is determined by the working of those at the lower level. In electronic systems, the starting elements are simple parts like resistors, capacitors, and transistors, and the operations are the connections that combine these parts into circuits, circuit boards, and devices. Here, too, in addition to the physical structure there is a structure that represents the performance of the system, and the operations in the latter are the ways in which the electronic functions at one level give rise to the functions we observe at the next higher level.

Turning now to software systems, consider a hypothetical application consisting of only one structure – the flow-control structure, just as structured programming says. The starting elements in this hierarchy are the statements permitted by a particular programming language, and the operations are the various ways in which statements are combined into blocks of statements, and blocks into larger blocks, modules, and so on. (Remember that the operations we are discussing here are the operations that define the hierarchical flow-control structure, which exists in time – *not* the operations we see as statements in a programming language; *those* operations function as the *starting elements* of the flow-control structure.) Clearly, if the flow of execution is to reflect the flow-control structure, the operations must be determined solely by the nesting scheme. Or, to put it differently, the only operations required in a software structure are the relations that create a nesting scheme of software elements. In particular, we need operations to delimit blocks of statements, and to invoke modules or subroutines. Ultimately, the operations in a software hierarchy must fulfil the same function as those in other types of hierarchies: combining the elements of one level to create the elements of the next higher level.

Note what is common to all these hierarchical systems: they are based on a set of starting elements and a set of operations, which constitute the definition of the hierarchy; and these sets can then generate any number of *actual* structures – different objects, or devices, or circuits, or software applications. Each actual structure is one particular implementation of a certain hierarchical system – a physical system, an electronic system, or a software system; that is, one combination of elements out of the many possible in that system. Note also that the actual structures are fixed: when we create a particular combination of elements, we end up with a *specific* device, circuit, or software application. The same structure – the same combination of elements – cannot represent two devices, circuits, or applications.

Given these common features, the second delusion ought to be obvious: the three standard constructs are *not* the set of operations that make up the definition of hierarchical software systems, as the theorists believe; and consequently, the resulting structures are not simple hierarchical software structures. *That* set of operations is found in the concept of sequential constructs, and in the concepts of blocks, modules, and subroutines. These are the only operations we need in order to generate hierarchical structures of software elements; that is, to generate any nesting scheme. With these operations, we create a higher level by combining several elements into a larger one: *consecutive* elements when using sequential constructs, and *separate*, distant elements when invoking modules and subroutines. (Subroutines, of course, also serve to create other *types* of structures, as we saw under the first delusion. But we must discuss one delusion at a time, so here we assume, with the theorists, that the flow-control structure is an independent structure.)

Of the three standard constructs, then, only the sequential construct performs the kind of operation that defines a hierarchical structure. We do not need conditional or iterative constructs to create software structures, so these two constructs do not perform ordinary operations, and are not part of the definition of a software hierarchy. Hierarchical systems, we just saw, generate actual structures that are *fixed*; and the structures formed with these two constructs are *variable*. While ordinary operations consist in *combining* elements, the operation performed by the conditional and iterative constructs consists in *selecting* elements. Specifically, instead of combining several elements into a higher-level element, the conditional and iterative constructs select one of two elements: in the conditional construct there is one selection, and one of the two elements may be empty; in the iterative construct the selection is performed in each iteration, and one of the two elements (the one selected when exiting the loop) is always empty.

So these two constructs do not treat software elements in the way a physical system treats the parts of a subassembly, or an electronic system treats the components of a circuit. In the other hierarchies, *all* the lower-level elements become part of the higher level, whereas in software hierarchies *only one* of the two elements that make up these constructs is actually executed. The real function of these constructs, therefore, is not to create higher-level elements within one nesting scheme, but to create multiple nesting schemes. Their function, in other words, is to turn the flow of execution from one structure into a system of structures.

2

If you still can't see how different they are from ordinary operations, note that both the conditional and the iterative constructs employ a *condition*. This is an important clue, and we can now analyze the second delusion with the method of simple and complex structures. Simple structures have no conditions in their operations. Hence, software structures that incorporate these constructs are complex, not simple. The condition, evaluated at run time and variously yielding *True* or *False*, is what generates the multiple structures.

Remember, again, that the structure we are discussing is the application's *flow of execution* (a structure that exists in time), not its *flow diagram* (a structure that exists in space). In flow diagrams these constructs do perhaps combine elements in a simple hierarchical way; but their run-time operation performs a selection, not a combination. And, since the running application includes all possible selections, it embodies all resulting structures.

Let us try, in our imagination, to identify and separate the structures that make up the *complex* flow-control structure – the one depicting the true manner in which the computer executes the application's elements. Let us start with the *static* structure (the flow diagram) and replace all the conditional and iterative constructs with the elements that are *actually* executed at run time. For simplicity, imagine an application that uses only one such construct (see figure 7-9). Thus, in the case of the conditional construct, instead of a condition and two elements, what we will see in the run-time structure is a sequential construct with one element – the element actually executed. And in the case of the iterative construct, instead of a condition and an element in a loop, what we will see is a sequential construct made up of several consecutive sequential constructs, their number being the number of times the element is executed at run time. More precisely, each iteration adds a sequential construct containing that element to the previous sequential construct, thereby generating a new, higher-level sequential construct. (Although this process occurs in time, it is similar to the way consecutive sequential constructs are merged in the static flow diagram.)

In the flow of execution, then, there is only a sequential construct. So, from the perspective of the flow of execution, the original structure can be represented as two or more overlapping structures, which differ only in the sequential construct that replaces the original conditional or iterative one. It is quite easy to visualize the two resulting structures in the case of the conditional construct, where the sequential construct contains one or the other of the two elements that can be selected. In the case of the iterative construct, though, there are *many* structures, as many as the possible number of iterations: the final construct can include none, one, two, three, etc., merged sequential constructs, depending on the condition. Each number gives rise to a slightly different final construct, and hence a different structure. Clearly, since the running application can perform a different number of iterations at different times, it embodies all these structures.

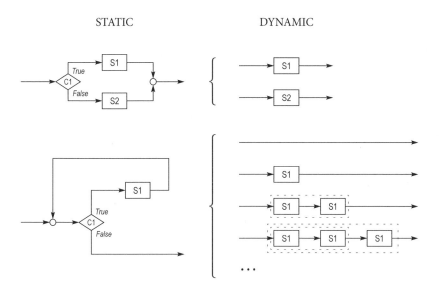

Figure 7-9

We can also explain the additional flow-control structures by counting the number of jumps implicit in a construct. Each jump in execution creates, as we know, a flow-control attribute, and hence a flow-control structure. The number of possible jumps reflects, therefore, the number of different sequences of execution that the application can display – the number of different paths that the execution can follow. In the conditional construct there are two possible paths, but only one needs a jump; the other is, in effect, the flow diagram itself. Let us decide, arbitrarily, that the path selected when the condition is *False* represents the flow diagram; then, the one selected when the condition is *True* represents the jump, and hence the *additional* structure.

In the iterative construct there are many possible paths, because the condition is evaluated in each iteration. For example, if in a particular situation the condition permits five iterations, this means that it is *True* five times, so there are five (backward) jumps. In another situation, the number of iterations, and hence the number of jumps generated by the construct, will be different. The number of possible structures is the largest number of iterations permitted by the condition, which is the same as the number of different paths. It is convenient to interpret these structures as those that are *additional* to the flow diagram; then, the flow diagram itself is represented by the path followed when ending the loop, when the condition is *False*.

❖

To summarize, ordinary operations – the kind we see in other types of hierarchical systems – give rise to *fixed* structures, whereas the conditional and iterative software constructs give rise to *variable* structures. A variable structure is logically equivalent to a family of structures that are almost identical, sharing all their elements except for one sequential construct. And, since these structures exist together in the running application, a variable structure is the same as a complex structure.

We can also describe the flow-control constructs as means of turning a simple static structure (the flow diagram, which reflects the nesting scheme) into a complex dynamic one (the flow-control structure of the running application). Through its condition, each construct creates from one nesting scheme several flow-control structures, and hence several sequences of execution. (We saw earlier how a hierarchical structure defines, through the nesting convention, a specific sequence of execution; see p. 545.) The construct does this by endowing elements with several flow-control attributes, thereby relating them, from the perspective of the flow of execution, in several ways. We can call the individual flow-control structures *dynamic nesting schemes*, since each one is a slightly different version, in the running application, of the static nesting scheme. The complex flow-control structure that reflects the performance of the application as a whole is then the totality of dynamic nesting schemes.

Complex structures cannot be reduced to simple ones, of course. We can perhaps study the individual structures when we assume one or two conditional or iterative constructs. But in real applications there are thousands of constructs, used at all levels, with elements and modules nested within one another. The links between structures are then too involved to analyze, and even to imagine.

So it is the *static* flow-control structure, not the dynamic one, that is the software equivalent of a physical structure. It is the *dynamic* structure that the theorists attempt to represent mathematically, though. Were their interest limited to flow diagrams, then strictly hierarchical methods like those used to build physical structures would indeed work. They work with the other types of systems because in those systems the dynamic structure usually mirrors the static one.[1]

We saw how each flow-control construct generates, through its condition, a system of flow-control structures. But in addition to the interactions between these structures, the flow-control constructs cause other interactions yet, with other *types* of structures. Here is how: The conditions employed by these constructs perform calculations and comparisons, so they necessarily involve memory variables, database fields, subroutines, or practices. They involve, thus, software processes; and, as we know, each process gives rise to a structure – the structure reflecting how the application's elements are affected by a particular variable, field, subroutine, or practice. Through their conditions, therefore, the flow-control constructs link the complex flow-control structure to some of the other structures that make up the application – structures that were supposedly isolated from the flow-control structure in the first delusion.

---

[1] Man-made physical systems that change over time (complicated mechanical or electronic systems) may well have a dynamic flow-control structure that is different from their static flow diagram and is, at the same time, complex – just like software systems. Even then, however, they remain relatively simple, so their dynamic behaviour can be usefully approximated with mechanistic means. They are equivalent, thus, to *trivial* software systems. We refrain from creating *physical* systems that we cannot fully understand and control, while being more ambitious with our *software* systems. But then, if we create software systems that are far more involved than our physical ones, we should be prepared to deal with the resulting complexity. It is absurd to attempt to represent them as we do the physical ones, mechanistically. Note that it is quite common for *natural* physical systems to display non-mechanistic behaviour (the three-body system, for instance, see pp. 109–110).

The links to those structures are officially reinstated in the third delusion, but they must be mentioned here too, just to demonstrate the great complexity created by the conditional and iterative constructs, even as the theorists believe that they are nothing but ordinary operations.

The complexity created by the conditional and iterative constructs is, in fact, even greater. For, in addition to the links to other *types* of structures, each construct creates links to other *flow-control* structures: to the families of structures generated by other constructs. The nesting process is what causes these links. Because these constructs are used at all levels, the links between the structures generated by a particular construct, at a particular level, also affect the structures generated by the constructs nested within it. So the links at the lower levels are *additional* to the links created by the lower-level constructs themselves.

3

The second delusion, we saw, consists in confusing the standard flow-control constructs with the set of operations that defines a simple hierarchical structure. The theorists are fascinated by the fact that three constructs are all we need, in principle, in order to create software applications; so they conclude, wrongly, that these constructs constitute a *minimal set of software operations.*

Now, a *real* minimal set of operations would indeed be an important discovery. If a set like this existed, then by restricting ourselves to these operations we could perhaps develop our applications mathematically. Even a minimal set defining just the flow-control structure (which is all we can hope for after the first delusion) would still be interesting. But if these constructs are not ordinary operations, the fact that they are a minimal set is irrelevant. If the flow-control structure is not a simple hierarchical structure, we cannot develop applications mathematically no matter what starting elements and operations we use.

The three constructs may well form a minimal set, but all we can say about it is that it is the minimal set of constructs that can generate enough *flow-control* structures to implement any software requirement. Here is why: The nesting scheme, as we know, endows all the elements in the application with one flow-control attribute; but each flow-control construct endows certain elements with *additional* flow-control attributes; finally, each one of these attributes gives rise to a flow-control structure, and this system of flow-control structures constitutes the application's flow of execution. To create serious applications, elements must be related through many different attributes, but only *some* of these attributes need to be of the flow-control type. What has been proved, thus, is that the three standard constructs – in conjunction with the nesting scheme – provide, in principle, the minimal set of *flow-control* attributes required to create any application. In principle, then, we can replace the extra flow-control attributes present in a given application with other *types* of attributes. It is possible, therefore, to reduce all flow-control structures to structures based on the three standard constructs – if we agree to add other types of structures. (This is the essence of the transformations prescribed in the third delusion.)

So the idea of a minimal set of flow-control constructs may be an interesting subject of research in computer science, and this is how it was perceived by the scientists who first studied it.[2] But it is meaningless as a method of programming. For, if the flow-control structure (to say nothing of the application as a whole) ceases to be a simple hierarchical structure as soon as we add *any* conditional or iterative constructs to the nesting scheme, the dream of mathematical programming is lost, so it doesn't matter whether the minimal set has three constructs or thirty, or whether we restrict ourselves to a minimal set or create our own constructs.

When misinterpreting the function of the flow-control constructs, the software mechanists are committing the same fallacy as all the mechanists before them: attempting to represent a complex phenomenon by means of a simple structure. These constructs are seen as mere operations within the traditional nesting concept, when in reality they constitute a *new* concept – a concept powerful enough to turn simple static structures into complex dynamic ones. The mechanists, though, continue to believe that the flow of execution can be represented with one structure. So the real function of these constructs is to restore some of the complexity that was lost in the first delusion, when the mechanists reduced applications to one structure. (The rest of that complexity is restored in the third and fourth delusions.)

The fallacy, thus, is in the belief that we can discover a simple structure that has the potency of a complex one. The software mechanists note that the hierarchical concept allows us to generate large structures with just a few operations and starting elements, and that this is useful in fields like manufacturing and construction; and they want to have the same qualities in

[2] See, for example, Corrado Böhm and Giuseppe Jacopini, "Flow Diagrams, Turing Machines and Languages with Only Two Formation Rules," in *Milestones in Software Evolution*, eds. Paul W. Oman and Ted G. Lewis (Los Alamitos, CA: IEEE Computer Society Press, ©1990 IEEE) – paper originally published in *Communications of the ACM* 9, no. 5 (1966): 366–371. We will return to this paper later.

software. They want software systems to be simple hierarchical structures, but to retain their power and versatility; that is, their ability to perform tasks which *cannot* be performed by mechanical or electronic systems. They fail to see that this ability derives precisely from the fact that software allows us to create a kind of structures which the other systems do not – complex structures.

Nothing stops us from restricting software applications to simple hierarchical structures, just like those we create with the other systems. We would be able to develop, however, only trivial applications – only those that could be represented as a nesting scheme of sequential constructs. To create a greater variety of applications, we must enhance the nesting concept with the concept of conditional and iterative constructs; but then the applications are no longer simple structures. In the end, it is only through self-deception that the mechanists manage to have a simple structure with the potency of a complex one: they are creating complex software structures while continuing to believe that they are working with simple ones.

The Third Delusion

1

The first delusion, we recall, was the belief that the flow-control structure can be isolated from the other structures that make up the application, and that it can be reduced to a simple structure. With the second delusion, the flow-control structure became a system of interacting flow-control structures; moreover, it was linked, through the conditions used in the flow-control constructs, to other *types* of structures. Thus, if after the first delusion the expectation of a mechanistic representation of the flow-control structure was still valid, this expectation was illogical after the second delusion, when it became a *complex* structure.

The third delusion is the belief that it is important to reduce the application – through a series of transformations – to the flow-control structure defined in the second delusion. It is important, the theorists insist, because *that* structure can be represented mechanistically. Through this reduction, therefore, we will represent the entire application mechanistically. Just as they succumbed to the second delusion when attempting to suppress the evidence of complexity after the first one, the theorists succumbed to the third delusion because they ignored the evidence of complexity after the second one.

I defined the four delusions as stages in a process of degradation, as distinct opportunities for the theorists and the practitioners to recognize the fallaciousness of structured programming. On this definition, the third delusion is a new development. The idea of structured programming could have ended with the second delusion, when the conditional and iterative constructs were introduced, since the very need for these constructs proves that the flow-control structure of a serious application is more than a simple hierarchical structure. Having missed the second opportunity to recognize their mistake, the theorists promoted now the idea of transformations: we must modify the application's requirements so as to limit the application to flow-control structures based on the three standard constructs; all other flow-control structures must be replaced with structures based on shared data or shared operations (see pp. 538–541).

Everyone could see that these transformations are artificial, that they complicate the application, that in most situations they are totally impractical, and that even when we manage to implement them we still cannot prove our applications mathematically. Yet no one wondered why, if the principle of hierarchical structures works so well in other fields, if we understand it so readily and implement it so easily with other systems, it is impractical for *software* systems. No one saw this as one more piece of evidence that software applications are not simple hierarchical structures. Thus, the theorists and the practitioners missed the third opportunity to recognize the fallaciousness of structured programming.

2

Let us review the motivation for the transformations. To perform a given task, the application's elements must be *related*; and, usually, they must be related in more than one way. It is by sharing attributes that software elements are related. Each attribute gives rise to a set of relations; namely, the structure representing how the application's elements are affected by that attribute.

There are several types of attributes and relations. A relation is formed, for example, when elements use the same memory variable or database field, when they perform the same operation or call the same subroutine, or when they are part of the same business practice. Elements can also be related through the flow of execution: the relative sequence in which they are executed constitutes a logical relation, so it acts as a shared attribute. And it is only this type of attributes and relations – the *flow-control* type – that structured programming recognizes.

A software element can possess more than one attribute. Thus, an element can use several variables, call several subroutines, and be part of several practices. Each attribute gives rise to a different set of relations between the application's elements, so each element can be related to the others in several ways at the same time. Since these sets of relations are the structures that make up the application, we can also express this by saying that each element is part of several structures at the same time. The multiplicity of software relations is necessary because this is how the *real* entities – the processes and events that make up our affairs, and which we want to represent in software – are related.

As is the case with the other types of attributes, elements can possess more than one *flow-control* attribute. Elements, therefore, can also be related to one another in more than one way through the flow of execution. Multiple flow-control relations are necessary when the relative position of an element in the flow of execution must change while the application is running.

The nesting scheme (the static arrangement we see in the application's flow diagram) provides *one* of these attributes. The nesting scheme defines a formal, precise set of relations, which constitutes in effect a *default* flow-control attribute – one shared by all the elements in the application. And if this were the *only* flow-control attribute, the application would have only one flow-control structure – a structure mirroring, in the actual flow of execution, the hierarchical structure that is the static nesting scheme.

In serious applications, though, elements must be related through more than one flow-control attribute, so the simple flow of execution established by the nesting scheme is insufficient. The additional flow-control attributes are implemented by performing *jumps* in the flow of execution; that is, by *overriding* the sequence dictated by the nesting scheme. The elements from which and to which a jump occurs, and the elements bypassed by the jump, are then related – when viewed from the perspective of the flow of execution – in two ways: through the nesting scheme, and through the connection created by the jump. Jumps provide an *alternative* to the sequence established by the nesting scheme: whether the flow of execution follows one jump or another, or the nesting scheme, depends on run-time conditions. So the execution of each element in the application reflects, in the end, both the nesting scheme and the various jumps that affect it.

Jumps can be explicit or implicit. Explicit jumps (typically implemented with GOTO statements) permit us to create any flow-control relations we want. Programming languages, though, also provide a number of *built-in* flow-control constructs. These constructs are basic syntactic units designed to create automatically, by means of implicit jumps, some of the more common flow-control relations. The best-known built-in constructs, and the only ones permitted by structured programming, are the elementary conditional and iterative constructs (also known as the standard constructs).

By eliminating the explicit jumps, these constructs simplify programming. But they are not versatile enough to satisfy all likely requirements; in fact, as we saw earlier, even some very simple requirements cannot be implemented with these constructs alone. The impossibility of implementing a given requirement means that some elements must have more flow-control attributes than what the nesting scheme and the standard constructs provide. Some elements, in other words, must be related to others – when viewed from the perspective of the flow of execution – in more ways than the number of jumps implicit in these constructs. (For the conditional construct, we recall, there is one possible jump, one way to override the nesting scheme; and for the iterative construct, the number of jumps equals the number of possible iterations. The sequential construct is not mentioned in this discussion, since it does not provide a jump that can override the nesting scheme; sequential constructs, in fact, are the entities that form the original nesting scheme, before adding conditional and iterative constructs.)

We shouldn't be surprised that software elements need more flow-control attributes for a difficult requirement than they do for a simple one; after all, we are not surprised that elements need more of the *other* types of attributes for a difficult requirement (they need to use more variables or database fields, for instance, or to call more subroutines).

Now, we could implement the additional flow-control relations by enhancing the standard conditional and iterative constructs, or by creating our own, specialized constructs. In either case, though, we would have to add flow-control attributes in the form of explicit jumps, and this is prohibited under structured programming. The reason it is prohibited, we saw under the second delusion, is the belief that applications restricted to the standard constructs have only one flow-control structure (the nesting scheme). And this, in turn, allows us to represent, develop, and prove them mathematically. Thus, the theorists say, since it is possible, in principle, to transform any requirements into a format programmable with the standard constructs alone, and since the benefits of this concept are so great, any effort invested in realizing it is worthwhile. This is the motivation for the transformations.

The transformations convert those flow-control relations that we need but cannot implement with the standard constructs, into relations based on shared data or shared operations. They convert, thus, some of the flow-control structures into other *types* of structures (so they create more structures of the types that have been ignored since the first delusion). When shared by several elements, data and operations can serve as attributes, since they relate the elements logically. (This, obviously, is why they can be used as substitutes for the *flow-control* attributes.)

Consider a simple example. If we want to override the nesting scheme by jumping across several elements and levels without resorting to GOTO, we can use a memory variable, like this: In the first element, instead of performing a jump, we assign the value 1 to a variable that is normally 0. Then, we enclose each element that would have been bypassed by the jump, inside a conditional construct where the condition is the value of this variable: if 1, the element is bypassed. So the flow of execution can follow the nesting scheme, as before, but those elements controlled by the condition will be bypassed rather than executed. In this way, *one* flow-control relation based on an explicit jump is replaced with *several* flow-control relations based on the standard conditional construct, plus *one* relation based on shared data.

The paper written by Corrado Böhm and Giuseppe Jacopini,[1] regarded by everyone as the mathematical foundation of structured programming, proved that we can always use pieces of storage (in ways similar to the foregoing example) to reduce an arbitrary flow diagram to a diagram based on the sequential, conditional, and iterative constructs. The paper proved, in other words, that any flow-control structure can be transformed into a functionally equivalent structure where the elements possess no more than three types of flow-control attributes: one provided by the nesting concept and by merging consecutive sequential constructs, and the others by the conditional and iterative constructs.[2]

Another way to put this is by stating that any flow of execution can be implemented by using no more than three types of flow-control relations. A simple nesting scheme, made up of sequential constructs alone, is insufficient. We need more than one type of relations between elements if we want the ability to implement any conceivable requirement. But we don't need more than a certain *minimal set* of relations. The minimal set includes the relations created by the nesting scheme, and those created by the standard conditional and iterative constructs. Any other flow-control relations can be replaced with relations based on other types of attributes; specifically, relations based on shared data or shared operations.

It is important to note that the paper only proved these facts *in principle*; that is, from a theoretical perspective. It did not prove that practical applications can actually be programmed in this fashion. This is an important point,

---

[1] Corrado Böhm and Giuseppe Jacopini, "Flow Diagrams, Turing Machines and Languages with Only Two Formation Rules," in *Milestones in Software Evolution*, eds. Paul W. Oman and Ted G. Lewis (Los Alamitos, CA: IEEE Computer Society Press, ©1990 IEEE) – paper originally published in *Communications of the ACM* 9, no. 5 (1966): 366–371.

[2] The paper proved, in fact, that conditional constructs can be further transformed into iterative constructs; so, in the end, only sequential and iterative constructs are necessary. I will return to this point later.

because the effort of performing the transformations – the essence of the third delusion – is justified by citing this paper, when in reality the paper is only a study in mathematical logic, unconcerned with the *practicality* of the transformations. (We will analyze this misrepresentation shortly.)

But regardless of their impracticality, the transformations would only make sense if the resulting flow-control structure were indeed a simple structure. The fallacies of the second delusion, thus, beget the fallacies of the third one: because they believe that a flow-control structure restricted to the standard constructs is a simple structure, the advocates of structured programming believe that the effort of performing the transformations is worthwhile.

The difficulty of programming – what demands skills and experience – is largely the need to deal with multiple structures, and hence with simultaneous relations. The theorists acknowledge this when they stress the importance of reducing the application to *one* flow-control structure: if every element in the application is restricted to one flow-control attribute, every element will be related to the others in only one way, and the application – viewed from the perspective of the flow of execution – will have only one structure. We will then be able to represent the application with a mechanistic model, and hence develop and prove it with the tools of mathematics. To put this differently, by eliminating the need to deal with simultaneous relations in our mind we will turn programming into a routine activity, and thereby eliminate the need for personal skills and experience.

This is the idea behind structured programming, but then the theorists contradict themselves and permit *several* flow-control relations per element, not one: the nesting scheme *plus* the relations generated by the standard conditional and iterative constructs. The flow-control structure, as a result, is a system of interacting structures. It was a simple hierarchical structure only when it was a nesting scheme of elements that were all sequential constructs. The *implicit* jumps that are part of the standard constructs create additional flow-control relations between the application's elements in exactly the same way that *explicit* jumps would. It is quite silly to think that, just because there are no explicit jumps – no GOTO statements – we have only one flow-control structure. After all, the very reason we added the conditional and iterative constructs is that the nesting scheme alone (a simple structure) could not provide all the flow-control relations we needed.

The theorists believe that transformations keep the flow-control structure simple because they eliminate the *non-standard* constructs. But if the *standard* constructs already make the flow-control structure complex, the use of non-standard ones is irrelevant, since we can no longer represent the flow-control structure mechanistically anyway. So, whether easy or difficult to implement, the transformations are futile if their purpose is to turn programming into a routine activity. Both with and without transformations, the flow-control structure is a system of interacting structures, so the most difficult aspect of programming – the need to process multiple structures in the mind – remains unchanged. Thus, because structured programming fails to reduce applications to a simple structure, it also fails to simplify programming.

And we must not forget that the transformations work by replacing flow-control structures with structures of other types, so in the end they add to the complexity of *other* systems of structures. Therefore, in those situations where an explicit jump provides the most effective relation between elements, the transformation will replace one structure with several, making the application as a whole *more* involved. (The impracticality of the transformations is finally acknowledged by the theorists in the fourth delusion.)

It is up to the programmer to select the most effective system of structures for a given requirement, and this system may well include some flow-control structures generated by means of explicit jumps. Discovering the best system and coping with the unavoidable interactions – this, ultimately, is the skill of programming. Since our affairs, and the software that mirrors them, consist of interacting structures, we *must* develop the capacity to deal with these interactions if we want to have useful applications. The aim of structured programming is to obviate the need for this expertise; specifically, to turn programming from an activity demanding skills and experience into one demanding only mechanistic knowledge. But now we see that, in their desire to simplify programming, the theorists *add* to the complexity of software, and end up making programming more difficult.

3

Let us examine next the mechanistic belief that it is possible to *actually* implement an idea that was only shown to be valid *in principle*. We saw that even when we manage to reduce the application to standard constructs, the flow of execution, and the application as a whole, remain complex structures; so the transformations are always futile. Let us ignore this fallacy, though, and assume with the theorists that by applying the transformations we *will* be able to represent the application mathematically, so the effort is worthwhile. But Böhm and Jacopini's paper only shows that applications can be reduced to the standard constructs *in principle*. The theorists, thus, are confidently promoting the idea of transformations when there is nothing – apart from a blind faith in mechanism – to guarantee that this idea can work with *practical* applications.

It is common for mathematical concepts to be valid in principle but not in practice, and many mechanistic delusions spring from confusing the theoretical with the practical aspects of an idea. The pseudosciences we studied in chapter 3, for instance, are founded upon the idea that it is possible to account for all the alternatives displayed by human minds and human societies. They claim, thus, that it is possible to discover a mechanistic model where the starting elements are some basic physiological entities, and the values of the top element represent every possible mental act, or behaviour pattern, or social phenomenon (see pp. 283–286). Now, it is perhaps true that every alternative of the top element is, ultimately, a combination of some elementary entities or propensities; but it doesn't follow that we can express these combinations in precise, mathematical terms. The mechanists invoke the principles of reductionism and atomism to justify their optimism, but they *cannot* discover a working mechanistic model; that is, a continuous series of reductions down to the basic entities. So, while it may be possible *in principle* to explain human intelligence or behaviour in terms of low-level physiological entities, we cannot *actually* do it.

The most fantastic mechanistic delusion is Laplacean determinism, which makes the following claim: the world is nothing but a system of particles of matter acting upon one another according to the mechanistic theory of gravitation; it should therefore be possible, *in principle*, to explain all current entities and phenomena, and to predict all future ones, simply by expressing the relations between all the particles in the universe in the form of equations and then solving these equations. The mechanists admit that this is only an idea, that we cannot *actually* do it; but this doesn't stop them from concluding that the world is deterministic. (We will discuss this fallacy in greater detail in chapter 8; see pp. 824–826.)

Returning to the domain of computer science, a well-known example of a mechanistic model that is only an idea is the Turing machine.[3] This theoretical device consists of a read-write head and a tape that moves under it in both directions, one position at a time. The device can be in one of a finite number of internal states, and its current state changes at each step. Also at each step, the device reads the symbol found on the tape in the current position, perhaps erases it or writes another one, and then advances the tape one position left or right. The operations performed at each step (erasing, replacing, or leaving the symbol unchanged; advancing the tape left or right; and selecting the

---

[3] Named after the mathematician and computer pioneer Alan Turing, who invented it while studying the concept of computable and non-computable functions.

next internal state) depend solely on the current state and the symbol found in the current position.

Turing machines can be programmed to execute algorithms. For example, if the permissible symbols are the digits *0* to *9*, a program could read a series of digits written in consecutive positions on the tape, interpret them as a number, calculate its square root by using the tape as working area, and finally erase the temporary symbols and write on the tape the digits that make up the result. (The program for a Turing machine is not a list of instructions, as for a computer, but a table specifying the operations to be performed for every possible combination of machine states and input symbols.)

There are many variations, but the most interesting Turing machines are those that define a *minimal* device: the machine with the smallest number of internal states, or the smallest alphabet of symbols, or the shortest tape, that can still solve any problem from a certain class of problems. It should be obvious, for instance, that we can always restrict Turing machines to two symbols, such as *0* and *1*, since we can reduce any data to this binary representation, just as we do in computers. Compared with devices that use a larger alphabet – the full set of letters and digits, for example – the minimal device would merely need a larger program and a longer tape to execute a given algorithm.

Now, it has been proved that a Turing machine can be programmed to execute, essentially, any algorithm. This simple computational device can represent, therefore, any deterministic phenomenon, any process that can be described precisely and completely. In particular, it can be programmed to execute any task that can be executed by more complicated devices – computers, for instance. Again, the program for the Turing machine would be larger and less efficient, and in most cases totally impractical, but the device is only an idea. We are only interested in the fact that, *in principle*, it can solve any problem. In principle, then, any problem, no matter how complicated, can be reduced to the simple operations possible on a basic Turing machine.

Thus, although the Turing machine is only a theoretical device, it is an interesting subject of study in computer science. Since we know that anything that can be computed can also be computed on a Turing machine, we can determine, say, whether a certain problem can be solved at all mathematically, by determining whether or not it can be programmed on a Turing machine. Often this is easier than actually finding a mathematical solution. The practicality of this program is irrelevant, since we don't have to run it, or even to develop it; all we need is the knowledge that such a program could be developed.

❖

Restricting software applications to the standard flow-control constructs is just like these other ideas: it is only possible *in principle*. Just like the theories that can explain only *in principle* any intelligent act, or those that can predict only *in principle* any future event, or the Turing machine that can execute only *in principle* any algorithm, it is possible only *in principle* to restrict software applications to the three standard constructs. The software theorists, thus, are promoting as a *practical* programming method an idea that is the software counterpart of well-known mechanistic fantasies.

Despite our mechanistic culture, not many scientists seriously claim that those other ideas have immediate, practical applications. But the software experts were enthusiastic about the possibility of mathematical programming. The idea of transformations – and hence the whole idea of structured programming, which ultimately depends on the practicality of these transformations – was taken seriously by every theorist, even though one could see from the start that it is the same type of fantasy as the other ideas.

But it is the Turing machine that is of greatest interest to us, not only because of its connection to programming in general, but also because Böhm and Jacopini actually discuss in their paper the link between Turing machines and standard flow-control constructs. (This link is clearly indicated even in the paper's title: "Flow Diagrams, Turing Machines and Languages with Only Two Formation Rules.")

Although computers can be reduced to Turing machines, everyone agrees that this is true only in principle, that most tasks would be totally impractical on a Turing machine. Thus, no one has suggested that, given the theoretical benefits of minimal computational devices, we replace our computers with Turing machines. Nor has anyone suggested that, given the theoretical benefits of minimal programming languages, we simulate the operation of a Turing machine on our computers, and then restrict programming languages to the instructions of the Turing machine.

At the same time, the software theorists perceive the transformations as a *practical* programming principle, and insist that we *actually* restrict our applications to the standard constructs. Their naivety is so great that, even in a mechanistic culture like ours, it is hard to find a precedent for such an absurd claim. And we must not forget that the delusion of transformations is *additional* to the two delusions we discussed earlier. This means that, since applications cannot be represented mechanistically in any case, the transformations would be futile even if they were practical.

It is important to emphasize that Böhm and Jacopini discussed the standard constructs and the transformations strictly as a concept in mathematical logic; they say nothing in their paper about grounding a programming theory on this concept. It was only the advocates of structured programming who, desperate to find a scientific foundation for their mechanistic fantasy, decided to interpret the paper in this manner. Having accepted as established fact what was only a wish – the idea that software applications can be represented mathematically – they saw in this paper something that its authors had not intended: the evidence for the possibility of a *practical* mechanistic programming theory.

The link between flow diagrams and Turing machines discussed by Böhm and Jacopini is this: They demonstrated that there exists a minimal Turing machine which is logically equivalent to a flow diagram restricted to the standard flow-control constructs. More specifically, they showed that a Turing machine restricted to the equivalent of the sequential, conditional, and iterative operations can still execute, essentially, any algorithm. In other words, any Turing machine, no matter how complicated, can be reduced, in principle, to this minimal configuration.

By discussing the link between flow diagrams and Turing machines, then, Böhm and Jacopini asserted in effect that they considered the transformation of flow diagrams to be, like the Turing machine, *a purely theoretical concept*. So it can be said that their study is the exact opposite of what the later theorists claimed it was: it is an *abstract* idea, not the basis of a *practical* programming theory. The study is *misrepresented* when invoked as the foundation of structured programming.

4

We saw that the advocates of structured programming misrepresent Böhm and Jacopini's paper when invoking it as the foundation of a practical programming theory. But this is not all. They also misrepresent the paper when saying that it proved that *only three* flow-control constructs – the sequential, the conditional, and the iterative – are necessary to create software applications. In reality, the paper proved that *only two* constructs are necessary – the sequential and the iterative ones. The conditional construct, it turns out, is merely a special case of the iterative construct. Just as we can reduce through transformations all non-standard constructs to conditional and iterative ones, we can *further* reduce, through similar transformations, all conditional constructs to iterative ones.

Thus, the paper is routinely depicted as the mathematical foundation of structured programming, and we are told that the only way to derive the benefits of mathematics is by restricting our applications to the elementary sequential, conditional, and iterative constructs – while the paper itself shows that the conditional construct is *not* an elementary construct. There are thousands of references to this paper – in casual as well as formal discussions of structured programming, in popular as well as professional publications – and it is difficult to find a single one stating what Böhm and Jacopini *actually* proved. According to all these references, they proved that applications can be built from three, not two, elementary constructs. We must study now this second aspect of the misrepresentation.

It is true that Böhm and Jacopini started by proving that any flow diagram can be reduced to the three elementary constructs. But they went on and proved that the conditional construct can be reduced to the iterative one. And they also proved that an equivalent reduction is possible for Turing machines (so the minimal Turing machine does not require conditional operations). Like the link to Turing machines, this final reduction is clearly indicated even in the paper's title ("... Languages with Only Two Formation Rules") and in its introduction ("... a language which admits as formation rules only composition [i.e., merging consecutive constructs] and iteration"[4]).

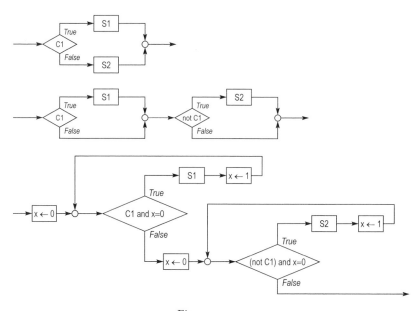

Figure 7-10

Although they proved it through mathematical logic, we can demonstrate this reduction with flow diagrams (see figure 7-10). In the first step, the conditional construct is reduced to two consecutive, simpler conditional

[4] Böhm and Jacopini, "Flow Diagrams," p. 3.

constructs. The new constructs have only one operation each, *S1* and *S2*, and the condition in the second one is the logical negation of the original condition. In the second step, the new constructs are transformed into two consecutive iterative constructs: the variable *x*, cleared before each loop and set in the first iteration, is part of the condition. In the end, either *S1* or *S2* is executed, and only once.[5]

The fallacy of the third delusion, we saw, is the idea of transformations. But now we see that, even *within* this idea, there is an inconsistency. And, even if we ignore the other delusions, and the other fallacies of the third delusion, this inconsistency alone is serious enough to cast doubt on the entire idea of structured programming.

The inconsistency is this: The theorists tell us that we must reduce our applications to the three standard flow-control constructs, because only if created with these elementary entities can applications be developed and proved mathematically. But if the most elementary software entities are *two* constructs, not three, the theorists claim in effect that even with some *unreduced* constructs we can derive the benefits of mathematical programming. It is *unimportant*, they tell us, to reduce our applications from three constructs to two; that is, from the conditional to the iterative construct. This reduction, though, as shown in figure 7-10, is similar to the reduction from any non-standard construct to the standard ones. (We saw examples of these other reductions earlier, from figure 7-5 to 7-6 and from figure 7-7 to 7-8, pp. 538–541.) So, if the mathematical benefits are preserved even without a complete reduction, if it is unimportant to reduce our applications from three constructs to two, why is it important to reduce them to three constructs in the first place?

Imagine an application that also employs a non-standard construct, for a total of *four* types of constructs. If this application can be reduced through similar transformations from four constructs to three and from three to two, and if at the same time it is unimportant to reduce it from three to two, then it must also be unimportant to reduce it from four to three. And, continuing this logic, it must also be unimportant to reduce an application from five constructs to four, from six to five, and so on. In other words, whatever mathematical benefits we are promised to gain from a reduction to the three standard constructs are ours to enjoy with any number of non-standard constructs. The transformations, therefore, and structured programming generally, are unnecessary, and we should be able to develop and prove our applications mathematically no matter how we choose to program them.

---

[5] The use of a memory variable as switch was explained earlier, for the transformation shown in figure 7-8 (see pp. 540–541).

The theory of structured programming, thus, is inconsistent if its principles prescribe a certain programming method, and the same principles lead to the conclusion that this method is irrelevant. The promoters of structured programming failed to notice what is, in fact, a blatant self-contradiction: claiming, at the same time, that it is important and that it is unimportant to reduce applications to three constructs. Having misrepresented Böhm and Jacopini's paper as the basis of a practical programming theory (as we saw earlier), they were now actually attempting to implement their fantasy. So, in their eagerness, they added to the misrepresentation. Moreover, they added to the theory's fallaciousness, by making it inconsistent.

It is impossible to prove mathematically the correctness of our applications – with or without transformations, with three or with two constructs. Since applications are not simple structures, the idea of mathematical programming is a fantasy, so there are no benefits in reducing them to *any* set of constructs. Let us ignore for a moment, though, this fallacy, and believe with the theorists that the transformations *are* worthwhile. But then, to be consistent – that is, to benefit from these transformations – we would have to seek a complete reduction, to two constructs. This shows that stopping the reduction at three constructs is a *separate* fallacy, *additional* to the fallacy of mathematical programming.

The following quotations are typical of how Böhm and Jacopini's work is misrepresented in programming books (that is, by mentioning the reduction to *three* constructs, not two): "In 1966, Böhm and Jacopini formally proved the basic theory of structured programming, that any program can be written using only three logical constructs."[6] "One of the theoretical milestones of systems science was Böhm and Jacopini's proof that demonstrated it was possible to build a good program using only three logical means of construction: sequences, alternatives, and repetition of instruction."[7] "The first major step toward structured programming was made in a paper published by C. Böhm and G. Jacopini.... They demonstrated that three basic control structures, or constructs, were sufficient for expressing any flowchartable program logic."[8] "According to Böhm and Jacopini, we need three basic building blocks in order to construct a program: 1. A process box. 2. A

[6] Victor Weinberg, *Structured Analysis* (Englewood Cliffs, NJ: Prentice Hall, 1980), p. 27.

[7] Ken Orr, *Structured Requirements Definition* (Topeka, KS: Ken Orr and Associates, 1981), p. 58.

[8] Randall W. Jensen, "Structured Programming," in *Software Engineering*, eds. Randall W. Jensen and Charles C. Tonies (Englewood Cliffs, NJ: Prentice Hall, 1979), p. 228.

generalized loop mechanism. 3. A binary-decision mechanism."⁹ "Böhm and Jacopini ... first showed that statement sequencing, IF-THEN-ELSE conditional branching, and DO-WHILE conditional iteration would suffice as a set of control structures for expressing *any* flow-chartable program logic."¹⁰ "In a now-classical paper, Böhm and Jacopini proved that any 'proper' program can be solved using only the three *logic structures* ... 1. Sequence. 2. Selection. 3. Iteration."¹¹ "Böhm and Jacopini provided the theoretical framework by showing it possible to write any program using only three logic structures: DOWHILE, IFTHENELSE, and SEQUENCE."¹² "A basic fact about structured programming is that it is known to be possible to duplicate the action of any flowchartable program by a program which uses as few as three basic program figures, namely, a SEQUENCE, an IFTHENELSE, and a WHILEDO.... This fact is due to C. Böhm and G. Jacopini."¹³ "Structured programming is a technique of writing programs that is based on the theorem (proved by Böhm and Jacopini) that any program's logic, no matter how complex, can be unambiguously represented as a sequence of operations, using only three basic structures."¹⁴

Even the *Encyclopedia of Computer Science*, in the article on structured programming, says the same thing: "... a seminal paper by Böhm and Jacopini, who proved that every 'flowchart' (program), however complicated, could be rewritten in an equivalent way using only repeated or nested subunits of no more than three different kinds – a *sequence* of executable statements, a *decision* clause ... and an *iteration* construct."¹⁵

Why did the theorists misrepresent the original study? Why did they not insist on a complete reduction, to two constructs, just as Böhm and Jacopini did in their paper? Why, in other words, do they permit us to use the conditional construct, when the paper proved that it is *not* an elementary construct, and that it can be reduced to the iterative one?

---

⁹ Edward Yourdon, *Techniques of Program Structure and Design* (Englewood Cliffs, NJ: Prentice Hall, 1975), p. 146.

¹⁰ Clement L. McGowan and John R. Kelly, *Top-Down Structured Programming Techniques* (New York: Petrocelli/Charter, 1975), p. 5.

¹¹ Robert T. Grauer and Marshal A. Crawford, *The COBOL Environment* (Englewood Cliffs, NJ: Prentice Hall, 1979), p. 4.

¹² Gary L. Richardson, Charles W. Butler, and John D. Tomlinson, *A Primer on Structured Program Design* (New York: Petrocelli Books, 1980), p. 4.

¹³ Richard C. Linger and Harlan D. Mills, "On the Development of Large Reliable Programs," in *Current Trends in Programming Methodology*, vol. 1, *Software Specification and Design*, ed. Raymond T. Yeh (Englewood Cliffs, NJ: Prentice Hall, 1977), p. 122.

¹⁴ Donald A. Sordillo, *The Programmer's ANSI COBOL Reference Manual* (Englewood Cliffs, NJ: Prentice Hall, 1978), pp. 296–297.

¹⁵ Anthony Ralston and Edwin D. Reilly, eds., *Encyclopedia of Computer Science*, 3rd ed. (New York: Van Nostrand Reinhold, 1993), p. 1309.

To understand the reason, recall that characteristic feature of structured programming – the continual blending of formal and informal concepts. The theorists like the formal, mechanistic principles, so they invoke them whenever they want to make their claims appear "scientific." But, because software applications are non-mechanistic phenomena, the formal principles are useless; so the theorists are compelled to revert to the informal concepts.

Thus, it would be embarrassing to ask programmers to avoid conditional constructs, just because they are not elementary (that is, to replace them, in the name of science, with their unwieldy transformation into iterative constructs), seeing that programming languages already include the simple IF statement, designed specifically for implementing conditional constructs.

But programming languages also include the simple GOTO statement, designed specifically for implementing jumps, and hence non-elementary flow-control constructs. And yet, while permitting us to use IF, the theorists prohibit us from using GOTO. The explanation for the discrepancy is that asking us to avoid GOTO can be made to look scientific, while asking us to avoid IF can only look silly.

Mathematically, a flow diagram with GOTO statements is no different from one with IF statements, since both can be reduced, through similar transformations, to the same two elementary flow-control constructs. The theorists, though, consider the former to be "unstructured" and the latter "structured." This attitude – invoking the formal, precise principles when practical, and reverting to informal guidelines when the formal principles are inconvenient – is the essence of the fourth delusion, as we will soon see. At that point, many other non-elementary flow-control constructs will be permitted.

The academics and the gurus who routinely cite Böhm and Jacopini's paper probably never set eyes on it. Most likely, only a handful of theorists actually studied it, and, blinded by their mechanistic obsession, saw in it the proof for the possibility of a *science* of programming. The other theorists, and the authors and the teachers, accepted then uncritically this distorted interpretation and helped to spread it further. By the time it reached the books and the periodicals, the programmers and the managers, and the general public, no one was questioning the interpretation, or verifying it against the original ideas. (Few would have understood the original paper anyway, written as it is in a formal, and rather difficult and laconic, language.) Everyone was convinced that structured programming is an important theory, mathematically grounded on Böhm and Jacopini's work, when in reality it is just another mechanistic fantasy, grounded on a *misrepresentation* of that work.

And so it is how Böhm and Jacopini – humble authors of an abstract study of flow diagrams – became unwitting pioneers of the structured programming revolution.

5

For twenty years, in thousands of books, articles, and lectures, the software experts were promoting structured programming. To understand how it is possible to promote an invalid theory for twenty years, it may help to analyze the style of this promotion. Typically, the experts start their discussion by presenting the formal principles and the mathematical foundation; and, often, they mention Böhm and Jacopini's paper explicitly, as in the passages previously quoted. This serves to set a serious, authoritative tone; but then they continue with informal, childish arguments.

For example, the *Encyclopedia of Computer Science*,[16] after citing Böhm and Jacopini's "seminal paper," includes the following "principles" in the definition of structured programming: "judicious use of embedded comments" (notes to explain the program's logic); "a preference for straightforward, easily readable code over slightly more efficient but obtuse code"; modules no larger than about one page, "mostly for the sake of the human reader"; "careful organization of each such page into clearly recognizable paragraphs based on appropriate indentation" of the nested constructs (again, for ease of reading).

Some of these "principles" make good programming sense, but what have they to do with the theory of structured programming? Besides, if the validity of structured programming has been proved mathematically, why are these informal guidelines mentioned here? Or, conversely, if structured programming is no longer a formal theory and "may be defined as a methodological style,"[17] why mention Böhm and Jacopini's mathematical foundation? The formal and the informal arguments overlap continually. They appear to support each other, but in fact the informal ones are needed only because the formal theory does not work.

Incredibly, we also find the following requirement listed as a structured programming principle: "the ability to make assertions about key segments of a structured program so as to 'prove' that the program is correct."[18] The editors enclosed the word "prove" in quotation marks presumably because the principle only stipulates an informal verification, not a real proof. This principle, thus, is quite ludicrous, seeing that structured programming is

---

[16] The quotations in this paragraph are ibid., pp. 1309–1311.   [17] Ibid., p. 1308.
[18] Ibid., p. 1311.

supposed to guarantee *mathematically* (that is, with no qualifications) the correctness of software; it is supposed to guarantee, moreover, the correctness of the entire program, not just "key segments."

Another absurd principle is the permission to deviate from the standard constructs if this "removes a gross inefficiency."[19] It is illogical to suggest that what is, in fact, the main tenet of this theory – the standard constructs – may cause inefficiency and must be forsaken. This principle is an excellent example of pseudoscientific thinking: every situation where one must deviate from the standard constructs is a *falsification* of structured programming; and the experts suppress these falsifications by turning them into *features* of the theory – non-standard constructs.

Lastly, we are told that "still further evolution of [structured programming] is to be expected."[20] The editors seem to have forgotten that structured programming is a formally defined theory, so it cannot evolve. What can evolve is only the *interpretations* of the theory. Only pseudosciences evolve – expand, that is, and become increasingly vague, as their defenders add more and more "principles" in order to suppress the endless falsifications.

Instead of all these arguments, formal and informal, why don't the theorists simply show us how to develop perfect applications using nothing but neat structures of standard constructs? This, after all, was the promise of structured programming. The theorists promote it as a practical programming concept, but all they can show us is some small, artificial examples (which, presumably, is the only type of software *they* ever wrote). They leave it to us to prove its benefits with real, fifty-thousand-line applications.

It is also worth repeating that, while this discussion is concerned with events that took place in the 1970s and 1980s, the principles of structured programming are being observed today as faithfully as they were then. Current textbooks and courses, for instance, avoid GOTO as carefully as did the earlier ones. In other words, despite their failure, these principles were incorporated into every programming theory and methodology that followed, and are now part of our programming culture. The irresistible appeal that structured programming has to the software bureaucrats, notwithstanding the popularity of more recent theories, can be understood only by recognizing its unique blend of mathematical pretenses and trivial principles. Thus, simply by talking about top-down design or about GOTO, ignorant academics, programmers, and managers can feel like scientists.

[19] Ibid., p. 1310.   [20] Ibid.

The Fourth Delusion

1

The fourth delusion is the absurd notion of *inconvenience*. The theorists continue to maintain that the principles of structured programming are sound, and the reason it is so difficult to follow them is just the inconvenience of the restriction to standard constructs. They note that structured programming works in simple situations – in their textbook illustrations, for instance. And they also note that the definition of structured programming guarantees its success for programs of any size: all we have to do is combine constructs and modules on higher and higher levels of nesting. So, they conclude, there is nothing wrong with the theory. If we find it increasingly difficult to follow its principles as we move to larger programs – and entirely impractical in serious business applications – we must simply disregard as many of these principles as is necessary to render the theory serviceable.

In particular, the theorists say, we don't have to *actually* restrict ourselves to standard constructs. Their justification for allowing non-standard constructs is this: We know that it is possible, in principle, to develop any application with standard constructs alone. And we know that, in principle, non-standard constructs can be reduced to standard ones through transformations. Why, then, restrict ourselves to the standard constructs? We will enjoy the benefits of structured programming even if we use the more convenient non-standard constructs.

Clearly, the theorists fail to appreciate the absurdity of this line of logic: if structured programming is promoted as a programming theory, the fact that its principles are impractical means that the theory is wrong. As was the case with the previous delusions, the theorists can deny this falsification of structured programming only by concocting an absurd explanation. The benefits of structured programming were only shown to emerge if we *actually* build our applications as hierarchies of standard constructs. If we agree to forgo its principles whenever found to be inconvenient, those benefits will vanish, and we no longer have a theory. What is left then is just some informal guidelines, not very different from what we had *before* structured programming.

The response should have been to determine *why* it is so difficult to apply these principles. We don't find it difficult to apply mechanistic principles in those fields where the mechanistic model is indeed practical – in engineering, for instance. We don't find these principles inconvenient with physical systems, or with electronic systems, so why are they inconvenient with *software* systems?

For mechanistic phenomena, the simple hierarchical structure works well no matter how large is the system. In fact, the larger the system, the more important it is to have a mechanistic model. When building a *toy* airplane, for example, we may well find it inconvenient to follow strictly the hierarchical principle of subassemblies, and impractical to adhere strictly to the mathematical principles of aerodynamics; but we couldn't build a jumbo jet without these principles. With software systems the problem is reversed: the mechanistic principles of structured programming seem to work in simple cases, but break down in large, serious applications.

The inconvenience is due, as we know, to the non-mechanistic nature of software applications. While the hierarchical structure is a good model for mechanistic phenomena, for non-mechanistic ones it is not: the approximation it provides is rarely close enough to be useful. What we notice with poor approximations is that the model works only in simple cases, or works in some cases but not in others. Thus, the fact that structured programming fails in serious applications while appearing to work in simple situations indicates that software systems cannot be usefully represented with a simple hierarchical structure.

Structured programming fails because it attempts to reduce software applications, which consist of many interacting structures, to *one* structure. It starts by taking into account only the flow-control structures and ignoring the others. And then it goes even further and recognizes only one flow-control structure – the nesting scheme. But this reified model cannot represent accurately enough the complex structure that is the actual application.

2

Let us examine some of the non-standard constructs that were incorporated into structured programming, and their justification. The simplest example is a loop where the terminating condition is tested *after* the operation – rather than before it, as in the standard iterative construct (see figure 7-11). Although this construct can be reduced to the standard one by means of a transformation,[1] most programming languages provide statements for both. And since these statements are equally simple, and the two types of loops are equally common in applications, the theorists could hardly ask us to use one construct and avoid the other. The justification for permitting the non-standard one, thus, is the inconvenience of the transformation: "Do we need both iteration

---

[1] There is one transformation based on memory variables, and another based on duplicating operations. The latter, for instance, is as follows: convert the non-standard construct into a standard one that has the same operation and condition, *S1* and *C1*, and add in front of it an operation identical to *S1*.

variants? The Böhm-Jacopini theorem says 'no,' but that theorem addresses only constructibility and not convenience. For this reason, programmers like to have both variants."[2]

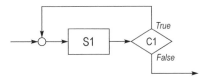

Figure 7-11

Another example is the conditional construct CASE, shown in figure 7-12. A variable, or the result of an expression, is compared with several values; a certain sequential construct (a statement, or a block of statements) is specified for each value, and only the one for which the comparison is successful is actually executed.[3]

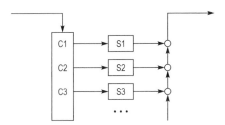

Figure 7-12

Again, we could use the standard conditional construct instead: we would specify a series of consecutive IF statements and perform the comparison with each value in turn. When only a few values are involved, this solution (or the alternative solution of nesting a second IF in the ELSE part of the previous one, and so on) is quite effective. But there are situations where we must specify many values, sometimes more than a hundred; the CASE construct is then more convenient (and also more efficient, because the compiler can optimize the comparisons).

[2] Anthony Ralston and Edwin D. Reilly, eds., *Encyclopedia of Computer Science*, 3rd ed. (New York: Van Nostrand Reinhold, 1993), p. 1310.
[3] The term "CASE" refers to the different cases, or alternatives, handled by this construct. An additional alternative (the default) is usually included to allow for the case when none of the comparisons is successful.

The most embarrassing problem for structured programming, however, is the ordinary loop, one of the most common software constructs. Practically every statement in a typical application is part of a loop of some sort, its execution repeated under the control of various conditions. And it is not just inconvenient, but totally impractical, to reduce all forms of repetitive execution to the standard iterative construct. We already saw how the need to specify the terminating condition at the end of the loop led to the acceptance of a new construct. But this is only *one* of the situations that cannot be managed with the standard construct. Just as common is the situation where the terminating condition is in the middle of the loop, or where there are conditions throughout the loop, or where a condition terminates the current iteration but not the loop. Since the standard construct cannot handle these situations, we must either perform some complicated transformations, or add to programming languages a new construct for each situation, or resort to explicit jumps (GOTO statements) and create our own, specialized constructs.

The problem is even more serious in the case of *nested* loops. A loop nested within another is nearly as frequent as a single loop, and even three and four levels of nesting are common. Thus, since the situations previously mentioned can occur at all levels, without explicit jumps even more complicated transformations would be required, or dozens of constructs would have to be added to cover all possible combinations.

In the end, the software theorists adopted all three methods: they incorporated into structured programming a small number of built-in constructs (typically, a statement that lets us terminate the iterations, and a statement that lets us terminate just the current iteration, from anywhere in the loop); they recommend transformations in the other situations; and they permit the use of GOTO when the first two methods are impractical.

Nearly as difficult as the combination of loops and conditions is the combination of conditions alone. Although we could, in principle, express all combinations by nesting IF-THEN-ELSE statements, this often leads to unwieldy transformations, or too many nesting levels, or huge blocks of statements in the THEN or ELSE part. A common requirement, for instance, is to terminate prematurely the current block or the current module. As in the case of loops, we can implement this requirement through transformations, or by adding to the language new constructs, or with explicit jumps. The theorists, in the end, incorporated into structured programming such constructs as EXIT and RETURN, which terminate a module; but we must still use transformations to terminate a block, unless the transformations are especially awkward, in which case we are permitted to use GOTO.

❖

The following quotations illustrate how the advocates of structured programming justify the adoption of non-standard constructs. The fact that we need these constructs at all proves that the theory of structured programming has failed. The constructs, though, are presented as "extensions" of the theory. They are substantially "in the spirit" of structured programming, we are told, and the only reason we need them is to make structured programming easier, or more practical, or more convenient. This explanation is illogical, of course: one cannot claim that non-standard constructs make structured programming easier, when the very essence of structured programming is the *absence* of non-standard constructs. What these experts are doing, in effect, is promoting the principles of structured programming, praising their benefits, and then showing us how to override them.

Edward Yourdon, one of the best-known experts, has this to say: "While the [three standard constructs] are sufficient to write any computer program, a number of organizations have found it practical to add some 'extensions.'"[4] And after describing some of these "extensions," Yourdon concludes: "A number of other modifications or compromises of the basic structured programming theory could be suggested and probably *will* be suggested as more programming organizations gain familiarity with the concept. As indicated, many of the compromises do not violate the black-box principle behind the original Böhm and Jacopini structures; other compromises *do* represent a violation and should be allowed only under extenuating circumstances."[5]

Note again the misrepresentation of Böhm and Jacopini's paper. What Yourdon calls the black-box principle – namely, the restriction to constructs with one entry and exit, which allows us to ignore their internal details and nest them hierarchically – is not a principle but a *consequence* of Böhm and Jacopini's theorem. (I will return to this point later.) Yourdon cites their work, but ignores the *real* principle – the restriction to nested *standard* constructs. Böhm and Jacopini did not say that we can use any construct that has one entry and exit. Yourdon invokes an exact theorem, but feels free to treat it as an informal rule: we can add to the theorem any "extensions," "modifications," and "compromises" (and, "under extenuating circumstances," violate even what is left of it), and the result continues to be called structured programming.

Here is another author who expresses the same view: "Although it is theoretically possible to write all well-formed programs using nothing more than the three basic logic structures shown here, we will find that programming is easier if we expand our repertoire a little. Extensions to the three basic logic structures are permitted as long as they retain the one-entry, one-exit

---

[4] Edward Yourdon, *Techniques of Program Structure and Design* (Englewood Cliffs, NJ: Prentice Hall, 1975), p. 149.   [5] Ibid., p. 152.

property."[6] And here is another misrepresentation of Böhm and Jacopini's work: "The legitimate code blocks using structured programming theory are as follows: 1. SEQUENCE .... 2. IFTHENELSE .... 3. DOWHILE .... 4. DOUNTIL .... 5. CASE .... This basic set of logic structures is a practical extension of Böhm and Jacopini's original form, which proved theoretically that any problem can be broken down into small subproblems whose equivalent form can be expressed with only the first three logic types described above. However, from a practical coding viewpoint, all five logic types outlined above facilitate the process without destroying its basic intent."[7] So the authors of this book have decided that, in order to make structured programming practical, the original theorem should be interpreted as the combination of a "basic intent," which must be respected, and some other parts, which may be ignored.

Some additional examples of the same justifications: "Usually the restriction to allow only these three control constructs in a structured program is relaxed to include extensions such as the nested IF, the CASE statement, and the escape. Allowing these extensions makes the program easier to code and to maintain."[8] "To the three basic figures SEQUENCE, IF-THEN-ELSE, and DO-WHILE we have added for programming convenience the ITERATIVE-DO ... and the REPEAT-UNTIL, LOOP-EXITIF-ENDLOOP, and the SELECT-CASE figures."[9] "One should always try to solve the problem using the basic composition rules (sequencing, conditionals, repetition and recursion). If this does not give a good solution, then use of some of the special types of jumps is justified."[10] "In general, the dogmatic use of only the structured constructs can introduce inefficiency when an escape from a set of nested loops or nested conditions is required."[11] The best solution, the author explains, is to redesign the module so as to avoid this requirement; alternatively, though, the structured programming restrictions may be "violated in a controlled manner,"[12] because such a violation "can be accommodated without violating the spirit of structured programming."[13]

---

[6] Dennie Van Tassel, *Program Style, Design, Efficiency, Debugging, and Testing*, 2nd ed. (Englewood Cliffs, NJ: Prentice Hall, 1978), p. 76.

[7] Gary L. Richardson, Charles W. Butler, and John D. Tomlinson, *A Primer on Structured Program Design* (New York: Petrocelli Books, 1980), pp. 46–47.

[8] James Martin and Carma McClure, *Structured Techniques: The Basis for CASE*, rev. ed. (Englewood Cliffs, NJ: Prentice Hall, 1988), p. 46. (Regarding "nested IF," the authors are wrong, of course: this is the nesting of standard conditional constructs, and hence not an extension but *within* the concept of structured programming.)

[9] Clement L. McGowan and John R. Kelly, *Top-Down Structured Programming Techniques* (New York: Petrocelli/Charter, 1975), p. 76.

[10] Suad Alagić and Michael A. Arbib, *The Design of Well-Structured and Correct Programs* (New York: Springer-Verlag, 1978), p. 226.

[11] Roger S. Pressman, *Software Engineering: A Practitioner's Approach* (New York: McGraw-Hill, 1982), p. 246.   [12] Ibid.   [13] Ibid., p. 247.

So, with all useful constructs again permitted, what was left of the theory of structured programming was just some informal bits of advice on disciplined programming, supplemented with the exhortation to use standard constructs and avoid GOTO "as much as possible."

In general, whenever a programming language included some new, useful constructs, these constructs were enthusiastically adopted, simply because they obviated the need for GOTO. The jumps implicit in these constructs could be easily implemented with GOTO; but this alternative was considered bad programming, even as the constructs themselves were praised as good programming. Many theorists went so far as to describe these constructs as modern language enhancements that help us adhere to the principles of structured programming, when their role, clearly, is to help us *override* those principles. (The only jumps allowed in structured programming, we recall, are those implicit in the standard conditional and iterative constructs.) The absence of the phrase "go to" was enough to turn their jumps from bad to good programming, and the resulting programs from unstructured to structured.

Thus, despite the insistence that structured programming is more than just GOTO-less programming, this concern – contriving transformations or new constructs in order to avoid GOTO, or debating whether GOTO is permissible in a particular situation – became in fact the main preoccupation of both the academics and the practitioners.

Their reaction to what is in reality a blatant falsification of structured programming – the need for explicit jumps – clearly reveals the theorists' ignorance and dishonesty. Not only were they naive enough to believe that we can program without jumps, but they refused to accept the evidence when this was tried in actual applications. Even more than the difficulties encountered under the first three delusions, the apparent inconvenience of the standard constructs should have motivated them to question the validity of structured programming. Instead, they suppressed this falsification by reinstating the very feature that the original theory had excluded (the use of non-standard constructs), and on the exclusion of which its promises were based. The original dream, thus, was now impossible even if we forget that the previous delusions had already negated it. The theorists, nevertheless, continued to advertise structured programming with the same promises.

3

Returning to the previous quotations, what is striking is the lack of explanation. The theorists mention rather casually that the reason we are permitted to violate the principles of structured programming is the inconvenience of the standard constructs. They are oblivious to the absurdity of this justification; it doesn't occur to them that this inconvenience is an important clue, that we ought to study it rather than avoid it. Incredibly, they are convinced that if the theory of structured programming does not work, we can make it work simply by disregarding some of its principles. Specifically, those important transformations we discussed earlier need to be performed now only when convenient. We will derive the same benefits, the theorists say, whether we *actually* reduce the application to standard constructs, or simply know that *in principle* we could do it.

When we do find an explanation, it is the black-box principle that is invoked. This principle, we are told now, is the only important one: since any flow-control construct with one entry and one exit will function, for all practical purposes, just like a standard construct, there is no need to restrict ourselves to the standard constructs. We will enjoy the benefits of structured programming with *any* constructs that have one entry and one exit.[14]

We saw the meaning of a software "black box" in figures 7-4 to 7-8 (pp. 527, 538–541). A program is deemed structured if its flow diagram can be represented with nested boxes. Each box encloses a standard construct and can be treated as a separate software element. And, since the standard constructs have only one entry and exit, from the perspective of the flow of execution each box is in effect a sequential construct. Moreover, when studying a certain box from higher nesting levels, its internal details are immaterial; each element, therefore, can be programmed independently of the others.

This principle applies at all nesting levels, so the entire application can be developed simply by creating standard constructs: one construct at a time, one level at a time. The restriction to software elements with one entry and exit guarantees that, regardless of the number of nesting levels, the application can be represented as a perfect hierarchical structure. The ultimate benefit of this restriction, then, is that we can develop and prove our applications with the formal methods of mathematics: if each element is correct, and if the relations between levels (reflected in the single entries and exits) are correct, the application as a whole is bound to be correct.

---

[14] The term *black box* refers to a device, real or theoretical, that consists of an input, an output, and an internal process that is unknown, or is immaterial in the current context. All we can see, and all we need to know, is how the output changes as a function of the input. Strictly speaking, then, since software flow-control constructs do not have input and output, the theorists are wrong to describe them as black boxes: the entry and exit points seen in the diagram do not depict an input value converted by a process into an output value, but rather a construct's place relative to the other constructs in the sequence of execution. Only if taken in its most general and informal sense, simply as a device whose internal operation is immaterial, can the concept of a black box be used at all with software flow-control constructs.

Suddenly, then, it seems that the principles of structured programming can be relaxed: from a restriction to the standard constructs, to a restriction to any constructs that have one entry and exit. Incredibly, structured programming can be expanded from three to an infinity of constructs without having to give up any of its original benefits. Still, as we just saw, there is no obvious fallacy in this expansion; those benefits appear indeed attainable through any constructs that have one entry and exit. But this sudden freedom, this ease of expanding the theory, is precisely what should have *worried* the advocates of structured programming, what should have prompted them to doubt its soundness. Instead, they interpreted this apparent freedom as a *good* thing, as evidence of its *power*: we can now combine in one theory, they concluded, the strictness of a mathematical concept and the convenience needed in a practical programming methodology.

This freedom is an illusion, of course. It appears logical only if we study the new claim in isolation, only if we forget that the principles of structured programming had been refuted *before* the theorists discovered the inconvenience of the standard constructs. Thus, to recognize the fallacies inherent in the new delusion we must bear in mind the previous ones.

We note, first, that what the theorists call the black-box principle is not a principle at all; it is a corollary, a *consequence* of the principles of structured programming. Since the standard constructs have only one entry and exit, if we restrict ourselves to standard constructs the flow diagram will display this characteristic at every nesting level. The main principle is the restriction to the standard constructs. The theorists take what is one of the *results* of this principle (constructs with only one entry and exit) and make *it* the main principle. Then, they substitute for what is the *actual* restriction (the three standard constructs) a new, vague restriction.

The new restriction merely states that we should use non-standard constructs "as little as possible." The number of constructs varies from expert to expert: some permit only three or four (the minimum needed to alleviate the inconvenience of the standard ones), others permit a dozen, and some go so far as permitting *any* constructs with one entry and exit. Whether permitting few or many, though, this restriction is specious; it is not an exact principle, as was the restriction to standard constructs. In reality, if permitted to use a construct just because it has one entry and exit, it matters little whether we use one or a hundred: the issue now is, at best, one of programming style. But by counting, studying, and debating the new constructs, and by describing them as extensions of structured programming, the experts can delude themselves that they still have a theory.

❖

So the experts embraced the black-box principle because it allowed them to bypass the rigours of structured programming. For, once we annul the *real* principle (the restriction to standard constructs), *any* flow-control construct can be said to have only one entry and exit. Take the CASE construct, for instance – one of the first to be permitted in structured programming (see figure 7-12, p. 582). Its flow diagram contains one component with several exits; but, if we draw a rectangular box around the whole diagram, *that box* will have only one entry and exit.

The same trick, obviously, can be performed with any piece of software: first, we create the most effective or convenient construct, which will likely violate the principles of structured programming by containing parts with more than one entry or exit; then, we draw a box around the whole thing and declare it an extension of structured programming, because now it has only one entry and exit. It is entirely up to us to decide at what point this structuring method becomes silly.

All non-standard constructs are based, ultimately, on this trick. And every expert was convinced that structured programming could be saved by extending it in this fashion. To pick just one case, Jensen allows six non-standard constructs in *his* definition of structured programming.[15] One of these constructs, for example, is called POSIT, and its purpose is to replace a particular combination of conditional statements, which involves an unusual jump.[16] Jensen shows us how much simpler his POSIT is than using standard constructs and transformations, and he considers this to be sufficient justification for including it in structured programming. (The jump, of course, is even easier to implement with GOTO; the sole reason for his new construct is to avoid the GOTO.) But Jensen may well be the only expert who deems this particular instance of explicit jumps important enough to become an official construct. Some experts would recommend transformations, others would permit the use of GOTO, and others yet would suggest more than six non-standard constructs. Still, no one saw how absurd these ideas were. Clearly, if each expert is free to interpret the theory of structured programming in his own way, there is no limit to the number of variants that can be invented. Is structured programming, then, this open-ended collection of variants?

Significantly, the experts did not replace the original principle with a more flexible, but equally precise, one. The original principle was strict and simple: in only two situations – *within* the standard conditional and iterative constructs – can the flow diagram include a component with more than one entry or exit.

---

[15] Randall W. Jensen, "Structured Programming," in *Software Engineering*, eds. Randall W. Jensen and Charles C. Tonies (Englewood Cliffs, NJ: Prentice Hall, 1979), p. 238.

[16] Ibid., p. 250.

By adopting the black-box principle, the experts increased the number of permitted situations from two to an infinity.

And with this permission, structured programming finally became a practical concept: whenever we want to avoid an awkward transformation, we can simply use a language-specific construct, or create a specialized flow-control construct, and justify this by claiming that it is a logical extension of structured programming.

We recognize in the black-box principle the pseudoscientific stratagem of turning falsifications into features (see "Popper's Principles of Demarcation" in chapter 3): the theory is expanded by permitting those situations that would otherwise falsify it, and calling them new features. Thus, the black-box principle permits almost any constructs, while the principle of standard constructs permitted only three. As a result, constructs whose usefulness originally *falsified* the theory are now *features* of the theory. This saves the idea of structured programming from refutation, but at the price of making it unfalsifiable, and hence worthless.

4

It is even easier to understand the fourth delusion when we represent applications as systems of interacting software structures. Recall our discussion under the second delusion. The purpose of the standard conditional and iterative constructs is to provide alternatives to the flow of execution defined by the nesting scheme. Each alternative endows the application with a unique flow-control structure. And, since the actual flow of execution is affected by all the flow-control constructs in the application, it is in reality a system comprising all the individual flow-control structures (see pp. 555–559).

So the two standard constructs already make the flow of execution a complex structure. When we study the application from the perspective of the nesting scheme alone – when we study the flow diagram, for instance – what we see is elements neatly related through one hierarchical structure. But if some of these elements are conditional or iterative constructs, the actual flow of execution will comprise *many* structures. Each one of these structures differs from the nesting scheme only slightly, in one element of one particular flow-control construct.

As far as their effect on the flow of execution is concerned, then, there is indeed no difference between the standard and the non-standard flow-control constructs. Just like the standard ones, any flow-control construct provides, by means of jumps, alternatives to the flow of execution defined by the nesting scheme: each possible jump creates a different flow-control attribute, and hence a flow-control structure. In the standard constructs, the jumps are implicit. In non-standard constructs, the jumps can be both implicit (when we use built-in, language-specific constructs) and explicit (when we create our own constructs with GOTO).

Thus, in a certain sense, the software theorists are right to claim that any construct with one entry and one exit is a valid structured programming extension. Since constructs possessing this quality can be elements in a hierarchical structure, a nesting scheme that includes non-standard constructs remains a correct hierarchy. There is no fallacy in the claim that, within the nesting scheme, non-standard constructs function just like the standard ones. The fallacy, rather, is in the belief that the nesting scheme alone represents the flow of execution.

The reason it seems that we can add an infinity of extensions and still enjoy the benefits promised by structured programming is that those benefits were *already* lost, since the first delusion. If the application consists of interacting flow-control structures even when restricted to the standard constructs, this means that it cannot be represented mathematically in any case. So it is true that there is nothing to lose by allowing non-standard constructs. The extensions are logical, just as the theorists say, but for a different reason: they are logical, not because structured programming is valid both with and without them, but because it is *invalid* both with and without them.

The dream of structured programming was always to establish a direct, one-to-one correspondence between the static flow diagram and the actual flow of execution (see pp. 546–547). Since flow diagrams can be drawn as hierarchical structures, and hence represented with the exact tools of mathematics, such a correspondence means that the same model that describes mathematically the flow diagram would also describe the flow of execution, and therefore the behaviour of the *running* application.

So the restriction to one entry and exit is important to the theorists because it guarantees that all the elements in the application are related through a simple hierarchical structure. And indeed, this restriction makes the *flow diagram* a hierarchical structure. The theorists then mistakenly conclude that the flow of execution, formed as it is from the same elements and relations, will mirror at run time the flow diagram; so it too will be a hierarchical structure. The flow of execution, though, is the combination of all the flow-control structures in the application. We could perhaps represent mathematically *each one* of those structures. But even if we accomplished this, we still could not represent mathematically the complex structure that is their totality, and which is the only true model of the application's flow of execution. And we must not forget the other *types* of structures – structures based on shared data or operations, and on business or software practices – all interacting with one another and with the flow-control structures, and therefore affecting the application's performance.

It is only when we recognize the great complexity of software that we can appreciate how ignorant the software experts are, and how naive is their belief that the nesting scheme represents the flow of execution. As I pointed out earlier, the *theory* of structured programming was refuted in the first delusion, when this belief was born. The *movement* known as structured programming was merely the pursuit of the various delusions that followed. It was, thus, a fraud: a series of dishonest and futile attempts to defend an invalid mechanistic theory.

5

Our concept of software structures can also help us to understand why the restriction to standard constructs is, indeed, inconvenient. The theorists, we saw, make no attempt to explain the reason for this inconvenience. They correctly note that non-standard constructs are more convenient, but they don't feel there is a need to understand this phenomenon. They invoke their convenience to justify their use, but, ultimately, it is precisely this phenomenon – the difference in convenience between the standard and the non-standard constructs – that must be explained.

The few theorists who actually attempt to explain this phenomenon seem to conclude that, since non-standard constructs can be reduced to standard ones, they function as software subassemblies: non-standard constructs consist of combinations of standard ones in the same way that subassemblies consist of simpler parts in a *physical* structure. So they are more convenient in building software structures for the same reason it is more convenient to start with subassemblies than with individual parts when building *physical* structures. In short, non-standard constructs are believed to be at a higher level of abstraction than the standard ones.[17] Let us analyze this fallacy.

We saw, under the second delusion, that the theorists confuse the operations performed by the three standard constructs with the operations that define a

---

[17] Knuth, for example, expresses this mistaken view when he says that the various flow-control constructs represent in effect different levels of abstraction in a given programming language, and that we can resolve the inconvenience of the standard constructs simply by inventing some new, higher-level constructs. Donald E. Knuth, "Structured Programming with *go to* Statements," in *Computing Surveys* 6, no. 4 (©1974 ACM, Inc.): 295–296.

hierarchical structure; they confuse these constructs, thus, with the operations that create the elements of one level from those of the lower level. Now it seems that this confusion extends to the non-standard constructs.

The only operations that define software structures, we saw, are those performed by the *sequential* constructs, and those that invoke modules and subroutines; in other words, the kind of operations that combine software elements into larger elements, one level at a time (see pp. 555–556). This is how the application's nesting scheme is formed, and we can create hierarchical software structures of any size with sequential constructs alone. The conditional and iterative constructs do not perform the same kind of operation; they do not combine elements into larger, higher-level elements. Their role, in fact, is to *override* the operations performed by the sequential constructs, by providing alternatives to the nesting scheme. And they do it by endowing the software elements with flow-control attributes (in the form of jumps): each attribute gives rise to an additional flow-control structure.

The non-standard constructs, too, endow elements with flow-control attributes; so their role, too, is to create additional flow-control structures. The two kinds of constructs fulfil a similar function, therefore, and their relationship is not one of high to low levels.

So the theorists are correct when noting that the non-standard constructs are more convenient, but they are wrong about the reason: the convenience is *not* due to starting from higher levels of abstraction. Let us try to find the real explanation.

Whether we employ non-standard constructs or restrict ourselves to the standard ones, the application will have multiple, interacting flow-control structures. In either case, then, it is our mind that must solve the most difficult programming problem – dealing with the interactions between structures. Thus, even when following the principles of structured programming, our success depends largely on our skills and experience, not on the soundness of these principles.

The defenders of structured programming delude themselves when maintaining that a perfectly structured program can be represented with an exact, mechanistic model. The static flow-control structure – the nesting scheme depicted by the flow diagram – has perhaps a mathematical representation. But this cannot help us, since we must ensure that the dynamic, complex flow-control structure is correct; we must ensure, in other words, that all the individual flow-control structures, *and* their interactions, are correct. So the most difficult aspect of programming is precisely that aspect which *cannot* be represented mathematically, and which lies therefore beyond the scope of structured programming (or any other mechanistic theory).

The goal of all mechanistic software theories is to eliminate our dependence on the non-mechanistic capabilities of the mind, on such imprecise qualities as talent, skill, and experience. And the only way to eliminate this dependence is by treating software applications as simple structures, or as systems of separable structures. This is an illogical quest, however, because software structures *must* interact. Our affairs consist of interacting processes and events; so, if we want our software to mirror our affairs accurately, the software entities that make up applications must be related in several ways at the same time. The only way for software entities to have multiple relations is by sharing more than one attribute. And, since each attribute gives rise to a different structure, these entities will belong to several structures at the same time, causing them to interact.

Even within that one aspect of the application that is the flow of execution, we find the need for multiple, interacting structures: to represent our affairs, the application's elements must possess and share several *flow-control* attributes. Each flow-control attribute serves to relate a number of elements, from the perspective of the flow of execution, in a unique way. The nesting scheme is, in effect, a flow-control attribute shared by all the elements in the application. And we create the other flow-control attributes by introducing jumps in the flow of execution: each possible jump, whether explicit or implicit, gives rise to a unique flow-control attribute, and hence a different flow-control structure.

The standard conditional and iterative constructs, useful as they are, can provide only two types of jumps; so they can create only *some* of the flow-control relations between the application's elements, only *some* of the attributes. In order to mirror in software our affairs, we need more types of relations, and hence more types of flow-control attributes. We need, in other words, more types of jumps than those provided by the standard constructs. We can provide the additional relations with our own, explicit jumps, or with the implicit jumps found in some language-specific constructs. Or, if we want to avoid jumps altogether, as structured programming recommends, we can resort to transformations: we provide the additional relations then, not through flow-control attributes, but through attributes based on shared data or shared operations.

And herein lies the explanation for the inconvenience of the standard constructs and the transformations. We usually need *several* relations of other types to replace *one* flow-control relation. That is, instead of one flow-control attribute, our elements must have several attributes of other types in order to implement a given requirement. More precisely, to replace *one* flow-control attribute deriving from non-standard constructs, we need *one or more* flow-control attributes deriving from standard constructs, plus *one or more* attributes deriving from shared data or shared operations. Thus, since each attribute gives rise to a structure, we end up with more structures, and more interactions. While the additional complexity may be insignificant with only a few elements and attributes, as in a small piece of software, it becomes prohibitive in a serious application, because the number of interactions grows exponentially relative to the number of structures.

To make matters worse, the substitute relations are *less intuitive* than the flow-control ones. They do not reflect the actual relations – those relations we observe in our activities, and which we wanted to implement in software. The substitute relations are unnatural, in that they exist only between software elements, and are necessary only in order to satisfy an illogical principle.

Our programming languages, as a matter of fact, do permit us to implement the actual relations simply and naturally, but only if we use both standard and non-standard constructs. It is the restriction to standard constructs that creates artificial relations, and makes the application larger and more complicated.

Let us analyze a specific case: the requirement to exit an iterative construct depending on a condition encountered in the middle of the loop. The simplest way to implement this requirement is by jumping out of the loop with a GOTO. This jump, moreover, simulates naturally in software what we do in our everyday activities when we want to end a repetitive act. If, however, we want to avoid the explicit jump, we must use a memory variable as switch (this transformation is similar to the one shown in figure 7-8, p. 541). Instead of simply terminating the loop, the condition only sets the switch; the operations to the end of the loop are placed in the other branch of this condition, so they are bypassed; then, the switch is checked in the main condition, so the loop will end before the next iteration. This method is more complicated than a GOTO, but it is the one recommended by the advocates of structured programming.

In our everyday activities, we terminate a repetitive act simply by ending the repetition; we don't make a note about ending the repetition, go back to the beginning of the act as if we intended to repeat it, pretend to discover the note we made a moment earlier, and only then decide to end the repetition. A person who regularly behaved in this manner would be considered stupid. Yet, we are asked to display this behaviour in our *programming* activities. No wonder we find the transformations inconvenient – unnatural and impractical.

We need *thousands* of such transformations in a serious application. Still, the real difficulty is not the large number of *individual* transformations, but their *interactions*. We saw that the application remains a system of interacting structures, and that the transformations add even more structures. Thus, in addition to the original interactions, we must now deal with the interactions between the new structures, and between these and the original ones. So, when multiplying, transformations that individually are merely inconvenient become a major part of the application's logic. In the end, it is the transformations, rather than the actual requirements, that govern the application's design.

Since it is quite easy to implement *isolated* transformations, we can justify the additional effort by calling this activity "software engineering." Software engineering, though, becomes increasingly awkward as our applications grow in size and detail. So what we perceive then as a new problem – the impracticality of the transformations – is in reality the same phenomenon as in simple situations, where structured programming appears to work. The only difference is that we can disregard the inconvenience when slight, but must face it when it becomes a handicap.

The inconvenience of the restriction to standard constructs indicates that our mental effort, even when developing "structured" software, entails more than just following mechanistic principles. It indicates that we are also using our *non-mechanistic* capabilities. It indicates, therefore, that we are dealing with systems of interacting structures; for, were applications mechanistic in nature, the restriction to standard constructs would be *increasingly helpful* as they grew in size.

The phenomenon of inconvenience proves, then, that it is not the mechanistic principles of structured programming but *our mind* – our skills and experience – that we are relying on. This phenomenon proves, in other words, that the theory of structured programming is invalid. So, by misinterpreting the inconvenience, the theorists missed the fourth opportunity to recognize the fallaciousness of structured programming.

In conclusion, non-standard constructs are more convenient because they result in fewer structures and interactions for implementing the same requirements. We need a certain number of flow-control attributes in order to mirror in software a given combination of processes and events; and we end up with more attributes, and hence more structures, when replacing the flow-control attributes with attributes of other types. There is a limit to our capacity to process interacting structures in our mind, and we reach this limit much sooner when following the principles of structured programming.

The best programming method, needless to say, is the one that results in the fewest interactions. The promise of structured programming is to eliminate the interactions altogether, and thereby obviate the need for non-mechanistic thinking. But now we see that the opposite is taking place: programmers need even greater non-mechanistic capabilities – an even greater capacity to process complex structures – with structured programming than without it.

A simple, ten-line piece of software will be changed by structured programming into a slightly more involved piece of software. Thus, if we believe in some ultimate benefits, we will gladly accept the small increase in complexity. But this self-deception cannot help us in real-world situations. Because the complexity induced by structured programming grows exponentially, a serious application will become, not *slightly* more, but *much* more, involved. Creating and maintaining such an application is not just inconvenient but totally impractical. Moreover, because it is still a system of interacting structures, the application will still be impossible to represent mathematically. There are no ultimate benefits, and no one ever developed a serious application while rigorously adhering to the principles of structured programming.

In the end, structured programming turned the activities of programmers into a kind of game: searching for ways to avoid GOTO. The responsibility of programmers shifted, from creating useful applications and improving their skills, to merely conforming to a certain dogma. They were pleased with their success in performing transformations on isolated pieces of software, while reverting to non-standard constructs whenever the transformations were inconvenient. And they believed that this senseless programming style was structured programming; after all, even the experts were recommending it. Thus, just as the experts were deluding themselves that structured programming was a valid theory, the programmers could delude themselves that what they were practising was structured programming.

6

Let us examine, lastly, that aspect of the fourth delusion that is the continued belief in an exact, mathematical representation of software applications, when in fact no one ever managed to represent mathematically anything but small and isolated pieces of software. When a phenomenon is mechanistic, mathematics works just as well for large systems as it does for small ones. Thus, the fact that a mathematical theory that works for small pieces of software becomes increasingly impractical as software grows in size should have convinced the theorists that software systems give rise to *non-mechanistic* phenomena.

Take a trivial case: an IF statement where, for instance, a memory variable is either incremented or decremented depending on a condition. Even this simple construct, with just one condition and two elements, is related to the rest of the application through more than one structure; so it is part of a complex system. In its static representation, there are at least two logical connections between the two elements, and between these elements and the rest of the application: the flow-control structure, the structure based on the memory variable, and further structures if the condition itself entails variables, subroutines, etc. And in the *dynamic* representation there are at least three logical connections, because the condition's branches generate an additional structure. (We studied these structures under the second delusion.) We are dealing with a complex system; but because it is such a small system, we can identify all the structures and even some of the interactions. In real applications, however, we must deal with *thousands* of structures, most of them interacting with one another; and, while *in principle* we can still study these systems, we cannot *actually* do it. Many mechanistic delusions, we saw earlier, spring from the failure to appreciate this difference between simple and real-world situations (see p. 569).

Thus, even at this advanced stage, even after all the falsifications, many theorists remained convinced that structured programming allows us to develop and prove applications mathematically. The success of this idea in simple situations gave them hope that, with further work, we would be able to represent mathematically increasingly large pieces of software. Entire books have been written with nothing more solid than this belief as their foundation. In one example after another, we are shown how to prove the validity of a piece of software by reducing it to simpler entities, just as we do with mathematical problems. But these demonstrations are worthless, because the theorists recognize only one structure – the static nesting scheme, typically – and ignore the other relations that exist between the same software elements; they only prove, therefore, the validity of *one aspect* of that piece of software. So, even when correct, these demonstrations remain abstract studies and have no practical value. Whether empirical (using software transformations) or analytical (using mathematical logic), they rely on the fact that, in simple situations, those structures and interactions that we can identify constitute a major portion of the system. Thus, although their study only *approximates* the complex software phenomenon, for small pieces of software the approximation may well be close enough to be useful.

The theorists take the success of these demonstrations as evidence that it is possible to represent software mathematically: if the method works in simple cases, they say, the principles of reductionism and atomism guarantee its success for larger and larger pieces of software, and eventually entire applications. But the number of structures and interactions in real-world situations grows very quickly, and any method that relies on identifying and studying them separately is bound to fail. No one ever managed to prove, either empirically or analytically, the validity of a significant piece of software, let alone a whole application. The software mechanists remain convinced that mathematical programming is a practical concept, when, like the other mechanistic delusions, it is only valid in principle.[18]

In principle, then, it is indeed possible to develop and prove applications mathematically – just as it is possible, in principle, to predict future events through Laplacean determinism, or to explain human acts with the theories of behaviourism, or to depict social phenomena with the theories of structuralism, or to represent languages with Chomskyan linguistics. But *actually* using a mathematical programming theory – just like using those other theories – is *inconvenient*.

The mathematical representation of software, thus, is treated by the theorists just like the restriction to standard constructs: they show that it works in simple, isolated cases; they believe that the principles of structured programming assure its success in *actual* applications; and they refuse to see its failure in actual applications as evidence that structured programming does *not* work.

So the conclusion we must draw from the fourth delusion is that structured programming *never* works, not even in those situations where we do *not* find it inconvenient. Even requirements simple enough to program with standard constructs alone, and simple enough to represent mathematically, give rise to multiple, interacting structures. But because in these situations we can identify the structures and the interactions, we can delude ourselves that we are dealing with a mechanistic phenomenon. The fourth delusion, then, can also be described as the belief that structured programming is inconvenient only in certain situations, while in reality the inconvenience is *always* present. We just don't notice it, or don't mind it, for simple requirements.

Simple requirements, in fact, can be programmed with mechanistic knowledge alone, if we follow a method that takes into account the most important structures and interactions. Thus, we often hear the remark that inexperienced programmers find it easier than experienced ones to adapt to the rigours of structured programming. As usual, the theorists misinterpret this fact. Experienced programmers dislike structured programming, the theorists say, because they are accustomed to the old-fashioned, undisciplined style of programming. Actually, experienced programmers dislike structured programming because they already possess superior, *non-mechanistic* knowledge, which

---

[18] It must be noted that this fallacy affected, not just the specific theory known as structured programming, but *all* theories based on structures of nested constructs. As example, here is a methodology that claims to validate mathematically entire applications, and an actual development system based on it: James Martin, *System Design from Provably Correct Constructs* (Englewood Cliffs, NJ: Prentice Hall, 1985).

exceeds the benefits of a mechanistic theory. Inexperienced programmers possess no knowledge at all, or a modicum of *mechanistic* knowledge; so they like structured programming because they indeed accomplish more with it than without it. But substituting rules and methods for skills and experience can benefit them only in *simple* situations. Ultimately, with serious applications, programmers possessing non-mechanistic knowledge easily outperform those who attempt to practise strict structured programming.

This, incidentally, explains also why CASE (the promise of automatic software generation) works in simple situations while failing for real-world applications. Only by following precise rules and methods – that is, by treating software as a mechanistic phenomenon – can a device convert requirements into applications. (Software devices, thus, display the same type of behaviour as inexperienced programmers.) In simple situations, the device can account for most interactions; but this method of programming breaks down when tried with serious applications, where the number of interactions is practically infinite.

Mathematics can represent large systems as easily as it can small ones. This is why phenomena that are truly mechanistic can be represented mathematically no matter how many elements, levels, and relations are involved. But, because software phenomena are *not* mechanistic, mechanistic theories only *appear* to represent software systems mathematically. When practical at all, they work merely by accounting for the individual interactions – not through general principles, like the truly useful mathematical theories.[19]

The *GOTO* Delusion

1

There is no better way to conclude our discussion of the structured programming delusions than with an analysis of the GOTO delusion – the prohibition and the debate.

We have already encountered the GOTO delusion: under the third delusion, we saw that the reason for transformations was simply to avoid GOTOs; and under the fourth delusion, we saw that the reason for introducing non-standard constructs into structured programming was, again, to avoid GOTOs.

---

[19] A related fallacy is the idea of *software metrics* – the attempt to measure the complexity of an application by counting and weighing in various ways the conditions, iterations, subroutines, etc., that make it up. Like the mathematical fallacy, these measurements reflect individual aspects of the application, not their interactions; so the result is a poor approximation of the *actual* complexity.

The GOTO delusion, however, deserves a closer analysis. The most famous problem in the history of programming, and unresolved to this day, this delusion provides a vivid demonstration of the ignorance and dishonesty of the software theorists. They turned what is the most blatant falsification of structured programming – the need for explicit jumps in the flow of execution – into its most important feature: new flow-control constructs that hide the jumps within them. The sole purpose of these constructs is to perform jumps without using GOTO statements. Thus, while purposely designed to help programmers *override* the principles of structured programming, these constructs were described as language enhancements that *facilitate* structured programming.

Turning falsifications into features is how fallacious theories are saved from refutation (see "Popper's Principles of Demarcation" in chapter 3). The GOTO delusion alone, therefore, ignoring all the others, is enough to characterize structured programming as a pseudoscience.

Clearly, if it was proved mathematically that structured programming needs no GOTOs, the very fact that a debate is taking place indicates that structured programming has failed as a practical programming concept. In the end, the GOTO delusion is nothing but the denial of this reality, a way for the theorists and the practitioners to cling to the idea of structured programming years and decades after its failure.

It is difficult for a lay person to appreciate the morbid obsession that was structured programming, and its impact on our programming practices. Consider, first, the direct consequence: programmers were more preoccupied with the "principles" of structured programming – with trivial concepts like top-down design and avoiding GOTO – than with the actual applications they were supposed to develop, and with improving their skills. A true mass madness possessed the programming community in the 1970s – a madness which the rest of society was unaware of. We can recall this madness today by studying the thousands of books and papers published during that period, something well worth doing if we want to understand the origins of our software bureaucracy. All universities, all software experts, all computer publications, all institutes and associations, and management in all major corporations were praising and promoting structured programming – even as its claims and promises were being falsified in a million instances every day, and the only evidence of usefulness consisted of a few anecdotal and distorted "success stories."

The worst consequence of structured programming, though, is not what happened in the 1970s, but what has happened *since* then. For, the incompetence and irresponsibility engendered by this worthless theory have remained the distinguishing characteristic of our software culture. As programmers and managers learned nothing from the failure of structured programming, they accepted with the same enthusiasm the following theories, which suffer in fact from the same fallacies.

2

Recall what is the GOTO problem. We need GOTO statements in order to implement explicit jumps in the flow of execution, and we need explicit jumps in order to create non-standard flow-control constructs. But explicit jumps and non-standard constructs are forbidden under structured programming. If we restrict ourselves to the three standard constructs, the theorists said at first, we will need no explicit jumps, and hence no GOTOs. We may have to subject our requirements to some awkward transformations, but the benefits of this restriction are so great that the effort is worthwhile.

The theorists started, thus, by attempting to replace the application's flow-control structures with structures based on shared data or shared operations; in other words, to replace the unwanted flow-control relations between elements with relations of other types. Then, they admitted that it is impractical to develop applications in this fashion, and rescued the idea of structured programming by permitting the use of *built-in* non-standard constructs; that is, constructs already present in a particular programming language. These constructs, specifically prohibited previously, were described now as *extensions* of the original theory, as *features* of structured programming. Only the use of GOTO – that is, creating our own constructs – continued to be prohibited.

The original goal of structured programming had been to eliminate *all* jumps, and thereby restrict the flow-control relations between elements to those defined by a single hierarchical structure. This is what the restriction to a nesting scheme of standard flow-control constructs was thought to accomplish – mistakenly, as we saw under the second delusion, because the *implicit* jumps present in these constructs already create multiple flow-control structures. Apart from this fallacy, though, it is illogical to permit *built-in* non-standard constructs while prohibiting *our own* constructs. For, just as there is no real difference between standard constructs and non-standard ones, there is no real difference between built-in non-standard constructs and those we create ourselves. All these constructs fulfil, in the end, the same function: they create additional flow-control structures in order to provide alternatives to the flow of execution established by the nesting scheme. Thus, all that the built-in constructs accomplish is to relate elements through implicit rather than explicit jumps. So they render the GOTOs unnecessary, not by *eliminating* the unwanted jumps, but by turning the *explicit* unwanted jumps into *implicit* unwanted ones. The unwanted relations between elements, therefore, and the multiple flow-control structures, remain.

The goal of structured programming, thus, was now reversed: from the restriction to standard constructs – the absence of GOTO being then merely a consequence – to searching for ways to replace GOTOs with implicit jumps; in other words, from *avoiding* non-standard constructs, to seeking and praising them. More and more constructs were introduced, but everyone agreed in the end that it is impractical to provide GOTO substitutes for all conceivable situations. So GOTO itself was eventually reinstated, with the severe admonition to use it "only when absolutely necessary." The theory of structured programming was now, in effect, defunct. Incredibly, though, it was precisely at this point that it generated the greatest enthusiasm and was seen as a programming revolution. The reason, obviously, is that it was only at this point – only after its fundamental principles were annulled – that it could be used at all in practical situations.

The GOTO delusion, thus, is the belief that the preoccupation with GOTO is an essential part of a structured programming project. In reality, the idea of structured programming had been refuted, and the use or avoidance of GOTO is just a matter of programming style. What had started as a precise, mathematical theory was now an endless series of arguments on whether GOTO or a transformation or a built-in construct is the best method in one situation or another. And, while engaged in these childish arguments, the theorists and the practitioners called their preoccupation structured programming, and defended it on the strength of the original, mathematical theory.[1]

Let us see first some examples of the GOTO prohibition – that part of the debate which claims, without any reservation, that GOTO leads to bad programming, and that structured programming means avoiding GOTO: "The primary *technique* of structured programming is the elimination of the GOTO statement

---

[1] For example, as late as 1986, and despite the blatant falsifications, the theorists were discussing structured programming just as they had been discussing it in the early 1970s: it allows us to prove mathematically the correctness of applications, write programs that work perfectly the first time, and so on. Then, as evidence, they mention a couple of "success stories" (using, thus, the type of argument used to advertise weight-loss gadgets on television). See Harlan D. Mills, "Structured Programming: Retrospect and Prospect," in *Milestones in Software Evolution*, eds. Paul W. Oman and Ted G. Lewis (Los Alamitos, CA: IEEE Computer Society Press, ©1990 IEEE), pp. 286–287 – paper originally published in *IEEE Software* 3, no. 6 (1986): 58–66. See also Harlan D. Mills, Michael Dyer, and Richard C. Linger, "Cleanroom Software Engineering," in *Milestones*, eds. Oman and Lewis, pp. 217–218 – paper originally published in *IEEE Software* 4, no. 5 (1987): 19–24.

and its replacement with a number of other, well-structured branching and control statements."[2] "The freedom offered by the GOTO statement has been recognized as not in keeping with the idea of structures in control flow. For this reason we will *never* use it."[3] "If a programmer actively endeavours to program without the use of GOTO statements, he or she is less likely to make programming errors."[4] "By eliminating *all* GOTO statements, we can do even better, as we shall see."[5] "In order to obtain a simple structure for each segment of the program, GOTO statements should be avoided."[6] "Using the techniques of structured programming, the GOTO or branch statement is avoided entirely."[7]

And the *Encyclopedia of Computer Science* offers us the following (wrong and silly) analogy as an explanation for the reason why we must avoid GOTO: it makes programs hard to read, just like those articles on the front page of a newspaper that are continued (with a sort of "go to") to another page. Then the editors conclude: "At least some magazines are more considerate, however, and always finish one thought (article) before beginning another. Why can't programmers? Their ability to do so is at the heart of structured programming."[8]

It is not difficult to understand why the subject of GOTO became such an important part of the structured programming movement. After all the falsifications, what was left of structured programming was just a handful of trivial concepts: top-down design, hierarchical structures of software elements, constructs with only one entry and exit, etc. These concepts were then supplemented with a few other, even less important ones: indenting the nested elements in the program's listing, inserting comments to explain the program's logic, restricting modules to a hundred lines, etc. The theorists call these concepts "principles," but these simple ideas are hardly the basis of a programming theory. Some are perhaps a *consequence* of the original structured programming principles, but they are not principles themselves.

[2] Edward Yourdon, *Techniques of Program Structure and Design* (Englewood Cliffs, NJ: Prentice Hall, 1975), p. 145.

[3] J. N. P. Hume and R. C. Holt, *Structured Programming Using PL/1*, 2nd ed. (Reston, VA: Reston, 1982), p. 82.

[4] Ian Sommerville, *Software Engineering*, 3rd ed. (Reading, MA: Addison-Wesley, 1989), p. 32.

[5] Gerald M. Weinberg et al., *High Level COBOL Programming* (Cambridge, MA: Winthrop, 1977), p. 43.

[6] Dennie Van Tassel, *Program Style, Design, Efficiency, Debugging, and Testing*, 2nd ed. (Englewood Cliffs, NJ: Prentice Hall, 1978), p. 78.

[7] Nancy Stern and Robert A. Stern, *Structured COBOL Programming*, 7th ed. (New York: John Wiley and Sons, 1994), p. 13.

[8] Anthony Ralston and Edwin D. Reilly, eds., *Encyclopedia of Computer Science*, 3rd ed. (New York: Van Nostrand Reinhold, 1993), p. 1308.

To appreciate this, imagine that the only structured programming concepts we ever knew were top-down design, hierarchical structures, indenting statements, etc. Clearly, no one would call it a programming revolution on the strength of these concepts. It was the promise of precision and rigour that made it famous – the promise of developing and proving software applications mathematically.

So, now that what was left of structured programming was only the trivial concepts, the preoccupation with GOTO provided a critical substitute for the original, strict principles: it allowed both the theorists and the practitioners to delude themselves that they were still pursuing a serious idea. GOTO-less programming is the only remnant of the formal theory, so it serves as a link to the original claims, to the promise of mathematical programming.

The formal theory, however, was about structures of standard constructs, not about avoiding GOTO. All the theory says is that, if we adhere to these principles, we will end up with GOTO-less programs. The defenders of structured programming violate the strict principles (because impractical), and direct their efforts instead to what was meant to be merely a *consequence* of those principles. By restricting and debating the use of GOTO, and by contriving substitutes, they hope now to attain the same benefits as those promised by the formal theory.

Here are some examples of the attempt to ground the GOTO prohibition on the original, mathematical principles: "A theorem proved by Böhm and Jacopini tells us that any program written using GOTO statements can be transformed into an equivalent program that uses only the [three] structured constructs."[9] "Böhm and Jacopini showed that essentially any control flow can be achieved without the GOTO by using appropriately chosen sequential, selection, and repetition control structures."[10] "Dijkstra's [structured programming] proposal could, indeed, be shown to be theoretically sound by previous results from [Böhm and Jacopini,] who had showed that the control logic of any flowchartable program ... could be expressed without GOTOs, using sequence, selection, and iteration statements."[11]

We saw under the third delusion that the theorists *misrepresent* Böhm and Jacopini's work (see pp. 571–575). Thus, invoking their work to support the GOTO prohibition is part of the misrepresentation.

---

[9] Doug Bell, Ian Morrey, and John Pugh, *Software Engineering: A Programming Approach* (Hemel Hempstead, UK: Prentice Hall, 1987), p. 14.

[10] Ralston and Reilly, *Encyclopedia*, p. 361.

[11] Harlan D. Mills, "Structured Programming: Retrospect and Prospect," in *Milestones in Software Evolution*, eds. Paul W. Oman and Ted G. Lewis (Los Alamitos, CA: IEEE Computer Society Press, ©1990 IEEE), p. 286 – paper originally published in *IEEE Software* 3, no. 6 (1986): 58–66.

606 STRUCTURED PROGRAMMING

❖

The GOTO preoccupation, then, was the answer to the failure of the formal theory. By degrading the definition of structured programming from exact principles to a preoccupation with GOTO, everyone appeared to be practising scientific programming while pursuing in reality some trivial and largely irrelevant ideas.

It is important to note that the absurdity of the GOTO delusion is not so much in the idea of avoiding GOTO, as in the never-ending debates and arguments *about* avoiding it: in which situations should it be permitted, and in which ones forbidden. Had the GOTO avoidance been a strict prohibition, it could have been considered perhaps a serious principle. In that case, we could have agreed perhaps to redefine structured programming as programming without the use of explicit jumps. But, since a strict GOTO prohibition is impractical, what started as a principle became an informal rule: the exhortation to avoid it "as much as possible." The prohibition, in other words, was to be enforced only when the GOTO alternatives were not too inconvenient.

An even more absurd manifestation of the GOTO delusion was the attempt to avoid GOTO by replacing it with certain built-in, language-specific constructs, which perform in fact the same jumps as GOTO. The purpose of avoiding GOTO had been to avoid all jumps in the flow of execution, not to replace explicit jumps with implicit ones. Thus, in their struggle to save structured programming, the theorists ended up interpreting the idea of avoiding GOTO as a requirement to avoid the *phrase* "go to," not the jumps. I will return to this point later.

Recognizing perhaps the shallowness of the GOTO preoccupation, some theorists were defending structured programming by insisting that the GOTO prohibition is only *one* of its principles. Thus, the statement we see repeated again and again is that structured programming is "more" than just GOTO-less programming: "The objective of structured programming is much more far reaching than the creation of programs without GOTO statements."[12] "There is, however, much more to structured programming than modularity and the elimination of GOTO statements."[13] "Indeed, there *is* more to structured programming than eliminating the GOTO statement."[14]

These statements, though, are specious. They sound as if "more" meant the original, mathematical principles. But, as we saw, those principles were falsified. So "more" can only mean the *trivial* principles – top-down design

[12] James Martin and Carma McClure, *Structured Techniques: The Basis for CASE*, rev. ed. (Englewood Cliffs, NJ: Prentice Hall, 1988), p. 39.
[13] L. Wayne Horn and Gary M. Gleason, *Advanced Structured COBOL: Batch and Interactive* (Boston: Boyd and Fraser, 1985), p. 1.   [14] Yourdon, *Techniques*, p. 140.

and nested constructs, writing and documenting programs clearly, etc. – which had replaced the original ones.

The degradation from a formal theory to trivial principles is also seen in the fact that the term "structured" was commonly applied now, not just to programs restricted to certain flow-control constructs, but to almost any software-related activity. Thus, in addition to structured programming, we had structured coding, structured techniques, structured analysis, structured design, structured development, structured documentation, structured flow-charts, structured requirements, structured specifications, structured English (for writing the specifications), structured walkthrough (visual inspection of the program's listing), structured testing, structured maintenance, and structured meetings.

3

To summarize, there are three aspects to the GOTO delusion. The first one is the reversal in logic: from the original principle that applications be developed as structures of standard constructs, to the stipulation that applications be developed without GOTO. The GOTO statement is not even mentioned in the original theory; its absence is merely a consequence of the restriction to standard constructs. Thus, the first aspect of the GOTO delusion is the belief that a preoccupation with ways to avoid GOTO can be a substitute for an adherence to the original principle.

The second aspect is the belief that avoiding GOTO need not be a strict, formal principle: we should strive to avoid it, but we may use it when its elimination is inconvenient. So, if the first belief is that we can derive the same benefits by avoiding GOTO as we could by restricting applications to standard constructs, the second belief is that we can derive the same benefits if we avoid GOTO only when it is convenient to do so. The second aspect of the GOTO delusion can also be described as the fallacy of making two contradictory claims: the claim that GOTO is harmful and must be banned (which sounds scientific and evokes the original theory), and the claim that GOTO is sometimes acceptable (which turns the GOTO prohibition from a fantasy into a practical method). Although in reality the two claims cancel each other, they appear to express important programming concepts.

Lastly, the third aspect of the GOTO delusion is the attempt to avoid GOTO, not by *eliminating* those programming situations that require jumps in the flow of execution, but by replacing GOTO with some new constructs, specifically designed to perform those jumps in its stead. The third aspect, thus, is the belief that we can derive the same benefits by converting explicit jumps into implicit ones, as we could with no jumps at all; in other words, the belief that it is not the jumps, but just the GO TO statement, that must be avoided.

❖

We already saw examples of the first aspect of the GO TO delusion – those statements simply asserting that structured programming means programming without GO TO (see pp. 603–604). Let us see now some examples of the second aspect; namely, claiming at the same time that GO TO must be avoided and that it may be used.

The best-known case is probably that of E. W. Dijkstra himself. One of the earliest advocates of structured programming, Dijkstra is the author of the famous paper "Go To Statement Considered Harmful." We have already discussed this paper (see pp. 522–523), so I will only repeat his remark that he was "convinced that the GO TO statement should be abolished from all 'higher level' programming languages"[15] (in order to make it *impossible* for programmers to use it, in *any* situation). He reasserted this on every opportunity, so much so that his "memorable indictment of the GO TO statement" is specifically mentioned in the citation for the Turing award he received in 1972.[16]

Curiously, though, *after* structured programming became a formal theory – that is, when it was claimed that Böhm and Jacopini's paper vindicated mathematically the abolition of GO TO – Dijkstra makes the following remark: "Please don't fall into the trap of believing that I am terribly dogmatical about [the GO TO statement]."[17]

Now, anyone can change his mind. Dijkstra, however, did not change his mind about the validity of structured programming, but only about the strictness of the GO TO prohibition. Evidently, faced with the impossibility of programming without explicit jumps, he now believes that we can enjoy the benefits of structured programming whether or not we restrict ourselves to the standard constructs. Thus, the popularity of structured programming was unaffected by his change of mind. Those who held that GO TO must be banned could continue to cite his former statement, while those who accepted GO TO could cite the latter. Whether against or in favour of GO TO, everyone could base his interpretation of structured programming on a statement made by the famous theorist Dijkstra.

[15] E. W. Dijkstra, "Go To Statement Considered Harmful," in *Milestones*, eds. Oman and Lewis, p. 9.   [16] Ralston and Reilly, *Encyclopedia*, p. 1396.

[17] E. W. Dijkstra, quoted as personal communication in Donald E. Knuth, "Structured Programming with *go to* Statements," in *Computing Surveys* 6, no. 4 (©1974 ACM, Inc.): 262 (brackets in the original).

One of those who chose Dijkstra's latter statement, and a famous theorist and Turing award recipient himself, is Donald Knuth: "I believe that by presenting such a view I am not in fact disagreeing sharply with Dijkstra's ideas"[18] (meaning his *new* idea, that GO TO is *not* harmful). Knuth makes this statement in the introduction to a paper that bears the striking title "Structured Programming with *go to* Statements" – a forty-page study whose goal is "to lay [the GO TO] controversy to rest."[19] It is not clear how Knuth hoped to accomplish this, seeing that the paper is largely an analysis of various programming examples, some with and others without GO TO, some where GO TO is said to be bad and others where it is said to be good; in other words, exactly what was being done by every other expert, in hundreds of other studies. The examples, needless to say, are typical textbook cases: trivial, isolated pieces of software (the largest has sixteen statements), where GO TO is harmless even if misused, and which have little to do, therefore, with the real reasons why jumps are good or bad in actual applications. One would think that if the GO TO controversy were simple enough to be resolved by such examples, it would have ended long before, through the previous studies. Knuth, evidently, is convinced that his discussion is better.

From the paper's title, and from some of his arguments, it appears at first that Knuth intends to "lay to rest" the controversy by boldly stating that the use of GO TO is merely a matter of programming style, or simplicity, or efficiency. But he only says this in certain parts of the paper. In other parts he tells us that it is important to avoid GO TO, shows us how to eliminate it in various situations, and suggests changes to our programming languages to help us program without GO TO.[20]

By the time he reaches the end of the paper, Knuth seems to have forgotten its title, and concludes that GO TO is not really necessary: "I guess the big question, although it really shouldn't be so big, is whether or not the ultimate language will have GO TO statements in its higher levels, or whether GO TO will be confined to lower levels. I personally wouldn't mind having GO TO in the highest level, just in case I really need it; but I probably would never use it, if the general iteration and situation constructs suggested in this paper were present."[21]

---

[18] Donald E. Knuth, "Structured Programming with *go to* Statements," in *Computing Surveys* 6, no. 4 (©1974 ACM, Inc.): 262.   [19] Ibid., p. 291.

[20] Knuth admits proudly that he deliberately chose "to present the material in this apparently vacillating manner" (ibid., p. 264). This approach, he explains, "worked beautifully" in lectures: "Nearly everybody in the audience had the illusion that I was largely supporting his or her views, regardless of what those views were!" (ibid.). What is the point of this approach, and this confession? Knuth and his audiences are evidently having fun debating GO TO, but are they also interested in solving this problem?   [21] Ibid., p. 295.

Note how absurd this passage is: "wouldn't mind ... just in case I really need it; but I probably would never use it ...." This is as confused and equivocal as a statement can get. Knuth is trying to say that it is possible to program without GOTO, but he is afraid to commit himself. So what was the point of this lengthy paper? Why doesn't he state, unambiguously, either that the ideal high-level programming language must include certain constructs but not GOTO, or, conversely, that it must include GOTO, because we will always encounter situations where it is the best alternative?

Knuth also says, at the end of the paper, that "it's certainly possible to write well-structured programs with GOTO statements,"[22] and points to a certain program that "used three GOTO statements, all of which were perfectly easy to understand." But then he adds that some of these GOTOs "would have disappeared" if that particular language "had had a WHILE statement." Again, he is unable to make up his mind. He notes that the GOTOs are harmless when used correctly, then he contradicts himself: he carefully counts them, and is pleased that more recent languages permit us to reduce their number.

One more example: In their classic book, *The C Programming Language*, Brian Kernighan and Dennis Ritchie seem unsure whether to reject or accept GOTO.[23] It was included in C, and it appears to be useful, but they feel they must conform to the current ideology and criticize it. First they reject it: "Formally, the GOTO is never necessary, and in practice it is almost always easy to write code without it. We have not used GOTO in this book."[24] We are not told how many situations are left outside the "almost always" category, but their two GOTO examples represent in fact a very common situation (the requirement to exit from a loop that is nested two or more levels within the current one).

At this point, then, the authors are demonstrating the *benefits* of GOTO. They even point out (and illustrate with actual C code) that any attempt to eliminate the GOTO in these situations results in an unnatural and complicated piece of software. The logical conclusion, thus, ought to be that GOTO *is* necessary in C. Nevertheless, they end their argument with this vague and ambiguous remark: "Although we are not dogmatic about the matter, it does seem that GOTO statements should be used sparingly, if at all."[25]

[22] The quotations in this paragraph are ibid., p. 294.

[23] Brian W. Kernighan and Dennis M. Ritchie, *The C Programming Language* (Englewood Cliffs, NJ: Prentice Hall, 1978), pp. 62–63.

[24] Ibid., p. 62. Incidentally, they managed to avoid GOTO in all their examples simply because, as in any book of this kind, the examples are limited to small, isolated, artificial bits of logic. But the very fact that the avoidance of GOTO in examples was a priority demonstrates the morbidity of this preoccupation.   [25] Ibid., p. 63.

It is the third aspect of the GOTO delusion, however, that is the most absurd: eliminating the GOTO statements by replacing them with new constructs that are designed to perform exactly the same jumps. At this point, it is no longer the *jumps* that we are asked to avoid, but just the *phrase* "go to."

At first, we saw under the fourth delusion, the idea of structured programming was modified to include a number of non-standard constructs – constructs already found in the existing programming languages. Originally, these constructs had been invented simply as language enhancements, as alternatives to the most common jumps. (They simplify the jumps, typically, by obviating the need for a destination label.) But, as they allowed practitioners to bypass the restriction to standard constructs, they were enthusiastically incorporated into structured programming and described as "extensions" of the theory.

Although the inclusion of language-specific constructs appeared to rescue the idea of structured programming, there remained many situations where GOTO could only be eliminated through some unwieldy transformations, and still others where GOTO-based constructs were the only practical alternative. So the concept of language-specific constructs – what had been originally intended merely as a way to improve programming languages – was expanded and turned by the theorists into a means to eliminate GOTO. Situations easily implemented with GOTO in any language became the subject of research, debate, and new constructs. More and more constructs were suggested as GOTO replacements, although, in the end, few were actually added to the existing languages.

The theorists hoped to discover a set of constructs that would eliminate forever the need for GOTO by providing built-in jumps for all conceivable programming situations. They hoped, in other words, to redeem the idea of structured programming by finding an alternative to the contrived and impractical transformations. No such set was ever found, but this failure was not recognized as the answer to the GOTO delusion, and the controversy continued.

The theorists justified their attempts to replace GOTO with language-specific constructs by saying that these constructs facilitate structured programming. But this explanation is illogical. If we interpret structured programming as the original theory, with its restriction to standard constructs, the role of the non-standard constructs is not to facilitate but to *override* structured programming. And if we interpret structured programming as the extended theory, which allows any construct with one entry and exit, we can implement all the constructs we need by combining standard constructs and GOTO statements; in this case, then, the role of the non-standard constructs is not to facilitate structured programming but to facilitate GOTO-less programming.

The theorists, therefore, were not inventing built-in constructs out of a concern for structured programming – no matter how we interpret this theory – but only in order to eliminate GOTO.

As an example of the attempts to define a set of flow-control constructs that would make GOTO unnecessary, consider Jensen's study.[26] Jensen starts by defining three "atomic" components: "We use the word *atomic* to characterize the lowest level constituents to which we can reduce the structure of a program."[27] The three atomic components are called process node, predicate node, and collector node, and represent lower software levels than do the three standard constructs of structured programming. Then, Jensen defines nine flow-control constructs based on these components (the three standard constructs plus six non-standard ones), proclaims structured programming to mean the restriction, not to the three standard constructs but to his nine constructs, and asserts that any application can be developed in this manner: "By establishing program structure building blocks (akin to molecules made from our three types of atoms) and a structuring methodology, we can scientifically implement structured programs."[28] But, even though Jensen discusses the practical implementation of this concept with actual programming languages and illustrates it with a small program, the concept remains a theoretical study, and we don't know how successful it would be with real-world applications.

An example of a set of constructs that was actually put into effect is found in a language called Bliss. One of its designers makes the following statement in a paper presented at an important conference: "The inescapable conclusion from the Bliss experience is that the purported inconvenience of programming without a GOTO is a myth."[29]

It doesn't seem possible that the GOTO delusion could reach such levels, but it did. That statement is ludicrous even if we overlook the fact that Bliss was just a special-purpose language (designed for systems software, so the conclusion about the need for GOTO is not at all inescapable in the case of other types of programs). The academics who created Bliss invented a number of constructs purposely in order to replace, one by one, various uses of GOTO. The constructs, thus, were specifically designed to perform *exactly* the same jumps as GOTO. To claim, then, that using these constructs instead of GOTO proves that it is possible to program without GOTO, and to have such claims published and debated, demonstrates the utter madness that had possessed the academic and the programming communities.

---

[26] Randall W. Jensen, "Structured Programming," in *Software Engineering*, eds. Randall W. Jensen and Charles C. Tonies (Englewood Cliffs, NJ: Prentice Hall, 1979).
[27] Ibid., p. 238.   [28] Ibid., p. 241.
[29] William A. Wulf, "A Case against the GOTO," *Proceedings of the ACM Annual Conference*, vol. 2 (1972), p. 795.

Here is how Knuth, in the aforementioned paper, describes this madness: "During the last few years several languages have appeared in which the designers proudly announced that they have abolished the GOTO statement. Perhaps the most prominent of these is Bliss, which originally replaced GOTO's by eight so-called 'escape' statements. And the eight weren't even enough.... Other GOTO-less languages for systems programming have similarly introduced other statements which provide 'equally powerful' alternative ways to jump.... In other words, it seems that there is widespread agreement that GOTO statements are harmful, yet programmers and language designers still feel the need for some euphemism that 'goes to' without saying GOTO."[30]

Unfortunately, Knuth ends his paper contradicting himself; now he *praises* the idea of replacing GOTO with new constructs designed to perform the same operation: "But GOTO is hardly ever the best alternative now, since better language features are appearing. If the invariant for a label is closely related to another invariant, we can usually save complexity by combining those two into one abstraction, using something other than GOTO for the combination."[31] What Knuth suggests is that we improve our programming languages by creating higher levels of abstraction: built-in flow-control constructs that combine several operations, including all necessary jumps. Explicit jumps, and hence GOTO, will then become unnecessary: "As soon as people learn to apply principles of abstraction consciously, they won't see the need for GOTO."[32]

Knuth's mistake here is the fallacy we discussed under the second and fourth delusions (see pp. 553–556, 592–593): he confuses the flow-control constructs with the *operations* of a hierarchical structure. In the static flow diagram – that is, in the nesting scheme – these constructs do indeed combine elements to form higher levels of abstraction. But because they employ conditions, their task in the flow of execution is not to create higher levels, but to create multiple, interacting nesting schemes.

The idea of replacing GOTO with higher-level constructs is, therefore, fallacious. Only an application restricted to a nesting scheme of sequential constructs has a flow of execution that is a simple hierarchical structure, allowing us to substitute one construct for several lower-level ones. And no serious application can be restricted to such a nesting scheme. This is why no one could invent a general-purpose language that eliminates the need for jumps. In the end, all flow-control constructs added to programming languages over the years are doing exactly what GOTO-based constructs are doing, but without using the *phrase* "go to."

---

[30] Knuth, "Structured Programming," pp. 265–266.   [31] Ibid., p. 294.
[32] Ibid., pp. 295–296.

4

Because of its irrationality, the GOTO prohibition acquired in the end the character of a superstition: despite the attempt to ground the debate on programming principles, avoiding GOTO became a preoccupation similar in nature to avoiding black cats, or avoiding the number 13.

People who cling to an unproven idea develop various attitudes to rationalize their belief. For example, since it is difficult to follow strictly the precepts of any superstition, we must find ways to make the pursuit of superstitions practical. Thus, even if convinced that certain events bring misfortune, we will tolerate them when avoiding them is inconvenient – and we will contrive an explanation to justify our inconsistency. Similarly, we saw, while GOTO is believed to bring software misfortune, most theorists agree that there is no need to be dogmatic: GOTO is tolerable when avoiding it is inconvenient.

Humour is an especially effective way to mask the irrationality of our acts. Thus, it is common to see people joke about their superstitions – about their habit of touching wood, for instance – even as they continue to practise them. So we shouldn't be surprised to find humorous remarks accompanying the most serious GOTO discussions. Let us study a few examples.

In his assessment of the benefits of structured programming, Yourdon makes the following comment: "Many programmers feel that programming without the GOTO statement would be awkward, tedious, and cumbersome. For the most part, this complaint is due to force of habit.... The only response that can be given to this complaint comes from a popular television commercial that made the rounds recently: 'Try it – you'll like it!'"[33] This is funny, perhaps, but what is the point of this quip? After explaining and praising GOTO-less programming, Yourdon admits that the only way to demonstrate its benefits is with the techniques of television advertising.

Another example of humour is the statement COME FROM, introduced as an alternative to GOTO. Although meant as a joke, this statement was actually implemented in several programming languages, and its merits are being discussed to this day in certain circles. Its operation is, in a sense, the reverse of GOTO; for instance, COME FROM L1 tells the computer to jump to the statement following it when the flow of execution encounters the label L1 somewhere in the program. (The joke is that, apart from being quite useless, COME FROM is even more difficult than GOTO to understand and to manage.) It is notable that the official introduction of this idea was in *Datamation*'s issue that proclaimed

---

[33] Yourdon, *Techniques*, p. 178.

structured programming a revolution (see p. 537). Thus, out of the five articles devoted to this revolution, one was meant in its entirety as a joke.[34]

One expert claims that the GOTO prohibition does not go far enough: the next step must be to abolish the ELSE in IF statements.[35] Since an IF-THEN-ELSE statement can be expressed as two consecutive IF-THEN statements where the second condition is the logical negation of the first, ELSE is unnecessary and complicates the program. The expert discusses in some detail the benefits of ELSE-less programming. The article, which apparently was *not* meant as a joke, ends with this sentence: "Structured programming, with elimination of the GOTO, is claimed to be a step toward changing programming from an art to a cost-effective science, but the ELSE will have to go, too, before the promise is a reality"[36] (note the pun, "go, too").

Knuth likes to head his writings with epigraphs, but from the quotations he chose for his aforementioned paper on GOTO, it is impossible to tell whether this is a serious study or a piece of entertainment. Two quotations, from a poem and from a song, were chosen, it seems, only because they include the word "go"; the third one is from an advertisement offering a remedy for "painful elimination." Also, we find the following remark in the paper: "The use of four-letter words like GOTO can occasionally be justified even in the best of company."[37]

The most puzzling part of Knuth's humour, however, is his allusion to Orwell's *Nineteen Eighty-Four*. He dubs the ideal programming language Utopia 84, as his "dream is that by 1984 we will see a consensus developing.... At present we are far from that goal, yet there are indications that such a language is very slowly taking shape.... Will Utopia 84, or perhaps we should call it Newspeak, contain GOTO statements?"[38]

Is this a joke or a serious remark? Does Knuth imply that the role of programming languages should be the same as the role of Newspeak in Orwell's totalitarian society – that is, to degrade knowledge and minds? (See "Orwell's Newspeak" in chapter 5.) Perhaps this *is* Knuth's dream, unless the following statement, too, is only a joke: "The question is whether we should ban [GOTO], or educate against it; should we attempt to legislate program morality? In this case I vote for legislation, with appropriate legal substitutes in place of the former overwhelming temptations."[39]

As the theorists and the practitioners recognized the shallowness of their preoccupation with GOTO, humour was the device through which they could

---

[34] R. Lawrence Clark, "A Linguistic Contribution to GOTO-less Programming," *Data-mation* 19, no. 12 (1973): 62–63.

[35] Allan M. Bloom, "The 'ELSE' Must Go, Too," *Datamation* 21, no. 5 (1975): 123–128.

[36] Ibid., p. 128.   [37] Knuth, "Structured Programming," p. 282.

[38] Ibid., pp. 263–264.   [39] Ibid., p. 296.

pursue two contradictory ideas: that the issue is important, and that it is irrelevant. Humour, generally, is a good way to deal with the emotional conflict arising when we must believe in two contradictory concepts at the same time. Thus, like people joking about their superstitions, the advocates of structured programming discovered that humour allowed them to denounce the irrational preoccupation with GOTO even while continuing to foster it.

5

The foregoing analysis has demonstrated that the GOTO prohibition had no logical foundation. It has little to do with the original structured programming idea, and can even be seen as a new theory: the theory of structured programming failed, and the GOTO preoccupation took its place. The theorists and the practitioners kept saying that structured programming is more than just GOTO-less programming, but in reality the elimination of GOTO was now the most important aspect of their work. What was left of structured programming was only some trivial concepts: top-down design, constructs with one entry and exit, indenting the levels of nesting in the program's listing, and the like.

To appreciate this, consider the following argument. First, within the original, *formal* theory of structured programming, we cannot even discuss GOTO; for, if we adhere to the formal principles we will never encounter situations requiring GOTO. So, if we have to debate the use of GOTO, it means that we are not practising structured programming.

It is only within the modified, *informal* theory that we can discuss GOTO at all. And here, too, the GOTO debate is absurd, because this degraded variant of structured programming can be practised both with and without GOTO. We can have structured programs either without GOTO (if we use only built-in constructs) or with GOTO (if we also design our own constructs). The only difference between the two alternatives is the presence of explicit jumps in some of the constructs, and explicit jumps are compatible with the informal principles. With both methods we can practise top-down design, create constructs with one entry and exit, restrict modules to a hundred lines, indent the levels of nesting in the program's listing, and so forth. *Every principle stipulated by the informal theory of structured programming can be rigorously followed whether or not we use GOTO.*

The use of GOTO, thus, is simply a matter of programming style, or programming standards, which can vary from person to person and from place to place. Since it doesn't depend on a particular set of built-in constructs, the informal style of structured programming can be practised with any programming language (even with low-level, assembly languages): we use built-in constructs when available and when effective, and create our own with explicit jumps when this alternative is better. (So we will have more GOTOs in COBOL, for example, than in C.)

Then, if GOTO does not stop us from practising the new, informal structured programming, why was its prohibition so important? As I stated earlier (see pp. 604–605), the GOTO preoccupation served as a substitute for the original theory: that theory restricted us to the three standard flow-control constructs (a rigorous principle that is all but impossible to follow), while the new theory permits us to use an arbitrary, larger set of constructs (in fact, any *built-in* constructs). Thus, the only restriction now is to use built-in constructs rather than create our own with GOTO. This principle is more practical than the original one, while still appearing precise. By describing this easier principle as an *extension* of structured programming, the theorists could delude themselves that they had a serious theory even after the actual theory had been refuted.

The same experts who had promised us the means to develop and prove applications mathematically were engaged now in the childish task of studying the use of GOTO in small, artificial pieces of software. And yet, no one saw this as evidence that the theory of structured programming had failed. While still talking about scientific programming, the experts were debating whether one trivial construct is easier or harder to understand than some other trivial construct. Is this the role of software theorists, to decide for us which style of programming is clearer? Surely, practitioners can deal with such matters on their own. We listened to the theorists because of their claim that software development can be a formal and precise activity. And if this idea turned out to be mistaken, they should have studied the reasons, admitted that they could not help us, and tried perhaps to discover what is the *true* nature of programming. Instead, they shifted their preoccupation to the GOTO issue, and continued to claim that programming would one day become a formal and precise activity.

The theorists knew, probably, that the small bits of software they were studying were just as easy to understand with GOTO as they were without it. But they remained convinced that this was a critical issue: it was important to find a set of ideal constructs because a flow-control structure free of GOTOs would eventually render the same benefits as a structure restricted to the three standard constructs. The dream of rigorous, scientific programming was still within reach.

The theorists fancied themselves as the counterpart of the old thinkers, who, while studying what looked like minute philosophical problems, were laying in fact the foundation of modern knowledge. Similarly, the theorists say, subjects like GOTO may seem trivial, but when studying the appearance of small bits of software with and without GOTO they are determining in fact some important software principles, and laying the foundation of the new science of programming.

❖

The GOTO issue was important to the theorists, thus, as a substitute for the formal principles of structured programming. But there was a second, even more important motivation for the GOTO prohibition.

Earlier in this chapter we saw that the chief purpose of structured programming, and of software engineering generally, was to get inexperienced programmers to perform tasks that require in fact great skills. The software theorists planned to solve the software crisis, not by promoting programming expertise, but, on the contrary, by eliminating the *need* for expertise: by turning programming from a difficult profession, demanding knowledge, experience, and responsibility, into a routine activity, which could be performed by almost anyone. And they hoped to accomplish this by discovering some exact, mechanistic programming principles – principles that could be incorporated in methodologies and development tools. The difficult skills needed to create software applications would then be reduced to the easier skills needed to follow methods and to operate software devices. Ultimately, programmers would only need to know how to use the tools provided by the software elite.

The GOTO prohibition was part of this ideology. Structured programs, we saw, can be written both with and without GOTO: we use only built-in flow-control constructs, or also create our own with GOTO statements. The difference is a matter of style and efficiency. So, if structured programming is what matters, all that the theorists had to do was to explain the principle of nested flow-control constructs. Responsible practitioners would appreciate its benefits, but the principle would not prevent them from developing an individual programming style. They would use custom constructs when better than the built-in ones, and the GOTOs would make their programs easier, not harder, to understand.

Thus, it was pointed out more than once that good programmers were practising structured programming even before the theorists were promoting it. And this is true: a programmer who develops and maintains large and complex applications inevitably discovers the benefits of hierarchical flow-control structures, indenting the levels of nesting in the program's listing, and other such practices; and he doesn't have to avoid GOTO in order to enjoy these benefits.

But the theorists had decided that programmers should not be expected to advance beyond the level attained by an average person after a few months of practice – beyond what is, in effect, the level of novices. The possibility of educating and training programmers as we do individuals in other professions – that is, giving them the time and opportunity to develop all the knowledge that human minds are capable of – was not even considered. It was simply assumed that if programmers with a few months of experience write bad software, the only way to improve their performance is by preventing them from dealing with the more difficult aspects of programming.

And, since the theorists believed that the flow-control structure is the most important aspect of the application, the conclusion was obvious: programmers must be forced to use built-in flow-control constructs, and prohibited from creating their own. In this way, even inexperienced programmers will create perfect flow-control structures, and hence perfect applications. Restricting programmers to built-in constructs, the theorists believed, is like starting with subassemblies rather than basic parts when building appliances: programming is easier and faster, and one needs lower skills and less experience to create the same applications. (We examined this fallacy earlier; see pp. 592–593.) Thus, simply by prohibiting mediocre programmers from creating their own flow-control constructs, we will attain about the same results as we would by employing expert programmers.

It is clear, then, why the theorists could not just *advise* programmers to follow the principles of structured programming. Since their goal was to control programming practices, it was inconceivable to allow the *programmers* to decide whether to use a built-in construct or a non-standard one, much less to allow them to *design* a construct. With its restriction to the three standard constructs, the original theory had the same goal, but it was impractical. So the theorists looked for a substitute, a different way to control the work of programmers. With its restriction to built-in constructs – constructs sanctioned by the theorists and incorporated into programming languages – the GO TO prohibition was the answer.

We find evidence that this ideology was the chief motivation for the GO TO prohibition in the reasons typically adduced for avoiding GO TO. The theorists remind us that its use gives rise to constructs with more than one entry or exit, thereby destroying the hierarchical nature of the flow-control structure; and they point out that it has been proved mathematically that GO TO is unnecessary. But despite the power of these formal explanations, they ground the prohibition, ultimately, on the idea that GO TO tempts programmers to write "messy" programs. It is significant, thus, that the theorists consider the informal observation that GOTO allows programmers to create bad software more convincing than the formal demonstration that GOTO is unnecessary.

Here are some examples: "The GOTO statement should be abolished" because "it is too much an invitation to make a mess of one's program."[40] "GOTO instructions in programs can go to *anywhere*, permitting the programmer to weave a tangled mess."[41] "It would be wise to avoid the GOTO statement altogether. Unconditional branching encourages a patchwork (spaghetti code) style of programming that leads to messy code and unreliable performance."[42] "The GOTO can be used to produce 'bowl-of-spaghetti' programs – ones in which the flow of control is involuted in arbitrarily complex ways."[43] "Unrestricted use of the GOTO encourages jumping around within programs, making them difficult to read and difficult to follow."[44] "One of the most confusing styles in computer programs involves overuse of the GOTO statement."[45] "GOTO statements make large programs very difficult to read."[46]

What these authors are saying is true. What they are describing, though, is not programming with GOTO, but simply *bad* programming. They believe that there are only two alternatives to software development: bad programmers allowed to use GOTO and writing therefore bad programs, and bad programmers prevented from using GOTO. The possibility of having *good* programmers, who write good programs with or without GOTO, is not considered at all.

The argument about messy programs is ludicrous. It is true that, if used incorrectly, GOTO can cause execution to "go to anywhere," can create an "arbitrarily complex" flow of control, and can make the program "difficult to follow." But the GOTO problem is no different from any other aspect of programming: bad programmers do *everything* badly, so the messiness of their flow-control constructs is not surprising. Had these authors studied other aspects of those programs, they would have discovered that the file operations, or the definition of memory variables, or the use of subroutines, or the calculations, were also messy. The solution, however, is not to prohibit bad programmers from using certain features of a programming language, but to teach them how to program; in particular, how to create simple and consistent

[40] Dijkstra, "Go To Statement," p. 9.

[41] Martin and McClure, *Structured Techniques*, p. 133.

[42] David M. Collopy, *Introduction to C Programming: A Modular Approach* (Upper Saddle River, NJ: Prentice Hall, 1997), p. 142.

[43] William A. Wulf, "Languages and Structured Programs," in *Current Trends in Programming Methodology*, vol. 1, *Software Specification and Design*, ed. Raymond T. Yeh (Englewood Cliffs, NJ: Prentice Hall, 1977), p. 37.

[44] Clement L. McGowan and John R. Kelly, *Top-Down Structured Programming Techniques* (New York: Petrocelli/Charter, 1975), p. 43.

[45] Weinberg et al., *High Level COBOL*, p. 39.   [46] Van Tassel, *Program Style*, p. 78.

flow-control constructs. And if they are incapable or unwilling to improve their work, they should be replaced with better programmers.

The very use of terms like "messy" to describe the work of programmers betrays the distorted attitude that the software elite has toward this profession. Programmers whose work is messy should not even be employed, of course. Incredibly, the fact that individuals considered professional programmers create messy software is perceived as a normal state of affairs. Theorists, employers, and society accept the incompetence of programmers as a necessary and irremediable situation. And we accept not only their incompetence, but also the fact that they are irresponsible and incapable of improving their skills. Thus, everyone agrees that it is futile to teach them how to use GOTO correctly; they cannot understand, or don't care, so it is best simply to prohibit them from using it.

To be considered a professional programmer, an individual ought to display the highest skill level attainable in the domain of programming. This is how we define professionalism in other domains, so why do we accept a different definition for programmers? The software theorists claim that programmers are, or are becoming, "software engineers." At the same time, they are redefining the notions of expertise and responsibility to mean something entirely different from what they mean for engineers and for other professionals. In the case of programmers, expertise means acquaintance with the latest theories and standards, and responsibility means following them blindly. And what do these theories and standards try to accomplish? To obviate the need for *true* expertise and responsibility. No one seems to note the absurdity of this ideology.

6

We must take a moment here to discuss some of the programming aspects of the GOTO problem; namely, what programming style creates excellent, rather than messy, GOTO-based constructs. Had the correct use of GOTO demanded great expertise – outstanding knowledge of computers or mathematics, for instance – the effort to prevent programmers from creating their own constructs might have been justified. I want to show, however, that the correct use of GOTO is a trivial issue: from the many kinds of knowledge involved in programming, this is one of the simplest.

The following discussion, thus, is not intended to promote a particular programming style, but to demonstrate the triviality of the GOTO problem, and hence the absurdity of its prohibition. This will serve as additional evidence for my argument that the GOTO prohibition was motivated, not by some valid software concerns, but by the corrupt ideology held by the software theorists. They had already decided that programmers must remain incompetent, and that it is they, the elite, who will control programming practices.

❖

The first step is to establish, within the application, the boundaries for each set of jumps: the whole program in the case of a small application, but usually a module, a subroutine, or some other section that is logically distinct. Thus, even when the programming language allows jumps to go anywhere in the program, we will restrict each set of jumps to the section that constitutes a particular procedure, report, data entry function, file updating operation, and the like.

The second step is to decide what types of jumps we want to implement with GOTO. The number of reasons for having jumps in the flow of execution is surprisingly small, so we can easily account for all the possibilities. We can agree, for example, to restrict the *forward* jumps to the following situations: bypassing blocks of statements (in order to create conditional constructs); jumping to the point past the end of a block that is at a lower nesting level than the current one (in order to exit from any combination of nested conditions and iterations); jumping to any common point (in order to terminate one logical process and start another). And we can agree to restrict the *backward* jumps to the following situations: jumping to the beginning of a block (in order to create iterative constructs, and also to end prematurely a particular iteration); jumping to any common point (in order to repeat the current process starting from a particular operation).

We need, thus, less than ten types of jumps; and by *combining* jumps we can create any flow-control constructs we like. We will continue to use whatever built-in constructs are available in a particular language, but we will not *depend* on them; we will simply use them when more effective than our own. Recall the failed attempts to replace all possible uses of GOTO with built-in constructs. Now we see that this idea is impractical, not because of the large number of *types* of jumps, but because of the large number of *combinations* of jumps. And the problem disappears if we can design our own constructs, because now we don't have to plan in advance all conceivable combinations; we simply create them as needed.

Lastly, we must agree on a good naming system for labels. Labels are those flow-control variables that identify the statement where execution is to continue after a jump. And, since each GOTO statement specifies a label, we can choose names that link logically the jump's origin, its destination, and the purpose of the jump. This simple fact is overlooked by those who claim that jumps unavoidably make programs hard to follow. If we adopt an intelligent naming system, the jumps, instead of confusing us, will *explain* the program's logic. (The compiler, of course, will accept any combination of characters as label names; it is the human readers that will benefit from a good naming convention.)

Here is one system: the first character or two of the name are letters identifying that section of the program where a particular set of jumps and labels are in effect; the next character is a letter identifying the type of jump; and these letters are followed by a number identifying the relative position of the label within the current set of jumps. In the name RKL3, for example, RK is the section, L identifies the start of a loop, and 3 means that the label is found after labels with numbers like 1 or 25, but before labels with numbers like 31 or 6. Similarly, T could identify the point past the end of a loop, S the point past a block bypassed by a condition, E the common point for dealing with an error, and so on.[47]

Note that the label numbers identify their order hierarchically, not through their values. For example, in a section called EM, the sequence of labels might be as follows: EMS2, EML3, EMS32, EMS326, EML35, EMT36, EMT4, EME82. The advantage of hierarchical numbering is that we can add new labels later without having to modify the existing ones. Note also that, while the numbers can be assigned at will, we can also use them to convey some additional information. For example, labels with one- or two-digit numbers could signify points in the program that are more important than those employing labels with three- or four-digit numbers (say, the main loop versus an ordinary condition).

Another detail worth mentioning is that we will sometimes end up with two or more consecutive labels. For example, a jump that terminates a loop and one that bypasses the block in which the loop is nested will go to the same point in the program, but for different reasons. Therefore, even though the compiler allows us to use one label for both jumps, each operation should have its own label. Also, while the *order* of consecutive labels has no effect on the program's execution, here it should match the nesting levels (for the benefit of the human readers); thus, the label that terminates the loop should come before the one that bypasses the whole block (EMT62, EMS64).

Simple as it is, this system is actually too elaborate for most applications. First, since the jump boundaries usually parallel syntactic units like subroutines, in many languages the label names need to be unique only within each

---

[47] In COBOL, labels are known as paragraph names, and paragraphs function also as procedures, or subroutines; but the method described here works the same way. (It is poor practice to use the same paragraph both as a GOTO destination and as a procedure, except for jumps within the procedure.)

section; so we can often dispose of the section identifier and start all label names in the program with the same letter. Second, in well-designed programs the purpose of most jumps is self-evident, so we can usually dispose of the type identifier too. (It is clear, for instance, whether a forward jump is to a common error exit or is part of a conditional construct.) The method I have followed for many years in my applications is to use even-numbered labels for forward jumps (EM4, EM56, EM836, etc.) and odd-numbered ones for backward jumps (EM3, EM43, EM627, etc.). I find this simplified identification of jump types adequate even in the most intricate situations.[48]

It is obvious that many other systems of jump types and label names are possible. It is also obvious that the consistent use of a particular system is more important than its level of sophistication. Thus, if we can be sure that every jump and label in a given application obeys a particular convention, we will have no difficulty following the flow of execution.

So the solution to the famous GOTO problem is something as simple as a consistent system of jump types and label names. All the problems that the software theorists attribute to GOTO have now disappeared. We can enjoy the benefits of a hierarchical flow-control structure and the versatility of explicit jumps at the same time.

The maintenance problem – the difficulty of understanding software created by others – has also disappeared: no matter how many GOTOs are present in the program, we know now for each jump where execution is going, and for each label where execution is coming from. We know, moreover, the *purpose* of each jump and label. Designing an effective flow-control structure, or following the logic of an existing one, may still pose a challenge; but, unlike the challenge of dealing with a messy structure, this is now a genuine programming problem. The challenge, in fact, is easier than it is with *built-in* constructs, because we have the actual, self-documented jumps and labels, rather than just the implicit ones. So, even when a built-in construct is available, the GOTO-based one is often a better alternative.

Now, it is hard to believe that any programmer can fail to understand a system of jumps and labels; and it is also hard to believe that no theorist ever thought of such a system. Thus, since a system of jumps and labels answers all the objections the theorists have to using GOTO, why were they trying to *eliminate* it rather than simply suggesting such a system? They describe the

---

[48] Figures 7-13 to 7-16 (pp. 694, 697–699) exemplify this style. Note that this method also makes the levels of nesting self-evident, obviating the need to indent the loops.

harmful effects of GOTO as if the only way to use it were with arbitrary jumps and arbitrary label names. They say nothing about the possibility of an intelligent and consistent system of jumps, or meaningful label names. They describe the use of GOTO, in other words, as if the only alternative were to have incompetent and irresponsible programmers. They appear to be describing a programming problem, but what they are describing is their distorted view of the programming profession: by stating that the best solution to the GOTO problem is avoidance, they are saying in effect that programmers will forever be too stupid even to follow a simple convention.

Structured programming, and the GOTO prohibition, did not make programming an exact activity and did not solve the software crisis. Programmers who had been writing messy programs before were now writing messy GOTO-less programs: they were messy in the way they were *avoiding* GOTO, and also in the way they were implementing subroutines, calculations, file operations, and everything else. Clearly, programmers who must be prohibited from using GOTO (because they cannot follow a simple system of jumps and labels) are unlikely to perform correctly any other programming task.

Recall what was the purpose of this discussion. I wanted to show that the GOTO prohibition, while being part of the structured programming movement, has little to do with its principles, or with any other programming principles. It is just another aspect of a corrupt ideology. The software elites claim that their theories are turning programming into a scientific activity, and programmers into engineers. In reality, the goal of these theories is to turn programmers into bureaucrats. The programming profession, according to the elites, is a large body of mediocre workers trained to follow certain methods and to use certain tools. Structured programming was the first attempt to implement this ideology, and the GOTO prohibition in particular is a blatant demonstration of it.

The Legacy

Because the theorists thought that the flow-control structure is the most important part of an application, they noticed at first only the GOTO messiness, and concluded that a restriction to built-in flow-control constructs would solve the problem of bad programming. Then, when this restriction was found to make no difference, they started to notice the other types of messiness. But the solution was thought to be, again, not helping programmers to improve their skills, but preventing them from dealing on their own with various aspects of programming. Thus, structured programming was followed by many other theories, languages, methodologies, and database systems, all having the same goal: to degrade the work of programmers by shifting it to higher and higher levels of abstraction; to replace programming skills with a dependence on development systems; and to reduce the contribution of programmers to simple acts that require practically no knowledge or experience.

Had the theorists tried to understand *why* structured programming failed, perhaps they would have discovered the true nature of software and programming. They would have realized then that no mechanistic theory can help us, because software applications consist of interacting structures. The mechanistic software delusions, thus, could have ended with structured programming. But because they denied its failure, and because they continued to claim that formal programming methods are possible, the theorists established a mechanistic software culture. After structured programming, the traditional idea of expertise – skills that are mainly the result of personal knowledge and experience – was no longer accepted in the field of programming.

Unlike structured programming, today's theories are embodied in *development environments*: large and complicated systems known as object-oriented, fourth-generation, database management, or CASE. Consequently, it is mainly the software companies behind these systems, rather than the theorists, that form now the software elite. No matter how impressive they are, though, the development environments are ultimately grounded on mechanistic principles. So, if the mechanistic programming theories cannot help us, these systems cannot help us either. The reason they appear to work is that their promoters continually "enhance" them: while praising their high-level features, they reinstate – *within* these systems, and under new names – the low-level, versatile capabilities of the traditional programming languages. In other words, instead of correctly interpreting a particular inadequacy as a falsification of the original principles, they eliminate the inadequacy by annulling those principles. Thus, the same stratagem that made structured programming appear successful – modifying the theory by reinstating the very features it was supposed to replace – also serves to cover up the failure of development environments. (See "The Delusion of High Levels" in chapter 6; see also "The Quest for Higher Levels" in the next section.)

Turning falsifications into features, we recall, is how pseudoscientists manage to rescue their theories from refutation. High-level programming aids, thus, are fraudulent: after all the "enhancements," using a development environment is merely a more complicated form of the same programming work that we had been performing all along, with the traditional languages.

We must also recall the other method employed by pseudoscientists to defend their theories: looking for confirmations instead of falsifications; that is, studying the few cases where the theory appears to work, and ignoring the many cases where it fails. All software theories are promoted with this simple trick, whether or not they also benefit from the more sophisticated stratagem of turning falsifications into features.

Thus, it is common to see a particular theory or development system praised in books and periodicals on the basis of just one or two "success stories." Structured programming, for example, was tried with thousands of applications, but the only evidence of usefulness comes from a handful of cases: we see the same stories repeated over and over everywhere structured programming is promoted. (And there is not a single case where a serious application was implemented by following the original, formal principles.)

The study of structured programming is more than the study of a chapter in the history of programming. If all mechanistic theories suffer from the same fallacy – the belief that software applications can be separated into independent structures – then what we learned in our analysis of structured programming can help us to recognize the fallaciousness of any other programming theory. All we need to do is identify the structures that each theory attempts to extract from the complex whole.

The failure of structured programming is the failure of all mechanistic programming theories, and hence the failure of the whole idea of software engineering. This is true because software engineering is, in the final analysis, the ideology of software mechanism; so one cannot say that the idea of software engineering is sound if the individual theories are failing. The dream of structured programming was to represent software applications mathematically, and to turn programming into a precise, predictable activity. And it is the same dream that we find in the other theories, and in the general idea of software engineering. Individual theories may come and go, but if they are all based on mechanistic principles, they are in effect different manifestations of the same delusion.

If the individual theories are failing, the whole project of software engineering – replacing personal skills with formal methods, developing software the way we build appliances, designing and proving applications mathematically – is failing. Each theory displays the characteristics of a pseudoscience; but, in addition, the failure of each theory constitutes a falsification of the very idea of software engineering. Thus, by denying the failure of the individual theories, software engineering as a whole has been turned into a pseudoscience.

Object-Oriented Programming

The Quest for Higher Levels

Mechanistic software theories attempt to improve programming productivity by raising the level of abstraction in software development; specifically, by introducing methods, languages, and systems where the starting elements are of a higher level than those found in the traditional programming languages. But the notion of higher starting levels is a delusion. It stems from the two mechanistic fallacies, reification and abstraction: the belief that we can separate the structures that make up a complex phenomenon, and the belief that we can represent a phenomenon accurately even while ignoring its low-level elements.

The similarity of software and language, we saw, can help us to understand this delusion. We cannot start from higher levels in software development for the same reason we cannot start with ready-made sentences in linguistic communication. In both cases, when we ignore the low levels we lose the ability to implement details and to link structures. The structures are the various *aspects* of an idea, or of a software application. In language, therefore, we must start with words, and create our own sentences, if we want to be able to express *any* idea; and in programming, we must start with the traditional software elements, and create our own constructs, if we want to be able to implement *any* application.

In a simple structure, the values displayed by the top element reflect the combinations of elements at the lower levels. So, the lower the starting elements, the more combinations are possible, and the larger is the number of alternatives for the value of the top element. In a *complex* structure even more values are possible, because the top element is affected by several interacting structures. Software applications are complex structures, so the impoverishment caused by starting from higher levels can be explained as a loss of both combinations and interactions: fewer combinations are possible between elements within the individual structures, and fewer interactions are possible between structures. As a result, there are fewer possible values for the top element – the application. (See "Abstraction and Reification" in chapter 1.)

While starting from higher levels may be practical for simple applications, or for applications limited to a narrow domain, for general business applications the starting level cannot be higher than the one found in the traditional programming languages. Any theory that attempts to raise this level must be "enhanced" later with features that restore the low levels. So, while praising the power of the high levels, the experts end up contriving more and more *low-level* expedients – without which their system, language, or method would be useless.

We already saw this charlatanism in the previous section, when non-standard flow-control constructs, and even GOTO, were incorporated into structured programming. But because structured programming was still based on the traditional languages, the return to low levels was not, perhaps, evident; all that the experts had to do to restore the low levels was to annul some of the restrictions they had imposed earlier. The charlatanism became blatant, however, with the theories that followed, because these theories restrict programming, not just to certain constructs, but to special development systems. Consequently, when the theories fail, the experts do not restore the low levels by returning to the traditional programming concepts, but by reproducing some of these concepts *within* the new systems. In other words, they now *prevent* us from regaining the freedom of the traditional languages, and *force* us to depend on their systems.

In the present section, we will see how this charlatanism manifests itself in the so-called object-oriented systems; then, in the next section, we will examine the same charlatanism in the relational database systems. Other systems belonging to this category are the fourth-generation languages and tools like spreadsheets and database query, which were discussed briefly in chapter 6 (see pp. 451–452, 454–455, 464–465).

If we recall the language analogy, and the hypothetical system that would force us to combine ready-made sentences instead of words, we can easily imagine what would happen. We would be unable to express a certain idea unless the system happened to include the required sentences. So the experts would have to offer us more and more sentences, and more and more methods to use them – means to modify a sentence, to combine sentences, and so forth. We would perceive every addition as a powerful new feature, convinced that this was the only way to have language. We would spend more and more time with these sentences and methods, and communication would become increasingly complicated. But, in the end, even with thousands of sentences, we would be unable to express ourselves as well as we do now, simply by combining words.

While it is hard to see how anyone could be persuaded to depend on a system that promises higher starting levels in language, the whole world is being fooled by the same promise in software. And when this idea turns out to be a delusion, we continue to be fooled: we agree to depend on development systems that praise the benefits of high starting levels, even as we see them being modified to reinstate the low levels.

At first, the software experts try to enhance the functionality of their system by adding more and more high-level elements: whenever we fail to implement a certain requirement by combining existing elements, they provide some new ones. But we need an infinity of alternatives in our applications, and it is impossible to provide enough high-level elements to generate them all. So the experts must also add some *low-level* elements, similar to those found in the traditional languages. By then, their system ceases to be the simple and elegant high-level environment they started with; it becomes an awkward mixture of high and low levels, built-in functions, and odd software concepts.

And still, many requirements remain impossible or difficult to implement. There are two reasons for this. First, the experts do not restore *all* the low-level elements we had before; and without enough low-level elements we cannot create all the combinations needed to implement details and to link the application's structures. Second, the low-level elements are provided as an artificial extension to the high-level features, so we cannot use them freely. Instead of the simple, traditional way of combining elements – from low to high levels – we must now use some contrived methods based on high-level features.

In conclusion, these systems are fraudulent: not only do they fail to provide the promised improvement (programming exclusively through high-level features), but they make application development even more difficult than before. Their true purpose is not to increase productivity, but to maintain programming incompetence and to prevent programming freedom. The software elites force us to depend on complicated, expensive, and inefficient development environments, when we could accomplish much more with ordinary programming languages. (The fallacy of high software levels was discussed in greater detail in "The Delusion of High Levels" in chapter 6.)

The Promise

Like structured programming before it, object-oriented programming was hailed as an entirely new approach to application development: "OOP – Object-Oriented Programming – is a revolutionary change in programming. Without a doubt, OOP is the most significant single change that has occurred in the software field."[1] "Object technology … represents a major watershed in the history of computing."[2] "Object-oriented technology promises to produce

---

[1] Peter Coad and Jill Nicola, *Object-Oriented Programming* (Englewood Cliffs, NJ: PTR Prentice Hall, 1993), p. xxxiii.

[2] Paul Harmon and David A. Taylor, *Objects in Action: Commercial Applications of Object-Oriented Technologies* (Reading, MA: Addison-Wesley, 1993), p. 15.

a software revolution in terms of cost and quality that will rival that of microprocessors and their integrated circuit technologies during the 1980s."[3] "The goal is not just to improve the programming process but to define an entirely new paradigm for software construction."[4] "Object orientation is … the technology that some regard as the ultimate paradigm for the modelling of information, be that information data or logic."[5] "The *paradigm shift* we'll be exploring … is far more fundamental than a simple change in tools or terminology. In fact, the shift to objects will require major changes in the way we think about and use business computing systems, not just how we develop the software for them."[6]

Thus, while structured programming had been just a revolution, object-oriented programming was also *a new paradigm*. Finally, claimed the theorists, we have achieved a breakthrough in programming concepts.

If the promise of structured programming had been to develop and prove applications mathematically, the promise of object-oriented programming was "reusable software components": employing pieces of software the way we employ subassemblies in manufacturing and construction. The new paradigm will change the nature of programming by turning the dream of software reuse into a practical concept. Programming – the "construction" of software – will be simplified by systematically eliminating all repetition and duplication. Software will be developed in the form of independent "objects": entities related and classified in such a way that no one will ever again need to program a piece of software that has already been programmed. One day, when enough classes of objects are available, the development of a new application will entail little more than putting together existing pieces of software. The only thing we will have to program is the *differences* between our requirements and the existing software.

Some of these ideas were first proposed in the 1960s, but it was only in the 1980s that they reached the mainstream programming community. And it was in the 1990s, when it became obvious that structured programming and the structured methodologies did not fulfil their promise, that object-oriented programming became a major preoccupation. A new madness possessed the universities and the corporations – a madness not unlike the one engendered

[3] Stephen Montgomery, *Object-Oriented Information Engineering: Analysis, Design, and Implementation* (Cambridge, MA: Academic Press, 1994), p. 11.

[4] David A. Taylor, *Object-Oriented Technology: A Manager's Guide* (Reading, MA: Addison-Wesley, 1990), p. 88.

[5] John S. Hares and John D. Smart, *Object Orientation: Technology, Techniques, Management and Migration* (Chichester, UK: John Wiley and Sons, 1994), p. 1.

[6] Michael Guttman and Jason Matthews, *The Object Technology Revolution* (New York: John Wiley and Sons, 1995), p. 13.

by structured programming in the 1970s. Twenty years later, we hear the same claims and the same rhetoric: There is a software crisis. Software development is inefficient because our current practices are based, like those of the old craftsmen, on personal skills. We must turn programming into a formal activity, like engineering. It is concepts like standard parts and prefabricated subassemblies that make our manufacturing and construction activities so successful, so we must emulate these concepts in our programming activities. We must build software applications the way we build appliances and houses.

Some examples: "A major theme of object technology is *construction from parts*, that is, the fabrication, customization, and assembly of component parts into working applications."[7] "The software-development process is similar in concept to the processes used in the construction and manufacturing industries."[8] "Part of the appeal of object orientation is the analogy between object-oriented software components and electronic integrated circuits. At last, we in software have the opportunity to build systems in a way similar to that of modern electronic engineers by connecting prefabricated components that implement powerful abstractions."[9] "Object-oriented techniques allow software to be constructed of *objects* that have a specified behavior. Objects themselves can be built out of other objects, that in turn can be built out of objects. This resembles complex machinery being built out of assemblies, subassemblies, sub-subassemblies, and so on."[10]

For some theorists, the object-oriented idea goes beyond software reuse. The ultimate goal of object-oriented programming, they say, is to reduce programming to mathematics, and thereby turn software development into an exact, error-free activity. Thus, because they failed to see why the earlier idea, structured programming, was mistaken despite its mathematical aspects, these theorists are committing now the same fallacy with the object-oriented idea. Here is an example: "For our work to become a true engineering discipline, we must base our practices on hard science. For us, that science is a combination of mathematics (for its precision in definition and reasoning) and a science of

[7] Daniel Tkach and Richard Puttick, *Object Technology in Application Development* (Redwood City, CA: Benjamin/Cummings, 1994), p. 4.

[8] Ed Seidewitz and Mike Stark, *Reliable Object-Oriented Software: Applying Analysis and Design* (New York: SIGS Books, 1995), p. 6.

[9] Meilir Page-Jones, *What Every Programmer Should Know about Object-Oriented Design* (New York: Dorset House, 1995), p. 66.

[10] James Martin, *Principles of Object-Oriented Analysis and Design* (Englewood Cliffs, NJ: PTR Prentice Hall, 1993), pp. 4–5.

information. Today we are starting to see analysis methods that are based on these concepts. The Shlaer-Mellor method of OOA [object-oriented analysis], for example, is constructed as a mathematical formalism, complete with axioms and theorems. These axioms and theorems have been published as 'rules'; we expect that as other methods become more fully developed, they, too, will be defined at this level of precision."[11]

And, once the analysis and design process is fully formalized, that elusive dream, the automation of programming, will finally be within reach. With the enormous demand for software, we can no longer afford to squander our skills constructing software by hand. We must alter the way we practise programming, from *handcrafting* software, to operating machines that make software for us: "We as practitioners must change. We must change from highly skilled artisans to being software manufacturing engineers.... We cannot afford to sit in front of our workstations and continue to build, fit, smooth, and adjust, making by hand each part of each subassembly, of each assembly, of each product.... How far away is this future? Not very far.... Our New Year's resolution is to continue this effort and, working with commercial toolmakers, to put meaningful automation in your hands by year's end. I think we can do it."[12]

Thus, the mechanistic software ideology – the belief that software development is akin to manufacturing, and the consequent belief that it is not better programmers that we need but better methods and tools – did not change. What was perceived as a shift in paradigms was in reality only a shift in preoccupations, from "structured" to "object-oriented."

This shift is also reflected in the accompanying rhetoric: as all the claims and promises made previously for structured programming were now being made for object-oriented programming, old slogans could be efficiently reused, simply by replacing the term "structured" with "object-oriented." Thus, we now have object-oriented techniques, object-oriented analysis, object-oriented design, object-oriented methodologies, object-oriented modeling, object-oriented tools, object-oriented user interface, object-oriented project management, and so forth.

There is one striking difference, though: the use of the term "technology." While structured programming was never called a technology, expressions like

---

[11] Sally Shlaer, "A Vision," in *Wisdom of the Gurus: A Vision for Object Technology*, ed. Charles F. Bowman (New York: SIGS Books, 1996), pp. 219–220.

[12] Ibid., pp. 222–223. These statements express perfectly that absurd, long-standing wish of the software theorists – to reduce software to mechanics: the "parts" that we build, fit, etc., in the quotation are *software* parts; and the "toolmakers" are making *software* tools, to be incorporated into software machines (development systems), which will then automatically make those parts for us.

"object technology" and "object-oriented technology" are widespread. What is just another programming concept is presented as a *technology*. But this is simply part of the general inflation in the use of "technology," which has affected all discourse (see "The Slogan 'Technology'" in chapter 5).

❖

To further illustrate the object-oriented propaganda, let as analyze a few passages from a book that was written as a guide for managers:[13] "We see object-oriented technology as an important step toward the industrialization of software, in which programming is transformed from an arcane craft to a systematic manufacturing process. But this transformation can't take place unless senior managers understand and support it."[14] This is why "this guide is written for managers, not engineers":[15] for individuals who need not "know how to program a computer or even use one."[16] The guide, in other words, is for individuals who can believe that, although they know nothing about program-ming, they will be able to decide, just by reading a few easy pages, whether this new "technology" can solve the software problems faced by their organization.

Taylor continues by telling us about the software crisis, in sentences that could have been copied directly from a text written twenty years earlier: development projects take longer than planned, and cost more; often, the resulting applications have so many defects that they are unusable; many of them are never completed; those that work cannot be modified later to meet their users' evolving needs.[17] Then, after describing some of the previous attempts to solve the crisis (structured programming, fourth-generation languages, CASE, various database models), Taylor concludes: "Despite all efforts to find better ways to build programs, the software crisis is growing worse with each passing year.... We need a new approach to building software, one that leaves behind the bricks and mortar of conventional programming and offers a truly better way to construct systems. This new approach must be able to handle large systems as well as small, and it must create reliable systems that are flexible, maintainable, and capable of evolving to meet changing needs.... Object-oriented technology can meet these challenges and more."[18]

The object-oriented revolution will transform programming in the same way the Industrial Revolution transformed manufacturing. Taylor reminds us how goods were produced earlier: Each product was a unique creation of a particular craftsman, and consequently its parts were not interchangeable with

---

[13] David A. Taylor, *Object-Oriented Technology: A Manager's Guide* (Reading, MA: Addison-Wesley, 1990).   [14] Ibid., p. iii.

[15] Ibid., p. vii ("engineers," of course, means programmers).   [16] Ibid.

[17] Ibid., pp. 1–2.   [18] Ibid., pp. 13–14.

those of another product, even when the products were alike. Goods made in this fashion were expensive, and their quality varied. Then, in 1798, Eli Whitney conceived a new way of building rifles: by using standard parts. This greatly reduced the overall time and cost of producing them; moreover, their quality was now uniform and generally better. Modern manufacturing is based on this concept.[19]

The aim of object-oriented technology is to emulate in programming the modern manufacturing methods. It is a radical departure from the traditional approach to software development – a paradigm shift, just as the concept of standard parts was for manufacturing: "Two hundred years after the Industrial Revolution, the craft approach to producing material goods seems hopelessly antiquated. Yet this is precisely how we fabricate software systems today. Each program is a unique creation, constructed piece by piece out of the raw materials of a programming language by skilled software craftspeople.... Conventional programming is roughly on a par with manufacturing two hundred years ago.... This comparison with the Industrial Revolution reveals the true ambition behind the object-oriented approach. The goal is not just to improve the programming process but to define an entirely new paradigm for software construction."[20]

Note, throughout the foregoing passages, the liberal use of terms like "build," "construct," "manufacture," and "fabricate" to describe software development, without any attempt to prove first that programming is similar to the activities performed in a factory. Taylor doesn't doubt for a moment that software applications can be developed with the methods we use to build appliances. It doesn't occur to him that the reason we still have a software crisis after all these years is precisely this fallacy, precisely because all theories are founded on mechanistic principles. He claims that object-oriented programming is different from the previous ideas; but it too is mechanistic, so it too will fail.

This type of propaganda works because few people remember the previous programming theories, and even fewer understand the reason for their failure. The assertions made in these passages – presenting the latest theory as salvation, hailing the imminent transition of programming from an arcane craft to an engineering process – are identical to those made twenty years earlier in behalf of structured programming. And they are also identical to those made in behalf of the so-called fourth-generation languages, and CASE. It is because they didn't study the failure of structured programming that the theorists and the practitioners fall prey to the same delusions with each new idea.

Also identical is calling incompetent programmers "skilled software crafts-people" (as in the last quotation), or "highly skilled artisans" (as in a previous

---

[19] Ibid., pp. 86–87.   [20] Ibid., p. 88.

quotation, see p. 633). We discussed this distortion earlier (see pp. 497–499). The same theorists who say that programmers are messy and cannot even learn to use GOTO correctly (see pp. 619–621) say at the same time that programmers have already attained the highest possible skills (and, hence, that new methods and tools are the only way to improve their work). Although absurd – because they are contradictory, and also untrue – these claims are enthusiastically accepted by the software bureaucrats with each new theory. Thus, at any given time, and just by being preoccupied with the latest fantasies, ignorant academics, managers, and programmers can flatter themselves that they are carrying out a software revolution.

The Theory

1

Let us examine the theory behind object-oriented programming. Software applications are now made up of *objects*, rather than modules. Objects are independent software entities that represent specific processes. The *attributes* of an object include various types of data and the operations that act on this data. The objects that make up an application communicate with one other through *messages*: by means of a message, one object invokes another and asks it to perform one of the operations it is capable of performing. Just as in calling traditional subroutines, a message may include parameters, and the invoked object may return a value. So it is this structure of objects and messages that determines the application's performance, rather than a structure of modules and flow-control constructs, as was the case under structured programming.

Central to the concept of objects is their hierarchical organization. Recall our discussion of hierarchical structures and levels of abstraction (in "Simple Structures" in chapter 1). When we move up from one level to the next, the complexity of the elements increases, because one element is made up of several lower-level elements. At each level we extract, or abstract, those attributes that define the relation between the two levels, and ignore the others; so the higher-level element retains only those attributes that are common to all the elements that make it up. Conversely, when we move down, each of the lower-level elements possesses all the attributes of the higher-level element, plus some new ones. There are more details as we move from high to low levels, and fewer as we move from low to high levels. Thus, the levels of a hierarchy function as both levels of complexity and levels of abstraction.

We saw how the process of abstraction works in classification systems. Take, for example, a classification of animals: we can divide animals into wild and domestic, the domestic into types like dogs, horses, and chickens, the dogs into breeds like spaniel, terrier, and retriever, and finally each breed into the individual animals. Types like dogs, horses, and chickens possess *specific* attributes, and in addition they *share* those attributes defining the higher-level element to which they all belong – domestic animals. Similarly, while each breed is characterized by specific attributes, all breeds share those attributes that distinguish them as a particular type of animal – dogs, for instance. Finally, each individual animal, in addition to possessing some unique attributes, shares with others the attributes of its breed.

Just like the elements in the classification of animals, software objects form a hierarchical structure. The elements at each level are known as *classes*, and the attributes relating one level to the next are the data types and the operations that make up the objects. A particular class, thus, includes the objects that possess a particular combination of data types and operations. And each class at the next lower level possesses, in addition to these, its own, unique data types and operations. The lower the level, the more data types and operations take part in the definition of a class. Conversely, the higher the level, the simpler the definition, since each level retains only those data types and operations that are common to all the classes of the lower level. So, as in any hierarchical structure, the levels in the classification of software objects also function as levels of abstraction.

This hierarchical relationship gives rise to a process called *inheritance*, and it is through inheritance that software entities can be systematically reused. As we just saw, the classes that make up a particular level *inherit* the attributes (the data types and operations) of the class that forms the next higher level. And, since the latter inherits in its turn the attributes of the next higher level, and so on, each class in the hierarchy inherits the attributes of all the classes above it. Each class, therefore, may possess many inherited attributes in addition to its own, unique attributes.

The process of inheritance is, obviously, the process of abstraction observed in reverse: when following the hierarchy from low to high levels, we note the *abstraction* of attributes (fewer and fewer are retained); from high to low levels, we note the *inheritance* of attributes (more and more are acquired).

Through the process of inheritance, we can create classes of objects with diverse combinations of attributes without having to define an attribute more than once. All we need to do for a new class is define the *additional* attributes – those that are not possessed by the higher-level classes. To put it differently, simply by defining the classes of objects hierarchically, as classes within classes, we eliminate the need to duplicate attributes: a data type or operation defined for a particular class will be inherited by all the classes below it. So, as we extend the software hierarchy with lower and lower levels of classes, we will have classes that, even if adding few attributes of their own, can possess a rich set of attributes – those of all the higher-level classes.

The classes are only templates, *definitions* of data types and operations. To create an application, we generate replicas, or instances of these templates, and it is these instances that become the *actual* objects. All classes, regardless of level, can function as templates; and each one can engender an unlimited number of actual objects. Thus, only in the application will the data types and operations defined in the class hierarchy become real objects – real data and operations.

2

These, then, are the principles behind the idea of object-oriented programming. And it is easy to see why they constitute a new programming paradigm, a radical departure from the traditional way of developing applications. It is not the idea of software reuse that is new, but the idea of taking software reuse to its theoretical limit: in principle, we will never again have to duplicate a programming task.

We always strove to avoid rewriting software – by copying pieces of software from previous applications, for example, and by relying on subroutine libraries. But the traditional methods of software reuse are not very effective. Their main limitation is that the existing module must fit the new requirements perfectly. This is why software reuse was limited to small pieces of code, and to subroutines that perform some common operations; we could rarely reuse a *significant* portion of an application. Besides, it was difficult even to *know* whether reusable software existed: a programmer would often duplicate a piece of software simply because he had no way of knowing that another programmer had already written it.

So code reuse was impractical before because our traditional development methods were concerned largely with *programming* issues. Hierarchical software classes, on the other hand, reflect our affairs, which are themselves related hierarchically. Thus, the hierarchical concept allows us to organize and relate the existing pieces of software logically, and to reuse them efficiently.

The object-oriented ideal is that all the software in the world be part of one giant hierarchy of classes, related according to function, and without any duplication of data types or operations. For a new application, we would start with some of the existing classes, and create the missing functions in the form of new classes that branch out of the existing ones. These classes would then join the hierarchy of existing software, and other programmers would be able to use them just as we used the older ones.

Realistically, though, what we should expect is not *one* hierarchy but a large number of *separate* hierarchies, created by different programmers on different occasions, and covering different aspects of our affairs. Still, because their classes can be combined, all these hierarchies together will act, in effect, as one giant hierarchy. For example, we can interpret a certain class in one hierarchy, together perhaps with some of its lower-level classes, as a new class that branches out of a particular class in another hierarchy. The only deviation from the object-oriented ideal is in the slight duplication of classes caused by the separation of hierarchies.

The explanation for the exceptional reuse potential in the object-oriented concept is that a class hierarchy allows us to start with software that is just *close*, in varying degrees, to a new requirement – whereas before we could only reuse software that fitted a new requirement *exactly*. It is much easier to find software that is *close* to our needs than software that *matches* our needs. We hope, of course, to find some *low-level* classes in the existing software; that is, classes which already include most of the details we have to implement. But even when no such classes exist, we can still benefit from the existing software. In this case, we simply agree to start from slightly higher levels of abstraction – from classes that resemble only broadly our requirements – and to create a slightly larger number of new classes and levels. Thus, regardless of how much of the required software already exists, the object-oriented approach guarantees that, in a given situation, we will only perform the minimum amount of work; specifically, we will only program what was not programmed before.

Let us take a specific situation. In many business applications we find data types representing the quantity in stock of various items, and operations that check and alter these values. Every day, thousands of programmers write pieces of software that are, in the end, nothing but variations of the same function: managing an item's quantity in stock. The object-oriented approach will replace this horrendous duplication with one hierarchy of classes, designed to handle the most common situations. Programmers will then start with these classes, and perhaps add a few classes of their own to implement some unique functions. Thus, the existing classes will allow us to increment and decrement the quantity, interpret a certain stock level as too high or too low, and the like. And if we need an unusual function – say, a history of the lowest monthly quantities left in stock – we will simply add to the hierarchy our own class, with appropriate data types and operations, just for this one function.

Clearly, we could have a hierarchy of this kind for every aspect of our work. But we could also have classes for entire processes, even entire applications. For example, we could have a hierarchy of specialized classes for inventory management systems. Then, starting with these classes, we could quickly create any inventory management application: we would take some classes from low levels and others from high levels; we would ignore some classes altogether; and we would add our own classes to implement details and unusual requirements. We could even combine classes from several inventory management hierarchies, supplied by different software vendors.

This is how the experts envisage the future of application development: "The term software industrial revolution has been used to describe the move to an era when software will be compiled out of reusable components. Components will be built out of other components and vast libraries of such components will be created."[1] "In the not-too-distant future, it will probably be considered archaic to design or code *any* application from scratch. Instead, the norm will be to grab a bunch of business object classes from a gigantic, worldwide assortment available on the meganet, create a handful of new classes that tie the reusable classes together, and – *voilà*! – a new application is born with no muss, no fuss, and very little coding."[2]

Programming as we know it will soon become redundant, and will be remembered as we remember today the old manufacturing methods. The number of available object classes will grow exponentially, so programmers will spend more and more time combining existing classes, and less and less time creating new ones. The skills required of programmers, thus, will change too: from knowing how to create new software, to knowing what classes are available and how to combine them. Since the new skills can be acquired more easily and more quickly, we will no longer depend on talented and experienced programmers. The object-oriented paradigm will solve the software crisis, therefore, both by reducing the time needed to create a new application and by permitting a larger number of people to create applications.

The Contradictions

1

We recognize in the object-oriented fantasy the software variant of the language fantasies we studied in chapter 4. The mechanistic language theories, we saw, assume that it is possible to represent the world with a simple hierarchical structure. Hence, if we invent a language that can itself be represented as a hierarchical structure, we will be able to mirror the world perfectly in language: the smallest linguistic elements (the words, for example) will mirror

[1] James Martin, *Principles of Object-Oriented Analysis and Design* (Englewood Cliffs, NJ: PTR Prentice Hall, 1993), p. 5.
[2] Michael Guttman and Jason Matthews, *The Object Technology Revolution* (New York: John Wiley and Sons, 1995), p. 76.

the smallest entities that make up the world; and the relations between linguistic elements will mirror the natural laws that govern the real things. The hierarchical structure of linguistic elements will then correspond on a one-to-one basis to the hierarchical structure of real objects, processes, and events. By combining sentences in this language as we do operations in mathematical logic, we will be able to explain any phenomenon. Thus, being logically perfect and at the same time a perfect picture of the world, a language designed as a simple hierarchical structure will allow us to represent and to understand the world.

From the theories of Leibniz, Dalgarno, and Wilkins in the seventeenth century to those of Russell and Carnap in the twentieth, the search for a logically perfect language has been one of the most persistent manifestations of the mechanistic myth. The fallacy, we saw, is not so much in the idea of a logically perfect language, as in the belief that such a language can accurately mirror the world. It is quite easy, in fact, to design a language in the form of a hierarchical structure, and to represent in it the entities and levels of abstraction that exist in the world. The problem, rather, is that there are *many* such structures – many different ways to represent the world – all correct and relevant.

The entities that make up the world possess many attributes, and are therefore connected through many structures at the same time, one structure for each attribute. Thus, if our language is to represent reality accurately, the linguistic elements too must be connected through more than one structure at the same time. The language mechanists attempt to find one classification, or one system, that would relate all objects, processes, and events that can exist in the world. But this is a futile quest. Even a simple object has many attributes – shape, dimensions, colour, texture, position, origin, age, and so forth. To place it in *one* hierarchy, therefore, we would have to choose *one* attribute and ignore the others. So, if we cannot represent with one hierarchy even ordinary objects, how can we hope to represent the more complex aspects of the world?

It is precisely because they are *not* logically perfect that our *natural* languages allow us to describe the world. Here is how: We use words to represent the real things that make up the world. Thus, since the real things share many attributes and are linked through many structures, the words that represent those things will also be linked through many structures. The words that make up a message, a story, or an argument will form one structure for each structure formed by the real things.

The mechanistic language theories fail to represent the world accurately because their elements can be connected in only one way: they attempt to represent with *one* linguistic structure the *system* of structures that is the world. The mechanists insist on a simple structure because this is the only way to have a deterministic system of representation. But if the world is a complex structure, and is therefore an indeterministic phenomenon, any theory that attempts to represent it through deterministic means is bound to fail.

❖

Since it is the same world that we have to represent through language and through software, what is true for language is also true for software. To represent the world, the software entities that make up an application must be related through many structures at the same time. If we restrict their relations to one hierarchy, the application will not mirror the world accurately. Thus, whether we classify all the existing software entities or just the entities of one application, we need a system of interacting structures. *One* structure, as in the object-oriented paradigm, can only represent the relations created by *one* attribute (or perhaps by *a few* attributes, if shared by the software entities in a limited way).

Recall our discussion of complex structures in chapter 1 (pp. 100–104) and in chapter 4 (pp. 356–363). We saw that any attempt to represent several attributes with one structure results in an incorrect hierarchy. Because the attributes must be shown *within one another*, all but the first will be repeated for each branch created by the previous ones; and this is not how entities possess attributes in reality.

Only when each attribute is possessed by just *some* of the entities can they all be included in one hierarchy. Here is how this can be done, if we agree to restrict the attributes (figure 1-6, p. 103, is an example of such a hierarchy): the class of all entities is shown as the top element, and one attribute can be shared by all the entities; on the basis of the values taken by this attribute, the entities are divided into several classes, thereby creating the lower level; then, in each one of these classes the entities can possess a second attribute (but they must all possess the same attribute, and this attribute cannot be shared with entities from the other classes); on the basis of the values taken by this attribute, each class is then divided into third-level classes, where the entities can possess a third attribute, again unique to each class; and so on. (On each level, instead of one attribute per class, we can have a set of several attributes, provided they are all unique to that class. The set as a whole will act in effect as one attribute, so the levels and classes will be the same as in a hierarchy with single attributes.)

The issue, then, is simply this: Is it possible to restrict software entities to the kind of relations that can be represented through a strict hierarchical structure, as described above? Do software entities possess their attributes in such a limited way that we can represent all existing software with one structure? Or, if not all existing software, can we represent at least each individual application with one structure? As we saw, the answer is *no*. To mirror the world, software entities must be related through all their attributes at the same time; and these attributes, which reflect the various processes implemented in the application (see pp. 347–348), only rarely exist *within one another*. Only rarely, therefore, can software entities be classified or related through *one* hierarchical structure. Whether the classification includes all existing software, or just the objects of one application, we need a *system* of structures – perhaps as many structures as there are attributes – to represent their relations.

The benefits promised by the object-oriented theory can be attained *only* with a simple hierarchical structure. Thus, since it assumes that the relations between software entities can be completely and precisely represented with one structure, the theory is fundamentally fallacious.

Let us recall some of the hierarchies we encountered in previous chapters. The biological classification of animals – classes, orders, families, genera, species – remains a perfect hierarchy only if we agree to take into account just *a few* of their attributes, and to ignore the others. We deliberately limit ourselves to those attributes that *can* be depicted within one another; then, obviously, the categories based on these attributes are related through a strict hierarchy. This classification is important to biologists (to match the theory of natural evolution, for instance); but we can easily create other classifications, based on other attributes.

The distinction between wild and domestic, for example, cannot be part of the biological classification. The reason is that those attributes we use to distinguish an animal as wild or domestic cannot be depicted *within* those attributes we use to distinguish it as mammal, or bird, or reptile; nor can the latter attributes be depicted *within* the former. The two hierarchies overlap. Thus, horses and foxes belong to different categories (domestic and wild) in one hierarchy, but to the same category (class of mammals) in the other; chickens and dogs belong to the same category (domestic) in one hierarchy, but to different categories (birds and mammals) in the other. Clearly, if we restricted ourselves to the biological classification we wouldn't be able to distinguish domestic from wild animals. Each classification is useful if we agree to view animals from one perspective at a time. But only a system of interacting structures can represent *all* their attributes and relations: a system consisting of several hierarchies that exist at the same time and share their terminal elements, the individual animals.

Similarly, organizations like corporations and armies can be represented as a strict hierarchy of people only if we take into account *one* attribute – the role or rank of these people. This is the hierarchy we are usually concerned with, but we can also create hierarchies by classifying the people according to their age, or gender, or height, or any other attribute. Each classification would likely be different, and only rarely can we combine two hierarchies by depicting one attribute *within* the other.

For example, only if the positions in an organization are gender-dependent can we combine gender and role in one hierarchy: we first divide the people into two categories, men and women, and then add their various roles as lower levels *within* these two categories. The final classification is a correct hierarchy, with no repetition of attributes. It is all but impossible, however, to add a *third* attribute to this hierarchy without repetition; that is, by depicting it strictly *within* the second one. We cannot add a level based on age, for instance, because people of the same age are very likely found in more than one of the categories established by the various combinations of gender and role.

Recall, lastly, the structure of subassemblies that make up a device like a car or appliance. This structure too is a strict hierarchy, and we can build devices as hierarchies of things within things because we purposely design them so that their parts are related mainly through one attribute – through their role in the construction and operation of the device. The levels of subassemblies are then the counterpart of the levels of categories in a classification hierarchy. But, just as entities can be the terminal elements in many classifications, the ultimate parts of a device can be the terminal elements of many hierarchies.

The hierarchy we are usually concerned with – the one we see in engineering diagrams and in bills of material, and which permits us to build devices as levels of subassemblies – is the structure established by their physical and functional relationship. But we can think of many other relations between the same parts – relations based on such attributes as weight, colour, manufacturer, date of manufacture, life expectancy, or cost. We can classify parts on the basis of any attribute, and each classification would constitute a different hierarchy. Besides, only rarely do parts possess attributes in such a way that we can depict their respective hierarchies as one *within* another. Only rarely, therefore, can we combine several hierarchies into one. (Parts made on different dates, for example, may be used in the same subassembly; and parts used in different subassemblies may come from the same manufacturer.)

The promise of object-oriented programming is *specifically* the concept of hierarchical classes. This concept is well-suited for representing our affairs in software, the experts say, because the entities that make up the world are themselves related hierarchically: "A model which is designed using an object-oriented technology is often easy to understand, as it can be directly related to reality."[1] "The object-oriented viewpoint attempts to more closely reflect the natural structure of the problem domain rather than the implicit structure of computer hardware."[2] "OOP [object-oriented programming] enables programmers to write software that is organized like the problem domain under consideration."[3] "One of the greatest benefits of an object-oriented structure is the direct mapping from objects in the problem domain to objects in the program."[4] "OOP design is less concerned with the underlying computer model than are most other design methods, as the intent is to produce a software system that has a natural relationship to the real world situation it is modelling."[5] "Object orientation ... should help to relate computer systems more closely to the real world."[6] "The intuitive appeal of object orientation is that it provides better concepts and tools with which to model and represent the real world as closely as possible."[7] "The models we build in OO [object-oriented] analysis reflect reality more naturally than the models in traditional systems analysis.... Using OO techniques, we build software that more closely models the real world."[8]

But, as we saw, the entities that make up the world are related through *many* hierarchies, not one. How, then, can software entities related through one classification mirror them accurately? The software mechanists want to have both the simplicity of a hierarchical structure and the ability to mirror the world. And in their attempt to realize this dream, they commit the fallacy of reification: they extract *one* structure from the complex phenomenon, expecting this structure alone to provide a useful approximation.

Now, it is obvious that hierarchical software classes allow us to implement such applications as the process of assembling an appliance, or the positions held by people in an organization, or the biological classification of animals.

[1] Ivar Jacobson et al., *Object-Oriented Software Engineering: A Use Case Driven Approach*, rev. pr. (Reading, MA: Addison-Wesley/ACM Press, 1993), p. 42.

[2] Ed Seidewitz and Mike Stark, *Reliable Object-Oriented Software: Applying Analysis and Design* (New York: SIGS Books, 1995), p. 26.

[3] Peter Coad and Jill Nicola, *Object-Oriented Programming* (Englewood Cliffs, NJ: PTR Prentice Hall, 1993), p. xxxiii.

[4] Greg Voss, *Object-Oriented Programming: An Introduction* (Berkeley, CA: Osborne McGraw-Hill, 1991), p. 30.

[5] Mark Mullin, *Object-Oriented Program Design* (Reading, MA: Addison-Wesley, 1989), p. 5.

[6] Daniel Tkach and Richard Puttick, *Object Technology in Application Development* (Redwood City, CA: Benjamin/Cummings, 1994), p. 17.

[7] Setrag Khoshafian and Razmik Abnous, *Object Orientation: Concepts, Languages, Databases, User Interfaces* (New York: John Wiley and Sons, 1990), p. 6.

[8] James Martin and James J. Odell, *Object-Oriented Analysis and Design* (Englewood Cliffs, NJ: Prentice Hall, 1992), p. 67.

But these are artificial structures, the result of a design that deliberately restricted the relations between elements to certain attributes: we can ignore the other structures because we *ensured* that the relations caused by the other attributes are much weaker. These structures, then, do not represent the actual phenomenon, but only one aspect of it – an aspect that can be depicted with one hierarchy. So, like any mechanistic concept, hierarchical software classes are useful when the problem can indeed be approximated with one structure.

The object-oriented promise, though, is that the concept of hierarchical classes will help us to implement *any* application, not just those that are *already* a neat hierarchy. Thus, since the parts that make up our affairs are usually related through several hierarchies at the same time, the object-oriented promise cannot possibly be met. Nothing stops us from restricting every application to what *can* be represented with one hierarchy; namely, relations based on one attribute, or a small number of carefully selected attributes. But then, our software will not mirror our affairs accurately.

As we saw under structured programming, an application in which all relations are represented with one hierarchy is useless, because it must always do the same thing (see p. 547). Such an application can have no conditions or iterations, for example. Whether the hierarchy is the nesting scheme of structured programming, or the object classification of object-oriented programming, each element must always be executed, always executed once, and always in the same relative sequence. This, after all, is what we expect to see in any system represented with one hierarchy; for instance, the parts and subassemblies that make up an appliance always exist, and are always connected in the same way.

Thus, after twenty years of structured programming delusions, the software experts started a new revolution that suffers, ultimately, from the same fallacy: the belief that our affairs can be represented with *one* hierarchical structure.

2

What we have discussed so far – the neatness of hierarchical classes, the benefits of code reuse, the idea of software concepts that match our affairs – is what we see in the *promotion* of object-oriented programming; that is, in advertisements, magazine articles, and the introductory chapters of textbooks. And this contrasts sharply with the *reality* of object-oriented programming: what we find when attempting to develop actual applications is difficult, non-intuitive concepts. Let us take a moment to analyze this contradiction.

As we saw, the theorists promote the new paradigm by claiming that it lets us represent our affairs in software *more naturally.* Here are some additional examples of this claim: "The models built during object-oriented analysis provide a more natural way to think about systems."[9] "Object-oriented programming is built around *classes* and *objects* that model real-world entities in a more natural way.... Object-oriented programming allows you to construct programs the way we humans tend to think about things."[10] "The object-oriented approach to computer systems is ... a more natural approach for people, since we naturally think in terms of objects and we classify them into hierarchies and divide them into parts."[11]

The illustrations, too, are simple and intuitive. One book explains the idea of hierarchical classes using the Ford Mustang car: there is a plain, generic model; then, there is a base model and an improved LX model, each one inheriting the features of the generic model but also adding its own; and there is the GT sports model, derived from the LX but with some features replacing or enhancing the LX features.[12] Another book explains the object-oriented concepts using the world of baseball: objects are entities like players, coaches, balls, and stadiums; they have attributes like batting averages and salaries, perform operations like pitching and catching, and belong to classes like teams and bases.[13]

The impression conveyed by the *promotion* of object-oriented programming, thus, is that all we have to do is define our requirements in a hierarchical fashion – an easy task in any event, since this is how we normally view the world and conduct our affairs – and the application is almost done. The power of this new technology is ours to enjoy simply by learning a few principles and purchasing a few tools.

When we study the *actual* object-oriented systems, however, we find an entirely different reality: huge development environments, complicated methodologies, and an endless list of definitions, rules, and principles that we must assimilate. Hundreds of books had to be written to help us understand the new paradigm. In one chapter after another, strange and difficult concepts are being introduced – concepts which have nothing to do with our programming or business needs, but which must be mastered if we want to use an object-oriented system. In other words, what we find when attempting

[9] James Martin, *Principles of Object-Oriented Analysis and Design* (Englewood Cliffs, NJ: PTR Prentice Hall, 1993), p. 3.

[10] Andrew C. Staugaard Jr., *Structured and Object-Oriented Techniques: An Introduction Using C++*, 2nd ed. (Upper Saddle River, NJ: Prentice Hall, 1997), p. 29.

[11] John W. Satzinger and Tore U. Ørvik, *The Object-Oriented Approach: Concepts, Modeling, and System Development* (Cambridge, MA: Course Technology, 1996), p. 11.

[12] Khoshafian and Abnous, *Object Orientation*, pp. 8–10.

[13] Donald G. Firesmith, *Object-Oriented Requirements Analysis and Logical Design: A Software Engineering Approach* (New York: John Wiley and Sons, 1993), pp. 5–9.

to *practise* object-oriented programming is the exact opposite of what its promotion says.

To make matters worse, the resulting applications are large, unwieldy, and difficult to manage. What can be programmed with just a few statements in a traditional language ends up as an intricate system of classes, objects, definitions, and relations when implemented in an object-oriented environment.

The theorists agree. After telling us that object-oriented programming is a natural, intuitive concept, they tell us that it is in fact difficult, and that it requires much time and effort to learn: "Many experienced and intelligent information systems developers have difficulty understanding and accepting this new point of view."[14] "Those who have programmed before may well find OOP [object-oriented programming] strange at first. It may take a while to forget the ways you have learned, and to [master] another method of programming."[15] "To use OO [object-oriented] technology well, much careful training is needed. It takes time for computer professionals to think in terms of encapsulation, inheritance, and the diagrams of OO analysis and design.... Good use of inheritance and reusable classes requires cultural and organizational changes."[16]

Claiming at the same time that the object-oriented principles are simple and that they are difficult is not as absurd as it sounds; for, in reality, the theorists are describing two different things. When praising the simplicity of these principles, they are referring to the *original* idea – the fantasy of combining and extending hierarchically classes of objects. And indeed, implementing applications as strict hierarchies of objects is easy and intuitive. Very few applications, however, *can* be implemented in this fashion, because very few aspects of the world are mechanistic. So, since most applications must be implemented as *systems* of hierarchies, the original idea was worthless. To make object-oriented programming practical, the means to create multiple, interacting hierarchies had to be restored. But this capability – a natural part of the *traditional* programming concepts – can only be added to an object-oriented system through contrived, awkward extensions. And it is these extensions, as opposed to the simple original idea, that the theorists have in mind when warning us that the object-oriented principles are hard to understand.

The difficulties caused by the object-oriented systems are due, thus, to the reversal of a fundamental programming principle: instead of creating high-level software elements by starting with low-level ones, we are asked to *start*

---

[14] Satzinger and Ørvik, *Object-Oriented Approach*, p. 3.

[15] David N. Smith, *Concepts of Object-Oriented Programming* (New York: McGraw-Hill, 1991), pp. 11–12.   [16] Martin, *Object-Oriented Analysis*, p. 45.

with high-level elements (classes of objects) and to add, where required, lower-level ones. But this is rarely practical. Only by starting with low-level elements can we create all the elements we need at the higher levels. Starting with low-level elements is, therefore, the only way to implement the interacting structures that make up a serious application. The object-oriented theory claimed that we can start with classes of objects because it assumed that we can restrict ourselves to isolated, non-interacting structures; but then, it was extended to permit us to *link* these structures. So now we must create the interactions by starting with high-level elements, which is much more complicated than the traditional way – starting with low-level ones.

3

If a theory expects us to represent our affairs with one hierarchy, while our affairs can only be represented with a system of interacting hierarchies, we must either admit that the theory is invalid, or modify it. The original object-oriented theory was falsified again and again, every time a programmer failed to represent with a strict hierarchical classification a real-world situation. The experts responded to these falsifications, however, not by doubting the theory, but by *expanding* it: they added more and more "features" to make it cope with those situations that would have otherwise refuted it. The theory became, thus, unfalsifiable. As is usually the case with a fallacious theory, the experts saved it from refutation by turning its falsifications into new features. And it is these features, rather than the original concepts, that constitute the *actual* theory – what is being practised under the object-oriented paradigm.

The new features take various forms, but their ultimate purpose is the same: to help us override the restrictions imposed by the original theory. The *actual* theory, thus, is the set of features that allow us to create *interacting* hierarchies. It is these features, the experts explain, that make the object-oriented paradigm such a powerful concept. In other words, the power of the theory derives from those features introduced in order to bypass the theory. We will examine some of these features shortly.

Structured programming, we recall, became practical only after restoring the means to create multiple, interacting flow-control structures – precisely what the original theory had condemned and claimed to be unnecessary. So, in the end, what was called structured programming was the exact opposite of the original theory. Similarly, the object-oriented concepts became practical only after restoring the means to create multiple, interacting class hierarchies. So what is called now object-oriented programming is the exact opposite of the original idea. To this day, the object-oriented concepts are being promoted by praising the benefits of strict hierarchical relations, and by demonstrating these benefits with trivial examples. At the same time, the *actual* object-oriented systems are specifically designed to help us *override* this restriction. But if the benefits are attainable only with a single hierarchy, just as the original theory said, the conclusion must be that the *actual* object-oriented systems offer no benefits.

So the object-oriented paradigm is no better than the other mechanistic software theories: it gives us nothing that we did not have before, with the traditional programming concepts and with any programming language. Each time, the elites promise us a dramatic increase in programming productivity by invoking the hierarchical model. Ultimately, these theories are nothing but various attempts to reduce the complex reality to a simple structure: an isolated flow-control structure, an isolated class structure, and so on. And when this naive idea proves to be worthless, the elites proceed to "enhance" the theories so as to allow us to create *complex* structures again: they restore both the lower levels and the means to link structures, which is the only way to represent our affairs in software.

But by the time a mechanistic theory is "enhanced" to permit multiple, interacting structures, the promised benefits – formal methods for reusing existing software, for building applications as we build appliances, for proving their validity mathematically – are lost. Now it is again our minds that we need, our personal skills and experience, because only minds can process complex structures. So we are back where we were before the theory. The theory, and also the methodologies, programming tools, and development environments based on it, are now senseless. They are even detrimental, because they force us to express our requirements in more complicated ways. We are told that the complications are worthwhile, that this is the only way to attain those benefits. But if the benefits were already lost, all we have now is a theory that makes programming more difficult than it was before.

Thus, by refusing to admit that their theory has failed, by repeatedly expanding it and asking us to depend on it, the elites are committing a fraud: they are covering up the fact that they have nothing to offer us; they keep promising us an increase in programming productivity, when in reality they are preventing us from practising this profession and improving our skills.

As we did for structured programming, we will study the object-oriented fantasy by separating it into several delusions: the belief that we can represent our affairs with a neat, hierarchical classification of software entities; the belief that, instead of one classification, we can represent the same affairs by combining many small, independent classifications; the belief that we can use the object-oriented concepts through traditional programming languages; the belief that we can modify the concepts of abstraction and inheritance in any way we like and still retain their benefits; and the belief that we no longer need to concern ourselves with the application's flow of execution.

Although the five delusions occurred at about the same time, they can be seen, like the delusions of structured programming, as stages in a process of degradation: repeated attempts to rescue the theory from refutation. Each stage was an opportunity for the software experts to recognize the fallaciousness of their theory; instead, at each stage they chose to *expand* it, by incorporating the falsifications and describing them as new features. The stages, thus, mark the evolution of the theory into a pseudoscience (see "Popper's Principles of Demarcation" in chapter 3).

Also as was the case with structured programming, when the object-oriented concepts were being promoted as a revolution and a new paradigm, all five delusions had *already* occurred. Thus, there never existed a serious, practical theory of object-oriented programming. What the experts were promoting was something entirely different: complicated development environments that helped us to create precisely what that theory had claimed to be unnecessary – multiple, interacting software hierarchies.

The First Delusion

The first object-oriented delusion is the belief that we can represent the world with a simple structure of software entities. In fact, only *isolated aspects* of the world can be represented with simple structures. To represent the world accurately we need a *system* of structures. We need, in other words, a complex structure: a set of software entities that belong to several hierarchies at the same time.

The first delusion is akin to the seventeenth-century belief that it is possible to represent all knowledge with one hierarchical structure (see pp. 313–317). What we need to do, said the rationalist philosophers, is depict knowledge in the form of concepts within concepts. The simplest concepts will function as terminal elements (the building blocks of the knowledge structure), while the most complex concepts will form the high levels. Everything that can be known will be represented, thus, in a kind of classification: a giant hierarchy of concepts, neatly related through their characteristics.

It is the principle of abstraction that makes a hierarchical classification possible: at each level, a concept retains only those characteristics common to all the concepts that make up the next lower level. This relationship is clearly seen in a tree diagram: the branches that connect several elements to form a higher-level element signify the operation that extracts the characteristics shared by those elements; then another operation relates the new element to others from the same level, forming an element of the next higher level, and so on.

Similarly, we believe that it is possible (in principle, at least) to design a giant hierarchy of all *software* entities. This hierarchy would be, in effect, a classification of those parts of human knowledge that we want to represent in software – a subset, as it were, of the hierarchy envisaged by the seventeenth-century philosophers. This idea, whether or not explicitly stated, forms the foundation of the object-oriented paradigm. For, only if we succeed in relating all software entities through one hierarchical structure can the benefits promised by this paradigm emerge. The benefits, we recall, include the possibility of formal, mechanistic methods for reusing and extending software entities.

No hierarchy has ever been found that represents all knowledge. This is because the concepts that make up knowledge are related, not through one, but through *many* hierarchies. Similarly, no hierarchy can represent all software, because the software entities that make up our applications are related through many hierarchies. So these theories fail, not because we cannot *find* a hierarchy, but because we can find *many*, and it is only this system of hierarchies, with their interactions, that can represent the world.

The mechanists are encouraged by the ease with which they discover one or another of these hierarchies, and are convinced that, with some enhancements, that hierarchy will eventually mirror the world. Any one hierarchy, however, can only relate concepts or software entities in one particular manner – based on one attribute, or perhaps on a small set of attributes. So one hierarchy, no matter how large or involved, can only represent *one* aspect of the world.

The theory of object-oriented programming was refuted, thus, even before it was developed. The theorists, however, misinterpreted the difficulty of relating all existing software entities through one giant hierarchy as a problem of management: it is impossible for one organization to create the whole hierarchy, and it is impractical to coordinate the work of thousands of individuals from different organizations. We must simplify the task, therefore, by dividing that hypothetical software hierarchy into many small ones. And this is quite easy to do, since any hierarchical structure can be broken down into smaller structures. For example, if we sever all the branches that connect a particular element to the elements at the lower level, that element will become a terminal element in the current structure, and each lower-level element will become the top element of a new, separate structure.

Thus, concluded the theorists, even if every one of us creates our own, smaller structures, rather than all of us adding elements to one giant structure, the *totality* of software entities will continue to form one giant structure. So the promise of object-oriented programming remains valid.

To save their theory, the advocates of object-oriented programming rejected the evidence that the idea of a giant software hierarchy is a delusion, and in so doing they succumbed to a second delusion.

The Second Delusion

If the first delusion is that it is possible to classify all existing software in one hierarchy, the second delusion – which emerged when this idea failed – is that it is *not* necessary, after all, to restrict ourselves to one classification: we can also create applications formally, as strict hierarchies of software entities, by combining many small, independent, specialized classifications. But this idea is even sillier than the first one. For, could we combine these structures, we would not have had to separate them in the first place. Let us analyze this problem.

The object-oriented theory assumes that each application is a hierarchy of software entities, and that this hierarchy is part of the larger hierarchy that is the classification of all existing software entities. In reality, just like the totality of existing software, each application is a system of interacting hierarchies. An application is indeed part of all existing software, but in an *indeterministic* way; namely, in the way a complex structure is part of a larger complex one, not in the way a simple structure is part of a larger simple one. There are no mechanistic means – no precise, completely specifiable methods – to derive an application from the system of entities that is the classification of all software. And this is why the idea of a formal classification of software entities, and a formal method of software reuse, is fundamentally mistaken.

The second delusion can also be described as the belief that there is a way around the problems created by the first delusion. But it is no easier to create an application by combining several smaller hierarchies, than it is to create one by extracting portions of a larger hierarchy. The difficulty that prevents us from building one hierarchical classification of all software – the need to relate software entities through *many* hierarchies, not one – is also the difficulty that prevents us from building individual applications as single hierarchies.

Let us see how this problem manifests itself in practice. Let us assume that we already have a large number of separate classifications, each one representing an isolated aspect of software applications: display functions, database functions, one type or another of accounting functions, one style or another of reporting, and the like. But it is impossible to create applications simply by combining these hierarchies; that is, by building a large hierarchy that incorporates somehow the individual ones. For, the only way to combine hierarchies in an object-oriented environment is mechanistically, as one *within* another. This is true because the only way for an element to possess attributes from both element *A* of one hierarchy and element *B* of another hierarchy is through inheritance: we make *A* a lower-level element in the latter hierarchy, thereby allowing it to inherit attributes from *B*.

A particular application may require, for example, display, database, and accounting operations. But even if the three separate hierarchies embodying these operations are complete and correct, even if they include all the details that we are likely to need, they are useless for generating serious accounting applications. The reason is that, in an application, the display operations are not always performed *within* the database or accounting operations; nor are the accounting operations performed *within* the display or database operations, or the database operations *within* the display or accounting operations. What we need is software entities that can invoke the three types of operations *freely*; and we cannot create such entities if restricted to hierarchical combinations. To put this differently, the hierarchical combinations represent only a fraction of all possible relations between the elements of the three structures. Missing are those combinations we would see in a system of *interacting* structures – the kind of system that is impossible to create through object-oriented programming.

We must also bear in mind that it is more than three hierarchies that we have to combine when creating an application. We may be able to represent with one hierarchy such functions as display or database, which are artificial and restricted by our mechanistic computing means in any case. But it is impossible to represent with one hierarchy all our accounting processes, for instance. These processes reflect business, social, and personal affairs, which can only be represented as *interacting* structures of entities. To create a serious accounting application, therefore, we must combine hundreds of different hierarchies, not three; and few of these combinations can be depicted as one hierarchy *within* another.

Another thing to bear in mind is that it doesn't matter whether we start with hierarchies that embody separately the three types of operations – display, database, and accounting – or with hierarchies that are already a combination of these operations. The best approach may well be to have whole accounting hierarchies, each one embodying a certain aspect of accounting. Each hierarchy would include, therefore, not just accounting operations, but also the associated display and database operations. Even then, however, to create an application we would have to combine these hierarchies by non-mechanistic means, because the various aspects of accounting do not exist as one within another.

The Third Delusion

We saw that the idea of combining several class hierarchies into one is a fallacy. Only very simple applications can be created in this fashion: those for which we can restrict ourselves to hierarchical combinations of elements. This idea, we recall, was thought to be a solution to the failure of the *original* object-oriented idea – which idea was to represent with one hierarchy *all* software, not just individual applications. (And the original idea is, in fact, the only way to derive the benefits promised by the object-oriented paradigm.)

Thus, to deal with the problems created by the first delusion, the theorists felt justified to modify the object-oriented concept; but the new idea is as fallacious as the first, so it became the second delusion. Just as they failed to recognize the first delusion as a falsification of the object-oriented concept, they failed to recognize the second one as a new falsification. And, just as they modified the theory in response to the first delusion, they now introduced additional modifications, to deal with the problems created by the second one.

Because it is impossible to generate enough relations through hierarchical relations alone, the theorists had to provide the means to build systems of *interacting* hierarchies. All the modifications, then, have one purpose: to enable us to relate software entities through several hierarchies at the same time; in other words, to bypass the restriction to one hierarchy. Faithful to the pseudoscientific tradition, these modifications – which are, in fact, blatant violations of the object-oriented principles – are described as new features, or enhancements. Here we will discuss only the simplest enhancement, the use of traditional programming languages; then, under the fourth and fifth delusions, we will study the others.

The traditional languages do provide, of course, the means to relate software entities freely. Each element in the application is affected by several processes (calling subroutines, using memory variables and database fields, being part of practices), and is therefore related to the other elements affected by these processes. Since the relations created by each process constitute a hierarchical structure, the application's elements are related through many hierarchies at the same time. (Software processes were introduced in chapter 4; see pp. 347–348.)

So the simplest way to combine hierarchies is by creating modules, blocks of statements, conditional constructs, and the like, by means of a *traditional* language, and *then* picking whatever classes we need from the various hierarchies. We use the class hierarchies, thus, not as originally intended – as a formal representation of the whole application – but in the manner of subroutine libraries. In this way, any element in the application can inherit attributes from several hierarchies, simply by invoking several classes. So, by using classes as we use subroutines, any element can possess any combination of attributes we need: we are no longer restricted to combining attributes hierarchically, one within another, as stipulated by the object-oriented principle of inheritance.

Recall the earlier problem: combining classes from three hierarchies – display, database, and accounting operations – but *not* as one within another. While impossible under the object-oriented paradigm, this requirement is easily implemented once we extend the use of classes so as to invoke them freely: directly rather than hierarchically, wherever needed, just as we invoke subroutines.

The first modification, then, was to turn the object-oriented concept from a formal, autonomous programming method, supported by special programming languages, into a mere extension to the *traditional* methods and languages. And this was accomplished by adding object-oriented capabilities to some of the popular languages (C and COBOL, for instance). The enhanced variants are known as *hybrid* languages. (The reverse is also true: special languages like Simula and Smalltalk, originally intended as pure object-oriented environments, were later enhanced with traditional capabilities.)

Thus, there are no strict object-oriented languages in existence, simply because one adhering to the object-oriented principles would be totally impractical. The theorists invented a new term to describe what is in reality not a new feature, but the reinstatement of old, well-established concepts: "hybrid" sounds as if these languages added a new quality to the object-oriented principles, when in fact they are a *reversal* of these principles. No one wondered why, if object-oriented programming is the revolutionary concept the experts say it is, we still need to rely on the old languages. The experts praise the power of the object-oriented paradigm, even as everyone can see that this paradigm is useless, and that its power derives from the freedom we regain when reverting to the traditional concepts.

In the end, no application was ever based on the *true* object-oriented principles. Programmers believe that they are practising object-oriented programming, when what they are practising in reality is *traditional* programming – supplemented here and there, when not too inconvenient, with some object-oriented concepts.

The Fourth Delusion

1

The most important "features" and "improvements" added to the object-oriented theory are those that alter the very nature of a hierarchical structure. We saw that the theory had to be modified in order to give us the means to combine class hierarchies, and that using class hierarchies from within a traditional language is the simplest way to accomplish this. But if we had to rely on this method alone to combine hierarchies, we would find little use for the *actual* object-oriented features. All we would have then is some class libraries that, apart from providing perhaps better hierarchical links, are identical to the traditional subroutine libraries.

In order to permit us to relate class hierarchies freely *within* the object-oriented paradigm, the very notion of a class hierarchy had to be modified. In the end, the theory of object-oriented programming was rescued by annulling its most celebrated principle – the restriction to classes related hierarchically through inherited attributes.

Inheritance, we recall, is that property of hierarchical structures whereby an element derives some of its attributes from the higher levels. Thus, in the case of software class hierarchies, each element, in addition to possessing its own attributes, inherits the attributes of the higher-level class – the class to which it is directly subordinate. And, since the latter inherits the attributes of the class to which *it* is subordinate, and so on, each element will possess the attributes of all the classes above it.

This property is not new to the object-oriented theory, but common to all hierarchical systems. This is so obvious, in fact, that inheritance is rarely mentioned as a hierarchical feature. It is the property of *abstraction* that is usually described as the distinguishing quality of hierarchical structures. Abstraction means that, as we move from low to high levels, an element at a given level retains only those attributes that are common to all the elements of the next lower level. Inheritance, therefore, is not a separate quality, but merely the process of abstraction observed in reverse. We can reverse the last sentence, for instance, and say that all the elements at a given level inherit the attributes possessed by the element of the next higher level. Both statements describe the same relationship.

The object-oriented theory, though, presents the property of inheritance as an important and powerful feature. We are left with the impression that this feature is somehow *additional* to the hierarchical relations between software classes. And, once inheritance is perceived as a separate feature, it is only natural to try to enhance it. But this idea is absurd. The property of inheritance cannot be enhanced; like abstraction, it is implicit in the notion of a hierarchy, a reflection of the relations between the structure's elements. One cannot have a hierarchy where the concept of inheritance is different in any way from its original meaning.

The first modification was to allow a class to *change*, and even to *omit*, an inherited attribute. The capability to add its own, unique attributes remains, but the class no longer needs to possess *all* the attributes possessed by the class of the next higher level. In other words, the attributes of a class, and hence its relations with the other classes, are no longer determined by its position in the class hierarchy. If what we need is indeed a hierarchical relationship with the higher-level classes, we let it inherit all their attributes, as before; but if what we need is a different relationship, we can change or omit some of these attributes.

The attributes of a class are its data types and operations. So what this modification means is that each class in the application can now have any data types and operations we like, not necessarily those inherited from the classes above it.

Attributes, as we know, relate entities by grouping them into hierarchical structures (see "Software Structures" in chapter 4). In a software application, each attribute generates a different structure by relating in a particular way the entities that make up the application. Clearly, then, what has been achieved with the new feature is to eliminate the restriction to one hierarchy. Since classes can now possess *any* attributes, they can be related in any way we want, so they can form many structures at the same time. The structure we started with – the class hierarchy – is no longer the only structure in the application. When we study this structure alone, the application's classes still appear to be related through a neat hierarchy. But if the relations that define the class hierarchy are now optional, if each class can also be related to the others through different attributes, the application is no longer a simple structure; it is a *complex* structure, and the class hierarchy is just one of the structures that make it up.

We can also appreciate the significance of the new feature by imagining that we had to implement the additional relations *without* the ability to change and omit attributes. Thus, for each inherited attribute that we were going to change or omit in a particular class, we would have to go up in the hierarchy, to the level just above the class where that attribute is defined. We would create there a new class, at the same level as the first one, and identical to it in all respects except for that attribute; in its stead, we would define the *changed* attribute (or we would *omit* the attribute). We would then duplicate, below the new class, the entire section of the hierarchy that lies below the first class. All the lower-level classes here would be identical to those in the original section, but they would inherit the new attribute instead of the original one (or no attribute, if omitted). The application would now be a larger hierarchy, consisting of both the original and the new sections. And in the new section, the counterpart of our original, low-level class would indeed possess the changed attribute (or no attribute), just as we wanted.

With this method, then, we can create classes with changed or omitted attributes but without the benefit of the new feature; that is, without modifying the concept of inheritance. We would have to repeat this procedure, however, for each attribute that must be changed or omitted. So the hierarchy would grow exponentially, because for most attributes we would have to duplicate a section of the hierarchy that is already the result of previous duplications.

It is not the impracticality of this method that concerns us here, though, but the repetition of attributes. Every time we duplicate a section, along with the classes defined in that section we must also duplicate their attributes. Moreover, some of the duplicated attributes will be duplicated again for the next attribute (when we duplicate a section of the new, larger hierarchy), and so on. And we already know that if we repeat attributes, we are creating an incorrect hierarchy: this repetition gives rise to relations that are additional to the strict hierarchical relations, and indicates that we are attempting to represent with one hierarchy a complex structure (see pp. 100–104, 360–362).

What we were trying to accomplish in this imaginary project was to implement through the *original* inheritance concept the kind of relations that we can so easily implement through the *modified* concept, by changing or omitting inherited attributes. Thus, if one method gives rise to a complex structure, the conclusion must be that the other method does too. The non-hierarchical relations may not be obvious when implemented by modifying the concept of inheritance, but we are only deluding ourselves if we believe that the class hierarchy is still the only structure. After all, the very reason for changing and omitting attributes is that we cannot create applications while restricted to one structure. The purpose of the new feature, thus, is to allow us to create multiple, interacting structures.

But even allowing us to change and omit inherited attributes did not make object-oriented programming a practical idea. A second feature had to be introduced – a second modification to the concept of inheritance. Through this feature, a class can inherit attributes, not just from the higher levels of its own hierarchy, but also from other hierarchies. Called *multiple inheritance,* this feature is seen as an especially powerful enhancement. There are no limitations, of course; a class is not restricted to inheriting only certain attributes from certain hierarchies, or required to inherit *all* the attributes above a certain level. We can now simply add, to any class we want, whichever attributes we need, from any class, from any hierarchy. And this feature can be combined with the first one; that is, after picking the attributes we need, we can change them in any way we like.

Recall the problem we discussed under the second delusion – the need to combine attributes from several hierarchies (database, display, and accounting, for instance). Multiple inheritance is the answer, as we can now select attributes from these hierarchies freely, and thereby create classes with any combination of data types and operations. Without this feature, we saw, the only way to combine attributes is by combining classes: we must employ a traditional language and invoke – in the same module, in the manner of subroutines – classes from several hierarchies.

In conclusion, modifying the concept of inheritance has *downgraded* it: from a formal property of hierarchical structures, to the informal act of copying an attribute from one class to another. And as a result, the relationship between the application's classes has been relaxed: from a strict hierarchy, to multiple and unrestricted connections. If the attributes of a class can be unique, or can be taken from the higher levels, or can be taken from higher levels but changed, or can even be taken from other hierarchies, then what we have is simply classes that can possess *any* attributes. The attributes of a class are no longer determined by its position in the hierarchy, or by the attributes of the other classes.

The theorists continue to use terms like "hierarchy" and "inheritance," but if a class can possess any attributes we like, these terms have lost their original meaning. What they describe now is not a formal class hierarchy, but software entities that possess whatever attributes we need, and are therefore related in whatever ways we need, to implement a particular application. What the modifications have accomplished, in other words, is to restore the programming freedom we had *before* object-oriented programming – the freedom that the new paradigm had attempted to eliminate in its quest for formality and precision.

2

We recognize in the modified concept of inheritance the pseudoscientific stratagem of turning falsifications into features: the theory is saved from refutation by *expanding* it – by incorporating, in the guise of new features, capabilities that were explicitly excluded originally. The original claim was that applications can be developed as strict hierarchies of software classes: either classes that already exist, or classes that can be generated hierarchically from existing ones. The only relations between the classes used in an application, then, would be those established by a hierarchical structure. This restriction is essential if we want to classify and extend software through exact principles, and, ultimately, turn software development into a formal and predictable activity.

The promise, thus, was to turn software development into an activity resembling the design and manufacture of appliances. But this promise can only be fulfilled if software applications, as well as their design and implementation, are restricted to entities and processes that can be represented with isolated hierarchical structures – as are indeed our appliances, and their design and manufacture.

Software applications, though, cannot be developed in this fashion, so the object-oriented theory was refuted. But instead of admitting that it has no practical value, its supporters modified it: they added, in the guise of enhancements, the means to create *multiple* structures – the very feature that the original theory had prohibited. The need to relate software entities through more than one hierarchy is a *falsification* of the object-oriented theory; but the modifications are presented as new and powerful *features* of the theory. These "features" make the theory practical, but they achieve this by contradicting its original principles. It is absurd, therefore, to say that these features enhance the theory, when their very purpose is to bypass the restrictions imposed by the theory.

The fourth delusion, thus, is the belief that what we are practising now, after these modifications, is still object-oriented programming; in other words, the belief that the "power" we gained from the new features is due to the object-oriented principles. In reality, the power derives from *abolishing* these principles, from lifting their restrictions and permitting us to create complex software structures again.

While regaining this freedom, however, we lose the promised benefits. For, those benefits can only emerge if we restrict ourselves to one hierarchy, or perhaps multiple but independent hierarchies – as we do in manufacturing and construction. The theorists praise the benefits of the hierarchical concept, and claim that the object-oriented paradigm is turning programming into a mechanistic activity, but at the same time they give us the means to bypass the mechanistic restrictions. They believe that we can enjoy the promised benefits – formal, exact programming methods – *without* the rigours demanded by the original theory.

So what we are doing after the fourth delusion is merely a more complicated version of what we were doing before the object-oriented paradigm. As was the case with structured programming earlier, what started as an ambitious, formal theory ended up as little more than a collection of programming tips. We are again creating complex software structures, and what is left of the object-oriented principles is just the exhortation to restrict software classes to hierarchical relations, and to avoid other links between them, "as much as possible."

It is indeed a good idea to relate software entities hierarchically. But because our applications consist of multiple, interacting hierarchies, this idea cannot be more than an informal guideline; and, in any case, we can also create hierarchical relations with *traditional* programming means.

In the end, since the idea of independent software structures is a fantasy, the object-oriented theory makes programming more complicated and more difficult, while offering us nothing that we did not already have. We are *not* developing applications through exact, formal methods – the way the experts had promised us. We are creating systems of interacting structures, just as before; so we depend on the non-mechanistic capabilities of our mind, on personal skills and experience, just as before. But by using terms like "objects," "classes," and "inheritance," we can delude ourselves that we are programming under a new paradigm.

The Fifth Delusion

1

The most fantastic object-oriented delusion is undoubtedly the fifth one. The fifth delusion is the belief that we no longer need to concern ourselves with the application's flow of execution: the important relations between the application's objects are those of the class hierarchy, so the relations determining the sequence of their execution can be disregarded.

The application's flow of execution, we recall, was the chief preoccupation of structured programming. The fallacy there was the belief that it is possible to represent applications with *one* flow-control structure. The flow-control structure, according to that theory, is the application's *nesting scheme*: the hierarchical arrangement of modules that makes up the application, plus the hierarchical arrangement of flow-control constructs that makes up each module. And the nesting scheme is depicted by the application's *flow diagram*. The theorists failed to see that the flow diagram depicts *only one* of the nesting schemes; that the *dynamic* structures created by conditional and iterative constructs at run time consist in fact of multiple, overlapping nesting schemes, so the application's flow-control structure is the complex structure that comprises *all* these nesting schemes; and that, moreover, the application's elements are connected through many other *types* of structures – the structures formed by the multitude of software *processes* that make up the application. (Software processes were introduced in chapter 4; see pp. 347–348. The dynamic structures were discussed under structured programming's second delusion; see pp. 556–560.)

The structured programming theory, thus, while mistaken, at least recognized the importance of the flow of execution. The object-oriented theory, on the other hand, ignores it completely. There are no flow diagrams in object-oriented programming. We don't find a single word about conditional and iterative constructs, or about constructs with one entry and exit, or about a restriction to standard constructs. All the problems that structured programming attempted to solve are now neglected. And if an expert mentions them at all, it is only in order to criticize them: It was wrong to represent applications with flow diagrams and flow-control constructs, because these are artificial concepts, designed to match the way *computers* work. These concepts force us to view our affairs unnaturally, and hence develop software that is very different, logically, from the way we deal with the *actual* issues. By replacing the structured programming principles with the concept of class hierarchies, the object-oriented paradigm helps us to build software structures that closely match the real world. Unlike the relations between modules and between flow-control constructs, the relations between software classes are very similar to the way we normally view our affairs.

To verify this claim, let us first recall what are the objects of an application. Each object is an instance of one of the classes defined in the class hierarchy; so the *static* relationship between objects reflects indeed the hierarchical relationship that links the classes. The sequence in which objects are executed, however, is determined, not by the class hierarchy, but by the *messages* they send and receive at run time. An object is executed only when receiving a message from another object in the application. The various operations that an object is designed to perform are called *methods*, and the particular method selected by the receiving object depends on the parameters accompanying the message. While performing its operations, an object may send messages to other objects, asking those objects to perform some of *their* operations, and so on. Following each message, execution returns to the object and operation that sent the message. Thus, messages, as well as the operations performed in response to messages, are nested hierarchically. And it is this hierarchy of messages and operations – which is *different* from the class hierarchy – that constitutes the application's flow of execution.

So, from the start, we note the same fallacy as in structured programming: the belief that the dynamic structure that represents the application's run-time performance can mirror the static structure of software entities that makes up the application (see pp. 546–547). The static structure – what was the hierarchical flow diagram of modules and constructs in structured programming – is now the hierarchy of classes; and the theorists believe that the neat relations they see in this structure are the only important links between objects. In structured programming, they failed to see the other *types* of structures – those formed by business or software practices, by shared data, and by shared operations; and they also failed to see the multiple *dynamic* flow-control structures. In object-oriented programming, the theorists again fail to see the many types of structures – they believe that each application, and even the totality of existing software, can be represented with one class hierarchy; and they fail to see the flow-control structures altogether, static or dynamic.

It is true that the theorists eventually removed the restriction to one hierarchy. They allowed interacting hierarchies, and they modified the concept of inheritance to create even more interactions. But these ideas contradict the object-oriented principles, negating therefore their benefits. To study the fifth delusion, then, we must separate it from the previous ones: we must assume, with the theorists, that even after modifying the object-oriented principles, even after expanding them to allow complex structures, we can still enjoy the promised benefits. In other words, we must forget that the object-oriented theory has already been refuted. What I want to show here is that the fifth delusion – the failure to deal with the application's flow of execution, and, moreover, the failure to note that it is the same as the flow of execution generated with any other programming method, including structured programming – would alone render the object-oriented theory worthless, even if the previous delusions had not already done this.

2

It is difficult to understand why the theorists ignore the application's flow of execution. For, even a simple analysis reveals that there are just as many deviations from a sequential flow as there were under structured programming. If, for example, we represented with a flow diagram all the conditions, iterations, and object invocations, we would end up with a diagram that looks just like the flow diagrams of structured programming. The theorists discuss the operations performed within each object, and the transfer of control between objects, but they don't see all this as a flow of execution.[1]

Clearly, to perform a particular task the application's elements must be executed by the computer in a specific sequence, no matter what method we use to develop that application. And, since the computer itself cannot be expected to know this sequence, *we* must design it. Now, it ought to be obvious that the relative sequence in which the objects are to be executed cannot be determined solely by the hierarchical relations between classes. This is true because class hierarchies are meant to be used in different applications, so the same objects may have to be executed in a different sequence on different occasions.[2] Thus, if the flow of execution is a critical part of the application's logic but is not determined by the class hierarchy, how are we designing it under the object-oriented paradigm?

There are two parts to the object-oriented flow of execution: *between* objects, and *within* objects. And, despite the new terminology, both parts are practically identical to the flow of execution familiar from earlier forms of programming – namely, between modules and within modules.

Between objects, the transfer of control is implemented by way of messages. And, clearly, sending a message from one object to another is logically and

---

[1] A half-hearted attempt to deal with the flow of execution is found in the so-called state transition diagrams, used by a few theorists to represent the effect of messages on individual objects. But, like the flow diagrams of structured programming, these diagrams can only depict the *static* aspects of the flow of execution. The *dynamic* aspects (the combined effect of messages in the running application) constitute a complex phenomenon, so they cannot be reduced to an exact, mechanistic representation.

[2] In fact, even if each application had its own class hierarchy, we would need more than a simple hierarchical structure to represent its flow of execution. As we saw under structured programming, if the sequence in which the application's elements are executed was determined solely by their relative position in the hierarchical nesting scheme, the application would be useless, because it would always do the same thing (see p. 547). Similarly now, the sequence in which the objects are executed must be determined by factors other than their relative position in the hierarchical class structure.

functionally identical to invoking a module or subroutine in traditional programming. *Within* objects, we can distinguish between the jump performed in order to select the so-called method (the object's response to a particular message) and the jumps performed by the operations that make up the method. Selecting a method is in effect a conditional flow-control construct (where the condition involves the values received as parameters with the message). Thus, while object-oriented languages may well offer a specialized construct, we could just as easily implement this selection with traditional constructs like IF or CASE. As for the operations that make up the methods, they are, of course, ordinary pieces of software: statements, blocks of statements, conditions, and iterations. These operations, therefore, are as rich in flow-control constructs as are the operations found in traditional languages.

But it is important to note that the messages themselves are, in effect, operations within methods. This is true because a message may be sent from within a conditional or iterative construct that is part of a method. Consequently, the execution of objects in a running application is not one nesting scheme but a *system* of nesting schemes. Just like the modules invoked in structured programming, the nested invocations of objects would form a simple hierarchical structure only if the methods included sequential constructs alone. Just as in structured programming, the purpose of conditional and iterative constructs is to create multiple dynamic nesting schemes (see pp. 555–558).

The role of the flow-control constructs, thus, is to create complex flow-control structures not just within methods, but also between objects. So, when disregarding the effect of the flow-control constructs on the operations within methods, the theorists also disregard their effect on the flow of execution between objects. In the end, not only are the application's objects subject to a flow of execution, but this execution forms a complex structure, just like the execution of modules in structured programming.

To conclude, the flow of execution in an application created through object-oriented programming is identical, for all practical purposes, to the one implemented through structured programming. And the latter, we recall, after annulling the restriction to standard flow-control constructs, was identical to the flow of execution implemented through any other programming method.[3]

---

[3] The object-oriented flow of execution is, in fact, even more complex than the one in structured programming (because a message may be sent to several objects simultaneously, an object may continue execution while waiting for the reply to a message, etc.). So the number of flow-control structures that we must deal with in our mind is even greater. Moreover, we must remember that the so-called hybrid languages (employed, actually, in all object-oriented systems) provide also the traditional concept of modules and subroutines, thereby adding to the number of flow-control structures.

❖

Both structured programming and object-oriented programming promised to revolutionize software development by restricting applications to a simple hierarchical structure. And when this idea turned out to be a fantasy, both theories were expanded so as to provide the means to create complex software structures again; in particular, complex *flow-control* structures. Thus, like all pseudoscientific theories, they ended up restoring the very features they had excluded in the beginning, and on the exclusion of which they had based their claims. So what we have in the end, after all the "enhancements," is some complicated programming concepts that offer us exactly what we had, in a much simpler form, before the theory. Still, no one sees this reversal as a failure of the theory. The promised benefits, possible *only* if applications are restricted to a simple structure, are now lost. The theory, nevertheless, continues to be promoted with the original claims.

The fifth delusion, thus, is similar to the previous ones: we believe that we can enjoy the benefits promised by the object-oriented paradigm even after annulling the object-oriented principles and reinstating the means to create complex structures. What we are creating now is complex *flow-control* structures. First, by introducing the concept of messages into object-oriented programming, we provide the means to link the application's objects through relations that are different from their relations in the class hierarchy. In other words, the sequence in which the objects are executed by the computer – the hierarchical nesting scheme that is the flow of execution – need not depend on their relative position in the class hierarchy. The application's objects, then, will belong to two different structures at the same time: a class hierarchy and a flow-control hierarchy. Second, by allowing messages to be controlled by conditional and iterative constructs, we turn the flow-control hierarchy itself into a complex structure: not *one* nesting scheme, but a *system* of nesting schemes.

3

Although we are discussing *flow-control* structures, we must not forget that objects, like their counterpart, subroutines, also give rise to a different *type* of structures. If an object is invoked from several other objects in the application, it necessarily links those objects logically. So, like subroutines, objects constitute a special case of shared operations (see pp. 353–356). For each object, we can represent with a hierarchical structure the unique way in which the application's other objects are affected by it. And the relations created by these structures will be different from those created by the flow-control structures or by the class hierarchies.

It is the concept of messages that makes all the additional structures possible. Without messages, the application's objects would be related only through class hierarchies, the way it was originally intended. So the concept of messages, described as an important object-oriented feature, was introduced specifically in order to override the limitations of the original principles. The theorists ignore completely the relations engendered by messages. They give us the means to link the application's objects through additional structures, but they continue to present the object-oriented concept as if the objects were linked only through class hierarchies. What is the point in designing strict class hierarchies if we are going to relate the same objects in many other ways, by means of messages, while the application is running?

In structured programming, the dream was to reduce the flow of execution to one structure, as this would permit us to represent the running application mathematically. And this idea failed because it was too restrictive, because applications must have *multiple* flow-control structures if they are to represent the world accurately. The object-oriented model is said to be more powerful. But when we examine this power, we find that it derives simply from lifting the restrictions introduced by structured programming; it derives from allowing us to link objects in any way we want, and in particular, to link them from the perspective of the flow of execution in any way we want. (Some of these restrictions had been lifted even under structured programming, when the theorists allowed us to use non-standard constructs and GO TO.)

By disregarding the effect of conditions and iterations, by refusing to draw flow diagrams, and by giving old concepts new names, the software experts managed to persuade us that the application's elements are related only through class hierarchies, so we no longer need to concern ourselves with the sequence of their execution. But, in the end, to create applications we are doing what we had been doing all along. The only real change is calling subroutines "objects," their invocation "messages," and their internal operations "methods."

So the power said to inhere in the object-oriented paradigm does not derive from the new programming concepts, but simply from having more opportunities to create complex software structures. What the theorists did was merely restore some of the programming freedom we had before structured programming, and invent some new terminology. The claim that this freedom is due to the object-oriented paradigm is a fraud. The freedom to connect the application's elements in any way we like is a freedom we always had, through any programming language – and, besides, without having to depend on complicated development environments.

The Final Degradation

1

We saw how, through several delusions, the idea of object-oriented programming was degraded from a strict theory to a set of informal concepts. These concepts, moreover, are practically identical to those we had *before* the theory. But the degradation did not end with those delusions. In addition to the traditional concepts, a number of new features and principles were added over the years to the object-oriented idea. Totally unrelated to the original theory, these enhancements were inspired by various concepts that were being introduced into programming languages in the same period. In other words, any concept found useful was labeled "object-oriented," and was incorporated into this theory too. Thus, the notion of object-oriented programming became increasingly vague, and the terms "object" and "object-oriented" were applied to almost any feature and principle.

The final degradation, then, was the degradation in expectations: from the original idea of finding a formal way to reuse software, to a preoccupation with isolated programming concepts. If the theory was promoted at first with the claim that it would revolutionize programming, in the end, when the revolution did not materialize, the same theory was promoted by praising merely its features and principles. Thus, the benefits of individual programming concepts replaced the benefits originally claimed for the theory, as the ultimate goal of object-oriented programming. Let us briefly study some of these fallacies.

I have already mentioned that the concept of hierarchies, and the related concepts of inheritance and abstraction, were known and appreciated long before the object-oriented theory. The concept of abstraction, in particular, is praised now as if the only way to benefit from it were with classes and objects. We are told, for example, that the object-oriented paradigm allows us to define abstract software entities, and then create actual instances of these entities by adding some lower-level attributes. The instances will differ from one another in their details, while sharing the broader attributes of the original entities.

Abstraction, however, is not peculiar to the object-oriented theory. It is, in fact, a fundamental programming principle. We make use of abstraction in any programming language, and in any programming task. The very essence of programming is to create data and operations of different levels of abstraction. Thus, merely using subroutines, and passing data by means of parameters, creates in effect levels of abstraction; and merely using variables and fields, which hold entities that differ in value while sharing certain attributes, is, again, a form of abstraction. It would be impossible to program serious applications if we restricted ourselves to software entities that cannot be altered, or extended, or grouped, or used in different contexts; in other words, if we did not make use of the concept of abstraction. Structured programming too, although criticized now, was based on abstraction: the flow-control constructs perform the same function at different levels of nesting.

Another object-oriented concept that is in reality a fundamental programming principle is *information hiding*, or *encapsulation*. We are told that the new paradigm allows us to hide inside an object the details of its operations, so that the other objects may know its capabilities without having to know how they are implemented. One of the benefits of this principle is that if we later modify an object, we won't have to modify also the objects that communicate with it. Object-oriented textbooks praise this principle and show us examples of situations where extensive modifications are avoided through object-oriented programming, alleging that this is the first time we can benefit from it. But the principle is a well-known one, and is found in every programming language (for example, in the use of subroutines and local variables). Experienced programmers always strive to keep software entities independent. Only the terms "information hiding" and "encapsulation" are new.

Along with encapsulation, we are told that keeping the data and the operations that act on it together, as one entity, is a new concept. This, we are told, is more natural than the traditional methods, which treated data and operations as separate entities. Actually, we always designed software in this fashion, when appropriate. And we didn't need a special development environment to do it: we simply ensured that a module uses local variables, or is the only one to use certain global variables. It is absurd to call this well-known programming style a new concept.

The very fact that notions like abstraction and encapsulation, understood and appreciated since the 1950s, are seen as a revolution and a new paradigm demonstrates the ignorance that the theorists and the practitioners suffer from. All that the object-oriented environments do is *formalize* these notions; that is, provide them in the form of built-in features, forcing us to depend on them. But, as we saw, this idea failed. It failed because, no matter how useful the hierarchical model is, we cannot *restrict* ourselves to hierarchical relations. So, in the end, the means to use and relate software entities freely – what we had been doing through traditional programming – had to be restored.

Other claims are even sillier. *Polymorphism* is the principle of implementing an operation in several different ways while providing a common interface. For example, different objects could be designed to print different types of documents, but this fact would be hidden from the rest of the application; we would always invoke one object, called "print," and the appropriate printing object would be invoked automatically, depending on the type of document to be printed. This is indeed a good programming technique, but what has it to do with the object-oriented theory? Polymorphism is described as one of the most important object-oriented principles, while being in reality a simple and common programming method, easily implemented in any language by means of subroutines and conditional constructs. And even if the concept of classes and objects simplifies sometimes its implementation, this is hardly a programming revolution. The object-oriented propaganda, though, presents this simple principle as if without classes and objects we would have to duplicate pieces of software all over the application every time we had to select one of several alternatives in a given operation.

Overloading is another concept described as an object-oriented principle, while being known, in fact, for a long time. Overloading allows us to redefine the function of a symbol or a name, in order to use it in different ways on different occasions. The operator *plus*, for example, is used with numbers; but we could also use it with character strings, by redefining its function as string concatenation. In a limited form, this feature is available in most programming languages; and, in any case, it can be easily implemented by means of subroutines and conditional constructs. Object-oriented languages do provide greater flexibility, but, again, this is just a language feature, not a programming revolution; and it has nothing to do with the object-oriented theory.

In conclusion, abstraction, information hiding, polymorphism, and the rest, are just a collection of programming principles. And, even when not directly available in a programming language, we can implement these principles by adopting an appropriate programming style. The software experts describe these principles as if *they* constituted the object-oriented theory; but if in one form or another we always had them, in what sense is this theory a new paradigm?

It is perhaps easier to implement some of these principles with an object-oriented language (that is, if we overlook the fact that we must first agree to depend on an enormously complex development environment). But this quality is not what the experts had promised us as the benefits of the theory. The promised benefits were not abstraction, encapsulation, or polymorphism, but the "industrialization" of software: the prospect of creating software applications the way we build appliances, through a process akin to the assembly of prefabricated components. It was its promises, not its principles, that made the object-oriented idea popular; the principles were merely the means to attain the promised benefits. In any case, after all the delusions, we no longer have the original theory; what we have now is just a more complicated way to program. So, since the promised benefits were lost with the original theory, the principles alone are perceived now as the benefits of object-oriented programming.

❖

We saw earlier how structured programming underwent a process of degradation: it started as a formal theory, promising us error-free software; and it ended as a preoccupation with trivial concepts like top-down design, constructs with one entry and exit, and avoiding GOTO. Now we see that a similar process of degradation, from an ambitious theory to a collection of trivial concepts, also affected object-oriented programming.

It is easy to understand the reason for this degradation. When the benefits promised by a theory are not forthcoming (we still don't create applications mathematically, or by assembling prefabricated software components), we can either admit that the theory has failed, or attempt to rescue it. The only way to rescue an invalid theory is by making it unfalsifiable; specifically, by *expanding* it, so that events which would normally falsify it no longer do so. And this can be accomplished by replacing the original principles with broader and simpler ones, which can be easily implemented. Thus, if we redefine structured programming or object-oriented programming to mean just a collection of programming principles, and if some of these principles are useful, then the *redefined* theory is indeed valid.

Both structured programming and object-oriented programming became in the end unfalsifiable, and hence pseudoscientific. Thanks to the various "enhancements," and to their degradation from a formal theory to a collection of principles, they became impossible to refute. Had they retained their original, exact definition, it would be obvious that they failed, simply because we are still not enjoying the claimed benefits. But by reducing them to an assortment of simple and well-known principles, they appear to work even if the claimed benefits never materialize. Indenting statements, expressing requirements hierarchically, information hiding, and the like, are indeed excellent principles; so, if *this* is what the theories are now, it is impossible to criticize them.

2

The degradation of the object-oriented idea can also be seen in the degradation of the *terms* "object" and "object-oriented." We saw earlier how the term "structured" was applied to almost any flow-control construct, and to almost any software-related activity. For example, the theorists allowed into structured programming any construct that was useful – simply because, after drawing around it a rectangular box with one entry and one exit, it looked like a structured construct. This trick worked so well for structured programming that the theorists repeated it with objects.

In the original theory, objects were formal, precisely defined entities. But the idea of an object has been degraded to such an extent that the term "object" can now be used to designate any piece of software. Such entities as data records, display screens, menus, subroutines, and utilities are called objects – simply because, like objects, they can be invoked, or possess attributes, or perform actions. In other words, we can take any software entity, draw a box around it, and call the result an object.

Even entire programs can be called, if we want, objects. For example, through a procedure called *wrapping*, an old application, or part of an application, written in a traditional language, can instantly become an object.[1] The application itself remains unchanged; but, by "wrapping" it (that is, adding a little software around it so that it can be *invoked* in a new fashion), it can become part of an object-oriented environment: "Wrapper technology ... provides an object-oriented interface to legacy code. The wrapped piece of legacy code behaves as an object."[2]

Along with the idea of an object, the object-oriented principles themselves were degraded. Thus, any programming feature, method, or technique that involves hierarchies, or abstraction, or encapsulation, and any development system that includes some of these principles, is called "object-oriented." We can see this degradation in books, articles, and advertising. And, since the use of these terms is perceived as evidence of expertise and modernity, ignorant academics, programmers, and managers employ them liberally in conversation. Thus, "object" and "object-oriented" are now little more than slogans, not unlike "technology," "power," and "solution."

In the end, the definition of object-oriented programming was degraded to the point where the original promises were forgotten altogether, and the criterion of success became merely whether an application can be developed at all through object-oriented concepts (or, rather, through what was left of these concepts after all the delusions). Thus, the success stories we see in the media are not about companies that achieved a spectacular reuse of existing software classes, or managed to reduce formally all their business requirements to a class

---

[1] See, for example, Daniel Tkach and Richard Puttick, *Object Technology in Application Development* (Redwood City, CA: Benjamin/Cummings, 1994), pp. 113–115.

[2] Ibid., p. 148. Note, again, the slogan "technology": what is in fact a simple programming concept (code wrapping) is presented as something important enough to name a whole domain of technology after it.

hierarchy, but about companies that are merely *using* a system, language, or methodology said to be object-oriented.

An example of this type of promotion is *Objects in Action*.[3] This book includes nineteen case studies of object-oriented development projects, from all over the world. For each project, those involved in its implementation describe in some detail the requirements and the work performed. These projects were selected, needless to say, because they were exceptional.[4] But, while presented as object-oriented successes, there is nothing in these descriptions to demonstrate the benefits of object-oriented programming. The only known fact is that certain developers implemented certain applications using certain object-oriented systems. There is no attempt to prove, for instance, that some other developers, experienced in traditional programming, could *not* have achieved the same results. Nor is there an attempt to understand why thousands of other object-oriented projects were *not* successful. In the end, there is nothing in these descriptions to exclude the possibility that the successes had nothing to do with the object-oriented principles, and were due to other factors (the type of applications, the particular companies where they were developed, unusual programming skills, etc.).

It is when encountering this kind of promotion that we get to appreciate the importance of Popper's idea; namely, that it is not the *confirmations* of a theory that we must study, but its *falsifications* (see "Popper's Principles of Demarcation" in chapter 3). As we just saw, if what we want to know is how useful the object-oriented principles really are, those success stories can tell us nothing. Promoters use success stories as evidence precisely because such stories can always be found and are so effective in fooling people. For, few of us understand why confirmations are worthless. The programming theories, in particular, are always promoted by pointing to isolated successes and ignoring the many failures. Thus, the very fact that the elites rely on this type of evidence demonstrates their dishonesty and the pseudoscientific nature of their theories.

3

The previous theory, structured programming, was promoted with the claim that it provides certain benefits; and we saw that, in fact, these benefits can be attained simply through good programming. In other words, those structured programming principles that are indeed useful can be implemented

---

[3] Paul Harmon and David A. Taylor, *Objects in Action: Commercial Applications of Object-Oriented Technologies* (Reading, MA: Addison-Wesley, 1993).

[4] This is acknowledged in the book: ibid., p. vii.

without the restrictions imposed by this theory. The motivation for structured programming, therefore, was not a desire to improve programming practices, but the belief that it is possible to get inexperienced programmers to perform tasks that demand expertise. What was promoted as an effort to turn programming into an exact activity was in reality an attempt to raise the level of abstraction in this work, so as to remove both the need and the possibility for programmers to make important decisions.

The software theorists assumed that the skills acquired after a year or two of practice represent the highest level that a typical programmer can attain. Thus, since these programmers create bad software, the conclusion was that the only way to improve their performance is by reducing programming to a routine activity. Anyone capable of acquiring mechanistic knowledge – capable, that is, of following rules and methods – would then create good software.

And this corrupt ideology was also the motivation for object-oriented programming. The true goal was, again, not to improve programming practices, but to raise the level of abstraction, in the hope of getting inexperienced programmers to perform tasks that lie beyond their capabilities. As we saw, those object-oriented principles that are indeed useful – abstraction, code reuse, information hiding, and the like – were always observed by good programmers. Those principles, moreover, can be implemented through any programming language. Just as they do not have to avoid GOTO in order to enjoy the benefits of hierarchical flow-control structures, good programmers do not have to use an object-oriented environment in order to create software that is easy to reuse, modify, and extend.

Ultimately, the object-oriented paradigm is merely another attempt to incorporate certain programming principles into development systems and methodologies, so as to allow programmers who are incapable of understanding these principles to benefit from them nonetheless. Just as the operator of a machine can use it to fabricate intricate parts without having to understand engineering principles, the new systems and methodologies would enable a programmer to fabricate software parts without having to understand the principles behind good programming.

Thus, like structured programming before it, object-oriented programming was not an attempt to turn bad programmers into good ones, but to eliminate the *need* for good ones. Each theory claimed to be the revolution that would turn programmers from craftsmen into modern engineers; but, in reality, programmers had neither the skills of the old craftsmen before the theory, nor the skills of engineers after it.

All that mechanistic theories can hope to accomplish is to turn ignorant programmers into ignorant operators of software devices. But we can only incorporate in devices *mechanistic* principles, while our applications must mirror *non-mechanistic* phenomena. So, to permit programmers to create useful applications, the theories must abandon in the end their restriction to mechanistic principles. They restore in roundabout and complicated ways the low levels of abstraction, and the means to link software structures, thereby bringing back the most challenging aspect of programming – the need to manage complex structures. Thus, not only do these theories fail to eliminate the need for non-mechanistic knowledge, but, by forcing programmers to depend on complicated concepts and systems, they make software development even more difficult than before.

Each time they get to depend on a mechanistic theory instead of simply practising, programmers forgo the only opportunity they have to improve their skills. Their performance remains at novice levels, and they believe that the only way to make progress is by adopting the *next* mechanistic theory. Professional programming, the elites keep telling them, means being familiar with the latest concepts and development systems.

Both structured programming and object-oriented programming are an expression of our mechanistic software ideology – an ideology promoted by universities and by the software companies. It is in the interest of these elites to prevent the evolution of a true programming profession. By redefining programming expertise as the capability to follow methods and to operate devices, the mechanistic ideology has reduced programmers to bureaucrats.

The Relational Database Model

The relational database model is the theoretical concept upon which the relational database systems are founded. Database systems are environments for data management, and among them the relational kind are the most popular. In this section we will try to determine how much of this popularity is due to their data management capabilities, and how much to our mechanistic delusions. What we will find is that, like the other mechanistic software theories, the relational database model is a pseudoscience; that it is worthless as a programming concept; and that the relational systems became practical only after *annulling* their relational features, and after *reinstating* – in a more complicated form, and under new names – the *traditional* data management principles.

The relational model belongs to the class of theories that promise us higher levels of abstraction than those offered by the traditional programming languages. Based on these theories, elaborate development systems are created and promoted. But instead of being abandoned when the idea of higher levels proves to be a fantasy, these systems undergo a series of "improvements." And the improvements, it turns out, consist in the addition of *low-level* capabilities; that is, precisely those features we had in the traditional languages, and which these systems were meant to supersede. So, in the end, all we accomplish is to replace efficient and straightforward languages with slow, complicated, and expensive development systems. (See "The Delusion of High Levels" in chapter 6; see also "The Quest for Higher Levels" in the previous section.)

The Promise

1

The idea of a database management system emerged in the late 1960s, when it was noticed that programmers had difficulty designing correct file relationships. Individually, the file operations are quite simple: reading a particular data record, writing a new record or modifying an existing one, and the like. The difficulty, rather, lies in creating correct *combinations* of operations. Applications need many files, and a file may have many records. Moreover, through the data present in their fields, the records form intricate relationships, and the file operations must exactly match these relationships if the application is to run correctly. It is the programmer's task to specify the iterations and conditions through which the application will create and use the various records at run time; and even a small error can have such consequences as reading or deleting the wrong record, corrupting the data stored in a record, or slowing down the application by performing unnecessary file operations.

The challenges that programmers face with file operations, thus, are similar to those they face with any other aspect of the application. So, as is the case with the other challenges, what they need is expertise: the knowledge and skills one develops over the years by programming increasingly complex applications. Programmers have difficulty designing correct and efficient file operations because they lack this expertise, because our programming culture prevents them from advancing past the level of novices.

The theories of structured programming and object-oriented programming, we saw, were invented by the software elite in an effort to obviate the need for programming expertise. Since programmers had difficulty creating correct flow-control constructs, restricting them to a few, standard constructs was seen as the answer; and since they had difficulty creating useful and modifiable applications, restricting them to ready-made modules was seen as the answer.

The solution to programming incompetence, in other words, was always thought to lie, not in encouraging programmers to *improve* their skills, but in discovering methods that would eliminate the *need* for skills; specifically, methods that would permit inexperienced programmers to accomplish tasks demanding expertise.

And it was the same ideology that prompted the invention of the relational database model. If programmers have difficulty designing combinations of file operations, let us provide these combinations in the form of built-in, high-level operations. For example, simply by specifying a few parameters, programmers would be able to read a set of logically related records. In contrast, to read the same records with the basic file operations, programmers must scan the file one record at a time, and control this process using iterative and conditional constructs.

Historically, the first database systems (which were based on the so-called hierarchical and network database models) were seen largely as management tools: means to take away from programmers the responsibility of designing and maintaining the application's database. The software experts hoped that, by keeping the most important database functions outside the application, database systems would eliminate our dependence on the skills of programmers: the database would become the responsibility of managers or analysts, and the programmers would simply be told, for each requirement, what database operations to invoke.

Now, the general trend was already to break down the application into smaller and smaller parts, in order to match the capabilities of inexperienced programmers. The trend, in other words, was to prevent programmers from *designing* software, and to reduce their work to little more than translating into a programming language the instructions received from a superior. So what the first database systems were promising was to reduce database programming to the same type of work. For all practical purposes, programmers would no longer need to know anything about the files used by the application, or about the relations between files. All they would have to do is translate some simple instructions into the equivalent database operations.

As was the case with the relational model later, attempting to simplify programming by raising the level of abstraction only made it more complicated. New software concepts, design methodologies, and languages (known as data definition and data manipulation languages) had to be introduced to support the hierarchical and network models; and in the end, the high-level operations turned out to be more difficult than the traditional ones. Database systems, thus, were a fraud from the start: they complicated programming instead of simplifying it, and did not provide any functions that could not be implemented through the traditional file operations. (In fact, certain file relationships, easily programmed using file operations, cannot be implemented at all with the hierarchical and network models.)

When judged from within our corrupt software culture, however, the appeal of the original promise is understandable. Once we accept the idea that the highest programming skills we can expect are those attained by an average person after a few months of practice, replacing programmers with software devices seems logical. The complexity created by database systems is a small price to pay, the software experts tell us, for what we gain: successful database management regardless of the skills of the available personnel. Surely, we cannot trust a *programmer* with the task of designing the complex relationships that make up a database. Besides, with so many programmers working on the same application, it is impractical to allow each one to modify the file definitions. A specialist should design the database, and the best way to separate this task from the programming tasks is with a database management system.

In reality, the programmer is the best person to design the application's database, just as he is the best person to deal with every other aspect of the application. However, this is true only of experienced, professional programmers. Everyone could see that the existing programmers were novices, not professionals. But instead of giving them the time and opportunity to develop their skills, the preferred solution was to employ hordes of these novices, and to create several levels of management – bureaucrats with titles like systems analyst and project manager – to supervise them.[1]

As I have already remarked, this ideology – the belief that programming skills can be replaced with management skills – was already accepted when the first database systems were being introduced. So the idea of transferring the responsibility for the application's *database* from programmers to managers, although just as absurd as the attempt to replace the other programming skills,

---

[1] Most business applications can be developed and supported by *one* person. Thus, working alone and only part-time, I designed, programmed, and maintained several business systems over the years – the kind of systems for which companies normally employ teams of programmers and analysts. Few people are aware of the immense inefficiency created when a number of inexperienced individuals work together on one software project. The resulting application can become, quite literally, hundreds of times larger than necessary, and also far more involved. The combination of large teams, incompetence, and the dependence on development environments and ready-made pieces of software gives rise to an inefficiency that feeds on itself. In the end, these bureaucrats spend most of their time solving specious problems, which they themselves keep creating, instead of genuine software and business problems.

appeared quite logical. (As it turned out, though, the complexity of the database systems exceeded the capacity of existing management, and a new type of software bureaucrat had to be invented – the database administrator.)

And so it is how, from a totally unnecessary tool, database systems became one of the main preoccupations, and a major contribution to the astronomic cost of data processing, in most computer installations.

2

Although all database models suffer from the same fallacies, it is the relational model that concerns us, because it was beginning with this model that the software experts presented the concept of database systems as a *scientific* theory. If the earlier systems were promoted as management tools, the relational systems were also seen as a step in the formalization of application development. Because the relational model is based on certain mathematical concepts, the experts were now convinced that the benefits of database systems had been proved. Accordingly, a manager who refused to adopt this model was guilty of more than just resisting software progress; he was guilty of rejecting science.

The relational model is much more ambitious than the earlier ones. What we are promised is that, if we keep the data in a particular format, and if we restrict ourselves to a particular type of operations, we will never again have to deal with *low-level* entities (indexes, individual records and fields, and the related iterative and conditional constructs). In addition, the relational model will eliminate all data inconsistencies. The files are treated now simply as tables with rows and columns, and all we have to do is select and combine logical portions of these tables. Any database requirement, we are told, can be implemented in this fashion – in the same way that any mathematical expression is, ultimately, a combination of some basic operations.

As they did for the other mechanistic ideas, the software experts failed to understand why the mathematical background of a theory does not guarantee its usefulness for application development. Its exact nature only means that a mechanistic model has been found for *one* aspect of the application. And this is a trivial accomplishment: We know that complex phenomena can be represented as systems of simple hierarchical structures; and we also know that it is possible to extract any one of these structures and to represent it with a mechanistic model. Software applications comprise many structures, so it is not difficult to find exact models if all we want is to represent these structures *individually*.

Thus, the theory of structured programming asked us to extract that aspect of the application that is its static flow diagram. Since it is possible to reduce this one aspect to a perfect hierarchy, and hence to represent it mathematically, the experts believed that the application as a whole can be represented mathematically. The theory of object-oriented programming asked us to identify the various aspects of our affairs, and to depict each one with a hierarchical classification of software entities. The experts believed that if each aspect is represented with a perfect hierarchy, whole applications can be developed simply by combining these hierarchies. Finally, the relational database theory asks us to extract that aspect of the application that is its database, and to reduce to perfect hierarchies the file relationships. This will permit us to represent mathematically the database structures, and hence the database operations.

What a mechanistic software theory does, in the final analysis, is model structures of a particular type, after separating them from the other structures that make up the application. So, no matter how successful these theories are in representing the individual structures, they are worthless as *programming* theories, because we cannot develop the application by dealing with each structure separately. The elements of these structures are the software entities that make up the application. Thus, since they share their elements, the structures interact, and we must deal with all of them at the same time. No theory that represents individual structures can model the whole application closely enough to be useful as a programming theory.

Like all mechanistic delusions, these theories are very naive. Since we already know that simple hierarchical structures can be represented mathematically, what these experts perceive as an important discovery is in reality a predictable achievement. All they are doing is breaking down software phenomena into smaller and smaller aspects, until they reach aspects that are simple enough to model with a hierarchical structure; and at that point they discover a mathematical theory for one of those aspects. But this is not surprising. The mathematical nature of the theory is a quality possessed by every hierarchical structure. We knew all along that they would find mathematical theories for the individual aspects. The very reason they separated the original, complex phenomenon into simpler phenomena is that simple structures can be represented with mathematical models while complex ones cannot.

Practitioners, though, must deal with whole applications, not isolated software phenomena. So, for these theories to have any value, we also need an exact theory for *combining* the various aspects – those neat hierarchical structures – into actual applications. And no such theory exists. The structures that represent the various aspects of an application are not related mechanistically, as one within another. They form complex structures.

The only way to create an application, therefore, is by relying on the non-mechanistic capabilities of our mind. But then, if we must have the expertise to deal with complex structures, why do we need theories that break down applications into simple structures in the first place? The software theorists are naive, thus, because they underestimate the difficulty of combining the isolated software structures into actual applications: they believe that we can combine them mechanistically, when the very reason for separating them was the impossibility of representing their totality mechanistically.

3

Like the other software theories, the delusion of the relational database model stems from the mechanistic fallacies of reification and abstraction: the belief that we can extract one aspect (the database structures, in this case) from the complex phenomenon that is a software application, and the belief that we can accomplish the same tasks by starting from high levels of abstraction as we can when starting from the lower levels.

So, as was the case with the ideas of structured programming and object-oriented programming, two great benefits are believed to emerge from the idea of a relational database. First, by reducing the application to strict hierarchical structures we will be able to represent software mathematically. Whether it is the flow of execution, the representation of a business process, or the database structures, we will deal with that aspect of the application formally, and thereby attain perfect, error-free software. Second, when we have strict hierarchical structures we can treat applications as systems of things within things. As we do in manufacturing, then, we will be able to use prefabricated software subassemblies, rather than depend on basic components. Application development will be easier and faster, since we will start our software projects from parts of a higher level of complexity – parts that already include other parts within them.

In the case of the relational model, this is accomplished by moving the low-level definitions and operations into the database system. All we need to do in the application is specify a relational operation, and the system will generate a database structure for us. In other words, not only do we have now a method that guarantees the correctness of the database, but this method consists of just a few simple, high-level operations. Instead of having to work with indexes and individual records, and with iterative and conditional constructs, we only need to understand now the concept of tables, of rows and columns: by extracting and combining portions of tables, we can generate all the database structures that we are likely to need in our applications.

Like the other software theories, the relational database model was seen as a critical step in the automation of programming. We only need to follow certain methods, and to use certain software systems; and because these methods and systems are based on mathematical concepts, we will end up with *provably* correct applications. It is already possible, we are told, to turn programming into a formal, routine activity. The concept of software engineering, if rigorously applied, already offers us the means to create perfect applications without depending on the skills or experience of individual programmers. And soon our systems will be powerful enough to eliminate the need for programmers altogether. Application development will then be completely automated: by means of sophisticated, interactive environments, managers and analysts will generate the application directly from the requirements.

❖

We have already discussed the fallacy of high-level starting elements. We saw, in particular, that even for a simple requirement like file maintenance we must link the file operations to the other types of operations – display and calculations, for instance. And consequently, if we want to be able to implement *any* file maintenance functions, we must start with the basic file operations and with the statements of a traditional programming language (see pp. 445–448).

Similarly, we can perhaps replace with a high-level operation the file operations and the logic needed to read a set of related records, but only for common requirements: comparing or totaling the values present in certain fields, displaying or printing these values, specifying some criteria for record selection or grouping, and the like. High-level operations are useless if what we need is a combination of file operations and logic peculiar to a particular requirement: displaying one field when a certain condition occurs and another field otherwise, performing one calculation for some records and another for other records, and so forth. Clearly, there is no limit to the number of situations that may require a particular combination of file operations and business requirements, so the idea of replacing the basic operations with high-level ones is absurd.

High-level database operations are useful, thus, if provided *in addition* to the basic file operations; that is, if we retain the means to create our own combinations of file operations, and use the high-level operations only when they are indeed more effective. But this is not how the relational database systems are presented. The concept of a database environment is promoted as a *replacement* of the basic file operations. We are told that these operations are no longer necessary, and that we must depend exclusively on the high-level relational ones.

It is easy to tell when starting from higher levels is indeed a practical alternative: the resulting operations are simple and beneficial. A good example is the idea of a mathematical function library: a collection of subroutines that evaluate for us, through built-in algorithms, various mathematical functions. Thus, simply by calling one of these subroutines, we can determine in the application such values as the logarithm or the sine of a variable. Because we seldom need to link the operations that make up these algorithms with the operations performed in the application, the calculations can be extracted from the rest of the application and replaced with independent modules – modules that interact with the application only through their input and output. And we notice the success of this idea in that the concept of a mathematical function library has remained practically unchanged over the years. One of the oldest programming concepts, the mathematical library is as simple and effective today as it was when first implemented. We didn't have to continually "improve" and "enhance" this concept, as we do our database systems.

But the best example of a practical move to higher levels is provided by the file operations themselves. The basic file operations are usually described as "low-level," but they are low-level only relative to the operations promised by database systems. The basic operations are executed by a file management system, and, relative to the operations performed internally by that system, their level is quite high. (The terms "basic file operations" and "file management system" will be discussed in greater detail in the next subsection; see pp. 686–687.) Thus, a simple statement that reads, writes, or deletes a record in the application becomes, when executed by the file management system, a complex set of operations involving indexes, buffers, search algorithms, and disk accesses. But because there are no links between these operations and the various operations performed by the application, they can be separated from the application and invoked by means of simple statements.

So, relative to the operations performed internally by the file management system, the basic file operations constitute in effect a library of file management functions, as do the mathematical functions relative to *their* internal operations. And, like the mathematical functions, the success of this concept is seen in the fact that it has remained practically unchanged since the 1960s, when it was introduced. But, just because we moved successfully from the low level of buffers and direct disk access to a level where all we need to do is read, write, and delete data records, it doesn't follow that we can move to an even higher level.

It is precisely because no higher levels are possible that the relational database systems evolved into such complicated environments. Were high-level database operations a practical idea, their use would be as straightforward as is the use of mathematical functions or basic file operations. The reason these systems became increasingly large and complicated is that, in order to make them practical, their designers had to add more and more "features." These features are perceived as *enhancements* of the relational concept, but their real function is to counteract the *falsifications* of this concept. They may have new and fancy names, but these are features we always had – in our programming languages.

Thus, in order to save the relational theory from refutation, the software pseudoscientists had to incorporate into database systems *programming* features: means to define integrity and security checks, to access individual records, to deal with run-time errors, and so forth. These, obviously, are the low-level, application-related processes which they had originally hoped to eliminate through high-level database operations.

So the relational database systems became in the end a fraud: instead of admitting that the idea of high-level database operations had failed, the theorists reinstated the low-level capabilities of the traditional programming languages while making them look like features of a database system. Entire new languages had to be invented, in order to let programmers perform *within the database system* those operations they had been performing all along, through traditional programming languages, *within the application*.

The reason for the complexity of the relational systems, thus, is that they ended up incorporating concepts which belong in the application. Programming problems that are quite easy to solve as part of the application become awkward and complicated when separated from the application and moved into a database environment. Besides, the new languages are not as versatile as the traditional, general-purpose ones: they provide only *some* of the low-level elements we need, and only as artificial extensions to the high-level features. So our work is complicated also by having to solve low-level programming problems in a high-level environment. Like other development environments, the relational systems have reversed a basic programming principle: instead of freely creating high-level elements by combining low-level ones, we are forced to start with high-level elements, and to treat the low-level ones as extensions.

The idea of a database system emerged, we recall, not because of any requirements that could not be implemented with the basic file operations, but as an answer to the lack of programmers who could use these operations correctly. So, if what programmers must do now is even more difficult than is the use of file operations, how can the database systems help them? High-level database operations cannot replace programming expertise any more than could the idea of structured programming, or the idea of object-oriented programming.

The Basic File Operations

1

To appreciate the inanity of the relational model, we must start by examining the basic file operations; that is, those operations which the relational systems are attempting to supplant. What I want to show is that these operations are *both necessary and sufficient* for implementing database management requirements, particularly in business applications. Thus, once we recognize the importance of the basic file operations, we will be in a better position to understand why the relational systems are fraudulent. For, as we will see, the only way to make them useful was by enhancing them with precisely those capabilities provided by the basic file operations; in other words, by restoring the very features that the database experts had claimed to be unnecessary.

Also, it is important to remember that the basic file operations have been available to programmers from the start, ever since mass storage devices with random access became popular. For example, they have been available through COBOL (a language specifically designed for business applications) since around 1970. So these operations have always been well known: COBOL was always a public language, was implemented on all major computers, and was adopted by most companies. Thus, in addition to being an introduction to the basic file operations, this discussion serves to support my claim that the only motivation for database systems in general, and for the relational systems in particular, was to find a substitute for the knowledge required of programmers to use these operations correctly.

Before examining the basic file operations, we must take a moment to clarify this term and the related terms "file operations" and "database operations." The basic file operations are a basic set of file management functions. They formed in the past an integral part of every major operating system, and were accessible through programming languages. These operations deal with *indexed data files* – the most versatile form of data storage; and, in conjunction with the features provided by the languages themselves, they allow us to use and to relate these files in any way we like.

"File operations" is a more general term. It refers to the basic file operations, but also to the various ways in which we combine them, using the flow-control constructs of a programming language, in order to implement file management requirements. "Database operations" is an even more general term. It refers to the file operations, but in the context of the whole application, so it usually means *combinations* of file operations; in particular, combinations involving several files. The terms "traditional file operations" and "low-level file operations" refer to any one of the operations defined above.

The term "database" refers to a set of related files; typically, the files used by a particular application. Hence, the term "database system" ought to mean any software system that helps us to manage a database.[1] Through their propaganda, though, the software elites have created in our minds a strong association between terms like "database," "database system," and "database management system" (or DBMS) and *high-level* database operations. And as a result, most people believe that the only way to manage a database is through high-level operations; that the current database systems provide indispensable features; and that it is impossible to implement a serious application without depending on such a system.

But we must not allow the software charlatans to control our language and our minds. Since we can implement any database functions through the basic file operations and a programming language, systems that provide high-level operations are not at all essential for database management. So we can continue to use the terms "database" and "database operations" even while rejecting the notion of a system that restricts us to high-level operations.

Strictly speaking, since the basic file operations permit us to manage a database, they too form a database system. But it would be confusing to use this term for the basic operations, now that it is associated with the high-level operations. Thus, I call the systems that provide basic file operations "*file* management systems," or "*file* systems" for short. This term is quite appropriate, in fact, seeing that these systems are limited to operations involving single files; it is *we* who implement the actual database management, by combining the operations provided by the file system with those provided by a programming language.

So I use the term "database," and terms like "database operations" and "database management," to refer to *any* set of related files – regardless of whether the files and relations are managed through the high-level operations of a *database* system, or through the basic operations of a *file* system.

The term "database structures" refers to the various hierarchical structures created by the files that make up the database: related files can be seen as the levels of a structure, and their records as the elements that make up these levels (see p. 702). In most applications, the totality of database structures is a complex structure.

---

[1] The term "database system" is used by everyone as an abbreviation of "database management system." It is somewhat misleading, though, since it sounds as if it refers to the database itself.

2

Two types of files make up the database structures of an application: *data* files and *index* files. The data files contain the actual data, organized as *records*; the index files (or indexes, for short) contain the pointers that permit us to access these records.

The record is the unit that the application typically reads from the file, or writes to the file. But within each record the data is broken down into *fields*, and it is the values present in the individual fields that we normally use in the application. For example, if each record in the file has 100 bytes, the first field may take the first 6 bytes, the second one the next 24 bytes, and so on. This is how the fields reside on disk, and in memory when the record is read from disk, but in most cases their relative order within the record is immaterial. For, in the application we assign names to these fields, and we refer to them simply by their names. Thus, once a record is read into memory, we treat database fields, for all practical purposes, as we do memory variables.

The records and fields of a data file reflect the structure and type of the information stored in the file. In an employee file, for example, there is a record for each employee, and each record contains such fields as employee number, name, salary, and year-to-date earnings and deductions; in a sales history file there is a record for each line in a sales order, with such fields as the customer and order numbers, date, price, and quantity sold. While in simple cases the required fields are self-evident, generally it takes some experience to design the most effective database for a given set of requirements. We must decide what information should be processed by the application, how to represent this information, how to distribute it among files, how to index the files, and how to relate them. Needless to say, it is impossible to predict all future requirements, so we must be prepared to alter the application's database structure later: we may need to add or delete fields, move fields from one file to another, and create new files or indexes.

We don't normally access data records directly, but through an index. Indexes, thus, are service files, means to access the data files. Indexes fulfil two essential functions: they allow us to identify a specific record, and to scan a series of records in a specific sequence. It is through *keys* that indexes perform these tasks. The key is one of the fields that make up the record, or a set of several fields. Clearly, if the combination of values present in these fields is different for each record in the file, each record can be uniquely identified. In addition, key uniqueness allows us to scan the records in a particular sequence – the sequence that reflects the current key values – regardless of their actual, physical sequence on disk. When the key is one field, the value present in the field is the value of the key. When the key consists of several fields, the value of the key is the combination of the field values, in the order in which they make up the key. The records are scanned, in effect, in a sorted sequence. For example, if the key is defined as the set of three fields, *A*, *B*, and *C*, the sorting sequence can be expressed as either "by *A* by *B* by *C*" or "by *C* within *B* within *A*."

Note that if we permit *duplicate* keys – if, that is, some combinations of values in the key fields are not unique – we will be unable to identify the individual records within a set of duplicates. Such an index is still useful, however, if all we need is to *scan* those records. The scanning sequence within a set of duplicate records is usually the order in which they were added to the file. Thus, for scanning too, if we want better control we must ensure key uniqueness.

An especially useful feature is the capability to create several indexes for the same data file. This permits us to access the same records in different ways – scan the file in one sequence or another, or read a record through one key or another. For example, we may scan a sales history file either by order number or by product number; or, we may search for a particular sales record through a key consisting of the customer number and order number, or through a key consisting of the product number and order date.

Another useful indexing feature is the option of *descending* keys. The normal scanning sequence is *ascending*, from low to high key values; but some file systems also allow indexes that scan records from high to low key values. Any one field, or all the fields in the key, can then be either ascending or descending. Simply by scanning the data file through such an index we can list, for instance, orders in ascending sequence by customer number, but within each customer those orders with a higher amount first; or we can list the sales history by ascending product number, but within each product by descending date (so those sold most recently come first), and within each date by ascending customer number. A related indexing feature, useful in its own right but also as an alternative to descending keys, is the capability to scan records backward.

In addition to indexed data files, most file management systems support two other types of files, *relative* and *sequential*. These files provide simpler record access, and are useful for data that does not require an elaborate indexing scheme. In relative data files, we access a record by specifying its relative position in the file (first, second, third, etc.). These files are useful, therefore, in situations where the individual records cannot, or need not, be identified by the values present in their fields (to store the entries of a large table, for instance). Sequential data files are organized as a series of consecutive records, which can only be accessed sequentially, starting from the beginning. These files are useful in situations where we don't need to access individual records directly, and where we normally read the whole file anyway (to store data that has no specific structure, for instance). Text data, too, is usually stored in sequential files. I will not discuss further the relative and sequential files. It is the indexed data files that interest us, because it is only *their* operations that the relational database systems are attempting to replace with high-level operations.

❖

File systems provide at least two types of fields, *alphanumeric* (or *alpha*, for short) and *numeric*. And, since these types are the same as the memory variables supported by most high-level languages (COBOL, in particular), database fields and memory variables can be used together, and in the same manner, in the application. In alphanumeric fields, data is stored as character symbols, so these fields are useful for names, addresses, descriptions, notes, identifiers, and the like. When these fields are part of an indexing key, the scanning sequence is alphabetical. In numeric fields, the data is stored as numeric values, so these fields can be used directly in calculations. Numeric fields are useful for any data that can be expressed as a numeric value: quantities, dollar amounts, codes, and the like. When part of an indexing key, the scanning sequence is determined by the numeric value.

Some file systems provide additional field types. *Date* fields, for instance, are useful for storing dates. In the absence of date fields, we must store dates in numeric fields, as six- or eight-digit values representing the combination of the month, day, and year; alternatively, we can store dates as values representing the number of days elapsed since some arbitrary, distant date in the past. (The latter method is preferable, as it simplifies date calculations, comparisons, and indexing.) Another field type is the *binary* field, used to store such data as text, graphics, and sound; that is, data which can be in any format whatsoever (hence "binary," or raw), and which may require many thousands of bytes. (Because of its large size, this data is stored in separate files, and only pointers to it are kept in the field itself.)

3

Now that we have examined the structure of indexed data files, let us review the basic file operations. Six operations, combined with the iterative and conditional constructs of high-level languages, are all we need in order to use indexed data files. I will first describe these operations, and then show how they are combined with language features to implement various requirements. The names I use for the basic operations are taken from COBOL. (There may be some small variations in the way these operations are implemented in a particular file system, or in a particular version of COBOL; for example, in the way multiple indexes or duplicate keys are supported.)

The following terms are used in the description of the file operations: The *current index* is the index file specified in the operation. *File* is a data file; although the file actually specified in the operation is an index file, the record read or written belongs to the data file (we always access a data file through one of its indexes). *Record area* is a storage area – the portion of memory where the fields that make up the record are specified; each file has its own record area, and this area is accessed by both the file system and the application (the application treats the fields as ordinary memory variables). *Key* is the field or set of fields, within the record area, that was defined as the key of a particular index; the *current key* is the key that was defined for the current index. The record *pointer* is an indicator maintained by the file system to identify the next record in the scanning sequence established by a particular index; each index has its own pointer, and the *current pointer* is the pointer corresponding to the current index.

WRITE: A new record is added to the file. Typically, the data in this record consists of the values previously placed by the application into the fields that make up the file's record area. The values present in the fields that make up the current key will become the new record's key in the current index. If the file has additional indexes, the values in their respective key fields will become the keys in those indexes. All indexes are updated together: following this operation, the new record can be accessed either through the current index or through another index. If one of the file's indexes does not permit duplicate keys and the new record would cause such a condition, the operation is aborted and the system returns an error code (so that the application can take appropriate action).

REWRITE: The data in the record area replaces the data in the record currently in the file. Typically, the application read previously the record into the record area through the current index, and modified some of the fields. The record is identified by the current key, so the fields that make up this key should not be modified. If there are other indexes, the fields that make up their keys may be modified, and REWRITE will update those indexes to reflect the change. REWRITE, however, can also be used without first reading the existing record: the application must place some values in all the fields, and REWRITE functions then like WRITE, except that it replaces an existing record. In either case, if no record is found with the current key, or if one of the file's indexes does not permit duplicate keys and the modified record would cause such a condition, the operation is aborted and the system returns an error code.

DELETE: The record identified by the current key is removed from the file. Only the values present in the current key fields are important for the operation; the rest of the record area is ignored. The application, therefore, can delete a record either by reading it first into the record area (through any one of its indexes) or just by placing the appropriate values into the current key fields. If no record is found with the current key, the system returns an error code.

READ: The record identified by the current key is read into the record area. The current index can be any one of the file's indexes, and only the values present in the current key fields are important for the operation. Following this operation, the fields in the record area contain the values present in that record in the file. If no record is found with the current key, the system returns an error code.

START: The current pointer is positioned at the record identified by the current key. The current index can be any one of the file's indexes, and only the values present in the current key fields are important for the operation. The specification for the operation includes a relation like *equal*, *greater*, or *greater or equal*, so the application need not indicate a valid key; the record identified is simply the first one, in the scanning sequence of the current index, whose key satisfies the condition specified (for example, the first one whose key is *greater* than the values present in the current key fields). If no record in the file satisfies that condition, the system returns an error code.

READ NEXT: The record identified by the current pointer is read into the record area. This operation, in conjunction with START, makes the file scanning feature available to the application. The application must first perform a START for the current index, in order to set the current pointer at the first record in the series of records to be scanned. (To indicate the first record in the file, null values are typically placed in the key fields, and the condition *greater* is specified.) READ NEXT will then read that record and advance the pointer to the next record in the scanning sequence of the current index. The subsequent READ NEXT will read the record indicated by the pointer's new position and advance the pointer to the next record, and so on. Through this process, then, the application can read a series of consecutive records without having to know their keys.[2] Typically, READ NEXT is part of a loop, and the application knows when the last record in the series is reached by checking a certain condition (for example, whether the key exceeds a particular value). If the pointer was already positioned past the last record in the file (the *end-of-file* condition), the

---

[2] Since no search is involved, it is not only simpler but also faster to read a record in this fashion, than by specifying its key. Thus, even when the keys are known, it is more efficient to read consecutive records with READ NEXT than with READ.

system returns an error code. (Simply checking for this code after each READ NEXT is how applications typically handle the situation where the last record in the series is also the last one in the file.)

These six operations form the minimal practical set of file operations: the set of operations that are both necessary and sufficient for using indexed data files in serious applications.[3] I will demonstrate now, with a few examples, how the basic file operations are used in conjunction with other types of operations to implement typical requirements. Again, I am describing COBOL constructs and statements, but the implementation would be very similar in other high-level languages.

A common requirement involves the *display* of data from a particular record: the user identifies the record by entering the value of its key (customer number, part number, invoice number, and the like), and the application responds by retrieving that record and displaying some of its fields. When the key consists of several fields, the user must enter several values. To implement this operation in the application, all we need is a READ: we place the values entered by the user into the current key fields, perform the READ, and then display for the user various fields from the record area. If, however, the system returns an error code, we display a message such as "record not found."

If the user wants to *modify* some of the fields in a particular record, we start by performing a READ and displaying the current values, as before; but then we allow the user to enter the new values, place them in the appropriate fields in the record area, and perform a REWRITE. And if what the user wants is to *delete* a particular record, we usually start with a READ, display some of the fields to allow the user to confirm it is the right record, and then perform a DELETE.

Lastly, to *add* a record, we display blank fields and allow the user to enter their actual values. (In a new record, some fields may have null values, or some default values; so these fields may be left out, or just displayed, or displayed with the option to modify them.) The user must also enter the value of the key fields, to identify the new record. We then perform a WRITE, and the system will add this record to the file. If, however, it returns an error code, we display a message such as "duplicate key" to tell the user why the record could not be added.

---

[3] I will not discuss here the various *support* operations – opening and closing files, locking and unlocking records in multiuser applications, and the like. Since there is little difference between these operations in file systems and in database systems, they have no bearing on my argument. Many of these operations can be performed automatically, in fact, in both types of systems.

Examples of this type of record access are found in the *file maintenance* operations – those operations that permit the user to add, delete, and modify records in the database. And, clearly, any maintenance requirement can be implemented through the basic file operations: any file, record, and field in the database can be read, displayed, or modified. If we must restrict this freedom (permit only a range of values for a certain field, permit the addition or deletion of a record only under certain conditions, etc.), all we have to do is add appropriate checks; then, if the checks fail, we bypass the file operation and display a message.

So far I have discussed the *interactive* access of individual records, but the basic file operations are used in the same way when the user is not directly involved. Thus, if we need to know at some point in the application the quantity on hand for a certain part, we place the part number in the key field, perform a READ, and then get the value from the quantity field; if we want to add a new transaction to the sales history file, we place the appropriate values in the key fields (customer number, invoice number, etc.) and in the non-key fields (date, price, quantity, etc.), and perform a WRITE; if we want to update a customer's balance, we place the customer number in the key field, perform a READ, calculate the new value, place it in the balance field, and then perform a REWRITE. Again, any conceivable requirement can be implemented through the basic file operations.

Accessing *individual* records, as described above, is one way of using indexed data files. The other way is by *scanning* records, an operation accomplished with an iterative construct based on START and READ NEXT. This construct, which may be called the basic file scanning loop, is used every time we read a series of records sequentially through an index. The best way to illustrate this loop is with a simple example (see figure 7-13). The loop here is designed to read the PART file in ascending part number sequence. The indexing key, P-KEY, consists of one field, P-NUM (part number). START positions the record pointer so that the first record read has a part number no less than P1, and the

```
    MOVE P1 TO P-NUM START PART KEY>=P-KEY INVALID GO TO L4.
  L3. READ PART NEXT END GO TO L4. IF P-NUM>P2 GO TO L4.
    IF P-QTY<Q1 GO TO L3.
    [various operations]
    GO TO L3.
  L4.
```

Figure 7-13

condition >P2 terminates the loop at the first record with a part number greater than P2. The loop will read, therefore, only the *range* of records, P1 through P2, inclusive.[4] In addition, within this range, the loop selects only those records where the quantity field, P-QTY, is no less than a certain value, Q1. The operations following the selection conditions will be performed for every record that satisfies these conditions. The labels L3 and L4 delimit the loop.[5]

We rarely perform the same operations with all the records in a file, so the selection of records is a common requirement in file scanning. The previous example illustrates the two selection methods – based on key fields, and on non-key fields. The method based on key fields is preferable when what we select is a range of records, as the records left out don't even have to be read. This can greatly reduce the processing time, especially if the file is large and the range selected is relatively small. In contrast, when the selection is based on non-key fields, each record in the file must be read. This is true because the value of non-key fields is unrelated to the record's position in the scanning sequence, so the only way to know what the values are is by reading the record. The two methods are often combined in the same loop, as illustrated in the example.

It should be obvious that these two selection methods are completely general, and can satisfy any requirement. For example, if the range must include all the records in the file, we specify null values for the key fields in START and omit the test for the end of the range. The loop also deals correctly with the case where no records should be selected (because there are none in the specified range, or because the selection based on non-key fields excludes all those in the range). It must be noted that the selection conditions can be as complex as we need: they can involve several fields, or fields from other files (by reading in the loop records from those files), or a combination of fields, memory variables, and constants. A complex condition can be formulated either as one complex IF statement or as several consecutive IF statements. And,

---

[4] Note the END clause in READ NEXT, specifying the action to take if the end of the file is reached before P2. (INVALID and END are the abbreviated forms of the COBOL keywords INVALID KEY and AT END. Similarly, GOTO can be abbreviated in COBOL as GO.)

[5] It is evident from this example that the most effective way to implement the basic file scanning loop in COBOL is with GOTO jumps. This demonstrates again the absurdity of the claim that GOTO is harmful and must be avoided (the delusion we discussed under structured programming). Modifying this loop to avoid the GOTOs renders the simple operations of file scanning and record selection complicated and abstruse; yet this is exactly what the experts have been advocating since 1970. It is quite likely that the complexity engendered by the delusions of structured programming contributed to the difficulty programmers had in using file operations, and was a factor in the evolution of database systems: because they tried to avoid the complications created by one pseudoscience, programmers must now deal with the greater complications created by another.

in addition to the conditions that affect all the operations in the loop, we can have conditions *within* the loop; any portion of the loop, therefore, can be restricted to certain records.

Let us see now how the basic file scanning loop is used to implement various file operations. In a typical file listing, or query, or report, the scanning sequence and the record selection criteria specified by the user become the index and the selection conditions for the scanning loop. And within the loop, for each record selected, we show certain fields and perhaps accumulate their values. Typically, one line is printed or displayed for each record, and the totals are shown at the end. When the indexing key consists of several fields, their value will change hierarchically, one within another, in the sorting sequence of the index; thus, we can have various levels of subtotals by noting within the loop when the value of these fields changes. In an orders file, for instance, if the key consists of order number within customer number, and if we need the quantity and amount subtotals for the orders belonging to each customer, we must show and then clear these subtotals every time the customer number changes.

Another use of the scanning loop is for *modifying* records. The reading and selection are performed as before, but here we modify the value stored in certain fields; then we perform a REWRITE (at the end of the loop, typically). This is useful when we have to modify a series of records according to some common logic. Not all the selected records need to be modified, of course; we can perform some calculations and display the results for all the records in a given range, for instance, but modify only those where the fields satisfy a certain condition. Rather than modify records, we can use the scanning loop to *delete* certain records; in this case we perform a DELETE at the end of the loop.

An interesting use of indexed data files is for sorting. If, for instance, we need a listing of certain values in a particular scanning sequence (values derived from files or from calculations), we create a temporary data file where the indexing key is the combination of fields for that scanning sequence, while the non-key fields are the other values to be listed. All we have to do then is perform a WRITE to add a record to the temporary file for each entry required in the listing. The system will build for us the appropriate index, and, once complete, we can scan the temporary file in the usual manner. Similarly, if we need to scan a portion of a data file in a certain sequence, but only occasionally, then instead of having a permanent index for that sequence we create a temporary data file that is a subset of the main data file: we read the main data file in a loop through one of its indexes, and for each selected record we copy the required fields to the record of the temporary file and perform a WRITE.

If we want to analyze certain fields in a data file according to the value present in some other fields (total the quantity by territory, total various amounts by the combination of territory and category, etc.), we must create a temporary data file where the indexing key is the field or combination of fields by which we want to group the records (the *analysis* fields in the main data file), while the non-key fields are the values to be totaled (the *analyzed* fields). We read the main file in a loop, and, for each record, we copy the analysis values and the analyzed values to the respective fields in record of the temporary file. We then perform a WRITE for this file and check the return code. If the system indicates that the record already exists, it means this is not the first time that combination of key values was encountered; the response then is to perform a READ, *add* the analyzed values to the respective fields, and perform a REWRITE. In other words, we create a new record in the temporary file only the first time a particular combination of analysis values is encountered, and *update* that record on subsequent occasions. At the end, the temporary file will contain one record for each unique combination of analysis values. This concept is illustrated in figure 7-14.

```
    MOVE C1 TO C-NUM START CUSTOMER KEY>=C-KEY INVALID GO TO L4.
  L3. READ CUSTOMER NEXT END GO TO L4. IF C-NUM>C2 GO TO L4.
    MOVE C-TER TO SR-TER MOVE C-QTY TO SR-QTY.
    WRITE SR-RECORD INVALID READ SORTFL
      ADD C-QTY TO SR-QTY REWRITE SR-RECORD.
    GO TO L3.
  L4.
```

Figure 7-14

In this example, a certain quantity in the CUSTOMER file is analyzed by territory for the customers in the range C1 through C2. SORTFL is the temporary file, and SR-RECORD is its record area. The simplicity of this operation is due to the fact that much of the logic is implicit in the READ, WRITE, and REWRITE.

4

One of the most important uses of the file scanning loop is to *relate* files. If we nest the scanning loop of one file within that of another, a logical relationship is created between the two files. From a programming standpoint, the nesting of file scanning loops is no different from the nesting of any iterative constructs: the whole series of iterations through the inner loop is repeated for every iteration through the outer loop. In the inner loop we can use fields from both files; any operation, therefore, including the record selection conditions, can depend on the record currently read in the outer loop.

Figure 7-15 illustrates this concept. The outer loop scans the CUSTOMER file and selects the range of customer numbers C1 through C2. The indexing key, C-KEY, consists of one field, C-NUM (customer number). Within this loop, in addition to any other operations performed for each customer record, we include a loop that scans the ORDERS file. The indexing key here, O-KEY, consists of two fields, O-CUS (customer number) and O-ORD (order number), in this sorting sequence. Thus, to restrict the inner loop to the orders belonging to one customer, we select only the range of records where the customer number equals the one currently read in the outer loop, while allowing the order number to be any value. (Note that the terminating condition, "IF O-CUS NOT=C-NUM," could be replaced with "IF O-CUS>C-NUM," since the first O-CUS read that is not equal to C-NUM is necessarily greater than it.) The inner loop here selects *all* the orders for the customer read in the outer loop; but we could have additional selection conditions, based on non-key fields, as in figure 7-13 (for example, to select only orders in a certain date range, or over a certain amount).

```
    MOVE C1 TO C-NUM START CUSTOMER KEY>=C-KEY INVALID GO TO L4.
L3. READ CUSTOMER NEXT END GO TO L4. IF C-NUM>C2 GO TO L4.
    [various operations]
    MOVE C-NUM TO O-CUS MOVE 0 TO O-ORD.
    START ORDERS KEY>O-KEY INVALID GO TO L34.
L33. READ ORDERS NEXT END GO TO L34. IF O-CUS NOT=C-NUM GO TO L34.
    [various operations]
    GO TO L33.
L34.
    [various operations]
    GO TO L3.
L4.
```

Figure 7-15

Although most file relations involve only two files, the idea of loop nesting can be used to relate hierarchically any number of files, simply by increasing the number of nesting levels. Thus, by nesting a third loop within the second one and using the same logic, the third file will be related to the second in the same way that the second is related to the first. With two files, we saw, the second file's key consists of two fields, and the range selected includes the records where the first field equals the first file's key. With three files, the third file's key must have three fields, and the range will include the records where the first two fields equal the second file's key. (The keys may have additional fields; two and three are the minimum needed to implement this logic.)

To illustrate this concept, figure 7-16 adds to the previous example a loop to scan the LINES file (the individual item lines associated with each order).

If ORDERS has fields like customer number, order number, date, and total amount, which apply to the whole order, LINES has fields like item number, quantity, and price, which are different for each line. Its indexing key consists of customer number, order number, and line number, in this sorting sequence. And the third loop isolates the lines belonging to a particular order by selecting the range of records where the customer and order numbers equal those of the order currently read in the second loop, while the line number is any value. Another example of a third nesting level is a transaction file, where each record is an invoice, payment, or adjustment pertaining to an order, and the indexing key consists of customer number, order number, and transaction number.[6]

```
MOVE C1 TO C-NUM START CUSTOMER KEY>=C-KEY INVALID GO TO L4.
L3. READ CUSTOMER NEXT END GO TO L4. IF C-NUM>C2 GO TO L4.
  [various operations]
  MOVE C-NUM TO O-CUS MOVE 0 TO O-ORD.
  START ORDERS KEY>O-KEY INVALID GO TO L34.
L33. READ ORDERS NEXT END GO TO L34. IF O-CUS NOT=C-NUM GO TO L34.
  [various operations]
  MOVE O-CUS TO L-CUS MOVE O-ORD TO L-ORD MOVE 0 TO L-LINE.
  START LINES KEY>L-KEY INVALID GO TO L334.
L333. READ LINES NEXT END GO TO L334.
  IF NOT(L-CUS=O-CUS AND L-ORD=O-ORD) GO TO L334.
  [various operations]
  GO TO L333.
L334.
  [various operations]
  GO TO L33.
L34.
  [various operations]
  GO TO L3.
L4.
```

Figure 7-16

Note that in the sections marked "various operations" we can access fields from all the currently read records: in the outer loop, fields from the current CUSTOMER record; in the second loop, fields from the current CUSTOMER and ORDERS records; and in the inner loop, fields from the current CUSTOMER, ORDERS, and LINES records.

Note also that the sections marked "various operations" may contain additional file scanning loops; in other words, we can have more than one

---

[6] Note, in figures 7-13 to 7-16, the numbering system used for labels in order to make the jumps self-explanatory (as discussed under the GOTO delusion, pp. 621–624).

scanning loop at a given nesting level. For instance, by creating two consecutive third-level loops, we can scan first the lines and then the transactions of the order read in the second-level loop.

The arrangement where the key used in the outer loop is part of the key used in the inner loop, as in these examples, is the most common and the most effective way to relate files, because it permits us to select records through their key fields (and to read therefore only a *range* of records). We can also relate files, though, by using non-key fields to select records (when it is practical to read the entire file in the inner loop).

Lastly, another way to relate files is by reading within the loop of one file just one record of another file, with no inner loop at all (or, as a special case, reading just one record in both files, with no outer loop either). Imagine that we are scanning an invoice file where the key is the invoice number and one of the key or non-key fields is the customer number, and that we need some data from the customer record – the name and address fields, for instance. (This kind of data is normally stored only in the customer record because, even though required in many operations, it is the same for all the transactions pertaining to a particular customer.) So, to get this data, we place the customer number from the currently read invoice record into the customer key field, and perform a READ. All the customer fields are then available within the loop, along with the current invoice fields.

❖

The relationship just described, where several records from one file point to the same record in another file, is called *many-to-one* relationship. And the relationship we discussed previously, where one record from the first file points to several records in the second file (because several records are read in the inner loop for each record read in the outer loop) is called *one-to-many* relationship. These two types of file relationships are the most common, but the other two, *one-to-one* and *many-to-many*, are also important.

We have a one-to-one relationship when the same field is used as a key in two files. For example, if in addition to the customer file we create a second file where the indexing key is the customer number (in order to store some of the customer data separately), then each record in one file corresponds to one record in the other. And we have a many-to-many relationship when one record in the first file points to several records in the second one, and at the same time one record in the second file points to several records in the first one. (We will study the four types of file relationships in greater detail later; see pp. 752–755.)

To understand the many-to-many relationship, imagine a factory where a number of different products are being built by assembling various parts from a common inventory. Thus, each product is made from a number of different parts, and at the same time a part may be used in different products. The product file has one record for each product, and the key is the product number. And the part file has one record for each part, and the key is the part number. We can use these files separately in the usual manner, but to implement the many-to-many relationship between products and parts we need an additional file – a service file for storing the cross-references. This file is a dummy data file that consists of key fields only. It has two indexes: in the first one the key is the product number and the part number, and in the second one it is the part number and the product number, in these sorting sequences. In the service file, therefore, there will be one record for each pair of product and part that are related in the manufacturing process (far more records, probably, than there are either products or parts). Now we can scan the product file in the outer loop, and the service file, through its first index, in the inner loop; or, we can scan the part file in the outer loop, and the service file, through its second index, in the inner loop. Then, by selecting in the inner loop a range of records in the usual manner, we will read in the first case the parts used by a particular product, and in the second case the products that use a particular part. What is left is to perform a READ in the inner loop using the part or product number, respectively, in order to read the actual records.

The Lost Integration

The preceding discussion was not meant to be an exhaustive study of indexed data files. My main intent was to show that any conceivable database requirement can be implemented with file operations, and that this is a fairly easy programming challenge: every one of the examples we examined takes just a few statements in COBOL. We only need to understand the two ways of using indexes (reading individual records or scanning a range of records) and the two ways of selecting records (through key fields or non-key fields). Then, simply by combining the basic file operations with the other operations available in a programming language, we can access and relate the files in the database in any way we like.

So the difficulties encountered by programmers are not caused by the basic file operations, nor by the selection of records, nor by the file scanning loops. The difficulties emerge, rather, when we combine file operations, and when we combine them with the other types of operations required by the application. The difficulties, in other words, are due to the need to deal with interacting software structures. Two kinds of structures, and hence two kinds of interactions, are generated: one through the file relationships we discussed earlier (one-to-many, many-to-many, etc.), the other through the links created between the application's elements by the file operations.

Regarding the first kind of structures, the file relationships are easy to understand individually, because we can view them as simple hierarchical structures. If we depict the nesting of files as a structure, each file can be seen as a different level of the structure, and its records as the various elements which make up that level. The relationship between files is then the relationship between the elements of one level and the next. But, even though each relationship is hierarchical, most files take part in several relationships, through different fields. In other words, a record in a certain file can be an element in several structures at the same time, so these structures interact. The totality of file relationships in the database is a complex structure.

As for the second kind of structures, we already know that the file operations give rise to processes based on shared data (see pp. 351–353). So they link the application's elements through many structures – one structure for each field, record, or file that is accessed by several elements. Thus, in addition to the interactions due to the file relationships, we must cope with the interactions between the structures generated by file operations. And we must also cope with the interactions between these structures and the structures formed by the other types of processes – practices, subroutines, memory variables, etc. To implement database requirements we must deal with complex software structures.

When replacing the basic file operations with higher-level operations, what are the database experts trying to accomplish? All that a database system can do is replace with a built-in process the two or three statements that constitute the use of a basic file operation. The experts misinterpret the difficulty that programmers have in implementing file operations as the problem of dealing with the relatively low levels. But, as we saw, the difficulty is not due to the individual file operations, nor to the individual relationships. The difficulty emerges when we deal with *interacting* operations and relationships, and with their interaction with the rest of the application. And these interactions cannot be eliminated; we must have them in a database system too, if the application is to do what we want it to do. Even with a database system, then, the difficult part of database programming remains. The database systems can perhaps replace the easy challenges – the individual operations; but they cannot eliminate the difficult part – the need to deal with interacting structures.

What is worse, database systems make the interactions even more complex, because some of the operations are now in the application while others are in the database system. The original idea was to have database functions akin to the functions provided by a mathematical library; that is, entities of a high level of abstraction, which interact with the application only through their input and output. But this is impossible, because database operations must interact with the rest of the application at a lower level – at the level of fields, variables, and conditions. Thus, the level of abstraction that a database system can provide while remaining a practical system is not as high as the one provided by a mathematical library. We cannot extract, for example, a complete file scanning loop, with all the operations in the loop, and move it into a database system – not if we want to retain the freedom of implementing *any* scanning loops and operations.

All we needed before was the six basic file operations. The database operations, and their interaction with the rest of the application, could then be implemented with the same programming languages, and with the same methods and principles, that we use for the other operations in the application. With a database system, on the other hand, we need new and complicated principles, languages, rules, and methods; we must deal with a new kind of operations in the database system, plus a new kind of operations in the application, the latter necessary in order to link the application to the database system. So, in the end, the difficulties faced by programmers in implementing database operations are even greater than before.

It is easy to see why the basic file operations are both necessary and sufficient for implementing database operations: for most applications – business applications, in particular – they are just the right level of abstraction. The demands imposed by our applications rarely permit us to move to higher levels, and we rarely need lower ones. An example of lower-level file operations is the requirement for a kind of fields, indexes, or records that is different from the one provided by the standard data files. And, in the rare situations where such a requirement is important, we can implement it in a language like C. Similarly, in those situations where we can indeed benefit from higher-level operations, we can create them by means of subroutines in the same language as the application itself: we design the appropriate combination of basic file operations and flow-control constructs, store it as a separate module, and invoke it whenever we need that particular combination.

For the vast majority of applications, however, we need neither lower nor higher levels, since the level provided by the basic file operations is just right. This level is similar to the level provided, for general programming requirements, by our high-level languages. With the features found in a language like COBOL, for instance, we can implement any business application. Thus, it is no coincidence that, in conjunction with the operations provided by a programming language, the basic file operations can be used quite naturally to implement practically all database operations, and also to link these operations to the other types of operations: iterative constructs are just right for scanning a data file sequentially through one of its indexes; nested iterations are just right for relating files hierarchically; conditional constructs are just right for selecting records; and assignment constructs are just right for moving data between fields, and between fields and memory variables. It is difficult to find a single database operation that cannot be easily and naturally implemented with the constructs found in the traditional languages.

This flexibility is due to the correct level of abstraction of both the basic file operations and the traditional languages. This level is sufficiently low to make all conceivable database operations possible, and at the same time sufficiently high to make them simple and convenient – for an experienced programmer, at least. We can so easily implement any database requirement using ordinary features, available in most languages, that it is silly to search for higher-level operations.

High-level database operations offer no benefits, therefore, for two reasons: first, because we can so easily implement database requirements using the basic file operations, and second, because it is impossible to have built-in operations for all conceivable situations. No matter how many high-level operations we are offered, and no matter how useful they are, we will always encounter requirements that cannot be implemented with high-level operations alone. We cannot give up the lower levels, thus, because we need them to implement details, and because the links between database operations, and also between database operations and the other types of operations, occur at the low level of these details.

So the idea of higher levels is fallacious for database operations in the same way it is fallacious for the other types of operations. This was also the idea behind the so-called fourth-generation languages (see pp. 464–465). And, like the 4GL systems, the relational systems became in the end a fraud.

The theorists start by promising us higher levels. Then, when it becomes clear that the restriction to high levels is impractical, they restore – in the guise of enhancements – the low levels. Thus, with 4GL systems we still use such concepts as conditions, iterations, and assigning values to variables; in other words, concepts of the same level of abstraction as those found in a traditional language. It is true that these systems provide *some* higher-level operations (in user interface, for instance), but they do not eliminate the lower levels. In any case, even in those situations where operations of a higher level are indeed useful, we don't need these systems; for, we can always provide the higher levels ourselves, in any language, through subroutines. Similarly, we will see in the present section, the relational database systems became practical only after restoring the low levels; that is, the traditional file management concepts.

In conclusion, the software elites promote ideas like 4GL and relational databases, not on the basis of any real benefits, but in order to deprive us of the programming freedom conferred by the traditional languages. Their real motive is to force us to depend on expensive and complicated development systems, which they control.

I want to stress again that remarkable quality found in the basic file operations, the fact that they are at the same level of abstraction as the operations provided by the traditional programming languages. This is why we can so easily link these operations and implement database requirements. One of the most successful of all software concepts, this simple feature greatly simplifies both programming and the resulting applications.

There is a *seamless integration* of the database and the rest of the application, for both data and operations. The fields, the record area, and the record keys function as both database entities and memory variables at the same time. Database fields can be mixed freely with memory variables in assignments, calculations, or comparisons. Transferring data between disk and memory is a logical extension of the data transfers performed in memory. Most statements, constructs, and methods we use in programming have the same form and meaning for file operations as they have for the other types of operations; iterative and conditional constructs, for example, are used in the same way to scan and select records from a file as they are to scan and select items from an array or table stored in memory.

Just by learning to use the six basic file operations, then, a programmer gains the means to design and control databases of any size and complexity. The most difficult part of this work is handled by the file management system, and what is left to the programmer is not very different from the challenges he faces when dealing with any other aspect of the application.

The seamless integration of the database and the application is such an important feature that, had we not already had it in the traditional file operations, we could have rightly called its introduction today a breakthrough in programming techniques. The ignorance of the academics and the practitioners is betrayed, thus, by their lack of appreciation of a feature that has been widely available (through COBOL, for instance) since the 1960s. Instead of studying it and learning how to make the most of it, the software experts have been promoting the relational model, whose express purpose is to *eliminate* the integration. In their attempt to simplify programming, they restrict the links between files, and between files and the rest of the application, to high levels of abstraction. But this is an absurd idea, as we saw, because serious applications require low-level links too.

Then, instead of admitting that the relational model had failed, the experts proceeded to *reestablish* the low-level links. For, in order to make the relational model practical, they had to restore the integration – the very quality that the relational model had tried to eliminate. But the only way to provide the low levels and the integration now, as part of a database system, is through a series of artificial enhancements. When examined, the new features turn out to be nothing but particular instances of the important quality of integration: they are means to link the database to the rest of the application in specific situations. What is the very nature of the traditional file operations, and in effect just one simple feature, is now being restored by annulling the relational principles and replacing them with a multitude of complicated features. Each new feature is, in reality, a substitute for a particular high-level software element (a particular database function) that can no longer be implemented naturally, by combining lower-level elements.

Like all development systems that promise a higher level of abstraction, the relational systems became increasingly large and complicated because they attempted to replace with built-in operations the infinity of alternatives that we need at high levels but can no longer create by starting from low levels. Recall the analogy of software with language: If we had to express ourselves through ready-made sentences, instead of creating our own starting with words, we would end up depending on systems that become increasingly large and complicated as they attempt to provide all necessary sentences. But even with thousands of sentences, we would be unable to express all possible ideas. So we would spend more and more time trying to communicate through these systems, even while being restricted to a fraction of the ideas that can be expressed by combining words.

Thus, the endless problems engendered by relational database systems, and the astronomic cost of using them, are due to the ongoing effort to overcome the restrictions imposed by the relational model. They are due, in the end, to the software experts, who not only failed to understand why this model is worthless, but continued to promote it while its claims were being falsified.

The relational model became a pseudoscience when the experts decided to "enhance" it, which they did by turning its falsifications into features; specifically, by restoring the traditional data management concepts. It is impossible, however, to restore the seamless integration we had before. So all we have in the end is some complicated and inefficient database systems that are struggling to emulate the simple, straightforward file systems.

The Theory

1

To understand the relational delusions, we must start with a brief review of *formal logic* – that branch of mathematics upon which the relational model is said to be founded.

Formal logic is treated as a branch of mathematics because its exact principles and its deductive methods are similar to those of traditional mathematics. For this reason, it is also called *mathematical logic*. But, whereas algebra and calculus deal with numerical values, and geometry with lines and planes, logic deals with *truth values*: assertions that can be either *True* or *False*. As in other branches of mathematics, the elements and formulas of logic are expressed as variables – abstract entities that stand for a large number of particular instances. Thus, we normally use symbols like x and y, rather than actual assertions. This is why formal logic is also known as *symbolic logic*.

The oldest system of formal logic is *syllogistics*. Created by Aristotle in the fourth century BC, and further developed over time, syllogistic logic is based on propositions of the form "all S are P," "no S is P," "some S are P," and "some S are not P." (Examples: all fishes are swimmers, some buildings are tall, some people are not nice.) These propositions consist of two terms (the subject S and the predicate P) and a quantifier (all, some, none). The propositions assert, therefore, that a certain thing, or a class of things, possess a certain attribute. Additional flexibility is attained by permitting negative terms: "all S are *not-P*," "some *not-S* are P," and so on. A syllogism consists of three such propositions: two are premises, and the third one is the conclusion. The premises are related through one of their terms, and the conclusion uses the other two terms. (Example: Some A are B, all A are C, therefore some C are B.)

Clearly, many combinations of propositions are possible, but not all constitute valid syllogisms. A syllogism is valid if the conclusion follows by logical necessity from the two premises, as in the classic inference "All men are mortal, Socrates is a man, therefore Socrates is mortal." An example of invalid syllogisms is "Some dogs are vicious, this animal is not a dog, therefore this animal is not vicious" (even if the two premises are true, the conclusion can be either true or false).[1]

The study of syllogisms involves the classification of the various combinations of propositions, their logical relationships and transformations, and the methods for determining their validity. It should be obvious that, if we can

---

[1] In syllogisms, a reference to an individual entity is interpreted as a class of things that comprises only one element, and therefore implies the quantifier *all*.

reduce an argument to a structure of propositions consisting of subjects and predicates, syllogistic logic allows us to determine *formally* whether a particular statement can or cannot be inferred from certain premises. In other words, if we know that the two premises are true, we can determine whether the conclusion is true or false strictly from the *structure* of the three propositions; we don't have to concern ourselves with the *meaning* of the terms that make them up.

Syllogistic logic is seen today as only one of the many systems comprising the field of formal logic. Modern logic, born in the nineteenth century, attempts to extend beyond the capabilities of syllogistics the range of discourse and the types of phenomena that can be represented formally. The benefits of a formal representation are well known: as with traditional mathematics, it allows us to build increasingly large and complex entities that are guaranteed to be valid – simply by combining hierarchically, level after level, entities whose validity is already established. Conversely, if confronted with an expression too complex to understand directly, we can determine its validity by reducing it to simpler entities, one level at a time, until we reach entities known to be valid. Formal logic, thus, permits us to apply the deductive methods of mathematics to any type of phenomena.

We also know what are the *limitations* of formal logic. We can reduce a phenomenon to an exact representation only when its links to other phenomena are weak enough to be ignored. If we recall the concept of simple and complex structures, logic systems allow us to create only *simple* structures; so they are useful only for phenomena that can be studied in isolation. While common in the natural sciences, this is rare for phenomena involving human minds and societies. In chapter 4, for example, we saw the attempts made by scientists to represent *knowledge* by means of logic systems. These attempts fail because the entities that make up knowledge are connected in many ways, not just through the hierarchical relations recognized by a particular logic system. These entities can only be represented, therefore, with a *complex* structure. To this day, few scientists are ready to admit that most human phenomena *cannot* be reduced to an exact, formal model. So they keep inventing one mechanistic theory after another, hoping to represent mathematically such phenomena as intelligence, language, and software.

Although differing in complexity and versatility, the modern systems of logic have a lot in common. To create a system of logic, we start by defining its basic entities – those entities that act as starting elements in the hierarchical structures created with that system: objects, propositions, etc. Logical *variables*

(single letters, usually) are used to represent these entities in definitions and expressions. Next, we define a set of logical *operations* – the means of creating the elements of one level by combining those from the lower level. We also need some *rules of inference* – principles that justify the various transformations performed when moving from one level to the next. These rules serve, in effect, to restrict the use of operations to those cases where the new element can be derived from the others only through logical deduction. (For example, the rule known as *modus ponens* states that, if we know that whenever *p* is true *q* is also true, then if *p* is found to be true we must conclude that *q* is true.) Lastly, we agree on a number of *axioms*. Axioms are assumptions taken to be valid by convention, and which can be employed therefore in logical expressions just as we do premises. (A common axiom, for example, is the assertion that any entity is identical to the negation of its negation.) The theorems of a logic system are the various assertions that can be proved deductively within the system by manipulating expressions. Clearly, increasingly complex expressions and theorems can be constructed by combining elements hierarchically, on higher and higher levels of abstraction.[2]

Despite their formality, there is considerable freedom in designing a logic system. For example, what is a rule in one system may be an axiom in another, and what is a theorem may be a rule. What matters is only that the system be *consistent*. A system is consistent when no contradictions can arise between the expressions derived by means of its operations, rules, and axioms. That is, if we can show that a certain expression or theorem is true, we should not be able to show in the same system, through a different deduction, that it is false. Another quality found in a correct logic system is that of *independence*: every one of its axioms and rules is necessary, and none can be derived from the others. To put this differently, if any one of them were omitted, we would no longer be able to determine the truth or falsity of some expressions or theorems.

The chief difference between logic systems, then, is in their basic entities, and in the way these entities are combined to create correct expressions (what is known as *well-formed formulas*). And, once we reach a hierarchical level where expressions can only yield truth values, *True* or *False*, the same operations can be used to manipulate them in any logic system. The starting elements themselves may be entities restricted to truth values, but many systems have starting elements of other types. In syllogistic logic, we saw, the

---

[2] Note that, when used with the simple structures created with logic systems, the term "complexity" is employed here (as it always is when discussing simple structures) to indicate the shift to a higher level within a structure, or to a structure with more levels. (The levels of complexity in a simple structure are its levels of abstraction.) So don't confuse this complexity with the complexity of complex structures, which is due to the interaction of structures.

starting elements are subjects and predicates (things and attributes), and only their combinations are propositions that can be true or false.

The most common logical operations, thus, are those that manipulate truth values. And among them, the best known are conjunction, disjunction, and negation (AND, OR, and NOT). Only conjunction and negation are usually defined as basic operations, though, since disjunction can be expressed in terms of them: A OR B is equivalent to NOT(NOT A AND NOT B). Additional operations (equivalence, implication, etc.) can be similarly defined in terms of conjunction and negation, or by combining previously defined operations. A *truth function* is an expression involving operands that have truth values, so its result is also a truth value. This result can then act as operand in other expressions.

One way of determining the result of a truth function is with *truth tables*. A truth table has a column for each operand used by the function, and a row for each possible combination of truth values (hence, two rows for one operand, four for two operands, eight for three operands, etc.). A final column depicts the truth value of the result, and there may be additional columns for intermediate results. (Figure 4-2, p. 332, illustrates the concept of truth tables.)

Another characteristic common to all logic systems is that the validity of their low-level elements, and of their axioms and premises, cannot be determined from *within* the system. A logic system only guarantees that, if certain expressions are known to be true or false, then the truth or falsity of other expressions – derived from the original ones strictly through the rules and operations permitted by the system – can be determined with certainty. It cannot verify for us whether the expressions we *start* with are true or not.

For example, a premise like "*A* is larger than *B*" could be used with numbers in one application and with animals in another. In either case, it would be true in some instances and false in others. But within the logic system, this statement appears simply as a symbol, say, *S*; and it is handled the same way regardless of what *A* and *B* stand for, or whether the statement is false while believed to be true. It is our responsibility to ensure that it is true – by means *external* to the system – before using it as premise in a particular application.

Logic systems, then, are only concerned with the *form* and *structure* of elements and expressions, not with their *interpretation*. Needless to say, though, both aspects are important in actual applications. If all we want is that the conclusion be sound logically, its correct deduction from premises is indeed sufficient. But for the system to be of practical value, the deduction *and* the premises must be correct.

Thus, along with their limitation to simple, isolated phenomena, their dependence on what is usually just an *informal* verification of premises and starting elements reduces considerably the usefulness of formal logic systems in real-world applications. The delusions of the relational database model, for instance, stem from overlooking the severity of these limitations, as we will soon see.

The simplest system of logic is the one known as *propositional calculus*. The basic elements in this system are whole propositions, and expressions are formed by combining propositions through logical operations, as described earlier. Although expressions of any complexity can be formed in this manner, this system is handicapped by its inability to analyze the individual propositions. For example, if two propositions comprise subject and predicate, as in syllogisms, the system cannot distinguish between the case where the propositions share their subject or predicate, and the case where they are unrelated. The chief quality of propositional calculus is its simplicity, so it is the system of choice in applications where the elements can be treated as either atomic entities or logical expressions built from these entities. The Boolean logic system, upon which digital circuits and many software concepts are founded, is a type of propositional calculus.

A more versatile system of logic, and the one that served as inspiration for the relational database model, is *predicate calculus*. The basic elements in this system are subjects and predicates, as in syllogistic logic, but a predicate can be shared by several subjects in one proposition. A predicate, in other words, is seen as an attribute that can be possessed by one, two, three, or generally n different elements. And when possessed by more than one, it serves not only as attribute, but also to relate them. Each set of n elements related through a predicate is known as an *n-tuple* (or *tuple*, for short).

An expression like $P(x,y,z)$ – which says that the elements x, y, and z are related and form a 3-tuple through the predicate P – is a basic proposition in predicate calculus. Since the elements are represented with variables, the expression stands for any number of such tuples. Each element has its own domain of permissible values, and when we substitute actual values for the three variables, the relationship will generally hold for some combinations of values but not for others. So the expression will be true for some tuples and false for others. The totality of tuples that share a particular predicate (or, usually, just those for which the expression is true) is called a *relation*.

An example of a relation is the sets of three integers, a, b, and c, each one selected perhaps from a different range of values, and fulfilling the condition that a is greater than b and b is greater than c. An expression like $G(a,b,c)$, representing this relationship, is then true for some sets of values and false for others. Another example is the sets of five men, p, c, b, n, and g, who could have been selected from various domains to act as crews in WWII B-25 bombers: pilot, co-pilot, bombardier, navigator, and gunner. An expression like $B(p,c,b,n,g)$, representing this relationship, is true only for those sets of men that formed actual crews.

Basic propositions can be combined by means of logical operations, in the usual manner, to form more complex propositions. Thus, we can form relations that are a logical function of other relations. Take, for example, these two relations: $P(x,y)$ as the sets of two elements, x and y, related through P, and $Q(y,z)$ as the sets of two elements, y and z, related through Q. The expression $P(x,y)$ AND $Q(y,z)$ may then be defined to mean, depending on the application, either the sets of two elements common to P and Q, or the sets of three elements, x, y, and z, for which both relations hold. Similarly, the expression $P(x,y)$ OR $Q(y,z)$ may be defined to mean either the sets of two elements that exist in either relation (excluding duplicates), or the sets of three elements for which either relation holds.

Additional flexibility can be achieved in expressions by binding each variable with the *universal* quantifier $\forall$ (which says that the relation holds for *all* instances of that variable) or with the *existential* quantifier $\exists$ (which says that the relation holds at least for *some* instances of that variable). These quantifiers become then part of the expression, and participate in operations and transformations, much like operators. Thus, if $\forall$ is applied to both x and y in the expression $R(x,y)$, the expression is true only if the relation R holds for all possible pairs of values of x and y; but if $\exists$ is applied to x and y, the expression is true even if the relation holds for just one pair of values.

This brief review will suffice for our purpose, to assess the mathematical merits of the relational database model. It is worth mentioning, though, that many other systems of logic have been designed. The system we have just examined, for example, is called *first-order* predicate calculus, and is only the simplest of the predicate calculi. (In higher-order systems, the quantified variables and the predicates can themselves be logical expressions.) Some logic systems include special axioms, rules, and operations to deal with such imprecise concepts as necessity, possibility, and contingency, which lie outside the scope of propositional and predicate calculi. Other systems attempt to deal with propositions whose truth value changes over time, and some systems even attempt to reduce to logic such moral issues as belief, obligation, and responsibility.

As I have already stated, the motivation for these systems is to bring phenomena involving minds and societies into the range of phenomena that can be represented with formal, mechanistic methods. And they have had very little success, because few human phenomena are simple enough to be reduced to a mechanistic representation.

Programming phenomena are largely human phenomena. So the relational model is, ultimately, an example of the attempts to find a mechanistic model for phenomena that are, in fact, too complex to represent mechanistically. Thus, apart from our interest in the theories of software engineering as pseudosciences in their own right, their analysis complements our study of mechanistic delusions, and serves to remind us of the degradation of the idea of research. We saw in chapters 3 and 4 the childish attempts made by some of our most famous scientists to represent behaviour, intelligence, and language with diagrams, or formulas, or logic. And the same fallacy is committed with *software* theories: the mechanists discover a model that explains *isolated aspects* of a complex phenomenon, and they interpret this trivial success as evidence that their theory is valid, and hence worth pursuing.

So, by invoking the official definition of science – which is simply the pursuit of mechanistic ideas, whether useful or not – academics can now spend their entire career developing worthless theories. Merely because mechanism works in fields like physics or chemistry, they feel justified to seek mechanistic explanations in psychology, or sociology, or linguistics, or economics, or programming. Then, because of our mechanistic culture, we admire and respect them, and regard their activities as serious research – even as we see that their theories never work, and that they resort to deception in order to defend them.

2

Let us see now how predicate calculus was adapted for database work. The inventor of the relational model is E. F. Codd, who presented his ideas in a series of papers starting in 1969.[3] We are not concerned here with the evolution of the model in the first few years, or with the specific contributions made by individual researchers, but only with the relational database ideas in general. And, in fact, apart from a few refinements, the theory presented by Codd in his original papers depicts quite accurately what became in the end the formal relational model. In 1981, Codd received the prestigious Turing award for his invention.

---

[3] The first paper was published in 1969 (as an IBM document), but it was only the second one, published the following year, that was widely read: E. F. Codd, "A Relational Model of Data for Large Shared Data Banks," *Communications of the ACM* 13, no. 6 (1970): 377–387.

Recall the organization of data files as records, and fields within records. To represent a file by means of predicate calculus, the fields are seen as the basic elements of a logic system, and the records as tuples – sets of n elements, where n is the number of fields in a record. Each field can possess a value from a domain of permissible values. Thus, if the field is a part number, the domain is all valid part numbers; if a vendor name, the names of all possible vendors; if a quantity, all numeric values that are valid quantities; and so on. Generally, some combinations of values exist as actual records in the file, and others do not; and, *by convention*, the relationship that links these fields holds only for those combinations that exist. In other words, an expression representing this relationship is deemed to yield the value *True* when the tuple actually exists in the file, and the value *False* otherwise. As in logic, the totality of tuples (i.e., records) in the file is called a relation.

To define an employee file with four fields, for instance, we would use a logical expression like $E(a,b,c,d)$, where a is the employee number, b the name, c the hourly rate, and d the number of hours worked. E stands then for the predicate that relates the four fields. E says, in effect, that each set of four values, taken from the respective domains of permissible values (all possible employee numbers, names, rates, and hours), are related in such a way that they represent a potential employee. The expression is true for the sets that actually exist in the file, and false for the others.

To this basic system, which matches the system of predicate calculus, a number of features were added in order to make the relational model suitable for database work. One feature is the idea of *field names*. In predicate calculus, the elements are identified by their relative position within the tuple, but this is impractical for database fields. Fields, therefore, are given names (QUANTITY, VENDOR-NO, INVOICE-DATE, etc.); we can then refer to them by their name, so their relative position within the physical record (as they are stored on disk, for example) is immaterial. These names are sometimes described as a special tuple that exists in every file but does not take part in operations; its function is similar to the top row in a typical table – the row that contains the column headers.

Another feature is the idea of a *key*: one field in the record is designated as key, and its value in each record must be unique within the file; alternatively, the key can consist of several fields, and then their combined values must be unique. The key, therefore, can be used to identify a specific record within the file, or to order the records in a logical sequence (so the actual sequence of records, as they are stored on disk or as they were added to the file, is irrelevant to the application). It is often useful to have several keys for the same record; in this case, one is designated as the *primary* key, and the others are called *candidate* keys. Lastly, in order to relate files, a field (or a group of fields) can be designated as a *foreign* key. This type of key is used to identify the records of another file, where that field usually functions as the primary key. The customer number in an invoice file, for example, is a foreign key that relates the invoice file to the customer file, where the customer number is the primary key. The values stored in a foreign key need not be unique in each record; thus, we can have several invoices with the same customer number.

It should be obvious, if you recall our discussion of indexed data files and the basic file operations, that the relational concepts we have examined so far are *identical* to the traditional data file concepts. The only difference is in the use of terms like "relation" and "tuple" instead of the terms traditionally associated with data files. The relational theory is rich in new terminology. Thus, in addition to the concepts and terms taken from logic, we are told that files are best perceived as tables: the rows of these tables are then the records, and the columns are the fields. Also, the term *attribute* is often used for columns. So the accepted relational terms are *tables* and *relations*, *rows* and *tuples*, *columns* and *attributes*.[4]

While tables still resemble the traditional data files, the way we access them is entirely different. The traditional file operations are based on indexes, and are used through the flow-control constructs of a programming language. The relational operations, on the other hand, are defined in the manner of logical operations. In predicate calculus, we saw, operations like AND and OR take relations as operands and produce a new relation; similarly, the relational operations take tables as operands and produce a new table.

In predicate calculus, the tuples in the resulting relation consist of variables that were elements in the tuples of the original relations. When the same values that made up the tuples of the original relations are substituted for the variables of the new tuples, the expression that represents the new relation may be true for some combinations and false for others; and the new relation is defined as those tuples for which the expression is true.

Similarly, the operations in the relational model are defined in such a manner that the columns of the resulting table are selected from among the columns of the original tables. Then, depending on the operation and the values present in the rows of the original tables, only *some* of the rows are retained in the new table. In other words, each operation has its own definition

---

[4] Generally, *tables*, *rows*, and *columns* are considered informal terms, while *relations*, *tuples*, and *attributes* are the formal ones. Since the entities described by these terms are identical to the traditional *files*, *records*, and *fields*, I am using both the new and the traditional terms in the discussion of relational databases.

of truth and falsity, and if we represent the rows with a logical expression, the new table is defined as those rows containing combinations of values for which the expression is true. For example, if we represent a customer table as *C(a,b,c,d)* and an orders table as *O(a,e,f)* (where the lower-case letters stand for columns, and *a* is the customer number), a particular operation could be defined as follows: create a new table *R(a,b,e)*, whose rows are those pairs of rows from the customer table and the orders table where *a* has the same value in both. The expression *R(a,b,e)* is said in this case to be true for these rows, and false for the others. This expression – that is, the new table – can then be combined with others in further operations.

There are five basic operations: The UNION of tables *A* and *B* is a table containing the rows present in either *A* or *B* or both (*A* and *B* must have the same number of columns, and rows common to *A* and *B* appear only once in the new table). The DIFFERENCE of tables *A* and *B* is a table containing those rows present in *A* but not in *B* (*A* and *B* must have the same number of columns). SELECTION takes one table, *A*, and produces a new table containing only those rows from *A* for which an expression involving one of the columns is evaluated as true (for example, only those rows where the value in a given column is greater than zero). PROJECTION takes one table, *A*, and produces a new table containing all the rows from *A*, but only some of its columns. The PRODUCT of tables *A* and *B* is a table whose columns are the columns of *A* plus those of *B*, and whose rows are every combination of rows from *A* and *B*; each row, thus, is built by taking a row from *A* and extending it with a row from *B* (so, for example, if *A* has 10 rows and *B* has 20 rows, the new table will have 200 rows).

Additional operations may be necessary in practice, but they can always be expressed as a combination of the five basic ones. For example, to reduce a table to only some of its rows and columns, we perform first a SELECTION to retain the specified rows, and then a PROJECTION on the resulting table to retain the specified columns. (Note that the order in which we perform these two operations is immaterial.) Most database systems, in line with their promise to give us higher levels of abstraction, provide some of the most common combinations in the form of built-in operations.

PRODUCT, in particular, is rarely useful on its own, and is normally employed as just the first step in a series of operations. JOIN, for instance, consists of PRODUCT followed by SELECTION and then by PROJECTION. JOIN selects from all the combinations of rows in tables *A* and *B* those rows where a particular column in *A* stands in a certain relationship to a particular column in *B*. Most often, JOIN is used to combine two tables on the basis of *equality* of values. For example, the JOIN of a customer table and an invoice table based on the customer number (present in both) will result in a table that has the combined customer and invoice columns, but (through SELECTION) only the rows where the customer number was the same in both tables. JOIN, thus, will match invoices and customers: it will have one row for each invoice, and each row will include the customer columns in addition to the invoice columns. (The PROJECTION in the last step serves to eliminate one of the two columns containing the customer number, since they are identical.) JOIN can be performed on key columns as well as non-key columns, and its chief use is to relate files.

For most operations and combinations of operations, we can understand intuitively how the resulting table is derived from the original ones. It is possible, though, to define these operations formally, as transformations based on the operations of formal logic. There are several ways to do it: the relational *algebra* describes them as operations on tables, as we just saw; the relational *calculus* – of which there are two versions, *tuple* calculus and *domain* calculus – describes them with logical expressions similar to those used in predicate calculus. The operations are the same; only the way they are described differs.

The value of the relational model is due to expressing the data in the resulting table as a logical expression of the data in the original tables. Thus, if the original data is correct, the final data will also be correct. When permitted to combine records and fields at will – with the traditional file operations, for instance – a programmer may make mistakes and generate files that do not reflect correctly the original data, or generate files containing inconsistent data. This cannot happen with a relational database. Because we are restricted to operations on whole tables, and because the relational operations introduce no spurious dependencies between fields, we can be certain that the final table will express the same data and relationships as the tables we start with. In a database query, for instance, no matter how many operations and combinations of tables are involved, the final entities are guaranteed to be the same as the original ones – only arranged differently. It is impossible, in fact, to generate wrong or inconsistent data if we restrict ourselves to the relational operations.

The relational model permits us to implement any database requirements that we are likely to encounter in applications. The restriction to whole tables is not really a handicap, because any portion of a table – any subset of rows and columns – is itself, in effect, a table. We can even isolate a single row (with appropriate SELECTIONs), and that row is treated as a table and can be used in further operations. Even one column of that row can be isolated (with a PROJECTION), and that single element still is, as far as the relational operations are concerned, a table.

Note that the resulting table need not be a real entity. When using SELECTION to answer a query, for example, the database system may simply *display* the selected rows, without actually creating a table. Generally, to perform a series of operations, the system may create some intermediate tables or use only the original ones, and may employ indexes or other expedients. But we don't have to concern ourselves with these details, because a good system will automatically discover the most effective alternative. All we need to do is specify, through the relational algebra or calculus, the original tables and the desired operations.

What we gain with the restriction to tables, then, is simplicity and accuracy: all we need now is a few operations, which are founded on formal logic and can be safely combined into more complex ones. Just as importantly, these operations permit us to view the data from a higher level of abstraction: we no longer need to access individual records, as in the traditional file systems; nor do we need file scanning loops, or intricate conditions to select records and to relate files. Whether our requirements involve single tables, or combinations of tables, or portions of tables, or just one row or column, all we need now is the high-level relational operations. Thus, a relational database is said to be "tables and nothing but tables."

3

It is not enough for the database *operations* to conform to a logic system. The relational theory also requires that the data be *stored* in a logical format. Specifically, the fields that make up the individual tuples must be simple, indivisible entities, with no unnecessary dependency between them. Tables that adhere to this format are said to be *normalized,* and the process of bringing them to this format is called *normalization.* There are several levels of normalization, each one a more stringent enforcement of these principles. The levels are known as first normal form, second normal form, third normal form, etc., and are abbreviated as 1NF, 2NF, 3NF, etc.

The fundamental requirement is 1NF. For a table to be in first normal form, each field must be a simple entity – a single, atomic value. In traditional data files, a field may consist of a series of values, or a multidimensional array of values, or a hierarchical structure of values. A twelve-month transaction history, for example, can be stored in one field of a customer record as an array of twelve rows by three columns – month, quantity, and amount. The relational model prohibits this format: data that comprises a set of related values must be stored in a separate table, where each value has its own column. Thus, to reduce the customer table just described to 1NF, we must create a separate table for the transaction history. The columns in this table will be the customer number, month, quantity, and amount, and the key will be the combination of customer number and month. For each row in the customer table there will be twelve rows in the transaction history table.

It should be obvious why the first normal form is so important. The relational operations expect to find tuples, and cannot process multiple values – data stored, in effect, as tuples within tuples. To deal with this format we need a more complex database model, and operations that can process more than just rows and columns.

The other normal forms deal with the problem of *field dependency*; specifically, the dependency of one field on another within a tuple. Since such a relationship is likely to cause data *redundancy* and *inconsistencies*, the only type of relationship permitted between fields within a tuple is the obvious dependency of the tuple's fields on the tuple's unique key. All other field relationships must be implemented by moving the fields to other tables and linking the tables logically.

An example of misplaced dependency is a customer orders table where the key is the combination of customer number and order number, and the other fields are the customer name and address, and the order date, quantity, and amount. All these fields depend on the customer number; but, whereas order-specific data like quantity and amount must indeed be included in each order, fixed customer data like name and address must not. This design is wrong because, while a customer's name and address are the same for all his orders, we *repeat* them in every order. The faulty design, thus, will cause data redundancy. Worse still, it will cause various inconsistencies ("anomalies," in relational terminology) when we run the application: first, if a customer's name or address changes, we may have to update not one but several rows – all his outstanding orders; second, we can store a customer's name and address in the database only if that customer has at least one outstanding order.

The solution, of course, is to store the name and address in a separate table, where the key is the customer number and there is only one row per customer. From the order rows we can then access the appropriate name and address by using the customer number as link. The process of normalization, thus, consists in creating two tables from one. In general, we eliminate a misplaced dependency by increasing the number of tables: we extract the fields with repeated values and place them in a separate table, where we discard the duplicate rows; then we choose a field (or a combination of fields) with unique values to act as a key for the new table and as a link to the original one.

The redundancy and inconsistencies were caused, obviously, by an incorrect design – a design that did not match the application's requirements: the name and address are the same for all orders, and yet we repeated them in every order. With the fields in a separate table, the design matches the requirements, and consequently there is no redundancy or inconsistency.

The normalization theory, however, describes the problem of incorrect design as a problem of misplaced dependency: the name and address depended on only a portion of the key (the customer number), instead of depending on the whole key (the combination of customer and order numbers), as do the order date, quantity, and amount. And we correct this dependency by placing the name and address in a separate table – a table where the customer number is the whole key. Clearly, what we do is the same as before, match the design to the requirements; but the normalization theory describes this process as the elimination of misplaced dependencies.

Few people would design a database with the kind of redundancy we have just examined. The theorists, nevertheless, treat the subject of normalization very seriously. Various types of field dependencies are defined and studied in great detail, along with the steps required to eliminate them. Thus, five types were discovered, each one more rare and more subtle. Tables, we saw, are already in first normal form when their fields are single elements. Then, after eliminating one type of dependency, they are in second normal form (2NF). After eliminating a second type, they are in third normal form (3NF). This is followed by a level known as Boyce/Codd normal form (BCNF), and then by the fourth and fifth normal forms (4NF and 5NF). When in fifth normal form, tables are in the ultimate relational format, devoid of any misplaced dependencies. Very few databases, however, require all five levels of normalization. If an application is not complicated, tables will likely be in their highest possible normal form after just one or two levels, simply because there are no other dependencies. In any case, many experts consider 3NF or BCNF adequate, and don't even mention 4NF and 5NF.

The second and higher normal forms are in reality very similar, and their differences need not concern us here. The reason for having several types of normalization and a numbering system is largely historical: while the first normal form was described by Codd in his original papers, the others were incorporated into the relational theory later – as they were discovered, one by one. (More specifically, the higher normal forms became necessary when the relational model was expanded to include *updating* operations.) Thus, it is worth noting that the theorists needed several years, and innumerable papers and conferences, to discover what an experienced programmer could have told them from the beginning. For, the problems caused by misplaced dependencies, as well as their solutions, are *identical* in relational databases and in databases created with traditional data files; only the attempt to treat these problems formally is new. We will return to this subject later, in our discussion of the relational delusions.

The Contradictions

1

To summarize, the relational model is an attempt to turn database programming, as well as database use, into an exact, formal activity. Since data records resemble the so-called tuples of predicate calculus, and since they can be manipulated with operations resembling logical operations, the theorists concluded that the rigour and exactness of mathematical logic can now be attained in database work. All we have to do is restrict the files and records to a certain format, and restrict the operations to a high level of abstraction; we have then a mathematical guarantee that the answers to queries will reflect accurately the data and relationships present in the database.

From the start, then, the relational theory was grounded on the curious principle that only *some* aspects of the database need to be covered by the formal, mathematical model; the others can remain informal. This principle is sometimes expressed with the statement that certain aspects lie *within* the scope of the formal model, while others are *outside* its scope. Thus, if we call "relational model" the whole body of relational principles and features, the "formal relational model" constitutes only a small part of it.

Within the scope of the formal model lie, as we just saw, the format of files and records, the concept of queries, and the use of high-level query operations. The theorists recognize, of course, that there is a lot more to databases and applications. So, while asking us to treat these aspects formally, they expect us to deal with the other aspects of the database *informally*: by relying on traditional programming methods and on personal skills.

In particular, operations that *update* the database – adding and deleting records, modifying the data in fields, creating and deleting files – cannot be treated formally, and therefore lie outside the scope of the formal model. Note that this is a necessary consequence of the model's mathematical foundation: predicate calculus is concerned with the logical expressions that *use* the tuples of a given relation, not with the way the tuples became part of that relation, or with the way the elements of these tuples acquired their current value. Thus, if the updating of tuples and relations lies outside the scope of predicate calculus, it must also be left out of the formal relational model.

Data normalization, too, is largely informal. Only the first normal form, which deals with the record format, is part of the formal model. The second and higher normal forms are only needed in order to prevent redundancy and inconsistencies when *updating* the files; thus, if the updating operations are informal, so must be the normalization. In any case, the process of normalization entails an *interpretation* of the application's requirements:

whether or not a certain field depends on another can be determined only from the way we intend to use them in the application, something that no formal system can know.

Another aspect of the database that cannot be formalized concerns *data integrity* – the countless rules that ensure the validity of the updating operations within the context of a particular application. Again, what is valid in one case may be invalid in another, and only *we* can decide how to interpret the result of a certain operation.

Lastly, the formal model does not include the means we use to *specify* the query and updating operations. These means – a set of commands, or a database language – can only be used informally. As is the case with any programming language, we can define with precision the commands or statements themselves, but not their effect when combined to perform a particular task in a given application.

In conclusion, the updating operations, the normalization process, the integrity rules, and the database language, even though needed in any application that uses relational databases, lie outside the scope of the formal relational model. So they can be no more formal or exact than they are in applications using traditional data files.

What, then, is the meaning of the relational model? What is the point, for instance, of including in the formal model the query operations while excluding the updating operations? Clearly, the two types of operations are equally important in an application. What is the value of a model that guarantees correct answers to queries while being unable to guarantee the correctness of the data upon which the queries are based?

The theorists acknowledge that the formal model is insufficient, that we must depend on some informal operations too, but they fail to appreciate the implication: if we must deal with certain aspects of the database by relying largely on personal knowledge, the inexactness of this method will annul the exactness of those aspects treated formally. The result of a process cannot be more exact than the least exact of its parts. The answer to a query may well be mathematically derivable from the original data, but this quality of the relational model has little value if we cannot prove that the original data is correct to begin with.

❖

We just saw how, in order to attain a practical relational model, the theorists were compelled to separate it into a formal and an informal part. But this is not all. There is one aspect of the database that is considered to lie, not only outside the scope of the *formal* model, but outside the scope of the relational model altogether: the actual, physical implementation of the database and operations.

Like the logic system that inspired it, the relational model is a mathematical, and hence abstract, concept. This limitation, however, is interpreted by the theorists as a *quality*: thanks to its abstract nature, they say, we no longer need to be concerned with such issues as the system's *performance* (the time required to execute the database operations). In general, the independence of the logical database structures from their physical implementation permits us to access the data from a higher level of abstraction. Here are some statements expressing this view: "The ideas of the relational model apply at the external and conceptual levels of the system, not the internal level. To put this another way, the relational model represents a database system at a level of abstraction that is somewhat removed from the details of the underlying machine."[1] "The eight relational operators express functionality without concern for (or knowledge of) technical implementation. An obvious benefit is that relational users apply relational operators without concern for storage and access techniques."[2] "The aim of the relational model is to represent logically all relationships, and hence alleviate the user from physical implementation details."[3] "The relational data model removes the details of storage structure and access strategy from the user interface."[4]

The operations of a mathematical system are assumed to occur instantaneously; we don't think of addition or multiplication, for instance, as physical processes that may take some time. Similarly, the high-level operations of the relational model – selection, projection, join, and the rest – are assumed to be executed instantaneously by the database system. Incredibly, while presenting the relational model as the foundation of practical database systems, the theorists insisted that the subject of performance lies outside the scope of the model. Everyone knew, of course, that the application's performance is limited by the speed of the computer's processor, and that databases rely on physical devices like disk drives, which impose additional speed limits on data access. Nevertheless, the claim that it is possible to design real databases without having to concern ourselves with their performance was received with enthusiasm. All we need to do, promised the theorists, is specify the relational

---

[1] C. J. Date, *An Introduction to Database Systems*, 6th ed. (Reading, MA: Addison-Wesley, 1995), p. 98.

[2] Candace C. Fleming and Barbara von Halle, *Handbook of Relational Database Design* (Reading, MA: Addison-Wesley, 1989), p. 38.

[3] M. Papazoglou and W. Valder, *Relational Database Management: A Systems Programming Approach* (Hemel Hempstead, UK: Prentice Hall, 1989), p. 30.

[4] Ken S. Brathwaite, *Relational Databases: Concepts, Design, and Administration* (New York: McGraw-Hill, 1991), p. 26.

operations, just as we do in mathematics. The database system will analyze the request, determine the most efficient implementation, and then execute the necessary low-level operations.

Separating the performance issue from the relational model is just as illogical as separating the updating operations from the query operations. It shouldn't come as a surprise, therefore, that the relational database systems have proved to be incurably slow, and that, in addition, their users have remained as preoccupied with the performance issue as those who use the traditional file operations.

It is absurd to expect the database system itself to know what is the most efficient implementation of a high-level request. It is absurd because most requests do not depend on database structures alone, but also on such other structures (i.e., aspects) of the application as its various processes (see pp. 347–348). To discover the most efficient implementation we must link, therefore, the database structures with the other structures that make up the application. These links, moreover, occur usually at the low level of database fields, memory variables, and individual statements; so the only way to implement them is through traditional programming means.

The inefficiency caused by the lack of low-level links, then, was the main reason for the continued preoccupation with the performance issue. And this inefficiency was also the reason for annulling, in the end, two fundamental relational principles: the restriction to normalized files, and the restriction to high-level operations.

❖

We know, of course, why the theorists separated the relational model into formal and informal aspects: because this is the only way to attain a precise, mechanistic representation of the database and the database operations. If we want to represent an indeterministic phenomenon with a deterministic theory, we must exclude from the phenomenon those aspects that prevent such a representation.

Thus, we can start with any phenomenon, no matter how complex, and invent an exact theory – a mathematical model – that depicts what we *wish* the phenomenon to be. Then, we match the phenomenon to the theory by eliminating, one by one, those aspects that contradict the theory – by branding them as "informal" parts of the phenomenon. If we eliminate enough aspects, we are certain to reduce the phenomenon eventually to a version that is simple enough to match the theory.

But this is a trivial accomplishment – we knew all along that it could be done. It is impossible, in fact, to *fail* in this project, if we place no limit on the number of aspects that we are willing to eliminate. Mechanistic projects of this nature are, therefore, intrinsically pseudoscientific. This is true because the concept of separating the phenomenon into aspects that are, and aspects that are not, within the scope of the model is unfalsifiable: since we are free at any moment to exclude any number of additional aspects in order to make the model work, there is no condition under which we can say that a mechanistic model *cannot* be found.

The issue, then, is not whether we can find a mathematical model for the phenomenon of a database, as this is always possible by simplifying the phenomenon. Rather, the issue is whether, by the time we simplify the phenomenon sufficiently to have an exact model, such a model is still meaningful. It is quite easy to discover mathematical models for *individual aspects* of software phenomena. The theorists happened to discover a database model grounded on predicate calculus, but with a little imagination we could find any number of other models. The real challenge, again, is not to discover a mathematical model by simplifying the phenomenon, but to discover a useful model for the original, complex phenomenon.

So, like all mechanistic delusions, the relational model failed because its mathematical foundation is insignificant: we can represent mathematically only a small fraction of the concepts involved in programming and using a database. If we were to rely on the original relational model, we would perhaps enjoy the promised benefits, but only with small and simple databases; we would be unable to develop the kind of databases we need in real applications.

Having failed as a practical concept, the relational model was rescued by expanding its *informal* aspects – precisely those aspects that had been excluded from the formal, mathematical model. The early works discuss in detail the formal model, including the various types of query operations, but mention only briefly the informal aspects – the updating operations, the integrity and performance problems, and the database language.[5] These aspects are presented merely as miscellaneous features needed to support the formal model in actual applications. In the end, however, it is precisely these features (the database language, in particular) that became the main concern of relational database systems, while the formal model declined in importance and became practically irrelevant.

Specifically, the restriction to normalized files and the restriction to high-level operations were both lifted; and no one, of course, is using databases through mathematical logic. Today's relational systems are promoted by praising the power of their programming language (usually SQL), the power of

---

[5] See, for example, Codd's original paper, "A Relational Model of Data for Large Shared Data Banks," *Communications of the ACM* 13, no. 6 (1970): 377–387. The other informal aspect (the second and higher normal forms) is not mentioned at all.

certain features described as integrity functions (but whose true role is to bypass the limitations of the high-level operations), and the power of a variety of new data formats and *low-level* file operations. In other words, while the power of the original model was said to derive from its formal, mathematical foundation, the power of what is seen today as the relational model derives entirely from *informal* concepts – concepts that are practically identical to the traditional ones. We will analyze this degradation in "The Third Delusion."

2

When studying the relational model and its evolution from a mechanistic fantasy to a pseudoscience, we can distinguish three major delusions. These delusions are summarized below; then, in the following subsections, we will study them in detail.

The first delusion is the belief that the relational model's mathematical background is an important quality. It is true that the model is grounded upon certain mathematical principles, and that these principles guarantee the soundness of certain database operations. But this quality constitutes an insignificant part of the phenomenon of a database: we can ground a database on mathematics only after limiting the data to a certain format, after separating the database from the rest of the application, and after restricting its use to queries expressed through high-level operations. Important aspects – the operations that modify the database, and the links to the rest of the application's logic – are not included in the mathematical model. Thus, we must deal with the most difficult aspects of database programming *informally*, just as we do when using the traditional file operations.

The second delusion is the belief that the principles of normalization are an essential part of the relational theory. In reality, data normalization is a totally useless concept, even *within* the relational model. It is a contrived theory that attempts to eliminate data redundancy and inconsistencies by identifying misplaced field dependencies. But misplaced dependencies occur only in an incorrectly designed database. So, in order to justify the need for normalization, the theorists ignore the application's requirements and deliberately create an incorrect database; then, they use normalization to convert it into a correct one. The theorists also delude themselves when claiming that they have turned database design into a formal, exact procedure. All they do, in fact, is discuss formally their invention, the various types of field dependencies; the design problem itself has remained as informal as before.

The third delusion emerged when the relational model was found to be impractical. In order to reduce them to a mathematical representation, the database format, relationships, and operations were simplified so much that very few actual requirements could be implemented. Consequently, the theorists were compelled to "enhance" the model. And this consisted in restoring, one by one, those features that had been eliminated in the first two delusions in order to attain the exact, formal representation. By the time the model was versatile enough to be practical, there was nothing left of the preciseness of the original theory, not even in that narrow domain where the database operations had indeed been mathematical. The third delusion, thus, is in the belief that the original restrictions are not really necessary; in other words, the belief that we can enjoy the benefits of an exact theory without having to adhere to its principles.

Historically, the first two delusions can be said to make up the original idea, while the third one emerged when trying to implement that idea. The first two are a manifestation of the mechanistic fallacies; that is, attempting to represent a complex phenomenon with simple structures. And the third one is the consequence of this attempt. Since the only way to save a fallacious theory from refutation is by making it a pseudoscience, the software experts rescued the relational model by turning its falsifications into what they describe as new relational features. But what they are doing is merely to restore those features which they had eliminated previously in order to make the theory mechanistic. So, if the first two delusions demonstrate the naivety of the software experts, the third one demonstrates their dishonesty: they continue to praise the benefits of the relational model even while annulling the relational concepts and replacing them with the traditional ones.

The relational database theory is an excellent example of what I have called *the new pseudosciences*. Even better than structured programming or object-oriented programming, it can serve as a model of the modern mechanistic delusions.

Recall how these delusions evolve. The scientists start by noticing *one* aspect of a complex phenomenon; so they extract, from the *system* of structures that make up the phenomenon, the structure depicting that one aspect. Then, they enthusiastically announce a formal, mathematical theory based on this structure alone – claiming, in effect, that a complex structure can be reduced to a simple one. A further benefit of having only one structure, they say, is that we can choose our starting elements from higher levels of abstraction – an expedient that makes it even easier to represent the phenomenon.

But the theory does not represent the phenomenon accurately enough to be useful. So, instead of trying to understand the reason for its failure, the scientists decide to "improve" it: they suppress the falsifications by reinstating, in the guise of new features, the very features they had previously excluded – features that must indeed be excluded if we seek a mechanistic theory. The purpose of the new features, thus, is to restore some of the original structures, and the links between them. In the end, the theory becomes useful only when enough of the old features are reinstated to allow us to represent the entire complex phenomenon again; that is, when we are allowed to represent it *informally*, the way we always did. The scientists, though, continue to praise the exact, mechanistic qualities of their theory – even as everyone can see that what made the theory useful is the *annulment* of these qualities, and their replacement with complex, indeterministic ones.

The First Delusion

1

The first delusion is the belief in the mathematical merits of the relational model. For over thirty years, we have been hearing the claim that the relational model is based on mathematical logic, and therefore relational databases benefit from the rigour and precision of mathematics. Although few people actually understand the connection between databases and mathematics, no one doubts this claim. After all, the mathematical benefits are being praised, not just by the vendors of relational systems, but also by university professors, database experts, and professional computer associations. In this subsection I want to show, however, that the claim is a fraud: relational databases do not benefit at all from mathematical logic.

Mathematical systems, which include logic systems, are artificial models invented by us in order to represent with precision various aspects of the world. It is not difficult to invent a mathematical system (see pp. 708–709). Essentially, we define its basic elements, the operations that combine elements from one level of complexity to the next, the rules that control the use of these operations, and the axioms (those assumptions taken by convention to be valid assertions). We can then build increasingly complex expressions and theorems by combining elements on higher and higher levels. For the system to be useful mathematically, it must be consistent: no contradictions should be possible between the expressions or the theorems derived within the system. The basic elements vary with the system: numerical values for the classical mathematical systems, or subjects, predicates, and propositions for the logic systems.

The more elaborate the system, the more complex its elements and operations. Differential calculus, for example, is more complex than arithmetic or algebra. Since mathematical systems are simple hierarchical structures, a higher complexity means only that the system can have more levels, and more intricate elements at the higher levels, within *one* structure. While still a simple structure, though, a more elaborate system allows us to represent more difficult phenomena.

To use a mathematical system as model, we start by translating the entities and processes that constitute the phenomenon into the entities and operations permitted by the system. Once this is accomplished, we can study the phenomenon by working strictly with the mathematical concepts. We create expressions and higher-level elements, manipulate them in various ways, and finally translate the results back into real entities and processes. With this method, we can explain and predict events that may be difficult or impossible to study directly.

A classic example of a mathematical model is Newton's theory of gravitation: if we represent with mathematical entities and operations the bodies that make up the solar system, their state at a given instant, and the natural laws that govern their motion, we can determine with accuracy their position at any other instant in the past or in the future. Clearly, it would be impossible to accomplish this without a mathematical model.

Imagine now a trivial system, a small subset of traditional mathematics: the basic elements in this system are integers, and the only operations are addition and subtraction. Thus, since expressions are limited to these two operations, the most complex elements possible are still integers. And, even though the system permits any number of levels and hence increasingly complex expressions, because of its simplicity it is unlikely that we will ever need more than a few levels. Nevertheless, while simple, this system is not without practical applications; we can employ it, for example, to create accounting models (if we agree to use only whole dollars). The chief difference between it and the mathematical systems of science and engineering is that the latter reach much higher levels, and much more complex elements and operations.[1]

Turning now to the relational model, we find a modification of the logic system known as predicate calculus. To this system, features like record keys and field names were added in order to adapt it for database work. The simplest

---

[1] It is worth stressing again that the term "complexity," when used with the simple structures of mathematical and logic systems, refers to *levels of complexity* (also known as levels of abstraction), and it must not be confused with the complexity of complex structures (which is due to the interaction of several simple structures).

elements in the relational model are the fields – called now columns, or attributes. Fields are combined to form records – called now rows, or tuples; and records are combined to form files – called now tables, or relations. Relations can then be combined into expressions by means of standard logical operations (AND, OR, and NOT) and some new, more complex operations (UNION, DIFFERENCE, SELECTION, PROJECTION, and PRODUCT). Relations can be combined in this manner to form increasingly high levels, but the result is still a relation. Relations, thus, are the most complex elements in a relational system. Although more intricate than our system of integers and two operations, it is still very simple – far simpler than the mathematical systems employed in science and engineering.

And herein lies the explanation for the first delusion, why the mathematical background of the relational model is irrelevant. It is true that the relational entities and operations can be defined rigorously, with the same methods and notation we use in mathematics. But this preciseness is specious. The relational definitions resemble perhaps the definitions found in the traditional mathematical systems, but, because the relational model is such a simple system, its formality is superfluous, even silly.

The operations of a mathematical system, and the rules that govern the use of these operations, determine how the elements that make up one level are combined to form the elements of the next level. These combinations become the theorems and expressions possible in the system, and, ultimately, the mathematical representation of a phenomenon when the system is used as model. A formal definition of entities, operations, and rules is important in the *traditional* systems, therefore, because this formality is our only guarantee that the theorems and expressions remain valid as we move to higher levels of complexity. But if in a relational system all we have is some simple elements and operations – some simple transformations of one file into another, or of two files into one – and if we rarely need more than a few levels, the formality is hardly necessary. The concept of files, records, and fields is so simple that we can accomplish the same tasks using nothing more than personal skills.

Let us divide the use of a mathematical system into two parts, *translation* and *manipulation*. The translation is the work required to convert into a mathematical representation the entities and processes that make up the phenomenon, and to convert the mathematical entities back into real entities and processes. The manipulation is the work performed *within* the system, with the mathematical entities alone.

When praising the power of mathematics, it is the manipulation that we have in mind, not the translation. The translation – an effort to represent a complex world with a neat, artificial system – is necessarily informal, and cannot benefit from the exactness of the mathematical system itself. Thus, there is no way to guarantee that we selected the right system and operations to model a particular phenomenon, or represented the phenomenon accurately, or interpreted the results correctly. All we have to guide us in the translation is our skills.

To take a simple example, we can use mathematics to model the relationship between the speed of a car and the distance traveled in a period of time. All we need to do is represent these entities with appropriate values, perform the operation of multiplication or division, and then translate the result back into an actual entity. So, if we know the car's speed, the mathematical model lets us predict the distance it will travel in a given period of time, or the time required to travel a given distance. But mathematics cannot verify for us that we employ the formulas correctly. It cannot stop us, for instance, from using an incorrect speed, or from measuring the speed in miles per hour and the distance in kilometers. We praise the power of mathematics to predict the distance or time, but, in reality, mathematics only guarantees that the higher-level element (the result) is indeed the product or quotient of the two elements we started with.

No mathematical system can also be a substitute for the expertise required to use it. Although no less important than the system itself, the work involved in using it – particularly the translation from real entities into mathematical ones and back – is largely informal, and hence open to errors despite the exactness of the system.

In relational systems, we saw earlier, this problem led to the separation between the formal and the informal aspects – those aspects deemed to be within, and those deemed to be outside, the scope of the formal model. The formal aspects, we see now, correspond to the manipulation, while the informal ones form the translation. The manipulation includes the definition of fields and tuples, and the query operations. And the translation includes everything else: the updating operations, the normalization, the integrity rules, and the database language. This separation is artificial, of course, since all aspects of the database are equally important. But it is inevitable if we want to have a mathematical model: if we must exclude from the model any database aspect that is too complex to treat formally, that aspect is bound to end up as part of the translation, where we can deal with it informally.

This limitation – the need to treat the translation informally – is inherent in all mathematical systems. No matter how rigorous and exact is the manipulation, we depend largely on personal skills when selecting a particular system for a given phenomenon, and when translating the real entities into mathematical ones. And the relational model is no different. What makes it silly, then, is not this limitation, which is universal, but the fact that it consists almost entirely of the informal translation. In the end, what is for the traditional mathematical systems the ultimate purpose – the formal, exact manipulation – plays in relational systems an insignificant part.

2

Recall the predicate calculus system, the logical foundation of the relational model. A logical expression like $P(x,y,z)$ describes the tuples of elements x, y, and z related through predicate P. When we substitute actual values for the three elements, the expression will be evaluated as *True* for some tuples and *False* for others. We retain then, usually, the set of tuples for which the expression is true (a relation); and, using logical operations, we combine it with other sets, which are based on different predicates and elements. Such a combination is an expression that describes a new set of tuples – a set that relates in a different and perhaps more complex way the elements of the original tuples. The new set may then be combined with others, and so on, to create higher levels of complexity.

Like all logic systems, predicate calculus is concerned with the *structure* of variables and expressions, not their meaning. All it can guarantee is that, if we restrict ourselves to combinations based on the operations permitted by the system, the result of each combination will be correct within the definition of the system. Thus, if we know that the tuples in the original sets are true, we can determine with certainty, level after level, whether those in the resulting sets are true or false.[2] The system guarantees the validity of the manipulation, but the translation remains our responsibility: it is up to us to determine – by means external to the system – whether the tuples we start with are true or false, and whether the expressions that define the tuples, along with the operations that combine them from one level to the next, match the relations between the entities we want to model in that system. A logic system, in the end, is only a tool. It is up to us to judge whether it is the right tool in a given situation, and to use it correctly.

The fallacy, thus, lies in the belief that if the database model resembles a logic system, database work will become an exact, mathematical activity. In reality, this new tool is inappropriate for database programming, because the

---

[2] Strictly speaking, it is not the tuples that are true or false, but the result of the logical expression that defines the tuples; the more accurate description, though, would make these sentences too complicated.

database structures are closely linked to the other structures that make up the application. Mathematical and logic systems can only model phenomena that can be represented with a simple structure. So their ability to model database structures has little value if these structures must interact with others.

Like the predicate calculus system, a relational system guarantees only that the sets of tuples generated from the previous ones, as we move from one level to the next, are correct within the system's definition. The elements are now fields, the tuples are records, the sets of tuples are files, and the logical expressions depict combinations of files or portions of files. The database and the relational operations can be represented, therefore, with the same formality and preciseness we enjoy in predicate calculus. An expression like *F(a,b,c)* defines a file by stating that the fields *a*, *b*, and *c* are related through the predicate *F*. When actual values are stored in these fields, the expression will be true for some tuples (i.e., records) and false for others; and the actual file consists of those tuples that are true.

In other words, we use simply the *existence* of the tuple to determine the truth or falsity of the expression that defines the tuple: a tuple is deemed "true" if it currently exists as a record in the file, and "false" if it does not. Thus, the definition of truth and falsity in a relational database is merely a *convention*. The convention states in effect that *the data in the original files is valid by default*, simply because the records present in the file are deemed to be "true." The absurdity of this convention is the root of the relational model's mathematical delusion, as we will see in a moment.

The relational operations are designed to create a new set of tuples from one or two existing sets; that is, to create a new file by selecting and combining records (or portions of records) from one or two existing files. So, if we restrict ourselves to the relational operations, the validity of the existing data guarantees the validity of the combinations: since the original records are true by default, the records in the new file will also be true. The new file can then be combined with others to create a higher level of complexity, and so on. No matter how we use the relational operations, we can be sure that the final result will reflect the data we started with. There can be no false records in the resulting files, because there were no false records in the original ones.

It should now be obvious why logic systems are inappropriate as database models. A logic system like predicate calculus cannot control the addition and deletion of tuples in the original sets, nor the modification of their elements. All it can do is create new sets of tuples from existing ones; that is, *read* the original data. And if predicate calculus is limited to reading its data, so must be the relational model. With a database, the limitation to reading is, of course, the limitation to queries. So the fact that the relational model is limited to queries follows *necessarily* from its logical grounding. In general-purpose applications, though, adding, deleting, and modifying records are as important as queries. It is absurd, therefore, to ground a database system on predicate calculus.

The great weakness of the relational model, then, is the need to ensure by *informal* means that the original tuples are true. Since it is the truth or falsity of each tuple that determines whether it can be a record in the file, what is merely the truth value of a logical expression in predicate calculus becomes the critical issue of data integrity in a relational system. This means that, before we add a new record to a file, we must ensure somehow that the record is true; similarly, when we modify the data in an existing record, we must ensure that it continues to be true; and before we delete a record, we must ensure that it is indeed false.

But the only way to perform these validity checks is by accessing the tuples from *outside* the relational model, with *traditional* programming methods. The software theorists underrate the significance of this weakness: they casually say that the database modifications and the associated integrity issue lie outside the scope of the formal model, as if this limitation were just a minor implementation detail.

Clearly, what the model offers us – the assurance that the files resulting from relational operations are correct if the original ones are – is meaningful only if we can be sure that the data in the database is correct at all times. But the values stored in database fields are not right or wrong in an absolute sense. Their validity can only be assessed within the context of the running application; that is, by performing certain operations that link the database structures with some of the other structures that make up the application. The database is one aspect of a complex structure, and the validation process cannot be represented with a formal, mechanistic model.

So, if the validation is an informal, error-prone process, how can anyone claim that the relational model guarantees the correctness of the resulting files? All it can guarantee is that the data in the resulting files reflects accurately the data in the original ones. Consequently, the validity of the resulting data can be no more certain than the validity of the original data. And ascertaining *that* validity is no different in a relational system than it is for traditional data files. Thus, since the ultimate precision of a system is limited by its least precise part, the belief that a relational database is more precise than a traditional one is a delusion.

Here are some of the mistakes that can be committed in applications based on a relational system – mistakes that would not be detected by the system:

adding a new record that has invalid values in fields like address, phone number, price, or part description; placing invalid values in the fields of an existing record; retrieving a part record using the vendor number as part number (record keys for parts, vendors, employees, customers, etc., may well share a common range of values, so this mistake would not result in an invalid key, and the wrong record would indeed be retrieved); adding the quantity purchased to the quantity in stock of a part, instead of subtracting it; deleting a record that must not, in fact, be deleted – and, generally, omitting a record that *should* be in the file (the convention that the records present in the file are true does not imply that all those not in the file are false, so the model cannot determine which records are *missing*).

The reason a relational system does not prevent us from performing such operations is that, within the relational model, these operations are perfectly correct. The only way to discover the mistakes is by performing these operations together with some *other* operations, which take into account both the database structures and the other aspects of the application; in particular, the business rules implemented in the application. In other words, we can only discover the mistakes by checking the data from *outside* the model.

It is not surprising, therefore, that the relational model had to be "enhanced" with informal means that allow us to discover such mistakes. We will study these enhancements under the third delusion, but it is worth noting at this point that, despite some new and impressive terminology, what we are doing with the new features – linking the database structures with the other structures of the application – is exactly what we had been doing all along, in a much simpler way, with ordinary programming languages.

3

Let us return to the formal model. To explain the relational theory, textbooks give us page after page of definitions and expressions in mathematical logic. Yet, as we just saw, this formality and preciseness cannot stop us from committing outrageous mistakes. No matter how rigorous the relational model is from a mathematical perspective, the only part that is formal and precise is the definition of database entities and operations; specifically, how we combine tuples into files, and files into other files, as we move from one level of complexity to the next. And these entities and operations are so simple that we can use them just as effectively without the formal definitions.

Recall the simple system that can handle only integers and two operations, addition and subtraction. In this system, all that mathematics does is ensure that the integer of the next level is indeed the sum or difference of the integers of the current level. Thus, the formal definitions in such a system offer very little beyond what we can accomplish using just common sense. For, we can also add and subtract integers correctly by replacing the formal definitions with an informal method, and carefully following that method. Because this system is so simple, the formal and the informal alternatives are equally practical. Even more importantly, the formal system cannot prevent us from committing such mistakes as using wrong values when translating an actual phenomenon into integers, or adding two integers when in fact we ought to subtract them. Whether we choose the formal system or an informal method, we must deal with these problems informally.

And the same is true of the relational model. All that mathematics does is assure us that each operation combines elements just as its definition says. It assures us, for example, that the selection operation indeed selects the specified records. Thus, an expression like $G(a,b,c) = F(a,b,c)$ AND $a>k$ defines a selection operation by saying that the new file G includes those tuples (a,b,c) which satisfy two conditions: they are true (i.e., are actual records) in file F, and the element a is greater than a certain value k. This formal definition is very impressive, but it is also very silly. Because record selection is such a simple concept, we can easily perform this operation by relying on common sense alone: we describe informally what we mean by record selection, and then carefully implement this concept using the basic file operations and a programming language (see figure 7-13, p. 694).

All mathematical systems appear silly, of course, if we study only the low levels. The low-level elements and operations are usually simple enough to understand intuitively, so the rigour and preciseness of their definition appear superfluous. But there is a reason for this formality. In serious mathematical systems there are *many* levels of complexity. We always start with simple elements, but we combine them so many times that we end up with very intricate ones at the higher levels. Since the elements and operations at these levels can no longer be understood intuitively, the formal definitions are our only assurance that the system functions correctly.

In a simple system, on the other hand, the elements do not increase in complexity as we move to higher levels, so there is no benefit in combining them more than a few times. With a simple system, therefore, we rarely create more than a few levels, and we can only model simple phenomena. In the system of integers and two operations, for instance, the sum or difference of two integers is still an integer. And there aren't many applications where all we need is to add or subtract integers while repeating these operations endlessly, level after level. Applications that require many levels also require an increase in the complexity of elements and operations.

In the relational model, too, the same type of elements (tuples and files) and the same type of operations (SELECTION, UNION, PRODUCT, etc.) are found at both the lowest and the highest levels. And as a result, there is no benefit in combining elements more than a few times. Thus, few requirements involve more than three or four files, or more than three or four operations, in the creation of a new file. It is difficult to imagine a situation where we have to perform a series of a dozen selections, products, and projections, each operation starting with the result of the previous ones.

The software theorists claim that the relational model offers benefits similar to those of the traditional mathematical systems, but this is not true. In science and engineering we start with simple elements like integers, and simple operations like addition, but after many levels we end up with such concepts as calculus and analytic geometry. The complexity of the elements, as well as the complexity of the operations, keeps increasing as we move to higher levels. With the traditional mathematical systems, therefore, we derive important benefits when adding levels; in particular, the higher complexity permits us to model more complex phenomena. Evidence of these benefits is also found in that the formality and preciseness are now critical: unlike the selection of records in a database, we can hardly replace concepts like differential equations with methods based on common sense alone.

In the relational model, it is the restriction to high-level operations that prevents us from using more than a few levels. Software applications do have many levels of complexity, starting with simple entities like statements and database fields, and ending with the logic of a whole business system. But these are not the levels of a simple structure. Unlike mathematical systems, which can be represented with one structure, software applications comprise *many* structures – structures that must share their elements if they are to model our affairs accurately. And it is often low-level elements like statements and database fields that must be shared.

Among these structures are also the database structures, but with a relational system the lowest-level elements that can be shared are the files. If we take the fields, records, and files to be the three lowest levels of a database structure, the relational operations only permit us to access files. Starting with files we can then create even higher levels – that is, further files. But the interactions with the other structures are not as versatile as those we could create by starting with records and fields. Most interactions, in fact, are now too awkward or inefficient to be practical.

Thus, we see no benefits in creating more than a few levels of relational operations, not because we do not *need* higher levels, but because the restriction to operations on whole files prevents us from creating the combinations of software entities needed to attain those levels. This is why the original model was useless, and why the features added later serve mainly to bypass the restriction to whole files: they restore the means to link the database structures to the rest of the application through lower-level elements (through individual records and fields), thus permitting more alternatives at the high levels.

4

With any mathematical system, we must perform the translation in order to attain the precise format required for the manipulation. But in itself the translation is a detriment: not only does it constitute additional work, but its informality detracts from the exactness of the manipulation. We can justify the use of a mathematical system, therefore, only if the manipulation confers significant benefits; that is, if it permits us to perform some important and difficult tasks. And this is indeed the case for the mathematical systems used in science and engineering: the manipulation in these systems is very elaborate, with many levels of complexity, while the translation may be as simple as converting things like weight, voltage, or time into numerical values.

In a relational system, the opposite is true: the manipulation is trivial, and it is the translation that ends up very elaborate. In order to have a mathematical database model, the part that is the manipulation had to be restricted so much that it involves in the end only trivial mathematics. The most difficult aspects of database programming – updating operations, integrity rules, the second and higher normal forms, the database language – were left out of the model and became part of the translation. They were left out, not because they do not entail manipulation, but because *that* manipulation cannot be represented mathematically.

So the manipulation includes only queries, and the queries permit only high-level operations on whole files. In any case, these queries are so simple that they can be implemented without mathematics. The basic file operations, we saw earlier, allow us to scan and relate files, and to select records and fields. Thus, the operations permitted by the relational model – selection, union, product, and the rest – can be easily programmed with ordinary iterative and conditional constructs.

To deal with those aspects of the database that make up the translation, and which were left out of the formal model, we need programming skills. So in the end we use the power of mathematics for the relatively simple manipulation, which hardly requires a formal system, while depending on informal programming methods for the difficult tasks.

Unlike the mathematical systems used in science and engineering, then, the relational model confers no benefits. In the traditional fields, mathematics permits us to accomplish tasks that are impossible without a formal system; so the translation, with its drawbacks, is worthwhile. Relational mathematics, on the other hand, is so simple that it can be replaced with a few lines of programming; so the drawbacks of the translation exceed the benefits of the manipulation. The idea behind the relational model is, therefore, senseless. What is the point in seeking a formal system for the query operations, if all the work required to prepare the database for these queries must remain informal? Since we must continue to depend on programming for the difficult translation, we may as well use programming also for the relatively simple manipulation.

The theorists promote the relational model by pointing to its mathematics, and implying that it provides the same benefits as the models of science and engineering. But if the relational model uses only trivial mathematics, the claim is a fraud. In reality, very little of the phenomenon of a database is amenable to an exact, mechanistic representation. Mathematics is useful for phenomena where changes are rare. Take the bodies in the solar system, for instance: we can represent their motion mathematically because their properties are fixed; so, with only a small investment in the translation, we gain the great benefits of the manipulation. In the database phenomenon, however, changes are very common. These changes include adding or deleting records, and modifying the data stored in fields. Each change produces a slightly different database – different data, and hence different relationships. No mathematical system can accurately represent such a changeable phenomenon, and it is for this reason that the theorists exclude the updating operations from the formal model.

The relational idea is worthless because we have to leave too much out of the manipulation in order to represent the database functions mathematically. What we leave out is far more than what we leave out in the traditional uses of mathematics. We must leave out of the formal model the database changes and all the related issues; in particular, the integrity rules and most of the normalization. These features are in reality as much part of the application as are the queries. So, for the model to be truly useful, they would have to be included in the manipulation. Only if we decide that databases are mainly query systems can we treat issues like updating, integrity, and normalization as part of the informal translation, rather than the formal manipulation; but then we must no longer claim that the relational model is useful for general applications.

The fact that so much had to be left out of their formal model ought to have worried the theorists. This was an opportunity to realize that the relational concept is fallacious, that databases cannot be usefully represented with a mathematical model. Instead, fascinated by the little that *could* be represented mathematically, they saw in the relational concept the beginning of a new science.

But an even greater deficiency than the separation of query operations from updating operations is the separation of the query operations from the other operations performed by the application. As we saw, the relational operations are restricted to manipulating whole files, rather than individual records and fields, like the traditional file operations. And, while in principle individual records and fields can be treated as tiny files and accessed with the relational operations, this method is far too awkward and inefficient to be practical. In effect, then, the relational model does not permit us to manipulate freely the low-level database entities. The immediate consequence of this limitation is that it is impossible to link, at the level of records and fields, the structures formed by database entities and operations with the structures formed by the other aspects of the application. And no serious application can be developed without these links.

Even for query systems, therefore, the relational model cannot be said to work if the only queries that can be implemented are those possible through operations on whole files. To be truly useful, a database system must allow us to manipulate database entities in any conceivable way.

In conclusion, the relational model is indeed a revolution in database concepts, in that it imparts to database programming the rigour and exactness of mathematics; but only *if* we restrict ourselves to queries; and *if* we restrict ourselves to queries that can be expressed through certain parameters (so that the database can be separated from the application and accessed only through operations performed on whole files); and *if* we restrict ourselves to normalized files (although it is possible, in principle, to implement any queries using normalized files, this is usually too complicated or too slow to be practical); and *if* we can ensure that all the operations that modify the database are performed correctly (so that the data upon which the queries are based is valid at all times).

Note that these restrictions describe the *original* model; so this model, absurd as it is, is in fact optimistic. As no practical uses were found for it, means had to be provided eventually to link the database structures with the other structures of the application. And the only way to do this was by permitting *low-level* database operations, which bypass the original restrictions. But if those restrictions are essential in order to attain an exact model, if we bypass them we will no longer enjoy the benefits of mathematics, not even in a narrow range of applications. So those benefits, which were insignificant in the original model already, were reduced in the end to zero.

5

There is no better way to conclude our discussion of the first delusion than by showing how the relational model is presented to the public. We just saw that there are no mathematical benefits in using a relational database. The database experts, however, promote the relational systems by praising *precisely* their mathematical background. Here are some examples: "The mathematical concept underlying the relational model is the set-theoretic *relation*."[3] "The relational model is founded on the mathematical disciplines of predicate calculus and set theory."[4] "The relational data model is based on the well developed mathematical theory of relations. The rigorous method of designing a data base (using normalization ...) gives this model a solid foundation. This kind of foundation does not exist for the other data models."[5] "The relational approach is based on the mathematical theory of relations.... The results of relational mathematics can be applied directly to relational data bases, and hence operations on data can be described with precision."[6] "The relational model is based on the mathematical notion of a relation. Codd and others have extended the notion to apply to database design."[7] "The solid theoretical foundation guarantees that results of relational requests are well defined and, therefore, predictable."[8] "One of the benefits of working with the relational approach to databases is that it can be couched within the formalism of first-order predicate logic. As a result a mathematical foundation is available for dealing with database issues when databases are all relational."[9] "The reason we could define rigorous approaches to relational database design is that the relational data model rests on a firm mathematical foundation."[10]

[3] Jeffrey D. Ullman, *Principles of Database Systems* (Potomac, MD: Computer Science Press, 1980), p. 73.

[4] Anthony Ralston and Edwin D. Reilly, eds., *Encyclopedia of Computer Science*, 3rd ed. (New York: Van Nostrand Reinhold, 1993), p. 1161.

[5] Shaku Atre, *Data Base: Structured Techniques for Design, Performance, and Management*, 2nd ed. (New York: John Wiley and Sons, 1988), p. 90.

[6] James Martin, *Computer Data-Base Organization*, 2nd ed. (Englewood Cliffs, NJ: Prentice Hall, 1977), p. 204.

[7] Catherine M. Ricardo, *Database Systems: Principles, Design, and Implementation* (New York: Macmillan, 1990), p. 177.

[8] Candace C. Fleming and Barbara von Halle, *Handbook of Relational Database Design* (Reading, MA: Addison-Wesley, 1989), p. 32.

[9] Barry E. Jacobs, *Applied Database Logic*, vol. 1, *Fundamental Database Issues* (Englewood Cliffs, NJ: Prentice Hall, 1985), p. 9.

[10] Henry F. Korth and Abraham Silberschatz, *Database System Concepts*, 2nd ed. (New York: McGraw-Hill, 1991), p. 209.

As we saw, it is not difficult to show that the model's mathematical foundation is irrelevant. Yet no one in the academic world – not the mathematicians, not the philosophers, not the engineers – ever challenged these claims. Nor did anyone challenge the other software theories. The computer scientists can invent any theories, thus, no matter how absurd, confident that the academic community, the software practitioners, and the rest of society will accept them unquestioningly.

Most people trust and respect the universities, without realizing that what the academics are promoting is not ideas that are useful, but ideas that help them maintain their privileged position even if useless; in particular, the idea that science means simply the pursuit of mechanistic theories – whether sound or not, whether useful or not.

Moreover, by fostering the mechanistic ideology, universities make it possible for everyone else to promote senseless ideas. The delusions that make up the activity we call advertising, for example, would not be possible if universities were teaching truth and rationality. These delusions are necessary because the advertised products are not, in fact, as useful as they appear. If our educators are permitted to promote useless ideas, then why not everyone else?

Universities and corporations, thus, prefer mechanistic concepts because they are easy to invent and to pursue. But when the actual phenomena are complex, these concepts are worthless. The mechanistic ideology benefits incompetents and charlatans, therefore, by making their activities look like serious research, or like legitimate business.

The Second Delusion

1

The second delusion is the idea of normalization: the belief that, within the relational model, the problem of database design has been turned into a formal theory. In reality, the principles of normalization do not constitute an exact procedure, but one that can only be implemented informally. (The concept of normalization was introduced earlier; see pp. 718–720.)

The delusion of normalization can be summarized by saying that it is an attempt to replace the simple process of *avoiding* incorrect file relationships, with the complicated process of *eliminating* them after allowing them into the database. To justify the need for normalization, the theorists misrepresent the design problem. Traditionally, we used methods that helped us to create a correct database, and thereby avoided data inconsistencies. Now we are expected to ignore those methods, deliberately create an incorrect database, discover the consequent problems, and then use normalization to convert the incorrect database into a correct one.

In the end, it is only this contrived, absurd procedure that the theorists managed to formalize, not the *actual* problem of database design. As we will see presently, even under normalization the correct database structures can only be discovered *informally*, by studying the application's requirements – just as we do when following the traditional design methods. The concept of normalization, thus, is a fraud. By inventing pompous terms to describe what are in fact senseless principles, and by discussing these principles with great seriousness, the relational experts delude themselves that they have turned database design into an exact theory.

❖

Note that here, in the discussion of the second delusion, I am using the term "normalization" to refer only to the second and higher normal forms; that is, to the problem of field dependency. The *first* normal form (which restricts fields to single values) is unrelated to the higher ones; it is part of the formal relational model, and hence part of the first delusion.

Note also that, although the mathematical pretenses of the second and higher normal forms resemble the first delusion, these transformations are not required at all by the formal model. A database, in other words, does not have to be normalized in order to satisfy the mathematical restrictions of the formal model (I will return to this point later). The higher normal forms are only needed in order to prevent problems that arise when *updating* the database; and the updating operations lie outside the scope of the formal model.

Thus, it would be wrong to treat the higher normal forms as part of the first delusion. Their *annulment* (the process known as *denormalization*) does constitute, however, the same kind of delusion as the annulment of the first normal form, or the annulment of the other aspects of the relational model. All annulments, therefore, are discussed under the third delusion.

Let us review the concept of normalization – how the relational theorists present the problem of data inconsistencies, and its solution.

Each piece of information in the database should exist in only one place, because data that is duplicated may cause various inconsistencies when records are added, deleted, or modified. The relational theorists call these inconsistencies "update anomalies." The unnecessary repetition of data also wastes storage space, but it is the anomalies that are the main reason for normalization. In fact, depending on the size of the duplicated fields and the number of records involved, normalization sometimes *increases* storage requirements. Still, the theorists say, the benefits are so important that we should normalize our files even at the cost of increased storage space.

It must also be noted that there is always an alternative to normalization: the inconsistencies can be avoided by performing additional operations in the application (additional checks and, when required, additional updating). Normalizing the files is generally a simpler and more efficient solution, but sometimes those operations are the better alternative. In the relational model, though, this too is unacceptable: we must *always* normalize our files.

Duplication, and hence redundancy, occurs when we store some data in several records in a certain file while that data could be stored in only one record in another file: repeating customer data like name or address in every order belonging to that customer, repeating product data like description or price in every order line with that product, and so on. Clearly, fixed data should be stored in a separate file – a customer file or a product file, in this case. Only data specific to an order should be stored in the orders file, and only data specific to an order line in the order lines file. A field in the orders file will contain the customer number, and a field in the order lines file will contain the product number. These fields will serve as links to the customer and product files. Thus, when processing an order, we can access the customer data by reading the customer record; and when processing an order line, we can access the product data by reading the product record. The same is true of an invoice file, a transaction file, a sales history file, and any other file that needs customer or product data.

With data separated in this manner, when there is a change in a customer's name or address, or in a product's description or price, we only need to modify the customer or product record, rather than all the orders for that customer, or all the order lines with that product. If there were no customer and product files, an anomaly would occur if we modified the customer data in an order, or the product data in an order line: any other orders for that customer, or any other lines with that product, would continue to have the old, and hence wrong, values. Another anomaly would occur if we had to store data for a customer that has no outstanding orders, or for a product that is not currently on order: we would have to create a dummy order just so that we had a place to store customer and product data.

Data redundancy can also be viewed as the result of a mistaken relationship between two fields in the same record; specifically, a *misplaced dependency* of one field on another. A field should depend only on the field or fields that make up the record's key. There is no need for other relationships *within* a record; and if such a relationship exists, some data will be redundant. This is true because, if one field can be determined from another, its value will be repeated unnecessarily in all the records where the other field has a particular value. We only need to specify the dependency between the two fields in one place. So the correct way to store this information is as a single record, in a separate file.

Generally, to eliminate the redundancy associated with one misplaced dependency (the dependency of one or several fields on a given field), we must create one extra file in the database.[1] Each level of normalization – the levels known as second, third, Boyce/Codd, fourth, and fifth normal forms – is a more stringent implementation of this principle. Each level, that is, will eliminate a more subtle type of dependency. These types – known as functional dependency, transitive dependency, multivalued dependency, and join dependency – differ in the types and combinations of fields that form the misplaced dependency: a non-key field depending on only some of the fields that make up the key (instead of depending on the whole key), or a non-key field depending on another non-key field, or a key field depending on another key field, or more than two fields depending on one another. The classification of the normal forms is such that, in addition to being more subtle and more rare, each level represents a broader category of misplaced dependencies – a category that includes as a special case the one at the next lower level.

2

One aspect of the second delusion is the belief that, because the ideals of normalization are discussed only with the relational model, they are exclusive to relational databases. The theorists present the concept of normalization as if no one had been aware of the problem of data redundancy and inconsistencies before we had relational databases, and as if the relational model and the normalization principles were the only way to deal with this problem. They never mention the fact that this problem and its solution are *identical* to their counterparts in databases created with the traditional file operations. And they are identical because they are concerned with files, records, fields, and keys – elements that are identical (despite the new terminology) in relational and in traditional databases. With one type of database or the other, redundancy and inconsistencies indicate a faulty design, a database that does not match the application's requirements. And the solution is to modify the design so as to satisfy the requirements.

---

[1] Several extra files are required when the relationship involves three or more inter-related fields (the kind of dependency resolved by the fifth normal form).

The issue of normalization, then, is perceived as an important part of the relational model while being, for all practical purposes, a separate theory. It was tacked on to the relational model because it was invented by the same theorists, but it could be applied to any database model that uses files, records, fields, and keys. For, what we are asked is simply to replace the traditional principle of designing a database so as to *avoid* redundancy and inconsistencies, with the absurd principle that we must start with a faulty design and then modify it so as to *eliminate* the redundancy and inconsistencies. Thus, nothing stops us from employing this absurd principle with a *traditional* database. All we have to do is deliberately create an incorrect database, and then normalize it in order to eliminate the consequent problems. The final, correct database would be identical to the one we create now simply by following the traditional design principle.

It is also worth noting that we can attain the ideals sought by normalization more effectively with traditional databases than we can with relational ones. Ironically, while the relational theory makes the problem of redundancy and inconsistencies look like a new discovery, insists on strict normalization, and overwhelms us with formality and new terminology, its restriction to high-level operations often *prevents* us from solving this problem. And it is with the traditional file operations, where we don't even use terms like "normal form," that we can more easily deal with it. This is true because those operations are more versatile and more efficient than JOIN, the operation that combines files in the relational model. Since the process of normalization separates fields by creating additional files, we must read and combine more files and more records later, when *accessing* the database. And it is when the performance degradation caused by these additional operations becomes unacceptable that we must leave some data unnormalized. Thus, since the traditional file operations permit us to combine files and records more efficiently than does JOIN, we can afford to separate more fields – and hence attain a higher level of normalization – in a traditional database than in a relational one.

We can appreciate even better why the problem of redundancy and inconsistencies is not part of the relational theory by recalling the mathematical foundation of the relational model, predicate calculus (see pp. 711–712). The relation described by the logical expression *P(x,y,z)*, for instance, consists of those tuples of elements *x*, *y*, and *z* that are related through the predicate *P*. Specifically, we substitute for the three elements certain values selected from their respective domains of permissible values, and we retain those combinations of values for which the expression yields *True*.

Now, there is nothing in this definition of a relation to prevent two elements in a tuple from forming an additional relationship. For example, if y depends on x in such a way that we can always derive its value from that of x, y is in effect redundant. But this redundancy is harmless; that is, if we combine this expression with other expressions, the redundancy will be reflected perhaps in the final result, but it will not cause a logical inconsistency.

The original, formal relational model is similar: even if mistaken, the dependency of one field on another in a given file does not cause an inconsistency when that file is combined with others through relational operations. The formal model is concerned only with the *structure* and *combination* of files. Thus, even if there is a misplaced dependency in that file, the consequent redundancy is harmless. All that will happen is that some fields in the resulting file will also be related through a misplaced dependency.

The reason we can have misplaced dependencies in predicate calculus and in the formal relational model is that these systems do not include *updating* operations. Predicate calculus is not concerned with the way tuples ended up in the relation, or the way elements acquired their current value, but only with the operations that *use* the tuples. And the formal relational model is not concerned with the way records are created, deleted, or modified, but only with the operations that *read* the records. Thus, since only updating operations can cause inconsistencies, we need not worry about misplaced dependencies when we restrict ourselves to the formal model. (The relational theorists acknowledge this fact by calling the inconsistencies *update* anomalies.) To put it differently, if we restrict ourselves to queries, and particularly to queries expressed through the relational operations, we need not worry about misplaced field dependencies.

So the theory of normalization is irrelevant for applications restricted to the formal model. It is only for the broader model, which includes various informal aspects, that it has any significance. The original papers mentioned only briefly the updating operations that would be required in an application, and the language through which they would be specified.[2] It was assumed that these operations, along with the problems they might cause and the checks needed to avoid these problems, would be similar to those used in other database systems. No one tried to extend the formal model by including, say, a formal set of updating operations. It was assumed, in other words, that the exact, formal model would provide all the important database operations. The updating operations, as well as the operations needed to protect the database from redundancy and inconsistencies, were seen as a minor issue; so the plan

[2] See, for example, E. F. Codd, "A Relational Model of Data for Large Shared Data Banks," *Communications of the ACM* 13, no. 6 (1970): 377–387.

was to implement them informally, just as they were implemented in other systems. We find evidence for this interpretation in that the second and higher normal forms are not mentioned at all in the original papers. The terms "normal form" and "normalization" in these papers refer only to what is called now the *first* normal form.

It was when the theorists turned the formal model – originally meant only for queries – into the basis of general database systems, that the idea of normalization had to be extended. By calling the new normal forms "second," "third," etc., the theorists made them look like a natural extension of the first one, although they are unrelated. While the first one is concerned with eliminating data structures *within* fields, the higher ones are concerned with eliminating misplaced dependencies *between* fields. The first one is needed in order to base the formal model on predicate calculus, but the higher ones are needed only if we perform updating operations. By making the latter look like an extension of the first one, though, the theorists managed to mask the fact that the relational model was changing from an exact theory into a collection of informal concepts. While everyone thought that the precision of the formal model was being extended to cover all aspects of database work, in reality the exact opposite was taking place: what had been originally the *informal* aspects of the model – the updating operations, the higher normalization, the integrity rules, the database language – was becoming the actual model, and the *formal* part was becoming irrelevant.

One wonders, if the updating operations constitute an informal aspect of the relational model, why is it so important to formalize the normalization process? Why do the theorists attempt to reduce the problem of redundancy and inconsistencies to an exact model, if the problem only concerns the updating operations, which are informal in any case? The answer is that the theorists saw in the normalization principles an extension of the original, formal model. The precision which that model offered for queries, they thought, can now be extended to the design phase, and to the updating operations; so we will soon have a mathematical model for the whole database concept.

As we will see later, the formality of the normalization process is specious. The theorists are indeed discussing the subject of dependencies in a formal manner, but, ultimately, we can determine the relationship between two given fields only by studying and interpreting the application's requirements; that is, informally. As is the case with all mechanistic pseudosciences, the relational theorists noticed a few patterns and regularities (the normal forms and the field dependencies), and jumped to the conclusion that an exact theory is possible for the design of file relationships. The same naivety that led earlier to the belief that the resemblance of records to the tuples of predicate calculus can be the basis of a practical database model, led now to the belief that a neat classification of field dependencies can be the basis of a formal model for database design.

3

When studying the problem of data redundancy and inconsistencies, we notice a marked discrepancy between the way it is presented by the relational theorists and its *actual* difficulty. The theorists discuss this subject with great seriousness, the way one would discuss the most difficult problems a programmer can encounter. In reality, this is one of the simplest programming problems. And it is a problem that does not lend itself to formal treatment, so an exact theory has no practical value in any case.

It is hard to think of anyone designing a database where the "anomalies" so seriously discussed by the theorists could occur at all. Even a novice can recognize the absurdity of storing fixed customer information only in the invoice records, or repeating fixed product information in every order line with that product. And if mistakes like these go undetected and end up in the working application, it is hard to imagine a place where the programmers or the users fail to understand why customer data is lost when an invoice is paid, or why two order lines with the same product show different descriptions. Then, once they understand the problem, it is hard to imagine them failing to discover the solution; that is, keeping the fixed data in a separate file. To put this differently, a person incapable of dealing with this simple problem would be unable to deal with any other programming problem. His applications wouldn't work, and those anomalies would be the least of his worries. Thus, it is highly unlikely that a place can exist at all where the theory of normalization can confer any benefits.

And indeed, before it was brought into the limelight by the relational experts, we treated the problem of redundancy and inconsistencies as we did every other programming problem: we recognized its importance, but we never tried to explain it with an exact theory, or to solve it with a formal method. As evidence of its simplicity, we didn't even think that the process of solving it needed a special name; it is only for the relational theory that terms like "normalization" and "normal form" had to be introduced. And for those of us who have continued to use the traditional database design method, the attempt to turn this subject into an exact theory has had no significance whatever. We are treating the problem of redundancy and inconsistencies exactly as we did thirty or forty years ago, simply because the theory of normalization is irrelevant.

Relational database books devote at least one chapter to the subject of normalization. And the more thorough among them intimidate us with their formal tone and lengthy explanations, the countless definitions and theorems, and the new terms and symbols. Thus, if we ignore its content and judge it solely by its style, the discussion of normalization in a database book resembles the kind of discussions found in engineering books. Readers new to the relational theory are impressed by this formality and expect to learn some important facts. Invariably, though, they find the discussion hard to follow. Then, when the book illustrates the theory with actual examples of unnormalized files and their conversion to normalized ones, these readers react by exclaiming, "But this is how I would have designed the database in the first place!" So it is only through actual examples that we can comprehend the theory of normalization at all, and at that point the reason for the earlier difficulty becomes clear: since we would intuitively create the correct, normalized files to begin with, we struggle to understand what is the problem that the theory is trying to solve. To most of us it doesn't even occur – until we read a relational book – that anyone would design a database by repeating, say, the customer address fields for each order, or the product description field for each order line.

The difficulty, then, is not in understanding the principles of database design, but in understanding the theory of normalization: the attempt to reduce database design to formal and exact methods. We must make an effort to understand the normalization problems and their solutions because we normally don't think in a way that can create these problems. The problems are contrived, unreal. They were *invented* by the theorists, in order to have a reason for seeking a formal solution.

Typically, the books start by showing us an incorrect design and its drawbacks. They continue then by showing us how to convert it into a correct design. But what is the point of this discussion if hardly anyone would even *consider* the incorrect alternative? The theorists are defining, classifying, and explaining in the style of mathematical analysis some implausible situations – situations we never encounter in real life. With just common sense and a little practice, we already know how to create correct databases. The normalization theory, on the other hand, asks us to study some strange problems (the difference between the second and third normal forms, why we have the so-called Boyce/Codd normal form between the third and fourth, how to convert a file from first to second or from second to third, etc.) and to assimilate an endless list of strange concepts (superkey, dependency preservation, nonloss decomposition, left-irreducible functional dependency, etc.).

It is the attempt to formalize the problem of field dependency, data redundancy, and data inconsistencies, and the need to fit the incorrect designs into the classification of normal forms, that we find hard to understand – not the actual principles of database design. And when we finally understand the new concepts, we realize that in practice we never encounter these problems. When we learn to program we don't learn two things – how to design incorrect databases, and how to convert incorrect databases into correct ones; we simply learn how to design correct ones. Thus, since the problems studied by the theory of normalization concern mostly the transition from bad to good design, it is not surprising that the theory is, for all practical purposes, irrelevant.

4

We saw earlier, in "The Basic File Operations," that the concept of records, fields, and keys allows us to implement any file relationships we need in our applications. And we also saw that this concept is identical in traditional and in relational databases. The difference lies mainly in the new terminology and in the way the files are used. In traditional databases, we use the basic file operations through the flow-control constructs of a programming language; and we specify, through indexes, the individual records. In relational databases, we use only the high-level relational operations; and, rather than individual records, we specify whole files or logical portions of files. But in both cases we must create the same files and fields, and the same relationships, in order to implement a particular set of requirements.

Thus, although our earlier discussion concerned traditional databases, the same design principles apply to relational ones. With one type of database or the other, the traditional principles permit us to create correct – that is, normalized – databases directly from the application's requirements. To appreciate the absurdity of the normalization theory, then, let us review the traditional design concepts.

The decision we must make when designing a database is what files, fields, and keys are needed; that is, what data to store in the database, how to distribute it among files, and how to relate the files, in order to satisfy the application's requirements. Thus, since the files depend on the application's logic, we usually implement them together with the various parts of the application. It is the file *relationships* that pose the greatest challenge. For, if all we needed were isolated files (a customer file, a product file, a history file, etc., with no links between them), designing the database would be trivial, little more than creating the respective fields.

Files are related through the values present in their fields. Typically, identifiers and codes are used to relate files (product number, invoice number, category, etc.). A relationship is established when two files use such a field, and some records in both files contain the same value in this field.[3] Depending on how the relationship is used in the application, we may use either key fields or non-key fields. Often, a combination of several fields, rather than a single field, is needed to relate files.

And it is the correct choice of relationships that ultimately determines whether or not there will be redundancy or inconsistencies in the database – what the theory of normalization is concerned with. The various normal forms, as we will see shortly, are nothing but a complicated way of expressing these relationships. In reality, all we have to do is create a database that correctly represents the application's requirements; and if we do this, there will be no redundancy or inconsistencies. In other words, if we understand the application's requirements, and if we implement them correctly, we don't need a theory of normalization (because we create "normalized" files from the start); and if we don't understand the requirements, or fail to implement them correctly, no theory can help us.

Four types of file relationships are possible between two files: one-to-one, one-to-many, many-to-one, and many-to-many. The terms "one" and "many" refer to the number of records in the first and second file that are logically linked.

Two files are in a *one-to-one* relationship when one record in the first file is related to no more than one record in the second file. Thus, the two files will have the same number of records when each record in the first one has a corresponding record in the second one, and they will have a different number of records when some records in either file have no corresponding records in the other. Files that are in a one-to-one relationship can always be combined into a single file, where each record comprises the two corresponding records: we simply merge their fields, and when there is no corresponding record we assign null values or default values to the respective fields. For practical reasons, though, it is sometimes preferable to have two files rather than one. For example, if a file has many fields but some operations involve only a few, we may decide to keep these fields in a separate, smaller record, in order to improve the application's performance.

An example of one-to-one relationship is an employee file and a special functions file, with the condition that a function may be performed by only one

---

[3] Relations based on field equality are the most common, but, strictly speaking, any values can be used to relate files. With a date field, for example, we can create a relationship where a record containing a certain date in the first file is logically linked to those records in the second file where a date is up to one year earlier.

employee, and an employee may select no more than one function. At some point in time we may have, say, 80 records in the employee file and 30 records in the functions file, but only 20 functions actually selected; thus, 60 employees will have no corresponding function, and 10 functions no corresponding employee. The two files are linked by adding a function number field to the employee record, or an employee number field to the function record (or both, if we need two-way links).

The most common relationship is *one-to-many*. Two files are in a one-to-many relationship when one record in the first file (the "one" file) is related to one, several, or no records in the second file (the "many" file), while each record in the second file is related to one or no records in the first file. Here are some examples: customer file and customer orders file (one customer may have one, several, or no outstanding orders, but each order belongs to one customer); orders file and order lines file (one order may include one or several order lines, but each line belongs to one order); employee file and payment history file (each employee has one record in the history file for each pay period, but each pay period record belongs to one employee). A one-to-many relationship is also a *many-to-one* relationship, when seen from the perspective of the second file: several orders are related to the same customer, several order lines to the same order, several pay periods to the same employee.

The one-to-many relationship is implemented by making the "many" file's key a combination of both files' identifying fields. For example, if we make the key in the orders file the combination of customer number and order number, we will be able to select for a given customer any one of the corresponding records in the orders file, and for a given order the single, corresponding record in the customer file. However, when the relationship is seen as many-to-one and a direct link is not required from the "one" file to the "many" file, the "one" file's identifying field can be just a non-key field in the "many" file. Thus, the key in the orders file would be just the order number, and we would access the customer records by including the customer number as a non-key field.

Two files are in a *many-to-many* relationship when one record in the first file is related to one, several, or no records in the second file, and at the same time one record in the second file is related to one, several, or no records in the first file. To implement such a relationship, we create a service file to act as a link between the main files. The service file has only key fields, and its key is simply the combination of the two main keys. For example, if some vendors supply several products, and certain products are supplied by several vendors, the vendor and product files form a many-to-many relationship. The key in the service file is the combination of vendor and product numbers, and we implement the two-way links between files (vendor to product, and product to vendor) by providing *both* sorting sequences: products within vendors, and vendors within products. (If using traditional file operations, we accomplish this by creating two indexes for the service file.) We can then select for a given vendor the corresponding records in the product file, and for a given product the corresponding records in the vendor file.

The four types of relationships can be combined to link more than two files. Thus, a set of *several* files can form a one-to-one relationship, when any two files in the set are in a one-to-one relationship. Also, a file can be in two many-to-many relationships at the same time: with one file through one field, and with another file through another field.

The most versatile relationship, however, is one-to-many. One way to combine one-to-many relationships is by having several "many" files share the "one" file, through the same field or through different fields. The customer file, for example, can be related through the customer number to both the orders and the sales history files. One-to-many relationships can also be combined to form hierarchies of more than two levels, by using the "many" file of one relationship as the "one" file of another. For example, for each order in the orders file we can have several lines. We store then the line-related data in an order lines file, and use the combination of customer, order, and line numbers as the key. The order records will function, at the same time, as "many" in their relationship with the customer records, and as "one" in their relationship with the order lines records. Most applications require a mixture of combinations: several levels, and several files on each level. Thus, several "many" files may share the "one" file while acting at the same time as "one" files in other relationships.

It is also possible for two "one" files to share the "many" file. For example, if a customer purchases several products and a product is purchased by several customers, there will be a set of records in the sales history file for each customer record, and another set for each product record. But these sets will overlap: each history record will be related at the same time to a certain customer and to a certain product. Thus, in addition to being the "many" file for both the customer and the product files, the history file serves to create a many-to-many relationship between them. (The many-to-many relationship, we see now, is merely a special case of two one-to-many relationships that share the "many" file – the case where this file's sole purpose is to link the "one" files.)

Although the four types of relationships are usually described as *file* relation-ships, they are also *field* relationships. When two files are related as one-to-one, or one-to-many, or many-to-many, it is through their records that the relationship exists: one or several records in one file correspond to one or several records in the other. But records are made up of fields, so the same correspondence exists between fields: the relationship between files is reflected in each pair of fields. Thus, when two files are related as one-to-one, each field in the first file is in a one-to-one relationship with each field in the second file; in addition, fields that belong to the same file are in effect in a one-to-one relationship with one another. When two files are related as one-to-many, each field in the first file is in a one-to-many relationship with each field in the second file. And when two files are related as many-to-many, each field in the first file is in a many-to-many relationship with each field in the second file.

For example, if the product and the orders files are related as one-to-many, a field like the product description or price in the former will be related as one-to-many to fields like the order date or quantity in the latter. What this means in practice is that the same product description or price may be associated with several order dates and quantities.

We can regard the four types of relationships, therefore, as either file or field relationships. So, rather than saying that two files are related and the field relationships reflect the file relationship, we can say that it is the fields that must be related, and the file relationship will reflect the field relationships. We design a database by creating relationships that match the requirements. In some situations we think in terms of *file* relationships; and once we create the files, it is obvious to which file each field must be assigned. In other situations it is better to think in terms of *field* relationships; and we implement the files and file links that will allow us to relate those fields as required.

Consider this example. We want to store some information about our products, so we start with a file that contains just the key field, the product number. If the requirements say that there may be several orders for each product, the product number is related as one-to-many to the order number. The order number must be, therefore, in a separate file, so we create an orders file with two fields: the order number as the key, and the product number as the link to the product file. Next, we need a product description field, which is always the same for a given product; it is related as one-to-one, therefore, to the product number, so we assign it to the product file. We then need an order date field, which is always the same for a given order; it is related as one-to-one to the order number, so we assign it to the orders file. (This also relates it as many-to-one to the product number and description, which is what we want.) Next, we need an order quantity field; like the date, it is related as one-to-one to the order number, so we assign it to the orders file.

This process, clearly, can be continued for each new field. And, since most requirements reflect common needs, an experienced programmer will easily design a correct database. Only in unusual situations do we have to analyze carefully the requirements to determine how to treat a new field.

The foregoing example, while very simple, already demonstrates that it is the application's requirements, not some database principles, that determine what is a correct database. Thus, if the requirements changed and the product description were permitted to differ from one order to the next, the description field would have to be in the orders file rather than the product file (because it would now be related as one-to-one to the order number, date, and quantity, and as many-to-one to the product number). Similarly, if the requirements permitted several lines in an order, the product number and quantity would be related as many-to-one to the order number. So they would be assigned to a separate file, order lines, where the key is the combination of order number and line number, and several records correspond to one order record. The order date, though, would stay in the orders file, because it continues to be related as one-to-one to the order number.

We know that relationships can be one-to-one, one-to-many (or many-to-one, if seen in reverse), many-to-many, and combinations of these. So, if we understand the role that a new field must play in the application, we already know what relationship to create, and hence to which file to assign it. (Key fields duplicated in another file in order to relate the two files are treated differently, of course.) All we need in order to design a correct database is to study the application's requirements. Then, we use an appropriate combination of relationships to represent these requirements. In other words, we create the database that matches the requirements – one field at a time. Ultimately, if we understand the requirements, we are bound to create a correct database.

And when we create a correct database, the problem of redundancy and inconsistencies does not arise. (The only time we must deal with this problem is when we *deliberately* introduce redundancy into the database; that is, when avoiding it would make the application too slow.) This is true because in a correct database all field relationships reflect actual requirements. Thus, in the foregoing example we assigned the product description to the product file because the requirements stated that it was the same for all orders. If we assigned it to the orders file instead, we would end up with unwanted duplication: a product's description would be repeated unnecessarily in each order that includes the product. The duplication can be explained by noting that this relationship does not reflect the requirements: the description field would be related as many-to-one to the fields in the product record, while the requirements called for a one-to-one relationship. (Alternatively, the error can be described as a one-to-one relationship with the fields in the orders record, while the requirements called for a one-to-many relationship with these fields.)

The most important lesson from this analysis is that data redundancy and inconsistencies can only be defined within the context of a particular set of requirements. So this is not a problem that can be solved by means of a formal database theory. This is a *programming* problem, one that can be solved only by taking into account both the database structures and the other structures that make up the application. It is the way we plan to use the files that determines what are the correct relationships. And with correct relationships, there will be no redundancy or inconsistencies.

A database, then, can be correct only for a specific set of requirements. With just a small change in requirements, the same database would no longer be correct. The incorrectness may manifest itself in the form of wrong values or unnecessarily duplicated values. In the earlier example, storing the description in the product record is correct if it must be the same in all orders, and wrong if it must change; conversely, storing it with each order is correct if it must change, and wrong if it must be the same in all orders. The presence of redundancy and inconsistencies, therefore, when unintended, is similar to any other programming error: we neglected the requirements, and consequently the application malfunctions. The error, in this case, is a discrepancy between the required file relationships and the actual ones.

It is worth repeating: the concept of file and field relationships applies to relational databases *exactly* as it does to traditional ones, because both types are based on files, records, fields, and keys. Thus, even those programmers who prefer the relational model can benefit from the traditional design methods. They too can avoid data redundancy and inconsistencies by creating a correct database directly from requirements. Even with a relational database system, therefore, there is no need for a theory of normalization – because, if we create correct relationships, there is no redundancy or inconsistency to eliminate. As is the case with the traditional databases, we simply need to understand the application's requirements and the four types of relationships.

We can appreciate even better the connection between file relationships and the application's requirements if we remember that requirements are in effect rules, or restrictions. Specifically, from all the operations that the application can perform, and from all possible values that memory variables and database fields can take, only a few must be permitted if the application is to run correctly. One type of restrictions concerns the *combinations* of values that the database fields will display at run time: how the value of one field depends on the value of another. And it is through the four types of file relationships that we implement these restrictions.

Two fields are related as one-to-one when they can have any combination of values; that is, when neither field depends on the other. Two fields are related as one-to-many when one field is restricted to a specific value by a series of values in the other. (Many-to-one is the same relationship seen in reverse.) And two fields are related as many-to-many when there are two simultaneous one-to-many restrictions: one field is restricted by the values of the other, and at the same time possesses values that restrict the other.

By interpreting the requirements as restrictions, we can explain the problem of redundancy as follows: we provide for all possible combinations of values in a situation where only a few can actually occur. If the requirement is for one-to-many and we place the two fields by mistake in the same file, they will be related as one-to-one. We provide for *any* combination of values when, in fact, the first field will have the *same* value for a series of values in the second. So that one value will be repeated unnecessarily every time the second field's value is in that series. We only need to specify their relationship once, and yet we do it several times.

There is an obvious correspondence between the various file relationships and the normal forms of the normalization theory: the relationship that is correct for a given requirement corresponds to the highest normal form attainable for that requirement (the one for which the files are deemed to be fully normalized). The relational theorists avoid the subject of file relationships – perhaps because this would reveal the shallowness of the normalization theory. Let us take a moment, though, to study this correspondence.

The first normal form is the highest one attainable when the application's requirements place no restriction on the combinations of values that two fields can take. From the perspective of the normalization theory, this means that there is no dependency between the two fields; so they can be assigned to the same file (or to separate files if those files are in a one-to-one relationship).

The second and higher normal forms can be attained when the application's requirements place some restrictions on the combinations of values. Because of these restrictions, the correct relationship is now one-to-many; and if we create one-to-one instead (by placing the fields in the same file), we will have a relationship that permits *any* combinations, while the actual data includes in fact only *some* combinations. The normalization theory describes this problem as a misplaced dependency: the only dependency permitted within a tuple is that of a non-key field on the field or fields that make up the key. We also note the mistake in that the file is only in first normal form, while a higher normal form is now attainable. The solution is to place its fields in separate files, thereby creating files that are in second, third, or Boyce/Codd normal form. (Which form is actually attainable depends on the combination of field types, key or non-key, that constitutes the misplaced dependency.) In traditional terms, what we do when using two files instead of one is replace the incorrect one-to-one relationship with a one-to-many relationship, which is what the requirements had called for to begin with.

Combinations of these three normal forms correspond to combinations of one-to-many relationships: two "many" files sharing the same "one" file, or two "one" files sharing the same "many" file. They also correspond, therefore, to a many-to-many relationship between two files. The more complicated fourth and fifth normal forms correspond to various many-to-many relationships involving three or more files, when some of the two-file relationships are restricted.

But this correspondence, while perhaps interesting, is irrelevant; for, in practice we don't need to know anything about field dependencies, or about the notion of normal forms. We can create the correct relationships directly from requirements, as we saw earlier. We don't have to start with an incorrect, one-to-one relationship (as the normalization theory says), note the redundancy and inconsistencies, and then try to attain the correct relationship by discovering misplaced dependencies.

5

We are now in a position to explain the fallacies behind the delusion of normalization. We saw that all we need in order to create correct file relationships is to understand the application's requirements. We can avoid data redundancy and inconsistencies, therefore, simply by implementing relationships that match the requirements. But, while not especially difficult, this task demands skills that most programmers lack.

Without exception, the mechanistic software theories attempt to solve the problem of programming incompetence, not by encouraging programmers to improve their skills, but by providing *substitutes* for skills. The relational theory, in particular, was meant to obviate the need for database programming skills. Instead of the traditional file operations, which must be used through a programming language, programmers will only need to understand the high-level relational operations. Moreover, the mathematical foundation of the theory will guarantee data correctness: since the relational operations are as exact as mathematical functions, and since any database requirement can be expressed as a combination of these operations, even inexperienced programmers will create correct database structures.

But, as we saw under the first delusion, the mathematical database model is a fantasy. To attain such a model, we must restrict it so much that it loses all practical value. If we divide the use of a mathematical system into translation (the conversion of the actual phenomenon into its mathematical representation) and manipulation (the work performed with the mathematical entities within the system), only the manipulation can be formal and exact. The translation entails an *interpretation* of the phenomenon, so it is necessarily informal. The relational model is senseless because it consists almost entirely of the translation. The manipulation, while indeed exact, forms a very small part of the model; and, besides, it is so simple that we can implement the same operations by relying on common sense alone. The theorists praise the mathematical benefits of the model, but these benefits can only help us to deal with a few, simple aspects of database work. Most work, including the most difficult aspects, lie outside the scope of the formal model. So, in the end, we need the same programming skills as before.

If the manipulation includes only the little that can be reduced to an exact representation, every other aspect of database work must become part of the translation. This includes the *design* of the database; that is, discovering the combinations of files and fields that correctly represent the real entities and the relationships between them. With a traditional database or a relational one, this is an informal activity: using our knowledge and experience, we study the application's requirements and ensure that the database entities and relationships match the real ones. And if we accomplish this, there will be no redundancy or inconsistencies. The relational theory never promised to replace this activity with an exact method; it simply left the issue out of the formal model (along with such other issues as integrity rules, updating operations, database language, and database performance).

The relational theory, thus, failed to eliminate the need for programming skills. Programmers continued to create incorrect database structures, but the theorists did not recognize this problem – the fact that so much had to be left out of the formal model – as a falsification of the relational concept. So, instead of studying the problem, they introduced an additional concept – the normalization theory. Their attitude, in other words, did not change: confronted with the evidence that mechanistic theories cannot be a substitute for expertise, they hoped to contend with the persisting incompetence by inventing yet another substitute. The second relational delusion (the delusion of normalization) emerged, therefore, because the theorists refused to face the first one (the delusion of a formal database model).

The normalization theory differs from the original relational theory in that it promises us exact methods for identifying the incorrect file relationships, not *before*, but *after* they are implemented. Rather than invoking the power of mathematics to *prevent* a bad design (something that everyone now agrees is impossible), we are told that the same power can be invoked to *correct* a bad design. Clearly, the theorists do not see the absurdity of this idea. For, were it possible to discover formally the incorrect relationships in an *existing* database, we could also discover them formally *while designing* the database. The phenomenon is the same in both cases: file relationships that do not match the application's requirements.

So the theorists still fail to understand why the original model could not help us to design correct file relationships. This is not a technical problem that might be solved with an additional theory, but a fundamental limitation: it is only through an informal interpretation of the requirements that we can determine what *are* the correct relationships. Thus, there is no difference between determining this *while* designing the database or *after*. In both cases, we must process the database structures together with the other structures that make up the application; in particular, the business practices reflected in the application. In both cases, then, we must deal with the complex structure that is the whole application, and this is something that only minds can do.

The normalization theory claims to eliminate the need for expertise by eliminating the need to design correct databases. Unlike the traditional design methods, which expect us to create file relationships that match the requirements, the new method permits us to create relationships that are as incorrect as we like. To take an extreme case, we can ignore the need for file relationships altogether: we create a database that consists of just one file, and assign *all* the fields to this file, regardless of their actual relationships. We can do this because the database we create now is only a starting point. By applying the principles of normalization, we will be able to transform the incorrect database, step by step, into a correct one.

As we know, files created within the formal model are already in first normal form. To attain the higher normal forms, we must modify the database by discovering and eliminating the misplaced field dependencies. And this can be accomplished, we are told, through the formal methods provided by the normalization theory. Through one procedure we eliminate one type of dependency, and thereby convert the files from first to second normal form; then, through another procedure we eliminate a different type of dependency, and convert them from second to third normal form, and so on. We continue this process until we find at a certain level – a level that varies from one database to another – that there are no misplaced dependencies left. At that point, the database is fully normalized. By eliminating all misplaced dependencies, we eliminated the possibility for any data redundancy or inconsistencies to emerge later, when the database is used.

The normalization theory, thus, claims to have solved the problem of programming incompetence by replacing the challenge of designing a correct database, with an easier challenge: eliminating the errors found in an existing, incorrect database. This shift, the theorists believe, reduces database design to a series of simple, mechanical activities. Their naivety is so great that, although the logic is the same (matching the file relationships to the application's requirements), and although the ultimate database is the same, they believe that the new principles are formal and exact while the old ones are not.

In the end, the problem of design became the problem of dependency: an elaborate system for defining, analyzing, and classifying the field dependencies found in a database. Date describes this shift perfectly: "The fact is, the theory of normalization and related topics – now usually known as *dependency theory* – has grown into a very considerable field in its own right, with several distinct (though of course interrelated) aspects and with a very extensive literature. Research in the area is continuing, and indeed flourishing."[4] But this research is a fraud: the theorists are distorting and complicating the problem of database design in order to have a reason for seeking an alternative. The delusion is not so much in the shift from design to dependency, as in the belief that this shift has turned the problem into a formal theory; specifically, the belief that we have now exact methods to prevent redundancy and inconsistencies.

In reality, redundancy, inconsistencies, and misplaced dependencies are different aspects of the same phenomenon: a discrepancy between the file relationships and the application's requirements. Thus, whether we wish to avoid redundancy and inconsistencies, or to eliminate misplaced dependencies, the only way to do it is by interpreting the requirements correctly; and this task cannot be formalized. What the theorists did is *add* to this task a complicated system of principles and procedures – the theory of normalization. And it is only this theory that is formal and exact. Their "research," then, is merely a preoccupation with this theory, with the problems they invented themselves. The real problem – creating a correct database – is as informal as before. So, if the normalization principles did not replace the original problem, if we continue to assess dependencies informally, the normalization theory is fraudulent.

---

[4] C. J. Date, *An Introduction to Database Systems*, 6th ed. (Reading, MA: Addison-Wesley, 1995), p. 337.

To repeat, dependency is indeed part of the same phenomenon that causes redundancy and inconsistencies. So the shift from design principles to dependency principles is wrong only because it is unnecessary, because it complicates the problem without providing any benefits in return. Recalling the earlier examples, repeating the unchangeable product description in every order entails redundancy. We can describe this redundancy as the result of an incorrect relationship: we created a one-to-one relationship between the description field and fields like order number, when their required relationship is one-to-many. But we can also describe the redundancy as the result of a misplaced dependency: the description depends on the part number, which is not the key in the orders file. Regardless of how we describe the redundancy, though, it is the incorrect relationship between the product description and the other fields that is the root of the problem. And in both cases it is this relationship that must be modified in order to solve the problem.

Generally, with the traditional design concept we create the correct relationships from the start. With the normalization theory, we start by creating one-to-one relationships – which are usually wrong, because most relationships are one-to-many or many-to-many; we then search for misplaced dependencies, which direct us to the incorrect relationships; and finally, we modify the relationships in order to eliminate those dependencies, and with them the redundancy and inconsistencies.

But with both the traditional method and the new one, we always reach the point where we must decide, for a given field, whether it must be in the same file as some other fields, or in another file. With the traditional method, this decision is also the design. With the normalization theory, this decision is only a small part in a long and complicated process. For, now we must also identify the current normal form, determine the type of dependency between fields and the higher normal form that would eliminate it, and convert the files to that normal form.

The decision itself, however, entails the same challenge: interpreting the application's requirements correctly. Thus, what is the critical step with both design methods – discovering the correct relationship between two fields – is necessarily an *informal* process. So the formality of the normalization theory is silly if normalization depends ultimately on an informal process, just like the traditional method. Before, we made that decision in order to create a correct file relationship. Now we make it in order to correct an incorrect one. But, if in the end it is only through our interpretation of the requirements that we can determine what *is* the correct relationship, we may as well use the traditional method, which is so much simpler.

❖

To conclude, there are two stages to the delusion of normalization. The first stage is the belief that we need a theory of normalization at all; namely, that preventing redundancy and inconsistencies is a special problem, which demands a formal theory. This problem, though, is no different from all the other problems that make up the challenge of programming. Regardless of which aspect of the application we are dealing with, we must create structures of software entities that correctly represent the structures of real entities. And to accomplish this task we must understand the application's requirements and the means of implementing them. Moreover, a given requirement usually affects *several* aspects of the application, so it is rarely possible to isolate these aspects and deal with them separately. The database structures, in particular, are always linked to the other structures that make up the application. Searching for a formal theory of database design is an absurd and futile quest.

The theorists assume that it is impossible, or very difficult, to design a correct database directly from requirements; that programmers cannot attain the necessary expertise, so this task must be replaced with a method which they can follow mechanically; and that it is possible to discover such a method. But, quite apart from the fact that no formal method can exist, the traditional design principles already provide a fairly simple method for creating correct databases. All we need to do is determine, for each new field, the appropriate relationship with the existing fields (one-to-one, one-to-many, many-to-one, or many-to-many). If we do this, we will end up with a correct database – a database that matches the requirements. And, among the many benefits of a correct design, there will be no redundancy or inconsistencies.

The second stage in the delusion of normalization is the belief that the body of principles that make up this theory constitutes indeed a formal solution to the problem of database design. In reality, the database structures are still based on the relationships between fields, and we can only determine the correct relationships by interpreting the requirements; in other words, informally, just as before. The theorists think that studying field dependencies rather than field relationships has resulted in a method that is formal and exact, but what is formal and exact is only the new principles. These principles did not replace the informal task of understanding the requirements; so that task – upon which the correctness of the database ultimately depends – has remained unchanged.

If we divide the design process into two parts, formal and informal, the traditional method is almost entirely informal, while the new one is almost entirely formal. But this improvement is an illusion. What confuses the theorists is that the part which they invented, and which is indeed formal, keeps growing, while the traditional part (understanding the requirements) remains the same. Recalling an earlier quotation, research in this area is flourishing. Thus, the more preoccupied they are with the dependency theory, the smaller the informal part appears to be. The informal part, after all, consists simply in determining, for a given field, its relationship with the other fields. In the end, though, this decision is the only thing that matters – what will make the database correct or incorrect – with both the traditional method and the new one. But, while this decision is practically the whole design process with the traditional method, with the new method it is such a small part that it goes unnoticed. So the theorists delude themselves that the new method is entirely formal.

The formal part, thus, did not eliminate the informal one in the new method; it is *additional* to it. The formal part, while impressive, is absurd if the correctness of the database depends ultimately on the small part that is informal – on the part that, with the traditional method, is the only thing we need.

So the conclusion must be that the concept of normalization is worthless. It is an artificial, unnecessary theory. The critical part is still the informal task of determining what field relationships match the application's requirements. But by spending most of their time with formal and complicated procedures, and only moments with that informal task, the relational enthusiasts can claim that database design is now an exact science.

We examined earlier the first stage of the delusion of normalization: the belief that we need some new, formal principles, when in fact the traditional concepts provide an excellent and relatively simple design method. In the following pages we examine the second stage: the belief that the principles of normalization provide indeed a formal design method, when in fact the critical part is as informal as before.

6

Like predicate calculus, which inspired it, the formal relational model is a true mathematical system, complete with operations and formulas. Its weakness, we saw under the first delusion, is only that it is irrelevant to database work: when we depict the use of a relational system as the *translation* of database entities into mathematical ones and their *manipulation* within the system, we find that the manipulation – the most important aspect in other mathematical systems, and the reason for performing the translation – plays an insignificant part.

The normalization theory, on the other hand, is not a mathematical system at all. The theorists discuss it as seriously as they do the formal relational model, but on closer analysis we discover that all they do is *present* it formally. There are no true operations or formulas in this theory, as there are in the formal model; all we have is a study of field dependencies, expressed through formal notation. The theory of normalization, in other words, consists *entirely* of a process of translation: from the real entities into the relational ones. There is no manipulation at all. The only operations available are those we had under the formal relational model.

An example of the specious mathematics of the normalization theory is found in a long paper written by E. F. Codd – a paper generally regarded as the most rigorous treatment of the second and third normal forms.[5] The paper provides an exhaustive analysis of field dependencies and their elimination, but despite the formal tone and terminology, this is not a mathematical theory. The paper describes various combinations of data elements, and represents their relationships and dependencies by means of a formal system of notation. The resulting expressions *look* perhaps like mathematical formulas, but they serve no purpose beyond this representation. Page after page of expressions are, in reality, only the *translation* of files and fields into the new notation. Once the translation is complete, we have no way to *manipulate* the expressions. All the system does, then, is represent field dependencies formally. Were this a true mathematical system, we would have some new relational operations, to replace the original ones.

We find the same style in thousands of other writings. What is described as mathematics is merely a system of definitions and theorems expressing in formal notation various issues pertaining to the subject of field dependency. Typically, the papers introduce new terms and define them through references to other terms, show how to derive certain parts of the system from other parts, prove that if certain conditions hold then other conditions will also hold, and so forth. And this is where the mathematics ends.

It is the introduction of new terms that the authors are especially fond of. The relational theory in general overwhelms us with new terminology, but the principles of normalization in particular seem to require some new terms at every step. Thus, along with the formal tone, the rich terminology helps to make the normalization theory appear important, no matter how shallow it actually is. But, while the mathematical style of these writings impresses naive readers, an intelligent person merely finds the writings incomprehensible. The reason is that, since we know that the whole theory is unnecessary, we have little motivation to assimilate the countless terms and definitions; and without understanding the new concepts it is impossible to follow the author's discussion.

To convey the flavour of this style, I will quote a few lines from Date's book (out of the seventy pages devoted to the subject of normalization). After

---

[5] E. F. Codd, "Further Normalization of the Data Base Relational Model," in *Data Base Systems*, ed. Randall Rustin (Englewood Cliffs, NJ: Prentice Hall, 1972), pp. 33–64.

presenting several related theorems, Date defines the fourth normal form as follows: "Relation R is in 4NF if and only if, whenever there exist subsets A and B of the attributes of R such that the (nontrivial) MVD $A \twoheadrightarrow B$ is satisfied, then all attributes of R are also *functionally* dependent on A."[6] Concepts like "nontrivial," "MVD," and "functionally dependent," used in this definition, are explained on previous pages. For example, MVD (multivalued dependency) is defined as follows: "Let R be a relation, and let A, B, and C be arbitrary subsets of the set of attributes of R. Then we say that B is *multidependent* on A – in symbols, $A \twoheadrightarrow B$ (read 'A multidetermines B,' or simply 'A double-arrow B') – if and only if the set of B-values matching a given (A-value, C-value) pair in R depends only on the A-value and is independent of the C-value."[7]

It is also worth mentioning the following warning: "We stress the point that the discussions that follow are intended to explain a *formal theory*, albeit in a fairly informal manner."[8] In other words, definitions and explanations like those quoted above, and the endless formulas and diagrams, are not the actual theory but a *simplified* version. For the *really* formal discussion we must consult the original papers, in academic journals.

To summarize, all that the normalization theory does is represent formally the relationships between fields. A true mathematical system would provide operations that combine entities to create increasingly high levels, as do the systems used in engineering. There are no such operations here, so the normalization theory does not describe a mathematical system. What it describes is *a formal system of representation*. This system may have its uses, but not in the way a mathematical system has. In the end, the only mathematical manipulation remains the one provided by the original relational model. The normalization theory is not a true enhancement of that model.

So what the relational theorists invented is akin to a game. The normalization work is *additional* to the task of studying and implementing the application's requirements. That task has remained as important – and as informal – as before. It is only the game that is formal and exact. This is a sophisticated and difficult game, demanding a special kind of knowledge. It is not surprising, therefore, that the academics who invented it, and the practitioners who learn it, feel that their normalization work is a sign of expertise. This is expertise in playing a game, though, not in programming.

[6] Date, *Database Systems*, p. 329.   [7] Ibid., p. 328.   [8] Ibid., p. 327.

7

The reason we cannot have a formal *and* useful theory of normalization is that the dependency of one field on another is not a *database* problem, but part of the application's logic. Formal normalization principles can only deal with the *database* structures. They cannot take into account the other structures that make up the application – the business practices, for instance. And it is these other structures that determine, ultimately, the relationships between database fields. A formal theory, thus, can deal with such issues as the definition and classification of dependencies, or the conversion from one normal form to another; but it cannot tell us whether the relationships are correct. In particular, no formal theory can tell us to which file to assign a given field. Only our knowledge of the application can do this.

Recalling the earlier examples, assigning the product description to the same file as the product number is not right or wrong in an absolute sense, but only relative to the requirements being implemented: if the description is fixed, it should be in the same file; if changeable, in the other file. We *must* understand the requirements. And when we do, we already know how to implement them: as a one-to-one or as a one-to-many relationship. Thus, a formal theory cannot replace the need to study the requirements, and is unnecessary once we understand them. It is, in other words, useless.

Let us take another example. An employee file usually includes such fields as department, position, salary, seniority code, and vacation code. Now, these fields may be related in one company, and unrelated in another. The salary, for instance, may be independent, or the same for all the employees with a particular position; the vacation code may be independent, or the same for all the employees with a particular seniority; the position and salary may be independent, or the same for all the employees in a particular department. Some of these fields, therefore, may be dependent on others, in which case they should be moved into separate files: a salary file where the key is the position, a vacation code file where the key is the seniority code, and so on. But only *we* can know whether a given field is or is not independent; and we would know this in the same way we know the other requirements that define the payroll application. The same application, in fact, may be used by two companies while a certain field is independent in one but not in the other. So, just like the business practices that make up an application, the normalization requirements may be different in each case; and as a result, a database that is deemed to be normalized for one company may not be for the other. Again, since it is only *we* that can discover the field relationships, a formal theory is useless.

Another situation where the need for normalization is determined largely by our knowledge of the application occurs when files are updated only under certain conditions. Thus, some files may be used by the application in such a way that a relationship of dependency between two fields in the same record would be harmless. For example, records may be added but not modified or deleted; or those fields alone may never be modified. Also, there are situations where it may be simpler or more efficient to deal with the problem of dependency through the application's logic, rather than through database restrictions. In all these situations, what we do is simplify the application or improve its performance by noting that not all conceivable database operations will *actually* be performed. Clearly, no formal theory can include such knowledge.

The only formal theory of normalization possible is one that assumes the worst case; namely, the case where *every* field may depend on another field. As we saw, we eliminate each dependency by separating the two fields: we place one field in a new file, where the records are linked through their key to the field left in the first file. Thus, if we want to be absolutely certain that there are no dependencies, and if we don't want to rely on an interpretation of the requirements, we must separate in this manner every field, in every file. In the end, every file in the database will have only one non-key field. This is an exact, formal procedure – a procedure that can even be automated. However, because many of the separated fields must be put back together in the running application, this overnormalization would make the application too complicated and too slow; so no one seriously suggests that we follow it. (In fact, as we will see under the third delusion, even minimal normalization – separating just a few fields – is often impractical and must be forsaken.)

A database where the smallest necessary number of fields (rather than an arbitrarily large number) were separated in an attempt to eliminate all dependencies is said to be in optimal second normal form. This sounds like a precise definition, but in reality it is only informally, through our knowledge of the application, that we can determine whether or not the normalization of a given database is "optimal." Again, the only way to have a formal theory is by separating *every* field in the database, regardless of how it is used in the application.

But even if we succeeded somehow in developing an exact and complete theory of normalization, it would still be inadequate. This is true because normalization deals only with dependencies that can be eliminated by separating fields. There are many other types of field dependencies in an application, all a natural part of the application's logic. Every application includes operations that relate fields in the same record, or fields in separate files. Some of these fields, therefore, depend on others; so they are, strictly speaking, unnecessary. But we cannot eliminate these dependencies through normalization, by separating fields.

Let us examine a simple example of the type of dependency that cannot be eliminated through normalization – the classic case of aged balances. The customer balance, for instance, is usually stored in several fields in the customer record: current, thirty-day, sixty-day, and ninety-day balances. And there is usually an additional field, for the total balance, which is the sum of the other four. But if the total balance is always the sum of the aged balances, its field can be eliminated. Instead of having a separate field, we can calculate the total balance (by adding the other fields) wherever we need it in the application. The reason we usually retain the total balance field is that this is simpler than calculating it: in most applications we modify it in only a couple of places (typically, when invoicing the customer and when receiving payments), but we show it in dozens of inquiries and reports. So it is simpler to update the total balance in the few places where an aged balance changes, and merely to *read* it in the other places.

It is obvious that the dependency of the total balance on the aged balances cannot be eliminated through normalization, by moving the total balance into a new file. What we do for this type of dependency, therefore, is similar to what we do when we decide *not* to normalize in situations where normalization *is* possible: we anticipate the problems that may be caused by the updating operations, and we add to the application's logic the necessary steps to prevent them. Thus, in the case of balances, we must remember to update the total balance too, when one of the aged ones is updated. And if we neglect this, we will face "update anomalies" (the total balance will no longer equal the sum of the aged ones) not unlike those that occur in unnormalized files when we ignore the effect of updating operations.

To continue this example, in most applications the aged balances themselves can be calculated, using a transactions file: we read the records belonging to a particular customer, and total the invoice and payment amounts under four different periods. So the aged balance fields too are dependent on other fields, and hence unnecessary (although the original data is now in another file). Also like the previous dependency, this dependency cannot be resolved through normalization. To prevent "update anomalies" (balance fields different from the sum of the transactions), we must either eliminate the balance fields, or ensure that they are updated whenever a record is added to the transactions file. (In this case, though, eliminating the fields is rarely practical, because it is too inefficient to calculate them by reading the transaction records every time.)

So what is the point in seeking a formal theory of normalization, if this theory would eliminate only *some* dependencies? Clearly, there is no limit to the types of field dependencies that can exist in an application – types like the ones we have just examined. In fact, we don't even think of these dependencies as a database problem, but as various aspects of the application's logic. Since most software requirements involve database fields – fields belonging to one file or to several files – it is natural to find relationships of dependency between fields. And it would be absurd to eliminate these relationships solely in order to avoid redundancy, or to avoid inconsistencies in updating operations. What we do in each case is seek the most effective design: we eliminate the dependency when practical, and deal with the updating problems as part of the application's logic when this is simpler or makes the application faster.

In the end, all field dependencies cause similar problems, and we can only deal with these problems by taking into account not just the database structures but *all* the structures that make up the application. These are not *database* problems but ordinary programming problems, similar to the many other problems we face when developing an application. And it is just as futile to search for an exact and complete theory of field dependency as it is to search for an exact and complete theory of programming. The relational theorists isolated *one type* of dependency – the type that can be eliminated by separating fields; and they naively concluded that, if we eliminate this one type, we will eliminate *all* the problems caused by dependency (or, at least, the most common problems).

This belief is reflected in the relational vocabulary (terms like "normalize" and "normal form" imply a particular, proper data format) and in the numbering system (the fifth normal form is said to be the last and most stringent one). Hardly ever are the other types of dependencies mentioned at all. Date discusses them briefly: "5NF is the *ultimate* normal form with respect to projection and join…. That is, a relation in 5NF is *guaranteed to be free of anomalies* that can be eliminated by taking projections [i.e., by separating fields]…. Of course, this remark does not mean that the relation is free of *all possible* anomalies. It just means (to repeat) that it is free of anomalies that can be removed by taking projections."[9] Most authors, however, depict the process of normalization as a final refinement, as a guarantee of database validity.

Thus, by emphasizing the few dependencies that can be eliminated through normalization while disregarding the many that cannot, the relational experts make the normalization principles appear more important than they really are. Then, they use this misrepresentation to rationalize their search for a theory of normalization.

[9] Ibid., p. 334 and footnote.

8

If the theory of normalization is unnecessary, if the traditional design method permits us to avoid redundancy and inconsistencies simply by understanding the application's requirements, how do the theorists justify their lengthy discussions? By distorting the problem of database design. They describe some contrived database structures that are incorrect but hardly ever occur in practice, and then they show us how to turn them into correct ones.

The only theory they can offer us is one that studies the so-called normal forms and gives us methods to convert files from one form to another. But we need such a theory only if we normally create incorrect databases. The theorists present the incorrect databases as a common occurrence, and the concept of normalization appears then important. In reality, we can create correct databases from the start, by selecting file relationships that match the application's requirements. So the classification of normal forms and the conversion procedures have no practical value.

I will illustrate this distortion now with a few examples taken from database books. In all these situations, we will see, the correct design can be easily determined from the requirements. The authors, however, *ignore* the requirements, and start with a *deliberately incorrect* design: a single file, when several are needed. They start, that is, with a one-to-one relationship when the requirements call for one-to-many or many-to-many. They point to the problems caused by the incorrect design, and *then* they study the requirements and show us how to arrive at the correct one: through normalization.

The examples, in other words, are presented so as to make the theory of normalization, which in reality is totally unnecessary, look like an indispensable concept in database design. Moreover, their method is so lengthy and complicated that the reader is likely to miss the fact that its preciseness and formality are specious: the most important decisions – identifying the misplaced field dependencies – are still being made, not mathematically, but through an *informal interpretation* of the requirements.

Brathwaite demonstrates the second normal form with this simple problem:[10] we want to store some information about students and about the classes they

[10] Ken S. Brathwaite, *Relational Databases: Concepts, Design, and Administration* (New York: McGraw-Hill, 1991), pp. 76–77.

attend; students are identified by a student number, and we must record their name and major; classes are identified by a class number, and we must record the class location and time; a student may attend several classes, and we must be able to identify these classes.

Ignoring all we know about normalization, we note that the students and classes form a many-to-many relationship (a student attends several classes, and a class is attended by several students). So the student number and class number must be in separate files: a student file, where the student number is the key, and a class file, where the class number is the key. The student name and major are both related as one-to-one to the student number, so they must be non-key fields in the student file. Similarly, the class location and time are related as one-to-one to the class number, so they must be non-key fields in the class file. Lastly, to link the two files, we need a service file where the key is the combination of student number and class number. In a traditional database, the service file could then have two indexes: class number within student number (to select the class records associated with a student), and student number within class number (to select the student records associated with a class). But the requirements call only for the link from student to classes, so we need in fact only the first index. (It is worth noting that in a real application the link file wouldn't be just a service file; it would also have some non-key fields, for data that is related as one-to-one to its key – the student's grade, for instance.)

Brathwaite, though, attempts to implement the requirements with *one* file: the combination of student number and class number is the key, while the student name and major, and the class location and time, are non-key fields. Then, he notes the problems caused by this design: no information can be stored about a particular student unless the student is enrolled in at least one class, or about a particular class unless at least one student attends it. Also, a certain name and major will be repeated for every class attended by that student, and a certain location and time will be repeated for every student attending that class; so if these values change, several records would have to be updated.

What causes these problems, Brathwaite explains, is the dependency of non-key fields on *part* of the key: while the key includes both the student and the class numbers, the student name and major depend only on the student number, and the class location and time only on the class number. Non-key fields must depend on the whole key, so the solution is to create a separate file for the two student-related fields, with the student number alone as the key, and another file for the two class-related fields, with the class number alone as the key. What will be left in the original file is just its key, the student and class numbers. This design eliminates all the aforementioned problems.

The final database, thus, is identical to the one we created earlier, directly from the requirements. We knew all along that it was correct, simply because it reflects accurately the requirements. Now, however, we are told that it is correct because the files are in second normal form (whereas the original file, with all fields bundled together, was only in first normal form).

What is the point of this approach? Starting with one file would make sense, perhaps, if the method used to reach the final design were indeed formal and exact (in which case we could even automate the design process). But the misplaced dependencies were discovered *informally*, by interpreting the requirements. For instance, when noting that the name and major depend only on the student number, we used the same information and the same logic as we used earlier, when noting that they are related as one-to-one to the student number. With normalization as much as with the traditional method, we relied on skill and common sense, not on mathematics. Thus, if we know how to determine the relationship between two fields, we may as well use this knowledge directly to assign them to the proper files. Why bundle them first in one file, and then use this knowledge to *separate* them?

So the part that is formal – the classification of field dependencies – did not replace the need for, nor the importance of, the part that is informal. The correctness of the normalization depends, ultimately, on the correct interpretation of the requirements. The fancy terminology makes the process of normalization seem more exact than the traditional method, when in reality it is merely more complicated.

Date starts his discussion of the second and third normal forms with the following problem.[11] Let us imagine that we purchase parts from a number of suppliers, located in different cities and identified by a supplier number; the cities are identified by the city name, and each city has a status associated with it; several suppliers may be located in the same city; a supplier can sell different parts, which are identified by a part number; and we want to record our purchase orders by storing for each order the supplier number, part number, and quantity. (The requirements assume, for the sake of simplicity, that only one order exists at a given time for each combination of supplier and part number, so we don't need order numbers. Also, the requirements call for the capability to identify directly the city of a given supplier, but not the suppliers in a given city.)

With our knowledge of file and field relationships, we can translate these

[11] Date, *Database Systems*, pp. 297–303.

requirements into the following design. We note first that the city is related as one-to-many to the supplier, so we need two files: a city file, where the key is the city name, and a supplier file. In one-to-many relationships, the key of the "many" file includes usually the "one" file's key; so here it would be the combination of city name and supplier number. But the present requirements do not call for selecting the suppliers in a given city, so the key in the supplier file can be just the supplier number. We do have to select the city associated with a supplier, though, so we include the city name as a non-key field. The status is related as one-to-one to the city, so we add it as a non-key field to the city file. The supplier number is related as one-to-many to the order-related fields, part number and quantity; so these fields must be in a third file, orders, where the key is the combination of supplier number and part number.

Date, however, says nothing about these relationships. He starts by bundling all five fields (supplier number, status, city name, part number, and quantity) in one file: the orders file, where the key is the combination of supplier number and part number. And immediately he notes the consequent redundancy and anomalies: Since there must be a record in this file for every order, the information that a certain supplier is located in a certain city will be repeated for every order from that supplier; so, if the supplier relocates to another city, we will have to modify several records. Similarly, the information that a certain city has a certain status will be repeated for every order from every supplier in that city; so, if the status changes, we will have to modify several records. Lastly, we cannot store the information that a certain supplier is located in a certain city unless an order exists for that supplier.

Date then presents the solution. The first step is to separate the fields by creating a new file: the supplier file, where the key is the supplier number, and the city name and status are non-key fields. The quantity is left in the orders file. Since each combination of supplier and city appears now in only one record, the redundancy associated with the city, along with the update anomalies, has been eliminated. The solution can be expressed in terms of misplaced dependencies: while non-key fields must depend on the whole key, the city and status in the original file were dependent only on the supplier (they are the same for all the orders from a given supplier). In terms of normalization, the problem was solved because the new files are in second normal form, while the original one was only in first normal form.

But this still leaves the other redundancy: the status of a certain city is repeated in the supplier file for every supplier located in that city. Although not as bad as in the original file (where the repetition was for every *order* from every supplier in that city), this redundancy will nevertheless cause the same kind of problems. The misplaced dependency that must be eliminated now is between the status and the city (two non-key fields). So we create a new file:

the city file, where the key is the city name, and the status is a non-key field. The supplier file will then be left with only the city as a non-key field. In terms of normalization, the problem was solved because these two files are in third normal form. In other words, while the second is the highest normal form attainable for the orders file, we can attain the third for the supplier file by creating a separate city file; and a database is fully normalized only when each file is in its highest attainable normal form. (The difference between the second and third is in the type of misplaced dependency that is eliminated: on only a portion of the key, and on a non-key field.)

So by the time he is done, Date ends up with exactly the same database as the one we created directly from requirements with the traditional design method. The normalization method is more complicated, and we *still* depend on an informal decision: we identify the misplaced field dependencies by interpreting the requirements, the same way we identified the correct field relationships before. What is formal is only the *analysis* of these dependencies and the *conversion* from one normal form to another; that is, the work that is *additional* to the task of identifying them.

Carter uses the example of an employee file to demonstrate the fourth normal form.[12] Specifically, we have to store for each employee, in addition to his name, some data about his children and about his salary history. Thus, we need a set of fields for each child (identified by the child's name), and a set of fields for the salary of each past year (identified by the year). We will have an employee file where the employee number is key, and the name (related as one-to-one to the number) is a non-key field. And we will have two one-to-many relationships, with the employee file acting as shared "one" file: between employee and children, and between employee and salary history. In the children file, the key will be the combination of employee number and child name; and in the salary history file, the combination of employee number and year. We will then be able to select for a given employee the corresponding child records and history records; and for a given child or year, the corresponding employee record.

Carter, however, starts by showing us what would happen if we placed the child and salary history fields in the same file – a file where the key is the combination of employee number, child name, and year: we would have to repeat the entire salary history for each child. For instance, for an employee with 3 children and 10 years of history, there would be 30 records in this file:

---

[12] John Carter, *The Relational Database* (London: Chapman and Hall, 1995), pp. 135–150.

one record for each combination of child and year. This design, therefore, would cause redundancy and anomalies: to add or modify the data for one child, we would have to add or modify 10 records (because the same child data is stored for each year); and to add or modify the history data for one year, we would have to add or modify 3 records (because the same history data is stored for each child).

Now, *no one* would try to combine child data and salary history in one file. Carter must start with this absurd design in order to demonstrate the benefits of normalization. It is pointless to describe his actual analysis – fifteen pages of complicated principles, definitions, and diagrams related to the fourth normal form, not to mention nearly forty prior pages dealing with the lower normal forms. Briefly, that file suffers from multivalued dependencies (i.e., several fields dependent on one another). The solution is to separate it into two files, one for child data and the other for salary history – which is exactly how *we* designed the database to begin with.

The redundancy and anomalies were eliminated, we are told, because these files are in fourth normal form, while the original file was only in Boyce/Codd normal form. But *we* know that the database is correct simply because it expresses two one-to-many relationships, which is what the requirements actually called for. Carter needs an enormously complicated procedure to reach the same design that *we* reached simply by implementing, directly from requirements, the appropriate file relationships. Moreover, the critical observation that the child data and history data must be separated could only be made *informally*, by studying the requirements – just as we identified the file relationships with the traditional design method.

Date explains the fourth normal form with a more difficult example.[13] We are asked to design a database to express the relationships between the courses, teachers, and textbooks in a certain school, with the following requirements: a particular course may be taught by one or more teachers, and a teacher may teach one or more courses; a particular course may use one or more textbooks, and a textbook may be used in one or more courses; a particular course always uses the same textbooks, regardless of the teacher.

Studying the requirements, we note two many-to-many relationships: between courses and teachers, and between courses and textbooks. We need, therefore, three main files (courses, teachers, and textbooks) linked through two service files. To satisfy the requirement that a teacher may teach several

[13] Date, *Database Systems*, pp. 325–329.

courses and at the same time a course may be taught by several teachers, we create a service file where the key is the combination of course and teacher; and to satisfy the requirement that a course may use several textbooks and at the same time a textbook may be used in several courses, we create a service file where the key is the combination of course and textbook.

As usual, in order to implement the two-way links between files (course to teacher and teacher to course, course to textbook and textbook to course), the service files must provide *both* sorting sequences: teachers within courses and courses within teachers, textbooks within courses and courses within textbooks. (Thus, if we use a traditional database, there will be two indexes for each service file.) We will then be able to select for a given course the corresponding records in the teachers file, and for a given teacher the corresponding records in the courses file; and we will also be able to select for a given course the corresponding records in the textbooks file, and for a given textbook the corresponding records in the courses file.

This, then, is how a sensible database book would present the example – the problem and the solution. Let us see now how Date presents it. He starts by attempting to implement all the relationships with *one* service file – a file where the key is the combination of course, teacher, and textbook. (So there is one record in the file for each combination of values in the three fields.) But this design is absurd; it is deliberately incorrect in order to demonstrate the transition from one normal form to another. The file, Date explains, is only in Boyce/Codd normal form, and this gives rise to redundancy and anomalies. For instance, if a particular course uses two textbooks, we will need two records for every teacher who teaches that course, although all teachers use the same textbooks. In addition to this duplication, we would have to add, delete, or modify several records (one for each teacher) when adding, deleting, or modifying the information about a textbook. Expressing the problem in terms of dependencies, the design is incorrect because it permits a multivalued dependency.

But this is a gross simplification of Date's actual explanation – four pages of complicated pseudo-mathematical analysis, which is in fact incomprehensible without a good understanding of some fifty prior pages on the subject of normalization.

The solution, Date concludes, is to have two service files rather than one, and to separate the three key fields into two sets of two fields.[14] More specifically, it is the teacher and textbook fields that must be separated.

---

[14] It must be noted that Date does not call these files *service* files, thus suggesting that they are the main data files (i.e., tables). A real application, though, would also require some non-key fields, to store details about courses, teachers, and textbooks; and such fields would not be added to these files, because that would cause much redundancy.

The result, needless to say, is the two service files we created previously, when we implemented the database as two many-to-many relationships. The redundancy and anomalies were eliminated, we learn now, because these files are in fourth normal form.

The design method based on file relationships, we saw, leads directly to the correct database. Date describes a situation that is a good example of a fundamental database concept, the many-to-many relationship. But instead of discussing this concept, he presents a silly, deliberately incorrect design. Then, he uses this design to justify the need for the normalization theory.

And, as in the previous examples, the complexity of the normalization masks the fact that the critical step (the observation that it is the teachers and textbooks fields that must be separated) was based on an *informal* interpretation of the requirements – exactly the same interpretation that helped us to determine the correct relationships with the traditional method.

9

We saw earlier that the principles of normalization are not, in fact, required by the original relational model: they are not an extension of the formal model, but an attempt to formalize the process of database design (see pp. 746–748). The normalization theory is, in effect, an independent theory – a theory that can be applied to any system based on records, fields, and keys. Thus, we can study the normalization theory on its own, ignoring the relational model altogether. And when doing so, its character as a mechanistic delusion becomes even clearer. By way of summary, therefore, I want to recapitulate the normalization fallacies and to show how they arose from the mechanistic way of thinking that pervades the academic world.

Mechanists attempt to explain a complex phenomenon, which can only be represented with a complex structure, by breaking it down into simpler phenomena: they extract smaller and smaller aspects of it, until they reach an aspect that can be represented with a simple structure. And at that point they discover an exact theory – a theory based on that aspect alone. But this discovery is a trivial, predictable achievement; for, if we keep reifying *any* phenomenon, we are bound to reach, eventually, aspects simple enough to allow an exact theory. The discovery, nevertheless, generates a great deal of excitement, so the mechanists initiate a research program. The more elaborate their research becomes, the more confident they are about its importance. Although it is obvious to everyone that the theory explains only that one isolated aspect, the mechanists promote it as if what it explained were the original, complex phenomenon.

The phenomenon of a database comprises many aspects, of which the most important are the application's *requirements* and the *file relationships*; that is, the *actual* entities and relationships, and their *representation in software*. And these two aspects consist, in their turn, of many aspects. Among the other aspects of this phenomenon are the field dependencies, the data redundancy, and the inconsistencies (the so-called update anomalies).

The aim of the normalization theory is to find a formal, exact method for designing the file relationships from a knowledge of the requirements (or, at least, for determining whether a given set of relationships matches the requirements). Now, it may be possible to represent with one structure the relationships on their own, or the dependencies, or the redundancy, or the inconsistencies, or perhaps even a combination of them. But the database phenomenon as a whole is complex, because these aspects interact with the requirements, which in turn interact with many other aspects of the application. Thus, no mechanistic theory can represent the system that consists of the file relationships *plus* the requirements. No formal method can exist, therefore, to determine whether or not a given set of relationships matches the requirements.

Because they could not discover a theory for the *actual* database phenomenon, the software mechanists tried to discover a theory by breaking down the phenomenon into simpler ones. They noticed that the inconsistencies occur when the file relationships are incorrect; and they also noticed that the inconsistencies are related to data redundancy and to field dependencies. It is the misplaced dependencies, they concluded, that cause redundancy and inconsistencies. And since this one aspect of the original phenomenon is simple enough to represent with an exact theory, they made *it* their subject of research. The *dependency* theory is believed to be the answer to the original problem: if we study, analyze, and classify the various types of field dependencies, the mechanists say, we will discover a formal method for avoiding misplaced ones; this will then prevent data redundancy and inconsistencies; and the lack of redundancy and inconsistencies will indicate that the file relationships match the requirements.

But this logic is fallacious. The dependencies, like the redundancy and the inconsistencies, are merely one aspect of the database phenomenon. They are not the *cause* of correct or incorrect file relationships, but just a different way of viewing them. So it is absurd to study the dependencies in the hope of determining from them the correct relationships. The *requirements* are the real determinant in this phenomenon. It is only from the requirements, therefore, that we can determine other aspects of the phenomenon: when there is no discrepancy between the requirements and the file relationships, there are no misplaced dependencies, no redundancy, and no inconsistencies; and when there is a discrepancy, we note misplaced dependencies, redundancy, and inconsistencies.

It is indeed possible to explain the relationships, the redundancy, and the inconsistencies in terms of dependencies; but this is true because they are closely related aspects of the same phenomenon, not because the dependencies *cause* the other aspects. Thus, instead of a dependency theory we could develop an equally elaborate redundancy theory, to study, analyze, and classify the various types of data redundancy; or an inconsistency theory, for the various types of data inconsistency; or a relationship theory, for the various types of file relationships. And each theory could then be used to "explain" the other three aspects, just as the dependency theory is said to explain the redundancy, the inconsistencies, and the relationships.

From the requirements, then, we can determine the other aspects, but not the other way around. The mechanists base their theory on dependencies because they mistakenly interpret them as the cause of correct or incorrect file relationships. The dependencies on their own, though, are meaningless; for, we cannot decide from a dependency alone whether or not it is misplaced. Similarly, the redundancy or inconsistencies or relationships on their own, or all aspects together, are meaningless. The real cause – what can explain all four aspects – is the requirements. The dependency theory, thus, suffers from the fallacy of confusing cause and effect. It is fundamentally wrong.

Each aspect of the phenomenon of a database has its own representation: the requirements are represented by means of business practices, the file relationships by means of diagrams or programming languages, and the dependencies by means of a system of notation peculiar to the normalization theory. Similar systems could be invented to represent the redundancy and the inconsistencies, if we wanted. Each aspect provides a different view of the database, but neither is complete; only a system embodying *all* these aspects, plus those aspects we are not even discussing here, can represent the phenomenon of a database accurately. Thus, because they form a complex phenomenon, it is impossible to describe these aspects and their relationships exactly and completely. We *can* design correct databases, but this is largely an informal procedure.

Database design entails the conversion from one system of representation to another. What we want to attain, of course, is the *software* representation; that is, the file relationships. So, if it is the requirements that ultimately determine what are the correct relationships, the only conversion worth studying is the traditional one, from requirements to relationships. Because they failed to discover a formal and exact procedure for *this* conversion, the relational mechanists shifted their attention to the study of field dependencies. Their theory does offer a formal and exact conversion, but only from dependencies to relationships. Its exactness is illusory, therefore, because to benefit from it we must ensure first that we have correct dependencies. And the only way to attain the correct dependencies is by performing the conversion from requirements to dependencies, which is as informal as the traditional one, from requirements to relationships (see figure 7-17).

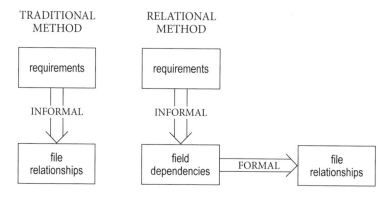

Figure 7-17

The dependency theory may appear impressive to the casual observer, but in reality an exact theory that explains relationships in terms of dependencies is a trivial accomplishment. It is not surprising that one aspect of a phenomenon can be shown to depend on another, if they are closely related. Thus, we could also discover similar theories to explain relationships in terms of redundancy, inconsistencies in terms of dependencies, dependencies in terms of redundancy, and so on. But that first step – from requirements to one of the other aspects – is always necessary, and is always informal. So we may as well use the traditional method, which entails *only* that one step – from requirements to relationships.

Of the five aspects of this phenomenon, the requirements and the file relationships are the most intuitive, and the field dependencies are the least intuitive. This is why, before the relational theory, we had no interest in dependencies; we only studied the requirements and the relationships, and sometimes the redundancy and the inconsistencies. We are asked now to replace what is the simplest method – the intuitive conversion from requirements to relationships – with a method that involves two steps, each one more complicated than our one-step method: the conversion from requirements to dependencies – which the mechanists must perform but don't like to discuss, because it is informal – is less intuitive and already more difficult than requirements to relationships; and in addition, we have now the intricate dependency theory, for the conversion from dependencies to relationships. (It is, perhaps, precisely because the study of field dependencies is so complicated that the mechanists think it is an important discovery.)

The dependency theory is typical of the mechanistic pseudosciences. The relational mechanists settled for a dependency theory only because this is one narrow aspect of the database phenomenon for which they *could* find an exact explanation. They never proved that this theory could model the whole phenomenon. But then they forgot this limitation, and proceeded to treat the theory as if it *did* provide a formal method for database design.

In conclusion, the dependency theory – a major, thirty-year-old research program involving thousands of academics and generating a vast literature – is a worthless, senseless pursuit. No matter how exact it is, it cannot help us to determine what are the correct relationships. Thus, recalling an earlier example, the theory cannot tell us whether to assign the product description field to the product file or to the orders file. We must decide which alternative is correct during the conversion from requirements to dependencies, before we even get to use the theory. The theory may well offer us a formal, faultless conversion from dependencies to relationships, but we can only apply it after determining – informally – what *are* the correct dependencies.

The Third Delusion

1

The third delusion consists of those modifications to the relational model that are presented as *enhancements*, while being in reality *reversals* of the relational principles. These modifications were introduced when it was discovered that the model worked only with small and simple databases, and was totally impractical for serious applications. Thus, while the need for reversals constitutes an obvious refutation of the relational model, the theorists describe these reversals as *new relational features*.

The original theory defined a complete database model, and, although generally worthless, was a falsifiable concept. So, had it remained an academic treatise, it could have been regarded perhaps as a serious study. But because its supporters believed that it could have practical applications, the theory had to be modified again and again. The modifications, as we will see shortly, serve largely to restore the low-level capabilities of the traditional file operations –

capabilities which the relational model had attempted to replace with high-level features. Clearly, by the time we restore these capabilities we no longer have a relational model. The third delusion is in the belief that we can continue to enjoy the benefits promised by the original model even while reversing its principles.

The relational theory, thus, was turned into a pseudoscience when its supporters, instead of admitting that it had been refuted, decided to "improve" it: they suppressed the falsifications, one by one, by incorporating them into the model in the guise of new features. This practice rendered the theory unfalsifiable. (We examined earlier the pseudoscientific nature of the relational theory; see pp. 724–726, 727–728.) The relational model was indeed rescued, but this was accomplished by annulling the relational principles and reinstating the traditional ones. And because they were reinstated *within* the relational model, the traditional principles are now far more complicated than they were on their own. Moreover, relational systems still lack the flexibility and efficiency we enjoy with the traditional file operations.

From its simple origin, and from its mathematical ambitions, the relational theory was degraded in the end to a complicated and messy concept. What is perceived today as the relational model has little to do with the original ideas. And, although we still see the claim that the model is founded upon mathematical principles, relational systems are promoted now on the strength of features that were described originally as *informal* aspects of the model. Today's relational systems consist of large, cumbersome, inefficient, and expensive development environments, which include special programming languages and an endless list of features, definitions, principles, standards, rules, and procedures that we must assimilate. And what is the purpose of this complexity? To provide a substitute for what any programmer should be able to do by using just the six basic file operations.

2

Let us start with the concept of normalization. There are two kinds of normalization: the first normal form (1NF), and the second and higher normal forms (2NF, 3NF, etc.). 1NF was, from the start, part of the *formal* relational model; its purpose is to restrict the data stored in each field to a single item, so that the records and files match the tuples and relations of predicate calculus. The second and higher normal forms were added later, and belong to the *informal* aspects of the relational model; their purpose is to eliminate data redundancy and inconsistencies.

As we saw, whether the goal is to avoid multiple items in a field or to eliminate redundancy and inconsistencies, we must separate the fields of the file in question into two sets, and move one set into a new file. Each normalizing step will generally increase by one the number of files in the database. Thus, although it is quite easy to normalize files, this process makes it more difficult to *access* the data. For, we must read more files and more records, in order to put back together the fields that were separated by normalization.

The idea of separating and recombining fields looks neat when presented as mathematical logic; that is, when we assume that data records can be accessed instantaneously, just like the tuples of predicate calculus. And the additional complexity caused by the separations and combinations can be justified by invoking the ultimate benefits of normalization. In real applications, however, even if we are willing to accept the additional complexity, normalization is often impractical, because of the excessive time needed to access the data.

Whether the fields were separated in order to attain the first or the higher normal forms, the only way to recombine them is with the JOIN relational operation (see 716–717). JOIN creates one file from two: it combines the records of the two files, retaining only those records where certain fields relate the files in a particular way. But, while easy to use as a high-level operation, JOIN is very inefficient and hard to optimize. This may go unnoticed with small files, but in most databases its execution takes far too long to be practical. Also, applications usually need *many* normalization steps, and hence *many* JOINs later. Even a simple query may need two or three JOINs, and perhaps hundreds of times the number of disk accesses that the traditional file operations would need.[1]

So the idea of strict normalization had to be abandoned. But the theorists refer to this reversal with such euphemisms as database "optimization," or "tuning," or "tailoring." They discuss now the benefits of *denormalization* with the same seriousness, and with the same technical, impressive language, as they did the benefits of normalization before. This makes the reversal appear like progress, like an *enhancement* of the relational model. No one mentions the fact that the abandonment of strict normalization means simply a return to the informal design principles we had followed *before* the relational model: we compare in each situation the benefits and drawbacks of keeping data together in one file, with those of using two files, and we choose the more effective alternative. This is what we routinely do when creating databases with the traditional file operations.

[1] As I remarked earlier (see p. 746), we can attain the ideals sought by normalization more effectively with *traditional* databases. As a result, what is perceived as a fundamental relational principle – normalized files – is found more often in applications using the traditional file operations than in applications using relational databases.

❖

The abandonment of the first normal form comes by way of a feature called – incredibly – *non-first-normal-form*. Abbreviated with scientific-looking terms like non-1NF, NFNF, and NF², this feature is so advanced that only a few database systems support it at present. Those that do are known as *extended relational* systems.

The name chosen by the experts for the new feature betrays their attitude: instead of simply stating that the first normal form – one of the fundamental principles of the relational model – has been abandoned, they present the abandonment as a new principle; and they call this principle, literally, the opposite of the original one. 1NF is still important, but now we need to impose this restriction only when convenient. Thus, the experts suppressed the falsification of an important principle by introducing a new one. In effect, the two principles, 1NF and non-1NF, cancel each other; that is, taken together they cannot possibly be serious principles. So the first normal form is now just an informal recommendation. But the experts describe this falsification of the relational model as a new, advanced relational feature.

To appreciate the significance of non-1NF, recall the 1NF restriction and its implications. For a file to be in first normal form, its fields must contain single, atomic values. Each field, in other words, must contain only one value at a time – not a list of items, or an array, or any other structure. This restriction is usually expressed by saying that the columns of a relational table must not contain *repeating groups*. The restriction to a single item per field is critical if we want to base the relational model on mathematical logic (because the elements of a tuple in predicate calculus are single items).

In most applications, however, we encounter sets of values that are so closely related that the most effective way to store and use them is as a list, or array. For example, in a file of purchased parts, we may want to store for each part a list of up to three vendor numbers, or three vendors and their selling price, or three vendors with their last price and purchase date. With the traditional file operations and a language like COBOL, we define these values, respectively, as an array of 3×1, or 3×2, or 3×3 elements. In the part record, the whole array will be treated as one field. It will be read into memory or written to disk along with the record, and, when in memory, its elements can be conveniently accessed with the same operations that programming languages provide for manipulating *memory* arrays. Thus, we can easily display or update one element or a subset of the elements, compare the three prices, change the relative position of the vendors, and so on.

In a relational database, the only way to store these values is as a separate file. The fields in the new file will be, for instance, the vendor number, price, and date; and the key will consist of the part number and a sequence number, 1 to 3. For each record in the part file, there will be up to three records in the new file. Operations like comparing prices or exchanging the relative position of vendors, which can be performed with a couple of statements in a traditional database, will now be small programming projects (since we must combine the two files with JOINs, access the three sets of elements as separate rows but save them somehow so that we can use them together, and so on). What is worse, these operations will now take longer to execute, because of the additional disk accesses.

For a few fields, it is possible to bypass the 1NF principle; and the simplest way to do it is by simulating arrays with ordinary fields. In the previous example, we would add to the part record three, six, or nine fields, each one with its own name, and access them through whatever means a relational system provides for accessing individual fields. This method obviates the need for a second file and separate records, and solves therefore the performance problem; but it makes programming even more complicated. Simulating arrays with ordinary fields, thus, is an awkward trick that programmers must employ if they want to bypass the 1NF principle while pretending to like the relational model.[2]

The fact that we have to resort to tricks in order to avoid the inefficiency of a relational principle constitutes a falsification of the relational theory. And the final abandonment of 1NF, after thirty years of struggling to fit real-world problems into relational systems, is in effect an acknowledgment of this falsification. Presenting non-1NF as a new relational feature is how the relational charlatans suppress the falsification.

With non-1NF, a field in one file acts as a pointer to records in a second file. For example, if the first file contains customer records, one field may be used for that customer's invoices. But the field itself contains no information. It only points to another file: an invoice file, where the records are identified through the combination of customer and invoice numbers, and the set of invoice records associated with a particular customer record are those with the same customer number.

---

[2] The 1NF principle is impractical, not because it requires a second file, but because it requires a second file in *any* situation. In contrast, with the traditional operations we are free to choose, in each situation, the most effective alternative. Thus, we may decide to use a second file even to replace a *small* array, if the application must access those elements in such a way that the use of indexed data records is simpler. Conversely, if access time is critical, we may decide to use an array even if this results in a very large record size.

With this method, a record in the first file can point to any number of records in the second file. In some database systems, more than one field can act as a pointer to another file; for example, in addition to the invoice field, we can have an order field and a history field in the customer record, pointing to records in an orders file and a sales history file, respectively.

Non-1NF allows us to relate files hierarchically, by logically *nesting* one file within another. Thus, databases that utilize this feature are also known as *nested relational* databases. Nesting is not limited to one level: fields in the second file can act as pointers to further files, which become then logically nested within the second one, and so on. Non-1NF allows us, therefore, to create hierarchical file structures. And, since the original relational model does not support these relationships, new relational operations were introduced for defining and accessing the records of nested files.

The concept of file nesting, however, is not new; it is practically identical, in fact, to the way we relate files when using the traditional file operations (see pp. 697–700). The only real difference is the higher level of abstraction of the non-1NF operations. What this means in practice is that, instead of creating explicit file scanning loops like those in figures 7-15 and 7-16, we invoke some built-in functions that generate the loops for us.

But, as we know, a higher level of abstraction also has drawbacks: we are restricted to fewer alternatives. So in the end, even with non-1NF, the relational systems are not as flexible or efficient as the basic file operations. For example, with the basic operations we can nest – in different places in the application, through different fields – the same files in different ways; we can create, therefore, several relationships between the same files. Also, with the basic operations we still have the option of storing arrays directly in a record – a method that is both simpler and faster than file nesting.

The main objection to non-1NF, however, is that it is presented as a new feature while being an abandonment of the relational file-relating method and a reinstatement of the traditional one. Even the term "nesting" is old: with the traditional operations, the files are nested by nesting their scanning loops; with relational systems, the files are nested through *implicit* scanning loops. The logical relationship between files is the same.

The term "non-1NF," then, is not only silly but also misleading. For, the intent of the new feature is not to avoid the problems caused by the 1NF principle, but to replace the impractical JOIN operation. Let us examine this misrepresentation more closely.

To promote non-1NF, the experts point to the inefficiency of certain file combinations in the original relational model. But the combinations they describe were never thought to be a consequence of the 1NF restriction. Specifically, non-1NF is recommended for files of any size, not just as a substitute for the small arrays that we may want to store directly in a record. Thus, referring to the earlier examples, we can use file nesting not just to replace an array of three vendors associated with one part, but also for a whole invoice file, where hundreds of invoices may be associated with one customer. For this type of data, though, we have *always* resorted to a second file, even with the traditional file operations, because this is the only practical way to store it. The difference between non-1NF and 1NF, then, is simply in the way we combine files: through nesting instead of JOINs. So what the experts are recommending in reality is not the replacement of 1NF with non-1NF, but the replacement of JOIN operations with the traditional concept of file nesting.

Non-1NF, in other words, is not promoted as a solution to the inefficiency of 1NF, but as a solution to the inefficiency of JOIN; that is, for any situation where we have to combine files. Thus, if we adopt non-1NF we can dispose of the JOIN operation altogether. If we want, we can replace with nested files every situation that would normally require JOINs: not just files that would be created when enforcing the first normal form, but also files that would be created when enforcing the second and higher normal forms, and even files that would be kept separate in any case. Non-1NF eliminates, therefore, the inefficiency caused by combining *any* files in a relational database. So, if it is a general substitute for the relational way of combining files, what we have now is *a different database model.*

Far from being just a new feature, then, non-1NF cancels the whole relational model. To understand this, let us take a moment and recall the importance of the first normal form. And there is no better way to start than by citing the experts themselves.

Date says that 1NF is so fundamental that the term "normalized," when unqualified, means "first normal form": "It follows that *every* normalized relation is in first normal form ...; it is this fact that accounts for the term 'first.' In other words, 'normalized' and '1NF' mean *exactly the same thing*."[3] In Codd's original papers, too, the term "normalized" means what we call now first normal form;[4] the higher normal forms are not even mentioned. Recall also that the first normal form is the only one that is part of the *formal* relational model.

[3] C. J. Date, *An Introduction to Database Systems*, 6th ed. (Reading, MA: Addison-Wesley, 1995), pp. 289–290.
[4] See, for example, E. F. Codd, "A Relational Model of Data for Large Shared Data Banks," *Communications of the ACM* 13, no. 6 (1970): 377–387.

Here are some additional statements: "At each intersection of a row and column there is exactly one value. This is the principle of *first normal form*, fundamental in the relational model."[5] "This property implies that columns do not contain repeating groups. Often, such tables are referred to as 'normalized' or as being in 'first normal form (1NF).' It is important that you understand the significance and effects of this property because it is a cornerstone of the relational data structure."[6] "Occasionally there might be good reasons for flouting the principles of normalization.... The only hard requirement is that relations be in at least first normal form."[7] "All data in a relational database is represented in *one and only one way*, namely by explicit value (this feature is sometimes referred to as 'the basic principle of the relational model' ...). In particular, logical connections within and across relations are represented by such explicit values."[8]

It is not difficult to see why the first normal form is so important to the relational model – why it is "fundamental," a "cornerstone," a "hard requirement," and a "basic principle." It is not so much the restriction to single values that is important, as the *purpose* of this restriction. By preventing us from creating any data structures within a record, 1NF forces us to keep all data in the form of tables. And if the data is restricted to tables, the methods used to access and combine the data can be restricted to operations on tables; that is, to high-level operations based on mathematical logic.

Accordingly, by annulling 1NF we also annul these restrictions: we can store, access, and combine data in other ways too. In effect, we have regained some of the freedom we enjoyed when using files through the traditional file operations: we can now relate them through the versatile hierarchical concept, as data within data. And we can use this method, not just with small arrays or structures, but with files of any size, and on any number of nesting levels. In the end, annulling 1NF permits us to create database structures that are more flexible and more efficient than those possible with the relational model.

In conclusion, the restriction imposed by the first normal form is far more significant than what it appears to be – merely preventing multiple values in a field. Its annulment, therefore, means far more than just permitting multiple values; it means the annulment of the relational model. It also demonstrates the pseudoscientific nature of this theory, as well as the dishonesty of its supporters: the impracticality of 1NF, along with the impracticality of JOIN, is

---

[5] Anthony Ralston and Edwin D. Reilly, eds., *Encyclopedia of Computer Science*, 3rd ed. (New York: Van Nostrand Reinhold, 1993), p. 1162.

[6] Candace C. Fleming and Barbara von Halle, *Handbook of Relational Database Design* (Reading, MA: Addison-Wesley, 1989), pp. 32–33.

[7] Date, *Database Systems*, p. 291.   [8] Ibid., p. 99.

a falsification of the model; but instead of being abandoned, the theory is expanded – by turning this falsification into a new relational feature, non-1NF.

The mathematical foundation of the original model was predicate calculus, with its relations and tuples. Thus, if our databases no longer consist of this type of relations and tuples, it is absurd to continue to call them relational. Terms like "extended relational" and "nested relational" are simply incorrect if the new model is not "relational." The term "relational" derives from the mathematical concept of a relation; namely, a set of tuples, where each tuple is composed of single elements. And in predicate calculus the only operations are those performed on such sets through mathematical logic. It is these relations, tuples, and elements that become the files, records, and fields of a relational database. So, if we want a different database organization, or different operations, we need a different model.

As we saw under the first delusion, the mathematical claims of the relational model were tenuous in any case, since only a small part (those aspects that constitute the formal model) had indeed a mathematical grounding. And with the annulments we are discussing in this subsection – non-1NF, in particular – even that small part has disappeared. What we have now is neither an enhanced nor an extended relational model. What we have is not a relational model at all.

Non-1NF systems, then, are indeed as useful as their promoters claim; but they are useful because they are no longer relational. This is why some experts, embarrassed perhaps by this fraud, suggest terms like "post-relational," and even "object-relational," for the database systems that include non-1NF or a similar "enhancement."

Still, if not predicate calculus, perhaps another mathematical system can serve as a foundation for the new database model. And indeed, some theorists have attempted to extend the formal relational model to include non-1NF. But this is silly. For, if a mathematical system could guarantee the correctness of nested databases, then the same system would also guarantee the correctness of the nesting performed through the traditional file operations – which is identical, logically.

This, of course, is true for the original model too: nothing stops us from using the traditional data files and operations while limiting ourselves to the subset of features that parallel the relational model; and our databases would then be founded on predicate calculus, just like the relational ones.

The conclusion must be that, no matter how rigorous a formal database model is, it offers no mathematical benefits that we do not also enjoy with the informal traditional operations.[9] The answer to this apparent contradiction is that the formal part plays such a small role in a database system that it is practically irrelevant. So, for the application as a whole, the mathematical benefits are about the same with a formal database model as they are without one. (This is the essence of the first delusion.)

❖

By way of summary, I want to show how the software elites are presenting the non-1NF feature. A good example is the white paper published by IBM to promote one of their new database systems.[10] This paper, we are told, "discusses technical advances represented by nested relational database technology."[11] And just in case we were not sufficiently impressed by this statement, a few sentences later we are reminded that nested relational databases represent an "advanced technology."

Now, the advanced technology that is file nesting has been available since around 1970 to anyone capable of writing a few lines of COBOL. So it is clear that IBM addresses individuals who, while being perhaps programmers or managers, have very little programming knowledge. These incompetents try to develop applications, not through programming, but by buying programming substitutes. They can be impressed by a feature like non-1NF because they are always dependent on the elites for solutions to their software problems. They have problems now because they trusted the elites in the past and adopted a relational system. But they believe that the solution must also come from the elites, in the form of a new system.

The paper continues by describing the problems caused by the restriction to 1NF: "Database conformance with 1NF often increases the amount of storage used, makes maintenance more difficult, and most importantly greatly increases the processing required to produce results, while still making the schema more complex.... For some potential users of relational databases, the joins [i.e., JOIN operations] that would be required to resolve relationship relations [i.e., cross-references] in 1NF databases would affect performance

---

[9] Because they are restricted to higher levels, the relational operations are logically a subset of the basic, traditional file operations. Thus, we can always simulate a relational database system using a traditional file system, but not vice versa. Many relational systems, in fact, are designed simply as a high-level environment based on an underlying file management system: the relational operations are implemented as subroutines that employ the basic file operations in conjunction with appropriate loops and conditions.

[10] IBM Corporation, *Nested Relational Databases*, white paper (2001).

[11] Ibid., p. 3. Note, again, the slogan "technology," used to make something appear more important than it really is.

enough to preclude the use of relational databases.... Apart from performance considerations, 1NF relational databases also have practical limitations for many applications."[12]

This is an excellent description of the restrictions imposed by the first normal form, and by the relational model in general. Reading this, one is liable to forget that the same institutions that are so harshly attacking this model now had been promoting it for the previous thirty years as an expression of database science, and as an important aspect of software engineering. These problems had been noticed from the start, of course. So how were the millions of programmers and users who had adopted relational systems coping all these years? By constantly seeking ways to bypass the restrictions; by spending most of their time dealing with these spurious problems instead of the actual business problems; and, ultimately, by being content with inadequate and inefficient applications.

The nested relational model, the paper tells us, eliminates the 1NF problems. Non-1NF is such an important feature, in fact, that all relational systems will soon support it: "Because of the limitations of 1NF relational databases, especially for storing complex data structures, all commercial relational databases have begun adopting extended relational technology; however, IBM has a technological lead of several years over its closest competitor."[13]

The shallowness of the non-1NF issue is seen in the pretentious description of file nesting. For example, one of the reasons why IBM's "extended relational technology" is more advanced than the competing ones is that "the IBM nested relational implementation, unlike others, is not limited to a single nested table."[14] With the basic file operations, as we know, it is just as easy to nest several file scanning loops as it is to nest one, simply because programming languages allow us to combine file scanning loops in any way we like. But with nested relational databases, this trivial capability is presented as a major technological advance, currently available only from IBM. Again, only ignorant practitioners can be impressed by such claims.

Finally, the paper reminds us (three times[15]) that the relational model has a rigorous mathematical foundation, which guarantees correct results when using the relational operations. And, the paper assures us, research has shown that this guarantee is not compromised by the annulment of the 1NF principle: "Analysis has proven that the resulting model is equally robust."[16] Such analysis and proof are senseless, though, because the relational model is *not* robust even *with* 1NF. As we saw under the first delusion, its mathematical foundation is irrelevant in practice. It is precisely because the mathematical foundation is

---

[12] Ibid., p. 7.   [13] Ibid., p. 14.   [14] Ibid.   [15] Ibid., pp. 3, 7, 14.
[16] Ibid., p. 7. The paper cites several sources, where presumably the proof can be found.

irrelevant that annulling an important principle like 1NF indeed makes no difference.

And we are expected to feel even better after reading that nested relational databases have been "accepted by the academic community as adhering to a valid relational model."[17] But we saw that it is wrong even to *call* the new model relational. In any case, this statement is hardly reassuring if we remember that the same academic community also advocated other theories that failed (structured programming and object-oriented programming, in particular), and that, just like the relational model, those theories were rescued by being turned into pseudosciences.

Thus, by promoting pseudoscientific software theories, the universities help software companies to sell worthless development systems, and help incompetent programmers and managers to control corporate computing.

3

I began the discussion of the third delusion with the non-1NF issue because this is the most flagrant of the relational reversals – a reversal that marks, in effect, the end of the relational theory. But 1NF is merely the latest principle to be annulled. At this point, most relational principles had already been forsaken, because, like 1NF, they had been found to be impractical. In the remainder of this subsection, I propose to study the other reversals.

❖

The abandonment of the second and higher normal forms (2NF, 3NF, etc.) came by way of a new relational principle, called *denormalization*. At first, database designers and programmers simply ignored the stipulation to fully normalize their files, when this was too complicated or too inefficient. But the theorists were condemning this practice. Before long, though, even they realized that strict normalization is impractical, and that the decision whether or not to normalize a particular set of files depends ultimately on the situation: on the type of data stored in these files, on the file relationships, and on the way we plan to use the files in the application.[18]

But instead of admitting that the idea of strict normalization had failed, the theorists reacted, as pseudoscientists do, by turning this falsification of the

---

[17] Ibid., p. 14.
[18] The term "normalization" refers usually to *all* normal forms; but here, in the discussion of the second and higher normal forms, I use "normalization" to refer only to them.

relational model into a new relational principle – denormalization. The new principle says that we must first normalize all files, as before; then, we must denormalize (that is, restore to their previous state) those files that should not have been normalized in the first place.

Both the principle and the term, "denormalization," are absurd. All we needed was a statement acknowledging that normalization was annulled as a relational principle and is now just an informal concept. The very term "normalization" should have been abandoned, in fact. After all, normalizing some files and not others is what we had been doing all along, with the traditional file operations, and we didn't need a special term to describe this activity. With the relational model we have now *two* principles for this activity, and *two* terms. We are told that normalization is as important as before, and that denormalization is the process of *improving* the results of normalization.

Clearly, the theorists invented the second principle in order to suppress the fact that the first one had failed. The two principles, normalization and denormalization, in effect cancel each other. But the theorists managed to make this return to what we had before the relational model look like an *enhancement* of the model.

Here is a typical explanation of the new principle: "Denormalization is the 'undoing' of the normalization process. It does not, however, imply omission of the normalization process. Rather, *denormalization* is the process whereby, after defining a stable, fully normalized data structure, you selectively introduce duplicate data to facilitate specific performance requirements."[19] What this sophistic verbiage is trying to say is that, while normalization is generally desirable, strict normalization is impractical; in other words, what we always knew. Now, however, we can no longer simply allow some data duplication from the start (when we know from experience that the application would otherwise be too slow). Instead, we must first normalize the whole database, and then "selectively introduce duplicate data to facilitate specific performance requirements." Actually, in both cases we address the same problem and end up with the same database. The pompous language serves to mask the fact that the principle of strict normalization – a fundamental relational requirement – has been falsified.

Here is how two other experts present this reversal: "The general idea of normalization is that the database designer should aim for relations in the 'ultimate' normal form (5NF). However, this recommendation should not be

---

[19] Fleming and von Halle, *Relational Database Design*, p. 440.

construed as law. Occasionally there might be good reasons for flouting the principles of normalization."[20] "There are, however, exceptions to [strict normalization].... We recommend that data models *always* be designed in third normal form, but that the physical data-base designer be permitted to deviate from it if he has good reasons and if the data administrator agrees that no serious harm will be done."[21]

A critical aspect of the idea of denormalization, then, and what the experts keep stressing, is that denormalization does *not* constitute the annulment of normalization. Normalization remains as important as before, and what we must do is both normalize and denormalize the database.

Here is another example of this doubletalk: "Data denormalization is constrained so that it does not alter the basic structure of the conceptual schema. It only makes adjustments to the basic structure for operational efficiency."[22] Denormalization, thus, consists in *adjusting* the database design, but without *altering* it. This is silly, of course, since adjusting something will also alter it. A database either is or is not normalized; so, if we denormalize a normalized database we necessarily end up with an unnormalized one, regardless of whether we call this process "adjustment" or "alteration." Not so, says Brackett: "A common misconception about data denormalization is that it results in a return to the unnormalized business schema that began the data normalization process.... However, this is not the situation. Data denormalization produces denormalized data, not unnormalized data."[23] In reality, there is no difference between the two: both "denormalized" and "unnormalized" mean simply data that is not fully normalized, violating therefore this relational principle.

The theorists, thus, are defending their deviation from strict normalization by claiming that denormalizing the database after fully normalizing it is different from simply leaving some of the files unnormalized in the first place. One method, they tell us, constitutes an exact design process, while the other is merely an informal decision. But this would be true if denormalization were indeed an exact process. In practice, though, the decision to denormalize a file can be no more exact than the decision to leave a file unnormalized to begin with. Recall the previous quotations: "[the designer is] permitted to deviate from [strict normalization] if he has good reasons and if the data administrator agrees that no serious harm will be done," and "occasionally there might be good reasons for flouting the principles of normalization."

---

[20] Date, *Database Systems*, p. 291.

[21] James Martin, *Managing the Data-Base Environment* (Englewood Cliffs, NJ: Prentice Hall, 1983), p. 216.

[22] Michael H. Brackett, *Practical Data Design* (Englewood Cliffs, NJ: Prentice Hall, 1990), pp. 155–156.   [23] Ibid., p. 156.

Informal comments like these can hardly be described as an exact method of denormalization.

Brackett starts by promising us an exact method: "Conceptual schema are converted to internal schema through a denormalization process following a precise set of rules depending on the physical operating environment."[24] But the "precise set of rules" never materializes. All we find on the subsequent pages is a list of cases where denormalization is beneficial, and a reminder to deal carefully with the consequent problem (redundancy and inconsistencies). For instance, this is how Brackett describes one of the cases of denormalization: "This situation creates redundant data and those redundant data must be consistently updated or the quality of the database will deteriorate rapidly.... Other data entities may be denormalized for operational efficiency based on these criteria.... Each situation must be carefully evaluated to assure that the logical model is not compromised and that any redundant data are routinely and consistently updated."[25]

So what Brackett is describing as denormalization is not "a precise set of rules" but an informal process – a process no different from what we do with *traditional* databases: we study the application's requirements, allow redundancy and inconsistencies when it is impractical to eliminate them, and deal with the consequent problems by adding special checks and operations to the application's logic.

Thus, to cover up the failure of strict normalization, the theorists were compelled to invent the absurd principle that we must first normalize the database and then denormalize it. And they defended the principle with the absurd claim that this method is exact while the traditional, simpler method – creating the correct database directly from the requirements – is not. In reality, both methods entail the same decisions and result in the same design.

We saw under the second delusion that the process of normalization is presented by the theorists as a formal design method, while being in fact as informal as the traditional method. It is informal because it must be based, ultimately, on the same decisions as those we make when designing the database directly from the requirements. Now we see that the process of denormalization too is informal, despite the claims that it is exact. Only we, by studying and interpreting the requirements, can determine whether strict normalization is practical in a given situation, and, if not, what operations must be added to maintain data integrity.

[24] Ibid., p. 155.   [25] Ibid., pp. 157–158.

In conclusion, both normalization and denormalization are perceived as formal design methods, when in fact both are informal. So, to appreciate the new delusion, denormalization, we must ignore the previous one: we must believe, with the theorists, that normalization is indeed an exact process. Judging it from *their* perspective, therefore, denormalization is a delusion; for they did not stop promoting normalization when they introduced the concept of denormalization. They continue their research in what they believe to be formal and exact concepts – the dependency theory, the classification of normal forms – even while praising the virtues of denormalization, which is informal. They are oblivious to the absurdity of promoting these two methods at the same time: no matter how exact is the process of normalization, when we modify its result by adding the inexact process of denormalization the final result is bound to be inexact. So what is the point in seeking a formal and exact normalization theory while also permitting denormalization?

It is in order to resolve this self-contradiction that the theorists introduced the principle that we must denormalize the database only after fully normalizing it. This principle appears to justify the need for both processes, when in reality it shows that we need neither.

Earlier, to justify the need for normalization, the theorists distorted the problem of database design. Instead of determining the correct design simply by studying the application's requirements, we were asked to do two things: create a deliberately incorrect database, and then normalize it to make it correct. And now, to justify both normalization and denormalization, we are asked to do *three* things: create an incorrect database, normalize it to make it correct, and, finally, denormalize it to make it practical.

The traditional design method allows us to create, not only correct databases, but also efficient ones. For, the same skills that help us to create a correct, fully normalized database also help us to decide when this would be inefficient. Thus, we can create a correct *and* efficient database at the same time, directly from the requirements. We don't need a denormalization theory any more than we need a normalization one.

Finally, and quite apart from the delusions already discussed, the need for denormalization means that we are again preoccupied with the *efficiency* of the database operations – contrary to the claim that the relational model shields us from the physical implementation of the database. We must study each situation and seek the most effective solution, instead of implementing the requirements through formal methods and high-level operations, as the relational theory had promised us. We must accept, rather than avoid, the "update anomalies"; and we must add special checks and operations to deal with them. In other words, we have returned to what we had been doing all along, with the traditional databases. The theorists describe denormalization as database "optimization"; but if the optimization consists in a deviation from fundamental relational principles, this description is merely a way of denying that the relational model has failed.

4

One of the relational model's promises was that we could restrict ourselves, in all database work, to the high-level relational operations. And this promise too had to be annulled. In the end, the relational systems became practical only after reinstating the low-level capabilities of the traditional file operations; specifically, the means to manipulate fields and records through traditional programming methods, and the means to link them to other low-level entities in the application. Let us examine this reversal.

Recall the original relational model. The database, we are told, must be perceived as "tables and nothing but tables." The relational operations can be assumed to occur instantaneously, and can therefore be treated like the operations of mathematical logic: all we have to do is reduce the database requirements to logical expressions where the operands are tables, and the relational operations (along with standard logical operations) combine in various ways tables and portions of tables. No matter how large or how small, a data file can be treated simply as a table with a number of rows and columns. In particular, if we need just one record of a given file, we must create a new table with just one row; and if we need one field, we must create a table with one row and one column. Also, there is no way to modify the tables. Updating the database was thought to be a relatively simple and infrequent aspect of database work, so the operations that add, delete, or modify records were expected to be informal, like the traditional ones. We must be careful when modifying the database, of course; but we don't need the formality and precision of mathematics, as we do for queries.

The original model, thus, permits only database queries. Consequently, the only database language we need is one that provides the means to formulate queries through the relational operations. In their naivety, the theorists believed that a model shown to satisfy some simple queries on small files could serve as the foundation of practical database systems: for applications with files of any size and queries of any complexity. Moreover, they later believed that the same model could be extended to cover all aspects of database work, including the updating operations and the design process. The fact that simple queries look neat when expressed as mathematical logic was enough to convince the theorists that all database programming could be restricted to high-level operations and to the notion of tables.

Today, after all the reversals, the relational systems are no longer restricted to "tables and nothing but tables." Rather, they provide, in a very complicated manner, the means to link individual fields and records to the other entities in the application. In addition, the database language, SQL, has grown from a set of simple query operations into an elaborate (although quite primitive) programming language. The relational systems, thus, have restored the means to manipulate, through programming, the low-level database entities. So they have restored exactly what the traditional file operations and programming languages had been doing all along, in a much simpler way – and what the original relational model had claimed to be unnecessary.

We need to access low-level database entities for two reasons: because this is the only way to implement the *details* of a database operation, and because this is the only way to *link* the database structures to the other structures that make up the application. It is obvious, therefore, why the traditional file operations are indispensable: in addition to allowing us to access the low-level database entities, they can be used from a programming language; and through this language we can create the critical, low-level links between database entities and the other types of entities in the application.

These two qualities are both necessary and sufficient for implementing any database requirement; and it is precisely these two qualities that are lost in the relational model. Thus, since it is impossible to implement serious applications without accessing and linking the low-level elements of the application, it is not surprising that the modifications needed to make the relational systems practical consisted in restoring both the low-level operations and the means to use these operations through a programming language.

So, like all systems that offer us high-level starting elements, the relational systems became in the end a fraud. When promising us higher levels, the software charlatans tempt us to commit the two mechanistic fallacies, reification and abstraction (see "The Delusion of High Levels" in chapter 6). In the case of relational systems, the claim was that we could separate the database structures from the other structures that make up the application; this would allow us to start from higher levels of abstraction within these structures, greatly simplifying database work.

With the traditional development method, all we need is a programming language and a few libraries of subroutines (for mathematical functions, display operations, database management, and the like). The software charlatans have replaced this simple concept with the concept of *development environments*: large and complicated systems that lure ignorant practitioners with the promise of high-level, built-in operations. These operations, we are told, function as prefabricated software subassemblies: they already contain within them many of the low-level operations that we would otherwise have to program ourselves. But, in fact, only trivial requirements can be implemented by combining high-level operations. So the systems must be continually enhanced, with more and more features. And what are these features? They are means to deal with low-level entities, precisely what the systems had originally attempted to eliminate.

Thus, instead of admitting that the restriction to high-level operations failed as a substitute for traditional programming, the software charlatans rescue these systems by turning their falsifications, one by one, into new features. The systems keep growing and appear to become more and more "powerful," but this power derives from reinstating the low-level, traditional concepts. By the time enough of these concepts are reinstated to make the systems practical, there is nothing left of the original promise. For now we must deal with the low levels again. What is worse, because the low levels were introduced within the high-level environment, they are much more complicated than they are when available directly, through a traditional language. So, in the end, programming is even more difficult than before.

Returning to the relational systems, the need for low levels emerged when the notion of *data integrity* was introduced. Data integrity became an issue in the relational model only when the model was expanded to include *updating* operations. As long as it permitted only queries, there was no need for integrity checks, because, within the scope of the model, the data never changed. Since the operations that add, delete, or modify data records were expected to be similar to the traditional ones, and to be performed outside the model, the validity checks accompanying these operations were also expected to be performed outside the model. Once the relational model was adopted for serious database work, however, the updating operations, along with the problem of data integrity, could no longer be ignored.

The normalization principles too, we saw earlier, were needed only when the relational model was expanded to include updating operations. Tables did not have to be normalized in the original model, because no data inconsistencies can arise when we restrict ourselves to queries and to the high-level relational operations. We also saw how both the attempt to formalize the process of normalization, and the idea of strict normalization, failed. In the end, the only way to design a correct database is informally, by studying the application's requirements. All that the theory of normalization accomplished was to add to the traditional design problems the complicated concepts of normal forms and field dependencies. The critical part – the need to determine whether two given fields must be in the same file or in separate files – remained unchanged. With the traditional design method or with the relational one, we can decide in which file to place a new field only by discovering the low-level links between the database entities and the other entities in the application.

The formality and the neat classification of normal forms can be seen, therefore, as a failed attempt to raise the level of abstraction in database design: instead of having to study and understand the application's requirements, it was believed that we could attain the same goal by knowing only how to convert files from one normal form into another – an easier, largely mechanical, task.

But regardless of its failure, the normalization theory was silly because it addressed only a small number of data inconsistencies; specifically, only those that can be prevented by placing fields in separate files (see pp. 769–771). Since most data inconsistencies cannot be eliminated simply by separating fields, we must deal with them through the application's logic: to ensure that an updating operation does not cause inconsistencies, we add various checks, restrictions, or further updating operations. An example of a situation where the updating problems cannot be solved through normalization, we saw, is the requirement for the balance field in the customer record to match at all times the amounts present in that customer's transaction records. Although technically redundant, the balance field is useful because it obviates the need to recalculate the balance by reading the transaction records every time. Thus, instead of avoiding the redundancy, we ensure that the field remains correct by adding to the application's logic some operations to update it whenever a transaction is added, deleted, or modified.

The requirement to match the balance field and the transaction records is, in effect, a database integrity rule. So the notion of integrity was the answer to the updating problems that could not be solved through normalization; that is, to practically *all* the updating problems that can arise in an application. A whole new class of relational features had to be invented – features totally unrelated to the original model – in order to move the data validity operations from the application, where they are normally performed, into the database system. The sole purpose of these features is to permit us to do through a new language, in the database system, what we had been doing all along through a traditional language in the application. Thus, the operations that update the customer balance field, previously mentioned, would no longer be part of the main program; they would be written instead in a special language, and made part of the database environment.

❖

The problem of data validity is well known. Whenever a database field is modified, the application must verify that the new value is correct within the current context. Similarly, when a record is added, the value of each field in the record must be correct. But there is more to the validity problem than verifying the value of individual fields. For example, the application must verify that a record may be modified at all, or added or deleted, in a given situation. Also, adding, deleting, or modifying a given record often affects other records and other files, so the application must perform additional operations if the database as a whole is to remain correct. Generally, all the specifications and restrictions known as business rules – which are reflected in the various processes implemented in the application – can be described, if we want, as integrity rules.

Data validity, thus, is closely related to the application's requirements: what is correct in one situation may be incorrect in another. Just like the "anomalies" they tried to eliminate through normalization, the problems that the relational theorists are discussing under "integrity" are problems we always faced. And we never thought of them as *database* problems, but as a natural part of application development. The so-called integrity problems are merely one aspect of the challenge of programming: if we fail to take into account certain requirements, some data may become incorrect – inconsistent, redundant, invalid – when the application is used. The problems that cause incorrect data are similar to those that cause incorrect operations. In both cases the application will malfunction, and in both cases the reason is that it does not reflect the requirements accurately.

We saw earlier that files cannot be said to be normalized in an absolute sense, but only relative to the application's requirements. For example, if the product description does not change from one order to the next, the product and orders files are normalized when the description field is in the product file; but when the description may change, they are normalized when the description field is in the orders file. Similarly, the validity criteria cannot be defined in an absolute sense, but only relative to the application's requirements. Some examples: A certain date may be deemed too old in one part of the application, but not in another. Deleting a transaction record may be permitted if certain conditions hold, but deemed invalid otherwise; elsewhere in the application, though, we may have to prevent the deletion under all conditions. Creating a new transaction record may generally entail adding a record to the history file too, and failing to do so would result in an incorrect history file; sometimes, though, when this is not a requirement, it is *adding* the history record that would result in an incorrect file.

Clearly, validity issues like these are part of the application's logic. It is absurd to treat them as a special class of operations just because they are concerned with the correctness of database entities. We also modify *memory* variables in the application, and they too must remain correct; yet no one has suggested that – in order to safeguard the correctness of memory-based entities – we extract these operations from the application, restrict them to high levels, and design special systems and languages to perform them. If we were to do this for every type of entities and operations, we would no longer need applications and general-purpose languages. Performing and combining various types of operations, including those concerned with data validity, is precisely what applications are for, and what programming languages are designed to do. In any case, the operations that validate the database, as much as those that modify it, must necessarily access *low-level* entities. So the idea of separating them from the application, incorporating them into a database system, and restricting them to high levels is senseless, and bound to fail.

In conclusion, the integrity features added to the relational database systems were totally unnecessary. Their real purpose was to rescue the relational model from refutation. Here is how: The promise had been a model that satisfies all our database needs through high-level operations. The existing data validity functions, however, required *low-level* operations. Moreover, they required *programming*, so they could not be implemented at all in a relational system. Asking us to depend on traditional programming for a critical aspect of database management was, thus, a falsification of the relational model. To save the model, the theorists were compelled to move these functions *from* the application, where they belong naturally and logically, *into* the database system. The integrity features are a fraud because this move is said to complement the high-level database operations, when in reality the new functions require low levels, and programming.

The integrity features, then, were the expedient through which low-level capabilities could be added to a relational system. Instead of recognizing the need to deal with low-level entities as a falsification, the theorists solved the problem by annulling the restriction to high-level operations. Using the issue of data integrity as pretext, they turned a blatant falsification into an important new feature. This feature is so important, in fact, that no serious database requirements can be implemented without it. And all this time, they kept praising the power of the relational model: annulling the restriction to high levels, they say, is an *enhancement* of the model.

❖

The first integrity functions were limited to simple validity checks. Here are some examples: The *attribute integrity* functions check that the value placed in a field is correct with respect to the definition of the field (valid numbers in a numeric field, valid dates in a date field, etc.). The *domain integrity* functions check that the value placed in a field is correct when the field is restricted to a range of values (a number must not be larger than 1,000, for instance, a date must not be older than 30 days ago, etc.). The *referential integrity* functions check that the relationship between two files remains correct when the files are modified; typically, they are used to prevent the deletion of a record in one file while there exist records in the other file related to it through their key.

To use an integrity function, the programmer specifies the event that is to invoke the function at run time (this event is known as *trigger*), the conditions and values that make up the constraint, and the action to take in case of error (display a message, prevent a change or deletion, etc.). Triggers may be included in the application when a certain field is modified, after a record is added to a certain file, before a record is deleted, and so on.

Validity checks like these can be easily implemented in the application, of course, using the conditional constructs or exception-handling features available in most languages. So it is not at all clear why a database system must provide these checks in the form of built-in functions. Still, if we agree that higher levels of abstraction are sometimes beneficial, these functions do provide a good alternative for specifying and enforcing certain validity criteria.

Only simple checks, however, can be implemented through standard, built-in functions. This is true because all we can do in a standard function is specify a few conditions and values and the action to take, while most integrity checks entail *combinations* of conditions, values, and actions. Thus, the checks we need in a typical application may affect several fields and files, may require a unique piece of logic, and may need some data that resides in the application, not in the database.

So, like all high-level operations, the concept of standard integrity functions can be useful if provided as an *option*, to be employed only when better than *programming* the same checks. The relational theorists, though, hoped to turn *all* integrity checks into standard functions. Their naivety is betrayed by their attempt to *classify* the integrity functions – referential integrity, domain integrity, and so forth. They actually believed that they could discover a set of standard functions that would encompass all conceivable data validation requirements (or, at least, the most common ones). Note also the pretentious names they invented to describe what are in reality simple operations. Clearly, they believed that the concept of built-in integrity functions represents an important contribution to database science. But preventing the deletion of a particular record, or ensuring that a field's value lies within a certain range, are operations we routinely perform in every application, using ordinary programming languages; and we don't need scientific-sounding terms like "referential integrity" and "domain integrity" to describe them.

The concept of built-in integrity functions failed, of course. After devising a few standard functions, the theorists had no choice but to give us the means to create freely our own functions, which is the only way to satisfy real-world data validation requirements. And, since it is only through programming that one can create such functions, new programming languages were invented – languages whose only purpose was to allow programmers to implement these functions as part of the database, rather than part of the application. Then the languages started to grow, as programmers demanded greater functionality. Means were introduced to perform calculations, to create flow-control constructs, to call subroutines, to access memory variables, to use general-purpose function libraries, and so forth. These languages provided, in other words, more and more of the very same features that were already available in the *traditional* languages.

No one noticed the absurdity of this situation. *Programming* our own functions is an alternative we always had. The promise had been, not a new language, but a higher level of abstraction. And if this turned out to be impossible, the theorists should have admitted that the only way to implement versatile data validation is through a programming language – the way we always did – and encouraged us to return to the traditional methods. What is the point in inventing specialized languages, indicating by means of "triggers" where in the application we need the integrity functions, and placing the functions in the database, when we could simply keep them as part of the application? After all, despite the multiplying features, the new languages remain inferior to the traditional ones, even in the narrow domain of database work that is their specialty. So programmers must now assimilate and depend on some new languages without deriving any real benefits. In the end, not only do the relational systems fail to provide the promised higher level of abstraction, but they make the task of data validation more complicated than before.[26]

The theorists, of course, could not admit that the concept of high-level integrity functions had failed, and that we must return to the traditional methods, because this would have been tantamount to admitting that the relational model had been falsified. So, inventing new languages was the way to cover up this falsification. Imagine an application written in COBOL, and a database system that asks us to write the data validation functions also in COBOL, but to store them in the database. Since we know that we can

---

[26] We hear sometimes the argument that storing the integrity functions outside the application facilitates the implementation of corporate standards, as all validity criteria are specified in one place. But this argument is tenuous. First, we can accomplish the same thing with ordinary subroutines. Second, even with the functions outside the application, why do we need new languages?

accomplish the same thing by making those functions an integral part of the application, we would reject the database alternative as absurd. If, however, it is not in COBOL but in a new language that we must write these functions – and if the language is accompanied by some new and impressive terminology, and if it is provided through a large and intricate development environment – the absurd alternative can be made to look like an important programming concept. And if we add to this the enthusiasm of the experts and the media, and the urgent needs of the companies that already depend on relational systems, everyone would perceive this concept as progress. Thus, what is in reality a *falsification* of the relational model is made to appear as an *enhancement* of the model.

Reinstating the programming capabilities, then, is what made the relational systems practical. *All* relational principles had to be annulled, as we saw earlier; but the other annulments would have amounted to nothing had the restriction to high-level database operations been maintained. The idea of programmable integrity functions was so well received because it provides the means to bypass the restriction to relational operations. Although not as useful as the traditional file operations, the operations available through the new languages do have similar capabilities. So they allow us to implement many database requirements that would be impractical through relational operations alone.

Thus, in the guise of integrity functions, programmers could now add to their applications a great variety of *low-level* file operations. Whenever a database requirement was too complicated or too inefficient to express through the relational operations, they could program it in the form of an integrity function and define a "trigger" in the application to invoke it. After all, with a little imagination any database requirement can be associated with some integrity checks or rules. For example, if we have to modify a record in such a way that a field's value is the result of calculations and conditions involving some other files and some memory variables – a task impossible or impractical through relational operations – we can program all this in a database language and call it an integrity function.

Understandably, this stratagem was very popular. Programmers praised the virtues of the relational model, but resorted to "integrity" functions and "triggers" whenever the requirements called for low-level file operations, or low-level links between database entities and other types of entities; in other words, whenever they needed the capabilities of the *traditional* file operations. They appeared to like the relational model, but what they liked in reality was the new, low-level capabilities – which contradict the relational principles.

In the end, all pretences of integrity and triggers were discarded, and these functions were expanded into the broader concept known as *stored procedures*. These procedures are general-purpose pieces of software that can be employed freely in the application. They are stored in the database, but are used like ordinary subroutines: they can be invoked from the application or from other stored procedures, can have parameters, and can return values. And, since there is no limit to the size or number of stored procedures, larger and larger portions of the application were being developed in this new fashion, in order to take advantage of the low-level capabilities of the database languages. Thus, while programmers were convinced that they were using the relational model, their applications resembled more and more those developed with the traditional languages and file operations.

So, by allowing programmers to bypass completely the relational principles, the concept of stored procedures was the final answer to the need for low-level file operations and low-level links to the other aspects of the application.

5

Although there are many relational database languages, it is SQL that became the official one. And it is through SQL, more than through the others, that the fraud of reinstating the traditional concepts was committed. Today's relational systems would be unusable without SQL. From its modest beginning as a query language, SQL has achieved its current status, and has grown to its enormous size, as a result of the enhancements introduced in order to provide programming and low-level capabilities – precisely those capabilities that the relational model had claimed to be unnecessary. Thus, today's official relational language is in reality the official means, not of *implementing*, but of *overriding*, the relational principles. Let us study this evolution.

The original relational model, we recall, was meant only for queries. And SQL (which stands for Structured *Query* Language) was the language through which programmers and users alike were expected to access the database. The original SQL, thus, allowed us to select and combine subsets of tables by specifying various criteria in the form of relational operations.

The SQL statement for queries is SELECT. This one statement, however, contains many clauses, which permit us to specify various details: the files involved in the query, the operations required to relate these files, the sorting sequence, the record selection criteria, which fields to display, and how to group the selected records for showing subtotals and the like. Thus, while neat and straightforward for trivial queries, a SELECT statement can become very long and complicated for intricate queries or queries involving several files.

The reason is that, no matter how complex, a query must be expressed in its entirety in *one* statement. Specifications that in a traditional language would be implemented naturally by combining some simple constructs must be expressed now by means of clauses and further SELECTs awkwardly nested within the various parts of the main SELECT. Moreover, in order to support real-world queries, some contrived features had to be added to SELECT. The features are, in reality, substitutes for ordinary programming concepts. But, while the traditional languages provide these concepts naturally, as diverse statements, in SQL they must all be crammed, artificially, into the SELECT statement. SQL, thus, while perceived as a modern, high-level database language, is in fact a primitive, ugly language.

Another way to include traditional operations in the SELECT statement was by making them look similar to the relational operations. For example, an operation that results in one value for a group of selected records (the sum of the values present in certain fields, or their average, or minimum) can be included through an option that creates a temporary file of one record where the fields contain the result; and an operation performed on a certain field in every record in the group (calculating the square root, multiplying by a constant, etc.) can be included through an option that creates a temporary file with the same number of records as the original group, but where the fields contain the new value. Many operations easily performed in traditional languages (mathematical and statistical functions, character string manipulation, date and time calculations, etc.) were artificially added to the SELECT statement in this fashion.

Clearly, if we have to develop real-world applications while being unable to create our own file scanning loops, and if SELECT is the only statement available, every operation that we will ever need must be included somehow in this one statement. Thus, the reason for the growing complexity of SELECT is the desire to keep SQL "non-procedural"; specifically, the attempt to provide programming capabilities while restricting these capabilities to a higher level of abstraction than a traditional language. This is an absurd quest, since, if we want the ability to implement any conceivable queries, the language must provide low-level file operations. (We examined in chapter 6 the fallacy of non-procedural languages; see pp. 452–453.) So, in the end, the entities and operations that became part of the SELECT statement had to be of the same level of abstraction as those used in traditional languages: fields, records, keys, comparisons, calculations, and so on.

What the relational theorists are trying to avoid at any cost, even if the cost is increased complexity, is code like that shown in figures 7-13 to 7-16 (pp. 694, 697–699); that is, traditional programming, where the file operations are managed through explicit flow-control constructs. An SQL SELECT statement may well be a little shorter than the equivalent COBOL code, but it does not provide a higher level of abstraction.[27] What is different between SQL and COBOL – *implicit* loops and conditions as opposed to *explicit* ones – is the easy, mechanical part of programming. The difficult part – the overall logic, the file relations, the concept of nested loops and conditions, the links between database entities and the other entities in the application – is necessarily the same in both. With SQL or with COBOL, since the computer cannot know what we want, the only way to implement a given query is by specifying all the details. It is futile to seek a higher level of abstraction.

Thus, even when restricted to queries (and hence still within the relational model), we already note the need to enhance SQL in order to extend its usefulness beyond trivial requirements, as well as the effort to cover up the fact that this is achieved by introducing *programming* capabilities. A complex SQL query is in reality a little program, and what we are doing when creating a complex SELECT statement is programming. We would be better off, therefore, to implement that requirement as several simpler statements, linked through a flow-control structure that follows naturally and intuitively the query's logic, as we do in most languages. But then we could no longer delude ourselves that SQL is non-procedural, or that we are using only high-level relational operations. In the end, as in all mechanistic software delusions, not only did SQL fail to eliminate the need for programming, but in attempting to do this it made programming more difficult.

When the relational systems were expanded to include updating operations, SQL was enhanced with the capability to add, modify, and delete records. The respective statements are INSERT, UPDATE, and DELETE. And these statements are very similar to SELECT, in that they create an implicit file scanning loop and include clauses for various details (record selection criteria, for instance). Updating operations, we recall, are not part of the formal relational model. Thus, regardless of how we feel about SQL as a *query* relational language, the new statements cannot be judged at all by relational principles. So the fact that they are in the same contrived style as SELECT, or the fact that INSERT also permits us to bypass the relational principles altogether and process individual records, can easily be overlooked.

Recall the traditional file operations (pp. 690–693): WRITE, REWRITE, DELETE,

[27] SQL code corresponding to the COBOL code of figure 7-13 might be: SELECT P-NUM FROM PART WHERE P-NUM>=P1 AND P-NUM<=P2 AND P-QTY>=Q1 ORDER BY P-NUM. For the operations in figures 7-14 to 7-16, however, the SQL code would be far more involved, especially if we have to access individual fields from two or three files at the same time.

READ, START, and READ NEXT. We concluded that this is the minimal practical set of file operations – the operations that are both necessary and sufficient for using indexed data files in serious applications. In conjunction with the flow-control constructs provided by the traditional languages, these operations permit us to implement any conceivable database requirement. Putting it in reverse, to permit us to implement any database requirement, a database system *must* provide these operations, or their equivalent.

After the various enhancements, SQL provided four of these operations: INSERT, UPDATE, DELETE, and SELECT correspond, respectively, to the traditional WRITE, REWRITE, DELETE, and READ. Only START and READ NEXT had no SQL counterpart. READ NEXT instructs the file system to retrieve the current record in the indexing sequence and advance the pointer to the next record. It is normally used, therefore, in a file scanning loop (and START is used once, before the loop, to indicate the first record). READ NEXT was thought to be unnecessary in SQL because the four other statements create their own, implicit file scanning loops.

So, with the traditional operations we use READ to access *individual* records, and READ NEXT to access in a loop a series of *consecutive* records; and to modify or delete records we use REWRITE or DELETE, either for individual records or in a READ NEXT loop. With the SQL statements, on the other hand, we access records *only* in a loop – the *implicit* loop generated by each one of the four statements. (Consequently, if we need to access a single record in SQL, we must specify selection criteria that will result in a trivial loop of one iteration.)

The most striking difference between SQL statements and the traditional operations, then, is the implicit file scanning loop as opposed to the loop that we create ourselves. So SQL statements are a little simpler, but to benefit from this simplicity we must give up all flexibility. When we create our own scanning loop, in a traditional language, we can include in the loop additional operations (to perform various tasks related to the file operation). In SQL, the only operations we can have in the loop are those provided by the statement itself, through its clauses. For example, in SQL we can specify with UPDATE the record selection criteria and how to modify the fields in these records. But with a traditional language, a loop based on READ NEXT and REWRITE can also include display operations, subroutine calls, and calculations involving both database fields and memory variables. Thus, when we create our own file scanning loop we can easily link the file entities to the other entities in the application. This is the seamless integration of the database and the application that we discussed earlier (see "The Lost Integration").

We saw how the relational theorists crammed into SELECT various features in an attempt to restore some of the flexibility that was lost in the implicit SQL loops. But there is a limit to the number of operations that can be specified in this fashion, and in the end they had to admit that the capability to create *explicit* file scanning loops, and to control the operations in the loop, is an indispensable database feature. So they added this feature to SQL too, by way of a new enhancement: the FETCH statement.

FETCH is the true counterpart of the traditional READ NEXT: it lets us create explicit loops, and retrieve one record at a time, just as we do in a traditional language. (There is no equivalent of the traditional START: in SQL we always start from the beginning of the file, and the system will deliver only those records that passed the selection criteria previously specified with a SELECT.) FETCH, of course, is not independent. To use it we also need the capability to create explicit loops, and this capability was added to SQL by means of further enhancements: actual loop-control constructs, and a way to perform SQL statements from within a traditional language. (We will examine these enhancements in a moment.)

The mechanism through which we read one record at a time in a loop is known in SQL as *cursor,* and is identical to the mechanism known as *pointer* in the traditional file operations (see pp. 691, 692). The cursor is the indicator that keeps track of records in the current indexing sequence: each time we perform a FETCH, the system retrieves the record identified by the cursor and advances the cursor to the next record – just as it does in the case of the traditional READ NEXT. And if we do this at the beginning of each iteration, all the operations in the loop will be able to access the fields in that record. Thus, in SQL too we can now include in a file scanning loop any operations we want, and thereby link the database fields to other types of entities (memory variables, display fields, etc.). Also, when used in conjunction with FETCH, UPDATE and DELETE can now modify or delete individual records in a scanning loop – just as REWRITE and DELETE can in conjunction with READ NEXT in a traditional loop.

With the concept of a cursor, then, all the capabilities of the traditional file operations were finally available in relational systems. But this was accomplished by abolishing the relational principles: the way we use data files in SQL is now practically identical to the way we use them in a traditional language.

It is even easier to appreciate the importance of this new feature if we ignore the enhancements related to updating operations. For, even if SQL had remained strictly a query language, it would have been almost useless without the means to create explicit file scanning loops. Let us see, therefore, how this feature helped the query operations.

The relational model, we recall, specifically restricts us to high-level operations: all we can do is extract and combine logical portions of tables (i.e., records and fields). The permitted operations are PROJECTION, SELECTION,

UNION, JOIN, and the like (see p. 716). The original SQL SELECT statement, with its implicit file scanning loop, follows this principle: we specify the operations through the various clauses of a SELECT, and combine them by nesting SELECTs within one another. At every step we manipulate only tables – tables that contain, usually, just some of the records and fields of an actual data file.

So the original SELECT statement is *all we need* in order to implement the relational model in SQL. This is true because in high-level queries, as the model was originally intended, all we do for each record in the scanning loop (the outer loop in the case of nested SELECTs) is list some of its fields. We only need, therefore, the means to specify which fields to list, and such details as their order and format. But if we want to employ the model for *any* conceivable query, in the context of *any* application, we need the means to perform additional operations with these fields, not just list them. Also, we need the means to use the fields together with other data types – display and data entry fields, and memory variables. The theorists hoped at first to satisfy these two demands by adding more and more options to the SELECT statement; that is, by inventing a high-level feature for every conceivable situation. This is an absurd idea, however, and they realized in the end that the only practical solution is to permit *low-level* operations.

Thus, even if all we need is queries, only trivial requirements can be implemented if restricted to the implicit file scanning loops of SELECT. It was by adding to SQL the concept of a cursor, and the means to create *explicit* file scanning loops, that we gained the two critical qualities: the capability to perform additional operations in the loop, and the capability to link low-level database entities (individual fields and records) to other entities in the application.

As SQL was used for more and more demanding tasks, it had to be enhanced with the kind of features found in general-purpose programming languages. And software vendors increasingly used *these* features – which have nothing to do with the relational principles, or with database operations – as a way to promote their database systems and attract buyers. For example, some vendors enhanced their version of SQL with the means to create conditional, iterative, and other flow-control constructs (officially abandoning, therefore, the idea of a non-procedural language). And, in addition to those functions similar to the traditional operations and subroutine libraries, already mentioned, countless expedients were provided to assist programmers in developing applications: functions for creating reports, for data entry and display, for system management, and so forth.

What is the point of these enhancements? We already had these features, in a hundred languages. The relational promise had been mathematical logic and a higher level of abstraction, not a new programming language. And if this idea turned out to be impractical, it should have been abandoned. Instead, like all pseudoscientists, the relational experts rescued their theory by reinstating precisely those concepts that the theory had attempted to replace. As a result, software vendors are competing today, not by stressing the *relational* capabilities of their systems, but by adding more and more low-level, programming features; that is, features meant to help us bypass the rigours imposed by the relational model. In other words, the value of a relational system is measured today by how good it is at overriding the relational principles.

But despite the enhancements, SQL remained inferior to the traditional languages. It was still too awkward and too inefficient for serious applications, so one more feature had to be invented: the capability to use SQL from within a traditional language. This feature, called *embedded SQL*, is the ultimate relational degradation: the most effective way for a programmer to enjoy the benefits of the traditional database concepts while pretending to use the relational model.

With embedded SQL, we implement in a traditional language the entire application, including all database requirements; then, we invoke isolated SQL statements here and there in the form of subroutines. The relational system, thus, is relegated to the role of subroutine library, and works similarly to a traditional file system. A typical use of this concept is with the FETCH statement, as explained earlier: we create a file scanning loop in COBOL or any other language, and use FETCH within the loop to read one record at a time – exactly the way we use the traditional READ NEXT. Every other operation in the loop is implemented in the traditional language. The resulting code is identical, for all practical purposes, although we employ in one case a relational system and in the other a traditional file system. We have come a long way from the idea of "tables and nothing but tables," accessed through high-level operations.

An important promise of the relational model had been that the result of a query is mathematically guaranteed to be correct: if we restrict ourselves to the relational operations – to extracting and combining portions of tables – the data in the final table will always reflect accurately the data in the tables we started with. So, if we bypass the restriction to relational operations, this promise no longer holds. Whether the new operations are added in the form of SELECT options or in the form of explicit file scanning loops, the benefits promised by the relational model are now lost. Without the restriction to relational operations, what we have is no longer a relational model, so the resulting tables may or may not reflect accurately the starting ones.

The SQL fallacy, thus, is the belief that the relational model can be enhanced with features that contradict its most fundamental principles, and still retain its original qualities. The mathematical benefits were shown to emerge only if we restrict ourselves to the relational operations. The theorists keep adding features designed specifically to bypass this restriction, but they continue to promote the model with the original claims.

We already know that the *updating* operations lie outside the scope of the formal model, so the model's mathematical grounding is irrelevant when a relational system is used for general database work. And now we see that the model's mathematical grounding has become irrelevant even for queries. As was the case with the other modifications, the SQL features do not *enhance* the relational model but *annul* it.

The Verdict

In the end, what has the relational model accomplished? After thirty years of "enhancements," relational database programming is more or less the same as *traditional* database programming: we manipulate fields, keys, records, and files in order to create database structures. The only real difference is that the database operations have been separated from the rest of the application, and are now possible only through complicated, inefficient, and expensive database environments.

If we disregard that extreme degradation, embedded SQL, applications are now divided into two parts: the part written in an ordinary language, where the application's main logic resides, and the part written in SQL (in the form of integrity functions, stored procedures, and the like), where the database-related operations reside. More and more pieces of the application have been moved into the SQL part; this is not because they are easier to implement in SQL, though, but because they are closely related to the database operations, and keeping them together is the only practical way to link them. And this artificial separation obscures the fact that the part dealing with the database-related operations is now very similar to what it was when integrated with the application's main logic.

The relational charlatans, thus, claimed at first that we must separate the database operations from the application, and restrict the links between the two to a high level of abstraction, because this is the only way to benefit from the relational model. Then, when the separation proved to be impractical, they restored the low-level links. They did it, though, not by moving the database operations back into the application, but by bringing into the SQL procedures further pieces of the application. They restored the links, thus, by reinstating in the SQL procedures the same low-level programming concepts that we had used in the application before the separation. So the benefits believed to emerge from the relational model are now lost even if we forget that they had already been lost, in the other annulments of the relational principles. The separation of the application into two parts is absurd because what we are doing in the SQL procedures is about the same as what we were doing before, in a much simpler way, in the application.

So, after all the "enhancements," there remains very little that is relational in the relational database systems. Programmers use SQL in about the same way that the traditional file operations are used. Only now and then, when not too inconvenient or too inefficient, do they employ the relational operations as they were defined in the original theory. But by calling files "tables," records "rows," and fields "columns," they can delude themselves that they are programming under the relational model.

It must be noted that some features are indeed found only in relational systems. But these features could easily be added also to the traditional file systems, simply because they have nothing to do with the relational model. These are the kind of features made possible by hardware and software advances – larger files, new types of fields, enhanced caching and buffering, better security or backup facilities, and the like. So, if these feature are missing in a file system, it is deliberate: in their effort to make everyone dependent on complicated and expensive development environments, the software elites are doing everything in their power to discredit the straightforward, traditional languages and file systems; and refusing to keep them up to date is part of this manipulation.

It is all the more remarkable, thus, that the traditional languages and file systems, while remaining practically unchanged for the last thirty years, have been the chief source of inspiration for the features added to the relational systems. This shows, again, just how little the relational model itself had to offer.

The relational model is still described as an application of mathematical logic. And those monstrous database systems are promoted with the claim that the relational model is the only way to have rigorous databases, even as everyone can see that these systems have little to do with the relational model, and that their only practical features are those taken from the traditional languages and file operations. So, like the theories of structured program- ming and object-oriented programming, and like all other pseudosciences, the relational theory continues to be promoted on the basis of its original principles even after these principles were abandoned, and hence their benefits were lost.

If we have to bypass the relational restrictions and revert to operations that are practically identical to the traditional ones, in what sense is the relational model beneficial? The theorists are committing a fraud when promoting the relational systems if, at the same time, they enhance these systems with means to override the relational principles.

The multibillion-dollar relational database industry thrives on the incompetence of the software practitioners, whose skills are limited to knowing how to use programming aids and substitutes. To repeat, the six basic file operations and an ordinary language are all we need in order to implement database requirements. Thus, only a programmer incapable of designing some simple loops and conditions can be impressed by the relational features. Every one of these features has been available – in a much simpler form, through file management systems and languages like COBOL – since the early 1970s.

CHAPTER 8

From Mechanism
to Totalitarianism

The End of Responsibility

The irresponsibility that characterizes the world of programming, and the apathy of the rest of society, form an extraordinary phenomenon – a phenomenon that warrants closer analysis. Why are we ready to tolerate, in the domain of programming, failures that in other domains would be easily recognized to be due to incompetence or corruption? In the present section, I will try to explain this phenomenon by showing that it is an inevitable consequence of our mechanistic culture.

Software Irresponsibility

1

"No one ever got fired for buying IBM." This famous saying illustrates perfectly the irresponsibility that defines corporate computing. The saying dates from the 1970s, and perhaps even earlier, so it also serves to remind us that corporate computing was always controlled by bureaucrats.

What the saying implied was that buying IBM hardware and software was a *safe* decision. If the project failed, no one would be blamed; the conclusion would be that everything humanly possible had been done, and the project would also have failed with any other kind of hardware or software. Buying another brand, on the other hand, was a *risky* decision. A failure in this case might have led to the conclusion that the project would have succeeded had IBM been chosen instead. (In reality, the saying exaggerates IBM's role in absolving decision makers from their responsibility: there were many cases where managers did *not* buy IBM, the project failed, and still no one got fired. Hardly anyone in the world of corporate computing is blamed for failures.)

The saying is about IBM because it was coined at a time when IBM was dominating the computer industry. Here we are concerned, however, with the mentality behind it – a mentality that has not changed.

Because of their ignorance, software practitioners perceive application development as a dangerous phenomenon, over which human beings have little control. Primitive people, when recognizing their own ignorance, invent superstitions and magic systems to cope with difficult situations. Similarly, managers and programmers have created a rich culture of *computer* beliefs, myths, and magic systems. (We discussed this in "Anthropology and Software" in the introductory chapter.) They attribute the success of computing projects, not to knowledge and skills, but to selecting the correct systems and performing the proper acts. Their ignorance has given rise to the idea that the success of a project is due to some unexplainable power, which appears to inhere in certain types of hardware or software but not in others. The bureaucratic mentality is similar to the primitive mentality: both stem from ignorance, and both result in intellectual stagnation. Instead of expanding their knowledge to deal with difficult problems, the software bureaucrats, like the primitives, develop elaborate systems of belief.

IBM's high profits in the early period (profits which allowed it to establish its monopolistic position) were due in large measure to the systematic exploitation of this bureaucratic mentality. IBM was aware of the ignorance of its customers, and their perception of computers not as business tool but as status symbol. Thus, as corporate decision makers could not assess rationally the cost and benefits of business computing, IBM was able to maintain arbitrarily high prices. Instead of helping companies to develop expertise in the programming and use of computers, IBM fostered ignorance and irresponsibility by encouraging everyone to view the perpetual adoption of new equipment, regardless of cost, as a business necessity.[1]

[1] Joan M. Greenbaum, *In the Name of Efficiency: Management Theory and Shopfloor Practice in Data-Processing Work* (Philadelphia: Temple University Press, 1979), pp. 133–135. These issues were brought up at IBM's antitrust trial.

Thus, the attitudes we see in today's decision makers were born in the first years of business computing. Recognizing that customer ignorance is more profitable than expertise, the computer companies played an important part in the evolution of the software bureaucracy. It was against their interest that software practitioners be knowledgeable, responsible, and creative, so they did all they could to reduce business computing to trivial tasks – tasks that appealed *only* to people with a bureaucratic mentality. This ensured that no talented individuals, no true professionals, could remain in the world of corporate computing. In particular, the computer companies contributed greatly to the redefinition of programming expertise as expertise in ways to *avoid* programming, and to depend instead on complicated development tools and ready-made pieces of software.[2]

As a result of this scheme, the typical programmer or data-processing manager emerging from that period is a person who knows very little about computers, programming, or business, but who enjoys a position of prestige in society thanks to the propaganda conducted on his behalf by the elites. These incompetents induce their employers to spend large amounts of money on hardware and software novelties, and in exchange, the elites flatter them by depicting them (with the assistance of the media) as skilled professionals whose expertise is vital to their company's success. Everyone gets to respect them and to depend on them, and they themselves are convinced that what they are doing is important and difficult, when in reality they are puppets manipulated by the elites.

Although IBM no longer dominates the computer industry, the saying can still be used to describe the software bureaucrats. Today no one gets fired for buying Microsoft, or for buying client/server, or object-oriented, or 4GL, or relational, or cloud, or data warehouse, or anything else deemed to be the correct choice.

Take CASE, for example – the idea that it is possible to develop business applications without programming. For many years, CASE was promoted by the software companies, by professors and gurus, by the business and computer media, and by professional associations, as the indisputable next

---

[2] It is an old maxim in the computer industry that good software sells hardware. But, even if the promotion of various types of software to help sell hardware started as an honest business strategy, the computer companies realized very quickly that, while good software indeed sells hardware, *bad* software sells even more hardware. Most hardware expenses are induced by bad software; and since bad software is the result of programming incompetence, it is not surprising that the computer companies never encouraged programming expertise. There are many ways for programming incompetence to demand more expensive hardware; for example, a more powerful computer is needed to compensate for the inefficiency of an inferior application, or to permit the use of large development environments, database systems, and packaged applications – all intended as substitutes for programming expertise.

stage in "software engineering." We will never know how many billions of dollars were wasted by businesses on this idea, before abandoning it. And the fact that they could not recognize its absurdity just by looking at it demonstrates the ignorance that managers and programmers suffer from. CASE had to be actually tried in thousands of projects before they realized that it didn't work. Even then, they could not see why the idea was fundamentally mistaken, so they learned nothing from this experience. (We discussed the CASE fallacy in chapter 6; see pp. 479–483.)

Needless to say, no one got fired for buying CASE. Nor did its failure affect the credibility of the companies that sold CASE systems, or the experts that advocated it, or the publications that promoted it. They simply went on inventing and promoting other concepts and expedients, for the same managers and programmers who had bought CASE earlier. Like the primitives, the software bureaucrats are not perturbed by the failure of one magic system. Their belief in software magic unshaken, they are trying now other systems. And no one will get fired for buying those systems either.

2

Partial or total software failures are such a common spectacle that they are now taken for granted. Actually, we no longer think of these occurrences as failures: the failing application, or utility, or methodology, or theory, or development system is accepted anyway, or else is abandoned and another one tried, and all this is seen as a normal software-related activity. Anyone close to the world of "information technology" is familiar with disappointing projects – requirements that cannot be satisfied, applications that cannot be kept up to date, projects that take far longer and cost far more than anticipated – but these situations are not seen as failures. New software products are installed every year in millions of places without being seriously used – presumably because they are not, in fact, the "solutions" they were said to be – but they are not seen as failures either. Nor are seen as failures those software projects that were approved on the promise of increased profits, or savings, or efficiency, or productivity, or strategic advantages, or return on investment, when these promises are not even remembered, much less verified, years later.

More and more organizations are facing software-related problems, but no one is referring to them as software failures. If the problem is discussed at all, the next software change is described as an upgrade, or as a migration, or as deploying a more advanced application, or as rearchitecting the system, or as strategic business transformation, or simply as investing in technology. For obvious reasons, it is in no one's interest to dwell on a failure; besides, neither the programmers, nor the managers, nor the consultants, nor the software companies appear to be responsible for it. So the whole affair is quietly forgotten, and the next project is initiated.

The only events reported in the media are the "success stories": isolated situations carefully selected from the thousands available, and described so as to create in the public eye a bright image of the world of computers and software. In reality we may well have a hundred failures for each success, but one wouldn't think so from reading business and computer periodicals. Only when the loss is in the tens of millions of dollars is a software failure likely to be made public. And even then, no one is seriously reproved: after a brief investigation – conducted largely for the sake of appearances – the failure is forgotten.

We are *surrounded* by software failures, but the software propaganda has succeeded in convincing us that these are not failures but normal occurrences. Thus, since they are not failures, no one is to be blamed. Software is designed and programmed by people, is sold and bought by people, is installed and used by people, but when it fails no one is to be blamed. In most cases we know the actual individuals involved in its development, purchase, or installation; but we don't feel that these individuals must be reprimanded, that they are accountable for their work in the same way that physicians, pilots, or engineers are for theirs.

In other professions we have the notions of incompetence, negligence, and malpractice to describe performance levels that fall below expectations. In software-related matters, and particularly in programming activities, these notions do not exist. In other professions we have created codes of expertise based on high performance levels – levels usually attained only after much training and practice; and we have associations safeguarding these codes, watching over the practitioners' conduct, and issuing and revoking licences. No one expects equivalent codes and licences for software practitioners.[3]

For most products, we expect solid warranties regarding quality and

---

[3] Some attempts *have* been made to establish codes for programming expertise. What these codes promote, though, is not the difficult skills required to solve real problems, but the trivial skills required to use the programming aids prescribed by the software elites. And the purpose of these aids, we saw, is to act as *substitutes* for programming expertise. Such codes, therefore, while appearing to promote professionalism, are in reality a fraud: they are invented by the elites as part of their effort to *prevent* expertise, and to create a dependence on development systems which they control. These are codes befitting a software bureaucracy.

performance; for software, the only warranty we get is that the bytes in the box will be read successfully into our computer. Instead of warranty we get *disclaimers*, and we sign a software agreement which specifies that, regardless of the product's performance, we alone are responsible for the consequences of its use. When other products do not work as promised, we are outraged, complain, return them, and even consider a lawsuit. When software products have deficiencies, or fail to provide the promised "solutions," we gladly expend time and effort dealing with their shortcomings, pay for "technical support," and look forward to the next version – which, we are told, will solve the problems created by the present one.

What is extraordinary, again, is not so much the incompetence and irresponsibility of the software practitioners, as the apathy of the rest of society: our acceptance, our belief that what they are doing represents the utmost that human beings can accomplish in the domain of programming.

If this incompetence and irresponsibility are found today mainly in programming, it is safe to predict that, as our dependence on software is growing, the same incompetence and irresponsibility, and the same tolerance and apathy, will spread into other fields. At issue, therefore, is more than just the current exploitation of society by the software bureaucrats. The corruption we are witnessing today in only one field may be the reflection of a trend that is affecting the entire society, so the study of software irresponsibility may reveal important truths about ourselves and our social future.

Determinism versus Responsibility

1

The idea of responsibility, and the closely related ideas of free will and determinism, are subjects studied by that branch of philosophy known as ethics, or moral philosophy. The *conflict* between free will and determinism, in particular, has troubled thinkers for centuries, and is still being debated.

The problem is simply this: Are human actions, choices, and decisions free, or are they causally determined? Usually, we feel that what we did on a certain occasion was the result of our own volition, that we could have acted differently had we chosen to. This perception is perhaps gratifying, but it is hardly sufficient when our acts affect other persons – when what we do has moral or legal significance. We need, therefore, a dependable method of determining, for a given act, whether it was performed freely or not. When a person performs a wrongful act, must he be blamed? Can we be sure that he could have acted differently and chose the wrongful act freely? And conversely, are a person's right acts always worthy of praise? Can we be sure that he could have acted differently and made the right choice freely?

It is obvious, then, why the idea of responsibility is related to the conflict between free will and determinism: If we believe in free will, we admit that we are free to conduct ourselves according to our own will; so we must be held responsible for our acts. If, however, we believe in determinism, then our acts, like any event in the universe, are the result of previous events, over which we may have no control; so we must not be held responsible.

Determinism is the thesis that the future state of a system can be determined from its present state, because all events are necessarily caused by some other events. And a belief in mechanism entails a belief in determinism. The mechanistic doctrine is founded upon the principles of reductionism and atomism: it maintains that a complex phenomenon can be seen as the result of simpler phenomena, which in their turn can be broken down into even simpler ones, and so on, reaching ultimately some elementary phenomena that can be understood intuitively. Mechanism, thus, holds that everything can be explained: from phenomena involving objects and physical processes, to phenomena involving human beings and mental processes.

Every entity or event in the present is a result of past phenomena, so mechanism assures us that from a knowledge of the past we can explain fully and precisely the present. Similarly, since present phenomena are the cause of future ones, a knowledge of the present should allow us to predict fully and precisely every entity and event in the future. This fantastic claim is the essence of determinism, and a *necessary consequence* of mechanism. To put it differently, a person who believes in mechanism cannot believe at the same time in *indeterminism* without contradicting himself.

The best-known expression of determinism is the one formulated by Laplace some two centuries ago: The whole universe, and every occurrence in the universe, can be seen as a system of particles of matter acting upon one another according to Newton's law of gravitation. Thus, an infinitely intelligent being, capable of observing the state of all the particles at a particular instant and capable also of solving the pertinent equations, could determine their state – and hence the state of the universe – for any other instant in the past and in the future. This being (known as Laplace's demon) could, therefore, predict every future occurrence in the universe.

Note that it is irrelevant whether such a being exists; only the *idea* matters. The mechanists merely claim that it is possible to reduce to particle mechanics all physical, chemical, biological, psychological, and social phenomena, and hence omniscience – complete understanding of the past and present, and complete knowledge of the future – is within our reach. The mechanists admit that we are far from having achieved this reduction. Still, they say, we are making progress, and one day we may well become omniscient. This too, however, is irrelevant: even if human beings are incapable of omniscience, the mechanists say, and even if no omniscient beings exist anywhere, this does not alter the fact that the future can be completely determined from the present. The particles and the law of gravitation continue to exist even if Laplace's demon is no more than an idea.

Thus, the mechanists conclude, even if no real or hypothetical being can know everything in the world, it is still true that the world can be explained; it is still true that the state of the universe at any instant is the result of earlier states, that every occurrence is caused by previous occurrences. And, since we are part of the universe, it must also be true that every decision and action displayed by human beings is the result of past occurrences. But most occurrences in the universe are beyond our control; so perhaps all our thoughts, feelings, and acts are due in fact to external causes, not our own volition. The idea of free will is therefore an illusion. And it is not only the possibility of free will that is an illusion, but also the possibility of original deeds, and hence of individual responsibility. Human beings are just mechanical parts in the great machine that is the universe, and all aspects of human existence can be explained and predicted, in principle, with the same equations that describe the motion of bits of matter.

This view, fallacious and distasteful as it is, has dominated science and philosophy since the seventeenth century. The mechanistic doctrine has been a complete failure in the human sciences, where it cannot explain even the simplest phenomena, let alone thoughts and feelings. But its spectacular success in the natural sciences has inspired scientists and philosophers with confidence, and few doubt, even today, that reductionism and atomism will eventually prove to be just as successful in explaining *human* phenomena. Thus, even though mechanism has been shown to work only in a narrow range of physical phenomena, researchers in *all* disciplines see it as their professional duty to adhere faithfully to the mechanistic doctrine. At the same time, because determinism creates such a demeaning view of humanity, many scientists and philosophers are now reluctant to call themselves determinists; and some even deny that they are mechanists.

As I have pointed out, today's mechanistic theories only *appear* less naive than the earlier ones (see pp. 82–84). In reality, current academic research is grounded, just like seventeenth-century science, on the assumption that all phenomena can be reduced to particle mechanics. The theories have not changed, and are as fallacious as ever; but because determinism is no longer fashionable, the bold and straightforward claims of earlier times have been replaced with a mass of sophisticated rhetoric.

Today's mechanists are in a difficult position. They want to give up the idea of determinism, but to continue to practise mechanism. Mechanism, however, entails determinism, so the mechanists are caught in a self-contradiction. The only way out is to claim that mechanism can be reconciled with indeterminism, that we can have both. And indeed, countless theories have been advanced in the last one hundred years in an attempt to show that mechanism is, in fact, compatible with indeterminism. This notion is nonsensical, of course, but in a culture where so many absurdities have already been claimed in the name of mechanism, one more absurdity makes little difference. This is how Karl Popper puts it: "I personally find Laplacean determinism a most unconvincing and unattractive view.... But it is, perhaps, worth stressing that Laplace does draw the correct conclusions from his idea of a causally closed and deterministic [world]. If we accept Laplace's view, then we must not argue (as many philosophers do) that we are nevertheless endowed with genuine human freedom and creativity."[1]

2

The delusion of determinism is easy to understand if we recall the concept of simple and complex structures. All phenomena are in reality non-mechanistic, the result of many interacting processes; so they can be represented accurately only with *complex* structures. Still, some phenomena can be *approximated* with simple structures. If a phenomenon requires a system of interacting structures, we can usefully approximate it with one structure when the links between structures are weak enough to be ignored. But a simple structure provides both mechanistic and deterministic qualities; consequently, a phenomenon seen as mechanistic will be seen at the same time as deterministic. The determinism of a phenomenon, though, just like its mechanism, is an illusion, an *approximation* of reality. We find a deterministic approximation useful, presumably, for the same phenomena for which we find a mechanistic approximation useful.

We have discovered useful mechanistic approximations for many phenomena – physical ones, in particular; but these phenomena form only a small part of our world. The most important biological processes, and practically all mental and social processes, are complex phenomena; and for them no useful mechanistic representations have been found. Even some physical phenomena are only poorly approximated by mechanistic models (the apparently simple three-body system, for instance, see pp. 109–110). And, most

---

[1] Karl R. Popper, *The Open Universe: An Argument for Indeterminism* (London: Routledge, 1988), p. 124.

surprisingly perhaps, mechanism has not kept up with the discoveries of modern physics in the field of *elementary* particles, precisely where one would expect reductionism and atomism to work best: everyone agrees that the theory of quantum mechanics is incompatible with classical mechanics.

Mechanistic approximation, thus, fails at both low and high levels of complexity: for elementary physical phenomena as much as mental and social phenomena. Ultimately, only a narrow range of phenomena are amenable to mechanistic approximation. So, if the others are non-mechanistic, they must also be indeterministic.

❖

Recall the theories we studied in chapter 3, and their consequences. Those scientists claimed that all human phenomena can be explained with precision, so human beings are in reality deterministic systems. Scientists today are still working on this type of theories; but because the academic fashion has changed, we don't hear the claim that human beings are deterministic systems as often as we did in the past.

A recapitulation of these delusions will help us to understand how they affect our conception of individual responsibility. What I want to show is that, by degrading the concept of indeterminism, the theories of mind – and now also the theories of software and programming – are still claiming, in effect, that human beings are deterministic systems. The conclusion that we are not responsible for our acts follows then logically. Thus, there is no real difference between a theory that *denies* the existence of free will and creativity, as the older theories did, and one that *accepts* these qualities but *redefines* them to match a mechanistic model.

Minds and societies give rise to indeterministic phenomena, so mechanistic theories cannot explain them. The faith in mechanism, however, prevents the scientists from recognizing these failures as falsifications. So, instead of doubting and severely testing their theories, they end up *defending* them. The only way to defend a fallacious theory is by turning it into a pseudoscience: tests are restricted to situations that confirm it; and the theory is repeatedly expanded, by incorporating the falsifying instances and making them look like new features. Eventually, the theory becomes unfalsifiable, and hence worthless. But the scientists do not consider this activity to be dishonest, or unprofessional. On the contrary: because the principles of reductionism and atomism are accepted implicitly as the universal method of science, defending a mechanistic theory is perceived as important scientific work.

Then, even though their theories keep failing, the scientists draw demeaning conclusions about human beings and human societies – conclusions that would be warranted only if their theories were successful. They conclude, in particular, that all manifestations of human knowledge and behaviour can be deduced from some innate faculties, which constitute a sort of alphabet of human capabilities; so the knowledge and behaviour displayed by each one of us can be described with precision as a function of these innate faculties, just as the operation of a machine can be described as a function of its parts.

Mechanistic theories of mind and society, thus, *inevitably* lead to the view that human beings are deterministic systems: we have no control over our innate capabilities, of course; and if, in addition, our knowledge and behaviour can be precisely deduced from these capabilities, then we can have no greater control over our decisions and actions than machines have over theirs. It is impossible to separate mechanism from determinism.

But, to adhere to the current academic fashion, the scientists claim that mechanistic theories do *not* preclude indeterminism in human affairs. Specifically, they claim that it is possible to explain mathematically all human acts, and all aspects of a human society, without denying free will and creativity. They avoid the contradiction by *redefining* these concepts: from the absolute qualities we take them to be, to some relative qualities, which match their theories. They continue to use the terms "freedom" and "creativity," but instead of *unpredictable* acts, the terms mean now just the freedom and creativity to select any act from a range of known alternatives. Still, the scientists argue, if the number of alternatives is sufficiently large, the new definition does not deny indeterminism. *Their fallacy is to misinterpret indeterminism as a large number of alternatives.*

Mechanistic models are logically equivalent to simple hierarchical structures, as we know. Mechanistic theories, therefore, depict human phenomena as simple structures. Depending on the theory, the starting elements are various bits of knowledge or behaviour, or various propensities, while the values of the top element are the many alternatives displayed by a mind or by a society: all possible knowledge, behaviour patterns, language uses, social customs, and so forth. The mechanistic *software* theories, for their part, depict as simple structures *software* phenomena – the development and use of software. The starting elements are various software entities and various bits of software-related knowledge, while the values of the top element are all the alternatives possible for software applications and their use.

Now, it is quite easy to design a mechanistic model that displays an infinite number of alternatives. And the scientists misinterpret this trivial quality of mechanistic models as indeterminism: they believe that these alternatives are the same as the infinity of alternatives that make up the actual, complex phenomenon. So, they conclude, a model has been discovered that is both mechanistic and indeterministic.

Mechanistic theories, thus, assume that human minds and societies are akin to devices, in that they can be in a number of states, or can generate a number of alternatives – states and alternatives that we can account for. A device like a die, for example, behaves unpredictably when rolling; but we know that it will display, when stopped, one of six given symbols. Human phenomena are thought to be essentially the same, except for displaying many more alternatives, perhaps even an infinite number of alternatives. Let us use the analogy of the die to examine this fallacy.

A rolling die constitutes a complex phenomenon, the interaction of several phenomena; this interaction is what determines its movement and, consequently, which symbol will be displayed when it stops. The six alternatives form, in fact, only a small part of the actual phenomenon. To describe the complex phenomenon, we would have to take into account many details of the die itself, its movement when rolling, and its environment: its size, its material and weight, the shape of its edges and corners, its starting orientation in space, the form and texture of the surfaces it touches, how variables like the ambient temperature and humidity affect its movement, and the direction and magnitude of the force that sets it in motion. Also, the final state will be, not just the symbol displayed, but the exact position and orientation of the die in space when the rolling stops; that is, not one of six, but one of an infinite number of alternatives. The actual phenomenon, thus, consists of a large number of factors, which can display an infinite number of values, and lead to an infinite number of possible results.

It is not this infinity of alternatives that prevents us from predicting the final state, though, but the fact that the phenomenon is non-mechanistic: we cannot describe with precision how the final state depends on the various factors. Still, nothing stops us from representing the phenomenon with a mechanistic model: all we have to do is depict it with a simple structure where the starting elements are the six symbols, and the top element is the symbol displayed when the die stops rolling. The phenomenon can then be said to be both mechanistic (because we can account for all possible values of the top element from a knowledge of the starting elements) and indeterministic (because we don't know which symbol will actually be displayed).

What we did, obviously, is *simplify* the phenomenon: our model is an *approximation* of the actual die phenomenon. Rather than a complicated movement and a final state determined by the interaction of many factors, we described the phenomenon simply as the selection of one symbol out of six. And "indeterminism" is now, not the uncertainty of the actual phenomenon, but the uncertainty of not knowing which symbol will be selected. In other words, if we degrade the notion of indeterminism to mean just the uncertainty of not knowing which alternative will be selected from a known range of alternatives, we can claim that the phenomenon of the die is both mechanistic and indeterministic.

Scientists attempt to represent minds and societies with mechanistic models because they believe the indeterminism of human phenomena to be like the indeterminism of the *simplified* die phenomenon. The only difference, they say, is the larger number of alternatives. The indeterminism of human phenomena, however, is like the indeterminism of the *actual* die phenomenon. Minds and societies give rise to complex phenomena, and hence to *true* indeterminism, not the weak indeterminism displayed by a mechanistic model.

We can perhaps delude ourselves that we understand the die phenomenon when we depict it as the selection of one symbol out of six; but this delusion comes to an end when we study the great complexity of the *actual* phenomenon. Clearly, the unpredictability of the final state of the die as a result of all those factors is of a higher level than the unpredictability of selecting one symbol out of six. Thus, the simplified, mechanistic model is useless if what we need is to describe the relationship between those factors and the die's final state.

Similarly, the scientists keep simplifying the complex structure that is a human phenomenon until they manage to depict it with a mechanistic model. But this approximation is too crude to be useful, because it can display only a fraction of the alternatives that make up the actual phenomenon. The scientists stop their simplification at a point where there is still enough indeterminism left to make the mechanistic model somewhat unpredictable; and they misinterpret this unpredictability – which is just the trivial process of selecting one alternative out of many – as the indeterminism of the original, complex phenomenon.

In our analogy, the actual die phenomenon stands for a human phenomenon, and the simplified model stands for the mechanistic model of the human phenomenon. But unlike the six alternatives of the die, the mechanistic model of the human phenomenon, even though a simplified version of the actual phenomenon, still displays an infinite number of alternatives. And this is the source of the confusion. For, the infinity of alternatives found in the mechanistic model is only a fraction of the infinity found in the actual, complex phenomenon; and consequently, the indeterminism of the mechanistic model is only a weak version of the indeterminism displayed by the actual phenomenon. The number is infinite in both cases, but we are witnessing in fact different *kinds* of phenomena: one can be represented mathematically, while the other cannot.

It is the infinity of alternatives displayed by their mechanistic models, therefore, that confuses the scientists: they mistakenly conclude that, being infinite, these must be all possible alternatives, so their models can represent human phenomena.

Mechanistic models fail because they are incapable of displaying the same indeterminism as the actual phenomena. True indeterminism is, of course, the highest form of indeterminism. It is only by choosing a weaker definition that the scientists manage to contrive models that are both mechanistic and indeterministic. But if their goal is to explain human phenomena, degrading the concept of indeterminism cannot help them: all they can discover then is theories that do not work, models that do not approximate the human phenomena closely enough to be useful.

In conclusion, the difference between true indeterminism and its weaker version is not as mysterious as it appears. When attempting to represent a complex phenomenon with a simple structure, the scientists are committing the two mechanistic fallacies, abstraction and reification: they start from levels that are too high, and they ignore the links with the *other* structures that are part of the phenomenon. Their model, as a result, cannot account for all the alternatives: missing are those caused by interactions at levels lower than the level of the starting elements. The difference between the alternatives generated when starting from low-level physiological elements, and those generated by starting from the higher-level elements, is the difference between true indeterminism and its weaker version. (See also the related discussion in chapter 3, pp. 283–286.)

3

Just like the mechanistic theories of mind and society, the mechanistic *software* theories praise creativity while degrading this concept to match the weak version of indeterminism. Creativity in software-related matters, according to these theories, does not mean the utmost that human minds can accomplish, but merely the selection and combination of bits of knowledge within a predetermined range of alternatives.

Software mechanism holds that software-related phenomena can be represented as simple structures, and that it is possible to account for all the values of the top element in these structures. These values are, in effect, all the applications that can be implemented with software, and all aspects of software use. Software mechanism claims, thus, that it is possible to account for all the alternatives displayed by human minds when engaged in software-related activities. Accordingly, it should be possible to identify the elements that lie just a few levels below the top element. It is these elements, clearly, that give rise to all the alternatives, so there is no need to deal with lower-level ones. We should treat *these* elements as starting elements, and incorporate them in software devices. Then, by operating such a device, anyone will be able to generate all the values of the top element – all conceivable alternatives in software-related phenomena – simply by selecting and combining these elements.

What this means in practice is that we should be able to replace the knowledge and experience needed to create software applications, with the simple skills needed to operate software devices; that is, the skills needed to make selections. Software devices, thus, materialize the belief that what an experienced mind does is merely select and combine alternatives, so the indeterminism we observe in software-related phenomena is just the uncertainty caused by the large number of alternatives.

This interpretation also explains why the software devices provide their operations in the form of selections (menus, buttons, lists, etc.), and selections within selections, instead of allowing us to use them freely – as we use natural languages, or traditional programming languages. Their designers, obviously, are attempting to implement a simple hierarchical structure: the structure of knowledge that, according to their theories, exists in the mind of an experienced person.

So there is no longer a need for each one of us to develop structures in our mind starting from low-level bits of knowledge. Since the operations provided by devices can directly replace high-level knowledge elements, by combining these operations we will be able to generate any one of the knowledge alternatives that human minds can display (or, at least, the important alternatives) without having to possess that knowledge ourselves. The easy skill of selecting and combining those operations, the software mechanists assure us, can be a substitute for the complex knowledge developed in a mind by starting from low levels. The only thing that human beings need to know from now on is how to select and combine operations within the range of alternatives provided by software devices.

Like the mind mechanists, the software mechanists commit the two fallacies, reification and abstraction: they take into account only one structure, ignoring the other relations that exist between the same elements; and they start from levels that are too high. As a result, they lose the alternatives arising from the interactions occurring at levels lower than their starting elements. They note the infinity of alternatives possible even when starting from higher levels, and conclude that, since their software devices can generate these alternatives, they have attained their goal: a mechanistic model that can emulate indeterministic phenomena. Their infinity, however, is only a fraction of the infinity of alternatives found in the actual, complex phenomenon.

By restricting ourselves to simple structures, we are becoming a closed, deterministic society, where only certain alternatives can exist. The danger posed by our software ideology, therefore, is not just the loss of alternatives in software-related matters, but the degradation of minds. Our non-mechanistic capabilities do not simply exist – they develop; and they can develop only when we are exposed to low-level elements, because this is the only way to create all possible alternatives in our minds. If we restrict ourselves to mechanistic knowledge – to simple knowledge structures and high-level starting elements – our minds cannot develop above the intellectual level of machines.

Why is it so easy for the software elites to convince us that our minds are inferior to their devices? Our willingness to accept this notion, despite its obvious fallaciousness, may well be a symptom, an indication of how advanced our mental degradation *already* is. We must use our minds to judge the usefulness of software devices, but it is these very minds that remain undeveloped when we agree to depend on devices. So, if we trust the elites and get to depend on their devices, we are *bound* to lose our ability to recognize how useless these devices actually are. We will believe that the devices are superior to our minds, so we will continue to depend on them; our minds will then be further degraded, in a process that feeds on itself.

This collective mental degradation is an amazing spectacle. We are willingly renouncing our natural mental capabilities, and our responsibility as individuals, and replacing them with a dependence on devices and on the elites behind them. We are degrading our status from creative and responsible individuals to operators of devices. This process, which may well be irreversible, is the ultimate consequence of our mechanistic culture: when we agree to limit ourselves to mechanistic performance, and hence to a fraction of our mental capacity, what we do in effect is fulfil the wish of those scientists who have been telling us for a long time that our minds are nothing but complicated machines.

4

We must not be confused by words. No matter what the mechanists say, their theories necessarily lead to the view that there is no indeterminism in human phenomena. The scientists, and now also the software theorists, may use words like "indeterminism," "freedom," and "creativity," but they are degrading these concepts to mean the selection of acts from a known range of alternatives. This is how they manage to have mechanism and indeterminism at the same time.

Whether their theories describe minds and societies, or software development and use, if they claim that it is possible to account for all the alternatives in advance then what they are promoting is *deterministic* theories; and if they attempt to represent minds and societies with mechanistic models, or to replace knowledge with software devices, then what they are saying is that human beings *are* deterministic systems.

If the mechanists believe that we are deterministic systems, their conclusion *must* be that we are not free agents, and that we cannot be held responsible for our acts. The theories of mind and society manage to avoid this conclusion by maintaining that it is possible to have both mechanism and indeterminism. And, since these theories do not work anyway, few notice the absurdity of the claim. We didn't change the way we think or behave or speak, to match the mechanistic theories; so the fact that they are self-contradictory can be overlooked. The *software* theories make claims similar to the traditional mechanistic claims, but now we *are* modifying our conception of intelligence and creativity: we are mutating into deterministic beings.

I remarked at the beginning of this chapter that the incompetence and irresponsibility displayed by the software practitioners, and the tolerance and apathy of the rest of us – our belief that they need not be accountable for their deeds as other professionals are for theirs – constitute an extraordinary phenomenon. We are now in a position to explain this phenomenon.

These attitudes are a natural consequence of the mechanistic software culture. It is impossible to have at the same time a mechanistic, and hence deterministic, culture *and* responsibility. If people are seen as deterministic systems, we cannot expect them to possess non-mechanistic knowledge. So, if all they can do is follow theories and methodologies, or operate software devices, we must limit their accountability to the performance of these acts; we cannot hold them responsible for the *results*.

Increasingly, as programmers and as users, we depend on software devices that are based on mechanistic theories. And when we agree to depend on these devices, we agree in effect to modify our conception of human intelligence to correspond to the mechanistic dogma. We agree, in other words, to forgo our non-mechanistic capabilities: we restrict ourselves to mechanistic knowledge, and thereby keep our performance at the level of novices, or machines. This, clearly, is a new development, a new manifestation of the mechanistic myth.

The traditional mechanistic theories tried to explain and predict human acts; and they failed, because we ignored them and remained indeterministic systems. The software theories, when viewed as theories of human capabilities, appear to work; but this is because we have now agreed to restrict our perform-ance to mechanistic levels. Thus, the reason why irresponsibility is especially noticeable in software-related activities is that, in our capacity as programmers or software users, our transformation from indeterministic to deterministic systems is almost complete. In our software pursuits, we have renounced our non-mechanistic capabilities; so the world of software constitutes, in effect, a social system founded upon mechanistic principles. In this system, people have been absolved from accountability for the consequences of their acts, and the idea of responsibility has been degraded to mean simply adherence to the official ideology. Attitudes that used to exist only in fictional societies, or in totalitarian societies, can now be found in our software pursuits.

Today we can observe this phenomenon mainly in our software-related affairs – programming, in particular – because the mechanistic software theories affect our software pursuits directly. But we should expect to see the same irresponsibility and the same acceptance emerge in other domains, as these domains become dependent on mechanistic software notions. We cannot retain the concept of individual responsibility in a society where we consider individuals to be deterministic systems. Indeterminism is associated with free will, and hence responsibility; so determinism *logically* entails irresponsibility.

5

As our dependence on software is growing, our society is becoming increasingly totalitarian; and this progression can be observed in our attitude toward individual responsibility. Under totalitarianism, the responsibility of the individual is redefined to mean the responsibility of obeying the elite. Terms like "freedom," "creativity," "expertise," and "intelligence" are still used, but their meaning is degraded: individuals are expected to possess these qualities, but the qualities mean now merely the selection of certain acts from a predetermined range of alternatives. Whereas in their true sense the terms describe *absolute* values – the ability to select *any* alternative that can be conceived by human minds – under totalitarianism the terms describe *relative* values: the freedom to perform any activity sanctioned by the elite, the creativity to accomplish a task with the means supplied by the elite, expertise in the kind of knowledge taught by the elite, and the intelligence to appreciate the totalitarian ideology.

Note how similar these concepts are to the mechanistic *academic* ideology: the theories of mind claim that intelligence, creativity, and expertise mean the selection of acts from a predetermined range of alternatives – the range for which human minds are biologically wired; and the responsibility of scientists is redefined to mean the obligation of pursuing only this type of theories. Note also how similar these concepts are to the mechanistic *software* ideology: expertise in programming, and in software-related activities generally, has been redefined to mean familiarity with the mechanistic software theories, and with the development tools provided by the elite; and responsibility means simply the challenge of keeping up with these theories and tools.

But this is no coincidence. Recall the inevitable progression – mechanism, scientism, utopianism, totalitarianism. Mechanistic beliefs lead to scientistic theories – mechanistic theories of mind and society – which then lead to the utopian vision of a perfect society. The perfect society must be founded upon strict mechanistic principles, but human beings are currently non-mechanistic systems, undisciplined and unpredictable. They must be coerced, therefore, in the name of progress, to abandon the old-fashioned ideas of freedom and creativity, to admit that they are merely small parts in a great deterministic system, and to restrict themselves to mechanistic performance. It *is* possible to create a perfect society, but, unfortunately, only through totalitarianism. This is a passing phase, though. The coercion is only necessary until everyone gets to appreciate the benefits of mechanistic thinking; that is, until every person becomes a deterministic system, an automaton.

Mechanism and determinism are logically related to irresponsibility, as we saw. Thus, one way of judging how close a society is to being "perfect" is by studying its conception of individual responsibility: how people think of themselves, of their rights and responsibilities, is an indication of the stage their society has reached in the progression from a human system to a mechanistic one. What we notice is a shift: from the idea that we are directly responsible for our acts as individuals and as professionals, to the idea that we are only responsible for conforming to a certain ideology, while its validity or morality need not concern us. If mechanistic, and hence "scientific," the ideology is believed to embody the absolute truth.

Under Nazism, for example, countless individuals were involved in atrocious crimes, or were watching passively as crimes were being committed all around them, convinced that they were serving their country. By modifying the idea of responsibility, perfectly normal people – people with family and friends, and an appreciation of life, art, and logic – were induced to do almost anything. For an entire society, the idea of responsibility was redefined in just a few years to mean, simply, adherence to the ideology established by their leaders. Pseudoscientific theories on social, racial, and political matters, invented by a small elite, became unquestionable principles. People no longer saw themselves as independent human beings, but as parts of a great mechanistic system, a great historical process that was as inevitable as evolution itself.

When the mechanistic dogma is accepted implicitly, the shift in the meaning of responsibility follows logically. If we believe in mechanistic social notions – if, in other words, we hold certain developments to be historically inevitable – we cannot at the same time consider ourselves to be free agents. All our thoughts and acts must then conform to these notions, and any doubts seem as absurd as doubting the laws of nature. The way mechanism engenders irresponsibility, then, is by assuming that individuals and societies are parts of a great deterministic system, so everything can be explained precisely and completely – in principle, at least. Our common-sense conceptions of free will, intelligence, creativity, and responsibility are therefore mere illusions. In reality, we *cannot help* thinking, feeling, and acting as we do. Our knowledge, beliefs, and capabilities are determined largely by forces beyond our control. Although we do not yet understand that great system of which we are part, there can be no doubt that it is deterministic; so the conclusion that we are not really free, and hence cannot be held responsible for our acts, remains valid.

6

Nazism is only an extreme example of the progression of a society from liberalism to mechanistic thinking and irresponsibility. Because mechanistic theories of mind end up degrading the notion of responsibility, we can observe this progression, in a milder form, in our own society. Recall the mechanistic delusions we studied in chapter 3. While society has yet to reach the level of degradation depicted by these theories, we can already observe it in the attitude of the scientists themselves. They have degraded the definition of scientific responsibility, from discovering sound and useful theories, to discovering *mechanistic* theories.

Then, since what matters to them is not whether the theory is valid but whether it is mechanistic, the scientists draw from their *failing* theories the kind of conclusions that would be warranted only if the theories were successful. Specifically, they claim that human beings are nothing but complicated machines; that human acts are a function of innate propensities and can be explained with mathematical precision; and that, based on these facts, it is possible to design and implement a perfect society.

Thus, in addition to turning their disciplines into pseudosciences, the scientists promote theories that lead to totalitarianism. But they do it out of a sense of duty: their responsibility, they say, is to promote science, and science means mechanism. They perceive themselves as pioneers, as experts who understand what the rest of us cannot yet see, and who alone have the courage to accept the implications of these discoveries; namely, to accept the fact that human beings are in reality automatons. So it is their duty to enforce these ideas upon us, the ignorant masses. But there is nothing wrong in this, the scientists say; all they are doing is helping to speed up a process of social evolution that was going to take place anyway.

Since mechanism has distorted their own sense of responsibility, it is not surprising that their vision of the perfect society is a deterministic social system where everyone has been degraded just as they have degraded themselves. The only reason we have not yet been turned into automatons is that these scientists lack the power to implement their vision. But it is important to study their mechanistic obsessions and totalitarian attitudes, because the same obsessions and attitudes are now being displayed by our *software* elites; and these elites do have the power to put their ideas into practice – through software concepts and devices.

❖

Recall the linguistic theories we studied in chapters 3 and 4. Discussing the same theories, Roy Harris[2] traces their evolution over the last three centuries, and notes that their foundation on the mechanistic dogma has turned the study of language and mind into a system of belief, a mythology. The current theories, which are merely the latest in our tradition of mechanistic language delusions, claim that human beings have an innate language faculty and that this faculty can be explained with deterministic models. What the mind does when we communicate through language, then, must be akin to what a machine does. So we can view the language faculty as a sort of language machine that runs in the mind.

Because they are founded on mechanistic delusions, our theories end up resembling the mystical conceptions of language held by earlier civilizations. "But no other civilization than ours," Harris observes, "has envisaged language as the product of mysterious inner machinery, run by programs over which human beings have no control. That, it will be said, is just the mythology one might expect of a computer-age society; and so it is.... What is significant is that the new view of language promoted is not a conceptual enrichment of what preceded, but a conceptual impoverishment. A society whose academic establishment accepts with alacrity and even with enthusiasm the prospect of being able to treat verbal communication as a complex form of data-processing is a society which proclaims its linguistic immaturity."[3]

This mechanistic model of mind, Harris continues, leads *unavoidably* to the conclusion that human beings are not free and responsible agents. The ultimate consequence of language mechanism, thus, is not the promotion of invalid linguistic theories, but the undermining of the idea of individual responsibility. Because language fulfils such an important function in society, if we believe

---

[2] Roy Harris, *The Language Machine* (Ithaca, NY: Cornell University Press, 1987).
[3] Ibid., pp. 171–172.

that we have little control over what we say – if we feel that all we do in reality is operate a language machine – we will necessarily conclude that we cannot be held responsible for any acts involving language. Our speech, our knowledge, our decisions, our social and professional performance, are then largely the result of factors beyond our control.

Such conclusions, like the language theories themselves, "are aberrations which the myth of the language machine unavoidably promotes. Unavoidably, because the workings of the machine are envisaged as totally independent of any criteria of values entertained by the machine's human operators. Thus a form of discourse about language is created which serves either to disengage language from human motives and intentions, or to disguise the extent and nature of that engagement.... The myth of the language machine is a convenient myth because it absolves us from our day-to-day duties as language-makers, and blankets out for us all awkward questions concerning the exercise of authority through language. We purchase this linguistic security at cost price: and the cost is the removal of language from the domain of social morality altogether."[4]

We have already determined the similarity of language and software, so the preceding arguments can also be read by substituting software for language. What we note then is that this analysis describes our software culture even more accurately than it does our conception of language. Our software theories are degrading the notion of individual responsibility just like the language theories. Like the myth of the language machine, the software myth "serves either to disengage [software] from human motives and intentions, or to disguise the extent and nature of that engagement." It "absolves us from our day-to-day duties as [software] makers, and blankets out for us all awkward questions concerning the exercise of authority through [software]." As in the case of language, human beings are perceived as mere operators of software machines; so our responsibility is limited to knowing how to operate these machines. The cost of this security is "the removal of [software] from the domain of social morality altogether."

Unlike the language machine believed to run in the mind, though, the software machines are real: these are the devices supplied by the software elites. Thus, while our degradation through language is a relatively slow process, the same degradation is taking place, at a much faster rate, through software. Since we have agreed to depend on software in everything we do, and have also agreed to restrict ourselves to the kind of applications that can be created with software devices, we are asserting in effect that our knowledge, our capabilities, and our performance are the result of factors beyond our control.

[4] Ibid., p. 162.

❖

Isaiah Berlin[5] shows that, despite their differences, most social and political theories are founded on the premise that social evolution is a deterministic process; that all historical developments are, in fact, inevitable and predictable; and that the only reason we cannot explain them is our limited knowledge.

Not surprisingly, these theories conclude that the ideas of free will and responsibility are illusions, reflections of our present ignorance. Science will allow us, one day, to control minds and societies as effectively as we control machines: "All these theories are, in one sense or another, forms of determinism, whether they be teleological, metaphysical, mechanistic, religious, aesthetic, or scientific. And one common characteristic of all such outlooks is the implication that the individual's freedom of choice ... is ultimately an illusion, that the notion that human beings could have chosen otherwise than they did usually rests upon ignorance of facts.... The more we know, the farther the area of human freedom, and consequently of responsibility, is narrowed. For the omniscient being, who sees why nothing can be otherwise than as it is, the notions of responsibility or guilt, of right and wrong, are necessarily empty."[6]

To be as successful as are the theories of the natural sciences, the theories of mind and society would have to explain social phenomena through reductionism and atomism; specifically, they would have to show how social phenomena derive from the knowledge and acts of individual persons. Although they cannot discover such theories, the mechanists continue to believe in the possibility of exact explanations of social phenomena. So they claim that social evolution is brought about, not by people, but by *social forces*. While manifesting themselves through the acts of people, these forces have a character of their own, and are more important than the people themselves.

Depending on the theory, the forces may be described as social classes, political institutions, religions, cultures, economic conditions, or technological changes. All these concepts, however, serve in the end the same purpose: because the mechanists cannot explain social evolution in terms of individual persons, they attempt to explain it by replacing the persons with an abstract entity – a "whole." The theories appear then to explain the evolution, but this is an illusion, because the "whole" is merely an invention of the scientists. Those social forces remain unexplained, and their existence remains unproved. The forces are said to cause social evolution, but they are themselves described in terms of this evolution; so, being circular, the theories are fallacious.

---

[5] Isaiah Berlin, "Historical Inevitability," in *Four Essays on Liberty* (Oxford: Oxford University Press, 1969).   [6] Ibid., pp. 58–59.

All deterministic theories, thus, are alike: "Different though the tone of these forms of determinism may be ... they agree in this: that the world has a direction and is governed by laws, and that the direction and the laws can in some degree be discovered by employing the proper techniques of investigation: and moreover that the working of these laws can only be grasped by those who realize that the lives, characters, and acts of individuals, both mental and physical, are governed by the larger 'wholes' to which they belong."[7]

If we believe in the existence of some great social forces that control our life, the necessary conclusion is that it is not we, the individuals, but those forces, that are responsible for what happens in the world: "What the variants of either of these attitudes entail, like all forms of genuine determinism, is the elimination of the notion of individual responsibility.... If the history of the world is due to the operation of identifiable forces other than, and little affected by, free human wills and free choices (whether these occur or not), then the proper explanation of what happens must be given in terms of the evolution of such forces. And there is then a tendency to say that not individuals, but these larger entities, are ultimately 'responsible.'"[8]

These theories are popular because they are comforting. It is reassuring to hear that we must not blame ourselves for failures, that our knowledge and accomplishments are in reality part of a master plan, so whatever we do is necessarily right: "The growth of knowledge brings with it relief from moral burdens, for if powers beyond and above us are at work, it is wild presumption to claim responsibility for their activity or blame ourselves for failing in it.... And so individual responsibility and the perception of the difference between right and wrong choices, between avoidable evil and misfortune, are mere symptoms, evidences of vanity, of our imperfect adjustment, of human inability to face the truth. The more we know, the greater the relief from the burden of choice.... We escape moral dilemmas by denying their reality; and, by directing our gaze towards the greater wholes, we make them responsible in our place. All we lose is an illusion, and with it the painful and superfluous emotions of guilt and remorse. Freedom notoriously involves responsibility, and it is for many spirits a source of welcome relief to lose the burden of both."[9]

Until recently, the transition from determinism to irresponsibility could be observed only in totalitarian societies and in the mechanistic theories concocted by academics. In our time, however, a third possibility has emerged: the software culture. The basic tenets of the deterministic *social* theories can now be found in our *software* theories: the blind faith in mechanism; the belief in historical inevitability; the idea of the "whole" – the mighty forces of progress that are beyond our control even though we are parts of them; and the

---

[7] Ibid., p. 62.   [8] Ibid., pp. 63–64.   [9] Ibid., pp. 77–81.

comfort of knowing that, in the final analysis, we are not really responsible for our acts, nor for our failures.

The mechanistic software theories started by affecting only the software practitioners, but they are now spreading into all software-related activities. We have already discussed these theories, and how they have degraded our notions of knowledge, freedom, and creativity. What I want to show here is that, while concerned with software, these theories belong in fact to the same category as the deterministic social theories we have just examined.

The software counterpart of the social forces that control the history of humanity are the forces of *software evolution*. Although we take part in this evolution (by performing software-related activities), only the software elites actually understand it. It is their task, therefore, to help us assimilate software changes; and they do it by inventing concepts and devices that embody the power of software while remaining simple enough for us to use.

Our role in the process of software evolution, then, is to adopt the latest software devices provided by the elites – the latest theories, methodologies, development environments, and applications. And we must not attempt to judge these innovations with our naive standards of good and bad, of success and failure. If, for example, a software device does not provide the promised benefits, or if it creates several new problems for each problem it solves, or if we have to alter the way we run our affairs in order to use it, or if it demands more of our time than we had planned, or if it makes us unduly dependent on the elites, we must not think of these issues as shortcomings, but as a manifestation of software evolution. We must not blame the device, nor its maker, nor ourselves.

Each version of a device is a newer thing, so it constitutes software progress. This evolution is historically inevitable, so we must conform to it even if we do not understand it. Founded as they are on mechanistic principles, the devices are expressions of software science, and their perpetual changes reflect the never-ending process of software evolution. It is ignorance and vanity that prompt us to doubt the innovations, and tempt us to pursue personal ideas. It is presumptuous to think that we can accomplish more with our own minds than by conforming to the forces of progress. The belief in skills or creativity in software-related matters is evidence of immaturity, of imperfect adjustment. The more we learn about software and programming, the further the area of individual choice, and hence of responsibility, is narrowed. Whether programmers or users, we are parts of a "whole," of a great historical process that is beyond our control. All we can reasonably be expected to do is adapt to it, by accepting the devices provided by the elites.

This is what we are told, but the existence of the forces of software evolution, like the existence of the *social* forces of evolution, was never proved. The generations of software devices are said to be a reflection of this evolution, but software evolution is explained in terms of generations of devices. So, just like the argument for social evolution, the argument for software evolution is circular, and hence fallacious.

Totalitarian systems like Nazism and Communism were said to be an expression of the great forces of social progress; so they represented an inevitable social evolution, and the elites were merely helping to bring about a social transformation that, historically, was *bound* to happen. Similarly, the software devices are said to be an expression of technological forces; so they represent an inevitable evolution of software principles, and the elites are merely helping to bring about a technological transformation that was *bound* to happen. Like the political elites, the software elites see themselves as an enlightened vanguard: they alone can understand this evolution, and it is their duty to make us conform to it.

In reality, the mechanistic software theories are pseudoscientific, as are the social theories behind totalitarianism. The software elites, therefore, are the same kind of charlatans as the totalitarian elites. Like them, the software elites managed to assume control of society by entrancing us with their utopian visions – visions that are in fact absurd, and are accepted only because of our mechanistic tradition. Moreover, by accepting their deterministic theories we are *all* participating in the creation of a totalitarian society, just as the millions of people living under Nazism and Communism were by accepting the deterministic *social* theories promoted by *their* elites.

Totalitarian Democracy

The Totalitarian Elites

Our modernity and our mechanistic culture have engendered a new and dangerous phenomenon: educational and business institutions that have more power than our *political* institutions. This phenomenon is dangerous because, while engaged in teaching, or research, or marketing, these institutions are promoting totalitarianism. Thus, although politically our society is still democratic, in effect it is becoming totalitarian.[1]

[1] The expression "totalitarian democracy" (the present section's title) is explained in the next subsection, "Talmon's Model of Totalitarianism."

The totalitarianism promoted through education and through business is due to the mechanistic ideology. Mechanism has been so successful in the exact sciences, and in fields like engineering, that we are ready to accept it in any endeavour. As a result, these institutions have attained, undeservedly, an elitist position. For, we judge their importance, not by the *validity* of their ideas, but by the formality and precision with which they pursue these ideas; in other words, by the mechanistic nature, rather than the usefulness, of their activities.

Universities and corporations like the mechanistic ideology, therefore, because it affords them a privileged position in society regardless of whether their activities are useful or not. Our problems are becoming more and more complex – that is, less and less mechanistic; and yet, these institutions restrict themselves to mechanistic concepts. The reputation of mechanism was established long ago, when our problems were simpler, and mechanistic concepts were generally useful. Today, the mechanistic failures exceed the successes, but we continue to trust the mechanists just as we did in the past.

The reason we continue to embrace mechanism despite its failures is the propaganda conducted by universities and corporations. Since a widespread acceptance of mechanism is the only way to maintain their privileged position, these institutions are aggressively promoting it, while discrediting all other forms of thought. Thus, whereas in the past they were *practising* mechanism, today they are *enforcing* it. Clearly, the propaganda is necessary because mechanism is becoming less and less useful. Were mechanism indeed as beneficial as it is said to be, the mechanists would gain our respect simply by providing answers to our problems. As we saw in the previous chapters, however, mechanistic methods and theories are, in most fields, mere delusions.

Mechanism becomes totalitarian when its status changes from *method* to *myth*. Once it becomes a system of belief, its principles are accepted unquestioningly, and those who were already practising it become revered elites. At that point, mechanism is officially taught and promoted, and every member of society is expected to adopt it.

Thus, if previously the harm was limited to the exploitation of society by the mechanists, now society itself is becoming mechanistic. If previously only the mechanists were wasting their time by pursuing useless activities, now everyone does it. In every field and occupation, people are increasingly judged, not by the value of their work, but by how faithfully they adhere to the mechanistic ideology. Through systematic indoctrination, every person is turned into a bureaucrat – a worker whose task is, simply, to obey the mechanistic principles.

The academic elites carry out the mechanistic indoctrination through the process known as education. The academics, we saw, restrict themselves to mechanistic ideas, because this permits them to stress the *methods*, rather than the *results*, of their research programs. Worthless activities can then be made to look important. And they extend this attitude to education: what they teach is only mechanistic concepts, only what can be described with neat theories and methods. Whether these theories and methods are effective or not is unimportant. Disciplines whose phenomena are almost entirely non-mechanistic – psychology, sociology, linguistics, economics, programming – are taught like the exact sciences. And the notions of expertise, talent, and professional responsibility in these fields are being degraded accordingly: what practitioners are expected to know is, not the utmost that human minds can attain, but only how to apply certain methods.

The business elites, for their part, carry out the mechanistic indoctrination through the process known as marketing. Like the universities, corporations restrict themselves to mechanistic ideas, because this permits them to engage in activities that are predictable and profitable. For example, they prefer products that can be made largely by machines, and workers whose skills are very low or very narrow, in order to control the process of production "scientifically." Most goods and services, therefore, are restricted to whatever can be done efficiently, through exact methods; so they reflect the limitations of business rather than our real needs. This is why we must be *persuaded* to depend on these goods and services. The persuasion – what we call advertising – consists mainly in exploiting human weaknesses through deceptive messages. The deception is required, obviously, in order to make the limited options possible through mechanistic concepts appear more important than they actually are. The ultimate goal of this indoctrination, then, is to force us all to replace our genuine values with artificial, mechanistic ones.

So mechanism can be just as utopian, and just as totalitarian, as a *political* ideology. As in the case of a political system, if accepted as unquestionable truth – as myth – the entire society will modify itself to fit its dogmas. In fact, it is even easier to be mesmerized by mechanistic ideas than it is by political ones, because we are less likely to suspect their advocates of dishonesty. Mechanism, after all, is not promoted by political parties, but by such respected institutions as universities and corporations. And its dogmas are justified by invoking such notions as science, efficiency, and progress.

A society where various elites are free to promote their ideologies is intrinsically totalitarian, if these ideologies seek to control the values held by large numbers of people. Whether an ideology concerns politics, or religion, or business, or technology, the result is always a spreading bureaucracy: more and more people cease to live a normal life, and follow instead the ideology's precepts. But totalitarian ideologies are pseudoscientific, so their utopian promises cannot be fulfilled. The harm they cause, therefore, extends beyond the inevitable disillusionment. For, if too many people accept the promises and cease performing useful activities, the entire society may collapse. Thus, totalitarianism destroys individual lives by tempting people to pursue worthless ideas, and destroys societies by corrupting their human resources.

By describing the promotion of an ideology with terms like "education" and "marketing," instead of "indoctrination" and "propaganda," we can continue to call our system democratic even while making it increasingly totalitarian. Again, it is not so much the *promotion* of ideologies that is harmful, as the fact that they are pseudoscientific, and hence bound to fail. Were these ideologies useful, they could be promoted through logic – as are, for instance, our truly scientific theories – and there would be no need for lies and delusions. (We studied in previous chapters the methods employed by charlatans to defend useless concepts, theories, and products; and we saw that most promotions today rely, in fact, on these methods. So the conclusion must be that most concepts, theories, and products promoted today are not as useful as they are said to be.)

A society that tolerates the advancement of *any* ideas through deception is, in effect, out of control. For, as these ideas are worthless, such a society is actually expending its energies on projects that constitute its own destruction.

❖

The reason we fail to notice the totalitarian nature of our present-day culture is that our brand of totalitarianism is being enforced, not by one, but by many different elites. Thus, when we are indoctrinated by the academic elite to embrace mechanism, or by the fashion elite to wear certain clothes, or by the tobacco elite to smoke cigarettes, or by the soft-drink elite to consume beverages, or by the fitness elite to manipulate certain contraptions, or by the automotive elite to prefer certain types of vehicles, or by the entertainment elite to enjoy certain types of TV shows, or by the cosmetics elite to use various concoctions, or by the financial elite to trust certain investments, or by the technology elite to depend on devices, we may be dealing with different organizations, but their ideologies share a common goal: to control our minds. They prevent us from developing useful knowledge, and encourage us to accept instead senseless ideas.

So, just like a *political* totalitarian elite, our elites have the right to shape the lives of millions of people. Also like a political elite, they do this by distorting knowledge, in order to make reality fit their ideology. But if we call this process advertising, or marketing, or public relations, we can delude ourselves that our culture is different from a *politically* totalitarian one. In reality, totalitarianism based on a non-political ideology is just as harmful.

In addition to their diversity, it is the *weakness* of these elites that prevents us from noticing their totalitarian attitude. In the past, none of these organizations had the power to impose its particular ideology on more than a fraction of the population. And as a result, no one person was influenced by more than a few of them at a given time. Thus, although each elite believes that the whole world ought to accept its ideas, and is attempting to turn us all into the kind of bureaucrats needed to implement these ideas, none has had, so far, the power to carry out its plan. What we have had so far, therefore, is only mild, fragmentary totalitarianism.

Software, however, has changed this. Through software, it has finally become possible for a non-political elite, upholding a non-political ideology, to dominate the entire society. It is the *nature* of software that makes this possible. We mistakenly perceive software as a new kind of product, and hence the software elite as a risk no greater than the traditional elites. In reality, software is a new phenomenon, a new way for human beings to represent the world and to communicate with it. And consequently, the totalitarianism of a software ideology is far more virulent than the traditional ones. If software is like language (as we saw in chapter 4), an elite that controls software controls in effect the means to represent the world; so it controls the way we acquire knowledge, communicate, and conduct our affairs. Ultimately, the elite can control the way we think. For, by distorting our knowledge of software, it can distort our knowledge of everything else. Thus, while the traditional elites could affect only separate aspects of our life, a software elite can affect our entire existence. Through software, therefore, an elite can achieve complete totalitarianism.

As we saw earlier, what is needed to implement totalitarianism is a myth, an elite, and an expanding bureaucracy (see pp. 30–31). With this principle, we can explain why the other elites failed to achieve complete totalitarianism: because, through the traditional mechanistic myth, their bureaucracies could not expand beyond a certain point. And we can also explain why the software elite *can* achieve complete totalitarianism: because, through the mechanistic *software* myth, a bureaucracy can expand easily; it can expand, in principle, to include every member of society.

If the software variant of totalitarianism is as harmful as the political one, we must treat it the same way: we must be as worried about the theories promoted by the software elite, or the spread of a software bureaucracy, or the degradation of minds caused by software devices, as we would if these phenomena were part of a *political* movement. In previous chapters we studied the pseudoscientific nature of the mechanistic software theories, and the dishonesty of their promoters. Thus, if software mechanism is worthless, as we saw, we already have good reasons for fighting this ideology and the charlatanism it engenders. But full-fledged software totalitarianism will cause much greater harm. The incompetence and corruption found today in the world of programming is but a small problem compared with the widespread destruction of knowledge that we will suffer when our immersion in software mechanism is complete.

To combat software totalitarianism we must first understand it. However, this being a new phenomenon, we only have the studies of *political* totalitarianism as guide. Still, if the main characteristics of totalitarianism are the same in both variants, we should be able to identify in the political studies various aspects that parallel the trends we are witnessing in our software-related affairs. And this, in turn, will help us to appreciate the threat posed by the mechanistic software ideology; that is, to appreciate why the argument against software mechanism is more than just an argument against mistaken programming concepts.

What most political studies do is merely analyze various totalitarian societies and ideologies. To understand those aspects shared by the political and the software variants, however, what we need is an analysis of the fundamental, philosophical aspects of totalitarianism. This is why I have selected two particular studies. One is Talmon's model: a society that is founded on democratic values but is pursuing, in fact, a totalitarian dream – a dream stemming from mechanistic beliefs. The other is Orwell's model: a society where the elite is reducing language to its mechanistic aspects in order to degrade people's minds. We already know that our culture is mechanistic. Thus, since this culture permits us to pursue a totalitarian software ideology while living in a democracy, and since the role of software in society is similar to that of language, these two studies are especially relevant.

Talmon's Model of Totalitarianism

1

In his classic work, *The Origins of Totalitarian Democracy*, J. L. Talmon argues that modern totalitarianism derives from *democratic* ideas; specifically, from the ideas prevailing in the eighteenth century, and which led eventually to the French Revolution.[1] The French thinkers of that period were seeking an answer

[1] J. L. Talmon, *The Origins of Totalitarian Democracy* (New York: Praeger, 1960). Talmon continued this study in two later books, which discuss the evolution of the totalitarian ideology in the nineteenth and twentieth centuries.

to the age-old problem of human freedom: what kind of society can guarantee liberty, equality, and happiness for all its citizens? They were convinced that the oppression and misery pervading the world were due simply to ignorance, to man's failure to understand his own nature. If people agreed to explore this issue with an open mind, rather than allow one authority or another to influence them, they would be able to establish a perfect social system. That system would be democratic, and would constitute the best society that human beings can create.

While all thinkers shared this ideal, they differed in the method they recommended for achieving it. There were two schools: The first – which Talmon calls the *liberal* type of democracy – held that, left alone, people will one day discover, simply through trial and error, what is the best way to run a society. The second – which Talmon calls the *totalitarian* type of democracy – held that ordinary people are irrational and undisciplined, so they will never accomplish this on their own. The only practical solution is to endow a wise elite (the leaders, the rulers, the state) with absolute power, and allow it to control all human affairs. With this power, the elite could follow an exact plan, based on objective theories, and force every citizen to conform to it. The guarantee for a perfect society, it was believed, lies in this combination of scientific principles and complete conformism. The elite, of course, would never abuse its power. Since by definition a wise elite identifies itself with the people, it would only use its power benevolently.

The first opportunity a society had to put these ideas to the test was during the French Revolution. And, surprisingly perhaps, it was the *totalitarian* alternative that was chosen. Thus, because the revolution's leaders preferred a democracy based on scientific principles to one based on spontaneous decisions, the movement that started with the promise of universal liberty ended in a violent, totalitarian system. The advocates of scientific social planning learned nothing from this failure, however, and continued to promote their type of democracy ever since. In the twentieth century, the best-known implementation of totalitarian democracy was Communism, while Nazism was an extreme, especially brutal manifestation of the same idea. In the end, liberal democracy – which is what we understand today as "democracy" – proved to be a better alternative, and was adopted by one society after another. The struggle between the totalitarian and the liberal types of democracy, says Talmon, has shaped the history of civilization since the eighteenth century.

The purpose of this discussion is to show that today's academic and business elites hold ideologies that are very similar to the political ideology of *totalitarian* democracy. And this is no accident: like the traditional elites, our elites claim that their ideologies are scientific (because based on mechanistic principles) and democratic (because beneficial to the majority of people); at the same time, they ask us to renounce all individual freedom (because only through conformism can a scientific and democratic ideology succeed). Stemming as they do from the same mechanistic delusions, these ideologies suffer from the same self-contradictions. Thus, if we want to understand today's totalitarian tendencies, particularly in our software-related affairs, a brief analysis of the original totalitarian theories will be helpful.

The eighteenth-century thinkers believed in the existence of an ideal, natural order. Impressed by the scientific advances of those days, they assumed that similar advances were imminent in social and political matters. Now, the discoveries in physics, chemistry, and astronomy had revealed a simple and logical pattern in the laws of nature. Thus, those thinkers concluded, a similar pattern must exist in the natural *social* laws. Human beings and human societies evolved as part of nature, and, given the beauty and logic of the natural laws already discovered, it is inconceivable that the natural *social* laws would prescribe oppression or unhappiness. The current societies suffer from these evils, therefore, only because we have not yet discovered the natural social laws. Once we discover them, our social relations will be as logical and successful as are our exact sciences.

Those thinkers also believed that all human beings are basically alike. The great differences we note in personality, intelligence, or wealth are due to accident; or they are artificially fostered by certain institutions, which have vested interest in maintaining these differences. Nature could not possibly have intended that such great disparity emerge between creatures which are practically identical when born.

In conclusion, since there undoubtedly exist some logical, natural laws for running a society, and since all human beings are naturally alike, the only explanation for the current misery is that our societies do not reflect the natural order. Specifically, we permit variation and inequality to arise among individual citizens. Hence, once we correct this mistake – once we reduce human existence to those aspects common to all people – the only social principles required will be those based on natural laws. By definition, the resulting system will constitute a perfect society: "If there is such a being as Man in himself, and if we all, when we throw off our accidental characteristics, partake of the same substance, then a universal system of morality, based on the fewest and simplest principles, becomes not only a distinct possibility, but a certainty. Such a system would be comparable in its precision to geometry."[2]

---

[2] Ibid., pp. 29–30.

These ideas were expressed most forcefully by Jean-Jacques Rousseau, who also explained how to implement them: by divesting people of their personal qualities and endowing them instead with the common, natural ones – what he called the general will. Achieving this transformation is the task of a sovereign (in practice, the ruling elite). Although immanent in each individual, the natural qualities are masked by his current, selfish character, and must be brought out through special education. The individual, in fact, may be so corrupt that he would not appreciate the importance of the transformation, in which case the sovereign must *enforce* it. The revolution will succeed only when all citizens adopt without reservation the general will.

Thus, while the other thinkers saw the idea of a natural social order as little more than a theory, Rousseau presented it as a plan for immediate action. Through the absurd notion of a general will – said to be natural to people but at the same time requiring a powerful elite to enforce it – Rousseau gave rise to modern totalitarianism: a political system that is totalitarian even though grounded on democratic principles.[3]

So it is the idea of natural, innate qualities that is used to justify totalitarianism. The elite claims that, since its ideology reflects some natural, and hence superior, human qualities, forcing an individual to conform to it is not an act of coercion but a sort of teaching. In an ideal world, that individual would display those qualities on his own. It is the fact that he lives in a corrupt society that distorts his character and prevents him from attaining his higher, natural self. In effect, society has denatured him. All that the elite does, then, is restore him to what nature had intended him to be. Thus, we do not object when a teacher forces his pupils to learn rules of grammar or arithmetic, and punishes them if they forget those rules. We do not object because the rules reflect valid, natural laws. Similarly, forcing people to conform to a natural ideology is a form of education: instead of grammar or arithmetic, what we must assimilate now is some *social* rules – rules which reflect the natural human condition, and which will therefore help us to create a perfect society.

We can recognize in these ideas the circularity characteristic of mechanistic delusions. Totalitarian elites see themselves as social engineers, as experts who know how to design societies. Their ideas are a breakthrough in political thought, they say, and what they need now in order to create a perfect society is the authority to implement these ideas. What they need, in other words, is the power to control the lives of millions of people. And they invoke the

---

[3] Ibid., pp. 40–43.

mechanistic philosophy as justification: first, they *invent* some mechanistic theories that match their ideas; then, they offer these theories as *proof* of the validity of their ideas. Since mechanism is universally equated with science, few notice the circularity of this line of logic.

The first theory the elites invent to defend their ideas is that societies are deterministic systems. So, they say, we should be able to design a society by following rigorous methods, just as we do in engineering projects. The elites need such a theory because they intend to replace the current social order with a new one; and only if societies can indeed be created from plans, like buildings, can such a project succeed. In reality, there is no evidence that societies can be designed as we design buildings. The millions of individuals who make up a society are sufficiently different from one another to cause complex, unpredictable social phenomena. It is precisely this diversity that makes the notion of a perfect society a fantasy.

Since it is the differences between individuals that would prevent the elites from implementing their ideas, they are compelled to invent a second theory. They say that human beings are naturally identical and virtuous, and the differences between them are simply deviations from this ideal, due to the corrupt society they live in. And this theory too is mechanistic: it claims, in effect, that human beings are born as a sort of automatons, all driven by the same program. Also like the first theory, there is no evidence that this is true. The elites *wish* this to be true; for, only if human beings are indeed automatons can the plan for erasing the differences between them succeed. The plan calls, in effect, for deleting the diverse, wrong programs running now in millions of individual minds, and installing in all of them an identical, correct program.

So the totalitarian philosophy is not the serious political thesis it is claimed to be, but a mechanistic delusion. What the elites really want is the power to control society; and they rationalize this megalomania by making their arguments look like scientific theories. They invent a theory about individuals in order to support a theory about societies. Both are fantasies, but together they seem to express self-evident truths. What the elites do, in reality, is invoke one mechanistic hypothesis as support for another. Ultimately, they use the mechanistic philosophy to defend the mechanistic philosophy. Being circular, their arguments are fallacious; they do *not* prove that totalitarianism can help us to create a perfect society. The circularity can be detected, in fact, in the very definition of the general will: "There is such a thing as an objective general will, whether willed or not willed by anybody. To become a reality it must be willed by the people. If the people does not will it, it must be made to will it, for the general will is latent in the people's will."[4]

[4] Ibid., p. 43.

Talmon calls this delusion the paradox of freedom: the elites promise us freedom, but at the same time they tell us that the only way to have freedom is by giving up individuality, and by conforming to the great whole that is society. Conformism, though, is the opposite of freedom. So, to resolve the contradiction, the elites *redefine* the notion of freedom as *conforming to an ideal*: "On the one hand, the individual is said to obey nothing but his own will; on the other, he is urged to conform to some objective criterion. The contradiction is resolved by the claim that this external criterion is his better, higher, or real self.... Hence, even if constrained to obey the external standard, man cannot complain of being coerced, for in fact he is merely being made to obey his own true self. He is thus still free; indeed freer than before."[5]

The most striking feature of totalitarianism, then, is this insistence on shaping the character of millions of individuals to fit a common mould, while claiming that they continue to be free: "From the difficulty of reconciling freedom with the idea of an absolute purpose spring all the particular problems and antinomies of totalitarian democracy. This difficulty could only be resolved by thinking not in terms of men as they are, but as they were meant to be, and would be, given the proper conditions. In so far as they are at variance with the absolute ideal they can be ignored, coerced or intimidated into conforming, without any real violation of the democratic principle being involved."[6]

Absurd as they are, these question-begging arguments have been adduced to justify totalitarianism for more than two hundred years. From science-fiction authors to progressive sociologists, from paranoid dictators to learned philosophers, every apologist has defended his particular brand of totalitarianism through the same mechanistic delusions. Thus, since mechanism dominates our present-day culture no less than it did previous ones, we shouldn't be surprised that our own elites, in universities and in business, invoke it to justify *today's* brands of totalitarianism. In the end, all elites say the same thing: the only way to improve matters is through complete conformism; specifically, by implementing a mechanistic ideology and forcing everyone to adhere to it.

What the elites want, in reality, is power – the power that comes from controlling knowledge and minds. And they attain this power by promising to solve our non-mechanistic problems with simple, mechanistic methods. All *we* have to do, they tell us, is obey the ideology; that is, restrict ourselves to

[5] Ibid., p. 40.   [6] Ibid., pp. 2–3.

mechanistic concepts. Non-mechanistic problems, however, cannot have mechanistic solutions, so the promise is a fraud. But because it is so appealing, we believe it. And this is how, at any given time, one or more elites are exploiting us.

Thanks to their similarity, then, totalitarian ideologies are easy to recognize: An elite promotes certain ideas about people and societies – ideas that are precise and attractive, but very different from the way people normally live. For these ideas to succeed, therefore, everyone must change so as to conform to them. And if some of us resist the change, this can only mean that we are too ignorant to appreciate the promised benefits. After all, being mechanistic, the ideas themselves cannot possibly be wrong. So we must be *forced* to change. This is not coercion, though, but education: we are forced, in effect, to think and live correctly. Whether the ideas concern politics, or work, or personal life, with proper teaching anyone can learn to appreciate them. (See also the related discussion in the introductory chapter, pp. 17–18.)

2

Let us see now how Talmon's totalitarian model is reflected in today's ideologies. Starting with the academic elites, the idea promoted is that phenomena involving minds and societies can be represented mechanistically, just like physical phenomena. In other words, we should be able to explain all human phenomena from a knowledge of the basic human propensities, just as we explain the operation of a machine from a knowledge of its basic components. It *is* possible to discover exact theories of mind and society. One day, we will be as successful in fields like psychology, sociology, and linguistics as we are in physics and astronomy.

These theories, however, do not work. And they do not work because human beings and human societies are *not* the deterministic systems the mechanists assume them to be. In chapter 3 we saw that these theories are, in fact, pseudoscientific: when falsified by evidence, the mechanists resort to various stratagems in order to cover up the falsifications. So, if three hundred years of mechanistic philosophy have failed to produce a single working theory in the human sciences, and if it is so easy to show that the promoters of these theories are not scientists but charlatans, common sense alone ought to prompt us to question the academics' elitist position. The fact that we do not question it demonstrates how successful is the mechanistic propaganda conducted by the universities.

Academic mechanism, thus, is a totalitarian ideology – because it asks us to change so as to conform to its tenets. It does not earn its status through real achievements, but through coercion: we are *forced* to accept it, regardless of whether the theories work or not. We are intimidated by its successes in the exact sciences, and we allow charlatans to fool us into accepting it in every other field. Both education and research are now little more than mechanistic indoctrination: every aspect of reality is described in mechanistic terms, and we must restrict ourselves to mechanistic practices. As a result of this indoctrination, we treat mechanism as unquestionable truth, as the only valid form of thought. And we respect anyone who upholds a mechanistic idea, even if the idea is worthless.

So the change demanded by the mechanistic ideology consists in replacing our traditional perception of knowledge, science, and research with a degraded one: the pursuit of mechanistic ideas. Instead of admiring accomplishments, we admire conformism. What we expect to see in academic work is not expertise and originality, not the utmost that human beings can attain, but merely the faithful application of mechanistic methods. Thus, since anyone with a bureaucratic mind can follow methods, individuals incapable of doing anything useful are perceived as scientists.

And this is not all. The theories promoted by the mechanists are about human beings – that is, about *us*. So, when we accept them, we do more than just agree to treat the academic charlatans as elites. What we really do is accept their claim that we are deterministic systems. By respecting the mechanists and their work, we are saying in effect that we think their project is important, and likely to succeed. But this project is an attempt to prove that human beings are in reality automatons. So our acceptance means that, like the academics themselves, we believe this *is* what we are. Our acceptance shows, therefore, how advanced is our mechanistic indoctrination – our dehumanization. For, we would not respect researchers who try to prove that we are automatons unless we already thought and acted, to some degree, like automatons. The reason we accept their theories, then, is that we no longer see ourselves as free and responsible agents.

In the end, because we trust the mechanists and increasingly restrict ourselves to mechanistic performance, these theories are becoming more and more plausible: they describe human beings and human societies more and more accurately. This is not because the mechanists are right, though, but because *we* are becoming, little by little, the deterministic systems they say we are. Thus, while failing in human affairs as scientific concept, mechanism is successful as totalitarian ideology: we are indeed changing to conform to its tenets.

❖

Let us turn next to the corporate elites. The idea promoted now is that every problem can be solved by purchasing something. In personal or professional pursuits, in our kitchens or in our offices, in matters of health or intellect or finance, the solution to a problem can always be found in a product sold by a company. While the traditional view is that we must study if we want to gain knowledge, practise if we want to develop expertise, change our lifestyle if we want to be fit, do something useful if we want to get rich, and alter our world view if we want to be happy, modern companies can help us avoid these challenges: we can achieve the same results, immediately and effortlessly, simply by purchasing their latest products.[7]

These products, however, do not work – at least, not in the way we are promised. And they do not work because difficult challenges cannot be met simply by purchasing something. Ready-made products are limited, by their very nature, to mechanistic concepts: they embody specific combinations of features and capabilities, on the assumption that every problem can be reduced to such combinations. Our most important problems, though, are non-mechanistic, because they reflect the complex phenomena that make up our existence. They can only be solved, therefore, through our own knowledge, experience, and effort. Products alone cannot help us, because no set of products can embody enough combinations of details to satisfy our combinations of needs. We are impressed by their ability to solve isolated, mechanistic problems, and we are fooled by the claim that they can also solve the important, complex ones. So, although products usually *function* as promised, this doesn't mean that they can also improve our life as promised.

If a product is actually not as useful as we think it is, the only way for its maker to make us buy it is by deceiving us. The process whereby a useless thing is made to appear useful is known as advertising. And, since more and more products need to be sold in this manner, advertising has become the most important part of trade. To put it differently, if advertising were restricted to factual information about a product's features (similarly, for instance, to the arguments accepted in a court of law), perhaps only 10 percent of what is being bought today would continue to be bought: those products that are indeed as useful as we think they are. It is not too much to say, then, that our economy is almost entirely dependent on the permission that companies have to tell lies and to exploit people's ignorance.

This contrasts sharply with the situation, say, one hundred years ago, when most products were useful and very few had to be sold through deception. In the past, the promotion of a product needed only plain statements, and perhaps

---

[7] To extend the range of this ideology, many services (bank accounts, insurance plans, investment schemes) are now called products.

some flourishes and exaggerations. Today, on the other hand, promotion means a systematic generation of delusions. Thus, advertising techniques that are now universal were employed in the past only by charlatans. Some examples: presenting particular instances (testimonials, success stories, case studies) as evidence of the product's usefulness, which is logically equivalent to lying (see p. 220); describing the product with deliberately misleading sentences – sentences that appear to state important facts while saying in reality nothing meaningful or accountable (see "The Practice of Deceit" in chapter 5); arbitrarily displaying attractive, smiling faces, which compels us to associate the product with beauty, youth, health, and happiness; deceptive prices, like $19.99; adding background music and special effects on radio and television – in order to distract and confuse us, and to induce a favourable mood.

The reason for the incessant lies is the declining usefulness of mechanism. In the past, when our problems were simpler, ready-made products were quite effective, so there was no need for deception. But our world is becoming more and more complex, and complex problems cannot be solved mechanistically – that is, by separating them into simpler ones. Advertising, thus, serves as mechanistic indoctrination: the corporate elites must persuade us that their products, which are based on mechanistic concepts, can solve our complex problems.

Like academic mechanism, then, business mechanism is a totalitarian ideology – because it asks us to change so as to conform to its tenets. When we succumb to advertising, we do more than just agree to be exploited by charlatans: we agree to forgo our non-mechanistic capabilities, and to restrict ourselves to mechanistic performance. While the world consists of complex phenomena, we see only its mechanistic aspects. Ultimately, the change demanded of us is to simplify our lives to the point where all our needs can be satisfied by purchasing ready-made products, and to limit our knowledge so as to remain dependent, in everything we do, on these products.

The elites, for their part, tell us that the mechanistic concepts only *appear* to be restrictive: we fail to appreciate their value because of our current, inefficient habits. Mechanism means science, we are told, so it is silly to think that our minds can be better than products based on mechanistic concepts. What we interpret as creativity and originality – what these products are eliminating – is in reality an old-fashioned, undisciplined way of doing things. Thus, just as education often forces children to accept notions they don't understand, for their own good, *we* must be forced to depend on ready-made products, for our own good. In the end, the restriction to mechanistic concepts is no more coercive than any type of education. What we are taught now is how to live efficiently; in particular, how to replace the dependence on personal knowledge and skills with a dependence on modern products.

Also like academic mechanism, business mechanism is successful as totalitarian ideology; that is, we *are* becoming the automatons the elites say we are. For, if we are forced to spend more and more time with useless mechanistic solutions, we are bound to spend less and less time developing our non-mechanistic capabilities. As we get to depend on ready-made products in every activity, the only knowledge we acquire is the trivial, mechanistic type needed to use these products. So we are being reduced, little by little, to the level of machines. But the result of this transformation is that the claims made for ready-made products are becoming increasingly accurate: since we no longer care about complex phenomena, it no longer matters that our complex problems remain unsolved; since we are dealing only with the mechanistic problems, the products increasingly appear to be as useful as their promoters say they are.

Orwell's Model of Totalitarianism

1

George Orwell's conception of totalitarianism is best known from his last work, *Nineteen Eighty-Four*, which was published in 1949. But to appreciate his remarkable insight into the nature of totalitarianism, and his ongoing preoccupation with it, we must study his writings over the preceding ten years. Although in *Nineteen Eighty-Four* he depicts an established totalitarian state, his aim was not to expose the evils of Nazism and Communism (the totalitarian ideologies of the 1940s), but to draw attention to the totalitarian tendencies of the *democratic* cultures.

Because he died shortly after the book's publication, Orwell did not have the opportunity to clarify its links to his actual views and concerns. A letter he wrote at the time, and which was widely published, is probably the only record of these links: "I do not believe that the kind of society I describe necessarily *will* arrive, but I believe (allowing of course for the fact that the book is a satire) that something resembling it *could* arrive…. The scene of the book is laid in Britain in order to emphasize that the English-speaking races are not innately better than anyone else and that totalitarianism, *if not fought against*, could triumph anywhere."[1]

Orwell's model, then, involves not just a certain type of totalitarianism, but

---

[1] George Orwell, "Letter to Francis A. Henson," in *The Collected Essays, Journalism and Letters of George Orwell*, vol. 4, eds. Sonia Orwell and Ian Angus (London: Penguin Books, 1970), p. 564.

also the *progression* of a society toward totalitarianism. He noticed that many aspects of the degradation reached in the totalitarian countries could also be found, to some degree, in the democratic ones. And this degradation was growing and spreading. In *Nineteen Eighty-Four*, Orwell drew an exaggerated, unrealistic picture of totalitarianism, in order to stress its dehumanizing effects. But, he warns us, while *that* totalitarianism is indeed a fantasy, its milder counterpart in our own society is real. It would be instructive, therefore, to review some of the totalitarian aspects of our culture, and to see how they have evolved since Orwell's time. This will help us to recognize the totalitarian aspects of our software practices, which, of course, he could not have anticipated.

One thing Orwell noticed was the ease with which people could be persuaded to accept totalitarian ideas. Totalitarianism, we saw, is presented as a *scientific* doctrine, because it is derived from mechanism. Most people fail to recognize its fallacies, and succumb to its utopian promises. Thus, like all pseudo-sciences, totalitarianism is appealing because it seems to offer easy solutions to complex problems: people accept it for the same reason they accept astrology, superstitions, and magic systems. But Orwell was especially annoyed to see that the most ardent supporters of totalitarianism are found among *educated* people: "I believe ... that totalitarian ideas have taken root in the minds of intellectuals everywhere."[2] "What is sinister ... is that the conscious enemies of liberty are those to whom liberty ought to mean most.... The direct, conscious attack on intellectual decency comes from the intellectuals themselves."[3]

Recall the mechanistic pseudosciences we examined in chapter 3. Instead of trying to understand the true nature of minds and societies, the academics *assume* they are mechanistic phenomena. Theories based on this assumption never work, but the academics refuse to admit that they are wrong, that human phenomena are in fact non-mechanistic. Thus, the academics are not serious scientists. They have redefined their responsibility, from the difficult challenge of discovering useful theories, to the easier challenge of practising mechanism. And, since mechanistic ideas in human affairs are intrinsically totalitarian, the tendency among intellectuals to accept totalitarian ideas implicitly – what Orwell condemned – is a consequence of their tendency to accept *mechanistic* ideas implicitly. Orwell noticed this corruption even in the 1940s, and was right to warn us about its growth. For, this is indeed what has happened: while

[2] Ibid.
[3] George Orwell, "The Prevention of Literature," in *Collected Essays*, vol. 4, p. 93.

mechanistic theories were already a temptation in the human sciences, they have become, since then, the only type of theories officially accepted.

In the end, "a society becomes totalitarian when its structure becomes flagrantly artificial: that is, when its ruling class has lost its function but succeeds in clinging to power by force or fraud."[4] If we take the academic elite to be one of our ruling classes, this observation describes perfectly its degradation since Orwell's time. The mechanists have turned disciplines like linguistics, economics, and programming into pseudosciences. What they perceive as research is in reality a never-ending series of attempts to cover up the failure of mechanistic theories. Thus, they are deceiving society in order to maintain their elitist position. As Orwell said, they are clinging to power through fraud, and in so doing they are fostering totalitarianism.

Another thing Orwell noticed and warned about was the trend toward a centralized economy, or collectivism. While enthusiastically advocated by experts as a progressive and effective system, a state-directed economy is, in reality, the exact opposite: it corrupts both the economy and politics, and undermines liberal values by promoting conformism. Thus, Orwell was one of the few to recognize the link between a government-controlled economy and totalitarianism. Writing in 1941, he makes this observation: "When one mentions totalitarianism one thinks immediately of Germany, Russia, Italy, but I think one must face the risk that this phenomenon is going to be world-wide. It is obvious that the period of free capitalism is coming to an end and that one country after another is adopting a centralized economy that one can call Socialism or state capitalism according as one prefers."[5] A socialist himself, Orwell had by then realized that socialism is largely a theoretical concept, that in practice it leads to totalitarianism.

In practice, therefore, the *economic* philosophy of central planning cannot be distinguished from the *political* philosophy of totalitarianism. And it is hardly necessary to point out that the intervention of governments in their country's economy has been increasing steadily since Orwell's time, as he said it would. In the last twenty years, particularly, fantastic monetary and fiscal policies – politically motivated – have given rise to the kind of central control that feeds on itself. We have reached the point where many countries can no longer function as liberal, free economies, and depend for survival on a perpetual increase in central control and a continuation of the same

---

[4] Ibid., p. 89.
[5] George Orwell, "Literature and Totalitarianism," in *Collected Essays*, vol. 2, p. 162.

fantastic policies. Under these conditions, the drift toward totalitarianism is not surprising.

With our model of simple and complex structures it is not difficult to understand the delusions of central economic planning. A country's economy is a complex phenomenon. It is the result of an infinity of interactions between millions of individuals, who act in various capacities: consumers, producers, workers, managers, inventors, entrepreneurs, financiers, and so forth. Thus, by encouraging uninhibited interactions, a free economy is the most likely to reflect, in the long run, the true needs and capabilities of the people. Governments like the idea of central planning because they believe it to be an improvement over a disorganized, free economy: why wait for the results of some random interactions, when we have experts who can control this phenomenon scientifically, and thereby guarantee a stable, ideal economy?

To control the economy, though, the experts must understand it. And, as we know, a complex phenomenon cannot be understood as we understand the working of a machine; that is, precisely enough to predict its manifestations and to control it. The experts, therefore, are compelled to invent theories based on a simplified, mechanistic version of the economy. They ignore the infinity of low-level interactions that make it up, and study separately its high-level aspects: inflation, unemployment, growth, government debt, stock market, gross domestic product, and so forth. In other words, they attempt to depict a complex structure as a combination of several simple ones. At this point, it seems logical to represent those separated aspects with exact values (averages, percentages, formulas, charts), and, moreover, to attempt to control the economy by manipulating these values. They forget that what they are studying is no longer the real economy, but a simpler, imaginary version. They may even manage to improve one aspect or another. But because they ignored the interactions between them, this is accomplished at the expense of other aspects, which deteriorate.

So the mechanistic economic theories are pseudoscientific. In the end, because they are concerned with minds and societies, they suffer from the same fallacies as the theories we examined in chapter 3. All these theories fail for the same reason: their assumption that human beings and human societies are deterministic systems.

Our model also explains why the idea of central economic planning is totalitarian. Its most appealing element is the promise of financial security for every citizen: the state will take care of our basic needs, leaving us free to pursue our careers and lifestyles. This promise, however, is an illusion. To implement a centrally-controlled economy, the state must assume that the needs of millions of individuals can be analyzed and controlled. It must assume, in other words, that human beings are a sort of automatons, driven by known programs. So, because it is based on invalid premises, because our needs are in reality complex and diverse, this economy is bound to fail. The only way to make it work is by *enforcing* it; namely, by asking us to replace our actual needs with the kind of needs that make central planning possible. Through education and through propaganda, we are told what knowledge is correct, what facts are important, what career is appropriate, what things must be purchased, what conduct is desirable, what to expect in the future, and so on. In the end, our needs will be simple, uniform, and predictable – the needs of automatons. To put this differently, since mechanistic economic theories do not reflect human nature, to make them work we must modify the people to match the theories: we must turn them into deterministic systems.

We can have government-controlled financial security, then, only if we agree to obey certain standards. In exchange for security, we replace individuality with conformism. Thus, there is only one step from accepting central economic planning to accepting totalitarianism. And, again, Orwell saw this trend clearly: "With [centralized economy] the economic liberty of the individual, and to a great extent his liberty to do what he likes, to choose his own work, to move to and fro across the surface of the earth, comes to an end. Now, till recently the implications of this were not foreseen. It was never fully realized that the disappearance of economic liberty would have any effect on intellectual liberty. Socialism was usually thought of as a sort of moralized liberalism. The state would take charge of your economic life and set you free from the fear of poverty, unemployment and so forth, but it would have no need to interfere with your private intellectual life.... Now, on the existing evidence, one must admit that these ideas have been falsified. Totalitarianism has abolished freedom of thought to an extent unheard of in any previous age."[6]

2

The best-known aspect of Orwell's totalitarian model is the use of language to control minds. (Orwell is generally recognized as the first thinker to study seriously this phenomenon.) It is from his discussion in *Nineteen Eighty-Four* that most people are familiar with Orwell's ideas (see "Orwell's Newspeak" in chapter 5). Just as it exaggerates the other aspects of totalitarianism, though,

---

[6] Ibid. Note how Orwell is referring to socialism and to totalitarianism interchangeably. The most outspoken critic of central economic planning was probably philosopher and economist F. A. Hayek. For fifty years, in numerous studies, Hayek exposed the fallacies and the totalitarian tendencies of this idea. His best-known book on this subject is *The Road to Serfdom* (Chicago: University of Chicago Press, 1994, 50th anniversary ed.). It is worth noting that Orwell actually read this book and praised it in a brief review.

that book exaggerates the language abuses, in order to demonstrate the *potential* of language manipulation. Orwell's intent was not so much to attack the totalitarian ideology itself, as to warn us that any society can become totalitarian. Thus, when we study his earlier writings, we realize that the hypothetical language abuses depicted in *Nineteen Eighty-Four* are a reflection of *real* abuses – those he noticed in the society of his time. So they are not a wild fantasy, but a logical extrapolation of *existing* conditions.

In our analysis we concluded that Orwell's chief contribution has been to make us aware of the link between language, mechanism, and totalitarianism (see pp. 405–407). The three are inseparable. Thus, in a totalitarian society people must act like automatons, and language is an important part of this transformation: by reducing language to its mechanistic aspects, the elite can restrict knowledge and thought to the level of machines. Conversely, a society where various elites are permitted to manipulate language in this fashion will be restricted to mechanistic values, and will become in the end totalitarian. How a society uses language, therefore, is a good indication of its progression toward totalitarianism: the greater the manipulation of language, the more totalitarian the society.

Orwell studied the language employed in speeches, pamphlets, articles, and debates, and saw that it was designed largely to deceive, rather than inform. He also noticed that the deception was achieved by restricting discourse to high levels of abstraction. Instead of simple and precise statements, the propagandists use euphemisms, vague terms, slogans, and standard phrases: "The whole tendency of modern prose is away from concreteness."[7] "As soon as certain topics are raised, the concrete melts into the abstract and no one seems able to think of turns of speech that are not hackneyed: prose consists less and less of *words* chosen for the sake of their meaning, and more of *phrases* tacked together like the sections of a prefabricated hen-house."[8]

We recognize this style as mechanistic language. Recall our discussion in chapter 5. Only by starting with *low-level* linguistic elements can a message convey information. When communicating through high-level elements – through prefabricated linguistic parts – the deceivers force us in effect to commit the two mechanistic fallacies, abstraction and reification: they restrict us to a fraction of the alternatives present in the new knowledge, and they prevent us from linking their message to our previous knowledge.

The aim of mechanistic language, then, is to control minds. To discover the meaning of a message, we must combine the meaning of its words and phrases with the knowledge structures already present in the mind. And when this

---

[7] George Orwell, "Politics and the English Language," in *Collected Essays*, vol. 4, p. 163.
[8] Ibid., p. 159.

process starts at high levels of abstraction, very few combinations are possible. Moreover, if those words and phrases are purposely selected so as to mislead us, we will create only *wrong* combinations, those that do *not* reflect reality.

Charlatans prefer high levels of abstraction, therefore, because of their usefulness as means of deception. An acronym, for example, stands for a whole phrase – a phrase which in its turn stands for many combinations of facts. But by employing the acronym in a certain way, and by tempting us to adopt it in our own discourse, a charlatan can make us associate it with just *a few* combinations: those we already perceive as "good." So we end up interpreting the acronym itself, and everything involving it, as "good." Having lost the lower levels – the individual words, their meanings and associations – we can no longer judge how important or unimportant are the facts subsumed by the acronym. Thus, while the high level of abstraction of the acronym seems to function merely as abbreviation, its real purpose is to shape and restrict thought. (See the discussion in chapter 5, pp. 373–374, 395–396, 403–404.)

Like acronyms, any high-level linguistic form – standard phrases, slogans, and the rest – can be used to avoid details and to obscure facts. In the aforementioned essay, Orwell analyzes several instances of political writing, and notes that this style is widespread: "This mixture of vagueness and sheer incompetence is the most marked characteristic of modern English prose, and especially of any kind of political writing."[9] But, while found earlier mainly in political writing, this style is employed today in nearly every field. In business computing, for instance, an article may be nothing more than some bombastic sentences praising the latest fads, reinforced with fashionable acronyms, and interspersed with slogans like "IT strategic planning," "empowering the enterprise," "competitive advantage," "mission-critical applications," and "business agility."

Improper use of high levels of abstraction is a sign of bad English, of course. But those who employ this style do it deliberately. For, their intent is not to debate logically a particular issue, but on the contrary, to force their readers to accept a distorted view of that issue. So this kind of writing betrays not so much a linguistic deficiency as an effort to control minds, which is the essence of totalitarianism. Or, putting this in reverse, only writers with a totalitarian attitude need to employ such a style. Also, the style's prevalence – the fact that we accept it rather than condemn it – indicates that the entire society is becoming totalitarian. It is this link between language and totalitarianism that preoccupied Orwell: "There does seem to be a direct connexion between acceptance of totalitarian doctrines and the writing of bad English ...."[10]

---

[9] Ibid.
[10] George Orwell, "Editorial to *Polemic*," in *Collected Essays*, vol. 4, p. 190.

❖

"To be corrupted by totalitarianism one does not have to live in a totalitarian country."[11] What Orwell meant is that the totalitarian mentality – elitism, conformism, bureaucratization, mind control – is found everywhere, and can corrupt any society. He was describing mostly its effect on writers and commentators, but this mentality has been spreading, and it affects now every aspect of society.

In the end, non-political totalitarianism can be as harmful as the political kind. If every elite is permitted to promote its ideology, and to deceive and exploit society, their total effect can be significant even if the individual elites are not. This is true because all these ideologies are similar to the totalitarian one: they claim that ideas based on mechanistic principles can solve our complex, non-mechanistic problems. The elites must uphold such ideologies because they can *only* offer us mechanistic solutions. We alone, with our minds, can conceive the non-mechanistic ones; and for this we need no elites. To stay in power, therefore, the elites must incessantly persuade us that their mechanistic concepts are more important than our minds. And this is why, ultimately, all elites deceive and exploit society in the same way.

We can also understand now why all elites end up manipulating language. We use language to represent the world in our minds, and to communicate with it. This is possible because language permits us to create complex knowledge structures. Since the world consists of complex phenomena, we *must* develop complex structures if we want to mirror the world accurately in the mind. By restricting language to its mechanistic aspects, the elites hope to make us see only the *mechanistic* aspects of the world – only the simple, isolated phenomena. And this, in turn, would make us accept their mechanistic ideas.

Each elite misleads us in a few, specific situations; but if all of them do this, it means that we are being misled all the time. Each elite wants to control just one aspect of our life; but between them, they control our entire existence. While each elite is promoting a different idea, they all do it by restricting us to high levels of abstraction, so they all prevent us from developing complex knowledge structures. Their goal, again, is to make their mechanistic ideas appear more important than they actually are. But, even though individually the deceptive messages may be weak, their cumulative effect is pernicious. If we are restricted to mechanistic values in all our affairs – in personal and in professional matters, in education and in business – our non-mechanistic capabilities remain undeveloped. Ultimately, we will indeed see only the mechanistic aspects of the world, just as the elites intended. At that point, those

---

[11] Orwell, "Prevention of Literature," p. 90.

useless ideas will finally seem important to us, because we will only be able to judge them with limited, mechanistic knowledge.

Clearly, then, if we live in a society where various elites have the right to control our knowledge and our values, the fact that our *political* system is democratic is irrelevant. If these elites are shaping our minds so as to accept mechanistic ideas that serve their interests, and if between them they have more power than our political institutions, our system is in effect totalitarian. To appreciate this, imagine that we had, not many academic and business elites inducing us to accept mechanistic ideas, but only one, political elite doing it. We would easily recognize the system then as totalitarian. In practice, therefore, there is no real difference between the two alternatives.

Software Totalitarianism

1

Talmon's model, we saw, can explain why academic and business mechanism become totalitarian ideologies. As in the case of political ideologies, the elites ask us to change so as to conform to an exact theory. This combination of science and total conformism, they say, is what will bring about a perfect society.

Let us use Talmon's model to explain why *software* mechanism becomes totalitarian. Software mechanism is, ultimately, the marriage of academic mechanism and business mechanism: the mechanistic software theories are invented in universities, and the software companies invoke these theories to justify the idea of software *products*.

The software theories claim that software applications are nothing but modules within modules, so the most effective way to develop them is by emulating the process of manufacturing. Devices like cars and appliances are designed as hierarchical structures of smaller and smaller subassemblies, ending with parts that are simple enough to be made directly. With this method, the task of manufacturing is reduced to the easier task of *assembling*: no matter how complex the finished product, every stage in its manufacture is now as simple as combining a number of parts into a larger part. Similarly, if we design our software applications as hierarchical structures of modules, programming will be reduced to the easier task of assembling pieces of software: starting with some small parts, we will build larger and larger modules, until we reach the complete application. Working in this fashion, even the most complex applications can be developed with skills no greater than those required to combine pieces of software.

If software can be built as we build cars and appliances – if, in other words, software is merely a new kind of product – the conclusion is that what we need is not expert programmers but a software industry: companies that make software products just as manufacturing companies make the traditional products. By running, as it were, efficient software factories, these companies should be able to supply most applications that society needs. And to help us build on our own those applications that are too specialized to be made as mass-market products, the software companies can give us *development tools*. These sophisticated software devices simplify the development of applications by providing high-level starting elements; namely, relatively large software subassemblies, instead of the small parts used in traditional programming. With these devices, even the least experienced among us should be able to create unique, customized applications.

This mechanistic software dream, however, cannot be fulfilled. As we saw in previous chapters, the theories are wrong when assuming that software applications can be treated as simple hierarchical structures. The facts, processes, and events that make up our affairs give rise to complex phenomena, and hence interacting structures. So, to represent them accurately, our software applications too must consist of interacting structures. If we follow the theories and separate the software structures, our applications will not match reality; for, as simple structures, they cannot display all the alternatives displayed by the complex phenomena. And if, in addition, we start with high-level elements, there will be even fewer alternatives. When forcing us to separate structures and to start from higher levels, the software elites force us in effect to commit the two mechanistic fallacies, reification and abstraction. The reduction in alternatives, then, is not surprising.

Whether we buy ready-made applications or make our own with development tools, applications based on mechanistic concepts can represent only the simple, mechanistic aspects of our affairs. Thus, the claim that these expedients have replaced the need for traditional programming, and for programming expertise, is a fraud. Only by resorting to our non-mechanistic capabilities – that is, through personal skills and experience – can we create applications versatile enough to represent accurately our affairs.

If the ready-made applications and the development tools are not, in fact, as useful as we think they are, the only way to make us depend on them is through deception. And indeed, software products are advertised just like the traditional consumer products: through testimonials, success stories, misleading language, portrayal of happy faces, and so forth. Thus, while addressing mostly businesses, and while discussing such issues as productivity and efficiency, software advertising is merely exploiting human weaknesses and ignorance, just like traditional advertising.

The goal of traditional advertising, we saw, is to persuade us that products based on mechanistic concepts will also solve our *complex* problems. Similarly, the goal of software advertising is to persuade us that applications based on mechanistic software concepts can represent complex phenomena – our business, social, and personal affairs. Also like traditional advertising, if software advertising were restricted to verifiable claims, only a small fraction of the applications and tools being bought today would continue to be bought: those that are indeed as beneficial as we think they are (specifically, those addressing problems that can be usefully approximated through mechanistic methods). For software, however, this fraction is much smaller than it is for the traditional products, probably less than 1 percent.

Like business and academic mechanism, then, software mechanism asks us to change: we must limit ourselves, in all software-related activities, to what can be accomplished with mechanistic concepts alone. In reality, we *can* develop non-mechanistic capabilities – knowledge, skills, experience – so we *can* create non-mechanistic software. But, the elites tell us, these capabilities are unreliable, and it is best to forgo them. Software mechanism, thus, is totalitarian – because it asks us to conform to its tenets. We must replace our natural, non-mechanistic capabilities with mechanistic ones. And we must replace our intuitive definition of software expertise – the utmost that human minds can attain – with a degraded one: the capability to understand mechanistic software concepts.

Now, if software were indeed just a new kind of product, software totalitarianism would mean only that the elites have found one more way to impoverish our existence. The harm, in other words, would be no worse than the harm caused by the traditional forms of academic and business totalitarianism. Software, however, is not just another product. Because of its versatility, software must be treated as a new phenomenon – a phenomenon comparable in potency to the phenomenon of language. Like language, software permits us to represent the world through symbols, and to communicate with it. It is their ability to generate *complex* structures, and hence to represent the world as it actually is, that distinguishes language and software systems from ordinary products. And it is precisely this ability that is lost when they are reduced to mechanistic systems. They behave then just like ordinary products, and they cease to mirror the world accurately.

Software is different from the expedients promoted by the traditional elites, therefore, because of its potential as a means of domination. When restricting us to mechanistic software, the elites restrict us in effect to thinking like automatons. Before, a certain type of product could be used by an elite to restrict only one aspect of our life; and no one was affected by more than a few types of product at a time. But as we get to depend on computers in more and more activities, the software elites have the opportunity to restrict practically every aspect of our life.

In conclusion, a society can become totalitarian simply by pursuing mechanistic ideas. And we saw that Talmon's model of totalitarianism can explain this phenomenon. There is a clear progression: from mechanistic theories that affect just academic bureaucrats, to products that affect many individuals but in a limited way, to software concepts that affect all members of society, in all their activities. In the past, only political institutions could enforce an ideology on such a large scale, and this is why Talmon's model describes *political* mechanism. But if software is now comparable in its scope to politics – if, that is, software concepts affect society as drastically as do the traditional political concepts – this model should also depict *our* situation.

Politically, a society becomes totalitarian when millions of people are forced to conform to mechanistic social concepts. And if the same people are forced to conform instead to mechanistic *software* concepts, the result is bound to be the same. For, in both cases, the effect is to restrict these people to mechanistic performance in every aspect of their life. Thus, all we have to do in order to use Talmon's model for today's society is substitute software for politics. The model explains then why our widespread adoption of mechanistic software ideas is causing a drift toward totalitarianism.

2

Orwell's model, we saw, explains our progression toward totalitarianism by pointing to the steady degradation in social values: the growing politicization of the economy, the growing corruption of the elites, and, especially, the growing use of language to control minds. The elites are promoting mechanistic notions; in addition, they are restricting language to high levels of abstraction, and this prevents us from recognizing how limited the mechanistic notions actually are.

The greatest value of Orwell's model, however, lies in helping us to understand the phenomenon of *software* totalitarianism – a phenomenon that did not even exist in his time. Thus, while warning us about the growth of traditional totalitarianism in the 1940s, Orwell created a model that can be used to explain the growth of software totalitarianism today.

Recall the similarity of language and software. Both function as systems of representation and communication, so both allow us to create complex structures that mirror the world. But, above all, it is our capacity to process these structures together with the *other* knowledge structures present in our minds that permits language and software to represent the world. With language, we saw, only by starting at low levels of abstraction can a message represent the world accurately. And the same is true of software: only by starting with low-level elements can a software application represent our affairs accurately. With both systems, when starting from high levels we lose the low-level interactions between structures, and hence many combinations of elements. The values we see at the top level are then only a fraction of all possible values. Thus, our knowledge of the world can be impoverished by restricting *software* to high levels of abstraction just as it can be by restricting language.

Orwell criticized the use of high-level linguistic elements – expressing an idea by combining ready-made phrases instead of starting with words. But this style, the essence of language impoverishment, is precisely the style recommended by our software experts for *programming*. All programming theories claim that applications can be designed as modules within modules, just like the appliances built in a factory; so programming can be based on the idea of software subassemblies – ready-made, high-level pieces of software. We have reached, therefore, an absurd situation: what we recognize as harmful in language – the mechanistic mode of communication – we strive to attain in software. Take, for instance, the following remark: "Political writing in our time consists almost entirely of prefabricated phrases bolted together like the pieces of a child's Meccano set."[1] Orwell is using here the metaphor of a child's building blocks to mock the high-level, vacuous linguistic style employed by propagandists. He could not have imagined that a few decades later, in programming, similar metaphors would be *seriously* used by experts to *praise* the high-level style.

Mechanism, we saw, destroys minds by reducing knowledge and thought to the level of machines. And mechanistic language enhances this process, because language structures interact with all other knowledge structures. Restricted to mechanistic thinking, we cannot develop *complex* knowledge. We become, in effect, automatons. We also saw that it is in the interest of the elites to maintain a mechanistic culture, because this guarantees ignorance and dependence: the mechanistic concepts promoted by the elites prevent us from using our minds; we cannot solve our complex problems, and we believe that the only answer is to adopt even more of these concepts; but this only increases our dependence on the elites and on mechanistic concepts, further degrading our minds, in a vicious circle.

And if software fulfils the same social role as language, a dependence on mechanistic software is bound to have the same effect. The software elites

---

[1] George Orwell, "The Prevention of Literature," in *The Collected Essays, Journalism and Letters of George Orwell*, vol. 4, eds. Sonia Orwell and Ian Angus (London: Penguin Books, 1970), p. 89.

promote mechanistic software concepts in order to keep us ignorant and dependent on their devices. But it is not only in software-related matters that we remain ignorant. Because we depend on computers in every aspect of our life, software structures, like language structures, interact with all other knowledge structures present in the mind. So the software elites are controlling our minds through software just as the traditional elites are through the older concepts and through language. The traditional elites, we saw, have more power between them than our political institutions. And, since their ideologies are totalitarian, our society is becoming totalitarian despite its democratic foundation. But the software elites are even more powerful than the traditional ones, so our progression toward totalitarianism is now even faster. They are more powerful because they are permitted to control, not an ordinary concept, but software.

The manipulation of language by the traditional elites forms, in the end, only a small part of our entire use of language. The manipulation of software by the software elites, on the other hand, is almost total. Only in the imaginary society of *Nineteen Eighty-Four* is the enforcement of language mechanism comparable to the enforcement of software mechanism in our own society. Thus, while no elite in a real society can ever have enough power to manipulate *language* to such an extent, our software elites already have this power in manipulating *software*. And, if even the relatively mild *language* mechanism currently imposed on us can degrade our minds, and can foster a totalitarian culture, it is safe to predict that complete *software* mechanism will cause widespread ignorance, and will bring about full-fledged totalitarianism.

3

Recall Orwell's observation that even a democratic society can be corrupted by totalitarianism (p. 865). Under the guise of administration, or education, or marketing, every elite is distorting knowledge in order to promote its ideas. The process of communication becomes a process of indoctrination: people are seen as little more than automatons that must be programmed to accept whatever ideology serves the interests of the elites.

And now we must add to this the corruption caused by *software* totalitarianism: universities are teaching pseudoscientific software notions, instead of fostering professionalism and responsibility; programmers rely on worthless theories, development tools, and ready-made pieces of software, instead of improving their skills; software systems are routinely promoted through testimonials and success stories – means of deception traditionally employed to promote useless consumer products; important software decisions are being made following the advice of charlatans acting as consultants, or lecturers, or gurus; workers in all fields are spending more and more of their time with software-related problems, instead of practising their profession; respected computer associations are promoting software notions that serve the interests of the software elite, not society; major government projects are abandoned after spending vast amounts of public money, while the incompetents responsible for these failures continue to be seen as software experts.

So it is true that we can be corrupted by totalitarianism even if we don't live in a totalitarian country. But Orwell made this observation *before* we had a software elite and a software bureaucracy. To bring the observation up to date, we must say that the corruption caused by software totalitarianism can *exceed* that found in a totalitarian country. It is the *nature* of software, its similarity to language, that makes this possible: we are becoming dependent on software in practically every activity; and if at the same time we are being restricted to *mechanistic* software concepts, it is only natural that we are increasingly thinking like machines. The incompetence, the irresponsibility, the apathy, the delusions we suffer from – this is exactly what we should expect to find in a society where people are prevented from using their minds.

It should be obvious, then, why I chose Talmon's and Orwell's models of totalitarianism. While dealing with political matters, their generality makes them equally suitable for the study of *software* matters. All we have to do is substitute software for politics, and these models will depict *software* totalitarianism. In the past, only a political elite had sufficient power to control society. No one could have imagined that one day we would invent something as potent as software, and that we would permit an elite to control it. Thus, if the software elite has the same power as a political elite, it is not surprising that our software ideology can be depicted with political models.

Another fact explained by the two models is why modern societies, founded upon liberal and democratic principles, end up nevertheless drifting toward totalitarianism. The reason is that the modernity which engenders democracy tempts us at the same time to accept blindly all mechanistic notions. Because of its successes in the exact sciences, we also see mechanism as the answer to our political, social, and economic problems. An elite can gain our support, therefore, by promising us simple, mechanistic solutions to these problems. So mechanism leads to utopianism: the belief that the methods we use in science and in engineering can help us to create a perfect society. But the only way to make a mechanistic ideology work is by enforcing conformism. Utopianism, thus, leads to totalitarianism: since a mechanistic ideology does not reflect human nature, *we* must be modified to match the ideology. Still, the elite says, this is not coercion but education. The ideology is based on scientific principles; so, if we accept science we must also accept totalitarianism. In a modern, efficient society, preferring individuality to conformism is a sign of maladjustment.

It makes little difference, thus, what type of mechanistic ideology one starts with – political, religious, business, educational, or software; if implemented on a large scale, it is guaranteed to become totalitarian. And this is why the same model can depict any type of totalitarianism. To demonstrate this kinship for software, I include below a passage from Talmon's book – the text where he describes the difference between the liberal and the totalitarian types of democracy (we discussed this earlier, see pp. 848–849). Read the passage, however, by substituting the word "software" for the twelve occurrences of "politics" and "political" (which I emphasized). And, with this change, the text describes perfectly our totalitarian *software* ideology.

> The essential difference between the two schools of democratic thought as they have evolved is not, as is often alleged, in the affirmation of the value of liberty by one, and its denial by the other. It is in their different attitudes to *politics*. The liberal approach assumes *politics* to be a matter of trial and error, and regards *political* systems as pragmatic contrivances of human ingenuity and spontaneity. It also recognizes a variety of levels of personal and collective endeavour, which are altogether outside the sphere of *politics*.
>
> The totalitarian democratic school, on the other hand, is based upon the assumption of a sole and exclusive truth in *politics*. It may be called *political* Messianism in the sense that it postulates a preordained, harmonious and perfect scheme of things, to which men are irresistibly driven, and at which they are bound to arrive. It recognizes ultimately only one plane of existence, the *political*. It widens the scope of *politics* to embrace the whole of human existence. It treats all human thought and action as having social significance, and therefore as falling within the orbit of *political* action. Its *political* ideas are not a set of pragmatic precepts or a body of devices applicable to a special branch of human endeavour. They are an integral part of an all-embracing and coherent philosophy. *Politics* is defined as the art of applying this philosophy to the organization of society, and the final purpose of *politics* is only achieved when this philosophy reigns supreme over all fields of life.[2]

[2] J. L. Talmon, *The Origins of Totalitarian Democracy* (New York: Praeger, 1960), pp. 1–2 (italics added). A similar effect is achieved if substituting "software" for politics-related or language-related words in Orwell's writings (the quotations on pp. 863 and 870, for instance).

Let us analyze these statements. The "sole and exclusive truth" in software is the ideology of software mechanism; in particular, the belief that software is a kind of product, so the most effective way to create and use software is through the devices supplied by software companies. Just like the political theories, the software theories are defended by invoking their mechanistic foundation. Mechanism is invalid both in politics and in software, and its failure in these domains is obvious. But if we accept blindly the mechanistic ideology, we must also accept mechanistic political and software systems.

The state "to which men are irresistibly driven, and at which they are bound to arrive" is the state where software mechanism is universally accepted, and no other form of programming or software use is envisaged. And software messianism is the belief that such a state is imminent: at any given moment, the latest concept, theory, or system is perceived as the revolution that would finally deliver us from all software evils. Recall the notion of a general will – the hidden, natural qualities said to inhere in all of us (p. 851): by enforcing conformism, the political elite will bring out these superior qualities, and thereby create a perfect society. Similarly, we may call the mechanistic software concepts a general *software* will. We all possess from birth such qualities as the appreciation of ready-made applications, high-level environments, and graphic user interface. But these natural, superior qualities are masked by the inefficient habits we acquire as individuals. So, by enforcing software conformism, the software elite helps us to attain our natural, higher self. The secret for becoming perfect programmers and users is an unwavering acceptance of the mechanistic software ideology.

Similarly to its political counterpart, the *liberal* software view recognizes "a variety of levels of personal and collective endeavour" for which software devices are ineffective, or unnecessary; and the *totalitarian* software view recognizes "only one plane of existence," our software-dependent activities. Under *political* totalitarianism, all social and personal affairs are modified to reflect the prevailing ideology, in order to permit the elite to directly control the life of every citizen. But to make this possible, the scope of politics is extended to encompass every aspect of human life. Politics, therefore, becomes more important than it ought to be. It grows into an exaggerated, morbid preoccupation, and every other activity in society is made subordinate to it. Under *software* totalitarianism, it is software – as expressed through the mechanistic ideology – that becomes more important than it ought to be, and grows into a morbid preoccupation. The scope of software is extended "to embrace the whole of human existence."

Thus, by invoking progress, or efficiency, or standards, the software elite attempts to replace every type of human knowledge with a software device. The only thing we need to know from now on, we are told, is how to operate these devices. Through these devices, then, the elite directly controls our capabilities, our values, our beliefs. The notion of personal skills and experience is becoming obsolete, as we are all expected to accomplish about the same thing: whatever can be done by combining the features found in the latest software devices. Instead of using our time to gain knowledge and experience, we waste it with software-related preoccupations; instead of using it to solve real professional and personal problems, we waste it solving specious, software-related problems.

The software elite treats software, thus, not as "a set of pragmatic precepts or a body of devices applicable to a special branch of human endeavour," but as "an integral part of an all-embracing and coherent philosophy" – the mechanistic philosophy. More precisely, software is seen as "the art of applying this philosophy to the organization of society." The elite treats software, in other words, not as what it really is – the means to represent the world with computers – but as a way to control society. And it does this by enforcing the mechanistic software ideology; specifically, by making us dependent on software devices. Since this kind of software cannot solve our real, complex problems, we end up spending more and more time with senseless pursuits. Simply by inducing us to squander our time on useless activities, then, the elite ensures our permanent ignorance; and this in turn ensures a growing dependence on software devices, in a process that feeds on itself. But "the final purpose" of software will only be achieved "when this philosophy reigns supreme over all fields of life"; that is, when every aspect of human existence is controlled through software devices.

Index

O

X

Y